W9-DAA-938

A Select Library of the Christian Church

NICENE AND POST-NICENE FATHERS

Volume 7

Cyril of Jerusalem, Gregory Nazianzen

SECOND SERIES

Edited by

Philip Schaff, D.D., LL.D. and Henry Wace, D.D.

Hendrickson Publishers, Inc.
P. O. Box 3473
Peabody, Massachusetts 01961-3473

ISBN 1-56563-123-4

Printed in the United States of America

First printing 1994

This is a reprint edition of the American Edition of the *Nicene and Post-Nicene Fathers, Second Series, Volume 7, S. Cyril of Jerusalem, S. Gregory Nazianzen*, originally published in the United States by the Christian Literature Publishing Company, 1894.

CONTENTS OF VOLUME VII.

NOTE.—S. Cyril is issued under the Editorial supervision of Dr. Wace, and S. Gregory Nazianzen under that of the translators.

THE CATECHETICAL LECTURES OF S. CYRIL, ARCHBISHOP OF JERUSALEM,

WITH A REVISED TRANSLATION, INTRODUCTION, NOTES, AND INDICES,

BY

EDWIN HAMILTON GIFFORD, D.D.,

FORMERLY ARCHDEACON OF LONDON, AND CANON OF S. PAUL'S.

PREFACE.

THE present translation of the Catechetical Lectures of S. Cyril of Jerusalem is based on a careful revision of the English translation published in the "Library of the Fathers of the Holy Catholic Church," with a most interesting Preface by John Henry Newman, dated from Oxford, *The Feast of St. Matthew*, 1838.

In his Preface Mr. Newman stated with respect to the translation "that for almost the whole of it the Editors were indebted to Mr. Church, Fellow of Oriel College." Mr. Church was at that time a very young man, having taken his First Class in Michaelmas Term, 1836; and this his first published work gave abundant promise of that peculiar felicity of expression, which made him in maturer life one of the most perfect masters of the English tongue. Having received full liberty to make such use of his translation as I might deem most desirable for the purpose of the present Edition, I have been obliged to exercise my own judgment both in preserving much of Dean Church's work unaltered, and in revising it wherever the meaning of the original appeared to be less perfectly expressed.

In this constant study and use of Dean Church's earliest work I have had always before my mind a grateful and inspiring remembrance of one whose friendship it was my great privilege to enjoy during the few last saddened years of his saintly and noble life.

In the notes of this Edition one of my chief objects has been to illustrate S. Cyril's teaching by comparing it with the works of earlier Fathers to whom he may have been indebted, and with the writings of his contemporaries.

In the chapters of the Introduction which touch on S. Cyril's doctrines of Baptism, Chrism, and the Holy Eucharist, I have not attempted either to criticise or to defend his teaching, but simply to give as faithful a representation as I could of his actual meaning. The Eastern Church had long before S. Cyril's day, and still has its own peculiar Sacramental doctrines, which, notwithstanding the efforts of rival theologians, can never be reduced to exact conformity with the tenets of our own or other Western Churches.

The Indices have been revised, and large additions made to the lists of Greek words, and of texts of Scripture.

E. H. G.

OXFORD,
26 May, 1893.

CONTENTS OF THE INTRODUCTION.

INTRODUCTION

CHAPTER I

Life of S. Cyril.

THE works of S. Cyril of Jerusalem owe much of their peculiar interest and value to the character of the times in which he wrote. Born a few years before the outbreak of Arianism in A.D. 318, he lived to see its suppression by the Edict of Theodosius, 380, and to take part in its condemnation by the Council of Constantinople in the following year.

The story of Cyril's life is not told in detail by any contemporary author; in his own writings there is little mention of himself; and the Church historians refer only to the events of his manhood and old age. We have thus no direct knowledge of his early years, and can only infer from the later circumstances of his life what may probably have been the nature of his previous training. The names of his parents are quite unknown; but in the Greek Menaea, or monthly catalogues of Saints, and in the Roman Martyrology for the 18th day of March, Cyril is said to have been "born of pious parents, professing the orthodox Faith, and to have been bred up in the same, in the reign of Constantine."

This account of his parentage and education derives some probability from the fact that Cyril nowhere speaks as one who had been converted from paganism or from any heretical sect. His language at the close of the vii^th Lecture seems rather to be inspired by gratitude to his own parents for a Christian education: "The first virtuous observance in a Christian is to honour his parents, to requite their trouble, and to provide with all his power for their comfort: for however much we may repay them, yet we can never be to them what they as parents have been to us. Let them enjoy the comfort we can give, and strengthen us with blessings."

One member only of Cyril's family is mentioned by name, his sister's son Gelasius, who was appointed by Cyril to be Bishop of Cæsarea on the death of Acacius, A.D. 366 *circ.*

Cyril himself was probably born, or at least brought up, in or near Jerusalem, for it was usual to choose a Bishop from among the Clergy over whom he was to preside, a preference being given to such as were best known to the people generally[1].

That Cyril, whether a native of Jerusalem or not, had passed a portion of his childhood there, is rendered probable by his allusions to the condition of the Holy Places before they were cleared and adorned by Constantine and Helena. He seems to speak as an eye-witness of their former state, when he says that a few years before the place of the Nativity at Bethlehem had been wooded[2], that the place where Christ was crucified and buried was a garden, of which traces were still remaining[3], that the wood of the Cross had been distributed to all nations[4], and that before the decoration of the Holy Sepulchre by Constantine, there was a cleft or cave before the door of the Sepulchre, hewn out of the

---

1 Bingham, *The Antiquities of the Christian Church*, Book II. c. 10, § 2.

2 Cat. xii. 20. The wood had been cleared away about sixteen years before this Lecture was delivered.

3 Cat. xiii. 32; xiv. 5.

4 Cat. iv. 10; x. 19: xiii. 4. Gregor. Nyss. *Baptism of Christ*, p. 520, in this Series: "The wood of the Cross is of saving efficacy for all men, though it is, as I am informed, a piece of a poor tree, less valuable than most trees are."

rock itself, but now no longer to be seen, because the outer cave had been cut away for the sake of the recent adornments [5].

This work was undertaken by Constantine after the year 326 A.D.[6]; and if Cyril spoke from remembrance of what he had himself seen, he could hardly have been less than ten or twelve years old, and so must have been born not later, perhaps a few years earlier, than 315 A.D.

The tradition that Cyril had been a monk and an ascetic was probably founded upon the passages in which he seems to speak as one who had himself belonged to the order of Solitaries, and shared the glory of chastity [7]. We need not, however, suppose that the "Solitaries" (μονάζοντες) of whom he speaks were either hermits living in remote and desert places, or monks secluded in a monastery: they commonly lived in cities, only in separate houses, and frequented the same Churches with ordinary Christians. To such a life of perpetual chastity, strict asceticism, and works of charity, Cyril may probably, in accordance with the custom of the age, have been devoted from early youth.

A more important question is that which relates to the time and circumstances of his ordination as Deacon, and as Priest, matters closely connected with some of the chief troubles of his later life.

That he was ordained Deacon by Macarius, Bishop of Jerusalem, who died in 334 or 335, may be safely inferred from the unfriendly notice of S. Jerome, *Chron.* ann. 349 (350 A.D.): "Cyril having been ordained Priest by Maximus, and after his death permitted by Acacius, Bishop of Cæsarea, and the other Arian Bishops, to be made Bishop on condition of repudiating his ordination by Maximus, served in the Church as a Deacon: and after he had been paid for this impiety by the reward of the Episcopate (*Sacerdotii*), he by various plots harassed Heraclius, whom Maximus when dying had substituted in his own place, and degraded him from Bishop to Priest."

From this account, incredible as it is in the main, and strongly marked by personal prejudice, we may conclude that Cyril had been ordained Deacon not by Maximus, but by his predecessor Macarius; for otherwise he would have been compelled to renounce his Deacon's Orders, as well as his Priesthood.

Macarius died in or before the year 335; for at the Council of Tyre, assembled in that year to condemn Athanasius, Maximus sat as successor to Macarius in the See of Jerusalem [8]. This date is confirmed by the fact that after the accession of Maximus, a great assembly of Bishops was held at Jerusalem in the year 335, for the dedication of the Church of the Holy Resurrection [9].

It thus appears that Cyril's ordination as Deacon cannot be put later than 334 or the beginning of 335.

Towards the close of the latter year the Bishops who had deposed Athanasius at the Council of Tyre proceeded to Jerusalem "to celebrate the *Tricennalia* of Constantine's reign by consecrating his grand Church on Mount Calvary [1]." On that occasion "Jerusalem became the gathering point for distinguished prelates from every province, and the whole city was thronged by a vast assemblage of the servants of God. . . . . . In short, the whole of Syria and Mesopotamia, Phœnicia and Arabia, Palestine, Egypt, and Libya, with the dwellers in the Thebaid, all contributed to swell the mighty concourse of God's ministers, followed as they were by vast numbers from every province. They were attended by an imperial escort, and officers of trust had also been sent from the palace itself, with instructions to heighten the splendour of the festival at the Emperor's expense [2]." Eusebius proceeds to describe

5 Cat. xiv. 9. 6 Eusebius; *Vita Const.* iii. 29 ff. 7 Cat. xii. 1, 33, 34. Compare iv. 24, note 8
8 Hefele, *History of Councils*, ii. 17; Sozom. *H.E.* ii. 25. 9 Euseb. *Vita Const.* iv. 43.
1 Robertson, *Prolegomena to Athanasius*, p. xxxix. 2 Euseb. *V.C.* iv. 43.

the splendid banquets, the lavish distribution of money and clothes to the naked and destitute, the offerings of imperial magnificence, the "intellectual feast" of the many Bishops' discourses, and last, not least, his own "various public orations pronounced in honour of this solemnity." Among the Clergy taking part in this gorgeous ceremony, the newly ordained Deacon of the Church of Jerusalem would naturally have his place. It was a scene which could not fail to leave a deep impression on his mind, and to influence his attitude towards the contending parties in the great controversy by which the Church was at this time distracted. He knew that Athanasius had just been deposed, he had seen Arius triumphantly restored to communion in that august assembly of Bishops "from every province," with his own Bishop Maximus, and Eusebius of Cæsarea, the Metropolitan, at their head. It is much to the praise of his wisdom and steadfastness that he was not misled by the notable triumph of the Arians to join their faction or adopt their tenets.

In September, 346, Athanasius returning from his second exile at Trèves passed through Jerusalem. The aged Bishop Maximus, who had been induced to acquiesce in the condemnation of Athanasius at Tyre, and in the solemn recognition of Arius at Jerusalem, had afterwards refused to join the Eusebians at Antioch in 341, for the purpose of confirming the sentence passed at Tyre, and now gave a cordial welcome to Athanasius, who thus describes his reception[3]: "As I passed through Syria, I met with the Bishops of Palestine, who, when they had called a Council at Jerusalem, received me cordially, and themselves also sent me on my way in peace, and addressed the following letter to the Church and the Bishops[4]." The letter congratulating the Egyptian Bishops and the Clergy and people of Alexandria on the restoration of their Bishop is signed first by Maximus, who seems to have acted without reference to the Metropolitan Acacius, successor of Eusebius as Bishop of Cæsarea, and a leader of the Arians, a bitter enemy of Athanasius. Though Cyril in his writings never mentions Athanasius or Arius by name, we can hardly doubt that, as Touttée suggests[5], he must at this time have had an opportunity of learning the true character of the questions in dispute between the parties of the great heresiarch and his greater adversary.

We have already learned from Jerome that Cyril was admitted to the Priesthood by Maximus. There is no evidence of the exact date of his ordination: but we may safely assume that he was a Priest of some years' standing, when the important duty of preparing the candidates for Baptism was intrusted to him in or about the year 348[6]. There appears to be no authority for the statement (*Dict. Chr. Antiq.* "Catechumens," p. 319 a), that "the *Catecheses* of Cyril of Jerusalem were delivered by him partly as a Deacon, partly as a Presbyter[7]."

At the very time of delivering the lectures, Cyril was also in the habit of preaching to the general congregation on the Lord's day[8], when the candidates for Baptism were especially required to be present[9]. In the Church of Jerusalem it was still the custom for sermons to be preached by several Presbyters in succession, the Bishop preaching last. From Cyril's *Homily on the Paralytic* (§ 20) we learn that he preached immediately before the Bishop, and so must have held a distinguished position among the Priests. This is also implied in the fact, that within three or four years after delivering his Catechetical Lectures to the candidates for Baptism, he was chosen to succeed Maximus in the See of Jerusalem.

The date of his consecration is approximately determined by his own letter to Constantius concerning the appearance of a luminous cross in the sky at Jerusalem. The letter was written on the 7th of May, 351, and is described by Cyril as the first-fruit of his Episcopate. He must therefore have been consecrated in 350, or early in 351.

---

3 *Apolog. contra Arian.* § 57.
4 Cf. Athan. *Hist. Arian.* § 25.
5 Introductory note to Cyril's Letter to Constantius, § x.
6 On the exact date of the Lectures, see below, ch. ix.
7 See more below on the office of "Catechist," ch. ii. § 2.
8 Cat. x. 14.
9 Cat. i. 6.

Socrates and Sozomen agree in the assertion that Acacius, Patrophilus the Arian Bishop of Scythopolis, and their adherents ejected Maximus and put Cyril in his place[9a]. But according to the statement of Jerome already quoted[9b] Maximus, when dying, had not only nominated Heraclius to be his successor, which, with the consent of the Clergy and people, was not unusual, but had actually established him as Bishop in his stead (*in suum locum substituerat*). The two accounts are irreconcileable, and both improbable. Touttée argues not without reason, that the consecration of Heraclius, which Jerome attributes to Maximus, would have been opposed to the right of the people and Clergy to nominate their own Bishop, and to the authority of the Metropolitan and other Bishops of the province, by whom the choice was to be confirmed and the consecration performed, and that it had moreover been expressly forbidden seven years before by the 23rd Canon of the Council of Antioch.

Still more improbable is the charge that Cyril had renounced the priesthood conferred on him by Maximus, and after serving in the Church as a Deacon, had been rewarded by the Episcopate, and then himself degraded Heraclius from Bishop to Priest. As a solution of these difficulties, it is suggested by Reischl[9c] that Cyril had been designated in the lifetime of Maximus as his successor, and after his decease had been duly and canonically consecrated, but had incurred the calumnious charges of the party opposed to Acacius and the Eusebians, because he was supposed to have bound himself to them by accepting consecration at their hands. This view is in some measure confirmed by the fact that "in the great controversy of the day Cyril belonged to the Asiatic party, Jerome to that of Rome. In the Meletian schism also they took opposite sides, Cyril supporting Meletius, Jerome being a warm adherent of Paulinus[1]," by whom he had been recently ordained Priest. It is also worthy of notice that Jerome's continuation of the *Chronicle* of Eusebius was written at Constantinople in 380—381, the very time when the many injurious charges fabricated by Cyril's bitter enemies were most industriously circulated in popular rumour on the eve of a judicial inquiry by the second general Council which met there in 381, under the presidency of Meletius, Cyril, and Gregory of Nazianzum[2]. Had Jerome written of Cyril a year or two later, he must have known that these calumnies had been emphatically rejected by the Synod of Constantinople (382) consisting of nearly the same Bishops who had been present at the Council of the preceding year. In their Synodical letter[3] to Pope Damasus they wrote: "And of the Church in Jerusalem, which is the Mother of all the Churches, we notify that the most reverend and godly Cyril is Bishop: who was long ago canonically appointed by the Bishops of the Province, and had many conflicts in various places against the Arians."

The beginning of Cyril's Episcopate was marked by the appearance of a bright Cross in the sky, about nine o'clock in the morning of Whitsunday, the 7th of May, 351 A.D. Brighter than the sun, it hung over the hill of Golgotha, and extended to Mount Olivet, being visible for many hours. The whole population of Jerusalem, citizens and foreigners, Christians and Pagans, young and old, flocked to the Church, singing the praises of Christ, and hailing the phænomenon as a sign from heaven confirming the truth of the Christian religion.

Cyril regarded the occasion as favourable for announcing to the Emperor Constantius the commencement of his Episcopate; and in his extant letter described the sign as a proof of God's favour towards the Empire and its Christian ruler. The piety of his father Constantine had been rewarded by the discovery of the true Cross and the Holy places: and now the greater devotion of the Son had won a more signal manifestation of Divine approval.

9a Socr. *H.E.* ii. 38; Soz. iv. 20. The Bishops of Palestine, except two or three, had received Athanasius most cordially a few years before (Athan. *Hist. Arian.* § 25). 9b p. ii. 9c Vol. I. p. xli. note.

1 *Dict. Chr. Biogr.* "Cyrillus," p. 761: and for the Meletian Schism, see "Meletius," "Paulinus," "Vitalius."

2 Hefele, ii. 344. 3 Theodoret, *Hist. Eccl.* v. 9.

The letter ends with a prayer that God may grant to the Emperor long to reign as the protector of the Church and of the Empire, "ever glorifying the Holy and Consubstantial Trinity, our true God." The word ὁμοούσιον, it is alleged, had not at this time been accepted by Cyril, and its use has therefore been thought to cast doubt upon the genuineness of this final prayer, which is nevertheless maintained by the Benedictine Editor[4]. The letter as a whole is certainly genuine, and the phenomenon is too strongly attested by the historians of the period to be called in question. While, therefore, we must reject Cyril's explanation, we have no reason to suspect him of intentional misrepresentation. A parhelion, or other remarkable phenomenon, of which the natural cause was at that time unknown, might well appear "to minds excited by the struggle between the Christian Faith and a fast-declining heathenism to be a miraculous manifestation of the symbol of Redemption, intended to establish the Faith and to confute its gainsayers[5]."

The first few years of Cyril's episcopate fell within that so-called "Golden Decade," 346—355, which is otherwise described as "an uneasy interval of suspense rather than of peace[6]." Though soon to be engaged in a dispute with Acacius concerning the privileges of their respective Sees, Cyril seems to have been in the interval zealous and successful in promoting the peace and prosperity of his own Diocese.

We learn from a letter of Basil the Great that he had visited Jerusalem about the year 357, when he had been recently baptized, and was preparing to adopt a life of strict asceticism. He speaks of the many saints whom he had there embraced, and of the many who had fallen on their knees before him, and touched his hands as holy[7],—signs, as Touttée suggests, of a flourishing state of religion and piety. Cyril's care for the poor, and his personal poverty, were manifested by an incident, of which the substantial truth is proved by the malicious use to which it was afterwards perverted. "Jerusalem and the neighbouring region being visited with a famine, the poor in great multitudes, being destitute of necessary food, turned their eyes upon Cyril as their Bishop. As he had no money to succour them in their need, he sold the treasures and sacred veils of the Church. It is said, therefore, that some one recognised an offering of his own as worn by an actress on the stage, and made it his business to inquire whence she had it, and found that it had been sold to her by a merchant, and to the merchant by the Bishop[8]."

This was one of the charges brought against Cyril in the course of the disputes between himself and Acacius, which had commenced soon after he had been installed in the Bishopric of Jerusalem. As Bishop of Cæsarea, Acacius exercised Metropolitan jurisdiction over the Bishops of Palestine. But Cyril, as presiding over an Apostolic See, "the Mother of all the Churches," claimed exemption from the jurisdiction of Cæsarea, and higher rank than its Bishop. It is not alleged, nor is it in any way probable, that Cyril claimed also the jurisdiction over other Bishops. The rights and privileges of his See had been clearly defined many years before by the 7th Canon of the Council of Nicæa: "As custom and ancient tradition shew that the Bishop of Aelia ought to be honoured, let him have precedence in honour, without prejudice to the proper dignity of the Metropolitical See." Eusebius[9], in reference to a Synod concerning the time of Easter, says: "There is still extant a writing of those who were then assembled in Palestine (about 200 A.D.), over whom Theophilus, Bishop of Cæsarea, and Narcissus, Bishop of Jerusalem, presided." If one Synod only is here meant, it would appear that the Bishop of Cæsarea took precedence of the Bishop of Jerusalem, which would be the natural order in a Synod held at Cæsarea. Bishop Hefele, however, takes a different view[1]: "According to the *Synodicon*, two Synods were held in Palestine on the

4 *Epist. ad Constantium*—Monitum, § x. 5 *Dict. Chr. Biogr.* p. 761. 6 Gwatkin, p. 74. 7 Epist. iv. p. 12.
8 Sozom. *H.E.* iv. 25. 9 *Hist. Eccl.* v. 23. 1 *History of the Christian Councils*, Book I. Sec. ii. c.

subject of the Easter controversy: the one at Jerusalem presided over by Narcissus, and composed of fourteen Bishops; and the other at Cæsarea, comprising twelve Bishops, and presided over by Theophilus." In confirmation of this view we may observe that when next Eusebius mentions Narcissus and Theophilus, he reverses the previous order, and names the Bishop of Jerusalem first.

However this may have been, Acacius, who as an Arian was likely to have little respect for the Council of Nicæa, seems to have claimed both precedence and jurisdiction over Cyril. From [2] Socrates we learn that Cyril was frequently summoned to submit to the judgment of Acacius, but for two whole years refused to appear. He was therefore deposed by Acacius and the other Arian Bishops of Palestine on the charge of having sold the property of the Church, as before mentioned. Socrates, who confesses that he does not know for what Cyril was accused, yet suggests that he was afraid to meet the accusations [3]. But Theodoret, a more impartial witness, says [4] that Acacius took advantage of some slight occasion (ἀφορμάς) and deposed him. Sozomen [5] also describes the accusation as a pretext (ἐπὶ προφάσει τοιᾷδε), and the deposition as hastily decreed, to forestall any countercharge of heresy by Cyril (φθάνει καθελών). The deposition was quickly followed by Cyril's expulsion from Jerusalem, and a certain Eutychius was appointed to succeed him [6]. Passing by Antioch, which at this time, 357—358, was left without a Bishop by the recent decease of the aged Arian Leontius Castratus [7], Cyril took refuge in Tarsus with its Bishop the "admirable Silvanus," "one of the Semi-Arians, who, as Athanasius testifies, agreed almost entirely with the Nicene doctrine, only taking offence at the expression ὁμοούσιος, because in their opinion it contained latent Sabellianism [8]." Cyril now sent to the Bishops who had deposed him a formal notice that he appealed to a higher Court (μεῖζον ἐπεκαλέσατο δικαστήριον), and his appeal was approved by the Emperor Constantius [9]. Acacius, on learning the place of Cyril's retreat, wrote to Silvanus announcing his deposition. But Silvanus out of respect both to Cyril, and to the people, who were delighted with his teaching, still permitted him to exercise his ministry in the Church. Socrates finds fault with Cyril for his appeal: "In this," he says, "he was the first and only one who acted contrary to the custom of the Ecclesiastical Canon, by having recourse to appeals as in a civil court." The reproach implied in this statement is altogether undeserved. The question, as Touttée argues, is not whether others had done the like before or after, but whether Cyril's appeal was in accordance with natural justice, and the custom of the Church. On the latter point he refers to the various appeals of the Donatists, of Marcellus of Ancyra, and Asclepas of Gaza, and to the case of the notorious heretic Photinus, who after being condemned in many Councils appealed to the Emperor, and was allowed to dispute in his presence with Basil the Great as his opponent. Athanasius himself, in circumstances very similar to Cyril's, declined to appear before Eusebius and a Synod of Arian Bishops at Cæsarea, by whom he was condemned A.D. 334, and appealed in person to Constantine, requesting either that a lawful Council of Bishops might be assembled, or that the Emperor would himself receive his defence [1]."

In justification of Cyril's appeal it is enough to say that it was impossible for him to submit to the judgment of Acacius and his Arian colleagues. They could not be impartial in a matter where the jurisdiction of Acacius their president, and his unsoundness in the Faith, were as much in question as any of the charges brought against Cyril. He took the only course open to him in requesting the Emperor to remit his case to the higher juris-

[2] *Hist. Eccl.* ii. 40. [3] Ib. [4] Ib. ii. 26.

[5] *H.E.* iv. 25.

[6] There is much uncertainty and confusion in the names of the Bishops who succeeded Cyril on the three occasions of his being deposed. His successor in 357 is said by Jerome to have been a certain Eutychius, probably the same who was afterwards excommunicated at Seleucia (*Dict. Chr. Biogr.* Eutychius 13). The subject is discussed at length by Touttée (*Diss.* I. vii.).

[7] See the account of his remarkable career in the *Dict. Chr. Biogr.*

[8] Athan. *De Synodis*, c. xii.; Hefele, ii. 262.

[9] Socrates, *H.E.* ii. 40.

[1] Athan. *contr. Arianos Apol.* c. 36: Hefele, ii. p. 27, note.

diction of a greater Council, and in giving formal notice of this appeal to the Bishops who had expelled him.

While the appeal was pending, Cyril became acquainted with "the learned Bishop, Basil of Ancyra" (Hefele), with Eustathius of Sebaste in Armenia, and George of Laodicea, the chief leaders of the party "usually (since Epiphanius), but with some injustice, designated Semi-Arian [2]." One of the charges brought against Cyril in the Council of Constantinople (360, A.D.) was, as we shall see, that he held communion with these Bishops.

Cyril had not long to wait for the hearing of his appeal. In the year 359 the Eastern Bishops met at Seleucia in Isauria, and the Western at Ariminum. Constantius had at first wished to convene a general Council of all the Bishops of the Empire, but this intention he was induced to abandon by representations of the long journeys and expense, and he therefore directed the two Synods then assembled at Ariminum and at Seleucia "the Rugged" to investigate first the disputes concerning the Faith, and then to turn their attention to the complaints of Cyril, and other Bishops against unjust decrees of deposition and banishment [3]. This order of proceeding was discussed, and after much controversy adopted on the first day of meeting, the 27th of September [4]. On the second day Acacius and his friends refused to remain unless the Bishops already deposed, or under accusation, were excluded. Theodoret relates that "several friends of peace tried to persuade Cyril of Jerusalem to withdraw, but that, as he would not comply, Acacius left the assembly [5]." Three days afterwards, according to Sozomen, a third meeting was held at which the demand of Acacius was complied with; "for the Bishops of the opposite party were determined that he should have no pretext for dissolving the Council, which was evidently his object in order to prevent the impending examination of the heresy of Aetius and of the accusations which had been brought against him and his partisans [6]." A creed put forward by Acacius having been rejected, he refused to attend any further meetings, though repeatedly summoned to be present at an investigation of his own charges against Cyril.

In the end Acacius and many of his friends were deposed or excommunicated. Some of these, however, in defiance of the sentence of the Council, returned to their dioceses, as did also the majority who had deposed them.

It is not expressly stated whether any formal decision on the case of Cyril was adopted by the Council: but as his name does not appear in the lists of those who were deposed or excommunicated, it is certain that he was not condemned. It is most probable that the charges against him were disregarded after his accuser Acacius had refused to appear, and that he returned, like the others, to his diocese. But he was not to be left long in peace. Acacius and some of his party had hastened to Constantinople, where they gained over to their cause the chief men attached to the palace, and through their influence secured the favour of Constantius, and roused his anger against the majority of the Council. But what especially stirred the Emperor's wrath were the charges which Acacius concocted against Cyril: "For," he said that "the holy robe which the Emperor Constantine of blessed memory, in his desire to honour the Church of Jerusalem, had presented to Macarius, the Bishop of that city, to be worn when he administered the rite of Holy Baptism, all fashioned as it was with golden threads, had been sold by Cyril, and bought by one of the dancers at the theatre, who had put it on, and while dancing had fallen, and injured himself, and died. With such an ally as this Cyril," he said, "they undertake to judge and pass sentence upon the rest of the world [7]."

Ten deputies who at the close of the Council of Seleucia had been appointed to report its

---

2 Robertson, *Prolegomena ad Athanas.* ii. § 8 (2) c. 3 Soz. iv. 17. 4 Socrat. ii. 39. 5 *H.E.* ii. 26. 6 Sozom. iv. 22. 7 Theodoret, *H.E.* ii. 23.

proceedings to the Emperor, "met, on their arrival at the Court, the deputies of the Council of Ariminum, and likewise the partisans of Acacius[8]. After much controversy and many intrigues, a mutilated and ambiguous Creed adopted at Ariminum in which the ὁμοούσιος of Nicæa was replaced by "like to the Father that begat Him according to the Scriptures," and the mention of either "essence" (οὐσία) or "subsistence" (ὑπόστασις) condemned[9], was brought forward and approved by the Emperor. "After having, on the last day of the year 359, discussed the matter with the Bishops till far into the night[1], he at length extorted their signatures .... It is in this connexion that Jerome says: *Ingemuit totus orbis, et Arianum se esse miratus est*[2]." Early in the following year, 360 A.D., through the influence of Acacius a new Synod was held at Constantinople, in which, among other Semi-Arian Bishops, Cyril also was deposed on the charge of having held communion with Eustathius of Sebaste, Basil of Ancyra, and George of Laodicea. Cyril, as we have seen, had become acquainted with these Bishops during his residence at Tarsus in 358, at which time they were all zealous opponents of Acacius and his party, but differed widely in other respects.

George of Laodicea was a profligate in morals, and an Arian at heart, whose opposition to Acaçius and Eudoxius was prompted by self-interest rather than by sincere conviction. He had been deposed from the priesthood by Alexander, Bishop of Alexandria, both on the ground of false doctrine, and of the open and habitual irregularities of his life. Athanasius styles him "the most wicked of all the Arians," reprobated even by his own party for his grossly dissolute conduct[3].

Basil of Ancyra was a man of high moral character, great learning, and powerful intellect, a consistent opponent both of the Sabellianism of Marcellus, and of every form of Arian and Anomœan heresy, a chief among those of whom Athanasius wrote[4], "We discuss the matter with them as brothers with brothers, who mean what we mean, and dispute only about the word (ὁμοούσιος). . . . Now such is Basil who wrote from Ancyra concerning the Faith" (358 A.D., the same year in which Cyril met him at Tarsus).

Eustathius is described as a man unstable in doctrine, vacillating from party to party, subscribing readily to Creeds of various tendency, yet commanding the respect even of his enemies by a life of extraordinary holiness, in which active benevolence was combined with extreme austerity. "He was a man," says Mr. Gwatkin[5], "too active to be ignored, too unstable to be trusted, too famous for ascetic piety to be lightly made an open enemy."

S. Basil the Great, when travelling from place to place, to observe the highest forms of ascetic life, had met with Eustathius at Tarsus, and formed a lasting friendship with a man whom he describes as "exhibiting something above human excellence," and of whom, after the painful dissensions which embittered Basil's later life, that great saint could say, that from childhood to extreme old age he (Eustathius) had watched over himself with the greatest care, the result of his self-discipline being seen in his life and character[6].

Of any intimate friendship between Cyril and these Semi-Arian leaders, we have no evidence in the vague charges of Acacius: their common fault was that they condemned him in the Synod of Seleucia. The true reason of Cyril's deposition, barely concealed by the frivolous charges laid against him, was the hatred of Acacius, incurred by the refusal to acknowledge the Metropolitan jurisdiction of the See of Cæsarea. The deposition was confirmed by Constantius, and followed by a sentence of banishment. The place of Cyril's exile is not mentioned; nor is it known whether he joined in the protest of the other deposed Bishops, described by S. Basil, *Epist.* 75. His banishment was not of longer continuance than two years. Constantius died on the 3rd of November, 361, and the accession of Julian was soon

---

8 Sozom. iv. 23. 9 Athan. *de Syn.* § 30, where this Creed is given in full. 1 S. Hilar. ii. Num. 708. 2 Hefele, *Councils*, ii. 271. 3 *Dict. Chr. Biogr.* 4 *De Synodis*, § 41. 5 *The Arian Controversy*, p. 135. 6 Basil, *Epist.* 244. Compare Newman, *Preface to Catechetical Lectures*, p. iv.

followed by the recall of all the exiled Bishops, orthodox and heretical, and the restoration of their confiscated estates[7]. Julian's object, according to Socrates, was "to brand the memory of Constantius by making him appear to have been cruel towards his subjects." An equally amiable motive imputed to him is mentioned by Sozomen: "It is said that he issued this order in their behalf not out of mercy, but that through contention among themselves the Church might be involved in fraternal strife[8]." Cyril, returning with the other Bishops, seems to have passed through Antioch on his way home, and to have been well received by the excellent Bishop Meletius.

It happened that the son of a heathen priest attached to the Emperor's Court, having been instructed in his youth by a Deaconess whom he visited with his mother, had secretly become a Christian. On discovering this, his father had cruelly scourged and burnt him with hot spits on his hands, and feet, and back. He contrived to escape, and took refuge with his friend the Deaconess. "'She dressed me in women's garments, and took me in her covered carriage to the divine Meletius. He handed me over to the Bishop of Jerusalem, at that time Cyril, and we started by night for Palestine.' After the death of Julian, this young man led his father also into the way of truth. This act he told me with the rest[9]."

The next incident recorded in the life of S. Cyril is his alleged prediction of the failure of Julian's attempt to rebuild the Temple of Jerusalem. "The vain and ambitious mind of Julian," says Gibbon, "might aspire to restore the ancient glory of the Temple of Jerusalem. As the Christians were firmly persuaded that a sentence of everlasting destruction had been pronounced against the whole fabric of the Mosaic law, the Imperial sophist would have converted the success of his undertaking into a specious argument against the faith of prophecy and the truth of revelation." Again he writes: "The Christians entertained a natural and pious expectation, that in this memorable contest, the honour of religion would be vindicated by some signal miracle[1]." That such an expectation may have been shared by Cyril is not impossible: but there is no satisfactory evidence that he ventured to foretell any miraculous interposition. According to the account of Rufinus[2], "lime and cement had been brought, and all was ready for destroying the old foundations and laying new on the next day. But Cyril remained undismayed, and after careful consideration either of what he had read in Daniel's prophecy concerning the 'times,' or of our Lord's predictions in the Gospels, persisted that it was impossible that one stone should ever there be laid upon another by the Jews." This account of Cyril's expectation, though probable enough in itself, seems to be little more than a conjecture founded on his statement (*Cat.* xv. 15), that "Antichrist will come at the time when there shall not be left one stone upon another in the Temple of the Jews." That doom was not completed in Cyril's time, nor did he expect it to be fulfilled until the coming of the Jewish Antichrist, who was to restore the Temple shortly before the end of the world. It was impossible for Cyril to see in Julian such an Antichrist as he has described; and therefore, without any gift or pretence of prophecy, he might very well express a firm conviction that the attempted restoration at that time must fail. Though Gibbon is even more cynical and contemptuous than usual in his examination of the alleged miracles, he does not attempt to deny the main facts of the story[3]: with their miraculous character we are not here concerned, but only with Cyril's conduct on so remarkable an occasion.

In the same year, A.D. 363, Julian was killed in his Persian campaign on the 26th of June, and was succeeded by Jovian, whose universal tolerance, and personal profession of the Nicene faith, though discredited by the looseness of his morals, gave an interval

---

7 Socr. *H.E.* iii. 1. 8 Sozom. *H.E.* v. c. 5. Compare Gibbon, Ch. xxiii.: "The impartial Ammianus has ascribed this affected clemency to the desire of fomenting the intestine divisions of the Church." 9 Theodoret, *H.E.* iii. 10.

1 Gibbon, c. xxiii. 2 *Hist.* i. 37. 3 See Gibbon's remarks on the testimony of Ammianus, "a contemporary and a Pagan,' and on the explanation from natural causes suggested by Michaelis.

of comparative rest to the Church. In his reign Athanasius was recalled, and Acacius and his friends subscribed the Nicene Creed, with an explanation of the sense in which they accepted the word ὁμοούσιον[4]. As Cyril's name is not mentioned in any of the records of Jovian's short reign of seven months, we may infer that he dwelt in peace at Jerusalem.

Jovian died on the 17th of February, 364, and was succeeded by Valentinian, who in the following March gave over the Eastern provinces of the Empire to his brother Valens. During the first two years of the new reign we hear nothing of Cyril: but at the beginning of the year 366, on the death of his old enemy Acacius, Cyril assumed the right to nominate his successor in the See of Cæsarea, and appointed a certain Philumenus[5]. Whether this assumption of authority was in accordance with the 7th Canon of Nicæa may be doubted: Cyril's choice of his nephew was, however, in after times abundantly justified by the conduct and character of Gelasius, who is described by Theodoret as a man "distinguished by the purity of his doctrine, and the sanctity of his life," and is quoted by the same historian as "the admirable," and "the blessed Gelasius[6]."

Epiphanius relates[7] that "after these three had been set up, and could do nothing on account of mutual contentions," Euzoius was appointed by the Arians, and held the See until the accession of Theodosius in A.D. 379, when he was deposed, and Gelasius restored. In the meantime Cyril had been a third time deposed and driven from Jerusalem, probably in the year 367. For at that time Valens, who had fallen under the influence of Eudoxius, the Arian Bishop of Constantinople, by whom he was baptized, "wrote to the Governors of the provinces, commanding that all Bishops who had been banished by Constantius, and had again assumed their sacerdotal offices under the Emperor Julian, should be ejected from their Churches[8]." Of this third and longest banishment we have no particulars, but we may safely apply to it the words of the Synod at Constantinople, 382, that Cyril "had passed through very many contests with the Arians in various places."

The terrible defeat and miserable death of Valens in the great battle against the Goths at Adrianople (A.D. 378) brought a respite to the defenders of the Nicene doctrine. For Gratian "disapproved of the late persecution that had been carried on for the purpose of checking the diversities in religious Creeds, and recalled all those who had been banished on account of their religion[9]." Gratian associated Theodosius with himself in the Empire on the 19th of January, 379; and "at this period," says Sozomen[1], "all the Churches of the East, with the exception of that of Jerusalem, were in the hands of the Arians." Cyril, therefore, had been one of the first to return to his own See. During his long absence the Church of Jerusalem had been the prey both of Arianism and of the new heresy of Apollinarius, which had spread among the monks who were settled on Mount Olivet. Egyptian Bishops, banished for their orthodoxy, having taken refuge in Palestine, there found themselves excluded from communion. Jerusalem was given over to heresy and schism, to the violent strife of rival factions, and to extreme licentiousness of morals.

Gregory of Nyssa, who had been commissioned by a Council held at Antioch in 378 to visit the Churches in Arabia and Palestine, "because matters with them were in confusion, and needed an arbiter," gives a mournful account both of the distracted state of the Church, and of the prevailing corruption. "If the Divine grace were more abundant about Jerusalem than elsewhere, sin would not be so much the fashion among those who live there; but as it is, there is no form of uncleanness that is not perpetrated among them; rascality, adultery, theft, idolatry, poisoning, quarrelling, murder, are rife." In a letter[2] written after his return

---

4 Socr. iii. 25; Sozom. vi. 4. 5 Epiphanius, *Hær.* 73, § 37. 6 *Hist. Eccl.* V. 8; *Dialog.* i. iii.

7 *Hæres.* lxxiii. § 37. 8 Sozom. vi. 12. Cf. Tillemont, *Mémoires*, Tom. viii. p. 357: "As Cyril was, no doubt, then persecuted only on account of his firmness in the true Faith, the title of Confessor cannot be refused to him."

9 Soz. vii. 1. 1 Ib. 2. 2 Greg. Nyss. *Epist.* xvii. in this Series.

to Cæsarea in Cappadocia he asks, "What means this opposing array of new Altars? Do we announce another Jesus? Do we produce other Scriptures? Have any of ourselves dared to say "Mother of Man" of the Holy Virgin, the Mother of God?

In the year A.D. 381 Theodosius summoned the Bishops of his division of the Empire to meet in Council at Constantinople, in order to settle the disputes by which the Eastern Church had been so long distracted, and to secure the triumph of the Nicene Faith over the various forms of heresy which had arisen in the half-century which had elapsed since the first General Council. Among the Bishops present were Cyril of Jerusalem, and his nephew Gelasius, who on the death of Valens had regained possession of the See of Cæsarea from the Arian intruder Euzoius. Cyril is described by Sozomen[3] as one of three recognised leaders of the orthodox party, and, according to Bishop Hefele[4], as sharing the presidency with the Bishops of Alexandria and Antioch. This latter point, however, is not clearly expressed in the statement of Sozomen. Socrates writes that Cyril at this time recognised the doctrine of ὁμοούσιον, having retracted his former opinion: and Sozomen says that he had at this period renounced the tenets of the Macedonians which he previously held[5]. Touttée rightly rejects these reproaches as unfounded: they are certainly opposed to all his teaching in the Catechetical Lectures, where the doctrine of Christ's unity of essence with the Father is fully and frequently asserted, though the term ὁμοούσιος is not used, and the co-equal Deity of the Holy Ghost is everywhere maintained.

We find no further mention of Cyril in the proceedings of the Council itself. As consisting of Eastern Bishops only, its authority was not at first acknowledged, nor its acts approved in the Western Church. The two Synods held later in the same year at Aquileia and at Milan, sent formal protests to Theodosius, and urged him to summon a General Council at Alexandria or at Rome. But instead of complying with this request, the Emperor summoned the Bishops of his Empire to a fresh Synod at Constantinople; and there in the summer of 382 very nearly the same Bishops were assembled who had been present at the Council of the preceding year. Their Synodical letter addressed to the Bishops assembled at Rome is preserved by Theodoret[6], and in it we read as follows: "Of the Church in Jerusalem, the Mother of all the Churches, we make known that Cyril the most reverend and most beloved of God is Bishop; and that he was canonically ordained long ago by the Bishops of the province, and that he has very often fought a good fight in various places against the Arians." Thus justice was done at last to one whose prudence, moderation, and love of peace, had exposed him in those days of bitter controversy to undeserved suspicion and relentless persecution. His justification by the Council is the last recorded incident in Cyril's life. We are told by Jerome that he held undisturbed possession of his See for eight years under Theodosius. The eighth year of Theodosius was A.D. 386, and in the Roman Martyrology, the 18th of March in that year is marked as "The birthday ('Natalis,' i.e. of his heavenly life) of Cyril, Bishop of Jerusalem, who after suffering many wrongs from the Arians for the sake of the Faith, and having been several times driven from his See, became at length renowned for the glory of sanctity, and rested in peace: an Ecumenical Council in a letter to Damasus gave a noble testimony to his untarnished faith."

CHAPTER II.

Catechetical Instruction.

§ 1. *Catechesis.* The term "Catechesis" in its widest sense includes instruction by word of mouth on any subject sacred or profane[1], but is especially applied to Christian teaching,

3 *H.E.* vii. 7. 4 *Councils*, ii. 344. 5 Socrat. v. 8; Sozom. vii. 7. 6 *H.E.* v. 9.

1 Acts xviii. 25; xxi. 21, 24; Rom. ii. 18; Gal. vi. 6. Cf. Clem. Alex. *Fragm.* § 28: οὐκ ἔστι πιστεῦσαι ἄνευ κατηχήσεως.

whether of an elementary kind appropriate to new converts, or, as in the famous Catechetical School of Alexandria, extending to the higher interpretation of Holy Scripture, and the exposition of Christian philosophy.

The earliest known example of a Catechetical work is the "*Teaching of the Twelve Apostles*," which Athanasius names among the "books not included in the Canon, but appointed by the Fathers to be read by those who are just recently coming to us, and wish to be instructed in the word of godliness (κατηχεῖσθαι τὸν τῆς εὐσεβείας λόγον)[2]." This use of the Didache for the instruction of recent converts from Paganism agrees with its original purpose as stated in the longer title, "*Teaching of the Lord through the Twelve Apostles for the Gentiles.*" The first six chapters are evidently adapted for those who need elementary instruction, more particularly for Catechumens of Gentile descent, as distinct from Jewish candidates for Baptism[3]. The remaining chapters of the Didaché relate chiefly to the administration of Baptism, to Prayer, Fasting, and the services of the Lord's Day, and to the celebration of the Agape and Eucharist[4]. This same division of subjects is observed in the two classes of S. Cyril's Catechetical Lectures: the first class, including the Procatechesis, consists of XIX Lectures addressed to candidates for Baptism, and these are followed by five "Mystagogic" Lectures, so called as being explanations of the Sacramental Mysteries to the newly-baptized.

The Didaché was taken as the basis of other manuals of instruction, as is evident from the fact that the greater part of the first six chapters is imbedded in "The Apostolical Church Order," supposed to date from Egypt in the third century. The Greek text, with an English translation, of the part corresponding with the Didaché, is given in "The oldest Church Manual" as Document V.

A further development of the Didaché, "adapted to the state of the Eastern Church in the first half of the fourth century," is contained in the Seventh Book of the Apostolical Constitutions of Pseudo-Clement of Rome, chs. i.-xxxii. "Here the Didaché is embodied almost word for word, but with significant omissions, alterations, and additions, which betray a later age. . . . The Didaché was thus superseded by a more complete and timely Church Manual, and disappeared." Dr. Schaff has appended this document also to his edition of the Didaché, noting the borrowed passages on the margin, and distinguishing them by spaced type in the Greek text, and by italics in the English translation.

In this work the directions concerning the instruction of Catechumens and their Baptism are addressed to the Catechist and the Minister of Baptism. They contain only a short outline (c. xxxix.) of the subjects in which the Catechumens are to be instructed, most if not all of which are explained at large in Cyril's Lectures: and in the directions concerning Baptism, Chrism, and the Eucharist, the similarity is so close, that in many passages of the Constitutions the author seems to be referring especially to the use of the Church of Jerusalem.

From this close affinity with earlier works we may be assured that in the Catecheses of Cyril we have trustworthy evidence of the great care which the Church had from the beginning bestowed on the instruction and training of converts, before admitting them to the privilege of Baptism; but beyond this, Cyril's own work has a peculiar value as the earliest extant example of a full, systematic, and continuous course of such instruction.

§ 2. *Catechist.* The duty of catechizing was not limited to a class of persons permanently set apart for that purpose, but all orders of the Clergy were accustomed to take part in the work. Even laymen were encouraged to teach children or new converts the first elements of religion, as we learn from Cyril's exhortation: "If thou hast a child according to the flesh, admonish him of this now; and if thou hast begotten one through *catechizing*, put him also on

[2] *Festal Epist.* 39. Compare Clem. Alex. *Strom.* V. c. x. § 67. Γάλα μὲν ἡ κατήχησις οἱονεὶ πρώτη ψυχῆς τροφὴ νοηθήσεται.

[3] Schaff, *Oldest Church Manual*, p. 15. [4] Ib. p. 26.

his guard [5]." That this remark was addressed not to the Catechumens, but to such of the Faithful as happened to be present among his audience, appears from what he says elsewhere, "So thou likewise, though not daring before thy Baptism to wrestle with the adversaries, yet after thou hast received the grace, and art henceforth confident in *the armour of righteousness*, must then do battle, and preach the Gospel, if thou wilt [6]."

The more systematic instruction of those who had been already admitted to the order of Catechumens was entrusted to persons appointed to this special duty. Thus Origen "was in his eighteenth year when he took charge of the Catechetical School at Alexandria," which "was entrusted to him alone by Demetrius, who presided over the Church [7]:" and S. Augustine's Treatise, *De Catechizandis Rudibus*, was addressed to Deogratias, who being a Deacon at Carthage, and highly esteemed for his skill and success as a Catechist, felt so strongly the importance of the work and his own insufficiency, that he wrote to Augustine for advice as to the best method of instructing those who were brought to him to be taught the first elements of the Christian Faith.

The final training of the Φωτιζόμενοι, or candidates for Baptism, was undertaken in part by the Bishop himself, but chiefly by a Priest specially appointed by him. Of the part taken by the Bishop mention is made by S. Ambrose in a letter to his sister Marcellina (*Ep.* xx.): "On the following day, which was the Lord's day, after the Lessons and Sermon, the Catechumens had been dismissed, and I was delivering the Creed to some candidates (*Competentes*) in the Baptistery of the Basilica."

Of this "delivery of the Creed," which was usually done by a Presbyter, we have examples in S. Augustine's Sermons *In traditione Symboli*, ccxii.—ccxiv., each of which contains a brief recapitulation and explanation of the several articles of belief. In Serm. ccxiv., after a short introduction, we find the following note inserted by the preacher himself. ["*After this preface the whole Creed is to be recited, without interposing any discussion. 'I BELIEVE IN GOD THE FATHER ALMIGHTY,'* and the rest that follows. Which Creed, thou knowest, is not wont to be written: after it has been said, the following discussion (*disputatio*) is to be added."]

From the opening words of Sermon ccxiv., and of ccxvi., "*ad Competentes*," it is evident that these were delivered by S. Augustine as the first-fruits of his ministry very soon after he had been reluctantly ordained Priest (A.D. 391). Two other examples of addresses to Candidates for Baptism are the *Catecheses* I., II., πρὸς τοὺς μέλλοντας φωτίζεσθαι, delivered at Antioch by S. Chrysostom while a Presbyter.

Another duty often undertaken by the Bishop was to hear each Candidate separately recite the Creed, and then to expound to them all the Lord's Prayer [8].

§ 3. *Catechumens.* The term Catechumen denoted a person who was receiving instruction in the Christian religion with a view to being in due time baptized. Such persons were either converts from Paganism and Judaism, or children of Christian parents whose Baptism had been deferred. For though the practice of Infant-Baptism was certainly common in the Early Church [1], it was not compulsory nor invariable. "In many cases Christian parents may have shared and acted on the opinion expressed by Tertullian in the second century, and by Gregory Nazianzen in the fourth, and thought it well to defer the Baptism of children, cases of grave sickness excepted, till they were able to make answer in their own name to the interrogations of the baptismal rite [2]."

---

5 Cat. xv. 18. 6 Cat. iii. 13. 7 Euseb. *H.E.* vi. 3.

8 S. August. *Serm.* lviii. et ccxv.

1 Cf. Iren. II. c. xxii. § 4: "Omnes enim venit per semet ipsum salvare; omnes, inquam, qui per eum *renascuntur* in Deum, infantes, et parvulos, et pueros, et juvenes, et seniores. Cf. Concil. Carthag. iii. *Epist. Synod.* (Cypriani *Ep.* lix. vel lxiv. Routh. *R. S.* iii. p. 98.)

2 *Dict. Chr. Antiq.* "Baptism," § 101. Tertull. *De Baptismo*, c. xviii. "And so, according to the circumstances, and disposition, and even age of each individual, the delay of Baptism is preferable; principally, however, in the case of little children.' Cf. Gregor. Naz. *Orat.* 40 *De Baptismo*, quoted by Bingham, xi. c. 4, § 13.

It is stated by Bingham[3], but without any reference to ancient authors, that "the children of believing parents, as they were baptized in infancy, were admitted Catechumens as soon as they were capable of learning." Though the title "Catechumen" was not usually applied to those who had been already baptized, it is probable that such children were admitted to the Lectures addressed to Catechumens both in the earlier and later stage of their preparation: for it seems to be implied in the passage quoted above from *Cat.* xv. 18, that admission was not limited to the candidates for Baptism.

To believe and to be baptized are the two essential conditions of membership in Christ's Church[4]: but for the admission of new converts to the class of Catechumens nothing more could be required than evidence of a sincere desire to understand, to believe, and ultimately to be baptized.

We know that unbelievers, Jews, and Heathens were allowed in the Apostolic age to be present at times in the Christian assemblies[5]; and in Cyril's days they stood in the lower part of the Church (*νάρθηξ*) to hear the Psalms, Lessons, and Sermon[6].

Any persons who by thus hearing the word, or by other means, were brought to believe in the truth of Christianity, and to wish for further instruction, were strictly examined as to their character, belief, and sincerity of purpose. The care with which such examinations were conducted is thus described by Origen: "The Christians, however, having previously, so far as possible, tested the souls of those who wish to become their hearers, and having previously admonished them in private, when they seem, before entering the community, to have made sufficient progress in the desire to lead a virtuous life, they then introduce them, having privately formed one class of those who are just beginners, and are being introduced, and have not yet received the mark of complete purification; and another of those who have manifested to the best of their ability the purpose of desiring no other things than are approved by Christians[7]." Such as were thus found worthy of admission were brought to the Bishop or Presbyter, and received by the sign of the Cross[8], with prayer and imposition of hands, to the status of Catechumens.

We have a description by Eusebius[9] of some of these ceremonies in the case of Constantine: When the Emperor felt his life to be drawing to a close, "he poured forth his supplications and confessions to God, kneeling on the pavement in the Church itself, in which he also now for the first time received the imposition of hands with prayer." Soon after this the Bishops whom he had summoned to Nicomedia to give him Baptism, "performed the sacred ceremonies in the usual manner, and having given him the necessary instructions made him a partaker of the mystic ordinances."

Another ceremony used in the admission of Catechumens, at least in some Churches, is mentioned by S. Augustine[1]: "Sanctification is not of one kind only: for I suppose that Catechumens also are sanctified in a certain way of their own by the sign of Christ's Cross, and the Prayer of the Imposition of Hands; and that which they receive, though it be not the Body of Christ, is yet an holy thing, and more holy than the common food which sustains us, because it is a sacrament." From this passage it has been inferred that *consecrated bread*

3 *Antiq.* X. i. § 4.

4 Mark xvi. 16; Acts xviii. 8.

5 1 Cor. xiv. 23.

6 *Apostolic Constitutions*, VIII. i. § 5: "And after the reading of the Law and the Prophets, and our Epistles, and Acts, and Gospels, let him that is ordained . . . speak to the people the word of exhortation, and when he has ended his discourse of doctrine, all standing up, let the Deacon ascend upon some high seat, and proclaim, Let none of the hearers, let none of the *unbelievers* stay: and silence being made, let him say, Ye *Catechumens*, pray, and let all the *Faithful* pray for them."

7 *Contra Celsum*, iii. c. 51. Cf. *Const. Apost.* viii. 32: "Let them be examined as to the causes wherefore they come to the word of the Lord, and let those who bring them inquire exactly about their character, and give them their testimony. Let their manners and their life be inquired into, and whether they be slaves or free,' &c.

8 S. Aug. *De Symbolo, Serm. ad Catechumenos*, § 1: "Ye have not yet been born again by holy Baptism, but by the sign of the Cross ye have been already conceived in the womb of your mother the Church."

9 *Vita Const.* iv. c. 60.

1 *De Peccatorum meritis*, ii. 42.

(εὐλογίαι, *panis benedictus*), taken out of the oblations provided for the Eucharist, was given to the Catechumens,—an opinion which seemed to have some support in the comparison between "that which the Catechumens receive," and "the food which sustains us." But Bingham maintains[2] that S. Augustine here refers only to the symbolical use of salt, of which he says in his *Confessions*, I. xi., that while yet a boy he "used to be marked with the sign of His Cross, and seasoned with His salt." The meaning of this so-called "Sacrament of the Catechumens" was that by the symbol of salt "they might learn to purge and cleanse their souls from sin."

In the African Church in the time of S. Augustine it was customary to anoint the new convert with exorcised oil at the time of his admission, but in the Eastern Church there seems to have been no such anointing until immediately before Baptism.

Persons who had been thus admitted to the class of Catechumens were usually regarded as Christians, but only in a lower degree, being still clearly distinguished from the Faithful. "Ask a man, Art thou a Christian? If he is a Pagan or a Jew, he answers, I am not. But if he say, I am, you ask him further, Catechumen or Faithful? If he answer, Catechumen, he has been anointed, but not yet baptized[3]." Augustine, like Tertullian, complains that among heretics there was no sure distinction between the Catechumen and the Faithful[4]: and according to the second General Council, *Canon* 7, converts from certain heresies to the orthodox Faith were to be received only as heathen: "On the first day we make them Christians, on the second Catechumens, on the third we exorcise them by three times breathing on them on the face and on the ears; and so we instruct them (κατηχοῦμεν), and make them frequent the Church for a long time, and listen to the Holy Scriptures, and then we baptize them."

Whether Cyril calls his hearers Christians before they had been baptized is not very clear: in *Cat.* x. § 16, he seems to include them among those who are called by the "new name;" but in § 20 of the same Lecture he assumes that there may be present some one who "was before a believer (πιστός)," and to him he says "Thou wert called a Christian; be tender of the name;" and in Lect. xxi. 1, speaking to those who had now been baptized, he says, "Having therefore become *partakers of Christ*, ye are properly called Christs. Now ye have been made Christs by receiving the antitype of the Holy Ghost," that is, Chrism.

§ 4. *Candidates for Baptism.* Bingham, who himself makes four classes or degrees of Catechumens, acknowledges that "the Greek expositors of the ancient Canons," and other writers, "usually make but two sorts[5]." These were (1) the *imperfect* (ἀτελέστεροι), called also *hearers* (ἀκροώμενοι, *audientes*), because in Church they were only allowed to remain till the Holy Scriptures had been read, the Sermon preached, the special prayers of the Catechumens said, and the blessing given to each by the Bishop in the words of the "prayer of the imposition of hands[6]." After this the Deacon says, "Go out, ye Catechumens, in peace." (2) After the Energumens also have been dismissed, *the more perfect* (τελειότεροι, φωτιζόμενοι) remain on their knees in prayer (γονυκλίνοντες, εὐχόμενοι). Then the Deacon is to cry aloud, "Ye that are to be illuminated, pray. Let us the faithful all pray for them. And being sealed to God through His Christ, let them bow down their heads, and receive the blessing from the Bishop." The "Prayer of the Imposition of hands" is then pronounced over them by the Bishop.

The period of probation and instruction varied at different times and places: according to Canon 42 of the Synod of Elvira, 305, it was to be two years: "He who has a good name,

---

[2] *Antiq.* X. ii. § 16.

[3] S. August. *In Joh. Evang. Tract.* xliv. § 2.

[4] *Serm.* xlvi. *de Pastoribus*, c. 13: Tertull. *de Præscriptione Hæret.* c. 41: "Imprimis quis Catechumenus, quis Fidelis, incertum est."

[5] *Ant.* X. ii. 1—5. The Council of Nicæa, Canon xiv., seems to speak only of two classes.

[6] *Const. Apost.* viii. § 6.

and wishes to become a Christian, must be a Catechumen two years: then he may be baptized[7]." After this probation had been satisfactorily passed, the Catechumens were invited to give in their names as Candidates for Baptism. This invitation, described by Cyril as a call to military service (*κλῆσις στρατείας*)[8], appears to have been often repeated on the approach of Lent. Thus S. Ambrose, in his *Commentary on S. Luke*, v. 5; *We have toiled all night and have taken nothing*, complains, "I too, Lord, know that for me it is night, when I have not Thy command. No one yet has given his name: with my voice I have cast the net throughout Epiphany, and as yet I have taken nothing."

This preliminary "call to service" must be distinguished from the actual enlistment in the Christian army at Baptism, in anticipation of which Cyril prays for his hearers that God "may enlist them in His service, and put on them the armour of righteousness[9]." The same metaphorical language in reference to the Christian warfare recurs in many passages[1].

The next step for those who responded to the call was the registration of names (ὀνοματογραφία)[2]. It appears from passages of Dionysius Pseudo-Areopagites, quoted by Bingham[3], that the Bishop, after laying his hand on each Catechumen's head, commanded his Presbyters and Deacons to register his name, together with that of his sponsor (ἀνάδοχος) in the Diptychs of the living. This ceremony took place at Jerusalem at the beginning of Lent, as we learn from *Procat.* § 1: "Thou hast entered, been approved; thy name inscribed. . . . A long notice is allowed thee; thou hast forty days for repentance." Those who had been admitted as candidates for Baptism were in most Churches still reckoned among the Catechumens, being distinguished as *συναιτοῦντες*, "*competentes*." But from Cyril's language in several passages it appears that in the Church of Jerusalem they ceased to be regarded as Catechumens, and were reckoned among the Faithful. "Thou wert called a Catechumen, while the word echoed round thee from without. Think not that thou receivest a small thing: though a miserable man, thou receivest one of God's titles. Hear S. Paul saying, *God is faithful.* But beware, lest thou have the title of '*faithful*,' but the will of the faithless[4]." "Thou receivest a new name which thou hadst not before. Heretofore thou wast a Catechumen, but now thou wilt be called a Believer (Πιστός)[5]."

Again, "How great a dignity the Lord bestows on you in transferring you from the order of Catechumens to that of the Faithful, the Apostle Paul shews, when he affirms, *God is faithful*[6]."

Two passages in S. Cyril have been thought to imply that the newly-admitted Candidates for Baptism carried lighted torches in procession, perhaps on the first Sunday after the registration. He speaks of their having received "torches of the bridal procession[7];" and on this expression the Benedictine Editor observes that "Wax tapers" were perhaps given to the *Illuminandi* to carry, a custom which may also be indicated in the words, "Ye who have lately lighted the torches of faith, guard them carefully in your hands unquenched[8]."

Others are of opinion that the custom of carrying torches or tapers was observed only in the procession of the newly-baptized from the Baptistery to the Church[9], and that here Cyril means by the "bridal lamps," those motions of the Holy Ghost, and spiritual instructions, which had lighted their way to Christ, and to the entrance to His Kingdom[10]. This latter interpretation is rather vague and far-fetched, and it is evident that the words, "Ye who have lately lighted the torches of faith," gain much in clearness and force, if suggested by the visible symbolism of a ceremony in which the *Illuminandi* had just borne their part. The

7 Hefele, *Councils*, i. p. 155. *Const. Apost.* viii. 32: "Let him that is to be instructed be a catechumen three years."
8 *Procat.* § 1. 9 Ib. § 17. 1 See Cat. i. 3; iii. 3, 13; iv. 36; xvii. 36; xxi. 4. 2 *Procat.* § 1. 3 *Antiq.* X. ii. § 6.
4 *Procat.* § 6. 5 Cat. i. 4. 6 Ib. v. 1. 7 λαμπάδες νυμφαγωγίας, *Procat.* § 1. 8 Cat. i. § 1.
9 Bingham, *Ant.* X. ii. § 15. 10 *Dict. Chr. Antiq.* Vol. ii. p. 995, note.

lighted torches would be a significant symbol both of the marriage of the soul with Christ, and of its enlightenment by faith.

§ 5. Φωτιζόμενοι. In the first words of his Introductory Lecture Cyril addresses his hearers as *οἱ φωτιζόμενοι*, "Ye who are being enlightened," and from the Titles of the Catechetical Lectures i.-xviii., we see that this name was constantly used to distinguish the candidates preparing for immediate Baptism.

The Verb *φωτίζω* is frequently used by the LXX., both in a physical and in a spiritual sense. In the New Testament it is found but rarely in the physical sense [1], being generally applied to the light of spiritual truth, and to Christ as its source [2].

In two passages of the Epistle to the Hebrews, the Aorist (*φωτισθέντας*) marks "the decisive moment when the light was apprehended in its glory [3]," from which the thought easily passes on to the public profession of the truth thus received, that is, to Baptism.

That the word began very early to be used in this new sense, is evident from Justin Martyr's explanation of it in his *First Apology*, c. 61; where, after speaking of instruction in Christian doctrine, of the profession of faith, and the promise of repentance and holy living, as the necessary preparations for Baptism, he thus proceeds: "And this washing is called Illumination (*φωτισμός*), because they who learn these things are illuminated in their understanding [4]." The same transition of the meaning from instruction to Baptism is clearly implied by Clement of Alexandria: "Among the barbarian philosophers also to instruct and to enlighten is called to regenerate [5];" and again: "For this reason the teaching, which made manifest the hidden things, has been called illumination (*φωτισμός*) [6]."

That this is the sense in which Cyril uses the word is placed beyond doubt by a passage of the Lecture delivered immediately before the administration of Baptism: "that your soul being *previously illuminated* (*προφωτιζομένης*) by the word of doctrine, ye may in each particular discover the greatness of the gifts bestowed on you by God [7]."

We thus see that the Present Participle (*φωτιζόμενοι*) describes a process of gradual illumination during the course of instruction, to be completed in Baptism, a sense which is well expressed in the Latin Gerundive "Illuminandi." And as we have seen that the candidates are addressed as *οἱ φωτιζόμενοι* even before the course of instruction has commenced, the quasi-Future sense "follows necessarily from the context [8]."

The spiritual "Illumination," of which Baptism was to be the completion and the seal, thus became by a natural development one of the recognised names of Baptism itself. On the contrary, the inverse process assumed by the Benedictine Editor is entirely unnatural. Starting from the later ecclesiastical use of *φωτίζω* and *φωτισμός* as connoting Baptism, he supposes that this was the first application of those terms, and that they were transferred to the previous illumination acquired by instruction in Christian truth, only because this was a necessary preparation for Baptism. He therefore maintains that *φωτιζόμενοι* throughout the Catechetical Lectures is another term for *βαπτιζόμενοι*: and as a decisive proof of this he refers to *Cat.* xvi. 26: *μέλλει δὲ καὶ ἐπὶ σὲ τὸν βαπτιζόμενον φθάνειν ἡ χάρις*, not observing that the grace is to come upon "the person being baptized" at a time still future. This meaning of the passage is made absolutely certain by the words which immediately follow,—"But in what manner I say not, for I will not anticipate the proper season." We may conclude, therefore, that in Cyril's Lectures the term *οἱ φωτιζόμενοι* refers to the preparatory course of enlightenment rather than to Baptism. At the same time we must remember that in Cyril's day, and long before, *φωτίζω*, *φωτισμός*, and *φώτισμα* were constantly used to denote Baptism

---

1 Luke xi. 36; Apoc. xviii. 1. 2 Joh. i. 9; 1 Cor. iv. 5; 2 Cor. iv. 4, 6; Eph. i. 18; iii. 9; 2 Tim. i. 10; Apoc. xxi. 23; xxii. 5.
3 Westcott, "*Hebrews*," vi. 4; x. 32.
4 ὡς φωτιζομένων τὴν διάνοιαν τῶν ταῦτα μανθανόντων.
5 *Strom.* V.c. 2, § 15: τὸ κατηχῆσαί τε καὶ φωτίσαι ἀναγεννῆσαι λέγεται.
6 *Strom.* V. c. x. § 65. Cf. V. c. viii. § 49.
7 Cat. xviii. § 32.
8 Cf. Winer, *Grammar of N.T. Greek*, Sect xl. 22, note 3.

itself, as being the time of special illumination by the grace of the Holy Spirit then given. Thus Clement of Alexandria writes: "In Baptism we are illuminated. . . . This work is variously called grace, and illumination (φώτισμα), and perfection, and washing: . . . illumination, by which that holy light of salvation is beheld, that is, by which we see God clearly [9]." Gregory Nazianzen speaks in the same way: "We call it gift, grace, baptism, chrism, illumination, garment of incorruption, washing of regeneration, seal, all that is precious [10]."

CHAPTER III.

Special Preparation for Baptism.

§ 1. *Penitence.* The candidate for Baptism, having been duly admitted and registered, was required not only to be diligent in attending the course of Catechetical instruction [1], but also to enter at once upon a course of strict devotion and penitential discipline. "Those who are coming to Baptism," says Tertullian, "must be constantly engaged in prayers, fastings, kneelings, and watchings, together with confession of all past faults [2]."

On these subjects Cyril's teaching is earnest, wise, and sympathetic: he seeks to lead to repentance by gentle persuasion, and pleads for self-discipline as needful for the good of the soul [3]. One whole Lecture is devoted to the necessity of thorough repentance for all past sins, and forgiveness of all offences [4]: another to the sure efficacy of repentance for the remission of sins [5].

§ 2. *Confession.* 'Εξομολόγησις. Great stress is laid by Cyril on the necessity not only of sincere inward repentance, but also of open confession. The words ἐξομολογεῖσθαι, ἐξομολόγησις have a twofold meaning and a wide application.

(1.) In the Septuagint they occur very frequently, especially in the Psalms, in the sense of "giving thanks or praise" (Heb. הודה) [6], a meaning which is also found in the New Testament [7]. Perhaps the earliest instance in an Ecclesiastical writer is in Hermas, *Mandat.* X. iii. 2: ἐξομολογούμενος τῷ Θεῷ. I have not found any instance of this meaning in Cyril.

S. Chrysostom, commenting on the words, "*I will give thanks unto Thee, O Lord* [8]," says, "There are two kinds of *exomologesis;* for it is either a condemnation of our own sins, or a giving of thanks to God." The link between these two ideas is seen in Joshua's exhortation to Achan, *My son, give, I pray thee, glory to the Lord, the God of Israel, and make confession* [9] *unto Him.* R. V. Margin. Or, *give praise.*

(2.) In the sense of "confessing" sins, the Verb is not uncommon in the N. T. [1], and in the early Fathers [2]. Tertullian adopts the Greek word, and calls *exomologesis* "the handmaid of repentance [3]," adding that it will extinguish the fire of Gehenna in the heart, being a second remedy for sin, after Baptism.

Again, speaking of the outward act of repentance, he says: "This act, which is more usually expressed and commonly spoken of under a Greek name, is ἐξομολόγησις, whereby we confess our sins to the Lord, not indeed as if He were ignorant of them, but inasmuch as by confession satisfaction is appointed, and of confession repentance is born, and God appeared by repentance. Accordingly *exomologesis* is a discipline for man's prostration and humiliation, enjoining a demeanour calculated to move mercy. With regard also to the very dress and food, it commands (the penitent) to lie in sackcloth and ashes . . . to know no food and drink but such

---

9 *Pædag.* I. vi. § 25. (Syllb. 41). 10 *Orat.* xl. § 4.

1 *Procat.* § 9: "Let thy feet haste to the Catechisings," § 10: "Abide thou in the Catechisings: though our discourse be long, let not thy mind be wearied out." Cf. Cat. i. 5.

2 *De Baptismo,* c. 20. Cf. Justin M. *Apol.* I. c. 61; *Const. Apost.* vii. 22.

3 Compare his teaching on Prayer, *Procat.* § 16; Cat. ix. 7: and on Fasting Cat. iv. 27, 37; xviii. 17.

4 Cat. i. 5 Cat. ii.

6 Ps. xlii. 5; xliii. 4, 5 (ἐξομολογήσομαι); and Ps. c. 4 (ἐν ἐξομολογήσει). 7 Matt. xi. 25; Phil. ii. 11.

8 Ps. ix. 1: 'Εξομολογήσομαί σοι, Κύριε.

9 Joshua vii. 19, Sept. ἐξομολόγησιν.

1 Matt. iii. 6; Mark i. 5; James iii. 16.

2 Irenæus, I. xiii. § 5; III. iv. § 3; Clem. Alex. *Protrept.* ii § 41: ἐξομολογοῦνται οἱ δαίμονες τὴν γαστριμαργίαν τὴν αὐτῶν.

3 *De Pænitentia,* c. xii.

as is plain,—to feed prayers on fastings, to groan, to weep and roar (*mugire*) unto the Lord God; to roll before the feet of the presbyters, and kneel to God's dear ones, to enjoin on all the brethren embassies of intercession on his behalf. All this *exomologesis* does, that it may enhance repentance[4], &c."

In this highly rhetorical description of the ecclesiastical discipline so dear to Tertullian there are many features of extreme severity to which Cyril makes no allusion; yet he frequently and very earnestly insists on the necessity and the efficacy of confession. "The present is the season of confession: confess what thou hast done in word or in deed, by night or by day; confess *in an acceptable time, and in the day of salvation* receive the heavenly treasure[5]." "Tell the Physician thine ailment: say thou also, like David, *I said, I will confess me my sin unto the LORD;* and the same shall be done in thy case, which he says forthwith, *and Thou forgavest the wickedness of my heart*[6]." "Seest thou the humility of the king? Seest thou his confession? . . . . The deed was quickly done, and straightway the Prophet appeared as accuser, and the offender confessed his fault; and because he candidly confessed, he received a most speedy cure[7]."

"Ezekias prevailed to the cancelling of God's decree, and cannot Jesus grant remission of sins? Turn and bewail thyself, shut thy door, and pray to be forgiven, pray that He may remove from thee the burning flames. For confession has power to quench even fire, power to tame even lions[8]."

The confession to which Cyril attaches so high a value, whether made in the privacy of solitude, or openly before the Ministers of the Church and the Congregation, is a confession to God, and not to man. "Having therefore, brethren, many examples of those who have sinned and repented and been saved, do ye also heartily make confession unto the Lord[9]." Elsewhere he expressly disclaims the necessity of private confession to man: "Not that thou shouldest shew thy conscience to me, for thou art not to *be judged of man's judgment;* but that thou shew the sincerity of thy faith to God, *who trieth the reins and hearts,* and *knoweth the thoughts of men*[1]." He also limits the season of confession and repentance to this present life: "Therefore the just shall then offer praise; but they who have died in sins have no further season for confession[2]."

§ 3. *Exorcism.* One of the earliest ceremonies, after the registration of names, was Exorcism, which seems to have been often repeated during the Candidate's course of preparation. "Receive with earnestness the exorcisms: whether thou be breathed upon or exorcised, the act is to thee salvation[3]."

The power of casting out devils, promised by our Lord[4], and exercised by Apostles[5], and by Philip the Deacon and Evangelist[6], was long regarded in the early Church as a direct gift still bestowed by the Holy Ghost, apart from any human ordinance. Justin Martyr[7], Tertullian[8], Origen[9], all speak of exorcism as being practised by laymen, even by soldiers, and women, by means of prayer and invocation of the name of Jesus. Accordingly "an Exorcist is not ordained, for it is a gift of the spontaneous benevolence and grace of God through Christ by visitation of the Holy Ghost. For he who has received the gift of healing is declared by revelation from God, the grace which is in him being manifest to all[1]." When the extraordinary gift was found to have been withdrawn, exorcists are mentioned among the inferior officers of the Church, after readers and subdeacons[2]. From an early period certain set formulæ, such as the Divine names, "The God of Abraham, and God of Isaac, and God

4 *De Pœnitentia*, c. ix. 5 Cat. i. § 5. 6 Ib § 6. 7 Ib. § 11. 8 Cat. ii. 15. For similar statements, see Cat. i. 2; ii. 19, 20, &c. 9 Cat. ii. § 20. 1 Ib. v. § 2. 2 Ib. xviii. 14. 3 *Procat.* § 9. 4 Mark xvi. 17; Luke ix. 1; x. 17. 5 Acts v. 16; xvi. 18; xix. 12. 6 Acts viii. 7.

7 *Apologia* I. §§ 6, 8; *Tryph.* lxxxv. 8 *De Idolol.* c. xi.; *de Corona Mil.* xi.; *de Anima*, lvii. *de Spectac.* xxvi.; *de Præscript. Hæret.* xli. 9 *Contra Celsum.* vii. c. 57. 1 *Const. Apost.* viii. 26. 2 Euseb. *H.E.* vi. 43; Syn. Antioch. in Encæniis, Can. 10: Syn. Laod. Can. 24.

of Jacob," "The God of Israel," "The God who drowned the king of Egypt and the Egyptians in the Red Sea," were frequently invoked against demons and certain wicked persons [3].

Accordingly, when an exorcist was ordained the Bishop was directed to give him the book in which the exorcisms were written, with the words, "Receive thou these, and commit them to memory, and have thou power to lay hands upon the Energumens, whether they be baptized or only Catechumens [4]." Though this Canon speaks only of exorcising Energumens, or such persons as were supposed to be possessed by evil spirits, we must remember that the power of such spirits was believed to extend to the whole world outside the Christian Church. Thus all converts from Paganism and Judaism, and even the children of Christian parents were exorcised before being baptized. The practice was closely connected with the doctrine of original sin, as we see in many passages of S. Augustine, and is declared by him to be very ancient and universal [5]. In expounding the Creed to candidates for Baptism, he says: "Therefore, as you have seen this day, and as you know, even little children are breathed on and exorcised, that the hostile power of the devil may be driven out of them, which deceived one man in order that he might get possession of all men [6]."

We find accordingly that Cyril enforces the duty of attending the Exorcisms on all the candidates alike, and from his use of the Plural (Exorcisms) we see that the ceremony was often repeated for each person. Thus in the Clementine Homilies Peter is represented as saying, "Whoever of you wish to be baptized, begin from to-morrow to fast, and each day have hands laid upon you [7]," the imposition of hands being one of the ceremonies used in exorcism [8]. From expressions in the Introductory Lecture, "When ye have come in before the hour of the exorcisms [9]," and again, "when your exorcism has been done, until the others who are to be exorcised have come [1]," it seems that before each Catechizing the candidates were all exorcised, one by one [2], and that the earlier, after returning from their own exorcism, had to wait for those who came later. The catechizing was thus frequently delayed till late in the day, and Cyril often complains of the shortness of the time left at his disposal [3].

At Antioch, the Catechizing preceded the Exorcism, as we learn from S. Chrysostom: "After you have heard our instruction, they take off your sandals, and unclothe you, and send you on naked and barefoot, with your tunic only, to the utterances of the Exorcists [4]." Cyril says nothing of this unclothing, but mentions another ceremony as practised at Jerusalem: "Thy face has been veiled, that thy mind may henceforward be free, lest the eye by roving make the heart rove also. But when thine eyes are veiled, thine ears are not hindered from receiving the means of salvation [5]." The veil may also have been a symbol of the slavery and darkness of sin, as S. Augustine regards the removal of the veil on the octave of Easter as symbolising the spiritual liberty of the baptized [6]. Of this meaning Cyril makes no express mention.

In the Greek Euchologion, as quoted by Kleopas, the act of the Exorcist is thus described: "And the Priest breathes upon his mouth, his forehead, and his breast, saying, Drive forth from him every evil and unclean spirit, hidden and lurking in his heart, the spirit of error, the spirit of wickedness [7], &c."

---

3 Origen. *Contra Cels.* iv. c. 34 (p. 184).

4 Fourth Council of Carthage, *Can.* 7 (A D. 398).

5 *De Nupt. et Concup.* II. § 33: *de Pecc. Orig.* § 45; *contra Julian Pelag.* VI. § 11; *Op. Imperf. c. Julian.* I. § 50; III. § 144, &c.

6 *De Symbolo*, § 2. Cf. Cat. xx. (*Myst.* ii.) § 2.

7 *Hom.* iii. c. 73.

8 Orig. in Josu. xxiv. § 1: "exorcistarum manus impositione."

9 *Procat.* § 13.

1 Ib. § 14.

2 Aug. *Sermo de Symb.* ii. § 1: "ut ex locis secretis singuli produceremini." This may possibly refer only to the final exorcism immediately before Baptism.

3 Cat. xiii. 8: xv. 33; xviii. 16, &c.

4 *Ad Illuminandos*, Cat. i. § 2.

5 *Procat.* § 9.

6 S. Aug. *Serm.* 376. "Hodie octavæ dicuntur Infantium; revelanda sunt capita eorum, quod est indicium libertatis. Habet enim libertatem ista spiritualis nativitas, propriæ autem carnis nativitas servitutem."

7 *Procat.* § 14.

Besides such invocations of the names of God, as we have mentioned above, the Exorcist used set forms of prayer "collected out of the Holy Scriptures." Their effect, as described by Cyril, is to "set the soul, as it were, on fire," and scare the evil spirit away; and his meaning may be illustrated by a passage of Tertullian, who says[8]: "All the authority and power we have over them is from naming the name of Christ, and recalling to their memory the woes with which God threatens them at the hands of Christ as Judge. . . . So at our touch and breathing, overwhelmed by the thought of those judgment-fires, they leave the bodies they have entered, at our command, unwilling and distressed, and before your very eyes put to an open shame."

The Exorcisms were performed in the Church; where also the Lectures were delivered, Catechumens of the lower order being excluded, "and the doors looking towards the city closed[9], while those which looked towards the Holy Sepulchre, from which the ruins of the ancient Temple, Golgotha, and the old city could be seen, were left open[10]."

CHAPTER IV.

Ceremonies of Baptism and Chrism.

§ 1. *Renunciation.* We have seen that Cyril's last Catechetical Lecture was delivered in the early dawn of the Great Sabbath, Easter Eve. The additional instructions then promised[1] concerning the behaviour of the Candidates were given on the same day, probably in the evening, when they were all assembled immediately before the administration of Baptism. The most important parts of the Baptismal ceremony are described by Cyril in the first Mystagogic Lecture, delivered on the Monday of Easter week. Thus in § 1 he says, "Let us now teach you these things exactly, that ye may know the significance of the things done to you on that evening of your Baptism."

The first act was the renunciation of the Devil and all his works. This, as described by Tertullian, was done first in the Church "under the hand of the Bishop," and again immediately before entering the water[1a]. Cyril speaks of the latter occasion only. "First ye entered into the outer chamber of the Baptistery, and there facing towards the West (as the region of darkness) ye heard the command to stretch forth your hand, and as in the presence of Satan to renounce him[2]." For the formula of renunciation in the Apostolical Constitutions, see note 2 on *Mystag.* i. § 8; it corresponds closely with Cyril's, except that this is addressed to Satan as if personally present: "I renounce thee, Satan[3], and all thy works[4], and all thy pomp[5], and all thy worship[6]."

§ 2. *Profession of Faith.* After the renunciation of Satan the Candidate immediately turned to the East and said, "And I associate myself (συντάσσομαι) with Christ." Cyril does not give the words, but seems to allude to the custom, when he speaks of the Candidates "turning from the West to the East, the place of light[7]."

Then, still facing the East, the Candidate was bidden to say, "I believe in the Father, and in the Son, and in the Holy Ghost, and in one Baptism of repentance[8]." We have seen that in Cat. xviii. 22, 32, Cyril intimated to his Candidates that they would be required to profess publicly the Creed which he had delivered to them and which they had repeated after him. This public profession of faith (ὁμολογία, "Redditio Symboli") was in some Churches made on Holy Thursday, according to Canon 46 of the Synod of Laodicea: "Those to be baptized must learn the Creed by heart, and recite it to the Bishop or

8 *Apologet.* c. 23. 9 *Procat.* § 9. 10 Cat. xiii. 23: "Thou seest this spot of Golgotha? Thou answerest with a shout of praise, as if assenting." 1 Cat. xviii. § 32. 1a *De Cor. Mil.* c. 3.

2 *Myst.* i. § 2. 3 § 4. 4 § 5. 5 § 6. 6 § 8. 7 § 9, note 3.

8 Compare xviii. 22: "One Baptism of repentance for the remission of sins."

Presbyters on the fifth day of the week." But in the *Apostolic Constitutions*, c. xli., the Candidate is required to recite the whole Creed immediately after the Renunciation: "And after his renunciation let him in his consociation (συνταασσόμενος) say: 'And I associate myself to Christ, and believe and am baptized into One Unbegotten Being, the Only True God Almighty, the Father of Christ, ... and into the Lord Jesus Christ . . . . and I am baptized into the Holy Ghost, ... into the resurrection of the flesh, and into the remission of sins, and into the kingdom of heaven, and into the life of the world to come.' And after this vow, he comes in order to the anointing with oil."

Such appears to have been the custom of the Eastern Churches in general and of Jerusalem in Cyril's time, although he mentions only those articles of the Creed which were commonly held to be indispensable to a valid profession of Christian belief.

Dr. Swainson[9] represents the matter somewhat differently: "When we come to the profession of his own personal faith which was made at Jerusalem by the Candidate for Baptism, we find that this was far briefer not only than the collection of 'necessary things' (Cat. iv.), but also than the Creed of the Church of Jerusalem." Then after quoting the short form in Cyril, *Myst.* i. § 9, "I believe in the Father, and in the Son, and in the Holy Ghost, and in one Baptism of repentance," Dr. Swainson adds: "The words are clear and definite. In these words each answered the question of which we read elsewhere, 'Did he believe in the name of the Father, and the Son, and the Holy Spirit?' In this his reply the Candidate 'confessed' what Cyril called 'the saving confession.'"

It is evident that two separate parts of the Baptismal Service are here confused: the question to which Dr. Swainson alludes, and "the saving confession" of which Cyril speaks in *Mystag.* ii. § 4, belong, as we shall presently see, to a later stage of the ceremony.

§ 3. *First Unction.* On passing from the outer to the inner chamber of the Baptistery, the Candidate who had made his renunciation and profession barefoot and wearing his tunic (Χιτών)[1] only, now put off this inner garment also, as an emblem of putting off the old man with his deeds[2]. A further significance is ascribed by Cyril to this unclothing of the Candidate, as being an imitation both of Christ, who hung naked[3] on the Cross, and by His nakedness *put off from Himself the principalities and the powers*, and "of the first-formed Adam, who was naked in the garden, and was not ashamed."

"Then, when ye were stripped, ye were anointed with exorcised oil, from the very hairs of your head to your feet[3a]." The consecration of the "exorcised oil" is thus described[4]: "Now this is blessed by the chief-priest for the remission of sins, and the first preparation for Baptism. For he calls thus upon the Unbegotten God, the Father of Christ, the King of all sensible and intelligent natures, that He would sanctify the oil in the name of the Lord Jesus, and impart to it spiritual grace and efficacious strength, the remission of sins, and the first preparation for the confession of Baptism, that so the Candidate for Baptism, when he is anointed may be freed from all ungodliness, and may become worthy of initiation, according to the command of the Only-begotten."

Bingham's observation, that Cyril describes this first unction as used "between the renunciation and the confession[5]" is not quite accurate: in fact it came between two confessions, the one made, as we have seen, immediately after the renunciation in the outer

9 *Creeds of the Church*, p. 17.

1 Pseudo-Dionysius Areopag. *Eccl. Hierarch.* iii.

2 *Mystag.* ii. § 2.

3 This passage has recently (1891) acquired a special interest from the controversy concerning Mr. Calderon's picture, representing St. Elisabeth of Hungary as kneeling naked before the altar. The word "naked" (γυμνός, nudus) is not in itself decisive, but here in St. Cyril's account of Baptism absolute nakedness seems to be implied; for though women sometimes wore an under-tunic (χιτώνιον), men had nothing beneath the tunic proper (χιτών), which is here said to be put off. According to Theophylact, on Matt. v. 40, the chiton was properly τὸ παρ' ἡμῖν λεγόμενον ὑποκάμισοε. See *Dictionary of Biblical Antiquities*, "Baptism," § 48.

3a Ib. § 3.

4 *Const. Apost.* vii. c. 42.

5 *Ant.* XI. c. 9, § 1.

chamber, the other at the very time of immersion. Chrysostom[6] clearly distinguishes two Confessions, but places one before Baptism, and the other after: "What can be more beautiful than the words by which we renounce the devil? Or those by which we associate ourselves with Christ? Than that confession which comes before the washing? Or that which comes after the washing?"

This first unction is not mentioned by Tertullian, nor in any genuine work of Justin Martyr, but in the *Responsiones ad Orthodoxos*, a work which though still early is regarded as certainly spurious, we find the question put, "Why are we first anointed with oil, and then, having performed the before-mentioned symbolic acts in the Laver, are afterwards sealed with the ointment, and do not regard this as done in opposition to what took place in our Lord's case, who was first anointed with ointment and then suffered[7]?" And in the answer it is stated that "We are anointed with the simple oil that we may be made Christs (Χριστοί), but with the ointment in remembrance of our Saviour Christ, who regarded the anointing with ointment as His burial, and called us to the fellowship of His own sufferings and glory, typically in the present life but truly in the life to come."

Cyril attributes to this "exorcised oil" the same power as to Exorcism itself, "not only to burn and cleanse away the traces of sin, but also to chase away all the invisible powers of the evil one[8]."

According to the directions concerning this first unction in the *Apostolical Constitutions*[9], the Bishop was first to anoint the head only, the anointing of the whole body being then completed by the Deacon or Deaconess.

§ 4. *Baptism.* After this anointing the Candidates were "led by the hand to the sacred pool of Holy Baptism[1]." This pool (κολυμβήθρα) was supplied with water raised from the reservoirs, of which, as we shall see, the Bordeaux Pilgrim speaks in his description of the Basilica.

As great multitudes both of men and women were baptized at the special seasons, the Baptisteries were large buildings outside the Church, such as the Baptistery of the Lateran, said to have been originally built by Constantine. The font itself also was large enough for several persons to be baptized at the same time. In some places the men were baptized first, and then the women: in others different parts of the Baptistery were assigned to them, and curtains were hung across the Font itself[2].

The consecration of the water is not mentioned in the Didache or Justin Martyr; but Tertullian thus describes its effect: "The waters after invocation of God acquire the sacramental power of sanctification; for immediately the Spirit comes down from heaven upon the waters, and rests upon them, sanctifying them from Himself, and they being thus sanctified imbibe a power of sanctifying[3]."

In the prayer of consecration given in the *Apostolic Constitutions* the Bishop is directed first to offer adoration and thanksgiving to the Father and Son, and then to call upon the Father and say: "Look down from heaven, and sanctify this water, and give it grace and power, that so he that is to be baptized, according to the command of Thy Christ, may be crucified with Him, and may die with Him, and may be buried with Him, and may rise with Him to the adoption which is in Him, that he may be dead to sin, and live to righteousness[4]."

Cyril ascribes the like effect to the consecration of the water, as imparting to it a new power of holiness by "the invocation of the Holy Ghost, and of Christ, and of the Father[5]."

While standing in the water the Candidate made what Cyril calls "the saving con-

6 *Ephes.* i. Hom. i. § 3. 7 *Quæstio* 137. 8 *Mystag.* ii. § 3. 9 Lib. iii. c. 15.
1 *Mystag.* ii. § 4. 2 Bingham, *Ant.* VIII. c. 7, § 2; XI. c. 11, § 3. 3 *De Baptismo*, c. iv.
4 VII. c. 43. 5 Cat. iii. § 3. See also Introduction, ch. vi. § 2.

fession[6]." The whole Creed having been already recited (*Redditio Symboli*) in the outer chamber immediately after the Renunciation, a short form was now employed containing only the necessary declaration of faith in the Holy Trinity, and in the Baptism of Repentance for the remission of sins.

§ 5. *Trine Immersion.* This short confession appears to have been made by way of question and answer thrice repeated. "Thou wast asked, Dost thou believe in God the Father Almighty? Thou saidst, I believe, and dippedst thyself, that is, wast buried. Again thou wast asked, Dost thou believe in our Lord Jesus Christ and in His Cross? Thou saidst, I believe, and dippedst thyself; therefore thou wast buried with Christ also: for he who is buried with Christ, rises again with Christ. A third time thou wast asked, Dost thou believe also in the Holy Ghost? Thou saidst, I believe, a third time thou dippedst thyself; that the threefold confession might absolve the manifold fault of thy former life[7]." But Cyril of Alexandria, as quoted by Bingham[8], "makes these answers not only to be a confession of the three Persons of the Trinity, but a triple confession of Christ; which implies a repetition of the Creed (the shortened form?) three times over."

In which of these ways the threefold interrogation ("usitata et legitima verba interrogationis") was made at Jerusalem, is not quite certain from Cyril's words: "Each was asked, Dost thou believe in the name of the Father, and of the Son, and of the Holy Ghost, and ye made that saving confession, and went down thrice into the water[9]." The Didaché[1] enjoins baptism simply into the names of the Three Persons of the Holy Trinity. Justin Martyr[2] adds a few words only to the names "of God the Father and Lord of the universe, and of our Saviour Jesus Christ, and of the Holy Spirit;" and Tertullian[3] observes that "Wherever there are three, that is, the Father, the Son, and the Holy Spirit, there is the Church, which is a body of three." The trine immersion had reference not only to the Trinity, but was also a symbol of the three days of our Saviour's burial[4]. The use of the three Holy Names was made more strictly indispensable as heresies were multiplied: thus the 49th Apostolic Canon, which, Hefele says, "must be reckoned among the most ancient Canons of the Church," orders that "If any Bishop or Presbyter does not baptize, according to the Lord's command, into the Father, the Son, and the Holy Ghost, but into three Beings without beginning, or into three Sons, or three Comforters, he shall be deprived."

We see here that the power of administering Baptism was not restricted to the Bishop: and Cyril speaks of it as possessed by "Bishops, or Presbyters, or Deacons," assigning as the reason the great increase of believers, "for the grace is everywhere, in villages and in cities, on them of low as on them of high degree, on bondsmen and on freemen[5]."

Thus the rule of Ignatius[6], that "it is not lawful either to baptize or to hold a love-feast apart from the Bishop (χωρὶς τοῦ ἐπισκόπου)," must be understood to mean "without the authority and permission of the Bishop."

Of certain minor ceremonies connected with Baptism, such as the "Kiss of peace," and the taste of milk and honey administered to the neophyte[7], no mention is made by Cyril.

§ 6. *Chrism.* The custom of anointing the baptized with consecrated ointment is regarded by Cyril as a sacramental act representing the anointing of Jesus by the Spirit at His Baptism. "As the Holy Ghost in substance lighted on Him, like resting upon like, so, after you had come up from the pool of the sacred waters, there was given to you an unction the counterpart (τὸ ἀντίτυπον) of that wherewith He was anointed, and this is the Holy Ghost[8]." As "He was anointed with a spiritual oil of gladness, that is with the Holy Ghost,

[6] *Mystag.* ii. § 4. [7] Pseudo-Ambros. *de Sacramentis*, II. c. 7. [8] *Ant.* XI. c. 7, § 11. [9] *Mystag.* iii. § 4.
[1] Cap. vii. [2] *Apolog.* I. c. [3] *De Baptismo*, c. vi. [4] *Mystag.* ii. § 4, note 3. [5] Cat. xvii. 35. [6] *Ad Smyrn.* c. viii.
[7] Bingham, *Ant.* XII. c. 4, §§ 5, 6. [8] *Mystag.* iii. § 1.

called oil of gladness, because He is the author of spiritual gladness, so ye were anointed with ointment, and made partakers and fellows of the Christ[9]." The ceremony was very ancient: there is probably a reference to it in the words of Theophilus of Antioch[1] (*c.* A.D. 170): "We are called Christians, because we are anointed with the oil of God." Tertullian, a little later, after speaking of Baptism, says: "Immediately on coming out of the Laver we are thoroughly anointed with a consecrated unction[2];" and again, "After that, the hand is laid upon us in benediction, invoking and inviting the Holy Ghost[3]." In another passage[4] he mentions also the sign of the Cross: "The flesh is washed, that the soul may be cleansed; the flesh is anointed that the soul may be consecrated; the flesh is signed [with the Cross] that the soul also may be guarded; the flesh is overshadowed by imposition of the hand, that the soul also may be illuminated by the Spirit."

The consecration of the ointment is compared by Cyril to the consecration of the Eucharist; after the invocation of the Holy Ghost it is no longer simple or common ointment, but a gift (Χάρισμα) of Christ, and by the presence of the Holy Ghost is able to impart of His Divine Nature. And this ointment is symbolically applied to thy forehead, and thy other organs of sense[5]."

The ears, nostrils, and breast were each to be anointed, and Cyril explains the symbolical meaning in each case by appropriate passages of Scripture[6].

The consecration of the chrism could be performed by none but the Bishop, and he alone could anoint the forehead[7], Presbyters being allowed to anoint the breast, but only with chrism received from the Bishop[8]. The several ceremonies are thus explained in the *Apostolical Constitutions*[9]: "This baptism is given into the death of Jesus: the water is instead of the burial, and the oil instead of the Holy Ghost; the seal instead of the Cross; the ointment is the confirmation of the Confession[1]."

In like manner the chrism is explained again, "The ointment is the seal of the covenants[2]," that is, both of God's promises, and of the Baptismal vows.

The members to be anointed were not the same in all Churches, but everywhere the chief ceremony was the anointing of the forehead with the sign of the Cross. This is what Cyril calls "the Royal Sign[3]," and "the Royal Seal to be borne upon the forehead of Christ's soldiers[4]," and again, "The Seal of the fellowship of the Holy Ghost[5]."

These last were probably the very words pronounced by the Bishop in making the sign of the Cross on the forehead; for by Canon 7 of the Second General Council at Antioch (381), converts from heretical sects were to be "sealed or anointed with the holy ointment on the forehead, eyes, nostrils, mouth, and ears. And in sealing them we say, 'The seal of the gift of the Holy Ghost.'"

An additional prayer to be said by the Bishop is given in the Apostolical Constitutions[6]: "O Lord God, the Unbegotten, who hast no Lord, who art Lord of all, who madest the odour of the knowledge of the Gospel to go forth among all nations, grant also now that this ointment may be efficacious upon him that is baptized (βαπτιζομένῳ), that the sweet odour of thy Christ may remain firm and stable in him, and that having died with Him, he may arise and live with Him."

The whole ceremony was called by the Greeks "Chrism," the "Unction" being regarded by them as the chief part. In the Latin Church the name Confirmation is of later date, and indicates that greater importance was then attached to the "Laying on of Hands" with prayer.

---

9 *Mystag.* iii. § 2. 1 *Ad Autolycum*, i. 2 *De Bapt.* c. 7. 3 Ib. c. 8. 4 *De Resurr. Carnis*, c. 8. 5 Ib. § 3. 6 *Myst.* iii. § 4. 7 *Apost. Const.* iii. § 16: "Let the Bishop anoint those that are baptized with ointment (μύρῳ)." 8 See the authorities in Bingham, *Ant.* xii. c. 2, §§ 1, 2. 9 iii. 17. 1 *Const. Apost.* vii. c. 22. 2 Ib. vii. c. 43. Cf. Cat. iii. 17. 3 Cat. iv. § 14. 4 Ib. xii. § 8. 5 Ib. xviii. 33. 6 vii. c. 44.

Another ceremony, not alluded to by Cyril, was the saying of the Lord's Prayer by the neophyte, standing up, and facing towards the East [7], after which he was also to pray, "O God Almighty, the Father of Thy Christ, Thine Only-begotten Son, give me a body undefiled, a clean heart, a watchful mind, an unerring knowledge, the influence (ἐπιφοίτησιν) of the Holy Ghost for attainment and full assurance of the truth, through Thy Christ, by whom be glory to Thee in the Holy Ghost for ever. Amen."

CHAPTER V.

Eucharistic Rites. Liturgy.

§ 1. *First Communion.* When the rites of Baptism and Chrism were completed, the new-made Christians, clothed in white robes (*Myst.* iv. 8), and bearing each a lighted taper in his hand, passed in procession from the Baptistery into the great "Church of the Resurrection." The time was still night, as we gather from the allusion in *Procat.*, § 15: "May God at length shew you that night, that darkness which shines like the day, concerning which it is said, *The darkness shall not be hidden from thee, and the night shall be light as the day.*" As the newly-baptized entered the church, they were welcomed in the words of the 32nd Psalm. "Even now," says Cyril (*Procat.*, § 15), "let your ears ring, as it were, with that glorious sound, when over your salvation the Angels shall chant, *Blessed are they whose iniquities are forgiven, and whose sins are covered;* when like stars of the Church you shall enter in, bright in the body and radiant in the soul." During the chanting of the Psalm the neophytes seem to have stood in front of the raised 'bema' or sanctuary, as we learn from Cyril's eloquent contemporary, Gregory Nazianzen, *Orat.* XL. § 46: "The station in which presently after Baptism thou wilt stand before the great sanctuary prefigures the glory from yonder heaven; the psalmody, with which thou wilt be welcomed, is a prelude of those heavenly hymns; the lamps, which thou wilt light, are a mystic sign of the procession of lights, with which bright and virgin souls shall go forth to meet the Bridegroom, with the lamps of faith burning brightly."

From the Syriac "Treatise of Severus, formerly Patriarch of Alexandria (Antioch), concerning the rites of Baptism and of Holy Communion (Synaxis) as received among the Syrian Christians" (Resch, *Agrapha*, § 12, p. 361); we learn that it was the custom "to lift up the newly-baptized to the altar, and after giving them the mysteries the Bishop (*Sacerdos*) crowned them with garlands."

The white garments (*Procat.*, § 2: *Mystag.*, iv. 88) were worn until the Octave of Easter, Low Sunday, *Dominica in Albis* (Bingham, XII. c. iv. § 3).

§ 2. The Liturgy. In Cyril's last Lecture, *Mystagogic* V., he reminds his hearers of what they had witnessed at their first Communion on Easter-day, and thus gives a most valuable testimony to the prescribed form of administering the Holy Eucharist in the Eastern Church in the middle of the fourth century.

Passing over all the preparatory portion of the Liturgy, he tells us first that the Deacon brings water to the Bishop or Priest (τῷ ἱερεῖ) and to the Presbyters who stand round the altar, that they may wash their hands in token of the need of purification from sin; a ceremony which evidently had reference to the words of the Psalmist, "I will wash mine hands in innocency; so will I compass Thine altar, O Lord [1]." In some Churches, perhaps also at Jerusalem, the words were actually chanted during the ablution [2].

"Then the Deacon cries aloud, Receive ye one another: and let us salute (ἀσπαζώμεθα) one another." In the Clementine Liturgy [3] the "Kiss of Peace" precedes the "Ablution."

7 *Const. Apost.* vii. c. 44.   1 *Mystag.* v. § 2.   2 *Dict. Chr. Ant.* "Lavabo."   3 *Apost. Const.* viii. c. 11.

Sometimes these two sentences are combined: "Salute ye one another with the holy kiss[4]." In the Liturgy of S. James there are two separate rubrics, one immediately after the dismissal of the Catechumens, "Take knowledge one of another," and a second after the Creed, "Let us embrace (ἀγαπήσωμεν) one another with a holy kiss."

"After this the Priest (ἱερεύς) cries aloud, Lift up your hearts. Then ye answer, We lift them up unto the Lord[5]."

The meaning of this Preface, as explained by Cyril, is an exhortation by the Priest, or Bishop when present, and a promise by the people, to raise all their thoughts to God on high, in preparation for the great Thanksgiving to which they were further invited: "Let us give thanks unto the Lord,"—"It is meet and right[6]."

Then follows a very brief summary of the Eucharistic Preface, and after that the Trisagion[7], corresponding in part to the long Thanksgiving in the *Apostolic Constitutions* for all God's mercies in creation, providence, and redemption[8].

It is important to observe how S. Cyril in this and the following sections associates the people with the Priest, using throughout the Plural "We." That this is intentional and significant, we may learn from a passage of S. Chrysostom[9] which is so interesting that we may be allowed to translate it at length: "Sometimes moreover no difference is made between the Priest and those over whom he presides, as for example when we are to partake of the awful mysteries; for we are all alike deemed worthy of the same privileges: not as in the Old Covenant some parts were eaten by the Priest, and others by the governed (ὁ ἀρχόμενος), and it was not lawful for the people to share in what the Priest partook of. It is not so now: but one Body is set before all, and one Cup. And in the prayers also one may see the laity contributing much. For the prayers on behalf of the Energumens, and on behalf of those in Penitence are offered in common both by the Priest and by themselves; and all say one prayer, a prayer that is full of compassion. Again, after we have excluded from the sacred precincts those who are unable to partake of the Holy Table, there is another prayer to be made, and we all alike lie prostrate on the floor, and all alike rise up. When again we are to receive and give a kiss of peace, we all alike embrace each other. Again even amid the most tremendous Mysteries the Priest prays over the people, and the people over the Priest: for the formula, "With Thy Spirit," is nothing else than this. The words of the Thanksgiving again are common: for he does not give thanks alone, but also the whole people. For having first got their answer, and they agreeing that 'It is meet and right so to do,' he then begins the thanksgiving. And why wonder that the people sometimes speak with the Priest, when even with the very Cherubim and the Powers on high they send up those sacred hymns in common. Now all this I have said in order that each of the common people (τῶν ἀρχομένων) also may be vigilant, that we may learn that we are all one Body, having only as much difference between one and another, as between members and members, and may not cast the whole work upon the Priests, but ourselves also care for the whole Church even as for a common Body."

It is remarkable that in Cyril's account of the Eucharistic rites in this Lecture there is not the slightest reference to the words of Institution, though these hold so prominent a place before the Invocation both in the Clementine Liturgy and in the Liturgy of S. James. But we cannot justly assume, from a mere omission in so brief a summary, that the Commemoration of the Institution had no place in the Liturgy then in use at Jerusalem. It seems more probable that Cyril did not think it necessary, after his repeated references to the Institution in the preceding Lecture, to make further mention of a custom so well known as the recitation of Christ's own words in the course of the Prayer preceding the Invocation. On

4 *Apost. Const.* viii. c. 11. Compare Justin M. *Apolog.* I. c. 65. 5 *Mystag.* v. § 4. 6 § 5. 7 § 6. 8 *Apost. Const.* viii. c. 12. See the Eucharistic Preface of the Liturgy of S. James in note 4 on *Mystag.* v. § 6. 9 *In Epist. II. ad Cor.* Homil. xviii. § 3.

the previous day he had quoted S. Paul's account of the Institution, with the remark, "Since then He Himself has declared and said of the Bread, *This is My Body*, who shall dare doubt any longer? And since he has Himself affirmed and said, *This is My Blood*, who shall ever hesitate, saying that it is not His Blood[1]?" The like efficacy he again ascribes to "the Lord's declaration" concerning both the Bread and the Wine, that they are "the Body and Blood of Christ[2]."

In the Didaché, which gives the oldest elements of an Eucharistic Service, there is neither the Commemoration nor the Invocation, but only two short and simple forms of Thanksgiving "for the Holy Vine of David," and "for the broken Bread[3]."

Justin Martyr seems to imply that the consecration is effected by the Commemoration of Christ's own words in the Institution: "We have been taught," he says, "that the food which is blessed by the prayer of the word which comes from Him (τὴν δι' εὐχῆς λόγου τοῦ παρ' αὐτοῦ εὐχαριστηθεῖσαν τροφήν), and by which our blood and flesh are by transmutation nourished, is the Flesh and Blood of that Jesus who was made Flesh." He gives no separate Invocation of the Holy Ghost, but this may have been supplied in the "praise and glory" or in the "prayers and thanksgivings" sent up "to the Father of all through the name of the Son and of the Holy Ghost[4]."

Irenæus is apparently the earliest writer who represents the Invocation of the Holy Ghost as the immediate act of consecration: "We make an oblation to God of the bread and the cup of blessing, giving Him thanks for that He has commanded the earth to bring forth these fruits for our nourishment. And then, having completed the oblation, we call forth (ἐκκαλοῦμεν) the Holy Spirit, that He may exhibit this sacrifice, both the bread the Body of Christ, and the cup the Blood of Christ, in order that the partakers of these antitypes may obtain the remission of sins and life eternal[5]."

Mr. Hammond writes that, "By the Oriental Churches an Invocation of the Holy Spirit is considered necessary to complete the consecration. In the three Oriental Families of Liturgies such an Invocation is invariably found shortly after the Words of Institution[6]."

It is in accordance with this statement that, we find Cyril so frequently declaring that the elements which before the Invocation are simple bread and wine, become after the Invocation the Body and Blood of Christ[7]. In the first of the passages referred to below he speaks of "the Holy Invocation of the Adorable Trinity," in the others of the Holy Spirit only.

Cyril next describes the Invocation as "completing the Spiritual Sacrifice, the bloodless Service," and then gives a summary of the "Great Intercession" as made "over that Sacrifice of the Propitiation." The Intercession, as represented by Cyril, is not simply a prayer, but an offering of the Sacrifice[8], and this is in accordance with the usual language of the Liturgies. "We offer to Thee, O Lord, on behalf also of Thy holy places, which Thou hast glorified by the Theophany of Thy Christ, and by the visitation of Thine All-Holy Spirit: especially on behalf of glorious Sion, the Mother of all the Churches, and on behalf of Thy Holy Catholic and Apostolic Church throughout the whole world[1]." In the Liturgy of S. Chrysostom, as now commonly used in the Orthodox Eastern Church, we find the fuller phrase, "We offer unto Thee *this reasonable Service* on behalf of the world, on behalf of the Holy Catholic and Apostolic Church[2]."

In some particulars Cyril's summary agrees most nearly with the Clementine Liturgy, as, for example, in the prayer "for the King and those in authority, and for the whole army, that they may be at peace with us[3]." In others he follows the Liturgy of S. James,

---

1 *Mystag.* iv. § 1. 2 Ib. § 6: see also § 7. 3 Capp. ix., x. 4 *Apol.* I. cc. 65—67. 5 *Frag.* xxxviii. 6 *Liturgies*, p. 382. 7 *Mystag.* v. i. § 7; iii. § 3; v. § 7. 8 *Mystag.* v. § 8: ταύτην προσφέρομεν τὴν θυσίαν.

1 Hammond, *Liturgy of S. James*, p. 43. 2 Ib. p. 115. 3 Ib. p 18.

as in the intercession for "every Christian soul afflicted and distressed, that stands in need of Thy pity and succour [4]."

Cyril next describes the commemoration of departed Saints, and "of all who in past years have fallen asleep among us," that is, in the bosom of the Church, and states his belief "that it will be a very great benefit to the souls, for whom the supplication is put up while that holy and most awful Sacrifice is presented [5]." He refers to objections against this belief, and brings forward in defence of it a reason applicable only to sinners: "When we offer," he says, "our supplications for those who have fallen asleep, though they be sinners, we offer up Christ sacrificed for our sins, propitiating our merciful God for them as well as for ourselves [6]." His language on this subject seems in fact to shew an advance in doctrine beyond the earliest Liturgies. In those of S. James and S. Basil we find prayers that the offering may be acceptable as a propitiation "for the rest of the souls that have fallen asleep aforetime;" and again, "that we may find mercy and grace with all the Saints who have ever been pleasing in Thy sight from generation to generation, forefathers, fathers, Patriarchs, Prophets, Apostles, Martyrs, Confessors, Teachers, holy men, and every righteous spirit made perfect in the faith of Thy Christ."

There is nothing here, nor in the Clementine Liturgy, nor in that of S. Mark, corresponding to the purpose which Cyril ascribes to the commemoration, "that at their prayers and intercessions God would receive our petition." In the Anaphora of S. Chrysostom contained in the later form of the Liturgy of Constantinople we find, apparently for the first time, this prayer added to the commemoration of all Saints, "at whose supplications look upon us, O God."

There was much controversy on the subject of prayers for the dead in Cyril's time, and the objections which he notices were brought into prominence by Aerius, and rebuked by Epiphanius [7].

From the commemoration of the departed Cyril passes at once to the Lord's Prayer [8], omitting the Preface which is found in the Liturgies of S. James and S. Mark. In the Clementine Liturgy, contrary to general use, the Lord's Prayer is not said at all. Cyril adds an exposition of each petition, and gives an unusual explanation of ἐπιούσιος, for which see the footnote: he also explains τοῦ πονηροῦ as referring to "the wicked one," following in this the Embolismus of S. James, "deliver us from the wicked one and from his works."

"After this the Bishop says, Holy things for holy men [9]." Chrysostom explains this as being both an invitation to the Faithful in general to communicate, and a warning to the unholy to withdraw. "The Bishop, with loud voice and awe-inspiring cry, raising high his arm like a herald, and standing on high in sight of all, above that awful silence cries aloud, inviting some and repelling others, and doing this not with his hand, but with his tongue more clearly than with the hand. . . . . For when he says, Holy things for the holy, he means this: Whosoever is not holy, let him not draw near [1]."

In regard to the doctrinal significance of the formula, Dr. Waterland's remarks should be consulted [2].

The response of the people to the "Sancta Sanctis" is given by Cyril [3] in accordance with the Liturgy of S. James and the Clementine: "One is Holy, One is the Lord, Jesus Christ:" but he does not mention the "Gloria in excelsis" nor the "Hosanna," both of which follow here in the Clementine.

"After this," says Cyril, "ye hear the chanter inviting you with a sacred melody to the Communion of the Holy Mysteries, and saying, *O taste and see that the Lord is good* [4]. This

4 Hammond, *Liturgy of S. James*, p. 44. 5 § 9. 6 § 10. 7 *Hæres.* lxxv. § 7. Cf. Bingh. *Ant.* XV. c. 3, § 16; *Dict. Chr. Biog.* "Aerius." 8 *Mystag.* V. § 11. 9 Ib. § 19. 1 *Hom. xvii. in Hebr.* These Homilies were edited after Chrysostom's death. 2 *A Review of the Doctrine of the Eucharist*, c. x. 3 § 19. 4 § 20.

agrees with the Clementine rubric: "Let the 33rd Psalm be sung while all the rest are partaking." In the Liturgy of S. James, while the Bishop is breaking the Bread and dipping it in the Wine, the "Agnus Dei" and several Psalms were sung: but of these there is no mention in the Clementine Liturgy or in Cyril.

On Cyril's directions for receiving the Bread and the Cup with due reverence, see the foot-notes on the passages[5].

His final injunction to remain for the prayer and thanksgiving is taken from that in the Clementine Liturgy: "Having partaken of the precious Body and the precious Blood of Christ, let us give thanks to Him who hath counted us worthy to partake of His holy Mysteries." The thanksgiving, benediction, concluding prayers, and dismissal, vary much in the different Liturgies.

CHAPTER VI.

Effects of Baptism and of Chrism.

§ 1. *Baptism.* When we try to ascertain the exact relation between Baptism and the Unction or Chrism which immediately followed, we find that Cyril's teaching on the subject has been understood in very different senses. By some he is thought to regard the Unction as being merely an accessory rite of the one great Sacrament of Baptism; to others he seems to draw a clear distinction between them, assigning to each its proper grace and efficacy.

The former view is stated by the Oxford editor, Milles, in his note on the words: "And in like manner to you also, after you had come up from the pool of the sacred waters, there was given an unction, a figure (*ἀντίτυπον*) of that with which Christ was anointed; and that is the Holy Ghost[1]." "It is evident," says Milles, "from his words here, that the Chrism of which Cyril treats in this Lecture is not to be referred to the Unction which is administered by the Romanists in Confirmation. For every one sees that by Unction in this passage a ceremony of Baptism is indicated. The ancients employed two Unctions in Baptism, the first before the immersion in the water, of which he spoke in the preceding Lecture; the second immediately upon ascending from the water, of which he speaks in this Lecture."

This opinion is elaborately discussed by the Benedictine editor, Touttée, *Dissertatio* iii. c. 7, who argues that the Unction described by Cyril is a Sacrament distinct from Baptism, that it has for its proper grace the gift of the Holy Spirit, and further that this gift is not conferred in Baptism. Of these assertions the first and second appear to represent Cyril's view correctly: the last is an exaggeration and a mistake, the tendency of which is to identify the Chrism of the Eastern Church with that which is used in Confirmation by the Roman Church, and to exalt the rite of Confirmation as a proper Sacrament distinct from Baptism, and even superior to it. A view differing in some respects from both of these has been recently put forward by a learned and devout writer of our own Church, who has fully discussed the teaching of Cyril and other Eastern Fathers, and gives the result of his investigation in the following "Summary[2]:" "For very many centuries the Christians of the East have never been forced to define to themselves at all clearly the position of a person baptized but unconfirmed. Their mode of administering Confirmation (*Chrism?*) by the hands of the baptizing Presbyter—though among the Greeks and some others with chrism prepared by the Bishop—relieves them from the necessity which weighs upon us Westerns, of teaching Christian children what their status is between the two rites. Confirmation (*Chrism?*) is for them, far more than it has been for a long while in the West, a factor in Baptism. Only

5 §§ 21, 22.

1 *Mystag.* iii. § 1.

2 A. J. Mason, D.D., *The Relation of Confirmation to Baptism*, p. 389. Though I find myself compelled to differ widely from my friend Canon Mason in the interpretation of Cyril's teaching on this subject, I cannot refrain from expressing my sincere admiration of the tone and purpose of his treatise, and of the learning and research which it exhibits.

a more or less conscious desire not to fall behind Western teachers in honouring the perfecting Unction can have led their later authorities to treat that Unction as a sacrament numerically distinct from Baptism. To all the early doctors of the East the two things are one, and Baptism culminates in the Unction. The tendency among Oriental Christians was, not to attribute to Baptism in our modern sense the gift of the Holy Ghost, but rather to consider Baptism by itself as a bare rite, benefiting the body alone, and dependent for its spiritual efficacy upon other actions, after and before. Not that this tendency has its full way. The Greek Fathers may be said certainly on the whole to trace the forgiveness of sins, the preparatory cleansing, to the baptismal Laver; the gift of the Holy Ghost, for the ordinary purposes of Christian living, they trace, like S. Chrysostom, to that act which comes "immediately after Baptism, and before the Mysteries."

When we come to inquire how far these several theories agree with the teaching of Cyril himself, we must in the outset put aside altogether the name *Confirmation*: for as applied to the Unction used in the Eastern Church it is only confusing and misleading. In the early ages of the Church *Confirmation* was not known even by name. In the Latin Church "neither Tertullian, Cyprian, Ambrose, Augustine, Jerome, nor any of the Latin Fathers, makes mention of *Confirmation* in this sense. Nor have the Greeks any word to answer to this Latin term[3]." So far, therefore, Milles appears to be perfectly right in refusing to connect the Chrism of which Cyril treats with the Unction used in Confirmation by the Roman Church.

We may add that in Cyril's account of Chrism it is wholly unconnected with Confirmation, both in its symbolic reference and in its outward form. Chrism, he says, is the antitype of the Unction of Christ by the Holy Ghost at His Baptism: Confirmation is universally admitted to have been a following of the Apostles in their laying on of hands. But in that Apostolic rite there was no unction, and in Chrism there was no such laying on of hands.

In several passages Cyril clearly distinguishes the outward form of Baptism from the spiritual grace.

"If thy body be here, but not thy mind, it profiteth thee nothing. Even Simon Magus once came to the Laver: he was baptized, but was not enlightened; and though he dipped his body in water, he enlightened not his heart with the Spirit: his body went down and came up, but his soul was not buried with Christ, nor raised with Him[4]."

It is impossible here to regard "the Spirit" as referring to the grace of Unction: for (1) Baptism was not accompanied by Unction in the time of the Apostles, and (2) we should thus make a false antithesis between the *outward* part of the one rite ("he dipped his body in water"), and the *inward* part of the other. Here, therefore, Cyril attributes enlightenment of the heart by the Spirit to Baptism apart from Unction, and at the same time lays stress upon the difference between the worthy and unworthy recipient of the outward form.

The importance of this difference is further enforced throughout the next two sections, and at the close of § 4 the distinction between the outward sign and inward grace of Baptism, strictly so called, is again asserted, "though the water will receive thee, the Spirit will not accept thee."

"Some might suppose," it is said, "from these words that Cyril thought of water and the Spirit as the sign and the thing signified in Baptism respectively, and a passage in a later Lecture upon the subject of the Sacrament (of Baptism) at first confirms that impression[5]."

To suppose that Cyril had any other thought in the former passage, seems to me impossible for any ordinary reader; and the later passage, not only at first, but more fully the longer it is considered, confirms that impression beyond all doubt. The whole quotation, including Cat. iii. §§ 3, 4, is too long to repeat here, but may be read in its proper place.

---

3 Suicer, *Thesaurus*, Χρίσμα.   4 *Procat.* § 2.   5 Mason, *ubi supr.*, p. 337.

It will be sufficient to give the passages which are of chief importance in the question before us, according to Canon Mason's translation.

Cat. iii. § 3. "Do not attend to the laver as mere water, but to the spiritual grace given along with the water" . . . "the mere water, receiving the invocation of the Holy Ghost, and of Christ, and of the Father, acquires a power of sanctity. For since man is a two-fold being composed of soul and body, the cleansing element also is two-fold, the incorporeal for the incorporeal, the bodily for the body. And the water cleanses the body, but the Spirit seals the soul, in order that having our hearts sprinkled by the Spirit, and our bodies washed with pure water, we may draw nigh to God. When, therefore, you are about to go down into the water do not pay attention to the mere nature of the water, but expect salvation by the operation of the Holy Ghost. For without both it is impossible for thee to be perfected."

No words could state more clearly the distinction between the outward sign and the inward grace of Baptism, and the absolute necessity for both. There is no posssible reference to Unction, but "the operation of the Holy Ghost" in cleansing and sealing the soul is unmistakably connected with Baptism as "the grace given with the water" (μετὰ τοῦ ὕδατος), and below, as "the seal by water" (τὴν δι' ὕδατος σφραγῖδα), the latter phrase shewing that Baptism by water is the *signum efficax* of the grace in question.

Cyril then quotes our Lord's words, *Except a man be born of water and the Spirit, he cannot enter into the kingdom of God*, and explains them thus: "On the one hand he who is being baptized (βαπτιζόμενος) with the water, but has not had the Spirit vouchsafed to him (καταξιωθείς), has not the grace in perfection: on the other hand, even if a man be distinguished for virtue in his deeds, but does not receive the seal bestowed by means of water (τὴν δι' ὕδατος σφραγῖδα), he shall not enter into the kingdom of heaven." Canon Mason, whose translation I have followed, finds here a reference both to Baptism and to Unction as "the first baptismal act and the second," and in support of this interpretation gives a second and more emphatic version: "He who is in course of being baptized with the water, but has not yet had the Spirit vouchsafed to him, has not the grace in perfection." This introduction of the word "*yet*," in order to represent a distinction between two separate acts, is not justified either by the reading of the older editions (οὐδὲ τῷ ὕδατι βαπτιζόμενος μὴ καταξιωθεὶς δὲ τοῦ Πνεύματος), nor by that of Codices Monac. Roe, Casaub. adopted by Reischl (οὔτε ὁ βεβαπτισμένος κ.τ.λ.), nor by the Benedictine text (οὔτε ὁ βαπτιζόμενος κ.τ.λ.). The obvious meaning of the passage, with either reading, is that "the man who in Baptism did not receive the Holy Spirit, has not the grace (of Baptism) complete." The Benedictine Editor in his elaborate argument for regarding Chrism as a distinct sacrament [5a], does not even refer to this passage.

A statement which is important in this connexion is found in *Mystag.* ii. § 6: "Let no one then suppose that Baptism is the grace of remission of sins only, or further of adoption, as the Baptism of John conferred only remission of sins; but as we know full well that it cleanses from sins and procures a gift of the Holy Spirit, so also it is a counterpart (ἀντίτυπον) of the sufferings of Christ."

Here besides "the remission of sins, which no man receiveth without the Holy Spirit [6]," we find "a gift of the Holy Ghost," and the fellowship of Christ's Passion distinctly attributed to Baptism.

If the "adoption" mentioned at the beginning of this passage were identical (as Touttée thinks) with the "gift of the Holy Ghost," it would by no means follow that Cyril here means to include Unction in Baptism. For the grace which beyond all others is exclusively attached to Baptism, and not to Unction, is the new birth, and this is "the new birth into freedom

---

5a *Dissert.* iii. c. 8.

6 Hooker, *E.P.* V. lxvi. § 6.

and *adoption*[7]." In fact Cyril's teaching on this point is in strict accordance with that of St. Paul in Gal. iv. 4-6, that we first *receive the adoption of sons* (υἱοθεσίαν), and then "*because ye are sons, God sent forth the Spirit of His Son into our hearts, crying, Abba, Father.*" So again in Rom. viii. 15, 16, he says, "*Ye received the Spirit of adoption, whereby we cry, Abba, Father. The Spirit Himself beareth witness with our spirit that we are the children of God.*" In both passages St. Paul clearly distinguishes two things, "the adoption" itself, and the witness of it by "the Spirit of adoption." Cf. Bengel on *v.* 4: "Prius *adoptionem*, deinde *Spiritum adoptionis* accepimus;" and on *v.* 6: "*Filiorum statum* sequitur inhabitatio Spiritus Sancti, non hanc ille." The adoption itself belongs to Baptism strictly so called, in which we are made children of God and joint heirs with Christ (cf. Cat. iii. 15): the witness of the indwelling Spirit of adoption is the special grace ascribed to Chrism in the Eastern Church, and to Confirmation in the Western. There are many other passages in which Cyril ascribes to Baptism itself, as distinct from Chrism, a gift of the Spirit, such as the following: "But He trieth the soul: He casteth not His pearls before the swine: if thou dissemble, men will baptize thee now, but the Spirit will not baptize thee[8]."

"The Lord, preventing us according to His loving-kindness, has granted repentance at Baptism, in order that we may cast off the chief—nay, rather the whole burden of our sins, and having received the seal by the Holy Ghost, may be made heirs of eternal life[9]."

Again, after speaking of "the invocation of grace having sealed the soul," he adds: "Having gone down dead in sins, thou comest up quickened in righteousness. For if thou hast been *united with the likeness of the Saviour's death*, thou shalt also be deemed worthy of His Resurrection[1]." The benefits ascribed to Baptism in these several passages without any allusion to Chrism, are brought together with rhetorical effect in the Introductory Lecture, § 16: "Great is the Baptism that lies before you; a ransom to captives, a remission of offences, a death of sin, a new birth of the soul, a garment of light, a holy indissoluble seal, a chariot to heaven, the delight of Paradise, a welcome into the kingdom, the gift of adoption."

From such language it is clear beyond question that in Cyril of Jerusalem, not to speak of other Oriental Fathers, the tendency is not "to consider Baptism by itself as a bare rite, benefiting the body alone, and dependent for its spiritual efficacy upon other actions after and before," but as depending on the power of the Holy Ghost, and the sincerity of repentance and faith in man.

If further proof were needed, a glance at the Index under the word "Baptism" will shew the extraordinary richness, variety, and precision of Cyril's teaching, as to the gifts of the Holy Ghost conferred therein.

§ 2. *Chrism.* When spiritual blessings so many and so great have been ascribed to Baptism, in what light, it may be asked, does Cyril regard the Unction which follows? Does he treat it as being merely an additional ceremony subordinate to Baptism, or as having for its own proper grace some special gift of the Holy Ghost? We find no answer to this question in the earlier course of Lectures[2]. But that Chrism was not regarded by Cyril as a mere accessory to Baptism, as Milles thought[3], may be safely inferred from the fact that in announcing the subjects of his Mystagogic Lectures, he mentions first Baptism, then "the seal of the fellowship of the Holy Ghost," and then "the Mysteries at the altar of the New Covenant[4]:" and this inference is fully confirmed by his language elsewhere: "Ye have heard enough of Baptism, and Chrism, and partaking of the Body and Blood of Christ[5]." A mere additional

7 Cat. i. 2. 8 Ib. xvii. § 36. 9 Ib. iv 37. 1 Ib. iii. § 12. 2 Upon the supposed allusion to Chrism in Cat. xvi. § 26, see below, p. xxxiv. 3 Note on *Mystag.* iii. § 1. 4 Cat. xviii. § 33. 5 *Mystag.* v. § 1.

ceremony of Baptism could not have been so independently placed between the two great Sacraments, and, as it were, in the same rank with them.

The importance thus attached to Chrism is further shewn in the fact that Cyril uses the very same language in reference to the consecration of the ointment of Chrism and of the water of Baptism, and of the Eucharistic elements. "The bread and wine of the Eucharist before the Invocation of the Holy and Adorable Trinity are simple (λιτός) bread and wine, but after the Invocation the Bread becomes the Body and the Wine the Blood of Christ[6]." "Regard not the Laver as simple (λιτῷ) water, but rather regard the spiritual grace that is given with the water[7]." "The simple water having received the Invocation of the Holy Ghost, and of Christ, and of the Father, acquires a new power of holiness[8]."

"But see thou suppose not this to be plain (ψιλόν) ointment. For as the Bread of the Eucharist, after the Invocation of the Holy Ghost is no longer simple (λιτός) bread, but the Body of Christ; so also this holy ointment is no longer plain (ψιλόν) ointment, nor, as one might say, common, after Invocation, but Christ's gift of grace (χάρισμα), and is made effectual to impart the Holy Ghost by the presence of His own Godhead[9]."

The spiritual benefits which Cyril ascribes to the Unction are set forth in the same Lecture. "This holy thing is a spiritual safeguard of the body, and salvation of the soul" (§ 7): it sanctifies all the organs of sense: "the body is anointed with the visible ointment, and the soul is sanctified by the Holy and Life-giving Spirit" (§ 3). After being anointed the Christian is now entitled to that name in its fullest sense[1]; he is clothed with the whole armour of the Holy Ghost, that he may stand against the power of the adversary: he may say, "*I can do all things in Christ who strengtheneth me*" (§ 4).

In regard to the supposed identity of Chrism and Confirmation, it is important to notice carefully how Cyril speaks of the laying on of hands in the only passage where he mentions it[2].

He first illustrates the freedom of the Spirit, and His independence of human agency, by the gift of prophecy to the seventy elders, including Eldad and Medad: he then refers to the gift of the spirit of wisdom to Joshua by the laying on of Moses' hands[3], and adds, "Thou seest everywhere the figure (τύπον) in the Old Testament, and in the New the same. In Moses' time the Spirit was given by laying on of hands (χειροθεσίᾳ), and Peter gives the Spirit by laying on of hands[4]: and upon thee also, who art to be baptized, the grace is about to come; but the manner (τὸ πῶς) I tell thee not, for I do not forestall the time."

From this passage it has been inferred (1) that Cyril alludes to a gift of the Spirit by laying on of hands in immediate connexion with Baptism and Unction[5], and (2) that he refers this gift of the Spirit not to Baptism itself, but to the laying on of hands, or to the Unction as a figure that answers to it[6].

(1) The first of these inferences is opposed to the fact that Cyril neither mentions the laying on of hands as part of the actual ceremonial in Baptism or Unction, nor as the analogous rite in the old Testament, but on the contrary expressly says[7] that the symbol (τὸ σύμβολον) of this holy Chrism in the Old Testament lies in the consecration of Aaron to be High Priest, when Moses, "after the washing in water anointed him, and he was called '*anointed*,' evidently from this figurative unction (τοῦ χρίσματος δηλαδὴ τοῦ τυπικοῦ)."

(2) In support of the second inference the argument offered is as follows: "That the Spirit was to come upon them in the course of their Baptism is here again clearly stated; but that Cyril did not intend them to suppose that Baptism itself would convey the gift is equally clear. Again and again in earlier Lectures, as well as in the words actually before us, Cyril has taught them to expect the gift in Baptism; if therefore the immersion itself were to be the means of

---

6 *Mystag.* i. § 7. 7 Cat. iii. § 3. 8 *Ibidem.* 9 *Mystag.* iii. 3. 1 Ib. iii. § 1. 2 Cat. xvi. §§ 25, 26. 3 Deut. xxxiv. 9 4 Acts viii. 17. 5 Touttée. 6 Mason, p. 341, with note. 7 *Mystag.* iii. 6.

receiving it, *he has already told them his secret.* Yet now he says that he will not tell them 'how' they are to receive it. That remains for a future occasion[8]." The mistake, as I venture to consider it, lies in the words which I have marked with italics. For of the mysteries which were to be concealed from the unbaptized (ἀμύητοι) the first was *the manner of administering Baptism* itself, and the second, the unction of Chrism; and in the preceding Lectures Cyril has no more told the secret of the one than of the other. "Baptism, the Eucharist, and the oil of Chrism, were things that the uninitiated (ἀμύητοι) were not allowed to look upon[9]."

"We bless," says S. Basil[1], "both the water of Baptism and the oil of the Chrism, and moreover the baptized (βαπτιζόμενον) himself. From what written commands? Is it not from a secret (σιωπωμένης) and mystical tradition? Again, the very anointing with the oil, what word of Scripture taught that? And the dipping the man thrice, whence came it? And all the other accompaniments of Baptism, the renunciation of Satan and his angels, from what Scripture came they? Come they not from this unpublished and secret teaching, which our fathers guarded in a silence with which no prying curiosity might meddle, having been well taught to preserve the sanctity of the mysteries by silence? For how could it have been right to publish in writing the doctrine of these mysteries, which the unbaptized are not even allowed to look upon?"

As these secret ceremonies of Baptism and Unction are revealed by Cyril only in the Mystagogic Lectures, the supposed reason for saying, that in Cat. xvi. 26, the promised gift of the Spirit refers not to Baptism but only to Unction, at once falls to the ground.

The true state of the case is well expressed by Bingham[2], "Though the ancients acquainted the Catechumens with the doctrine of Baptism so far as to make them understand the spiritual nature and design of it, yet they never admitted them to the sight of the actual ceremony, nor so much as to hear any plain discourse about the manner of its administration, till they were fitted and prepared for the actual reception of it,"—or rather, till they actually received it.

There is in fact no reason to exalt the benefits of Unction, or Confirmation, by robbing Baptism of its proper grace. "It was this Unction, as the completion of Baptism, to which they ascribed the power of making every Christian in some sense partaker of a royal priesthood. To it they also ascribed the noble effects of confirming the soul with the strength of all spiritual graces on God's part, as well as the confirmation of the profession and covenant made on man's part[3]." We may well be satisfied that the doctrine of the early Church has been so fully retained in essential points in our own Office of Confirmation, recalling as it does by the ratification of the baptismal vows the immediate connexion of the ancient Unction with Baptism, and in its Prayers invoking the same gifts of the Holy Spirit,—"Strengthen them, we beseech Thee, O Lord, with the Holy Ghost the Comforter, and daily increase in them Thy manifold gifts of grace; the spirit of wisdom and understanding; the spirit of counsel and ghostly strength; the spirit of knowledge and true godliness; and fill them, O Lord, with the spirit of Thy holy fear, now and for ever. Amen."

CHAPTER VII.

Eucharistic Doctrine.

We have seen that Cyril makes the consecration of sacramental elements in every case consist in the Invocation of the Holy Ghost, after which the water of Baptism is no longer

---

8 Mason, p. 341. 9 Basil, *apud* Bingham, X. 5, § 4. 1 *De Spiritu S.* c. xxvii. 2 *Ant.* X. v. § 4.

3 Bingh. XII. iii. § 3. Cf. *Apost. Const.* III. c. 17. "This Baptism therefore is into the death of Jesus: the water is instead of the burial, and the oil instead of the Holy Ghost; the seal instead of the Cross; *the ointment is the confirmation of the Confession.*" VII. 22: "that the anointing with oil may be the participation of the Holy Spirit, and the water the symbol of the death, and the ointment the seal of the covenants."

mere simple water [1], the ointment no longer plain ointment [2], the bread and the wine no longer plain bread and wine, but the Body and Blood of Christ [3].

Upon these statements an argument against Transubstantiation has been founded by Bishop Cosin [4], and adopted both by Dr. Pusey [5] and Dean Goode [6]. It being universally admitted that the substance of the water and of the ointment remains unchanged, it is argued from the identity of the language employed in each case that, according to Cyril, no *substantial* change takes place in the Bread and Wine. Bishop Cosin quotes the following passage, of which the original is given below: "Take heed thou dost not think that this is a mere ointment only. For as the bread of the Eucharist after the invocation of the Holy Ghost is no longer ordinary bread, but is the body of Christ; so this holy ointment is no longer a bare common ointment after it is consecrated, but is the gift or grace of Christ, which, by His Divine Nature, and the coming of the Holy Ghost, is made efficacious; so that the body is anointed with the ointment, but the soul is sanctified by the holy and vivifying Spirit [7]."

Bishop Cosin proceeds to argue thus: "Can anything more clear be said? Either the ointment is transubstantiated by consecration into the spirit and grace of Christ, or the bread and wine are not transubstantiated by consecration into the Body and Blood of Christ. Therefore as the ointment retains still its substance, and yet is not called a mere or common ointment, but the Chrism or grace of Christ: so the bread and wine remaining so, as to their substance, yet are not said to be only bread and wine· common and ordinary, but also the Body and Blood of Christ."

Notwithstanding the great authority of Bishop Cosin, and the assent of Theologians of such opposite schools as Dr. Pusey and Dean Goode, it must be admitted that the argument, even as against Transubstantiation, is pressed beyond its just limits. The identity of language extends only to two points, (1) the mode of consecration by Invocation, (2) the effect negatively stated, that the material element in each case is no longer simply a material element. A change, therefore, of some kind has taken place, and we have still to inquire how the change in each case is described by Cyril. "The water acquires a power of sanctity," otherwise described as "the spiritual grace given with the water [8]."

"The ointment is Christ's gift of grace (Χάρισμα), and becomes effectual to impart by the presence of the Holy Ghost His Divine Nature [9]." "The Bread becomes the Body and the Wine the Blood of Christ [1]."

There is here no such identity of language as would justify the assertion that the change described is of the same nature in each case, that because it leaves the substance of the water and the ointment untouched, *therefore* the substance of the Bread also must, according to Cyril, remain unchanged: this must be proved by other arguments. We must also remember that if this argument based upon the identity of the language used on the two sides of a comparison is trustworthy, there is another passage in Cyril to which it may be applied: "He once, in Cana of Galilee, changed the water into wine akin to blood (οἰκεῖον αἵματι) [2], and is it incredible that He changed wine into blood?" The change of the water into wine was a change of substance: are we then prepared to agree with the Roman Church that the change of the bread also is a change of substance? Nay further, would the Roman Church itself accept the principle of the argument? For observe that in fact Bishop Cosin himself, when he comes to deal with this passage, gives up his former argument, and distinctly rejects it.

1 Cat. iii. § 3. 2 *Mystag.* iii. § 3.

3 *Mystag.* iii. § 3. In the same Lecture, § 7, the consecration of the bread and wine is said to follow "the Invocation of the Holy and Adorable Trinity."

4 *The History of Popish Transubstantiation*, Ch. v. § 14.

5 *The Doctrine of the Real Presence*, pp. 277—281.

6 *The Nature of Christ's Presence in the Eucharist*, p. 483.

7 Ἀλλ' ὅρα μὴ ὑπονοήσῃς ἐκεῖνο τὸ μύρον ψιλὸν εἶναι. ὥσπερ γὰρ ὁ ἄρτος τῆς εὐχαριστίας μετὰ τὴν ἐπίκλησιν τοῦ ἁγίου Πνεύματος οὐκ ἔτι ἄρτος λιτός, ἀλλὰ σῶμα Χριστοῦ, οὕτω καὶ τὸ ἅγιον τοῦτο μύρον οὐκ ἔτι ψιλόν, οὐδ' ὡς ἂν εἴποι τις κοινὸν μετ' ἐπίκλησιν, ἀλλὰ Χριστοῦ χάρισμα, καὶ Πνεύματος ἁγίου παρουσίᾳ τῆς αὐτοῦ θεότητος ἐνεργητικὸν γινόμενον.

8 Cat. iii. 3.

9 *Mystag.* iii. 3. On the translation see note on the passage.

1 Ib. i. § 7.

2 On this reading, see *Mystag.* iv. § 2, note 4.

"Protestants," he says, "do freely grant and firmly believe that the wine, in the sense already often mentioned, is changed into the Blood of Christ; but every change is not a transubstantiation; neither doth Cyril say that this change (*i.e.* of the wine) is like that of the water, for then it would appear to our senses; but that He who changed the water sensibly can also change the wine sacramentally, will not be doubted by any [3]." Again, in describing the act of consecration, Cyril says: "We beseech the merciful God to send forth His Holy Spirit upon the gifts lying before Him, that He may make the bread the Body of Christ, and the wine the Blood of Christ, for certainly whatsoever the Holy Ghost has touched, is sanctified and changed (ἡγίασται καὶ μεταβέβληται) [4]." Here again, as in the passage quoted from *Myst.* iii. § 3, a sacramental change of some sort is asserted, but its specific character is not defined.

There is, however, a passage which throws some light on Cyril's conception of the change in *Myst.* iv. § 3: "In the figure of Bread is given to thee His Body, and in the figure of Wine His Blood; that thou by partaking of the Body and Blood of Christ mightest be made of the same body and the same blood with Him. For thus we come to bear Christ in us, His Body and His Blood being distributed to our members (εἰς τὰ ἡμέτερα ἀναδιδομένου μέλη)." Several good MSS read ἀναδεδεγμένοι, which would give the meaning, "having received of His Body and of His blood into our members." This does not alter the general sense of the passage; but the reading ἀναδιδομένου is supported by another passage, *Myst.* v. § 15: "Our common bread is not substantial (ἐπιούσιος): but this Holy Bread is substantial, that is, appointed for the substance of the soul. This Bread *goeth* not *into the belly and is not cast out into the draught*, but is distributed (ἀναδίδοται) into thy whole system for the benefit of body and soul."

In order to accommodate these passages to the Roman doctrine of Transubstantiation the Benedictine Editor here introduces the idea of *species*, the outward forms or accidents of the bread. "We must not suppose," he says, "that Cyril thought the Body of Christ to be divided and digested (*digeri*) into our body; but by a customary way of speaking he attributes to the Holy Body what is suitable only to the species which conceal it. And he does not deny that the species pass into the draught, but only that the Body of Christ does so."

But Cyril draws no such distinction between the *species* and the Body of Christ: to him the Bread and Wine after consecration are the Body and the Blood of Christ. For how could it be said that the *species*, which in Transubstantiation are the mere outward accidents of bread and wine, are distributed into the whole system for the benefit of body and *soul?*

In whatever sense the bread and wine become by consecration the Body and Blood of Christ, in that same sense the Body and Blood of Christ are, according to Cyril, distributed to our whole system.

This was no new doctrine: Ignatius, *Ephes.* xxi., speaks of Christians as "breaking one Bread, which is the medicine of immortality, and the antidote that we should not die, but live for ever in Jesus Christ." This is perhaps the earliest expression of the belief that the resurrection of the body is secured by *the communion of the Body of Christ* in the Eucharist. The manner in which this communion is effected is described by Justin Martyr (*Apolog.* I. § 66) in language which shews clearly what Cyril meant: "We do not receive these things as common bread and common drink: but in the same way as Jesus Christ our Saviour was made flesh by the Word of God, and took both flesh and blood for our salvation, so we have been taught that the food over which thanksgiving has been made by prayer in the word received from Him (τὴν δι' εὐχῆς λόγου τοῦ παρ' αὐτοῦ εὐχαριστηθεῖσαν τροφήν), from which (food) our blood and flesh are by transmutation (κατὰ μεταβολήν) nourished, is both the Flesh and Blood of Him the Incarnate Jesus."

Here it is plainly taught that by consecration the Bread and Wine have become the Flesh and Blood of Christ, and that as such they nourish our "blood and flesh" (observe the

3 *Of Transubstantiation*, Ch. vi. § 14.

4 *Mystag.* v. § 7.

inverted order) by undergoing a change: in other words, the Eucharistic Body and Blood of Christ are changed into nourishment of our blood and flesh, by being distributed (as Cyril says) to all our members, that is by being subjected to the natural processes of digestion and assimilation. The unusual order of the words "our blood and flesh" is not accidental, but answers to the process of assimilation, in which the digested food first nourishes the blood, and then the blood nourishes the flesh.

The meaning is, as Otto says in his note, "that the divine food passes away into our bodies entire, so that nothing remains:" and Dr. Pusey seems to take the same view, in his note on the words, "from which (food) through transmutation our blood and flesh are nourished:" "*i.e.* the material parts are changed into the substance of the human body[5]."

Thus then, according to Cyril, the Eucharistic Body and Blood of Christ are distributed to all our members; His Flesh and Blood pass by a change into our blood and flesh, and we thereby become "of the same body and the same blood with Him[6]:" and "this Bread does not pass into the belly, and is not cast out into the draught[7]," but wastes away as the body itself wastes[8].

However much this view of the Sacramental mystery may differ from later theories, it was certainly held by many of the Greek Fathers. Irenæus, for example, in addition to those already mentioned, thus writes: "When therefore both the mingled cup and the created bread receive the Word of God, and the Eucharist becomes the Body of Christ, and from these the substance of our flesh increaseth and consisteth, how say they that the flesh is incapable of the gift of God which is eternal life, that flesh which is nourished from the Body and Blood of the Lord, and is already (*ὑπάρχουσα*) a member of Him?—even as the blessed Paul saith, that we are members of His Body, of His Flesh, and of His Bones[8a]."

That this was also the teaching of Cyril's contemporaries is clear from the famous passage of Gregory of Nyssa, in which this doctrine is fully developed. It will be sufficient to quote here the latter part of the passage, in which Gregory is speaking of the Wine. "Since then that God-containing flesh partook for its substance and support of this particular nourishment also, and since the God who was manifested infused Himself into perishable humanity for this purpose, viz. that by this communion with Deity mankind might at the same time be deified, for this end it is that, by dispensation of His grace, He disseminates Himself in every believer through that flesh whose substance comes from bread and wine, blending Himself with the bodies of believers, to secure that, by this union with the immortal, man too may be a sharer in incorruption. He gives these gifts by virtue of the benediction through which He transelements the natural quality of these visible things to that immortal thing[9]."

In another remarkable passage[1] Cyril gives a further explanation of the effect of consecration: "In the New Testament there is heavenly Bread and a Cup of salvation, sanctifying soul and body: for as the Bread corresponds to the body, so also the Word (*ὁ Λόγος*) is appropriate to the soul." With this language of Cyril we may compare further what is said by Gregory of Nyssa in the context of the passage already quoted: "Just then, as in the case of ourselves, as has been repeatedly said already, if a person sees bread he also in a kind of way looks on a human body, for by being within this it becomes this, so in that other case the Body into which God entered (*τὸ θεοδόχον σῶμα*), by partaking of the nourishment of bread was in a certain sense the same with it, since that nourishment, as we have said, is changed into the nature of the body: for that which is proper to all men is acknowledged also in the case of

---

5 *Real Presence*, p. 144. See note 8, below.

6 *Mystag.* iv. §§ 1, 3.

7 Ib. v. § 15.

8 See Pusey, *R. P.* p. 151, note 3: "Dr. Gaisford, on my applying to him, kindly answered me,—'συναναλίσκεσθαι. It appears to me that this word can only be explained by a periphrasis. The writer appears to me to mean that the elements are not thrown off like ordinary food, but that they become blended or assimilated to the body, and waste away as the body wastes away.' Mr. Field gives the same meaning."

8a V. ii. § 3.

9 *Oratio Catechetica*, c. xxxvii. The whole chapter should be read with the Rev. W. Moore's notes in this Series, Vol. V. pp. 504—506.

1 *Mystag.* iv. § 5.

That Flesh, namely, that That Body too was maintained by bread; which Body also by the indwelling of God the Word was changed into the dignity of Godhead. Rightly then do we believe that now also the bread which is sanctified by the Word of God is changed into the Body of God the Word. For even that Body was once virtually (τῇ δυνάμει) bread, but has been sanctified by the inhabitation of the Word that tabernacled in the flesh."

In this passage we have the full explanation of what Irenæus meant when he said that the elements "by receiving the Word of God become the Eucharist," and what Cyril meant by saying that "as the Bread corresponds to the body, so also the Word is appropriate to the soul." Their common doctrine is, that besides the Body and Blood of Christ, that is, His Humanity offered upon the Cross for our redemption, His Divine Nature, the Word, is also present, and that it is by receiving the Divine Word that the Bread is made the Body of Christ. "The fathers," says Touttée, "often play upon the ambiguity of the term, saying at one time that the Divine Word, at another that the word and oracles of God nourish our soul. Both are true. For the whole life-giving power of the Eucharist is derived from the Divine Word united with the flesh which He assumed: and the whole benefit (*fructus*) of Eucharistic eating consists in the union of our soul with the Word, by meditation on His mysteries and words, and conformation thereto [2]." *O si sic omnia!*

In this view the Bread and Wine are signs or figures of the natural Body of Christ crucified; but they are also much more, they are endued *by* the Divine Word, and through the operation of the Holy Ghost, with the life-giving power of the same Body and Blood of Christ,—a power which being imparted to the faithful recipient makes him to be "of the same body and the same blood with Christ," thereby assuring him of the resurrection of the body to eternal life, and at the same time strengthening and refreshing the soul by its being united through faith with the Word, and being thus made "*partaker of the Divine nature.*"

This is not the language of the Western Church, whether Roman, Lutheran, or Anglican, but it is the language of the earliest Greek Fathers, and of Cyril, as is partly and reluctantly admitted by so cautious a writer as Dr. Waterland. After referring to the passage quoted above from Justin Martyr (*Apol.* i. 66) he proceeds: "There is another the like obscure hint in Irenæus, which may probably be best interpreted after the same way. He supposes the elements to become *Christ's body* by receiving *the word* (Word). He throws two considerations into one, and does not distinguish so accurately as Origen afterwards did between the *symbolical* food and the *true food.*" The elements, Waterland adds, "are made the *representative* body of Christ; but they are at the same time, *to worthy receivers*, made the means of their spiritual union with Christ Himself; which Irenæus points at in what he says of the *bread's* receiving the *Logos*, but should rather have said it of the *communicants* themselves, as receiving the *spiritual* presence of Christ, in the worthy *use* of the *sacred* symbols [3]."

Again, in c. vii., he says more explicitly of Irenæus, what is equally true of Cyril; "Least of all does he favour the *figurists* or *memorialists;* for his doctrine runs directly counter to them almost in every line: he asserts over and over, that Christ's *body* and *blood* are eaten and drunk in the Eucharist, and our bodies thereby *fed;* and not only so, but *insured* thereby for a happy *resurrection:* and the reason he gives is, that our *bodies* are thereby made or continued members of Christ's *body, flesh, and bones.*"

From this view of Cyril's doctrine concerning the Sacramental elements we can easily understand in what sense he applies the terms "type" and "antitype" to the Eucharistic elements. "The Sacrament of the Holy Eucharist having two parts, an outward and an inward, and the outward part having been instituted by our Blessed Lord with a certain relation to the inward, and gifted with a certain significance of it, nothing is more natural than that the titles, type, antitype, symbol, figure, image, should be given to the outward part [4]."

---

[2] *Mystag.* iv. note 4.

[3] *Review of the Doctrine of the Eucharist*, c. V.

[4] Pusey, *R. P.* p. 94.

Add to this that, according to Cyril's doctrine as already explained, the bread after the Invocation, without ceasing to be bread, not only signifies but also *is* the Body, and we see how natural it was for him to say in one passage that "His Body bore the figure of bread [5]," and in another that "in the figure of bread the Body is given [6]." The Body which "is given" cannot be an *absent* Body of our Lord, but must be that Sacramental Body, of which Cyril goes on to say in the same sentence that it is "distributed to our members." Thus the Bread broken is a type or figure of Christ's Body as crucified for us; and by virtue of its union with the Divine Word it becomes the life-giving Body, which makes the faithful recipient to be, in Cyril's words, "of the same body and same blood with Christ."

Another term applied by Cyril and other Greek Fathers to the sacramental elements is "antitype."

In *Mystag.* ii. § 6, where Baptism is called "the counterpart (ἀντίτυπον) of Christ's sufferings," the meaning is clearly explained by the context: for in § 5 the reality of Christ's sufferings is emphatically and repeatedly contrasted with the figurative representation of the same; and this figurative representation no less emphatically contrasted with the real and actual bestowal of the grace of salvation: ἐν εἰκόνι ἡ μίμησις, ἐν ἀληθείᾳ δὲ ἡ σωτηρία, ... ἵνα τῇ μιμήσει τῶν παθημάτων αὐτοῦ κοινωνήσαντες, ἀληθείᾳ τὴν σωτηρίαν κερδήσωμεν.

We have thus a clear distinction of (1) the 'res sacramenti,' Christ's Death and Resurrection, (2) the 'sacramentum' or 'sign,' the outward form of Baptism, and (3) the 'virtus sacramenti,' our real participation in the benefits of Christ's Passion, "a death unto sin, and a new birth unto righteousness." Thus, as Cyril adds at the end of the section, Baptism "has the fellowship by representation of Christ's true sufferings," it is the spiritual counterpart in us of that which was actual in Him.

In *Mystag.* iii. § 1, speaking of the Chrism, Cyril says, "Now ye have been made Christs (Χριστοί) by receiving the antitype of the Holy Ghost, and all things have been wrought in you by imitation, because ye are images of Christ:" and again, "there was given to you an Unction, the antitype of that wherewith Christ was anointed, and this is the Holy Ghost."

Here again we have (1) the 'res sacramenti,' the anointing of Christ with the Holy Ghost at His Baptism, (2) the sacramental sign or figure, the anointing of the baptized, and (3) the spiritual benefit received in the gift of the Holy Ghost, for, as Cyril adds at the end of § 3, "while Thy body is anointed with the visible ointment, thy soul is sanctified by the Holy and Life-giving Spirit." In these passages we see a distinction between τύπος and ἀντίτυπος. The former is simply the outward sign or figure; the latter includes with the sign the spiritual counterpart in us of the thing signified, the benefits of Christ's Passion in the one case, the gift of the Holy Ghost in the other.

It only remains to inquire whether there is the same distinction in the meaning of the words as applied to the Holy Eucharist.

In *Mystag.* v. § 20, Cyril informs us that during the Administration the words, "O taste and see that the Lord is good," were sung: and in reference to that passage he adds, "In tasting we are bidden to taste not bread and wine, but the antitypical Body and Blood of Christ." To taste "the antitypical Body" is therefore to taste "that the Lord is good," whence it clearly follows that "the antitypical Body" is not the mere sign or figure of Christ's own natural Body, but the sacramental and spiritual counterpart of it, by which those who faithfully receive it are so united to Him, that their *spirit, and soul, and body, are to be preserved entire without blame* at His coming [6].

---

5 Cat. xiii. § 19: τὸ σῶμα αὔτου κατὰ τὸ εὐαγγέλιον τύπον ἔφερεν ἄρτου. 6 *Mystag.* iv. § 3: ἐν τύπῳ γὰρ ἄρτου δίδοταί σοι τὸ σῶμα.

7 1 Thess. v. 23, quoted at the end of *Mystag.* v. § 23.

CHAPTER VIII.

Place of S. Cyril's Lectures.

We have seen in a passage already quoted[1] that at Milan S. Ambrose expounded the Creed to Catechumens in the Baptistery. But whatever may have been the custom in other places, it is certain from numerous passages in Cyril's Lectures that they were delivered in the great Basilica, or Church of the Resurrection, built by Constantine on the site of the Holy Sepulchre, and consecrated, as we have seen, with great splendour in the year 335[2]. In a passage[3] where Cyril is speaking of the descent of the Holy Ghost on the day of Pentecost, he says, "as we discourse on Christ and Golgotha here in Golgotha, so it were most fitting that we should also speak concerning the Holy Ghost in the Upper Church; yet since He who descended there jointly partakes of the glory of Him who was crucified here, we here speak concerning Him also who descended there." It appears from a passage in the Introductory Lecture[4] that it was delivered in the Church itself before the whole congregation, after that portion of the daily Service to which Catechumens were usually admitted: "Dost thou behold this venerable constitution of the Church? Dost thou view her order and discipline, the reading of Scripture, the presence of the Ordained, the course of instruction?" The same custom was retained in Jerusalem in the time of John, Cyril's successor in the Bishopric, who in writing to Jerome says, "The custom with us is that we deliver the doctrine of the Holy Trinity publicly during forty days to those who are to be baptized[5]."

The Mystagogic Lectures were delivered not in the Church, but after the conclusion of the public Service "in the Holy Place of the Resurrection itself[6]," that is, in the small Chapel which contained the Holy Sepulchre, and to which the name "Anastasis" more properly belonged. Happily we are not required by the purpose of this work to enter into the disputed questions concerning the Holy Places. Whether the cave re-fashioned and adorned by Constantine was the actual sepulchre in which our Lord's body was laid, and whether the present Churches occupy the same site as the Basilica and Anastasis of Constantine, are matters still under discussion, and awaiting the result of further researches. What more properly concerns us is to collect the chief passages in which Cyril refers to these localities, and to try to give a fair representation of his testimony, comparing it with that of earlier or contemporary writers.

Next to Eusebius, and the Bordeaux Pilgrim who visited Jerusalem in 333, Cyril is the earliest and most important witness as to the site of Constantine's Churches.

In Cat. xiv. § 5, he says, "It was a garden where He was crucified. For though it has now been most highly adorned with royal gifts, yet formerly it was a garden, and the signs and the remnants of this remain." From this it is evident that the traces of a garden close to the Church were still visible both to Cyril and his hearers. Twice again in § 11 he mentions the garden, which he had most probably himself seen in its former state, before the ground was cleared at the time of the recovery of the Holy Sepulchre in 326.

On this point it may be well to quote the words of Mr. Walter Besant, Honorary Secretary of the Palestine Exploration Fund, who, in an article on "The Holy Sepulchre" in the *Dictionary of Christian Antiquities*, writes as follows: "While the temple of Venus with its foundations was being cleared away, there might have been, and most probably was present, a Christian lad, native of Jerusalem, eleven years of age, watching the discovery, which did as much as the great luminous cross which appeared in the sky four (? twenty-four) years later to confirm the doubtful and strengthen the faithful, that of the rock containing the

---

1 Ch. II. § 2.

2 See above, Ch. I. p. 2. Cf. Cat. iv. 10; x. 19; xiii. 4, 22, 39; xiv. 9, 14, 22, &c

3 Cat. xvi. § 4.

4 *Procat.* § 4.

5 Hieron. *Ep.* 61 (al. 38). The passage is quoted more fully below on p. xliv.

6 Cat. xviii. § 33.

sacred tomb. It was Cyril, afterwards Bishop of Jerusalem. One must not forget that he is the third eye-witness who speaks of these things; that though he was a boy at the time of the discovery, he lived in Jerusalem, and must have watched, step by step, the progress of the great Basilica; that he was ordained before the completion and dedication of the buildings, and that many, if not all, of his lectures were delivered in the Church of the Anastasis itself."

That Cyril's testimony concerning the Holy Places was in full accordance with the general belief of his contemporaries is clear from the fact that he so frequently points to the traditional sites as bearing witness to the truth of the Crucifixion and Resurrection. He speaks of Golgotha in eight separate passages, sometimes as near to the Church in which he and his hearers are assembled[7], and sometimes as standing up above in their sight[8]. In one place he asks, "Seest thou this spot of Golgotha?" and the hearers answer with a shout of approval[9]. In other passages he speaks as if the Church itself was *in* or rather *on* Golgotha[1], the same Preposition (ἐν) being repeated when he mentions "Him who was crucified thereon."

In explanation of these different modes of speaking, the Benedictine Editor comments thus[2]: "The Church of the Resurrection was built on part of the hill Golgotha (*intra montem G.*): but the actual rock on which our Lord was crucified was not within the limits of the Church, yet not far off, namely about "a stone's throw," as the author of the *Jerusalem Itinerary* says. For the Church had been built on the site of the Sepulchre. Some think that the place of Crucifixion was included in the vast area which was enclosed with colonnades between the Sepulchre and the Basilica, . . . that Golgotha was midway between the Basilica of the Crucifixion, and the Anastasis or Sepulchre. But the area in question Constantine paved with stones, and it must therefore have been flat, as we learn from Eusebius[3]; Golgotha, on the contrary, stood up high[4], and moreover shewed a cleft made there at Christ's death[5], which would either have been a hindrance to the paving or covered up by it. In addition to this, from the doors of the Basilica there seems to have been a view of the Sacred Tomb[6]. This would have been obstructed if Golgotha had been between them."

The cleft in the rock of Golgotha is mentioned in a fragment of the defence made before Maximinus in 311 or 312 by Lucian the Martyr of Antioch[7]: "If yet you believe not, I will also offer you the testimony of the very spot on which the thing was done. The place itself in Jerusalem vouches for these facts, and the rock of Golgotha broken asunder under the weight of the Cross: that cave also, which when the gates of hell were burst, gave back the Body in newness of life" On this passage Dr. Routh remarks that Maundrell, *Journey from Aleppo to Jerusalem, at Easter*, 1697, "shews that the rock had been rent not by any instrument, but by the force of an earthquake. Also it is related by Eusebius in his Theophania, a book now recovered, that there was one cave only in this cleft of the rock."

According to Eusebius in the passages of the *Life of Constantine* already referred to, the Emperor first beautified the monument or sepulchre with rare columns, then paved with finely polished stone a large area open to the sky, and enclosed on three sides with long colonnades, and lastly erected the Church itself "at the side opposite to the cave, which was the Eastern side."

---

7 xiii. § 4: οὗτος ὁ Γολγοθᾶς οὗ πλησίον νῦν πάντες πάρεσμεν.

8 x. § 19: ὁ Γ. ὁ ἅγιος οὗτος ὁ ὑπερανεστηκὼς μαρτυρεῖ φαινόμενος. Cf. xiii. 19.

9 xiii. § 23: Ὁρᾷς τοῦ Γολγοθᾶ τὸν τόπον; Ἐπιβοᾷς ἐπαίνῳ ὡς συντιθέμενος.

1 iv. § 10: ὁ μακάριος οὗτος Γ. ἐν ᾧ νῦν διὰ τὸν ἐν αὐτῷ σταυρωθέντα συγκεκροτήμεθα. Cf. § 14: ὁ ἐν τῷ Γ. τούτῳ σταυρωθείς. xiii. § 22: xvi. 4: ἐν τῷ Γ τούτῳ λέγομεν.

2 Cat. xiii. § 4, note 1.

3 *Vit. Const.* iii. c. 35.

4 Cat. x. § 19; xiii. § 39.

5 xiii. § 39.

6 Eus. *Vit. Const.* iii. c. 36.

7 The fragment is added by Rufinus to his Latin translation of Eusebius, *Hist. Eccl.* ix. 6, and is also given in Routh, *Rell. Sacr.* iv. p. 6.

The following is the statement of the Bordeaux Pilgrim: "From thence (the Palace of David) as you go out of the wall of Sion walking towards the gate of Neapolis, on the right side below in the valley are walls where the house or Prætorium of Pontius Pilate was: here our Lord was tried before His Passion. On the left hand is the little hill (*monticulus*) of Golgotha, where the Lord was crucified. About a stone's throw from thence is a vault (*crypta*) wherein His body was laid, and rose again on the third day. There by command of the Emperor Constantine has now been built a Basilica, that is to say, a Church of wondrous beauty, having at the side reservoirs (*exceptoria*) from which water is raised, and a bath behind in which infants are washed (baptized)." Neapolis was the name given by Vespasian to the ancient city of Shechem, now Nâbulus: the "porta Neapolitana" therefore was in the North wall of Sion.

In reference to the passage quoted above, Mr. Aubrey Stewart says: "The narrative is clear and connected, and it is hardly possible, for any one who knows the ground, to read it without feeling that the Pilgrim from Bordeaux actually saw Constantine's buildings standing on the site now occupied by the Church of the Holy Sepulchre [8]."

From these earlier testimonies, compared with the several passages already quoted from Cyril, we may safely draw the following inferences. (1) The Anastasis properly so called, or Church of the Holy Sepulchre, in which the five Mystagogic Lectures were delivered, was built by Constantine over the cave which, according to the evidence then existing, was fully believed to be the Burial-place of our Lord. (2) The Great Basilica, called also the Church of the Holy Cross, in which the Catechetical Lectures were delivered, was erected on the East of the Anastasis, and separated from it by a large open area. (3) The hill of Golgotha (on which at a later period there was built a third Church, called the Church of Golgotha, of Holy Calvary, or of Cranium) stood about a stone's throw on the North side of Constantine's two Churches, and about equidistant from them.

CHAPTER IX.

The Time and Arrangement of S. Cyril's Lectures.

§ 1. *The Year.* The incidental notes of time in the Catechetical Lectures are sufficient to determine with considerable probability the exact year in which they were delivered.

In Cat. xiv. 14, Cyril speaks in the Plural of the Emperors then reigning (οἱ νῦν βασιλεῖς) as having completed the building (ἐξειργάσαντο) and embellishment of the great Church of the Resurrection. This can only apply to the sons of Constantine, Constans and Constantius; and as Constans died early in 350, the Lectures must have been delivered before that year.

In Cat. xv. § 6, Cyril asks, "Is there at this time war between Persians and Romans, or no?" The time thus indicated was apparently that of the campaign which ended in the disastrous defeat of Constantius at Singara, 348, the battle being soon followed by a suspension of hostilities [1].

The Benedictine Editor tries to find another proof of the date of the Lectures in Cyril's description of the state of the Church in Cat. xv. § 7: "If thou hear that Bishops advance against Bishops, and clergy against clergy, and laity against laity, even unto blood, be not troubled." Touttée refers this account to the fierce dissensions which followed the Synod of Sardica, where Athanasius and Marcellus were declared innocent and received into communion, while the Encyclical of the dissentient Bishops, who had withdrawn to Philippopolis, condemned them both. But it is now ascertained that the Synod of Sardica was held not in 347, as Touttée supposed, but in 344 [2]: and Cyril's description may unhappily be applied to

---

8 *The Bordeaux Pilgrim*, Introd. p. ix.

1 See Gibbon, c. xviii. vol. ii. p. 370.

2 *Dict. Chr. Biogr.* "Athanasius," p. 190, note; Hefele, *Councils*, §§ 58, 66, 67.

the state of the Church at almost any time from the Council of Tyre, by which Athanasius had been deposed in 335, until long after any date which can possibly be assigned to Cyril's Lectures.

There is a much more definite note of time in Cat. vi. § 20, where speaking of Manes Cyril says: "The delusion began full seventy years ago." If we may assume that the outbreak of this heresy is to be dated from the famous disputation between Archelaus and Manes in 277[3], it follows that Cyril must have made this statement in 347 or 348. And further, if Dr. Routh[4] is correct in fixing the date of the Disputation between July and December 277, the Lent in which the Lectures were delivered must have been, as Touttée decides, that of 348, not of 347, as Tillemont had supposed.

§ 2. *The days.* It is expressly stated by Sozomen[5] that "the interval called Quadragesima" was made to consist of six weeks in Palestine, "whereas it comprised seven weeks in Constantinople and the neighbouring provinces."

It is certain the Catechetical Lectures i.-xviii. were all delivered in these six weeks, being preceded by the Procatechesis, which was addressed to the candidates before the whole congregation at the public Service on Sunday (§ 4). In the same context Cyril says, "Thou hast forty days for repentance," and again in Cat. i. § 5, "Hast thou not forty days to be free for thine own soul's sake?" It thus appears probable that the first of the eighteen Catechetical Lectures was delivered on the Monday of the first week of the Fast, the forty days being completed on the night preceding the Great Sabbath, that is to say, the night of Good Friday, when the fast was brought to an end at a late hour.

With regard to the date of Cat. iv., which contains a brief preliminary statement of all the articles of the Creed, we may obtain some evidence from an incident recorded in a letter of Jerome[6] to Pammachius. John, who had then succeeded Cyril as Bishop of Jerusalem, had on a certain occasion discoursed on the Creed and all the doctrines of the Church in the presence of Epiphanius and the whole congregation. Jerome, being ignorant of the peculiar custom of the Church of Jerusalem, rebukes the supposed presumption of the Bishop, "that a man deficient in eloquence should in one discourse in Church discuss all the doctrines concerning the Trinity, the Incarnation, the Crucifixion, the descent into hell, the nature of angels, the state of departed souls, the Resurrection of Christ, and of ourselves, and other subjects." The rebuke calls out a statement from John: "The custom among us is that for forty days we publicly deliver the doctrine of the Holy and Adorable Trinity to those who are to be baptized." This being the custom at Jerusalem in Cyril's time, we may conjecture that Cat. iv., which corresponds closely to the description of John's discourse, was delivered, like that, on a Sunday before the whole congregation: and this is in fact suggested by Cyril's own words in § 3: "Let those here present, whose habit of mind is mature, and who *have their senses already exercised to discern good and evil*, endure patiently to listen to things fitted rather for children." That this could not have been later than the Sunday following that on which the Procatechesis was delivered, is shewn by the mention in the same section of "the long interval of the days of all this holy Quadragesima," an expression which could not well have been used later than the second Sunday in Lent.

In Cat. iv. § 32, Cyril speaks of having discoursed on Baptism "the day before yesterday," that is, on the Friday.

In Cat. v. we have first a discourse on the nature of faith, and then towards the end, between § 12 and § 13, the actual words of the Creed are for the first time recited by Cyril to the candidates alone. In the next four Lectures there are no marks of time, except that

3 Cat. vi. § 27. 4 *Rell. Sac.* v. p. 12. 5 *Hist. Eccles.* vii. c. 19. 6 *Ep.* 61 (al. 38). Cf. Ben. Ed. *Praeloq. ad* Cat. iv. pp 49, 50.

vi., vii., viii., were delivered on successive days, as is proved by the word "yesterday" (τῇ χθὲς ἡμέρᾳ) in vii. § 1, and viii. § 1. It thus appears probable that the five Lectures, v.—ix., belong to the five days, Monday to Friday inclusive, of the second or third week.

In Cat. x. § 14 Cyril reminds his hearers that he had preached on the words *after the order of Melchizedek* at the public Service on the Lord's day. As he does not here employ his usual phrase "yesterday," we may infer that Cat. x. was delivered not earlier than the Tuesday following the 4th Sunday in Lent, the Epistle for that Sunday in the Eastern Church being Heb. vi. 13—20, which ends with the words on which Cyril had preached. The next two Lectures followed Cat. x. immediately on successive days, Wednesday and Thursday, the word "yesterday" recurring in xi. § 1, and xii. § 4.

Cat. xiii., which is occupied with the Crucifixion and Burial, seems to have followed them immediately on the Friday: it certainly came a few days only before Cat. xiv. § 1. For speaking there of the preceding Lecture, Cyril says, "I know the sorrow of Christ's friends in these past days; because, as our discourse stopped short at the Death and the Burial, and did not tell the good tidings of the Resurrection, your mind was in suspense to hear what you were longing for." Now we know that Cat. xiv. was delivered on the Monday after Passion Sunday: for the Epistle for that 5th Sunday in Lent was Heb. vi. 11—14, referring to the Ascension[7]: and in § 24 Cyril says, "The grace of God so ordered it, that thou heardest most fully concerning it, so far as our weakness allowed, yesterday on the Lord's day, since by the providence of divine grace the course of the Readings (ἀναγνωσμάτων) in Church included the account of our Saviour's going up into the heavens."

In Cat. xv. there is no note of time to determine on what day it was spoken; but in § 33 Cyril speaks as if his course of teaching was to be interrupted for a little while: "If the grace of God should permit us, the remaining Articles also of the Faith shall be in good time (κατὰ καιρόν) declared to you." We may therefore assign Cat. xv. to the early part of Passion week, and the three remaining Catechetical Lectures to the week before Easter. This arrangement seems to be confirmed by Cat. xvii. 34, where Cyril speaks of the two Lectures on the Holy Spirit, xvi. and xvii., as "these present Lectures," distinguishing them from "our previous discourses." In the same section he refers to "the fewness of the days," and in § 20 speaks of "the holy festival of the Passover" as being close at hand. We may therefore probably assign xvi. and xvii. to two consecutive days in the earlier part of the week before Easter.

Cat. xviii. contains many indications from which we may conclude with certainty that it was delivered either on the night of Good Friday, or in the early hours of the morning of the "Great Sabbath." Thus in § 17 he speaks of "the weariness caused by the prolongation (ὑπερθέσεως) of the fast of the Preparation (Friday), and the watching." In § 21 he calls upon the Candidates to recite the Creed, which he had dictated to them, and which they would be required to repeat more publicly immediately before their Baptism, as we learn from § 32: "Concerning the holy Apostolic Faith which has been delivered to you to profess (εἰς ἐπαγγελίαν), we have spoken through the grace of the Lord as many Lectures as was possible in these past days of Lent. . . . But now the holy day of the Passover is at hand, and ye, beloved in Christ, are to be enlightened *by the washing of regeneration.* Ye shall therefore again be taught what is requisite if God so will; with how great devotion and order you must enter in when summoned, for what purpose each of the holy mysteries of Baptism is performed, and with what reverence and order you must go from Baptism to the holy altar of God, and enjoy its spiritual and heavenly mysteries." The additional instructions here promised were to be given on the same day as the last Lecture, Cat. xviii., that is on Easter Eve immediately before Baptism. For it was forbidden to reveal the mysteries of Baptism, Chrism, and the

7 *Dict. Chr. Antiq.* "Lectionary," p. 958 b.

Holy Eucharist to the uninitiated, and yet it was necessary that the Candidates should not come wholly unprepared to perform what would be required of them. The full explanation of the various ceremonies and of the doctrines implied in them was reserved for the Mystagogic Lectures, which were to be delivered on Easter Monday and the four following days, after the public Service, not in the great Basilica, but in the Holy Sepulchre itself.

§ 3. *Arrangement.* The Lectures of S. Cyril have a peculiar value as being the first and only complete example of the course of instruction given in the early centuries to Candidates seeking admission to the full privileges of the Christian Church. "The Great Catechetical Oration" of Gregory of Nyssa is addressed not to the learner but to the teacher, in accordance with the opening statement of the Prologue, that "The presiding ministers of *the mystery of godliness* have need of a system in their instructions, in order that the Church may be replenished by the accession of such as should be saved, through the teaching of the word of Faith being brought home to the hearing of unbelievers." As an instruction to the Catechist how he should refute the opponents of Christianity, it is an apologetic work rather than a Catechism. S. Augustine's treatise *De catechizandis rudibus* is also addressed to the teacher, being an answer to Deogratias, a Deacon of Carthage, who on being appointed Catechist had written to Augustine for advice as to the best method of discharging the office. S. Augustine's Sermons *De traditione Symboli*, and *De redditione Symboli*, are not a connected series, but single addresses to Catechumens consisting of brief comments on a few chief articles of the Creed. Cyril's Lectures thus remain unique in character.

After the Procatechesis, which is simply an introductory exhortation to the newly admitted Candidates, he devotes three Lectures to the need of a sincere purpose of mind, the efficacy of repentance, and the general nature and importance of Baptism. The fourth Lecture gives "a short summary of necessary doctrines," stating with admirable clearness and brevity ten chief points of the Faith, and the arguments on each point, which are to be developed in the remaining Catechetical Lectures v.—xviii. He thus traverses the whole ground of Theology as expressed in the Creed of Jerusalem, of which the exact language is given in the titles of the successive Lectures. These instructions to the 'Illuminandi' (φωτιζομένων) were followed on Easter-day by the administration of Baptism, Chrism, and Holy Communion: and on the following days of Easter-week the ceremonies and doctrines proper to each of these Sacraments were explained in the five Lectures on the Mysteries (Μυσταγωγίαι) to the newly-baptized (πρὸς τοὺς Νεοφωτίστους). These Mystagogic Lectures thus form a most important record of the Sacramental Rites and Doctrines of the Eastern Church in the fourth Century, the most critical period of Ecclesiastical History.

CHAPTER X.

The Creed of Jerusalem: Doctrine of The Holy Trinity.

§ 1. *The Creed.* The ancient Creed which was used by the Church of Jerusalem in the middle of the fourth Century, and which Cyril expounded in his Catechetical Lectures, was recited by him to the Catechumens at the end of the fifth Lecture, to be committed to memory, but not to be written out on paper (§ 12). Accordingly it is not found in any of the MSS., but instead of it the Nicene Creed with the Anathema is there inserted in Codd. Roe, Casaub. This could only have been added after Cyril's time, when the motives for secrecy had ceased.

The Creed which Cyril really taught and expounded may be gathered from various passages in the Lectures themselves, and especially from the Titles prefixed to them.

With the Creed of Jerusalem thus ascertained, it will be instructive to compare the Nicene formula, and for this purpose we print them in parallel columns.

CREED OF S. CYRIL OF JERUSALEM.

Πιστεύομεν εἰς ἕνα Θεόν [1],
Πατέρα [2] Παντοκράτορα [3],
Ποιητὴν οὐρανοῦ καὶ γῆς
Ὁρατῶν τε πάντων καὶ ἀοράτων [4].

Καὶ εἰς ἕνα Κύριον Ἰησοῦν Χριστόν [5],
τὸν Υἱὸν τοῦ Θεοῦ
τὸν Μονογενῆ,
τὸν ἐκ τοῦ Πατρὸς γεννηθέντα,
Θεὸν ἀληθινὸν
πρὸ πάντων τῶν αἰώνων,
δι' οὗ τὰ πάντα ἐγένετο [6],

τὸν σαρκωθέντα καὶ ἐνανθρωπήσαντα [7],
σταυρωθέντα καὶ ταφέντα [8],
καὶ ἀναστάντα ἐκ νεκρῶν τῇ τρίτῃ ἡμέρᾳ,
καὶ ἀνελθόντα εἰς τοὺς οὐρανούς,
καὶ καθίσαντα ἐκ δεξιῶν τοῦ Πατρός [9],

καὶ πάλιν ἐρχόμενον ἐν δόξῃ
κρῖναι ζῶντας καὶ νεκρούς,
οὗ τῆς βασιλείας οὐκ ἔσται τέλος [1].

Καὶ εἰς ἓν ἅγιον Πνεῦμα
τὸν Παράκλητον,
τὸ λαλῆσαν ἐν τοῖς προφήταις [2].

καὶ εἰς ἓν βάπτισμα μετανοίας εἰς ἄφεσιν ἁμαρτιῶν [3],
καὶ εἰς μίαν ἁγίαν καθολικὴν ἐκκλησίαν,
καὶ εἰς σαρκὸς ἀνάστασιν,
καὶ εἰς ζωὴν αἰώνιον [4].

[1] Cat. vi. tit. [2] vii. tit.; § 4. [3] viii. tit. [4] ix. tit.; § 4. [5] x. tit.; vii. 4. [6] xi. tit.; § 21. [7] xii. tit. [8] xiii. tit. [9] xiv. tit., cf. § 27; xv. 3. [1] xv. tit.; § 2. [2] xvi. tit.; xviii. 3. [3] xviii. 22. [4] xviii. tit.; § 22.

CREED OF NICÆA.

From S. Athanasius, De Decretis Fidei Nicænæ.

Πιστεύομεν εἰς ἕνα Θεόν,
Πατέρα παντοκράτορα,
πάντων ὁρατῶν τε
καὶ ἀοράτων ποιήτην,

καὶ εἰς ἕνα Κύριον Ἰησοῦν Χριστόν,
τὸν Υἱὸν τοῦ Θεοῦ,
γεννηθέντα ἐκ τοῦ Πατρὸς μονογενῆ,
τουτέστιν ἐκ τῆς οὐσίας τοῦ Πατρός,
Θεὸν ἐκ Θεοῦ, φῶς ἐκ φωτός. Θεὸν ἀληθινὸν ἐκ Θεοῦ ἀληθινοῦ,
γεννηθέντα οὐ ποιηθέντα, ὁμοούσιον τῷ Πατρί,
δι' οὗ τὰ πάντα ἐγένετο,
τά τε ἐν τῷ οὐρανῷ καὶ τὰ ἐπὶ τῆς γῆς,
τὸν δι' ἡμᾶς τοὺς ἀνθρώπους καὶ διὰ τὴν ἡμετέραν σωτηρίαν [1]
κατελθόντα καὶ σαρκωθέντα, ἐνανθρωπήσαντα, παθόντα,
καὶ ἀναστάντα τῇ τρίτῃ ἡμέρᾳ,
ἀνελθόντα εἰς οὐρανούς,
καὶ ἐρχόμενον
κρῖναι ζῶντας καὶ νεκρούς,

καὶ εἰς τὸ ἅγιον Πνεῦμα.

Τοὺς δὲ λέγοντας· ἦν ποτε ὅτε οὐκ ἦν, καί πρὶν γεννηθῆναι οὐκ ἦν, καὶ ὅτι ἐξ οὐκ ὄντων ἐγένετο, ἢ ἐξ ἑτέρας ὑποστάσεως ἢ οὐσίας φάσκοντας εἶναι ἢ κτιστὸν ἢ τρεπτὸν ἢ ἀλλοιωτὸν τὸν Υἱὸν τοῦ Θεοῦ, ἀναθεματίζει ἡ καθολικὴ ἐκκλησία.

[1] Cyril, Cat. iv. 9; xii. 3; *Mystag.* ii. 7.

§ 2. *Doctrine of the Holy Trinity.* The doctrinal position of S. Cyril is admirably described, and his orthodoxy vindicated by Cardinal Newman in the following passage of his Preface to the Lectures in the Library of the Fathers. "There is something very remarkable and even startling to the reader of S. Cyril, to find in a divine of his school such a perfect agreement, for instance as regards the doctrine of the Trinity, with those Fathers who in his age were more famous as champions of it. Here is a writer, separated by whatsoever cause from what, speaking historically, may be called the Athanasian School, suspicious of its adherents, and suspected by them; yet he, when he comes to explain himself, expresses precisely the same doctrine as that of Athanasius or Gregory, while he merely abstains from the particular theological term in which the latter Fathers agreeably to the Nicene Council conveyed it. Can we have a clearer proof that the difference of opinion between them was not one of ecclesiastical and traditionary doctrine, but of practical judgment? that the Fathers at Nicæa wisely considered that, under the circumstances, the word in question was the only symbol which would secure the Church against the insidious heresy which was assailing it, while S. Cyril, with Eusebius of Cæsarea, Meletius and others shrank from it, at least for a while, as if an addition to the Creed, or a word already taken into the service of an opposite heresy, and likely to introduce into the Church heretical notions? Their judgment, which was erroneous, was their own; their faith was not theirs only, but shared with them by the whole Christian world [1]."

In regard to the doctrine of the Trinity in general the two great heresies which distracted the Church in S. Cyril's day were Sabellianism and Arianism, the one "confounding the Persons," the other "dividing the substance" of the indivisible Unity of the Godhead. Both these opposite errors Cyril condemns with equal energy: "Do thou neither separate the Son from the Father, nor by making a confusion believe in a Son-Fatherhood [2]." Again he says: "Our hope is in Father, and Son, and Holy Ghost. We preach not three Gods; let the Marcionites be silenced; but with the Holy Ghost through One Son we preach One God. The Faith is indivisible; the worship inseparable. We neither separate the Holy Trinity, like some (that is the Arians); nor do we, as Sabellius, work confusion [3]." "He says not, I am the Father, but *the Father is in Me, and I am in the Father*. And again He said not, *I and the Father* am *one*, but, *I and the Father are One*, that we should neither separate them, nor make a confusion of Son-Father [4]."

In the sequel of this last passage Cyril proceeds to argue that this unity of the Father and the Son lies in their Nature, "since God begat God," in their Kingdom [5], in their Will [6], and in their joint Creation [7], thus at each step rejecting some prominent heretical tenet.

The question, however, of Cyril's orthodoxy depends especially upon his supposed opposition to the Creed of Nicæa, of which no evidence is alleged except his attendance at the Council of Seleucia, and the absence from his Lectures of the word ὁμοούσιον.

The purpose of Cyril's attendance at Seleucia was to appeal against his deposition by Acacius, and there is apparently no evidence of his having taken part in the doctrinal discussions, or signed the Creed of Antioch [8]. What is certain is that Cyril's bitterest enemies who refused to sit with him in the Council were Acacius and his Arian allies, who expressly rejected both ὁμοούσιος and ὁμοιούσιος and "altogether denied the Nicene formula and censured the Council, while the others, who were the majority, accepted the whole proceedings of the Council, except that they complained of the word 'Co-essential,' as obscure, and so open to suspicion [9]." It thus appears that Cyril's friends at Seleucia were partly those who approved the word "Co-essential," and partly those of whom Athanasius speaks as "brothers, who mean what we mean, and dispute only about the word [1]." It needed in fact the profound insight of an Athanasius to foresee that in the end that word must triumph over all opposition, and be accepted by the Universal Church as the one true safeguard of the Christian Faith. Meanwhile it was the standard round which, debate, and strife, and hatred, and persecution, were to rage for fifty years with unexampled fury.

Was Cyril to be blamed, ought he not rather to be commended, for not introducing such a war-cry into the exposition of an ancient Creed, in which it had no place, the Creed of his own Church, the Mother of all the Churches, whose Faith he as a youthful Presbyter was commissioned to teach to the young Candidates for Baptism?

But if we compare his doctrine with that of the Nicene formula, we shall find that, as Dr. Newman says, "His own writings are most exactly orthodox, though he does not in the Catechetical Lectures use the word ὁμοούσιον [2]."

The first point to be noticed in the comparison is the use of the title "Son of God."

---

1 *Preface*, p. ix. 2 Cat. iv. § 8.

3 Cat. xvi. § 4. See the notes on this and the preeeding passage. 4 Cat. xi. § 16. 5 Cat. xv. § 27, note 3.

6 Athan. *Contra Arian.* Or. ii. § 31, 1: "For the Word of God is Framer and Maker, and He is the Father's Will. Cf. Or. iii. § 63 fin.

7 Ib. Or. iii. § 11, 3: "Such then being the Son, therefore when the Son works, the Father is the Worker."

8 There is, I believe, no extant list of signatures: "Whether the few Homoüsians and Hilary were among those who signed is not said" (Hefele, *Councils*, II. p. 264).

9 Athan. *De Synod.* c. 12. 1 Ib. c. 41. 2 *Preface*, p. 14.

For this Eusebius in his Creed had substituted "Word of God." Athanasius explains the significance of the change: "Uniting the two titles, Scripture speaks of 'Son' in order to herald the natural and true offspring of His essence (οὐσίας); and on the other hand that none may think of the offspring as human, in again indicating His essence it calls Him Word, and Wisdom, and Radiance; for from this we infer that the generation was impassible (ἀπαθές), and eternal, and becoming to God[3]."

Cyril is here in full accord with Athanasius: in his Creed he found "Son of God," and in his exposition he states that the Father is "by nature and in truth Father of One only, the Only-begotten Son[4]:" "One they are because of the dignity pertaining to the Godhead, since God begat God[5]:" "The Son then is VERY GOD, having the Father in Himself, not changed into the Father[6]." When he says that the Son is in all things like (ὅμοιος ἐν πᾶσιν) to Him who begat Him; begotten Life of Life, and Light of Light, Power of Power, God of God, and the characteristics of the Godhead are unchangeable (ἀπαράλλακτοι) in the Son[7]," he is using in all good faith the very words of the orthodox Bishops at Nicæa, "ὅμοιόν τε καὶ ἀπαράλλακτον αὐτὸν κατὰ πάντα τῷ Πατρί[8]."

The further significance which Athanasius ascribes to the title "Logos," is also expressed fully and repeatedly by Cyril: "Whenever thou hearest of God begetting, sink not down in thought to bodily things, nor think of a corruptible generation, lest thou be guilty of impiety[9]."

The "passionless generation," to which so much importance was attached at Nicæa and by Athanasius, is also asserted by Cyril when he says that God "became a Father not by passion (οὐ πάθει Πατὴρ γενόμενος)[1]." The eternal generation is most emphatically declared again and again: the Son, he says, "began not His existence in time, but was before all ages eternally and incomprehensibly begotten of the Father; the Wisdom, and the Power of God, and His Righteousness personally subsisting[2]:" "Throughout His being (ἐξ οὗπερ ἦν), a being by eternal generation, He holds His royal dignity, and shares His Father's seat[3]." "Believe that of One God there is One Only-begotten Son, who is before all ages God the Word; not the uttered word diffused into the air, nor to be likened to impersonal words; but the Word, the Son, Maker of all who partake of reason, the Word who heareth the Father, and Himself speaketh[4]."

The importance of such language is better understood when we remember that Marcellus, "another head of the dragon lately sprung up in Galatia[5]," entirely rejected the word "Begotten," as implying a beginning, and "contradicting the eternity of the Logos, so distinctly proclaimed by S. John." An eternal generation, as stated by Athanasius and others, was to him unimaginable. The Logos in His pre-existence was unbegotten, and could not be called Son, but only the Logos invested with human nature was Son of God and begotten[6]." These heretical opinions of Marcellus had been condemned in several Councils within a few years preceding Cyril's Lectures.

The next supposed proof of Cyril's opposition to the Nicene doctrine is that he has not adopted in his Lectures the phrases "of the essence (οὐσίας) of the Father," and "of one essence (ὁμοούσιον) with the Father." This omission is the chief ground of the reproaches cast upon the memory of Cyril by the writers of Ecclesiastical History; for this he was described by Jerome as an Arian, and by Rufinus as a waverer, while his formal acceptance of the terms used at Nicæa is called by Socrates and Sozomen an act of repentance. By others he was denounced as Ἀρειανόφρων because he had addressed his letter to Constantius as "the most religious king," and never used the word ὁμοούσιον in his Lectures.

---

3 *Contra Arianos*, Or. i. 28. 4 Cat. vii. § 5. 5 Ib. xi. § 16. 6 Ib. § 17. 7 Ib. § 18. 8 Athan. *De Decretis*, c. 20. 9 Cat. xi. § 7. 1 Ib. vii. 5: see note there. 2 Ib. iv. 7. 3 Ib. 4 Ib. iv. § 8. 5 Ib. xv. § 27. 6 Zahn, *Marcellus of Ancyra*, as quoted by Hefele, *Councils*, II. p. 31, slightly abridged. See also Hefele, p. 186.

We shall be better able to estimate the justice of these reproaches, if we consider first the history of these words οὐσία and ὁμοούσιος, and the reasons which Cyril may have had for not employing them in the instruction of youthful Candidates for Baptism.

It is strange to find that seven hundred years before the great controversy at Nicæa on the introduction of the word Οὐσία into the Creed, it had been the war-cry of almost as fierce a conflict between rival schools of philosophy.

"There appears," says Plato in the person of the Eleatic stranger, "to be a sort of war of the giants going on between them because of the dispute concerning οὐσία. Some of them are dragging all things down from heaven and from the invisible to earth, grasping rocks and oaks in their hands; for of all such things they lay hold, in obstinately maintaining that what can be touched and handled alone has being (εἶναι), because they define 'being' and 'body' as one; and if any one else says that what is not a body has being, they altogether despise him, and will hear of nothing but body. . . . Therefore their opponents cautiously defend themselves from above out of some invisible world, mightily contending that certain intelligible and incorporeal ideas are the true essence (οὐσίαν) [7]."

It is apparently to this passage of Plato that Aristotle refers in describing the ambiguity of the word οὐσία [8]: "Now Οὐσία seems to belong most manifestly to bodies: wherefore animals and plants and their parts we say are οὐσίαι, also natural bodies as fire and water and earth and all such things, and all either parts of these, or products either of parts or the whole, as the heaven and its parts, stars, moon, and sun. But whether these are the only οὐσίαι or there are others also, or none of these but others of a different kind, is a matter for inquiry. Some think that the boundaries of bodies, as a surface, and a line and a point and a unit (μονάς), are οὐσίαι, even more so than body and solid. Further, one class of persons thinks that besides things sensible there is no οὐσία, and another that there are many things, and these more enduring (ἀΐδια), as Plato thinks that the ideas (εἴδη) and the mathematical elements are two kinds of οὐσία, and that the οὐσία of sensible bodies is a third."

In proceeding to define the term, Aristotle says that οὐσία is used in four senses if not more: the essential nature (τὸ τί ἦν εἶναι), the universal (τὸ καθόλου) the genus, and a fourth the subject (τὸ ὑποκείμενον). Under this fourth sense he proceeds to discuss the application of the term ουσια to the matter, the form, and the resulting whole. Without going further we may see that the use of the word in philosophy was full of difficulty and ambiguity.

The ambiguity is thus expressed by Mr. Robertson [9]: "We may look at a concrete term as denoting either this or that individual simply (τόδε τι), or as expressing its nature, and so as *common* to more individuals than one. Now properly (πρώτως) οὐσία is only appropriate to the former purpose. But it may be employed in a secondary sense to designate the latter, in this sense species and genera are δεύτεραι οὐσίαι, the wider class being less truly οὐσίαι than the former." Perhaps the earliest use of οὐσία in Christian writings is in Justin M. [1], where he describes the Logos as "having been begotten from the Father, by His power and will, but not by abscission (ἀποτομήν), as if the οὐσία of the Father were divided, as all other things when divided and cut are no longer the same as before." His example was fire, from which other fires are kindled, while it remains undiminished and unchanged. According to Dr. Newman [2], οὐσία here means "substance, or being."

In Clement of Alexandria [3], οὐσία means a "nature" common to many, for he speaks of the Gnostic Demiurge as creating an irrational soul ὁμοούσιον with the soul of the beasts;" and again as implanting in man "something co-essential (ὁμοούσιον) with himself, inasmuch as he is invisible and incorporeal; his essence (οὐσίαν) he called "the breath of life," but the thing formed (μορφωθέν) became "a living soul," which in the prophetic Scriptures he

---

[7] Plato, *Sophist.* § 246. "The passage is quoted by Theodoret, *Græcarum affectionem Curatio*, ii. p. 732." (Heindorf.)
[8] *Metaph.* vi. § 2. [9] Athanasius, *Proleg.* p. xxxi., in this Series. [1] *Tryph.* c. 128 *. [2] *Arians*, p. 186. [3] *Fragm.* § 50, Sylb. 341.

confesses himself to be. Again in § 42 of the same Fragment, according to the Valentinians, "the body of Jesus is co-essential (ὁμοούσιον) with the Church."

So Hippolytus[4] speaks of the Son Incarnate as being "at one and the same time Infinite God and finite Man, having the nature (οὐσίαν) of each in perfection:" and again, "There has been effected a certain inexpressible and irrefragable union of the two (the Godhead and the Manhood) into one subsistence (ὑπόστασιν)."

In Origen we find the two words οὐσία (essence, or substance) and ὑπόστασις (individual subsistence) accurately distinguished. Quoting the description of Wisdom, as being the breath (ἀτμίς) of the power of God, and pure effluence (ἀπόρροια) from the glory of the Almighty, and radiance (ἀπαύγασμα) of the Eternal Light[5]," he says that "Wisdom proceeding from Him is generated of the very substance of God," and adds that "these comparisons most manifestly shew that there is community of substance between Father and Son. For an effluence appears to be ὁμοούσιος, that is, of one substance with that body from which it is an effluence or vapour."

On the other hand he writes, "We worship the Father of the Truth, and the Son who is the Truth, being in subsistence (τῇ ὑποστάσει) two[6]." On this passage Bishop Bull remarks: "The words ὑπόστασις and οὐσία in ancient times were variously used, at least by the Christians. That is to say, sometimes ὑπόστασις was taken by them for what we call οὐσία, and *vice versa*, οὐσία for what we call ὑπόστασις: sometimes the ancients even before the Council of Nicæa used ὑπόστασις for what we now call 'person' or 'subsistence[7].'" This Bishop Bull presently explains again as "an individual thing subsisting by itself, which in rational beings is the same as *person*."

For examples of these interchanges of meaning, we may notice that the Synod of Antioch (A.D. 269), in the Epistle addressed to Paul of Samosata before his deposition, speaking of the unity of Christ's *Person*, says that "He is one and the same in His οὐσίᾳ[8]." On this passage Routh remarks that "The words οὐσία and φύσις are sometimes employed by the ancients for a personal subsistence (*persona subsistente*), as is plainly testified by Photius."

In the earlier part[9] of the same Epistle the Son is described as "being before all ages, not in foreknowledge, but in essence and subsistence (ἐν οὐσίᾳ καὶ ὑποστάσει)."

The confusion arising from the uncertainty in the use of these two words is well illustrated in the account which Athanasius[1] himself gives of this same Synod of Antioch: "They who deposed the Samosatene, took Co-essential (ὁμοούσιος) in a bodily sense, because Paul had attempted sophistry and said, 'Unless Christ has of man become God, it follows that He is Co-essential with the Father; and if so, of necessity there are three essences (οὐσίαι), one the previous essence, and the other two from it;' and therefore guarding against this they said with good reason, that Christ was not Co-essential (ὁμοούσιον)." Athanasius then explains on what grounds the Bishops at Nicæa "reasonably asserted on their part, that the Son was Co-essential" Athanasius himself states that, in giving this explanation of the rejection of ὁμοούσιον by the Bishops who condemned the Samosatene, he had not their Epistle before him[2]; and his statement, that Paul used the term not to express his own view, but to refute that of the Bishops, is thought to be opposed to what Hilary says[3], "Male ὁμοούσιον Samosatenus confessus est: sed numquid melius Ariani negaverunt?"

That the statement of Athanasius himself is not free from difficulty is clear from the way in which so great a Theologian as Bishop Hefele endeavours to explain it: "Athanasius says that Paul argued in this way: If Christ is Ὁμοούσιος with the Father, then three subsistences (οὐσίαι) must be admitted—one first substance (the Father), and two more recent (the Son and

4 *Adv. Beron. et Hel.* Fragm. i. 5 Wisdom of Solomon, vii. 25, quoted by Origen, *Fragm. in Epist. ad Hebræos*, Lommatzsch, V. p. 300. 6 *Contra Celsum*, viii. p. 386. 7 *Def. Fid. Nic.* II. c. 9, § 11. 8 Routh, *Rel. Sacr.*, III. p. 299
9 Ib. p. 290. 1 *De Synodis*, c. 45, p. 474, in this Series. 2 Ib. c. 43. 3 *Liber de Synodis*, 513.

the Spirit); that is to say, that the Divine Substance is separated into three parts[4]." The logical subtlety of Paul was better understood by Basil the Great[5]: "For in truth they who met together about Paul of Samosata found fault with the phrase, as not being distinct; for they said that the word ὁμοούσιος gave the idea of an οὐσία and of those derived from it, so that the title ὁμοούσιον assigned the οὐσία separately to the subjects to which it was distributed: and this notion has some reason in the case of copper and the coins made from it; but in the case of God the Father, and God the Son, there is no substance conceived to be antecedent and superior to both: for to say and to think this surpasses all bounds of impiety."

The confusion arising from the uncertainty in the use of these words had been the cause of strife throughout the Christian Church for more than twenty years before the date of Cyril's Lectures; and though it was declared at the Council of Alexandria (362) to be but a controversy about words[5a], it had long been and long afterwards continued to be a fruitful cause of dissension between men who, when forced to explain their meaning, were found to be in substantial agreement. That Cyril abstained from introducing into his elementary teaching terms so provocative of dangerous controversy, is a reason for commendation, not for censure. But if it is alleged that he denied or doubted or failed to assert the essential Godhead of the Son, the suspicion is unfounded and easily refuted. To the many passages already quoted concerning the eternal generation of the Son, it will be enough to add one single sentence which ought to dispel all doubt of his orthodoxy. "The Only-begotten Son, together with the Holy Ghost, is partaker of the Godhead of the Father (τῆς θεότητος τῆς Πατρικῆς κοινωνός)." The word chosen by Cyril to express the Divine Essence (θεότης) common to the three Persons of the Godhead is at least as appropriate as οὐσία.

If we now look at the particular errors mentioned in the Anathema of the Nicene Council, we shall find that every one of them is earnestly condemned by Cyril.

"*Once He was not* (Ἦν ποτε ὅτε οὐκ ἦν). This famous Arian formula is expressly rejected in Cat. xi. § 17: "Neither let us say, There was a time when the Son was not." The eternity of the Son is asserted again and again, in reference, for instance, to His generation[6], His Priesthood[7], and His throne[8].

"*Before His generation He was not*" (πρὶν γεννηθῆναι οὐκ ἦν). Compare with this Cyril's repeated assertions that "the Son is eternally begotten, by an inscrutable and incomprehensible generation[9]," "the Son of God BEFORE ALL AGES, without beginning[1]," that "time intervenes not in the generation of the Son from the Father[2]."

"*He came to be from nothing*" (ἐξ οὐκ ὄντων ἐγένετο). Cyril's language is emphatic: "As I have often said, He did not bring forth the Son from non-existence (ἐκ τοῦ μὴ ὄντος) into being, nor take the non-existent into Sonship[3]."

"*That He is of other subsistence or essence*" (ἐξ ἑτέρας ὑποστάσεως ἢ οὐσίας). It is certain that Cyril has given no countenance to the error or errors condemned in this clause, but is in entire agreement with the Council.

On the question whether ὑπόστασις and οὐσία have in this passage the same or different meanings, see Bull, *Def. Fid. Nic.* II. 9, 11, p. 314 (*Oxf. Ed.*). Athanasius expressly states that they are perfectly equivalent: "Subsistence (ὑπόστασις) is essence (οὐσία), and means nothing else but very being, which Jeremiah calls existence (ὕπαρξις)." Basil distinguishes them, and is followed by Bishop Bull, whose opinion is controverted by Mr. Robertson in an Excursus on the meaning of the phrase, on p. 77 of his edition of Athanasius in this Series. The student who desires to pursue the subject may consult in addition to the works

4 Councils, I. p. 124. 5 *Epist.* 300 (al. 52), quoted by Bull, *D.F.N.* ii. 1, § 11. 5a Athan. *Tomus ad Antiochenos*, §§ 5, 6. 6 Cat. iv. § 7. 7 Ib. x. § 14. 8 Ib. xiv. § 27. 9 Cat. xi. § 4. 1 § 5. 2 § 7.

3 § 14. Cf. S. Alex. *Epist. apud Theodoret*, § 4: "That the Son of God was not made 'from things which are not,' and that 'there was no time when He was not,' the Evangelist John sufficiently shews" (Ante-Nic. Library).

just named, and the authorities therein mentioned, Dr. Newman's *Arians of the Fourth Century*, especially chap. v. sect. i. 3, and Appendix, note iv., on "the terms οὐσία and ὑπόστασις as used in the early Church;" Mr. Robertson's *Prolegomena*, ch. ii. § 3 (2) (b); and the Rev. H. A. Wilson's *Prolegomena* to Gregory of Nyssa, ch. iv., in this Series.

CHAPTER XI.

S. Cyril's Writings.

§ 1. *List of Works.* Besides the Catechetical and Mystagogic Lectures translated in this volume, the extant works of S. Cyril include (1) the "Letter to the Emperor Constantius concerning the appearance at Jerusalem of a luminous Cross in the sky:" (2) "The Homily on the Paralytic at the Pool of Bethesda:" and (3) Fragments of Sermons on the Miracle of the water changed into wine, and on Joh. xvi. 28, "I go to My Father."

Another work attributed by some authorities to Cyril of Jerusalem and by others to Cyril of Alexandria is a Homily *De Occursu Domini*, that is, On the Presentation of Christ in the Temple, and the meeting with Symeon, called in the Greek Church ἡ Ὑπαπαντή.

The other Fragments and Letters mentioned in the Benedictine Edition have no claim to be considered genuine.

§ 2. *Authenticity of the Lectures.* The internal evidence of the time and place at which the Lectures were delivered has been already discussed in chapters viii. and ix., and proves beyond doubt that they must have been composed at Jerusalem in the middle of the fourth century. At that date Cyril was the only person living in Jerusalem who is mentioned by the Ecclesiastical Historians as an author of Catechetical Lectures: and S. Jerome, a younger contemporary of Cyril, expressly mentions the Lectures which Cyril had written in his youth. In fact their authenticity seems never to have been doubted before the seventeenth century, when it was attacked with more zeal than success by two French Protestant Theologians of strongly Calvinistic opinions, Andrew Rivet (*Critic. Sacr.* Lib. iii. cap. 8, Genev. 1640), and Edmund Aubertin (*De Sacramento Eucharistiæ*, Lib. ii. p. 422, Ed. Davent., 1654). Their objections, which were reprinted at full length by Milles at the end of his Edition, were directed chiefly against the Mystagogic Lectures, and rested on dogmatic rather than on critical grounds. The argument most worthy of notice was that in a MS. of the Library of Augsburg the Mystagogic Lectures were attributed to John, Bishop of Jerusalem. This is admitted by Milles, who gives the title thus: Μυσταγωγικαὶ κατηχήσεις πέντε Ἰωάννου Ἐπισκόπου Ἱεροσολύμων, περὶ βαπτίσματος, χρίσματος, σώματος, καὶ αἵματος Χριστοῦ.

I do not find this Codex Augustinus mentioned elsewhere by any of the Editors under that name: but the Augsburg MSS. were removed to Munich in 1806, and in the older Munich MS. (Cod. Monac. 1), the title of the first Mystagogic Lecture is Μυσταγωγία πρώτη Ἰωάννου ἐπισκόπου Ἱεροσολύμων. Also in Codd. Monac. 2, Ottobon. there is added at the end of the Title, τοῦ αὐτοῦ Κυρίλλου καὶ Ἰωάννου ἐπισκόπου. That John, Cyril's successor, did deliver Catechetical Lectures, we know from his own correspondence with Jerome: and this very circumstance may account for his name having been associated with, or substituted for that of Cyril.

To Rivet's objection Milles makes answer that if the mistakes of a transcriber or the stumbling of an ignorant Librarian (*imperiti Librarii cæspitationes*) have in one or two MSS. ascribed the Lectures to John or any one else, this cannot be set against the testimony of those who lived nearest to the time when the Lectures were composed, as Jerome and Theodoret. Also the internal evidence proves that the Lectures could not have been delivered later than the middle of the fourth century, whereas John succeeded Cyril about 386.

Moreover it is quite impossible to assign the two sets of Lectures to different authors.

In Cat. xviii. § 33 the author promises, as we have seen, that he will fully explain the Sacramental Mysteries in other Lectures to be given in Easter week, in the Holy Sepulchre itself, and describes the subject of each Lecture; to which description the Mystagogic Lectures correspond in all particulars. Other promises of future explanations are given in Cat. xiii. § 19, and xvi. § 26, and fulfilled in *Myst.* iv. § 3, and ii. § 6, and iii. § 1. On the other hand the author of *Myst.* i. § 9, after quoting the words, "I believe in the Father, and in the Son, and in the Holy Ghost, and in one Baptism of repentance," adds, "Of which things I spoke to thee at length in the former Lectures."

By these and many other arguments drawn from internal evidence Touttée has shewn convincingly that all the Lectures must have had the same author, and that he could be no other than Cyril.

§ 3. *Early Testimony.* Under the title "Veterum Testimonia de S. Cyrillo Hierosolymitano ejusque Scriptis," Milles collected a large number of passages bearing on the life and writings of S. Cyril, of which it will be sufficient to quote a few which refer expressly to his Lectures.

S. Jerome, in his *Book of Illustrious Men*, or *Catalogue of Ecclesiastical Writers*, composed at Bethlehem about six years after Cyril's death, writes in Chapter 112: "Cyril, Bishop of Jerusalem, having been often driven out from the Church, afterwards in the reign of Theodosius held his Bishopric uudisturbed for eight years: by whom there are Catechetical Lectures, which he composed in his youth."

Theodoret, born six or seven years after the death of Cyril, in his *Dialogues* (p. 211 in this Series) gives the "Testimony of Cyril, Bishop of Jerusalem, from his fourth Catechetical Oration concerning the ten dogmas. Of the birth from a virgin, "Believe thou this, &c."

Theophanes (575 *circ.*) *Chronographia*, p. 34, Ed. Paris, 1655, defends the orthodoxy of Cyril, as follows: "It was right to avoid the word ὁμοούσιος, which at that time offended most persons, and through the objections of the adversaries deterred those who were to be baptized, and to explain clearly the co-essential doctrine by words of equivalent meaning: which also the blessed Cyril has done, by expounding the Creed of Nicæa word for word, and proclaiming Him VERY GOD OF VERY GOD."

Gelasius, Pope 492, *De duabus in Christo naturis*, quotes as from Gregory Nazianzen the words of Cyril, Cat. iv. § 9: Διπλοῦς ἦν ὁ Χριστός, κ.τ.λ.

Leontius Byzantinus (610 *circ.*), *Contra Nestor. et Eutychem*, Lib. I. quotes the same passage expressly as taken "From the 4th Catechetical Oration of Cyril, Bishop of Jerusalem."

Many other references to the Catecheses as the work of Cyril are given by Touttée, pp. 306—315.

§ 4. *Editions.* **1.** Our earliest information concerning the Greek text and translations of S. Cyril's Lectures is derived from John Grodecq, Dean of Glogau in Bohemia.

From his statement it appears that Jacob Uchanski, Archbishop of Gnessen and Primate of Poland, had obtained from Macedonia a version of the Catecheses in the Slavonic dialect, and had translated it into the Polish language some years before 1560.

2. In that year Grodecq himself published at Vienna an edition of the Mystagogic Lectures, thus described in the catalogue of the Imperial Library:—

"S. Cyril's Mystagogic Lectures to the newly baptized, which now for the first time are edited in Greek and Latin together, that he who doubts the Latin may have recourse to the Greek, and he who does not understand Greek well may read the Latin, translated by John Grodecq."

Nothing more is known of this edition: Fabricius, Milles, Touttée, and Reischl, all say that they have been unable to find any trace of it. Uchanski about this time sent to Grodecq his Slavonic and Polish versions, in order that they might be compared with the

Greek original. The result according to Grodecq was that the fidelity of both versions was clearly shewn, and "there could not possibly remain any doubt that these Lectures of Cyril are perfectly genuine."

Whether Uchanski's book was written or printed is unknown, as no trace of it has hitherto been found.

3. S. Cyrilli Hier. Catecheses ad Illuminandos et Mystagogicæ. Interpretatus est Joannes Grodecius. Romæ 1564. 8°.

Grodecq had come to Rome in the suite of Stanislaus Hosius, Cardinal Legate at the Council of Trent, who in the year 1562 had published in the Confession of Petricow the 4th and part of the 3rd Mystagogic Lectures from a Greek MS. belonging to Cardinal Sirlet. From this MS. Grodecq made his Latin translation, using also the work of Uchanski before mentioned. The preface is dated from Trent, on the 9th of July, 1563. The translation was published in the following year at Rome, Cologne, Antwerp, and Paris, and often elsewhere until superseded by the new Latin Version of Touttée in the Benedictine Edition.

4. In the same year, 1564, the Mystagogic Lectures and Catecheses iv., vi., viii.—x., xv., xviii. were published at Paris by William Morel, the King's Printer, under the following title:—

"S. Cyrilli Hier. Catecheses, id est institutiones ad res sacras, Græce editæ, ex bibliotheca Henrici Memmii, cum versione Latina. Cura Guil. Morellii. Paris. G. Morel., 1564. 4° min."

The Greek text depending on de Mesme's one MS., and that mutilated and faulty, is said by Touttée to have many faults and omissions, but to have been nevertheless very useful to him in correcting the text. The MS. itself had entirely disappeared. The Latin version, appended to the copy in the Royal (National) Library at Paris, but not always attached to the Greek, is said by Touttée to be a careful and elegant version, independent of Grodecq's.

A copy of Morel's Edition which formerly belonged to Du Fresne, containing various readings in the margin from two other MSS., was lent to Touttée from the Library of S. Geneviève (Genovef.).

Reischl describes the MS. as "Cod. Mesmianus (Montf. I. 185). Sec. xi."

5. "S. Cyrilli H. Catecheses Græce et Latine ex interpretatione Joan. Grodecii nunc primum editæ, ex variis bibliothecis, præcipue Vaticana, studio et opera Joan. Prevotii. Paris. (Claude Morellus), 1608." This was the first complete edition of the Greek text. Prevot, a native of Bordeaux, states in the Dedication to Pope Paul V., that by the help of MSS. "melioris notæ" found in the Vatican, he had both corrected the text of the Lectures previously published by Morel, and carefully transcribed the rest. He made, according to Touttée, many useful emendations, but did not mention the number, age, nor various readings of the MSS. employed.

6. "S. Cyrilli Hier. Arch. opera quæ supersunt omnia; quorum quædam nunc primum ex Codd. MSS. edidit, reliqua cum Codd. MSS. contulit, plurimis in locis emendavit, Notisque illustravit Tho. Milles S.T.B. ex Æde Christi. Oxoniæ, e Theatro Sheldoniano, Impensis Richardi Sare Bibliopol. *Lond.* MDCCIII."

The author of this fine Edition gives us in his Preface the following description of his work:—

"In the first place I wished to amend more thoroughly the text of J. Prevot, which, as I said, he himself largely corrected and supplied from MSS. in the Vatican, and which I have printed in this Edition: I have therefore compared it with all the other Editions that I could collect, and in this manner have easily removed many errors both of the printers and of Prevot himself. Afterwards I carefully compared all the Catecheses and the Epistle to Constantinus with two MSS. and some with three, namely iv., vi., viii.—x., xv., xvi., xviii. The first Codex, written on parchment apparently six hundred years ago, I found among those MSS. which Sir Tho. Roe, our first Ambassador from King James I. to the Great Mogul, brought from the East, and presented to the Bodleian Library. The second we owe to the diligence of Isaac Casaubon, who collated the Catecheses and Epistle to Constantius with a MS. which he chanced to find, I think, in some Library in France, and carefully noted all the various readings in the margin. This copy of Casaubon's the Right Reverend Father in Christ, John Bishop of Norwich, very kindly lent to me out of his well-furnished Library, and of his great love for learning did not disdain to shew the highest favour to my slight endeavours."

Touttée thinks that the MS. from which Casaubon drew his various readings was C. Roe itself, or that one of the two MSS. had been copied from the other, or both from the same.

7. "S. Cyrilli Arch. Hier. opera quæ exstant omnia et ejus nomine circumferuntur, ad MSS. codices necnon ad superiores Editiones castigata, Dissertationibus et Notis illustrata, cum nova interpretatione et copiosis indicibus. Cura et studio Domni Antonii-Augustini Touttéi, Presbyteri et Monachi Benedictini e Congregatione S. Mauri. Paris. Typis Jac. Vincent. 1720, fol. (Recusa Venet. 1763)."

Of the Greek text the Editor says, "I have collated it as carefully as I could with Grodecq's translation, Morel's and Prevot's Editions, and with MSS. to be found in this City. The various readings of the Roman MSS. I have obtained by the help of friends: those which Milles had collected from the English Codices I have adopted for my own use."

8. "S. Cyrilli Hier. Arch. opp. quæ supersunt omnia ad libros MSS. et impressos recensuit Notis criticis commentariis indicibusque locupletissimis illustravit Gulielm. Car. Reischl S. Th. D. et Reg. Lycei Ambergensis Professor. Vol. I. Monac. MDCCCXLVIII."

The Editor says in his Preface that he has altered the Benedictine text only when the evidence was very weighty, and has then given all the various readings in the critical notes. The exegetical commentary was to be reserved for the 2nd Volume, but this Dr. Reischl did not live to complete.

The Prolegomena contain (1) Touttée's inordinately long "Life of Cyril," (2) a Dissertation on the general character and authenticity of the Catecheses, and (3) an "Apparatus Litterarius," to which I have been indebted.

Vol. ii., containing Catecheses xii.—xviii., *Myst.* i.-v., and the other works, genuine and spurious, attributed to Cyril, was published by J. Rupp at Munich, 1860.

The MSS used in revising the text of this, the best critical edition, will be noticed below.

9. An Edition of the Catecheses only was published at Jerusalem in 1867, having been commenced in 1849 at the request of the Archbishop, Cyril II., by Dionysius Kleopas, Principal of the Theological School of Jerusalem, and, after his death in 1861, continued by his successor Photius Alexandrides, "Archdeacon of the Apostolic and Patriarchal See of Jerusalem, and Principal of the Theological School."

The Editor gives in the Preface an interesting account of the life of Kleopas, and of the work which he left unfinished.

§ 5. Manuscripts. From the preceding account of the various Editions of S. Cyril we may obtain the following list of authorities which have been hitherto used in revising the Text.

1. Codex Sirletianus, known only by Grodecq's Latin version, Rome, 1564. Cf. § i. 3.

2. C. Mesmianus, known only in Morel's edition, Paris, 1564. Cf. § i. 4.

3. Vatican MSS. used by Prevot, 1608, but not identified. Cf § i. 5.

4. C. Roe, Bibl. Bodleian. Oxon. "Codex membranaceus in folio, ff. 223, sec. xi., binis columnis bene exaratus;" [ol. 271].

5. C. Casaubon. On this and the preceding MS. see Milles as quoted above, § i. 6.

6. C. Ottobonianus (1) ol. Rom. iv. membran. sec. xi. "Continet Catecheses omnes et Epist. ad Constantium. Multas habet insignes ab editis varietates."

C. Ottob. (2), "Chartaceus et recens est, nihil fere ab editis discrepans."

These are the Roman MSS. mentioned by Touttée: see above, § i. 7.

7. C. Coislin. 227 (ol. 101). Membran. Sæc. xi. *circ.* "From this came many important emendations" (Touttée, *Notitia Codicum MSS.).*

In the descriptions of the following MSS. of the National Library at Paris there is so much discrepancy between Touttée and Reischl, that it is better to quote both.

8. "Catecheses xii., xiii., xiv., xv., comparavi cum Codice Reg. bibliothecæ num. 2503. Scriptus est in bombycina charta an. 1231, quam anni notam apposuit calligraphus" (Touttée, *Not. Codd. MSS.*).

Reischl has no notice of a MS. at all answering to this description.

9. Cod. Reg. alter, "ol. 1260, nunc 1824, qui S. Basilii opera complectitur, sub ejus nomine Procatechesin continet" (Touttée, *Not. Codd. MSS.*) : *aliter*, "Cod. Reg. ol. 260, nunc 1284, pag. 254, qui duodecimi circiter est sæculi, in quo habetur Procatechesis hæc sub nomine S. Basilii" (Id. *Monit. in Procatechesin*).

"Cod. Reg. 467 (apud Toutteum, 1824) Fonteblandensis, chartac. fol. sec. x. Continet sub S. Basilii nomine *Orationem de Baptismo*, quæ est S. Cyrilli Hier. Procatechesis. C. Reg. Touttéi" (Reischl).

10. "Cod. Reg. 969 (ol. Mazarin.) Epistolarum S. Basilii. 4°. Sec. xiv. Exhibet sub n. 7 Basilii homiliam *quo* (sic) *ostenditur Deum esse incomprehensibilem*, quæ non S. Basilii, sed Cyrilli est Procatechesis" (Reischl).

This description agrees in substance with Touttée's.

11. C. Colbert. "Catecheses iv., vi., viii., ix., x., xv., xviii., contuli cum cod. Colbert. Biblioth. chartaceo et recenti 4863 notato . . . In omnibus pene cum Morelliana editione consentit" (Touttée, *Notitia Codd. MSS.*).

Reischl makes no mention of this MS.

12. C. Colbert. alter. "membran. sign. 1717, Sec. xiii. diversas Patrum homilias continet, et Cat. xiii. exhibet sub nomine Cyrillianæ in Crucem et Porasceven homiliæ" (Touttée, *Notitia*).

This is described by Reischl as "Cod. Reg. 771 (ol. 1717) Colbertinus. Membran. fol. seculi xiii.—xiv."

The following MSS have been used in Editions later than the Benedictine.

13. "C. Monacensis I. 394 membran. fol., titulis et initialibus miniatis, f. 261 nitidissime uncialibus minutis circiter seculo decimo in Oriente scriptus."

This was regarded both by Reischl and by Rupp as the most important authority for the text: it is much older than Codd. Roe, Casaub., and seems to be related to Codd. Ottobon. Coislin.

C. Mon. 2 of the 16th Century is of little value.

14. "C. Vindobonensis, 55, membran. fol antiquissimus, sed incerto sæculo"

A full account is given by Rupp in the Preface to Vol. ii. It was collated by Joseph Müller, 1848, and contains all Cyril's Lectures, except the Procatechesis.

15. Codex A, found by Kleopas in the Library of the Archbishop of Cyprus, and used as the basis of his text, sometimes stands alone in preserving the true reading.

§ 6. *Versions.* Besides the Latin Translations published with the Greek text, as mentioned above, Reischl mentions the first three of the following :—

(*a*) Les catéchèses de Sainct Cyrille. Traduit par Louis Ganey. Paris, 1564.

(*b*) Cyrill's Schriften übersetzt und mit Anmerkungen versehen von J. Mich. Feder. Bamberg, 1786.

(*c*) Cyrilli Hier Catecheses in Armen. Linguam versæ. Viennæ 1832.

(*d*) The Catechetical Lectures of S. Cyril, Archbishop of Jerusalem, Translated, with Notes and Indices (Library of Fathers of the Holy Catholic Church.) Parker, Oxford, 1838. See Preface.

(*e*) S. Cyril on the Mysteries. (The five Mystagogic Lectures.) H. de Romestin. Parker, Oxford, 1887.

(*f*) On Faith and the Creed. C. A. Heurtley, D.D., Margaret Professor of Divinity, and Canon of Christ Church, Oxford. Parker, 3rd Ed., 1889. Contains, with other Treatises, the Fourth Catechetical Lecture of S. Cyril.

In the present volume the translation given in the Oxford "Library of Fathers" has been carefully revised throughout. Where it has been found necessary to depart from the Benedictine text, the Editor has consulted the readings and critical notes of Milles, Reischl, and Rupp, and the Jerusalem edition of Kleopas and Anaxandrides.

A few additions have been made to the Index of Subjects: the Indices of Greek Words and of Scripture Texts have been much enlarged, and carefully revised. For any errors which may have escaped observation the indulgence of the critical reader will not, it is hoped, be asked in vain.

E. H. G.

THE

CATECHETICAL LECTURES

OF

S. CYRIL,

ARCHBISHOP OF JERUSALEM.

CONTENTS.

PROCATECHESIS,

OR,

PROLOGUE TO THE CATECHETICAL LECTURES OF OUR HOLY FATHER, CYRIL, ARCHBISHOP OF JERUSALEM.

---

1. ALREADY there is an odour of blessedness upon you, O ye who are soon to be enlightened[1]: already ye are gathering the spiritual[2] flowers, to weave heavenly crowns: already the fragrance of the Holy Spirit has breathed upon you: already ye have gathered round the vestibule of the King's palace[3]; may ye be led in also by the King! For blossoms now have appeared upon the trees[4]; may the fruit also be found perfect! Thus far there has been an inscription of your names[5], and a call to service, and torches[6] of the bridal train, and a longing for heavenly citizenship, and a good purpose, and hope attendant thereon. For he lieth not who said, *that to them that love God all things work together for good.* God is lavish in beneficence, yet He waits for each man's genuine will: therefore the Apostle added and said, *to them that are called according to a purpose*[7]. The honesty of purpose makes thee called: for if thy body be here but not thy mind, it profiteth thee nothing.

2. Even Simon Magus once came to the Laver[8]: he was baptized, but was not enlightened; and though he dipped his body in water, he enlightened not his heart with the Spirit: his body went down and came up, but his soul was not buried with Christ, nor raised with Him[9]. Now I mention the statements[1] of (men's) falls, that thou mayest not fall: for these things happened to them by way of example, *and they are written for the admonition*[2] of those who to this day draw near. Let none of you be found tempting His grace, *lest any root of bitterness spring up and trouble you*[3]. Let none of you enter saying, Let us see what the faithful[4] are doing: let me go in and see, that I may learn what is being done. Dost thou expect to see, and not expect to be seen? And thinkest thou, that whilst thou art searching out what is going on, God is not searching thy heart?

3. A certain man in the Gospels once pried into the marriage feast[5], and took an unbecoming garment, and came in, sat down, and ate: for the bridegroom permitted it. But when he saw them all clad in white[6], he ought to have assumed a garment of the same kind himself: whereas he partook of the like food, but was unlike them in fashion and in purpose. The bridegroom, however, though bountiful, was not undiscerning: and in going round to each of the guests and observing them (for his care was not for their eating, but for their seemly behaviour), he saw a stranger *not having on a wedding garment*, and said to him, *Friend, how camest thou in hither?* In what a colour[7]! With what a conscience! What though the door-keeper forbade thee not, because of the bountifulness of the entertainer? what though thou wert ignorant in what fashion thou shouldest come in to the banquet?—thou

---

1 The "blessedness" is the grace of Baptism, the hope of which is as a fragrant odour already borne towards the Candidates. These were called no longer Catechumens, but φωτιζόμενοι, as already on the way "to be enlightened." Compare xvi. 26, the last sentence, and see Index, "enlighten."

2 *νοητά*. The word is much used by Plato to distinguish things which can be discerned only by the mind from the objects of sight and sense. Here "the spiritual (or, mental) flowers" are the Divine truths in which "the fragrance of the Holy Spirit" breathes.

3 By "the vestibule" is meant "the outer hall of the Baptistery" (xix. 2). and by "the King's Palace" the Baptistery itself, which Cyril calls "the inner chamber" (xx. 1) and "the bride-chamber" (iii. 2; xxii. 2). See Index, "Baptistery." Here the local terms have also an allegorical sense, Baptism being regarded as the marriage of the Soul to Christ.

4 Another allegory, from the season of Spring, when the Lectures were delivered.

5 *ὀνοματογραφία*. See Index.

6 That the Candidates on their first admission carried torches or lighted tapers in procession is a conjecture founded on this passage and Lect. I. 1: "Ye who have just lighted the torches of faith, preserve them in your hands unquenched." But see Index, "Lights."

7 Rom. viii. 28. In S. Paul's argument the "purpose" is God's eternal purpose of salvation through Christ (Eph. i. 11; iii. 11): but Cyril applies it here to sincerity of purpose in coming to Baptism.

8 Acts viii. 13.

9 Rom. vi. 4; Col. ii. 12.

1 Greek, *ὑπογραφή*, meaning either an "indictment," or a descriptive "sketch." For the former meaning, see Plato, *Theaet.* 172, E. *ὑπογραφὴν . . . ἣν ἀντωμοσίαν καλοῦσιν.*

2 1 Cor. x. 11.

3 Heb. xii. 15.

4 "The faithful" are those who have been already baptized, and instructed in those mysteries of the Christian Faith which were reserved for the initiated. See Index, "Faithful."

5 Matt. xxii. 12. The same passage is applied to Baptism in Cat. iii. 2.

6 See Cat. xxii. 8. and Index, "White."

7 The Greek word (*χρῶμα*) is used by Ignatius in the beginning of his *Epistle to the Romans* of a discolouring stain.

didst come in, and didst see the glittering fashions of the guests: shouldest thou not have been taught even by what was before thine eyes? Shouldest thou not have retired in good season, that thou mightest enter in good season again? But now thou hast come in unseasonably, to be unseasonably cast out. So he commands the servants, *Bind his feet*, which daringly intruded: *bind his hands*, which knew not how to put a bright garment around him: *and cast him into the outer darkness*; for he is unworthy of the wedding torches[8]. Thou seest what happened to that man: make thine own condition safe.

4. For we, the ministers of Christ, have admitted every one, and occupying, as it were, the place of door-keepers we left the door open: and possibly thou didst enter with thy soul bemired with sins, and with a will defiled. Enter thou didst, and wast allowed: thy name was inscribed. Tell me, dost thou behold this venerable constitution of the Church? Dost thou view her order and discipline[9], the reading of Scriptures[1], the presence of the ordained[2], the course of instruction[3]? Be abashed at the place, and be taught by what thou seest[4]. Go out opportunely now, and enter most opportunely to-morrow.

If the fashion of thy soul is avarice, put on another fashion and come in. Put off thy former fashion, cloke it not up. Put off, I pray thee, fornication and uncleanness, and put on the brightest robe of chastity. This charge I give thee, before Jesus the Bridegroom of souls come in and see their fashions. A long notice[5] is allowed thee; thou hast forty[6] days for repentance: thou hast full opportunity both to put off, and wash, and to put on and enter. But if thou persist in an evil purpose, the speaker is blameless, but thou must not look for the grace: for the water will receive, but the Spirit will not accept thee[7]. If any one is conscious of his wound, let him take the salve; if any has fallen, let him arise. Let there be no Simon among you, no hypocrisy, no idle curiosity about the matter.

5. Possibly too thou art come on another pretext. It is possible that a man is wishing to pay court to a woman, and came hither on that account[8]. The remark applies in like manner to women also in their turn. A slave also perhaps wishes to please his master, and a friend his friend. I accept this bait for the hook, and welcome thee, though thou camest with an evil purpose, yet as one to be saved by a good hope. Perhaps thou knewest not whither thou wert coming, nor in what kind of net thou art taken. Thou art come within the Church's nets[9]: be taken alive, flee not: for Jesus is angling for thee, not in order to kill, but by killing to make alive: for thou must die and rise again. For thou hast heard the Apostle say, *Dead indeed unto sin, but living unto righteousness*[1]. Die to thy sins, and live to righteousness, live from this very day.

6. See, I pray thee, how great a dignity Jesus bestows on thee. Thou wert called a Catechumen, while the word echoed[2] round thee from without; hearing of hope, and knowing it not; hearing mysteries, and not understanding them; hearing Scriptures, and not knowing their depth. The echo is no longer around thee, but within thee; for *the indwelling Spirit*[3] henceforth makes thy mind a house of God. When thou shalt have heard what is written concerning the mysteries, then wilt thou understand things which thou knewest not. And think not that thou receivest a small thing: though a miserable man, thou receivest one of God's titles. Hear St. Paul saying, *God is faithful*[4]. Hear another Scripture saying, *God is faithful and just*[5]. Foreseeing this, the Psalmist, because men are to receive a title of God, spake thus in the person of God: *I said, Ye are Gods, and are all sons of the Most High*[6]. But beware lest thou have the title of "*faithful*," but the will of the faithless. Thou hast entered into a contest, toil on through the race: another such opportunity thou canst not have[7]. Were it thy wedding-day before thee, wouldest thou not have disregarded all else, and set about the preparation for the feast? And on the eve of consecrating thy soul to the heavenly Bridegroom, wilt thou not cease from carnal things, that thou mayest win spiritual?

---

8 Compare § 1, note 6.

9 The Greek word (ἐπιστήμη) which commonly means "knowledge" or "understanding," is applied here and in vi. 35 to the intelligence and skill displayed in the arrangement of the public services of the Church. Compare *Apostolic Constitutions*, ii. 57, where the Bishop is exhorted to have the assemblies arranged μετὰ πάσης ἐπιστήμης.

1 In the same passage of the Apostolic Constitutions precise directions are given for reading a Lesson from the Old Testament, singing the Psalms, and reading the Epistle and Gospel.

2 By "the ordained" (κανονικῶν) are meant all whose names were registered as bearing office in the Church, Priests, Deacons, Deaconesses, Monks, Virgins, Widows, all having their appointed places and proper duties. *Apost. Canon.* 70, εἴ τις ἐπίσκοπος, ἢ πρεσβύτερος, ἢ διάκονος, ἢ ὅλως τοῦ καταλόγου τῶν κληρικῶν, κ.τ.λ.

3 Compare *Apost. Const.* as above: "Let the Presbyters one by one, not all together, exhort the people; and the Bishop last, as being the commander."

4 S. Aug. *de Civit. Dei*, ii. 28: "Though some come to mock at such admonitions, all their insolence is either humbled by a sudden conversion (immutatio) or suppressed by fear or shame."

5 Greek, προθεσμία. Compare Gal. iv. 2: "the time appointed of the father." At Athens it meant a "limitation," or fixed period within which a debt must be claimed or paid, or an action commenced.

6 Index, "Lent."

7 Compare xvii. 36.

8 S. Ambrose on the 119th Psalm, *Serm.* xx. § 48, speaks of some who pretended to be Christians in order to marry one whose parents would not give her in marriage to a heathen.

9 Matt. xiii. 47.

1 Rom. vi 11, 14.

2 S. Cyril plays upon the word "Catechumen," which has the same root as "echo."

3 Rom. viii. 9, 11.

4 1 Cor. i. 9.

5 1 John i. 9.

6 Ps. lxxxi. 6.

7 Compare xvii. 36.

7. We may not receive Baptism twice or thrice; else it might be said, Though I have failed once, I shall set it right a second time: whereas if thou fail once, the thing cannot be set right; for there is *one Lord, and one faith, and one baptism*[8]: for only the heretics are re-baptized[9], because the former was no baptism.

8. For God seeks nothing else from us, save a good purpose. Say not, How are my sins blotted out? I tell thee, By willing, by believing[1]. What can be shorter than this? But if, while thy lips declare thee willing, thy heart be silent, He knoweth the heart, who judgeth thee. Cease from this day from every evil deed. Let not thy tongue speak unseemly words, let thine eye abstain from sin, and from roving[2] after things unprofitable.

9. Let thy feet hasten to the catechisings; receive with earnestness the exorcisms[3]: whether thou be breathed upon or exorcised, the act is to thee salvation. Suppose thou hast gold unwrought and alloyed, mixed with various substances, copper, and tin, and iron, and lead: we seek to have the gold alone; can gold be purified from the foreign substances without fire? Even so without exorcisms the soul cannot be purified; and these exorcisms are divine, having been collected out of the divine Scriptures. Thy face has been veiled[4], that thy mind may henceforward be free, lest the eye by roving make the heart rove also. But when thine eyes are veiled, thine ears are not hindered from receiving the means of salvation. For in like manner as those who are skilled in the goldsmith's craft throw in their breath upon the fire through certain delicate instruments, and blowing up the gold which is hidden in the crucible stir the flame which surrounds it, and so find what they are seeking; even so when the exorcists inspire terror by the Spirit of God, and set the soul, as it were, on fire in the crucible of the body, the hostile demon flees away, and there abide salvation and the hope of eternal life, and the soul henceforth is cleansed from its sins and hath salvation. Let us then, brethren, abide in hope, and surrender ourselves, and hope, in order that the God of all may see our purpose, and cleanse us from our sins, and impart to us good hopes of our estate, and grant us repentance that bringeth salvation. God hath called, and His call is to thee.

10. Attend closely to the catechisings, and though we should prolong our discourse, let not thy mind be wearied out. For thou art receiving armour against the adverse power, armour against heresies, against Jews, and Samaritans[5], and Gentiles. Thou hast many enemies; take to thee many darts, for thou hast many to hurl them at: and thou hast need to learn how to strike down the Greek, how to contend against heretic, against Jew and Samaritan. And the armour is ready, and most ready *the sword of the Spirit*[6]: but thou also must stretch forth thy right hand with good resolution, that thou mayest war the Lord's warfare, and overcome adverse powers, and become invincible against every heretical attempt.

11. Let me give thee this charge also. Study our teachings and keep them for ever. Think not that they are the ordinary homilies[7]; for though they also are good and trustworthy, yet if we should neglect them to-day we may study them to-morrow. But if the teaching concerning the laver of regeneration delivered in a consecutive course be neglected to-day, when shall it be made right? Suppose it is the season for planting trees: if we do not dig, and dig deep, when else can that be planted rightly which has once been planted ill? Suppose, pray, that the Catechising is a kind of building: if we do not bind the house together by regular bonds in the building, lest some gap be found, and the building become unsound, even our former labour is of no use. But stone must follow stone by course, and corner match with corner, and by our smoothing off inequalities the building must thus rise evenly. In like manner we are bringing to thee stones, as it were, of knowledge. Thou must hear concerning the living God, thou must hear of Judgment, must hear of Christ, and of the Resurrection. And many things there are to be discussed in succession, which though now dropped one by one are afterwards to be presented in harmonious connexion. But unless thou fit them together in the one whole, and remember what is first, and what is second, the builder may build, but thou wilt find the building unsound.

12. When, therefore, the Lecture is delivered,

---

8 Eph. iv. 5.

9 This sentence is omitted in one MS. (Paris, 1824), but probably only through the repetition of the word "baptism." On the laws of the Church against the repetition of Baptism, and concerning the re-baptism of heretics, see Tertull. *de Baptismo*, c. xv.: *Apost. Const.* xv.: Bingham, xii. 5: Hefele, *Councils*, Lib. I. c. 2: Dictionary Christian Antiq. I. p. 167 a.

1 Rufinus, in the *Exposition of the Creed*, on the *Remission of sins*: "The Pagans are wont to say in derision of us, that we deceive ourselves in thinking that crimes which have been committed in deed can be washed out by words."

2 The reading in the Benedictine Edition, μηδὲ ὁ νοῦς σου ῥεμβέσθω, has little authority, and is quite unsuitable. See below, τὸ βλέμμα ῥεμβόμενον.

3 Index, "Exorcism."

4 Index, "Veiling"

5 The Samaritans are frequently mentioned by Epiphanius and other writers of the 4th century among the chief adversaries of Christianity. "In their humble synagogue, at the foot of the mountain (Gerizim), the Samaritans still worship, the oldest and the smallest sect in the world." (Stanley, *Sinai and Palestine*, p. 240.)

6 Eph. vi. 17.

7 See above, § 4, note 3.

if a Catechumen ask thee what the teachers have said, tell nothing to him that is without[8]. For we deliver to thee a mystery, and a hope of the life to come. Guard the mystery for Him who gives the reward. Let none ever say to thee, What harm to thee, if I also know it? So too the sick ask for wine; but if it be given at a wrong time it causes delirium, and two evils arise; the sick man dies, and the physician is blamed. Thus is it also with the Catechumen, if he hear anything from the believer: both the Catechumen becomes delirious (for he understands not what he has heard, and finds fault with the thing, and scoffs at what is said), and the believer is condemned as a traitor. But thou art now standing on the border: take heed, pray, to tell nothing out; not that the things spoken are not worthy to be told, but because his ear is unworthy to receive. Thou wast once thyself a Catechumen, and I described not what lay before thee. When by experience thou hast learned how high are the matters of our teaching, then thou wilt know that the Catechumens are not worthy to hear them.

13. Ye who have been enrolled are become sons and daughters of one Mother. When ye have come in before the hour of the exorcisms, let each one of you speak things tending to godliness: and if any of your number be not present, seek for him. If thou wert called to a banquet, wouldest thou not wait for thy fellow-guest? If thou hadst a brother, wouldest thou not seek thy brother's good?

Afterwards busy not thyself about unprofitable matters: neither, what the city has done, nor the village, nor the King[9], nor the Bishop, nor the Presbyter. Look upward; that is what thy present hour needeth. *Be still*[10], *and know that I am God.* If thou seest the believers ministering, and shewing no care, they enjoy security, they know what they have received, they are in possession of grace. But thou standest just now in the turn of the scale, to be received or not: copy not those who have freedom from anxiety, but cherish fear.

14. And when the Exorcism has been done, until the others who are being exorcised have come[11], let men be with men, and women with women. For now I need the example of Noah's ark: in which were Noah and his sons, and his wife and his sons' wives. For though the ark was one, and the door was shut, yet had things been suitably arranged. If the Church is shut, and you are all inside, yet let there be a separation, men with men, and women with women[1]: lest the pretext of salvation become an occasion of destruction. Even if there be a fair pretext for sitting near each other, let passions be put away. Further, let the men when sitting have a useful book; and let one read, and another listen: and if there be no book, let one pray, and another speak something useful. And again let the party of young women sit together in like manner, either singing or reading quietly, so that their lips speak, but others' ears catch not the sound: *for I suffer not a woman to speak in the Church*[2]. And let the married woman also follow the same example, and pray; and let her lips move, but her voice be unheard, that a Samuel[3] may come, and thy barren soul give birth to the salvation of "God who hath heard thy prayer;" for this is the interpretation of the name Samuel.

15. I shall observe each man's earnestness, each woman's reverence. Let your mind be refined as by fire unto reverence; let your soul be forged as metal: let the stubbornness of unbelief be hammered out: let the superfluous scales of the iron drop off, and what is pure remain; let the rust of the iron be rubbed off, and the true metal remain. May God sometime shew you that night, the darkness which shines like the day, concerning which it is said, *The darkness shall not be hidden from thee, and the night shall shine as the day*[4]. Then may the gate of Paradise be opened to every man and every woman among you. Then may you enjoy the Christ-bearing waters in their fragrance[5]. Then may you receive the name of Christ[6], and the power of things divine. Even now, I beseech you, lift up the eye of the

---

8 On the Disciplina Arcani, or rule against publishing the Christian Creed and Mysteries to Catechumens and Gentiles, see Index, "*Mysteries.*"

9 The title "King" (Βασιλεύς) is used in the Greek Liturgies and Fathers of the Roman Emperor, as in the Clementine Liturgy: ὑπὲρ τοῦ βασιλέως, καὶ τῶν ἐν ὑπεροχῇ, where it is taken from 1 Tim. ii. 2. Compare Cat. xiv. 14, and 22: Κωνσταντίνου τοῦ βασιλέως.

10 Ps. xlvi. 10. Sept. σχολάσατε, "give attention freely."

11 From S. Augustine, *de Symbolo*, i. 1 (Migne T. vi. p. 930), we learn that the Candidates were brought in before the Congregation one by one for exorcism; and so, as Cyril here shews, they had to wait outside till the others returned.

1 Chrys. *in Matt. Hom.* lxxiv. § 3: "You ought to have within, you the wall that separates you from the women: but since ye will not, our fathers have thought it necessary to separate you at least by these boards; for I have heard from my elders that there were not these walls in old times." These barriers had not yet been introduced at Jerusalem, or Cyril's admonition would have been needless. Compare *Apostolic Constitutions*, II. 57.

2 1 Cor. xiv. 34; 1 Tim. ii. 12.

3 1 Sam. i. 13, 20. On the various interpretations of the name Samuel, see *Dict. Bib.* "Samuel," and Driver on the passage. Cyril adopts the meaning "heard of God."

4 Ps. cxxxix. 12. On Easter Eve the Church was full of lights which were kept burning all night, and the newly-baptized carried torches. Gregory of Nyssa, preaching on the Resurrection (*Orat.* iv.), describes the scene: "This brilliant night, by mingling the flames of torches with the morning rays of the sun, has made one continuous day, not divided by the interposition of darkness."

5 Or, as the Benedictine Editor conjectures, "the waters which have a Christ-bearing (χριστοφόρον) fragrance." On the epithet χριστοφόρος, see Bishop Lightfoot's note on Ignat. *ad Eph.* § 1 and § 9. Its meaning, as well as that of Θεοφόρος is defined in the answer of Ignatius to Trajan, Ὁ Χριστὸν ἔχων ἐν στέρνοις (*Martyr. Ign. Ant.* § 2).

6 Cat. xxi. 1: "made partakers therefore of Christ, ye are rightly called Christs."

mind: even now imagine the choirs of Angels, and God the Lord of all there sitting, and His Only-begotten Son sitting with Him on His right hand, and the Spirit present with them; and Thrones and Dominions doing service, and every man of you and every woman receiving salvation. Even now let your ears ring, as it were, with that glorious sound, when over your salvation the angels shall chant, *Blessed are they whose iniquities are forgiven, and whose sins are covered*[7]: when like stars of the Church you shall enter in, bright in the body and radiant in the soul.

16. Great is the Baptism that lies before you[8]: a ransom to captives; a remission of offences; a death of sin; a new-birth of the soul; a garment of light; a holy indissoluble seal; a chariot to heaven; the delight of Paradise; a welcome into the kingdom; the gift of adoption! But there is a serpent by the wayside watching those who pass by: beware lest he bite thee with unbelief. He sees so many receiving salvation, and is *seeking whom he may devour*[9]. Thou art coming in unto the Father of Spirits, but thou art going past that serpent. How then mayest thou pass him? Have *thy feet shod with the preparation of the gospel of peace*[1]; that even if he bite, he may not hurt thee. Have faith in-dwelling, stedfast hope, a strong sandal, that thou mayest pass the enemy, and enter the presence of thy Lord. Prepare thine own heart for reception of doctrine, for fellowship in holy mysteries. Pray more frequently, that God may make thee worthy of the heavenly and immortal mysteries. Cease not day nor night: but when sleep is banished from thine eyes, then let thy mind be free for prayer. And if thou find any shameful thought rise up in thy mind, turn to meditation upon Judgment to remind thee of Salvation. Give thy mind wholly to study, that it may forget base things. If thou find any one saying to thee, Art thou then going in, to descend into the water? Has the city just now no baths? take notice that it is *the dragon of the sea*[2] who is laying these plots against thee. Attend not to the lips of the talker, but to God who worketh in thee. Guard thine own soul, that thou be not ensnared, to the end that abiding in hope thou mayest become an heir of everlasting salvation.

17. We for our part as men charge and teach you thus: but make not ye our building *hay and stubble* and chaff, lest we *suffer loss*, from our *work being burnt up*: but make ye our work *gold, and silver, and precious stones*[3]! For it lies in me to speak, but in thee to set thy mind[4] upon it, and in God to make perfect. Let us nerve our minds, and brace up our souls, and prepare our hearts. The race is for our soul: our hope is of things eternal: and God, who knoweth your hearts, and observeth who is sincere, and who a hypocrite, is able both to guard the sincere, and to give faith to the hypocrite: for even to the unbeliever, if only he give his heart, God is able to give faith. So may He *blot out the handwriting that is against you*[5], and grant you forgiveness of your former trespasses; may He plant you into His Church, and enlist you in His own service, and put on you *the armour of righteousness*[6]: may He fill you with the heavenly things of the New Covenant, and give you the seal of the Holy Spirit indelible throughout all ages, in Christ Jesus Our Lord: to whom be the glory for ever and ever! Amen.

(*To the Reader*[7].)

These Catechetical Lectures for those who are to be enlightened thou mayest lend to candidates for Baptism, and to believers who are already baptized, to read, but give not at all[8], neither to Catechumens, nor to any others who are not Christians, as thou shalt answer to the Lord. And if thou make a copy, write this in the beginning, as in the sight of the Lord.

7 Ps. xxxii. 1, which verse is still chanted in the Greek Church as soon as the Baptism is completed.

8 S. Basil has a passage in praise of Baptism almost the same, word for word, with this. It is more likely to have been borrowed from Cyril by Basil and other Fathers, than to be a later interpolation here.

9 1 Pet v. 8. 1 Eph. vi. 15. 2 Is. xxvii. 1.

3 1 Cor. iii. 12, 15.

4 Greek προσθέσθαι, Sept. Deut. xiii. 4, "cleave unto Him." Compare Josh. xxiii. 12; Ps. lxii. 10, "Set not your heart upon them." 5 Col. ii. 14. 6 2 Cor. vi. 7; Rom. vi. 13.

7 It is doubtful whether this caution proceded from Cyril himself when issuing a written copy of his Lectures, or from some later editor. Eusebius (*E.H.* v. 20) has preserved an adjuration by Irenæus at the end of his treatise, *On the Ogdoad:* I adjure thee, who mayest transcribe this book, by Our Lord Jesus Christ, and by His glorious advent, when He cometh to judge the quick and the dead, to compare what thou hast written and correct it carefully by this copy, from which thou hast transcribed it; this adjuration also thou shalt write in like manner, and set it in the copy.

8 Gr. τὸ σύνολον. Plat. Leg. 654 B; Soph. 220 B.

FIRST CATECHETICAL LECTURE

OF

OUR HOLY FATHER CYRIL,

ARCHBISHOP OF JERUSALEM,

To those who are to be Enlightened, delivered extempore at Jerusalem, as an Introductory Lecture to those who had come forward for Baptism[1]:

WITH A READING FROM ISAIAH,

Wash you, make you clean; put away your iniquities from your souls, from before mine eyes, and the rest[2].

1. Disciples of the New Testament and partakers of the mysteries of Christ, as yet by calling only, but ere long by grace also, *make you a new heart and a new spirit*[3], that there may be gladness among the inhabitants of heaven: for *if over one sinner that repenteth there is joy*, according to the Gospel[4], how much more shall the salvation of so many souls move the inhabitants of heaven to gladness. As ye have entered upon a good and most glorious path, run with reverence the race of godliness. For the Only-begotten Son of God is present here most ready to redeem you, saying, *Come unto Me all that labour and are heavy laden, and I will give you rest*[5]. Ye that are clothed with the rough garment[6] of your offences, who are *holden with the cords of your own sins*, hear the voice of the Prophet saying, *Wash you, make you clean, put away your iniquities from before Mine eyes*[7]: that the choir of Angels may chant over you, *Blessed are they whose iniquities are forgiven, and whose sins are covered*[8]. Ye who have just lighted the torches of faith[9], guard them carefully in your hands unquenched; that He, who erewhile on this all-holy Golgotha opened Paradise to the robber on account of his faith, may grant to you to sing the bridal song.

2. If any here is a slave of sin, let him promptly prepare himself through faith for the new birth into freedom and adoption; and having put off the miserable bondage of his sins, and taken on him the most blessed bondage of the Lord, so may he be counted worthy to inherit the kingdom of heaven. *Put off*, by confession[1], *the old man, which waxeth corrupt after the lusts of deceit*, that ye may *put on the new man, which is renewed according to knowledge of Him that created him*[2]. Get you *the earnest of the Holy Spirit*[3] through faith, that ye may be able to be received *into the everlasting habitations*[4]. Come for the mystical Seal, that ye may be easily recognised by the Master; be ye numbered among the holy and spiritual flock of Christ, to be set apart on His right hand, and inherit the life prepared for you. For they to whom the rough garment[5] of their sins still clings are found on the left hand, because they came not to the grace of God which is given through Christ at the new birth of Baptism: new birth I mean not of bodies, but the spiritual new birth of the soul. For our bodies are begotten by parents who are seen, but our souls are begotten anew through faith: *for the Spirit bloweth where it listeth*[6]: and then, if thou be found worthy, thou mayest hear, *Well done, good and faithful servant*[7], when thou art found to have no defilement of hypocrisy in thy conscience.

3. For if any of those who are present should think to tempt God's grace, he deceives himself, and knows not its power. Keep thy soul free from hypocrisy, O man, because of Him *who searcheth hearts and reins*[8]. For as those who are going to make a levy for war examine the ages and the bodies

[1] The title prefixed to this Lecture is given in full. In the following Lectures the form will be abbreviated. See Index, ἀνάγνωσις and σχεδιασθεῖσα.
[2] Is. i. 16.
[3] Ezek. xviii. 31.
[4] Luke xv. 7.
[5] Matt. xi. 28.
[6] Compare xv. 25.
[7] Is. i. 16.
[8] Ps. xxxii. 1. See Procat. 15.
[9] Procat. 1, note 6.

[1] See Index, "Confession."
[2] Eph. iv. 22; Col. iii. 10.
[3] 2 Cor. i. 22.
[4] Luke xvi. 9.
[5] Compare xv. 25.
[6] John iii. 8.
[7] Matt. xxv. 21.
[8] Ps. vii. 10.

of those who are taking service, so also the Lord in enlisting souls examines their purpose: and if any has a secret hypocrisy, He rejects the man as unfit for His true service; but if He finds one worthy, to him He readily gives His grace. He gives not holy things to the dogs[9]; but where He discerns the good conscience, there He gives the Seal of salvation, that wondrous Seal, which devils tremble at, and Angels recognise; that the one may be driven to flight, and the others may watch around it as kindred to themselves. Those therefore who receive this spiritual and saving Seal, have need also of the disposition akin to it. For as a writing-reed or a dart has need of one to use it, so grace also has need of believing minds.

4. Thou art receiving not a perishable but a spiritual shield. Henceforth thou art planted in the invisible[1] Paradise. Thou receivest a new name, which thou hadst not before. Heretofore thou wast a Catechumen, but now thou wilt be called a Believer. Thou art transplanted henceforth among the spiritual[2] olive-trees, being grafted from the wild into the good olive-tree[3], from sins into righteousness, from pollutions into purity. Thou art made partaker of the Holy Vine[4]. Well then, if thou abide in the Vine, thou growest as a fruitful branch; but if thou abide not, thou wilt be consumed by the fire. Let us therefore bear fruit worthily. God forbid that in us should be done what befell that barren fig-tree[5], that Jesus come not even now and curse us for our barrenness. But may all be able to use that other saying, *But I am like a fruitful olive-tree in the house of God: I have trusted in the mercy of God for ever*[6],—an olive-tree not to be perceived by sense, but by the mind[7], and full of light. As then it is His part to plant and to water[8], so it is thine to bear fruit: it is God's to grant grace, but thine to receive and guard it. Despise not the grace because it is freely given, but receive and treasure it devoutly.

5. The present is the season of confession: confess what thou hast done in word or in deed, by night or by day; confess *in an acceptable time, and in the day of salvation*[9] receive the heavenly treasure. Devote thy time to the Exorcisms: be assiduous at the Catechisings, and remember the things that shall be spoken, for they are spoken not for thine ears only, but that by faith thou mayest seal them up in the memory. Blot out from thy mind all earthly[1] care: for thou art running for thy soul. Thou art utterly forsaking the things of the world: little are the things which thou art forsaking, great what the Lord is giving. Forsake things present, and put thy trust in things to come. Hast thou run so many circles of the years busied in vain about the world, and hast thou not forty days to be free (for prayer[2]), for thine own soul's sake? *Be still*[3], *and know that I am God*, saith the Scripture. Excuse thyself from talking many idle words: neither backbite, nor lend a willing ear to backbiters; but rather be prompt to prayer. Shew in ascetic exercise that thy heart is nerved[4]. Cleanse thy vessel, that thou mayest receive grace more abundantly. For though remission of sins is given equally to all, the communion of the Holy Ghost is bestowed in proportion to each man's faith. If thou hast laboured little, thou receivest little; but if thou hast wrought much, the reward is great. Thou art running for thyself, see to thine own interest.

6. If thou hast aught against any man, forgive it: thou comest here to receive forgiveness of sins, and thou also must forgive him that hath sinned against thee. Else with what face wilt thou say to the Lord, Forgive me my many sins, if thou hast not thyself forgiven thy fellow-servant even his little sins. Attend diligently the Church assemblies[5]; not only now when diligent attendance is required of thee by the Clergy, but also after thou hast received the grace. For if, before thou hast received it, the practice is good, is it not also good after the bestowal? If before thou be grafted in, it is a safe course to be watered and tended, is it not far better after the planting? Wrestle for thine own soul, especially in such days as these. Nourish thy soul with sacred readings; for the Lord hath prepared for thee a spiritual table; therefore say thou also after the Psalmist, *The Lord is my shepherd, and I shall lack nothing: in a place of grass, there hath He made me rest; He hath fed me beside the waters of comfort, He hath converted my soul*[6]:—that Angels also may share your joy, and Christ Himself the great High Priest, having accepted your resolve, may present you all to the Father, saying, *Behold, I and the children whom God hath given Me*[7]. May He keep you all well-pleasing in His sight! To whom be the glory, and the power unto the endless ages of eternity. Amen.

---

9 Matt. vii. 6.
1 Gr. νοητόν, i.e. the true Paradise, to be seen by the mind, not by the eye. Apoc. xii. 7, 17.
2 See preceding note.
3 Rom. xi. 24.
4 John xv. 1, 4, 5.
5 Matt. xxi. 19.
6 Ps. lii. 10.
7 νοητῇ, see note 1, above.
8 1 Cor. iii. 6. When Paul plants and Apollos waters, it is God Himself who works through His ministers.
9 2 Cor. vi. 2.

1 Literally "human."
2 Some MSS. omit τῇ προσευχῇ after σχολάζεις.
3 Ps. xlvi. 10: σχολάσατε. Compare Procat. 13.
4 Compare Procat. 17: xviii. 1.
5 See Index, σύναξις.
6 Ps. xxiii. 1—3.
7 Is. viii. 18; Heb. ii. 13.

LECTURE II.

On Repentance and Remission of Sins, and concerning the Adversary.

Ezekiel xviii. 20—23.

The righteousness of the righteous shall be upon him, and the wickedness of the wicked shall be upon him. But if the wicked will turn from all his sins, &c.

1. A fearful thing is sin, and the sorest disease of the soul is transgression, secretly cutting its sinews, and becoming also the cause of eternal fire; an evil of a man's own choosing, an offspring of the will[1]. For that we sin of our own free will the Prophet says plainly in a certain place: *Yet I planted thee a fruitful vine, wholly true: how art thou turned to bitterness, (and become) the strange vine[2]?* The planting was good, the fruit coming from the will is evil; and therefore the planter is blameless, but the vine shall be burnt with fire; since it was planted for good, and bore fruit unto evil of its own will. *For God*, according to the Preacher, *made man upright, and they have themselves sought out many inventions*[3]. *For we are His workmanship*, says the Apostle, *created unto good works, which God afore prepared, that we should walk in them*[4]. So then the Creator, being good, created for good works; but the creature turned of its own free will to wickedness. Sin then is, as we have said, a fearful evil, but not incurable; fearful for him who clings to it, but easy of cure for him who by repentance puts it from him. For suppose that a man is holding fire in his hand; as long as he holds fast the live coal he is sure to be burned, but should he put away the coal, he would have cast away the flame also with it. If however any one thinks that he is not being burned when sinning, to him the Scripture saith, *Shall a man wrap up fire in his bosom, and not burn his clothes*[5]*?* For sin burns the sinews of the soul, [and breaks the spiritual bones of the mind, and darkens the light of the heart[6]].

2. But some one will say, What can sin be? Is it a living thing? Is it an angel? Is it a demon? What is this which works within us? It is not an enemy, O man, that assails thee from without, but an evil shoot growing up out of thyself. *Look right on with thine eyes*[7], and there is no lust. [Keep thine own, and[8]] seize not the things of others, and robbery has ceased[9]. Remember the Judgment, and neither fornication, nor adultery, nor murder, nor any transgression of the law shall prevail with thee. But whenever thou forgettest God, forthwith thou beginnest to devise wickedness and to commit iniquity.

3. Yet thou art not the sole author of the evil, but there is also another most wicked prompter, the devil. He indeed suggests, but does not get the mastery by force over those who do not consent. Therefore saith the Preacher, *If the spirit of him that hath power rise up against thee, quit not thy place*[1]. Shut thy door, and put him far from thee, and he shall not hurt thee. But if thou indifferently admit the thought of lust, it strikes root in thee by its suggestions, and enthrals thy mind, and drags thee down into a pit of evils.

But perhaps thou sayest, I am a believer, and lust does not gain the ascendant over me, even if I think upon it frequently. Knowest thou not that a root breaks even a rock by long persistence? Admit not the seed, since it will rend thy faith asunder: tear out the evil by the root before it blossom, lest from being careless at the beginning thou have afterwards to seek for axes and fire. When thine eyes begin to be diseased, get them cured in good time, lest thou become blind, and then have to seek the physician.

4. The devil then is the first author of sin, and the father of the wicked: and this is the Lord's saying, not mine, *that the devil sinneth*

---

1 For references to Cyril's doctrine of Free-will, see Index, "Soul."

2 Jer. ii. 21.

3 Eccles. vii. 29.

4 Eph. ii. 10.

5 Prov. vi. 27.

6 Milles and the Benedictine Editor omit these clauses, but the more recent editions of Reischl and Alexandrides insert them on the authority of the Munich, Jerusalem, and other good MSS.

7 Prov. iv. 25.

8 Omitted by recent editors with the best MSS.

9 Gr. κεκοίμηται, "has fallen asleep."

1 Eccles. x. 4. Compare Eph. iv. 27: "Neither give place to the devil."

from the beginning[2]: none sinned before him. But he sinned, not as having received necessarily from nature the propensity to sin, since then the cause of sin is traced back again to Him that made him so; but having been created good, he has of his own free will become a devil, and received that name from his action. For being an Archangel[3] he was afterwards called a devil from his slandering: from being a good servant of God he has become rightly named Satan; for "Satan" is interpreted *the adversary*[4]. And this is not my teaching, but that of the inspired prophet Ezekiel: for he takes up a lamentation over him and says, *Thou wast a seal of likeness, and a crown of beauty; in the Paradise of God wast thou born*[5]: and soon after, *Thou wast born blameless in thy days, from the day in which thou wast created, until thine iniquities were found in thee.* Very rightly hath he said, *were found in thee;* for they were not brought in from without, but thou didst thyself beget the evil. The cause also he mentions forthwith: *Thine heart was lifted up because of thy beauty: for the multitude of thy sins wast thou wounded, and I did cast thee to the ground.* In agreement with this the Lord says again in the Gospels: *I beheld Satan as lightning fall from heaven*[6]. Thou seest the harmony of the Old Testament with the New. He when cast out drew many away with him. It is he that puts lusts into them that listen to him: from him come adultery, fornication, and every kind of evil. Through him our forefather Adam was cast out for disobedience, and exchanged a Paradise bringing forth wondrous fruits of its own accord for the ground which bringeth forth thorns.

5. What then? some one will say. We have been beguiled and are lost. Is there then no salvation left? We have fallen: Is it not possible to rise again? We have been blinded: May we not recover our sight? We have become crippled: Can we never walk upright? In a word, we are dead: May we not rise again? He that woke Lazarus who was four days dead and already stank, shall He not, O man, much more easily raise thee who art alive? He who shed His precious blood for us, shall Himself deliver us from sin. Let us not despair of ourselves, brethren; let us not abandon ourselves to a hopeless condition. For it is a fearful thing not to believe in a hope of repentance. For he that looks not for salvation spares not to add evil to evil: but to him that hopes for cure, it is henceforth easy to be careful over himself. The robber who looks not for pardon grows desperate; but, if he hopes for forgiveness, often comes to repentance. What then, does the serpent cast its slough[7], and shall not we cast off our sin? Thorny ground also, if cultivated well, is turned into fruitful; and is salvation to us irrecoverable? Nay rather, our nature admits of salvation, but the will also is required.

6. God is loving to man, and loving in no small measure. For say not, I have committed fornication and adultery: I have done dreadful things, and not once only, but often: will He forgive? Will He grant pardon? Hear what the Psalmist says: *How great is the multitude of Thy goodness, O Lord*[8]*!* Thine accumulated offences surpass not the multitude of God's mercies: thy wounds surpass not the great Physician's skill. Only give thyself up in faith: tell the Physician thine ailment: say thou also, like David: *I said, I will confess me my sin unto the Lord:* and the same shall be done in thy case, which he says forthwith: *And thou forgavest the wickedness of my heart*[9].

7. Wouldest thou see the loving-kindness of God, O thou that art lately come to the catechising? Wouldest thou see the loving-kindness of God, and the abundance of His long-suffering? Hear about Adam. Adam, God's first-formed man, transgressed: could He not at once have brought death upon him? But see what the Lord does, in His great love towards man. He casts him out from Paradise, for because of sin he was unworthy to live there; but He *puts him to dwell over against Paradise*[1]: that seeing whence he had fallen, and from what and into what a state he was brought down, he might afterwards be saved by repentance. Cain the first-born man became his brother's murderer, the inventor of evils, the first author of murders, and the first envious man. Yet after slaying his brother to what is he condemned? *Groaning and trembling shalt thou be upon the earth*[2]. How great the offence, the sentence how light!

8. Even this then was truly loving-kindness in God, but little as yet in comparison with what follows. For consider what happened in the days of Noe. The giants sinned, and

---

2 1 John iii. 8; John viii. 44.

3 On Cyril's doctrine of the Angels, see Index, "Angels."

4 1 Kings v. 4, &c.

5 Ezek. xxviii. 12—17, an obscure passage, addressed to the Prince of Tyre, and meaning that he was "the perfect pattern" of earthly glory, set in a condition like that of Adam in Paradise, and, seemingly, blameless as Adam before his fall. Cyril seems to regard the Prince of Tyre as an embodiment of Satan, because he was deified as the object of national worship: v. 1, "Thou hast said, I am a God, I sit in the seat of God."

6 Luke x. 18.

7 Literally, "its old age" (τὸ γῆρας). Compare iii. 7, and Dict. Chr. Biogr., *Macarius*, p. 770 a.

8 Ps. xxxi. 20. 9 Ps. xxxii. 5.

1 This is the reading of the Septuagint instead of—"He placed at the east of the garden of Eden."

2 Gen. iv. 12: "A fugitive and a vagabond shalt thou be upon the earth.

much wickedness was then spread over the earth, and because of this the flood was to come upon them: and in the five hundredth year God utters His threatening; but in the six hundredth He brought the flood upon the earth. Seest thou the breadth of God's loving-kindness extending to a hundred years? Could He not have done immediately what He did then after the hundred years? But He extended (the time) on purpose, granting a respite for repentance. Seest thou God's goodness? And if the men of that time had repented, they would not have missed the loving-kindness of God.

9. Come with me now to the other class, those who were saved by repentance. But perhaps even among women some one will say, I have committed fornication, and adultery, I have defiled my body by excesses of all kinds: is there salvation for me? Turn thine eyes, O woman, upon Rahab, and look thou also for salvation; for if she who had been openly and publicly a harlot was saved by repentance, is not she who on some one occasion before receiving grace committed fornication to be saved by repentance and fasting? For inquire how she was saved: this only she said: *For your God is God in heaven and upon earth*[3]. *Your God;* for her own she did not dare to say, because of her wanton life. And if you wish to receive Scriptural testimony of her having been saved, you have it written in the Psalms: *I will make mention of Rahab and Babylon among them that know me*[4]. O the greatness of God's loving-kindness, making mention even of harlots in the Scriptures: nay, not simply *I will make mention of Rahab and Babylon*, but with the addition, *among them that know me.* There is then in the case both of men and of women alike the salvation which is ushered in by repentance.

10. Nay more, if a whole people sin, this surpasses not the loving-kindness of God. The people made a calf, yet God ceased not from His loving-kindness. Men denied God, but God denied not Himself[5]. *These be thy gods, O Israel*[6], they said: yet again, as He was wont, the God of Israel became their Saviour. And not only the people sinned, but also Aaron the High Priest. For it is Moses that says: *And the anger of the Lord came upon Aaron: and I prayed for him*, saith he, *and God forgave him*[7]. What then, did Moses praying for a High Priest that sinned prevail with God, and shall not Jesus, His Only-begotten, prevail with God when He prays for us? And if He did not hinder Aaron, because of his offence, from entering upon the High Priesthood, will He hinder thee, who art come out from the Gentiles, from entering into salvation? Only, O man, repent thou also in like manner, and grace is not forbidden thee. Render thy way of life henceforth unblameable; for God is truly loving unto man, nor can all time[8] worthily tell out His loving kindness; nay, not if all the tongues of men unite together will they be able even so to declare any considerable part of His loving-kindness. For we tell some part of what is written concerning His loving-kindness to men, but how much He forgave the Angels we know not: for them also He forgives, since One alone is without sin, even Jesus who purgeth our sins. And of them we have said enough.

11. But if concerning us men thou wilt have other examples also set before thee[9], come on to the blessed David, and take him for an example of repentance. Great as he was, he fell: after his sleep, walking in the eventide on the housetop, he cast a careless look, and felt a human passion. His sin was completed, but there died not with it his candour concerning the confession of his fault. Nathan the Prophet came, a swift accuser, and a healer of the wound. *The Lord is wroth*, he says, *and thou hast sinned*[1]. So spake the subject to the reigning king. But David the king[2] was not indignant, for he regarded not the speaker, but God who had sent him. He was not puffed up[3] by the array of soldiers standing round: for he had seen in thought the angel-host of the Lord, and he trembled *as seeing Him who is invisible*[4]; and to the messenger, or rather by him in answer to God who sent him, he said, *I have sinned against the Lord*[5]. Seest thou the humility of the king? Seest thou his confession? For had he been convicted by any one? Were many privy to the matter? The deed was quickly done, and straightway the Prophet appeared as accuser, and the offender confesses the fault. And because he candidly confessed, he received a most speedy cure. For Nathan the Prophet who had uttered the threat, said immediately, *The Lord also hath put away thy sin.* Thou seest the swift relenting of a merciful God. He says, however, *Thou hast greatly provoked the enemies of the*

3 Josh. ii. 11.
4 Ps. lxxxvii. 4. "Rahab" is there a poetical name of Egypt, and the passage has nothing to do with Rahab the harlot. The Benedictine Editor rightly disregards S. Jerome's suggestion, that Rahab is, like Egypt, a type of the Gentile Church.
5 2 Tim. ii. 13. 6 Ex. xxxii. 4. 7 Deut. ix. 20.

8 For "all time," the reading of the best MSS., the Benedictine text has "all mankind."
9 The Benedictine has, "But if thou wilt I will set before thee other examples also of our state? Come on to the blessed David."
1 2 Sam. xii.
2 Bened. "The king, the wearer of the purple."
3 Bened. "blinded." 4 Heb. xi. 27. 5 2 Sam. xii. 13.

Lord. Though thou hadst many enemies because of thy righteousness, thy self-control protected thee; but now that thou hast surrendered thy strongest armour, thine enemies are risen up, and stand ready against thee.

12. Thus then did the Prophet comfort him, but the blessed David, for all he heard it said, *The LORD hath put away thy sin*, did not cease from repentance, king though he was, but put on sackcloth instead of purple, and instead of a golden throne, he sat, a king, in ashes on the ground; nay, not only sat in ashes, but also had ashes for his food, even as he saith himself, *I have eaten ashes as it were bread*[6]. His lustful eye he wasted away with tears, saying, *Every night will I wash my couch, and water my bed with my tears*[7]. When his officers besought him to eat bread he would not listen. He prolonged his fast unto seven whole days. If a king thus made confession, oughtest not thou, a private person, to confess? Again, after Absalom's insurrection, though there were many roads for him to escape, he chose to flee by the Mount of Olives, in thought, as it were, invoking the Redeemer who was to go up thence into the heavens[8]. And when Shimei cursed him bitterly, he said, *Let him alone*, for he knew that "to him that forgiveth it shall be forgiven[9]."

13. Thou seest that it is good to make confession. Thou seest that there is salvation for them that repent. Solomon also fell: but what saith he? *Afterwards I repented*[10]. Ahab, too, the King of Samaria, became a most wicked idolater, an outrageous man, the murderer of the Prophets[1], a stranger to godliness, a coveter of other men's fields and vineyards. Yet when by Jezebel's means he had slain Naboth, and the Prophet Elias came and merely threatened him, he rent his garments, and put on sackcloth. And what saith the merciful God to Elias? *Hast thou seen how Ahab is pricked in the heart before Me*[2]*?* as if almost He would persuade the fiery zeal of the Prophet to condescend to the penitent. For He saith, *I will not bring the evil in his days.* And though after this forgiveness he was sure not to depart from his wickedness, nevertheless the forgiving God forgave him, not as being ignorant of the future, but as granting a forgiveness corresponding to his present season of repentance. For it is the part of a righteous judge to give sentence according to each case that has occurred.

14. Again, Jeroboam was standing at the altar sacrificing to the idols: his hand became withered, because he commanded the Prophet who reproved him to be seized: but having by experience learned the power of the man before him, he says, *Entreat the face of the Lord thy God*[3]; and because of this saying his hand was restored again. If the Prophet healed Jeroboam, is Christ not able to heal and deliver thee from thy sins? Manasses also was utterly wicked, who sawed Isaiah asunder[4], and was defiled with all kinds of idolatries, and *filled Jerusalem with innocent blood*[5]; but having been led captive to Babylon he used his experience of misfortune for a healing course of repentance: for the Scripture saith that Manasses *humbled himself before the Lord, and prayed, and the Lord heard him, and brought him back to his kingdom.* If He who sawed the Prophet asunder was saved by repentance, shalt not thou then, having done no such great wickedness, be saved?

15. Take heed lest without reason thou mistrust the power of repentance. Wouldst thou know what power repentance has? Wouldst thou know the strong weapon of salvation, and learn what the force of confession is? Hezekiah by means of confession routed a hundred and fourscore and five thousand of his enemies. A great thing verily was this, but still small in comparison with what remains to be told: the same king by repentance obtained the recall of a divine sentence which had already gone forth. For when he had fallen sick, Esaias said to him, *Set thine house in order; for thou shalt die, and not live*[6]. What expectation remained, what hope of recovery, when the Prophet said, *for thou shalt die?* Yet Hezekiah did not desist from repentance; but remembering what is written, *When thou shalt turn and lament, then shalt thou be saved*[7], he turned to the wall, and from his bed lifting his mind to heaven (for thickness of walls is no hindrance to prayers sent up with devotion), he said, "Remember me, O Lord, for it is sufficient for my healing that Thou remember me. Thou art not subject to times, but art Thyself the giver of the law of life. For our life depends not on a

6 Ps. cii. 10. 7 Ib. vii. 7. 8 2 Sam. xvi. 10, 11.

9 Resch. (*Agrapha*, p. 137) quotes various forms of this saying from early writers, and regards it as a fragment of an extra-canonical Gospel. But see Lightfoot, *Clem. Rom.* c. xiii.

10 Prov. xxiv. 32, Sept. Heb. "Set my heart." The passage has no reference to repentance: it means, "I considered the field of the slothful." Hilary, Ps. lii.; Ambrose, *Apolog.* 1, *Prophetæ David*, c. iii. and other Fathers affirm the repentance of Solomon. Augustine (*c. Faustum*, Lib. xxii. c. 88) maintains that Scripture says nothing of his repentance or forgiveness. See Dante, *Paradiso*, *Canto* x. 109.

1 1 Kings xviii. 4. 2 Ib. xxi. 29.

3 1 Kings xiii. 6.

4 Justin Martyr, *Dialogue with Trypho*, § 120, charges the Jews with having cut out a passage referring to the death of Isaiah. Theophylact commenting on Heb. xi. 37, says: "They were sawn asunder, as Isaiah by Manasses: and they say that he was sawn with a wooden saw, that his punishment might be the more painful to him from being prolonged." Jerome on Is. i. 10, says that he was slain because of his calling the Jews "princes of Sodom and people of Gomorra," and because he said, "I saw the Lord sitting upon a throne, high and lifted up."

5 2 Chron. xxxiii. 12, 13. 6 2 Kings xx. 1. 7 Is. xxx. 15.

nativity, nor on a conjunction of stars, as some idly talk; but both of life and its duration. Thou art Thyself the Lawgiver according to Thy Will." And he, who could not hope to live because of the prophetic sentence, had fifteen years added to his life, and for the sign the sun ran backward in his course Well then, for Ezekias' sake the sun turned back, but for Christ the sun was eclipsed, not retracing his steps, but suffering eclipse [8], and therefore shewing the difference between them, I mean between Ezekias and Jesus. The former prevailed to the cancelling of God's decree, and cannot Jesus grant remission of sins? Turn and bewail thyself, shut thy door, and pray to be forgiven, pray that He may remove from thee the burning flames. For confession has power to quench even fire, power to tame even lions [9].

16. But if thou disbelieve, consider what befel Ananias and his companions. What streams did they pour out [1]? How many vessels [2] of water could quench the flame that rose up forty-nine cubits high [3]? Nay, but where the flame mounted up a little [4] too high, faith was there poured out as a river, and there spake they the spell against all ills [5]: *Righteous art Thou, O Lord, in all the things that Thou hast done to us: for we have sinned, and transgressed Thy law* [6]. And their repentance quelled the flames [7]. If thou believest not that repentance is able to quench the fire of hell, learn it from what happened in regard to Ananias [8]. But some keen hearer will say, Those men God rescued justly in that case: because they refused to commit idolatry, God gave them that power. And since this thought has occurred, I come next to a different example of penitence [9].

17. What thinkest thou of Nabuchodonosor? Hast thou not heard out of the Scriptures that he was bloodthirsty, fierce [1], lion-like in disposition? Hast thou not heard that he brought out the bones of the kings from their graves into the light [2]? Hast thou not heard [3] that he carried the people away captive? Hast thou not heard that he put out the eyes of the king, after he had already seen his children slain [4]? Hast thou not heard that he brake in pieces [5] the Cherubim? I do not mean the invisible [6] beings;—away with such a thought, O man [7],—but the sculptured images, and the mercy-seat, in the midst of which God spake with His voice [8]. The veil of the Sanctuary [9] he trampled under foot: the altar of incense he took and carried away to an idol-temple [1]: all the offerings he took away: the Temple he burned from the foundations [2]. How great punishments did he deserve, for slaying kings, for setting fire to the Sanctuary, for taking the people captive, for setting the sacred vessels in the house of idols? Did he not deserve ten thousand deaths?

18. Thou hast seen the greatness of his evil deeds: come now to God's loving-kindness. He was turned into a wild beast [3], he abode in the wilderness, he was scourged, that he might be saved. He had claws as a lion [4]; for he was a ravager of the Sanctuary. He had a lion's mane: for he was a ravening and a roaring lion. He ate grass like an ox: for a brute beast he was, not knowing Him who had given him the kingdom. His body was wet from the dew; because after seeing the fire quenched by the dew he believed not [5]. And what happened [6]? *After this*, saith he, *I, Nabuchodonosor, lifted up*

8 Isaiah xxxviii. 8.

9 From this point the MSS. differ so widely that the Benedictine Editor gives two complete recensions of the whole Lecture. The Codd. Coislin, Ottob. 2, and Grodec, with the editions of Prevot and Milles, forming as it were one family of MSS., constitute the received text. On the other hand the older Munich Codex, with Codd. Roe and Casaubon, exhibit a recension of the Lecture differing from the editions. Reischl wishing to retain the received text unaltered, though preferring the other in particular passages, intended to append the other recension complete, but having left his work half finished, failed to do so. The chief variations are given in the following notes.

1 Roe and Casaubon (R. C.) add: "into the furnace of fire."

2 R. C. "What measure."

3 Song of the Three Children, v. 24.

4 R. C. "Much."

5 R.C. "A great stream of repentance was poured forth, when they said, For Thou art righteous," &c.

6 Song of the Three Children, v. 4.

7 R. C. "Did then repentance quench the flames of the furnace, and dost thou disbelieve that it is able also to quench the fire of hell?"

8 The Gospel only says, "There was darkness over all the land." An eclipse of the sun was impossible at the time of the Paschal full moon.

9 R. C. "That the narrative is not appropriate to those who are here present. For it was because Ananias and his companions refused to worship the idol, that God gave them that marvellous power. Adapting myself, therefore, to such a hearer, and looking to the profusion of instances, I come next to a different example of repentance."

1 R.C. "most impious, and most fierce in temper."

2 Jer. viii. 1; Baruch ii. 25.

3 "Knowest thou not..."

4 2 Kings xxv. 7.

5 R. C. "carried off."

6 νοητά. R. C. add "and heavenly."

7 Omitted by R. C.

8 R. C. "But those which had been constructed in the Temple. which were over the mercy-seat of the Ark." Besides the two Cherubim of solid gold which Moses placed on the two ends of the Mercy-seat (Ex. xxxvii. 7 ff.), Solomon set "within the oracle" two Cherubim of olive wood overlaid with gold, ten feet high with outstretched wings overshadowing the Ark (1 Kings vi. 23—26; viii. 6, 7). All these were either carried off or destroyed, when Nebuchadnezzar took away "all the treasures of the house of the Lord" and "cut in pieces all the vessels of gold which Solomon, King of Israel, had made in the Temple of the Lord" (2 Kings xxiv. 13; 1 Esdras i. 54; 2 Esdras x. 22). The Benedictine editor is concerned because Cyril has paid no attention to the strange fiction in 2 Maccabees ii. 4, that Jeremy the Prophet "commanded the Tabernacle and the Ark to go with him" to Mount Horeb, and there hid them, with the Altar of Incense, in a hollow cave, to remain "unknown until the time that God gathers His people again together."

9 The Greek word rendered "Sanctuary" is ἡ ἁγιωσύνη, literally "the holiness."

1 2 Chron. xxxvi. 7.

2 R. C. "The veil of the Sanctuary he tore down, he overturned the altar, and took all the vessels and carried them away to an idol temple. The Temple itself he burned."

3 R. C. Afterwards he was turned into a wild beast: "he who was like a wild beast and most cruel in disposition; but he was turned into a wild beast, not that he might perish, but that by repentance he might be saved."

4 R. C. "of birds." See Dan. iv. 33.

5 R. C. "after the midst of the furnace had become to Ananias and his companions as the tinkling breath of rain, he saw and believed not."

6 R. C. "But afterwards he came to his senses and repented, as he says himself."

mine eyes unto heaven, and I blessed the Most High, and to Him that liveth for ever I gave praise and glory[7]. When, therefore, he recognised the Most High[8], and sent up these words of thankfulness to God, and repented himself for what he had done, and recognised his own weakness, then God gave back to him the honour of the kingdom.

19. What then[9]? When Nabuchodonosor, after having done such deeds, had made confession, did God give him pardon and the kingdom, and when thou repentest shall He not give thee the remission of sins, and the kingdom of heaven, if thou live a worthy life? The LORD is loving unto man, and swift to pardon, but slow to punish. Let no man therefore despair of his own salvation. Peter, the chiefest and foremost of the Apostles, denied the Lord thrice before a little maid: but he repented himself, and wept bitterly. Now weeping shews the repentance of the heart: and therefore he not only received forgiveness for his denial, but also held his Apostolic dignity unforfeited.

20. Having therefore, brethren, many examples of those who have sinned and repented and been saved, do ye also heartily make confession unto the Lord, that ye may both receive the forgiveness of your former sins, and be counted worthy of the heavenly gift, and inherit the heavenly kingdom with all the saints in Christ Jesus; to Whom is the glory for ever and ever. Amen[1].

7 Dan. iv. 34.

8 R. C. "And after he had been scourged many years, he gave praise to Him that liveth for ever, and acknowledged Him that had given him the kingdom, and recognised the King of kings. And though he had often sinned in deeds, on making confession only in words, he received the benefit of God's unspeakable loving-kindness. He who was of all men most wicked, by the Divine judgment and loving-kindness of God who chastised him, crowned himself again with the royal diadem, and recovered his imperial throne."

9 R. C. "If then there is present among you any from among the Heathen who has ever spoken evil against Christians, or in times of persecution plotted against the Holy Churches, let him take Nabuchodonosor as an example of salvation: let him confess in like manner, that he may also find the like forgiveness. If any has been defiled by lust and passions, let him take up the repentance of the blessed David: if any has denied like Peter, let him die like him for the sake of the Lord Jesus. For He who to his tears begrudged not the Apostleship, will not refuse thee the gospel mysteries. And for women let Rahab be a pattern unto salvation, and for men the manifold examples mentioned of the men of old times.

1 R. C. "And be ye all of good hope, having regard to the loving-kindness of God; not that we may fall back into the same sins, but that having had the benefit of redemption, and lived in a manner worthy of His grace, we may be able to blot out the hand-writing that is against us by good works; in the power of the Only-begotten, the Son of God, and our Lord Jesus Christ, with whom be glory to the Father, with the Holy Ghost, both now and ever, and unto all the ages of eternity. Amen."

LECTURE III.

On Baptism.

Romans vi. 3, 4.

Or know ye not that all we who were baptized into Christ Jesus were baptized into His death? were buried therefore with Him by our baptism into death, &c.

1. *Rejoice, ye heavens, and let the earth be glad*[1], for those who are to be sprinkled with hyssop, and cleansed with the spiritual[2] hyssop, the power of Him to whom at His Passion drink was offered on hyssop and a reed[3]. And while the Heavenly Powers rejoice, let the souls that are to be united to the spiritual Bridegroom make themselves ready. For *the voice* is heard *of one crying in the wilderness, Prepare ye the way of the Lord*[4]. For this is no light matter, no ordinary and indiscriminate union according to the flesh[5], but the All-searching Spirit's election according to faith. For the intermarriages and contracts of the world are not made altogether with judgment: but wherever there is wealth or beauty, there the bridegroom speedily approves: but here it is not beauty of person, but the soul's clear conscience; not the condemned Mammon, but the wealth of the soul in godliness.

2. Listen then, O ye children of righteousness, to John's exhortation when he says, *Make straight the way of the Lord.* Take away all obstacles and stumbling-blocks, that ye may walk straight onward to eternal life. Make ready the vessels[6] of the soul, cleansed by unfeigned faith, for reception of the Holy Ghost. Begin at once to wash your robes in repentance, that when called to the bride-chamber ye may be found clean. For the Bridegroom invites all without distinction, because His grace is bounteous; and the cry of loud-voiced heralds assembles them all: but the same Bridegroom afterwards separates those who have come in to the figurative marriage. O may none of those whose names have now been enrolled hear the words, *Friend, how camest thou in hither, not having a wedding garment*[7]*?* But may you all hear, *Well done, good and faithful servant; thou wast faithful over a few things, I will set thee over many things: enter thou into the joy of thy lord*[8].

For now meanwhile thou standest outside the door: but God grant that you all may say, *The King hath brought me into His chamber*[9]. *Let my soul rejoice in the Lord: for He hath clothed me with a garment of salvation, and a robe of gladness: He hath crowned me with a garland as a bridegroom*[1], *and decked me with ornaments as a bride:* that the soul of every one of you may be found *not having spot or wrinkle or any such thing*[2]; I do not mean before you have received the grace, for how could that be? since it is for remission of sins that ye have been called; but that, when the grace is to be given, your conscience being found uncondemned may concur with the grace.

3. This is in truth a serious matter, brethren, and you must approach it with good heed. Each one of you is about to be presented to God before tens of thousands of the Angelic Hosts: the Holy Ghost is about to seal[3] your souls: ye are to be enrolled in the army of the Great King. Therefore make you ready, and equip yourselves, by putting on I mean, not bright apparel[4], but piety of soul with a good conscience. Regard not the Laver as simple water, but rather regard the spiritual grace that is given with the water. For just as the offerings brought to the heathen altars[5], though simple in their nature, become defiled by the invocation of the idols[6], so contrariwise

---

1 Ps. xcvi. 11.

2 The invisible or spiritual (νοητός) hyssop is the cleansing power of the Holy Ghost in Baptism. Compare Ps. li. 7.

3 S. Cyril here, and still more emphatically in xiii. 39, distinguishes the hyssop (John xix. 29) from the reed (Matt. xxvii. 48), implying that the sponge filled with vinegar was bound round with hyssop, and then fixed on a reed. Another opinion is that the reed itself was that of hyssop. See Dictionary of the Bible, "Hyssop."

4 Is. xl. 3.

5 σωμάτων.

6 So in § 15, the soul is regarded as a vessel for receiving grace.

7 Matt. xxii. 12.

8 Matt. xxv. 12.

9 Cant. i. 4.

1 Is. lxi. 10. Compare Cant. iii. 11: *Go forth, O ye daughters of Zion, and behold King Solomon, with the crown wherewith his mother hath crowned him in the day of his espousals.* In the pssage of Isaiah the bridegroom's crown is likened to the priestly mitre.

2 Eph. v. 7.

3 See Index, "Seal."

4 Index, "White."

5 βωμοῖς used of heathen altars only, in Septuagint and N.T.

6 Both here and in xix. 7, Cyril speaks of things offered to idols just as S. Paul in 1 Cor, x. 20. The Benediction of the water of Baptism is found in the *Apostolic Constitutions*, vii. 43: "Look down from heaven, and sanctify this water, and give it grace and power, that so he that is to be baptized according to the command of Thy Christ, may be crucified with Him, and may die with Him, and be buried with Him, and may rise with Him to the adoption which is in Him, that he may be dead to sin and live to righteousness."

the simple water having received the invocation of the Holy Ghost, and of Christ, and of the Father, acquires a new power of holiness.

4. For since man is of twofold nature, soul and body, the purification also is twofold, the one incorporeal for the incorporeal part, and the other bodily for the body: the water cleanses the body, and the Spirit seals the soul; that we may draw near unto God, *having onr heart sprinkled* by the Spirit, *and our body washed with pure water*[7]. When going down, therefore, into the water, think not of the bare element, but look for salvation by the power of the Holy Ghost: for without both thou canst not possibly be made perfect[8]. It is not I that say this, but the Lord Jesus Christ, who has the power in this matter: for He saith, *Except a man be born anew* (and He adds the words) *of water and of the Spirit, he cannot enter into the kingdom of God*[9]. Neither doth he that is baptized with water, but not found worthy of the Spirit, receive the grace in perfection; nor if a man be virtuous in his deeds, but receive not the seal by water, shall he enter into the kingdom of heaven. A bold saying, but not mine, for it is Jesus who hath declared it: and here is the proof of the statement from Holy Scripture. Cornelius was a just man, who was honoured with a vision of Angels, and had set up his prayers and almsdeeds as a good memorial[1] before God in heaven. Peter came, and the Spirit was poured out upon them that believed, and they spake with other tongues, and prophesied: and after the grace of the Spirit the Scripture saith that Peter *commanded them to be baptized in the name of Jesus Christ*[2]: in order that, the soul having been born again by faith[3], the body also might by the water partake of the grace.

5. But if any one wishes to know why the grace is given by water and not by a different element, let him take up the Divine Scriptures and he shall learn. For water is a grand thing, and the noblest of the four visible elements of the world. Heaven is the dwelling-place of Angels, but the heavens are from the waters[4]: the earth is the place of men, but the earth is from the waters: and before the whole six days' formation of the things that were made, *the Spirit of God moved upon the face of the water*[5]. The water was the beginning of the world, and Jordan the beginning of the Gospel tidings: for Israel deliverance from Pharaoh was through the sea, and for the world deliverance from sins *by the washing of water with the word*[6] of God. Where a covenant is made with any, there is water also. After the flood, a covenant was made with Noah: a covenant for Israel from Mount Sinai, but *with water, and scarlet wool, and hyssop*[7]. Elias is taken up, but not apart from water: for first he crosses the Jordan, then in a chariot mounts the heaven. The high-priest is first washed, then offers incense; for Aaron first washed, then was made high-priest: for how could one who had not yet been purified by water pray for the rest? Also as a symbol of Baptism there was a laver set apart within the Tabernacle.

6. Baptism is the end of the Old Testament, and beginning of the New. For its author was John, than whom was *none greater among them that are born of women*. The end he was of the Prophets: *for all the Prophets and the law were until John*[8]: but of the Gospel history he was the first-fruit. For it saith, *The beginning of the Gospel of Jesus Christ*, &c.: *John came baptizing in the wilderness*[9]. You may mention Elias the Tishbite who was taken up into heaven, yet he is not greater than John: Enoch was translated, but he is not greater than John: Moses was a very great lawgiver, and all the Prophets were admirable, but not greater than John. It is not I that dare to compare Prophets with Prophets: but their Master and ours, the Lord Jesus, declared it: *Among them that are born of women there hath not risen a greater than John*[1]: He saith not "among them that are born of virgins," but *of women*[2]. The comparison is between the great servant and his fellow-servants: but the pre-eminence and the grace of the Son is beyond comparison with servants. Seest thou how great a man God chose as the first minister of this grace?—a man possessing nothing, and a lover of the desert, yet no hater of mankind: who ate locusts, and winged his soul for heaven[3]: feeding upon honey, and speaking things both sweeter and more salutary than honey: clothed with a garment of camel's hair, and shewing in himself the pattern of the ascetic life; who also was sanctified by the Holy Ghost while yet he was carried in his mother's womb. Jeremiah was sanctified, but

7 Heb. x. 22.

8 See the note on "the twofold grace perfected by water and the Spirit," at the end of this Lecture.

9 John iii. 3.

1 στηλή. Sept. A pillar of stone, bearing an inscription, was a common form of memorial among the Israelites and other ancient nations. See Dictionary of the Bible, "Pillar."

2 Acts x. 48.

3 S. Cyril considers that Cornelius and his friends were regenerated, as the Apostles were, apart from Baptism; as August. *Serm.* 269, *n.* 2, and Chrysost. *in Act. Apost. Hom.* 25, seem to do. R. W. C.

4 Compare ix. 5.

5 Gen. i, 2.

6 Ephes. v. 26.

7 Heb. ix. 19.

8 Matt. xi. 13.

9 Mark i. 1, 4.

1 Matt. xi. 11.

2 From the Clementine Recognitions, I. 54 and 60, we learn that there were some who asserted that John was the Christ, and not Jesus, inasmuch as Jesus Himself declared that John was greater than all men, and all Prophets. The answer is there given, that John was greater than all who are born of women, yet not greater than the Son of Man.

3 The locust being winged suggests the idea of growing wings for the soul. Is. xl. 31: πτεροφυήσουσιν ὡς ἀετοί.

did not prophesy, in the womb[4]: John alone while carried in the womb leaped for joy[5], and though he saw not with the eyes of flesh, knew his Master by the Spirit: for since the grace of Baptism was great, it required greatness in its founder also.

7. This man was baptizing in Jordan, and *there went out unto him all Jerusalem*[6], to enjoy the first-fruits of baptisms: for in Jerusalem is the prerogative of all things good. But learn, O ye inhabitants of Jerusalem, how they that came out were baptized by him: *confessing their sins*, it is said[7]. First they shewed their wounds, then he applied the remedies, and to them that believed gave redemption from eternal fire. And if thou wilt be convinced of this very point, that the baptism of John is a redemption from the threat of the fire, hear how he says, *O generation of vipers, who hath warned you to flee from the wrath to come*[8]*?* Be not then henceforth a viper, but as thou hast been formerly a viper's brood, put off, saith he, the slough[9] of thy former sinful life. For every serpent creeps into a hole and casts its old slough, and having rubbed off the old skin, grows young again in body. In like manner *enter thou also through the strait and narrow gate*[1]*:* rub off thy former self by fasting, and drive out that which is destroying thee. *Put off the old man with his doings*[2], and quote that saying in the Canticles, *I have put off my coat, how shall I put it on*[3]*?*

But there is perhaps among you some hypocrite, a man-pleaser, and one who makes a pretence of piety, but believes not from the heart; having the hypocrisy of Simon Magus; one who has come hither not in order to receive of the grace, but to spy out what is given: let him also learn from John: *And now also the axe is laid unto the root of the trees, Every tree therefore that bringeth not forth good fruit is hewn down, and cast into the fire*[4]. The Judge is inexorable; put away thine hypocrisy.

8. What then must you do? And what are the fruits of repentance? *Let him that hath two coats give to him that hath none*[5]*:* the teacher was worthy of credit, since he was also the first to practise what he taught: he was not ashamed to speak, for conscience hindered not his tongue: *and he that hath meat, let him do likewise.* Wouldst thou enjoy the grace of the Holy Spirit, yet judgest the poor not worthy of bodily food? Seekest thou the great gifts, and impartest not of the small? Though thou be a publican, or a fornicator, have hope of salvation: *the publicans and the harlots go into the kingdom of God before you*[6]. Paul also is witness, saying, *Neither fornicators, nor adulterers, nor* the rest, *shall inherit the kingdom of God. And such were some of you: but ye were washed, but ye were sanctified*[7]. He said not, *such are some of you*, but *such were some of you.* Sin committed in the state of ignorance is pardoned, but persistent wickedness is condemned.

9. Thou hast as the glory of Baptism the Son Himself, the Only-begotten of God. For why should I speak any more of man? John was great, but what is he to the Lord? His was a loud-sounding voice, but what in comparison with the Word? Very noble was the herald, but what in comparison with the King? Noble was he that baptized with water, but what to Him that baptizeth *with the Holy Ghost and with fire*[8]*?* The Saviour baptized the Apostles with the Holy Ghost and with fire, when *suddenly there came a sound from heaven as of the rushing of a mighty wind, and it filled all the house where they were sitting. And there appeared unto them cloven tongues like as of fire: and it sat upon each one of them, and they were all filled with the Holy Ghost*[9].

10. If any man receive not Baptism, he hath not salvation; except only Martyrs, who even without the water receive the kingdom. For when the Saviour, in redeeming the world by His Cross, was pierced in the side, He shed forth blood and water; that men, living in times of peace, might be baptized in water, and, in times of persecution, in their own blood. For martyrdom also the Saviour is wont to call a baptism, saying, *Can ye drink the cup which I drink, and be baptized with the baptism that I am baptized with*[1]*?* And the Martyrs confess, by *being made a spectacle unto the world, and to Angels, and to men*[2]*;* and thou wilt soon confess:—but it is not yet the time for thee to hear of this.

11. Jesus sanctified Baptism by being Himself baptized. If the Son of God was baptized, what godly man is he that despiseth Baptism? But He was baptized not that He might receive remission of sins, for He was sinless; but being sinless, He was baptized, that He might give to them that are baptized a divine and excellent grace. For *since the children are partakers of flesh and blood, He also Himself likewise partook of the same*[3], that having been

4 Jer. i. 5. 5 Luke i. 44. 6 Matt. iii. 5.
7 Matt. iii. 6. 8 Ib. iii. 7.
9 The Greek word (ὑπόσταωις) is used by Polybius (xxxiv. 9) for the deposit of silver from crushed ore, and by Hippocrates for any sediment or deposit Here it means, as the context clearly shews, the old skin cast by a snake. Compare ii. 5.
1 Matt. vii. 13, 14. 2 Col. iii. 9.
3 Cant. v. 3. In the Song, this saying is an excuse for not rising from bed. S. Cyril applies it in a different way.
4 Matt. iii. 10. 5 Luke iii. 11.

6 Matt. xxi. 31. 7 1 Cor. vi. 9, 10. 8 Matt. iii. 11.
9 Acts ii. 2 1 Mark x. 38. 2 1 Cor. iv. 9.
3 Heb. ii. 14.

made partakers of His presence in the flesh, we might be made partakers also of His Divine grace: thus Jesus was baptized, that thereby we again by our participation might receive both salvation and honour. According to Job, there was in the waters the dragon that *draweth up Jordan into his mouth*[4]. Since, therefore, it was necessary to *break the heads of the dragon in pieces*[5], He went down and bound the strong one in the waters, that we might receive power to *tread upon serpents and scorpions*[6]. The beast was great and terrible. *No fishing-vessel was able to carry one scale of his tail*[7]: *destruction ran before him*[8], ravaging all that met him. The Life encountered him, that the mouth of Death might henceforth be stopped, and all we that are saved might say, *O death, where is thy sting? O grave, where is thy victory*[9]? The sting of death is drawn by Baptism.

12. For thou goest down into the water, bearing thy sins, but the invocation of grace[1], having sealed thy soul, suffereth thee not afterwards to be swallowed up by the terrible dragon. Having gone down dead in sins, thou comest up quickened in righteousness. For if thou hast been *united with the likeness of the Saviour's death*[2], thou shalt also be deemed worthy of His Resurrection. For as Jesus took upon Him the sins of the world, and died, that by putting sin to death He might rise again in righteousness; so thou by going down into the water, and being in a manner buried in the waters, as He was in the rock, art raised again *walking in newness of life*[3].

13. Moreover, when thou hast been deemed worthy of the grace, He then giveth thee strength to wrestle against the adverse powers. For as after His Baptism He was tempted forty days (not that He was unable to gain the victory before, but because He wished to do all things in due order and succession), so thou likewise, though not daring before thy baptism to wrestle with the adversaries, yet after thou hast received the grace and art henceforth confident in *the armour of righteousness*[4], must then do battle, and preach the Gospel, if thou wilt.

14. Jesus Christ was the Son of God, yet He preached not the Gospel before His Baptism. If the Master Himself followed the right time in due order, ought we, His servants, to venture out of order? *From that time Jesus began to preach*[5], when *the Holy Spirit had descended upon Him in a bodily shape, like a dove*[6]; not that Jesus might see Him first, for He knew Him even before He came in a bodily shape, but that John, who was baptizing Him, might behold Him. For *I*, saith he, *knew Him not: but He that sent me to baptize with water, He said unto me, Upon whomsoever thou shalt see the Spirit descending and abiding on Him, that is He*[7]. If thou too hast unfeigned piety, the Holy Ghost cometh down on thee also, and a Father's voice sounds over thee from on high—not, "*This is My Son*," but, "This has now been made My son;" for the "*is*" belongs to Him alone, because *In the beginning was the Word, and the Word was with God, and the Word was God*[8]. To Him belongs the "*is*," since He is always the Son of God: but to thee "has now been made:" since thou hast not the sonship by nature, but receivest it by adoption. He eternally "*is*;" but thou receivest the grace by advancement.

15. Make ready then the vessel of thy soul, that thou mayest become a son of God, and *an heir of God, and joint-heir with Christ*[9]; if, indeed, thou art preparing thyself that thou mayest receive; if thou art drawing nigh in faith that thou mayest be made faithful; if of set purpose thou art putting off the old man. For all things whatsoever thou hast done shall be forgiven thee, whether it be fornication, or adultery, or any other such form of licentiousness. What can be a greater sin than to crucify Christ? Yet even of this Baptism can purify. For so spake Peter to the three thousand who came to him, to those who had crucified the Lord, when they asked him, saying, *Men and brethren, what shall we do*[1]? For the wound is great. Thou hast made us think of our fall, O Peter, by saying, *Ye killed the Prince of Life*[2]. What salve is there for so great a wound? What cleansing for such foulness? What is the salvation for such perdition? *Repent*, saith he, *and be baptized every one of you in the name of Jesus Christ our Lord, for the remission of sins, and ye shall receive the gift of the Holy Ghost*[3]. O unspeakable loving-kindness of God! They have no hope of being saved, and yet they are thought worthy of the Holy Ghost. Thou seest the power of Baptism! If any of you has crucified the Christ by blasphemous words; if any of you in ignorance has denied Him before men; if any by wicked works has caused the doctrine to be blasphemed; let him repent and be of good hope, for the same grace is present even now.

4 Job xl. 23. 5 Ps. lxxiv. 14. 6 Luke x. 19.
7 Job xl. 26, in the Sept. in place of xli. 7: Canst thou fill his skin with barbed irons, or his head with fish spears? (A.V. and R.V.)
8 Job xli. 13, Sept. but in R.V. xli. 22: And terror danceth before him. 9 1 Cor. xv. 55.
1 Compare III. 3, and see Index, "Baptism." 2 Rom. vi. 5.
3 Rom. vi. 4. Instead of "might rise again" (Roe. Casaub. Mon.), the older Editions have "might raise thee up," which is less appropriate in this part of the sentence.
4 2 Cor. vi. 7.

5 Matt. iv. 17. 6 Luke iii. 22. 7 John i. 33. 8 Ib. i. 1.
9 Rom. viii. 17. 1 Acts ii. 37. 2 Ib. iii. 15. 3 Ib. ii. 58.

16. *Be of good courage, O Jerusalem; the Lord will take away all thine iniquities*[4]. *The Lord will wash away the filth of His sons and of His daughters by the Spirit of judgment, and by the Spirit of burning*[5]. *He will sprinkle clean water upon you, and ye shall be cleansed from all your sin*[6]. Angels shall dance around you, and say, *Who is this that cometh up in white array, leaning upon her beloved*[7]*?* For the soul that was formerly a slave has now adopted her Master Himself as her kinsman: and He accepting the unfeigned purpose will answer: *Behold, thou art fair, my love; behold, thou art fair: thy teeth are like flocks of sheep new shorn,* (because of the confession of a good conscience: and further) *which have all of them twins*[8]*;* because of the twofold grace, I mean that which is perfected of water and of the Spirit[9], or that which is announced by the Old and by the New Testament. And God grant that all of you when you have finished the course of the fast, may remember what I say, and bringing forth fruit in good works, may stand blameless beside the Spiritual Bridegroom, and obtain the remission of your sins from God; to whom with the Son and Holy Spirit be the glory for ever. Amen.

4 Zeph. iii. 14, 15. 5 Is. iv. 4. 6 Ezek. xxxvi. 25.
7 Cant. viii. 5, Gr. ἀδελφιδόν, "brother," "kinsman."
8 Ib. iv. 1, 2.

9 The Fathers sometimes speak as if Baptism was primarily the Sacrament of remission of sins, and *upon* that came the gift of the Spirit, which notwithstanding was but begun in Baptism and completed in Confirmation. Vid. Tertullian. *de Bapt.* 7, 8, *supr.* i. 5 *fin.* Hence, as in the text, Baptism may be said to be made up of *two* gifts, Water, which is Christ's blood, and the Spirit. There is no real difference between this and the ordinary way of speaking on the subject;—Water, which *conveys* both gifts, is considered as a *type* of one especially,—*conveys* both remission of sins through Christ's blood and the grace of the Spirit, but is the *type* of one, *viz.* the blood of Christ, as the Oil in Confirmation is of the other. And again, remission of sins is a complete gift given at once. sanctification an increasing one. (R. W. C.) See Index, "Baptism."

LECTURE IV.

On the Ten[1] points of Doctrine.

Colossians ii. 8.

Beware lest any man spoil you through philosophy and vain deceit, after the tradition of men, after the rudiments of the world, &c.

1. Vice mimics virtue, and the tares strive to be thought wheat, growing like the wheat in appearance, but being detected by good judges from the taste. *The devil also transfigures himself into an angel of light*[2]; not that he may reascend to where he was, for having made *his heart hard as an anvil*[3], he has henceforth a will that cannot repent; but in order that he may envelope those who are living an Angelic life in a mist of blindness, and a pestilent condition of unbelief. Many wolves are going about *in sheeps' clothing*[4], their clothing being that of sheep, not so their claws and teeth: but clad in their soft skin, and deceiving the innocent by their appearance, they shed upon them from their fangs the destructive poison of ungodliness. We have need therefore of divine grace, and of a sober mind, and of eyes that see, lest from eating tares as wheat we suffer harm from ignorance, and lest from taking the wolf to be a sheep we become his prey, and from supposing the destroying Devil to be a beneficent Angel we be devoured: for, as the Scripture saith, *he goeth about as a roaring lion, seeking whom he may devour*[5]. This is the cause of the Church's admonitions, the cause of the present instructions, and of the lessons which are read.

2. For the method of godliness consists of these two things, pious doctrines, and virtuous practice: and neither are the doctrines acceptable to God apart from good works, nor does God accept the works which are not perfected with pious doctrines. For what profit is it, to know well the doctrines concerning God, and yet to be a vile fornicator? And again, what profit is it, to be nobly temperate, and an impious blasphemer? A most precious possession therefore is the knowledge of doctrines: also there is need of a wakeful soul, since there are many *that make spoil through philosophy and vain deceit*[6]. The Greeks on the one hand draw men away by their smooth tongue, *for honey droppeth from a harlot's lips*[7]: whereas they of the Circumcision deceive those who come to them by means of the Divine Scriptures, which they miserably misinterpret though *studying them from childhood to old age*[8], and growing old in ignorance. But the children of heretics, *by their good words and smooth tongue, deceive the hearts of the innocent*[9], disguising with the name of Christ as it were with honey the poisoned arrows[10] of their impious doctrines: concerning all of whom together the Lord saith, *Take heed lest any man mislead you*[1]. This is the reason for the teaching of the Creed and for expositions upon it.

3. But before delivering you over to the Creed[2], I think it is well to make use at present of a short summary of necessary doctrines; that the multitude of things to be spoken, and the long interval of the days of all this holy Lent, may not cause forgetfulness in the mind of the more simple among you; but that, having strewn some seeds now in a summary way, we may not forget the same when afterwards more widely tilled. But let those here present whose habit of mind is mature, and

1 The number "ten" is confirmed by Theodoret, who quotes the article on Christ's "Birth of the Virgin" as from Cyril's fourth Catechetical Lecture "On the ten Doctrines." The MSS. vary between "ten" and "eleven," and differ also in the special titles and numeration of the separate Articles.

2 2 Cor. xi. 14.

3 Job xli. 24, Sept.; xli. 15: ἡ καρδία αὐτοῦ .. ἕστηκεν ὥσπερ ἄκμων ἀνήλατος. These statements concerning the Devil seem to be directed against Origen's opinion (*De Principiis* I. 2), that the Angels "who have been removed from their primal state of blessedness have not been removed irrecoverably." The question is discussed, and the opinions of several Fathers quoted, by Huet, *Origeniana*, II. c. 25.

4 Matt. vii. 15. The same text is applied to Heretics by Ignatius, *Philadelph.* ii., and by Irenæus, L. I. c. i. § 2.

5 1 Pet. v. 8.

6 Col. ii. 8.

7 Prov. v. 3.

8 Is. xlvi. 3. Sept. παιδευόμενοι ἐκ παιδίου ἕως γήρως.

9 Rom. xvi. 17. Cyril has εὐγλωττίας in place of εὐλογίας.

10 Compare Ignatius, *Trall.* vi.

1 Matt. xxiv. 4.

2 Compare Rom. vi. 17: "*that form of teaching whereunto ye were delivered.*" The instruction of Catechumens in the Articles of the Faith was commonly called the "Traditio Symboli," or "Delivery of the Creed."

who *have their senses already exercised to discern good and evil*[3], endure patiently to listen to things fitted rather for children, and to an introductory course, as it were, of milk: that at the same time both those who have need of the instruction may be benefited, and those who have the knowledge may rekindle the remembrance of things which they already know.

I. Of God.

4. First then let there be laid as a foundation in your soul the doctrine concerning God; that God is One, alone unbegotten, without beginning, change, or variation[4]; neither begotten of another, nor having another to succeed Him in His life; who neither began to live in time, nor endeth ever: and that He is both good and just; that if ever thou hear a heretic say, that there is one God who is just, and another who is good[5], thou mayest immediately remember, and discern the poisoned arrow of heresy. For some have impiously dared to divide the One God in their teaching: and some have said that one is the Creator and Lord of the soul, and another of the body[6]; a doctrine at once absurd and impious. For how can a man become the one servant of two masters, when our Lord says in the Gospels, *No man can serve two masters*[7]? There is then One Only God, the Maker both of souls and bodies: One the Creator of heaven and earth, the Maker of Angels and Archangels: of many the Creator, but of One only the Father before all ages,—of One only, His Only-begotten Son, our Lord Jesus Christ, by Whom He made *all things visible and invisible*[8].

5. This Father of our Lord Jesus Christ is not circumscribed in any place[9], nor is He less than the heaven; but *the heavens are the works of His fingers*[10], and *the whole earth is held in His grasp*[11]: He is in all things and around all. Think not that the sun is brighter than He[1], or equal to Him: for He who at first formed the sun must needs be incomparably greater and brighter. He foreknoweth the things that shall be, and is mightier than all, knowing all things and doing as He will; not being subject to any necessary sequence of events, nor to nativity, nor chance, nor fate; in all things perfect, and equally possessing every absolute form[2] of virtue, neither diminishing nor increasing, but in mode and conditions ever the same; who hath prepared punishment for sinners, and a crown for the righteous.

6. Seeing then that many have gone astray in divers ways from the One God, some having deified the sun, that when the sun sets they may abide in the night season without God; others the moon, to have no God by day[3]; others the other parts of the world[4]; others the arts[5]; others their various kinds of food[6]; others their pleasures[7]; while some, mad after women, have set up on high an image of a naked woman, and called it Aphrodite[8], and worshipped their own lust in a visible form; and others dazzled by the brightness of gold have deified it[9] and the other kinds of matter;—whereas if one lay as a first foundation in his heart the doctrine of the unity[10] of God, and trust to Him, he roots out at once the whole crop[1] of the evils of idolatry, and of the error of the heretics: lay thou, therefore, this first doctrine of religion as a foundation in thy soul by faith.

Of Christ.

7. Believe also in the Son of God, One and Only, our Lord Jesus Christ, Who was be-

---

3 Heb. v. 14.

4 Compare Hermas, *Mandat.* i. Athan. *Epist. de Decretis Nic. Syn.* xxii.: οὕτω καὶ τὸ ἄτρεπτον καὶ ἀναλλοίωτον αὐτὸν εἶναι σωθήσεται. So Aristotle (*Metaphys.* XI. c. iv. 13) describes the First Cause as ἀπαθὲς καὶ ἀναλλοίωτον.

5 Irenæus, I. c. xxvii. says that Cerdo taught that the God of the Law and the Prophets was not the Father of our Lord Jesus Christ: for that He is known, but the other unknown, and the one is just, but the other good. Also III. c. 25, § 3: "Marcion himself, therefore, by dividing God into two, and calling the one good, and the other judicial, on both sides puts an end to Deity." Compare Tertullian, *c. Marcion.* I. 2, and 6; Origen, *c. Cels.* iv. 54.

6 This tenet was held by the Manichæans and other heretics, and is traced back to the Apostolic age by Bishop Pearson (*Exposition of the Creed*, Art. i. p. 79, note c). Compare Athanasius (*c. Apollinarium*, I. 21; II. 8; *c. Gentes*, § 6; *de Incarnatione*, § 2, in this series, and Augustine (*c. Faustum*, xx. 15, 21, and xxi. 4).

7 Matt. vi. 24; Luke xvi. 13.

8 John i. 3; Col. i. 16.

9 S. Aug. *in Ps.* lxxv. 6: Si in aliquo loco esset, non esset Deus. *Sermo* 342: Deus habitando continet non continetur. Origen, *c. Cels.* vii. 34: "God is of too excellent a nature for any place: He holds all things in His power, and is Himself not confined by anything whatever.' Compare the quotation from Sir Isaac Newton's *Principia*, in the note on Cat. vi. 8.

10 Ps. viii. 3.

11 Is. xl. 12.

1 See Cat. xv. 3, and note there.

2 ἰδέαν. Cyril uses the word in the Platonic sense, as in the next sentence he adopts the formula, which Plato commonly uses in describing the "idea:" ἀεὶ κατὰ τὰ αὐτὰ καὶ ὡσαύτως ἔχειν. Phaed. 78 c.

3 Job xxxi. 26, 27. The worship of Sun and Moon under various names was almost universal.

4 Gaea or Tellus, the earth; Zeus or Jupiter, the sky; rivers, fountains, &c.

5 Music, Medicine, Hunting, War, Agriculture, Metallurgy, &c., represented by Apollo, Aesculapius, Diana, Mars, Ceres, Vulcan.

6 Herodotus, Book II., describes the Egyptian worship of various birds, fishes, and quadrupeds. Leeks and onions also were held sacred: Porrum et caepe nefas violare, Juv. *Sat.* xv. 9. Compare Clement of Alexandria, *Protrept.* c. ii. § 39, Klotz.

7 Eros, Dionysus.

8 Clement of Alexandria (*Protrept.* c. iv. § 53, Klotz) states that the courtesan Phryne was taken as a model for Aphrodite. "Praxiteles when fashioning the statue of Aphrodite of Cnidus made it like the form of Cratine his paramour." *Ibid.*

9 Plutus.

10 τῆς μοναρχίας τοῦ θεοῦ. See note on the title of Cat. VI. Praxeas made use of the term "Monarchy" to exclude the Son (and the Spirit) from the Godhead. Tertullian in his treatise against Praxeas maintains the true doctrine that the Son is no obstacle to the "Monarchy," because He is of the substance of the Father, does nothing without the Father's will, and has received all power from the Father, to Whom He will in the end deliver up the kingdom. In this sense Dionysius, Bishop of Rome, speaks of the Divine Monarchy as "that most sacred doctrine of the Church of God." Compare Athanas. *de Decretis, Nic. Syn.* c. vi. § 3. and Dr. Newman's note. In *Orat.* iv. *c. Arian.* p. 606 (617). Athanasius derives the term from ἀρχή, in the sense of "beginning:" οὕτως μία ἀρχὴ θεότητος καὶ οὐ δύο ἀρχαί, ὅθεν κυρίως καὶ μοναρχία ἐστίν. See the full discussion of Monarchianism in *Athanasius*, p. xxiii. ff. in this series, and Newman's Introduction to *Athan. Or.* iv.

1 For φοράν (Bened.) many MSS. read φθοράν, "corruption."

gotten God of God, begotten Life of Life, begotten Light of Light[2], Who is in all things like[3] to Him that begat, Who received not His being in time, but was before all ages eternally and incomprehensibly begotten of the Father: The Wisdom and the Power of God, and His Righteousness personally subsisting[4]: Who sitteth on the right hand of the Father before all ages.

For the throne at God's right hand He received not, as some have thought, because of His patient endurance, being crowned as it were by God after His Passion; but throughout His being,—a being by eternal generation[5],—He holds His royal dignity, and shares the Father's seat, being God and Wisdom and Power, as hath been said; reigning together with the Father, and creating all things for the Father, yet lacking nothing in the dignity of Godhead, and knowing Him that hath begotten Him, even as He is known of Him that hath begotten; and to speak briefly, remember thou what is written in the Gospels, that *none knoweth the Son but the Father, neither knoweth any the Father save the Son*[6].

8. Further, do thou neither separate[7] the Son from the Father, nor by making a confusion believe in a Son-Fatherhood[8]; but believe that of One God there is One Only-begotten Son, who is before all ages God the Word; not the uttered[9] word diffused into the air, nor to be likened to impersonal words[1]; but the Word the Son, Maker of all who partake of reason, the Word who heareth the Father, and Himself speaketh. And on these points, should God permit, we will speak more at large in due season; for we do not forget our present purpose to give a summary introduction to the Faith.

Concerning His Birth of the Virgin.

9. Believe then that this Only-begotten Son of God for our sins came down from heaven upon earth, and took upon Him this human nature of like passions[2] with us, and was begotten of the Holy Virgin and of the Holy Ghost, and was made Man, not in seeming and mere show[3], but in truth; nor yet by passing through the Virgin as through a channel[4]; but was of her made truly flesh, [and truly nourished with milk[5]], and did truly eat as we do, and truly drink as we do. For if the Incarnation was a phantom, salvation is a phantom also. The Christ was of two natures, Man in what was seen, but God in what was not seen; as Man truly eating like us, for He had the like feeling of the flesh with us; but as God feeding the five thousand from five loaves; as Man truly dying, but as God raising him that had been dead four days; truly sleeping in the ship as Man, and walking upon the waters as God.

Of the Cross.

10. He was truly crucified for our sins. For if thou wouldest deny it, the place refutes thee visibly, this blessed Golgotha[6], in which we are now assembled for the sake of Him who was here crucified; and the whole world has since been filled with pieces of the wood of the Cross[7]. But He was crucified not for sins of His own, but that we might be delivered from *our* sins. And though as Man He was at that time *despised of men*, and was buffeted, yet He was acknowledged by the Creation as God: for when the sun saw his Lord dishonoured, he grew dim and trembled, not enduring the sight.

---

2 Compare xi. 4, 9, 18.

3 Τὸν ὅμοιον κατὰ πάντα τῷ γεννήσαντι. On the meaning and history of this phrase, proposed by the Semi-Arians at the Council of Ariminum as a substitute for ὁμοούσιον, see Athan. *de Syn.* § 8, *sqq.*

4 ἐνυπόστατος. Cf. xi 10; Athan. *c. Apollinar.* I. 20, 21.

5 The MSS. vary much, but I have followed the Benedictine text.

6 Matt. xi. 27; John x. 15; xvii. 25.

7 This was a point earnestly maintained by the orthodox Bishops at Nicæa, that the Son begotten of the substance of the Father is ever inseparably in the Father. Athan. *de Decretis Syn.* c. 20; Tertullian *c. Marc.* IV. c. 6. Cf. Ignat. *ad Trall.* vi. (Long Recension): τὸν μὲν γὰρ Χριστὸν ἀλλοτριουσι τοῦ Πατρός.

8 υἱοπατορία. A term of derision applied to the doctrine of Sabellius. Compare Athanasius. *Expositio Fidei*, c. 2: "neither do we imagine a Son-Father, as the Sabellians." See Index, Υἱοπάτωρ.

9 Λόγος προφορικός, the term used by Paul of Samosata, implied that the Word was impersonal, being conceived as a particular activity of God. See Dorner, *Person of Christ*, Div. I. vol. ii. p. 436 (English Tr.): and compare Athanasius, *Expositio Fidei*, c. 1; υἱὸν ἐκ τοῦ Πατρὸς ἀνάρχως καὶ ἀϊδίως γεγεννημένον, λόγον δὲ οὐ προφορικόν, οὐκ ἐνδιάθετον. Cardinal Newman (*Athan. c. Arianos*, I. 7, note) observes that some Christian writers of the 2nd century "seem to speak of the Divine generation as taking place immediately before the creation of the world, that is as if not eternal, though at the same time they teach that our Lord existed before that generation. In other words they seem to teach that He was the Word from eternity, and became the Son at the beginning of all things; some of them expressly considering Him, first as the λόγος ἐνδιάθετος, or Reason, in the Father, or (as may be speciously represented) a mere attribute; next, as the λόγος προφορικός, or Word.'

The terms λόγος ἐνδιάθετος, or 'word conceived in the mind,' and λόγος προφορικός, or 'word expressed' (*emissum*, or *prolativum*), were in use among the Gnostics (*Iren.* II. c. 12, § 5). As applied to the Son both terms, though sometimes used in a right sense, were condemned as inadequate. Compare xi. 10.

1 ἀνυποστάτοις λόγοις. Athan. *c. Arianos Orat.* iv. c. 8: πάλιν οἱ λέγοντες μόνον ὄνομα εἶναι υἱοῦ, ἀνούσιον δὲ καὶ ἀνυπόστατον εἶναι τὸν υἱὸν τοῦ Θεοῦ, κ.τ.λ.

2 ὁμοιοπαθῆ. Compare Acts xiv. 15; Jas. v. 17.

3 On the origin of the Docetic heresy, see vi. 14.

4 Valentinus the Gnostic taught that God produced a Son of an animal nature who "passed through Mary just as water through a tube, and that on him the Saviour descended at his Baptism." Irenæus, I. vii. 2.

5 The words which the Benedictine Editor introduces in brackets are found in Theodoret, and adopted by recent Editors, with Codd. M.A.

6 Eusebius, *Life of Constantine*, iii. 28.

7 The discovery of the "True Cross" is related with many marvellous particulars by Socrates, *Eccles. Hist.* i. 17; and Sozomen, *E.H.* ii. 1. A portion was said to have been left by Helena at Jerusalem, enclosed in a silver case; and another portion sent to Constantinople, where Constantine privately enclosed it in his own statue, to be a safeguard to the city. Eusebius, *Life of Constantine*, iii. 25—30, gives a long account of the discovery of the Holy Sepulcare, but makes no mention of the Cross. Cyril seems to have been the first to record it, 25 years after. Cf. Greg. Nyss. *Bapt. Christi* (p. 519).

Of His Burial.

11. He was truly laid as Man in a tomb of rock; but rocks were rent asunder by terror because of Him. He went down into the regions beneath the earth, that thence also He might redeem the righteous[8]. For, tell me, couldst thou wish the living only to enjoy His grace, and that, though most of them are unholy; and not wish those who from Adam had for a long while been imprisoned to have now gained their liberty? Esaias the Prophet proclaimed with loud voice so many things concerning Him; wouldst thou not wish that the King should go down and redeem His herald? David was there, and Samuel, and all the Prophets[9], John himself also, who by his messengers said, *Art thou He that should come, or look we for another*[10]? Wouldst thou not wish that He should descend and redeem such as these?

Of the Resurrection.

12. But He who descended into the regions beneath the earth came up again; and Jesus, who was buried, truly rose again the third day. And if the Jews ever worry thee, meet them at once by asking thus: Did Jonah come forth from the whale on the third day, and hath not Christ then risen from the earth on the third day? Is a dead man raised to life on touching the bones of Elisha, and is it not much easier for the Maker of mankind to be raised by the power of the Father? Well then, He truly rose, and after He had risen was seen again of the disciples: and twelve disciples were witnesses of His Resurrection, who bare witness not in pleasing words, but contended even unto torture and death for the truth of the Resurrection. What then, *shall every word be established at the mouth of two or three witnesses*[1], according to the Scripture, and, though twelve bear witness to the Resurrection of Christ, art thou still incredulous in regard to His Resurrection?

Concerning the Ascension.

13. But when Jesus had finished His course of patient endurance, and had redeemed mankind from their sins, He ascended again into the heavens, a cloud receiving Him up: and as He went up Angels were beside Him, and Apostles were beholding. But if any man disbelieves the words which I speak, let him believe the actual power of the things now seen. All kings when they die have their power extinguished with their life: but Christ crucified is worshipped by the whole world. We proclaim The Crucified, and the devils tremble now. Many have been crucified at various times; but of what other who was crucified did the invocation ever drive the devils away?

14. Let us, therefore, not be ashamed of the Cross of Christ; but though another hide it, do thou openly seal it upon thy forehead, that the devils may behold the royal sign and flee trembling far away[2]. Make then this sign at eating and drinking, at sitting, at lying down, at rising up, at speaking, at walking: in a word, at every act[3]. For He who was here crucified is in heaven above. If after being crucified and buried He had remained in the tomb, we should have had cause to be ashamed; but, in fact, He who was crucified on Golgotha here, has ascended into heaven from the Mount of Olives on the East. For after having gone down hence into Hades, and come up again to us, He ascended again from us into heaven, His Father addressing Him, and saying, *Sit Thou on My right hand, until I make Thine enemies Thy footstool*[4].

Of Judgment to come.

15. This Jesus Christ who is gone up shall come again, not from earth but from heaven: and I say, "not from earth," because there are many Antichrists to come at this time from earth. For already, as thou hast seen, many have begun to say, *I am the Christ*[5]: and *the abomination of desolation*[6] is yet to come, assuming to himself the false title of Christ. But look thou for the true Christ, the Only-begotten Son of God, coming henceforth no more from earth, but from heaven, appearing to all more bright than any lightning and brilliancy of light, with angel guards attended, that He may judge both quick and dead, and reign in a heavenly, eternal kingdom, which shall have no end. For on this point also, I pray thee, make thyself sure, since there are many who say that Christ's Kingdom hath an end[7].

8 Compare xiv. 18, 19, on the Descent into Hades.

9 The same Old Testament saints are named in xiv. 19, as redeemed by Christ in Hades.

10 Matt. xi. 3.

1 Deut. xix. 15.

2 Justin M. *Dialogue with Trypho*, 247 C: We call Him Helper and Redeemer, the power of whose Name even demons do fear; and at this day, when exorcised in the name of Jesus Christ, crucified under Pontius Pilate, Governor of Judæa, they are overcome.

3 Tertullian, *de Coronâ*, 3: At every forward step and movement, at every going in and out, when we put on our clothes and shoes, when we bathe, when we sit at table, when we light the lamps, on couch, on seat, in all the ordinary actions of daily life, we trace upon the forehead the Sign. If for these, and other such rules, you insist upon having positive Scripture injunction, you will find none. Tradition will be held forth to you as the originator of them, custom as their strengthener, and faith as their observer.

4 Ps. cx. 1.

5 Matt. xxiv. 5.

6 Matt. xxiv. 15. Compare Cat. xv. 9, 15.

7 Compare xv. 27, where the followers of Marcellus of Ancyra are indicated as holding this opinion.

Of the Holy Ghost.

16. Believe thou also in the Holy Ghost, and hold the same opinion concerning Him, which thou hast *received to hold* concerning the Father and the Son, and follow not those who teach blasphemous things of Him[8]. But learn thou that this Holy Spirit is One, indivisible, of manifold power; having many operations, yet not Himself divided; Who knoweth the mysteries, Who *searcheth all things, even the deep things of God*[9]: Who descended upon the Lord Jesus Christ in form of a dove; Who wrought in the Law and in the Prophets; Who now also at the season of Baptism sealeth thy soul; of Whose holiness also every intellectual nature hath need: against Whom *if any dare to blaspheme, he hath no forgiveness, neither in this world, nor in that which is to come*[1]: "Who with the Father and the Son together[2]" is honoured with the glory of the Godhead: of Whom also *thrones, and dominions, principalities, and powers* have need[3]. For there is One God, the Father of Christ; and One Lord Jesus Christ, the Only-begotten Son of the Only God; and One Holy Ghost, the sanctifier and deifier of all[4], Who spake in the Law and in the Prophets, in the Old and in the New Testament.

17. Have thou ever in thy mind this seal[5], which for the present has been lightly touched in my discourse, by way of summary, but shall be stated, should the Lord permit, to the best of my power with the proof from the Scriptures. For concerning the divine and holy mysteries of the Faith, not even a casual statement must be delivered without the Holy Scriptures; nor must we be drawn aside by mere plausibility and artifices of speech. Even to me, who tell thee these things, give not absolute credence, unless thou receive the proof of the things which I announce from the Divine Scriptures. For this salvation which we believe depends not on ingenious reasoning[6], but on demonstration of the Holy Scriptures.

Of the Soul.

18. Next to the knowledge of this venerable and glorious and all-holy Faith, learn further what thou thyself art: that as man thou art of a two-fold nature, consisting of soul and body; and that, as was said a short time ago, the same God is the Creator both of soul and body[7]. Know also that thou hast a soul self-governed, the noblest work of God, made after the image of its Creator[8]: immortal because of God that gives it immortality; a living being, rational, imperishable, because of Him that bestowed these gifts: having free power to do what it willeth[9]. For it is not according to thy nativity that thou sinnest, nor is it by the power of chance that thou committest fornication, nor, as some idly talk, do the conjunctions of the stars compel thee to give thyself to wantonness[1]. Why dost thou shrink from confessing thine own evil deeds, and ascribe the blame to the innocent stars? Give no more heed, pray, to astrologers; for of these the divine Scripture saith, *Let the star-gazers of the heaven stand up and save thee*, and what follows: *Behold, they all shall be consumed as stubble on the fire, and shall not deliver their soul from the flame*[2].

19. And learn this also, that the soul, before it came into this world, had committed no sin[3], but having come in sinless, we now sin of our free-will. Listen not, I pray thee, to any one perversely interpreting the words, *But if I do that which I would not*[4]: but remember Him who saith, *If ye be willing, and hearken unto Me, ye shall eat the good things of the land: but if ye be not willing, neither hearken unto Me, the sword shall devour you, &c.*[5]: and again, *As ye presented your members as servants to uncleanness and to iniquity unto iniquity, even so now present your members as servants to righteousness unto sanctification*[6]. Remember also the Scripture, which saith, *Even as they did not like to retain God in their knowledge*[7]: and, *That which may be known of God is mani-*

---

8 In xvi. 6—10, Cyril gives a long list of heresies concerning the Holy Ghost.

9 1 Cor. ii. 10.

1 Matt. xii. 32.

2 This clause is not in the Creed of Nicæa, but is added in the Creed of Constantinople, A.D. 381.

3 Col. i. 16.

4 θεοποιόν is omitted in Codd. Roe, Casaubon, and A.

5 The Benedictine Editor argues from Cat. i. 5, "that thou mayest by faith seal up the things that are spoken;" and xxiii. 18: "sealing up the Prayer by the Amen," that Cyril means by "this seal" the firm belief of Christian doctrine. Compare John iii. 33. But Milles understands by the "seal" the Creed itself, which agrees better with the following context.

6 ἡ σωτηρία γὰρ αὕτη τῆς πίστεως ἡμῶν, which might be rendered, "this our salvation by faith," or, with Milles, "this safety of our Faith." For the rendering in the text, compare Heb. iii. 1: ἀρχιερέα τῆς ὁμολογίας ἡμῶν. On εὑρεσιλογία, see Polybius xviii. 29, § 3: διὰ τῆς προς ἀλλήλους εὑρεσιλογίας.

7 iv. 4.

8 In the Clementine Homily xvi. 16, the soul having come forth from God, clothed with His breath, is said to be of the same substance, and yet not God. In Tertull. *c. Marcion* II. c. 9, the soul is the *afflatus* (πνοή not πνεῦμα) of God, i.e. the image of the Spirit, and inferior to it, though possessing the true lineaments of divinity, immortality, freedom, its own mastery over itself.

9 Tertull. *c. Marc.* II. 6: It was proper that he who is the image and likeness of God should be formed with a free will, and a mastery of himself, so that this very thing, namely freedom of will and self-command, might be reckoned as the image and likeness of God in him.

1 Compare Aug. *de Civ. Dei.* v. 1, where he says that the astrologers (Mathematici) say, not merely such or such a position of Mars signifies that a man will be a murderer, but makes him a murderer. See Dict. of Christian Antiq., "Astrology."

2 Is. xlvii. 13.

3 "The Orphic poets were under the impression that the soul is suffering the punishment of sin, and that the body is an enclosure or prison in which the soul is incarcerated and kept (σώζεται) as the name σῶμα implies, until the penalty is paid." Plato, *Cratyl.* 400. Clement of Alexandria (*Strom.* III. iii. 17), after referring to this passage of Plato, quotes Philolaus the Pythagorean, as saying: "The ancient theologians and soothsayers also testify that the soul has been chained to the body for a kind of punishment, and is buried in it as in a tomb."

4 Rom. vii. 16.

5 Is. i. 19, 20.

6 Rom. vi. 19.

7 Rom. i. 28.

fest in them[8]; and again, *their eyes they have closed*[9]. Also remember how God again accuseth them, and saith, *Yet I planted thee a fruitful vine, wholly true: how art thou turned to bitterness, thou the strange vine*[1] *?*

20. The soul is immortal, and all souls are alike both of men and women; for only the members of the body are distinguished[2]. There is not a class of souls sinning by nature, and a class of souls practising righteousness by nature[3]: but both act from choice, the substance of their souls being of one kind only, and alike in all. I know, however, that I am talking much, and that the time is already long: but what is more precious than salvation? Art thou not willing to take trouble in getting provisions for the way against the heretics? And wilt thou not learn the bye-paths of the road, lest from ignorance thou fall down a precipice? If thy teachers think it no small gain for thee to learn these things, shouldest not thou the learner gladly receive the multitude of things told thee?

21. The soul is self-governed: and though the devil can suggest, he has not the power to compel against the will. He pictures to thee the thought of fornication: if thou wilt, thou acceptest it; if thou wilt not, thou rejectest. For if thou wert a fornicator by necessity, then for what cause did God prepare hell? If thou wert a doer of righteousness by nature and not by will, wherefore did God prepare crowns of ineffable glory? The sheep is gentle, but never was it crowned for its gentleness: since its gentle quality belongs to it not from choice but by nature.

Of the Body.

22. Thou hast learned, beloved, the nature of the soul, as far as there is time at present: now do thy best to receive the doctrine of the body also. Suffer none of those who say that this body is no work of God[4]: for they who believe that the body is independent of God, and that the soul dwells in it as in a strange vessel, readily abuse it to fornication[5]. And yet what fault have they found in this wonderful body? For what is lacking in comeliness? And what in its structure is not full of skill? Ought they not to have observed the luminous construction of the eyes? And how the ears being set obliquely receive the sound unhindered? And how the smell is able to distinguish scents, and to perceive exhalations? And how the tongue ministers to two purposes, the sense of taste, and the power of speech? How the lungs placed out of sight are unceasing in their respiration of the air? Who imparted the incessant pulsation of the heart? Who made the distribution into so many veins and arteries? Who skilfully knitted together the bones with the sinews? Who assigned a part of the food to our substance, and separated a part for decent secretion, and hid away the unseemly members in more seemly places? Who when the human race must have died out, rendered it by a simple intercourse perpetual?

23. Tell me not that the body is a cause of sin[6]. For if the body is a cause of sin, why does not a dead body sin? Put a sword in the right hand of one just dead, and no murder takes place. Let beauties of every kind pass before a youth just dead, and no impure desire arises. Why? Because the body sins not of itself, but the soul through the body. The body is an instrument, and, as it were, a garment and robe of the soul: and if by this latter it be given over to fornication, it becomes defiled: but if it dwell with a holy soul, it becomes a temple of the Holy Ghost. It is not I that say this, but the Apostle Paul hath said, *Know ye not, that your bodies are the temple of the Holy Ghost which is in you*[7] *?* Be tender, therefore, of thy body as being a temple of the Holy Ghost. Pollute not thy flesh in fornication: defile not this thy fairest robe: and if ever thou hast defiled it, now cleanse it by repentance: get thyself washed, while time permits.

24. And to the doctrine of chastity let the first to give heed be the order of Solitaries[8] and of Virgins, who maintain the angelic life in the world; and let the rest of the Church's people follow them. For you, brethren, a great crown is laid up: barter not away a great dignity for a petty pleasure: listen to the Apostle speaking: *Lest there be any fornicator or profane person, as Esau, who for one mess of*

8 Rom. i. 19. 9 Matt. xiii. 15. 1 Jer. ii. 21.

2 Apelles, the heretic, attributed the difference of sex to the soul, which existing before the body impressed its sex upon it. Tertull. *On the Soul*, c. xxxvi.

3 Irenæus I. vii. 5: "They (the Valentinians) conceive of three kinds of men, spiritual, material, and animal....These three natures are no longer found in one person, but constitute various kinds of men. . . . And again subdividing the animal souls themselves, they say that some are by nature good, and others by nature evil." Origen *on Romans*, Lib. VIII. § 10: "I know not how those who come from the School of Valentinus and Basilides . . . suppose that there are souls of one nature which are always safe and never perish, and others which always perish, and are never saved."

4 See iv. 18.

5 On the impure practices of the Manichees, see vi. 33, 34.

6 Fortunatus, the Manichee, in August. *Disput.* ii. 20. *contra Fortunat.* is represented as saying, What we assert is this, that the soul is compelled to sin by a substance of contrary nature.

7 1 Cor. vi. 19.

8 μονάζοντες. Compare xii. 33; xvi. 22. The origin of Monasticism is usually traced to the time of the Decian persecution, the middle of the third century. Previously "there were no monks, but only ascetics in the Church; from that time to the reign of Constantine, Monachism was confined to the anchorets living in private cells in the wilderness: but when Pachomius had erected monasteries in Egypt, other countries presently followed the example. . . . Hilarion, who was scholar to Antonius, was the first monk that ever lived in Palestine or Syria." Bingham, VII. i. 4.

meat sold his own birthright[9]. Enrolled henceforth in the Angelic books for thy profession of chastity, see that thou be not blotted out again for thy practice of fornication.

25. Nor again, on the other hand, in maintaining thy chastity be thou puffed up against those who walk in the humbler path of matrimony. For as the Apostle saith, *Let marriage be had in honour among all, and let the bed be undefiled*[1]. Thou too who retainest thy chastity, wast thou not begotten of those who had married? Because thou hast a possession of gold, do not on that account reprobate the silver. But let those also be of good cheer, who being married use marriage lawfully; who make a marriage according to God's ordinance, and not of wantonness for the sake of unbounded license; who recognise seasons of abstinence, *that they may give themselves unto prayer*[2]; who in our assemblies bring clean bodies as well as clean garments into the Church; who have entered upon matrimony for the procreation of children, but not for indulgence.

26. Let those also who marry but once not reprobate those who have consented to a second marriage[3]: for though continence is a noble and admirable thing, yet it is also permissible to enter upon a second marriage, that the weak may not fall into fornication. For *it is good for them*, saith the Apostle, *if they abide even as I. But if they have not continency, let them marry: for it is better to marry than to burn*[4]. But let all the other practices be banished afar, fornication, adultery, and every kind of licentiousness: and let the body be kept pure for the Lord, that the Lord also may have respect unto the body. And let the body be nourished with food, that it may live, and serve without hindrance; not, however, that it may be given up to luxuries.

Concerning Meats.

27. And concerning food let these be your ordinances, since in regard to meats also many stumble. For some deal indifferently with things offered to idols[5], while others discipline themselves, but condemn those that eat: and in different ways men's souls are defiled in the matter of meats, from ignorance of the useful reasons for eating and not eating. For we fast by abstaining from wine and flesh, not because we abhor them as abominations, but because we look for our reward; that having scorned things sensible, we may enjoy a spiritual and intellectual feast; and that *having now sown in tears we may reap in joy*[6] in the world to come. Despise not therefore them that eat, and because of the weakness of their bodies partake of food: nor yet blame those who *use a little wine for their stomach's sake and their often infirmities*[7]: and neither condemn the men as sinners, nor abhor the flesh as strange food; for the Apostle knows some of this sort, when he says: *forbidding to marry, and commanding to abstain from meats, which God created to be received with thanksgiving by them that believe*[8]. In abstaining then from these things, abstain not as from things abominable[9], else thou hast no reward: but as being good things disregard them for the sake of the better spiritual things set before thee.

28. Guard thy soul safely, lest at any time thou eat of things offered to idols: for concerning meats of this kind, not only I at this time, but ere now Apostles also, and James the bishop of this Church, have had earnest care: and the Apostles and Elders write a Catholic epistle to all the Gentiles, that they should *abstain* first *from things offered to idols, and* then *from blood* also *and from things strangled*[1]. For many men being of savage nature, and living like dogs, both lap up blood[2], in imitation of the manner of the

9 Heb. xii. 16. 1 Heb. xiii. 4. 2 1 Cor. vii. 5.

3 The condemnation of a second marriage, which the Benedictine Editor and others import into this passage, is not to be found in it. τοὺς δευτέρῳ γάμῳ συμπεριενεχθέντας neither means "qui ad secundas nuptias ultro se dejecere," nor even "who have *involved* themselves" (R.W.C.), but simply "who have consented to,"—or, "consented together in—a second marriage,' without any intimation of censure. See V. 9; VI. 13; Ecclus. xxv. 1; γυνὴ καὶ ἀνὴρ ἑαυτοῖς συμπεριφερόμενοι); 2 Macc. ix. 27; Euseb. *H.E.* ix. 9, 7: ἀνεξικάκως καὶ συμμέτρως συμπεριφέροιντο αὐτοῖς; Zeno, *ap. Diog. Laert.* vii. 18; τὸ συμπεριφέρεσθαι τοῖς φίλοις. *Diog. Laert.* vii. 13: εὐσυμπερίφορος. Polyb. IV. 35, § 7, and II. 17, § 12. The gentleness with which Cyril here speaks of second marriages is in striking contrast with the passionate vehemence of Tertullian in the treatise *de Monogamia*, and elsewhere. Aug. *de Hæresibus*, cc. 26, 38, reckons the condemnation of second marriage among the heretical doctrines of the Montanists and Cathari. In the treatise *de Bono Viduitatis, c.* 6, he argues that a second marriage is not to be condemned, but is less honourable than widowhood, and severely rebukes the heretical teaching on this point of Tertullian, the Montanists, and the Novatians. *De Bono Conjugali*, c. 21: Sacramentum nuptiarum temporis nostri sic ad unum virum et unam uxorem redactum est, ut Ecclesiæ dispensatorem non liceat ordinare nisi unius uxoris virum. On the practice of the Church at various times see Bingham, IV. v. 1—4; Suicer, *Thesaur.* Διγαμία.

4 1 Cor. vii. 8, 9.

5 The Nicolaitans (*Apocal.* ii. 14, 20); and the Valentinians, of whom Irenæus (II. xiv. 5), says that they derived their opinion as to the indifference of meats from the Cynics. See also Irenæus I. vi. 3; and xxvi. 3.

6 Ps. cxxvi. 5. 7 1 Tim. v. 23. 8 1 Tim. iv. 3.

9 The various sects of Gnostics, and the Manichees, considered certain meats and drinks, as flesh and wine, to be polluting. Vid. Iren. *Hær.* i. 28. Clem. *Pæd.* ii. 2. p. 186. Epiph. *Hær.* xlvi. 2, xlvii. 1, &c., &c. August. *Hær.* 46, vid. Canon. *Apost.* 43. "If any Bishop, &c., abstain from marriage, flesh, and wine, not for discipline (δι' ἄσκησιν) but as abhorring them, forgetting that they are all very good, &c., and speaking blasphemy against the creation, let him amend or be deposed," &c. R. W. C.

1 Acts xv. 20, 29. The prohibition of blood and things strangled has continued to the present day in the Eastern Church, though already disregarded by the Latins in the time of S. Augustine (*c. Faustum.* xxxii. 13).

2 Tertullian (*Apologeticus*, c. 9) speaks of those "who at the gladiator shows, for the cure of epilepsy, quaff with greedy thirst the blood of criminals slain in the arena," and of others "who make meals on the flesh of wild beasts at the place of combat:" and contrasts the habits of Christians, who abstain from things strangled, to avoid pollution by the blood.

fiercest beasts, and greedily devour things strangled. But do thou, the servant of Christ, in eating observe to eat with reverence. And so enough concerning meats.

Of Apparel.

29. But let thine apparel be plain, not for adornment, but for necessary covering: not to minister to thy vanity, but to keep thee warm in winter, and to hide the unseemliness of the body: lest under pretence of hiding the unseemliness, thou fall into another kind of unseemliness by thy extravagant dress.

Of the Resurrection.

30. Be tender, I beseech thee, of this body, and understand that thou wilt be raised from the dead, to be judged with this body. But if there steal into thy mind any thought of unbelief, as though the thing were impossible, judge of the things unseen by what happens to thyself. For tell me; a hundred years ago or more, think where wast thou thyself: and from what a most minute and mean substance thou art come to so great a stature, and so much dignity of beauty[3]. What then? Cannot He who brought the non-existent into being, raise up again that which already exists and has decayed[4]? He who raises the corn, which is sown for our sakes, as year by year it dies,—will He have difficulty in raising us up, for whose sakes that corn also has been raised[5]? Seest thou how the trees stand now for many months without either fruit or leaves: but when the winter is past they spring up whole into life again as if from the dead[6]: shall not we much rather and more easily return to life? The rod of Moses was transformed by the will of God into the unfamiliar nature of a serpent: and cannot a man, who has fallen into death, be restored to himself again?

31. Heed not those who say that this body is not raised; for it is raised: and Esaias is witness, when he says: *The dead shall arise, and they that are in the tombs shall awake*[7]: and according to Daniel, *Many of them that sleep in the dust of the earth shall arise, some to everlasting life, and some to everlasting shame*[8]. But though to rise again is common to all men, yet the resurrection is not alike to all: for the bodies received by us all are eternal, but not like bodies by all: for the just receive them, that through eternity they may join the Choirs of Angels; but the sinners, that they may endure for ever the torment of their sins.

3 XVIII. 9.

4 Compare xviii. 6, 9; Athenagoras, *On the Resurrection of the Dead*, c. 3.

5 XVIII. 6. John xii. 24; 1 Cor. xv. 36.

6 XVIII. 7.

7 Is. xxvi. 19.

8 Dan. xii. 2.

Of the Laver.

32. For this cause the Lord, preventing us according to His loving-kindness, has granted repentance at Baptism[9], in order that we may cast off the chief—nay rather the whole burden of our sins, and having received the seal by the Holy Ghost, may be made heirs of eternal life. But as we have spoken sufficiently concerning the Laver the day before yesterday, let us now return to the remaining subjects of our introductory teaching.

Of the Divine Scriptures.

33. Now these the divinely-inspired Scriptures of both the Old and the New Testament teach us. For the God of the two Testaments is One, Who in the Old Testament foretold the Christ Who appeared in the New; Who by the Law and the Prophets led us to Christ's school. *For before faith came, we were kept in ward under the law*, and, *the law hath been our tutor to bring us unto Christ*[1]. And if ever thou hear any of the heretics speaking evil of the Law or the Prophets, answer in the sound of the Saviour's voice, saying, Jesus *came not to destroy the Law, but to fulfil it*[2]. Learn also diligently, and from the Church, what are the books of the Old Testament, and what those of the New. And, pray, read none of the apocryphal writings[3]: for why dost thou, who knowest not those which are acknowledged among all, trouble thyself in vain about those which are disputed? Read the Divine Scriptures, the twenty-two books of the Old Testament, these that have been translated by the Seventy-two Interpreters[4].

9 Gr. λουτροῦ μετάνοιαν. Other readings are λύτρον μετανοίας, "redemption by repentance," and λουτρὸν μετανοίας "a laver (baptism) of repentance."

1 Gal. iii. 24. The Παιδαγωγός is described by Clement of Alexandria (*Paedag.* i. 7) as one who both conducts a boy to school, and helps to teach him,—an usher: "under-master" (Wicliff).

2 Matt. v. 17.

3 τῶν ἀποκρύφων. The sense in which Cyril uses this term may be learned from Rufinus (*Expositio Symboli*, § 38), who distinguishes three classes of books: (1) The Canonical Books of the Old and New Testaments, which alone are to be used in proof of doctrine: (2) Ecclesiastical, which may be read in Churches, including Wisdom, Ecclesiasticus, Tobit, Judith, and the Books of the Maccabees, in the Old Testament, and *The Shepherd* of Hermas, and *The Two Ways* in the New Testament. (3) The other writings they called "Apocryphal," which they would not have read in Churches. The distinction is useful, though the second class is not complete.

4 The original source of this account of the Septuagint version is a letter purporting to have been written by Aristeas, or Aristæus, a confidential minister of Ptolemy Philadelphus, to his brother Philocrates. Though the letter is not regarded as genuine its statements are in part admitted to be true, being confirmed by a fragment, preserved by Eusebius (*Præparatio Evangelica*, ix. 6), of a work of Aristobulus. a Jewish philosopher who wrote in the reign of Ptolemy Philometor, 181—146, B.C. Upon these testimonies it is generally admitted that "the whole Law," i.e. the Pentateuch was translated into Greek at Alexandria in the reign

34. For after the death of Alexander, the king of the Macedonians, and the division of his kingdom into four principalities, into Babylonia, and Macedonia, and Asia, and Egypt, one of those who reigned over Egypt, Ptolemy Philadelphus, being a king very fond of learning, while collecting the books that were in every place, heard from Demetrius Phalereus, the curator of his library, of the Divine Scriptures of the Law and the Prophets, and judged it much nobler, not to get the books from the possessors by force against their will, but rather to propitiate them by gifts and friendship; and knowing that what is extorted is often adulterated, being given unwillingly, while that which is willingly supplied is freely given with all sincerity, he sent to Eleazar, who was then High Priest, a great many gifts for the Temple here at Jerusalem, and caused him to send him six interpreters from each of the twelve tribes of Israel for the translation[5]. Then, further, to make experiment whether the books were Divine or not, he took precaution that those who had been sent should not combine among themselves, by assigning to each of the interpreters who had come his separate chamber in the island called Pharos, which lies over against Alexandria, and committed to each the whole Scriptures to translate. And when they had fulfilled the task in seventy-two days, he brought together all their translations, which they had made in different chambers without sending them one to another, and found that they agreed not only in the sense but even in words. For the process was no word-craft, nor contrivance of human devices: but the translation of the Divine Scriptures, spoken by the Holy Ghost, was of the Holy Ghost accomplished.

35. Of these read the two and twenty books, but have nothing to do with the apocryphal writings. Study earnestly these only which we read openly in the Church. Far wiser and more pious than thyself were the Apostles, and the bishops of old time, the presidents of the Church who handed down these books. Being therefore a child of the Church, trench[6] thou not upon its statutes. And of the Old Testament, as we have said, study the two and twenty books, which, if thou art desirous of learning, strive to remember by name, as I recite them. For of the Law the books of Moses are the first five, Genesis, Exodus, Leviticus, Numbers, Deuteronomy. And next, Joshua the son of Nave[7], and the book of Judges, including Ruth, counted as seventh. And of the other historical books, the first and second books of the Kings[8] are among the Hebrews one book; also the third and fourth one book. And in like manner, the first and second of Chronicles are with them one book; and the first and second of Esdras are counted one. Esther is the twelfth book; and these are the Historical writings. But those which are written in verses are five, Job, and the book of Psalms, and Proverbs, and Ecclesiastes, and the Song of Songs, which is the seventeenth book. And after these come the five Prophetic books: of the Twelve Prophets one book, of Isaiah one, of Jeremiah one, including Baruch and Lamentations and the Epistle[9]; then Ezekiel, and the Book of Daniel, the twenty-second of the Old Testament.

36. Then of the New Testament there are the four Gospels only, for the rest have false titles[1] and are mischievous. The Manichæans also wrote a Gospel according to Thomas, which being tinctured with the fragrance of the evangelic title corrupts the souls of the simple sort. Receive also the Acts of the Twelve Apostles; and in addition to these the seven

either of Ptolemy Soter (323—285, B.C.), or of his son Ptolemy Philadelphus (285—247, B.C.), under the direction of Demetrius Phalereus, curator of the King's library.

5 Up to this point Cyril's account is based upon the statements of the Pseudo-Aristeas. The fabulous incidents which follow, concerning the separate cells, the completion of the whole version by each translator, the miraculous agreement in the very words, proving a Divine inspiration, are found in Philo Judæus, *Life of Moses*, II. 7. Josephus, *Antiquities*, XII. *c.* ii. 3—14, following the letter of Aristeas, gives long descriptions of the magnificent presents sent by Philadelphus to Jerusalem, and of his splendid hospitality to the translators, but makes no allusion to the separate cells or miraculous agreement. On the contrary he represents the 72 interpreters as meeting together for consultation, agreeing on the text to be adopted, and completing their joint labours in 72 days. The slightest comparison of the Version with the original Hebrew must convince any reasonable person that the idea of divine inspiration or supernatural assistance, borrowed by Justin Martyr, Irenæus, and other Fathers, apparently from Philo, is a mere invention of the imagination, disproved by the facts. Compare the article "Septuagint" in Murray's Dictionary of the Bible.

6 The rendering "trench not" (R.W.C.) agrees well with the etymology of the verb (παραχαράσσω). Its more usual signification seems to be "counterfeit," "forge." The sense required here, apart from any metaphor, is "transgress" (Heurtley).

7 The name "Nun" is represented by "Nave" in the Septuagint, which Cyril used.

8 The two books of Samuel.

9 The Epistle of Jeremy, which now appears in the Apocrypha as the last chapter of Baruch. On the number and arrangement of the Books of the Old and New Testaments the student should consult an interesting Essay by Professor Sanday (*Studia Biblica*, vol. iii.), who traces the introduction of a fixed order to the time when papyrus *rolls* were superseded by *codices*, in which the sheets of skin were folded and bound together, as in printed books. This change had commenced before the Diocletian persecution, A.D. 303, when among the sacred books taken from the Christians *codices* were much more numerous than *rolls*. On the contents of the Jewish Canon, see Dictionary of the Bible, "Canon." B.F.W. "Josephus enumerates 20 books 'which are justly believed to be divine.'" One of the earliest attempts by a Christian to ascertain correctly the number and order of the Books of the O.T. was made by Melito, Bishop of Sardis, who travelled for this purpose to Palestine, in the latter part of the 2nd Century. His list is as follows:—"Of Moses five (books); Genesis, Exodus, Numbers, Leviticus, Deuteronomy, Jesus son of Nave, Judges, Ruth, four Books of Kings, two of Chronicles, Psalms of David, Solomon's Proverbs, which is also called Wisdom, Ecclesiastes, Song of Songs, Job, Prophets, Isaiah, Jeremiah, the Twelve in one Book, Daniel, Ezekiel, Esdras." (Eusebius, *H.E.* III. cap. 10, note 1, in this series.) Cyril's List agrees with that of Athanasius (*Festal Epistle*, 373 A.D.), except that Job is placed by Ath. after Canticles instead of before Psalms.

1 Gr. ψευδεπίγραφα. For an account of the many Apocryphal Gospels, see the article by Lipsius in the "*Dictionary of Christian Biography*," Smith and Wace, and the English translations in Clark's Ante-Nicene Library.

Catholic Epistles of James, Peter, John, and Jude; and as a seal upon them all, and the last work of the disciples, the fourteen Epistles of Paul [2]. But let all the rest be put aside in a secondary rank. And whatever books are not read in Churches, these read not even by thyself, as thou hast heard me say. Thus much of these subjects.

37. But shun thou every diabolical operation, and believe not the apostate Serpent, whose transformation from a good nature was of his own free choice: who can overpersuade the willing, but can compel no one. Also give heed neither to observations of the stars nor auguries, nor omens, nor to the fabulous divinations of the Greeks [3]. Witchcraft, and enchantment, and the wicked practices of necromancy, admit not even to a hearing. From every kind of intemperance stand aloof, giving thyself neither to gluttony nor licentiousness, rising superior to all covetousness and usury. Neither venture thyself at heathen assemblies for public spectacles, nor ever use amulets in sicknesses; shun also all the vulgarity of tavern-haunting. Fall not away either into the sect of the Samaritans, or into Judaism: for Jesus Christ henceforth hath ransomed thee. Stand aloof from all observance of Sabbaths [4], and from calling any indifferent meats *common or unclean*. But especially abhor all the assemblies of wicked heretics; and in every way make thine own soul safe, by fastings, prayers, almsgivings, and reading the oracles of God; that having lived the rest of thy life in the flesh in soberness and godly doctrine, thou mayest enjoy the one salvation which flows from Baptism; and thus enrolled in the armies of heaven by God and the Father, mayest also be deemed worthy of the heavenly crowns, in Christ Jesus our Lord, to Whom be the glory for ever and ever. Amen.

[2] Cyril includes in this list all the books which we receive, except the Apocalypse. See Bishop Westcott's Article, "Canon," in the *Dictionary of the Bible*, and Origen's Catalogue in Euseb. *Hist.* vi. 25 (Nicene and Post-Nicene Fathers. vol. i.).

[3] Compare xix. 8, where all such acts of divination are said to be service of the devil.

[4] Compare Gal. iv. 10, "Ye observe days."

LECTURE V.

Of Faith.

Hebrews xi. 1, 2.

Now faith is the substance of things hoped for, the evidence of things not seen. For by it the elders obtained a good report.

1. How great a dignity the Lord bestows on you in transferring you from the order of Catechumens to that of the Faithful, the Apostle Paul shews, when he affirms, *God is faithful, by Whom ye were called into the fellowship of His Son Jesus Christ*[1]. For since God is called Faithful, thou also in receiving this title receivest a great dignity. For as God is called Good, and Just, and Almighty, and Maker of the Universe, so is He also called Faithful. Consider therefore to what a dignity thou art rising, seeing thou art to become partaker of a title of God[2].

2. Here then it is further required, that each of you be found faithful in his conscience: for *a faithful man it is hard to find*[3]: not that thou shouldest shew thy conscience to me, for thou art not to *be judged of man's judgment*[4]; but that thou shew the sincerity of thy faith to God, *who trieth the reins and hearts*[5], and *knoweth the thoughts of men*[6]. A great thing is a faithful man, being richest of all rich men. For *to the faithful man belongs the whole world of wealth*[7], in that he disdains and tramples on it. For they who in appearance are rich, and have many possessions, are poor in soul: since the more they gather, the more they pine with longing for what is still lacking. But the faithful man, most strange paradox, in poverty is rich: for knowing that we need only to have *food and raiment*, and being *therewith content*[8], he has trodden riches under foot.

3. Nor is it only among us, who bear the name of Christ, that the dignity of faith is great[9]: but likewise all things that are accomplished in the world, even by those who are aliens[1] from the Church, are accomplished by faith.

By faith the laws of marriage yoke together those who have lived as strangers: and because of the faith in marriage contracts a stranger is made partner of a stranger's person and possessions. By faith husbandry also is sustained, for he who believes not that he shall receive a harvest endures not the toils. By faith sea-faring men, trusting to the thinnest plank, exchange that most solid element, the land, for the restless motion of the waves, committing themselves to uncertain hopes, and carrying with them a faith more sure than any anchor. By faith therefore most of men's affairs are held together: and not among us only has there been this belief, but also, as I have said, among those who are without[1]. For if they receive not the Scriptures, but bring forward certain doctrines of their own, even these they accept by faith.

4. The lesson also which was read to-day invites you to the true faith, by setting before you the way in which you also must please God: for it affirms that *without faith it is impossible to please Him*[2]. For when will a man resolve to serve God, unless he believes that *He is a giver of reward*? When will a young woman choose a virgin life, or a young man live soberly, if they believe not that for chastity there is *a crown that fadeth not away*[3]? Faith is an eye that enlightens every conscience, and

---

1 1 Cor. i. 9. 2 See Procatechesis 6, and Index, *Faithful*.
3 Prov. xx. 6. 4 1 Cor. iv. 3. See Index, *Confession*.
5 Ps. vii. 9. 6 Ps. xciv. 11.

7 This sentence is a spurious addition to the text of the Septuagint, variously placed after Prov. xvii. 4, and xvii. 6. The thought is there completed by the antithesis, *but to the faithless not even an obol*. The origin of the interpolation is unknown.

8 1 Tim. vi. 8.

9 It was a common objection of Pagan philosophers that the Christian religion was not founded upon reason but only on faith. Cyril's answer that faith is necessary in the ordinary affairs of life is the same which Origen had employed against Celsus (I. 11): "Why should it not be more reasonable, since all human affairs are dependent upon faith, to believe God rather than men? For who takes a voyage, or marries, or begets children, or casts seeds into the ground, without believing that better things will result, although the contrary might and sometimes does happen?" See also Arnobius, *adversus Gentes*, II. 8; and Hooker's allusion to the scornful reproach of Julian the Apostate, "The highest point of your wisdom is *believe*" (*Eccles. Pol.* V. lxiii. 1.).

1 By "aliens from the Church," and "those who are without," S. Cyril here means Pagans: so Tertullian, *de Idololatriâ*, c. xiv. But the latter term is applied to a Catechumen in Procatechesis, c. 12, and was also a common description of heretics: see Tertullian, *de Baptismo*, c. xv. 2 Heb. xi. 6.

3 1 Pet. v. 4.

imparts understanding; for the Prophet saith, *And if ye believe not, ye shall not understand*[4].

Faith *stoppeth the mouths of lions*[5], as in Daniel's case: for the Scripture saith concerning him, that *Daniel was brought up out of the den, and no manner of hurt was found upon him, because he believed in his God*[6]. Is there anything more fearful than the devil? Yet even against him we have no other shield than faith[7], an impalpable buckler against an unseen foe. For he sends forth divers arrrows, and *shoots down in the dark night*[8] those that watch not; but, since the enemy is unseen, we have faith as our strong armour, according to the saying of the Apostle, *In all things taking the shield of faith, wherewith ye shall be able to quench all the fiery darts of the wicked one*[9]. A fiery dart of desire of base indulgence is often cast forth from the devil: but faith, suggesting a picture of the judgment, cools down the mind, and quenches the dart.

5. There is much to tell of faith, and the whole day would not be time sufficient for us to describe it fully. At present let us be content with Abraham only, as one of the examples from the Old Testament, seeing that we have been made his sons through faith. He was justified not only by works, but also by faith[1]: for though he did many things well, yet he was never called the friend of God[2], except when he believed. Moreover, his every work was performed in faith. Through faith he left his parents; left country, and place, and home through faith[3]. In like manner, therefore, as he was justified be thou justified also. In his body he was already dead in regard to offspring, and Sarah his wife was now old, and there was no hope left of having children. God promises the old man a child, and Abraham *without being weakened in faith, though he considered his own body now as good as dead*[4], heeded not the weakness of his body, but the power of Him who promised, because *he counted Him faithful who had promised*[5], and so beyond all expectation gained the child from bodies as it were already dead. And when, after he had gained his son, he was commanded to offer him up, although he had heard the word, *In Isaac shall thy seed be called*[6], he proceeded to offer up his son, his only son, to God, believing *that God is able to raise up even from the dead*[7]. And having bound his son, and laid him on the wood, he did in purpose offer him, but by the goodness of God in delivering to him a lamb instead of his child, he received his son alive. Being faithful in these things, he was sealed for righteousness, *and received circumcision as a seal of the faith which he had while he was in uncircumcision*[8], having received a promise *that he should be the father of many nations*[9].

6. Let **us** see, then, how Abraham is the father of many nations[1]. Of Jews he is confessedly the father, through succession according to the flesh. But if we hold to the succession according to the flesh, we shall be compelled to say that the oracle was false. For according to the flesh he is no longer father of us all: but the example of his faith makes us all sons of Abraham. How? and in what manner? With men it is incredible that one should rise from the dead; as in like manner it is incredible also that there should be offspring from aged persons as good as dead. But when Christ is preached as having been crucified on the tree, and as having died and risen again, we believe it. By the likeness therefore of our faith we are adopted into the sonship of Abraham. And then, following upon our faith, we receive like him the spiritual seal, being circumcised by the Holy Spirit through Baptism, not in the foreskin of the body, but in the heart, according to Jeremiah, saying, *And ye shall be circumcised unto God in the foreskin of your heart*[2]: and according to the Apostle, *in the circumcision of Christ, having been buried with Him in baptism*, and the rest[3].

7. This faith if we keep we shall be free from condemnation, and shall be adorned with all kinds of virtues. For so great is the strength of faith, as even to buoy men up in walking on the sea. Peter was a man like ourselves, made up of flesh and blood, and living upon like food. But when Jesus said, *Come*[4], he believed, and walked upon the waters, and found his faith safer upon the waters than any ground; and his heavy body was upheld by the buoyancy of his faith. But though he had safe footing over the water as long as he believed, yet when he doubted, at once he began to sink: for as

4 Is. vii. 9, according to the Septuagint. But A.V. and R.V. both render: *If ye will not believe, surely ye shall not be established.*

5 Heb. xi. 34.

6 Dan. vi. 23.

7 1 Pet. v. 9: *Whom resist, stedfast in the faith.*

8 Ps. xi. 2, *that they may shoot in darkness at the upright in heart* (R.V.). The Hebrew word אֹפֶל, signifying deep darkness (Job iii. 6; x. 22) is vigorously rendered by the Seventy σκοτομήνη, which is explained by the Scholiast on Homer (Od. xiv. 457: Νὺξ δ' ἄρ' ἐπῆλθε κακὴ σκοτομήνιος) to be the deep darkness of the night preceding the new moon.

9 Eph. vi. 16.

1 James ii. 21. Casaubon omitted *μόνον*, which is found in every MS., thus making the meaning to be, "He was justified not by works but by faith," which directly contradicts the statement of S. James, and is inconsistent with the following context in S. Cyril.

2 James ii. 23; 2 Chron. xx. 7; Is. xli. 8; Gen. xv. 6.

3 Heb. xi. 8—10.

4 Rom. iv. 19.

5 Heb. xi. 11, 12.

6 Gen. xxi. 12; xxii. 2.

7 Heb. xi. 19.

8 Rom. iv. 11.

9 Gen. xvii. 5.

1 Rom. iv. 17, 18.

2 Jer. iv. 4: *Circumcise yourselves to the Lord, and take away the foreskins of your heart.* The Septuagint agrees closely with the Hebrew, but Cyril quotes freely from memory.

3 Col. ii. 11, 12.

4 Matt. xiv. 29.

his faith gradually relaxed, his body also was drawn down with it. And when He saw his distress, Jesus who remedies the distresses of our souls, said, *O thou of little faith, wherefore didst thou doubt*[5]? And being nerved again by Him who grasped his right hand, he had no sooner recovered his faith, than, led by the hand of the Master, he resumed the same walking upon the waters: for this the Gospel indirectly mentioned, saying, *when they were gone up into the ship*[6]. For it says not that Peter swam across and went up, but gives us to understand that, after returning the same distance that he went to meet Jesus, he went up again into the ship.

8. Yea, so much power hath faith, that not the believer only is saved, but some have been saved by others believing. The paralytic in Capernaum was not a believer, but they believed who brought him, and let him down through the tiles[7]: for the sick man's soul shared the sickness of his body. And think not that I accuse him without cause: the Gospel itself says, *when Jesus saw*, not his faith, but *their faith, He saith to the sick of the palsy, Arise*[8]! The bearers believed, and the sick of the palsy enjoyed the blessing of the cure.

9. Wouldest thou see yet more surely that some are saved by others' faith? Lazarus died[9]: one day had passed, and a second, and a third; his sinews[1] were decayed, and corruption was preying already upon his body. How could one four days dead believe, and entreat the Redeemer on his own behalf? But what the dead man lacked was supplied by his true sisters. For when the Lord was come, the sister fell down before Him, and when He said, *Where have ye laid him?* and she had made answer, *Lord, by this time he stinketh; for he hath been four days dead*, the Lord said, *If thou believe, thou shalt see the glory of God;* as much as saying, Supply thou the dead man's lack of faith: and the sisters' faith had so much power, that it recalled the dead from the gates of hell. Have then men by believing, the one on behalf of the other, been able to raise[2] the dead, and shalt not thou, if thou believe sincerely on thine own behalf, be much rather profited? Nay, even if thou be faithless, or of little faith, the Lord is loving unto man; He condescends to thee on thy repentance: only on thy part say with honest mind, *Lord, I believe, help thou mine unbelief*[3]. But if thou thinkest that thou really art faithful, but hast not yet the fulness of faith, thou too hast need to say like the Apostles, *Lord, increase our faith*[4]: for some part thou hast of thyself, but the greater part thou receivest from Him.

10. For the name of Faith is in the form of speech[5] one, but has two distinct senses. For there is one kind of faith, the dogmatic, involving an assent of the soul on some particular point: and it is profitable to the soul, as the Lord saith: *He that heareth My words, and believeth Him that sent Me, hath everlasting life, and cometh not into judgment*[6]: and again, *He that believeth in the Son is not judged, but hath passed from death unto life*[7]. Oh the great loving-kindness of God! For the righteous were many years in pleasing Him: but what they succeeded in gaining by many years of well-pleasing[8], this Jesus now bestows on thee in a single hour. For if thou shalt believe that Jesus Christ is Lord, and that God raised Him from the dead, thou shalt be saved, and shalt be transported into Paradise by Him who brought in thither the robber. And doubt not whether it is possible; for He who on this sacred Golgotha saved the robber after one single hour of belief, the same shall save thee also on thy believing[9].

11. But there is a second kind of faith, which is bestowed by Christ as a gift of grace. *For to one is given through the Spirit the word of wisdom, and to another the word of knowledge according to the same Spirit: to another faith, by the same Spirit, and to another gifts of healing*[1]. This faith then which is given of grace from the Spirit is not merely doctrinal, but also worketh things above man's power. For whosoever hath this faith, *shall say to this mountain, Remove hence to yonder place, and it shall remove*[2]. For whenever any one shall say this in faith, *believing that it cometh to pass, and shall not doubt in his heart*, then receiveth he the grace.

And of this faith it is said, *If ye have faith as a grain of mustard seed*[3]. For just as the grain of mustard seed is small in size, but fiery in its operation, and though sown in a small space has a circle of great branches, and when grown up is able even to shelter the fowls[4]; so, likewise, faith in the swiftest moment works the greatest effects in the

5 Mark xiv. 31. 6 Ib. 32.
7 Mark ii. 4. 8 Matt. ix. 2, 6. 9 John xi. 14—44.
1 *νεῦρα*. "Sinews" is the original meaning, the application to "nerves," as distinct organs of sensation, being later.
2 For *ἀναστῆναι*, retained by the Benedictine Editor and Reischl, read *ἀναστῆσαι*, with Roe, Casaubon, and Alexandrides.
3 Mark ix. 24.

4 Luke xvii. 5.
5 *κατὰ τὴν προσηγορίαν*. Compare Aristotle, *Categories*, V. 30: *τῷ σχήματι τῆς προσηγορίας*. Cyril's description of faith as two-fold, and of dogmatic faith as an assent (*συγκατάθεσις*) of the soul to something as credible, seems to be derived from Clement of Alexandria, Strom. II. c. 12. Compare by all means Pearson on the Creed, Art. I. and his Notes a, b, c.
6 John v. 24. 7 Ib. iii. 18; v. 24.
8 *εὐαρεστήσεως*, Bened. and Reischl, with best MSS. Milles and the earlier editions have *ἐρευνήσεως*, "searching."
9 Luke xxiii. 43; the argument is used again in Cat. xiii. 31.
1 1 Cor. xii. 8, 9. 2 Mark xi. 23. 3 Matt. xvii. 20.
4 Matt. xiii. 32.

soul. For, when enlightened by faith, the soul hath visions of God, and as far as is possible beholds God, and ranges round the bounds of the universe, and before the end of this world already beholds the Judgment, and the payment of the promised rewards. Have thou therefore that faith in Him which cometh from thine own self, that thou mayest also receive from Him that faith which worketh things above man[5].

12. But in learning the Faith and in professing it, acquire and keep that only, which is now delivered[6] to thee by the Church, and which has been built up strongly out of all the Scriptures. For since all cannot read the Scriptures, some being hindered as to the knowledge of them by want of learning, and others by a want of leisure, in order that the soul may not perish from ignorance, we comprise the whole doctrine of the Faith in a few lines. This summary I wish you both to commit to memory when I recite it[7], and to rehearse it with all diligence among yourselves, not writing it out on paper[8], but engraving it by the memory upon your heart[9], taking care while you rehearse it that no Catechumen chance to overhear the things which have been delivered to you. I wish you also to keep this as a provision[1] through the whole course of your life, and beside this to receive no other, neither if we ourselves should change and contradict our present teaching, nor if an adverse angel, *transformed into an angel of light*[2], should wish to lead you astray. *For though we or an angel from heaven preach to you any other gospel than that ye have received, let him be to you anathema*[3]. So for the present listen while I simply say the Creed[4], and commit it to memory; but at the proper season expect the confirmation out of Holy Scripture of each part of the contents. For the articles of the Faith were not composed as seemed good to men; but the most important points collected out of all the Scripture make up one complete teaching of the Faith. And just as the mustard seed in one small grain contains many branches, so also this Faith has embraced in few words all the knowledge of godliness in the Old and New Testaments. Take heed then, brethren, and *hold fast the traditions*[5] which ye now receive, and *write them on the table of your heart*[6].

13. Guard them with reverence, lest perchance the enemy despoil any who have grown slack; or lest some heretic pervert any of the truths delivered to you. For faith is like putting money into the bank[7], even as we have now done; but from you God requires the accounts of the deposit. *I charge you*, as the Apostle saith, *before God, who quickeneth all things, and Christ Jesus, who before Pontius Pilate witnessed the good confession, that ye keep* this faith which is committed to you, *without spot, until the appearing of our Lord Jesus Christ*[8]. A treasure of life has now been committed to thee, and the Master demandeth the deposit at His appearing, *which in His own times He shall shew, Who is the blessed and only Potentate, the King of kings, and Lord of lords; Who only hath immortality, dwelling in light which no man can opproach unto; Whom no man hath seen nor can see. To Whom be glory, honour, and power*[9] for ever and ever. Amen.

5 S. Chrysostom (Hom. xxix. in 1 Cor. xii. 9, 10) in like manner distinguishes dogmatic faith from the faith which is "the mother of miracles." The former S. Cyril calls our own, not meaning that God's help is not needed for it, but because, as he has shewn in § 10, it consists in the mind's assent, and voluntary approval of the doctrines set before it: but the latter is a pure gift of grace working in man without his own help. Compare *Apostolic Constitutions*, VIII. c. 1.

6 This Lecture was to be immediately followed by a first recitation of the Creed. See Index, *Creed*.

7 ἐπ' αὐτῆς τῆς λέξεως. "in ipsâ lectione" (Milles): "ipsis verbis" (Bened.): "in the very phrase" (R. W. C.). See below, note 4.

8 Compare S. August. Serm. ccxii., "At the delivery of the Creed," and Index, *Creed*.

9 Compare Aeschylus, *Prometheus* V. 789: ἣν ἐγγράφου σὺ μνήμοσιν δέλτοις φρενῶν.

1 ἐφόδιον, *Viaticum*, i.e. provision for a journey, and here for the journey through this life. It is applied metaphorically by other Fathers (a) in this general sense, to the reading of Holy Scripture, Prayer, and Baptism, and (b) in a special sense to the Holy Eucharist when administered to the sick and dying, as a preparation for departure to the life after death. Council of Nicæa (A.D. 325), Canon xiii. "With respect to the dying, the old rule of the Church should continue to be observed, which forbids that any one who is on the point of death should be deprived of the last and most necessary *viaticum* (ἐφόδιον)."

2 2 Cor. xi. 14.

3 Gal. i. 8, 9.

4 ἐπ' αὐτῆς τῆς λέξεως. (Bened. Reischl. with best MSS.). ταύτης τῆς λέξεως, "this my recitation," (Milles).

5 2 Thess. ii. 15. Compare Cat. xxiii. 23.

6 Prov. vii. 3. Note 9, above.

7 Matt. xxv. 27; Luke xix. 23. See note on Catech. vi. 36: "Be thou a good banker."

8 1 Tim. v. 21; vi. 13, 14.

9 1 Tim. vi. 15, 16.

LECTURE VI.

Concerning the Unity of God[1]. On the Article, I Believe in One God. Also concerning Heresies.

Isaiah xlv. 16, 17. (Sept.)

Sanctify yourselves unto Me, O islands. Israel is saved by the Lord with an everlasting salvation; they shall not be ashamed, neither shall they be confounded for ever, &c.

1. *Blessed be the God and Father of our Lord Jesus Christ*[2]. Blessed also be His Only-begotten Son[3]. For with the thought of *God* let the thought of *Father* at once be joined, that the ascription of glory to the Father and the Son may be made indivisible For the Father hath not one glory, and the Son another, but one and the same, since He is the Father's Only-begotten Son; and when the Father is glorified, the Son also shares the glory with Him, because the glory of the Son flows from His Father's honour: and again, when the Son is glorified, the Father of so great a blessing is highly honoured.

2. Now though the mind is most rapid in its thoughts, yet the tongue needs words, and a long recital of intermediary speech. For the eye embraces at once a multitude of the 'starry quire;' but when any one wishes to describe them one by one, which is the Morning-star, and which, the Evening-star, and which each one of them, he has need of many words. In like manner again the mind in the briefest moment compasses earth and sea and all the bounds of the universe; but what it conceives in an instant, it uses many words to describe[4]. Yet forcible as is the example I have mentioned, still it is after all weak and inadequate. For of God we speak not all we ought (for that is known to Him only), but so much as the capacity of human nature has received, and so much as our weakness can bear. For we explain not what God is but candidly confess that we have not exact knowledge concerning Him. For in what concerns God to confess our ignorance is the best knowledge[5]. Therefore *magnify the Lord with me, and let us exalt His Name together*[6],—all of us in common, for one alone is powerless; nay rather, even if we be all united together, we shall yet not do it as we ought. I mean not you only who are here present, but even if all the nurslings of the whole Church throughout the world, both that which now is and that which shall be, should meet together, they would not be able worthily to sing the praises of their Shepherd.

3. A great and honourable man was Abra-

1 Περὶ Θεοῦ Μοναρχίας. The word μοναρχία, as used by Plato (*Polit.* 291 C), Aristotle (*Polit.* III. xiv. 11. εἶδος μοναρχίας βασιλικῆς), Philo Judæus (*de Circumcisione*, § 2; *de Monarchia*, Titul.), means "sole government." Compare Tertullian (*adv. Praxean.* c. iii.): "If I have gained any knowledge of either language, I am sure that Μοναρχία has no other meaning than 'single and individual rule.'" Athanasius (*de Decretis Nicænæ Synodi*, § 26) has preserved part of an Epistle of Dionysius, Bishop of Rome (259—269, A.D.), against the Sabellians: "It will be natural for me now to speak against those who divide, and cut into pieces, and destroy that most sacred doctrine of the Church of God, the Monarchia, making it, as it were, three powers and divided hypostases, and three Godheads;" (*ibid.*): "It is the doctrine of the presumptuous Marcion to sever and divide the Monarchia into three origins (ἀρχάς)." We see here the sense which Μοναρχία had acquired in Christian Theology: it meant the "Unity of God," as the one principle and origin of all things. "By the Monarchy is meant the doctrine that the Second and Third Persons in the Ever-blessed Trinity are ever to be referred in our thoughts to the First, as the Fountain of Godhead" (Newman, Athanas. *de Decretis Nic. Syn.* § 26, note h). Justin Martyr (Euseb. *H.E.* IV. 18), and Irenæus (*ibid.* V. 20), had each written a treatise περὶ Μοναρχίας. On the history of Monarchianism see, in this Series, Athanasius, *Prolegomena*, p. xxiii. *sqq.*

2 2 Cor. i. 3.

3 This clause is omitted in some MSS. Various forms of the Doxology were adopted in Cyril's time by various parties in the Church. Thus Theodoret (*Hist. Eccles.* II. c. 19) relates that Leontius, Bishop of Antioch, A.D. 348—357, observing that the Clergy and the Congregation were divided into two parties, the one using the form "and to the Son, and to the Holy Ghost," the other "through the Son, in the Holy Ghost," used to repeat the Doxology silently, so that those who were near could hear only "world without end."

The form which was regarded as the most orthodox, and adopted in the Liturgies, ran thus: "Glory to the Father, and to the Son, and to the Holy Ghost, now and ever, and to the ages of the ages." See Suicer's Thesaurus, Δοξολογία.

4 Irenæus II. xxviii. 4: "But since God is all mind, all reason, all active Spirit, all light, and always exists as one and the same, such conditions and divisions (of operation) cannot fittingly be ascribed to Him. For our tongue, as being made of flesh, is not able to minister to the rapidity of man's sense, because that is of a spiritual nature; for which reason our speech is restrained (*suffocatur*) within us, and is not at once expressed as it has been conceived in the mind, but is uttered by successive efforts, just as the tongue is able to serve it."

5 Tertullian, *Apologeticus*, § 17: "That which is infinite is known only to itself. This it is which gives some notion of God, while yet beyond all our conceptions—our very incapacity of fully grasping Him affords us the idea of what He really is. He is presented to our minds in His transcendent greatness, as at once known and unknown." Cf. Phil. Jud. *de Monarch.* I. 4; Hooker, *Eccles. Pol.* I. ii. 3: "Whom although to know be life, and joy to make mention of His name; yet our soundest knowledge is to know that we know Him not as He is, neither can know Him."

6 Ps. xxxiv. 3.

ham, but only great in comparison with men; and when he came before God, then speaking the truth candidly he saith, *I am earth and ashes*[7]. He did not say '*earth*,' and then cease, lest he should call himself by the name of that great element; but he added '*and ashes*,' that he might represent his perishable and frail nature. Is there anything, he saith, smaller or lighter than ashes? For take, saith he, the comparison of ashes to a house, of a house to a city, a city to a province, a province to the Roman Empire, and the Roman Empire to the whole earth and all its bounds, and the whole earth to the heaven in which it is embosomed;—the earth, which bears the same proportion to the heaven as the centre to the whole circumference of a wheel, for the earth is no more than this in comparison with the heaven[8]: consider then that this first heaven which is seen is less than the second, and the second than the third, for so far Scripture has named them, not that they are only so many, but because it was expedient for us to know so many only. And when in thought thou hast surveyed all the heavens, not yet will even the heavens be able to praise God as He is, nay, not if they should resound with a voice louder than thunder. But if these great vaults of the heavens cannot worthily sing God's praise, when shall '*earth and ashes*,' the smallest and least of things existing, be able to send up a worthy hymn of praise to God, or worthily to speak of God, *that sitteth upon the circle of the earth, and holdeth the inhabitants thereof as grasshoppers*[9].

4. If any man attempt to speak of God, let him first describe the bounds of the earth. Thou dwellest on the earth, and the limit of this earth which is thy dwelling thou knowest not: how then shalt thou be able to form a worthy thought of its Creator? Thou beholdest the stars, but their Maker thou beholdest not: count these which are visible, and then describe Him who is invisible, *Who telleth the number of the stars, and calleth them all by their names*[1]. Violent rains lately came pouring down upon us, and nearly destroyed us: number the drops in this city alone: nay, I say not in the city, but number the drops on thine own house for one single hour, if thou canst: but thou canst not. Learn then thine own weakness; learn from this instance the mightiness of God: for *He hath numbered the drops of rain*[2], which have been poured down on all the earth, not only now but in all time. The sun is a work of God, which, great though it be, is but a spot in comparison with the whole heaven; first gaze stedfastly upon the sun, and then curiously scan the Lord of the sun. *Seek not the things that are too deep for thee, neither search out the things that are above thy strength: what is commanded thee, think thereupon*[3].

5. But some one will say, If the Divine substance is incomprehensible, why then dost thou discourse of these things? So then, because I cannot drink up all the river, am I not even to take in moderation what is expedient for me? Because with eyes so constituted as mine I cannot take in all the sun, am I not even to look upon him enough to satisfy my wants? Or again, because I have entered into a great garden, and cannot eat all the supply of fruits, wouldst thou have me go away altogether hungry? I praise and glorify Him that made us; for it is a divine command which saith, *Let every breath praise the Lord*[4]. I am attempting now to glorify the Lord, but not to describe Him, knowing nevertheless that I shall fall short of glorifying Him worthily, yet deeming it a work of piety even to attempt it at all. For the Lord Jesus encourageth my weakness, by saying, *No man hath seen God at any time*[5].

6. What then, some man will say, is it not written, *The little ones' Angels do always behold the face of My Father which is in heaven*[6]? Yes, but the Angels see God not as He is, but as far as they themselves are capable. For it is Jesus Himself who saith, *Not that any man hath seen the Father, save He which is of God, He hath seen the Father*[7]. The Angels therefore behold as much as they can bear, and Archangels as much as they are able; and Thrones and Dominions more than the former, but yet less than His worthiness: for with the Son the Holy Ghost alone can rightly behold Him: for He *searcheth all things, and knoweth even the deep things of God*[8]: as indeed the Only-begotten Son also, with the Holy Ghost, knoweth the Father fully: For *neither*, saith He, *knoweth any man the Father, save the Son, and he to whom the Son will reveal Him*[9]. For He fully beholdeth, and, according as each can bear, revealeth God through the Spirit: since the Only-begotten Son together with the Holy Ghost is a partaker of the Father's Godhead.

7 Gen. xviii. 27.

8 The opinion of Aristarchus of Samos, as stated by Archimedes (*Arenarius*, p. 320, Oxon), was that the sphere of the fixed stars was so large, that it bore to the earth's orbit the same proportion as a sphere to its centre, or more correctly (as Archimedes explains) the same proportion as the earth's orbit round the sun to the earth itself. Compare Cat. xv. 24.

9 Is. xl. 22.

1 Ps. cxlvii. 4.

2 Job xxxvi. 27: ἀριθμηταὶ δὲ αὐτῷ σταγόνες ὑετοῦ. R.V. *For He draweth up the drops of water*.

3 Ecclus. iii. 21, 22.

4 Ps. cl. 6.

5 John i. 18. They are the Evangelist's own words.

6 Matt. xviii. 10.

7 John vi. 46.

8 1 Cor. ii. 10.

9 Matt. xi. 27.

He, who[1] was begotten knoweth Him who begat; and He Who begat knoweth Him who is begotten. Since Angels then are ignorant (for to each according to his own capacity doth the Only-begotten reveal Him through the Holy Ghost, as we have said), let no man be ashamed to confess his ignorance. I am speaking now, as all do on occasion: but how we speak, we cannot tell: how then can I declare Him who hath given us speech? I who have a soul, and cannot tell its distinctive properties, how shall I be able to describe its Giver?

7. For devotion it suffices us simply to know that we have a God; a God who is One, a living[2], an ever-living God; always like unto Himself[3]; who has no Father, none mightier than Himself, no successor to thrust Him out from His kingdom: Who in name is manifold, in power infinite, in substance uniform[4]. For though He is called Good, and Just, and Almighty and Sabaoth[5], He is not on that account diverse and various; but being one and the same, He sends forth countless operations of His Godhead, not exceeding here and deficient there, but being in all things like unto Himself. Not great in loving-kindness only, and little in wisdom, but with wisdom and loving-kindness in equal power: not seeing in part, and in part devoid of sight; but being all eye, and all ear, and all mind[6]: not like us perceiving in part and in part not knowing; for such a statement were blasphemous, and unworthy of the Divine substance. He foreknoweth the things that be; He is Holy, and Almighty, and excelleth all in goodness, and majesty, and wisdom: of Whom we can declare neither beginning, nor form, nor shape. For *ye have neither heard His voice at any time, nor seen His shape*[7], saith Holy Scripture. Wherefore Moses saith also to the Israelites: *And take ye good heed to your own souls, for ye saw no similitude*[8]. For if it is wholly impossible to imagine His likeness, how shall thought come near His substance?

8. There have been many imaginations by many persons, and all have failed. Some have thought that God is fire; others that He is, as it were, a man with wings, because of a true text ill understood, *Thou shalt hide me under the shadow of Thy wings*[9]. They forgot that our Lord Jesus Christ, the Only-begotten, speaks in like manner concerning Himself to Jerusalem, *How often would I have gathered thy children together, even as a hen doth gather her chickens under her wings, and ye would not*[10]. For whereas God's protecting power was conceived as wings, they failing to understand this sank down to the level of things human, and supposed that the Unsearchable exists in the likeness of man. Some again dared to say that He has seven eyes, because it is written, *seven eyes of the Lord looking upon the whole earth*[1]. For if He has but seven eyes surrounding Him in part, His seeing is therefore partial and not perfect: but to say this of God is blasphemous; for we must believe that God is in all things perfect, according to our Saviour's word, which saith, *Your Father in heaven is perfect*[2]*:* perfect in sight, perfect in power, perfect in greatness, perfect in foreknowledge, perfect in goodness, perfect in justice, perfect in loving-kindness: not circumscribed in any space, but the Creator of all space, existing in all, and circumscribed by none[3]. *Heaven is His throne*, but higher is He that sitteth thereon: *and earth is His footstool*[4], but His power reacheth unto things under the earth.

9. One He is, everywhere present, beholding all things, perceiving all things, creating all things through Christ: *For all things were made by Him, and without Him was not anything made*[5]. A fountain of every good, abundant and unfailing, a river of blessings, an eternal light of never-failing splendour, an insuperable power condescending to our infirmities: whose very Name we dare not hear[6]. *Wilt thou find a footstep of the Lord?* saith Job, *or hast thou attained unto the least things which the Almighty hath made*[7]*?* If the least of His works are incomprehensible, shall He be

1 The Benedictine and earlier printed texts read ὁ γεννηθεὶς [ἀπαθῶς πρὸ τῶν χρόνων αἰωνίων]: but the words in brackets are not found in the best MSS. The false grammar betrays a spurious insertion, which also interrupts the sense. On the meaning of the phrase ὁ γεννηθεὶς ἀπαθῶς, see note on vii. 5: οὐ πάθει πατὴρ γενόμενος.

2 Gr. ὄντα, ἀεὶ ὄντα.

3 Iren. II. xiii. 3: "He is altogether like and equal to Himself; since He is all sense, and all spirit, and all feeling, and all thought, and all reason, and all hearing, and all ear, and all eye, and all light, and all a fount of every good,—even as the religious and pious are wont to speak of God."

4 μονοειδῆ. A Platonic word. *Phædo*, 80 B: τῷ μὲν θείῳ καὶ ἀθανάτῳ καὶ νοητῷ καὶ μονοειδεῖ καὶ ἀδιαλύτῳ καὶ ἀεὶ ὡσαύτως κατὰ τὰ αὐτὰ ἔχοντι ἑαυτῷ ὁμοιότατον εἶναι ψυχήν. See Index, "Hypostasis."

5 Iren. II. xxxv. 3: "If any object that in the Hebrew language different expressions occur, such as Sabaoth, Elöe, Adonai, and all other such terms, striving to prove from these that there are different powers and Gods, let them learn that all expressions of this kind are titles and announcements of one and the same Being."

6 See the passages of Irenæus quoted above, § 2 note 4, and § 7 note 3.

7 John v. 37.

8 Deut. iv. 15.

9 Ps. xvii. 8.

10 Matt. xxiii. 37.

1 Zech. iv. 10.

2 Matt. v. 48.

3 Philo Judæus (*Leg. Alleg.* I. 14, p. 52). Θεοῦ γὰρ οὐδὲ ὁ σύμπας κόσμος ἀξίον ἂν εἴη χωρίον καὶ ἐνδιαίτημα, ἐπεὶ αὐτὸς ἑαυτῷ τήπος. So Sir Isaac Newton, at the end of the Principia, asserts that God by His eternal and infinite existence constitutes Time and Space: "Non est duratio vel spatium, sed durat et adest, et existendo semper et ubique spatium et durationem constituit."

4 Is. lxvi. 1.

5 John i. 3.

6 The sacred name (יהוה) was not pronounced, but Adonai was substituted.

7 Job xi. 7 (R.V.): *Canst thou by searching find out God? Canst thou find out the Almighty unto perfection?* Cyril seems to have understood τὰ ἔσχατα as "the least," not as "the utmost."

comprehended who made them all? *Eye hath not seen, and ear hath not heard, neither have entered into the heart of man, the things which God hath prepared for them that love Him*[8]. If the things which God hath prepared are incomprehensible to our thoughts, how can we comprehend with our mind Himself who hath prepared them? *O the depth of the riches, and wisdom, and knowledge of God! How unsearchable are His judgments, and His ways past finding out*[9]! saith the Apostle. If His judgments and His ways are incomprehensible, can He Himself be comprehended?

10. God then being thus great, and yet greater, (for even were I to change my whole substance into tongue, I could not speak His excellence: nay more, not even if all Angels should assemble, could they ever speak His worth), God being therefore so great in goodness and majesty, man hath yet dared to say to a stone that he hath graven, *Thou art my God*[10]! O monstrous blindness, that from majesty so great came down so low! The tree which was planted by God, and nourished by the rain, and afterwards burnt and turned into ashes by the fire,—this is addressed as God, and the true God is despised. But the wickedness of idolatry grew yet more prodigal, and cat, and dog, and wolf[1] were worshipped instead of God: the man-eating lion[2] also was worshipped instead of God, the most loving friend of man. The snake and the serpent[3], counterfeit of him who thrust us out of Paradise, were worshipped, and He who planted Paradise was despised. And I am ashamed to say, and yet do say it, even onions[4] were worshipped among some. Wine was given *to make glad the heart of man*[5]: and Dionysus (Bacchus) was worshipped instead of God. God made corn by saying, *Let the earth bring forth grass, yielding seed after his kind and after his likeness*[6], that *bread may strengthen man's heart*[7]: why then was Demeter (Ceres) worshipped? Fire cometh forth from striking stones together even to this day: how then was Hephaestus (Vulcan) the creator of fire?

11. Whence came the polytheistic error of the Greeks[8]? God has no body: whence then the adulteries alleged among those who are by them called gods? I say nothing of the transformations of Zeus into a swan: I am ashamed to speak of his transformations into a bull: for bellowings are unworthy of a god. The god of the Greeks has been found an adulterer, yet are they not ashamed: for if he is an adulterer let him not be called a god. They tell also of deaths[9], and falls[1], and thunder-strokes[2] of their gods. Seest thou from how great a height and how low they have fallen? Was it without reason then that the Son of God came down from heaven? or was it that He might heal so great a wound? Was it without reason that the Son came? or was it in order that the Father might be acknowledged? Thou hast learned what moved the Only-begotten to come down from the throne at God's right hand. The Father was despised, the Son must needs correct the error: for He THROUGH WHOM ALL THINGS WERE MADE must bring them all as offerings to the Lord of all. The wound must be healed: for what could be worse than this disease, that a stone should be worshipped instead of God?

Of Heresies.

12. And not among the heathen only did the devil make these assaults; for many of those who are falsely called Christians, and wrongfully addressed by the sweet name of Christ, have ere now impiously dared to banish God from His own creation. I mean the brood of heretics, those most ungodly men

---

8 1 Cor. ii. 9. 9 Rom xi. 33. 10 Is. xliv. 17.

1 The cat was sacred to the goddess Pasht, called by the Greeks Bubastis, and identified by Herodotus (ii. 137) with Artemis or Diana. Cats were embalmed after death, and their mummies are found at various places, but especially at Bubastis (*Herod.* ii 67).

"The Dogs are interred in the cities to which they belong, in sacred burial-places" (*Herod.* ii. 67), but chiefly at Cynopolis ("City of Dogs") where the dog-headed deity Anubis was worshipped.

Mummies of wolves are found in chambers excavated in the rocks at Lycopolis, where Osiris was worshipped under the symbol of a wolf.

2 The lion was held sacred at Leontopolis (Strabo, xvii. p. 812).

3 "In the neighbourhood of Thebes there are sacred serpents perfectly harmless to man. These they bury in the temple of Zeus, the god to whom they are sacred." (*Herod.* ii. 74.)

At Epidaurus in Argolis the serpent was held sacred as the symbol of Aesculapius. Clement of Alexandria (*Exhort.* c. ii.) gives a fuller list of animals worshipped by various nations. Compare also *Clement. Recogn.* V. 20.

4 Juvenal *Sat.* xv. 7.

> Illic aeluros, hic piscem fluminis, illic
> Oppida tota canem venerantur, nemo Dianam.
> Possum et caepe nefas violare et frangere morsu.

5 Ps. civ. 15. 6 Gen. i. 11. 7 Ps. civ. 15.

8 The early Creeds of the Eastern Churches, like that which Eusebius of Cæsarea proposed at Nicæa, expressly declare the unity of God, in opposition both to the heathen Polytheism, and to the various heresies which introduced two or more Gods. See below in this Lecture, §§ 12—18; and compare Athan. (*contra Gentes*, § 6, *sqq.*).

9 Clement of Alexandria (*Exhort.* cap. ii. § 37), quotes a passage from a hymn of Callimachus, implying the death of Zeus:

> "For even thy tomb, O king,
> The Cretans fashioned."

Adonis, or "Thammuz yearly wounded," was said to live and die in alternate years.

1 By the word "falls" (ἀποπτώσεις) Cyril evidently refers to the story of Hephæstus, or Vulcan, to which Milton alludes (*Paradise Lost*, I. 740):—

> "Men call'd him Mulciber, and how he fell
> From heaven they fabled, thrown by angry Jove
> Sheer o'er the crystal battlements: from morn
> To noon he fell, from noon to dewy eve,
> A summer's day."

2 The "thunder-strokes" refer to "Titan heaven's first-born, With his enormous brood" (*Par. Lost*, I. 510). Cf. Virgil, *Aen.* vi. 580:—

> "Hic genus antiquum Terræ, Titania pubes,
> Fulmine dejecti fundo volvuntur in imo."

Ibid. *v.* 585:—

> "Vidi et crudeles dantem Salmonea pœnas,
> Dum flammas Jovis et sonitus imitatur Olympi."

Clem. Alex. (*Exhort.* II. § 37):—"Aesculapius lies struck with lightning in the regions of Cynosuris." Cf. Virg. *Aen.* vii. 770 *ss.*

of evil name, pretending to be friends of Christ but utterly hating Him. For he who blasphemes the Father of the Christ is an enemy of the Son. These men have dared to speak of two Godheads, one good and one evil[3]! O monstrous blindness! If a Godhead, then assuredly good. But if not good, why called a Godhead? For if goodness is an attribute of God; if loving-kindness, beneficence, almighty power, are proper to God, then of two things one, either in calling Him God let the name and operation be united; or if they would rob Him of His operations, let them not give Him the bare name.

13. Heretics have dared to say that there are two Gods, and of good and evil two sources, and these unbegotten. If both are unbegotten it is certain that they are also equal, and both mighty. How then doth the light destroy the darkness? And do they ever exist together, or are they separated? Together they cannot be; for *what fellowship hath light with darkness?* saith the Apostle[4]. But if they are far from each other, it is certain that they hold also each his own place; and if they hold their own separate places, we are certainly in the realm of one God, and certainly worship one God. For thus we must conclude, even if we assent to their folly, that we must worship one God. Let us examine also what they say of the good God. Hath He power or no power? If He hath power, how did evil arise against His will? And how doth the evil substance intrude, if He be not willing? For if He knows but cannot hinder it, they charge Him with want of power; but if He has the power, yet hinders not, they accuse Him of treachery. Mark too their want of sense. At one time they say that the Evil One hath no communion with the good God in the creation of the world; but at another time they say that he hath the fourth part only. Also they say that the good God is the Father of Christ, but Christ they call this sun. If, therefore, according to them, the world was made by the Evil One, and the sun is in the world, how is the Son of the Good an unwilling slave in the kingdom of the Evil? We bemire ourselves in speaking of these things, but we do it lest any of those present should from ignorance fall into the mire of the heretics. I know that I have defiled my own mouth and the ears of my listeners: yet it is expedient. For it is much better to hear absurdities charged against others, than to fall into them from ignorance: far better that thou know the mire and hate it, than unawares fall into it. For the godless system of the heresies is a road with many branches, and whenever a man has strayed from the one straight way, then he falls down precipices again and again.

14. The inventor of all heresy was Simon Magus[5]: that Simon, who in the Acts of the Apostles thought to purchase with money the unsaleable grace of the Spirit, and heard the words, *Thou hast neither part nor lot in this matter*[6], and the rest: concerning whom also it is written, *They went out from us, but they were not of us; for if they had been of us, they would have remained with us*[7]. This man, after he had been cast out by the Apostles, came to Rome, and gaining over one Helena a harlot[8], was the first that dared with blasphemous mouth to say that it was himself who appeared on Mount Sinai as the Father, and afterwards appeared among the Jews, not in real flesh but in seeming[9], as Christ Jesus, and afterwards as the Holy Spirit whom Christ promised to send as the Paraclete[10]. And he so deceived the City of Rome that Claudius set up his statue, and wrote beneath it, in the language of the Romans, "Simoni Deo Sancto," which being interpreted signifies, "To Simon the Holy God[1]."

3 The theory of two Gods, one good and the other evil, was held by Cerdo, and Marcion (Hippolytus, *Refut. omnium Hær.* VII. cap. 17: Irenæus, III. xxv. 3, quoted in note on Cat. iv. 4). The Manichees also held that the Creator of the world was distinct from the Supreme God (Alexander Lycop. *de Manichæorum Sententiis*, cap. iii.).

4 2 Cor. vi. 14. Cyril's description applies especially to the heresy of Manes. See § 36, note 3, at the end of this Lecture; also Cat. xi. 21. and Cat. xv. 3.

5 So Irenæus (I. xxiii. 2) says that "from this Simon of Samaria all kinds of heresies derive their origin."

6 Acts viii. 18—21.

7 1 John ii. 19.

8 Irenæus (I. xxiii. 2): "Having purchased from Tyre, a city of Phœnicia, a certain harlot named Helena, he used to carry her about with him, declaring that this woman was the first conception of his mind, the mother of all, by whom in the beginning he conceived in his mind the creation of Angels and Archangels."

9 Cf. Epiphan. (*Hæres.* p. 55, B): "He said that he was the Son, and had not really suffered, but only in appearance (δοκήσει)."

10 Irenæus (I. xxiii. 1): "He taught that it was himself who appeared among the Jews as the Son, and descended in Samaria as the Father, but came to other nations as the Holy Spirit."

Cyril here departs from his authority by substituting Mount Sinai for Samaria, and thereby falls into error. Simon had first appeared in Samaria, being a native of Gitton: moreover in claiming to be the Father he meant to set himself far above the inferior Deity who had given the Law on Sinai, saying that he was "the highest of all Powers, that is the Father who is over all."

1 "Justin Martyr in his first Apology, addressed to Antoninus Pius, writes thus (c. 26): 'There was one Simon a Samaritan, of the village called Gitton, who in the reign of Claudius Cæsar, and in your royal city of Rome, did mighty feats of magic by the art of dæmons working in him. He was considered a god, and as a god was honoured among you with a statue, which statue was set up in the river Tiber between the two bridges, and bears this inscription in Latin:

Simoni Deo Sancto;

which is,

To Simon the holy God.

"The substance of this story is repeated by Irenæus (*adv. Hær.* I. xxiii. 1), and by Tertullian (*Apol. c.* 13), who reproaches the Romans for installing Simon Magus in their Pantheon, and giving him a statue and the title 'Holy God.'

"In A.D. 1574, a stone, which had formed the base of a statue, was dug up on the site described by Justin, the Island in the Tiber, bearing an inscription—'Semoni Sanco Deo Fidio Sacrum, &c.' Hence it has been supposed that Justin mistook a statue of the Sabine God, 'Semo Sancus,' for one of Simon Magus. See the notes in Otto's Justin Martyr, and Stieren's Irenæus.

"On the other hand Tillemont (*Memoires*, t. ii. p. 482) maintains that Justin in an Apology addressed to the emperor and written in Rome itself cannot reasonably be supposed to have fallen into

15. As the delusion was extending, Peter and Paul, a noble pair, chief rulers of the Church, arrived and set the error right[2]; and when the supposed god Simon wished to shew himself off, they straightway shewed him as a corpse. For Simon promised to rise aloft to heaven, and came riding in a dæmons' chariot on the air; but the servants of God fell on their knees, and having shewn that agreement of which Jesus spake, that *If two of you shall agree concerning anything that they shall ask, it shall be done unto them*[3], they launched the weapon of their concord in prayer against Magus, and struck him down to the earth. And marvellous though it was, yet no marvel. For Peter was there, who carrieth the keys of heaven[4]: and nothing wonderful, for Paul was there[5], who was *caught up to the third heaven*, and *into Paradise, and heard unspeakable words, which it is not lawful for a man to utter*[6]. These brought the supposed God down from the sky to earth, thence to be taken down to the regions below the earth. In this man first the serpent of wickedness appeared; but when one head had been cut off, the root of wickedness was found again with many heads.

16. For Cerinthus[7] *made havoc of the Church*, and Menander[8], and Carpocrates[9], Ebionites[1] also, and Marcion[2], that mouthpiece of ungodliness. For he who proclaimed different gods, one the Good, the other the Just, contradicts the Son when He says, *O righteous Father*[3]. And he who says again that the Father is one, and the maker of the world another, opposes the Son when He says, *If then God so clothes the grass of the field which to-day is, and to-morrow is cast into the furnace of fire*[4]; and, *Who maketh His sun to rise on the evil and on the good, and sendeth rain on the just and on the unjust*[5]. Here again is a second inventor of more mischief, this Marcion. For being confuted by the testimonies from the Old Testament which are quoted in the New, he was the first who dared to cut those testimonies out[6], and leave the preaching of the word of faith without witness, thus effacing the true God: and sought to undermine the Church's faith, as if there were no heralds of it.

17. He again was succeeded by another, Basilides, of evil name, and dangerous character, a preacher of impurities[7]. The contest of wickedness was aided also by Valentinus[8], a preacher of thirty gods. The Greeks tell of but few: and the man who was called—but more truly was not—a Christian extended the delusion to full thirty. He says, too, that Bythus the Abyss (for it became him as being an abyss of wickedness to begin his teaching from the Abyss) begat Silence, and of Silence begat the Word. This Bythus was worse than the Zeus of the Greeks, who was united to his sister: for Silence was said to be the child of Bythus. Dost thou see the absurdity invested with a show of Christianity? Wait a little, and thou wilt be shocked at his impiety; for he asserts that of this Bythus were begotten eight Aeons; and of them, ten; and of them, other twelve, male and female. But whence is the proof of these things? See their silliness from their fabrications. Whence hast thou the proof of the thirty Aeons? Because, saith he, it is written, that *Jesus was baptized*,

---

so manifest an error. Whichever view we take of Justin's accuracy concerning the inscription and the statue, there is nothing improbable in his statement that Simon Magus was at Rome in the reign of Claudius." (Extracted by permission from the Speaker's Commentary, *Introduction to the Epistle to the Romans*, p. 4.)

2 "Justin says not one word about St. Peter's alleged visit to Rome, and his encounter with Simon Magus." But "Eusebius in his *Ecclesiastical History* (c. A.D. 325), quotes Justin Martyr's story about Simon Magus (*E.H.* ii. c. 13), and then, without referring to any authority, goes on to assert (c. 14) that 'immediately in the same reign of Claudius divine Providence led Peter the great Apostle to Rome to encounter this great destroyer of life,' and that he thus brought the light of the Gospel from the East to the West' (*ibidem*).

Eusebius probably borrowed this story "from the strange fictions of the *Clementine Recognitions* and *Homilies*, and *Apostolic Constitutions*." See *Recogn.* III. 63–65; *Hom.* I. 15; III. 58; *Apost. Constit.* VI. 7, 8, 9. Cyril's account of Simon's death is taken from the same untrustworthy sources.

3 Matt. xviii. 19. 4 Ib. xvi. 19.

5 It is certain that S. Paul was not at Rome at this time. This story of Simon Magus and his 'fiery car' is told, with variations, by Arnobius (*adv. Gentes*, II. 12), and in *Apost. Constit.* VI. 9.

6 2 Cor. xii. 2, 4.

7 Cerinthus taught that the world was not made by the supreme God, but by a separate Power ignorant of Him. See Irenæus, *Hær.* I. xxvi., Euseb. *E.H.* iii. 28, with the notes in this Series.

8 Menander is first mentioned by Justin M. (*Apolog.* I. cap. 26): "Menander, also a Samaritan, of the town Capparetæa, a disciple of Simon, and inspired by devils, we know to have deceived many while he was in Antioch by his magical art. He persuaded those who adhered to him that they should never die." Irenæus (I. xxiii. 5) adds that Menander announced himself as the Saviour sent by the Invisibles, and taught that the world was created by Angels. See also Tertullian (*de Animâ*, cap. 50.)

9 Carpocrates, a Platonic philosopher, who taught at Alexandria (125 A.D. *circ.*), held that the world and all things in it were made by Angels far inferior to the unbegotten (unknown) Father (Iren. I. xxv. 1; Tertullian, *Adv. Hær.* cap. 3).

1 Irenæus, I. 26: "Those who are called Ebionites agree that the world was made by God: but their opinions with respect to the Lord are like those of Cerinthus and Carpocrates."

2 On Marcion, see note 5, on Cat. iv. 4.

3 John xvii. 25. 4 Luke xii. 28. 5 Matt. v. 45.

6 Marcion accepted only St. Luke's Gospel, and mutilated that (Tertullian, *Adv. Marcion.* iv. 2). He thus got rid of the testimony of the Apostles and eye-witnesses, Matthew and John, and represented the Law and the Gospel as contradictory revelations of two different Gods. For this Cyril calls him 'a second inventor of mischief,' Simon Magus (§ 14) being the first.

7 Basilides was earlier than Marcion, being the founder of a Gnostic sect at Alexandria in the reign of Hadrian (A.D. 117—138). His doctrines are described by Irenæus (I. xxvii. 3—7), and very fully by Hippolytus (*Refut. omn. Hær.* VII. 2—15). The charge of teaching licentiousness attaches rather to the later followers of Basilides than to himself or his son Isidorus (Clem. Alex. *Stromat.* III. cap. 1). Basilides wrote a Commentary on the Gospel in 24 books (*Exegetica*), of which the 23rd is quoted by Clement of Alexandria (*Stromat.* IV. cap. 12), and against which Agrippa Castor wrote a refutation. Origen (*Hom.* i. *in Lucam.*) says that Basilides wrote a Gospel bearing his own name. See Routh, *Rell. Sacr.* I. p. 85; V. p. 106: Westcott, *History of Canon of N.T.* iv. § 3.

8 "The doctrines of Valentinus are described fully by Irenæus (I. cap. i.), from whom S. Cyril takes this account. "Valentinus, and Basilides, and Bardesanes, and Harmonius, and those of their company admit Christ's conception and birth of the Virgin, but say that God the Word received no addition from the Virgin, but made a sort of passage through her, as through a tube, and made use of a phantom in appearing to men." (Theodoret, *Epist.* 145.)

being thirty years old[9]. But even if He was baptized when thirty years old, what sort of demonstration is this from the thirty years? Are there then five gods, because He brake five loaves among five thousand? Or because he had twelve Disciples, must there also be twelve gods?

18. And even this is still little compared with the impieties which follow. For the last of the deities being, as he dares to speak, both male and female, this, he says, is Wisdom[1]. What impiety! For *the Wisdom of God*[2] is Christ His Only-begotten Son: and he by his doctrine degraded the Wisdom of God into a female element, and one of thirty, and the last fabrication. He also says that Wisdom attempted to behold the first God, and not bearing His brightness fell from heaven, and was cast out of her thirtieth place. Then she groaned, and of her groans begat the Devil[3], and as she wept over her fall made of her tears the sea. Mark the impiety. For of Wisdom how is the Devil begotten, and of prudence wickedness, or of light darkness? He says too that the Devil begat others, some of whom created the world: and that the Christ came down in order to make mankind revolt from the Maker of the world.

19. But hear whom they say Christ Jesus to be, that thou mayest detest them yet more. For they say that after Wisdom had been cast down, in order that the number of the thirty might not be incomplete, the nine and twenty Aeons contributed each a little part, and formed the Christ[4]: and they say that He also is both male and female[5]. Can anything be more impious than this? Anything more wretched? I am describing their delusion to thee, in order that thou mayest hate them the more Shun, therefore, their impiety, and *do not even give greeting to*[6] a man of this kind, lest thou have *fellowship with the unfruitful works of darkness*[7]: neither make curious inquiries, nor be willing to enter into conversation with them.

20. Hate all heretics, but especially him who is rightly named after mania[8], who arose not long ago in the reign of Probus[9]. For the delusion began full seventy years ago[1], and there are men still living who saw him with their very eyes. But hate him not for this, that he lived a short time ago; but because of his impious doctrines hate thou the worker of wickedness, the receptacle of all filth, who gathered up the mire of every heresy[2]. For aspiring to become pre-eminent among wicked men, he took the doctrines of all, and having combined them into one heresy filled with blasphemies and all iniquity, he makes havoc of the Church, or rather of those outside the Church, roaming about like a lion and devouring. Heed not their fair speech, nor their supposed humility: for they are serpents, *a generation of vipers*[3]. Judas too *said Hail! Master*[4], even while he was betraying Him. Heed not their kisses, but beware of their venom.

21. Now, lest I seem to accuse him without reason, let me make a digression to tell who this Manes is, and in part what he teaches: for all time would fail to describe adequately the whole of his foul teaching. But *for help in time of need*[5], store up in thy memory what I have said to former hearers, and will repeat to those now present, that they who know not may learn, and they who know may be reminded. Manes is not of Christian origin, God forbid! nor was he like Simon cast out of the Church, neither himself nor the teachers who were before him. For he steals other men's wickedness, and makes their wickedness his own: but how and in what manner thou must hear.

22. There was in Egypt one Scythianus[6], a

---

9 Luke iii. 23. 1 Irenæus I. ii. 2. 2 1 Cor. i. 24.

3 Irenæus, l. c., and Hippolytus, who gives an elaborate account of the doctrines of Valentinus (L. VI. capp. xvi.—xxxii.), both represent Sophia, "Wisdom," as giving birth not to Satan, but to a shapeless abortion, which was the origin of matter. According to Irenæus (I. iv. 2), Achamoth, the enthymesis of Sophia, gave birth to the Demiurge, and "from her tears all that is of a liquid nature was formed."

In Tertullian's Treatise *against the Valentinians* chap. xxii., Achamoth is said as by Cyril to have given birth to Satan: but in chap. xxiii. Satan seems to be identified (or interchanged) with the Demiurge.

4 The account in Irenæus (I. ii. 6) is rather different: "The whole Pleroma of the Aeons, with one design and desire, and with the concurrence of the Christ and the Holy Spirit, their Father also setting the seal of His approval on their conduct, brought together whatever each one had in himself of the greatest beauty and preciousness; and uniting all these contributions so as skilfully to blend the whole, they produced, to the honour and glory of Bythus, a being of most perfect beauty, the very star of the Pleroma, and its perfect fruit, namely Jesus."

Tertullian, *Against the Valentinians*, chap. 12, gives a sarcastic description of this strange doctrine, deriving his facts (chap. 5) from Justin, Miltiades, "Irenæus, that very exact inquirer into all doctrines," and Proculus.

5 This statement does not agree with Irenæus (I. vii. 1), who says that the Valentinians represented the Saviour, that is Jesus, as becoming the bridegroom of Achamoth or Sophia.

6 2 John 10, 11: "Neither bid him God speed" (A.V.): "give him no greeting" (R.V).

7 Ephes. v. 11.

8 Eusebius in his brief notice of the Manichean heresy (*Hist. Eccles.* vii. 31) plays, like S. Cyril, upon the name Manes as well suited to a madman.

9 Marcus Aurelius Probus, Emperor A.D. 276—282, from being an obscure Illyrian soldier came to be universally esteemed the best and noblest of the Roman Emperors.

1 Routh (*R. S.* V. p. 12) comes to the conclusion that the famous disputation between Manes and Archelaus took place between July and December, A.D. 277. Accordingly these Lectures, being "full 70 years" later, could not have been delivered before the Spring of A.D. 348.

2 Leo the Great (*Serm.* xv. cap. 4) speaks of the madness of the later Manichees as including all errors and impieties: "all profanity of Paganism, all blindness of the carnal Jews, the illicit secrets of the magic art, the sacrilege and blasphemy of all heresies, flowed together in that sect as into a sort of cess-pool of all filth." Leo summoned those whom they called the "elect," both men and women, before an assembly of Bishops and Presbyters, and obtained from these witnesses a full account of the execrable practices of the sect, in which, as he declares, "their law is lying, their religion the devil, their sacrifice obscenity."

3 Matt. iii. 7. 4 Ib. xxvi. 49. 5 Heb. iv. 16.

6 Cyril takes his account of Manes from the "Acta Archelai et Manetis Disputationis," of which Routh has edited the Latin

Saracen[7] by birth, having nothing in common either with Judaism or with Christianity. This man, who dwelt at Alexandria and imitated the life of Aristotle[8], composed four books[9], one called a Gospel which had not the acts of Christ, but the mere name only, and one other called the book of Chapters, and a third of Mysteries, and a fourth, which they circulate now, the Treasure[1]. This man had a disciple, Terebinthus by name. But when Scythianus purposed to come into Judæa, and make havoc of the land, the Lord smote him with a deadly disease, and stayed the pestilence[2].

23. But Terebinthus, his disciple in this wicked error, inherited his money and books and heresy[3], and came to Palestine, and becoming known and condemned in Judæa[4] he resolved to pass into Persia: but lest he should be recognised there also by his name, he changed it and called himself Buddas[5]. However, he found adversaries there also in the priests of Mithras[6]: and being confuted in the discussion of many arguments and controversies, and at last hard pressed, he took refuge with a certain widow. Then having gone up on the housetop, and summoned the dæmons of the air, whom the Manichees to this day invoke over their abominable ceremony of the fig[7], he was smitten of God, and cast down from the housetop, and expired: and so the second beast was cut off.

24. The books, however, which were the records of his impiety, remained; and both these and his money the widow inherited. And having neither kinsman nor any other friend, she determined to buy with the money a boy named Cubricus[8]: him she adopted and educated as a son in the learning of the Persians, and thus sharpened an evil weapon against mankind. So Cubricus, the vile slave, grew up in the midst of philosophers, and on the death of the widow inherited both the books and the money. Then, lest the name of slavery might be a reproach, instead of Cubricus he called himself Manes, which in the language of the Persians signifies discourse[9]. For as he thought himself something of a disputant, he surnamed himself Manes, as it were an excellent master of discourse. But though he contrived for himself an honourable title according to the language of the Persians, yet the providence of God caused him to become a self-accuser even against his will, that through thinking to honour himself in Persia, he might proclaim himself among the Greeks by name a maniac.

25. He dared too to say that he was the Paraclete, though it is written, *But whosoever shall blaspheme against the Holy Ghost, hath no forgiveness*[1]. He committed blasphemy therefore by saying that he was the Holy Ghost: let him that communicates with those heretics see with whom he is enrolling himself. The slave shook the world, since *by three things the earth is shaken, and the fourth it cannot bear,—if a slave become a king*[2]. Having come into public he now began to promise things above man's power. The son of the King of the Persians was sick, and a multitude of physicians were in attendance: but Manes promised, as if he were a godly man, to cure him by prayer. With the departure of the physicians, the life of the child departed: and the man's impiety was detected. So the would-be philosopher was a prisoner, being cast into prison not for reproving the king in the cause of truth, not for destroying the idols, but for promising to save and lying, or rather, if the truth must be told, for committing murder. For the child who might have been saved by medical treatment, was murdered by this man's driving away the physicians, and killing him by want of treatment.

26. Now as there are very many wicked things which I tell thee of him, remember first his blasphemy, secondly his slavery (not that slavery is a disgrace, but that his pretending to be free-born, when he was a slave, was wicked), thirdly, the falsehood of his promise, fourthly, the murder of the child, and fifthly,

translation, together with the Fragments of the Greek preserved by Cyril in this Lecture and by Epiphanius. There is an English translation of the whole in Clark's "Ante-Nicene Christian Library."

7 The Saracens are mentioned by both Pliny and Ptolemy. See *Dict. of Greek and Roman Geography*.

8 There is no mention of Aristotle in the *Acta Archelai*, but Scythianus is stated (cap. li.) to have founded the sect in the time of the Apostles, and to have derived his duality of Gods from Pythagoras, and to have learned the wisdom of the Egyptians.

9 These four books are stated by Archelaus (*Acta*, cap. lii.), to have been written for Manes by his disciple Terebinthus.

1 In allusion to this name the history of the Disputation is called (*Acta*, cap. i.) "The true Treasure."

2 The true reading of this sentence, *προαιρούμενον τὸν Σκυθιανόν*, instead of *τὸν πρόειρημένον Σκ.*, has been restored by Cleopas from the MS. in the Archiepiscopal library at Jerusalem. This reading agrees with the statement in *Acta Archel.* cap. li.: "Scythianus thought of making an excursion into Judæa, with the purpose of meeting all those who had a reputation there as teachers; but it came to pass that he suddenly departed this life, without having been able to make any progress."

3 This statement agrees with the reading of the Vatican MS. of the *Acta Archelai*, "omnibus quæcunque ejus fuerunt congregatis."

4 In the *Acta* there is no mention of Palestine, but only that he "set out for Babylonia, a province which is now held by the Persians."

5 Clem. Alex. (*Strom.* i. 15): "Some also of the Indians obey the precepts of Boutta, and honour him as a god for his extraordinary sanctity."

6 Cf. *Acta Arch.* cap. lii.: "A certain Parcus, however, a prophet, and Labdacus, son of Mithras, charged him with falsehood." On the names Parcus and Labdacus, see *Dict. Chr. Biogr.*, "Barcabbas," and on the Magian worship of the Sun-god Mithras, see Rawlinson (*Herodot.* Vol. I. p. 426).

7 See below, § 33.

8 Cf. *Acta Arch.* cap. liii. "A boy about seven years old, named Corbicius."

9 See a different account in *Dict. Chr. Biogr.*, "Manes."

1 Mark iii. 29.

2 Prov. xxx. 21, 22.

the disgrace of the imprisonment. And there was not only the disgrace of the prison, but also the flight from prison. For he who called himself the Paraclete and champion of the truth, ran away: he was no successor of Jesus, who readily went to the Cross, but this man was the reverse, a runaway. Moreover, the King of the Persians ordered the keepers of the prison to be executed: so Manes was the cause of the child's death through his vain boasting, and of the gaolers' death through his flight. Ought then he, who shared the guilt of murder, to be worshipped? Ought he not to have followed the example of Jesus, and said, *If ye seek Me, let these go their way*[3]? Ought he not to have said, like Jonas, *Take me, and cast me into the sea: for this storm is because of me*[4]?

27. He escapes from the prison, and comes into Mesopotamia: but there Bishop Archelaus, a shield of righteousness, encounters him[5]: and having accused him before philosophers as judges, and having assembled an audience of Gentiles, lest if Christians gave judgment, the judges might be thought to shew favour,—Tell us what thou preachest, said Archelaus to Manes. And he, whose *mouth was as an open sepulchre*[6], began first with blasphemy against the Maker of all things, saying, The God of the Old Testament is the author of evils, as He says of Himself, *I am a consuming fire*[7]. But the wise Archelaus undermined his blasphemous argument by saying, "If the God of the Old Testament, as thou sayest, calls Himself a fire, whose Son is He who saith, *I came to send fire on the earth*[8]? If thou findest fault with Him who saith, *The Lord killeth, and maketh alive*[9], why dost thou honour Peter, who raised up Tabitha, but struck Sapphira dead? If again thou findest fault, because He prepared fire, wherefore dost thou not find fault with Him who saith, *Depart from Me into everlasting fire*[1]? If thou findest fault with Him who saith, *I am God that make peace, and create evil*[2], explain how Jesus saith, *I came not to send peace but a sword*[3]. Since both speak alike, of two things one, either both are good, because of their agreement, or if Jesus is blameless in so speaking, why blamest thou Him that saith the like in the Old Testament?"

28. Then Manes answers him: "And what sort of God causes blindness? For it is Paul who saith, *In whom the God of this world hath blinded the minds of them that believe not, lest the light of the Gospel should shine unto them*[4]." But Archelaus made a good retort, saying, "Read a little before: *But if our Gospel is veiled, it is veiled in them that are perishing*[5]. Seest thou that in them that are perishing it is veiled? For it is not right *to give the things which are holy unto the dogs*[6]. Again, Is it only the God of the Old Testament that hath blinded the minds of them that believe not? Hath not Jesus Himself said, *For this cause speak I unto them in parables, that seeing they may not see*[7]? Was it from hating them that He wished them not to see? Or because of their unworthiness, since *their eyes they had closed*[8]. For where there is wilful wickedness, there is also a withholding of grace: *for to him that hath shall be given; but from him that hath not shall be taken even that which he seemeth to have*[9].

29. "But if some are right in their interpretation, we must say as follows[1] (for it is no unworthy expression)—If indeed He blinded the thoughts of them that believe not, he blinded them for a good purpose, that they might look with new sight on what is good. For he said not, He blinded their soul, but, *the thoughts of them that believe not*[2]. And the meaning is something of this kind: 'Blind the lewd thoughts of the lewd, and the man is saved: blind the grasping and rapacious thought of the robber, and the man is saved.' But wilt thou not understand it thus? Then there is yet another interpretation. The sun also blinds those whose sight is dim: and they whose eyes are diseased are hurt by the light and blinded. Not that the sun's nature is to blind, but that the substance of the eyes is incapable of seeing. In like manner unbelievers being diseased in their heart cannot look upon the radiance of the Godhead. Nor hath he said, '*He hath blinded their thoughts*, that they should not hear the Gospel:' but, *that the light of the glory of the Gospel of our Lord Jesus Christ should not shine unto them.* For to hear the Gospel is permitted to all: but the glory of the Gospel is reserved for Christ's

3 John xviii. 8. 4 Jonah i. 12.

5 The account of the discussion in this and the two following chapters is not now found in the Latin Version of the "Disputation," but is regarded by Dr. Routh as having been derived by Cyril from some different copies of the Greek. The last paragraph of § 29, "These mysteries, &c.," is evidently a caution addressed to the hearers by Cyril himself (Routh, *Rell. Sac.* V. 199).

6 Ps. v. 9. 7 Deut. iv. 24. 8 Luke xii. 49.

9 1 Sam. ii. 6. 1 Matt. xxv. 41. 2 Is. xlv. 7.

3 Matt. x. 34.

4 2 Cor. iv. 4, *νοήματα*, "thoughts." 5 2 Cor. iv. 3.

6 Matt. vii. 6.

7 Matt. xiii. 13. Both A.V. and R.V. follow the better reading: "because seeing they see not, &c."

8 Matt. xiii. 15. 9 Ib. xxv. 29: Luke viii. 18.

1 Instead of the reading of the Benedictine and earlier editions, εἰ δὲ δεῖ καὶ ὥς τινες ἐξηγοῦνται τοῦτο εἰπεῖν, the MSS. Roe and Casaubon combine δει και ως into the one word δικαιως, which is probably the right reading. Something, however, is still wanted to complete the construction, and Petrus Siculus (*circ.* A.D. 870) who quotes the passage in his *History of the Manichees*, boldly conjectures ἔστι καὶ οὕτως εἰπεῖν. A simpler emendation would be—εἰ δὲ δικαίως τινὲς ἐξηγοῦνται, δεῖ τουτο εἰπεῖν—which both completes the construction and explains the reading δεῖ καὶ ὡς.

2 νοήματα, 2 Cor. iv. 4.

true children only. Therefore the Lord spake in parables to those who could not hear[3]: but to the Disciples he explained the parables in private[4]: for the brightness of the glory is for those who have been enlightened, the blinding for them that believe not." These mysteries, which the Church now explains to thee who art passing out of the class of Catechumens, it is not the custom to explain to heathen. For to a heathen we do not explain the mysteries concerning Father, Son, and Holy Ghost, nor before Catechumens do we speak plainly of the mysteries: but many things we often speak in a veiled way, that the believers who know may understand, and they who know not may get no hurt[5].

30. By such and many other arguments the serpent was overthrown: thus did Archelaus wrestle with Manes and threw him. Again, he who had fled from prison flees from this place also: and having run away from his antagonist, he comes to a very poor village, like the serpent in Paradise when he left Adam and came to Eve. But the good shepherd Archelaus taking forethought for his sheep, when he heard of his flight, straightway hastened with all speed in search of the wolf. And when Manes suddenly saw his adversary, he rushed out and fled: it was however his last flight. For the officers of the King of Persia searched everywhere, and caught the fugitive: and the sentence, which he ought to have received in the presence of Archelaus, is passed upon him by the king's officers. This Manes, whom his own disciples worship, is arrested and brought before the king. The king reproached him with his falsehood and his flight: poured scorn upon his slavish condition, avenged the murder of his child, and condemned him also for the murder of the gaolers: he commands him to be flayed after the Persian fashion. And while the rest of his body was given over for food of wild beasts, his skin, the receptacle of his vile mind, was hung up before the gates like a sack[6]. He that called himself the Paraclete and professed to know the future, knew not his own flight and capture.

31. This man has had three disciples, Thomas, and Baddas, and Hermas. Let none read the Gospel according to Thomas[7]: for it is the work not of one of the twelve Apostles, but of one of the three wicked disciples of Manes. Let none associate with the soul-destroying Manicheans, who by decoctions of chaff counterfeit the sad look of fasting, who speak evil of the Creator of meats, and greedily devour the daintiest, who teach that the man who plucks up this or that herb is changed into it. For if he who crops herbs or any vegetable is changed into the same, into how many will husbandmen and the tribe of gardeners be changed[8]? The gardener, as we see, has used his sickle against so many: into which then is he changed? Verily their doctrines are ridiculous, and fraught with their own condemnation and shame! The same man, being the shepherd of a flock, both sacrifices a sheep and kills a wolf. Into what then is he changed? Many men both net fishes and lime birds: into which then are they transformed?

32. Let those children of sloth, the Manicheans, make answer; who without labouring themselves eat up the labourers' fruits: who welcome with smiling faces those who bring them their food, and return curses instead of blessings. For when a simple person brings them anything, "Stand outside a while," saith he, "and I will bless thee." Then having taken the bread into his hands (as those who have repented and left them have confessed), "I did not make thee," says the Manichee to the bread: and sends up curses against the Most High; and curses him that made it, and so eats what was made[9]. If thou hatest the food, why didst thou look with smiling countenance on him that brought it to thee? If thou art thankful to the bringer, why dost thou utter thy blasphemy to God, who created and made it? So again he says, "I sowed thee not: may he be sown who sowed thee! I reaped thee not with a sickle: may he be reaped who reaped thee! I baked thee not with fire: may he be baked who baked thee!" A fine return for the kindness!

33. These are great faults, but still small in comparison with the rest. Their Baptism I dare not describe before men and women[1]. I dare not say what they distribute to their wretched communicants[2].... Truly we pollute

3 Matt. xiii. 13. 4 Mark iv. 34.

5 See the note at the end of the Procatechesis.

6 Disput. § 55. Compare the account of Manes in Socrates, Eccles. Hist. I. 22, in this series.

7 The Gospel of Thomas, an account of the Childhood of Jesus, is extant in three forms, two in Greek and one in Latin: these are all translated in Clark's Ante-Nicene Library. The work is wrongly attributed by Cyril to a disciple of Manes, being mentioned long before by Hippolytus (*Refutation of all Heresies*, V. 2) and by Origen (*Hom. i. in Lucam*): "There is extant also the Gospel according to Thomas."

8 In the Disputation, § 9, Turbo describes these transformations: "Reapers must be transformed into hay, or beans, or barley, or corn, or vegetables, that they may be reaped and cut. Again if any one eats bread, he must become bread, and be eaten. If one kills a chicken, he will be a chicken himself. If one kills a mouse, he also will be a mouse."

9 See Turbo's confession, Disput. § 9: "And when they are going to eat bread, they first pray, speaking thus to the bread: 'I neither reaped thee, nor ground thee, nor kneaded thee, nor cast thee into the oven: but another did these things, and brought thee to me, and I am not to blame for eating thee.' And when he has said this to himself, he says to the Catechumen, 'I have prayed for thee,' and so he goes away."

1 On the rites of Baptism and Eucharist employed by the Manichees, see Dict. Chr. Biogr., *Manicheans*.

2 The original runs: *Οὐ τολμῶ εἰπεῖν, τίνι ἐμβάπτοντες τὴν*

our mouth in speaking of these things. Are the heathen more detestable than these? Are the Samaritans more wretched? Are Jews more impious? Are fornicators more impure[3]? But the Manichee sets these offerings in the midst of the altar as he considers it[4]. And dost thou, O man, receive instruction from such a mouth? On meeting this man dost thou greet him at all with a kiss? To say nothing of his other impiety, dost thou not flee from the defilement, and from men worse than profligates, more detestable than any prostitute?

34. Of these things the Church admonishes and teaches thee, and touches mire, that thou mayest not be bemired: she tells of the wounds, that thou mayest not be wounded. But for thee it is enough merely to know them: abstain from learning by experience. God thunders, and we all tremble; and they blaspheme. God lightens, and we all bow down to the earth; and they have their blasphemous sayings about the heavens[5]. These things are written in the books of the Manichees. These things we ourselves have read, because we could not believe those who told of them: yes, for the sake of your salvation we have closely inquired into their perdition.

35. But may the Lord deliver us from such delusion: and may there be given to you a hatred against the serpent, that as they lie in wait for the heel, so you may trample on their head. Remember ye what I say. What agreement can there be between our state and theirs? *What communion hath light with darkness*[6]? What hath the majesty of the Church to do with the abomination of the Manichees? Here is order, here is discipline[7], here is majesty, here is purity: here even *to look upon a woman to lust after her*[8] is condemnation. Here is marriage with sanctity[9], here stedfast continence, here virginity in honour like unto the Angels: here partaking of food with thanksgiving, here gratitude to the Creator of the world. Here the Father of Christ is worshipped: here are taught fear and trembling before Him who sends the rain: here we ascribe glory to Him who makes the thunder and the lightning.

36. Make thou thy fold with the sheep: flee from the wolves: depart not from the Church. Hate those also who have ever been suspected in such matters: and unless in time thou perceive their repentance, do not rashly trust thyself among them. The truth of the Unity of God has been delivered to thee: learn to distinguish the pastures of doctrine. Be an approved banker[1], *holding fast that which is good, abstaining from every form of evil*[2]. Or if thou hast ever been such as they, recognise and hate thy delusion. For there is a way of salvation, if thou reject the vomit, if thou from thy heart detest it, if thou depart from them, not with thy lips only, but with thy soul also: if thou worship the Father of Christ, the God of the Law and the Prophets, if thou acknowledge the Good and the Just to be one and the same God[3]. And may He preserve you all, guarding you from falling or stumbling, stablished in the Faith, in Christ Jesus our Lord, to Whom be glory for ever and ever. Amen.

ἰσχάδα, διδόασι τοῖς ἀθλίοις. διὰ συσσήμων δὲ μόνον δηλούσθω. ἄνδρες γὰρ τὰ ἐν τοῖς ἐνυπνιασμοῖς ἐνθυμείσθωσιν, καὶ γυναῖκες τὰ ἐν ἀφέδροις. Μιαίνομεν ἀληθῶς τὸ στόμα κ.τ.λ.

3 Ὁ μὲν γὰρ πορνεύσας, πρὸς μίαν ὥραν δ ἐπιθυμίαν τελεῖ τὴν πρᾶξιν· καταγινώσκων δὲ τῆς πράξεως ὡς μιανθεὶς οἶδε λουτροῦ ἐπιδεόμενος, καὶ γινώσκει τῆς πρὰξεως τὸ μυσαρόν. Ὁ δὲ Μανιχαῖος θυσιαστηρίου μέσον, οὗ νομίζει, τίθησι ταῦτα, καὶ μιαίνει καὶ τὸ στόμα καὶ τὴν γλῶτταν. παρὰ τοιούτου στόματος, ἄνθρωπε κ.τ.λ.

4 οὗ νομίζει. The Manichees boasted of their superiority to the Pagans in not worshipping God with altars, temples, images, victims, or incense (August. *contra Faustum* XX. cap. 15). Yet they used the names, as Augustine affirms (*l.c.* cap. 18): "Nevertheless I wish you would tell me why you call all those things which you approve in your own case by these names, temple, altar, sacrifice."

5 Κἀκεῖνοι περὶ οὐρανῶν τὰς δυσφήμους ἔχουσι γλώσσας. Ἰησοῦς λέγει περὶ τοῦ πατρὸς αὐτοῦ, Ὅστις τὸν ἥλιον αὐτοῦ ἀνατέλλει ἐπὶ δικαίους καὶ ἀδίκους, καὶ βρέχει ἐπὶ πονηροὺς καὶ ἀγαθούς. κἀκεῖνοι λέγουσιν, ὅτι οἱ ὑετοὶ ἐξ ἐρωτικῆς μανίας γίνονται, καὶ τολμῶσι λέγειν, ὅτι ἐστί τις παρθένος ἐν οὐρανῷ εὐειδὴς μετὰ νεανίσκου εὐειδοῦς, καὶ κατὰ τὴν τῶν καμηλῶν ἢ λύκων καιρὸν, τοὺς τῆς αἰσχρᾶς ἐπιθυμίας καιροὺς ἔχειν, καὶ κατὰ τὴν τοῦ χειμῶνος καιρὸν, μανιωδῶς αὐτὸν ἐπιτρέχειν τῇ παρθένῳ, καὶ τὴν μὲν φεύγειν φασί, τὸν δὲ ἐπιτρέχειν, εἶτα ἐπιτρέχοντα ἱδροῦν, ἀπὸ δὲ τῶν ἱδρώτων αὐτοῦ εἶναι τὸν ὑετόν. Ταῦτα γέγραπται ἐν τοῖς τῶν Μανιχαίων βιβλίοις· ταῦτα ἡμεῖς ἀνέγνωμεν, κ.τ.λ.

6 2 Cor. vi. 14.

7 Gr. ἐπιστήμη. See note on Introductory Lect. § 4.

8 Matt. v. 28.

9 σεμνότατος is the reading of the chief MSS. But the printed editions have σεμνότητος, comparing it with such phrases as στόμα ἀθεότητος (vi. 15), and μετάνοια τῆς σωτηρίας (xiv. 17).

1 This saying is quoted three times in the Clementine Homilies as spoken by our Lord. See Hom. II. § 51; III. § 50; XVIII. § 20: "Every man who wishes to be saved must become, as the Teacher said, a judge of the books written to try us. For thus He spake: *Become experienced bankers*. Now the need of bankers arises from the circumstance that the spurious is mixed up with the genuine."

On the same saying, quoted as Scripture in the Apostolic Constitutions (II. § 36), Cotelerius suggests that in oral tradition, or in some Apocryphal book, the proverb was said to come from the Old Testament, and was added by some transcriber as a gloss in the margin of Matt. xxv. 27, or Luke xix. 23. Dionysius of Alexandria, Epist. VII., speaks of "the Apostolic word, which thus urges all who are endowed with greater virtue, 'Be ye skilful money-changers,'" referring apparently as here to 1 Thess. v. 21, 22, "try all things, &c." (See Euseb. *E.H.* VII. ch. 6 in this series: Suicer. *Thesaurus*, Τραπεζίτης: and Resch. (*Agrapha*, pp. 233—239.)

2 1 Thess. v. 21, 22.

3 Compare § 13 of this Lecture, where Cyril seems to refer especially to the heresy of Manes, as described in the *Disputatio Archelai*, cap. 6: "If you are desirous of being instructed in the faith of Manes, hear it briefly from me. That man worships two gods, unbegotten, self-originate, eternal, opposed one to the other. The one he represents as good, and the other as evil, naming the one Light, and the other Darkness."

LECTURE VII.

THE FATHER.

EPHESIANS iii. 14, 15.

For this cause I bow my knees unto the Father, . . . of whom all fatherhood in heaven and earth is named, &c.

1. OF God as the sole Principle we have said enough to you yesterday[1]: by "enough" I mean, not what is worthy of the subject, (for to reach that is utterly impossible to mortal nature), but as much as was granted to our infirmity. I traversed also the bye-paths of the manifold error of the godless heretics: but now let us shake off their foul and soul-poisoning doctrine, and remembering what relates to them, not to our own hurt, but to our greater detestation of them, let us come back to ourselves, and receive the saving doctrines of the true Faith, connecting the dignity of Fatherhood with that of the Unity, and believing IN ONE GOD THE FATHER: for we must not only believe in one God; but this also let us devoutly receive, that He is the Father of the Only-begotten, our Lord Jesus Christ.

2. For thus shall we raise our thoughts higher than the Jews[2], who admit indeed by their doctrines that there is One God, (for what if they often denied even this by their idolatries?); but that He is also the Father of our Lord Jesus Christ, they admit not; being of a contrary mind to their own Prophets, who in the Divine Scriptures affirm, *The Lord said unto me, Thou art My Son, this day have I begotten thee*[3]. And to this day they *rage and gather themselves together against the Lord, and against His Anointed*[4], thinking that it is possible to be made friends of the Father apart from devotion towards the Son, being ignorant that *no man cometh unto the Father but by*[5] the Son, who saith, *I am the Door*, and *I am the Way*[6]. He therefore that refuseth the Way which leadeth to the Father, and he that denieth the Door, how shall he be deemed worthy of entrance unto God? They contradict also what is written in the eighty-eighth Psalm, *He shall call Me, Thou art my Father, my God, and the helper of my salvation. And I will make him my first-born, high among the kings of the earth*[7]. For if they should insist that these things are said of David or Solomon or any of their successors, let them shew how *the throne* of him, who is in their judgment described in the prophecy, is *as the days of heaven, and as the sun before God, and as the moon established for ever*[8]. And how is it also that they are not abashed at that which is written, *From the womb before the morning-star have I begotten thee*[9]: also this, *He shall endure with the sun, and before the moon, from generation to generation*[1]. To refer these passages to a man is a proof of utter and extreme insensibility.

3. Let the Jews, however, since they so will, suffer their usual disorder of unbelief, both in these and the like statements. But let us adopt the godly doctrine of our Faith, worshipping one God the Father of the Christ, (for to deprive Him, who grants to all the gift of generation, of the like dignity would be impious): and let us BELIEVE IN ONE GOD THE FATHER, in order that, before we touch upon our teaching concerning Christ, the faith concerning the Only-begotten may be implanted in the soul of the hearers, without being at all interrupted by the intervening doctrines concerning the Father.

4. For the name of the Father, with the very utterance of the title, suggests the thought of the Son: as in like manner one who names the Son thinks straightway of the Father also[2]. For if a Father, He is certainly

---

1 See Lecture VI. 1, and 5.

2 "In Athanasius, *Quæstio* i. *ad Antiochum*, tom. II. p. 331, Monarchia is opposed to Polytheism: 'If we worship One God, it is manifest that we agree with the Jews in believing in a Monarchia: but if we worship three gods, it is evident that we follow the Greeks by introducing Polytheism, instead of piously worshipping One Only God.'" (Suicer, *Thesaurus*, Μοναρχία.)

3 Ps. ii. 7.

4 Ib. ii. 2.

5 John xiv. 6.

6 Ib. x. 9.

7 Ps. lxxxix. 26, 27.

8 *vv.* 29, 36, 37.

9 Ps. cx. 3: "From the womb of the morning thou hast the dew of thy youth" (R.V.).

1 Ps. lxxii. 5.

2 Compare Athanasius (*de Sententiâ Dionysii*, § 17): "Each of the names I have mentioned is inseparable and indivisible from that next to it. I spoke of the Father, and before bringing in the

the Father of a Son; and if a Son, certainly the Son of a Father. Lest therefore from our speaking thus, IN ONE GOD, THE FATHER ALMIGHTY, MAKER OF HEAVEN AND EARTH, AND OF ALL THINGS VISIBLE AND INVISIBLE, and from our then adding this also, AND IN ONE LORD JESUS CHRIST, any one should irreverently suppose that the Only-begotten is second in rank to heaven and earth,—for this reason before naming them we named GOD THE FATHER, that in thinking of the Father we might at the same time think also of the Son: for between the Son and the Father no being whatever comes.

5. God then is in an improper sense[3] the Father of many, but by nature and in truth of One only, the Only-begotten Son, our Lord Jesus Christ; not having attained in course of time to being a Father, but being ever the Father of the Only-begotten[4]. Not that being without a Son before, He has since by change of purpose become a Father: but before every substance and every intelligence, before times and all ages, God hath the dignity of Father, magnifying Himself in this more than in His other dignities; and having become a Father, not by passion[5], or union, not in ignorance, not by effluence[6], not by diminution, not by alteration, for *every good gift and every perfect gift is from above, coming down from the Father of lights, with whom can be no variation, neither shadow of turning*[7]. Perfect Father, He begat a perfect Son, and delivered all things to Him who is begotten: (for *all things*, He saith, *are delivered unto Me of My Father*[8]:) and is honoured by the Only-begotten: for, *I honour My Father*[9], saith the Son; and again, *Even as I have kept My Father's commandments, and abide in His love*[1]. Therefore we also say like the Apostle, *Blessed be the God and Father of our Lord Jesus Christ, the Father of mercies, and God of all consolation*[2]: and, *We bow our knees unto the Father, from whom all fatherhood in heaven and on earth is named*[3]: glorifying Him with the Only-begotten: for *he that denieth the Father, denieth the Son also*[4]: and again, *He that confesseth the Son, hath the Father also*[5]; knowing *that Jesus Christ is Lord to the glory of God the Father*[6].

6. We worship, therefore, as the Father of Christ, the Maker of heaven and earth, *the God of Abraham, Isaac, and Jacob*[7]; to whose honour the former temple also, over against us here, was built. For we shall not tolerate the heretics who sever the Old Testament from the New[8], but shall believe Christ, who says concerning the temple, *Wist ye not that I must be in My Father's house*[9]? and again, *Take these things hence, and make not my Father's house a house of merchandise*[1]: whereby He most clearly confessed that the former temple in Jerusalem was His own Father's house. But if any one from unbelief wishes to receive yet more proofs as to the Father of Christ being the same as the Maker of the world, let him hear Him say again, *Are not two sparrows sold for a farthing, and not one of them shall fall on the ground without My Father which is in heaven*[2]; this also, *Behold the fowls of the heaven that they sow not, neither do they reap, nor gather into barns; and your heavenly Father feedeth them*[3]; and this, *My Father worketh hitherto, and I work*[4].

7. But lest any one from simplicity or perverse ingenuity should suppose that Christ is but equal in honour to righteous men, from His saying, *I ascend to My Father, and your*[5] *Father*, it is well to make this distinction beforehand, that the name of the Father is one, but the power of His operation[6] manifold. And Christ Himself knowing this has spoken unerringly, *I go to My Father, and your Father*: not saying 'to our Father,' but distinguishing, and saying first what was proper to Himself, *to My Father*, which was by nature; then adding, *and your Father*, which was by adoption. For however high the privilege we have received of saying in our prayers, *Our Father*,

---

Son, I designated Him also in the Father. I brought in the Son, and even if I had not previously mentioned the Father, in any wise He would have been presupposed in the Son."

3 καταχρηστικῶς. A technical term in Grammar, applied to the use of a word in a derived or metaphorical sense See Aristotle's description of the various kinds of metaphor, *Poet.* § xxi. 7—16. The opposite to καταχρηστικῶς is κυρίως, as used in a parallel passage by Athanasius, *Oratio* i. *contra Arianos*, § 21 fin. "It belongs to the Godhead alone, that the Father is properly (κυρίως) Father, and the Son properly Son."

4 "And in Them, and Them only, does it hold, that the Father is ever Father, and the Son ever Son." (Athan., *as above*.)

5 Compare vi. 6: ὁ γεννηθεὶς ἀπαθῶς. The importance attached to the assertion of a "passionless generation" arose from the objections offered by Eusebius of Nicomedia and others to the word ὁμοούσιος when proposed by Constantine at Nicæa. We learn from Eusebius of Cæsarea (*Epist. ad suæ parœciæ homines*, § 4) that the Emperor himself explained that the word was used "not in the sense of the affections (πάθη) of bodies," because "the immaterial, and intellectual, and incorporeal nature could not be the subject of any corporeal affection." Again, in § 7, Eusebius admits that "there are grounds for saying that the Son is 'one in essence' with the Father, not in the way of bodies, nor like mortal beings, for He is not such by division of essence, or by severance, no, nor by any affection, or alteration, or changing of the Father's essence and power." (See the next note.)

6 Athanasius (*Expos. Fidei*, § 1): "Word not pronounced nor mental, nor an effluence of the Perfect, nor a dividing of the passionless nature." Also (*de Decretis*, § 11): "God being without parts is Father of the Son without partition or passion; for there is neither effluence of the Immaterial, nor influx from without, as among men."

7 James i. 17. 8 Matt. xi. 27. 9 John viii. 49.

1 John xv. 10. 2 2 Cor. i. 3. 3 Eph. iii. 14, 15.

4 1 John ii. 22: "This is the Antichrist, even he that denieth the Father and the Son" (R V.).

5 *v.* 23, bracketed in the A.V. as spurious, but rightly restored in R.V.

6 Phil. ii. 11. 7 Ex. iii. 6. 8 Compare Lect. iv. 33.

9 Luke ii. 49. 1 John ii. 16.

2 Matt. x. 29. S. Cyril instead of "your Father" writes "my Father which is in heaven:" so Origen and Athanasius.

3 Matt. vi. 26. 4 John v. 17.

5 John xx. 17. On this text, quoted again in Cat. xi. 19, see the three Sermons of Bishop Andrewes *On the Resurrection*.

6 ἐνεργείᾳ, meaning here, the operation of God, by nature in begetting His Son, by adoption in making many sons.

which art in heaven, yet the gift is of loving-kindness. For we call Him Father, not as having been by nature begotten of Our Father which is in heaven; but having been transferred from servitude to sonship by the grace of the Father, through the Son and Holy Spirit, we are permitted so to speak by ineffable loving-kindness.

8. But if any one wishes to learn how we call God "Father," let him hear Moses, the excellent schoolmaster, saying, *Did not this thy Father Himself buy thee, and make thee, and create thee*[7]*?* Also Esaias the Prophet, *And now, O Lord. Thou art our Father: and we all are clay, the works of Thine hands*[8]. For most clearly has the prophetic gift declared that not according to nature, but according to God's grace, and by adoption, we call Him Father.

9. And that thou mayest learn more exactly that in the Divine Scriptures it is not by any means the natural father only that is called father, hear what Paul says:—*For though ye should have ten thousand tutors in Christ, yet have ye not many fathers: for in Christ Jesus I begat you through the Gospel*[9]. For Paul was father of the Corinthians, not by having begotten them after the flesh, but by having taught and begotten them again after the Spirit. Hear Job also saying, *I was a father of the needy*[1]*:* for he called himself a father, not as having begotten them all, but as caring for them. And God's Only-begotten Son Himself, when nailed in His flesh to the tree at the time of crucifixion, on seeing Mary, His own Mother according to the flesh, and John, the most beloved of His disciples, said to him, *Behold! thy mother*, and to her, *Behold! thy Son*[2]*:* teaching her the parental affection due to him[3], and indirectly explaining that which is said in Luke, *and His father and His mother marvelled at Him*[4]*:* words which the tribe of heretics snatch up, saying that He was begotten of a man and a woman. For like as Mary was called the mother of John, because of her parental affection, not from having given him birth, so Joseph also was called the father of Christ, not from having begotten Him (for *he knew her not*, as the Gospel says, *until she had brought forth her first-born Son*[5]), but because of the care bestowed on His nurture.

10 Thus much then at present, in the way of a digression, to put you in remembrance. Let me, however, add yet another testimony in proof that God is called the Father of men in an improper sense. For when in Esaias God is addressed thus, *For Thou art our Father, though Abraham be ignorant of us*[6], and *Sarah travailed not with us*[7], need we inquire further on this point? And if the Psalmist says, *Let them be troubled from His countenance, the Father of the fatherless, and Judge of the widows*[8], is it not manifest to all, that when God is called the Father of orphans who have lately lost their own fathers, He is so named not as begetting them of Himself, but as caring for them and shielding them. But whereas God, as we have said, is in an improper sense the Father of men, of Christ alone He is the Father by nature, not by adoption: and the Father of men in time, but of Christ before all time, as He saith, *And now, O Father, glorify Thou Me with Thine own self, with the glory which I had with Thee before the world was*[9].

11. We believe then IN ONE GOD THE FATHER the Unsearchable and Ineffable, *Whom no man hath seen*[1], but *the Only-begotten alone hath declared Him*[2]. *For He which is of God, He hath seen God*[3]*:* whose face the Angels do alway behold in heaven[4], behold, however, each according to the measure of his own rank. But the undimmed vision of the Father is reserved in its purity for the Son with the Holy Ghost.

12. Having reached this point of my discourse, and being reminded of the passages just before mentioned, in which God was addressed as the Father of men, I am greatly amazed at men's insensibility. For God with unspeakable loving-kindness deigned to be called the Father of men,—He in heaven, they on earth,—and He the Maker of Eternity, they made in time,—He *who holdeth the earth in the hollow of His hand*, they upon the earth *as grasshoppers*[5]. Yet man forsook his heavenly Father, and said to the stock, *Thou art my father, and to the stone, Thou hast begotten me*[6]. And for this reason, methinks, the Psalmist says to mankind, *Forget also thine own people, and thy father's house*[7], whom thou hast chosen for a father, whom thou hast drawn upon thyself to thy destruction.

13. And not only stocks and stones, but even Satan himself, the destroyer of souls, have some ere now chosen for a father; to whom the Lord said as a rebuke, *Ye do the deeds of your father*[8], that is of the devil, he being the father of men not by nature, but by fraud.

---

7 Deut. xxxii. 6. 8 Is. lxiv. 8. 9 1 Cor. iv. 15.
1 Job xxix. 16. 2 John xix. 26, 27.
3 φιλοστοργία might be applied to the mutual affection of mother and son, but the context shews that it refers here to parental love only; see Polybius, V. § 74, 5; Xenoph. *Cyrop.* I. § 3, 2. 4 Luke ii. 33. 5 Matt. i. 25.

6 Is. lxiii. 16. 7 Ib. li. 2.
8 Ps. lxviii. 5. Cyril quotes as usual from the Septuagint (Ps. lxvii. 6), where the clause ταραχθήσονται ἀπὸ προσώπου αὐτοῦ, answering to nothing in the Hebrew, is evidently an interpolation, and may have crept in from a marginal quotation of Is. lxiv. 2.
9 John xvii. 5. 1 1 Tim. ii. 16. 2 John i. 18.
3 John vi. 46: *He hath seen the Father.* The weight of authority is against the reading (τὸν θεόν) which Cyril follows.
4 Matt. xviii. 10. 5 Is. xl. 12 and 22. 6 Jer. ii. 27.
7 Ps. xlv. 10. 8 John viii. 41.

For like as Paul by his godly teaching came to be called the father of the Corinthians, so the devil is called the father of those who of their own will *consent unto him*[9].

For we shall not tolerate those who give a wrong meaning to that saying, *Hereby know we the children of God, and the children of the devil*[1], as if there were by nature some men to be saved, and some to be lost. Whereas we come into such holy sonship not of necessity but by choice: nor was the traitor Judas by nature a son of the devil and of perdition; for certainly he would never have cast out devils at all in the name of Christ: for *Satan casteth not out Satan*[2]. Nor on the other hand would Paul have turned from persecuting to preaching. But the adoption is in our own power, as John saith, *But as many as received Him, to them gave He power to become the children of God, even to them that believe in His name*[3]. For not before their believing, but from their believing they were counted worthy to become of their own choice the children of God.

14. Knowing this, therefore, let us walk spiritually, that we may be counted worthy of God's adoption. *For as many as are led by the Spirit of God, they are the sons of God*[4]. For it profiteth us nothing to have gained the title of Christians, unless the works also follow; lest to us also it be said, *If ye were Abraham's children, ye would do the works of Abraham*[5]. *For if we call on Him as Father, who without respect of persons judgeth according to every man's work, let us pass the time of our sojourning here in fear*[6], *loving not the world, neither the things that are in the world: for if any man love the world, the love of the Father is not in him*[7]. Wherefore, my beloved children, let us by our works offer glory to *our Father which is in heaven, that they may see our good works, and glorify our Father which is in heaven*[8]. *Let us cast all our care upon Him, for our Father knoweth what things we have need of*[9].

9 Ps. l. 18. 1 1 John iii. 10. 2 Mark iii. 23. 3 John i. 12. 4 Rom. viii. 14. 5 John viii. 39. 6 1 Pet. i. 17. 7 1 John ii. 15. 8 Matt. v. 16. 9 1 Pet. v. 7; Matt. vi. 8.

15. But while honouring our heavenly Father let us honour also *the fathers of our flesh*[1]: since the Lord Himself hath evidently so appointed in the Law and the Prophets, saying, *Honour thy father and thy mother, that it may be well with thee, and thy days shall be long in the land*[2]. And let this commandment be especially observed by those here present who have fathers and mothers. *Children, obey your parents in all things: for this is well pleasing to the Lord*[3]. For the Lord said not, *He that loveth father or mother is not worthy of Me*, lest thou from ignorance shouldest perversely mistake what was rightly written, but He added, *more than Me*[4]. For when our fathers on earth are of a contrary mind to our Father in heaven, then we must obey Christ's word. But when they put no obstacle to godliness in our way, if we are ever carried away by ingratitude, and, forgetting their benefits to us, hold them in contempt, then the oracle will have place which says, *He that curseth father or mother, let him die the death*[5].

16. The first virtue of godliness in Christians is to honour their parents, to requite the troubles of those who begat them[6], and with all their might to confer on them what tends to their comfort (for if we should repay them ever so much, yet we shall never be able to return their gift of life[7]), that they also may enjoy the comfort provided by us, and may confirm us in those blessings which Jacob the supplanter shrewdly seized; and that our Father in heaven may accept[8] our good purpose, and judge us worthy *to shine amid the righteous as the sun in the kingdom of our Father*[9]: To whom be the glory, with the Only-begotten our Saviour Jesus Christ, and with the Holy and Life-giving Spirit, now and ever, to all eternity. Amen.

1 Heb. xii. 9. 2 Deut. v. 16. 3 Col. iii. 20. 4 Matt. x. 37. 5 Ex. xxi. 17; Lev. xx. 9; Matt. xv. 4.

6 Compare for the thought Euripides, *Medea*, 1029—1035.

7 ἀντιγεννῆσαι. Jeremy Taylor (*Ductor Dubitantium*, Book III. cap. ii. § 17) mentions several stories in which a parent is nourished from a daughter's breast, who thus 'saves the life she cannot give.'

8 On the change of Moods, see Jelf, *Greek Grammar*, § 809. The second verb (καταξιώσειεν) expresses a wish and a consequence which *might* follow, if the first (στηρίξωσιν) wish be realized, as it probably may be. Cf. Herod. ix. 51.

9 Matt. xiii. 43.

LECTURE VIII.

ALMIGHTY.

JEREMIAH xxxix. 18, 19 (Septuagint).

The Great, the strong God, Lord of great Counsel, and mighty in His works, the Great God, the Lord Almighty and of great name[1].

1. BY believing IN ONE GOD we cut off all misbelief in many gods, using this as a shield against Greeks, and every opposing power of heretics; and by adding, IN ONE GOD THE FATHER, we contend against those of the circumcision, who deny the Only-begotten Son of God. For, as was said yesterday, even before explaining the truths concerning our Lord Jesus Christ, we made it manifest at once, by saying "The Father," that He is the Father of a Son: that as we understand that God is, so we may understand that He has a Son. But to those titles we add that He is also "ALMIGHTY;" and this we affirm because of Greeks and Jews[2] together, and all heretics.

2. For of the Greeks some have said that God is the soul of the world[3]: and others that His power reaches only to heaven, and not to earth as well. Some also sharing their error, and misusing the text which says, "*And Thy truth unto the clouds*[4]," have dared to circumscribe God's providence by the clouds and the heaven, and to alienate from God the things on earth; having forgotten the Psalm which says, *If I go up into heaven, Thou art there: if I go down into hell, Thou art present*[5]. For if there is nothing higher than heaven, and if hell is deeper than the earth, He who rules the lower regions reaches the earth also.

3. But heretics again, as I have said before, know not One Almighty God. For He is Almighty who rules all things, who has power over all things. But they who say that one God is Lord of the soul, and some other of the body, make neither of them perfect, because either is wanting to the other[6]. For how is he almighty, who has power over the soul, but not over the body? And how is he almighty who has dominion over bodies, but no power over spirits? But these men the Lord confutes, saying on the contrary, *Rather fear ye Him which is able to destroy both soul and body in hell*[7]. For unless the Father of our Lord Jesus Christ has the power over both, how does He subject both to punishment? For how shall He be able to take the body which is another's and cast it into hell, *except He first bind the strong man, and spoil his goods*[8]*?*

4. But the Divine Scripture and the doctrines of the truth know but One God, who rules all things by His power, but endures many things of His will. For He rules even over the idolaters, but endures them of His forbearance: He rules also over the heretics who set Him at nought, but bears with them because of His long-suffering: He rules even over the devil, but bears with him of His long-suffering, not from want of power, as if defeated. For *he is the beginning of the Lord's creation, made to be mocked*[9], not by Himself,

---

[1] The text is translated from the Septuagint, in which S. Cyril found the title ALMIGHTY (Παντοκράτωρ), one of the usual equivalents in the Septuagint for *Lord of Hosts* (*Sabaoth*). In the English A.V. and R.V. the passage stands thus: Jer. xxxii. 18, 19: *The Great, the Mighty God, the LORD of Hosts, is His name, Great in counsel, and mighty in work.*

[2] "For even the Jewish nation had wicked heresies: for of them were . . . the Pharisees, who ascribe the practice of sinners to fortune and fate; and the Basmotheans, who deny providence and say that the world is made by spontaneous motion" (*Apost. Const.* VI. 6). Compare Euseb. (*E.H.* IV. 22.)

[3] Cicero, *De Natura Deorum*, Lib. I. 27: "Pythagoras thought that God was the soul pervading all nature." The doctrine was accepted both by Stoics and Platonists, and became very general. Cf. Virg. *Georg.* iv. 221:

Deum namque ire per omnis
Terrasque, tractusque maris, cælumque profundum.

and *Aen.* vi. 726:

Spiritus intus alit, totamque infusa per artus
Meus agitat molem, et magno se corpore miscet.

[4] Ps. xxxvi. 5. Cyril appears to have borrowed this statement from Clement of Alexandria, who states (*Stromat.* V. xiv. § 91) that from this Psalm the thought occurred to Aristotle to let Providence come down as far as to the Moon.

[5] Ps. cxxxix. 8.

[6] See note on Lect. IV. 4.

[7] Matt. x. 28.

[8] Ib. xii. 29.

[9] Job xl. 14, τοῦτ' ἔστιν ἀρχὴ πλάσματος Κυρίου, πεποιημένον ἐγκαταπαίζεσθαι ὑπὸ τῶν ἀγγέλων αὐτοῦ. In this description of Behemoth the Septuagint differs much from the Hebrew, which is thus rendered in our English Versions, xl. 19: *He is the chief of the ways of God: he* (*only*, R.V.) *that made him can make his sword to approach unto him.* Compare Job xli. 5: *Wilt thou play with him as with a bird?* and Ps. civ. 26: *There is that Leviathan whom thou hast formed to play therein* (Sept. *to take thy pastime with him*). See Baruch iii. 17, with the note in the Speaker's Commentary.

for that were unworthy of Him, but *by the Angels* whom He hath made. But He suffered him to live, for two purposes, that he might disgrace himself the more in his defeat, and that mankind might be crowned with victory. O all wise providence of God! which takes the wicked purpose for a groundwork of salvation for the faithful. For as He took the unbrotherly purpose of Joseph's brethren for a groundwork of His own dispensation, and, by permitting them to sell their brother from hatred, took occasion to make him king whom He would; so he permitted the devil to wrestle, that the victors might be crowned; and that when victory was gained, he might be the more disgraced as being conquered by the weaker, and men be greatly honoured as having conquered him who was once an Archangel.

5. Nothing then is withdrawn from the power of God; for the Scripture says of Him, *for all things are Thy servants*[10]. All things alike are His servants, but from all these One, His only Son, and One, His Holy Spirit, are excepted; and all the things which are His servants serve the Lord through the One Son and in the Holy Spirit. God then rules all, and of His long-suffering endures even murderers and robbers and fornicators, having appointed a set time for recompensing every one, that if they who have had long warning are still impenitent in heart, they may receive the greater condemnation. They are kings of men, who reign upon earth, but not without the power from above: and this Nebuchadnezzar once learned by experience, when he said; *For His kingdom is an everlasting kingdom, and His power from generation to generation*[1].

6. Riches, and gold, and silver are not, as some think, the devil's[2]: for *the whole world of riches is for the faithful man, but for the faithless not even a penny*[3]. Now nothing is more faithless than the devil; and God says plainly by the Prophet, *The gold is Mine, and the silver is Mine, and to whomsoever I will I give it*[4]. Do thou but use it well, and there is no fault to be found with money: but whenever thou hast made a bad use of that which is good, then being unwilling to blame thine own management, thou impiously throwest back the blame upon the Creator. A man may even be justified by money: *I was hungry, and ye gave Me meat*[5]*:* that certainly was from money. *I was naked, and ye clothed Me:* that certainly was by money. And wouldest thou learn that money may become a door of the kingdom of heaven? *Sell*, saith He, *that thou hast, and give to the poor, and thou shalt have treasure in heaven*[6].

7. Now I have made these remarks because of those heretics who count possessions, and money, and men's bodies accursed[7]. For I neither wish thee to be a slave of money, nor to treat as enemies the things which God has given thee for use. Never say then that riches are the devil's: for though he say, *All these will I give thee, for they are delivered unto me*[8], one may indeed even reject his assertion; for we need not believe the liar: and yet perhaps he spake the truth, being compelled by the power of His presence: for he said not, *All these will I give thee*, for they are mine, but, *for they are delivered unto me.* He grasped not the dominion of them, but confessed that he had been entrusted[9] with them, and was for a time dispensing them. But at a proper time interpreters should inquire whether his statement is false or true[1].

8. God then is One, the Father, the Almighty, whom the brood of heretics have dared to blaspheme. Yea, they have dared to blaspheme the Lord of Sabaoth[2], *who sitteth above the Cherubim*[3]*:* they have dared to blaspheme the Lord Adonai[4]: they have dared to blaspheme Him who is in the Prophets the Almighty

---

10 Ps. cxix. 91. 1 Dan. iv. 34.

2 On this doctrine of the Manicheans see Archelaus (*Disputatio*, cap. 42), Epiphanius (*Hæres.* lxvi. § 81). Compare Clement. Hom. xv. cap. 9: "To all of us possessions are sins." Plato (*Laws*, V. 743): "I can never agree with them that the rich man will be really happy, unless he is also good: but for one who is eminently good to be also extremely rich is impossible."

3 Prov. xvii. 6, according to the Septuagint. See note on Cat. V. 2, where the same passage is quoted. Clement of Alexandria (*Stromat.* II. 5) refers to it in connexion with the passage of Plato quoted in the preceding note. S Augustine also quotes and explains it in *Epist.* 153, § 26.

4 The former clause is from Haggai ii. 8; the latter, taken from the words of the Tempter in Luke iv. 6, is quoted both by Cyril and by other Fathers as if from Haggai. Chrysostom (*Hom.* xxxiv. § 5, in 1 Cor. xiii.) treats the use which some made of the misquotation as ridiculous.

5 Matt. xxv. 35, 36. 6 Ib. xix. 21.

7 The connexion of σώματα with money and possessions suggests the not uncommon meaning "slaves." See Polyb. xviii. 18, § 6: καὶ τὴν ἐνδουχίαν ἀπέδοντο καὶ τὰ σώματα, καὶ σὺν τουτοις ἔτι τινὰς τῶν κτήσεων, "household furniture, and slaves, and besides these some also of their lands." See *Dictionary of Christian Antiquities*, "Slavery," where it is shewn that Christians generally and even Bishops still possessed slaves throughout the 4th Century.

But here it is perhaps more probable that Cyril refers, as before, Cat. iv. § 23, to the Manichean doctrine of the body as the root of sin.

8 Matt. iv. 9; Luke iv. 6.

9 For ἐγκεχειρῆσθαι, the reading of all the printed Editions, which hardly yields a suitable sense, we should probably substitute ἐγκεχειρίσθαι. A similar confusion of the two verbs occurs in Polybius (*Hist.* VIII. xviii. 6); the proper use of the latter is seen in Joh. Damasc. (*De Fide Orthod.* II. 4, quoted by Cleopas), who speaks of Satan as being "of these Angelic powers the chief of the earthly order, and entrusted by God with the guardianship of the earth" (τῆς γῆς τὴν φυλακὴν ἐγχειρισθεὶς παρὰ Θεοῦ).

1 On this point compare Irenæus (*Hær.* V. xxi.—xxiv.), and Gregory of Nyssa (*Orat. Catech.* § 5).

2 The reference is to Manes, of whom his disciple Turbo says (*Archelai Disput.* § 10), "The name Sabaoth, which is honourable and mighty with you, he declares to be the nature of man, and the parent of lust: for which reason the simple, he says, worship lust, and think it to be a god."

3 Ps. lxxx. 1.

4 'Αδωναΐ, Heb. אֲדֹנָי, "the Lord," an old form of the Plural of majesty, used of God only.

God[5]. But worship thou One God the Almighty, the Father of our Lord Jesus Christ. Flee from the error of many gods, flee also from every heresy, and say like Job, *But I will call upon the Almighty Lord, which doeth great things and unsearchable, glorious things and marvellous without number*[6], and, *For all these things there is honour from the Almighty*[7]: to Whom be the glory for ever and ever. Amen.

5 παντοκράτορα, Heb. אֵל שַׁדַּי, El-Shaddai, "God Almighty."

6 Job v. 8, 9. Cyril's quotation agrees with the Codex Alexandrinus of the Septuagint, which has παντοκράτορα, "Almighty," while the Vatican and other MSS. read τὸν πάντων δεσπότην.

7 Job xxxvii. 23: *God hath upon Him terrible majesty* (R.V.) The Vatican and Alexandrine MSS. of the Septuagint read ἐπὶ τούτοις μεγάλη ἡ δόξα καὶ τιμὴ παντοκράτορος. (*For these things great is the glory and honour of the Almighty.*) But Cyril's text is the same as the Aldine and Complutensian.

LECTURE IX.

On the words, Maker of heaven and earth, and of all things visible and invisible.

Job xxxviii. 2—3.

Who is this that hideth counsel from Me, and keepeth words in his heart, and thinketh to hide them from Me[1]*?*

1. To look upon God with eyes of flesh is impossible: for the incorporeal cannot be subject to bodily sight: and the Only begotten Son of God Himself hath testified, saying, *No man hath seen God at any time*[2]. For if according to that which is written in Ezekiel any one should understand that Ezekiel saw Him, yet what saith the Scripture? *He saw the likeness of the glory of the Lord*[3]*;* not the Lord Himself, but *the likeness of His glory*, not the glory itself, as it really is. And when he saw merely *the likeness of the glory*, and not the glory itself, he fell to the earth from fear. Now if the sight of the likeness of the glory brought fear and distress upon the prophets, any one who should attempt to behold God Himself would to a certainty lose his life, according to the saying, *No man shall see My face and live*[4]. For this cause God of His great loving-kindness spread out the heaven as a veil of His proper Godhead, that we should not perish. The word is not mine, but the Prophet's · *If Thou shalt rend the heavens, trembling will take hold of the mountains at sight of Thee, and they will flow down*[5]. And why dost thou wonder that Ezekiel fell down on seeing *the likeness of the glory?* when Daniel at the sight of Gabriel, though but a servant of God, straightway shuddered and fell on his face, and, prophet as he was, dared not answer him, until the Angel transformed himself into the likeness of a son of man[6]. Now if the appearing of Gabriel wrought trembling in the Prophets, had God Himself been seen as He is, would not all have perished?

2. The Divine Nature then it is impossible to see with eyes of flesh: but from the works, which are Divine, it is possible to attain to some conception of His power, according to Solomon, who says, *For by the greatness and beauty of the creatures proportionably the Maker of them is seen*[7]. He said not that from the creatures the Maker is seen, but added *proportionably*. For God appears the greater to every man in proportion as he has grasped a larger survey of the creatures: and when his heart is uplifted by that larger survey, he gains withal a greater conception of God.

3. Wouldest thou learn that to comprehend the nature of God is impossible? The Three Children in the furnace of fire, as they hymn the praises of God, say *Blessed art thou that beholdest the depths, and sittest upon the Cherubim*[8]. Tell me what is the nature of the Cherubim, and then look upon Him who sitteth upon them. And yet Ezekiel the Prophet even made a description of them, as far as was possible, saying that *every one has four faces*, one of a man, another of a lion, another of an eagle, and another of a calf; and that each one had six wings[9], and they had eyes on all sides; and that under each one was a wheel of four sides. Nevertheless though the Prophet makes the explanation, we cannot yet understand it even as we read. But if we cannot understand the throne, which he has described, how shall we be able to comprehend Him who sitteth thereon, the Invisible and Ineffable God? To scrutinise then the nature of God is impossible: but it is in our power to send up praises of His glory for His works that are seen.

4. These things I say to you because of the

---

1 The Septuagint, from which Cyril quotes the text, differs much from the Hebrew, and from the English Versions: *Who is this that darkeneth counsel by words without knowledge? Gird up now thy loins like a man: for I will demand of thee, and answer thou Me.*

2 John i. 18. 3 Ezekiel i. 28. 4 Exod. xxxiii. 20.

5 Is. lxiv. 1, Septuagint. R.V. *Oh that Thou wouldest rend the heavens, that Thou wouldest come down, that the mountains might flow down.* 6 Dan. x. 9, 16, 18.

7 Wisdom xiii. 5. Compare Theophilus of Antioch *To Autolycus*, I. 5, 6: "God cannot indeed be seen by human eyes, but is beheld and perceived through His providence and works. . . . He is not visible to eyes of flesh, since He is incomprehensible."

8 Song of the Three Children, 32.

9 In Ezekiel i. 6—11, the four living creatures have each *four* wings, as also in x. 21 according to the Hebrew. But in the latter passage, according to the Vatican text of the Septuagint, each has *eight* wings, as Codd. R. and Casaub. read here. Cyril seems to have confused the number in Ezekiel with that in Is. vi. 2: *each one had six wings.* By "a wheel of four sides" Cyril explains Ez. i. 16: *a wheel in the midst of a wheel*, as meaning two circles set at right angles to each other, like the equator and meridian on a globe.

following context of the Creed, and because we say, WE BELIEVE IN ONE GOD, THE FATHER ALMIGHTY, MAKER OF HEAVEN AND EARTH, AND OF ALL THINGS VISIBLE AND INVISIBLE; in order that we may remember that the Father of our Lord Jesus Christ is the same as He that made the heaven and the earth[1], and that we may make ourselves safe against the wrong paths of the godless heretics, who have dared to speak evil of the Allwise Artificer of all this world[2], men who see with eyes of flesh, but have the eyes of their understanding blinded.

5. For what fault have they to find with the vast creation of God?—they, who ought to have been struck with amazement on beholding the vaultings of the heavens: they, who ought to have worshipped Him who reared the sky as a dome, who out of the fluid nature of the waters formed the stable substance of the heaven. For *God said, Let there be a firmament in the midst of the water*[3]. God spake once for all, and it stands fast, and falls not. The heaven is water, and the orbs therein, sun, moon, and stars are of fire: and how do the orbs of fire run their course in the water? But if any one disputes this because of the opposite natures of fire and water, let him remember the fire which in the time of Moses in Egypt flamed amid the hail, and observe the all-wise workmanship of God. For since there was need of water, because the earth was to be tilled, He made the heaven above of water, that when the region of the earth should need watering by showers, the heaven might from its nature be ready for this purpose.

6. But what? Is there not cause to wonder when one looks at the constitution of the sun? For being to the sight as it were a small body he contains a mighty power; appearing from the East, and sending forth his light unto the West: whose rising at dawn the Psalmist described, saying: *And he cometh forth out of his chamber as a bridegroom*[4]. He was describing the brightness and moderation of his state on first becoming visible unto men: for when he rides at high noon, we often flee from his blaze: but at his rising he is welcome to all as a bridegroom to look on.

Observe also his arrangement (or rather not his, but the arrangement of Him who by an ordinance determined his course), how in summer he rises higher and makes the days longer, giving men good time for their works: but in winter contracts his course, that the period of cold may be increased, and that the nights becoming longer may contribute to men's rest, and contribute also to the fruitfulness of the products of the earth[5]. See also how the days alternately respond each to other in due order, in summer increasing, and in winter diminishing; but in spring and autumn granting equal intervals one to another. And the nights again complete the like courses; so that the Psalmist also says of them, *Day unto day uttereth speech, and night unto night proclaimeth knowledge*[6]. For to the heretics who have no ears, they all but cry aloud, and by their good order say, that there is none other God save the Creator who hath set them their bounds, and laid out the order of the Universe[7].

7. But let no one tolerate any who say that one is the Creator of the light, and another of darkness[8]: for let him remember how Isaiah says, *I am the God who made the light, and created darkness*[9]. Why, O man, art thou vexed thereat? Why art thou offended at the time that is given thee for rest[1]? A servant would have had no rest from his masters, had not the darkness necessarily brought a respite. And often after wearying ourselves in the day, how are we refreshed in the night, and he who was yesterday worn with toils, rises vigorous in the morning because of the night's rest[2]? And what more helpful to wisdom than the night[3]? For herein oftentimes we set before our minds the things of God; and herein we read and contemplate the Divine Oracles. And when is our mind most attuned to Psalmody and

1 Compare Cat. iv. 4. Irenæus (I. x. 1): "The Church, though dispersed throughout the whole world, even to the ends of the earth, yet received from the Apostles and their disciples the Faith in One God the Father Almighty, Maker of heaven, and earth, and the sea and all that therein is." Tertullian (*de Præscriptione Hæret.* cap. xiii.) "The rule of faith is that whereby we believe that there is One God only, and none other than the Creator of the world, who brought forth all things out of nothing through His own Word first of all sent forth."

2 Compare Cat. vi. 13, 27. 3 Gen. i. 6. 4 Ps. xix. 5.

5 The common reading ἵνα μὴ τοῦ ψύχους πλείων γένηται ὁ χρόνος, ἀλλ' ἵνα αἱ νύκτες, κ.τ.λ. gives a meaning contrary to the facts. The translation follows the MSS. Roe, Casaubon, which omit μή and for ἀλλά read καί. Compare Whewell's *Astronomy*, p. 22: "The length of the year is so determined as to be adapted to the constitution of most vegetables: or the construction of vegetables is so adjusted as to be suited to the length which the year really has, and unsuited to a duration longer or shorter by any considerable portion. The vegetable clock-work is so set as to go for a year." *Ibid.* p. 34: "The terrestrial day, and consequently the length of the cycle of light and darkness, being what it is, we find various parts of the constitution both of animals and vegetables, which have a periodical character in their functions, corresponding to the diurnal succession of external conditions, and we find that the length of the period, as it exists in their constitution, coincides with the length of the natural day."

6 Ps. xix. 2. Compare a beautiful passage of Theophilus of Antioch (*To Autolycus*, vi.).

7 Lucretius, V. 1182:

"They saw the skies in constant order run,
The varied seasons and the circling sun,
Apparent rule, with unapparent cause,
And thus they sought in gods the source of laws."

8 See note 3 on Cat. iii. 33.

9 Is. xlv. 7. Compare the Homily of Chrysostom on this text.

1 Whewell, *Astronomy*. p. 38: "Animals also have a period in their functions and habits; as in the habits of waking, sleeping, eating, &c., and their well-being appears to depend on the coincidence of this period with the length of the natural day."

2 Chrysostom, VI. p. 171: "As the day brings man out to his work, so the night succeeding releases him from his countless toils and thoughts, and lulling his weary eyes to sleep, and closing their lids, prepares him to welcome the sunbeam again with his force in full vigour."

3 Clement of Alexandria (*Stromat.* IV. 22, E. Tr.): "And in this way they seem to have called the night Euphrone, since then the soul released from the perceptions of sense turns in on itself, and has a truer hold of intelligence (φρόνησις)."

Prayer? Is it not at night? And when have we often called our own sins to remembrance? Is it not at night[4]? Let us not then admit the evil thought, that another is the maker of darkness: for experience shews that this also is good and useful.

8. They ought to have felt astonishment and admiration not only at the arrangement of sun and moon, but also at the well-ordered choirs of the stars, their unimpeded courses, and their risings in the seasons due to each: and how some are signs of summer, and others of winter; and how some mark the season for sowing, and others shew the commencement of navigation[5]. And a man sitting in his ship, and sailing amid the boundless waves, steers his ship by looking at the stars. For of these matters the Scripture says well, *And let them be for signs, and for seasons, and for years*[6], not for fables of astrology and nativities. But observe how He has also graciously given us the light of day by gradual increase: for we do not see the sun at once arise; but just a little light runs on before, in order that the pupil of the eye may be enabled by previous trial to look upon his stronger beam: see also how He has relieved the darkness of the night by rays of moonlight.

9. *Who is the father of the rain? And who hath begotten the drops of dew*[7]*?* Who condensed the air into clouds, and bade them carry the waters of the rain[8], now *bringing golden-tinted clouds from the north*[9], now changing these into one uniform appearance, and again transforming them into manifold circles and other shapes? *Who can number the clouds in wisdom*[1]*?* Whereof in Job it saith, *And He knoweth the separations of the clouds*[2], *and hath bent down the heaven to the earth*[3]: and, *He who numbereth the clouds in wisdom*: and, *the cloud is not rent under Him*[4]. For so many measures of waters lie upon the clouds, yet they are not rent: but come down with all good order upon the earth. Who *bringeth the winds out of their treasuries*[5]*? And who*, as we said before, *is he that hath begotten the drops of dew? And out of whose womb cometh the ice*[6]*?* For its substance is like water, and its strength like stone. And at one time the water becomes *snow like wool*, at another it ministers to Him *who scattereth the mist like ashes*[7], and at another it is changed into a stony substance; since *He governs the waters as He will*[8]. Its nature is uniform, and its action manifold in force. Water becomes in vines *wine that maketh glad the heart of man*: and in olives *oil that maketh man's face to shine*: and is transformed also into *bread that strengtheneth man's heart*[9], and into fruits of all kinds which He hath created[1].

10. What should have been the effect of these wonders? Should the Creator have been blasphemed? Or worshipped rather? And so far I have said nothing of the unseen works of His wisdom. Observe, I pray you, the spring, and the flowers of every kind in all their likeness still diverse one from another; the deepest crimson of the rose, and the purest whiteness of the lily: for these spring from the same rain and the same earth, and who makes them to differ? Who fashions them? Observe, pray, the exact care: from the one substance of the tree there is part for shelter, and part for divers fruits: and the Artificer is One. Of the same vine part is for burning[2], and part for shoots, and part for leaves, and part for tendrils, and part for clusters.

Admire also the great thickness of the knots which run round the reed, as the Artificer hath

---

4 Chrysostom (Tom. II. p. 793): "We usually take the reckoning of our money early in the morning, but of our actions, of all that we have said and done by day, let us demand of ourselves the account after supper, and even after nightfall, as we lie upon our bed, with none to trouble, none to disturb us. And if we see anything done amiss, let us chastise our conscience, let us rebuke our mind, let us so vehemently impugn our account, that we may no more dare to rise up and bring ourselves to the same pit of sin, being mindful of the scourging at night."

5 Clem. Alex. (*Stromat.* VI. 11): "The same is true also of Astronomy, for being engaged in the investigation of the heavenly bodies, as to the form of the universe, and the revolution of the heaven, and the motion of the stars, it brings the soul nearer to the Creative Power, and teaches it to be quick in perceiving the seasons of the year, the changes of the atmosphere, and the risings of the stars; since navigation also and husbandry are full of benefit from this science." Compare Lactantius (*De Irâ Dei*, cap. xiii.).

6 Gen. i. 14.

7 Job xxxviii. 28.

8 Whewell, *Astronomy*, p. 88: "*Clouds* are produced by aqueous vapour when it returns to the state of water." p. 89: "Clouds produce *rain*. In the formation of a cloud the precipitation of moisture probably forms a fine watery *powder*, which remains suspended in the air in consequence of the minuteness of its particles: but if from any cause the precipitation is collected in larger portions, and becomes *drops*, these descend by their weight and produce a shower." Compare Aristotle, *Meteorologica*, I. ix. 3; Ansted, *Physical Geography*, p. 210.

9 Job xxxvii. 22: "Out of the north cometh golden splendour" (R.V.).

1 Job xxxviii. 37.

2 Job xxxvii. 16: "Dost thou know the balancings of the clouds?" In the Septuagint διάκρισιν νεφῶν may mean "the separate path of the clouds" (Vulg. "semitas nubium,") or "the dissolving," as in Aristotle (*Meteorol.* I. vii. 10: διακρίνεσθαι καὶ διαλύεσθαι τὸ διάτμίζον ὑγρὸν ὑπὸ τοῦ πλήθους τῆς θερμῆς ἀναθυμιάσεως, ὥστε μὴ συνίστασθαι ῥαδίως εἰς ὕδωρ. "The moist vapour is separated and dissolved by the great heat of the evaporation, so that it does not easily condense into water." Cf. Plato, *Sophistes* 243 B: διακρίσεις καὶ συγκρίσεις.

3 Job xxxviii. 37 (according to the Septuagint): "And who is he that numbereth the clouds by wisdom, and bent down the heaven to the earth?" A.V., R.V. "Or who can pour out the bottles of heaven?"

4 Job xxvi. 8: "He bindeth up the waters in His thick clouds; and the cloud is not rent under them."

5 Ps. cxxxv. 7.

6 Job xxxviii. 28.

7 Ps. cxlvii. 16: "He scattereth the hoar frost like ashes." The Hebrew כְּפוֹר is rendered by πάχνη, "hoar frost," in Job xxxviii. 29, but here by ὀμιχλη, "mist."

8 Job xxxvii. 10: "the breadth of the waters is straitened" (Marg. R.V. "congealed"). The word οἰακίζει in the Septuagint means to "steer," Lat. "gubernare" to "turn as by a helm."

9 Ps. civ. 15.

1 There is a similar passage on the various effects of water in Cat. xvi. 12. Chrysostom (*de Statuis*, Hom. xii. 2), Epiphanius (*Ancoratus*, p. 69), and other Fathers, appear to reproduce both the thoughts and words of Cyril.

2 For καῦσιν, "burning," Morel and Milles, with Cod. Coisl., read καῦστιν, a rare word explained by Hesychius as the "growth" or "foliage" of the vine: but this is fully expressed in what follows, and the reading καῦσιν is confirmed by Virgil (*Georg.* ii. 408): "Primus devecta cremato sarmenta" (Reischl).

made them. From one and the same earth come forth creeping things, and wild beasts, and cattle, and trees, and food; and gold, and silver, and brass, and iron, and stone. The nature of the waters is but one, yet from it comes the substance of fishes and of birds; whereby[3] as the former swim in the waters, so the birds fly in the air.

11. *This great and wide sea, therein are things creeping innumerable*[4]. Who can describe the beauty of the fishes that are therein? Who can describe the greatness of the whales, and the nature[5] of its amphibious animals, how they live both on dry land and in the waters? Who can tell the depth and the breadth of the sea, or the force of its enormous waves? Yet it stays at its bounds, because of Him who said, *Hitherto shalt thou come, and no further, but within thyself shall thy waves be broken*[6]. Which sea also clearly shews the word of the command imposed upon it, since after it has run up, it leaves upon the beach a visible line made by the waves, shewing, as it were, to those who see it, that it has not passed its appointed bounds.

12. Who can discern the nature of the birds of the air? How some carry with them a voice of melody, and others are variegated with all manner of painting on their wings, and others fly up into mid air and float motionless, as the hawk: for by the Divine command *the hawk spreadeth out his wings and floateth motionless, looking towards the south*[7]. What man can behold the eagle's lofty flight? If then thou canst not discern the soaring of the most senseless of the birds, how wouldest thou understand the Maker of all?

13. Who among men knows even the names of all wild beasts? Or who can accurately discern the physiology of each? But if of the wild beasts we know not even the mere names, how shall we comprehend the Maker of them? God's command was but one, which said, *Let the earth bring forth wild beasts, and cattle, and creeping things, after their kinds*[8]: and from one earth[9], by one command, have sprung diverse natures, the gentle sheep and the carnivorous lion, and various instincts[1] of irrational animals, bearing resemblance to the various characters of men; the fox to manifest the craft that is in men, and the snake the venomous treachery of friends, and the neighing horse the wantonness of young men[2], and the laborious ant, to arouse the sluggish and the dull: for when a man passes his youth in idleness, then he is instructed by the irrational animals, being reproved by the divine Scripture saying, *Go to the ant, thou sluggard, see and emulate her ways, and become wiser than she*[3]. For when thou seest her treasuring up her food in good season, imitate her, and treasure up for thyself fruits of good works for the world to come. And again, *Go to the bee, and learn how industrious she is*[4]: how, hovering round all kinds of flowers, she collects her honey for thy benefit: that thou also, by ranging over the Holy Scriptures, mayest lay hold of salvation for thyself, and being filled with them mayest say, *How sweet are thy words unto my throat, yea sweeter than honey and the honeycomb unto my mouth*[5].

14. Is not then the Artificer worthy the rather to be glorified? For what? If thou knowest not the nature of all things, do the things that have been made forthwith become useless? Canst thou know the efficacy of all herbs? Or canst thou learn all the benefit which proceeds from every animal? Ere now even from venomous adders have come antidotes for the preservation of men[6]. But thou wilt say to me, "The snake is terrible." Fear thou the Lord, and it shall not be able to hurt thee. "A scorpion stings." Fear the Lord, and it shall not sting thee. "A lion is bloodthirsty." Fear thou the Lord, and he shall lie down beside thee, as by Daniel. But truly wonderful also is the action of the animals: how some, as the scorpion, have the sharpness in a sting; and others have their power in their teeth; and others do battle with their claws; while the basilisk's power is his gaze[7]. So then from this varied workmanship understand the Creator's power.

---

3 For the construction of ἵνα with the Indicative ἵπτανται, see Bernhardy, *Syntax*, p. 401. Winer (*Gram. N.T.* III. sect. xli. c).

4 Ps. civ. 25.

5 Gr. ὑπόστασιν, literally "substance."

6 Job xxxviii. 11.

7 Ib. xxxix. 26.

8 Gen. i. 24.

9 Instead of φωνῆς (Milles), or πηγῆς (Bened. Roe, Casaub.) the recent Editors have restored τῆς γῆς with the Jerusalem and Munich MSS., and Basil.

1 Gr. κινήσεις "movements," "impulses." Aristotle (*Historia Animalium.* IX. vii. 1) remarks that many imitations of man's mode of life may be observed in the habits of other animals.

2 Jer. v. 8.

3 Prov. vi. 6. Instead of the epithet "laborious" (γεωργότατος) some MSS. have "agile" or "restless" (γοργότατος).

4 After the description of the ant, Prov. vi. 6—8, there follows in the Septuagint a similar reference to the bee: "Or go to the bee, and learn how industrious she is, and how comely she makes her work, and the produce of her labours kings and commons adopt for health, and she is desired and esteemed by all, and though feeble in strength has been exalted by her regard for wisdom." The interpolation is supposed to be of Greek origin, as containing "idiomatic Greek expressions which would not occur to a translator from the Hebrew" (Delitzsch).

5 Ps. cxix. 103.

6 Compare Bacon (*Natural Hist.* 965): "I would have trial made of two other kinds of bracelets, for comforting the heart and spirits: one of the trochisch of vipers, made into little pieces of beads; for since they do great good inwards (especially for pestilent agues), it is like they will be effectual outwards, where they may be applied in greater quantity. There would be trochisch likewise made of snakes; whose flesh dried is thought to have a very good opening and cordial virtue." *Ib.* 969: "The writers of natural magic commend the wearing of the spoil of a snake, for preserving of health." Thomas Jackson (*On the Creed*, VIII. 8, § 4): "The poisonous bitings of the scorpion are usually cured by the oil of scorpions."

7 Shakespeare (*Richard III.* Act. I. Sc. ii.).

Glo. "Thine eyes, sweet lady, have infected mine."

Anne. "'Would they were basilisks to strike thee dead."

15. But these things perhaps thou knowest not: thou wouldest have nothing in common with the creatures which are without thee. Enter now into thyself, and from thine own nature consider its Artificer. What is there to find fault with in the framing of thy body? Be master of thyself, and nothing evil shall proceed from any of thy members. Adam was at first without clothing in Paradise with Eve, but it was not because of his members that he deserved to be cast out. The members then are not the cause of sin, but they who use their members amiss; and the Maker thereof is wise. Who prepared the recesses of the womb for child-bearing? Who gave life to the lifeless thing within it? Who *knitted us with sinews and bones, and clothed us with skin and flesh*[8], and, as soon as the child was born, brought streams of milk out of the breasts? How grows the babe into a boy, and the boy into a youth, and then into a man; and, still the same, passes again into an old man, while no one notices the exact change from day to day? Of the food, how is one part changed into blood, and another separated for excretion, and another part changed into flesh? Who gives to the heart its unceasing motion? Who wisely guarded the tenderness of the eyes with the fence of the eyelids[9]? For as to the complicated and wonderful contrivance of the eyes, the voluminous books of the physicians hardly give us explanation. Who distributes the one breath to the whole body? Thou seest, O man, the Artificer, thou seest the wise Creator.

16. These points my discourse has now treated at large, having left out many, yea, ten thousand other things, and especially things incorporeal and invisible, that thou mayest abhor those who blaspheme the wise and good Artificer, and from what is spoken and read, and whatever thou canst thyself discover or conceive, *from the greatness and beauty of the creatures mayest proportionably see the maker of them*[1], and bending the knee with godly reverence to the Maker of the worlds, the worlds, I mean, of sense and thought, both visible and invisible, thou mayest with a grateful and holy tongue, with unwearied lips and heart, praise God and say, *How wonderful are Thy works, O Lord; in wisdom hast Thou made them all*[2]. For to Thee belongeth honour, and glory, and majesty, both now and throughout all ages. Amen.

Compare Bacon (*De Augmentis*, VII. cap. ii.): "The fable goes of the basilisk, that if he see you first, you die for it, but if you see him first, he dies." Bacon refers to Pliny (*Nat. Hist.* viii. 33).

8 Job x. 11.

9 Xenophon (*Memor. Socratis*, I. cap iv.): "And moreover does not this also seem to thee like a work of providence, that, whereas the sight is weak, the Creator furnished it with eyelids for doors, which are opened whenever there is need to use the sight, but are closed in sleep."

1 Wisdom xiii. 5.

2 Ps. civ. 24.

APPENDIX TO LECTURE IX.

NOTE.—In the manuscripts which contain this discourse under the name of "A Homily of S. Basil *on God as Incomprehensible*," some portions are changed to suit that subject: but the conclusion especially is marked by great addition and variation, which it is well to reproduce here. Accordingly in place of the words in §15: τί μεμπτόν, "What is there to find fault with?" and the following, the manuscripts before mentioned have it thus:

"What is there to find fault with in the framing of the body? Come forth into the midst and speak. Control thine own will, and nothing evil shall proceed from any of thy members. For every one of these has of necessity been made for our use. Chasten thy reasoning unto piety, submit to God's commandments, and none of these members sin in working and serving in the uses for which they were made. If thou be not willing, the eye sees not amiss, the ear hears nothing which it ought not, the hand is not stretched out for wicked greed, the foot walketh not towards injustice, thou hast no strange loves, committest no fornication, covetest not thy neighbour's wife. Drive out wicked thoughts from thine heart, be as God made thee, and thou wilt rather give thanks to thy Creator.

Adam at first was without clothing, faring daintily in Paradise: and after he had received the commandment, but failed to keep it, and wickedly stretched forth his hand (not because the hand wished this, but because his will stretched forth his hand to that which was forbidden), because of his disobedience he lost also the good things he had received. Thus the members are not the cause of sin to those who use them, but the wicked mind, as the Lord says, *For out of the heart proceed evil thoughts, fornications, adulteries, envyings, and such like.* In what things thou choosest, therein thy limbs serve thee; they are excellently made for the service of the soul: they are provided as servants to thy reason. Guide them well by the motion of piety; bridle them by the fear of God; bring them into subjection to the desire of temperance and abstinence, and they will never rise up against thee to tyrannise over thee; but rather they will guard thee, and help thee more mightily in thy victory over the devil, while expecting also the incorruptible and everlasting crown of the victory. Who openeth the chambers of the womb? Who, &c."

At the end of the same section, after the words "Wise Creator," this is found: "Glorify Him in His unsearchable works, and concerning Him whom thou art not capable of knowing inquire not curiously what His essence is. It is better for thee to keep silence, and in faith adore, according to the divine Word, than daringly to search after things which neither thou canst reach, nor Holy Scripture hath delivered to thee. These points my discourse has now treated at large, that thou mayest abhor those who blaspheme the wise and good Artificer, and rather mayest thyself also say, *How wonderful are Thy works O Lord; in wisdom hast Thou made them all.* To Thee be the glory, and power, and worship, with the Holy Spirit, now and ever, and throughout all ages. Amen."

LECTURE X.

On the Clause, And in one Lord Jesus Christ, with a reading from the First Epistle to the Corinthians.

For though there be that are called gods, whether in heaven or on earth[1]*; yet to us there is One God, the Father, of whom are all things, and we in Him; and One Lord Jesus Christ, through whom are all things, and we through Him.*

1. They who have been taught to believe "in One God the Father Almighty," ought also to believe in His Only-begotten Son. For *he that denieth the Son, the same hath not the Father*[2]. *I am the Door*[3], saith Jesus; *no one cometh unto the Father but through Me*[4]. For if thou deny the Door, the knowledge concerning the Father is shut off from thee. *No man knoweth the Father, save the Son, and he to whomsoever the Son shall reveal Him*[5]. For if thou deny Him who reveals, thou remainest in ignorance. There is a sentence in the Gospels, saying, *He that believeth not on the Son, shall not see life; but the wrath of God abideth on him*[6] For the Father hath indignation when the Only-begotten Son is set at nought. For it is grievous to a king that merely his soldier should be dishonoured; and when one of his nobler officers or friends is dishonoured, then his anger is greatly increased: but if any should do despite to the king's only-begotten son himself, who shall appease the father's indignation on behalf of his only-begotten son?

2. If, therefore, any one wishes to shew piety towards God, let him worship the Son, since otherwise the Father accepts not his service. The Father spake with a loud voice from heaven, saying, *This is My beloved Son, in whom I am well pleased*[7]. The Father was well pleased; unless thou also be well pleased in Him, thou hast not life. Be not thou carried away with the Jews when they craftily say, There is one God alone; but with the knowledge that God is One, know that there is also an Only-begotten Son of God. I am not the first to say this, but the Psalmist in the person of the Son saith, *The Lord said unto Me, Thou art My Son*[8]. Heed not therefore what the Jews say, but what the Prophets say. Dost thou wonder that they who stoned and slew the Prophets, set at nought the Prophets' words?

3. Believe thou in One Lord Jesus Christ, the Only-begotten Son of God. For we say "One Lord Jesus Christ," that His Sonship may be "Only-begotten:" we say "One," that thou mayest not suppose another: we say "One," that thou mayest not profanely diffuse the many names[9] of His action among many sons. For He is called a Door[1]; but take not the name literally for a thing of wood, but a spiritual, a living Door, discriminating those who enter in. He is called a Way[2], not one trodden by feet, but leading to the Father in heaven; He is called a Sheep[3], not an irrational one, but the one which through its precious blood cleanses the world from its sins, which is led before the shearers, and knows when to be silent. This Sheep again is called a Shepherd, who says, *I am the Good Shepherd*[4]*:* a Sheep because of His manhood, a Shepherd because of the loving-kindness of His Godhead. And wouldst thou know that there are rational sheep? the Saviour says to the Apostles, *Behold, I send you as sheep in the midst of wolves*[5]. Again, He is called a Lion[6], not as a devourer of men, but indicating as it were by the title His kingly, and stedfast, and confident nature: a Lion He is also called in opposition to the lion our adver-

---

1 1 Cor. viii. 5, 6. Cyril omits the clause: *as there be gods many and lords many.* 2 1 John ii. 23. 3 Ib. x. 9. 4 Ib. xiv. 6. 5 Matt. xi. 27. 6 John iii. 36. 7 Matt. iii. 17.

8 Ps. ii. 7.

9 τὸ πολυώνυμον, a word used by the Greek Poets of their gods, as by Homer (*Hymn to Demeter*, 18, 32) of Zeus, Κρόνου πολυώνυμος υἱός. Cf. Soph. *Ant.* 1115; Aeschyl. *Prom.* V. 210.

1 John x. 7, 9. Cyril calls Christ a "spiritual," or "rational (λογική) door," and applies the same term to His sheep, below. Origen (*In Evang. Joh.* Tom. i. cap. 29): Θύρα ὁ Σωτηρ ἀναγέγραπται, *ibid.* φιλάνθρωπος δὲ ὢν . . . ποιμὴν γινεται.

2 John xiv. 6. 3 Ib. i. 29; Is. liii. 7, 8; Acts viii. 32. 4 John x. 11 5 Matt. x. 10, 16. 6 Gen. xlix. 9; Apoc. v. 5.

sary, who roars and devours those who have been deceived[7]. For the Saviour came, not as having changed the gentleness of His own nature, but as the strong *Lion of the tribe of Judah*[8], saving them that believe, but treading down the adversary. He is called a Stone, not a lifeless stone, cut out by men's hands, but a *chief corner-stone*[9], on whom *whosoever believeth shall not be put to shame.*

4. He is called CHRIST, not as having been anointed by men's hands, but eternally anointed by the Father to His High-Priesthood on behalf of men[1]. He is called Dead, not as having abode among the dead, as all in Hades, but as being alone *free among the dead*[2]. He is called Son of Man, not as having had His generation from earth, as each of us, but as coming upon the clouds TO JUDGE BOTH QUICK AND DEAD[3]. He is called LORD, not improperly as those who are so called among men, but as having a natural and eternal Lordship[4]. He is called JESUS by a fitting name, as having the appellation from His salutary healing. He is called SON, not as advanced by adoption, but as naturally begotten. And many are the titles of our Saviour; lest, therefore, His manifold appellations should make thee think of many sons, and because of the errors of the heretics, who say that Christ is one, and Jesus another, and the Door another, and so on[5], the Faith secures thee beforehand, saying well, IN ONE LORD JESUS CHRIST: for though the titles are many, yet their subject is one.

5. But the Saviour comes in various forms to each man for his profit[6]. For to those who have need of gladness He becomes a Vine; and to those who want to enter in He stands as a Door; and to those who need to offer up their prayers He stands a mediating High Priest. Again, to those who have sins He becomes a Sheep, that He may be sacrificed for them. He is *made all things to all men*[7], remaining in His own nature what He is. For so remaining, and holding the dignity of His Sonship in reality unchangeable, He adapts Himself to our infirmities, just as some excellent physician or compassionate teacher; though He is Very Lord, and received not the Lordship by advancement[8], but has the dignity of His Lordship from nature, and is not called Lord improperly[9], as we are, but is so in verity, since by the Father's bidding[1] He is Lord of His own works. For our lordship is over men of equal rights and like passions, nay often over our elders, and often a young master rules over aged servants. But in the case of our Lord Jesus Christ the Lordship is not so; but He is first Maker, then Lord[2]: first He made all things by the Father's will, then, He is Lord of the things which were made by Him.

6. *Christ the Lord* is He who was ***born in the city of David***[3]. And wouldest thou know

7 1 Pet. v. 8. 8 Ps. cxviii. 22. 9 Is. xxviii. 16; 1 Pet. ii. 4—6.

1 The reading of the earlier Editions ὑπὲρ ἀνθρώπων is free from all difficulty, and so the more likely to have been substituted for what is at first sight more difficult ὑπὲρ ἄνθρωπον, the reading of Cod. Coislin. adopted by the Benedictine and subsequent Editors. The idea of a super-human Priesthood to which the Son in His Divine nature was anointed by the Father from eternity is repeated by Cyril in § 14 of this Lecture, and in Cat. xi. 1, 14. See Index, "Priesthood," and the reference there given to a fuller consideration of the subject in the Introduction.

2 Ps. lxxxviii. 5.

3 John v. 27. Comparing what Cyril says here with Cat. iv. 15, and xv. 10, we see that he means to explain why Christ is called the "Son of Man" when "He cometh again from heaven," and "no more from earth." The preceding clause refers to His first coming in the flesh, as differing in the manner of His conception and birth from other men.

4 Cf. Athanas. (*c. Arian.* II. xv. 14), "That very Word who was by nature Lord, and was then made man, hath by means of a servant's form been made Lord of all and Christ."

5 Cf. Irenæus (III. xvi. 8): "All therefore are outside the Dispensation, who under pretence of knowledge understand that Jesus was one, and Christ another, and the Only-begotten another (from whom again is the Word), and the Saviour another." The Cerinthians, Ebionites, Ophites, and Valentinians are mentioned by Irenæus as thus separating the Christ from Jesus.

6 Cf. Athanas. (*Epist.* X.): "Since He is rich and manifold, He varies Himself according to the individual capacity of each soul."

7 1 Cor. ix. 22.

8 ἐκ προκοπῆς. We learn from Athanasius (*c. Arian.* i. 37, 38, 40), that from St. Paul's language *Philipp.* ii. 9: "Wherefore also God highly exalted Him, &c.," and from Ps. xlv. 7: "Thou hast loved righteousness and hated iniquity: therefore God, thy God, hath anointed thee with the oil of gladness above thy fellows," the Arians argued that Christ first received Divine honour as Son and Lord as the reward of His obedience as Man. Athanasius replies (c. 40): "He was not from a lower state promoted; but rather, existing as God, He took the form of a servant, and in taking it was not promoted but humbled Himself. Where then is there here any reward of virtue, or what advancement (προκοπή) and promotion in humiliation?"

The same doctrine had been previously held by the disciples of Paul of Samosata, who said that Christ was not originally God, but after His Incarnation was by advance (ἐκ προκοπῆς) made God, from being made by nature a mere man: see Athanas. (*de Decretis*, § 24, *c. Arian.* i. 38). S. Cyril refers to the error, and uses the same word, in xi. 1, 7, 13, 15, 17, and xiv. 27.

9 καταχρηστικῶς, i.e. in a secondary or metaphorical sense. Cf. vii. 5.

1 νεύματι, "command" or "bidding," as expressed by nodding the head.

2 Origen (*De Principiis*, I. ii. 10) had argued that "even God cannot be called Omnipotent, unless there exist those over whom He may exercise His power," and therefore creation must have been eternal, or God could not have been eternally Omnipotent. In other passages Origen declares it an impiety to hold that matter is co-eternal with God (*De Princip.* II. i. 4), and yet maintains that there were other worlds before this, and that there was never a time when there was no world existing.

Methodius, in a fragment of his work *On things Created*, preserved by Photius, and quoted by Bishop Bull (*Def. Fid. Nic.* II. xiii. 9), argues against these theories of Origen, that in John i. 2 the words "The same was in the beginning with God" indicate the authority (τὸ ἐξουσιαστικόν) of the Word which He had with the Father before the world came into existence; since from all eternity God the Father, together with His Word, possessed the Almighty power whereby whenever He would He could create worlds to rule over.

Dean Church remarks that "On the other hand Tertullian, *contra Hermog.* 3, considering the attributes in question to belong not to the Divine Nature, but Office, denies that God was Almighty (Lord?) from eternity; while the Greeks affirmed this (vid. Cyril Alex. *in Joann.* xvii. 8, p. 963; Athan. *Orat.* ii. 12—14), as understanding by the term the inherent but latent attribute of doing what He had not yet done, τὸ ἐξουσιαστικόν."

Cleopas, the Jerusalem Editor, regards the passage as directed against Paul of Samosata, who asserted that Christ had become God, and received His kingdom and Lordship only after His Incarnation, and remarks:—"S. Cyril evidently regards the Lordship of Jesus Christ as twofold: one that which from eternity belonged to Him as God, which he calls natural, according to which 'He was ever both Lord and King, as being by nature God' (Cyril Alex. *in Johann.* cap. xvii.); and the other the Lordship in time relative to the creatures, by which He exercises dominion over the works created by Him, as being their Maker."

3 Luke ii. 11.

that Christ is Lord with the Father even before His Incarnation[4], that thou mayest not only accept the statement by faith, but mayest also receive proof from the Old Testament? Go to the first book, Genesis: God saith, *Let us make man*, not 'in My image,' but, *in Our image*[5]. And after Adam was made, the sacred writer says, *And God created man; in the image of God created He him*[6]. For he did not limit the dignity of the Godhead to the Father alone, but included the Son also: that it might be shewn that man is not only the work of God, but also of our Lord Jesus Christ, who is Himself also Very God. This Lord, who works together with the Father, wrought with Him also in the case of Sodom, according to the Scripture: *And the Lord rained upon Sodom and Gomorrah fire and brimstone from the Lord out of heaven*[7]. This Lord is He who afterwards was seen of Moses, as much as he was able to see. For the Lord is loving unto man, ever condescending to our infirmities.

7. Moreover, that you may be sure that this is He who was seen of Moses, hear Paul's testimony, when he says, *For they all drank of a spiritual rock that followed them; and the rock was Christ*[8]. And again: *By faith Moses forsook Egypt*[9], and shortly after he says, *accounting the reproach of Christ greater riches than the treasures in Egypt*[1]. This Moses says to Him, *Shew me Thyself.* Thou seest that the Prophets also in those times saw the Christ, that is, as far as each was able. *Shew me Thyself, that I may see Thee with understanding*[2]. But He saith, *There shall no man see My face, and live*[3]. For this reason then, because no man could see the face of the Godhead and live, He took on Him the face of human nature, that we might see this and live. And yet when He wished to shew even that with a little majesty, when *His face did shine as the sun*[4], the disciples fell down affrighted. If then His bodily countenance, shining not in the full power of Him that wrought, but according to the capacity of the Disciples, affrighted them, so that even thus they could not bear it, how could any man gaze upon the majesty of the Godhead? 'A great thing,' saith the Lord, 'thou desirest, O Moses: and I approve thine insatiable desire, *and I will do this thing*[5] for thee, but according as thou art able. *Behold, I will put thee in the clift of the rock*[6]*:* for as being little, thou shalt lodge in a little space.'

8. Now here I wish you to make safe what I am going to say, because of the Jews. For our object is to prove that the Lord Jesus Christ was with the Father. The LORD then says to Moses, *I will pass by before thee with My glory, and will proclaim the name of the* LORD *before thee*[7]. Being Himself the LORD, what LORD doth He proclaim? Thou seest how He was covertly teaching the godly doctrine of the Father and the Son. And again, in what follows it is written word for word: *And the* LORD *descended in the cloud, and stood with him there, and proclaimed the name of the* LORD. *And the* LORD *passed by before him, and proclaimed, The* LORD, *the* LORD *God, merciful and gracious, long-suffering, and abundant in goodness and truth, both keeping righteousness and shewing mercy unto thousands, taking away iniquities, and transgressions, and sins*[8]. Then in what follows, *Moses bowed his head and worshipped*[9] before the Lord who proclaimed the Father, and said: *Go Thou then, O Lord, in the midst of us*[1].

9. This is the first proof: receive now a second plain one. *The* LORD *said unto my Lord, sit Thou on My right hand*[2]. The LORD says this to the Lord, not to a servant, but to the Lord of all, and His own Son, to whom He put all things in subjection. *But when He saith that all things are put under Him, it is manifest that He is excepted, which did put all things under Him*, and what follows; *that God may be all in all*[3]. The Only-begotten Son is Lord of all, but the obedient Son of the Father, for He grasped not the Lordship[4], but received it by nature of the Father's own will. For neither did the Son grasp it, nor the Father grudge to impart it. He it is who saith, *All things are delivered unto Me of My Father*[5]; "delivered unto Me, not as though

---

4 Among those who denied the Divine præ-existence of Christ Cleopas enumerates Ebion, Carpocrates, Theodotus, Artemon, Paul of Samosata, Marcellus, and Photinus.

5 Gen. i. 26. 6 Ib. i. 27. 7 Ib. xix. 24.

8 1 Cor. x. 4. 9 Heb. xi. 27.

1 Heb. xi. 26. Quoting from memory Cyril mistakes the order of the two sentences.

2 Ex. xxxiii. 13. Cyril means that even before His Incarnation Christ was seen as far as was possible by Prophets such as Moses. This view was held by many of the Fathers before Cyril. See Justin M. (*Tryph.* § 56 ff.); Tertull. (*adv. Praxean,* § 16); Euseb. (*Demonstr. Evang.* V. 13—16).

3 Ex. xxxiii. 20. 4 Matt. xvii. 2.

5 Ex. xxxiii. 17. Gr. λόγον, "word," in imitation of the Hebrew idiom.

6 Ex. xxxiii. 22.

7 Ex. xxxiii. 19. Literally "will call in the name of the LORD (Jehovah):" compare Gen. iv. 26.

8 Ex. xxxiv. 5—7. For "keeping righteousness and shewing mercy," the Hebrew has only "keeping mercy."

9 Ex. xxxiv. 8. 1 Ib. xxxiv. 9.

2 Ps. cx. 1. Heb. "An oracle of Jehovah unto my lord." Cyril's argument is based upon the common mistake of supposing that Κύριος represents the same Hebrew word in both parts of the sentence. 3 1 Cor. xv. 27, 28.

4 Cyril evidently alludes to Philipp. ii. 6, "Who being in the form of God thought it not a prize to be on an equality with God:" for the right interpretation of which passage, see Dean Gwynn's notes in the *Speaker's Commentary*.

5 Matt. xi. 27; Luke x. 22. On this text Athanasius wrote a special treatise (*In illud 'Omnia,' &c.*), against the arguments of Arius, Eusebius, and their fellows, who said,—"If all things were delivered (meaning by 'all' the Lordship of Creation), there was once a time when He had them not. But if He had them not, He is not of the Father, for if He were, He would on that account have had them always."

Again (*contr. Arian. Orat.* III. cap. xxvii. § 36), Athanasius argues: "Lest a man, perceiving that the Son has all that the Father hath, from the exact likeness and identity of what He

I had them not before; and I keep them well, not robbing Him who hath given them."

10. The Son of God then is Lord: He is Lord, who was born in Bethlehem of Judæa, according to the Angel who said to the shepherds, *I bring you good tidings of great joy, that unto you is born this day in the city of David Christ the Lord*[6]: of whom an Apostle says elsewhere, *The word which God sent unto the children of Israel, preaching the gospel of peace by Jesus Christ: He is Lord of all*[7]. But when he says, *of all*, do thou except nothing from His Lordship: for whether Angels, or Archangels, or principalities, or powers, or any created thing named by the Apostles, all are under the Lordship of the Son. Of Angels He is Lord, as thou hast it in the Gospels, *Then the Devil departed from Him, and the Angels came and ministered unto Him*[8]; for the Scripture saith not, they succoured Him, but they *ministered unto Him*, that is, like servants. When He was about to be born of a Virgin, Gabriel was then His servant, having received His service as a peculiar dignity. When He was about to go into Egypt, that He might overthrow the gods of Egypt made with hands[9], again *an Angel appeareth to Joseph in a dream*[1]. After He had been crucified, and had risen again, an Angel brought the good tidings, and as a trustworthy servant said to the women, *Go, tell His disciples that He is risen, and goeth before you into Galilee; lo, I have told you*[2]: almost as if he had said, "I have not neglected my command, I protest that I have told you; that if ye disregard it, the blame may not be on me, but on those who disregard it." This then is the One Lord Jesus Christ, of whom the lesson just now read speaks: *For though there be many that are called gods, whether in heaven or in earth*, and so on, *yet to us there is One God, the Father, of whom are all things, and we in Him; and One Lord, Jesus Christ, through whom are all things, and we through Him*[3].

11. And He is called by two names, Jesus Christ; Jesus, because He saves,—Christ, because He is a Priest[4]. And knowing this the inspired Prophet Moses conferred these two titles on two men distinguished above all[5]: his own successor in the government, Auses[6], he renamed Jesus; and his own brother Aaron he surnamed Christ[7], that by two well-approved men he might represent at once both the High Priesthood, and the Kingship of the One Jesus Christ who was to come. For Christ is a High Priest like Aaron; since He *glorified not Himself to be made a High Priest, but He that spake unto Him, Thou art a Priest for ever after the order of Melchizedek*[8]. And Jesus the son of Nave was in many things a type of Him. For when he began to rule over the people, he began from Jordan[9], whence Christ also, after He was baptized, began to preach the gospel. And the son of Nave appoints twelve to divide the inheritance[1]; and twelve Apostles Jesus sends forth, as heralds of the truth, into all the world. The typical Jesus saved Rahab the harlot when she believed: and the true Jesus says, *Behold, the publicans and the harlots go before you into the kingdom of God*[2]. With only a shout the walls of Jericho fell down in the time of the type: and because Jesus said, *There shall not be left here one stone upon another*[3], the Temple of the Jews opposite to us is fallen, the cause of its fall not being the denunciation but the sin of the transgressors.

12. There is One Lord Jesus Christ, a wondrous name, indirectly announced beforehand by the Prophets. For Esaias the Prophet says, *Behold, thy Saviour cometh, having His own reward*[4]. Now Jesus in Hebrew is by interpretation *Saviour*. For the Prophetic gift, foreseeing the murderous spirit of the Jews against their Lord[5], veiled His name, lest from knowing it plainly beforehand they might plot against Him readily. But He was openly called Jesus not by men, but by an Angel, who came not by his own authority, but was sent by the power of God, and said to Joseph, *Fear not to take unto thee Mary thy wife; for that which is con-*

hath, should wander into the impiety of Sabellius, considering Him to be the Father, therefore He has said, *Was given unto Me*, and *I received*, and *Were delivered to Me*, only to shew that He is not the Father, but the Father's Word, and the Eternal Son, who, because of His likeness to the Father, has eternally what He has from Him, and, because He is the Son, has from the Father what eternally He hath."

6 Luke ii. 10, 11. 7 Acts x. 36. 8 Matt. iv. 11.

9 Isa. xix. 1. "Behold, the Lord rideth upon a swift cloud, and cometh unto Egypt: and the idols of Egypt shall be moved at His presence." The prophecy was supposed by many of the Fathers to have been fulfilled by the flight into Egypt. Cf. Athanas. (*Ep.* LXI. *ad Maximum*, § 4): "As a child He came down to Egypt, and brought to nought its idols made with hands:" and (*de Incarn.* § 36): "Which of the righteous men or kings went down into Egypt, so that at his coming the idols of Egypt fell?" On the passage of Isaiah see Delitzsch, and Kay (*Speaker's Commentary*).

1 Matt. ii. 13. 2 Ib. xxviii. 7. 3 1 Cor. viii. 5, 6.

4 Compare Eusebius (*Eccl. Hist.* I. cap. iii.), a passage which Cyril seems to have followed in his explanation of the names 'Jesus' and 'Christ.'

5 For the common reading ἐγκρίτοις πάντων Cod. Mon. I. has ἐκκρίτοις π. which is required both by the construction and the sense. The change may have been caused by the occurrence of ἐγκρίτων just below.

6 Eusebius (*u.s.*): "His successor, therefore, who had not hitherto borne the name Jesus, but had been called by another name, Auses, which had been given him by his parents, he now called Jesus, bestowing the name upon him as a gift of honour far greater than any kingly diadem." Auses is a common corruption of the name Oshea. See the note on the passage of Eusebius in this series.

7 Eusebius: "He consecrated a man high-priest of God, in so far as that was possible, and him he called Christ." Cf. Lev. iv. 5, 16; vi. 22: ὁ ἱερεὺς ὁ Χριστός.

8 Heb. v. 4, 5, 6. Cyril omits from his quotation the reference to Ps. ii. 7: "Thou art My Son: this day have I begotten Thee.'

9 Josh. iii. 1. 1 Ib. xiv. 1. 2 Matt. xxi. 31.

3 Matt. xxiv. 2.

4 Isa. lxii. 11: "Behold, thy salvation cometh; behold, his reward is with him." 5 τὸ κυριοκτόνον τῶν Ἰουδαίων.

ceived in her is of the Holy Ghost. And she shall bring forth a Son, and thou shalt call His name Jesus[6]. And immediately he renders the reason of this name, saying, *for He shall save His people from their sins.* Consider how He who was not yet born could have a *people*, unless He was in being before He was born[7]. This also the Prophet says in His person, *From the bowels of my mother hath He made mention of My name*[8]*;* because the Angel foretold that He should be called Jesus. And again concerning Herod's plot again he says, *And under the shadow of His hand hath He hid Me*[9].

13. Jesus then means according to the Hebrew "Saviour," but in the Greek tongue "The Healer;" since He is physician of souls and bodies, curer of spirits, curing the blind in body[1], and leading minds into light, healing the visibly lame, and guiding sinners' steps to repentance, saying to the palsied, *Sin no more*, and, *Take up thy bed and walk*[2]. For since the body was palsied for the sin of the soul, He ministered first to the soul that He might extend the healing to the body. If, therefore, any one is suffering in soul from sins, there is the Physician for him: and if any one here is of little faith, let him say to Him, *Help Thou mine unbelief*[3]. If any is encompassed also with bodily ailments, let him not be faithless, but let him draw nigh; for to such diseases also Jesus ministers[4], and let him learn that Jesus is the Christ.

14. For that He is Jesus the Jews allow, but not further that He is Christ. Therefore saith the Apostle, *Who is the liar, but he that denieth that Jesus is the Christ*[5]? But Christ is a High Priest, *whose priesthood passes not to another*[6], neither having begun His Priesthood in time[7], nor having any successor in His High-Priesthood: as thou heardest on the Lord's day, when we were discoursing in the congregation[8] on the phrase, *After the Order of Melchizedek.* He received not the High-Priesthood from bodily succession, nor was He anointed with oil prepared by man[9], but before all ages by the Father; and He so far excels the others as *with an oath* He is made Priest: *For they are priests without an oath, but He with an oath by Him that said, The Lord sware, and will not repent*[1]. The mere purpose of the Father was sufficient for surety: but the mode of assurance is twofold, namely that with the purpose there follows the oath also, *that by two immutable things, in which it was impossible for God to lie, we might have strong encouragement*[2] for our faith, who receive Christ Jesus as the Son of God.

15. This Christ, when He was come, the Jews denied, but the devils confessed. But His forefather David was not ignorant of Him, when he said, *I have ordained a lamp for mine Anointed*[3]*:* which lamp some have interpreted to be the brightness of Prophecy[4], others the flesh which He took upon Him from the Virgin, according to the Apostle's word, *But we have this treasure in earthen vessels*[5]. The Prophet was not ignorant of Him, when He said, *and announceth unto men His Christ*[6]. Moses also knew Him, Isaiah knew Him, and Jeremiah; not one of the Prophets was ignorant of Him. Even devils recognised Him, for He rebuked them, and the Scripture says, *because they knew that He was Christ*[7]. The Chief-priests knew Him not, and the devils confessed Him: the Chief Priests knew Him not, and a woman of Samaria proclaimed Him, saying, *Come, see a man which told me all things that ever I did. Is not this the Christ*[8]*?*

16. This is Jesus Christ who came *a High-Priest of the good things to come*[9]*;* who for the bountifulness of His Godhead imparted His own title to us all. For kings among men have their royal style which others may not share: but Jesus Christ being the Son of God gave us the dignity of being called Christians. But some one will say, The name of "Christians" is new, and was not in use aforetime[1]: and new-fashioned phrases are often objected to

---

6 Matt. i. 20.

7 The Anathema appended to the Creed of Nicæa condemns those who said πρὶν γεννηθῆναι οὐκ ἦν On this Eusebius of Cæsarea (*Epist.* § 9) remarks: "Moreover to anathematize 'Before His generation He was not,' did not seem preposterous, in that it is confessed by all, that the Son of God was before the generation according to the flesh."

8 Isa. xlix. 1. 9 Ib. xlix. 2. 1 τυφλῶν αἰσθητῶν.

2 John v. 14, 8. 3 Mark ix. 24.

4 Compare the fragment of the Apology of Quadratus presented to Hadrian 127 A.D., preserved by Eusebius (*H.E.* IV. iii.): "But the works of our Saviour were always present, for they were genuine:—those that were healed, and those that arose from the dead, who were seen not only, when they were healed and when they were raised, but were also always present; and not merely while the Saviour was on earth, but also after His death they were alive for a long while, so that some of them survived even to our times." See the notes on the passage of Eusebius, in this series.

5 1 John ii. 22. 6 Heb. vii. 24.

7 On the opinion that Christ was from all eternity the true High Priest of the Creation, see Index, *Priesthood*, and the reference there given to the Introduction. Cf. x. 4: xi. 1. Athan. (c. Arian. *Or.* ii. 12, *J.H.N.*).

8 The word 'synaxis' was used by the early Christians to distinguish their assemblies from the Jewish 'synagogue,' a word formed from the same root and more regularly. 'Synaxis' came to be used more especially of a celebration of the Eucharist. See Suicer, *Thesaurus*, Σύναξις.

9 σκευαστῷ, Ex. xxx. 22—25: "a perfume compounded (μυρεψικόν) after the art of the perfumer" (R.V.).

1 Heb. vii. 21. 2 Ib. vi. 18.

3 Ps. cxxxii. 17. The "lamp for the Anointed" was commonly applied by the Fathers to John the Baptist. Compare John v. 35, and Bishop Westcott's note there.

4 2 Pet. i. 19. The supposed reference in the Psalm to the lamp of prophecy is mentioned by Eusebius (*Demonstr. Evang.* IV. cap. 16).

5 2 Cor. iv. 7. The reference of the 'lamp' to Christ's Incarnation is mentioned by Eusebius (*u.s.*) and other Fathers.

6 Amos. iv. 13: "and declareth unto man what is his thought." For מַה־שֵּׂחוֹ, 'what is his thought,' the LXX. read מְשִׁיחוֹ, 'His Anointed,' τὸν Χριστὸν αὐτοῦ.

7 Luke iv. 41. 8 John iv. 29. 9 Heb. ix. 11.

1 οὐκ ἐπολιτεύετο, "was not in citizenship," "not naturalised." Cf. Sueton. *Nero.* cap. 16: "Christiani, genus hominum superstitionis novae et maleficae."

on the score of strangeness[2]. The prophet made this point safe beforehand, saying, *But upon My servants shall a new name be called, which shall be blessed upon the earth*[3]. Let us question the Jews: Are ye servants of the Lord, or not? Shew then your new name. For ye were called Jews and Israelites in the time of Moses, and the other prophets, and after the return from Babylon, and up to the present time: where then is your new name? But we, since we are servants of the Lord, have that new name: *new* indeed, but the *new name, which shall be blessed upon the earth*. This name caught the world in its grasp: for Jews are only in a certain region, but Christians reach to the ends of the world: for it is the name of the Only-begotten Son of God that is proclaimed.

17. But wouldest thou know that the Apostles knew and preached the name of Christ, or rather had Christ Himself within them? Paul says to his hearers, *Or seek ye a proof of Christ that speaketh in me*[4]? Paul proclaims Christ, saying, *For we preach not ourselves, but Christ Jesus as Lord, and ourselves your servants for Jesus' sake*[5]. Who then is this? The former persecutor. O mighty wonder! The former persecutor himself preaches Christ. But wherefore? Was he bribed? Nay there was none to use this mode of persuasion. But was it that he saw Him present on earth, and was abashed? He had already been taken up into heaven. He went forth to persecute, and after three days the persecutor is a preacher in Damascus. By what power? Others call friends as witnesses for friends: but I have presented to you as a witness the former enemy: and dost thou still doubt? The testimony of Peter and John, though weighty, was yet of a kind open to suspicion: for they were His friends. But of one who was formerly his enemy, and afterwards dies for His sake, who can any longer doubt the truth?

18. At this point of my discourse I am truly filled with wonder at the wise dispensation of the Holy Spirit; how He confined the Epistles of the rest to a small number, but to Paul the former persecutor gave the privilege of writing fourteen. For it was not because Peter or John was less that He restrained the gift; God forbid! But in order that the doctrine might be beyond question, He granted to the former enemy and persecutor the privilege of writing more, in order that we all might thus be made believers. For *all were amazed* at Paul, *and said, Is not this he that* was formerly a persecutor[6]? Did he not come hither, that he might lead us away bound to Jerusalem? Be not amazed, said Paul, I know that *it is hard for me to kick against the pricks*: I know that *I am not worthy to be called an Apostle, because I persecuted the Church of God*[7]; but I did it *in ignorance*[8]: for I thought that the preaching of Christ was destruction of the Law, and knew not that He came Himself to fulfil the Law and not to destroy it[9]. *But the grace of God was exceeding abundant in me*[1].

19. Many, my beloved, are the true testimonies concerning Christ. The Father bears witness from heaven of His Son: the Holy Ghost bears witness, descending bodily in likeness of a dove: the Archangel Gabriel bears witness, bringing good tidings to Mary: the Virgin Mother of God[2] bears witness: the blessed place of the manger bears witness. Egypt bears witness, which received the Lord while yet young in the body[3]: Symeon bears witness, who received Him in his arms, and said, *Now, Lord, lettest Thou Thy servant depart in peace, according to Thy word; for mine eyes have seen Thy salvation, which Thou hast prepared before the face of all people*[4]. Anna also, the prophetess, a most devout widow, of austere life, bears witness of Him. John the Baptist bears witness, the greatest among the Prophets, and leader of the New Covenant, who in a manner united both Covenants in Himself, the Old and the New. Jordan is His witness among rivers; the sea of Tiberias among seas: blind and lame bear witness, and dead men raised to life, and devils saying, *What have we to do with Thee, Jesus? we know Thee, who Thou art, the Holy One of God*[5]. Winds bear witness, silenced at His bidding: five loaves multiplied into five

---

2 τὸ ξένον.

3 Isa. lxv. 15, 16. The LXX. here depart from the meaning of the Hebrew: "*He shall call His servants by another name: so that he who blesseth himself in the earth shall bless himself in the God of truth*" (R.V.).

4 2 Cor. xiii. 3.

5 Ib. iv. 5.

6 Acts ix. 21.

7 1 Cor. xv. 9.

8 1 Tim. i. 13.

9 Matt. v. 17.

1 1 Tim. i. 14.

2 ἡ θεοτόκος—*Deipara*. Gibbon (Chap. xlvii. 34) says, "It is not easy to fix the invention of this word, which La Croze (*Christianisme des Indes*, tom. i. p. 16) ascribes to Eusebius of Cæsarea and the Arians. The orthodox testimonies are produced by Cyril (of Alexandria) and Petavius (*Dogmat. Theolog.* tom. v. L. v. cap. 15, p. 254, &c.), but the veracity of the Saint is questionable, and the epithet of θεοτόκος so easily slides from the margin to the text of a Catholic MS." This passage is justly described as "Gibbon's calumny" by Dr. Newman: see his notes on the title θεοτόκος (*Athan. c. Arian. Or.* ii. cap. 12, n.; *Or.* iii. capp. 14, 29, 33). The word is certainly used by Origen (*Deut.* xxii. 13, Lommatzsch. Tom. x. p. 378): "She that is already betrothed is called a wife, as also in the case of Joseph and the Theotokos." Cf. Archelaus (*Disput. cum Mane*, cap. xxxiv. "qui de Maria Dei Genetrice natus est"); Eusebius (*de Vita Constantini*, III. cap. 43: "The pious Empress adorned with rare memorials the place of the travail of the Theotokos"). For other examples see Suicer's *Thesaurus*, θεοτόκος, Pearson, *Creed*, Art. iii. notes l, m, n, o, and Routh, *Reliq. Sacr.* ii. p. 332.

3 "Chrysostom describing the flourishing state of the Church in Egypt in those times, says: 'Egypt welcomes and saves Him when a fugitive and plotted against, and receives a beginning as it were of its appropriation to Him, in order that when it shall hear Him proclaimed by the Apostles, it may in their day also be honoured as having been first to welcome Him'" (Cleopas).

4 Luke ii. 29, 30.

5 Mark i. 24.

thousand bear Him witness. The holy wood of the Cross bears witness, seen among us to this day, and from this place now almost filling the whole world, by means of those who in faith take portions from it[6]. The palm-tree[7] on the ravine bears witness, having supplied the palm-branches to the children who then hailed Him. Gethsemane[8] bears witness, still to the thoughtful almost shewing Judas. Golgotha[9], the holy hill standing above us here, bears witness to our sight: the Holy Sepulchre bears witness, and the stone which lies there[1] to this day. The sun now shining is His witness, which then at the time of His saving Passion was eclipsed[2]: the darkness is His witness, which was then from the sixth hour to the ninth: the light bears witness, which shone forth from the ninth hour until evening. The Mount of Olives bears witness, that holy mount from which He ascended to the Father: the rain-bearing clouds are His witnesses, having received their Lord: yea, and the gates of heaven bear witness [having received their Lord[3]], concerning which the Psalmist said, *Lift up your doors, O ye Princes, and be ye lift up, ye everlasting doors; and the King of Glory shall come in*[4]. His former enemies bear witness, of whom the blessed Paul is one, having been a little while His enemy, but for a long time His servant: the Twelve Apostles are His witnesses, having preached the truth not only in words, but also by their own torments and deaths: *the shadow of Peter*[5] bears witness, having healed the sick in the name of Christ. The handkerchiefs and aprons bear witness, as in like manner by Christ's power they wrought cures of old through Paul[6]. Persians[7] and Goths[8], and all the Gentile converts bear witness, by dying for His sake, whom they never saw with eyes of flesh: the devils, who to this day[9] are driven out by the faithful, bear witness to Him.

20. So many and diverse, yea and more than these, are His witnesses: is then the Christ thus witnessed any longer disbelieved? Nay rather if there is any one who formerly believed not, let him now believe: and if any was before a believer, let him receive a greater increase of faith, by believing in our Lord Jesus Christ, and let him understand whose name he bears. Thou art called a Christian: be tender of the name; let not our Lord Jesus Christ, the Son of God, be blasphemed through thee: but rather *let your good works shine before men*[1] that they who see them may in Christ Jesus our Lord glorify the Father which is in heaven: To whom be the glory, both now and for ever and ever. Amen.

---

6 See Cat. iv. 10, note 7.

7 The Bordeaux Pilgrim, who visited the Holy Places of Jerusalem, A.D. 333, *c.* speaks of this palm-tree as still existing. The longevity of the palm was proverbial: cf. Aristot. (*De Longitudine Vitae*, c. iv. 2).

8 The same Pilgrim (as quoted by the Benedictine Editor) says, "There is also the rock where Judas Iscariot betrayed Christ." Compare Cat. xiii. 38.

9 See Index, *Golgotha.*

1 See the passage of the Introduction referred to in Index, *Sepulchre.*

2 See Cat. ii. 15, note 8, and xiii. 25, 34, 38. On the supernatural character of the darkness mentioned in the Gospels see Meyer, *Commentary*, Matt. xxvii. 45. An eclipse of the sun was of course impossible, as the moon was full. Mr. J. R. Hind (*Historical Eclipses*, "Times," 19th July, 1872) states that the solar eclipse, mentioned by Phlegon the freedman of Hadrian, which occurred on Nov. 24, A.D. 29, and was partial at Jerusalem, is "the only solar eclipse that could have been visible at Jerusalem during the period usually fixed for the ministry of Christ." He adds, "The Moon was eclipsed on the generally received date of the Crucifixion, 3 April, A.D. 33. I find she had emerged from the earth's dark shadow a quarter of an hour before she rose at Jerusalem (6.36 p.m.), but the penumbra continued upon her disc for an hour afterwards." Thus the "darkness from the sixth hour unto the ninth" cannot be explained as the natural effect of an eclipse either solar or lunar.

3 This clause is omitted in Codd. Mon. 1, 2, Roe, Casaub., and is probably repeated from the preceding line: such repetitions, however, are not uncommon in Cyril's style.

4 Ps. xxiv. 7. The first clause is mistranslated by the LXX. from whom Cyril quotes.

5 Acts v. 15.

6 Ib. xix. 12.

7 The persecution of the Christians in Persia by Sapor II. is described at length by Sozomen (*E.H.* II. cc. ix.—xv., in this Series). It commenced in A.D. 343, and was going on at the date of these Lectures and long after. "During fifty years the Cross lay prostrate in blood and ashes" (*Dict. Bib.* 'Sassanidæ'). Compare Neander. *Church History*, Tom. III. p. 148, Bohn.)

8 The Goths here mentioned are the *Gothi minores* dwelling on the north of the Danube, where Ulfilas, "the Apostle of the Goths" (311—381), converted many of his countrymen to Christianity. After suffering severe persecution, he was allowed by Constantius to take refuge with his Arian converts in Mœsia and Thrace. This migration took place in 348 A.D., the same year in which Cyril's Lectures were delivered.

9 See Index, *Exorcism.*

1 Matt. v. 16.

LECTURE XI.

On the words, The Only-Begotten Son of God, Begotten of the Father Very God before all ages, By Whom all things were made.

Hebrews i. 1.

God, who at sundry times and in divers manners spake in times past unto the Fathers by the Prophets, hath in these last days spoken unto us by His Son.

1. That we have hope in Jesus Christ has been sufficiently shewn, according to our ability, in what we delivered to you yesterday. But we must not simply believe in Christ Jesus nor receive Him as one of the many who are improperly called Christs[1]. For they were figurative Christs, but He is the true Christ; not having risen by advancement[2] from among men to the Priesthood, but ever having the dignity of the Priesthood from the Father[3]. And for this cause the Faith, guarding us beforehand lest we should suppose Him to be one of the ordinary Christs, adds to the profession of the Faith, that we believe In One Lord Jesus Christ, The Only-Begotten Son of God.

2. And again on hearing of a "Son," think not of an adopted son but a Son by nature[4], an Only-begotten Son, having no brother. For this is the reason why He is called "Only-begotten," because in the dignity of the Godhead, and His generation from the Father, He has no brother. But we call Him the Son of God, not of ourselves, but because the Father Himself named Christ[5] His Son[6]: and a true name is that which is set by fathers upon their children[7].

3. Our Lord Jesus Christ erewhile became Man, but by the many He was unknown. Wishing, therefore, to teach that which was not known, He called together His disciples, and asked them, *Whom do men say that I, the Son of Man, am*[8]*?*—not from vain-glory, but wishing to shew them the truth, lest dwelling with God, the Only-begotten of God[9], they should think lightly of Him as if He were some mere man. And when they answered that some said Elias, and some Jeremias, He said to them, They may be excused for not knowing, but ye, My Apostles, who in My name cleanse lepers, and cast out devils, and raise the dead, ought not to be ignorant of Him, through whom ye do these wondrous works. And when they all became silent (for the matter was too high for man to learn), Peter, the foremost of the Apostles and chief herald[1] of the Church, neither aided by cunning invention, nor persuaded by human reasoning, but enlightened in his mind from the Father, says to Him, *Thou art the Christ*, not only so, but *the Son of the living God.* And there follows a blessing upon his speech (for in truth it was above man), and as a seal upon what he had said, that it was the Father who had revealed it to him. For the Saviour says, *Blessed art thou, Simon Barjona, for flesh and blood hath not revealed it to thee, but My Father which is in heaven*[2]. He therefore who acknowledges our Lord Jesus Christ the Son of God, partakes of this blessedness; but he who denies the Son of God is a poor and miserable man.

4. Again, I say, on hearing of a Son, under-

---

1 Compare x. 11, 15; xvi. 13: xxi. 1.

2 ἐκ προκοπῆς. See x. 5, note 8.

3 Compare x. 14, note 9.

4 θετόν. Athanasius (*de Sententiâ Dionysii*, § 23), represents Arius as saying that the Word "is not by nature (κατὰ φύσιν) and in truth Son of God, but is called Son, He too, by adoption (κατὰ θέσιν), as a creature." Again (*c. Arian. Orat.* iii. 19), he says, "This is the true God and the Life eternal, and we are made sons through Him by adoption and grace (θέσει καὶ χάριτι)." Cf. vii. 10, and § 4, below.

5 The MSS. all read αὐτὸν Χριστόν which might mean "Christ and no other." But Χριστόν is probably a gloss introduced from the margin.

6 Compare the passages in which Cyril quotes Ps. ii. 7, as Cat. vii. 2; x. 2; xi. 5; xii. 18.

7 "It was one of the especial rights of a father to choose the names for his children, and to alter them if he pleased" (*Dict. Greek and Roman Antiq.* "Nomen. 1 Greek.") The right to the name given by the father is the subject of one of the Private Orations of Demosthenes (Πρὸς Βοιωτὸν περὶ τοῦ ὀνόματος).

8 Matt. xiii. 16.

9 Compare iv. 7: "God of God begotten:" xiii. 3, and 13: "God the Son of God." Here, however, the MSS. vary, and the reading of Cod. Coisl. Υἱῷ Θεοῦ μονογενεῖ is approved by the Benedictine Editor, though not adopted. The confusion of Υἱῷ and Θεῷ is like that in John i. 18.

1 ὁ πρωτοστάτης τῶν Ἀποστόλων καὶ τῆς Ἐκκλησίας κορυφαῖος κῆρυξ. Cf. ii. 19.

2 Matt. xvi. 17.

stand it not merely in an improper sense, but as a Son in truth, a Son by nature, without beginning[3]; not as having come out of bondage into a higher state of adoption[4], but a Son eternally begotten by an inscrutable and incomprehensible generation. And in like manner on hearing of the First-born[5], think not that this is after the manner of men; for the first-born among men have other brothers also. And it is somewhere written, *Israel is My son, My first-born*[6]. But Israel is, as Reuben was, a first-born son rejected: for Reuben went up to his father's couch; and Israel cast his Father's Son out of the vineyard, and crucified Him.

To others also the Scripture says, *Ye are the sons of the Lord your God*[7]*:* and in another place, *I have said, Ye are gods, and ye are all sons of the Most High*[8]. *I have said*, not, "I have begotten." They, when God so *said*, received the sonship, which before they had not: but He was not begotten to be other than He was before; but was begotten from the beginning Son of the Father, being above all beginning and all ages, Son of the Father, in all things like[9] to Him who begat Him, eternal of a Father eternal, Life of Life begotten, and Light of Light, and Truth of Truth, and Wisdom of the Wise, and King of King, and God of God, and Power of Power[1].

5. If then thou hear the Gospel saying, *The book of the generation of Jesus Christ, the Son of David, the Son of Abraham*[2], understand "according to the flesh." For He is the Son of David *at the end of the ages*[3], but the Son of God BEFORE ALL AGES, without beginning[4]. The one, which before He had not, He received; but the other, which He hath, He hath eternally as begotten of the Father. Two fathers He hath: one, David, according to the flesh, and one, God, His Father in a Divine manner[5]. As the Son of David, He is subject to time, and to handling, and to genealogical descent: but as Son according to the Godhead[6], He is subject neither to time nor to place, nor to genealogical descent: for *His generation who shall declare*[7]*? God is a Spirit*[8]*;* He who is a Spirit hath spiritually begotten, as being incorporeal, an inscrutable and incomprehensible generation. The Son Himself says of the Father, *The Lord said unto Me, Thou art My Son, to-day have I begotten Thee*[9]. Now this *to-day* is not recent, but eternal: a timeless *to-day*, before all ages. *From the womb, before the morning star, have I begotten Thee*[1].

6. Believe thou therefore on JESUS CHRIST, SON OF the living GOD, and a Son ONLY-BEGOTTEN, according to the Gospel which

3 Athanasius (*de Synodis*, § 15) quotes a passage from the *Thalia* of Arius, in which he says: "We praise Him as without beginning, because of Him who has a beginning: and adore Him as eternal, because of Him who in time has come to be. He who is without beginning made the Son a beginning of things created."

It is important, therefore, to notice the sense in which Cyril here calls the Son ἄναρχος. The word has two meanings, which should be clearly distinguished, (i) *unoriginate*, (ii) *without beginning in time*. The former referring to origin, or cause, can properly be applied to the One true God, or to God the Father only, as it is used by Clement of Alexandria (*Protrept.* cap. v. § 65: τὸν πάντων ποιητὴν . . . ἀγνοοῦντες, τὸν ἄναρχον Θεόν. [*Strom.* IV. cap. xxv. § 164: ὁ Θεὸς δὲ ἄναρχος ἀρχὴ τῶν ὅλων παντελὴς ἀρχῆς ποιητικός]. [*Stromat.* V. cap. xiv. § 142: ἐξ ἀρχῆς ἀνάρχου]. Methodius (*ob.* 312 A.D. *circ.*) in a fragment (*On things created*, § 8, English Trans. Clark's Ante-Nic. Libr.) comments thus on Joh. i. 1—3: "And so after *the peculiar unbeginning beginning*, who is the Father, He (the Word) is the beginning of other things, 'by whom all things are made.'"

In this sense Cyril has said (iv. 4) that God alone is "unbegotten, unoriginate:" and in xi. 20 he explains this more fully,—"Suffer none to speak of a beginning of the Son in time (χρονικὴν ἀρχήν), but as a timeless beginning acknowledge the Father. For the Father is the beginning of the Son, timeless, incomprehensible, without beginning." From a confusion of the two meanings the word came to be improperly applied in the sense of "unoriginate" to the Son, and to the Spirit; and this improper usage is condemned in the 49th *Apostolic Canon*, which Hefele regards as amongst the most ancient Canons, and taken from the *Apostolic Constitutions*, vi. 11: "If any Bishop or Presbyter shall baptize not according to our Lord's ordinance into the Father, and Son, and Spirit, but into *three Unoriginates*, or three Sons, or three Paracletes, let him be deposed." (ii.) Athanasius frequently calls the Son ἄναρχος in the sense of 'timeless,' as being the co-eternal brightness (ἀπαύγασμα) of the Eternal Light: see *de Sent. Dionys.* §§ 15, 16, 22; "God is the Eternal Light, which never either began or shall cease: accordingly the Brightness is ever before Him, and co-exists with Him, without beginning and ever-begotten (ἄναρχον καὶ ἀειγενές)."

4 εἰς προκοπὴν υἱοθεσίας. Cf. § 2, note 4.

5 Πρωτότοκον. The word occurs in Heb. i. 6, which had been read in the Lesson before this Lecture. The exact dogmatic sense of the word is carefully explained by Athanasius (*c. Arian.* Or. ii. 62): "The same cannot be both Only-begotten and First-born, except in different relations;—that is, Only-begotten, because of His generation from the Father, as has been said; and First-born, because of His condescension to the creation, and His making the many His brethren." See Mr. Robertson's discussion of the word πρωτότοκος (*Athan.* p. 344, in this series), and Bp. Bull (*Def. Fid. Nic.* iii. 5—8).

6 Ex. iv. 22. 7 Deut. xiv. 1. 8 Ps. lxxxii. 6.

9 ἐν πᾶσιν ὅμοιος. See the note on iv. 7. That the phrase was not equivalent to ὁμοούσιος, and did not adequately express the relation of the Son to the Father is clearly shewn by Athanasius (*de Synodis*, cap. iii. § 53).

1 The additions which the Benedictine Editor has here made to the earlier text, as represented by Milles, may be conveniently shewn in brackets. ἀλλὰ Υἱὸς [τοῦ Πατρὸς]* ἐξ ἀρχῆς ἐγεννήθη, [ὑπεράνω πάσης ἀρχῆς καὶ αἰώνων τυγχάνων]*, Υἱὸς τοῦ Πατρὸς [ἐν πᾶσιν]† ὅμοιος τῷ γεγεννηκότι· [ἀΐδιος ἐξ ἀϊδίου Πατρός,]* ζωὴ ἐκ ζωῆς γεγεννημένος . . . . καὶ Θεὸς ἐκ Θεοῦ, [καὶ δύναμις ἐκ δυνάμεως]‡.

* Codd. Coisl. Ottob. Mon. 2. † Coisl. Ottob. Roe, Casaub Mon. 1, 2. ‡ Coisl. Ottob. Mon. 1, 2.

2 Matt. i. 1. 3 Heb. ix. 26. 4 See § 4, note 3.

5 Θεϊκῶς.

6 τὸ μὲν κατὰ τὸν Δαβίδ . . . . τὸ δὲ κατὰ τὴν Θεότητα.

7 Isa. liii. 8. Compare § 7, below. 8 John iv. 24.

9 Ps. ii. 7.

1 Ps. cx. 3. "From the womb of the morning thou hast the dew of thy youth" (R.V.). There is a remarkable various reading in Codd. Roe, Casaub. Τό εἶ σύ, ἄχρονον καὶ ἀΐδιον· τὸ δὲ σήμερον πρόσφατον, ἀλλ' οὐκ ἀΐδιον, οἰκειουμένου τοῦ Πατρὸς καὶ τὴν κάτω γέννησιν. Καὶ πάλιν λέγει· Ἐκ γαστρὸς πρὸ ἑωσφόρου γεγέννηκά σε· τοῦτο μόνον τῆς Θεότητος· Πίστευσον, κ.τ.λ. The words "*Thou art My Son*," are thus referred to the eternal generation, and "*This day*" to the birth in time: whereas in the received text, followed in our translation, σήμερον refers to the timeless and eternal generation of the Son. The former interpretation of Ps. ii. 7 is found in many Fathers, as for example in Tertullian (*adv. Prax.* vii. xi.), and Methodius (*Conviv. Virg.* VIII. cap. ix.): "He says 'Thou art,' and not 'Thou hast become,' shewing that He had not recently attained to the position of Son. . . . But the expression, 'This day have I begotten Thee,' signifies that He willed that existing already before the ages in heaven He should also be begotten for the world, that is that He who was before unknown should be made known." The same interpretation was held by many Fathers, some referring σήμερον to the Nativity, as Cyprian (*adv. Judæos Testim.* ii. 8), others to the Baptism (Justin M. *Dialog.* cap. lxxxviii.; Tertullian, *adv. Marcion.* iv. 22). Athanasius (*c. Arian.* iv. § 27), has a long discussion on the question whether Ps. cx. 3, ἐκ γαστρὸς πρὸ ἑωσφόρου γεγέννηκά σε, refers to the eternal generation of the Son, or to His Nativity.

says, *For God so loved the world, that He gave His Only-begotten Son, that whosoever believeth on Him should not perish, but have everlasting life*[2]. And again, *He that believeth on the Son is not judged, but hath passed out of death into life*[3]. *But he that believeth not the Son shall not see life, but the wrath of God abideth on him*[4]. And John testified concerning Him, saying, *And we beheld His glory, glory as of the only-begotten from the Father,—full of grace and truth*[5]: at whom the devils trembled and said, *Ah! what have we to do with Thee, Jesus, Thou Son of the living God*[6].

7. He is then the Son of God by nature and not by adoption[7], begotten of the Father. *And he that loveth Him that begat, loveth Him also that is begotten of Him*[8]; but he that despiseth Him that is begotten casts back the insult upon Him who begat. And whenever thou hear of God begetting, sink not down in thought to bodily things, nor think of a corruptible generation, lest thou be guilty of impiety. *God is a Spirit*[9], His generation is spiritual: for bodies beget bodies, and for the generation of bodies time needs must intervene; but time intervenes not in the generation of the Son from the Father. And in our case what is begotten is begotten imperfect: but the Son of God was begotten perfect; for what He is now, that is He also from the beginning[1], begotten without beginning. We are begotten so as to pass from infantine ignorance to a state of reason: thy generation, O man, is imperfect, for thy growth is progressive. But think not that it is thus in His case, nor impute infirmity to Him who hath begotten. For if that which He begat was imperfect, and acquired its perfection in time, thou art imputing infirmity to Him who hath begotten; if so be, the Father did not bestow from the beginning that which, as thou sayest, time bestowed afterwards[2].

8. Think not therefore that this generation is human, nor as Abraham begat Isaac. For in begetting Isaac, Abraham begat not what he would, but what another granted. But in God the Father's begetting there is neither ignorance nor intermediate deliberation[3]. For to say that He knew not what He was begetting is the greatest impiety; and it is no less impious to say, that after deliberation in time He then became a Father. For God was not previously without a Son, and afterwards in time became a Father; but hath the Son eternally, having begotten Him not as men beget men, but as Himself only knoweth, who begat Him before all ages VERY GOD.

9. For the Father being Very God begat the Son like unto Himself, Very God[4]; not as teachers beget disciples, not as Paul says to some, *For in Christ Jesus I begat you through the Gospel*[5]. For in this case he who was not a son by nature became a son by discipleship, but in the former case He was a Son by nature, a true Son. Not as ye, who are to be illuminated, are now becoming sons of God: for ye also become sons, but by adoption of grace, as it is written, *But as many as received Him, to them gave He the right to become children of God, even to them that believe on His name: which were begotten not of blood, nor of the will of the flesh, nor of the will of man, but of God*[6]. And we indeed are begotten of water and of the Spirit, but not thus was Christ begotten of the Father. For at the time of His Baptism addressing Him, and saying, *This is My Son*[7], He did not say, "This has now become My Son," but, *This is My Son*; that He might make manifest, that even before the operation of Baptism He was a Son.

10. The Father begat the Son, not as among men mind begets word. For the mind is substantially existent in us; but the word when spoken is dispersed into the air and comes to an end[8]. But we know Christ to have been begotten not as a word pronounced[9], but as a Word substantially existing[1] and living; not spoken by the lips, and dispersed, but begotten of the Father eternally and ineffably, in substance[2]. For, *In the beginning was the Word, and the Word was with God, and the Word was God*[3], sitting at God's right

2 John iii. 16. 3 Ib. iii. 18; v. 24. 4 Ib. iii. 36.
5 Ib. i. 14. 6 Luke iv. 34.
7 φύσει καὶ οὐ θέσει. Cf. § 2, note 4.
8 1 John v. 1. 9 John iv. 24. Cf. § 5.
1 γεγεννημένος ἀνάρχως. Cf. § 5, note 4.
2 ὁ χρόνος. Bened. c. Codd. Roe, Casaub. Coisl. ὁ χρόνοις Ottob. Mon. 1. 2. A. With the latter reading, the meaning will be—"if He did not bestow from the beginning, as thou sayest, what He bestowed in after times." Cyril does not here address his auditor, but an imaginary opponent,—"O man."

Compare Athan. (*de Synodis*, § 26).

3 The Arians appear to have made use of a dilemma: If God begat with will and purpose, these preceded the begetting, and so ἦν ποτε ὅτε οὐκ ἦν, there was a time when the Son was not: if without will and purpose, then He begat in ignorance and of necessity. The answer is fully given by Athanasius (*c. Arian.* iii. 58—67, pp. 425—431 in this Series).

4 Athanasius (*ad Episcopos Ægypti*, § 13), referring to 1 John v. 20, *This is the true* (ἀληθινός) *God*, writes: "But these men (the Arians), as if in contradiction to this, allege that Christ is not the true God, but that He is only called God, as are other creatures, in regard of His participation in the Divine nature." Again (*c. Arian.* iii. 9), "He gave us to know that of the true Father He is the true Offspring (ἀληθινὸν γέννημα).

5 1 Cor. iv. 15. 6 John i. 12, 13. 7 Matt. iii. 17.

8 Compare Athanasius (*de Sententiâ Dionysii*, § 23): "the mind creates the word, being manifested in it, and the word shews the mind, having originated therein." Tertullian (*adv. Prax.* vii.): "You will say what is a word but a voice and sound of the mouth, and (as the Grammarians teach) air when struck against, intelligible to the ear, but for the rest a sort of void, empty, and incorporeal thing." Cf. Athan. (*de Synodis*, § 12): ἀνυπόστατον.

9 προφορικόν. See Cat. iv. 8, note 9.

1 ἐνυπόστατον. *ibid.* So the Spirit is described in Cat. xvii. 5 "not uttered or breathed by the mouth and lips of the Father and the Son, nor dispersed into the air, but personally subsisting (ἐνυπόστατον)."

2 ἐν ὑποστάσει. 3 John i. 1.

hand;—the Word understanding the Father's will, and creating all things at His bidding: the Word, which came down and went up; for the word of utterance when spoken comes not down, nor goes up; the Word speaking and saying, *The things which I have seen with My Father, these I speak*[4]: the Word possessed of power, and reigning over all things: for *the Father hath committed all things unto the Son*[5].

11. The Father then begat Him not in such wise as any man could understand, but as Himself only knoweth. For we profess not to tell in what manner He begat Him, but we insist that it was not in this manner. And not we only are ignorant of the generation of the Son from the Father, but so is every created nature. *Speak to the earth, if perchance it may teach thee*[6]: and though thou inquire of all things which are upon the earth, they shall not be able to tell thee. For the earth cannot tell the substance of Him who is its own potter and fashioner. Nor is the earth alone ignorant, but the sun also[7]: for the sun was created on the fourth day, without knowing what had been made in the three days before him; and he who knows not the things made in the three days before him, cannot tell forth the Maker Himself. Heaven will not declare this: for at the Father's bidding *the heaven also was like smoke established*[8] by Christ. Nor shall *the heaven of heavens* declare this, *nor the waters which are above the heavens*[9]. Why then art thou cast down, O man, at being ignorant of that which even the heavens know not? Nay, not only are the heavens ignorant of this generation, but also every angelic nature. For if any one should ascend, were it possible, into the first heaven, and perceiving the ranks of the Angels there should approach and ask them how God begat His own Son, they would say perhaps, "We have above us beings greater and higher; ask them." Go up to the second heaven and the third; attain, if thou canst, to Thrones, and Dominions, and Principalities, and Powers: and even if any one should reach them, which is impossible, they also would decline the explanation, for they know it not.

12. For my part, I have ever wondered at the curiosity of the bold men, who by their imagined reverence fall into impiety. For though they know nothing of Thrones, and Dominions, and Principalities, and Powers, the workmanship of Christ, they attempt to scrutinise their Creator Himself. Tell me first, O most daring man, wherein does Throne differ from Dominion, and then scrutinise what pertains to Christ. Tell me what is a Principality, and what a Power, and what a Virtue, and what an Angel: and then search out their Creator, for *all things were made by Him*[1]. But thou wilt not, or thou canst not ask Thrones or Dominions. What else is there that *knoweth the deep things of God*[2], save only the Holy Ghost, who spake the Divine Scriptures? But not even the Holy Ghost Himself has spoken in the Scriptures concerning the generation of the Son from the Father. Why then dost thou busy thyself about things which not even the Holy Ghost has written in the Scriptures? Thou that knowest not the things which are written, busiest thou thyself about the things which are not written? There are many questions in the Divine Scriptures; what is written we comprehend not, why do we busy ourselves about what is not written? It is sufficient for us to know that God hath begotten One Only Son.

13. Be not ashamed to confess thine ignorance, since thou sharest ignorance with Angels. Only He who begat knoweth Him who was begotten, and He who is begotten of Him knoweth Him who begat. He who begat knoweth what He begat: and the Scriptures also testify that He who was begotten is God[3]. For *as the Father hath life in Himself, so also hath He given to the Son to have life in Himself*[4]; and, *that all men should honour the Son, even as they honour the Father*[5]; and, *as the Father quickeneth* whom He will, *even so the Son quickeneth whom He will*[6]. Neither He who begat suffered any loss, nor is anything lacking to Him who was begotten (I know that I have said these things many times, but it is for your safety that they are said so often): neither has He who begat, a Father, nor He who was begotten, a brother. Neither was He who begat changed into the Son[7], nor did He who was begotten become the Father[8]. Of One Only Father there is One

4 John viii. 38. 5 Matt. xi. 27; John v. 22.

6 Job xii. 8.

7 In saying that the earth, the sun, and the heavens know not their Maker, Cyril is simply using figurative language like that of the passage of Job just quoted. There is no reason to suppose that he accepted Origen's theory (*de Principiis*, II. cap. 7), that the heavenly bodies are living and rational beings, capable of sin.

8 Isa. li. 6: *the heavens shall vanish away like smoke.*

9 Ps. cxlviii. 4.

1 John i. 3. 2 1 Cor. ii. 10, 11.

3 I have followed the reading of Codd. Coisl. Roe, Casaub. Mon. A, which is approved though not adopted by the Benedictine Editor. The common text is manifestly interpolated: "And the Holy Spirit of God testifies in the Scriptures, that He who was begotten without beginning is God. *For what man knoweth, &c.*" This insertion of 1 Cor. ii. 11 interrupts the argument, and is a useless repetition of the allusion to the same passage in § 12.

4 John v. 26. 5 Ib. v. 23. 6 Ib. v. 21.

7 See iv. 8, note 8, on the Sabellian doctrine, and Athanas. (*de Synodis*, § 16, note 10 in this series).

8 The doctrine of Sabellius might be expressed in two forms, either the Father became the Son, or the Son became the Father. Both forms are here denied. The Jerusalem Editor thinks there is an allusion to the Arian argument mentioned by Athanasius (*c. Arian. Or.* I. cap. vi. 22): "If the Son is the Father's offspring and Image, and is like in all things to the Father, then it necessarily holds that as He is begotten so He begets, and He too becomes father of a son." But the close connexion of the two clauses is in favour of the reference to the Sabellian υἱοπατορία.

Only-begotten Son: neither two Unbegotten [9], nor two Only-begotten; but One Father, Unbegotten (for He is Unbegotten who hath no father); and One Son, eternally begotten of the Father; begotten not in time, but before all ages; not increased by advancement, but begotten that which He now is.

14. We believe then IN THE ONLY-BEGOTTEN SON OF GOD, WHO WAS BEGOTTEN OF THE FATHER VERY GOD. For the True God begetteth not a false god, as we have said, nor did He deliberate and afterwards beget [1]; but He begat eternally, and much more swiftly than our words or thoughts: for we speaking in time, consume time; but in the case of the Divine Power, the generation is timeless. And as I have often said, He did not bring forth the Son from non existence into being, nor take the non-existent into sonship [2]: but the Father, being Eternal, eternally and ineffably begat One Only Son, who has no brother. Nor are there two first principles; but the Father is *the head of the Son* [3]; the beginning is One. For the Father begat the Son VERY GOD, called Emmanuel; and Emmanuel *being interpreted is, God with us* [4].

15. And wouldest thou know that He who was begotten of the Father, and afterwards became man, is God? Hear the Prophet saying, *This is our God, none other shall be accounted of in comparison with Him. He hath found out every way of knowledge, and given it to Jacob His servant, and to Israel His beloved. Afterwards He was seen on earth, and conversed among men* [5]. Seest thou herein God become man, after the giving of the law by Moses? Hear also a second testimony to Christ's Deity, that which has just now been read, *Thy throne, O God, is for ever and ever* [6]. For lest, because of His presence here in the flesh, He should be thought to have been advanced after this to the Godhead, the Scripture says plainly, *Therefore God, even Thy God, hath anointed Thee with the oil of gladness above Thy fellows* [7]. Seest thou Christ as God anointed by God the Father?

16. Wouldest thou receive yet a third testimony to Christ's Godhead? Hear Esaias saying, *Egypt hath laboured, and the merchandise of Ethiopia:* and soon after, *In Thee shall they make supplication, because God is in Thee, and there is no God save Thee. For Thou art God, and we knew it not, the God of Israel, the Saviour* [8]. Thou seest that the Son is God, having in Himself God the Father: saying almost the very same which He has said in the Gospels: *The Father is in Me, and I am in the Father* [9]. He says not, I am the Father, but *the Father is in Me, and I am in the Father.* And again He said not, I and the Father am [1] one, but, *I and the Father are one*, that we should neither separate them, nor make a confusion of Son-Father [2]. One they are because of the dignity pertaining to the Godhead, since God begat God. One in respect of their kingdom; for the Father reigns not over these, and the Son over those, lifting Himself up against His Father like Absalom: but the kingdom of the Father is likewise the kingdom of the Son. One they are, because there is no discord nor division between them: for what things the Father willeth, the Son willeth the same. One, because the creative works of Christ are no other than the Father's; for the creation of all things is one, the Father having made them through the Son: *For He spake, and they were made; He commanded, and they were created*, saith the Psalmist [3]. For He who speaks, speaks to one who hears; and He who commands, gives His commandment to one who is present with Him.

17. The Son then is VERY GOD, having the Father in Himself, not changed into the Father; for the Father was not made man, but the Son. For let the truth be freely spoken [4]. The Father suffered not for us, but the Father sent Him who suffered. Neither let us say, There was a time when the Son was not; nor let us admit a Son who is the Father [5]: but let us walk in the king's highway; let us turn aside neither on the left hand nor on the right. Neither from thinking to honour the Son, let us call Him the Father; nor from

---

9 ἀγέννητοι. The context shews that this, not ἀγένητοι, is here the right form. Athanasius seems to have used ἀγέννητος in both senses "Un-begotten," as here, and "unoriginate." Thus (*c. Arian. Or.* i. cap. ix. § 30) he says of the Arians: "Their further question 'whether the Unoriginate be one or two,' shews how false are their views." Compare Bp. Lightfoot's Excursus on Ignatius, *Ephes.* § 7, and Mr. Robertson's notes on Athanasius in this Series.

1 See above, § 8, note 3.

2 Athan. (*c. Arian.* I. ix. 31) "speaking against the Lord, 'He is of nothing,' and 'He was not before His generation.'"

3 1 Cor. xi. 3.

4 Matt. i. 23.

5 Baruch iii. 35—37. The last verse was understood by Cyril, as by many of the Greek and Latin Fathers, to be a prophecy of the Incarnation: but in reality it refers to "knowledge" (ἐπιστήμη, *v.* 36), and should be translated "she was seen upon earth." See notes on the passage in the *Speaker's Commentary.*

6 Heb. i. 8.

7 Ib. i. 9. See x. 14, note 9.

8 Isa. xlv. 14, 15: "They shall make supplication unto thee, saying, surely God is in thee." The words are addressed to Jerusalem as the city of God. Cyril applies them to the Son, misled by the Septuagint.

9 John xiv. 11.

1 Athanasius (*c. Arian. Or.* iv. § 9), arguing for the ὁμοούσιον says: "There are two, because there is Father and Son, that is the Word; and one, because one God. For if this is not so, He would have said, I am the Father, or, I and the Father am."

2 See iv. 8, notes 7 and 8.

3 Pss. xxxiii. 9; cxlviii. 5. S. Cyril explains the creative "Fiat" in Gen. i. as addressed by the Father to the Son.

4 We learn from Socrates (*Eccl. Hist.* I. 24), that after the Nicene Council "those who objected to the word ὁμοούσιος conceived that those who approved it favoured the opinion of Sabellius." Marcellus of Ancyra, who was deposed on a charge of Sabellianism, and who did not in fact make clear the distinct personality of the Son, had been warmly supported by the friends of Athanasius. Cyril apparently fears to incur their censure, if he too strongly condemned the Sabellian view.

5 Cyril here rejects both the opposite errors, Arianism, "There was a time when the Son was not," and Sabellianism, "a Son who is the Father."

thinking to honour the Father, imagine the Son to be some one of the creatures. But let One Father be worshipped through One Son, and let not their worship be separated. Let One Son be proclaimed, sitting at the right hand of the Father before all ages: sharing His throne not by advancement in time after His Passion, but by eternal possession.

18. *He who hath seen the Son, hath seen the Father*[6]: for in all things the Son is like to Him who begat Him[7]; begotten Life of Life, and Light of Light, Power of Power, God of God; and the characteristics of the Godhead are unchangeable[8] in the Son; and he who is counted worthy to behold Godhead in the Son, attains to the fruition of the Father. This is not my word, but that of the Only-begotten: *Have I been so long time with you, and hast thou not known Me, Philip? He that hath seen Me, hath seen the Father*[9]. And to be brief, let us neither separate them, nor make a confusion[1]: neither say thou ever that the Son is foreign to the Father, nor admit those who say that the Father is at one time Father, and at another Son: for these are strange and impious statements, and not the doctrines of the Church. But the Father, having begotten the Son, remained the Father, and is not changed. He begat Wisdom, yet lost not wisdom Himself; and begat Power, yet became not weak: He begat God, but lost not His own Godhead: and neither did He lose anything Himself by diminution or change; nor has He who was begotten any thing wanting. Perfect is He who begat, Perfect that which was begotten: God was He who begat, God He who was begotten; God of all Himself, yet entitling the Father His own God. For He is not ashamed to say, *I ascend unto My Father and your Father, and to My God and your God*[2].

19. But lest thou shouldest think that He is in a like sense Father of the Son and of the creatures, Christ drew a distinction in what follows. For He said not, "I ascend to our Father," lest the creatures should be made fellows of the Only-begotten; but He said, *My Father and your Father;* in one way Mine, by nature; in another yours, by adoption. And again, *to my God and your God*, in one way Mine, as His true and Only-begotten Son, and in another way yours, as His workmanship[3]. The Son of God then is VERY GOD, ineffably begotten before all ages (for I say the same things often to you, that it may be graven upon your mind). This also believe, that God has a Son: but about the manner be not curious, for by searching thou wilt not find. Exalt not thyself, lest thou fall: *think upon those things only which have been commanded thee*[4]. Tell me first what He is who begat, and then learn that which He begat; but if thou canst not conceive the nature of Him who hath begotten, search not curiously into the manner of that which is begotten.

20. For godliness it sufficeth thee to know, as we have said, that God hath One Only Son, One naturally begotten; who began not His being when He was born in Bethlehem, but BEFORE ALL AGES. For hear the Prophet Micah saying, *And thou, Bethlehem, house of Ephrata, art little to be among the thousands of Judah. Out of thee shall come forth unto Me a Ruler, who shall feed My people Israel: and His goings forth are from the beginning, from days of eternity*[5]. Think not then of Him who is now come forth out of Bethlehem[6], but worship Him who was eternally begotten of the Father. Suffer none to speak of a beginning of the Son in time, but as a timeless Beginning acknowledge the Father. For the Father is the Beginning of the Son, timeless, incomprehensible, without beginning[7]. The fountain of the river of righteousness, even of the Only-begotten, is the Father, who begat Him as Himself only knoweth. And wouldest thou know that our Lord Jesus Christ is King Eternal? Hear Him again saying, *Your father Abraham rejoiced to see My day, and he saw it, and was glad*[8]. And then, when the Jews received this hardly, He says what to them was still harder, *Before Abraham was, I am*[9]. And again He saith to the Father, *And now, Father, glorify Thou Me with Thine own self, with the glory which I had with Thee before the world was*[1]. He says plainly, "before the world was, I had the glory which is with Thee." And again when

---

6 John xiv. 9. 7 See above, § 4, note 9.

8 ἀπαράλλακτοι. The word was used by the Orthodox Bishops at Nicæa, who said that "the Word must be described as the True power and Image of the Father, in all things like the Father and Himself incapable of change." See the notes of Dr. Newman and Mr. Robertson on Athanasius (*de Decretis*, § 20).

9 John xiv. 9. 1 See iv. 8, note 8.

2 John xx. 17.

3 Compare Cat. vii. 7. The Jerusalem Editor observes that the expression "My God" is understood by the Fathers generally as spoken by Christ in reference to His human nature, but Cyril applies this, as well as the other expression "My Father," to the Divine nature. So Hilary (*de Trinit.* iv. 53): "idcirco Deus ejus est, quia ex eo natus in Deum est." Compare Epiphanius (*Hær.* lxix. 55).

4 Ecclus iii. 22.

5 Micah v. 2; on the various readings ὀλιγοστὸς εἶ, μὴ ὀλ, εἶ, οὐκ ὀλ. εἶ, found in the MSS. of Cyril, see the Commentaries on the quotation of the passage in Matt. ii. 6.

6 Codd. Roe, Casaub. have a different reading—"Think not then of His having now been born in Bethlehem, and (nor) suppose Him as the Son of Man to be altogether recent, but worship, &c." This is rightly regarded by the Benedictine and other Editors as an interpolation intended to avoid the apparent tendency of Cyril's language in the received text to separate the Virgin's Son from the Eternal Word. Had Cyril so written after the Nestorian controversy arose, he would have appeared to favour the Nestorian formula that "Mary did not give birth to the Deity." Compare Swainson (*Nicene Creed*, Ch. ix. § 7.) What Cyril really means is that we are not to think of Christ simply as man, but to worship Him as God.

7 Compare § 4, note 3. 8 John viii. 56. 9 Ib. viii. 58.

1 Ib. xvii. 5.

He says, *For Thou lovedst Me before the foundation of the world*[2], He plainly declares, "The glory which I have with thee is from eternity."

21. We believe then IN ONE LORD JESUS CHRIST, THE ONLY-BEGOTTEN SON OF GOD, BEGOTTEN OF HIS FATHER VERY GOD BEFORE ALL WORLDS, BY WHOM ALL THINGS WERE MADE. For *whether they be thrones, or dominions, or principalities, or powers, all things were made through Him*[3], and of things created none is exempted from His authority. Silenced be every heresy which brings in different creators and makers of the world; silenced the tongue which blasphemes the Christ the Son of God; let them be silenced who say that the sun is the Christ, for He is the sun's Creator, not the sun which we see[4]. Silenced be they who say that the world is the workmanship of Angels[5], who wish to steal away the dignity of the Only-begotten. For whether visible or invisible, whether thrones or dominions, or anything that is named, all things were made by Christ. He reigns over the things which have been made by Him, not having seized another's spoils, but reigning over His own workmanship, even as the Evangelist John has said, *All things were made by Him, and without Him was not anything made*[6]. All things were made by Him, the Father working by the Son.

22. I wish to give also a certain illustration of what I am saying, but I know that it is feeble; for of things visible what can be an exact illustration of the Divine Power? But nevertheless as feeble be it spoken by the feeble to the feeble. For just as any king, whose son was a king, if he wished to form a city, might suggest to his son, his partner in the kingdom, the form of the city, and he having received the pattern, brings the design to completion; so, when the Father wished to form all things, the Son created all things at the Father's bidding, that the act of bidding might secure to the Father His absolute authority[7], and yet the Son in turn might have authority over His own workmanship, and neither the Father be separated from the lordship over His own works, nor the Son rule over things created by others, but by Himself. For, as I have said, Angels did not create the world, but the Only-begotten Son, begotten, as I have said, before all ages, BY WHOM ALL THINGS WERE MADE, nothing having been excepted from His creation. And let this suffice to have been spoken by us so far, by the grace of Christ.

23. But let us now recur to our profession of the Faith, and so for the present finish our discourse. Christ made all things, whether thou speak of Angels, or Archangels, of Dominions, or Thrones. Not that the Father wanted strength to create the works Himself, but because He willed that the Son should reign over His own workmanship, God Himself giving Him the design of the things to be made. For honouring His own Father the Only-begotten saith, *The Son can do nothing of Himself, but what He seeth the Father do; for what things soever He doeth, these also doeth the Son likewise*[8]. And again, *My Father worketh hitherto, and I work*[9], there being no opposition in those who work. *For all Mine are Thine, and Thine are Mine*, saith the Lord in the Gospels[1]. And this we may certainly know from the Old and New Testaments. For He who said, *Let us make man in our image and after our likeness*[2], was certainly speaking to some one present. But clearest of all are the Psalmist's words, *He spake and they were made; He commanded, and they were created*[3], as if the Father commanded and spake, and the Son made all things at the Father's bidding. And this Job said mystically, *Which alone spread out the heaven, and walketh upon the sea as on firm ground*[4]; signifying to those who understand that He who when present here walked upon the sea is also He who aforetime made the heavens. And again the Lord saith, *Or didst Thou take earth, and fashion clay into a living being*[5]? then afterwards, *Are the gates of death opened to Thee through fear, and did the door-keepers of hell shudder at sight of Thee*[6]? thus signifying that He who through loving-kindness descended into hell, also in the beginning made man out of clay.

24. Christ then is the Only-begotten Son of God, and Maker of the world. For *He was in the world, and the world was made by Him*; and *He came unto His own*, as the Gospel teaches us[7]. And not only of the things which are seen, but also of the things which are not seen, is Christ the Maker at the Father's bidding. For *in Him*, according to the Apostle, *were all things created that are in the heavens, and that are upon the earth, things visible and invisible, whether thrones, or dominions, or principalities, or powers; all things have been created by Him and for Him; and He is before all, and*

---

2 John xvii. 24.
3 Col. i. 16.
4 Compare Cat. vi. 13, and xv. 3: "Here let converts from the Manichees gain instruction, and no longer make those lights their gods; nor impiously think that this sun which shall be darkened is Christ."
5 The creation of the world was ascribed to Angels by the Gnostics generally. *e.g.* by Simon Magus (Irenæus, *adv. Hæres.* I. xxiii. § 2), Menander (*ibid.* § 5), Saturninus (*ibid.* xxiv. 1), Basilides (*ibid.* § 3), Carpocrates (*ibid.* xxv. 1).
6 John i. 3.
7 On the doctrine of Creation by the Son as held by Cyril, see the reference to the Introduction in the Index, *Creation*.

8 John v. 19.
9 Ib. v. 17.
1 Ib. xvii. 10.
2 Gen. i. 26.
3 Ps. cxlviii. 5.
4 Job ix. 8.
5 Ib. xxxviii. 14.
6 Ib. xxxviii. 17.
7 John i. 10, 11.

in Him all things consist[8]. Even if thou speak of the worlds, of these also Jesus Christ is the Maker by the Father's bidding. For *in these last days God spake unto us by His Son, whom He appointed heir of all things, by whom also He made the worlds*[9]. To whom be the glory, honour, might, now and ever, and world without end. Amen.

8 Col. i. 16 17.

9 Heb. i. 2.

LECTURE XII.

On the words Incarnate, and made Man. Isaiah vii. 10—14.

"*And the Lord spake again unto Ahaz, saying, Ask thee a sign, &c.:*" and "*Behold! a virgin shall conceive, and bear a son, and shall call His name Emmanuel, &c.*"

1. Nurslings of purity and disciples of chastity, raise we our hymn to the Virgin-born God[1] with lips full of purity. Deemed[2] worthy to partake of the flesh of the Spiritual Lamb[3], let us take the head together with the feet[4], the Deity being understood as the head, and the Manhood taken as the feet. Hearers of the Holy Gospels, let us listen to John the Divine[5]. For he who said, *In the beginning was the Word, and the Word was with God, and the Word was God*[6], went on to say, *and the Word was made flesh*[7]. For neither is it holy to worship the mere man, nor religious to say that He is God only without the Manhood. For if Christ is God, as indeed He is, but took not human nature upon Him, we are strangers to salvation. Let us then worship Him as God, but believe that He also was made Man. For neither is there any profit in calling Him man without Godhead, nor any salvation in refusing to confess the Manhood together with the Godhead. Let us confess the presence of Him who is both King and Physician. For Jesus the King when about to become our Physician, *girded Himself with the linen* of humanity[8], and healed that which was sick. The perfect Teacher of babes[9] became a babe among babes, that He might give wisdom to the foolish. The Bread of heaven came down on earth[1] that He might feed the hungry.

2. But the sons of the Jews by setting at nought Him that came, and looking for him who cometh in wickedness, rejected the true Messiah, and wait for the deceiver, themselves deceived; herein also the Saviour being found true, who said, *I am come in My Father's name, and ye receive Me not: but if another shall come in his own name, him ye will receive*[2]. It is well also to put a question to the Jews. Is the Prophet Esaias, who saith that Emmanuel shall be born of a virgin, true or false[3]? For if they charge him with falsehood, no wonder: for their custom is not only to charge with falsehood, but also to stone the Prophets. But if the Prophet is true, point to the Emmanuel, and say, Whether is He who is to come, for whom ye are looking, to be born of a virgin or not? For if He is not to be born of a virgin, ye accuse the Prophet of falsehood: but if in Him that is to come ye expect this, why do ye reject that which has come to pass already?

3. Let the Jews, then, be led astray, since they so will: but let the Church of God be glorified. For we receive God the Word made Man in truth, not, as heretics say[4], of the will of man and woman, but of the Virgin and the Holy Ghost[5] according to the

---

1 This passage supplies a complete answer to the suspicion of a quasi-Nestorian tendency referred to in note 6, on xi. 20. See x. 19, note 2, on the title Θεοτόκος.

2 The Present Participle (καταξιούμενοι) means that the Candidates for Baptism were already on the way to be admitted to Holy Communion. Compare Cat. i. 1, where the same Candidates are addressed as "partakers of the mysteries of Christ, as yet by calling only, but ere long by grace also."

3 Aubertin remarks on this passage that "this spiritual Lamb, consisting of head and feet, can be received only by the spiritual mouth." This explanation, however true in itself, cannot fairly be held to express fully the meaning of Cyril. See the section of the Introduction referred to in the Index, "Eucharist."

4 Ex. xii. 9: *the head with the feet.* The same figurative interpretation is given by Eusebius (*Eccl. Hist.* I. ii. § 1): "In Christ there is a twofold nature; and the one—in so far as He is thought of as God—resembles the head of the body, while the other may be compared with the feet,—in so far as He, for the sake of our salvation, put on human nature with the same passions as our own."

5 Ἰωάννῃ τῷ Θεολόγῳ. The title is given to Moses by Philo Judæus (*Vita Mos.* III. § 11), to Prophets by Eusebius (*Demostr. Evang.* ii. 9), to Apostles by Athanasius (*de Incarn.* § 10: *τῶν αὐτοῦ τοῦ Σωτῆρος θεολόγων ἀνδρῶν*), and especially to St. John, because the chief purpose of his Gospel was to set forth the Deity of Christ. See note on Revel. i. 1, in *Speaker's Commentary*, and Suicer, *Thesaurus*, Θεολόγος.

6 John i. 1. 7 Ib. i. 14. 8 Ib. xiii. 4.

9 Rom. ii. 20. 1 John vi. 32, 33, 50. 2 Ib. v. 43. Cf. 2 John 7. 3 Isa. vii. 14.

4 Carpocrates, Cerinthus, the Ebionites, &c. See Irenæus (*Hær.* I. xxv. § 1; xxvi. §§ 1, 2).

5 Dr. Swainson (*Creeds*, Chap. vii. § 7), speaking of the Creed of Cyril of Jerusalem, says that "the words *σαρκωθέντα καὶ ἐνανθρωπήσαντα* are found in it, but no reference whatever is made to the birth from the Virgin." The present passage, and that in Cat. iv. § 9, "begotten of the Holy Virgin and the Holy Ghost," seem to shew that such a clause formed part of the Creed which Cyril was expounding. The genuineness of both passages is attested by all the MSS., and Dr. Swainson was mistaken in charging the Editors of the Oxford Translation with having omitted to "mention that Touttée was himself doubtful as to the words within the brackets" [ἐκ Παρθένου καὶ Πνεύματος Ἁγίου]. The brackets are added by Dr. Swainson himself, and Touttée had no doubt of the genuineness of the words: on the contrary he believed them to be part of the Creed itself. His note is as follows: "The words *of the Virgin and Holy Ghost* I have caused to be printed in larger letters as if taken from the Symbol: although they are

Gospel, MADE MAN[6], not in seeming but in truth. And that He was truly Man made of the Virgin, wait for the proper time of instruction in this Lecture, and thou shalt receive the proofs[7]: for the error of the heretics is manifold. And some have said that He has not been born at all of a virgin[8]: others that He has been born, not of a virgin, but of a wife dwelling with a husband. Others say that the Christ is not God made Man, but a man made God[9]. For they dared to say that not He—the pre-existent Word—was made Man; but a certain man was by advancement crowned.

4. But remember thou what was said yesterday concerning His Godhead. Believe that He the Only-begotten Son of God—He Himself was again begotten of a Virgin. Believe the Evangelist John when he says, *And the Word was made flesh, and dwelt among us*[1]. For the Word is eternal, BEGOTTEN OF THE FATHER BEFORE ALL WORLDS: but the flesh He took on Him recently for our sake. Many contradict this, and say: "What cause was there so great, for God to come down into humanity? And, is it at all God's nature to hold intercourse with men? And, is it possible for a virgin to bear, without man?" Since then there is much controversy, and the battle has many forms, come, let us by the grace of Christ, and the prayers of those who are present, resolve each question.

5. And first let us inquire for what cause Jesus came down. Now mind not my argumentations, for perhaps thou mayest be misled: but unless thou receive testimony of the Prophets on each matter, believe not what I say: unless thou learn from the Holy Scriptures concerning the Virgin, and the place, the time, and the manner, *receive not testimony from man*[2]. For one who at present thus teaches may possibly be suspected: but what man of sense will suspect one that prophesied a thousand and more years beforehand? If then thou seekest the cause of Christ's coming, go back to the first book of the Scriptures. In six days God made the world: but the world was for man. The sun however resplendent with bright beams, yet was made to give light to man, yea, and all living creatures were formed to serve us: herbs and trees were created for our enjoyment. All the works of creation were good, but none of these was an image of God, save man only. The sun was formed by a mere command, but man by God's hands: *Let us make man after our image, and after our likeness*[3]. A wooden image of an earthly king is held in honour; how much more a rational image of God?

But when this the greatest of the works of creation was disporting himself in Paradise, the envy of the Devil cast him out. The enemy was rejoicing over the fall of him whom he had envied: wouldest thou have had the enemy continue to rejoice? Not daring to accost the man because of his strength, he accosted as being weaker the woman, still a virgin: for it was after the expulsion from Paradise that *Adam knew Eve his wife*[4].

6. Cain and Abel succeeded in the second generation of mankind: and Cain was the first murderer. Afterwards a deluge was poured abroad because of the great wickedness of men: fire came down from heaven upon the people of Sodom because of their transgression. After a time God chose out Israel: but Israel also turned aside, and the chosen race was wounded. For while Moses stood before God in the mount, the people were worshipping a calf instead of God. In the lifetime of Moses, the law-giver who had said, *Thou shalt not commit adultery*, a man dared to enter a place of harlotry and transgress[5]. After Moses, Prophets were sent to cure Israel: but in their healing office they lamented that they were not able to overcome the disease, so that one of them says, *Woe is me! for the godly man is perished out of the earth, and there is none that doeth right among men*[6]: and again, *They are all gone out of the way, they are together become unprofitable; there is none that doeth good, no, not one*[7]: and again, *Cursing and stealing, and adultery, and murder are poured out upon the land*[8]. *Their sons and their daughters*

wanting in the Title of this Lecture and in § 13, where the third Article of the Creed is referred to. But they are read in nearly all the Latin and Greek Symbols, and are referred to in Cat. iv. § 9."

6 ἐνανθρωπήσαντα. The word occurs in the true Nicene formula, where, as Dr. Swainson thinks, it is "scarcely ambiguous," "it is defective." Both the Verb and the Substantive ἐνανθρώπησις are constantly used by Athanasius to denote the Incarnation in a perfectly general way, without any indication of ambiguity or defect. In the Creed proposed by Eusebius of Cæsarea instead of ἐνανθρωπήσαντα we find ἐν ἀνθρώποις πολιτευσάμενον; and in the *Expositio Fidei* ascribed to Athanasius, but of somewhat doubtful authenticity, the Incarnation is described thus ἐκ τῆς ἀχράντου παρθένου Μαρίας τὸν ἡμέτερον ἀνείληφεν ἄνθρωπον Χριστὸν Ἰησοῦν. In the Apollinarian controversy the attempt was made to interpret ἐνηνθρώπησεν as meaning not that "He became Man," but that "He assumed a man," *i.e.* that "the man was first formed and then assumed" (Gregory, *Epist. ad Cledon.* quoted by Swainson, p. 83), or else merely that "He dwelt among men." But the context of the passages in which Cyril uses the word (iv. 9; xii. 3) clearly shews that he employed it in the perfectly orthodox sense which it has in the Nicene Formula and in Athanasius.

7 See below, § 21 ff. Cyril means that the direct proof cannot be given at once, because there are many errors to be set aside first. Compare the end of § 4.

8 See Cat. iv. 9, notes 3, 4.

9 Athanasius (*contra Arian. Or.* I. § 9) quotes as from Arius, *Thalia*, "Christ is not Very God, but He, as others, was made God (ἐθεοποιήθη) by participation." The Eusebians in the Confession of Faith called Macrostichos (A.D. 344) condemned this view as being held by the disciples of Paul of Samosata, "who say that after the incarnation He was by advance made God, from being made by nature a mere man." The orthodox use of the word Θεοποιεῖσθαι is seen in Athan. *de Incarnat.* § 54: αὐτὸς ἐνηνθρώπησεν, ἵνα ἡμεῖς θεοποιηθῶμεν.

1 John i. 14.

2 John v. 34. 3 Gen. i. 26. 4 Ib. iv. 1. 5 Numb. xxv. 6. 6 Micah vii. 2. 7 Ps. xiv. 3 Rom. iii. 12. 8 Hosea iv. 2.

they sacrificed unto devils[9]. *They used auguries, and enchantments, and divinations*[1]. *And again, they fastened their garments with cords, and made hangings attached to the altar*[2].

7. Very great was the wound of man's nature; *from the feet to the head there was no soundness in it; none could apply mollifying ointment, neither oil, nor bandages*[3]. Then bewailing and wearying themselves, the Prophets said, *Who shall give salvation out of Sion*[4]*?* And again, *Let Thy hand be upon the man of Thy right hand, and upon the son of man whom Thou madest strong for Thyself: so will not we go back from Thee*[5]. And another of the Prophets entreated, saying, *Bow the heavens, O Lord, and come down*[6]. The wounds of man's nature pass our healing. *They slew Thy Prophets, and cast down Thine altars*[7]. The evil is irretrievable by us, and needs thee to retrieve it.

8. The Lord heard the prayer of the Prophets. The Father disregarded not the perishing of our race; He sent forth His Son, the Lord from heaven, as healer: and one of the Prophets saith, *The Lord whom ye seek, cometh, and shall suddenly come*[8]. Whither? *The Lord* shall come *to His own temple*, where ye stoned Him. Then another of the Prophets, on hearing this, saith to him: In speaking of the salvation of God, speakest thou quietly? In preaching the good tidings of God's coming for salvation, speakest thou in secret? *O thou that bringest good tidings to Zion, get thee up into the high mountain. Speak to the cities of Judah.* What am I to speak? *Behold our God! Behold! the Lord cometh with strength*[9] *!* Again the Lord Himself saith, *Behold! I come, and I will dwell in the midst of thee, saith the Lord. And many nations shall flee unto the Lord*[1]. The Israelites rejected salvation through Me: *I come to gather all nations and tongues*[2]. For *He came to His own, and His own received Him not*[3]. Thou comest, and what dost Thou bestow on the nations? *I come to gather all nations, and I will leave on them a sign*[4]. For from My conflict upon the Cross I give to each of My soldiers a royal seal to bear upon his forehead. Another also of the Prophets said, *He bowed the heavens also, and came down; and darkness was under His feet*[5]. For His coming down from heaven was not known by men.

9. Afterwards Solomon hearing his father David speak these things, built a wondrous house, and foreseeing Him who was to come into it, said in astonishment, *Will God in very deed dwell with men on the earth*[6]*?* Yea, saith David by anticipation in the Psalm inscribed *For Solomon*, wherein is this, *He shall come down like rain into a fleece*[7]*: rain*, because of His heavenly nature, and *into a fleece*, because of His humanity. For rain, coming down into a fleece, comes down noiselessly: so that the Magi, not knowing the mystery of the Nativity, say, *Where is He that is born King of the Jews*[8]*?* and Herod being troubled inquired concerning Him who was born, and said, *Where is the Christ to be born*[9]*?*

10. But who is this that cometh down? He says in what follows, *And with the sun He endureth, and before the moon generations of generations*[1]. And again another of the Prophets saith, *Rejoice greatly, O daughter of Sion, shout, O daughter of Jerusalem. Behold! thy King cometh unto thee, just and having salvation*[2]. Kings are many: of which speakest thou, O Prophet? Give us a sign which other Kings have not. If thou say, A king clad in purple, the dignity of the apparel has been anticipated. If thou say, Guarded by spear-men, and sitting in a golden chariot, this also has been anticipated by others. Give us a sign peculiar to the King whose coming thou announcest. And the Prophet maketh answer and saith, *Behold! thy King cometh unto thee, just, and having salvation: He is meek, and riding upon an ass and a young foal*, not on a chariot. Thou hast a unique sign of the King who came. Jesus alone of kings sat upon an unyoked[3] foal, entering into Jerusalem with acclamations as a king. And when this King is come, what doth He? *Thou also by the blood of the covenant hast sent forth thy prisoners out of the pit wherein is no water*[4].

11. But He might perchance even sit upon a foal: give us rather a sign, where the King that entereth shall stand. And give the sign not far from the city, that it may not be unknown to us: and give us the sign plain before our eyes, that even when in the city we may behold the place. And the Prophet again makes answer, saying: *And His feet shall stand in that day upon the Mount of Olives which is before Jerusalem on the east*[5]. Does

---

9 Ps. cvi. 37. 1 2 Chron. xxxiii. 6.

2 Amos ii. 8: *they lay themselves down beside every altar upon clothes taken in pledge* (R.V.).

3 Isa. i. 6. 4 Ps. xiv. 7. 5 Ib. lxxx. 17, 18.

6 Ps. cxliv. 5. 7 1 Kings xix. 10. 8 Mal. iii. 1.

9 Isa. xl. 9, 10. 1 Zech. ii. 10, 11. 2 Isa. lxvi. 18.

3 John i. 11.

4 Isa. lxvi. 19, a passage interpreted by the Fathers of the sign of the Cross. Eusebius (*Demonstr. Evang.* vi. 25): "Who, on seeing that all who have believed in Christ use as a seal the symbol of salvation, would not reasonably be astonished at hearing the Lord's saying of old time, *And they shall come, and see My glory, and I will leave a sign upon them?*" Cf. Cat. iv. 14; xiii. 36.

5 Ps. xviii. 9. The "feet," interpreted allegorically, mean the Humanity, and the "darkness" the mystery of the Incarnation. See Euseb. *Demonstr. Evang.* vi. 1, § 2.

6 1 Kings viii. 27; 2 Chron. vi 18. 7 Ps. lxxii. Title, and *v.* 6. 8 Matt. ii. 2. 9 Ib. ii. 4. 1 Ps. lxxii. 5.

2 Zech. ix. 9. 3 ἀσαγῆ, a rare word, formed from σάγη, "harness." 4 Zech. ix. 11.

5 Zech. xiv. 4. "There is an excellent view from the city

any one standing within the city fail to behold the place?

12. We have two signs, and we desire to learn a third. Tell us what the Lord doth when He is come. Another Prophet saith, *Behold! our God*, and afterwards, *He will come and save us. Then the eyes of the blind shall be opened, and the ears of the deaf shall hear: then shall the lame man leap as an hart, and the tongue of the stammerers shall be distinct*[6]. But let yet another testimony be told us. Thou sayest, O Prophet, that the Lord cometh, and doeth signs such as never were: what other clear sign tellest thou? *The Lord Himself entereth into judgment with the elders of His people, and with the princes thereof*[7]. A notable sign! The Master judged by His servants, the elders, and submitting to it.

13. These things the Jews read, but hear not: for they have stopped the ears of their heart, that they may not hear. But let us believe in Jesus Christ, as having come in the flesh and *been made Man*, because we could not receive Him otherwise. For since we could not look upon or enjoy Him as He was, He became what we are, that so we might be permitted to enjoy Him. For if we cannot look full on the sun, which was made on the fourth day, could we behold God its Creator[8]? The Lord came down in fire on Mount Sinai, and the people could not bear it, but said to Moses, *Speak thou with us, and we will hear; and let not God speak to us, lest we die*[9]: and again, *For who is there of all flesh that hath heard the voice of the living God speaking out of the midst of the fire, and shall live*[1]? If to hear the voice of God speaking is a cause of death, how shall not the sight of God Himself bring death? And what wonder? Even Moses himself saith, *I exceedingly fear and quake*[2].

14. What wouldest thou then? That He who came for our salvation should become a minister of destruction because men could not bear Him? or that He should suit His grace to our measure? Daniel could not bear the vision of an Angel, and wert thou capable of the sight of the Lord of Angels? Gabriel appeared, and Daniel fell down: and of what nature or in what guise was he that appeared? *His countenance was like lightning*[3]; not like the sun: *and his eyes as lamps of fire*, not as a furnace of fire: *and the voice of his words as the voice of a multitude*, not as the voice of twelve legions of angels; nevertheless the Prophet fell down. And the Angel cometh unto him, saying, *Fear not, Daniel, stand upright: be of good courage, thy words are heard*[4]. And Daniel says, *I stood up trembling*[5]: and not even so did he make answer, until the likeness of a man's hand touched him. And when he that appeared was changed into the appearance of a man, then Daniel spake: and what saith he? *O my Lord, at the vision of Thee my inward parts were turned within me, and no strength remaineth in me, neither is there breath left in me*[6]. If an Angel appearing took away the Prophet's voice and strength, would the appearance of God have allowed him to breathe? And until *there touched me as it were a vision of a man*[7], saith the Scripture, Daniel took not courage. So then after trial shewn of our weakness, the Lord assumed that which man required: for since man required to hear from one of like countenance, the Saviour took on Him the nature of like affections, that men might be the more easily instructed.

15. Learn also another cause. Christ came that He might be baptized, and might sanctify Baptism: He came that He might work wonders, walking upon the waters of the sea. Since then before His appearance in flesh, *the sea saw Him and fled, and Jordan was turned back*[8], the Lord took to Himself His body, that the sea might endure the sight, and Jordan receive Him without fear. This then is one cause; but there is also a second. Through Eve yet virgin came death; through a virgin, or rather from a virgin, must the Life appear: that as the serpent beguiled the one, so to the other Gabriel might bring good tidings[9]. Men forsook God, and made carved images of men. Since therefore an image of man was falsely worshipped as God, God became truly Man, that the falsehood might be done away. The Devil had used the flesh as an instrument against us; and Paul knowing this, saith, *But I see another law in my members warring against the law of my mind, and bringing me into captivity*[1], and the rest. By the very same weapons, therefore, wherewith the Devil used to vanquish us, have we been saved. The Lord took on Him from us our likeness, that He might save man's nature: He took our likeness, that He might give greater grace to that which lacked; that sinful humanity might become partaker of God. *For where sin abounded, grace did much more abound*[2]. It

of the Mount of Olives which stands up over against it, especially from the height of Golgotha where Cyril was delivering his Lectures" (Cleopas). 6 Isa. xxxv. 4—6. 7 Ib. iii. 14.

8 Cf. Epist. Barnab. § 13: "For had He not come in flesh, how could we men have been safe in beholding Him? For in beholding the Sun, which being the work of His hands shall cease to be, men have no strength to fix their eyes upon him."

9 Exod. xx. 19. 1 Deut. v. 26. 2 Heb. xii. 21.

3 Dan. x. 6.

4 Dan. x. 12. 5 Ib. x. 11.

6 Ib. x. 16, 17. 7 Ib. x. 18. 8 Ps. cxiv. 3.

9 Justin M. (*Tryph.* § 100): "Eve, when she was a virgin and undefiled, having conceived the word of the serpent, brought forth disobedience and death: but the Virgin Mary received faith and joy, when the Angel Gabriel announced the good tidings to her."

1 Rom. vii 23. 2 Ib. v. 20.

behoved the Lord to suffer for us; but if the Devil had known Him, he would not have dared to approach Him. *For had they known it, they would not have crucified the Lord of Glory*[3]. His body therefore was made a bait to death, that the dragon[4], hoping to devour it, might disgorge those also who had been already devoured[5]. For *Death prevailed and devoured;* and again, *God wiped away every tear from off every face*[6].

16. Was it without reason that Christ was made Man? Are our teachings ingenious phrases and human subtleties? Are not the Holy Scriptures our salvation? Are not the predictions of the Prophets? Keep then, I pray thee, this deposit[7] undisturbed, and let none remove thee: believe that God became Man. But though it has been proved possible for Him to be made Man, yet if the Jews still disbelieve, let us hold this forth to them: What strange thing do we announce in saying that God was made Man, when yourselves say that Abraham received the Lord as a guest[8]? What strange thing do we announce, when Jacob says, *For I have seen God face to face, and my life is preserved*[9]? The Lord, who ate with Abraham, ate also with us. What strange thing then do we announce? Nay more, we produce two witnesses, those who stood before the Lord on Mount Sinai: Moses was in a *clift of the rock*[1], and Elias was once in a clift of the rock[2]: they being present with Him at His Transfiguration on Mount Tabor, *spake* to the Disciples *of His decease which He should accomplish at Jerusalem*[3]. But, as I said before, it has been proved possible for Him to be made man: and the rest of the proofs may be left for the studious to collect.

17. My statement, however, promised to declare[4] also the time of the Saviour's advent, and the place: and I must not go away convicted of falsehood, but rather send away the Church's novices[5] well assured. Let us therefore inquire the time when our Lord came: because His coming is recent, and is disputed; and because *Christ Jesus is the same yesterday, and to-day, and for ever*[6]. Moses then, the prophet, saith, *A Prophet shall the Lord your God raise up unto you of your brethren, like unto me*[7]: but let that "*like unto me*" be reserved awhile to be examined in its proper place[8]. But when cometh this Prophet that is expected? Recur, he says, to what has been written by me: examine carefully Jacob's prophecy addressed to Judah: *Judah, thee may thy brethren praise*, and afterwards, not to quote the whole, *A prince shall not fail out of Judah, nor a ruler from his loins, until He come, for whom it is reserved; and He is the expectation*, not of the Jews but *of the Gentiles*[9]. He gave, therefore, as a sign of Christ's advent the cessation of the Jewish rule. If they are not now under the Romans, the Christ is not yet come: if they still have a prince of the race of Judah and of David[1], he is not yet come that was expected. For I am ashamed to tell of their recent doings concerning those who are now called Patriarchs[2] among them, and what their descent is, and who their mother: but I leave it to those who know. But He that cometh as *the expectation of the Gentiles*, what further sign then hath He? He says next, *Binding his foal unto the vine*[3]. Thou seest that foal which was clearly announced by Zachariah[4].

18. But again thou askest yet another testimony of the time. *The* LORD *said unto Me, Thou art My Son; this day have I begotten Thee:* and a few words further on, *Thou shalt rule them with a rod of iron*[5]. I have said before that the kingdom of the Romans is clearly called *a rod of iron;* but what is wanting concerning this let us further call to mind out of Daniel. For in relating and interpreting to Nebuchadnezzar the image of the statue, he tells also his whole vision concerning it: and that a stone cut out of a mountain without hands, that is, not set up by human contrivance, should overpower the whole world: and he speaks most clearly thus; *And in the days of*

---

3 1 Cor. ii. 8.

4 Death is here called "the dragon," as in xiv. 17 he is called "the invisible whale," in allusion to the case of Jonah.

5 On Christ's descent into Hades compare iv. 11; xiv. 19; and Eusebius (*Dem. Evang.* x. 50). and Athanasius (*c. Arian. Or.* iii. 56): "The Lord, at Whom the keepers of hell's gates shuddered and set open hell. The Lord, Whom death as a dragon flees."

6 Isa. xxv. 8. The first clause, *He hath swallowed up death for ever* (R V.), is mistranslated in the Septuagint.

7 *ταύτην τὴν παρακαταθήκην*. 1 Tim. vi. 20; 2 Tim. i. 14.

8 Gen. xviii. 1 ff. 9 Ib. xxxii. 30.

1 Ex. xxxiii. 22. 2 1 Kings xix. 8

3 Luke ix. 30, 31. On the tradition that Mt. Tabor was the place of the Transfiguration, accepted by S. Jerome and other Fathers, compare Lightfoot (*Hor. Hebr.* in Marc. ix. 2).

4 Cat. xii. 5. For *εὑρεῖν* the recent Editors with MSS. A.R.C. and Grodecq. have *ἐρεῖν*. 5 *νεήλυδας*.

6 Heb. xiii. 8. Cyril is supposed to refer to two objections to the Incarnation, one founded on the lateness of Christ's coming, the other on the Divine immutability. But the meaning of the passage is not clear, and the construction of the second sentence is incomplete.

7 Deut. xviii. 15; Acts vii. 37.

8 *ἐξεταζόμενον*, a clear instance of the Gerundive, or quasi-Future, sense of the Present Participle, common in Cyril. "This intention is not fulfilled in the sequel of these Lectures" (R.W.C.).

9 Gen. xlix. 8, 10.

1 According to Cyril (§ 19, below) and other Fathers, the continuance of Jewish rulers ceased on the accession of Herod an Idumean. Compare Justin M. (*Tryphon.* §§ 52, 120); Eusebius (*Demonstr. Evang.* VIII. 1). On modern interpretations of the passage see Delitzsch (*New Commentary on Genesis*), Briggs (*Messianic Prophecy*, p. 93), Cheyne (*Isaiah*, Vol. II. p. 189), Driver (*Journal of Philology*, No. 27, 1885).

2 A full and interesting account of the Jewish Patriarchs of the West established at Tiberias from the time of Antoninus Pius till the close of the 4th century is contained in Dean Milman's *History of the Jews*, Vol. III. Compare Epiphanius (*Hæres.* xxx. § 3 ff.). 3 Gen. xlix. 11.

4 Zechar. ix. 9, quoted above, § 10.

5 Ps. ii. 7, 9. The passage is interpreted by Cyril (xi. 5) of the eternal generation of the Son: here it refers to His Incarnation, or perhaps is meant only to identify the Son of God with him who "shall rule with a rod of iron."

those kingdoms the God of heaven shall set up a kingdom, which shall never be destroyed, and His kingdom shall not be left to another people[6].

19. But we seek still more clearly the proof of the time of His coming. For man being hard to persuade, unless he gets the very years for a clear calculation, does not believe what is stated. What then is the season, and what the manner of the time? It is when, on the failure of the kings descended from Judah, Herod a foreigner succeeds to the kingdom? The Angel, therefore, who converses with Daniel says, and do thou now mark the words, *And thou shalt know and understand: From the going forth of the word for making answer*[7], *and for the building of Jerusalem, until Messiah the Prince are seven weeks and three score and two weeks*[8]. Now three score and nine weeks of years contain four hundred and eighty-three years. He said, therefore, that after the building of Jerusalem, four hundred and eighty-three years having passed, and the rulers having failed, then cometh a certain king of another race, in whose time the Christ is to be born. Now Darius the Mede[9] built the city in the sixth year of his own reign, and first year of the 66th Olympiad according to the Greeks. Olympiad is the name among the Greeks of the games celebrated after four years, because of the day which in every four years of the sun's courses is made up of the three[1] (supernumerary) hours in each year. And Herod is king in the 186th Olympiad, in the 4th year thereof. Now from the 66th to the 186th Olympiad there are 120 Olympiads intervening, and a little over. So then the 120 Olympiads make up 480 years: for the other three years remaining are perhaps taken up in the interval between the first and fourth years. And there thou hast the proof according to the Scripture which saith, *From the going forth of the word that Jerusalem be restored and built until Messiah the Prince are seven weeks and sixty-two weeks.* Of the times, therefore, thou hast for the present this proof, although there are also other different interpretations concerning the aforesaid weeks of years in Daniel.

20. But now hear the place of the promise, as Micah says, *And thou, Bethlehem, house of Ephrathah, art thou little to be among the thousands of Judah? For out of thee shall come forth unto Me a ruler, to be governor in Israel: and His goings forth are from the beginning, from the days of eternity*[2]. But assuredly as to the places, thou being an inhabitant of Jerusalem, knowest also beforehand what is written in the hundred and thirty-first psalm. *Lo! we heard of it at Ephrathah, we found it in the plains of the wood*[3]. For a few years ago the place was woody[4]. Again thou hast heard Habakkuk say to the Lord, *When the years draw nigh, thou shalt be made known, when the time is come, thou shalt be shewn*[5]. And what is the sign, O Prophet, of the Lord's coming? And presently he saith, *In the midst of two lives shalt thou be known*[6], plainly saying this to the Lord, "Having come in the flesh thou livest and diest, and after rising from the dead thou livest again." Further, from what part of the region round Jerusalem cometh He? From east, or west, or north, or south? Tell us exactly. And he makes answer most plainly and says, *God shall come from Teman*[7] (now Teman is by interpretation 'south') *and the Holy One from Mount Paran*[8], *shady, woody:* what the Psalmist

---

6 Dan. ii. 44.

7 Sept. τοῦ ἀποκριθῆναι, a frequent meaning of the Hebrew לְהָשִׁיב, by which the Greek Translators understood the answer of Darius to the letter of Tatnai and his companions. Both A.V. and R.V. render the word "to restore."

8 Dan. ix. 25.

9 Darius the Mede (Dan. v. 31) succeeded Belshazzar as king in Babylon B.C. 538, the date assigned in Dan. ix. 1 to the prophecy of the 70 years. But "Darius the king" in whose 6th year (B.C. 516) the Temple was finished (Ezra vi. 15) was Darius Hystaspis, king of Persia, whom Cyril here confounds with "Darius the Mede." He also fails to distinguish the rebuilding of the Temple, B.C. 516, from the rebuilding of the City by permission of Artaxerxes Longimanus, B.C. 444 (*Nehemiah*, ii. 1).

1 In speaking of three supernumerary hours in the year instead of nearly six, Cyril seems to follow the division of the diurnal period into twelve parts, not twenty-four. The Jews had derived this division either from the Egyptians, or more probably from the Babylonians: see Herodotus, II. 109.

2 Micah v. 2, quoted also in Cat. xi. 20, where see note.

3 Ps. cxxxii. 6. The Psalmist refers to the recovery of the Ark, but Cyril interprets the passage mystically of Christ, and the place of His Nativity.

4 The Benedictine Editor thinks that in calling the place "woody" Cyril refers to a grove planted by Hadrian in honour of Adonis, which had been destroyed about sixteen years before, when Helena built the Church at Bethlehem: see Eusebius, *Life of Constantine*, III. 43. But Cyril evidently means that the wood of which the Psalmist speaks had remained till a few years before. Ephrâthah is the ancient name of Bethlehem (Gen. xxxv. 19; xlviii. 7), and by "the fields of the wood" is probably meant Kirjath-Jearim, "the city of woods," where the Ark was found by David (2 Sam. vi. 2; 1 Chron. xiii. 6).

5 Hab. iii. 2: (R.V.) *O Lord, revive Thy work in the midst of the years, in the midst of the years make it known.* The Septuagint gives a different sense: *In the midst of two lives* (or, *living beings*) *shalt Thou be known: when the years draw nigh Thou shalt be recognised: when the time is come, Thou shalt be shewn.* The two latter clauses seem to be different renderings of the same Hebrew words.

6 ἑξῆς. This clause comes before the preceding quotation: Cyril misplaces them. In the Vatican and other MSS. of the Sept. and in some Fathers ζώων ("living creatures") is found in place of ζωῶν "lives;" but the latter reading is evidently required by the interpretation which follows in Cyril. Origen (*de Principiis*, I. 4), who recognises both readings ("In medio vel duorum animalium, vel duarum vitarum, cognosceris,") interprets the "two living beings" of the Son and the Spirit. Eusebius (*Demonstr. Evang.* VI. 15) observes that ζωων is to be read as perispomenon from the Singular ζωή, and interprets it of Christ's life with God, and life on earth. Theodoret says, in commenting on the passage, "To me it seems that the Prophet means not "living beings" (ζῶα) but "lives" (ζωάς), the present life, and that which is to come, between which is the appearance of the Righteous Judge."

7 Hab. iii. 3. Cyril interprets the word Θαιμάν (Heb. תֵּימָן) as a common Noun meaning "South," and the Vulgate has here "ab Austro veniet." The prophecy is thus referred to Bethlehem, as lying to the South of Jerusalem. Eusebius (*Dem. Evang.* VI. 15) mentions this as the rendering of Theodotion in his Greek Version, about 180 A.D. As a proper name Teman denotes a district and town in the southern part of Idumea, so called from a grandson of Esau (Gen. xxxvi. 11, 15, 42; Jer. xlix. 7, 20; Ezek. xxv. 13; Amos i. 12; Obad. 9).

8 The following note is slightly abridged from the Edition

spake in like words, *We found it in the plains of the wood.*

21. We ask further, of whom cometh He and how? And this Esaias tells us: *Behold! the virgin shall conceive in her womb, and shall bring forth a Son, and they shall call His name Emmanuel*[9]. This the Jews contradict, for of old it is their wont wickedly to oppose the truth: and they say that it is not written "the virgin," but "the damsel." But though I assent to what they say, even so I find the truth. For we must ask them, If a virgin be forced, when does she cry out and call for helpers, after or before the outrage? If, therefore, the Scripture elsewhere says, *The betrothed damsel cried, and there was none to save her*[1], doth it not speak of a virgin?

But that you may learn more plainly that even a virgin is called in Holy Scripture a "damsel," hear the Book of the Kings, speaking of Abishag the Shunamite, *And the damsel was very fair*[2]*:* for that as a virgin she was chosen and brought to David is admitted.

22. But the Jews say again, This was said to Ahaz in reference to Hezekiah. Well, then, let us read the Scripture: *Ask thee a sign of the Lord thy God, in the depth or in the height*[3]. And the sign certainly must be something astonishing. For the water from the rock was a sign, the sea divided, the sun turning back, and the like. But in what I am going to mention there is still more manifest refutation of the Jews. (I know that I am speaking at much length, and that my hearers are wearied: but bear with the fulness of my statements, because it is for Christ's sake these questions are moved, and they concern no ordinary matters.) Now as Isaiah spake this in the reign of Ahaz, and Ahaz reigned only sixteen years, and the prophecy was spoken to him within these years, the objection of the Jews is refuted by the fact that the succeeding king, Hezekiah, son of Ahaz, was twenty-five years old when he began to reign: for as the prophecy is confined within sixteen years, he must have been begotten of Ahaz full nine years before the prophecy. What need then was there to utter the prophecy concerning one who had been already begotten even before the reign of his father Ahaz[4]? For he said not, *hath conceived*, but "*the virgin shall conceive*," speaking as with foreknowledge[5].

23. We know then for certain that the Lord was to be born of a Virgin, but we have to shew of what family the Virgin was. *The Lord sware in truth unto David, and will not set it aside. Of the fruit of thy body will I set upon thy throne*[6]*:* and again, *His seed will I establish for ever, and his throne as the days of heaven*[7]. And afterwards, *Once have I sworn by My holiness that I will not lie unto David. His seed shall endure for ever, and his throne as the sun before Me, and as the moon established for ever*[8]. Thou seest that the discourse is of Christ, not of Solomon. For Solomon's throne endured not as the sun. But if any deny this, because Christ sat not on David's throne of wood, we will bring forward that saying, *The Scribes and the Pharisees sit in Moses' seat*[9]*:* for it signifies not his wooden seat, but the authority of his teaching. In like manner then I would have you seek for David's throne not the throne of wood, but the kingdom itself. Take, too, as my witnesses the children who cried aloud, *Hosanna to the Son of David*[1], *blessed is the King of Israel*[2]. And the blind men also say, *Son of David, have mercy on us*[3]. Gabriel too testifies plainly to Mary, saying, *And the Lord God shall give unto Him the throne of His father David*[4]. Paul also saith, *Remember Jesus Christ raised from the dead, of the seed of David, according to my Gospel*[5]*:* and in the beginning of the Epistle to the Romans he saith, *Which was made of the seed of David according to the flesh*[6]. Receive thou therefore Him that was born of David, believing the prophecy which saith, *And in that day there shall be a root of Jesse, and He that shall rise to rule over the Gentiles: in Him shall the Gentiles trust*[7].

24. But the Jews are much troubled at these things. This also Isaiah foreknew, saying, *And they shall wish that they had been burnt with fire: for unto us a child is born* (not unto them), *unto us a Son is given*[8]. Mark thou

---

of Alexandrides of Jerusalem. "Previous Editions read ἐξ ὄρους Φαρὰν κατασκίου δασέος. This reading is found in Cod. Vat. and other MSS. of the Septuagint, but Φαράν is omitted in the Aldine and many other copies nor was it read in the MSS. of the Sept. in Jerome's time, as is clear from his comments on the passage. In the MSS. of Cyril, Ottob. R.C.V. Monac. I. and II. it is wanting. Paran is the name of the desert towards the S. of Palestine lying between it and Egypt (Gen. xxi. 21; Num. i. 12). There was also a Mount Paran (Deut. xxxiii. 2). But since Cyril applies the prophecy to Bethlehem, and the "shady thickly-wooded mountain" of Habakkuk is identified with "the plains of the wood" of David, we may safely conclude that Cyril did not read Φαράν in his copies of the Septuagint, nor write it in his Lecture: but the reading crept in from the later copyists, accustomed to the reading Φαράν in the Septuagint.'

9 Isa. vii. 14. The objection of the Jews that the Hebrew word "Almah" means "a young woman," whether married or not, is mentioned by Justin M. (*Tryph.* 43, 67, 71), and by Eusebius (*Dem. Evang.* VII. i. 315).

1 Deut. xxii. 27.

2 1 Kings i. 4. Cyril's argument is fully justified by the actual usage of "Almah," which certainly refers to unmarried women in *Gen.* xxiv. 43; *Ex.* ii. 8; *Cant.* i. 3. The same is probably the meaning in Ps. lxviii. 25: "in the midst were the damsels playing with the timbrels." There is no passage in which the word can be shewn to mean a married woman.

3 Isa. vii. 11.

4 Compare Justin M. (*Tryph.* § 77), Euseb. (*Demonstr. Evang.* L. VII. c. i. 317).

5 In the Hebrew the word used is a Participle, and describes what Isaiah sees in a prophetic vision; "*Behold, the damsel—with child.*"

6 Ps. cxxxii. 11. 7 Ib lxxxix. 22. 8 *vv.* 35—37. 9 Matt. xxiii. 2. 1 Ib. xxi. 9. 2 Joh. xii. 13. 3 Matt. xx. 30. 4 Luke i. 32 5 2 Tim. ii. 8. 6 Rom. i. 3. 7 Is. xi. 10; Rom. xv. 12. 8 Isa. ix. 5,

that at first He was the Son of God, then was given to us. And a little after he says, *And of His peace there is no bound*[9]. The Romans have bounds: of the kingdom of the Son of God there is no bound. The Persians and the Medes have bounds, but the Son has no bound. Then next, *upon the throne of David, and upon his kingdom to order it.* The Holy Virgin, therefore, is from David.

25. For it became Him who is most pure, and a teacher of purity, to have come forth from a pure bride-chamber. For if he who well fulfils the office of a priest of Jesus abstains from a wife, how should Jesus Himself be born of man and woman? *For thou*, saith He in the Psalms, *art He that took Me out of the womb*[1]. Mark that carefully, *He that took Me out of the womb*, signifying that He was begotten without man, being taken from a virgin's womb and flesh. For the manner is different with those who are begotten according to the course of marriage.

26. And from such members He is not ashamed to assume flesh, who is the framer of those very members. But then who telleth us this? The Lord saith unto Jeremiah: *Before I formed thee in the belly, I knew thee: and before thou camest forth out of the womb, I sanctified thee*[2]. If, then, in fashioning man He was not ashamed of the contact, was He ashamed in fashioning for His own sake the holy Flesh, the veil of His Godhead? It is God who even now creates the children in the womb, as it is written in Job, *Hast thou not poured me out as milk, and curdled me like cheese? Thou hast clothed me with skin and flesh, and hast knit me together with bones and sinews*[3]. There is nothing polluted in the human frame, except a man defile this with fornication and adultery. He who formed Adam formed Eve also, and male and female were formed by God's hands. None of the members of the body as formed from the beginning is polluted. Let the mouths of all heretics be stopped who slander their bodies, or rather Him who formed them. But let us remember Paul's saying, *Know ye not that your bodies are the temples of the Holy Ghost which is in you*[4]? And again the Prophet hath spoken before in the person of Jesus, *My flesh is from them*[5]: and in another place it is written, *Therefore will He give them up, until the time that she bringeth forth*[6]. And what is the sign? He tells us in what follows, *She shall bring forth, and the remnant of their brethren shall return.* And what are the nuptial pledges of the Virgin, the holy bride? *And I will betroth thee unto Me in faithfulness*[7]. And Elizabeth, talking with Mary, speaks in like manner: *And blessed is she that believed; for there shall be a performance of those things which were told her from the Lord*[8].

27. But both Greeks and Jews harass us and say that it was impossible for the Christ to be born of a virgin. As for the Greeks we will stop their mouths from their own fables. For ye who say that stones being thrown were changed into men[9], how say ye that it is imposssible for a virgin to bring forth? Ye who fable that a daughter was born from the brain[1], how say ye that it is impossible for a son to have been born from a virgin's womb? Ye who falsely say that Dionysus was born from the thigh of your Zeus[2], how set ye at nought our truth? I know that I am speaking of things unworthy of the present audience: but in order that thou in due season mayest rebuke the Greeks, we have brought these things forward answering them from their own fables.

28. But those of the circumcision meet thou with this question: Whether is harder, for an aged woman, barren and past age, to bear, or for a virgin in the prime of youth to conceive? Sarah was barren, and though it had ceased to be with her after the manner of women, yet, contrary to nature, she bore a child. If, then, it is against nature for a barren woman to conceive, and also for a virgin, either, therefore, reject both, or accept both. For it is the same God[3] who both wrought the one and appointed the other. For thou wilt not dare to say that it was possible for God in that former case, and impossible in this latter. And again: how is it natural for a man's hand to be changed in a single hour into a different appearance and restored again? How then was the hand of Moses made white as snow, and at once restored again? But thou sayest that God's will made the change. In that case God's will has the power, and has it then no power in this case? That moreover was a sign concerning the Egyptians only, but this was a sign given to the whole world. But whether is the more difficult, O ye Jews? For a virgin to bear, or for a rod to be quickened into a living creature? Ye confess that in the case of Moses a perfectly straight rod became

9 *v.* 7. 1 Ps. xxii. 9. 2 Jer. i. 5.
3 Job x. 10, 11. 4 1 Cor. vi. 19.
5 Hos. ix. 12. R.V. *Woe also to them, when I depart from them.* The Seventy mistook בְּשׂוּרִי, "at my departure," for בְּשָׂרִי, "my flesh.' 6 Mic v. 3

7 Hos. ii. 20. 8 Luke i. 45.
9 See the story of Pyrrha and Deucalion in Pindar, *Ol.* ix. 60: ἄτερ δ' εὐνᾶς κτησάσθαν λίθινον γόνον, and in Ovid. *Metam.* i. 260 ff.
1 Athena was said to have sprung armed from the head of Zeus: Pindar, *Ol.* vii. 65: κορυφὰν κατ' ἄκραν ἀνορούσαισ' ἀλάλαξεν ὑπερμάκει βοᾷ. Cf. Hes. *Theog.* 924.
2 Eurip. *Bacchae.* 295; Ovid. *Metam.* iv. 11.
3 Codd. Mon. i, A: ὁ γὰρ αὐτὸς Θεός. Bened. ὁ γὰρ Θεὸς αὐτός.

like a serpent, and was terrible to him who cast it down, and he who before held the rod fast, fled from it as from a serpent; for a serpent in truth it was: but he fled not because he feared that which he held, but because he dreaded Him that had changed it. A rod had teeth and eyes like a serpent: do then seeing eyes grow out of a rod, and cannot a child be born of a virgin's womb, if God wills? For I say nothing of the fact that Aaron's rod also produced in a single night what other trees produce in several years. For who knows not that a rod, after losing its bark, will never sprout, not even if it be planted in the midst of rivers? But since God is not dependent on the nature of trees, but is the Creator of their natures, the unfruitful, and dry, and barkless rod budded, and blossomed, and bare almonds. He, then, who for the sake of the typical high-priest gave fruit supernaturally to the rod, would He not for the sake of the true High-Priest grant to the Virgin to bear a child?

29. These are excellent suggestions of the narratives: but the Jews still contradict, and do not yield to the statements concerning the rod, unless they may be persuaded by similar strange and supernatural births. Question them, therefore, in this way: of whom in the beginning was Eve begotten? What mother conceived her the motherless? But the Scripture saith that she was born out of Adam's side. Is Eve then born out of a man's side without a mother, and is a child not to be born without a father, of a virgin's womb? This debt of gratitude was due to men from womankind: for Eve was begotten of Adam, and not conceived of a mother, but as it were brought forth of man alone. Mary, therefore, paid the debt of gratitude, when not by man but of herself alone in an immaculate way she conceived of the Holy Ghost by the power of God.

30. But let us take what is yet a greater wonder than this. For that of bodies bodies should be conceived, even if wonderful, is nevertheless possible: but that the dust of the earth should become a man, this is more wonderful. That clay moulded together should assume the coats and splendours of the eyes, this is more wonderful. That out of dust of uniform appearance should be produced both the firmness of bones, and the softness of lungs, and other different kinds of members, this is wonderful. That clay should be animated and travel round the world self-moved, and should build houses, this is wonderful. That clay should teach, and talk, and act as carpenter, and as king, this is wonderful. Whence, then, O ye most ignorant Jews, was Adam made? Did not God take dust from the earth, and fashion this wonderful frame? Is then clay changed into an eye, and cannot a virgin bear a son. Does that which for men is more impossible take place, and is that which is possible never to occur?

31. Let us remember these things, brethren: let us use these weapons in our defence. Let us not endure those heretics who teach Christ's coming as a phantom. Let us abhor those also who say that the Saviour's birth was of husband and wife; who have dared to say that He was the child of Joseph and Mary, because it is written, *And he took unto him his wife*[4]. For let us remember Jacob, who before he received Rachel, said to Laban, *Give me my wife*[5]. For as she before the wedded state, merely because there was a promise, was called the wife of Jacob, so also Mary, because she had been betrothed, was called the wife of Joseph. Mark also the accuracy of the Gospel, saying, *And in the sixth month the Angel Gabriel was sent from God unto a city of Galilee, named Nazareth, to a virgin espoused to a man whose name was Joseph*[6], and so forth. And again when the census took place, and Joseph went up to enrol himself, what saith the Scripture? *And Joseph also went up from Galilee, to enrol himself with Mary who was espoused to him, being great with child*[7]. For though she was with child, yet it said not "with his wife," but with her *who was espoused to him*. For *God sent forth His Son*, says Paul, not made of a man and a woman, but *made of a woman*[8] only, that is of a virgin. For that the virgin also is called a woman, we shewed before[9]. For He who makes souls virgin, was born of a Virgin.

32. But thou wonderest at the event: even she herself who bare him wondered at this. For she saith to Gabriel, *How shall this be to me, since I know not a man?* But he says, *The Holy Ghost shall come upon thee, and the power of the Highest shall overshadow thee: wherefore also the holy thing which is to be born shall be called the Son of God*[1]. Immaculate and undefiled was His generation: for where the Holy Spirit breathes, there all pollution is taken away: undefiled from the Virgin was the incarnate generation of the Only-begotten. And if the heretics gainsay the truth, the Holy Ghost shall convict them: that overshadowing power of the Highest shall wax wroth: Gabriel shall stand face to face against them in the day of judgment: the place of the manger, which received the Lord, shall put them to shame. The shepherds, who then received the good tidings, shall bear witness; and the host of the Angels who sang praises and hymns, and said,

4 Matt. i. 24. 5 Gen. xxix. 21. 6 Luke i. 26, 27. 7 Ib. ii. 4, 5. 8 Gal. iv. 4. 9 See above, § 21. 1 Luke i. 34, 35.

Glory to God in the highest, and on earth peace among men of His good pleasure[2]*:* the Temple into which He was then carried up on the fortieth day: the pairs of turtle-doves, which were offered on His behalf[3]: and Symeon who then took Him up in his arms, and Anna the prophetess who was present.

33. Since God then beareth witness, and the Holy Ghost joins in the witness, and Christ says, *Why do ye seek to kill me, a man who has told you the truth*[4]*?* let the heretics be silenced who speak against His humanity, for they speak against Him, who saith, *Handle me, and see; for a spirit hath not flesh and bones, as ye see me have*[5]. Adored be the Lord the Virgin-born, and let Virgins acknowledge the crown of their own state: let the order also of Solitaries acknowledge the glory of chastity; for we men are not deprived of the dignity of chastity. In the Virgin's womb the Saviour's period of nine months was passed: but the Lord was for thirty and three years a man: so that if a virgin glories[6] because of the nine months, much more we because of the many years.

34. But let us all by God's grace run the race of chastity, *young men and maidens, old men and children*[7]*;* not going after wantonness, but praising the name of Christ. Let us not be ignorant of the glory of chastity: for its crown is angelic, and its excellence above man. Let us be chary of our bodies which are to shine as the sun: let us not for short pleasure defile so great, so noble a body: for short and momentary is the sin, but the shame for many years and for ever. Angels walking upon earth are they who practise chastity: the Virgins have their portion with Mary the Virgin. Let all vain ornament be banished, and every hurtful glance, and all wanton gait, and every flowing robe, and perfume enticing to pleasure. But in all for perfume let there be the prayer of sweet odour, and the practice[8] of good works, and the sanctification of our bodies: that the Virgin-born Lord may say even of us, both men who live in chastity and women who wear the crown, *I will dwell in them; and walk in them, and I will be their God, and they shall be My people*[9]. To whom be the glory for ever and ever. Amen.

2 Luke ii. 14.

3 Ib. ii. 24. In Lev. xii. 8 one pair only of turtles is prescribed, to be offered for the mother, not for the child. But the reading τὰ ζεύγη in Cyril is confirmed by that in St. Luke, τοῦ καθαρισμοῦ αὐτῶν. See the authorities in Tischendorf.

4 John vii. 19; viii. 40.

5 Luke xxiv. 39.

6 σεμνύνεται. Rivet, misled by a double error in the old Latin version, "veneratur," accused Cyril of approving the worship of the Virgin Mary.

7 Ps. cxlviii. 12.

8 ἡ τῶν ἀγαθῶν πρᾶξις, Cod. A.

9 2 Cor. vi. 16.

LECTURE XIII.

On the Words, Crucified and Buried.

Isaiah liii. 1, 7.

Who hath believed our report? and to whom is the arm of the Lord revealed? . . . He **is** *brought as a lamb to the slaughter, &c.*

1. Every deed of Christ is a cause of glorying to the Catholic Church, but her greatest of all glorying is in the Cross; and knowing this, Paul says, *But God forbid that I should glory, save in the Cross of Christ*[1]. For wondrous indeed it was, that one who was blind from his birth should receive sight in Siloam[2]; but what is this compared with the blind of the whole world? A great thing it was, and passing nature, for Lazarus to rise again on the fourth day; but the grace extended to him alone, and what was it compared with the dead in sins throughout the world? Marvellous it was, that five loaves should pour forth food for the five thousand; but what is that to those who are famishing in ignorance through all the world? It was marvellous that she should have been loosed who had been bound by Satan eighteen years: yet what is this to all of us, who were fast bound in the chains of our sins? But the glory of the Cross led those who were blind through ignorance into light, loosed all who were held fast by sin, and ransomed the whole world of mankind.

2. And wonder not that the whole world was ransomed; for it was no mere man, but the only-begotten Son of God, who died on its behalf. Moreover one man's sin, even Adam's, had power to bring death to the world; but *if by the trespass of the one death reigned* over the world, how shall not life much rather reign *by the righteousness of the One*[3]*?* And if because of the tree of food they were then cast out of paradise, shall not believers now more easily enter into paradise because of the Tree of Jesus? If the first man formed out of the earth brought in universal death, shall not He who formed him out of the earth bring in eternal life, being Himself the Life? If Phinees, when he waxed zealous and slew the evil-doer, stayed the wrath of God, shall not Jesus, who slew not another, but *gave up Himself for a ransom*[4], put away the wrath which is against mankind?

3. Let us then not be ashamed of the Cross of our Saviour, but rather glory in it. *For the word of the Cross is unto Jews a stumbling-block, and unto Gentiles foolishness*, but to us salvation: and *to them that are perishing it is foolishness, but unto us which are being saved it is the power of God*[5]. For it was not a mere man who died for us, as I said before, but the Son of God, God made man. Further; if the lamb under Moses drove the destroyer[6] far away, did not much rather the *Lamb of God, which taketh away the sin of the world*[7], deliver us from our sins? The blood of a silly sheep gave salvation; and shall not the Blood of the Only-begotten much rather save? If any disbelieve the power of the Crucified, let him ask the devils; if any believe not words, let him believe what he sees. Many have been crucified throughout the world, but by none of these are the devils scared; but when they see even the Sign of the Cross of Christ, who was crucified for us, they shudder[8]. For those men died for their own sins, but Christ for the sins of others; for He *did no sin, neither was guile found in His mouth*[9]. It is not Peter who says this, for then we might suspect that he was partial to his Teacher; but it is Esaias who says it, who was not indeed present with Him in the flesh, but in the Spirit foresaw His coming in the flesh. Yet why now bring the Prophet only as a witness? take for a witness Pilate himself, who gave sentence upon Him, saying, *I find no fault in this Man*[1]*:* and when he gave Him up, and had washed his

---

1 Gal. vi. 14.
2 Cf. Athanas. (*de Incarn.* § 18, 49).
3 Rom. v. 17, 18.

4 1 Tim. ii. 6.
5 1 Cor. i. 18, 23.
6 Ex. xii. 23
7 John i. 29.
8 Cf. Cat. i. 3; xvii. 35, 36.
9 1 Pet. ii. 22, quoted from Isa. liii. 9.
1 Luke xxiii. 14.

hands, he said, *I am innocent of the blood of this just person*[2]. There is yet another witness of the sinlessness of Jesus,—the robber, the first man admitted into Paradise; who rebuked his fellow, and said, "*We receive the due reward of our deeds; but this man hath done nothing amiss*[3]; for we were present, both thou and I, at His judgment."

4. Jesus then really suffered for all men; for the Cross was no illusion[4], otherwise our redemption is an illusion also. His death was not a mere show[5], for then is our salvation also fabulous. If His death was but a show, they were true who said, *We remember that that deceiver said, while He was yet alive, After three days I rise again*[6]. His Passion then was real: for He was really crucified, and we are not ashamed thereat; He was crucified, and we deny it not, nay, I rather glory to speak of it. For though I should now deny it, here is Golgotha to confute me, near which we are now assembled; the wood of the Cross confutes me, which was afterwards distributed piecemeal from hence to all the world[7]. I confess the Cross, because I know of the Resurrection; for if, after being crucified, He had remained as He was, I had not perchance confessed it, for I might have concealed both it and my Master; but now that the Resurrection has followed the Cross, I am not ashamed to declare it.

5. Being then in the flesh like others, He was crucified, but not for the like sins. For He was not led to death for covetousness, since He was a Teacher of poverty; nor was He condemned for concupiscence, for He Himself says plainly, *Whosoever shall look upon a woman to lust after her, hath committed adultery with her already*[8]; not for smiting or striking hastily, for He turned the other cheek also to the smiter; not for despising the Law, for He was the fulfiller of the Law; not for reviling a prophet, for it was Himself who was proclaimed by the Prophets; not for defrauding any of their hire, for He ministered without reward and freely; not for sinning in words, or deeds, or thoughts, He *who did no sin, neither was guile found in His mouth; who when He was reviled, reviled not again; when He suffered, threatened not*[9]; who came to His passion, not unwillingly, but willingly; yea, if any dissuading Him say even now, *Be it far from Thee, Lord*, He will say again, *Get thee behind Me, Satan*[1].

6. And wouldest thou be persuaded that He came to His passion willingly? others, who foreknow it not, die unwillingly; but He spake before of His passion: *Behold, the Son of man is betrayed to be crucified*[2]. But knowest thou wherefore this Friend of man shunned not death? It was lest the whole world should perish in its sins. *Behold, we go up to Jerusalem, and the Son of man shall be betrayed, and shall be crucified*[3]; and again, *He stedfastly set His face to go to Jerusalem*[4]. And wouldest thou know certainly, that the Cross is a glory to Jesus? Hear His own words, not mine. Judas had become ungrateful to the Master of the house, and was about to betray Him. Having but just now gone forth from the table, and drunk His cup of blessing, in return for that draught of salvation he sought to shed righteous blood. *He who did eat of His bread, was lifting up his heel against Him*[5]; his hands were but lately receiving the blessed gifts[6], and presently for the wages of betrayal he was plotting His death. And being reproved, and having heard that word, *Thou hast said*[7], he again went out: then said Jesus, *The hour is come, that the Son of man should be glorified*[8]. Seest thou how He knew the Cross to be His proper glory? What then, is Esaias not ashamed of being sawn asunder[9], and shall Christ be ashamed of dying for the world? *Now is the Son of man glorified*[1]. Not that He was without glory before: for He was *glorified with the glory* which was *before the foundation of the world*[2]. He was ever glorified as God; but now He was to be glorified in wearing the Crown of His patience. He gave not up His life by compulsion, nor was He put to death by murderous violence, but of His own accord. Hear what He says: *I have power to lay down My life, and I have power to take it again*[3]: I yield it of My own choice to My enemies; for unless I chose, this could

---

2 Matt. xxvii. 24.

3 Luke xxiii. 41. Cf. Cat. xiii. 30, 31. The Benedictine Editor remarks, "We know not whence Cyril took the notion that the two robbers were present at the trial of Jesus." He may have inferred from the words ἐν τῷ αὐτῷ κρίματι that the sentence of crucifixion was pronounced on them at the same time as on Jesus.

4 δόκησις. Cf. Ignat. *Smyrn.* § 2: "He suffered truly, as also He raised Himself truly: not as certain unbelievers say, that He suffered in semblance (τὸ δοκεῖν αὐτὸν πεπονθέναι)." See § 37, below.

5 φαντασιώδης. Athanas. *c. Apollinar.* § 3: "Supposing the exhibition and the endurance of the Passion to be a mere show (φαντασίαν)."

6 Matt. xxvii. 63.

7 Cf. iv. 10; x. 19.

8 Matt. v. 28.

9 1 Pet. ii. 22, 23.

1 Matt. xvi. 22, 23.

2 Ib. xxvi. 2.

3 Ib. xx. 18.

4 Luke ix. 5.

5 Ps. xli. 9.

6 "τὰς εὐλογίας. The word has this meaning in Chrysostom and Cyril of Alexandria also; afterwards it came to signify consecrated bread, distinct from that of the Eucharist. Vid. Bingham, *Antiq.* xv. 4, § 3." (R. W. C.)

The custom of sending the bread of the Eucharist was forbidden in the latter part of the 4th century by the Synod of Laodicea, Canon 14: "At Easter the Host shall no more be sent into foreign dioceses as *eulogiae*." Bp. Hefele (*Councils* II. p. 308) says—"It was a custom in the ancient Church, not indeed to consecrate, but to bless those of the several breads of the same form laid on the altar which were not needed for the Communion, and to employ them partly for the maintenance of the Clergy, and partly for distributing them to those of the faithful who did not communicate at the Mass." See Eusebius (*Hist. Eccles.* V. 24), with the note thereon in this Series.

7 Matt. xxvi. 25.

8 John xii. 23.

9 See Cat. ii. 14, note 4.

1 John xiii. 31.

2 Ib. xvii. 5.

3 Ib. x. 18.

not be. He came therefore of His own set purpose to His passion, rejoicing in His noble deed, smiling at the crown, cheered by the salvation of mankind; not ashamed of the Cross, for it was to save the world. For it was no common man who suffered, but God in man's nature, striving for the prize of His patience.

7. But the Jews contradict this[4], ever ready, as they are, to cavil, and backward to believe; so that for this cause the Prophet just now read says, *Lord, who hath believed our report*[5]? Persians believe[6], and Hebrews believe not; *they shall see, to whom He was not spoken of, and they that have not heard shall understand*[7], while they who study these things shall set at nought what they study. They speak against us, and say, "Does the Lord then suffer? What? Had men's hands power over His sovereignty?" Read the Lamentations; for in those Lamentations, Jeremias, lamenting you, wrote what is worthy of lamentations. He saw your destruction, he beheld your downfall, he bewailed Jerusalem which then was; for that *which now is*[8] shall not be bewailed; for that Jerusalem crucified the Christ, but that *which now is* worships Him. Lamenting then he says, *The breath of our countenance, Christ the Lord was taken in our corruptions*[9]. Am I then stating views of my own? Behold he testifies of the Lord Christ seized by men. And what is to follow from this? Tell me, O Prophet. He says, *Of whom we said, Under His shadow we shall live among the nations*[1]. For he signifies that the grace of life is no longer to dwell in Israel, but among the Gentiles.

8. But since there has been much gainsaying by them, come, let me, with the help of your prayers, (as the shortness of the time may allow,) set forth by the grace of the Lord some few testimonies concerning the Passion. For the things concerning Christ are all put into writing, and nothing is doubtful, for nothing is without a text. All are inscribed on the monuments of the Prophets; clearly written, not on tablets of stone, but by the Holy Ghost. Since then thou hast heard the Gospel speaking concerning Judas, oughtest thou not to receive the testimony to it? Thou hast heard that He was pierced in the side by a spear; oughtest thou not to see whether this also is written? Thou hast heard that He was crucified in a garden; oughtest thou not to see whether this also is written? Thou hast heard that He was sold for thirty pieces of silver; oughtest thou not to learn what prophet spake this? Thou hast heard that He was given vinegar to drink; learn where this also is written. Thou hast heard that His body was laid in a rock, and that a stone was set over it; oughtest thou not to receive this testimony also from the prophet? Thou hast heard that He was crucified with robbers; oughtest thou not to see whether this also is written? Thou hast heard that He was buried; oughtest thou not to see whether the circumstances of His burial are anywhere accurately written? Thou hast heard that He rose again; oughtest thou not to see whether we mock thee in teaching these things? For *our speech and our preaching is not in persuasive words of man's wisdom*[2]. We stir now no sophistical contrivances; for these become exposed; we do not conquer words with words[3], for these come to an end; but *we preach Christ Crucified*[4], who has already been preached aforetime by the Prophets. But do thou, I pray, receive the testimonies, and seal them in thine heart. And, since they are many, and the rest of our time is narrowed into a short space, listen now to a few of the more important as time permits; and having received these beginnings, be diligent and seek out the remainder. Let not thine hand be only stretched out to receive, but let it be also ready to work[5]. God gives all things freely. *For if any of you lack wisdom, let him ask of God who giveth*[5(bis)], and he shall receive. May He through your prayer grant utterance to us who speak, and faith to you who hear.

9. Let us then seek the testimonies to the Passion of Christ: for we are met together, not now to make a speculative exposition of the Scriptures, but rather to be certified of the things which we already believe. Now thou hast received from me first the testimonies concerning the coming of Jesus; and concerning His walking on the sea, for it is written, *Thy way is in the sea*[6]. Also concerning divers

4 There is so close a resemblance between the remainder of this Lecture and the explanation of the same Article of the Creed by Rufinus, that "I have no doubt," says the Benedictine Editor, 'that Rufinus drew from Cyril's fountains." Cf. Rufin. *de Symbolo*, § 19, *sqq.*

5 Isa. lii. 15.

6 Cf. Acts ii. 9: *Parthians and Medes and Elamites.* These Jewish converts of the day of Pentecost would naturally be the first heralds of the Gospel in their respective countries. On the dispersion of the Apostles, "Parthia, according to tradition, was allotted to Thomas as his field of labour" (Euseb. *Hist. Eccl.* III. 1; cf. I. 13). An earlier notice of the tradition is found in the *Clementine Recognitions*, L. IX. c. 29, where the Pseudo-Clement professes to have received a letter from "Thomas, who is preaching the Gospel among them."

7 Rom. xv. 21, quoted from Isaiah, *u s.*

8 Gal. iv. 25.

9 Lam. iv. 20: *The breath of our nostrils, the anointed of the Lord, was taken in their pits.*

1 Ibid.

2 1 Cor. ii. 4. The simple style of the New Testament is defended by Origen, *c. Celsum*, iii. 68, and in many other passages.

3 Cyril alludes to the same proverb in the *Homily on the Paralytic*, c. 14: "Word resists word, but a deed is irresistible." The Jerusalem Editor refers to Gregory Nazianzen (Tom. II. p. 596): Λόγῳ παλαίει πᾶς λόγος.

4 1 Cor. i. 23.

5 Ecclus. iv. 31: *Let not thine hand be stretched out to receive, and shut when thou shouldest repay.* The passage is quoted in the *Didaché*, c. iv., Barnab. *Epist.* c. xix., and *Constit. Apost.* VII. 11.

5(bis) James i. 5.

6 Ps. lxxvii. 19. The Benedictine Editor, with no authority

cures thou hast on another occasion received testimony. Now therefore I begin from whence the Passion began. Judas was the traitor, and he came against Him, and stood, speaking words of peace, but plotting war. Concerning him, therefore, the Psalmist says, *My friends and My neighbours drew near against Me, and stood*[7]. And again, *Their words were softer than oil, yet be they spears*[8]. *Hail, Master*[9]; yet he was betraying his Master to death; he was not abashed at His warning, when He said, *Judas, betrayest thou the Son of Man with a kiss*[1]? for what He said to him was just this, Recollect thine own name; Judas means *confession*[2]; thou hast covenanted, thou hast received the money, make confession quickly. *O God, pass not over My praise in silence; for the mouth of the wicked, and the mouth of the deceitful, are opened against Me; they have spoken against Me with a treacherous tongue, they have compassed Me about also with words of hatred*[3]. But that some of the chief-priests also were present, and that He was put in bonds before the gates of the city, thou hast heard before, if thou rememberest the exposition of the Psalm, which has told the time and the place; how *they returned at evening, and hungered like dogs, and encompassed the city*[4].

10. Listen also for the thirty pieces of silver. *And I will say to them, If it be good in your sight, give me my price, or refuse*[5]; and the rest. One price is owing to Me from you for My healing the blind and lame, and I receive another; for thanksgiving, dishonour, and for worship, insult. Seest thou how the Scripture foresaw these things? *And they weighed for My price thirty pieces of silver*[6]. How exact the prophecy! how great and unerring the wisdom of the Holy Ghost! For he said, not ten, nor twenty, but thirty, exactly as many as there were. Tell also what becomes of this price, O Prophet! Does he who received it keep it? or does he give it back? and after he has given it back, what becomes of it? The Prophet says then, *And I took the thirty pieces of silver, and cast them into the house of the Lord, into the foundry*[7]. Compare the Gospel with the Prophecy: *Judas*, it says, *repented himself, and cast down the pieces of silver in the temple, and departed*[8].

11. But now I have to seek the exact solution of this seeming discrepancy. For they who make light of the prophets, allege that the Prophet says on the one hand, *And I cast them into the house of the Lord, into the foundry*, but the Gospel on the other hand, *And they gave them for the potter's field*[9]. Hear then how they are both true. For those conscientious Jews forsooth, the high-priests of that time, when they saw that Judas repented and said, *I have sinned, in that I have betrayed innocent blood*, reply, *What is that to us, see thou to that*[1]. Is it then nothing to you, the crucifiers? but shall he who received and restored the price of murder see to it, and shall ye the murderers not see to it? Then they say among themselves, *It is not lawful to cast them into the treasury, because it is the price of blood*[2]. Out of your own mouths is your condemnation; if the price is polluted, the deed is polluted also; but if thou art fulfilling righteousness in crucifying Christ, why receivest thou not the price of it? But the point of inquiry is this: how is there no disagreement, if the Gospel says, *the potter's field*, and the Prophet, *the foundry*? Nay, but not only people who are goldsmiths, or brass-founders, have a foundry, but potters also have foundries for their clay. For they sift off the fine and rich and useful earth from the gravel, and separate from it the mass of the refuse matter, and temper the clay first with water, that they may work it with ease into the forms intended. Why then wonderest thou that the Gospel says plainly *the potter's field*, whereas the Prophet spoke his prophecy like an enigma, since prophecy is in many places enigmatical?

12. They bound Jesus, and brought Him into the hall of the High-priest. And wouldest thou learn and know that this also is written? Esaias says, *Woe unto their soul, for they have taken evil counsel against themselves, saying, Let us bind the Just, for He is troublesome to us*[3]. And truly, *Woe unto their soul!* Let us see how. Esaias was sawn asunder, yet after this the people was restored. Jeremias was cast into the mire of the cistern, yet was the wound of the Jews healed; for the sin was less, since it was against man. But when the Jews sinned, not against man, but against God in man's nature, *Woe unto their soul!—Let us bind the Just;* could He not then set Himself free, some one will say; He, who freed Lazarus from the bonds of death on the fourth day, and loosed Peter

but the Latin version by Grodecq, inserts a quotation of Job **ix. 8**: *Who walketh on the sea, as on a pavement.* Cf. xi. 23.

7 Ps. xxxviii. 11. 8 Ib. lv. 21.

9 Matt. xxvi. 49. 1 Luke xxii. 48.

2 Cf. Phil. Jud. *de Plantatione Noë*, II § 33: "And his name was called Judah, which being interpreted is "confession to the Lord." In Gen. xlix. 8 the name is differently interpreted: "Judah, thou art he whom thy brethren shall praise." The root has both senses "to confess," and "to praise," which are closely allied, since to "confess" is to "give God the glory" (Josh. vii. 19). 3 Ps. cix. 1—3.

4 Ps. lix. 6. The exposition was probably given in a sermon preached to the whole congregation, not in these Lectures.

5 Zech. xi. 12. 6 Ib. 7 Ib. xi. 13.

8 Matt. xxvii. 3, 5.

9 Matt. xxvii. 3, 7. 1 Ib. *v.* 4. 2 Ib. *v.* 6.

3 Isa. iii. 9: (R.V.) *they have rewarded evil unto themselves. Say ye of the righteous, that it shall be well with him.* In the Septuagint, from which Cyril quotes, there is an evident interpolation of Wisdom ii. 12: *Let us lie in wait for the righteous; because he is not for our turn* (δύσχρηστος, as in Cyril).

from the iron bands of a prison? Angels stood ready at hand, saying, *Let us burst their bands in sunder*[4]; but they hold back, because their Lord willed to undergo it. Again, He was led to the judgment-seat before the Elders; thou hast already the testimony to this, *The Lord Himself will come into judgment with the ancients of His people, and with the princes thereof*[5].

13. But the High-priest having questioned Him, and heard the truth, is wroth; and the wicked officer of wicked men smites Him; and the countenance, which had shone as the sun, endured to be smitten by lawless hands. Others also come and spit on the face of Him, who by spittle had healed the man who was blind from his birth. *Do ye thus requite the Lord? This people is foolish and unwise*[6]. And the Prophet greatly wondering, says, *Lord, who hath believed our report*[7]*?* for the thing is incredible, that God, the Son of God, and *the Arm of the Lord*[8], should suffer such things. But that they who are being saved may not disbelieve, the Holy Ghost writes before, in the person of Christ, who says, (for He who then spake these things, was afterward Himself an actor in them,) *I gave My back to the scourges*; (for Pilate, *when he had scourged Him, delivered Him to be crucified*[9];) *and My cheeks to smitings; and My face I turned not away from the shame of spittings*; saying, as it were, "Though knowing before that they will smite Me, I did not even turn My cheek aside; for how should I have nerved My disciples against death for truth's sake, had I Myself dreaded this?" I said, *He that loveth his life shall lose it*[1]: if I had loved My life, how was I to teach without practising what I taught? First then, being Himself God, He endured to suffer these things at the hands of men; that after this, we men, when we suffer such things at the hands of men for His sake, might not be ashamed. Thou seest that of these things also the prophets have clearly written beforehand. Many, however, of the Scripture testimonies I pass by for want of time, as I said before; for if one should exactly search out all, not one of the things concerning Christ would be left without witness.

14. Having been bound, He came from Caiaphas to Pilate,—is this too written? yes; *And having bound Him, they led Him away as a present to the king of Jarim*[2]. But here some sharp hearer will object, "Pilate was not a king," (to leave for a while the main parts of the question,) "how then having bound Him, led they Him as a present to the king?" But read thou the Gospel; *When Pilate heard that He was of Galilee, he sent Him to Herod*[3]; for Herod was then king, and was present at Jerusalem. And now observe the exactness of the Prophet; for he says, that He was sent as a present; for *the same day Pilate and Herod were made friends together, for before they were at enmity*[4]. For it became Him who was on the eve of making peace between earth and heaven, to make the very men who condemned Him the first to be at peace; for the Lord Himself was there present, *who reconciles*[5] *the hearts of the princes of the earth.* Mark the exactness of the Prophets, and their true testimony.

15. Look with awe then at the Lord who was judged. He suffered Himself to be led and carried by soldiers. Pilate sat in judgment, and He who sitteth on the right hand of the Father, stood and was judged[6]. The people whom He had redeemed from the land of Egypt, and ofttimes from other places, shouted against Him, *Away with Him, away with Him, crucify Him*[7]. Wherefore, O ye Jews? because He healed your blind? or because He made your lame to walk, and bestowed His other benefits? So that the Prophet in amazement speaks of this too, *Against whom have ye opened your mouth, and against whom have ye let loose your tongue*[8]*?* and the Lord Himself says in the Prophets, *Mine heritage became unto Me as a lion in the forest; it gave its voice against Me; therefore have I hated it*[9]. I have not refused them, but they have refused Me; in consequence thereof I say, *I have forsaken My house*[1].

16. When He was judged, He held His peace; so that Pilate was moved for Him, and said, *Hearest Thou not what these witness against Thee*[2]*?* Not that He knew Him who was judged, but he feared his own wife's dream which had been reported to him. And Jesus held His peace. The Psalmist says, *And I became as a man that heareth not; and in whose mouth are no reproofs*[3]; and again, *But I was as a deaf man and heard not; and as a dumb man that openeth not his mouth*[4]. Thou

---

4 Ps. ii. 3. 5 Isa. iii. 14. 6 Deut. xxxii. 6.
7 Isa. liii. 1. 8 Ibid. 9 Isa. l. 6; Matt. xxvii. 26.
1 John xii. 25.
2 Hosea x. 6: (R.V.) *It also shall be carried unto Assyria for a present to king Jareb.* This passage is applied in the same manner to Luke xxiii. 7 by Justin M. (*Tryph.* § 103), Tertullian (*c. Marcion.* iv. 42), and Rufinus (*de Symbolo*, § 21), who adds,—"And rightly does the Prophet add the name 'Jarim,' which means 'a wild vine,' for Herod was . . . a wild vine, i.e. of an alien stock." For the various interpretations of the name see the Commentaries on Hosea v. 13, and x. 6; Schrader, *Cuneiform Inscriptions*, II. § 439, Driver, *Introduction to O.T. Literature*, p. 283.
3 Luke xxiii. 6, 7. 4 Ibid. xxiii. 12.
5 Job xii. 24: (R.V.) *He taketh away the heart of the chiefs of the people of the earth.* The rendering "who reconciles" (ὁ διαλλάσσων. Sept.) is forbidden by the context.
6 Some MSS. have ἠνέσχετο or ἠνείχετο, "He submitted to stand."
7 Josh. xix. 15. 8 Isa. lvii. 4.
9 Jer. xii. 8. 1 Ibid. *v.* 7. 2 Matt. xxvii. 13.
3 Ps. xxxviii. 14. 4 Ibid. *v.* 13.

hast before heard concerning this[5], if thou rememberest.

17. But the soldiers who crowd around mock Him, and their Lord becomes a sport to them, and upon their Master they make jests. *When they looked on Me, they shaked their heads*[6]. Yet the figure of kingly state appears; for though in mockery, yet they bend the knee. And the soldiers before they crucify Him, put on Him a purple robe, and set a crown on His head; for what though it be of thorns? Every king is proclaimed by soldiers; and Jesus also must in a figure be crowned by soldiers; so that for this cause the Scripture says in the Canticles, *Go forth, O ye daughters of Jerusalem, and look upon King Solomon in the crown wherewith His mother crowned Him*[7]. And the crown itself was a mystery; for it was a remission of sins, a release from the curse.

18. Adam received the sentence, *Cursed is the ground in thy labours; thorns and thistles shall it bring forth to thee*[8]. For this cause Jesus assumes the thorns, that He may cancel the sentence; for this cause also was He buried in the earth, that the earth which had been cursed might receive the blessing instead of a curse. At the time of the sin, they clothed themselves with fig-leaves; for this cause Jesus also made the fig-tree the last of His signs. For when about to go to His passion, He curses the fig-tree, not every fig-tree, but that one alone, for the sake of the figure; saying, *No more let any man eat fruit of thee*[9]; let the doom be cancelled. And because they aforetime clothed themselves with fig-leaves, He came at a season when food was not wont to be found on the fig-tree. Who knows not that in winter-time the fig-tree bears no fruit, but is clothed with leaves only? Was Jesus ignorant of this, which all knew? No, but though He knew, yet He came as if seeking; not ignorant that He should not find, but shewing that the emblematical curse extended to the leaves only.

19. And since we have touched on things connected with Paradise, I am truly astonished at the truth of the types. In Paradise was the Fall, and in a Garden was our Salvation. From the Tree came sin, and until the Tree sin lasted. *In the evening, when the Lord walked in the Garden, they hid themselves*[1]; and in the evening the robber is brought by the Lord into Paradise. But some one will say to me, "Thou art inventing subtleties; shew me from some prophet the Wood of the Cross; except thou give me a testimony from a prophet, I will not be persuaded. Hear then from Jeremias, and assure thyself; *I was like a harmless lamb led to be slaughtered; did I not know it*[2]*?* (for in this manner read it as a question, as I have read it; for He who said, *Ye know that after two days comes the passover, and the Son of Man is betrayed to be crucified*[3], did He not know?) *I was like a harmless lamb led to be slaughtered; did I not know it?* (but what sort of lamb? let John the Baptist interpret it, when he says, *Behold the Lamb of God, that taketh away the sin of the world*[4].) *They devised against Me a wicked device, saying*[5],—(He who knows the devices, knew He not the result of them? And what said they?)—*Come, and let us place a beam upon His bread*[6]—(and if the Lord reckon thee worthy, thou shalt hereafter learn, that His body according to the Gospel bore the figure of bread;)—*Come* then, *and let us place a beam upon His bread, and cut Him off out of the land of the living;*—(life is not cut off, why labour ye for nought?)—*And His name shall be remembered no more.* Vain is your counsel; for *before the sun His Name*[7] abideth in the Church. And that it was Life, which hung on the Cross, Moses says, weeping, *And thy life shall be hanging before thine eyes; and thou shalt be afraid day and night, and thou shalt not trust thy life*[8]. And so too, what was just now read as the text, *Lord, who hath believed our report?*

20. This was the figure which Moses completed by fixing the serpent to a cross, that whoso had been bitten by the living serpent, and looked to the brasen serpent, might be saved by believing[9]. Does then the brazen serpent save when crucified, and shall not the Son of God incarnate save when crucified also? On each occasion life comes by means of wood. For in the time

5 "Perhaps in some Homily" (Ben. Ed.). 6 Ps. cix. 25.
7 Cant. iii. 11.
8 Gen. iii. 17, 18. By mistaking one letter in the Hebrew, the Seventy give the meaning "in thy labours" instead of "for thy sake." 9 Mark xi. 1 1 Gen. iii. 8.

2 Jer. xi. 19: *I was like a tame* (R.V. *gentle*) *lamb that is led to the slaughter; and I knew not that they had devised devices against me.* Cyril's interrogative rendering is not admissible.
3 Matt. xxvi. 2. 4 John i. 29. 5 Jer. xi. 19.
6 Ibid. R.V. *Let us destroy the tree with the fruit thereof.* The word rendered *fruit* is literally *bread.* The phrase is evidently proverbial. The Hebrew word which means "destroy" is misinterpreted by ἐμβάλωμεν in the Greek. Hence arose the fanciful application of the passage to the Cross laid on the body of Christ to be borne by Him. Justin M. (*Tryph.* lxxii.) charges the Jews with having recently cut out the passage because of the supposed reference to Christ. Tertullian (*adv. Judæos*, c. 10) writes: "Of course on His body that 'wood' was put; for so Christ has revealed, calling His body 'bread.'" He gives the same interpretation elsewhere (*adv. Marcion.* III. 19; IV. 40). Cf. Cyprian (*Testimonia ad Quirinum*, Lib. II. 15); Athanas. (*de Incarn.* § 33).
7 Ps. lxxii. 17. 8 Deut. xxviii. 66.
9 Num. xxi. 9; John iii. 14. The Jerusalem Editor asks, "How did Moses complete the figure by fixing the serpent to a cross? First he set up the wood and fixed it in the earth as a post: then by putting the brazen serpent athwart (πλαγίως), he formed a figure of the Cross." Cf. Barnab. *Epist.* c. xii.; Justin M. (*Apol.* i. c. 60); Iren. (*Hæres.* IV. c. 2); Tertull. (*adv. Judæos*, c. 10).

of Noe the preservation of life was by an ark of wood. In the time of Moses the sea, on beholding the emblematical rod, was abashed at him who smote it; is then Moses' rod mighty, and is the Cross of the Saviour powerless? But I pass by the greater part of the types, to keep within measure. The wood in Moses' case sweetened the water; and from the side of Jesus the water flowed upon the wood.

21. The beginning of signs under Moses was blood and water; and the last of all Jesus' signs was the same. First, Moses changed the river into blood; and Jesus at the last gave forth from His side water with blood. This was perhaps on account of the two speeches, his who judged Him, and theirs who cried out against Him; or because of the believers and the unbelievers. For Pilate said, *I am innocent*, and washed his hands in water; they who cried out against Him said, *His blood be upon us*[1]: there came therefore these two out of His side; the water, perhaps, for him who judged Him; but for them that shouted against Him, the blood. And again it is to be understood in another way; the blood for the Jews, and the water for the Christians: for upon them as plotters came the condemnation from the blood; but to thee who now believest, the salvation which is by water. For nothing has been done without a meaning. Our fathers who have written comments have given another reason of this matter. For since in the Gospels the power of salutary Baptism is twofold, one which is granted by means of water to the illuminated, and a second to holy martyrs, in persecutions, through their own blood, there came out of that saving Side blood and water[2], to confirm the grace of the confession made for Christ, whether in baptism, or on occasions of martyrdom. There is another reason also for mentioning the Side. The woman, who was formed from the side, led the way to sin; but Jesus who came to bestow the grace of pardon on men and women alike, was pierced in the side for women, that He might undo the sin.

22. And whoever will inquire, will find other reasons also; but what has been said is enough, because of the shortness of the time, and that the attention of my hearers may not become sated. And yet we never can be tired of hearing concerning the crowning of our Lord, and least of all in this most holy Golgotha. For others only hear, but we both see and handle. Let none be weary; take thine armour against the adversaries in the cause of the Cross itself; set up the faith of the Cross as a trophy against the gainsayers. For when thou art going to dispute with unbelievers concerning the Cross of Christ, first make with thy hand the sign of Christ's Cross, and the gainsayer will be silenced. Be not ashamed to confess the Cross; for Angels glory in it, saying, *We know whom ye seek, Jesus the Crucified*[3]. Mightest thou not say, O Angel, "I know whom ye seek, my Master?" But, "I," he says with boldness, "I know the Crucified." For the Cross is a Crown, not a dishonour.

23. Now let us recur to the proof out of the Prophets which I spoke of. The Lord was crucified; thou hast received the testimonies. Thou seest this spot of Golgotha! Thou answerest with a shout of praise, as if assenting. See that thou recant not in time of persecution. Rejoice not in the Cross in time of peace only, but hold fast the same faith in time of persecution also; be not in time of peace a friend of Jesus, and His foe in time of wars. Thou receivest now remission of thy sins, and the gifts of the King's spiritual bounty; when war shall come, strive thou nobly for thy King. Jesus, the Sinless, was crucified for thee; and wilt not thou be crucified for Him who was crucified for thee? Thou art not bestowing a favour, for thou hast first received; but thou art returning a favour, repaying thy debt to Him who was crucified for thee in Golgotha. Now Golgotha is interpreted, "the place of a skull." Who were they then, who prophetically named this spot Golgotha, in which Christ the true Head endured the Cross? As the Apostle says, *Who is the Image of the Invisible God;* and a little after, *and He is the Head of the body, the Church*[4]. And again, *The Head of every man is Christ*[5]; and again, *Who is the Head of all principality and power*[6]. The Head suffered in "the place of the skull." O wondrous prophetic appellation! The very name also reminds thee, saying, "Think not of the Crucified as of a mere man; He is *the Head of all principality and power.* That Head which was crucified is the Head of all power, and has for His Head the Father; *for the Head of the man is Christ, and the Head of Christ is God*[7]."

24. Christ then was crucified for us, who was judged in the night, when it was cold, and therefore a *fire of coals*[8] was laid. He was crucified at the third hour; *and from the sixth*

---

1 Matt. xxvii. 24, 25.

2 John xix. 34. Cf. Cat. iii. 10. Origen (*In Lib. Judic.* Hom. vii. § 2): "It is the Baptism of blood alone that can render us purer than the Baptism of water has done." Cf. Origen (*in Ev. Matt.* Tom. xvi. 6): "If Baptism promises remission of sins, as we have received concerning Baptism in water and the Spirit, and if one who has endured the Baptism of Martyrdom receives remission of sins, then with good reason martyrdom may be called a Baptism" For a summary of the "Patristic Interpretation" of the passage, see Bp. Westcott, *Speaker's Commentary*.)

3 Matt. xxviii. 5.

4 Col. i. 15, 18.

5 1 Cor. xi. 3.

6 Col. ii. 10.

7 1 Cor. xi. 3.

8 John xviii. 18.

hour there was darkness until the ninth hour[9]; but from the ninth hour there was light again. Are these things also written? Let us inquire. Now the Prophet Zacharias says, *And it shall come to pass in that day, that there shall not be light, and there shall be cold and frost one day*; (the cold on account of which Peter warmed himself;) *And that day shall be known unto the Lord*[1]; (what, knew He not the other days? days are many, but *this is the day* of the Lord's patience, *which the Lord made*[2];)—*And that day shall be known unto the Lord, not day, and not night*: what is this dark saying which the Prophet speaks? That day is neither day nor night? what then shall we name it? The Gospel interprets it, by relating the event. It was not day; for the sun shone not uniformly from his rising to his setting, but from the sixth hour till the ninth hour, there was darkness at mid-day. The darkness therefore was interposed; but *God called the darkness night*[3]. Wherefore it was neither day nor night: for neither was it all light, that it should be called day; nor was it all darkness, that it should be called night; but after the ninth hour the sun shone forth. This also the Prophet foretels; for after saying, *Not day, nor night*, he added, *And at evening time it shall be light*[4]. Seest thou the exactness of the prophets? Seest thou the truth of the things which were written aforetime?

25. But dost thou ask exactly at what hour the sun failed[5]? was it the fifth hour, or the eighth, or the tenth? Tell, O Prophet, the exact time thereof to the Jews, who are unwilling to hear; when shall the sun go down? The Prophet Amos answers, *And it shall come to pass in that day, saith the Lord God, that the sun shall go down at noon* (for there was darkness from the sixth hour;) *and the light shall grow dark over the earth in the day*[6]. What sort of season is this, O Prophet, and what sort of day? *And I will turn your feasts into mourning*; for this was done in the days of unleavened bread, and at the feast of the Passover: then afterwards he says, *And I will make Him as the mourning of an Only Son, and those with Him as a day of anguish*[7]; for in the day of unleavened bread, and at the feast, their women were wailing and weeping, and the Apostles had hidden themselves and were in anguish. Wonderful then is this prophecy.

26. But, some one will say, "Give me yet another sign; what other exact sign is there of that which has come to pass? Jesus was crucified; and He wore but one coat, and one cloak: now His cloak the soldiers shared among themselves, having rent it into four; but His coat was not rent, for when rent it would have been no longer of any use; so about this lots are cast by the soldiers; thus the one they divide, but for the other they cast lots. Is then this also written? They know, the diligent chanters[8] of the Church, who imitate the Angel hosts, and continually sing praises to God: who are thought worthy to chant Psalms in this Golgotha, and to say, *They parted My garments among them, and upon My vesture they did cast lots*[9]. The "lots" were what the soldiers cast[1].

27. Again, when He had been judged before Pilate, He was clothed in red; for there they put on Him a purple robe. Is this also written? Esaias saith, *Who is this that cometh from Edom? the redness of His garments is from Bosor*[2]; (who is this who in *dishonour* weareth purple? For Bosor has some such meaning in Hebrew[3].) *Why are Thy garments red, and Thy raiment as from a trodden wine-press?* But He answers and says, *All day long have I stretched forth Mine hands unto a disobedient and gainsaying people*[4].

28. He stretched out His hands on the Cross, that He might embrace the ends of the world; for this Golgotha is the very centre of the earth. It is not my word, but it is a prophet who hath said, *Thou hast wrought salvation in the midst of the earth*[5]. He stretched forth human hands, who by His spiritual hands had established the heaven; and they were fastened with nails, that His manhood, which bore the sins of men, having been nailed to the tree, and having died, sin might die with it, and we might rise again in righteousness. *For since by* one *man came death, by* One *Man came also* life[6]; by One Man, the Saviour, dying of His own accord: for remember what He said, *I have power to*

---

9 Matt. xxvii. 45. 1 Zech. xiv. 6, 7. 2 Ps. cxviii. 24.

3 Gen. i. 5.

4 Zech. xiv. 7. Cf. Euseb. (*Dem. Evang*. x. 7): "It was not day, because of the noon-tide darkness: and again it was not night, because of the day which followed upon it, which he represented by a sign in saying, *at evening time there shall be light*.

5 ἐξέλιπεν. See Cat. x. 19, note 2. *Acta Pilati*. c. xi.

6 Amos viii. 9. Cf Euseb. (*Dem. Ev*. x. 6). 7 Amos viii. 10.

8 Synod of Laodicea, Can. xvi. 15: "Besides the appointed singers, who mount the ambo and sing from the book, others shall not sing in the Church." Hefele thinks that this was not intended to forbid the laity to take any part in the Church music, but only to forbid those who were not cantors to take the lead. See Bingham, *Antiquities*, III. c. 7; XIV. c. 1.

9 Ps. xxii 18, quoted in John xix 24.

1 κλῆρος δὲ ἦν ὁ λαχμός. Bishop Hall. *Contemplations*, Book IV. 32, speaks of the soldiers' "barbarous *sortitions*." The technical term is "sortilege." Cf. *Evang. Pet*. § 4; Justin M. *Dial*. 97.

2 Isa. lxiii. 1, 2.

3 Bozrah means a "sheepfold," and is the name of a city in Idumea. Cyril's interpretation rests on a false derivation.

4 Isa. lxv. 2. "It is a commonplace in patristic literature that the Crucifixion was prefigured by Isa. lxv. 2." (Dr. C. Taylor, *Hermas and the Four Gospels*, p. 49.) Cf. Barnab. *Epist*. c. xii.; *Didache* xvi.; Justin M. (*Apolog*. I. c. 35; *Tryph*. cc. 97, 114); Tertull. (*contra Jud*. xii.); Irenæ. IV. xxxiii. 12.

5 Ps. lxxiv. 12. The passage does not refer to Palestine especially: "in the midst of the earth" is equivalent to "in the sight of all nations." Cf. *Orac. Sibyll*. viii. 302: "He shall spread out His hands, and span the whole world," quoted by Dr. Taylor, "The Teaching," p. 103.

6 Rom. v. 12, 17.

lay down My life, and I have power to take it again[7].

29. But though He endured these things, having come for the salvation of all, yet the people returned Him an evil recompense. Jesus saith, *I thirst*[8],—He who had brought forth the waters for them out of the craggy rock; and He asked fruit of the Vine which He had planted. But what does the Vine? This Vine, which was by nature of the holy fathers, but of Sodom by purpose of heart;—(for *their Vine is of Sodom, and their tendrils of Gomorrah*[9];)—this Vine, when the Lord was athirst, having filled a sponge and put it on a reed, offers Him vinegar. *They gave Me also gall for My meat, and in My thirst, they gave Me vinegar to drink*[1]. Thou seest the clearness of the Prophets' description. But what sort of gall put they into My mouth? *They gave Him*, it says, *wine mingled with myrrh*[2]. Now myrrh is in taste like gall, and very bitter. Are these things what ye recompense unto the Lord? Are these thy offerings, O Vine, unto thy Master? Rightly did the Prophet Esaias aforetime bewail you, saying, *My well-beloved had a vineyard in a hill in a fruitful place;* and (not to recite the whole) *I waited*, he says, *that it should bring forth grapes;* I thirsted that it should give wine; *but it brought forth thorns*[3]; for thou seest the crown, wherewith I am adorned. What then shall I now decree? *I will command the clouds that they rain no rain upon it*[4]. For the clouds which are the Prophets were removed from them, and are for the future in the Church; as Paul says, *Let the Prophets speak two or three, and let the others judge*[5]; and again, *God gave in the Church, some, Apostles, and some, Prophets*[6]. Agabus, who bound his own feet and hands, was a prophet.

30. Concerning the robbers who were crucified with Him, it is written, *And He was numbered with the transgressors*[7]. Both of them were before this transgressors, but one was so no longer. For the one was a transgressor to the end, stubborn against salvation; who, though his hands were fastened, smote with blasphemy by his tongue. When the Jews passing by wagged their heads, mocking the Crucified, and fulfilling what was written, *When they looked on Me, they shaked their heads*[8], he also reviled with them. But the other rebuked the reviler; and it was to him the end of life and the beginning of restoration; the surrender of his soul a first share in salvation. And after rebuking the other, he says, *Lord, remember me*[9]; for with Thee is my account. Heed not this man, for the eyes of his understanding are blinded; but remember me. I say not, remember my works, for of these I am afraid. Every man has a feeling for his fellow-traveller; I am travelling with Thee towards death; remember me, Thy fellow-wayfarer. I say not, Remember me now, but, *when Thou comest in Thy kingdom.*

31. What power, O robber, led thee to the light? Who taught thee to worship that despised Man, thy companion on the Cross? O Light Eternal, which gives light to them that are in darkness! Therefore also he justly heard the words, *Be of good cheer*[1]; not that thy deeds are worthy of good cheer; but that the King is here, dispensing favours. The request reached unto a distant time; but the grace was very speedy. *Verily I say unto thee, This day shalt thou be with Me in Paradise;* because *to-day* thou hast *heard My voice*, and hast not *hardened thine heart*[2]. Very speedily I passed sentence upon Adam, very speedily I pardon thee. To him it was said, *In the day wherein ye eat, ye shall surely die*[3]; but thou to-day hast obeyed the faith, to-day is thy salvation. Adam by the Tree fell away; thou by the Tree art brought into Paradise. Fear not the serpent; he shall not cast thee out; for he is *fallen from heaven*[4]. And I say not unto thee, This day shalt thou depart, but, *This day shalt thou be with Me.* Be of good courage: thou shalt not be cast out. Fear not the flaming sword; it shrinks from its Lord[5]. O mighty and ineffable grace! The faithful Abraham had not yet entered, but the robber enters[6]! Moses and the Prophets had not yet entered, and the robber enters though a breaker of the law. Paul also wondered at this before thee, saying, *Where sin abounded, there grace did much more abound*[7]. They who had borne the heat of the day had not yet entered; and he of the eleventh hour entered. Let none murmur against the goodman of the house, for he says, *Friend, I do thee no wrong; is it not*

7 John x. 18. 8 Ib. ix. 28. 9 Deut. xxxii. 32.
1 Ps. lxix. 21. 2 Mark xv. 23. 3 Isa. v. 1, 2.
4 Ib. *v.* 6. Cf. Tertull. *adv. Marcion.* III. c. 23; *contra Jud.* c. 13: "The clouds being celestial benefits which were commanded not to be forthcoming to the house of Israel; for it 'had borne *thorns*,' whereof that house of Israel had wrought a crown for Christ." *Constitt. Apost.* VI. § 5: "He has taken away from them the Holy Spirit, and the prophetic rain, and has replenished His Church with spiritual grace."
5 1 Cor. xiv. 29. 6 Eph. iv. 11. 7 Isa. liii. 12.
8 Ps. cix. 25.

9 Luke xxiii. 40 ff.
1 θάρσει. An addition to the text of Luke xxiii. 43 in Codex Bezae.
2 Ps. xcv. 7, 8. 3 Gen. ii. 17. 4 Luke x. 18.
5 Gen. iii. 24. S. Ambrose (*Ps.* cxix. Serm. xx. § 12): "All who desire to return to Paradise must be tried by fire: for not in vain the Scripture saith, that when Adam and Eve were driven out of their abode in Paradise, God placed at the gate of Eden a flaming sword which turned every way."
6 Cf. Iren. V. c. 5, § 1; Athan. (*Expos. Fid.* c. i.): "He shewed us .... an entrance into Paradise from which Adam was cast out, and into which he entered again by means of the thief." S. Leo (*de Pass. Dom.* Serm. II. c. 1): "Excedit humanam conditionem ista promissio: nec tam de ligno Crucis, quam de throno editur potestatis."
7 Rom. v. 20.

lawful for Me to do what I will with Mine own[8]? The robber has a will to work righteousness, but death prevents him; I wait not exclusively for the work, but faith also I accept. I am come who *feed* My sheep *among the lilies*[9], I am come to feed them in the gardens. I have *found* a *sheep that was lost*[10], but I lay it on My shoulders; for he believes, since he himself has said, *I have gone astray like a lost sheep*[1]; *Lord, remember me when Thou comest in Thy kingdom.*

32. Of this garden I sang of old to My spouse in the Canticles, and spake to her thus. *I am come into My garden, My sister, My spouse*[2]; (*now in the place where He was crucified was a garden*[3];) and what takest Thou thence? *I have gathered My myrrh;* having drunk wine mingled with myrrh, and vinegar, after receiving which, He said, *It is finished*[4]. For the mystery has been fulfilled; the things that are written have been accomplished; sins are forgiven. For *Christ being come an High-Priest of the good things to come, by the greater and more perfect tabernacle, not made with hands, that is to say, not of this creation, nor yet by the blood of goats and calves, but by His own blood, entered in once for all into the holy place, having obtained eternal redemption; for if the blood of bulls and of goats, and the ashes of an heifer, sprinkling the defiled, sanctifieth to the purifying of the flesh, how much more the blood of Christ*[5]? And again, *Having therefore, brethren, boldness to enter into the holiest by the blood of Jesus, by a new and living way, which He hath consecrated for us, through the veil, that is to say, His flesh*[6]. And because His flesh, this veil, was dishonoured, therefore the typical veil of the temple was rent asunder, as it is written, *And, behold, the veil of the temple was rent in twain from the top to the bottom*[7]; for not a particle of it was left; for since the Master said, *Behold, your house is left unto you desolate*[8], the house brake all in pieces.

33. These things the Saviour endured, *and made peace through the Blood of His Cross, for things in heaven, and things in earth*[9]. For we were enemies of God through sin, and God had appointed the sinner to die. There must needs therefore have happened one of two things; either that God, in His truth, should destroy all men, or that in His loving-kindness He should cancel the sentence. But behold the wisdom of God; He preserved both the truth of His sentence, and the exercise of His loving-kindness. Christ took our sins *in His body on the tree, that we by His death might die to sin, and live unto righteousness*[1]. Of no small account was He who died for us; He was not a literal sheep; He was not a mere man; He was more than an Angel; He was God made man. The transgression of sinners was not so great as the righteousness of Him who died for them; the sin which we committed was not so great as the righteousness which He wrought who laid down His life for us,—who laid it down when He pleased, and took it again when He pleased. And wouldest thou know that He laid not down His life by violence, nor yielded up the ghost against His will? He cried to the Father, saying, *Father, into Thy hands I commend My spirit*[2]; I commend it, that I may take it again. And having said these things, *He gave up the ghost*[3]; but not for any long time, for He quickly rose again from the dead.

34. The Sun was darkened, because of *the Sun of Righteousness*[4]. Rocks were rent, because of the spiritual Rock. Tombs were opened, and the dead arose, because of Him who was *free among the dead*[5]; *He sent forth His prisoners out of the pit wherein is no water*[6]. Be not then ashamed of the Crucified, but be thou also bold to say, *He beareth our sins, and endureth grief for us, and with His stripes we are healed*[7]. Let us not be unthankful to our Benefactor. And again; *for the transgression of my people was He led to death; and I will give the wicked for His burial, and the rich for His death*[8]. Therefore Paul says plainly, *that Christ died for our sins according to the Scriptures, and that He was buried, and that He hath risen again the third day according to the Scriptures*[9].

35. But we seek to know clearly where He has been buried. Is His tomb made with hands? Is it, like the tombs of kings, raised above the ground? Is the Sepulchre made of stones joined together? And what is laid upon it? Tell us, O Prophets, the exact truth concerning His tomb also, where He is laid, and where we shall seek Him? And they say, *Look into the solid rock which ye have hewn*[1]. *Look in* and behold. Thou hast in the Gospels *In a sepulchre hewn in stone, which was hewn out of a rock*[2]. And what happens next? What kind of door has the sepulchre? Again another Prophet says, *They cut off My life in a dungeon*[3], *and cast a stone upon Me.* I, who am *the Chief corner-stone, the elect, the precious*[4], lie for a little time within a stone—I who am a stone of stumbling to the Jews, and of salvation to

8 Matt. xx. 12 ff. 9 Cant. vi. 3. 10 Luke xv. 5, 6.
1 Ps. cxix. 176. 2 Cant. v. 1. 3 John xix. 41.
4 Ib. 30. 5 Heb. ix. 11. 6 Ib. x. 19.
7 Matt. xxvii. 51. 8 Ib. xxiii. 38. 9 Col. i. 20.

1 1 Pet. ii. 24. 2 Luke xxiii. 46.
3 Matt. xxvii. 50. 4 Mal. iv. 2. 5 Ps. lxxxviii. 5.
6 Zech. ix. 11. 7 Isa. liii. 4, 5. 8 Ib. *vv.* 8, 9.
9 1 Cor. xv. 3, 4. 1 Isa. li. 1.
2 Matt. xxvii. 60; Mark xv. 46; Luke xxiii. 50.
3 Lam. iii. 53: ἐν λάκκῳ, "in a pit," or "well." Cf. Jer. xxxvii. 16. 4 1 Pet. ii. 6.

them who believe. *The Tree of life*[5], therefore was planted in the earth, that the earth which had been cursed might enjoy the blessing, and that the dead might be released.

36. Let us not then be ashamed to confess the Crucified. Be the Cross our seal made with boldness by our fingers on our brow, and on everything; over the bread we eat, and the cups we drink; in our comings in, and goings out; before our sleep, when we lie down and when we rise up; when we are in the way, and when we are still[6]. Great is that preservative; it is without price, for the sake of the poor; without toil, for the sick; since also its grace is from God. It is the Sign of the faithful, and the dread of devils: for He *triumphed over them in it, having made a shew of them openly*[7]; for when they see the Cross, they are reminded of the Crucified; they are afraid of Him, who *bruised the heads of the dragon*[8]. Despise not the Seal, because of the freeness of the gift; but for this the rather honour thy Benefactor.

37. And if thou ever fall into disputation, and hast not the grounds of proof, yet let Faith remain firm in thee; or rather, become thou well learned, and then silence the Jews out of the prophets, and the Greeks out of their own fables. They themselves worship men who have been thunderstricken[9]: but the thunder when it comes from heaven, comes not at random. If they are not ashamed to worship men thunderstricken and abhorred of God, art thou ashamed to worship the beloved Son of God, who was crucified for thee? I am ashamed to tell the tales about their so-called Gods, and I leave them because of time; let those who know, speak. And let all heretics also be silenced. If any say that the Cross is an illusion, turn away from him. Abhor those who say that Christ was crucified to our fancy[1] only; for if so, and if salvation is from the Cross, then is salvation a fancy also. If the Cross is fancy, the Resurrection is fancy also; but *if Christ be not risen, we are yet in our sins*[2]. If the Cross is fancy, the Ascension also is fancy; and if the Ascension is fancy, then is the second coming also fancy, and everything is henceforth unsubstantial.

38. Take therefore first, as an indestructible foundation, the Cross, and build upon it the other articles of the faith. Deny not the Crucified; for, if thou deny Him, thou hast many to arraign thee. Judas the traitor will arraign thee first; for he who betrayed Him knows that He was condemned to death by the chief-priests and elders. The thirty pieces of silver bear witness; Gethsemane bears witness, where the betrayal occurred; I speak not yet of the Mount of Olives, on which they were with Him at night, praying. The moon in the night bears witness; the day bears witness, and the sun which was darkened; for it endured not to look on the crime of the conspirators. The fire will arraign thee, by which Peter stood and warmed himself; if thou deny the Cross, the eternal fire awaits thee. I speak hard words, that thou may not experience hard pains. Remember the swords that came against Him in Gethsemane, that thou feel not the eternal sword. The house of Caiaphas[3] will arraign thee, shewing by its present desolation the power of Him who was erewhile judged there. Yea, Caiaphas himself will rise up against thee in the day of judgment, the very servant will rise up against thee, who smote Jesus with the palm of his hand; they also who bound Him, and they who led Him away. Even Herod shall rise up against thee; and Pilate; as if saying, Why deniest thou Him who was slandered before us by the Jews, and whom we knew to have done no wrong? For I Pilate then washed my hands. The false witnesses shall rise up against thee, and the soldiers who arrayed Him in the purple robe, and set on Him the crown of thorns, and crucified Him in Golgotha, and cast lots for His coat. Simon the Cyrenian will cry out upon thee, who bore the Cross after Jesus.

39. From among the stars there will cry out upon thee, the darkened Sun; among the things upon earth, the Wine mingled with myrrh; among reeds, the Reed; among herbs, the Hyssop; among the things of the sea, the Sponge; among trees, the Wood of the Cross;—the soldiers, too, as I have said, who nailed Him, and cast lots for His vesture; the soldier who pierced His side with the spear; the women who then were present; the veil of the

5 Gen. ii. 9; iii. 22. Methodius (*Sympos.* ix. c. 3): "He that hath not believed in Christ, nor hath understood that He is the first principle and the Tree of Life, &c."

6 Cf. Cat. iv. 14, note 3; Euseb. (*Dem. Ev.* ix. 14).

7 Col. ii. 15.

8 Ps. lxxiv. 13.

9 See Cat. vi. 11, note 2.

1 κατὰ φαντασίαν. Cf. Ignat. *Trall.* 9, 10; Cat. iv. 9; xiii. 4.

2 1 Cor. xv. 17.

3 The house of Caiaphas and Pilate's Prætorium (§ 41), and Mount Zion itself (Cat. xvi. 18), on which they both stood, are described by Cyril as being in his time ruined and desolate. Eusebius (*Dem. Ev.* VIII. 406), referring to the prophecy of Micah (iii. 12), repeated by Jeremiah (xxvi. 18), that *Zion shall be plowed as a field, and Jerusalem shall become heaps*, testifies that he had seen with his own eyes the place being ploughed and sown by strangers, and adds that in his own time the stones for both public and private buildings were taken from the ruins. The Bordeaux Pilgrim (333 A.D.) says, "It is evident where the house of Caiaphas the Priest was; and there is still the pillar at which Christ was scourged:" this pillar is described by Jerome (*Ep.* 86) as supporting the portico of the Church which by his time had been built on the spot. Prudentius (*circ.* 400 A.D.):—

"Impia blasphemi cecidit domus alta Caiphae . . . .
Vinctus in his Dominus stetit ædibus atque columnae
Annexus tergum dedit ut servile flagellis.
Perstat adhuc, templumque gerit veneranda columna."

(Benedictine Editor.)

temple then rent asunder; the hall of Pilate, now laid waste by the power of Him who was then crucified; this holy Golgotha, which stands high above us, and shews itself to this day, and displays even yet how because of Christ the rocks were then riven[4]; the sepulchre nigh at hand where He was laid; and the stone which was laid on the door, which lies to this day by the tomb; the Angels who were then present; the women who worshipped Him after His resurrection; Peter and John, who ran to the sepulchre; and Thomas, who thrust his hand into His side, and his fingers into the prints of the nails. For it was for our sakes that he so carefully handled Him; and what thou, who wert not there present, wouldest have sought, he being present, by God's Providence, did seek.

40. Thou hast Twelve Apostles, witnesses of the Cross; and the whole earth, and the world of men who believe on Him who hung thereon. Let thy very presence here now persuade thee of the power of the Crucified. For who now brought thee to this assembly? what soldiers? With what bonds wast thou constrained? What sentence held thee fast here now? Nay, it was the Trophy of salvation, the Cross of Jesus that brought you all together. It was this that enslaved the Persians, and tamed the Scythians; this that gave to the Egyptians, for cats and dogs and their manifold errors, the knowledge of God; this, that to this day heals diseases; that to this day drives away devils, and overthrows the juggleries of drugs and charms.

41. This shall appear again with Jesus from heaven[5]; for the trophy shall precede the king: that seeing *Him whom they pierced*[6], and knowing by the Cross Him who was dishonoured, the Jews may repent and mourn; (but *they shall mourn tribe by tribe*[7], for they shall repent, when there shall be no more time for repentance;) and that we may glory, exulting in the Cross, worshipping the Lord who was sent, and crucified for us, and worshipping also God His Father who sent Him, with the Holy Ghost: To whom be glory for ever and ever. Amen.

4 Cf. Lucian. Antioch. ap. Rufin. *Hist. Eccl.* ix. c. 6; "Golgothana rupes sub patibuli onere disrupta."

5 Cf. Cat. xv. 22. 6 Zech. xii. 10. 7 Ib. *v.* 12.

LECTURE XIV.

On the words, And rose again from the dead on the third day, and ascended into the Heavens, and sat on the right hand of the Father.

1 Cor. xv. 1—4.

Now I make known unto you, brethren, the gospel which I preached unto you . . . . that He hath been raised on the third day according to the Scriptures, &c.

Rejoice, O Jerusalem, and keep high festival, all ye that love Jesus; for He is risen. *Rejoice, all ye that mourned before*[1], when ye heard of the daring and wicked deeds of the Jews: for He who was spitefully entreated of them in this place is risen again. And as the discourse concerning the Cross was a sorrowful one, so let the good tidings of the Resurrection bring joy to the hearers. Let mourning be turned into gladness, and lamentation to joy: and let our mouth be filled with joy and gladness, because of Him, who after His resurrection, said *Rejoice*[2]. For I know the sorrow of Christ's friends in these past days; because, as our discourse stopped short at the Death and the Burial, and did not tell the good tidings of the Resurrection, your mind was in suspense, to hear what you were longing for.

Now, therefore, the Dead is risen, He who was *free among the dead*[3], and the deliverer of the dead. He who in dishonour wore patiently the crown of thorns, even He arose, and crowned Himself with the diadem of His victory over death.

2. As then we set forth the testimonies concerning His Cross, so come let us now verify the proofs of His Resurrection also: since the Apostle before us[4] affirms, *He was buried, and has been raised on the third day according to the Scriptures.* As an Apostle, therefore, has sent us back to the testimonies of the Scriptures, it is good that we should get full knowledge of the hope of our salvation; and that we should learn first whether the divine Scriptures tell us the season of His resurrection, whether it comes in summer or in autumn, or after winter; and from what kind of place the Saviour has risen, and what has been announced in the admirable Prophets as the name of the place of the Resurrection, and whether the women, who sought and found Him not, afterwards rejoice at finding Him; in order that when the Gospels are read, the narratives of these holy Scriptures may not be thought fables nor rhapsodies.

3. That the Saviour then was buried, ye have heard distinctly in the preceding discourse, as Isaiah saith, *His burial shall be in peace*[5]*:* for in His burial He made peace between heaven and earth, bringing sinners unto God: and, *that the righteous is taken out of the way of unrighteousness*[6]*:* and, *His burial shall be in peace:* and, *I will give the wicked for His burial*[7]. There is also the prophecy of Jacob saying in the Scriptures, *He lay down and couched as a lion, and as a lion's whelp: who shall rouse Him up*[8]*?* And the similar passage in Numbers, *He couched, He lay down as a lion, and as a lion's whelp*[9]. The Psalm also ye have often heard, which says, *And Thou hast brought me down into the dust of death*[1]. Moreover we took note of the spot, when we quoted the words, *Look unto the rock, which ye have hewn*[2]. But now let the testimonies concerning His resurrection itself go with us on our way.

4. First, then, in the 11th Psalm He says, *For the misery of the poor, and the sighing of the needy, now will I arise, saith the Lord*[3]. But this passage still remains doubtful with some: for He often rises up also in anger[4], to take vengeance upon His enemies.

Come then to the 15th Psalm, which says distinctly: *Preserve Me, O Lord, for in Thee*

---

1 Is. lxvi. 10.

2 Matt. xxviii. 9, "All hail." The usual greeting, Χαίρετε, "Rejoice."

3 Ps. lxxxviii. 5: *Cast off among the dead* (R.V.); *Cast away* (Margin).

4 ὁ παρών, i.e. in the text. 1 Cor xv. 4.

5 Is. lvii. 2: *He entereth into peace* (R.V.).

6 Is. lvii. 1: *that the righteous is taken away from the evil to come* (R.V.).

7 Is. liii. 9: *they made His grave with the wicked* (R.V.).

8 Gen. xlix. 9. 9 Num. xxiv. 9. 1 Ps. xxii. 15.

2 ἐπεσημειωσάμεθα, "noted for ourselves;" Middle Voice. Is. li. 1: quoted in Cat. xiii. 35.

3 Ps. xii. 5. 4 Ib. vii. 6: "Arise, O Lord, in Thine anger

have I put my trust[5]*:* and after this, *their assemblies of blood will I not join, nor make mention of their names between my lips*[6]*;* since they have refused me, and chosen Cæsar as their king[7]: and also the next words, *I foresaw the* LORD *alway before Me, because He is at My right hand, that I may not be moved*[8]*:* and soon after, *Yea and even until night my reins chastened me*[9]. And after this He says most plainly, *For Thou wilt not leave My soul in hell*[1]*; neither wilt Thou suffer Thine Holy One to see corruption.* He said not, neither wilt Thou suffer Thine Holy One to see death, since then He would not have died; but *corruption*, saith He, I see not, and shall not abide in death. *Thou hast made known to Me the ways of life*[2]. Behold here is plainly preached a life after death. Come also to the 29th Psalm, *I will extol Thee, O* LORD, *for Thou hast lifted Me up, and hast not made My foes to rejoice over Me*[3]. What is it that took place? Wert thou rescued from enemies, or wert thou released when about to be smitten? He says himself most plainly, *O* LORD, *Thou hast brought up My soul from hell*[4]. There he says, *Thou wilt not leave*, prophetically: and here he speaks of that which is to take place as having taken place, *Thou hast brought up. Thou hast saved Me from them that go down into the pit*[5]. At what time shall the event occur? *Weeping shall continue for the evening, and joy cometh in the morning*[6]*:* for in the evening was the sorrow of the disciples, and in the morning the joy of the resurrection.

5. But wouldst thou know the place also? Again He saith in Canticles, *I went down into the garden of nuts*[7]*;* for it was a garden where He was crucified[8]. For though it has now been most highly adorned with royal gifts, yet formerly it was a garden, and the signs and the remnants of this remain. *A garden enclosed, a fountain sealed*[9], by the Jews who said, *We remember that that deceiver said while He was yet alive, After three days, I will rise: command, therefore, that the sepulchre be made sure;* and further on, *So they went, and made the sepulchre sure, sealing the stone with the guard*[1]. And aiming well at these, one saith, *and in rest Thou shalt judge them*[2]. But who is the fountain that is sealed, or who is interpreted as being *a well-spring of living water*[3]*?* It is the Saviour Himself, concerning whom it is written, *For with Thee is the fountain of life*[4].

6. But what says Zephaniah in the person of Christ to the disciples? *Prepare thyself, be rising at the dawn: all their gleaning is destroyed*[5]*:* the gleaning, that is, of the Jews, with whom there is not a cluster, nay not even a gleaning of salvation left; for their vine is cut down. See how He says to the disciples, *Prepare thyself, rise up at dawn:* at dawn expect the Resurrection.

And farther on in the same context of Scripture He says, *Therefore wait thou for Me, saith the* LORD, *until the day of My Resurrection at the Testimony*[6]. Thou seest that the Prophet foresaw the place also of the Resurrection, which was to be surnamed "the Testimony." For what is the reason that this spot of Golgotha and of the Resurrection is not called, like the rest of the Churches, a Church, but a Testimony? Why, perhaps, it was because of the Prophet, who had said, *until the day of My Resurrection at the Testimony*.

7. And who then is this, and what is the sign of Him that rises? In the words of the Prophet that follow in the same context, He says plainly, *For then will I turn to the peoples a language*[7]*:* since, after the Resurrection, when the Holy Ghost was sent forth the gift of tongues was granted, *that they might serve the* LORD *under one yoke*[8]. And what other token is set forth in the same Prophet, that they should *serve the* LORD *under one yoke? From beyond the rivers of Ethiopia they shall bring me offerings*[9]. Thou knowest what is written in the Acts, when the Ethiopian eunuch came from beyond the rivers of Ethiopia[1]. When therefore the Scriptures tell both the time and the peculiarity of the place, when they tell also the signs which followed the Resurrection, have thou henceforward a firm faith in the Resurrection, and let no one stir thee from confessing *Christ risen from the dead*[2].

8. Now take also another testimony in the

5 Ps. xvi. 1.

6 Ib. xvi. 4: "their drink-offerings of blood will I not offer." The Psalmist abhors the bloody rites, and the very names of the false gods.

7 John xix. 15. Cyril applies to the Jews what the Psalmist says concerning those that hasten after another god.

8 Ps. xvi. 8.

9 Ib. 7. Quoting from memory, Cyril transposes these sentences.

1 Ib. 10. R.V. *in Sheol*, Sept. *in Hades*.

2 Ib. 11. 3 Ib. xxx. 1.

4 Ib. 3. R.V. *from Sheol*, Sept. *from Hades*.

5 Ib. 3. 6 Ib. 5. 7 Cant. vi. 11.

8 John xix. 41. See Index, *Golgotha*. 9 Cant. iv. 12.

1 Matt. xxvii. 63, 65.

2 Job vii. 18: .... *try him every moment.* Heb. רֶגַע, "a wink," as in Job xxi. 13, misinterpreted in both passages by the LXX. as meaning "rest."

3 Cant. iv. 15. 4 Ps. xxxvi. 9.

5 Zeph. iii. 7: *they rose early and corrupted all their doings.* The passage is wholly misunderstood by the Seventy, whom S. Cyril follows.

6 Zeph. iii. 8: *until the day that I rise up to the prey.* For לְעַד, *to the prey*, the LXX. seem to have read לְעֵד, *to the testimony.* About ten years before these Lectures were delivered, Eusebius (*Life of Constantine*, III. c. xxviii.), speaking of the discovery of the Holy Sepulchre, A.D. 326, calls it "a testimony to the Resurrection of the Saviour clearer than any voice could give."

7 Zeph. iii. 9: *a pure language.*

8 Ib. *to serve him with one consent* (Marg. *shoulder*).

9 Ib. *v.* 10. 1 Acts viii. 27. 2 2 Tim. ii. 8.

87th Psalm, where Christ speaks in the Prophets, (for He who then spake came afterwards among us): *O* LORD, *God of My salvation, I have cried day and night before Thee*, and a little farther on, *I became as it were a man without help, free among the dead*[3]. He said not, I became a man without help; but, *as it were a man without help*. For indeed He was crucified not from weakness, but willingly: and His Death was not from involuntary weakness. *I was counted with them that go down into the pit*[4]. And what is the token? *Thou hast put away Mine acquaintance far from Me*[5] (for the disciples have fled). *Wilt Thou shew wonders to the dead*[6]*?* Then a little while afterwards: *And unto Thee have I cried, O* LORD*; and in the morning shall my prayer come before Thee*[7]. Seest thou how they shew the exact point of the Hour, and of the Passion, and of the Resurrection?

9. And whence hath the Saviour risen? He says in the Song of Songs: *Rise up, come, My neighbour*[8]*:* and in what follows, *in a cave of the rock*[9]*!* A cave of the rock He called the cave which was erewhile before the door of the Saviour's sepulchre, and had been hewn out of the rock itself, as is wont to be done here in front of the sepulchres. For now it is not to be seen, since the outer cave was cut away at that time for the sake of the present adornment. For before the decoration of the sepulchre by the royal munificence, there was a cave in the front of the rock[1]. But where is the rock that had in it the cave? Does it lie near the middle of the city, or near the walls and the outskirts? And whether is it within the ancient walls, or within the outer walls which were built afterwards? He says then in the Canticles: *in a cave of the rock, close to the outer wall*[2].

10. At what season does the Saviour rise? Is it the season of summer, or some other? In the same Canticles immediately before the words quoted He says, *The winter is past, the rain is past and gone*[3]*; the flowers appear on the earth; the time of the pruning is come*[4]. Is not then the earth full of flowers now, and are they not pruning the vines? Thou seest how he said also that the winter is now past. For when this month Xanthicus[5] is come, it is already spring. And this is the season, the first month with the Hebrews, in which occurs the festival of the Passover, the typical formerly, but now the true. This is the season of the creation of the world: for then God said, *Let the earth bring forth herbage of grass, yielding seed after his kind and after his likeness*[6]. And now, as thou seest, already every herb is yielding seed. And as at that time God made the sun and moon and gave them courses of equal day (and night), so also a few days since was the season of the equinox.

At that time God said, *Let us make man after our image and after our likeness*[7]. And the *image* he received, but the *likeness* through his disobedience he obscured. At the same season then in which he lost this the restoration also took place. At the same season as the created man through disobedience was cast out of Paradise, he who believed was through obedience brought in. Our Salvation then took place at the same season as the Fall: when *the flowers appeared*, and *the pruning was come*.

11. A garden was the place of His Burial, and a vine that which was planted there: and He hath said, *I am the vine*[8]*!* He was planted therefore in the earth in order that the curse which came because of Adam might be rooted out. The earth was condemned to *thorns and thistles:* the true Vine sprang up out of the earth, that the saying might be fulfilled, *Truth sprang up out of the earth, and righteousness*

3 Ps. lxxxviii. 1, 4, 5. 4 Ib. *v.* 4. 5 Ib. *v.* 8.
6 Ib. *v.* 10. 7 Ib. *v.* 13.
8 Cant. ii. 10: *Rise up, my love, my fair one, and come away.*
9 *v.* 14: *in the clefts of the rock.* 1 See Index, *Sepulchre.*
2 Cant. ii. 14: *in the clefts of the rock, in the secret places of the stairs.* The Revised Version reads, *in the covert of the steep place.*
3 Cant. ii. 11. In παρῆλθεν, ἐπορεύθη ἑαυτῷ the LXX. have imitated the pleonastic use of לְךָ after verbs of motion, corresponding to our idiom "Go away with you," and to the *Dativus Ethicus* in Greek and Latin. See Gesenius *Lexicon* on this use of לְ, and Ewald, *Introductory Grammar*, § 217, l. 2.
4 Cant. ii. 12: *the singing of birds.* The Hebrew word (זָמִיר) means either "cutting," as in the LXX. τομῆς, Symmachus κλαδεύσεως, and R.V. Marg. "pruning," or as in A.V. "singing."

5 Xanthicus is the name of the sixth month in the Macedonian Calendar, corresponding nearly to the Jewish Nisan (Josephus, *Antiq.* II. xiv. 6), and to the latter part of Lent and Easter. On the tradition that the Creation took place at this season, see S. Ambrose, *Hexæmeron*, I. c. 4, § 13.
6 Gen. i. 11: *grass, the herb yielding seed.*
The LXX. give an irregular construction,
Βοτανὴν χόρτου σπεῖρον σπέρμα.
7 Gen. i. 26. "The ancient Church very accurately distinguished between εἰκών (*image*) and ὁμοίωσις (*likeness*), and the Greek Church does the same in its Confession. The latter phrase expresses man's destination, which is not to be regarded as carried out at the moment of creation. (Dorner, *System of Christian Doctrine*, *E.Tr.* II. p. 78). The *image* lies in the permanent capacities of man's nature (Gen. ix. 6: 1 Cor. xi. 7: Jas. iii. 9), the *likeness* in their realisation in moral conformity with God (ὁμοήθειαν Θεοῦ, Ignatius, *Magnes* vi). "The image of God is a comprehensive thing. . . . To this belongs man's intellective power, his liberty of will, his dominion over the other creatures flowing from the two former. These make up the τὸ οὐσιῶδες, that part of that divine image which is natural and essential to man, and consequently can never be wholly blotted out, defaced, or extinguished, but still remains even in man fallen. But beside these the Church of God hath ever acknowledged, in the first man, certain additional ornaments, and as it were complements of the divine image, such as immortality, grace, holiness, righteousness, whereby man approached more nearly to the similitude and likeness of God. These were (if I may so speak) the lively colours wherein the grace, the beauty, and lustre of the divine image principally consisted; these colours faded, yea, were defaced and blotted out by man's transgression. (Bull, *The State of Man before the Fall*, Vol. ii. p. 114, *Ox.*). Cf. Iren. (V. vi. § 1; xvi. § 2); Tertullian (*de Baptismo*, c. 5); Clem. Alex. (*Exhort.* c. 12); Origen (*c. Cels.* IV. 30).
8 John xv. 1. The Benedictine Editor has a different punctuation: "and the vine which was planted there hath said, *And I am he Vine.*"

looked down from heaven[9]. And what will He that is buried in the garden say? *I have gathered My myrrh with My spices:* and again, *Myrrh and aloes, with all chief spices*[1]. Now these are the symbols of the burying; and in the Gospels it is said, *The women came unto the sepulchre bringing the spices which they had prepared*[2]*: Nicodemus also bringing a mixture of myrrh and aloes*[3]. And farther on it is written, *I did eat My bread with My honey*[4]*:* the bitter before the Passion, and the sweet after the Resurrection. Then after He had risen He entered through closed doors: but they believed not that it was He: for *they supposed that they beheld a spirit*[5]. But He said, *Handle Me and see.* Put your fingers into the print of the nails, as Thomas required. *And while they yet believed not for joy, and wondered, He said unto them, Have ye here anything to eat? And they gave Him a piece of a broiled fish and honeycomb*[6]. Seest thou how that is fulfilled, *I did eat My bread with My honey.*

12. But before He entered through the closed doors, the Bridegroom and Suitor[7] of souls was sought by those noble and brave women. They came, those blessed ones, to the sepulchre, and sought Him Who had been raised, and the tears were still dropping from their eyes, when they ought rather to have been dancing with joy for Him that had risen. Mary came seeking Him, according to the Gospel, and found Him not: and presently she heard from the Angels, and afterwards saw the Christ. Are then these things also written? He says in the Song of Songs, *On my bed I sought Him whom my soul loved.* At what season? *By night on my bed I sought Him Whom my soul loved: Mary,* it says, *came while it was yet dark. On my bed I sought Him by night, I sought Him, and I found Him not*[8]. And in the Gospels Mary says, *They have taken away my Lord, and I know not where they have laid Him*[9]. But the Angels being then present cure their want of knowledge; for they said, *Why seek ye the living among the dead*[1]*?* He not only rose, but had also the dead with Him when He rose[2]. But she knew not, and in her person the Song of Songs said to the Angels, *Saw ye Him Whom my soul loved? It was but a little that I passed from them* (that is, from the two Angels), *until I found Him Whom my soul loved. I held Him, and would not let Him go*[3].

13. For after the vision of the Angels, Jesus came as His own Herald; and the Gospel says, *And behold Jesus met them, saying, All hail! and they came and took hold of His feet*[4]. They took hold of Him, that it might be fulfilled, *I will hold Him, and will not let Him go.* Though the woman was weak in body, her spirit was manful. *Many waters quench not love, neither do rivers drown it*[5]*;* He was dead whom they sought, yet was not the hope of the Resurrection quenched. And the Angel says to them again, *Fear not ye;* I say not to the soldiers, *fear not,* but to you[6]; as for them, let them be afraid, that, taught by experience, they may bear witness and say, *Truly this was the Son of God*[7]*;* but you ought not to be afraid, *for perfect love casteth out fear*[8]. *Go, tell His disciples that He is risen*[9]*;* and the rest. And they depart with joy, yet full of fear; is this also written? yes, the second Psalm, which relates the Passion of Christ, says, *Serve the Lord with fear, and rejoice unto Him with trembling*[1]*;—rejoice,* because of the risen Lord; but *with trembling,* because of the earthquake, and the Angel who appeared as lightning.

14. Though, therefore, Chief Priests and Pharisees through Pilate's means sealed the tomb; yet the women beheld Him who was risen. And Esaias knowing the feebleness of the Chief Priests, and the women's strength of faith, says, *Ye women, who come from beholding, come hither*[2]*; for the people hath no understanding;*—the Chief Priests want understanding, while women are eye-witnesses. And when the soldiers came into the city to them, and told them all that had come to pass, they said to them, *Say ye, His disciples came by night, and stole Him away while we slept*[3]*?* Well therefore did Esaias foretell this also, as in their persons, *But tell us, and relate to us another deceit*[4]. He who rose again, is up, and for a gift of money they persuade the soldiers; but they persuade not the kings of our time. The soldiers then surrendered the truth for silver; but the kings of this day have, in their piety, built this holy Church of the Resurrection of God our Saviour, inlaid with silver and wrought with gold, in which we are assembled[5]; and embellished it with the treasures of silver and gold and precious stones. *And if this come to the governor's ears,* they say, *we will persuade him*[6]. Yea, though ye persuade the soldiers, yet ye will not persuade the world; for why, as Peter's guards were condemned when he escaped out of the prison, were not

9 Ps. lxxxv. 11.
1 Cant. v. 1; iv. 14. Compare Cat. xiii. 32.
2 Luke xxiv. 1. 3 John xix. 39.
4 Cant. v. 1: *my honeycomb with my honey.*
5 Luke xxiv. 37. 6 Ib. v. 41.
7 ὁ θεραπευτής. In connexion with "Bridegroom," and "Him whom my soul loveth" the meaning "Suitor" is more appropriate than "Physician." 8 Cant. iii. 1: Joh. xx. 1.
9 John xx. 13. 1 Luke xxiv. 5. 2 Matt. xxvii. 52.
3 Cant. iii. 3, 4.

4 Matt. xxviii. 9. 5 Cant. viii. 7.
6 Matt. xxviii. 5. The emphatic ὑμεῖς is rightly interpreted by Cyril as distinguishing the women from the frightened sentinels. 7 Matt. xxvii. 54.
8 1 John iv. 18. 9 Matt. xxviii. 7. 1 Ps. ii. 11.
2 Isa. xxvii. 11: *The women shall come, and set them on fire.*
3 Matt. xxviii. 13. 4 Isa. xxx. 10.
5 Cf. Euseb. (*Life of Const.* III. 36). 6 Matt. xxxviii. 14.

they also who watched Jesus Christ condemned? Upon the former, sentence was pronounced by Herod, for they were ignorant and had nothing to say for themselves; while the latter, who had seen the truth, and concealed it for money, were protected by the Chief Priests. Nevertheless, though but a few of the Jews were persuaded at the time, the world became obedient. They who hid the truth were themselves hidden; but they who received it were made manifest by the power of the Saviour, who not only rose from the dead, but also raised the dead with Himself. And in the person of these the Prophet Osee says plainly, *After two days will He revive us, and in the third day we shall rise again, and shall live in His sight*[7].

15. But since the disobedient Jews will not be persuaded by the Divine Scriptures, but forgetting all that is written gainsay the Resurrection of Jesus, it were good to answer them thus: On what ground, while you say that Eliseus and Elias raised the dead, do you gainsay the Resurrection of our Saviour? Is it that we have no living witnesses now out of that generation to what we say? Well, do you also bring forward witnesses of the history of that time. But that is written;—so is this also written: why then do ye receive the one, and reject the other? They were Hebrews who wrote that history; so were all the Apostles Hebrews: why then do ye disbelieve the Jews[8]? Matthew who wrote the Gospel wrote it in the Hebrew tongue[9]; and Paul the preacher was a Hebrew of the Hebrews; and the twelve Apostles were all of Hebrew race: then fifteen Bishops of Jerusalem were appointed in succession from among the Hebrews[1]. What then is your reason for allowing your own accounts, and rejecting ours, though these also are written by Hebrews from among yourselves.

16. But it is impossible, some one will say, that the dead should rise; and yet Eliseus twice raised the dead,—when he was alive, and also when dead. Do we then believe, that when Eliseus was dead, a dead man who was cast upon him and touched him, arose; and is Christ not risen? But in that case, the dead man who touched Eliseus, arose, yet he who raised him continued nevertheless dead: but in this case both the Dead of whom we speak Himself arose, and many dead were raised without having even touched Him. For *many bodies of the Saints which slept arose, and they came out of the graves after His Resurrection, and went into the Holy City*[2], (evidently this city, in which we now are[3],) *and appeared unto many.* Eliseus then raised a dead man, but he conquered not the world; Elias raised a dead man, but devils are not driven away in the name of Elias. We are not speaking evil of the Prophets, but we are celebrating their Master more highly; for we do not exalt our own wonders by disparaging theirs; for theirs also are ours; but by what happened among them, we win credence for our own.

17. But again they say, "A corpse then lately dead was raised by the living; but shew us that one three days dead can possibly arise, and that a man should be buried, and rise after three days." If we seek for Scripture testimony in proof of such facts, the Lord Jesus Christ Himself supplies it in the Gospels, saying, *For as Jonas was three days and three nights in the whale's belly; so shall the Son of man be three days and three nights in the heart of the earth*[4]. And when we examine the story of Jonas, great is the force[5] of the resemblance. Jesus was sent to preach repentance; Jonas also was sent: but whereas the one fled, not knowing what should come to pass; the other came willingly, to give repentance unto salvation. Jonas was asleep in the ship, and snoring amidst the stormy sea; while Jesus also slept, the sea, according to God's providence[6], began to rise, to shew in the sequel the might of Him who slept. To the one they said, *Why art thou snoring? Arise, call upon thy God, that God may save us*[7]; but in the other case they say unto the Master, *Lord, save us*[8]. Then they said, *Call upon thy God;* here they say, *save Thou.* But the one says, *Take me, and cast me into the sea; so shall the sea be calm unto you*[9]; the other, Himself *rebuked the winds and the sea, and there was a great calm*[8]. The one was cast into a whale's belly: but the other of His own accord went down thither, where the invisible whale of death is. And He went down of His own accord, that death

---

7 Hos. vi. 2.

8 Instead of τοῖς Ἰουδαίοις the Jerusalem Editor adopts from Cod. A. τοῖς ἰδίοις, "Your own countrymen," a better reading in this place, if it had more support from MSS. The Latin in Milles has only "Cur igitur non creditis?"

9 The statements of Papias, Irenæus, Origen, Eusebius, Epiphanius, and Jerome, concerning a Hebrew Gospel of S. Matthew are ably discussed by Dr. Salmon (*Introduction to N.T.* Lect. X.), who comes to the conclusion that the Canonical Gospel was not translated from Hebrew (Aramaic), but originally written in Greek.

1 This statement may have been derived either from Eusebius (*Hist. Eccl.* IV. c. 5), or from the "written records" (ἐγγράφων), from which he had learned that "until the siege of the Jews which took place under Adrian (135 A.D.), there were fifteen bishops in succession there, all of whom are said to have been of Hebrew descent." See the list of names, and the notes on the passage in this Series.

2 Matt. xxvii. 52, 53.

3 The Archdeacon of Jerusalem, Photius Alexandrides, observes that "by this parenthetic explanation Cyril perhaps wished to refute the opinion which some favoured that these saints which slept and were raised entered into the heavenly Jerusalem." See Euseb. *Dem. Evang.* IV. 12.

4 Matt. xii. 40.

5 "ἐνέργεια [Forte ἐνάργεια, Edit.]." This conjecture of the Benedictine Editor is recommended by the very appropriate sense "distinctness of the resemblance," but seems to have no MS. authority.

6 *κατ' οἰκονομίαν.*

7 Jonah i. 6.

8 Matt. viii. 25, 26.

9 Jonah i. 12.

might cast up those whom he had devoured, according to that which is written, *I will ransom them from the power of the grave; and from the hand of death I will redeem them*[1].

18. At this point of our discourse, let us consider whether is harder, for a man after having been buried to rise again from the earth, or for a man in the belly of a whale, having come into the great heat of a living creature, to escape corruption. For what man knows not, that the heat of the belly is so great, that even bones which have been swallowed moulder away? How then did Jonas, who was three days and three nights in the whale's belly, escape corruption? And, seeing that the nature of all men is such that we cannot live without breathing, as we do, in air, how did he live without a breath of this air for three days? But the Jews make answer and say, The power of God descended with Jonas when he was tossed about in hell. Does then the Lord grant life to His own servant, by sending His power with him, and can He not grant it to Himself as well? If that is credible, this is credible also; if this is incredible, that also is incredible. For to me both are alike worthy of credence. I believe that Jonas was preserved, for *all things are possible with God*[2]; I believe that Christ also was raised from the dead; for I have many testimonies of this, both from the Divine Scriptures, and from the operative power even at this day[3] of Him who arose,—who descended into hell alone, but ascended thence with a great company; for He went down to death, *and many bodies of the saints which slept arose*[4] through Him.

19. Death was struck with dismay on beholding a new visitant descend into Hades, not bound by the chains of that place. Wherefore, O porters of Hades, were ye scared at sight of Him? What was the unwonted fear that possessed you? Death fled, and his flight betrayed his cowardice. The holy prophets ran unto Him, and Moses the Lawgiver, and Abraham, and Isaac, and Jacob; David also, and Samuel, and Esaias, and John the Baptist, who bore witness when he asked, *Art Thou He that should come, or look we for another*[5]? All the Just were ransomed, whom death had swallowed; for it behoved the King whom they had proclaimed, to become the redeemer of His noble heralds. Then each of the Just said, *O death, where is thy victory? O grave, where is thy sting*[6]? For the Conqueror hath redeemed us.

20. Of this our Saviour the Prophet Jonas formed the type, when he prayed out of the belly of the whale, and said, *I cried in my affliction*, and so on; *out of the belly of hell*[7], and yet he was in the whale; but though in the whale, he says that he is in Hades; for he was a type of Christ, who was to descend into Hades. And after a few words, he says, in the person of Christ, prophesying most clearly, *My head went down to the chasms of the mountains*[8]; and yet he was in the belly of the whale. What mountains then encompass thee? I know, he says, that I am a type of Him, who is to be laid in the Sepulchre hewn out of the rock. And though he was in the sea, Jonas says, *I went down to the earth*, since he was a type of Christ, who went down into the heart of the earth. And foreseeing the deeds of the Jews who persuaded the soldiers to lie, and told them, *Say that they stole Him away*, he says, *By regarding lying vanities they forsook their own mercy*[9]. For He who had mercy on them came, and was crucified, and rose again, giving His own precious blood both for Jews and Gentiles; yet say they, *Say that they stole Him away*, having regard to *lying vanities*[1]. But concerning His Resurrection, Esaias also says, *He who brought up from the earth the great Shepherd of the sheep*[2]; he added the word, *great*, lest He should be thought on a level with the shepherds who had gone before Him.

21. Since then we have the prophecies, let faith abide with us. Let them fall who fall through unbelief, since they so will; but thou hast taken thy stand on the rock of the faith in the Resurrection. Let no heretic ever persuade thee to speak evil of the Resurrection. For to this day the Manichees say, that the resurrection of the Saviour was phantom-wise, and not real, not heeding Paul who says, *Who was made of the seed of David according to the flesh*; and again, *By the resurrection of Jesus Christ our Lord from the dead*[3]. And again he aims at them, and speaks thus, *Say not in*

---

1 Hosea xiii. 14. 2 Matt. xix. 26. 3 Cf. Cat. iv. 13; xiii. 3. 4 Matt. xxvii. 52. 5 Ib. xi. 3.

6 1 Cor. xv. 55. On the opinion that the Patriarchs, Prophets, and Righteous men were redeemed by Christ in Hades, compare Irenæus (*Hær.* I. xxvii. § 3; IV. xxvii. § 2), Clem. Alex. (*Stromat.* vi. c. 6), Origen (*In Genes.* Hom. xv. § 5).

7 Jonah ii. 2.

8 Ib. *v.* 6: (R.V.) *I went down to the bottoms of the mountains: the earth with her bars closed upon me for ever.*

9 *v.* 8.

1 By *lying vanities* are meant in the original "vain idols."

2 Isa. lxiii. 11; (R.V.), *Where is He that brought them up out of the sea with the shepherds* (Marg. *shepherd*) *of His flock?* Cyril's reading, ἐκ τῆς γῆς instead of ἐκ τῆς θαλάσσης is found in the Alexandrine MS. of the Septuagint. Athanasius (*Ad Serapion*, Ep. i. 12) has the same reading and interpretation as Cyril. By "*the shepherds*" are probably meant Moses and Aaron: cf. Ps. lxxvii. 20: *Who leddest Thy people like sheep by the hand of Moses and Aaron.*

Heb. xiii. 20: *Now the God of peace, that brought again from the dead our Lord Jesus, that great Shepherd of the sheep*, &c. The word "great" is added by the Author of the Epistle to the Hebrews not by Isaiah.

3 Rom. i. 3, 4. Cyril in his incomplete quotation of *v.* 4 makes Ἰησοῦ Χριστοῦ τοῦ Κ. ἡμ. depend on ἀναστάσεως. The right order and construction is given in R.V., *who was declared to be the Son of God .... by the resurrection of the dead; even Jesus Christ our Lord.*

thine heart, who shall ascend into heaven; or, who shall descend into the deep? that is, to bring up Christ from the dead[4]; and in like manner warning as he has elsewhere written again, *Remember Jesus Christ raised from the dead*[5]; and again, *And if Christ be not risen, then is our preaching vain, and your faith is also vain. Yea, and we are found false witnesses of God; because we testified of God that He raised up Christ, whom He raised not up*[6]. But in what follows he says, *But now is Christ risen from the dead, the first fruits of them that are asleep*[7];—*And He was seen of Cephas, then of the twelve;* (for if thou believe not the one witness, thou hast twelve witnesses;) *then He was seen of above five hundred brethren at once*[8]; (if they disbelieve the twelve, let them admit the five hundred;) *after that He was seen of James*[9], His own brother, and first Bishop of this diocese. Seeing then that such a Bishop originally[1] saw Christ Jesus when risen, do not thou, his disciple, disbelieve him. But thou sayest that His brother James was a partial witness; *afterwards He was seen also of me*[2] Paul, His enemy; and what testimony is doubted, when an enemy proclaims it? "I, *who was before a persecutor*[3], now preach the glad tidings of the Resurrection."

22. Many witnesses there are of the Saviour's resurrection.—The night, and the light of the full moon; (for that night was the sixteenth[4];) the rock of the sepulchre which received Him; the stone also shall rise up against the face of the Jews, for it saw the Lord; even the stone which was then rolled away[5], itself bears witness to the Resurrection, lying there to this day. Angels of God who were present testified of the Resurrection of the Only-begotten: Peter and John, and Thomas, and all the rest of the Apostles; some of whom ran to the sepulchre, and saw the burial-clothes, in which He was wrapped before, lying there after the Resurrection; and others handled His hands and His feet, and beheld the prints of the nails; and all enjoyed together that Breath of the Saviour, and were counted worthy to forgive sins in the power of the Holy Ghost. Women too were witnesses, who took hold of His feet, and who beheld the mighty earthquake, and the radiance of the Angel who stood by: the linen clothes also which were wrapped about Him, and which He left when He rose;—the soldiers, and the money given to them; the spot itself also, yet to be seen;—and this house of the holy Church, which out of the loving affection to Christ of the Emperor Constantine of blessed memory, was both built and beautified as thou seest.

23. A witness to the resurrection of Jesus is Tabitha also, who was in His name raised from the dead[6]; for how shall we disbelieve that Christ is risen, when even His Name raised the dead? The sea also bears witness to the resurrection of Jesus, as thou hast heard before[7]. The draught of fishes also testifies, and the fire of coals there, and the fish laid thereon. Peter also bears witness, who had erst denied Him thrice, and who then thrice confessed Him; and was commanded to feed His spiritual[8] sheep. To this day stands Mount Olivet, still to the eyes of the faithful all but displaying Him Who ascended on a cloud, and the heavenly gate of His ascension. For from heaven He descended to Bethlehem, but to heaven He ascended from the Mount of Olives[9]; at the former place beginning His conflicts among men, but in the latter, crowned after them. Thou hast therefore many witnesses; thou hast this very place of the Resurrection; thou hast also the place of the Ascension towards the east; thou hast also for witnesses the Angels which there bore testimony; and the cloud on which He went up, and the disciples who came down from that place.

24. The course of instruction in the Faith would lead me to speak of the Ascension also; but the grace of God so ordered[1] it, that thou heardest most fully concerning it, as far as our weakness allowed, yesterday, on the

---

4 Rom. x. 6, 7. 5 2 Tim. ii. 8. 6 1 Cor. xv. 14, 15.
7 Ib. *v.* 20. 8 Ib. 5, 6.
9 Ib. 7. This appearance of Christ to James is not mentioned in the Gospels. Jerome (*Catalog. Script. Eccles.* p. 170 D) mentions a tradition that James had taken an oath that he would eat no bread from the hour in which he had drunk the Cup of the Lord, until he should see Him rising from the dead. Wherefore the Saviour immediately after He had risen appeared to James and commanded him to eat.
1 For τοιούτου τοίνυν ἐπισκόπου πρωτοτύπως ἰδόντος Codd. Roe, Casaub. have τοῦ τοίνυν πρωτοτύπου ἐπισκόπου ἰδόντος, which gives the better sense—"since therefore the primary Bishop saw, &c." On the meaning of παροικία, and the extent of a primitive Diocese, see Bingham. IX. c. 2.
2 1 Cor. xv. 8. 3 1 Tim. i. 13.
4 If the Crucifixion took place on the 14th of Nisan, the following night would begin the 15th, and the next night the 16th.
5 Cf. Cat. xiii. 39.

6 Acts ix. 41. 7 See § 17, above. 8 νοητά.
9 St. Luke (xxiv. 50) describes the Ascension as taking place at Bethany, but the tradition, which Cyril follows, had long since fixed the scene on the summit of the Mount of Olives, a mile nearer to Jerusalem; and here the Empress Helena had built the Church of the Ascension (Eusebius, *Life of Constantine*, III. 43; *Demonstr. Evang.* VI. xviii. 26). There is nothing in Cyril's language to warrant the Benedictine Editor's suggestion that he alludes to the legend, according to which the marks of Christ's feet were indelibly impressed on the spot from which He ascended. In the next generation St. Augustine seems to countenance the miraculous story (*In Joh. Evang.* Tract xlvii.): "There are His footsteps, now adored, where last He stood, and whence He ascended into heaven." The supposed trace of one foot is still shewn on Mount Olivet; "the other having been removed by the Turks is now to be found in the Chapel of S. Thecla, which is in the Patriarch's Palace" (Jerusalem Ed.). Compare Stanley, *Sinai and Palestine*, c. xiv.; Dictionary of Bible, *Olives, Mount of.*
1 ᾠκονόμησε. In this word, as also in the phrase below, κατ' οἰκονομίαν τῆς Θείας χάριτος, Cyril refers to the order of reading the Scriptures as part of a dispensation established by Divine grace.

Lord's day; since, by the providence of divine grace, the course of the Lessons[2] in Church included the account of our Saviour's going up into the heavens[3]; and what was then said was spoken principally for the sake of all, and for the assembled body of the faithful, yet especially for thy sake[4]. But the question is, didst thou attend to what was said? For thou knowest that the words which come next in the Creed teach thee to believe in Him "Who ROSE AGAIN THE THIRD DAY, AND ASCENDED INTO HEAVEN, AND SAT DOWN ON THE RIGHT HAND OF THE FATHER." I suppose then certainly that thou rememberest the exposition; yet I will now again cursorily put thee in mind of what was then said. Remember what is distinctly written in the Psalms, *God is gone up with a shout*[5]; remember that the divine powers also said to one another, *Lift up your gates, ye Princes*[6], and the rest; remember also the Psalm which says, *He ascended on high, He led captivity captive*[7]; remember the Prophet who said, *Who buildeth His ascension unto heaven*[8]; and all the other particulars mentioned yesterday because of the gainsaying of the Jews.

25. For when they speak against the ascension of the Saviour, as being impossible, remember the account of the carrying away of Habakkuk: for if Habakkuk was transported by an Angel, being carried by the hair of his head[9], much rather was the Lord of both Prophets and Angels, able by His own power to make His ascent into the Heavens on a cloud from the Mount of Olives. Wonders like this thou mayest call to mind, but reserve the pre-eminence for the Lord, the Worker of wonders; for the others were borne up, but He bears up all things. Remember that Enoch was translated[1]; but Jesus ascended: remember what was said yesterday concerning Elias, that Elias was taken up in a chariot of fire[2]; but that *the chariots of* Christ *are ten thousand-fold even thousands upon thousands*[3]: and that Elias was taken up, towards the east of Jordan; but that Christ ascended at the east of the brook Cedron: and that Elias went *as into heaven*[4]; but Jesus, into heaven: and that Elias said that a double portion in the Holy Spirit should be given to his holy disciple; but that Christ granted to His own disciples so great enjoyment of the grace of the Holy Ghost, as not only to have It in themselves, but also, by the laying on of their hands, to impart the fellowship of It to them who believed.

26. And when thou hast thus wrestled against the Jews,—when thou hast worsted them by parallel instances, then come further to the pre-eminence of the Saviour's glory; namely, that they were the servants, but He the Son of God. And thus thou wilt be reminded of His pre-eminence, by the thought that a servant of Christ was caught up to the third heaven. For if Elias attained as far as the first heaven, but Paul as far as the third, the latter, therefore, has obtained a more honourable dignity. Be not ashamed of thine Apostles; they are not inferior to Moses, nor second to the Prophets; but they are noble among the noble, yea, nobler still. For Elias truly was taken up into heaven; but Peter has the keys of the kingdom of heaven, having received the words, *Whatsoever thou shalt loose on earth shall be loosed in heaven*[5]. Elias was taken up only to heaven; but Paul both into *heaven*, and into *paradise*[6] (for it behoved the disciples of Jesus to receive more manifold grace), and *heard unspeakable words, which it is not lawful for man to utter*. But Paul came down again from above, not because he was unworthy to abide in the third heaven, but in order that after having enjoyed things above man's reach, and descended in honour, and having preached Christ, and died for His sake, he might receive also the crown of martyrdom. But I pass over the other parts of this argument, of which I spoke yesterday in the Lord's-day congregation; for with understanding hearers, a mere reminder is sufficient for instruction.

27. But remember also what I have often said[7] concerning the Son's sitting at the right

---

2 **ἀναγνωσμάτων**, a term including the portions of Scripture (περικοπαί) appointed for the Epistle and Gospel as well as the daily lessons from the Old and New Testaments.

3 The section Luke xxiv. 36—53, which in the Eastern Church is the Gospel for Ascension Day, is also one of the "eleven morning Gospels of the Resurrection (εὐαγγέλια ἀναστασιμὰ ἑωθινά), which were read in turn, one every Sunday at Matins." *Dictionary of Chr. Antiq.* "Lectionary." This Lecture being delivered on Monday, the Section in question had been read on the preceding day.

4 μάλιστα μὲν . . . ἐξαιρέτως δέ.

5 Ps. xlvii. 5.

6 Ps. xxiv. 7: *Lift up, O gates, your heads.* The order of the Hebrew words misled the Greek Translators.

7 Ps. lxviii. 18. On the reading ἀνέβη, found in a few MSS. of the Septuagint, see Tischendorf's note on Eph. iv. 8.

8 Amos ix. 6: (R.V.) *It is He that buildeth His chambers in the heaven.* (A.V.) *His stories.* Marg. *ascensions*, or *spheres.* Sept. τὴν ἀνάβασιν αὐτοῦ.

9 Bel and the Dragon, *v.* 33: Compare Ezek. viii. 3.

1 Heb. xi. 5.

2 2 Kings ii. 11.

3 Ps. lxviii. 17: χιλιάδες εὐθηνούντων. The Hebrew means literally "thousands of repetition," i.e. many thousands: εὐθηνεῖν, "to abound."

4 Sept. ὡς εἰς τὸν οὐρανόν. In 1 Macc. ii. 58 the MSS. vary between ἕως and ὡς, but the latter (says Fritzsche) "is an alteration made to agree with 2 Kings ii. 11. But there the reference is to the *intended* exaltation of Elijah into heaven, and therefore ὡς is rightly used (Kühner, *Gramm.* § 604, note; Jelf, § 626, Obs. 1), while here the thing is referred to as an *accomplished historical fact.*" The distinction here drawn by Cyril is therefore hypercritical, as is seen below in § 26, where he writes, Ἠλίας μὲν γὰρ ἀνελήφθη εἰς οὐρανόν.

5 Matt. xvi. 19.

6 2 Cor. xii. 2, 4.

7 See Cat. iv. 7; xi. 17. The clause, καὶ καθίσαντα ἐκ δεξιῶν τοῦ Πατρός, does not occur in the original form of the Nicene Creed, but is found in the Confession of Faith contained in *Const. Apost.* c. 41, in the four Eusebian Confessions of Antioch (341, 2 A.D.), and in the Macrostichos (344 A.D.). An equivalent clause is found in the brief Confession of Hippolytus (circ. 220 A.D.) *Contra Hæres. Noeti*, c. 1: "καὶ ὄντα ἐν δεξιᾷ τοῦ Πατρός," and in Tertullian, *De Virgin. Veland.* c. 1: "Regula quidem Fidei una omnino est, sola immobilis et irreformabilis, ... sedentem nunc ad dextram Patris:" *de Præscriptione*, c. 13: "Regula est

hand of the Father; because of the next sentence in the Creed, which says, "AND ASCENDED INTO HEAVEN, AND SAT DOWN AT THE RIGHT HAND OF THE FATHER." Let us not curiously pry into what is properly meant by the throne; for it is incomprehensible: but neither let us endure those who falsely say, that it was after His Cross and Resurrection and Ascension into heaven, that the Son began to sit on the right hand of the Father. For the Son gained not His throne by advancement[8]; but throughout His being (and His being is by an eternal generation[9]) He also sitteth together with the Father. And this throne the Prophet Esaias having beheld before the incarnate coming of the Saviour, says, *I saw the Lord sitting on a throne, high and lifted up*[1], and the rest. For the Father *no man hath seen at any time*[2], and He who then appeared to the Prophet was the Son. The Psalmist also says, *Thy throne is prepared of old; Thou art from everlasting*[3]. Though then the testimonies on this point are many, yet because of the lateness of the time, we will content ourselves even with these.

28. But now I must remind you of a few things out of many which are spoken concerning the Son's sitting at the right hand of the Father. For the hundred and ninth Psalm says plainly, *The LORD said unto my Lord, Sit Thou on My right hand, until I make Thine enemies Thy footstool*[4]. And the Saviour, confirming this saying in the Gospels, says that David spake not these things of himself, but from the inspiration of the Holy Ghost, saying, *How then doth David in the Spirit call Him Lord, saying, The LORD said unto my Lord, Sit Thou on My right hand*[5]*?* and the rest. And in the Acts of the Apostles, Peter on the day of Pentecost standing with the Eleven[6], and discoursing to the Israelites, has in very words cited this testimony from the hundred and ninth Psalm.

29. But I must remind you also of a few other testimonies in like manner concerning the Son's sitting at the right hand of the Father. For in the Gospel according to Matthew it is written, *Nevertheless, I say unto you, Henceforth ye shall see the Son of Man sitting on the right hand of power*[7], and the rest: in accordance with which the Apostle Peter also writes, *By the Resurrection of Jesus Christ, who is on the right hand of God, having gone into heaven*[8]. And the Apostle Paul, writing to the Romans, says, *It is Christ that died, yea rather, that is risen again, who is even at the right hand of God*[9]. And charging the Ephesians, he thus speaks, *According to the working of His mighty power, which He wrought in Christ when He raised Him from the dead, and set Him at His own right hand*[1]*;* and the rest. And the Colossians he taught thus, *If ye then be risen with Christ, seek the things above, where Christ is seated at the right hand of God*[2]. And in the Epistle to the Hebrews he says, *When He had made purification of our sins, He sat down on the right hand of the Majesty on high*[3]. And again, *But unto which of the Angels hath He said at any time, Sit thou at My right hand, until I make thine enemies thy footstool*[4]*?* And again, *But He, when He had offered one sacrifice for all men, for ever sat down on the right hand of God; from henceforth expecting till His enemies be made His footstool*[5]. And again, *Looking unto Jesus, the author and perfecter of our faith; Who for the joy that was set before Him endured the Cross, despising shame, and is set down on the right hand of the throne of God*[6].

30. And though there are many other texts concerning the session of the Only-begotten on the right hand of God, yet these may suffice us at present; with a repetition of my remark, that it was not after His coming in the flesh[7] that He obtained the dignity of this seat; no, for even before all ages, the Only-begotten Son of God, our Lord Jesus Christ, ever possesses the throne on the right hand of the Father. Now may He Himself, the God of all, who is Father of the Christ, and our Lord Jesus Christ, who came down, and ascended, and sitteth together with the Father, watch over your souls; keep unshaken and unchanged your hope in Him who rose again; raise you together with Him from your dead sins unto His heavenly gift; count you worthy to be *caught up in the clouds, to meet the Lord in the air*[8], in His fitting time; and, until that time arrive of His glorious second advent, write all your names in the Book of the living, and having written them, never blot them out (for the names of many, who fall away, are blotted out); and may He grant to all of you to believe on Him who rose again, and to look for Him who is gone up, and is to come again, (to come, but not from the earth; for be on your guard, O man, because of the deceivers who are to come;) Who sitteth on high, and is here present together with us, *beholding the*

autem fidei .... sedisse ad dexteram Patris:" *adversus Praxean*, c. 2: "sedere ad dexteram Patris."

8 ἐκ προκοπῆς. Cf. Cat. x. 5, note 8.

9 ἀφ' οὗπερ ἔστιν, (ἔστι δὲ ἀεὶ γεννηθείς). In both clauses ἔστιν is emphatic.

1 Is. vi. 1. 2 Joh. i. 18. 3 Ps. xciii. 2. 4 Ps. cx. 1. 5 Matt. xxii. 43. 6 Acts ii. 34. 7 Matt. xxvi. 64. 8 1 Pet. iii. 22.

9 Rom. viii. 34. 1 Eph. i. 19, 20. 2 Col. iii. 1. 3 Heb. i. 3. 4 Ib. v. 13. 5 Ib. x. 12.

6 Ib. xii. 2. On Cyril's omission cf Mark xvi. 19. see Westcott and Hort.

7 τὴν ἔνσαρκον παρουσίαν. Cf. § 27. 8 1 Thess. iv. 17.

order of each, and the steadfastness of his faith[9]. For think not that because He is now absent in the flesh, He is therefore absent also in the Spirit. He is here present in the midst of us, listening to what is said of Him, and beholding thine inward thoughts, and *trying the reins and hearts*[1];—who also is now ready to present those who are coming to baptism, and all of you, in the Holy Ghost to the Father, and to say, *Behold, I and the children whom God hath given Me*[2]:—To whom be glory for ever. Amen.

9 Col. ii. 5.

1 Ps. vii. 9.

2 Isa. viii. 18; Heb. ii. 13.

LECTURE XV.

On the clause, And shall come in glory to judge the quick and the dead; of whose kingdom there shall be no end.

Daniel vii. 9—14.

I beheld till thrones were placed, and one that was ancient of days did sit, and then, *I saw in a vision of the night, and behold one like unto the Son of Man came with the clouds of heaven, &c.*

1. We preach not one advent only of Christ, but a second also, far more glorious than the former. For the former gave a view of His patience; but the latter brings with it the crown of a divine kingdom. For all things, for the most part, are twofold in our Lord Jesus Christ: a twofold generation; one, of God, before the ages; and one, of a Virgin, at the close of the ages: His descents twofold; one, the unobserved, *like rain on a fleece*[1]; and a second His open coming, which is to be. In His former advent, He was wrapped in swaddling clothes in the manger; in His second, He *covereth Himself with light as with a garment*[2]. In His first coming, *He endured the Cross, despising shame*[3]; in His second, He comes attended by a host of Angels, receiving glory[4]. We rest not then upon His first advent only, but look also for His second. And as at His first coming we said, *Blessed is He that cometh in the Name of the Lord*[5], so will we repeat the same at His second coming; that when with Angels we meet our Master, we may worship Him and say, *Blessed is He that cometh in the Name of the Lord.* The Saviour comes, not to be judged again, but to judge them who judged Him; He who before held His peace when judged[6], shall remind the transgressors who did those daring deeds at the Cross, and shall say, *These things hast thou done, and I kept silence*[7]. Then, He came because of a divine dispensation, teaching men with persuasion; but this time they will of necessity have Him for their King, even though they wish it not.

2. And concerning these two comings, Malachi the Prophet says, *And the Lord whom ye seek shall suddenly come to His temple*[8]; behold one coming. And again of the second coming he says, *And the Messenger of the covenant whom ye delight in. Behold, He cometh, saith*[9] *the Lord Almighty. But who shall abide the day of His coming? or who shall stand when He appeareth? Because He cometh in like a refiner's fire, and like fullers' herb; and He shall sit as a refiner and purifier.* And immediately after the Saviour Himself says, *And I will draw near to you in judgment; and I will be a swift witness against the sorcerers, and against the adulteresses, and against those who swear falsely in My Name*[1], and the rest. For this cause Paul warning us beforehand says, *If any man buildeth on the foundation gold, and silver, and precious stones, wood, hay, stubble; every man's work shall be made manifest; for the day shall declare it, because it shall be revealed in fire*[2]. Paul also knew these two comings, when writing to Titus and saying, *The grace of God hath appeared which bringeth salvation unto all men, instructing us that, denying ungodliness and worldly lusts, we should live soberly, and godly, and righteously in this present world; looking for the blessed hope, and appearing of the glory of the great God and our Saviour Jesus Christ*[3]. Thou seest how he spoke of a first, for which he gives thanks; and of a second, to which we look forward. Therefore the words also of the Faith which we are announcing were just now delivered thus[4]; that we believe in Him, who also ascended into the heavens, and sat

---

1 Ps. lxxii. 6. See xii. 9; and § 10, below.
2 Ps. civ. 2.
3 Heb. xii. 2.
4 Cyril's contrast of the two Advents seems to be partly borrowed from Justin M. (*Apol.* i. 52; *Tryph.* 110). See also Tertullian (*Adv. Judaeos,* c. 14); Hippolytus (*De Antichristo,* 44).
5 Matt. xxi. 9; xxiii. 39.
6 Ib. xxvi. 63.
7 Ps. l. 21.
8 Mal. iii. 1—3.

---

9 The Benedictine Editor by omitting λέγει, obtains the sense, *He cometh, even the Lord Almighty.* But λέγει is supported by the MSS. of Cyril, as well as by the Septuagint and Hebrew.

1 Mal. iii. 5.
2 1 Cor. iii. 12.

3 Titus ii. 11. The Benedictine Editor adopts τοῦ Σωτῆρος instead of ἡ σωτήριος, against the authority of the best MSS. of Cyril.

4 νῦν παρεδόθη. Cyril means that at the beginning of this present Lecture he had delivered to the Catechumens those articles of the Creed which he was going to explain. Compare Cat. xviii. 21, where we see that Cyril first announces (ἐπαγγέλλω) the words which the learners repeat after him (ἀπαγγέλλω).

The clause, Whose Kingdom shall have no end, was not contained in the original form of the Creed of Nicæa, A.D. 325, but its substance is found in many earlier writings. Compare Justin M. (*Tryph.* § 46: καὶ αὐτοῦ ἐστιν ἡ αἰώνιος βασιλεία); *Const. Apost.* vii. 41; the Eusebian Confessions 1st and 4th of Antioch, and the Macrostich, A.D. 341, 342, 344. Bp. Bull asserts that the Creed of Jerusalem, containing this clause, was no other than the ancient Eastern Creed, first directed against the Gnostics of the Sub-Apostolic age (*Judicium Eccl. Cathol.* vi. 16).

DOWN ON THE RIGHT HAND OF THE FATHER, AND SHALL COME IN GLORY TO JUDGE QUICK AND DEAD; WHOSE KINGDOM SHALL HAVE NO END.

3. Our Lord Jesus Christ, then, comes from heaven; and He comes with glory at the end of this world, in the last day. For of this world there is to be an end, and this created world is to be re-made anew[5]. For since corruption, *and theft, and adultery*, and every sort of sins *have been poured forth over the earth, and blood has been mingled with blood*[6] in the world, therefore, that this wondrous dwelling-place may not remain filled with iniquity, this world passeth away, that the fairer world may be made manifest. And wouldest thou receive the proof of this out of the words of Scripture? Listen to Esaias, saying, *And the heaven shall be rolled together as a scroll; and all the stars shall fall, as leaves from a vine, and as leaves fall from a fig-tree*[7]. The Gospel also says, *The sun shall be darkened, and the moon shall not give her light, and the stars shall fall from heaven*[8]. Let us not sorrow, as if we alone died; the stars also shall die; but perhaps rise again.. And the Lord rolleth up the heavens, not that He may destroy them, but that He may raise them up again more beautiful. Hear David the Prophet saying, *Thou, Lord, in the beginning didst lay the foundations of the earth, and the heavens are the work of Thy hands; they shall perish, but Thou remainest*[9]. But some one will say, Behold, he says plainly that *they shall perish.* Hear in what sense he says, *they shall perish;* it is plain from what follows; *And they all shall wax old as doth a garment; and as a vesture shalt Thou fold them up, and they shall be changed.* For as a man is said to "perish," according to that which is written, *Behold, how the righteous perisheth, and no man layeth it to heart*[1], and this, though the resurrection is looked for; so we look for a resurrection, as it were, of the heavens also. *The sun shall be turned into darkness, and the moon into blood*[2]. Here let converts from the Manichees gain instruction, and no longer make those lights their gods; nor impiously think, that this sun which shall be darkened is Christ[3]. And again hear the Lord saying, *Heaven and earth shall pass away, but My words shall not pass away*[4]; for the creatures are not as precious as the Master's words.

4. The things then which are seen shall pass away, and there shall come the things which are looked for, things fairer than the present; but as to the time let no one be curious. For *it is not for you*, He says, *to know times or seasons, which the Father hath put in His own power*[5]. And venture not thou to declare when these things shall be, nor on the other hand supinely slumber. For he saith, *Watch, for in such an hour as ye expect not the Son of Man cometh*[6]. But since it was needful for us to know the signs of the end, and since we are looking for Christ, therefore, that we may not die deceived and be led astray by that false Antichrist, the Apostles, moved by the divine will, address themselves by a providential arrangement to the True Teacher, and say, *Tell us, when shall these things be, and what shall be the sign of Thy coming, and of the end of the world*[7]? We look for Thee to come again, but *Satan transforms himself into an Angel of light;* put us therefore on our guard, that we may not worship another instead of Thee. And He, opening His divine and blessed mouth, says, *Take heed that no man mislead you.* Do you also, my hearers, as seeing Him now with the eyes of your mind, hear Him saying the same things to you; *Take heed that no man mislead you.* And this word exhorts you all to give heed to what is spoken; for it is not a history of things gone by, but a prophecy of things future, and which will surely come. Not that we prophesy, for we are unworthy; but that the things which are written will be set before you, and the signs declared. Observe thou, which of them have already come to pass, and which yet remain; and make thyself safe.

5. *Take heed that no man mislead you: for many shall come in My name, saying, I am Christ, and shall mislead many.* This has happened in part: for already Simon Magus has said this, and Menander[8], and some others of the godless leaders of heresy; and others will say it in our days, or after us.

6. A second sign. *And ye shall hear of wars and rumours of wars*[9]. Is there then at this time war between Persians and Romans for Mesopotamia, or no? Does nation rise up against nation and kingdom against kingdom, or no? *And there shall be famines and pesti-*

5 The Benedictine Editor suggests that Cyril "is refuting those who said that the Universe was to perish utterly, an opinion which seems to be somehow imputed to Origen by Methodius, or Proclus, in Epiphanius (*Hæres.* lxiv. 31, 32)." On Origen's much controverted opinions concerning the beginning and end of the world, see Huet. *Origeniana*, II. 4—6: and Bp. Westcott, *Dictionary of Christian Biography*, "Origen," pp. 137, 138.

6 Hos. iv. 2.

7 Is. xxxiv. 4.

8 Matt. xxiv. 29.

9 Ps. cii. 25, 26; Heb. i. 10—12.

1 Is. lvii. 1.

2 Joel ii. 31.

3 Cat. vi. 13; xi. 21.

4 Matt. xxiv. 35.

5 Acts i. 7.

6 Matt. xxiv. 42, 44; Ib. *v.* 3.

7 Ib. *vv* 3 and 4.

8 Cat. vi. 14, 16.

9 Matt. xxiv. 6. The war with Sapor II., King of Persia, which broke out immediately on the death of Constantine, and continued throughout the reign of Constantius, was raging fiercely at the date of these Lectures, the great battle of Singara being fought in the year 348 A.D.

lences and earthquakes in divers places. These things have already come to pass; and again, *And fearful sights from heaven, and mighty storms*[1]. *Watch therefore*, He says; *for ye know not at what hour your Lord doth come*[2].

7. But we seek our own sign of His coming; we Churchmen seek a sign proper to the Church[3]. And the Saviour says, *And then shall many be offended, and shall betray one another, and shall hate one another*[4]. If thou hear that bishops advance against bishops, and clergy against clergy, and laity against laity even unto blood, be not troubled[5]; for it has been written before. Heed not the things now happening, but the things which are written; and even though I who teach thee perish, thou shalt not also perish with me; nay, even a hearer may become better than his teacher, and he who came last may be first, since even those about the eleventh hour the Master receives. If among Apostles there was found treason, dost thou wonder that hatred of brethren is found among bishops? But the sign concerns not only rulers, but the people also; for He says, *And because iniquity shall abound, the love of the many shall wax cold*[6]. Will any then among those present boast that he entertains friendship unfeigned towards his neighbour? Do not the lips often kiss, and the countenance smile, and the eyes brighten forsooth, while the heart is planning guile, and the man is plotting mischief with words of peace?

8. Thou hast this sign also: *And this Gospel of the kingdom shall be preached in all the world for a witness unto all nations, and then shall the end come*[7]. And as we see, nearly the whole world is now filled with the doctrine of Christ.

9. And what comes to pass after this? He says next, *When therefore ye see the abomination of desolation, which was spoken of by Daniel the Prophet, standing in the Holy Place, let him that readeth understand*[8]. And again, *Then if any man shall say unto you, Lo, here is the Christ, or, Lo, there; believe it not*[9]. Hatred of the brethren makes room next for Antichrist; for the devil prepares beforehand the divisions among the people, that he who is to come may be acceptable to them. But God forbid that any of Christ's servants here, or elsewhere, should run over to the enemy! Writing concerning this matter, the Apostle Paul gave a manifest sign, saying, *For that day shall not come, except there come first the falling away, and the man of sin be revealed, the son of perdition, who opposeth and exalteth himself against all that is called God, or that is worshipped; so that he sitteth in the temple of God, shewing himself that he is God. Remember ye not that when I was yet with you, I told you these things? And now ye know that which restraineth, to the end that he may be revealed in his own season. For the mystery of iniquity doth already work, only there is one that restraineth now, until he be taken out of the way. And then shall the lawless one be revealed, whom the Lord Jesus shall slay with the breath of His mouth, and shall destroy with the brightness of His coming. Even him, whose coming is after the working of Satan, with all power and signs and lying wonders, and with all deceit of unrighteousness for them that are perishing*[1]. Thus wrote Paul, and now is the *falling away*. For men have fallen away from the right faith[2]; and some preach the identity of the Son with the Father[3], and others dare to say that Christ

---

1 Luke xxi. 11. Jerome in the *Chronicon* mentions a great earthquake in 346 A.D., by which Dyrrachium was destroyed, and Rome and other cities of Italy greatly injured (Ben. Ed.).

Cyril substitutes χειμῶνες for σημεῖα, the better reading in Luke xxi. 11.

2 Matt. xxiv. 42.

3 ἐκκλησιαστικός, when applied to persons, means either, as here, an orthodox member of the Church in contrast to a heretic, pagan, or Jew (Origen. *in Job* xx. 6), or more particularly a Cleric as opposed to a layman (Cat. xvii. 10).

4 Matt. xxiv. 10.

5 "S. Cyril here describes the state of the Church, when orthodoxy was for a while trodden under foot, its maintainers persecuted, and the varieties of Arianism, which took its place, were quarrelling for the ascendancy. Gibbon quotes two passages, one from a pagan historian of the day, another from a Father of the Church, which fully bear out S. Cyril's words. What made the state of things still more deplorable, was the defection of some of the orthodox party, as Marcellus, into opposite errors; while the subsequent secessions of Apollinaris and Lucifer show what lurking disorders there were within it at the time when S. Cyril wrote. (Vid. *infr.* 9.) The passages referred to are as follows: 'The Christian Religion,' says Ammianus, 'in itself plain and simple, he (Constantius) confounded by the dotage of superstition. Instead of reconciling the parties by the weight of his authority, he cherished and propagated, by vain disputes, the differences which his vain curiosity had excited. The highways were covered with troops of Bishops, galloping from every side to the assemblies, which they called synods; and while they laboured to reduce the whole sect to their own particular opinions, the public establishment of the posts was almost ruined by their hasty and repeated journeys.' *Hist.* xxi. 16. S. Hilary of Poictiers thus speaks of Asia Minor, the chief seat of the Arian troubles: 'It is a thing equally deplorable and dangerous, that there are as many creeds as opinions among men, as many doctrines as inclinations, and as many sources of blasphemy as there are faults among us; because we make creeds arbitrarily, and explain them as arbitrarily. The Homoousion is rejected and received and explained away by successive synods. The partial or total resemblance of the Father and of the Son is a subject of dispute for these unhappy divines. Every year, nay, every moon, we make new creeds to describe invisible mysteries. We repent of what we have done, we defend those who repent, we anathematize those whom we defended. We condemn either the doctrine of others in ourselves, or our own in that of others; and reciprocally tearing one another to pieces, we have been the cause of each other's ruin,' *ad Constant.* ii. 4, 5. Gibbon's translations are used, which, though diffuse, are faithful in their matter. What a contrast do these descriptions present to Athanasius' uniform declaration, that the whole question was really settled at Nicæa, and no other synod or debate was necessary!"—(R.W.C.). Compare, for example, the account of the seditions in Antioch and in Constantinople, in Socrates, *Eccles. Hist.* i. 24; i., 12—14, and Athanas. *Hist. Arianorum*, passim.

6 Matt. xxiv. 12.

7 Matt. xxiv. 14.

8 Ib. *v.* 15.

9 Ib. *v.* 23.

1 2 Thess. ii. 3—10.

2 The prediction was supposed by earlier Fathers to refer to a personal Antichrist, whom they expected to come speedily. See Justin M. (*Tryph.* § 110: ὁ τῆς ἀποστασίας ἄνθρωπος; *ib.* § 32: "He who is to speak blasphemous and daring things against the Most High is already at the doors." Iren. *Hær.* V. 25. Cyril in this passage regards the heresies of his time as the apostasy in general, but looks also for a personal Antichrist: (§§ 11, 12).

3 *υἱοπατορία.* On this contemptuous name for Sabellianism, see Cat. iv. 8; xi. 16. The Third (Eusebian) Confession, or Third of Antioch, A.D. 341, anathematizes any who hold the doctrines of Marcellus of Ancyra or Sabellius, or Paul of Samosata (Athan. *de Synodis*, § 24, note 10, p. 462, in this Series, and Mr. Robert-

was brought into being out of nothing[4]. And formerly the heretics were manifest; but now the Church is filled with heretics in disguise[5]. For men have fallen away from the truth, and *have itching ears*[6]. Is it a plausible discourse? all listen to it gladly. Is it a word of correction? all turn away from it. Most have departed from right words, and rather choose the evil, than desire the good[7]. This therefore is *the falling away*, and the enemy is soon to be looked for: and meanwhile he has in part begun to send forth his own forerunners[8], that he may then come prepared upon the prey. Look therefore to thyself, O man, and make safe thy soul. The Church now charges thee before the Living God; she declares to thee the things concerning Antichrist before they arrive. Whether they will happen in thy time we know not, or whether they will happen after thee we know not; but it is well that, knowing these things, thou shouldest make thyself secure beforehand.

10. The true Christ, the Only-begotten Son of God, comes no more from the earth. If any come making false shows[9] in the wilderness, go not forth; if they say, *Lo, here is the Christ, Lo, there, believe it not*[1]. Look no longer downwards and to the earth; for the Lord descends from heaven; not alone as before, but with many, escorted by tens of thousands of Angels; nor secretly as the dew on the fleece[2]; but shining forth openly as the lightning. For He hath said Himself, *As the lightning cometh out of the east, and shineth even unto the west, so shall also the coming of the Son of Man be*[3]; and again, *And they shall see the Son of Man coming upon the clouds with power and great glory, and He shall send forth His Angels with a great trumpet*[4]; and the rest.

11. But as, when formerly He was to take man's nature, and God was expected to be born of a Virgin, the devil created prejudice against this, by craftily preparing among idol-worshippers[5] fables of false gods, begetting and begotten of women, that, the falsehood having come first, the truth, as he supposed, might be disbelieved; so now, since the true Christ is to come a second time, the adversary, taking occasion by[6] the expectation of the simple, and especially of them of the circumcision, brings in a certain man who is a magician[7], and most expert in sorceries and enchantments of beguiling craftiness; who shall seize for himself the power of the Roman empire, and shall falsely style himself Christ; by this name of Christ deceiving the Jews, who are looking for the Anointed[8], and seducing those of the Gentiles by his magical illusions.

12. But this aforesaid Antichrist is to come when the times of the Roman empire shall have been fulfilled, and the end of the world is now drawing near[9]. There shall rise up together ten kings of the Romans, reigning in different parts perhaps, but all about the same time; and after these an eleventh, the Antichrist, who by his magical craft shall seize upon the Roman power; and of the kings who reigned before him, *three he shall humble*[1], and the remaining seven he shall keep in subjection to himself. At first indeed he will put on a show of mildness (as though he were a learned and discreet person), and of soberness and benevolence[2]: and by the lying

son's *Prolegomena*, p. xliv.). In the *Ecthesis*, or *Statement of Faith*, § 2, Athanasius writes: "Neither do we hold a Son-Father, as do the Sabellians, calling Him of one but (*a sole and?*) not the same essence, and thus destroying the existence of the Son." As to Marcellus, see Athanasius, *Hist. Arian.* § 6 (p. 271), and the letter of Julius in the *Apologia c. Arian.* § 32 (p. 116): also notes 3, 4 on § 27 below.

4 See Athanasius, *De Synod.* § 15: "Arius and those with him thought and professed thus: 'God made the Son out of nothing, and called Him His Son:"' and *Expos. Fidei*, § 2: "We do not regard as a creature, or thing made, or as made out of nothing, God the Creator of all, the Son of God, the true Being from the true Being, the Alone from the Alone, inasmuch as the like glory and power was eternally and conjointly begotten of the Father." The 4th (Eusebian) Confession, or 4th of Antioch, A.D. 342, ends thus: "Those who say that the Son was from nothing, ... the Catholic Church regards as aliens."

5 Athan. *Adversus Arianos*, *Or.* i. 1: "One heresy and that the last which has now risen as forerunner of Antichrist, the Arian as it is called, considering that other heresies, her elder sisters, have been openly proscribed, in her craft and cunning affects to array herself in Scripture language, like her father the devil, and is forcing her way back into the Church's paradise, &c." The supposed date of this Oration is 8 or 10 years later than that of Cyril's Lectures.

6 2 Tim. iv. 3.

7 A reading supported by the best MSS. and approved by the Benedictine Editor gives a different sense, "and rather choose to seem than resolve to be," inverting the proverb "esse quam videri."

8 In the passage quoted above in note 5 the Arian heresy is called a "forerunner" (πρόδρομος) of Antichrist.

9 φαντασιοκοπῶν, a rare word, rendered "frantic" in Ecclus. iv. 30: its more precise meaning seems to be "making a false show," which is here applied to a false Christ, and again in § 14 to the father of lies who makes a vain show of false miracles.

1 Matt. xxiv. 23.

2 Ps. lxxii. 6. Cf. § 1, note 1.

3 Matt. xxiv. 27.

4 Matt. xxiv. *v.* 30.

5 ἐν εἰδωλολατρείᾳ may mean either "in idol-worship," or "among idolaters," the abstract being used for the concrete, as in Rom. iii. 30: δικαιώσει περιτομήν.

6 ἐφόδιον, "provision for a journey," is here equivalent in meaning to ἀφορμή, "a starting point," or favourable occasion."

7 Antichrist is described by Hippolytus (*De Christo et Antichristo*, § 57, as "a son of the devil, and a vessel of Satan," who will rule and govern "after the manner of the law of Augustus, by whom the Roman empire was established, sanctioning everything thereby." Cf. Iren. *Hær.* V. 30, § 3; Dictionary of Christian Biography, *Antichrist*: "The sharp precision with which St. Paul had pointed to '*the* man of sin,' '*the* lawless one,' '*the* adversary,' '*the* son of perdition,' led men to dwell on that thought rather than on the many ψευδόχριστοι of whom Christ Himself had spoken."

8 τὸν 'Ηλειμμένον, Aquila's rendering of משיח, adopted by the Jews in preference to τὸν Χριστόν, from hatred of the name Christ or Christian. Hippolytus, *ubi supra*, § 6: "The Saviour came into the world in the Circumcision, and he (Antichrist) will come in the same manner:" ib. § 14: "As Christ springs from the tribe of Judah, so Antichrist is to spring from the tribe of Dan." This expectation was grounded by Hippolytus on Gen. xlix. 17.

9 The fourth kingdom in the prophecy of Daniel (vii. 7, 23) was generally understood by early Christian writers to be the Roman Empire; and its dissolution was to be speedily followed by the end of the world. See § 13 below; Irenæus, V. 26; and Hippolytus, *ubi supra*, §§ 19, 28.

1 Dan. vii. 24: *and he shall put down three kings* (R.V.).

2 The Jerusalem Editor quotes as from Hippolytus a similar description of Antichrist (§ 23): "In his first steps he will be gentle, loveable, quiet, pious, pacific, hating injustice, detesting gifts, not allowing idolatry, &c.' But the treatise is a forgery of unknown date, apparently much later than Cyril.

signs and wonders of his magical deceit[3] having beguiled the Jews, as though he were the expected Christ, he shall afterwards be characterized by all kinds of crimes of inhumanity and lawlessness, so as to outdo all unrighteous and ungodly men who have gone before him; displaying against all men, but especially against us Christians, a spirit murderous and most cruel, merciless and crafty[4]. And after perpetrating such things for three years and six months only, he shall be destroyed by the glorious second advent from heaven of the only-begotten Son of God, our Lord and Saviour Jesus, the true Christ, who shall slay Antichrist *with the breath of His mouth*[5], and shall deliver him over to the fire of hell.

13. Now these things we teach, not of our own invention, but having learned them out of the divine Scriptures used in the Church[6], and chiefly from the prophecy of Daniel just now read; as Gabriel also the Archangel interpreted it, speaking thus: *The fourth beast shall be a fourth kingdom upon earth, which shall surpass all kingdoms*[7]. And that this kingdom is that of the Romans, has been the tradition of the Church's interpreters. For as the first kingdom which became renowned was that of the Assyrians, and the second, that of the Medes and Persians together, and after these, that of the Macedonians was the third, so the fourth kingdom now is that of the Romans[8]. Then Gabriel goes on to interpret, saying, *His ten horns are ten kings that shall arise; and another king shall rise up after them, who shall surpass in wickedness all who were before him*[9]; (he says, not only the ten, but also all who have been before him;) *and he shall subdue three kings*; manifestly out of the ten former kings: but it is plain that by subduing three of these ten, he will become the eighth king; *and he shall speak words against the Most High*[10]. A blasphemer the man is and lawless, not having received the kingdom from his fathers, but having usurped the power by means of sorcery.

14. And who is this, and from what sort of working? Interpret to us, O Paul. *Whose coming*, he says, *is after the working of Satan, with all power and signs and lying wonders*[1]; implying, that Satan has used him as an instrument, working in his own person through him; for knowing that his judgment shall now no longer have respite, he wages war no more by his ministers, as is his wont, but henceforth by himself more openly[2]. And *with all signs and lying wonders*; for the father of falsehood will make a show[3] of the works of falsehood, that the multitudes may think that they see a dead man raised, who is not raised, and lame men walking, and blind men seeing, when the cure has not been wrought.

15. And again he says, *Who opposeth and exalteth himself against all that is called God, or that is worshipped*; (*against every God*; Antichrist forsooth will abhor the idols,) *so that he seateth himself in the temple of God*[4]. What temple then? He means, the Temple of the Jews which has been destroyed. For God forbid that it should be the one in which we are! Why say we this? That we may not be supposed to favour ourselves. For if he comes to the Jews as Christ, and desires to be worshipped by the Jews, he will make great account of the Temple, that he may more completely beguile them; making it supposed that he is the man of the race of David, who shall build up the Temple which was erected by Solomon[5]. And Antichrist will come at the time when there shall not be left one stone upon another in the Temple of the Jews, according to the doom pronounced by our Saviour[6]; for when, either

3 Iren. V. 28, § 2: "Since the demons and apostate spirits are at his service, he through their means performs wonders, by which he leads the inhabitants of the earth astray."

4 Iren. V. 25, § 4: "He shall remove his kingdom into that city (Jerusalem), and shall sit in the Temple of God, leading astray those who worship him as if he were Christ."

According to the genuine treatise of Hippolytus Antichrist was to restore the kingdom of the Jews (*De Antichristo*, § 25), to collect the Jews out of every country of the Dispersion, making them his own, as though they were his own children, and promising to restore their country, and establish again their kingdom and nation, in order that he may be worshipped by them as God (§ 54), and he will lead them on to persecute the saints, i.e. the Christians (§ 56). Compare the elaborate description of Antichrist and his cruelty in Lactantius, *Div. Inst.* vii. 17; *Epit.* § 71.

5 2 Thess. ii. 8. Cf. Iren. V. 25, § 3: Hippol. § 64.

6 ἐκκλησιαζομένων. Cf. Cat. iv. 35, 36, where Cyril distinguishes the Scriptures ἃς καὶ ἐν Ἐκκλησίᾳ μετὰ παρρησίας ἀναγινώσκομεν from ὅσα ἐν Ἐκκλησίαις μὴ ἀναγινώσκεται.

7 Dan. vii. 23: (R.V.) *shall be diverse from all the kingdoms.*

8 Irenæus (V. 26) identifies the fourth kingdom with "the empire which now rules." Hippolytus, *de Antichristo*, § 25: "*A fourth beast dreadful and terrible: it had iron teeth and claws of brass.* And who are these but the Romans?"

9 Dan. vii. 24.

10 Dan. v. 25. Dean Church compares Rev. xvii. 11: *And the beast that was, and is not, even he is the eighth, and is of the seven, and goeth into perdition.* See also Iren. V. 26, § 1.

1 2 Thess. ii. 9. Lactantius (A.D. 300 *circ.*), *Div. Inst.* vii. 17: "That king . . . . will also be a prophet of lies; and he will constitute and call himself God, and will order himself to be worshipped as the Son of God; and power will be given him to do signs and wonders, by the sight of which he may entice men to adore him." Cf. *Epitome*, lxxi.

2 "Vid. Iren. *Hær.* V. 26, 2," (R.W.C.). The passage is quoted by Eusebius (*Eccl. Hist.* iv. 18), from a lost work of Justin M. *Against Marcion*: "Justin well said that before the coming of the Lord Satan never dared to blaspheme God, as not yet knowing his own condemnation, because it was stated by the prophets in parables and allegories. But after our Lord's advent having learnt plainly from His words and those of the Apostles that everlasting fire is prepared for him, ... he by means of such men as these blasphemes the Lord who brings the judgment upon him, as being already condemned."

S. Cyril seems to expect that Antichrist will be an incarnation of Satan, as did Hippolytus (*de Antichr.* § 6): "The Saviour appeared in the form of man, and he too will come in the form of a man."

3 φαντασιοκοπεῖ. See above, § 10, note 9, and the equivalent phrase in § 17: σημείων καὶ τεράτων φαντασίας ἐδείκνυον.

4 2 Thess. ii. 4.

5 See § 12, notes 3, 4, and Hippolytus, *ubi supra*: "The Saviour raised up and shewed His holy flesh like a temple; and he will raise a temple of stone in Jerusalem." "Cyril wrote this before Julian's attempt to rebuild the Jewish Temple" (R.W.C.).

6 Matt. xxiv. 2. Cyril refers the whole prophecy to the time of Christ's second coming at the end of the world, not regarding the destruction of Jerusalem and its Temple by Titus as fulfilling any part of the prediction.

decay of time, or demolition ensuing on pretence of new buildings, or from any other causes, shall have overthrown all the stones, I mean not merely of the outer circuit, but of the inner shrine also, where the Cherubim were, then shall he come *with all signs and lying wonders*, exalting himself against all idols; at first indeed making a pretence of benevolence, but afterwards displaying his relentless temper, and that chiefly against the Saints of God. For he says, *I beheld, and the same horn made war with the saints*[7]; and again elsewhere, *there shall be a time of trouble, such as never was since there was a nation upon earth, even to that same time*[8]. Dreadful is that beast, a mighty dragon, unconquerable by man, ready to devour; concerning whom though we have more things to speak out of the divine Scriptures, yet we will content ourselves at present with thus much, in order to keep within compass.

16. For this cause the Lord knowing the greatness of the adversary grants indulgence to the godly, saying, *Then let them which be in Judæa flee to the mountains*[9]. But if any man is conscious that he is very stout-hearted, to encounter Satan, let him stand (for I do not despair of the Church's nerves), and let him say, *Who shall separate us from the love of Christ and the rest*[1]? But, let those of us who are fearful provide for our own safety; and those who are of a good courage, stand fast: *for then shall be great tribulation, such as hath not been from the beginning of the world until now, no, nor ever shall be*[2]. But thanks be to God who hath confined the greatness of that tribulation to a few days; for He says, *But for the elect's sake those days shall be shortened*[3]; and Antichrist shall reign for three years and a half only. We speak not from apocryphal books, but from Daniel; for he says, *And they shall be given into his hand until a time and times and half a time*[4]. *A time* is the one year in which his coming shall for a while have increase; and *the times* are the remaining two years of iniquity, making up the sum of the three years; and *the half a time* is the six months. And again in another place Daniel says the same thing, *And he sware by Him that liveth for ever that it shall be for a time, and times, and half a time*[5]. And some peradventure have referred what follows also to this; namely, *a thousand two hundred and ninety days*[6]; and this, *Blessed is he that endureth and cometh to the thousand three hundred and five and thirty days*[7]. For this cause we must hide ourselves and flee; for perhaps *we shall not have gone over the cities of Israel, till the Son of Man be come*[8].

17. Who then is the blessed man, that shall at that time devoutly witness for Christ? For I say that the Martyrs of that time excel all martyrs. For the Martyrs hitherto have wrestled with men only; but in the time of Antichrist they shall do battle with Satan in his own person[9]. And former persecuting kings only put to death; they did not pretend to raise the dead, nor did they make false shows[10] of signs and wonders. But in his time there shall be the evil inducement both of fear and of deceit, *so that if it be possible the very elect shall be deceived*[1]. Let it never enter into the heart of any then alive to ask, "What did Christ more? For by what power does this man work these things? Were it not God's will, He would not have allowed them." The Apostle warns thee, and says beforehand, *And for this cause God shall send them a working of error; (send*, that is, *shall allow to happen;)* not that they might make excuse, but *that they might be condemned*[2]. Wherefore? *They*, he says, *who believed not the truth*, that is, the true Christ, *but had pleasure in unrighteousness*, that is, in Antichrist. But as in the persecutions which happen from time to time, so also then God will permit these things, not because He wants power to hinder them, but because according to His wont He will through patience crown His own champions like as He did His Prophets and Apostles; to the end that having toiled for a little while they may inherit the eternal kingdom of heaven, according to that which Daniel says, *And at that time thy people shall be delivered, every one that shall be found written in the book* (manifestly, the book of life); *and many of them that sleep in the dust of the earth shall awake, some to everlasting life, and some to shame and everlasting contempt; and they that be wise shall shine as the brightness of the firmament; and of the many righteous*[3], *as the stars for ever and ever.*

---

7 Dan. vii. 21. Here again Cyril follows Hippolytus, § 25: "And under this (horn) was signified none other than Antichrist.

8 Ib. xii. 1.

9 Matt. xxiv. 16.

1 Rom. viii. 35.

2 Matt. xxiv. 21.

3 Ib. *v.* 22.

4 Dan. vii. 25. By "apocryphal" books Cyril probably means all such as were not allowed to be read in the public services of the Church: see Cat. iv. 33. note 3; and Bp. Westcott's note on the various meanings of the word ἀπόκρυφος, *Hist. of the Canon*, P. III. c. 1. That the Apocalypse of St. John is included under this term by Cyril, appears probable from the following reasons suggested by the Benedictine Editor. (1) It is not mentioned in the list of the Canonical Scriptures in iv. 36. (2) The earlier writers whom Cyril follows in this Lecture, Irenæus, *Hær.* V., 26, § 1, and Hippolytus, *De Antichristo*, § 34, combine the testimony of the Apocalypse with that of Daniel. The omission in Cyril therefore cannot have been accidental.

5 Dan. xii. 7.

6 Ib. *v.* 11.

7 Ib. *v.* 12.

8 Matt. x. 23.

9 αὐτοπροσώπως. See above, § 14, note 2. Some MSS. read ἀντιπροσώπως, "face to face," as in xii. 32, ἀντιπρόσωπος.

10 See above, § 14, note 3.

1 Matt. xxiv. 24.

2 2 Thess. ii. 11, 12: (R.V.) *That they all might be judged.* Cyril has κατακριθῶσι

3 Dan. xii. 1, 2: (R.V.) *they that turn many to righteousness.* Cyril follows the rendering of the Septuagint, ἀπὸ τῶν δικαίων τῶν πολλῶν, which gives no proper construction.

18. Guard thyself then, O man; thou hast the signs of Antichrist; and remember them not only thyself, but impart them also freely to all. If thou hast a child according to the flesh, admonish him of this now; if thou hast begotten one through catechizing[4], put him also on his guard, lest he receive the false one as the True. For the *mystery of iniquity doth already work*[5]. I fear these wars of the nations[6]; I fear the schisms of the Churches; I fear the mutual hatred of the brethren. But enough on this subject; only God forbid that it should be fulfilled in our days; nevertheless, let us be on our guard. And thus much concerning Antichrist.

19. But let us wait and look for the Lord's coming upon the clouds from heaven. Then shall Angelic trumpets sound; *the dead in Christ shall rise first*[7],—the godly persons who are alive shall be caught up in the clouds, receiving as the reward of their labours more than human honour, inasmuch as theirs was a more than human strife; according as the Apostle Paul writes, saying, *For the Lord Himself shall descend from heaven with a shout, with the voice of the Archangel, and with the trump of God: and the dead in Christ shall rise first. Then we which are alive and remain shall be caught up together with them in the clouds, to meet the Lord in the air; and so shall we ever be with the Lord*[8].

20. This coming of the Lord, and the end of the world, were known to the Preacher; who says, *Rejoice, O young man, in thy youth*, and the rest[9]; *Therefore remove anger*[1] *from thy heart, and put away evil from thy flesh; . . . and remember thy Creator . . . or ever the evil days come*[2], *. . . . or ever the sun, and the light, and the moon, and the stars be darkened*[3], *. . . . and they that look out of the windows be darkened*[4]; (signifying the faculty of sight;) *or ever the silver cord be loosed*; (meaning the assemblage of the stars, for their appearance is like silver;) *and the flower of gold be broken*[5]; (thus veiling the mention of the golden sun; for the camomile is a well-known plant, having many ray-like leaves shooting out round it;) *and they shall rise up at the voice of the sparrow, yea, they shall look away from the height, and terrors shall be in the way*[6]. What shall they see? *Then shall they see the Son of man coming on the clouds of heaven; and they shall mourn tribe by tribe*[7]. And what shall come to pass when the Lord is come? *The almond tree shall blossom, and the grasshopper shall grow heavy, and the caper-berry shall be scattered abroad*[8]. And as the interpreters say, the blossoming almond signifies the departure of winter; and our bodies shall then after the winter blossom with a heavenly flower[9]. *And the grasshopper shall grow in substance* (that means the winged soul clothing itself with the body[1],) and *the caper-berry shall be scattered abroad* (that is, the transgressors who are like thorns shall be scattered[2]).

21. Thou seest how they all foretell the coming of the Lord. Thou seest how they know *the voice of the sparrow*. Let us know what sort of voice this is. *For the Lord Himself shall descend from heaven with a shout, with the voice of the Archangel, and with the trump of God*[3]. The Archangel shall make proclamation and say to all, *Arise to meet the Lord*[4]. And fearful will be that descent of our Master. David says, *God shall manifestly come, even our God, and shall not keep silence; a fire shall burn before Him, and a fierce tempest round about Him*, and the rest[5]. The Son of Man shall come to the Father, according to the Scripture which was just now read, *on the clouds of heaven*, drawn by *a stream of fire*[6], which is to make trial of men. Then if any man's works are of gold, he shall be made brighter; if any man's course of life be like stubble, and unsubstantial, it shall be burnt up by the fire[7]. And the Father *shall sit*, having *His garment white as snow, and the hair of His head like pure wool*[8]. But this is spoken after the manner of men; wherefore? Because He is the King of those who

---

4 Compare 1 Cor. iv. 15: *I begat you through the gospel.* Clem. Alex. *Strom.* iii. c. 15: τῷ διὰ τῆς ἀληθοῦς κατηχήσεως γεννήσαντι κεῖταί τις μισθός.

5 2 Thess. ii. 7.

6 See above, §§ 6, 7.

7 1 Thess. iv. 16.

8 Ib. *vv.* 16, 17.

9 Eccles. xi. 9. The Preacher's description of old age and death is interpreted by Cyril of the end of the world, as it had been a century before by Gregory Thaumaturgus, in his paraphrase of the book.

1 Ib. *v.* 10: (R.V.) *sorrow.* Marg. Or, *vexation*, Or, *provocation.*

2 Ib. xii. 1.

3 Ib. *v.* 2.

4 Ib. *v.* 3.

5 Ib. *v.* 6. According to the usual interpretation death is here represented by the breaking of a chain and the lamp which hangs from it. Cf. Delitzsch, and *Speaker's Commentary*, in loc. for other interpretations.

τὸ ἀνθέμιον τοῦ χρυσιόυ (Sept.), by which Cyril understood camomile' (ἀνθεμίς), more probably meant a pattern of flowers embossed on the vessel of gold: *vid.* Xenoph. *Anab.* V. 4, § 32: ἐστιγμένους ἀνθέμια, "damasked with *flowers.*"

6 Eccles. xii. 5. Cyril means rightly that the aged shrink from a giddy height, and from imaginary dangers of the road. For *the voice of the sparrow*, see below, § 21, note 4.

7 Matt. xxiv. 30: Zech. xii. 12.

8 Eccles. xii. 5.

9 "Dr. Thomson (*The Land and the Book*, p. 319,) says of the almond tree, "It is the type of old age, whose hair is white" (Speaker's Commentary).

1 The step, once as active as a *grasshopper*, or locust, shall grow heavy and slow. For other interpretations see Delitzsch.

2 *The caper-berry* (κάππαρις) *shall fail*, i.e. no longer stimulate appetite. But διασχεδασθήσεται (Sept. Cyril) means that the old man shall be like a caper-berry which when fully ripe bursts its husks and scatters its seeds: so R.V. (Margin); *The caper-berry shall burst.* Greg. Thaumat. *Metaphr. Eccles.* "The transgressors are cast out of the way, like a black and despicable caper-plant."

3 1 Thess. ii. 16.

4 Compare the spurious *Apocalypse of John*: "And at the voice of the bird every plant shall arise; that is, At the voice of the Archangel all the human race shall arise" (English Trs. *Ante-Nic. Libr.* p. 496). According to the Talmud the meaning is, "Even a bird awakes him" (Delitzsch).

5 Ps. l. 3.

6 Dan. vii. 13, 10.

7 1 Cor. iii. 12, 13. On ἀνυπόστατον, see Index. On δοκιμαστικόν, compare *The Teaching of the Apostles*, § 16: "Then all created mankind shall come to the fire of testing (δοκιμασίας), and many shall be offended and perish."

8 Dan. vii. 9.

have not been defiled with sins; *for*, He says, *I will make your sins white as snow, and as wool*[9], which is an emblem of forgiveness of sins, or of sinlessness itself. But the Lord who shall come from heaven on the clouds, is He who ascended on the clouds; for He Himself hath said, *And they shall see the Son of Man coming on the clouds of heaven, with power and great glory*[1].

22. But what is the sign of His coming? lest a hostile power dare to counterfeit it. *And then shall appear*, He says, *the sign of the Son of Man in heaven*[2]. Now Christ's own true sign is the Cross; a sign of a luminous Cross shall go before the King[3], plainly declaring Him who was formerly crucified: that the Jews who before *pierced Him* and plotted against Him, when they see it, may *mourn tribe by tribe*[4], saying, "This is He who was buffeted, this is He whose face they spat on, this is He whom they bound with chains, this is He whom of old they crucified, and set at nought[5]. Whither, they will say, shall we flee from the face of Thy wrath?" But the Angel hosts shall encompass them, so that they shall not be able to flee anywhere. The sign of the Cross shall be a terror to His foes; but joy to His friends who have believed in Him, or preached Him, or suffered for His sake. Who then is the happy man, who shall then be found a friend of Christ? That King, so great and glorious, attended by the Angel-guards, the partner of the Father's throne, will not despise His own servants. For that His Elect may not be confused with His foes, *He shall send forth His Angels with a great trumpet, and they shall gather together His elect from the four winds*[6]. He despised not Lot, who was but one; how then shall He despise many righteous? *Come, ye blessed of My Father*[7], will He say to them who shall then ride on chariots of clouds, and be assembled by Angels.

23. But some one present will say, "I am a poor man," or again, "I shall perhaps be found at that time sick in bed;" or, "I am but a woman, and I shall be taken at the mill: shall we then be despised?" Be of good courage, O man; the Judge is no respecter of persons; *He will not judge according to a man's appearance, nor reprove according to his speech*[8]. He honours not the learned before the simple, nor the rich before the needy. Though thou be in the field, the Angels shall take thee; think not that He will take the landowners, and leave thee the husbandman. Though thou be a slave, though thou be poor, be not any whit distressed; He who *took the form of a servant*[9] despises not servants. Though thou be lying sick in bed, yet it is written, *Then shall two be in one bed; the one shall be taken, and the other left*[1]. Though thou be of compulsion put to grind, whether thou be man or woman[2]; though thou be in fetters[3], and sit beside the mill, yet He *who by His might bringeth out them that are bound*[4], will not overlook thee. He who brought forth Joseph out of slavery and prison to a kingdom, shall redeem thee also from thy afflictions into the kingdom of heaven. Only be of good cheer, only work, only strive earnestly; for nothing shall be lost. Every prayer of thine, every Psalm thou singest is recorded; every alms-deed, every fast is recorded; every marriage duly observed is recorded; continence[5] kept for God's sake is recorded; but the first crowns in the records are those of virginity and purity; and thou shalt shine as an Angel. But as thou hast gladly listened to the good things, so listen again without shrinking to the contrary. Every covetous deed of thine is recorded; thine every act of fornication is recorded, thine every false oath is recorded, every blasphemy, and sorcery, and theft, and murder. All these things are henceforth to be recorded, if thou do the same now after having been baptized; for thy former deeds are blotted out.

24. *When the Son of Man*, He says, *shall come in His glory, and all the Angels with Him*[6]. Behold, O man, before what multitudes thou shalt come to judgment. Every race of mankind will then be present. Reckon, therefore, how many are the Roman nation; reckon how many the barbarian tribes now living, and how many have died within the last hundred years; reckon how many nations have been buried during the last thousand years; reckon all from Adam to this day. Great indeed is the multitude; but yet it is

---

9 Is. i. 18. 1 Matt. xxiv. 30. 2 Ib.

3 Cat. xiii. 41. In the letter to Constantius, three or four years later than this Lecture, Cyril treats the appearance at that time of a luminous Cross in the sky as a fulfilment of Matt. xxiv. 30: but he there adds (*Ep. ad Constantium*, § 6) that our Lord's prediction "was both fulfilled at that present time, and shall again be fulfilled more largely." On the opinion that "the sign of the Son of Man in heaven" should be the Cross, see Suicer, *Thesaurus*, Σταυρός. It is not improbable that the earliest trace of this interpretation is found in *The Teaching of the Apostles*, § 16: "Then shall appear the signs of the Truth: the first the sign of a (cross) spreading out (ἐκπετάσεως) in heaven."

4 Zech. xii. 12.

5 Cf. Barnab. *Epist.* c. vii.: "For they shall see Him in that day wearing the long scarlet robe about His flesh, and shall say, Is not this He, whom once we crucified, and set at nought, and spat upon (*al.* and pierced, and mocked)?"

6 Matt. xxiv. 31. 7 Ib. xxv. 34.

8 Is. xi. 3: (R.V.) *He shall not judge after the sight of his eyes, nor reprove after the hearing of his ears.*

9 Phil. ii. 7. 1 Luke xvii. 34. 2 Ib. *v.* 35.

3 The Jerusalem MS. (A) alone has the true reading πέδας, which is confirmed by πεπεδημένους in the quotation following, instead of παῖδας, which is quite inappropriate, and evidently an itacism. 4 Ex. xi. 5.

5 Ἐγκράτεια. "Id est viduitas" (Ben. Ed.). This special reference of the word to widowhood is to some extent confirmed by 1 Cor. vii. 9: εἰ δὲ οὐκ ἐγκρατεύονται, and is rendered highly probable by Cyril's separate mention of marriage and virginity.

6 Matt. xxv. 31.

little, for the Angels are many more. They are *the ninety and nine sheep*, but mankind is the single *one*[7]. For according to the extent of universal space, must we reckon the number of its inhabitants. The whole earth is but as a point in the midst of the one heaven, and yet contains so great a multitude; what a multitude must the heaven which encircles it contain? And must not the heaven of heavens contain unimaginable numbers[8]? And it is written, *Thousand thousands ministered unto Him, and ten thousand times ten thousand stood before Him*[9]; not that the multitude is only so great, but because the Prophet could not express more than these. So there will be present at the judgment in that day, God, the Father of all, Jesus Christ being seated with Him, and the Holy Ghost present with Them; and an angel's trumpet shall summon us all to bring our deeds with us. Ought we not then from this time forth to be sore troubled? Think it not a slight doom, O man, even apart from punishment, to be condemned in the presence of so many. Shall we not choose rather to die many deaths, than be condemned by friends?

25. Let us dread then, brethren, lest God condemn us; who needs not examination or proofs, to condemn. Say not, In the night I committed fornication, or wrought sorcery, or did any other thing, and there was no man by. Out of thine own conscience shalt thou be judged, thy *thoughts the meanwhile accusing or else excusing, in the day when God shall judge the secrets of men*[1]. The terrible countenance of the Judge will force thee to speak the truth; or rather, even though thou speak not, it will convict thee. For thou shalt rise clothed with thine own sins, or else with thy righteous deeds. And this has the Judge Himself declared,—for it is Christ who judges—*for neither doth the Father judge any man, but he hath given all judgment unto the Son*[2], not divesting Himself of His power, but judging through the Son; the Son therefore judgeth by the will[3] of the Father; for the wills of the Father and of the Son are not different, but one and the same. What then says the Judge, as to whether thou shalt bear thy works, or no? *And before Him shall they gather all nations*[4]: (for in the presence of Christ *every knee must bow, of things in heaven, and things in earth, and things under the earth*[5]:) *and He shall separate them one from another, as the shepherd divideth his sheep from the goats.* How does the shepherd make the separation? Does he examine out of a book which is a sheep and which a goat? or does he distinguish by their evident marks? Does not the wool show the sheep, and the hairy and rough skin the goat? In like manner, if thou hast been just now cleansed from thy sins, thy deeds shall be henceforth as pure wool; and thy robe shall remain unstained, and thou shalt ever say, *I have put off my coat, how shall I put it on*[6]? By thy vesture shalt thou be known for a sheep. But if thou be found hairy, like Esau, who was rough with hair, and wicked in mind, who for food lost his birthright and sold his privilege, thou shalt be one of those on the left hand. But God forbid that any here present should be cast out from grace, or for evil deeds be found among the ranks of the sinners on the left hand!

26. Terrible in good truth is the judgment, and terrible the things announced. The kingdom of heaven is set before us, and everlasting fire is prepared. How then, some one will say, are we to escape the fire? And how to enter into the kingdom? *I was an hungred*, He says, *and ye gave Me meat.* Learn hence the way; there is here no need of allegory, but to fulfil what is said. *I was an hungred, and ye gave Me meat; I was thirsty, and ye gave Me drink; I was a stranger, and ye took Me in; naked, and ye clothed Me; I was sick, and ye visited Me; I was in prison, and ye came unto Me*[7]. These things if thou do, thou shalt reign together with Him; but if thou do them not, thou shalt be condemned. At once then begin to do these works, and abide in the faith; lest, like the foolish virgins, tarrying to buy oil, thou be shut out. Be not confident because thou merely possessest the lamp, but constantly keep it burning. Let the light of thy good works shine before men[8], and let not Christ be blasphemed on thy account. Wear thou a garment of incorruption[9], resplendent in good works; and whatever matter thou receivest from God to administer as a steward, administer profitably. Hast thou been put in trust with riches? Dispense them well. Hast thou been entrusted with the word of teaching? Be a good steward thereof. Canst thou attach the souls of the hearers[1]? Do this diligently.

7 Matt. xviii. 12; Luke xv. 4. Ambrose, *Expos. in Luc.* VII. 210: "Rich is that shepherd of whose flock we are but the one hundredth part. Of Angels and Archangels, of Dominions, Powers, Thrones, and others He hath countless flocks, whom He hath left upon the mountains." Cf. Gregor. Nyss. *Contra Eunom. Or.* xii.

8 There is much variation in the reading and punctuation of this passage. I have followed the text adopted by the Jerusalem Editor with Codd. A. Roe. Casaub. and Grodecq, in preference to the Benedictine text, with which the Editor himself is dissatisfied.

9 Dan. vii. 10.

1 Rom. ii. 15, 16.

2 John v. 22.

3 νεύματι. Cat. xi. 22.

4 Matt. xxv. 32.

5 Phil. ii. 10.

6 Cant. V. 3. Compare Cat. iii. 7; xx. (Mystag. ii.) 2.

7 Matt. xxv. 35.

8 Matt. v. 16.

9 The prayer for the Catechumens in the *Apostolic Constitutions*, viii. 6, contains a petition that God would "vouchsafe to them the laver of regeneration, and the garment of incorruption, which is the true life."

1 προσθεῖναι. Cf. Acts ii. 41: προσετέθησαν. According to some MSS. the sentence would run thus: "Hast thou been entrusted with the word of teaching? Be a good steward of thy hearers' souls. Hast thou power to rule (προστῆναι)? Do this diligently."

There are many doors of good stewardship. Only let none of us be condemned and cast out; that we may with boldness meet Christ the Everlasting King, who reigns for ever. For He doth reign for ever, who shall be judge of quick and dead, because for quick and dead He died. And as Paul says, *For to this end Christ both died and lived again, that He might be Lord both of the dead and living*[2].

27. And shouldest thou ever hear any say that the kingdom of Christ shall have an end, abhor the heresy; it is another head of the dragon, lately sprung up in Galatia. A certain one has dared to affirm, that after the end of the world Christ shall reign no longer[3]; he has also dared to say, that the Word having come forth from the Father shall be again absorbed into the Father, and shall be no more[4]; uttering such blasphemies to his own perdition. For he has not listened to the Lord, saying, *The Son abideth for ever*[5]. He has not listened to Gabriel, saying, *And He shall reign over the house of Jacob for ever, and of His kingdom there shall be no end*[6]. Consider this text. Heretics of this day teach in disparagement of Christ, while Gabriel the Archangel taught the eternal abiding of the Saviour; whom then wilt thou rather believe? wilt thou not rather give credence to Gabriel? Listen to the testimony of Daniel in the text[7]; *I saw in a vision of the night, and behold, one like the Son of Man came with the clouds of heaven, and came to the Ancient of days. . . . . And to Him was given the honour, and the dominion, and the kingdom: and all peoples, tribes, and languages shall serve Him; His dominion is an everlasting dominion, which shall not pass away, and His kingdom shall not be destroyed*[8]. These things rather hold fast, these things believe, and cast away from thee the words of heresy; for thou hast heard most plainly of the endless kingdom of Christ.

28. The like doctrine thou has also in the interpretation of the *Stone, which was cut out of a mountain without hands*, which is *Christ according to the flesh*[9]; *And His kingdom shall not be left to another people.* David also says in one place, *Thy throne, O God, is for ever and ever*[1]; and in another place, *Thou, Lord, in the beginning hast laid the foundations of the earth, &c., they shall perish, but Thou remainest, &c.; but Thou art the same, and Thy years shall not fail*[2]: words which Paul has interpreted of the Son[3].

29. And wouldest thou know how they who teach the contrary ran into such madness? They read wrongly that good word of the Apostle, *For He must reign, till He hath put all enemies under His feet*[4]; and they say, when His enemies shall have been put under His feet, He shall cease to reign, wrongly and foolishly alleging this. For He who is king before He has subdued His enemies, how shall He not the rather be king, after He has gotten the mastery over them.

30. They have also dared to say that the Scripture, *When all things shall be subjected unto Him, then shall the Son also Himself be subjected unto Him that subjected all things unto Him*[5],—that this Scripture shews that the Son also shall be absorbed into the Father. Shall ye then, O most impious of all men, ye the creatures of Christ, continue? and shall Christ perish, by whom both you and all things were made? Such a word is blasphemous. But further, how shall all things be made subject unto Him? By perishing, or by abiding? Shall then the other things, when subject to the Son, abide, and shall the Son, when subject to the Father, not abide? For He shall be subjected, not because He shall then begin to do the Father's will (for from eternity He *doth* always *those things that please Him*[6]), but because, then as before, He obeys the Father, yielding, not a forced obedience, but a self-chosen accordance; for He is not a servant, that He should be subjected by force, but a Son, that He should comply of His free choice and natural love.

---

2 Rom. xiv. 9.

3 Marcellus, Bishop of Ancyra, and his pupil Photinus, are anathematized in the Creed called Μακρόστιχος as holding that Christ first became "Son of God when He took our flesh from the Virgin. . . . For they will have it that then Christ began His Kingdom, and that it will have an end after the consummation of all and the judgment. Such are the disciples of Marcellus and Scotinus of Galatian Ancyra, &c." See Newman on Athanasius, *de Synodis*, § 26, (5), notes *a* and *b*. Compare the description of Marcellus in the Letter of the Oriental Bishops who had withdrawn from the Council of Sardica to Philippopolis (A.D. 344). "There has arisen in our days a certain Marcellus of Galatia, the most execrable pest of all heretics, who with sacrilegious mind, and impious mouth, and wicked argument seeks to set bounds to the perpetual, eternal, and timeless kingdom of our Lord Christ, saying that He began to reign four hundred years since, and shall end at the dissolution of the present world" (Hilar. Pictav. *Ex Opere Hist.* Fragm. iii.).

4 "The person meant by Cyril, though he withholds the name, is Marcellus of Ancyra; who having written a book against the Arian Sophist Asterius to explain the Apostle's statement concerning the subjection of the Son to the Father, was thought to be renewing the heresy of Paul of Samosata. On this account he was reproved by the Bishops at the Council of Jerusalem, A.D. 335, for holding false opinions, and being ordered to recant his opinions promised to burn his book. Afterwards he applied to Constantine, by whom he was remitted to the Council of Constantinople, A.D. 336, and deposed by the Bishops. As however he was acquitted by the Councils of Rome, A.D 342, and of Sardica, A.D. 347, it became a matter of dispute whether he was really heretical. . . . From the fragments of his books transcribed by Eusebius, you may possibly acquit him of the Sabellian heresy and the confusion of the Father and the Son, but certainly not of the heresy concerning the end of Christ's kingdom, and the abandonment by the Word of the human nature which He assumed for our sake; so express are his words recorded by Eusebius in the beginning of the 2nd Book *Contra Marcellum*, pp. 50, 51." (Ben. Ed.) Cf. *Dict. Chr. Biogr.* "Eusebius of Cæsarea," p. 341; and note 3 on § 9 above.

5 John viii. 25.

6 Luke i. 33.

7 τὴν παροῦσαν.

8 Dan. vii. 13, 14.

9 Ib. ii. 45; Rom. ix. 5.

1 Ps xlv. 6.

2 Ib. cii. 25—27.

3 Heb. i. 10—12.

4 1 Cor. xv. 25.

5 1 Cor. xv. *v.* 28. Theodoret. *Comment. in Epist. i. ad Cor.* xv. 28: "This passage the followers of Arius and Eunomius carry continually on their tongue, thinking in this way to disparage the dignity of the Only-begotten."

6 John viii. 29.

31. But let us examine them; what is the meaning of "until" or "as long as?" For with the very phrase will I close with them, and try to overthrow their error. Since they have dared to say that the words, *till He hath put His enemies under His feet*, shew that He Himself shall have an end, and have presumed to set bounds to the eternal kingdom of Christ, and to bring to an end, as far as words go, His never-ending sovereignty, come then, let us read the like expressions in the Apostle: *Nevertheless, death reigned from Adam till Moses*[7]. Did men then die up to that time, and did none die any more after Moses, or after the Law has there been no more death among men? Well then, thou seest that the word "unto" is not to limit time; but that Paul rather signified this,—"And yet, though Moses was a righteous and wonderful man, nevertheless the doom of death, which was uttered against Adam, reached even unto him, and them that came after him; and this, though they had not committed the like sins as Adam, by his disobedience in eating of the tree."

32. Take again another similar text. *For until this day . . . when Moses is read, a vail lieth upon their heart*[8]. Does *until this day* mean only "until Paul?" Is it not *until this day* present, and even to the end? And if Paul say to the Corinthians, *For we came even as far as unto you in preaching the Gospel of Christ, having hope when your faith increases to preach the Gospel in the regions beyond you*[9], thou seest manifestly that *as far as* implies not the end, but has something following it. In what sense then shouldest thou remember that Scripture, *till He hath put all enemies under His feet*[1]*?* According as Paul says in another place, *And exhort each other daily, while it is called to-day*[2]*;* meaning, "continually." For as we may not speak of the "beginning of the days" of Christ, so neither suffer thou that any should ever speak of the end of His kingdom. For it is written, *His kingdom is an everlasting kingdom*[3].

33. And though I have many more testimonies out of the divine Scriptures, concerning the kingdom of Christ which has no end for ever, I will be content at present with those above mentioned, because the day is far spent. But thou, O hearer, worship only Him as thy King, and flee all heretical error. And if the grace of God permit us, the remaining Articles also of the Faith shall be in good time declared to you. And may the God of the whole world keep you all in safety, bearing in mind the signs of the end, and remaining unsubdued by Antichrist. Thou hast received the tokens of the Deceiver who is to come; thou hast received the proofs of the true Christ, who shall openly come down from heaven. Flee therefore the one, the False one; and look for the other, the True. Thou hast learnt the way, how in the judgment thou mayest be found among those on the right hand; guard *that which is committed to thee*[4] concerning Christ, and be conspicuous in good works, that thou mayest stand with a good confidence before the Judge, and inherit the kingdom of heaven:—Through whom, and with whom, be glory to God with the Holy Ghost, for ever and ever. Amen.

7 Rom. v. 14. "ἄχρι from ἄκρος, as μέχρι from μῆκος, μακρός" (L. and Sc.). It is not always possible to mark this distinction in translation: cf. Lobeck, *Phrynichus*, p. 14; Viger, *De Idiot. Gr.* p. 419.

8 2 Cor. iii. 14, 15.

9 Ib. x. 14, 15, 16.

1 1 Cor. xv. 25.

2 Heb. iii. 13.

3 Dan. vii. 14, 27.

4 1 Tim. vi. 20.

LECTURE XVI.

On the Article, And in one Holy Ghost, the Comforter, which spake in the Prophets.

1 Corinthians xii. 1, 4.

Now concerning spiritual gifts, brethren, I would not have you ignorant. . . . Now there are diversities of gifts, but the same Spirit, &c.

1. Spiritual in truth is the grace we need, in order to discourse concerning the Holy Spirit; not that we may speak what is worthy of Him, for this is impossible, but that by speaking the words of the divine Scriptures, we may run our course without danger. For a truly fearful thing is written in the Gospels, where Christ has plainly said, *Whosoever shall speak a word against the Holy Ghost, it shall not be forgiven him, neither in this world, nor in that which is to come*[1]. And there is often fear, lest a man should receive this condemnation, through speaking what he ought not concerning Him, either from ignorance, or from supposed reverence. The Judge of quick and dead, Jesus Christ, declared that he hath no forgiveness; if therefore any man offend, what hope has he?

2. It must therefore belong to Jesus Christ's grace itself to grant both to us to speak without deficiency, and to you to hear with discretion; for discretion is needful not to them only who speak, but also to them that hear, lest they hear one thing, and misconceive another in their mind. Let us then speak concerning the Holy Ghost nothing but what is written; and whatsoever is not written, let us not busy ourselves about it. The Holy Ghost Himself spake the Scriptures; He has also spoken concerning Himself as much as He pleased, or as much as we could receive. Let us therefore speak those things which He has said; for whatsoever He has not said, we dare not say.

3. There is One Only Holy Ghost, the Comforter; and as there is One God the Father, and no second Father;—and as there is One Only-begotten Son and Word of God, who hath no brother;—so is there One Only Holy Ghost, and no second spirit equal in honour to Him. Now the Holy Ghost is a Power most mighty, a Being divine and unsearchable; for He is living and intelligent, a sanctifying principle of all things made by God through Christ. He it is who illuminates the souls of the just; He was in the Prophets, He was also in the Apostles in the New Testament. Abhorred be they who dare to separate the operation of the Holy Ghost! There is One God, the Father, Lord of the Old and of the New Testament: and One Lord, Jesus Christ, who was prophesied of in the Old Testament, and came in the New; and One Holy Ghost, who through the Prophets preached of Christ, and when Christ was come, descended, and manifested Him[2].

[1] Matt. xii. 32.

[2] At the end of this section there follows in the Coislin MS. a long interpolation consisting of two parts. The former is an extract taken word for word from Gregory of Nyssa, *Oratio Catechetica*, ii. c, which may be read in this series: Ἀλλ' ὡς Θεοῦ Λόγον ἀκούσαντες . . . . σύνδρομον ἔχουσαν τῇ βουλήσει τὴν δύναμιν. Of the second passage the Benedictine Editor says: "I have not been able to discover who is the author. No one can assign it to our Cyril, although the doctrine it contains is in full agreement with his: but he explains all the same points more at large in his two Lectures (xvi. xvii.). The passage is very ancient and undoubtedly older than the eleventh century, which is the date of the Cod. Coislin. Therefore in the controversy of the Latins against the Greeks concerning the Procession of the Holy Ghost it is important to notice what is taught in this passage, and also brought forward as a testimony by S. Thomas (Aquinas), that "The Holy Ghost is of the Godhead of the Father and the Son (ex Patris et Filii divinitate existere)." To me indeed these words seem to savour altogether not of the later but of the more ancient theology of the Greeks, and to be earlier than the controversies of the Greeks against the Latins."

This second passage is as follows:—

"For the Spirit of God is good. *And Thy good Spirit*, says David, *shall lead me in the land of righteousness*. This then is the Spirit of God in which we believe: the blessed Spirit, the eternal, immutable, unchangeable, ineffable: which rules and reigns over all productive being, both visible and invisible natures: which is Lord both of Angels and Archangels, Powers, Principalities, Dominions, Thrones: the Creator of all being, enthroned with the glory of the Father and the Son, reigning without beginning and without end with the Father and the Son, before the created substances: Who sanctifies the *ministering spirits sent forth for the sake of those who are to inherit salvation*: Who came down upon the holy and blessed Virgin Mary, of whom

4. Let no one therefore separate the Old from the New Testament[3]; let no one say that the Spirit in the former is one, and in the latter another; since thus he offends against the Holy Ghost Himself, who with the Father and the Son together is honoured, and at the time of Holy Baptism is included with them in the Holy Trinity. For the Only-begotten Son of God said plainly to the Apostles, *Go ye, and make disciples of all the nations, baptizing them into the name of the Father, and of the Son, and of the Holy Ghost*[4]. Our hope is in Father, and Son, and Holy Ghost. We preach not three Gods[5]; let the Marcionites be silenced; but with the Holy Ghost through One Son, we preach One God. The Faith is indivisible; the worship inseparable. We neither separate the Holy Trinity, like some; nor do we as Sabellius work confusion[6]. But we know according to godliness One Father, who sent His Son to be our Saviour; we know One Son, who promised that He would send the Comforter from the Father; we know the Holy Ghost, who spake in the Prophets, and who on the day of Pentecost descended on the Apostles in the form of fiery tongues, here, in Jerusalem, in the Upper Church of the Apostles[7]; for in all things the choicest privileges are with us. Here Christ came down from heaven; here the Holy Ghost came down from heaven. And in truth it were most fitting, that as we discourse concerning Christ and Golgotha here in Golgotha, so also we should speak concerning the Holy Ghost in the Upper Church; yet since He who descended there jointly partakes of the glory of Him who was crucified here, we here speak concerning Him also who descended there: for their worship is indivisible.

5. We would now say somewhat concerning the Holy Ghost; not to declare His substance with exactness, for this were impossible; but to speak of the diverse mistakes of some concerning him, lest from ignorance we should fall into them; and to block up the paths of error, that we may journey on the King's one highway. And if we now for caution's sake repeat any statement of the heretics, let it recoil on their heads, and may we be guiltless, both we who speak, and ye who hear.

6. For the heretics, who are most profane in all things, have *sharpened their tongue*[8] against the Holy Ghost also, and have dared to utter impious things; as Irenæus the interpreter has written in his injunctions against heresies[9]. For some of them have dared to say that they were themselves the Holy Ghost;—of whom the first was Simon[1], the sorcerer spoken of in the Acts of the Apostles; for when he was cast out, he presumed to teach such doctrines: and they who are called Gnostics, impious men, have spoken other things against the Spirit[2], and the wicked Valentinians[3] again something else; and the profane Manes dared to call himself the Paraclete sent by Christ[4]. Others again have taught that the Spirit is different in the Prophets and in the New Testament[5]. Yea, and great is their error, or rather their blasphemy. Such therefore abhor, and flee from them who blaspheme the Holy Ghost, and have no forgiveness. For what fellowship hast thou with the desperate, thou, who art now to be baptized, into the Holy Ghost also[6]? If he who attaches himself to a thief, and consenteth with him, is subject to punishment, what hope shall he have, who offends against the Holy Ghost?

7. Let the Marcionists also be abhorred, who tear away from the New Testament the sayings of the Old[7]. For Marcion first, that most impious of men, who first asserted three Gods[8], knowing that in the New Testament are

---

was born Christ according to the flesh; came down also upon the Lord Himself in bodily form of a dove in the river Jordan: Who came upon the Apostles on the day of Pentecost in form of fiery tongues; Who gives and supplies all spiritual gifts in the Church, WHO PROCEEDETH FROM THE FATHER: Who is of the Godhead of the Father and the Son; Who is of one substance with the Father and the Son, inseparable and indivisible."

3 Cf. Cat. iv. 33; vii. 6. Irenæus, *Hæres.* III. xxi. 4; IV. ix. 1. In Eusebius, *E.H.* V. 13, Rhodon says that Apelles attributed the prophecies to an adverse spirit, and rejected them as false and self-contradictory. Similar blasphemies against the holy Prophets are imputed to Manes by Epiphanius (*Hæres.* lxvi. 30).

4 Matt. xxviii. 19. The same text is used with much force by S. Basil (*De Spir. S.* cap. xxiv.).

5 Cat. xi. 4, note 3. See Newman's notes on Athanasius, *Contra Arian. Or.* I. viii. 1; Ib. *Or.* III. xxv. 9; Ib. xxvii. 3. Marcion's doctrine of three first principles (τριῶν ἀρχῶν λόγος) is discussed by Epiphanius (*Hæres.* xlii. 6, 7). See also Tertull. *Contra Marcion.* I. 15; Euseb. *Hist. Eccles.* V. 13.

6 συναλοιφήν, iv. 8; xi. 16; xv. 9.

7 Cat. xvii. 13. Epiphanius (*De Mensuris et Ponder.* c. 14): "And he (Hadrian) found the city all levelled to the ground, except a few houses, and the Church of God which was small: where the Disciples, on their return after the Saviour was taken up from the Mount of Olives, went up into the upper chamber: for there it had been built, that is on Sion." Cf. Stanley, *Sinai and Palestine*, c. xiv. 3: "Within the precincts of that Mosque (of the Tomb of David) is a vaulted Gothic chamber, which contains within its four walls a greater confluence of traditions than any other place of like dimensions in Palestine. It is startling to hear that this is the scene of the Last Supper, of the meeting after the Resurrection, of the miracle of Pentecost, of the residence and death of the Virgin, of the burial of Stephen."

8 Ps. cxl. 3.

9 Irenæus is called "the interpreter" in the same general sense as other ecclesiastical authors (Cat. xiii. 21; xv. 20), on account of his frequent comments upon the Scriptures. The full title of his work was *A Refutation and Subversion of Knowledge falsely so called* (Euseb. *Hist. Eccles.* V. c. 7). Cyril's expression (ἐν τοῖς προστάγμασι) is sufficiently appropriate to the hortatory purpose professed by Irenæus in his preface. But the Benedictine Editor thinks that the word προστάγμασι may be an interpolation arising from the following words πρὸς τὰς . . . . The meaning would then be "in his writings *Against Heresies*," the usual short title of the work.

1 Cat. vi. 14, note 10.

2 Irenæus (I. xxix. § 4; xxx. § 1).

3 Ib. I. ii. §§ 5, 6.

4 Cat. vi. 25.

5 Cat. iv. 33. See § 3, note 3, above.

6 i.e. as well as into the Father and the Son.

7 See *Dict. Christ. Biography*, Marcion, p. 283; and Tertullian (*Adv. Marcion.* IV. 6): "His whole aim centres in this that he may establish a diversity between the Old and New Testaments, so that his own Christ may be separate from the Creator, as belonging to the rival god, and as alien from the Law and the Prophets.

8 Cf. § 4, note 5, above.

contained testimonies of the Prophets concerning Christ, cut out the testimonies taken from the Old Testament, that the King might be left without witness. Abhor those above-mentioned Gnostics, men of knowledge by name, but fraught with ignorance; who have dared to say such things of the Holy Ghost as I dare not repeat.

8. Let the Cataphrygians[9] also be thy abhorrence, and Montanus, their ringleader in evil, and his two so-called prophetesses, Maximilla and Priscilla. For this Montanus, who was out of his mind and really mad (for he would not have said such things, had he not been mad), dared to say that he was himself the Holy Ghost,—he, miserable man, and filled with all uncleanness and lasciviousness; for it suffices but to hint at this, out of respect for the women who are present. And having taken possession of Pepuza, a very small hamlet of Phrygia, he falsely named it Jerusalem; and cutting the throats of wretched little children, and chopping them up into unholy food, for the purpose of their so-called mysteries[1],—(wherefore till but lately in the time of persecution, we were suspected of doing this, because these Montanists were called, falsely indeed, by the common name of Christians;)—yet he dared to call himself the Holy Ghost, filled as he was with all impiety and inhuman cruelty, and condemned by an irrevocable sentence.

9. And he was seconded, as was said before, by that most impious Manes also, who combined what was bad in every heresy[2]; who being the very lowest pit of destruction, collected the doctrines of all the heretics, and wrought out and taught a yet more novel error, and dared to say that he himself was the Comforter, whom Christ promised to send. But the Saviour when He promised Him, said to the Apostles, *But tarry ye in the city of Jerusalem, until ye be endued with power from on high*[3]. What then? did the Apostles who had been dead two hundred years, wait for Manes, *until they should be endued with the power;* and will any dare to say, that they were not forthwith full of the Holy Ghost? Moreover it is written, *Then they laid their hands on them, and they received the Holy Ghost*[4]*;* was not this before Manes, yea, many years before, when the Holy Ghost descended on the day of Pentecost?

10. Wherefore was Simon the sorcerer condemned? Was it not that he came to the Apostles, and said, *Give me also this power, that on whomsoever I lay hands, he may receive the Holy Ghost?* For he said not, "Give me also the fellowship of the Holy Ghost," but "Give me the power;" that he might sell to others that which could not be sold, and which he did not himself possess. He offered money also to them who had no possessions[5]; and this, though he saw men bringing the prices of the things sold, and laying them at the Apostles' feet. And he considered not that they who trod under foot the wealth which was brought for the maintenance of the poor, were not likely to give the power of the Holy Ghost for a bribe. But what say they to Simon? *Thy money perish with thee, because thou hast thought to purchase the gift of God with money*[6]*;* for thou art a second Judas, for expecting to buy the grace of the Spirit with money. If then Simon, for wishing to get this power for a price, is to *perish*, how great is the impiety of Manes, who said that he was the Holy Ghost? Let us hate them who are worthy of hatred; let us turn away from them from whom God turns away; let us also ourselves say unto God with all boldness concerning all heretics, *Do not I hate them, O Lord, that hate Thee, and am not I grieved with Thine enemies*[7]*?* For there is also an enmity which is right, according as it is written, *I will put enmity between thee and her seed*[8]*;* for friendship with the serpent works enmity with God, and death.

11. Let then thus much suffice concerning those outcasts; and now let us return to the divine Scriptures, and let us *drink waters out of our own cisterns* [that is, the holy Fathers[9]], *and out of our own springing wells*[1]. Drink we of *living water, springing up into everlasting life*[2]*; but this spake* the Saviour *of the Spirit, which they that believe on Him should receive*[3]. For observe what He says, *He that believeth on Me* (not simply this, but), *as the Scripture hath said* (thus He hath sent thee back to the Old Testament), *out of his belly shall flow rivers of living water*, not rivers perceived by sense, and merely watering the earth with its thorns and trees, but bringing souls to the light. And in another place He says, *But the water that I shall give him, shall be in him a well of living water springing up*

9 Phrygians, or Cataphrygians (οἱ κατὰ Φρύγας) was the name given to the followers of the Phrygian Montanus. See the account of Montanism in Eusebius, *Hist. Eccl.* V. xvi., and the note there in this Series.

1 The charges of lust and cruelty brought against the Montanists by Cyril and Epiphanius (*Hær.* 48) seem to rest on no trustworthy evidence, and are not mentioned by Eusebius, a bitter foe to the sect.

2 On Manes, see Cat. vi. 20 ff.

3 Luke xxiv. 49.

4 Acts viii. 17.

5 Acts viii. 19. ἀκτήμοσι. Cf. § 19: ἀκτημονοῦσι, and § 22: ἀκτημοσύνην.

6 Ib. *v.* 20.

7 Ps. cxxxix. 21.

8 Gen. iii. 15.

9 The words ἁγίων πατέρων are not found in the MSS. Mon. 1. Mon. 2. Vind. Roe. Casaub. nor in Grodecq. Whether meant to refer, as the Benedictine Editor thinks, to the writers of the Old Testament, or to Christian authors, they are an evident gloss.

1 Prov. v. 15.

2 John iv. 14, quoted more fully at the end of the section.

3 Ib. vii. 38, 39.

into everlasting life,—a new kind of water, living and springing up, springing up unto them who are worthy.

12. And why did He call the grace of the Spirit water? Because by water all things subsist; because water brings forth grass and living things; because the water of the showers comes down from heaven; because it comes down one in form, but works in many forms. For one fountain watereth the whole of Paradise, and one and the same rain comes down upon all the world, yet it becomes white in the lily, and red in the rose, and purple in violets and hyacinths, and different and varied in each several kind: so it is one in the palm-tree, and another in the vine, and all in all things; and yet is one in nature, not diverse from itself; for the rain does not change itself, and come down first as one thing, then as another, but adapting itself to the constitution of each thing which receives it, it becomes to each what is suitable [4]. Thus also the Holy Ghost, being one, and of one nature, and indivisible, divides to each His grace, *according as He will* [5]: and as the dry tree, after partaking of water, puts forth shoots, so also the soul in sin, when it has been through repentance made worthy of the Holy Ghost, brings forth clusters of righteousness. And though He is One in nature, yet many are the virtues which by the will of God and in the Name of Christ He works. For He employs the tongue of one man for wisdom; the soul of another He enlightens by Prophecy; to another He gives power to drive away devils; to another He gives to interpret the divine Scriptures. He strengthens one man's self-command; He teaches another the way to give alms; another He teaches to fast and discipline himself; another He teaches to despise the things of the body; another He trains for martyrdom: diverse in different men, yet not diverse from Himself, as it is written, *But the manifestation of the Spirit is given to every man to profit withal. For to one is given through the Spirit the word of wisdom; and to another the word of knowledge according to the same Spirit; to another faith, in the same Spirit; and to another gifts of healing, in the same Spirit; and to another workings of miracles; and to another prophecy; and to another discernings of spirits; and to another divers kinds of tongues; and to another the interpretation of tongues: but all these worketh that one and the same Spirit, dividing to every man severally as He will* [6].

13. But since concerning spirit in general many diverse things are written in the divine Scriptures, and there is fear lest some out of ignorance fall into confusion, not knowing to what sort of spirit the writing refers; it will be well now to certify you, of what kind the Scripture declares the Holy Spirit to be. For as Aaron is called Christ, and David and Saul and others are called Christs [7], but there is only one true Christ, so likewise since the name of spirit is given to different things, it is right to see what is that which is distinctively called the Holy Spirit. For many things are called spirits. Thus an Angel is called spirit, our soul is called spirit, and this wind which is blowing is called spirit; great virtue also is spoken of as spirit; and impure practice is called spirit; and a devil our adversary is called spirit. Beware therefore when thou hearest these things, lest from their having a common name thou mistake one for another. For concerning our soul the Scripture says, *His spirit shall go forth, and he shall return to his earth* [8]: and of the same soul it says again, *Which formeth the spirit of man within him* [9]. And of the Angels it is said in the Psalms, *Who maketh His Angels spirits, and His ministers a flame of fire* [1]. And of the wind it saith, *Thou shalt break the ships of Tarshish with a violent spirit* [2]; and, *As the tree in the wood is shaken by the spirit* [3]; and, *Fire, hail, snow, ice, spirit of storm* [4]. And of good doctrine the Lord Himself says, *The words that I have spoken unto you, they are spirit* [5], *and they are life*; instead of, "are spiritual." But the Holy Spirit is not pronounced by the tongue; but He is a Living Spirit, who gives wisdom of speech, Himself speaking and discoursing.

14. And wouldest thou know that He discourses and speaks? Philip by revelation of an Angel went down to the way which leads to Gaza, when the Eunuch was coming; and the Spirit said to Philip, *Go near, and join thyself to this chariot* [6]. Seest thou the Spirit talking to one who hears Him? Ezekiel also speaks thus, *The Spirit of the Lord came upon me, and said unto me, Thus saith the Lord* [7]. And again, *The Holy Ghost said* [8], unto the Apostles who were in Antioch, *Separate me now Barnabas and Saul for the work whereunto I have called them.* Beholdest thou the Spirit living, separating, calling, and with authority sending forth? Paul also said, *Save that the Holy Ghost witnesseth in every city, saying that bonds and afflictions await me* [9]. For this good Sanctifier of the Church, and her Helper, and Teacher, the Holy Ghost, the Comforter, of whom the Saviour said, *He shall*

4 Compare a similar passage on rain in Cat. ix. 9, 10.
5 1 Cor. xii. 11. 6 Ib. *vv.* 7—11.

7 See Cat. x. 11; xi. 1. 8 Ps. cxlvi. 4. 9 Zech. xii. 1.
1 Ps. civ. 4. 2 Ps. xlviii. 7. 3 Is. vii. 2.
4 Ps. cxlviii. 8. 5 John vi. 63. 6 Acts viii. 29.
7 Ezek. xi. 5. 8 Acts xiii. 2. 9 Ib. xx. 23.

teach you all things (and He said not only, *He shall teach*, but also, *He shall bring to your remembrance whatever I have said unto you* [1]; for the teachings of Christ and of the Holy Ghost are not different, but the same)—He, I say, testified before to Paul what things should befall him, that he might be the more stout-hearted, from knowing them beforehand. Now I have spoken these things unto you because of the text, *The words which I have spoken unto you, they are spirit;* that thou mayest understand this, not of the utterance of the lips [2], but of the good doctrine in this passage.

15. But sin also is called spirit, as I have already said; only in another and opposite sense, as when it is said, *The spirit of whoredom caused them to err* [3]. The name "spirit" is given also to the *unclean spirit*, the devil; but with the addition of, "the unclean;" for to each is joined its distinguishing name, to mark its proper nature. If the Scripture speak of the soul of man, it says *the spirit* with the addition, *of the man;* if it mean the wind, it says, *spirit of storm;* if sin, it says, *spirit of whoredom;* if the devil, it says, *an unclean spirit:* that we may know which particular thing is spoken of, and thou mayest not suppose that it means the Holy Ghost; God forbid! For this name of spirit is common to many things; and every thing which has not a solid body is in a general way called spirit [4]. Since, therefore, the devils have not such bodies, they are called spirits: but there is a great difference; for the unclean devil, when he comes upon a man's soul (may the Lord deliver from him every soul of those who hear me, and of those who are not present), he comes like a wolf upon a sheep, ravening for blood, and ready to devour. His coming is most fierce; the sense of it most oppressive; the mind becomes darkened; his attack is an injustice also, and so is his usurpation of another's possession. For he makes forcible use of another's body, and another's instruments, as if they were his own; he throws down him who stands upright (for he is akin to him who *fell from heaven* [5]); he twists the tongue and distorts the lips; foam comes instead of words; the man is filled with darkness; his eye is open, yet the soul sees not through it; and the miserable man gasps convulsively at the point of death. The devils are verily foes of men, using them foully and mercilessly.

16. Such is not the Holy Ghost; God forbid! For His doings tend the contrary way, towards what is good and salutary. First, His coming is gentle; the perception of Him is fragrant; His burden most light; beams of light and knowledge gleam forth before His coming [6]. He comes with the bowels of a true guardian; for He comes to save, and to heal, to teach, to admonish, to strengthen, to exhort, to enlighten the mind, first of him who receives Him, and afterwards of others also, through him. And as a man, who being previously in darkness then suddenly beholds the sun, is enlightened in his bodily sight, and sees plainly things which he saw not, so likewise he to whom the Holy Ghost is vouchsafed, is enlightened in his soul, and sees things beyond man's sight, which he knew not; his body is on earth, yet his soul mirrors forth the heavens. He sees, like Esaias, *the Lord sitting upon a throne high and lifted up* [7]; he sees, like Ezekiel, *Him who is above the Cherubim* [8]; he sees like Daniel, *ten thousand times ten thousand, and thousands of thousands* [9]; and the man, who is so little, beholds the beginning of the world, and knows the end of the world, and the times intervening, and the successions of kings,—things which he never learned: for the True Enlightener is present with him. The man is within the walls of a house; yet the power of his knowledge reaches far and wide, and he sees even what other men are doing.

17. Peter was not with Ananias and Sapphira when they sold their possessions, but he was present by the Spirit; *Why*, he says, *hath Satan filled thine heart to lie to the Holy Ghost* [1]? There was no accuser; there was no witness; whence knew he what had happened? *Whiles it remained was it not thine own? and after it was sold, was it not in thine own power? why hast thou conceived this thing in thine heart* [2]? The *unlettered* [3] Peter, through the grace of the Spirit, learnt what not even the wise men of the Greeks had known. Thou hast the like in the case also of Elisseus. For when he had freely healed the leprosy of Naaman, Gehazi received the reward, the reward of another's achievement; and he took the money from Naaman, and bestowed it in a dark place. But the *darkness is not* hidden from the Saints [4]. And when he came, Elisseus asked him; and like Peter, when he said, *Tell me whether ye*

---

1 John xiv. 26.
2 Ib. vi. 63. The Holy Spirit is more than words pronounced by the tongue, even than our Lord's own words, which he called *spirit*.
3 Hosea iv. 12.
4 Origen, *de Principiis*, i. § 2: "It is the custom of Holy Scripture, when it would designate anything contrary to this more dense and solid body, to call it spirit."
5 Luke x. 18.

6 In this contrast between the evil spirit and the Spirit of God Cyril's language rises to true eloquence, far surpassing a somewhat similar description, which may have been known to him, in Euseb. *Dem. Evang.* V. 132.
7 Is. vi. 1. 8 Ezek. x. 1. 9 Dan. vii. 10.
1 Acts v. 3. 2 Ib. *v.* 4. 3 Ib. iv. 13.
4 Ps. cxxxix. 12.

sold the land for so much[5]*?* he also enquires, *Whence comest thou, Gehazi*[6]*?* Not in ignorance, but in sorrow ask I *whence comest thou?* From darkness art thou come, and to darkness shalt thou go; thou hast sold the cure of the leper, and the leprosy is thy heritage. I, he says, have fulfilled the bidding of Him who said to me, *Freely ye have received, freely give*[7]*;* but thou hast sold this grace; receive now the condition of the sale. But what says Elisseus to him? *Went not mine heart with thee?* I was here shut in by the body, but the spirit which has been given me of God saw even the things afar off, and shewed me plainly what was doing elsewhere. Seest thou how the Holy Ghost not only rids of ignorance, but invests with knowledge? Seest thou how He enlightens men's souls?

18. Esaias lived nearly a thousand years ago; and he beheld Zion *as a booth.* The city was still standing, and beautified with public places, and robed in majesty; yet he says, *Zion shall be ploughed as a field*[8], foretelling what is now fulfilled in our days[9]. And observe the exactness of the prophecy; for he said, *And the daughter of Zion shall be left as a booth in a vineyard, as a lodge in a garden of cucumbers*[1]. And now the place is filled with gardens of cucumbers. Seest thou how the Holy Spirit enlightens the saints? Be not therefore carried away to other things, by the force of a common term, but keep fast the exact meaning.

19. And if ever, while thou hast been sitting here, a thought concerning chastity or virginity has come into thy mind, it has been His teaching. Has not often a maiden, already at the bridal threshold[2], fled away, He teaching her the doctrine of virginity? Has not often a man distinguished at court[3], scorned wealth and rank, under the teaching of the Holy Ghost? Has not often a young man, at the sight of beauty, closed his eyes, and fled from the sight, and escaped the defilement? Askest thou whence this has come to pass? The Holy Ghost taught the soul of the young man. Many ways of covetousness are there in the world; yet Christians refuse possessions: wherefore? because of the teaching of the Holy Ghost. Worthy of honour is in truth that Spirit, holy and good; and fittingly are we baptized into Father, Son, and Holy Ghost. A man, still clothed with a body, wrestles with many fiercest demons; and often the demon, whom many men could not master with iron bands, has been mastered by the man himself with words of prayer, through the power which is in him of the Holy Ghost; and the mere breathing of the Exorcist[4] becomes as fire to that unseen foe. A mighty ally and protector, therefore, have we from God; a great Teacher of the Church, a mighty Champion on our behalf. Let us not be afraid of the demons, nor of the devil; for mightier is He who fighteth for us. Only let us open to Him our doors; *for He goeth about seeking such as are worthy*[5], and searching on whom He may confer His gifts.

20. And He is called the Comforter, because He comforts and encourages us, and *helpeth our infirmities; for we know not what we should pray for as we ought; but the Spirit Himself maketh intercession for us, with groanings which cannot be uttered*[6], that is, makes intercession to God. Oftentimes a man for Christ's sake has been outraged and dishonoured unjustly; martyrdom is at hand; tortures on every side, and fire, and sword, and savage beasts, and the pit. But the Holy Ghost softly whispers to him, "*Wait thou on the Lord*[7], O man; what is now befalling thee is a small matter, the reward will be great. Suffer a little while, and thou shalt be with Angels for ever. *The sufferings of this present time are not worthy to be compared with the glory which shall be revealed in us*[8]." He portrays to the man the kingdom of heaven; He gives him a glimpse of the paradise of delight; and the martyrs, whose bodily countenances are of necessity turned to their judges, but who in spirit are already in Paradise, despise those hardships which are seen.

21. And wouldest thou be sure that by the power of the Holy Ghost the Martyrs bear their witness? The Saviour says to His disciples, *And when they bring you unto*

---

5 Acts v. 8. 6 2 Kings v. 25.

7 Matt. x. 8. 8 Micah iii. 12; ascribed by Cyril to Isaiah.

9 Cf. Euseb. *Dem. Evang.* vi. 13: "In our own time we have seen with our eyes the Sion of old renown being ploughed by Romans with yokes of oxen, and Jerusalem in a state of utter desolation, as the oracle itself says, like a lodge in a garden of cucumbers. As Cyril at that time saw the Prophet's prediction fulfilled, so we also to the present day see most plainly the fulfilment of the divine oracle, and Sion ploughed before our eyes: for except the Church of the Apostles, with the houses lying around it, and the house of Caiaphas and the cemeteries, all the remaining space of this hill, lying without the city, is under plough." (Jerusalem Editor).

1 Isa. i. 8. ὀπωροφυλάκιον is the hut of the watchman who guarded the crop when ripening for harvest. Σικυήλατον is explained by Basil in his comment on the passage of Isaiah as "A place that produces quick-growing and perishable fruits." This agrees with the etymological sense of the word as "a forcing-bed for cucumbers" (Hippocrates apud Fritzsche, "*Der Brief des Jeremia*," *v.* 70). On the form σικυηράτῳ, see the notes on the Epistle of Jeremy in the Speaker's Commentary.

2 παστάδας. On the meaning of παστάς see the notes on Herodotus, II. 148, 169 in Bähr, and Rawlinson. Here it appears to mean the cloister or colonnade which gave access to the bridal chamber, θάλαμος. 3 ἐν παλατίοις

4 Compare Procat. § 9; Cat. xx. 3.

5 Wisdom vi. 16. Compare the saying in Clem. Alex. *Quis dives salvetur?* § 31: αὐτὸν ζητεῖν τοὺς εὖ πεισομένους ἀξίους τε ὄντας τοῦ Σωτῆρος μαθητάς. The Jerusalem Editor quotes from Origen (*Prolog. in Cantic.*) a passage which may have been known to Cyril: "This Comforter therefore goeth about seeking if He may discover any worthy and receptive souls, to whom He may reveal the greatness of the love which is in God."

6 Rom. viii. 26. 7 Ps. xxvii. 14; xxxvii. 34.

8 Rom. viii. 18.

the synagogues, and the magistrates, and authorities, be not anxious how ye shall answer, or what ye shall say; for the Holy Ghost shall teach you in that very hour, what ye ought to say[9]. For it is impossible to testify as a martyr for Christ's sake, except a man testify by the Holy Ghost; for if *no man can say that Jesus Christ is the Lord, but by the Holy Ghost*[1], how shall any man give his own life for Jesus' sake, but by the Holy Ghost?

22. Great indeed, and all-powerful in gifts, and wonderful, is the Holy Ghost. Consider, how many of you are now sitting here, how many souls of us are present. He is working suitably for each, and being present in the midst, beholds the temper of each, beholds also his reasoning and his conscience, and what we say, and think, and believe[2]. Great indeed is what I have now said, and yet is it small. For consider, I pray, with mind enlightened by Him, how many Christians there are in all this diocese, and how many in the whole province[3] of Palestine, and carry forward thy mind from this province, to the whole Roman Empire; and after this, consider the whole world; races of Persians, and nations of Indians, Goths and Sarmatians, Gauls and Spaniards, and Moors, Libyans and Ethiopians, and the rest for whom we have no names; for of many of the nations not even the names have reached us. Consider, I pray, of each nation, Bishops, Presbyters, Deacons, Solitaries, Virgins, and laity besides; and then behold their great Protector, and the Dispenser of their gifts;—how throughout the world He gives to one chastity, to another perpetual virginity, to another almsgiving, to another voluntary poverty, to another power of repelling hostile spirits. And as the light, with one touch of its radiance sheds brightness on all things, so also the Holy Ghost enlightens those who have eyes; for if any from blindness is not vouchsafed His grace, let him not blame the Spirit, but his own unbelief.

23. Thou hast seen His power, which is in all the world; tarry now no longer upon earth, but ascend on high. Ascend, I say, in imagination even unto the first heaven, and behold there so many countless myriads of Angels. Mount up in thy thoughts, if thou canst, yet higher; consider, I pray thee, the Archangels, consider also the Spirits; consider the Virtues, consider the Principalities, consider the Powers, consider the Thrones, consider the Dominions[4];—of all these the Comforter is the Ruler from God, and the Teacher, and the Sanctifier. Of Him Elias has need, and Elisseus, and Esaias, among men; of Him Michael and Gabriel have need among Angels. Nought of things created is equal in honour to Him: for the families of the Angels, and all their hosts assembled together, have no equality with the Holy Ghost. All these the all-excellent power of the Comforter overshadows. And they indeed are *sent forth to minister*[5], but He searches even the deep things of God, according as the Apostle says, *For the Spirit searcheth all things, yea, the deep things of God. For what man knoweth the things of a man, save the spirit of the man which is in him? even so the things of God knoweth no man, but the Spirit of God*[6].

24. He preached concerning Christ in the Prophets; He wrought in the Apostles; He to this day seals the souls in Baptism. And the Father indeed gives to the Son; and the Son shares with the Holy Ghost. For it is Jesus Himself, not I, who says, *All things are delivered unto Me of My Father*[7]; and of the Holy Ghost He says, *When He, the Spirit of Truth, shall come*, and the rest . . . . *He shall glorify Me; for He shall receive of Mine, and shall shew it unto you*[8]. The Father through the Son, with the Holy Ghost, is the giver of all grace; the gifts of the Father are none other than those of the Son, and those of the Holy Ghost; for there is one Salvation, one Power, one Faith; One God, the Father; One Lord, His only-begotten Son; One Holy Ghost, the Comforter. And it is enough for us to know these things; but inquire not curiously into His nature or substance[9]: for had it been written, we would have spoken of it; what is not written, let us not venture on; it is sufficient for our salvation to know, that there is Father, and Son, and Holy Ghost.

25. This Spirit descended upon the seventy Elders in the days of Moses. (Now let not the length of the discourse, beloved, produce weariness in you: but may He the very subject of our discourse grant strength to every one, both to us who speak, and to you who listen!) This Spirit, as I was saying, came down upon the seventy Elders in the time of Moses; and this I say to thee, that I may now prove, that He knoweth all things, and worketh *as He will*[1].

---

9 Luke xii. 11, 12.

1 1 Cor. xii. 3. Μαρτυρῆσαι, "to bear witness by death."

2 Codd. Monac. Vind. Roe. Casaub. add καὶ τί πιστεύομεν.

3 The terms παροικία, the See of a Bishop, and ἐπαρχία, the Province of a Metropolitan, were both adopted from the corresponding divisions of the Roman Empire. See Bingham, *Antt.* Book IX. i. §§ 2—6.

4 S. Basil (*De Spiritu S.* c. xvi. § 38), after quoting the same passage, Col. i. 16, proceeds—εἴτε κυριότητες, καὶ εἴ τινές εἰσιν ἕτεραι λογικαὶ φύσεις ἀκατονόμαστοι. The last word shews that Basil had in mind this passage of Cyril, who after the names of nations in § 22, adds καὶ τοὺς λοίπους ἀκατονομάστους ἡμῖν.

5 Heb. i. 14.

6 1 Cor. ii. 10, 11.

7 Matt. xi. 27.

8 John xvi. 13, 14.

9 In regard to the caution with which St. Cyril here speaks, we must remember that the heresy of Macedonius had not yet given occasion to the formal discussion and determination of the "nature and substance" of the Holy Ghost.

1 1 Cor. xii. 11.

The seventy Elders were chosen; *And the Lord came down in a cloud, and took of the Spirit that was upon Moses, and put it upon the seventy Elders*[2]; not that the Spirit was divided, but that His grace was distributed in proportion to the vessels, and the capacity of the recipients. Now there were present sixty and eight, and they prophesied; but Eldad and Modad were not present: therefore that it might be shewn that it was not Moses who bestowed the gift, but the Spirit who wrought, Eldad and Modad, who though called, had not as yet presented themselves, did also prophesy[3].

26. Jesus the Son of Nun, the successor of Moses, was amazed; and came to him and said, "Hast thou heard that Eldad and Modad are prophesying? They were called, and they came not; *my lord Moses, forbid them*[4]." "I cannot forbid them," he says, "for this grace is from Heaven; nay, so far am I from forbidding them, that I myself am thankful for it. I think not, however, that thou hast said this in envy; *art* thou *jealous for my sake*, because that they prophesy, and thou prophesiest not yet? Wait for the proper season; *and oh that all the Lord's people may be prophets, whenever the Lord shall give His Spirit upon them*[5]!" saying this also prophetically, *whenever the Lord shall give;* "For as yet then He has not given it; so thou hast it not yet."—Had not then Abraham this, and Isaac, and Jacob, and Joseph? And they of old, had they it not? Nay, but the words, "*whenever the Lord shall give*" evidently mean "give it upon all; as yet indeed the grace is partial, then it shall be given lavishly." And he secretly alluded to what was to happen among us on the day of Pentecost; for He Himself came down among us. He had however also come down upon many before. For it is written, *And Jesus the son of Nun was filled with a spirit of wisdom; for Moses had laid his hands upon him*[6]. Thou seest the figure everywhere the same in the Old and New Testament;—in the days of Moses, the Spirit was given by laying on of hands; and by laying on of hands Peter[7] also gives the Spirit. And on thee also, who art about to be baptized, shall His grace come; yet in what manner I say not, for I will not anticipate the proper season.

27. He also came down upon all righteous men and Prophets; Enos, I mean, and Enoch, and Noah, and the rest; upon Abraham, Isaac, and Jacob; for as regards Joseph, even Pharaoh perceived that he had *the Spirit of God within him*[8]. As to Moses, and the wonderful works wrought by the Spirit in his days, thou hast heard often. This Spirit Job also had, that most enduring man, and all the saints, though we repeat not all their names. He also was sent forth when the Tabernacle was in making, and filled with wisdom the wise-hearted men who were with Bezaleel[9].

28. In the might of this Spirit, as we have it in the Book of Judges, Othniel judged[1]; Gideon[2] waxed strong; Jephtha conquered[3]; Deborah, a woman, waged war; and Samson, so long as he did righteously, and grieved Him not, wrought deeds above man's power. And as for Samuel and David, we have it plainly in the Books of the Kingdoms, how by the Holy Ghost they prophesied themselves, and were rulers of the prophets;—and Samuel was called *the Seer*[4]; and David says distinctly, *The Spirit of the Lord spake by me*[5], and in the Psalms, *And take not thy Holy Spirit from me*[6], and again, *Thy good Spirit shall lead me in the land of righteousness*[7]. And as we have it in Chronicles, Azariah[8], in the time of King Asa, and Jahaziel[9] in the time of King Jehoshaphat, partook of the Holy Ghost; and again, another Azariah, he who was stoned[1]. And Ezra says, *Thou gavest also Thy good Spirit to instruct them*[2]. But as touching Elias who was taken up, and Elisseus, those inspired[3] and wonder-working men, it is manifest, without our saying so, that they were full of the Holy Ghost.

29. And if further a man peruse all the books of the Prophets, both of the Twelve, and of the others, he will find many testimonies concerning the Holy Ghost; as when Micah says in the person of God, *surely I will perfect power by the Spirit of the Lord*[4]; and Joel cries, *And it shall come to pass afterwards*, saith God, *that I will pour out My Spirit upon all flesh*[5], and the rest; and Haggai, *Because I am with you, saith the Lord of Hosts*[6]; and *My Spirit remaineth in the midst of you*[7]; and in like manner Zechariah, *But receive My words and My statutes which I command by My Spirit, to My servants the Prophets*[8]; and other passages.

30. Esaias too, with his majestic voice, says, *And the Spirit of God shall rest upon Him,*

---

2 Num. xi. 24, 25. "Modad" is the form of the name in the LXX.

3 The apocryphal book of Eldad and Modad is mentioned by Hermas, *Shepherd*, Vis. ii. § 3. S. Basil, *Liber de Spir. S.* cap. 61, referring to Num. xi. 26, says that the Spirit rested permanently only upon Eldad and Modad.

4 Num. xi. 28.

5 Num. xi. 29.

6 Deut. xxxiv. 9.

7 Acts viii. 18. On this passage of Cyril, see the section on "*Chrism*" in the Introduction.

8 Gen. xli. 38.

9 Ex. xxxi. 1—6; xxxvi. 1.

1 Judges iii. 10.

2 Ib. vi. 34.

3 Ib. xi. 29.

4 1 Sam. ix. 9.

5 2 Sam. xxiii. 2.

6 Ps. li. 11.

7 Ps. cxliii. 10.

8 2 Chron. xv. 1.

9 Ib. xx. 14.

1 Ib. xxiv. 20, 21.

2 Neh. ix. 20. Ezra and Nehemiah form one book "Ezra" in the Hebrew Canon.

3 πνευματοφόρων, used only twice in the Sept. (Hosea ix. 7; Zeph. iii. 4), and in an unfavourable sense. With Cyril's use of it compare Theophilus, *Ad Autolyc.* ii. 9: Θεοῦ ἀνθρώπους πνευματοφόρους Πνεύματος ἁγίου.

4 Mic. iii. 8.

5 Joel ii. 28.

6 Haggai ii. 4.

7 Ib. v. 5.

8 Zech. i. 6.

the spirit of wisdom and understanding, the spirit of counsel and might, the spirit of knowledge and godliness; and the Spirit of the fear of God shall fill Him[9]; signifying that the Spirit is one and undivided, but His operations various. So again, *Jacob My servant, ... I have put My Spirit upon Him*[1]. And again, *I will pour My Spirit upon thy seed*[2]; and again, *And now the Lord Almighty and His Spirit hath sent Me*[3]; and again, *This is My covenant with them, saith the Lord, My Spirit which is upon thee*[4]; and again, *The Spirit of the Lord is upon Me, because He hath anointed Me*[5], and the rest; and again in his charge against the Jews, *But they rebelled and vexed His Holy Spirit*[6], and, *Where is He that put His Holy Spirit within them*[7]? Also thou hast in Ezekiel (if thou be not now weary of listening), what has already been quoted, *And the Spirit fell upon me, and said unto me, Speak; Thus saith the Lord*[8]. But the words, *fell upon me* we must understand in a good sense, that is "lovingly;" and as Jacob, when he had found Joseph, fell upon his neck; as also in the Gospels, the loving father, on seeing his son who had returned from his wandering, *had compassion, and ran and fell on his neck, and kissed him*[9]. And again in Ezekiel, *And he brought me in a vision by the Spirit of God into Chaldæa, to them of the captivity*[1]. And other texts thou heardest before, in what was said about Baptism; *Then will I sprinkle clean water upon you*[2], and the rest; *a new heart also will I give you, and a new spirit will I put within you*[3]; and then immediately, *And I will put My Spirit within you*[4]. And again, *The hand of the Lord was upon me, and carried me out in the Spirit of the Lord*[5].

31. He endued with wisdom the soul of Daniel, that young as he was he should become a judge of Elders. The chaste Susanna was condemned as a wanton; there was none to plead her cause; for who was to deliver her from the rulers? She was led away to death, she was now in the hands of the executioners. But her Helper was at hand, the Comforter, the Spirit who sanctifies every rational nature. Come hither to me, He says to Daniel; young though thou be, convict old men infected with the sins of youth; for it is written, *God raised up the Holy Spirit upon a young stripling*[6]; and nevertheless, (to pass on quickly,) by the sentence of Daniel that chaste lady was saved. We bring this forward as a testimony; for this is not the season for expounding. Nebuchadnezzar also knew that the Holy Spirit was in Daniel; for he says to him, *O Belteshazzar, master of the magicians, of whom I know, that the Holy Spirit of God is in thee*[7]. One thing he said truly, and one falsely; for that he had the Holy Spirit was true, but he was not the *master of the magicians*, for he was no magician, but was wise through the Holy Ghost. And before this also, he interpreted to him the vision of the Image, which he who had seen it himself knew not; for he says, Tell me the vision, which I who saw it know not[8]. Thou seest the power of the Holy Ghost; that which they who saw it, know not, they who saw it not, know and interpret.

32. And indeed it were easy to collect very many texts out of the Old Testament, and to discourse more largely concerning the Holy Ghost. But the time is short; and we must be careful of the proper length of the lecture. Wherefore, being for the present content awhile with passages from the Old Testament, we will, if it be God's pleasure, proceed in the next Lecture to the remaining texts out of the New Testament. And may the God of peace, through our Lord Jesus Christ, and through the love of the Spirit, count all of you worthy of His spiritual and heavenly gifts:—To whom be glory and power for ever and ever. Amen.

---

9 Is. xi. 2. 1 Ib. xliv. 1; xlii. 1. 2 Ib. xliv. 3. 3 Ib. xlviii. 16. 4 Is. lix. 21. 5 Is. lxi. 1. 6 Ib. lxiii. 10. 7 *v.* 11. 8 Ezek. xi. 5. 9 Gen. xlvi. 29; Luke xv. 20. 1 Ezek. xi. 24. 2 Ib. xxxvi. 25; Cat. iii. 16. 3 Ib. *v.* 26. 4 Ib. *v.* 27. 5 Ezek. xxxvii. 1.

6 Susanna, *v.* 45. 7 Dan. iv. 9 8 Ib. ii. 26, 31.

LECTURE XVII.

Continuation of the Discourse on the Holy Ghost.

1 Corinthians xii. 8.

For to one is given by the Spirit the word of wisdom, &c.

1. In the preceding Lecture, according to our ability we set before you, our beloved hearers[1], some small portion of the testimonies concerning the Holy Ghost; and on the present occasion, we will, if it be God's pleasure, proceed to treat, as far as may be, of those which remain out of the New Testament: and as then to keep within due limit of your attention we restrained our eagerness (for there is no satiety in discoursing concerning the Holy Ghost), so now again we must say but a small part of what remains. For now, as well as then, we candidly own that our weakness is overwhelmed by the multitude of things written. Neither to-day will we use the subtleties of men, for that is unprofitable; but merely call to mind what comes from the divine Scriptures; for this is the safest course, according to the blessed Apostle Paul, who says, *Which things also we speak, not in words which man's wisdom teacheth, but which the Holy Ghost teacheth, comparing spiritual things with spiritual*[2]. Thus we act like travellers or voyagers, who having one goal to a very long journey, though hastening on with eagerness, yet by reason of human weakness are wont to touch in their way at divers cities or harbours.

2. Therefore though our discourses concerning the Holy Ghost are divided, yet He Himself is undivided, being one and the same. For as in speaking concerning the Father, at one time we taught how He is the one only Cause[3]; and at another, how He is called Father[4], or Almighty[5]; and at another, how He is the Creator[6] of the universe; and yet the division of the Lectures made no division of the Faith, in that He, the Object of devotion, both was and is One;—and again, as in discoursing concerning the Only-begotten Son of God we taught at one time concerning His Godhead[7], and at another concerning His Manhood[8], dividing into many discourses the doctrines concerning our Lord Jesus Christ, yet preaching undivided faith towards Him;—so now also though the Lectures concerning the Holy Spirit are divided, yet we preach faith undivided towards Him. For it is one and the Self-same Spirit who *divides* His gifts *to every man severally as He will*[9], Himself the while remaining undivided. For the Comforter is not different from the Holy Ghost, but one and the self-same, called by various names; who lives and subsists, and speaks, and works; and of all rational natures made by God through Christ, both of Angels and of men, He is the Sanctifier[1].

3. But lest any from lack of learning, should suppose from the different titles of the Holy Ghost that these are divers spirits, and not one and the self-same, which alone there is, therefore the Catholic Church guarding thee beforehand hath delivered to thee in the profession of the faith, that thou "believe in one Holy Ghost the Comforter, who spake by the Prophets;" that thou mightest know, that though His names be many, the Holy Spirit is but one;—of which names, we will now rehearse to you a few out of many.

4. He is called the Spirit, according to the Scripture just now read, *For to one is given by the Spirit the word of wisdom*[2]. He is called the Spirit of Truth, as the Saviour says, *When He, the Spirit of Truth, is come*[3]. He is called also the Comforter, as He said, *For if I go not away, the Comforter will not come unto you*[4].

---

[1] ταῖς τῆς ὑμετέρας ἀγάπης ἀκοαῖς. Compare § 30, below: συγγώμην αἰτῶ παρὰ τῆς ὑμετέρας ἀγάπης. Ignat. *Philadelph.* c. iv. (Long recension): θαρρῶν γράφω τῇ ἀξιοθέῳ ἀγάπῃ ὑμῶν. "Caritas" is constantly used in the same manner.

[2] 1 Cor. ii. 13. [3] Cat. vi. [4] Ib. vii. [5] Ib. viii.

[6] Ib. ix.

[7] Cat. x. xi. [8] Ib. xii. xv. [9] 1 Cor. xii. 11.

[1] Compare Basil. *de Sp. Sancto*, c. 38: "By the Father's will the ministering spirits subsist, and by the operation of the Son they are brought into existence, and by the presence of the Holy Ghost are perfected: and the perfection of Angels is sanctification and continuance therein."

[2] 1 Cor. xii. 8. [3] John xvi. 13. [4] Ib *v.* 7.

But that He is one and the same, though called by different titles, is shewn plainly from the following. For that the Holy Spirit and the Comforter are the same, is declared in those words, *But the Comforter, which is the Holy Ghost*[5]; and that the Comforter is the same as the Spirit of Truth, is declared, when it is said, *And I will give you another Comforter, that He may abide with you for ever, even the Spirit of Truth*[6]; and again, *But when the Comforter is come whom I will send unto you from the Father, even the Spirit of Truth*[7]. And He is called the Spirit of God, according as it is written, *And I saw the Spirit of God descending*[8]; and again, *For as many as are led by the Spirit of God, they are the sons of God*[9]. He is called also the Spirit of the Father, as the Saviour says, *For it is not ye that speak, but the Spirit of your Father which speaketh in you*[1]; and again Paul saith, *For this cause I bow my knees unto the Father*, and the rest; . . . *that He would grant you to be strengthened by His Spirit*[2]. He is also called the Spirit of the Lord, according to that which Peter spake, *Why is it that ye have agreed together to tempt the Spirit of the Lord*[3]? He is called also the Spirit of God and Christ, as Paul writes, *But ye are not in the flesh, but in the Spirit, if so be that the Spirit of God dwell in you. But if any man have not the Spirit of Christ, he is none of His*[4]. He is called also the Spirit of the Son of God, as it is said, *And because ye are sons, God hath sent forth the Spirit of His Son*[5]. He is called also the Spirit of Christ, as it is written, *Searching what or what manner of time the Spirit of Christ which was in them did signify*[6]; and again, *Through your prayer, and the supply of the Spirit of Jesus Christ*[7].

5. Thou wilt find many other titles of the Holy Ghost besides. Thus He is called the Spirit of Holiness, as it is written, *According to the Spirit of Holiness*[8]. He is also called the Spirit of adoption, as Paul saith, *For ye received not the spirit of bondage again unto fear, but ye received the Spirit of adoption, whereby we cry, Abba, Father*[9]. He is also called the Spirit of revelation, as it is written, *May give you the Spirit of wisdom and revelation in the knowledge of Him*[1]. He is also called the Spirit of promise, as the same Paul says, *In whom ye also after that ye believed, were sealed with the Holy Spirit of promise*[2]. He is also called the Spirit of grace, as when he says again, *And hath done despite to the Spirit of grace*[3]. And by many other such-like titles is He named.

5 John xiv. 26. 6 Ib. *vv.* 16, 17. 7 Ib. xv. 26.
8 John i. 32. 9 Rom. viii. 14. 1 Matt. x. 20.
2 Eph. iii. 14—16. 3 Acts v. 9. 4 Rom. viii. 9.
5 Gal. iv. 6. 6 1 Pet. i. 11. 7 Phil. i. 19.
8 Rom. i. 4. 9 Ib. viii. 15. 1 Eph. i. 17.
2 Ib. *v.* 13. 3 Heb. x. 29.

And thou heardest plainly in the foregoing Lecture, that in the Psalms He is called at one time the *good Spirit*[4], and at another the *princely Spirit*[5]; and in Esaias He was styled *the Spirit of wisdom and understanding, of counsel, and might, of knowledge, and of godliness, and of the fear of God*[6]. By all which Scriptures both those before and those now alleged, it is established, that though the titles of the Holy Ghost be different, He is one and the same; living and subsisting, and always present together with the Father and the Son[7]; not uttered or breathed from the mouth and lips of the Father or the Son, nor dispersed into the air, but having a real substance[8], Himself speaking, and working, and dispensing, and sanctifying; even as the Economy of salvation which is to usward from the Father and the Son and the Holy Ghost, is inseparable and harmonious and one, as we have also said before. For I wish you to keep in mind those things which were lately spoken, and to know clearly that there is not one Spirit in the Law and the Prophets, and another in the Gospels and Apostles; but that it is One and the Self-same Holy Spirit, which both in the Old and in the New Testament, spake the divine Scriptures[9].

6. This is the Holy Ghost, who came upon the Holy Virgin Mary; for since He who was conceived was Christ the Only-begotten, the *power of the Highest overshadowed her*, and the *Holy Ghost came upon her*[1], and sanctified her, that she might be able to receive Him, *by whom all things were made*[2]. But I have no need of many words to teach thee that that generation was without defilement or taint, for thou hast learned it. It is Gabriel who says to her, I am the herald of what shall be done, but have no part in the work. Though an Archangel, I know my place; and though I joyfully bid thee All hail, yet how thou shalt bring forth, is not of any grace of mine. *The Holy Ghost shall come upon thee, and the power of the Highest shall overshadow thee; therefore also that Holy Thing which shall be born of thee shall be called the Son of God*[3].

7. This Holy Spirit wrought in Elisabeth; for He recognises not virgins only, but matrons also, so that their marriage be lawful. *And*

4 Cat. xvi. 28; Ps. cxliii. 10.

5 ἡγεμονικῷ, Sept. Ps. li. 12: R.V. *Uphold me with a free spirit.* 6 Is. xi. 2.

7 Origen, in the Catena on St. John iii. 8: "This also shews that the Spirit is a Being (οὐσίαν): for He is not, as some suppose an energy of God, having according to them no individuality of subsistence. And the Apostle also, after enumerating the gifts of the Spirit, immediately added, *But all these worketh the one and the same Spirit, dividing to each one severally as He will.* Now if He willeth and worketh and divideth, He is surely an energizing Being, but not an energy" (Suicer, *Thesaurus*, Πνευμα).

8 ἐνυπόστατον. Cf. Cat. xi. 10; xvi. 13, note 5.

9 Cat. iv. 16; xvi. 4. 1 Luke i. 35. 2 John i. 3.

3 Luke i. 35.

Elisabeth was filled with the Holy Ghost[4], and prophesied; and that noble hand-maiden says of her own Lord, *And whence is this to me, that the Mother of my Lord should come to me*[5]*?* For Elisabeth counted herself blessed. Filled with this Holy Spirit, Zacharias also, the father of John, prophesied[6], telling how many good things the Only-begotten should procure, and that John should be His harbinger[7] through baptism. By this Holy Ghost also it was revealed to just Symeon, *that he should not see death, till he had seen the Lord's Christ*[8]*;* and he received Him in his arms, and bore clear testimony in the Temple concerning Him.

8. And John also, who had been filled with the Holy Ghost from his mother's womb[9], was for this cause sanctified, that he might baptize the Lord; not giving the Spirit himself, but preaching glad tidings of Him who gives the Spirit. For he says, *I indeed baptize you with water unto repentance, but He that cometh after me*, and the rest; *He shall baptize you with the Holy Ghost and with fire*[1]. But wherefore with fire? Because the descent of the Holy Ghost was in fiery tongues; concerning which the Lord says joyfully, *I am come to send fire on the earth; and what will I, if it be already kindled*[2]*?*

9. This Holy Ghost came down when the Lord was baptized, that the dignity of Him who was baptized might not be hidden; as John says, *But He which sent me to baptize with water, the same said unto me, Upon whomsoever thou shalt see the Spirit descending and remaining upon Him, the same is He which baptizeth with the Holy Ghost*[3]. But see what saith the Gospel; *the heavens were opened;* they were opened because of the dignity of Him who descended; for, *lo*, he says, *the heavens were opened, and he saw the Spirit of God descending as a dove, and lighting upon Him*[4]*:* that is, with voluntary motion in His descent. For it was fit, as some have interpreted, that the primacy and first-fruits[5] of the Holy Spirit promised to the baptized should be conferred upon the manhood of the Saviour, who is the giver of such grace. But perhaps He came down in the form of a dove, as some say, to exhibit a figure of that dove who is pure and innocent and undefiled, and also helps the prayers for the children she has begotten, and for forgiveness of sins[6]; even as it was emblematically foretold that Christ should be thus manifested in the appearance of His eyes; for in the Canticles she cries concerning the Bridegroom, and says, *Thine eyes are as doves by the rivers of water*[7].

10. Of this dove, the dove of Noe, according to some, was in part a figure[8]. For as in his time by means of wood and of water there came salvation to themselves, and the beginning of a new generation, and the dove returned to him towards evening with an olive branch; thus, say they, the Holy Ghost also descended upon the true Noe, the Author of the second birth, who draws together into one the wills of all nations, of whom the various dispositions of the animals in the ark were a figure:—Him at whose coming the spiritual wolves feed with the lambs, in whose Church the calf, and the lion, and the ox, feed in the same pasture, as we behold to this day the rulers of the world guided and taught by Churchmen. The spiritual dove therefore, as some interpret, came down at the season of His baptism, that He might shew that it is He who by the wood of the Cross saves them who believe, He who at eventide should grant salvation through His death.

11. And these things perhaps should be otherwise explained; but now again we must hear the words of the Saviour Himself concerning the Holy Ghost. For He says, *Except a man be born of water and of the Spirit, he cannot enter into the kingdom of God*[9]. And that this grace is from the Father, He thus states, *How much more shall your heavenly Father give the Holy Spirit to them that ask him*[1]. And that we ought to worship God in the Spirit, He shews thus, *But the hour cometh and now is, when the true worshippers shall worship the Father in Spirit and in truth; for the Father also seeketh such to worship Him. God is a Spirit; and they that worship Him must worship Him in spirit and in truth*[2]. And again, *But if I by the*

---

4 Luke i. 41. 5 Ib. *v.* 43. 6 Ib. *v.* 67. 7 Ib. *v.* 76.
8 Luke ii. 26—35. 9 Cat. iii. 6. 1 Matt. iii. 11.
2 Luke xii. 49. 3 John i. 33. 4 Matt. iii. 16.

5 τὰς ἀπαρχὰς καὶ τὰ πρωτεῖα. The order is inverted in the translation. Cf. Hermas, *Sim.* viii. 7 ἔχοντες ζῆλόν τινα ἐν ἀλλήλοις περὶ πρωτείων.

6 The Benedictine Editor adds the two ast words τύπον παραδηλοῦν from MSS. Roe. Casaub. as necessary to the construction, and adds the following note. "The text thus emended is capable of two senses. The first, that the Holy Spirit came down in the form of a dove, a pure and harmless bird, to shew that He is Himself as it were a mystic dove in His simplicity and love of children, for whose new birth and remission of sins at Baptism He unites His prayers with Christ's, as Cyril teaches in Cat. xvi. 20: and that Christ was for the like cause mystically foreshown in Canticles as having eyes like a dove's. The other sense is, that the Spirit descended in the form of a dove on Christ's Humanity in order to shew this to be as it were a dove in innocence, holiness, love of children, and concurrence with the Holy Spirit in their regeneration. . . . Either sense is admissible, and maintained by many of the Fathers: but I prefer the former." This interpretation is confirmed by Tertullian (*de Baptismo*, c. viii.), who says that the Holy Spirit glided down on the Lord "in the shape of a dove" in order that the nature of the Holy Spirit might be declared by means of a creature of simplicity and innocence."

7 Cant. v. 12. ἐπὶ πληρώματα ὑδάτων (Sept.). The usual meaning of ὀφθαλμοφανῶς is "manifestly to the eyes," Esther viii. 13.

8 Tertullian, *ibid* "Just as after the waters of the deluge, by which the old iniquity was purged—after the baptism, so to say, of the world—a dove was the herald which announced to the earth the assuagement of celestial wrath, ... so to our flesh, as it emerges from the font after its old sins, flies the dove of the Holy Spirit, bringing us the peace of God, sent out from heaven where the Church is, the typified ark." Compare also Hippolytus. *The Holy Theophany*, §§ 8, 9, a treatise with which Cyril has much in common.

9 John iii. 5. 1 Luke xi. 13. 2 John iv. 23.

Spirit of God cast out devils[3]; and immediately afterwards, *Therefore I say unto you, All manner of sin and blasphemy shall be forgiven unto men; but the blasphemy against the Holy Ghost shall not be forgiven. And whosoever shall speak a word against the Son of man, it shall be forgiven him; but whosoever shall speak a word against the Holy Ghost, it shall not be forgiven him, neither in this world, neither in the world to come*[4]. And again He says, *And I will pray the Father, and He shall give you another Comforter, that He may be with you for ever, the Spirit of Truth; whom the world cannot receive, because it seeth Him not, neither knoweth Him; but ye know Him, for He abideth with you, and shall be in you*[5]. And again He says, *These things have I spoken unto you being yet present with you. But the Comforter, which is the Holy Ghost, whom the Father will send in My name, He shall teach you all things, and bring to your remembrance all things that I said unto you*[6]. And again He says, *But when the Comforter is come, whom I will send unto you from the Father, even the Spirit of Truth, which proceedeth from the Father, He shall testify of Me*[7]. And again the Saviour says, *For if I go not away, the Comforter will not come unto you*[8]..... *And when He is come, He will convince the world of sin, of righteousness, and of judgment*[9]; and afterwards again, *I have yet many things to say unto you, but ye cannot bear them now. Howbeit, when He the Spirit of Truth is come, He will declare unto you all the truth; for He shall not speak from Himself; but whatsoever He shall hear that shall He speak, and He shall announce unto you the things to come. He shall glorify Me, for He shall take of Mine, and shall announce it unto you. All things that the Father hath are mine; therefore said I, That He shall take of Mine, and shall announce it unto you*[1]. I have read to thee now the utterances of the Only-begotten Himself, that thou mayest not give heed to men's words.

12. The fellowship of this Holy Spirit He bestowed on the Apostles; for it is written, *And when He had said this, He breathed on them, and saith unto them, Receive ye the Holy Ghost: whose soever sins ye remit, they are remitted unto them; and whose soever sins ye retain, they are retained*[2]. This was the second time He breathed on man (His first breath[3] having been stifled through wilful sins); that the Scripture might be fulfilled, *He went up breathing upon thy face, and delivering thee from affliction*[4]. But whence went He up? From Hades; for thus the Gospel relates, that then after His resurrection He breathed on them. But though He bestowed His grace then, He was to lavish it yet more bountifully; and He says to them, "I am ready to give it even now, but the vessel cannot yet hold it; for a while therefore receive ye as much grace as ye can bear; and look forward for yet more; *but tarry ye in the city of Jerusalem, until ye be clothed with power from on high*[5]. *Receive* it in part now; then, ye shall wear it in its fulness. For he who receives, often possesses the gift but in part; but he who is clothed, is completely enfolded by his robe. "Fear not," He says, "the weapons and darts of the devil; for ye shall bear with you the power of the Holy Ghost." But remember what was lately said, that the Holy Ghost is not divided, but only the grace which is given by Him.

13. Jesus therefore went up into heaven, and fulfilled the promise. For He said to them, *I will pray the Father, and He shall give you another Comforter*[6]. So they were sitting, looking for the coming of the Holy Ghost; *and when the day of Pentecost was fully come*, here, in this city of Jerusalem,—(for this honour also belongs to us[7]; and we speak not of the good things which have happened among others, but of those which have been vouchsafed among ourselves,)—on the day of Pentecost, I say, they were sitting, and the Comforter came down from heaven, the Guardian and Sanctifier of the Church, the Ruler of souls, the Pilot of the tempest-tossed, who leads the wanderers to the light, and presides over the combatants, and crowns the victors.

14. But He came down to clothe the Apostles with power, and to baptize them; for the Lord says, *ye shall be baptized with the Holy Ghost not many days hence*[8]. This grace was not in part, but His power was in full perfection; for as he who plunges into the waters and is baptized is encompassed on all sides by the waters, so were they also baptized completely by the Holy Ghost. The water however flows round the outside only, but the Spirit baptizes also the soul within, and that completely. And wherefore wonderest thou? Take an example from matter; poor indeed and common, yet useful for the simpler sort. If the fire passing in through the mass of the iron makes the whole of it

3 Matt. xii. 28. 4 Ib. *v.* 31. 5 John xiv. 16.
6 Ib. *v.* 25. 7 Ib. xv. 26. 8 Ib. xvi. 7.
9 Ib. *v.* 8. 1 Ib. *v.* 12—15. 2 John xx. 22.

3 Gen. ii. 7: *and breathed into his nostrils the breath of life.* Compare Cat. xiv. 10.

4 Nahum ii. 1. The Septuagint, followed by Cyril, differs widely from the Hebrew: (R.V.) *He that dasheth in pieces is come up before thy face.*

5 Luke xxiv. 39. 6 John xiv. 16.

7 Cat. iii. 7; xvi. 5. Bp. Pearson (*Lectiones in Acta Apost.* I. § 18): "Rightly said Cyril, Bishop of Jerusalem, 'All prerogatives are with us.' And the Emperor Justin called her 'Mother of the Christian name.' Jerome also (*Ep.* 17, 3), said: 'The whole mystery of our Faith is native of that province and city.'"

8 Acts i. 5.

fire, so that what was cold becomes burning and what was black is made bright,—if fire which is a body thus penetrates and works without hindrance in iron which is also a body, why wonder that the Holy Ghost enters into the very inmost recesses of the soul?

15. And lest men should be ignorant of the greatness of the mighty gift coming down to them. there sounded as it were a heavenly trumpet, For *suddenly there came from heaven a sound as of the rushing of a mighty wind*[9], signifying the presence of Him who was to grant power unto men to seize with violence the kingdom of God; that both their eyes might see the fiery tongues, and their ears hear the sound. *And it filled all the house where they were sitting;* for the house became the vessel of the spiritual water; as the disciples sat within, the whole house was filled. Thus they were entirely baptized according to the promise, and invested soul and body with a divine garment of salvation. *And there appeared unto them cloven tongues like as of fire, and it sat upon each of them; and they were all filled with the Holy Ghost.* They partook of fire, not of burning but of saving fire; of fire which consumes the thorns of sins, but gives lustre to the soul. This is now coming upon you also, and that to strip away and consume your sins which are like thorns, and to brighten yet more that precious possession of your souls, and to give you grace; for He gave it then to the Apostles. And He sat upon them in the form of fiery tongues, that they might crown themselves with new and spiritual diadems by fiery tongues upon their heads. A fiery sword barred of old the gates of Paradise; a fiery tongue which brought salvation restored the gift.

16. *And they began to speak with other tongues as the Spirit gave them utterance*[1]. The Galilean Peter or Andrew spoke Persian or Median. John and the rest of the Apostles spake every tongue to those of Gentile extraction; for not in our time have multitudes of strangers first begun to assemble here from all quarters, but they have done so since that time. What teacher can be found so great as to teach men all at once things which they have not learned? So many years are they in learning by grammar and other arts to speak only Greek well; nor yet do all speak this equally well; the Rhetorician perhaps succeeds in speaking well, and the Grammarian sometimes not well, and the skilful Grammarian is ignorant of the subjects of philosophy. But the Holy Spirit taught them many languages at once, languages which in all their life they never knew. This is in truth vast wisdom, this is power divine. What a contrast of their long ignorance in time past to their sudden, complete and varied and unaccustomed exercise of these languages!

17. The multitude of the hearers was confounded;—it was a second confusion, in the room of that first evil one at Babylon. For in that confusion of tongues there was division of purpose, because their thought was at enmity with God; but here minds were restored and united, because the object of interest was godly. The means of falling were the means of recovery. Wherefore they marvelled, saying[2], *How hear we them speaking?* No marvel if ye be ignorant; for even Nicodemus was ignorant of the coming of the Spirit, and to him it was said, *The Spirit breatheth where it listeth, and thou hearest the voice thereof, but canst not tell whence it cometh, and whither it goeth*[3]*;* but if, even though I hear His voice, I know not whence he cometh, how can I explain, what He is Himself in substance?

18. *But others mocking said, They are full of new wine*[4], and they spoke truly though in mockery. For in truth the wine was new, even the grace of the New Testament; but this new wine was from a spiritual Vine, which had oftentimes ere this borne fruit in Prophets, and had budded in the New Testament. For as in things sensible, the vine ever remains the same, but bears new fruits in its seasons, so also the self-same Spirit continuing what He is, as He had often wrought in Prophets, now manifested a new and marvellous work. For though His grace had come before to the Fathers also, yet here it came exuberantly; for formerly men only partook of the Holy Ghost, but now they were baptized completely.

19. But Peter who had the Holy Ghost, and who knew what he possessed, says, "*Men of Israel*, ye who preach Joel, but know not the things which are written, *these men are not drunken as ye suppose*[5]. Drunken they are, not however as ye suppose, but according to that which is written, *They shall be drunken with the fatness of thy house; and thou shalt make them drink of the torrents of thy pleasure*[6]. They are drunken, with a sober drunkenness, deadly to sin and life-giving to the heart, a drunkenness contrary to that of the body; for this last causes forgetfulness even of what was known, but that bestows the knowledge even of what was not known. They are drunken, for they have drunk the wine of the spiritual vine, which says, *I am the vine and ye*

9 Acts ii. 2.

1 Ib. *v.* 4.

2 Acts ii. 8.

3 John iii. 8: (R.V.) *The wind bloweth:* (Marg.) Or, *The Spirit breatheth.* It is impossible to preserve the double meaning in English.

4 Acts ii. 13.

5 Ib. *v.* 15.

6 Ps. xxxvi. 8.

are the branches[7]. But if ye are not persuaded by me, understand what I tell you from the very time of the day; for *it is the third hour of the day*[8]. For He who, as Mark relates, was crucified at the third hour, now at the third hour sent down His grace. For His grace is not other than the Spirit's grace, but He who was then crucified, who also gave the promise, made good that which He promised. And if ye would receive a testimony also, *Listen*, he says: "*But this is that which was spoken by the prophet Joel; And it shall come to pass after this, saith God, I will pour forth of My Spirit*[9]"—(and this word, *I will pour forth*, implied a rich gift; *for God giveth not the Spirit by measure, for the Father loveth the Son, and hath given all things into His hand*[1]; and He has given Him the power also of bestowing the grace of the All-holy Spirit on whomsoever He will);—*I will pour forth of My Spirit upon all flesh, and your sons and your daughters shall prophesy;* and afterwards, *Yea, and on My servants and on My handmaidens I will pour out in those days of My Spirit, and they shall prophesy*[2]." The Holy Ghost is no respecter of persons; for He seeks not dignities, but piety of soul. Let neither the rich be puffed up, nor the poor dejected, but only let each prepare himself for reception of the Heavenly gift.

20. We have said much to-day, and perchance you are weary of listening; yet more still remains. And in truth for the doctrine of the Holy Ghost there were need of a third lecture; and of many besides. But we must have your indulgence on both points. For as the Holy Festival of Easter is now at hand, we have this day lengthened our discourse; and yet we had not room to bring before you all the testimonies from the New Testament which we ought. For many passages are still to come from the Acts of the Apostles in which the grace of the Holy Ghost wrought mightily in Peter and in all the Apostles together; many also from the Catholic Epistles, and the fourteen Epistles of Paul; out of all which we will now endeavour to gather a few, like flowers from a large meadow, merely by way of remembrance.

21. For in the power of the Holy Ghost, by the will of Father and Son, Peter stood with the Eleven, and lifting up his voice, (according to the text, *Lift up thy voice with strength, thou that bringest good tidings to Jerusalem*[3]), captured in the spiritual net of his words, *about three thousand souls.* So great was the grace which wrought in all the Apostles together, that, out of the Jews, those crucifiers of Christ, this great number believed, and were baptized in the Name of Christ, and *continued steadfastly in the Apostles' doctrine and in the prayers*[4]. And again in the same power of the Holy Ghost, *Peter and John went up into the Temple at the hour of prayer, which was the ninth hour*[5], and in the Name of Jesus healed the man at the Beautiful gate, who had been lame from his mother's womb for forty years; that it might be fulfilled which was spoken, *Then shall the lame man leap as an hart*[6]. And thus, as they captured in the spiritual net of their doctrine five thousand believers at once, so they confuted the misguided rulers of the people and chief priests, and that, not through their own wisdom, for *they were unlearned and ignorant men*[7], but through the mighty power of the Holy Ghost; for it is written, *Then Peter filled with the Holy Ghost said to them*[8]. So great also was the grace of the Holy Ghost, which wrought by means of the Twelve Apostles in them who believed, that *they were of one heart and of one soul*[9], and their enjoyment of their goods was common, the possessors piously offering the prices of their possessions, and no one among them wanting aught; while Ananias and Sapphira, who attempted to lie to the Holy Ghost, underwent their befitting punishment.

22. *And by the hands of the Apostles were many signs and wonders wrought among the people*[1]. And so great was the spiritual grace shed around the Apostles, that gentle as they were, they were the objects of dread; for *of the rest durst no man join himself to them; but the people magnified them; and multitudes were added of those who believed on the Lord, both of men and women;* and the streets were filled with the sick on their beds and couches, *that as Peter passed by, at least his shadow might overshadow some of them.* And *the multitude also of the cities round about came* unto this holy Jerusalem, *bringing sick folk, and them that were vexed with unclean spirits, and they were healed every one* in this power of the Holy Ghost[2].

23. Again, after the Twelve Apostles had been cast into prison by the chief priests for preaching Christ, and had been marvellously delivered from it at night by an Angel, and were brought before them in the judgment hall from the Temple, they fearlessly rebuked them in their discourse to them concerning Christ, and added this, that *God hath also given His Holy Spirit to them that obey Him*[3]. And

7 John xv. 5. 8 Acts ii. 25, and 15. 9 Joel ii. 28. 1 John iii. 34, 35. 2 Joel ii. 29. 3 Is. xl. 9.

4 Acts ii. 42. 5 Ib. iii. 1. 6 Is. xxxv. 6. 7 Acts iv. 13. 8 Ib. *v.* 8. 9 Ib. *v.* 32. 1 Acts v. 12. 2 Ib. *vv.* 13—16. 3 Ib. *v.* 32.

when they had been scourged, they went their way rejoicing, and ceased not to *teach and preach Jesus as the Christ*[4].

24. And it was not in the Twelve Apostles only that the grace of the Holy Spirit wrought, but also in the first-born children of this once barren Church, I mean the seven Deacons; for these also were chosen, as it is written, being *full of the Holy Ghost and of wisdom*[5]. Of whom Stephen, rightly so named[6], the first fruits of the Martyrs, a man *full of faith and of the Holy Ghost, wrought great wonders and miracles among the people*, and vanquished those who disputed with him; *for they were not able to resist the wisdom and the Spirit by which he spake*[7]. But when he was maliciously accused and brought to the judgment hall, he was radiant with angelic brightness; for *all they who sat in the council, looking steadfastly on him, saw his face, as it had been the face of an Angel*[8]. And having by his wise defence confuted the Jews, those *stiffnecked men, uncircumcised in heart and ears, ever resisting the Holy Ghost*[9], he beheld *the heavens opened*, and saw *the Son of Man standing on the right hand of God.* He saw Him, not by his own power, but, as the Divine Scripture says, *being full of the Holy Ghost, he looked up steadfastly into heaven, and saw the glory of God, and Jesus standing on the right hand of God*[1].

25. In this power of the Holy Ghost, Philip also in the Name of Christ at one time in the city of Samaria drove away the unclean spirits, *crying out with a loud voice;* and healed the palsied and the lame, and brought to Christ great multitudes of them that believe. To whom Peter and John came down, and with prayer, and the laying on of hands, imparted the fellowship of the Holy Ghost, from which Simon Magus alone was declared an alien, and that justly. And at another time Philip was called by the Angel of the Lord in the way, for the sake of that most godly Ethiopian, the Eunuch, and heard distinctly the Spirit Himself saying, *Go near, and join thyself to this chariot*[2]. He instructed the Eunuch, and baptized him, and so having sent into Ethiopia a herald of Christ, according as it is written, *Ethiopia shall soon stretch out her hand unto God*[3], he was caught away by the Angel, and preached the Gospel in the cities in succession.

26. With this Holy Spirit Paul also had been filled after his calling by our Lord Jesus Christ. Let godly Ananias come as a witness to what we say, he who in Damascus said to him, *The Lord, even Jesus who appeared to thee in the way which thou camest, hath sent me, that thou mayest receive thy sight, and be filled with the Holy Ghost*[4]. And straightway the Spirit's mighty working changed the blindness of Paul's eyes into newness of sight; and having vouchsafed His seal unto his soul, made him *a chosen vessel* to *bear the Name* of the Lord who had appeared to him, *before kings and the children of Israel*, and rendered the former persecutor an ambassador and good servant,—one, who *from Jerusalem, and even unto Illyricum, fully preached the Gospel*[5], and instructed even imperial Rome, and carried the earnestness of his preaching as far as Spain, undergoing conflicts innumerable, and performing signs and wonders. Of him for the present enough.

27. In the power of the same Holy Spirit Peter also, the chief of the Apostles and the bearer of the keys[6] of the kingdom of heaven, healed Æneas the paralytic in the Name of Christ at Lydda, which is now Diospolis, and at Joppa raised from the dead Tabitha rich in good works. And being on the housetop in a trance, he saw heaven opened, and by means of the vessel let down as it were a sheet full of beasts of every shape and sort, he learnt plainly to call no man common or unclean, though he should be of the Greeks[7]. And when he was sent for by Cornelius, he heard clearly the Holy Ghost Himself saying, *Behold, men seek thee; but arise and get thee down, and go with them, nothing doubting; for I have sent them*[8]. And that it might be plainly shewn that those of the Gentiles also who believe are made partakers of the grace of the Holy Ghost, when Peter was come to Cesarea, and was teaching the things concerning Christ, the Scripture says concerning Cornelius and them who were with him; *While Peter yet spake these words, the Holy Ghost fell on all them which heard the word; so that they of the circumcision also which came with Peter were astonished, and when they understood it said that on the Gentiles also was poured out the gift of the Holy Ghost*[9].

28. And in Antioch also, a most renowned city of Syria, when the preaching of Christ took effect, Barnabas was sent hence as far as Antioch to help on the good work, being a *good man, and full of the Holy Ghost, and of faith*[1]; who seeing a great harvest of believers in Christ, brought Paul from Tarsus to Antioch, as his fellow-combatant. And when crowds had been instructed by them and assembled in the Church, *it came to pass that the disciples were called Christians first in Antioch*[2]; the Holy Ghost, methinks, bestowing on the believers that new Name, which had been promised be-

4 Acts v. 42. 5 Ib. vi. 3. 6 Ib. *v.* 8. Στέφανος, "a crown." 7 Ib. *v.* 10. 8 Ib. *v.* 15. 9 Ib. vii. 51. 1 Ib. *v.* 55. 2 Ib. viii. 5. 3 Ps. lxviii. 31.

4 Acts ix. 17. 5 Rom. xv. 19. 6 κλειδοῦχος. Cf. Matt. xvi. 19; Cat. ii. 19; xi. 3. 7 Acts x. 11–16. 8 Ib. *v.* 19 9 Ib. *v.* 44. 1 Ib. xi. 24. 2 Ib. *v.* 26. Cf. Is. lxv. 15.

fore by the Lord. And the grace of the Spirit being shed forth by God more abundantly in Antioch, there were there prophets and teachers of whom Agabus was one[3]. And *as they ministered to the Lord and fasted, the Holy Ghost said, Separate Me Barnabas and Saul for the work whereunto I have called them.* And after hands had been laid on them, *they were sent forth by the Holy Ghost*[4]. Now it is manifest, that the Spirit which speaks and sends, is a living Spirit, subsisting, and operating, as we have said.

29. This Holy Spirit, who in unison with Father and Son has established the New Covenant in the Church Catholic, has set us free from the burdens of the law grievous to be borne,—those I mean, concerning things common and unclean, and meats, and sabbaths, and new moons, and circumcision, and sprinklings, and sacrifices; which were given for a season, and *had a shadow of the good things to come*[5], but which, when the truth had come, were rightly withdrawn. For when Paul and Barnabas were sent to the Apostles, because of the question moved at Antioch by them who said that it was necessary to be circumcised and to keep the customs of Moses, the Apostles who were here at Jerusalem by a written injunction set free the whole world from all the legal and typical observances; yet they attributed not to themselves the full authority in so great a matter, but send an injunction in writing, and acknowledge this: *For it hath seemed good unto the Holy Ghost and to us, to lay upon you no greater burden than these necessary things; that ye abstain from things sacrificed to idols, and from blood, and from things strangled, and from fornication*[6]; shewing evidently by what they wrote, that though the writing was by the hands of human Apostles, yet the decree is universal from the Holy Ghost: which decree Paul and Barnabas took and confirmed unto all the world.

30. And now, having proceeded thus far in my discourse, I ask indulgence from your love[7], or rather from the Spirit who dwelt in Paul, if I should not be able to rehearse everything, by reason of my own weakness, and your weariness who listen. For when shall I in terms worthy of Himself declare the marvellous deeds wrought by the operation of the Holy Ghost in the Name of Christ? Those wrought in Cyprus upon Elymas the sorcerer, and in Lystra at the healing of the cripple, and in Cilicia and Phrygia and Galatia and Mysia and Macedonia? or those at Philippi (the preaching, I mean, and the driving out of the spirit of divination in the Name of Christ; and the salvation by baptism of the jailer with his whole house at night after the earthquake); or the events at Thessalonica; and the address at Areopagus in the midst of the Athenians; or the instructions at Corinth, and in all Achaia? How shall I worthily recount the mighty deeds which were wrought at Ephesus through Paul, by the Holy Ghost[8]? Whom they of that City knew not before, but came to know Him by the doctrine of Paul; and when Paul had laid his hands on them, and the Holy Ghost had come upon them, *they spake with tongues, and prophesied.* And so great spiritual grace was upon him, that not only his touch wrought cures, but even the *handkerchiefs and napkins*[9], brought from his body, healed diseases, and scared away the evil spirits; and at last *they also who practised curious arts brought their books together, and burned them before all men*[1].

31. I pass by the work wrought at Troas on Eutychus, who *being borne down by his sleep fell down from the third loft, and was taken up dead;* yet was saved alive by Paul[2]. I also pass by the prophecies addressed to the Elders of Ephesus whom he called to him in Miletus, to whom he openly said, *That the Holy Ghost witnesseth in every city, saying*[3],—and the rest; for by saying, *in every city*, Paul made manifest that the marvellous works done by him in each city, were from the operative power of the Holy Ghost, by the will of God, and in the Name of Christ who spake in him. By the power of this Holy Ghost, the same Paul was hastening to this holy city Jerusalem, and this, though Agabus by the Spirit foretold what should befall him; and yet he spoke to the people with confidence, declaring the things concerning Christ. And when brought to Cesarea, and set amid tribunals of justice, at one time before Felix, and at another before Festus the governor and King Agrippa, Paul obtained of the Holy Ghost grace so great, and triumphant in wisdom, that at last Agrippa himself the king of the Jews said, *Almost thou persuadest me to be a Christian*[4]. This Holy Spirit granted to Paul, when he was in the island of Melita also, to receive no harm when bitten by the viper, and to effect divers cures on the diseased. This Holy Spirit guided him, the persecutor of old, as a herald of Christ, even as far as imperial Rome, and there he persuaded many of the Jews to believe in Christ, and to them who gainsaid he said plainly, *Well spake the Holy Ghost by Esaias the Prophet, saying unto your fathers*, and the rest[5].

3 Acts xi. 28. 4 Ib. xiii. 2—4. 5 Heb. x. 1.

6 Acts xv. 28, 29. ἐπιστολή means a *message* or *injunction* whether verbal or written.

7 See note 1 on § 1, above.

8 Acts xix. 1—6. 9 Ib. *v.* 12. 1 Ib. *v.* 19.

2 Ib. xx. 9—12. 3 Ib. *v.* 23.

4 Ib. xxvi. 28. Cyril evidently understood ἐν ὀλίγῳ to mean "*almost*" (A.V.): but the more correct rendering is, "In brief thou wouldest persuade me to become a Christian."

5 Ib. xxviii. 25.

32. And that Paul was full of the Holy Ghost, and all his fellow Apostles, and they who after them believed in Father, Son, and Holy Ghost, hear from himself as he writes plainly in his Epistles; *And my speech*, he says, *and my preaching was not in persuasive words of man's wisdom, but in demonstration of the Spirit and of power*[6]. And again, *But He who sealed us for this very purpose is God, who gave us the earnest of the Spirit*[7]. And again, *He that raised up Jesus from the dead shall also quicken your mortal bodies by His Spirit which dwelleth in you*[8]. And again, writing to Timothy, *That good thing which was committed to thee guard through the Holy Ghost which was given to us*[9].

33. And that the Holy Ghost subsists, and lives, and speaks, and foretells, I have often said in what goes before, and Paul writes it plainly to Timothy: *Now the Spirit speaketh expressly, that in later times some shall depart from the faith*[1],—which we see in the divisions not only of former times but also of our own; so motley and diversified are the errors of the heretics. And again the same Paul says, *Which in other generations was not made known unto the sons of men, as it hath now been revealed unto His Holy Apostles and Prophets in the Spirit*[2]. And again, *Wherefore, as saith the Holy Ghost*[3]; and again, *The Holy Ghost also witnesseth to us*[4]. And again he calls unto the soldiers of righteousness, saying, *And take the helmet of salvation, and the sword of the Spirit, which is the Word of God, with all prayer and supplication*[5]. And again, *Be not drunk with wine, wherein is excess; but be filled with the Spirit, speaking to yourselves in psalms, and hymns, and spiritual songs*[6]. And again, *The grace of the Lord Jesus, and the love of God, and the communion of the Holy Ghost be with you all*[7].

34. By all these proofs, and by more which have been passed over, is the personal, and sanctifying, and effectual power of the Holy Ghost established for those who can understand; for the time would fail me in my discourse if I wished to quote what yet remains concerning the Holy Ghost from the fourteen Epistles of Paul, wherein he has taught with such variety, completeness, and reverence. And to the power of the Holy Ghost Himself it must belong, to grant to us forgiveness for what we have omitted because the days are few, and upon you the hearers to impress more perfectly the knowledge of what yet remains; while from the frequent reading of the sacred Scriptures those of you who are diligent come to understand these things, and by this time, both from these present Lectures, and from what has before been told you, hold more steadfastly the Faith in "ONE GOD THE FATHER ALMIGHTY; AND IN OUR LORD JESUS CHRIST, HIS ONLY-BEGOTTEN SON; AND IN THE HOLY GHOST THE COMFORTER." Though the word itself and title of Spirit is applied to Them in common in the sacred Scriptures,—for it is said of the Father, *God is a Spirit*[8], as it is written in the Gospel according to John; and of the Son, *A Spirit before our face, Christ the Lord*[9], as Jeremias the prophet says; and of the Holy Ghost, *the Comforter, the Holy Ghost*[1], as was said;—yet the arrangement of articles in the Faith, if religiously understood, disproves the error of Sabellius also[2]. Return we therefore in our discourse to the point which now presses and is profitable to you.

35. Beware lest ever like Simon thou come to the dispensers of Baptism in hypocrisy, thy heart the while not seeking the truth. It is ours to protest, but it is thine to secure thyself. If *thou standest in faith*[3], blessed art thou; if thou hast fallen in unbelief, from this day forward cast away thine unbelief, and receive full assurance. For, at the season of baptism, when thou art come before the Bishops, or Presbyters, or Deacons[4],—(for its grace is everywhere, in villages and in cities, on them of low as on them of high degree, on bondsmen and on freemen, for this grace is not of men, but the gift is from God through men,)—approach the Minister of Baptism, but approaching, think not of the face of him thou seest, but remember this Holy Ghost of whom we are now speaking. For He is present in readiness to seal thy soul, and He shall give thee that Seal at which evil spirits tremble, a heavenly and sacred seal, as also it is written, *In whom also ye believed, and were sealed with the Holy Spirit of promise*[5].

36. Yet He tries the soul. He casts not His pearls before swine; if thou play the hypocrite, though men baptize thee now, the Holy Spirit will not baptize thee[6]. But if thou approach with faith, though men minister in what is seen, the Holy Ghost bestows that which is unseen. Thou art coming to a great trial,

6 1 Cor. ii. 4. 7 2 Cor. i. 22. 8 Rom. viii. 11.
9 2 Tim. i. 14: (R.V.) *by the Holy Ghost which dwelleth in us.*
1 1 Tim. iv. 1. 2 Eph. iii. 5. 3 Heb. iii. 7.
4 Ib. x. 15. 5 Eph. vi. 17. 6 Ib. v. 18, 19.
7 2 Cor. xiii. 14.

8 John iv. 24.
9 Lam. iv. 20. *The breath of our nostrils, the anointed of the Lord:* referring to the captive king. 1 John xiv. 25.
2 The distinct mention in the Creed of three Persons excludes the error of Sabellius in confusing them. Cf. Cat. iv. 8; xvi. 14.
3 Rom. xi. 20.
4 Cf. Bingham, *Antiquities*, II. xx. 9. "When Cyril directs his Catechumens how they should behave themselves at the time of Baptism, when they came either before a bishop, or presbyter, or deacon, in city or village,—this may be presumed a fair intimation that then deacons were ordinarily allowed to minister Baptism in country places." See further 'Of the power granted anciently to deacons to baptize,' Bingham, *Lay Baptism*, I. i. 5.
5 Eph. i. 13. Cf. Cat. i. 2, 3.
6 Cf. Procat. § 4: "The water will receive, but the Spirit will not accept thee."

to a great muster[7], in that one hour, which if thou throw away, thy disaster is irretrievable; but if thou be counted worthy of the grace, thy soul will be enlightened, thou wilt receive a power which thou hadst not, thou wilt receive weapons terrible to the evil spirits; and if thou cast not away thine arms, but keep the Seal upon thy soul, no evil spirit will approach thee; for he will be cowed; for verily by the Spirit of God are the evil spirits cast out.

37. If thou believe, thou shalt not only receive remission of sins, but also do things which pass man's power[8]. And mayest thou be worthy of the gift of prophecy also! For thou shalt receive grace according to the measure of thy capacity and not of my words; for I may possibly speak of but small things, yet thou mayest receive greater; since faith is a large affair[9]. All thy life long will thy guardian the Comforter abide with thee; He will care for thee, as for his own soldier; for thy goings out, and thy comings in, and thy plotting foes. And He will give thee gifts of grace of every kind, if thou grieve Him not by sin; for it is written, *And grieve not the Holy Spirit of God, whereby ye were sealed unto the day of redemption*[1]. What then, beloved, is it to preserve grace? Be ye ready to receive grace, and when ye have received it, cast it not away.

38. And may the very God of All, who spake by the Holy Ghost through the prophets, who sent Him forth upon the Apostles on the day of Pentecost in this place, Himself send Him forth at this time also upon you; and by Him keep us also, imparting His benefit in common to us all, that we may ever render up the fruits of the Holy Ghost, *love, joy, peace, long-suffering, gentleness, goodness, faith, meekness, temperance*[2], in Christ Jesus our Lord:—By whom and with whom, together with the Holy Ghost, be glory to the Father, both now, and ever, and for ever and ever. Amen.

---

7 *στρατολογία.* Cf. Cat. iii. 3, *μέλλετε στρατολογεῖσθαι.*

8 The same twofold grace is ascribed to Baptism in Cat. xiii. 23: "Thou receivest now remission of thy sins, and the gifts of the King's spiritual bounty."

9 *πραγματεία.* Cf. 2 Tim. ii. 4; and Luke xix. 13: *Trade (πραγματεύεσθε) till I come.*

1 Eph. iv. 30.

2 Gal. v. 22, 23.

LECTURE XVIII.

On the Words, And in One Holy Catholic Church, And in the Resurrection of the Flesh, And the Life Everlasting.

Ezekiel xxxvii. 1.

The hand of the Lord was upon me, and carried me out in the Spirit of the Lord, and set me down in the midst of the valley which was full of bones.

1. The root of all good works is the hope of the Resurrection; for the expectation of the recompense nerves the soul to good works. For every labourer is ready to endure the toils, if he sees their reward in prospect; but when men weary themselves for nought, their heart soon sinks as well as their body. A soldier who expects a prize is ready for war, but no one is forward to die for a king who is indifferent about those who serve under him, and bestows no honours on their toils. In like manner every soul believing in a Resurrection is naturally careful of itself; but, disbelieving it, abandons itself to perdition. He who believes that his body shall remain to rise again, is careful of his robe, and defiles it not with fornication; but he who disbelieves the Resurrection, gives himself to fornication, and misuses his own body, as though it were not his own. Faith therefore in the Resurrection of the dead, is a great commandment and doctrine of the Holy Catholic Church; great and most ncessary, though gainsaid by many, yet surely warranted by the truth. Greeks contradict it[1], Samaritans[2] disbelieve it, heretics[3] mutilate it; the contradiction is manifold, but the truth is uniform.

2. Now Greeks and Samaritans together argue against us thus. The dead man has fallen, and mouldered away, and is all turned into worms; and the worms have died also; such is the decay and destruction which has overtaken the body; how then is it to be raised? The shipwrecked have been devoured by fishes, which are themselves devoured. Of them who fight with wild beasts the very bones are ground to powder, and consumed by bears and lions. Vultures and ravens feed on the flesh of the unburied dead, and then fly away over all the world; whence then is the body to be collected? For of the fowls who have devoured it some may chance to die in India, some in Persia, some in the land of the Goths. Other men again are consumed by fire, and their very ashes scattered by rain or wind; whence is the body to be brought together again[4]?

3. To thee, poor little feeble man, India is far from the land of the Goths, and Spain from Persia; but to God, who holds the whole *earth in the hollow of His hand*[5], all things are near at hand. Impute not then weakness to God, from a comparison of thy feebleness, but rather dwell on His power[6]. Does then the sun, a small work of God, by one glance of his beams give warmth to the whole world; does the atmosphere, which God has made, encompass all things in the world; and is God, who is the Creator both of the sun, and of the atmosphere, far off from the world? Imagine a mixture of seeds of different plants (for as thou art weak concerning the faith, the examples which I allege are weak also), and that these different seeds are contained in thy single hand; is it then to thee, who art a man, a difficult or an easy matter to separate what is in thine hand, and to collect each seed according to its nature, and restore it to its own kind? Canst thou then separate the things in thine hand, and cannot God separate the things contained in His hand, and restore them to their proper place? Consider what I say, whether it is not impious to deny it?

4. But further, attend, I pray, to the very principle of justice, and come to thine own case. Thou hast different sorts of servants: and some are good and some bad;

1 Acts xvii. 32; xxvi. 24.

2 Cf. § 12, below.

3 Tertull. *De Resurr. carnis*, cap. 2: "They acknowledge a half-resurrection, to wit of the soul only." Compare Iren. I. xxiii. 5, on Menander's assertion that his disciples attain to the resurrection by being baptized into him, and can die no more, but retain immortal youth: *ib.* xxiv. 5. Basilides taught that "salvation belongs to the soul alone." On other forms of heresy concerning the Resurrection, see Suicer, *Thesaurus*, Ἀνάστασις.

4 The objections noticed in § 2 are discussed by Athenagoras, *De Resurr.* capp. ii., iv.—viii.; Tatian. *Or. ad Graecos*, cap. vi., Tertull. *De Resurr. Carn.* cap. 63.

5 Is. xl. 12.

6 On the argument from God's power compare Athenagor *De Resurr.* c. ix; Justin. M. *De Resurr.* c. v; Theophil. *ad Autolyc.* c. xiii.; Iren. V. iii. 2.

thou honourest therefore the good, and smitest the bad. And if thou art a judge, to the good thou awardest praise, and to the transgressors, punishment. Is then justice observed by thee a mortal man; and with God, the ever changeless King of all, is there no retributive justice[7]? Nay, to deny it is impious. For consider what I say. Many murderers have died in their beds unpunished; where then is the righteousness of God? Yea, ofttimes a murderer guilty of fifty murders is beheaded once; where then shall he suffer punishment for the forty and nine? Unless there is a judgment and a retribution after this world, thou chargest God with unrighteousness. Marvel not, however, because of the delay of the judgment; no combatant is crowned or disgraced, till the contest is over; and no president of the games ever crowns men while yet striving, but he waits till all the combatants are finished, that then deciding between them he may dispense the prizes and the chaplets[8]. Even thus God also, so long as the strife in this world lasts, succours the just but partially, but afterwards He renders to them their rewards fully.

5. But if according to thee there is no resurrection of the dead, wherefore condemnest thou the robbers of graves? For if the body perishes, and there is no resurrection to be hoped for, why does the violator of the tomb undergo punishment? Thou seest that though thou deny it with thy lips, there yet abides with thee an indestructible instinct of the resurrection.

6. Further, does a tree after it has been cut down blossom again, and shall man after being cut down blossom no more? And does the corn sown and reaped remain for the threshing floor, and shall man when reaped from this world not remain for the threshing? And do shoots of vine or other trees, when clean cut off and transplanted, come to life and bear fruit; and shall man, for whose sake all these exist, fall into the earth and not rise again? Comparing efforts, which is greater, to mould from the beginning a statue which did not exist, or to recast in the same shape that which had fallen? Is God then, who created us out of nothing, unable to raise again those who exist and are fallen[9]? But thou believest not what is written of the resurrection, being a Greek: then from the analogy of nature consider these matters, and understand them from what is seen to this day. Wheat, it may be, or some other kind of grain, is sown; and when the seed has fallen, it dies and rots, and is henceforth useless for food. But that which has rotted, springs up in verdure; and though small when sown, springs up most beautiful. Now wheat was made for us; for wheat and all seeds were created not for themselves, but for our use; are then the things which were made for us quickened when they die, and do we for whom they were made, not rise again after our death[1]?

7. The season is winter[2], as thou seest; the trees now stand as if they were dead: for where are the leaves of the fig-tree? where are the clusters of the vine? These in winter time are dead, but green in spring; and when the season is come, there is restored to them a quickening as it were from a state of death. For God, knowing thine unbelief, works a resurrection year by year in these visible things; that, beholding what happens to things inanimate, thou mayest believe concerning things animate and rational. Further, flies and bees are often drowned in water, yet after a while revive[3]; and species of dormice[4], after remaining motionless during the winter, are restored in the summer (for to thy slight thoughts like examples are offered); and shall He who to irrational and despised creatures grants life supernaturally, not bestow it upon us, for whose sake He made them?

8. But the Greeks ask for a resurrection of the dead still manifest; and say that, even if these creatures are raised, yet they had not utterly mouldered away; and they require to see distinctly some creature rise again after complete decay. God knew men's unbelief, and provided for this purpose a bird, called a Phœnix[5]. This bird, as Clement writes, and

7 The argument from God's justice is treated by Athenagor. *De Resurr.* c. x. and xx.—xxiii.; Justin M. *De Resurr.* c. viii.

8 τὴν στεφανηφορίαν. Roe. Cas. A. Cf. Pind. *Ol.* viii. 13; Eurip. *Electr.* 862.

9 Athenag. *De Resurr.* c. iii.: "If, when they did not exist, He made at their first formation the bodies of men, and their original elements, He will, when they are dissolved, in whatever manner that may take place, raise them again with equal ease." Lactant. *Institt.* VII. 23 fin.: *Apost. Const.* V 7.

1 An eloquent statement of the argument for the resurrection from the analogies of nature occurs in Tertull. *De Resurr.* c. xii. That it was not unknown to Cyril, seems probable from the concluding sentence: "And surely if all things rise again for man, for whom they have been provided—but not for man unless for his flesh also—how can the flesh itself perish utterly, for the sake and service of which nothing is allowed to perish." Tertullian himself was probably indebted, as Bp. Lightfoot suggests, to Clemens. Rom. *Epist. ad Corinth.* xxiv. Cf. Lactant. *Div. Inst.* vii. 4.

2 Cf. Cat. iv. 30. These passages shew that the Lectures were delivered in a year when Easter fell early, as was the case in 348 A.D.

3 In such cases there is, of course, no actual death.

4 The μυοξός is supposed by the Benedictine Editor to be the toad ("Inventusque cavis bufo," Virg. *Georg.* i. 185), by others the marmot (mus Alpinus). More probably it is the dormouse (myoxis glis), which stores up provisions for the winter, though it sleeps through much of that season.

5 The story of the Phœnix as told by Herodotus, II. 73, is as follows: "They have also another sacred bird called the phœnix, which I myself have never seen, except in pictures. Indeed it is a great rarity even in Egypt, only coming there (according to the accounts of the people of Heliopolis) once in five hundred years, when the old phœnix dies.... They tell a story of what this bird does, which does not seem to me to be credible; that he comes all

as many more relate, being the only one of its kind [6], arrives in the land of the Egyptians at periods of five hundred years, shewing forth the resurrection, not in desert places, lest the occurrence of the mystery should remain unknown, but appearing in a notable city [7], that men might even handle what would otherwise be disbelieved. For it makes itself a coffin [8] of frankincense and myrrh and other spices, and entering into this when its years are fulfilled, it evidently dies and moulders away. Then from the decayed flesh of the dead bird a worm is engendered, and this worm when grown large is transformed into a bird;—and do not disbelieve this, for thou seest the offspring of bees also fashioned thus out of worms [9], and from eggs which are quite fluid thou hast seen wings and bones and sinews of birds issue. Afterwards the aforesaid Phœnix, becoming fledged and a full-grown Phœnix, like the former one, soars up into the air such as it had died, shewing forth to men a most evident resurrection of the dead. The Phœnix indeed is a wondrous bird, yet it is irrational, nor ever sang praise to God; it flies abroad through the sky, but it knows not who is the Only-begotten Son of God. Has then a resurrection from the dead been given to this irrational creature which knows not its Maker, and to us who ascribe glory to God and keep His commandments, shall there no resurrection be granted?

9. But since the sign of the Phœnix is remote and uncommon, and men still disbelieve our resurrection, take again the proof of this from what thou seest every day. A hundred or two hundred years ago, we all, speakers and hearers, where were we? Know we not the groundwork of the substance of our bodies? Knowest thou not how from weak and shapeless and simple [1] elements we are engendered, and out of what is simple and weak a living man is formed? and how that weak element being made flesh is changed into strong sinews, and bright eyes, and sensitive nose, and hearing ears, and speaking tongue, and beating heart, and busy hands, and swift feet, and into members of all kinds [2]? and how that once weak element becomes a shipwright, and a builder, and an architect, and a craftsman of various arts, and a soldier, and a ruler, and a lawgiver, and a king? Cannot God then, who has made us out of imperfect materials, raise us up when we have fallen into decay? He who thus frames a body out of what is vile, cannot He raise the fallen body again? And He who fashions that which is not, shall He not raise up that which is and is fallen?

10. Take further a manifest proof of the resurrection of the dead, witnessed month by month in the sky and its luminaries [3]. The body of the moon vanishes completely, so that no part of it is any more seen, yet it fills again, and is restored to its former state [4]; and for the perfect demonstration of the matter, the moon at certain revolutions of years suffering eclipse and becoming manifestly changed into blood, yet recovers its luminous body: God having provided this, that thou also, the man who art formed of blood, mightest not refuse credence to the resurrection of the dead, but mightest believe concerning thyself also what thou seest in respect of the moon. These therefore use thou as arguments against the Greeks; for with them who receive not what is written fight thou with unwritten weapons, by reasonings only and demonstrations; for these men know not who Moses is, nor Esaias, nor the Gospels, nor Paul.

11. Turn now to the Samaritans, who, receiving the Law only, allow not the Prophets. To them the text just now read from Ezekiel appears of no force, for, as I said, they admit no Prophets; whence then shall we persuade the Samaritans also? Let us go to the writings of the Law. Now God says to Moses, *I am the God of Abraham, and of Isaac, and of Jacob* [5]; this must mean of those who have being and subsistence. For if Abraham has

the way from Arabia, and brings the parent bird, all plastered over with myrrh, to the temple of the Sun, and there buries the body."

The many variations and fabulous accretions of the story are detailed by Suicer, *Thesaurus.* Φοῖνιξ, and by Bp. Lightfoot in a long and interesting note on Clemens Rom. *Epist. ad Cor.* xxv. Cyril borrows the story from Clement almost verbally, yet not without some variations, which will be noticed below. The legend with all its miraculous features is told by Ovid, *Metamorph.* xv. 392, by Claudian, *Phœnix*, and by the Pseudo-Lactantius in an Elegiac poem, *Phœnix*, included in Weber's *Corpus Poetarum Latinorum*, and literally translated in Clark's *Ante-Nicene Library.* See also Tertull. *De Resurr. Carn.* c. xiii.

6 μονογενὲς ὕπαρχον, Clem. Rom. *ubi supra.* Cf. Origen. *contra Celsum*, iv. 98: *Apost. Const.* V. 7: "a bird single in its kind, which they say is without a mate, and the only one in the creation." Pseudo-Lactant. *v.* 30.

"Hoc nemus hos lucos avis incolit unica, phœnix,
Unica, sed vivit morte refecta suâ."

7 "By day, in the sight of all" (Clem. R.) The city was Heliopolis, according to Herodotus and the other ancient authors. But Milton, "*Paradise Lost*, V. 272—

'A phœnix gaz'd by all, as that *sole* bird,
When to enshrine his reliques in the Sun's
Bright temple to Ægyptian Thebes he flies.'

Why does Milton despatch his bird to Thebes rather than Heliopolis?" (Lightfoot).

8 Ovid, *Met.* xv. 405: "Fertque pius cunasque suas patriumque sepulcrum." See the Commentaries on Job xxix. 18: *I shall die in my nest, and I shall multiply my days as the sand.* Margin R.V. Or, *the phœnix.*

9 The mode of reproduction in bees was regarded by Aristotle as mysterious, having in it something supernatural (θεῖον): *De Generatione Animal.* III. 10. 1, 27. In the story of the phœnix Herodotus makes no mention of the "worm."

1 μονοειδής.

2 For a similar argument, see Lactant. *De Resurr.* c. xvii.

3 Clem. Rom. *Epist. ad Cor.* xxiv: "Day and night shew unto us the resurrection. The night falleth asleep, and day ariseth; the day departeth, and night cometh on."

4 Tertull. *de Resurr. Carnis*, xii.: "Readorned also are the mirrors of the moon, which her monthly course had worn away."... "The whole of this revolving order of things bears witness to the resurrection of the dead."

5 Ex iii. 6. Cf. Matt. xxii. 32: *He is not the God of the dead, but of the living.*

come to an end, and Isaac and Jacob, then He is the God of those who have no being. When did a king ever say, I am the king of soldiers, whom he had not? When did any display wealth which he possessed nct? Therefore Abraham and Isaac and Jacob must subsist, that God may be the God of those who have being; for He said not, "I was their God," but *I am*. And that there is a judgment, Abraham shews in saying to the Lord, *He who judgeth all the earth, shall He not execute judgment*[6]?

12. But to this the foolish Samaritans object again, and say that the souls possibly of Abraham and Isaac and Jacob continue, but that their bodies cannot possibly rise again. Was it then possible that the rod of righteous Moses should become a serpent, and is it impossible that the bodies of the righteous should live and rise again? And was that done contrary to nature, and shall they not be restored according to nature? Again, the rod of Aaron, though cut off and dead, budded, *without the scent of waters*[7], and though under a roof, sprouted forth into blossoms as in the fields; and though set in dry places, yielded in one night the flowers and fruit of plants watered for many years. Did Aaron's rod rise, as it were, from the dead, and shall not Aaron himself be raised? And did God work wonders in wood, to secure to him the high-priesthood, and will He not vouchsafe a resurrection to Aaron himself? A woman also was made salt contrary to nature; and flesh was turned into salt; and shall not flesh be restored to flesh? Was Lot's wife made a pillar of salt, and shall not Abraham's wife be raised again? By what power was Moses' hand changed, which even within one hour became as snow, and was restored again? Certainly by God's command. Was then His command of force then, and has it no force now?

13. And whence in the beginning came man into being at all, O ye Samaritans, most senseless of all men? Go to the first book of the Scripture, which even you receive; *And God formed man of the dust of the ground*[8]. Is dust transformed into flesh, and shall not flesh be again restored to flesh? You must be asked too, whence the heavens had their being, and earth, and seas? Whence sun, and moon, and stars? How from the waters were made the things which fly and swim? And how from earth all its living things? Were so many myriads brought from nothing into being, and shall we men, who bear God's image, not be raised up? Truly this course is full of unbelief, and the unbelievers are much to be condemned; when Abraham addresses the Lord as *the Judge of all the earth*, and the learners of the Law disbelieve; when it is written that man is of the earth, and the readers disbelieve it[9].

14. These questions, therefore, are for them, the unbelievers: but the words of the Prophets are for us who believe. But since some who have also used the Prophets believe not what is written, and allege against us that passage, *The ungodly shall not rise up in judgment*[1], and, *For if man go down to the grave he shall come up no more*[2], and, *The dead shall not praise Thee, O Lord*[3],—for of what is well written, they have made ill use—it will be well in a cursory manner, and as far as is now possible, to meet them. For if it is said, that *the ungodly shall not rise up in judgment*, this shews that they shall rise, not in judgment, but in condemnation; for God needs not long scrutiny, but close on the resurrection of the ungodly follows also their punishment. And if it is said, *The dead shall not praise Thee, O Lord*, this shews, that since in this life only is the appointed time for repentance and pardon, for which they who enjoy it shall *praise the Lord*, it remains not after death for them who have died in sins to give praise as the receivers of a blessing, but to bewail themselves; for praise belongs to them who give thanks, but to them who are under the scourge, lamentation. Therefore the just then offer praise; but they who have died in sins have no further season for confession[4].

15. And respecting that passage, *If a man go down to the grave, he shall come up no more*, observe what follows, for it is written, *He shall come up no more, neither shall he return to his own house*. For since the whole world shall pass away, and every house shall be destroyed, how shall he return to his own house, there being henceforth a new and different earth? But they ought to have heard Job, saying, *For there is hope of a tree; for if it be cut down, it will sprout again, and the tender branch thereof will not cease. For though the root thereof wax old in the earth, and the stock thereof die in the rocky ground; yet from the scent of water it will bud, and bring forth a crop like a new plant. But man when he dies, is gone; and when mortal man falls, is he no more*[5]? As it were remonstrating and reproving (for thus ought we to

6 Gen. xviii. 25. 7 Job xiv. 9. 8 Gen. ii. 7.

9 The anomalous construction ὅταν γέγραπται . . . . καὶ ἀπιστῶσιν may be explained by the consideration, that the uncertainty expressed in ὅταν attaches only to the latter Verb. See Winer's *Grammar of N. T. Greek*, P. III. sect. xlii. 5.

1 Ps. i. 5: *The wicked shall not stand in the judgment* (R.V.).

2 Job vii. 9. 3 Ps. cxv. 17.

4 As to the bearing of this passage on the doctrine of Purgatory and prayer for the dead see note on xxiii. 10.

5 Job xiv. 7—10.

read the words *is no more* with an interrogation[6]); he says since a tree falls and revives, shall not man, for whom all trees were made, himself revive? And that thou mayest not suppose that I am forcing the words, read what follows; for after saying by way of question, *When mortal man falls, is he no more?* he says, *For if a man die, he shall live again*[7]; and immediately he adds, *I will wait till I be made again*[8]; and again elsewhere, *Who shall raise up on the earth my skin, which endures these things*[9]. And Esaias the Prophet says, *The dead men shall rise again, and they that are in the tombs shall awake*[1]. And the Prophet Ezekiel, now before us, says most plainly, *Behold I will open your graves, and bring you up out of your graves*[2]. And Daniel says, *Many of them that sleep in the dust of the earth shall arise, some to everlasting life, and some to everlasting shame*[3].

16. And many Scriptures there are which testify of the Resurrection of the dead; for there are many other sayings on this matter. But now, by way of remembrance only, we will make a passing mention of the raising of Lazarus on the fourth day; and just allude, because of the shortness of the time, to the widow's son also who was raised, and merely for the sake of reminding you, let me mention the ruler of the synagogue's daughter, and the rending of the rocks, and how *there arose many bodies of the saints which slept*[4], their graves having been opened. But specially be it remembered that *Christ has been raised from the dead*[5]. I speak but in passing of Elias, and the widow's son whom he raised; of Elisseus also, who raised the dead twice; once in his lifetime, and once after his death. For when alive he wrought the resurrection by means of his own soul[6]; but that not the souls only of the just might be honoured, but that it might be believed that in the bodies also of the just there lies a power, the corpse which was cast into the sepulchre of Elisseus, when it touched the dead body of the prophet, was quickened, and the dead body of the prophet did the work of the soul, and that which was dead and buried gave life to the dead, and though it gave life. yet continued itself among the dead. Wherefore? Lest if Elisseus should rise again, the work should be ascribed to his soul alone; and to shew, that even though the soul is not present, a virtue resides in the body of the saints, because of the righteous soul which has for so many years dwelt in it, and used it as its minister[7]. And let us not foolishly disbelieve, as though this thing had not happened: for if handkerchiefs and aprons, which are from without, touching the bodies of the diseased, raised up the sick, how much more should the very body of the Prophet raise the dead?

17. And with respect to these instances we might say much, rehearsing in detail the marvellous circumstances of each event; but as you have been already wearied both by the superposed fast of the Preparation[8], and by the watchings[9], let what has been cursorily spoken concerning them suffice for a while; these words having been as it were sown thinly, that you, receiving the seed like richest ground, may in bearing fruit increase them. But be it remembered, that the Apostles also raised the dead; Peter raised Tabitha in Joppa, and Paul raised Eutychus in Troas; and thus did all the other Apostles, even though the wonders wrought by each have not all been written. Further, remember all the sayings in the first Epistle to the Corinthians, which Paul wrote against them who said, *How are the dead raised, and with*

6 There is no indication of a question in the Septuagint version of the passage, which means in the Hebrew, *and where is he?* (A.V. and R.V.): Vulg. *ubi, quæso, est?*

7 Job xiv. 14: *For if a man die, shall he live again?* (A.V. and R.V.). By omitting the interrogation here, and inserting it above in *v.* 10, Cyril exactly inverts the meaning.

8 Ib. *v.* 14: (A.V.) *All the days of my appointed time* (R.V. *of my warfare*) *will I wait, till my change* (R.V. *release*) *come.*

9 Job xix. 26: (R.V.) *and that he shall stand up at the last upon the earth: and after my skin hath been thus destroyed, &c.* Cyril, as usual, follows the Septuagint.

1 Is. xxvi. 19.

2 Ezek. xxxvii. 12.

3 Dan. xii. 2.

4 Matt. xxvii. 52.

5 1 Cor. xv. 20.

6 2 Kings iv. 34.

7 "The worship of relics, and the belief in them as remedies and a protection against evil, originated in the 4th century. They first (?) appear in writings, none of which are earlier than the year 370: but they prevailed rapidly when they had once taken root" (Scudamore, *Dict. Chr. Antiq.* "Relics," p. 1770). Bingham (*Ant.* xxiii. 4, § 7) quotes a law of Theodosius, "that no one should remove any dead body that was buried, from one place to another; that no one should sell or buy the relics of Martyrs: but if any one was minded to build over the grave, where a martyr was buried, a church to be called a *martyrium*, in respect to him, he should have liberty to do it." The law wholly failed to suppress a superstition which was sanctioned by such men as Cyril, Basil, Chrysostom, Ambrose, and Augustine.

8 ἐκ τῆς ὑπερθέσεως τῆς νηστείας τῆς παρασκευῆς, Ed. Bened. "The ecclesiastical term τῆς ὑπερθέσεως we have rendered, according to the interpretation received among the Latins, by the word 'superpositio.' The ancients meant by it a fast continued for two or three days without food. Moreover, since the great week was observed with severer fastings, there were many who passed either the whole week or four, three, or two days, namely the Preparation and the Holy Sabbath (Easter Eve), entirely fasting, as is testified by S. Irenæus (Euseb. *Hist.* V. 24) and others. The continuance of the fast throughout the Friday and Saturday was highly approved, as may be seen from the *Apostolical Constitutions*, V. 18." The passage referred to is as follows: "Do you therefore fast on the days of the Passover, beginning from the second day of the week until the Preparation and the Sabbath, six days, making use only of bread, and salt, and herbs, and water for your drink: but abstain on these days from wine and flesh, for they are days of lamentation and not of fasting. Do ye who are able fast throughout the Preparation and the Sabbath entirely, tasting nothing till the cockcrowing at night; but if any one is not able to combine them both, let the Sabbath at least be observed."

9 The fast of the Great Sabbath was to be continued through the night, as prescribed in the *Apost. Const.* V. 19: "Continue until cock-crowing and break off your fast at dawn of the first day of the week, which is the Lord's day, keeping awake from evening until cock-crowing: and assembling together in the Church, watch and pray and beseech God, in your night-long vigil, reading the Law, the Prophets. and the Psalms. until the crowing of the cocks: and after baptizing your Catechumens, and reading the Gospel in fear and trembling, and speaking to the people the things pertaining to salvation, so cease from your mourning." A chief reason for the watching was that Christ was expected to return at the same hour in which He rose. On the meaning of "superposition" see Routh's note on the Synodical Epistle of Irenæus to Victor of Rome (*Rell. Sac.* ii. p. 45, ss.), and the passage of Dionysius of Alexandria there quoted.

what manner of body do they come[1]? And how he says, *For if the dead rise not, then is not Christ raised*[2]; and how he called them *fools*[3], who believed not; and remember the whole of his teaching there concerning the resurrection of the dead, and how he wrote to the Thessalonians, *But we would not have you to be ignorant, brethren, concerning them which are asleep, that ye sorrow not, even as the rest which have no hope*[4], and all that follows: but chiefly that, *And the dead in Christ shall rise first*[5].

18. But especially mark this, how very pointedly[6] Paul says, *For this corruptible must put on incorruption, and this mortal must put on immortality*[7]. For this body shall be raised, not remaining weak as now; but raised the very same body, though by putting on incorruption it shall be fashioned anew[8],—as iron blending with fire becomes fire, or rather as He knows how, the Lord who raises us. This body therefore shall be raised, but it shall abide not such as it now is, but an eternal body; no longer needing for its life such nourishment as now, nor stairs for its ascent, for it shall be made *spiritual*, a marvellous thing, such as we cannot worthily speak of. *Then*, it is said, *shall the righteous shine forth as the sun*[9], and the moon, *and as the brightness of the firmament*[10]. And God, foreknowing men's unbelief, has given to little worms in the summer to dart beams of light from their body[1], that from what is seen, that which is looked for might be believed; for He who gives in part is able to give the whole also, and He who made the worm radiant with light, will much more illuminate a righteous man.

19. We shall be raised therefore, all with our bodies eternal, but not all with bodies alike: for if a man is righteous, he will receive a heavenly body, that he may be able worthily to hold converse with Angels; but if a man is a sinner, he shall receive an eternal body, fitted to endure the penalties of sins, that he may burn eternally in fire, nor ever be consumed[2]. And righteously will God assign this portion to either company; for we do nothing without the body. We blaspheme with the mouth, and with the mouth we pray. With the body we commit fornication, and with the body we keep chastity. With the hand we rob, and by the hand we bestow alms; and the rest in like manner. Since then the body has been our minister in all things, it shall also share with us in the future the fruits of the past[3].

20. Therefore, brethren, let us be careful of our bodies, nor misuse them as though not our own. Let us not say like the heretics, that this vesture of the body belongs not to us, but let us be careful of it as our own; for we must give account to the Lord of all things done through the body. Say not, none seeth me; think not, that there is no witness of the deed. Human witness oftentimes there is not; but He who fashioned us, an unerring *witness*, abides *faithful in heaven*[4], and beholds what thou doest. And the stains of sin also remain in the body; for as when a wound has gone deep into the body, even if there has been a healing, the scar remains, so sin wounds soul and body, and the marks of its scars remain in all; and they are removed only from those who receive the washing of Baptism. The past wounds therefore of soul and body God heals by Baptism; against future ones let us one and all jointly guard ourselves, that we may keep this vestment of the body pure, and may not for practising fornication and sensual indulgence or any other sin for a short season, lose the salvation of heaven, but may inherit the eternal kingdom of God; of which may God, of His own grace, deem all of you worthy.

21. Thus much in proof of the Resurrection of the dead; and now, let me again recite to you the profession of the faith, and do you with all diligence pronounce it while I speak[5], and remember it.

---

22. The Faith which we rehearse contains in order the following, "AND IN ONE BAPTISM OF REPENTANCE FOR THE REMISSION OF SINS; AND IN ONE HOLY CATHOLIC CHURCH; AND IN THE RESURRECTION OF THE FLESH; AND IN ETERNAL LIFE." Now of Baptism and repentance I have spoken in the earliest Lectures; and my present remarks concerning the resurrection of the dead have been made with reference to the Article "In the resurrection of the flesh." Now then let me finish what still remains to be said for the Article, "In one Holy Catholic Church," on which, though one might say many things, we will speak but briefly.

23. It is called Catholic then because it

---

1 1 Cor. xv. 35. 2 Ib. *v.* 16. 3 Ib. *v.* 36.
4 1 Thess. iv. 13. 5 Ib. *v.* 16.
6 μονονουχὶ δακτυλοδεικτῶν.
7 1 Cor. xv. 53.
8 μεταποιεῖται. The meaning of this word as applied to the Eucharistic elements is fully discussed, and illustrated from its use by Cyril and other Fathers, by Dr. Pusey (*Real Presence*, p. 189).
9 Matt. xiii. 43. 10 Dan. xii. 3.
1 Cyril refers to the glow-worm (πυγολαμπίς, Aristot *Hist. Animal.* V. 19. 14), or some other species of Lampyris (Arist. *de Partibus Animal.* I. 3. 3). 2 Cf. Cat. iv. 31.

3 τῶν γενομένων. With the reading γινομένων (Codd. Monn. Vind.), the meaning will be—"share with us in the future what shall happen to us then." On the argument of this section compare the passages quoted on § 4, note 7.
4 Ps. lxxxix. 37.
5 Cat. V. 12, notes 7 and 4. Cf. Plat. Theaet. 204 C: ἐφ' ἑκάστης λέξεως, "each time we speak."

extends over all the world, from one end of the earth to the other; and because it teaches universally and completely one and all the doctrines which ought to come to men's knowledge, concerning things both visible and invisible, heavenly and earthly[6]; and because it brings into subjection to godliness the whole race of mankind, governors and governed, learned and unlearned; and because it universally treats and heals the whole class of sins, which are committed by soul or body, and possesses in itself every form of virtue which is named, both in deeds and words, and in every kind of spiritual gifts.

24. And it is rightly named (Ecclesia) because it calls forth[7] and assembles together all men; according as the Lord says in Leviticus, *And make an assembly for all the congregation at the door of the tabernacle of witness*[8]. And it is to be noted, that the word *assemble*, is used for the first time in the Scriptures here, at the time when the Lord puts Aaron into the High-priesthood. And in Deuteronomy also the Lord says to Moses, *Assemble the people unto Me, and let them hear My words, that they may learn to fear Me*[9]. And he again mentions the name of the Church, when he says concerning the Tables, *And on them were written all the words which the Lord spake with you in the mount out of the midst of the fire in the day of the Assembly*[10]; as if he had said more plainly, in the day in which ye were called and gathered together by God. The Psalmist also says, *I will give thanks unto Thee, O Lord, in the great Congregation; I will praise Thee among much people*[1].

25. Of old the Psalmist sang, *Bless ye God in the congregations, even the Lord, (ye that are) from the fountains of Israel*[2]. But after the Jews for the plots which they made against the Saviour were cast away from His grace, the Saviour built out of the Gentiles a second Holy Church, the Church of us Christians, concerning which he said to Peter, *And upon this rock I will build My Church, and the gates of hell shall not prevail against it*[3]. And David prophesying of both these, said plainly of the first which was rejected, *I have hated the Congregation of evil doers*[4]; but of the second which is built up he says in the same Psalm, *Lord, I have loved the beauty of Thine house*[5]; and immediately afterwards. *In the Congregations will I bless thee, O Lord*[6]. For now that the one Church in Judæa is cast off, the Churches of Christ are increased over all the world; and of them it is said in the Psalms, *Sing unto the Lord a new song, His praise in the Congregation of Saints*[7]. Agreeably to which the prophet also said to the Jews, *I have no pleasure in you, saith the Lord Almighty*[8]; and immediately afterwards, *For from the rising of the sun even unto the going down of the same, My name is glorified among the Gentiles*[9]. Concerning this Holy Catholic Church Paul writes to Timothy, *That thou mayest know how thou oughtest to behave thyself in the House of God, which is the Church of the Living God, the pillar and ground of the truth*[1].

26. But since the word Ecclesia is applied to different things (as also it is written of the multitude in the theatre of the Ephesians, *And when he had thus spoken, he dismissed the Assembly*[2]), and since one might properly and truly say that there is a *Church of evil doers*, I mean the meetings of the heretics, the Marcionists and Manichees, and the rest, for this cause the Faith has securely delivered to thee now the Article, "And in one Holy Catholic Church;" that thou mayest avoid their wretched meetings, and ever abide with the Holy Church Catholic in which thou wast regenerated. And if ever thou art sojourning in cities, inquire not simply where the Lord's House is (for the other sects of the profane also attempt to call their own dens houses of the Lord), nor merely where the Church is, but where is the Catholic Church. For this is the peculiar name of this Holy Church, the mother of us all, which is the spouse of our Lord Jesus Christ, the Only-begotten Son of God (for it is written, *As Christ also loved the Church and gave Himself for it*[3], and all the rest,) and is a figure and copy of *Jerusalem which is above, which is free, and the mother of us all*[4]; which before was barren, but now has many children.

27. For when the first Church was cast off, in the second, which is the Catholic Church, God *hath set*, as Paul says, *first Apostles, secondly Prophets, thirdly teachers, then miracles, then gifts of healings, helps, governments, divers kinds of tongues*[5], and every sort of virtue, I mean wisdom and understanding, temperance and justice, mercy and loving-kindness, and patience unconquerable

6 Bishop Lightfoot (*Ignatius*, ad Smyrnæos, viii.) traces the original and later senses of the word "Catholic" very fully. "In its earliest usages, therefore, as a fluctuating epithet of ἐκκλησία, 'catholic' means 'universal,' as opposed to 'individual,' 'particular.' In its later sense, as a fixed attribute, it implies orthodoxy as opposed to heresy, conformity as opposed to dissent." Commenting on this passage of Cyril, the Bishop adds that "these two latter reasons, that it (the Church) is comprehensive in doctrine, and that it is universal in application, can only be regarded as secondary glosses."

7 ἐκκαλεῖσθαι. Cf. Heb. xii. 23.

8 Lev. viii. 3: ἐκκλησίασον.

9 Deut. iv. 10.

10 Ib. ix. 10: ἐκκλησίας.

1 Ps. xxxv. 18; Heb. ii. 12.

2 Ps. lxviii. 26: ἐν ἐκκλησίαις.

3 Matt. xvi. 18.

4 Ps. xxvi. 5.

5 Ps. xxvi. 8: Sept. εὐπρέπειαν. R.V. and A.V. "habitation."

6 Ib. *v.* 12.

7 Ps. cxlix. 1.

8 Mal. i. 10.

9 Ib. *v.* 11.

1 1 Tim. iii. 15.

2 Acts xix. 14.

3 Eph. v. 25.

4 Gal. iv. 26.

5 1 Cor. xii. 28.

in persecutions. She, *by the armour of righteousness on the right hand and on the left, by honour and dishonour* [6], in former days amid persecutions and tribulations crowned the holy martyrs with the varied and blooming chaplets of patience, and now in times of peace by God's grace receives her due honours from *kings and those who are in high place* [7], and from every sort and kindred of men. And while the kings of particular nations have bounds set to their authority, the Holy Church Catholic alone extends her power without limit over the whole world; *for God*, as it is written, *hath made her border peace* [8]. But I should need many more hours for my discourse, if I wished to speak of all things which concern her.

---

28. In this Holy Catholic Church receiving instruction and behaving ourselves virtuously, we shall attain the kingdom of heaven, and inherit ETERNAL LIFE; for which also we endure all toils, that we may be made partakers thereof from the Lord. For ours is no trifling aim, but our endeavour is for eternal life. Wherefore in the profession of the Faith, after the words, "AND IN THE RESURRECTION OF THE FLESH," that is, of the dead (of which we have discoursed), we are taught to believe also "IN THE LIFE ETERNAL," for which as Christians we are striving.

29. The real and true life then is the Father, who through the Son in the Holy Spirit pours forth as from a fountain His heavenly gifts to all; and through His love to man, the blessings of the life eternal are promised without fail to us men also. We must not disbelieve the possibility of this, but having an eye not to our own weakness but to His power, we must believe; *for with God all things are possible.* And that this is possible, and that we may look for eternal life, Daniel declares, *And of the many righteous shall they shine as the stars for ever and ever* [9]. And Paul says, *And so shall we be ever with the Lord* [1]: for the *being for ever with the Lord* implies the life eternal. But most plainly of all the Saviour Himself says in the Gospel, *And these shall go away into eternal punishment, but the righteous into life eternal* [2].

30. And many are the proofs concerning the life eternal. And when we desire to gain this eternal life, the sacred Scriptures suggest to us the ways of gaining it; of which, because of the length of our discourse, the texts we now set before you shall be but few, the rest being left to the search of the diligent. They declare at one time that it is by faith; for it is written, *He that believeth on the Son hath eternal life* [3], and what follows; and again He says Himself, *Verily, verily, I say unto you, He that heareth My word, and believeth Him that sent Me, hath eternal life* [4], and the rest. At another time, it is by the preaching of the Gospel; for He says, that *He that reapeth receiveth wages, and gathereth fruit unto life eternal* [5]. At another time, by martyrdom and confession in Christ's name; for He says, *And he that hateth his life in this world, shall keep it unto life eternal* [6]. And again, by preferring Christ to riches or kindred; *And every one that hath forsaken brethren, or sisters* [7], and the rest, *shall inherit eternal life.* Moreover it is by keeping the commandments, *Thou shalt not commit adultery, Thou shalt not kill* [8], and the rest which follow; as He answered to him that came to Him, and said, *Good Master, what shall I do that I may have eternal life* [9]*?* But further, it is by departing from evil works, and henceforth serving God; for Paul says, *But now being made free from sin, and become servants to God, ye have your fruit unto sanctification, and the end eternal life* [1].

31. And the ways of finding eternal life are many, though I have passed over them by reason of their number. For the Lord in His loving-kindness has opened, not one or two only, but many doors, by which to enter into the life eternal, that, as far as lay in Him, all might enjoy it without hindrance. Thus much have we for the present spoken within compass concerning THE LIFE ETERNAL, which is the last doctrine of those professed in the Faith, and its termination; which life may we all, both teachers and hearers, by God's grace enjoy!

---

32. And now, brethren beloved, the word of instruction exhorts you all, to prepare your souls for the reception of the heavenly gifts. As regards the Holy and Apostolic Faith delivered to you to profess, we have spoken through the grace of the Lord as many Lectures, as was possible, in these past days of Lent; not that this is all we ought to have said, for many are the points omitted; and these perchance are thought out better by more excellent teachers. But now the holy day of the Passover is at hand, and ye, beloved [2] in Christ, are to be enlightened *by the Laver of regeneration.* Ye shall therefore again be taught what is requi-

6 2 Cor. vi. 7, 8. 7 1 Tim. ii. 2. 8 Ps. cxlvii. 14. 9 Dan. xii. 3, Sept. 1 1 Thess. iv. 17. 2 Matt. xxv. 46.

3 John iii. 36. 4 Ib. v. 24. 5 Ib. iv. 36. 6 Ib. xii. 25. 7 Matt. xix. 29. 8 Ib. *vv.* 16—18. 9 Mark x. 17. 1 Rom. vi. 22.

2 τῆς ὑμετέρας ἐν Χριστῷ ἀγάπης. Cf. Cat. xvii. 1, note 1. Athan. *Epist. ad Epict.* § 2: παρὰ τῇ σῇ θεοσεβ.ίᾳ. *ad Serap.* iv. 1: παρὰ τῆς σῆς εὐλαβείας.

site, if God so will; with how great devotion and order you must enter in when summoned, for what purpose each of the holy mysteries of Baptism is performed, and with what reverence and order you must go from Baptism to the Holy Altar of God, and enjoy its spiritual and heavenly mysteries; that your souls being previously enlightened by the word of doctrine, ye may discover in each particular the greatness of the gifts bestowed on you by God.

33. And after Easter's Holy Day of salvation, ye shall come on each successive day, beginning from the second day of the week, after the assembly into the Holy Place of the Resurrection[3], and there, if God permit, ye shall hear other Lectures; in which ye shall again be taught the reasons of every thing which has been done, and shall receive the proofs thereof from the Old and New Testaments,—first, of the things done just before Baptism,—next, how ye were cleansed from your sins by the Lord, *by the washing of water with the word*[4],—and how like Priests ye have become partakers of the Name of Christ,—and how the Seal of the fellowship of the Holy Ghost was given to you,—and concerning the mysteries at the Altar of the New Testament, which have taken their beginning from this place, both what the Divine Scriptures have delivered to us, and what is the power of these mysteries, and how ye must approach them, and when and how receive them;—and at the end of all, how for the time to come ye must behave yourselves worthily of this grace both in words and deeds, that you may all be enabled to enjoy the life everlasting. And these things shall be spoken, if it be God's pleasure.

34. *Finally, my brethren, rejoice in the Lord alway; again I will say, Rejoice: for your redemption hath drawn nigh*[5], and the heavenly host of the Angels is waiting for your salvation. And there is now *the voice of one crying in the wilderness, Prepare ye the way of the Lord*[6]; and the Prophet cries, *Ho, ye that thirst, come ye to the water*[7]; and immediately afterwards, *Hearken unto me, and ye shall eat that which is good, and your soul shall delight itself in good things*[8]. And within a little while ye shall hear that excellent lesson which says, *Shine, shine, O thou new Jerusalem; for thy light is come*[9]. Of this Jerusalem the prophet hath said, *And afterwards thou shalt be called the city of righteousness, Zion, the faithful mother of cities*[1]; *because of the law which went forth out of Zion, and the word of the Lord from Jerusalem*[2], which word has from hence been showered forth on the whole world. To her the Prophet also says concerning you, *Lift up thine eyes round about, and behold thy children gathered together*[3]; and she answers, saying, *Who are these that fly as a cloud, and as doves with their young ones to me*[4]? (*clouds*, because of their spiritual nature, and *doves*, from their purity). And again, she says, *Who knoweth such things? or who hath seen it thus? did ever a land bring forth in one day? or was ever a nation born all at once? for as soon as Zion travailed, she brought forth her children*[5]. And all things shall be filled with joy unspeakable because of the Lord who said, *Behold, I create Jerusalem a rejoicing, and her people a joy*[6].

35. And may these words be spoken now again over you also, *Sing, O heavens, and be joyful, O earth;* and then; *for the Lord hath had mercy on His people, and comforted the lowly of His people*[7]. And this shall come to pass through the loving-kindness of God, who says to you, *Behold, I will blot out as a cloud thy transgressions, and as a thick cloud thy sins*[8]. But ye who have been counted worthy of the name of Faithful (of whom it is written, *Upon My servants shall be called a new name which shall be blessed on the earth*[9],) ye shall say with gladness, *Blessed be the God and Father of our Lord Jesus Christ, who hath blessed us with every spiritual blessing in the heavenly places in Christ*[1]: *in whom we have our redemption through His blood, the forgiveness of our sins, according to the riches of His grace, wherein He abounded towards us*[2], and what follows; and again, *But God being rich in mercy, for His great love wherewith He loved us, when we were dead through our trespasses, quickened us together with Christ*[3], and the rest. And again in like manner praise ye the Lord of all good things, saying, *But when the kindness of God our Saviour, and His love towards man appeared, not by works of righteousness which we had done, but according to His mercy He saved us, through the washing of regeneration, and renewing of the Holy Ghost, which He shed on us abundantly through Jesus Christ our Saviour, that being*

3 The place meant is not the Church of the Resurrection in which the Service had been held, but the Anastasis or actual cave of the Resurrection, which Constantine had so enlarged by additional works that a discourse to the people could be held there: for Jerome (*Epist.* 61) relates that Epiphanius had preached in that place in front of the Lord's sepulchre to clergy and people in the hearing of John the Bishop (Ben. Ed.).

4 Eph. v. 26.

5 Phil. iii. 1; and iv. 4; Luke xxi. 28.

6 Is. xl. 3.

7 Ib. lv. 1.

8 Ib. *v.* 2.

9 Is. lx. 1.

1 Ib. i. 26.

2 Ib. ii. 3.

3 Ib. xlix. 18.

4 Ib. lx 8.

5 Ib. lxvi. 8.

6 Ib. lxv. 18.

7 Ib. xlix. 13.

8 Is. xliv. 22.

9 Ib. lxv. 15.

1 Eph. i. 3.

2 Ib. *v.* 7.

3 Ib. ii. 4.

justified by His grace, we might be made heirs, according to hope, of eternal life[4]. And may God Himself the Father of our Lord Jesus Christ, the Father of glory, *give unto you a spirit of wisdom and revelation in the knowledge of Himself, the eyes of your understanding being enlightened*[5], and may He ever keep you in good works, and words, and thoughts; to Whom be glory, honour, and power, through our Lord Jesus Christ, with the Holy Ghost, now and ever, and unto all the endless ages of eternity. Amen[6].

4 Tit. iii. 4.

5 Eph. i. 17, 18.

6 "At the end of this Lecture in the older of the Munich MSS. there is the following addition: Many other Lectures were delivered year by year, both before Baptism and after the neophytes had been baptized. But these alone were taken down when spoken and written by some of the earnest students in the year 352 of the advent of our Lord and Saviour Jesus Christ. And in these you will find partly discussions of all the necessary doctrines of the Faith which ought to be known to men, and answers to the Greeks, and to those of the Circumcision, and to the Heresies, and the moral precepts of Christians of all kinds, by the grace of God. The year 352 according to the computation of the Greeks is the year 360 of the Christian era" (Rupp).

The date at which the Lectures were delivered cannot possibly be so late as is here stated. See the section of the Introduction on the "Date."

FIVE CATECHETICAL LECTURES

OF

THE SAME AUTHOR,

TO THE NEWLY BAPTIZED[1].

LECTURE XIX.

FIRST LECTURE ON THE MYSTERIES.

WITH A LESSON FROM THE FIRST GENERAL EPISTLE OF PETER, BEGINNING AT *Be sober, be vigilant*, to the end of the Epistle.

1. I HAVE long been wishing, O true-born and dearly beloved children of the Church, to discourse to you concerning these spiritual and heavenly Mysteries; but since I well knew that seeing is far more persuasive than hearing, I waited for the present season; that finding you more open to the influence of my words from your present experience, I might lead you by the hand into the brighter and more fragrant meadow of the Paradise before us; especially as ye have been made fit to receive the more sacred Mysteries, after having been found worthy of divine and life-giving Baptism[2]. Since therefore it remains to set before you a table of the more perfect instructions, let us now teach you these things exactly, that ye may know the effect[3] wrought upon you on that evening of your baptism.

2. First ye entered into the vestibule[4] of the Baptistery, and there facing towards the West ye listened to the command to stretch forth your hand, and as in the presence of Satan ye renounced him. Now ye must know that this figure is found in ancient history. For when Pharaoh, that most bitter and cruel tyrant, was oppressing the free and high-born people of the Hebrews, God sent Moses to bring them out of the evil bondage of the Egyptians. Then the door-posts were anointed with the blood of a lamb, that the destroyer might flee from the houses which had the sign of the blood; and the Hebrew people was marvellously delivered. The enemy, however, after their rescue, *pursued after them*[5], and saw the sea wondrously parted for them; nevertheless he went on, following close in their footsteps, and was all at once overwhelmed and engulphed in the Red Sea.

3. Now turn from the old to the new, from the figure to the reality. There we have Moses sent from God to Egypt; here, Christ, sent forth from His Father into the world: there, that Moses might lead forth an afflicted people out of Egypt; here, that Christ might rescue those who are oppressed in the world under sin: there, the blood of a lamb was the spell against[6] the destroyer; here, the blood of the Lamb without blemish Jesus Christ is made the charm to scare[7] evil spirits: there, the tyrant

---

1 This general title of the five following Lectures is omitted in many MSS. "In Cod. Ottob. at the end of the special title of this first Mystagogic Lecture, after the words "to the end of the Epistle," there follows the statement "Of the same author Cyril, and of John the Bishop" (Bened. Ed.). See Index, *Authenticity*.

2 This Lecture was delivered on the Monday after Easter in the Holy Sepulchre: see Cat. xviii. 33.

3 τὴν ἔμφασιν τὴν . . . . γεγενημένην, is found in all the MSS. "Nevertheless it would seem that we ought to read τῶν . . . . γεγενημένων, which Grodecq either read or substituted" (Ben. Ed.). With the proposed reading the meaning would be—"the significance of the things done to you," which agrees better with the meaning of ἔμφασις.

4 τὸν προαύλιον, called below in § 11 "the outer chamber." Cf. Procat. § 1, note 3. It appears from Tertullian, *De Corona*, § 3, that the renunciation was made first in the Church, and afterwards in the Baptistery: "When we are going to enter the water, at that moment as well as just before in the Church under the hand of the President, we solemnly profess that we disown the devil, and his pomp, and his angels."

5 Ex. xiv. 9, 23.

6 ἀποτρόπαιον.

7 φυγαδευτήριον, the word commonly used in the Septuagint

was pursuing that ancient people even to the sea; and here the daring and shameless spirit, the author of evil, was following thee even to the very streams of salvation. The tyrant of old was drowned in the sea; and this present one disappears in the water of salvation.

4. But nevertheless thou art bidden to say, with arm outstretched towards him as though he were present, "I renounce thee, Satan." I wish also to say wherefore ye stand facing to the West; for it is necessary. Since the West is the region of sensible darkness, and he being darkness has his dominion also in darkness, therefore, looking with a symbolical meaning towards the West, ye renounce that dark and gloomy potentate. What then did each of you stand up and say? "I renounce thee, Satan,"—thou wicked and most cruel tyrant! meaning, "I fear thy might no longer; for that Christ hath overthrown, having partaken with me of flesh and blood, that through these He *might by death destroy death*[8], that I might not be made *subject to bondage* for ever." "I renounce thee,"—thou crafty and most subtle serpent. "I renounce thee,"—plotter as thou art, who under the guise of friendship didst contrive all disobedience, and work apostasy in our first parents. "I renounce thee, Satan,"—the artificer and abettor of all wickedness.

5. Then in a second sentence thou art taught to say, "and all thy works." Now the works of Satan are all sin, which also thou must renounce;—just as one who has escaped a tyrant has surely escaped his weapons also. All sin therefore, of every kind, is included in the works of the devil. Only know this; that all that thou sayest, especially at that most thrilling hour, is written in God's books; when therefore thou doest any thing contrary to these promises, thou shalt be judged as *a transgressor*[9]. Thou renouncest therefore the works of Satan; I mean, all deeds and thoughts which are contrary to reason.

6. Then thou sayest, "And all his pomp[1]." Now the pomp of the devil is the madness of theatres[2], and horse-races, and hunting, and all such vanity: from which that holy man praying to be delivered says unto God, *Turn away mine eyes from beholding vanity*[3]. Be not interested in the madness of the theatre, where thou wilt behold the wanton gestures of the players[4], carried on with mockeries and all unseemliness, and the frantic dancing of effeminate men[5];—nor in the madness of them who in hunts[6] expose themselves to wild beasts, that they may pamper their miserable appetite; who, to serve their belly with meats, become themselves in reality meat for the belly of untamed beasts; and to speak justly, for the sake of their own god, their belly, they cast away their life headlong in single combats[7]. Shun also horse-races that frantic and soul-subverting spectacle[8]. For all these are the pomp of the devil.

7. Moreover, the things which are hung up at idol festivals[9], either meat or bread, or other such things polluted by the invocation of the unclean spirits, are reckoned in the pomp of the devil. For as the Bread and Wine of the Eucharist

---

for "a city of refuge." But the Verb φυγαδεύω is Transitive in 2 Macc. ix. 4, as well as in Xenophon and Demosthenes. The application of the blood of Christ in Baptism is represented by marking the sign of the Cross on the forehead. Compare the lines of Prudentius quoted by the Benedictine Editor:

"Passio quæ nostram defendit sanguine frontem,
Corporeamque domum signato collinit ore."

8 Heb. ii. 14, 15. 9 Gal. ii. 18.

1 Herod. II. 58: "The Egyptians were the first to introduce solemn assemblies (πανηγύρις) and processions (πομπάς)." At Rome the term "pompa" was applied especially to the procession with which the Ludi Circenses were opened, and also to any grand ceremony or pageant.

2 θεατρομανίαι. Cf. Tertull. *Apologet.* 38; "We renounce all your spectacles. . . . Among us nothing is ever said, or seen, or heard, which has anything in common with the madness of the Circus, the immodesty of the theatre, the atrocities of the arena, the useless exercises of the wrestling-ground." He calls the theatre "that citadel of all impurities," *De Spectaculis*, c. 10, "immodesty's peculiar abode," c. 17, and gives a vivid description of the rage and fury of the Circus in c. 16.

3 Ps. cxix. 37.

4 μίμων, the name either of a species of low comedy, "consisting more of gestures and mimicry than of spoken dialogue," or of the persons who acted in them. Cyril's description of the coarse and indecent character of the mimes is more than justified by the impartial testimony of Ovid, *Trist.* ii. 497:

"Quid si scripsissem mimos obscœna jocantes,
Qui semper vetiti crimen amoris habent;
In quibus assidue cultus procedit adulter,
Verbaque dat stulto callida nupta viro.
Nubilis hos virgo, matronaque, virque, puerque
Spectat, et e magna parte Senatus adest.
Nec satis incestis temerari vocibus aures;
Assuescunt oculi multa pudenda pati."

A theatre is mentioned as one of the buildings erected by Hadrian in his new city Aelia Capitolina built on the site of Jerusalem; and that theatrical performances were continued in the time of Cyril we know from the accusation that in a time of famine he had sold one of the Church vestments, which was afterwards used upon the stage.

5 Lactantius, *Epitome*, § 63: "Histrionici etiam impudici gestus, quibus infames fœminas imitantur, libidines, quæ saltando exprimunt, docent."

6 κυνηγεσίαις, the so-called "venationes" of the Circus in which the "bestiarii" fought with wild beasts.

7 The "bestiarii" were feasted in public on the day before their encounter with the beasts. See Tertull. *Apologet.* § 42: "I do not recline in public at the feast of Bacchus, after the manner of the beast-fighters at their last banquet." Ib. § 9: "Those also who dine on the flesh of wild beasts from the arena, who have keen appetites for bear and stag." These latter, however, were chiefly the poor, to whom flesh was a rarity: Apuleius *Metam.* iv. 14, quoted by Oehler.

8 ψυχὰς ἐκτραχήλιζον, an allusion to the risk of a broken neck in the chariot-race. Tertull. *de Spectaculis*, § 9: "Equestrianism was formerly practised in a simple way on horseback, and certainly its ordinary use was innocent: but when it was dragged into the games, it passed from a gift of God into the service of demons." The presiding deity of the chariot-race was Poseidon (Hom. *Il.* xxiii. 307; Pind. *Ol.* i. 63; *Pyth.* vi. 50; Soph. Œdip. Col. 712), and both this and the other shows of the Circus, and of the theatre, were connected with the worship of the gods of Greece and Rome, and therefore forbidden as idolatrous: "What high religious rites, what sacrifices precede, intervene, and follow, how many guilds, how many priesthoods, how many services are set astir" (Tert. *de Spect.* § 7).

9 πανηγύρεσι. The Panegyris was strictly a religious festival, but was commonly accompanied by a great fair or market, in which were sold not only such things as the worshippers might need for their offerings, e.g. frankincense, but also the flesh of the animals which had been sacrificed. Cf. *Dictionary of Greek and Rom. Antiq.* "Panegyris." Tertull. *Apolog.* § 42: "We do not go to your spectacles: yet the articles that are sold there, if I need them, I shall obtain more readily at their proper places. We certainly buy no frankincense."

before the invocation of the Holy and Adorable Trinity were simple bread and wine, while after the invocation the Bread becomes the Body of Christ, and the Wine the Blood of Christ [1], so in like manner such meats belonging to the pomp of Satan, though in their own nature simple, become profane by the invocation of the evil spirit.

8. After this thou sayest, "and all thy service [2]." Now the service of the devil is prayer in idol temples; things done in honour of lifeless idols; the lighting of lamps [3], or burning of incense by fountains or rivers [4], as some persons cheated by dreams or by evil spirits do [resort to this [5]], thinking to find a cure even for their bodily ailments. Go not after such things. The watching of birds, divination, omens, or amulets, or charms written on leaves, sorceries, or other evil arts [6], and all such things, are services of the devil; therefore shun them. For if after renouncing Satan and associating thyself with Christ [7], thou fall under their influence, thou shalt find [8] the tyrant more bitter; perchance, because he treated thee of old as his own, and relieved thee from his hard bondage, but has now been greatly exasperated by thee; so thou wilt be bereaved of Christ, and have experience of the other. Hast thou not heard the old history which tells us of Lot and his daughters? Was not he himself saved with his daughters, when he had gained the mountain, while his wife became a pillar of salt, set up as a monument for ever, in remembrance of her depraved will and her turning back. Take heed therefore to thyself, and turn not again to *what is behind* [9], having put thine hand to the plough, and then turning back to the salt savour of this life's doings; but escape to the mountain, to Jesus Christ, that *stone hewn without hands* [1], which has filled the world.

9. When therefore thou renouncest Satan, utterly breaking all thy covenant with him, that ancient *league with hell* [2], there is opened to thee the paradise of God, which He planted towards the East, whence for his transgression our first father was banished; and a symbol of this was thy turning from West to East, the place of light [3]. Then thou wert told to say, "I believe in the Father, and in the Son, and in the Holy Ghost, and in one Baptism of repentance [4]." Of which things we spoke to thee at length in the former Lectures, as God's grace allowed us.

10. Guarded therefore by these discourses, *be sober. For* our *adversary the devil*, as was just now read, *as a roaring lion, walketh about, seeking whom he may devour* [5]. But though in former times death was mighty and devoured, at the holy Laver of regeneration God has *wiped away every tear from off all faces* [6]. For thou shalt no more mourn, now that thou hast put off the old man; but thou shalt keep holyday [7], *clothed in the garment of salvation* [8], even Jesus Christ.

11. And these things were done in the outer chamber. But if God will, when in the succeeding lectures on the Mysteries we have entered into the Holy of Holies [9], we shall there know the symbolical meaning of the things which are there performed. Now to God the Father, with the Son and the Holy Ghost, be glory, and power, and majesty, for ever and ever. Amen.

---

1 Compare St. Paul's argument against meats offered to idols, 1 Cor. x. 14—21: and on Cyril's Eucharistic doctrine, see notes on Cat. xxii.

2 The form of renunciation before Baptism is given in the *Apostolic Constitutions*, VII. 41: "I renounce Satan, and his works, and his pomps, and his services, and his angels, and his inventions, and all things that are under him." Cf. Tertull. *De Spectaculis*, § 4: "When on entering the water, we make profession of the Christian faith in the words of its rule, we bear public testimony that we have renounced the devil, his pomp, and his angels."

3 Herod. ii. 62: "At Sais, when the assembly takes place for the sacrifices (to Minerva, or Neith), there is one night on which the inhabitants all burn a multitude of lights in the open air round their houses. . . . These burn the whole night, and give to the festival the name of the Feast of Lamps (Λυχνοκαΐη)."

4 Fountains and rivers had each its own deity or nymph, to whom sacrifices were offered, and incense burned.

5 ἐς τοῦτο διέβησαν. These words are omitted in many MSS., and regarded by the Benedictine Editor as a spurious addition made to complete the construction. The words ἢ τοιαῦτα at the end of the sentence are better omitted, as in several good MSS.

6 Cat. iv. 37; *Apost. Const.* vi.: "Be not a diviner, for that leads to idolatry. . . . Thou shalt not use enchantments or purgations for thy child. Thou shalt not be a soothsayer nor a diviner by great or little birds. Nor shalt thou learn wicked arts; for all these things has the Law forbidden." Deut. xviii. 10, 11.

7 *Apost. Const.* vii. 41: "And after his renunciation let him in his association (συντασσόμενος) say, I associate myself with Christ."

8 πειραθήσῃ (Cod. Mon. 1) is a better reading than πειρασθήσῃ. Cf. Plat. *Laches*, 188 E: τῶν ἔργων ἐπειράθην.

9 Phil. iii. 13. On the pillar of salt, see *Wisd.* x. 7: "Of whose wickedness even to this day the waste land that smoketh is a testimony, . . . and a standing pillar of salt is a monument of an unbelieving soul." Joseph. *Ant.* I. xi. 4: "Moreover I have seen it, for it remains even unto this day." Bp. Lightfoot, *Clem. Rom. Ep. ad Cor.* xi. remarks that the region abounds in pillars of salt, and "Mediæval and even modern travellers have delighted to identify one or other of these with Lot's wife."

1 Dan. ii. 35, 45.

2 Is. xxviii. 15.

3 Cf. S. Ambros. *De Mysteriis*, c. ii. 7: "Ad orientem converteris; qui enim renunciat diabolo ad Christum convertitur:" "Where he plainly intimates . . . . that turning to the East was a symbol of their aversion from Satan and conversion unto Christ, that is, from darkness to light, from serving idols, to serve Him, who is the Sun of Righteousness and Fountain of Light" (Bingh. *Ant.* xi. vii. 7).

4 Cf. Didaché, vii. 1; Justin M. *Apolog.* I. c. 61 A; Swainson, *Creeds*, c. iii. on the short Baptismal Professions. "The writings of S. Cyprian distinctly tell us, that in his day the form of interrogation at Baptism was fixed and definite. He speaks of the "usitata et legitima verba interrogationis,"—and we know as distinctly that the interrogation included the words, "Dost thou believe in God the Father, in His Son Christ, in the Holy Spirit? Dost thou believe in remission of sins and eternal life through the Church?"

5 1 Pet. v. 9.

6 Is. xxv. 8; Rev. vii. 17.

7 πανηγυρίσεις.

8 Is. lxi. 10.

9 These words seem to imply that the Lectures on the Eucharist were to be delivered in the Holy Sepulchre, though the Mysteries themselves may be called metaphorically "the Holy of Holies."

LECTURE XX.

(ON THE MYSTERIES. II.)

OF BAPTISM.

ROMANS vi. 3—14.

Know ye not, that so many of us as were baptized into Jesus Christ, were baptized into His death? &c. . . . . for ye are not under the Law, but under grace.

1. THESE daily introductions into the Mysteries[1], and new instructions, which are the announcements of new truths, are profitable to us; and most of all to you, who have been renewed from an old state to a new. Therefore, I shall necessarily lay before you the sequel of yesterday's Lecture, that ye may learn of what those things, which were done by you in the inner chamber[2], were symbolical.

2. As soon, then, as ye entered, ye put off your tunic; and this was an image of *putting off the old man with his deeds*[3]. Having stripped yourselves, ye were naked; in this also imitating Christ, who was stripped naked on the Cross, and by His nakedness *put off from Himself the principalities and powers, and openly triumphed over them on the tree*[4]. For since the adverse powers made their lair in your members, ye may no longer wear that old garment; I do not at all mean this visible one, but the *old man, which waxeth corrupt in the lusts of deceit*[5]. May the soul which has once put him off, never again put him on, but say with the Spouse of Christ in the Song of Songs, *I have put off my garment, how shall I put it on*[6]*?* O wondrous thing! ye were naked in the sight of all, and were not ashamed[7]; for truly ye bore the likeness of the first-formed Adam, who was naked in the garden, and was not ashamed.

3. Then, when ye were stripped, ye were anointed with exorcised oil[8], from the very hairs of your head to your feet, and were made partakers of the good olive-tree, Jesus Christ. For ye were cut off from the wild olive-tree[9], and grafted into the good one, and were made to share the fatness of the true olive-tree. The exorcised oil therefore was a symbol of the participation of the fatness of Christ, being a charm to drive away every trace of hostile influence. For as the breathing of the saints, and the invocation of the Name of God, like fiercest flame, scorch and drive out evil spirits[1], so also this exorcised oil receives such virtue by the invocation of God and by prayer, as not only to burn and cleanse away the traces of sins, but also to chase away all the invisible powers of the evil one.

4. After these things, ye were led to the holy pool[2] of Divine Baptism, as Christ was carried from the Cross to the Sepulchre which is before our eyes. And each of you was asked, whether he believed in the name of the Father, and of the Son, and of the Holy Ghost, and ye made that saving confession,

---

1 μυσταγωγίαι.

2 The renunciation and the profession of faith were made in the outer chamber or vestibule of the Baptistery.

3 Col. iii. 9.

4 Ib. ii. 15. Cyril's use of this passage agrees best with the interpretation that Christ, having been clothed with the likeness of sinful flesh during His life on earth, submitted therein to the assaults of the powers of evil, but on the Cross threw off from Himself both it and them.

5 Eph. iv. 22.

6 Cant. v. 3.

7 See *Dict. Christ. Antiq.* "Baptism," § 48: *The Unclothing of the Catechumens:* Bingh. *Ant.* XI. xi. 1: All "persons were baptized naked, either in imitation of Adam in Paradise, or our Saviour upon the Cross, or to signify their putting off the body of sin, and the old man with his deeds."

8 Apost. Const. vii. 22: "But thou shalt beforehand anoint the person with holy oil (ἐλαίῳ), and afterward baptize him with water, and in the conclusion shalt seal him with the ointment (μύρῳ), that the anointing (χρῖσμα) may be a participation of the Holy Spirit, and the water a symbol of the death, and the ointment the seal of the Covenants. But if there be neither oil nor ointment, water suffices both for anointing, and for a seal, and for a confession of Him who died, or indeed is dying with us." The previous anointing "with oil sanctified by prayer" is mentioned in the *Clementine Recognitions*, III. c. 67, and in the Pseudo-Justin, *Quæstiones ad Orthodoxos*, Qu. 137. It was not however universal, and seems to have been unknown in Africa, not being mentioned by Clement of Alexandria (*Pæd.* II. c. viii. *On the use of ointments*), nor Tertullian, nor Augustine.

9 On the significance of the wild olive-tree, see Irenæus, V. 10.

1 See Index, "Exorcism."

2 κολυμβήθραν. The pool or piscina was deep enough for total immersion, and large enough for many to be baptized at once. Cf. Bingh. Ant. VIII. vii. 2; XI. xi. 2, 3. For engravings of the very ancient Baptisteries at Aquileia and Ravenna, shewing the form of the font or piscina, see *Dict. Christian Ant.* "Baptistery."

and descended three times into the water, and ascended again; here also hinting by a symbol at the three days burial of Christ[3]. For as our Saviour passed three days and three nights in the heart of the earth, so you also in your first ascent out of the water, represented the first day of Christ in the earth, and by your descent, the night; for as he who is in the night, no longer sees, but he who is in the day, remains in the light, so in the descent, as in the night, ye saw nothing, but in ascending again ye were as in the day. And at the self-same moment ye were both dying and being born; and that Water of salvation was at once your grave and your mother. And what Solomon spoke of others will suit you also; for he said, in that case, *There is a time to bear and a time to die*[4]; but to you, in the reverse order, there was a time to die and a time to be born; and one and the same time effected both of these, and your birth went hand in in hand with your death.

5. O strange and inconceivable thing! we did not really die, we were not really buried, we were not really crucified and raised again; but our imitation was in a figure, and our salvation in reality. Christ was actually crucified, and actually buried, and truly rose again; and all these things He has freely bestowed upon us, that we, sharing His sufferings by imitation, might gain salvation in reality. O surpassing loving-kindness! Christ received nails in His undefiled hands and feet, and suffered anguish; while on me without pain or toil by the fellowship of His suffering He freely bestows salvation.

6. Let no one then suppose that Baptism is merely the grace of remission of sins, or further, that of adoption; as John's was a baptism[5] conferring only remission of sins: whereas we know full well, that as it purges our sins, and ministers[6] to us the gift of the Holy Ghost, so also it is the counterpart[7] of the sufferings of Christ. For this cause Paul just now cried aloud and said, *Or are ye ignorant that all we who were baptized into Christ Jesus, were baptized into His death? We were buried therefore with Him by baptism into His death*[8]. These words he spake to some who were disposed to think that Baptism ministers to us the remission of sins, and adoption, but has not further the fellowship also, by representation, of Christ's true sufferings.

7. In order therefore that we might learn, that whatsoever things Christ endured, FOR US AND FOR OUR SALVATION[9] He suffered them in reality and not in appearance, and that we also are made partakers of His sufferings, Paul cried with all exactness of truth, *For if we have been planted together with the likeness of His death, we shall be also with the likeness of His resurrection.* Well has he said, *planted together*[10]. For since the true Vine was planted in this place, we also by partaking in the Baptism of death have been *planted together* with Him. And fix thy mind with much attention on the words of the Apostle. He said not, "For if we have been planted together with His death," but, *with the likeness of His death.* For in Christ's case there was death in reality, for His soul was really separated from His body, and real burial, for His holy body was wrapt in pure linen; and everything happened really to Him; but in your case there was only a likeness of death and sufferings, whereas of salvation there was not a likeness but a reality.

8. Having been sufficiently instructed in these things, keep them, I beseech you, in your remembrance; that I also, unworthy though I be, may say of you, *Now I love you*[1], *because ye always remember me, and hold fast the traditions, which I delivered unto you.* And God, who has presented you *as it were alive from the dead*[2], is able to grant unto you *to walk in newness of life*[3]: because His is the glory and the power, now and for ever. Amen.

3 The same significance is attributed to the trine immersion by many Fathers, but a different explanation is given by Tertullian (*Adv. Praxean,* c. xxvi.): "Not once only, but three times, we are immersed into the several Persons at the mention of their several names." Gregory of Nyssa (*On the Baptism of Christ*, p. 520 in this Series) joins both reasons together; "By doing this thrice we represent for ourselves that grace of the Resurrection which was wrought in three days: and this we do, not receiving the Sacrament in silence, but while there are spoken over us the Names of the Three Sacred Persons on whom we believed, &c." Compare p. 529. Cf. *Apost. Const.* VIII. § 47, Can. 50: "If any Bishop or Presbyter does not perform the three immersions of one initiation, but one immersion made into the death of Christ, let him be deprived."

Milles in his note on this passage mentions that "this form of Baptism is still used in the Greek Church. See Euchology. p. 355. Ed. Jac. Goar. and his notes p. 365."

4 Eccles. iii. 2.

5 Tertullian (*De Baptismo*, c. 10) denies that John's Baptism availed for the remission of sins: "If repentance is a thing human, its baptism must necessarily be of the same nature: else if it had been celestial, it would have given both the Holy Spirit and the remission of sins." Cyril's doctrine is more in accordance with the language of the Fathers generally, and of St. Mark i. 4, Luke iii. 3.

6 προξενον.

7 ἀντίτυπον. The "Antitype" is here the sign or memorial of that which is past, and no longer actually present: See note 6 on xxi. 1. Cf. Heb. ix. 24.

8 Rom. vi. 3. In the following sentence several MSS. have a different reading: "These things perhaps he said to some who were disposed to think that Baptism ministers remission of sins only, and not adoption, and that further it has not the fellowship, &c." Against this reading, approved by Milles, the Benedictine Editor argues that in Rom. vi. 3, 4, there is no reference to adoption, but only to the fellowship of Christ's Passion, and that Cyril quotes the passage only to prove the latter, the gift of adoption being generally admitted, and therefore not in question.

9 This clause is contained in the Nicene Creed, and in that which was offered to the Council by Eusebius as the ancient Creed of Cæsarea. It probably formed part of the Creed of Jerusalem, though it is not found in the titles of the Lectures, nor specially explained.

10 Ib. vi. 5. Cyril gives the phrase "*planted together*" a special application to those who had been baptized in the same place where Christ had been buried.

1 1 Cor. xi. 2: *Now I praise you, &c.*

2 Rom. vi. 13.

3 Ib. *v.* 4.

LECTURE XXI.

(ON THE MYSTERIES. III.)

ON CHRISM.

1 JOHN ii. 20—28.

But ye have an unction from the Holy One, &c. . . . . that, when He shall appear, we may have confidence, and not be ashamed before Him at His coming.

1. HAVING been *baptized into Christ*, and *put on Christ*[1], ye have been made conformable to the Son of God; for God having *foreordained us unto adoption as sons*[2], made us *to be conformed to the body of Christ's glory*[3]. Having therefore become *partakers of Christ*[4], ye are properly called Christs, and of you God said, *Touch not My Christs*[5], or anointed. Now ye have been made Christs, by receiving the antitype[6] of the Holy Ghost; and all things have been wrought in you by imitation[7], because ye are images of Christ. He washed in the river Jordan, and having imparted of the fragrance[8] of His Godhead to the waters, He came up from them; and the Holy Ghost in the fulness of His being[9] lighted on Him, like resting upon like[10]. And to you in like manner, after you had come up from the pool of the sacred streams, there was given an Unction[1], the anti-type of that wherewith Christ was anointed; and this is the Holy Ghost; of whom also the blessed Esaias, in his prophecy respecting Him, said in the person of the Lord, *The Spirit of the Lord is upon Me. because He hath anointed Me: He hath sent Me to preach glad tidings to the poor*[2].

2. For Christ was not anointed by men with oil or material ointment, but the Father having before appointed Him to be the Saviour of the whole world, anointed Him with the Holy Ghost, as Peter says, *Jesus of Nazareth, whom God anointed with the Holy Ghost*[3]. David also the Prophet cried, saying, *Thy throne, O God, is for ever and ever; a sceptre of righteousness is the sceptre of Thy kingdom; Thou hast loved righteousness and hated iniquity; therefore God even Thy God hath anointed Thee with the oil of gladness above Thy fellows*[4]. And as Christ was in reality crucified, and buried, and raised, and you are in Baptism accounted worthy of being crucified, buried, and raised together with Him in a likeness, so is it with the unction also. As He was anointed with an ideal[5] oil of gladness, that is, with the Holy Ghost, called oil of gladness, because He is the author of spiritual gladness, so ye were anointed with ointment, having been made partakers and *fellows of Christ*.

---

1 Gal. iii. 27. 2 Eph. i. 5. 3 Phil. iii. 21.
4 Heb. iii. 14. 5 Ps. cv. 15.

6 ἀντίτυπον. Cat. xx. 6; xxiii. 20. Twice in this section, as in Heb. ix. 24 (ἀντίτυπα τῶν ἀληθινῶν), ἀντίτυπον is the copy or figure representing the original pattern (τύπος, cf. Acts vii. 44). Otherwise (as in Cat. x. 11; xiii. 19; xxii. 3) τύπος is the figure to be subsequently realised in the antitype.

7 εἰκονικῶς . . . . εἰκόνες τοῦ Χριστοῦ.

8 χρώτων, literally "tinctures." The Ben. Ed. writes: "For φώτων we have written χρώτων with Codd. Coisl. Ottob. Roe, Casaub., &c. .. But we must write χρώτων from χρῶτα, not χρῶτων from χρῶτες. Authors use the word χρῶτα to signify the effluence of an odour. So Gregory of Nyssa takes it in his 3rd *Homily on the Song of Songs*, p. 512; and S. Maximus in *Question* 37 *on Scripture*: 'χρῶτα we say is the godliness (εὐσέβειαν) whereby S. Paul was *to the one a savour of life unto life.*' . . . In the *Procatechesis*, § 15, Cyril calls the waters of Baptism ὑδάτων χριστοφόρων ἐχόντων εὐωδίαν. If however any one prefers the reading φώτων, he may defend himself by the authority of Epiphanius, who in the *Exposition of the Faith*, c. 15, says that Christ descending into the water gave rather than received, ... illuminating them, and empowering them for a type of what was to be accomplished in Him." According to the Ebionite Gospel of St. Matthew in Epiphanius (*Hær.* xxx. *Ebionitæ* c. 13), when Jesus came up out of the water a great light shone around the place: a tradition to which the Benedictine Editor thinks the reading φώτων may refer. Justin M. (*Dialog.* c. lxxxviii.): "When Jesus had stepped into the water, a fire was kindled in the Jordan." Otto quotes the legend, as found in *Orac. Sibyll.* vii. 81—83:—

Ὅς σε Λόγον γέννησε Πατήρ Πνεῦμ' ὄρνιν ἄφηκεν,
Ὀξὺν ἀπαγγελτῆρα λόγων, Λόγον ὕδασιν ἁγνοῖς
Ῥαίνων, σὸν βάπτισμα, δι' οὗ πυρὸς ἐξεφαάνθης.

9 οὐσιώδης ἐπιφοίτησις ἐγένετο. The Benedictine Editor understands this phrase as an allusion to the descent of the Holy Ghost on Jesus in a substantial bodily form. So Gregory Nazianzen (*Orat.* xliv. 17), says that the Holy Ghost descended on the Apostles οὐσιωδῶς καὶ σωματικῶς. But Anastasius Sinaita interprets οὐσιωδῶς in this latter passage as meaning "in the essence and reality of His (Divine) Person:" and this latter sense agreeing with the frequent use of οὐσιωδής by Athanasius is well rendered by Canon Mason (*The Relation of Confirmation to Baptism*, p. 343, "in the fulness of His being."

10 Cf. Greg. Naz. *Orat.* xxxix: "The Spirit also bears witness to His Godhead, for He comes to that which is like Himself."

1 Cf. Tertullian, *De Baptismo*, c. 7: "Exinde egressi de lavacro perungimur benedictâ unctione." It is clear that the Unction mentioned in these passages was conferred at the same time and place as Baptism. Whether it formed part of that Sacrament, or was regarded by Cyril as a separate and independent rite, has been made a matter of controversy. See Index, "Chrism."

2 Is. lxi. 1. 3 Acts x. 38. 4 Ps. xlv. 6, 7.

5 νοητῷ cannot here be translated "spiritual" because of πνευματικῆς immediately following. Cf. i. 4, note.

3. But beware of supposing this to be plain ointment. For as the Bread of the Eucharist, after the invocation of the Holy Ghost, is mere bread no longer[6], but the Body of Christ, so also this holy ointment is no more simple ointment, nor (so to say) common, after invocation, but it is Christ's gift of grace, and, by the advent of the Holy Ghost, is made fit to impart His Divine Nature[7]. Which ointment is symbolically applied to thy forehead and thy other senses[8]; and while thy body is anointed with the visible ointment, thy soul is sanctified by the Holy and life-giving Spirit.

4. And ye were first anointed on the forehead, that ye might be delivered from the shame, which the first man who transgressed bore about with him everywhere; and that *with unveiled face ye might reflect as a mirror the glory of the Lord*[9]. Then on your ears; that ye might receive the ears which are quick to hear the Divine Mysteries, of which Esaias said, *The Lord gave me also an ear to hear*[1]; and the Lord Jesus in the Gospel, *He that hath ears to hear let him hear*[2]. Then on the nostrils; that receiving the sacred ointment ye may say, *We are to God a sweet savour of Christ, in them that are saved*[3]. Afterwards on your breast; that having put on the *breast-plate of righteousness*, ye may *stand against the wiles of the devil*[4]. For as Christ after His Baptism, and the visitation of the Holy Ghost, went forth and vanquished the adversary, so likewise ye, after Holy Baptism and the Mystical Chrism, having put on the whole armour of the Holy Ghost, are to stand against the power of the adversary, and vanquish it, saying, *I can do all things through Christ which strengtheneth me*[5].

5. Having been counted worthy of this Holy Chrism, ye are called Christians, verifying the name also by your new birth. For before you were deemed worthy of this grace, ye had properly no right to this title, but were advancing on your way towards being Christians.

6. Moreover, you should know that in the old Scripture there lies the symbol of this Chrism. For what time Moses imparted to his brother the command of God, and made him High-priest, after bathing in water, he anointed him; and Aaron was called Christ or Anointed, evidently from the typical Chrism. So also the High-priest, in advancing Solomon to the kingdom, anointed him after he had bathed in Gihon[6]. To them however these things happened in a figure, but to you not in a figure, but in truth; because ye were truly anointed by the Holy Ghost. Christ is the beginning of your salvation; for He is truly the First-fruit, and ye the mass[7]; but if the First-fruit be holy, it is manifest that Its holiness will pass to the mass also.

7. Keep This unspotted: for it shall teach you all things, if it abide in you, as you have just heard declared by the blessed John, discoursing much concerning this Unction[8]. For this holy thing is a spiritual safeguard of the body, and salvation of the soul. Of this the blessed Esaias prophesying of old time said, *And on this mountain*,—(now he calls the Church a mountain elsewhere also, as when he says, *In the last days the mountain of the Lord's house shall be manifest*[9];)—*on this mountain shall the Lord make unto all nations a feast; they shall drink wine, they shall drink gladness, they shall anoint themselves with ointment*[1]. And that he may make thee sure, hear what he says of this ointment as being mystical; *Deliver all these things to the nations, for the counsel of the Lord is unto all nations*[2]. Having been anointed, therefore, with this holy ointment, keep it unspotted and unblemished in you, pressing forward by good works, and being made well-pleasing to the Captain of your salvation, Christ Jesus, to whom be glory for ever and ever. Amen.

---

6 Compare xix. 7; xxiii. 7, 19; and the section on "*Eucharist*" in the Introduction.

7 Χριστοῦ χάρισμα καὶ Πνεύματος ἁγίου παρουσίᾳ τῆς αὐτοῦ Θεότητος ἐνεργητικὸν γινόμενον. The meaning of this passage seems to have been obscured by divergent views of the order and construction of the words. In the Oxford translation, followed by Dr. Pusey (*Real Presence*, p. 357), the Chrism is "the gift of Christ, and by the presence of His Godhead it causes in us the Holy Ghost." The order of the operations proper to the two Divine Persons seems thus to be inverted.

According to the Benedictine Editor, and Canon Mason (*Relation of Confirmation to Baptism*, p. 344), it is "Christ's gracious gift, and is made effectual to convey the Holy Ghost by the presence of His own Godhead,"—i.e. apparently, the Godhead of the Holy Ghost conveys the Holy Ghost.

But according to the context "the presence" must be that of the Divine Person who has been invoked, namely the Holy Ghost: and this is clearly expressed in the order of the words Πνεύματος ἁγίου παρουσίᾳ τῆς αὐτοῦ θεότητος ἐνεργητικόν. The connexion of the words Πν. ἁγ. παρουσίᾳ is put beyond doubt by the Invocation in the Liturgy of S. James quoted in *Myst*. V. 7, note 8. The true meaning thus seems to be that the Chrism is Christ's gift of grace, and imparts His Divine nature by the presence of the Holy Ghost after the Invocation. This meaning is confirmed by the formula given in *Apost. Const.* vii. 44, for the consecration of the Chrism: "Grant also now that this ointment may be made effectual in the baptized, that the sweet savour of Thy Christ may remain firm and stable in him, and that, having died with Him, he may rise again and live with Him." The Chrism is thus regarded as "the Seal" which confirms the proper benefits of Baptism.

8 ἐπὶ μετώπου καὶ τῶν ἄλλων σου αἰσθητηρίων. The forehead may be regarded as representing the sense of touch; or we may translate, according to the idiomatic use of ἄλλος, "thy forehead and thine organs of sense besides." See Winer, *Grammar of N. T. Greek*, P. III. Sect. lix. 7: Riddell, *Digest of Platonic Idioms*, § 46.

9 2 Cor. iii. 18.

1 Is. l. 4.

2 Matt. xi. 15.

3 2 Cor. ii. 15.

4 Eph. vi. 14, and 11.

5 Phil. iv. 13.

6 1 Kings i. 39.

7 Rom. xi. 16.

8 1 John ii. 20: *But ye have an unction* (χρῖσμα) *from the Holy One*.

9 Is. ii. 2.

1 Ib. xxv. 6. The Septuagint differs much from the Hebrew, both here and in the following verse. R.V. "And in this mountain shall the Lord of hosts make unto all peoples a feast of fat things, a feast of wines on the lees, of fat things full of marrow, of wines on the lees well refined."

2 Ib. *v.* 7. R.V. "And He will destroy in this mountain the face of the covering that is cast over all peoples, and the veil that is spread over all nations."

LECTURE XXII.

(ON THE MYSTERIES. IV.)

ON THE BODY AND BLOOD OF CHRIST.

1 COR. xi. 23.

I received of the Lord that which also I delivered unto you, how that the Lord Jesus, in the night in which He was betrayed, took bread, &c.

1. EVEN of itself[1] the teaching of the Blessed Paul is sufficient to give you a full assurance concerning those Divine Mysteries, of which having been deemed worthy, ye are become of *the same body*[2] and blood with Christ. For you have just heard him say distinctly, *That our Lord Jesus Christ in the night in which He was betrayed, took bread, and when He had given thanks He brake it, and gave to His disciples, saying, Take, eat, this is My Body: and having taken the cup and given thanks, He said, Take, drink, this is My Blood*[3]. Since then He Himself declared and said of the Bread, *This is My Body*, who shall dare to doubt any longer? And since He has Himself affirmed and said, *This is My Blood*, who shall ever hesitate, saying, that it is not His blood?

2. He once in Cana of Galilee, turned the water into wine, akin to blood[4], and is it incredible that He should have turned wine into blood? When called to a bodily marriage, He miraculously wrought[5] that wonderful work; and *on the children of the bride-chamber*[6], shall He not much rather be acknowledged to have bestowed the fruition of His Body and Blood[7]?

3. Wherefore with full assurance let us partake as of the Body and Blood of Christ: for in the figure[8] of Bread is given to thee His Body, and in the figure of Wine His Blood; that thou by partaking of the Body and Blood of Christ, mayest be made of the same body and the same blood with Him. For thus we come to bear Christ[9] in us, because His Body and Blood are distributed[1] through our members; thus it is that, according to the blessed Peter, *we become partakers of the divine nature*[2].

4. Christ on a certain occasion discoursing with the Jews said, *Except ye eat My flesh and drink My blood, ye have no life in you*[3]. They not having heard His saying in a spiritual

---

1 *αὐτή* found in all MSS. is changed for the worse into *αὔτη* by the Benedictine Editor.

2 Introduction, "*Eucharist.*" The word *σύσσωμοι* has a different sense in Eph. iii. 6, where it is applied to the Gentiles as having been made members of Christ's body the Church.

3 1 Cor. xi. 23. The clause "and gave to His disciples" is an addition taken from Matt. xxvi. 26. The part relating to the cup does not correspond exactly either with St. Paul's language or with the Evangelists'.

4 *οἰκεῖον αἵματι.* Cod. Scirlet. (Grodecq), Mesm. (Morel), Vindob.; Ben. Ed. *οἰκείῳ νεύματι*, Codd. Monac. 1, 2, Genovef. Vatt. (Prevot.). Rupp. The whole passage is omitted in Codd. Coisl. R. Casaub. owing to the repetition of *αἷμα*

The reading *οἰκείῳ νεύματι*, "by His own will," introduces a superfluous thought, and destroys the very point of Cyril's argument, in which the previous change of water into an element so different as wine is regarded as giving an *a fortiori* probability to the change of that which is already "akin to blood" into blood itself.

If Cyril thus seems to teach a physical change of the wine, it must be remembered that we are not bound to accept his view, but only to state it accurately. See however the section of the Introduction on his Eucharistic doctrine.

5 *ἐθαυματούργησε τὴν παραδοξοποιίαν.* Cf. Chrysost. *Epist.* i. *ad Olympiad. de Deo*, § 1, c.: *τότε θαυματουργεῖ καὶ παραδοξοποιεῖ.*

6 Matt. ix. 15.

7 Ben. Ed.: "That the force of Cyril's argument may be the better understood, we must observe that in Baptism is celebrated the marriage of Christ with the Christian soul; and that the consummation of this marriage is perfected through the union of bodies in the mystery of the Eucharist. Read Chrysostom's *Hom.* xx. *in Ephes.*" Chrysostom's words are: "In like manner therefore we become one flesh with Christ by participation (*μετουσίας*)." But the participation expressed by *μετουσία* does not necessarily refer to the Eucharist. From the use of the word in Cat. xxiii. 11, and in Athanasius (*Contra Arianos*, *Or.* i.; *de Synodis*. 19. 22, 25) the meaning rather seems to be that we are one flesh with Christ not by nature but by His gift.

8 See Index, *Τύπος*, and the references there, and Waterland, *On the Eucharist*, c. vii.

9 *Χριστοφόροι γινόμεθα.* Procat. 15.

1 Ben. Ed.: "'*Ἀναδιδομένου.* The Codices Coisl. Roe, Casaub. Scirlet. Ottob. 2. Genovef. have *ἀναδεδεγμένοι*, which does not agree well with the Genitives *τοῦ σώματος* and *τοῦ αἵματος*. It is evident that it was an ill-contrived emendation of *ἀναδιδομένου*, the transcribers being offended at the distribution of Christ's Body among our members. But Cyril uses even the same word in Cat. xxiii. 9: *Οὗτος ὁ ἄρτος. . . . εἰς πᾶσάν σου τὴν σύστασιν ἀναδίδοται, εἰς ὠφέλειαν σώματος καὶ ψυχῆς*, 'This Bread is distributed into thy whole system, to the benefit of body and soul.'" '*Ἀναδιδομένου* is the reading of Milles and Rupp. For similar language see Justin M. *Apol.* i. 66; Iren. V. ii. 2.

2 2 Pet. i. 4.

3 John vi. 53.

sense were offended, and went back, supposing that He was inviting them to eat flesh.

5. In the Old Testament also there was shew-bread; but this, as it belonged to the Old Testament, has come to an end; but in the New Testament there is Bread of heaven, and a Cup of salvation, sanctifying soul and body; for as the Bread corresponds to our body, so is the Word[4] appropriate to our soul.

6. Consider therefore the Bread and the Wine not as bare elements, for they are, according to the Lord's declaration, the Body and Blood of Christ; for even though sense suggests this to thee, yet let faith establish thee. Judge not the matter from the taste, but from faith be fully assured without misgiving, that the Body and Blood of Christ have been vouchsafed to thee.

7. Also the blessed David shall advise thee the meaning of this, saying, *Thou hast prepared a table before me in the presence of them that afflict me*[5]. What he says, is to this effect: Before Thy coming, the evil spirits prepared a table for men[6], polluted and defiled and full of devilish influence[7]; but since Thy coming. O Lord, *Thou hast prepared a table before me.* When the man says to God, *Thou hast prepared before me a table*, what other does he indicate but that mystical and spiritual Table, which God hath prepared for us *over against*, that is, contrary and in opposition to the evil spirits? And very truly; for that had communion with devils, but this, with God. *Thou hast anointed my head with oil*[8]. With oil He anointed thine head upon thy forehead, for the seal which thou hast of God; that thou mayest be made *the engraving of the signet, Holiness unto God*[9]. And *thy cup intoxicateth me, as very strong*[1]. Thou seest that cup here spoken of, which Jesus took in His hands, and gave thanks, and said, *This is My blood, which is shed for many for the remission of sins*[2].

8. Therefore Solomon also, hinting at this grace, says in Ecclesiastes, *Come hither, eat thy bread with joy* (that is, the spiritual bread; *Come hither*, he calls with the call to salvation and blessing), *and drink thy wine with a merry heart* (that is, the spiritual wine); *and let oil be poured out upon thy head* (thou seest he alludes even to the mystic Chrism); *and let thy garments be always white, for the Lord is well pleased with thy works*[3]; for before thou camest to Baptism, thy works were *vanity of vanities*[4]. But now, having put off thy old garments, and put on those which are spiritually white, thou must be continually robed in white: of course we mean not this, that thou art always to wear white raiment; but thou must be clad in the garments that are truly white and shining and spiritual, that thou mayest say with the blessed Esaias, *My soul shall be joyful in my God; for He hath clothed me with a garment of salvation, and put a robe of gladness around me*[5].

9. Having learnt these things, and been fully assured that the seeming bread is not bread, though sensible to taste, but the Body of Christ; and that the seeming wine is not wine, though the taste will have it so, but the Blood of Christ[6]; and that of this David sung of old, saying, *And bread strengtheneth man's heart, to make his face to shine with oil*[7], "strengthen thou thine heart," by partaking thereof as spiritual, and "make the face of thy soul to shine." And so having it unveiled with a pure conscience, mayest thou *reflect as a mirror the glory of the Lord*[8], and proceed from *glory to glory*, in Christ Jesus our Lord:—To whom be honour, and might, and glory, for ever and ever. Amen.

---

4 Ben. Ed.: "Here we are to understand (by ὁ Λόγος) the Divine Word, not the bare discourse of God, but the second Person of the Holy Trinity, Christ Himself, the Bread of Heaven, as He testifies of Himself, John vi. 51: Him Cyril contrasts with the earthly shew-bread in the O. T.; otherwise he could not rightly from this sentence infer, by the particle οὖν, "therefore," that the Eucharist is truly the Body and Blood of Christ. And since he says, in Cat. xxiii. 15, that the Eucharistic food is "appointed for the substance of the soul," for its benefit, that cannot be said of Christ's body cr of His soul, but only of the Word which is conjoined with both. Moreover that the Divine Word is the food of Angels and of the soul, is a common mode of speaking with all the Fathers. They often play on the ambiguity of this word (λόγος), saying sometimes that the Divine Word, sometimes the word and oracles of God, are the food of our souls: both statements are true. For the whole life-giving power of the Eucharist is derived from the Word of God united to the flesh which He assumed: and the whole benefit of Eucharistic eating consists in the union of our soul with the Word, in meditation on His mysteries and sayings, and conformity thereto."

5 Ps. xxiii. 5.

6 ἠλισγημένην, a good restoration by Milles, with Codd. Roe, Casaub. Coislin. The earlier printed texts had ἠλυγισμένην, "overshadowed." Cf. Mal. i. 7: ἄρτους ἠλισγημένους, ... Τράπεζα Κυρίου ἠλισγημένη ἐστίν.

7 Cyril refers to the idolatrous feasts, which St. Paul calls "the table of devils," 1 Cor. x. 21.

8 Ps. xxiii. 5.

9 Ex. xxviii. 36; Ecclus. xlv. 12. The plate of pure gold on the forefront of Aaron's mitre was engraved with the motto, *Holy unto the Lord.* This symbolism Cyril transfers to the sacramental Chrism, in which the forehead is signed with ointment, and the soul with the seal of God.

1 Ps. xxiii. 5: *My cup runneth over.* Eusebius (*Dem. Evang.* I. c. 10, § 28) applies the Psalm, as Cyril does, to the Eucharist.

2 Matt. xxvi. 28.

3 Eccles. ix. 7, 8.

4 For προσέλθῃς (Bened.) we must read προσῆλθες, or, with Monac. 1, προσελθεῖν.

5 Is. lxi. 10.

6 On this passage see the section of the Introduction referred to in the Index, "*Eucharist.*"

7 Ps. civ. 15.

8 2 Cor. iii. 18.

LECTURE XXIII.

(ON THE MYSTERIES. V.)

ON THE SACRED LITURGY AND COMMUNION[1].

1 PET. ii. 1.

Wherefore putting away all filthiness, and all guile, and evil speaking[2], *&c.*

1. BY the loving-kindness of God ye have heard sufficiently at our former meetings concerning Baptism, and Chrism, and partaking of the Body and Blood of Christ; and now it is necessary to pass on to what is next in order, meaning to-day to set the crown on the spiritual building of your edification.

2. Ye have seen then the Deacon who gives to the Priest water to wash[3], and to the Presbyters who stand round God's altar. He gave it not at all because of bodily defilement; it is not that; for we did not enter the Church at first[4] with defiled bodies. But the washing of hands is a symbol that ye ought to be pure from all sinful and unlawful deeds; for since the hands are a symbol of action, by washing[5] them, it is evident, we represent the purity and blamelessness of our conduct. Didst thou not hear the blessed David opening this very mystery, and saying, *I will wash my hands in innocency, and so will I compass Thine Altar, O Lord*[6]*?* The washing therefore of hands is a symbol of immunity[7] from sin.

3. Then the Deacon cries aloud, "Receive ye one another; and let us kiss one another[8]." Think not that this kiss is of the same character with those given in public by common friends. It is not such: but this kiss blends souls one with another, and courts entire forgiveness for them. The kiss therefore is the sign that our souls are mingled together, and banish all remembrance of wrongs. For this cause Christ said, *If thou art offering thy gift at the altar, and there rememberest that thy brother hath aught against thee, leave there thy gift upon the altar, and go thy way; first be reconciled to thy brother, and then come and offer thy gift*[9]. The kiss therefore is reconciliation, and for this reason holy: as the blessed Paul somewhere cried, saying, *Greet ye one another with a holy kiss*[1]; and Peter, *with a kiss of charity*[2].

4. After this the Priest cries aloud, "Lift up your hearts[3]." For truly ought we in that most awful hour to have our heart on high with God, and not below, thinking of earth and earthly things. In effect therefore the Priest bids all in that hour to dismiss all cares of this life, or household anxieties, and to have

---

1 This title is added by the Benedictine Editor. There is nothing corresponding to it in the Greek.

2 The text is made up from memory of James i. 21: διὸ ἀποθέμενοι πᾶσαν ῥυπαρίαν, and 1 Pet. ii. 1: ἀποθέμενοι οὖν πᾶσαν κακίαν καὶ πάντα δόλον καὶ ὑποκρίσεις καὶ πάσας καταλαλίας.

3 In the *Apostolic Constitutions*, VIII. xi. this duty is assigned to a sub-deacon: "Let one of the sub-deacons bring water to wash the hands of the Priests, which is a symbol of the purity of those souls that are devoted to God." See *Dictionary of Christian Antiquities*, "Lavabo." The Priest who celebrates the Eucharist is here distinguished by the title ἱερεύς from the other Presbyters who stood round the altar.

4 Cyril evidently refers to the custom of placing vessels of water outside the entrance of the Church. Bingham, *Antiquities*, VIII. iii. 6. Chrysost. *In Johannem Hom.* lxxiii. 3: "Do we then wash our hands when going into Church, and shall we not wash our hearts also?" That the same custom was observed in heathen Temples appears from Herod. I. 51: περιῤῥαντήρια δύο ἀνέθηκε (See Bähr's note). Compare also Joseph. *Ant. Jud.* III. vi. 2.

5 [τῷ] νίψασθαι. Rupp: "Τῷ ex conjectura addidi." Possibly the original reading was νιψάμενοι, which would easily become altered through the presence of νίψασθαι in the preceding line. This washing is not mentioned in the Liturgy of St. James.

6 Ps. xxvi. 6. In the Liturgy of Constantinople this Psalm was chanted by the Priest and Deacon while washing their hands at the Prothesis or Credence.

7 ἀνυπεύθυνος.

8 These two directions by the Deacon are separated in the Liturgy of St. James: after the dismissal of the Catechumens, the Deacon says, "Take note one of another;" and after the Incense, Cherubic Hymn, Oblation, Creed. and a short prayer "that we may be united one to another in the bond of peace and charity," the Deacon says, "Let us salute (ἀγαπῶμεν) one another with a holy kiss." In the *Apostolic Constitutions*, VIII. 11, there is but one such direction, and this comes before the washing of hands and the dismissal of the Catechumens, "Salute (ἀσπάσασθε) ye one another with a holy kiss."

9 Matt. v. 23. From Cyril's reference to this passage "it may be inferred that the kiss of peace had been given before the gifts were brought to the altar, according to ancient custom attested by Justin M. *Apolog.* i. c. 65: 'Having ended the prayers' (for the newly baptized) 'we salute one another with a kiss. Then there is brought to the President of the brethren bread, and a cup of wine mixed with water'" (Ben. Ed.). There is the same order in the *Apost. Const.* VIII. 12, and in the 19th Canon of the Synod of Laodicea; but in the Liturgy of S. James the gifts are offered before the kiss of peace.

1 1 Cor. xvi. 20.

2 1 Pet. iii. 15.

3 The words are slightly varied in the Liturgies: thus in the Liturgy of St. James, "Let us lift up our mind and hearts;" in the *Apost. Const.* viii. 12, "Lift up your mind."

their heart in heaven with the merciful God. Then ye answer, "We lift them up unto the Lord:" assenting to it, by your avowal. But let no one come here, who could say with his mouth, "We lift up our hearts unto the Lord," but in his thoughts have his mind concerned with the cares of this life At all times, rather, God should be in our memory; but if this is impossible by reason of human infirmity, in that hour above all this should be our earnest endeavour.

5. Then the Priest says, "Let us give thanks unto the Lord." For verily we are bound to give thanks, that He called us, unworthy as we were, to so great grace; that He reconciled us when we were His foes; that He vouchsafed to us the Spirit of adoption. Then ye say, "It is meet and right:" for in giving thanks we do a meet thing and a right; but He did not right, but more than right, in doing us good, and counting us meet for such great benefits.

6. After this, we make mention of heaven, and earth, and sea[4]; of sun and moon; of stars and all the creation, rational and irrational, visible and invisible; of Angels, Archangels, Virtues, Dominions, Principalities, Powers, Thrones; of the Cherubim with many faces: in effect repeating that call of David's, *Magnify the Lord with me*[5]. We make mention also of the Seraphim, whom Esaias in the Holy Spirit saw standing around the throne of God, and with two of their wings veiling their face, and with twain their feet, while with twain they did fly, crying *Holy, Holy, Holy, is the Lord of Sabaoth*[6]. For the reason of our reciting this confession of God[7], delivered down to us from the Seraphim, is this, that so we may be partakers with the hosts of the world above in their Hymn of praise.

7. Then having sanctified ourselves by these spiritual Hymns, we beseech the merciful God to send forth His Holy Spirit upon the gifts lying before Him; that He may make the Bread the Body of Christ, and the Wine the Blood of Christ[8]; for whatsoever the Holy Ghost has touched, is surely sanctified and changed.

8. Then, after the spiritual sacrifice, the bloodless service, is completed, over that sacrifice of propitiation[9] we entreat God for the common peace of the Churches, for the welfare of the world[1]; for kings; for soldiers and allies; for the sick; for the afflicted; and, in a word, for all who stand in need of succour we all pray and offer this sacrifice.

9. Then we commemorate also those who have fallen asleep before us, first Patriarchs, Prophets, Apostles, Martyrs, that at their prayers and intercessions God would receive our petition[2]. Then on behalf also of the Holy Fathers and Bishops who have fallen asleep before us, and in a word of all who in past years have fallen asleep among us, believing that it will be a very great benefit to the souls[3], for whom the supplication is put up, while that holy and most awful sacrifice is set forth.

10. And I wish to persuade you by an illustration. For I know that many say, what is a soul profited, which departs from this world either with sins, or without sins, if it be commemorated in the prayer? For if a king were to banish certain who had given him offence, and then those who belong to them[4]

4 Compare the noble Eucharistic Preface in the Liturgy of St. James: "It is verily meet, right, becoming, and our bounden duty to praise Thee. to sing of Thee, to bless Thee, to worship Thee, to glorify Thee, to give thanks to Thee the Maker of every creature, visible and invisible, the Treasure of eternal blessings; the Fount of life and immortality, the God and Lord of all, whom the heavens of heavens do praise, and all the powers thereof, sun and moon and all the choir of the stars, earth, sea, and all that in them is, Jerusalem the heavenly assembly, Church of the first-born that are written in the heavens, spirits of righteous men and prophets, souls of martyrs and Apostles. Angels, Archangels, Thrones, Dominions, Principalities, Authorities, and Powers dread, also the many-eyed Cherubim, and the six-winged Seraphim, which with twain of their wings cover their faces, and with twain their feet, and with twain do fly, crying one to another with unresting lips, in unceasing praises, singing with loud voice the triumphant hymn of Thy majestic glory, shouting, and glorifying, and crying aloud, and saying,—Holy, Holy, Holy, O Lord of Hosts, heaven and earth are full of Thy glory. Hosanna in the highest; blessed is He that cometh in the name of the Lord; Hosanna in the highest."

5 Ps. xxxiv. 3.

6 Is. vi. 2, 3.

7 θεολογίαν, "the doctrine of the Godhead," either of the Son in particular, or, as here, of the whole Trinity: cf. Athanas. *contra Arianos*, Or. i. § 18: *νῦν ἐν τριάδι ἡ θεολογία τελεία ἐστίν.*

8 In the Liturgy of St. James the Triumphal Hymn is followed by the 'Recital of the work of Redemption,' and of 'the Institution.' by the 'Great Oblation,' and then by the 'Invocation,' as follows: "Have mercy upon us, O God, after Thy great mercy, and send forth on us, and on these gifts here set before Thee, Thine all-holy Spirit, ... that He may come, and by His holy, good, and glorious advent (παρουσίᾳ) may sanctify this Bread and make it the holy Body of Thy Christ (*Amen*), and this Cup the precious Blood of Thy Christ" (*Amen*). In Cat. xix. 7, Cyril calls this prayer "the holy Invocation of the Adorable Trinity," and in xxi. 3, "the Invocation of the Holy Ghost."

9 See Index, "Sacrifice," and the reference there to the Introduction. Compare Athenagoras (*Apol.* c. xiii.): "What have I to do with burnt-offerings, of which God has no need? Though indeed it behoves us to bring a bloodless sacrifice, and the *reasonable service*."

1 Cyril here gives a brief summary of the "Great Intercession," in which, according to the common text of the Liturgy of St. James, there is a suffrage "for the peace and welfare (εὐστάθεια) of the whole world, and of the holy Churches of God." Mr. Hammond thinks that it has been taken from the Deacon's Litany, and repeated by mistake in the Great Intercession. But from Chrysostom's language (*In Ep. ad Phil.* Hom. iii. p. 218; Gaume, T. xi. p. 251), we must infer that the prayer ὑπὲρ εἰρήνης καὶ εὐσταθείας τοῦ κόσμου formed part of the 'Great Intercession' in his Liturgy, as it does in the Clementine (*Apost. Constit.* VIII. § 10).

2 In the Liturgies of St. James and St. Mark, and in the Clementine, there are similar commemorations of departed saints, especially "patriarchs, prophets, apostles, martyrs," but nothing corresponding to the words, "that at their prayers and intercessions God would receive our petition." See Index, *Prayer* and *Intercession.*

3 So Chrysostom (*In* 1 *Cor.* Hom. 41, p. 457 A): "Not in vain was this rule ordained by the Apostles, that in the dread Mysteries remembrance should be made of the departed: for they knew that it is a great gain to them, and a great benefit.

4 οἱ τούτοις διαφέροντες. "Hesychius, Διαφέρει, ἀνήκει. Ubi Kusterus ait, ἀνήκει, id est. "*pertinet*," vel "*attinet*' Routh, *Scriptor. Eccles. Opuscula*, p. 441). Dr. Routh's note

should weave a crown and offer it to him on behalf of those under punishment, would he not grant a remission of their penalties? In the same way we, when we offer to Him our supplications for those who have fallen asleep, though they be sinners, weave no crown, but offer up Christ sacrificed for our sins[5], propitiating our merciful God for them as well as for ourselves.

11. Then, after these things, we say that Prayer which the Saviour delivered to His own disciples, with a pure conscience entitling God our Father, and saying, *Our Father, which art in heaven.* O most surpassing loving-kindness of God! On them who revolted from Him and were in the very extreme of misery has He bestowed such a complete forgiveness of evil deeds, and so great participation of grace, as that they should even call Him Father. *Our Father, which art in heaven;* and they also are a heaven who *bear the image of the heavenly*[6], in whom is God, *dwelling and walking in them*[7].

12. *Hallowed be Thy Name.* The Name of God is in its nature holy, whether we say so or not; but since it is sometimes profaned among sinners, according to the words, *Through you My Name is continually blasphemed among the Gentiles*[8], we pray that in us God's Name may be hallowed; not that it comes to be holy from not being holy, but because it becomes holy in us, when we are made holy, and do things worthy of holiness.

13. *Thy kingdom come.* A pure soul can say with boldness, *Thy kingdom come;* for he who has heard Paul saying, *Let not therefore sin reign in your mortal body*[9], and has cleansed himself in deed, and thought, and word, will say to God, *Thy kingdom come.*

14. *Thy will be done as in heaven so on earth.* God's divine and blessed Angels do the will of God, as David said in the Psalm, *Bless the Lord, all ye Angels of His, mighty in strength, that do His pleasure*[1]. So then in effect thou meanest this by thy prayer, "as in the Angels Thy will is done, so likewise be it done on earth in me, O Lord."

15. *Give us this day our substantial bread.* This common bread is not substantial bread, but this Holy Bread is substantial, that is, appointed for the substance of the soul[2]. For this Bread *goeth* not *into the belly and is cast out into the draught*[3], but is distributed into thy whole system for the benefit of body and soul[4]. But by *this day*, he means, "each day," as also Paul said, *While it is called to-day*[5].

16. *And forgive us our debts as we also forgive our debtors.* For we have many sins. For we offend both in word and in thought, and very many things we do worthy of condemnation; and *if we say that we have no sin*, we lie, as John says[6]. And we make a covenant with God, entreating Him to forgive us our sins, as we also forgive our neighbours their debts. Considering then what we receive and in return for what, let us not put off nor delay to forgive one another. The offences committed against us are slight and trivial, and easily settled; but those which we have committed against God are great, and need such mercy as His only is. Take heed therefore, lest for the slight and trivial sins against thee thou shut out for thyself forgiveness from God for thy very grievous sins.

17. *And lead us not into temptation, O Lord.* Is this then what the Lord teaches us to pray, that we may not be tempted at all? How then is it said elsewhere, "a man untempted, is a man unproved[7];" and again, *My brethren, count it all joy when ye fall into divers temptations*[8]? But does perchance the entering into temptation mean the being overwhelmed by the temptation? For temptation is, as it were, like a winter torrent difficult to cross. Those therefore who are not overwhelmed in temptations, pass through, shewing themselves excellent swimmers, and not being swept away by them at all; while those who are not such, enter into them and are overwhelmed. As for example, Judas having entered into the temptation of the love of money, swam not through it, but was overwhelmed and was strangled[9] both in body and spirit. Peter entered into the temptation of the denial; but having entered, he was not over-

---

refers to *Nicæni Conc.* Can. xvi.: ὑφαρπάσαι τὸν τῷ ἑτέρῳ διαφέροντα. Cf. *Synodi Nic. ad Alexandrinos Epist.*: διαφέροντα τῇ Αἰγύπτῳ καὶ τῇ ἁγιωτάτῃ Ἀλεξανδρέων ἐκκλησίᾳ.

5 According to the Ben. Ed. the meaning is not "We offer Christ, who was sacrificed for our sins," but "We offer for our sins Christ sacrificed." i.e "Christ lying on the altar as a victim sacrificed," in allusion to Apoc. V. 6, 12. See Index, "Sacrifice."

6 1 Cor. xv. 49. 7 2 Cor. vi. 16.

8 Is. lii. 5; Rom. ii. 24. 9 Rom. vi. 12.

1 Ps. ciii. 20.

2 "It is manifest that the author derives the word ἐπιούσιος from the two words ἐπί and οὐσία, as do many others: although the explanation which derives it from ἐπιούσῃ ἡμέρᾳ is more probable. We render it "substantial" in accordance with Cyril's meaning, with which the word "super-substantial does not agree" (Ben. Ed).

3 Matt. xv. 17.

4 Cat. xxii. § 3, note 1. Ben. Ed. "We are not to think that Cyril supposed the Body of Christ to be distributed and digested into our body; but in the usual way of speaking he attributes to the Holy Body that which belongs only to the species under which It is hidden. Nor does he deny that those species pass into the draught, but only the Body of Christ." Cf. Iren. V. ii. 2, 3, and "Eucharistic Doctrine" in the Introduction.

5 Heb. iii. 15. 6 1 John i. 8. *We deceive ourselves.*

7 Tertull. *De Bapt.* c. 20: "For the word had gone before 'that no one untempted should attain to the celestial kingdoms.'" *Apost. Const.* II. viii.: "The Scripture says, 'A man that is a reprobate (ἀδόκιμος) is not tried (ἀπείραστος) by God.'" Resch, *Agrapha*, Logion 26, p. 188, quotes allusions to the saying in Jas. i. 12, 13; 2 Cor. xiii. 5, 6, 7, and concludes that it was recorded as a saying of our Lord in one of the un-canonical gospels (Luke i. 1), where it occurred in the context of the incident narrated in Matt. xxvi. 41, Mark xiv. 38.

8 Jas. i. 2. 9 ἀπεπνίγη. Matt. xxvii. 5: ἀπήγξατο.

whelmed by it, but manfully swam through it, and was delivered from the temptation[1]. Listen again, in another place, to a company of unscathed saints, giving thanks for deliverance from temptation, *Thou, O God. hast proved us; Thou hast tried us by fire like as silver is tried. Thou broughtest us into the net; Thou layedst afflictions upon our loins. Thou hast caused men to ride over our heads; we went through fire and water; and thou broughtest us out into a place of rest*[2]. Thou seest them speaking boldly in regard to their having passed through and not been pierced[3]. *But Thou broughtest us out into a place of rest;* now their coming into a place of rest is their being delivered from temptation.

18. *But deliver us from the evil.* If *Lead us not into temptation* implied the not being tempted at all, He would not have said, *But deliver us from the evil.* Now evil is our adversary the devil, from whom we pray to be delivered[4]. Then after completing the prayer thou sayest, *Amen*[5]; by this *Amen*, which means "So be it," setting thy seal to the petitions of the divinely-taught prayer.

19. After this the Priest says, "Holy things to holy men." Holy are the gifts presented, having received the visitation of the Holy Ghost; holy are ye also, having been deemed worthy of the Holy Ghost; the holy things therefore correspond to the holy persons[6]. Then ye say, "One is Holy, One is the Lord, Jesus Christ[7]." For One is truly holy, by nature holy; we too are holy, but not by nature, only by participation, and discipline, and prayer.

20. After this ye hear the chanter inviting you with a sacred melody to the communion of the Holy Mysteries, and saying, *O taste and see that the Lord is good*[8]. Trust not the judgment to thy bodily palate[9]; no, but to faith unfaltering; for they who taste are bidden to taste, not bread and wine, but the antitypical[1] Body and Blood of Christ.

21. In approaching[2] therefore, come not with thy wrists extended, or thy fingers spread; but make thy left hand a throne for the right, as for that which is to receive a King[3]. And having hollowed thy palm, receive the Body of Christ, saying over it, *Amen.* So then after having carefully hallowed thine eyes by the touch of the Holy Body, partake of it; giving heed lest thou lose any portion thereof[4]; for whatever thou losest, is evidently a loss to thee as it were from one of thine own members. For tell me, if any one gave thee grains of gold, wouldest thou not hold them with all carefulness, being on thy guard against losing any of them, and suffering loss? Wilt thou not then much more carefully keep watch, that not a crumb fall from thee of what is more precious than gold and precious stones?

22. Then after thou hast partaken of the Body of Christ, draw near also to the Cup of His Blood; not stretching forth thine hands, but bending[5], and saying with an air of worship and reverence, *Amen*[6], hallow thyself by partaking also of the Blood of Christ. And while the moisture is still upon thy lips, touch it with thine hands, and hallow thine eyes and brow and the other organs of sense[7]. Then wait for the prayer, and give thanks unto God, who hath accounted thee worthy of so great mysteries[8].

---

1 Compare the description of Peter's repentance in Cat. ii. 19.

2 Ps. lxvi. 10—12.

3 For ἐμπαρῆναι the Ben. Ed. conjectures ἐμπαγῆναι "to have been stuck fast."

4 Cyril is here a clear witness for the reference of τοῦ πονηροῦ to "the wicked one."

5 From § 14, εὐχόμενος τοῦτο λέγεις, it seems probable that the whole Prayer was said by the people as well as by the Priest. See Introduction, "Eucharistic Rites."

6 Compare Waterland on this passage, c. X. p. 688.

7 *Apost. Const.* VIII. c. xiii: "Let the Bishop speak thus to the people: Holy things for holy persons. And let the people answer: There is One that is holy; there is one Lord, one Jesus Christ, blessed for ever, to the glory of God the Father." The Liturgies of St. James and of Constantinople have nearly the same words: in the Liturgy of St Mark the answer of the people is: One Father holy, one Son holy, one Spirit holy, in the unity of the Holy Spirit.

8 Ps. xxxiv. 9. In the *Apostolic Constitutions* the "Sancta Sanctis" and its response are immediately followed by the "Gloria in excelsis," and the "Hosanna." Then the Clergy partake, and there follows a direction that this Psalm xxxiv. is to be said while all the rest are partaking. In the Liturgy of Constantinople there is the direction: "The Choir sings the communion-antiphon (τὸ κοινωνικόν) of the day or the saint."

9 For μὴ ἐπιτρέπητε, probably an itacism, we should read μὴ ἐπιτρέπεται, as a question, the propriety of the change being indicated by the answer οὐχί. "Is the judgment of this entrusted to the bodily palate? No, but, &c."

1 ἀντιτύπου σώματος, "the antitypical Body," not "the antitype of the Body," which would require τοῦ σώματος. Cf. Cat. xxi. § 1, note 6.

2 Cat. xviii. 32: "with what reverence and order you must go from Baptism to the Holy Altar of God."

3 Cyril appears to be the earliest authority for thus placing the hands in the form of a Cross. A similar direction is given in the 101st Canon of the Trullan Council (692), and by Joh. Damasc. (*De Fid. Orthod.* iv. 14). *Dict. Chr. Ant.* "*Communion.*" That the communicant was to receive the Bread in his own hands is clear from the language of Cyril and other Fathers. Cf. Clem. Alex. *Strom.* I. c. i. § 5: "Some after dividing the Eucharist according to custom allow each of the laity himself to take his part." See the passage of Origen quoted in the next note, and Tertull. *Cor. Mil.* c. iii. "The Sacrament of the Eucharist, which the Lord commanded both (to be taken) at meal-times and by all, we take even in assemblies before dawn, and from the hand of none but the presidents."

4 Origen, *Hom. xiii. in Exod.* § 3: "I wish to admonish you by examples from your own religion: ye, who have been accustomed to attend the Sacred Mysteries, know how, when you receive the Body of the Lord, you guard it with all care and reverence, that no little part of it fall down, no portion of the consecrated gift slip away. For you believe yourselves guilty, and rightly so believe, if any part thereof fall through carelessness."

5 κύπτων, not kneeling, but standing in a bowing posture. Cf. Bingham, XV. c. 5, § 3.

6 *Apost. Const.* VIII. c. 13: "Let the Bishop give the Oblation (προσφοράν) saying, *The Body of Christ*. And let him that receiveth say, *Amen*. And let the Deacon hold the Cup, and when he delivers it say, *The Blood of Christ, the Cup of Life*. And let him that drinketh say, *Amen*."

7 Cat. xxi. 3, note 8.

8 In the Liturgy of St. James, after all have communicated, "*The Deacons and the People say:* Fill our mouths with Thy praise, O Lord, and fill our lips with joy, that we may sing of Thy glory, of Thy greatness, all the day. *And again:* We render

23. Hold fast these traditions undefiled and, keep yourselves free from offence. Sever not yourselves from the Communion; deprive not yourselves, through the pollution of sins, of these Holy and Spiritual Mysteries. *And the God of peace sanctify you wholly; and may your spirit, and soul, and body be preserved entire without blame at the coming of our Lord Jesus Christ*[9]:—To whom be glory and honour and might, with the Father and the Holy Spirit, now and ever, and world without end. Amen.

thanks to Thee, Christ our God, that Thou hast accounted us worthy to partake of Thy Body and Blood, &c."

9 1 Thess. v. 23.

INDICES.

INDEX OF SUBJECTS.

The References are to the Lectures and numbered Sections of each Lecture.

INDEX OF GREEK WORDS.

An asterisk marks a reference to a note : for other passages refer to the Greek Text.

S. CYRIL.

INDEX OF TEXTS.

The references are to the pages.

SELECT ORATIONS

OF

SAINT GREGORY NAZIANZEN,

SOMETIME ARCHBISHOP OF CONSTANTINOPLE.

TRANSLATED BY

CHARLES GORDON BROWNE, M.A.,

Rector of Lympstone, Devon;

AND

JAMES EDWARD SWALLOW, M.A.,

Chaplain of the House of Mercy, Horbury.

CONTENTS.

PROLEGOMENA.

ORATIONS.

LETTERS.

PROLEGOMENA.

SECTION I.

The Life.

S. Gregory Nazianzen, called by the Ecumenical Council of Ephesus "The Great," and universally known as "The Theologian" or "The Divine," a title which he shares with S. John the Evangelist alone among the Fathers of the Church, was, like the great Basil of Cæsarea and his brother Gregory, Bishop of Nyssa, by birth a Cappadocian. He was born at Arianzus, a country estate belonging to his father, in the neighbourhood of Nazianzus.

This latter, sometimes called Nazianzum, is a place quite unknown to early writers, and derives all its importance from its connection with our Saint. The Romans seem to have called it Diocæsarea. This would place it in the south-western portion of the district called Cappadocia Secunda, a sub-division of the Province, which had previously included the whole country of Cappadocia under the Prefect of Cæsarea. The Emperor Valens made the division for financial purposes about A.D. 371, and assigned Tyana as its civil Metropolis, and, as we shall see, thereby caused an ecclesiastical quarrel which had considerable effect on the life of S. Gregory. Tyana was situated at no great distance south and east of Nazianzus, which place is usually identified with some interesting ruins about eighteen miles south-east of Ak Serai, on a rocky platform at the foot of the mountains called Hassan Dagh. Amongst other ruined buildings here are the remains of three Byzantine churches of great age, but more recent than the rest of the town.

His father, who bore the same name with himself, had originally belonged to an obscure sect called Hypsistarians or Hypsistians, of whom we know little except what we learn from Gregory of Nazianzus and his namesake of Nyssa. They seem to have held a sort of syncretist doctrine, containing elements derived from heathen, Christian, and Jewish sources. They were very strict monotheists, rejecting both polytheism and the doctrine of the Trinity, and worshipping the One Supreme Being under the names of The Most High and The Almighty, and the emblems of Fire and Light, but with no external cultus; for they rejected sacrifice and every outward form of worship, holding adoration to be an exclusively interior and spiritual act. With singular inconsistency, however, they adopted the observance of the Jewish Sabbath, and the Levitical prohibition of certain kinds of food. They were but few in number, and their influence was insignificant even in Cappadocia, which was the headquarters of the sect.[1] From this form of error the elder Gregory was converted by the influence of his wife, Nonna; and soon after his conversion was consecrated to the bishopric of Nazianzus.

Nonna, the mother of our Saint, was the daughter of Christian parents, and had been very carefully brought up. Like S. John Chrysostom and S. Augustine, Gregory had the inestimable advantage of being reared at the knee of a mother of conspicuous holiness. There

[1] ἐκ δύοιν ἐναντιωτάτοιν συγκεκραμένης, ἑλληνικῆς τε καὶ νομικῆς τερατείας· ὧν αμφοτέρων τὰ μέρη φυγὼν, ἐκ μέρων συνετέθη. Τῆς μέν γὰρ τὰ εἴδωλα καὶ τὰς θυσίας ἀποπεμπόμενοι, τιμῶσι τὸ πῦρ καὶ τὰ λύχνα· τῆς δὲ τὸ σάββατον αἰδούμενοι καὶ τὰ περὶ τὰ βρώματά ἐστιν ἃ μικρολογίαν, τὴν περιτομὴν ἀτιμάζουσιν.—Or. xviii. 5.

were three children of the marriage—a sister, Gorgonia, probably somewhat older than Gregory, who was devotedly fond of her; and a brother, Cæsarius, perhaps younger, who was a distinguished physician, and occupied a post of confidence at the Court of Constantinople. Gregory was certainly born at a late period of the life of his mother. He tells us that, like so many other holy men of whom we read both in the Bible and outside its pages, he was consecrated to God by his mother even before his birth. The precise date is uncertain. There are two lines in his poem on his own life which seem to indicate clearly that it took place after his father's elevation to the Episcopate, or at any rate after his ordination to the Priesthood. Speaking of the great desire of the elder Gregory to see his son ordained to the Priesthood, in order that he might have him as a coadjutor and aid to his own declining years and failing strength, he gives the arguments by which the old man sought to persuade him to take upon himself a burden which he dreaded; and among them we find the father saying to the son: [2] "You have not been yet so long in life as I have spent in sacrifice." And though the Roman Catholic writers on the subject strain every nerve to get rid of the obvious meaning, by ingenious manipulation of the text or by far-fetched interpretations, yet the conclusion remains unshaken, and is supported also by another passage, to be cited presently, that he was at any rate born during the Priesthood of his father. He tells us that he left Athens in or about his thirtieth year,[3] and also that the Emperor Julian was his contemporary there. Now Julian was at Athens in 355; so that we must place Gregory's birth not earlier than 325; and if we give its natural meaning to the first passage quoted, not earlier than 330, the latest date available for his father's consecration as Bishop. This is not inconsistent with the Athenian chronology of his life, as he certainly spent many years there, and probably did not leave the place till 357.

As soon as the children's age permitted, Gregory and his brother Cæsarius were sent to school at Cæsarea, under the care of a good man named Carterius, who as long as he lived retained a great influence over the mind of his elder pupil. This is perhaps the same Carterius who afterwards presided over the monasteries of Antioch in Syria, and was one of the instructors of S. John Chrysostom. The following is a free rendering of one of four funeral epigrams written in later years by our Saint in honour of his old friend and tutor:

"Whither, Carterius, best beloved of friends,
O whither hast thou gone, and left me here
Alone amid the many toils of earth?
Thou who didst hold the rudder of my youth,
When in another land I learned to weigh
The words and stories of a learned age;
Thou who didst bind me to the uncarnal life.
Truly the Christ, whom thou possessest now,
Took thee unto Himself, the King thou lov'st.
O thou bright lightning of most glorious Christ,
Thou best protection of my early days,
Thou charioteer of all my younger life;
Remember now the Gregory whom erst
Thou trainedst in the ways of virtuous life,
Carterius, master of the life of grace."

It was probably at Cæsarea that the acquaintance between Gregory and S. Basil the Great began, which was afterwards to ripen into a lifelong friendship. But their association did

[2] Carm. de vita sua, 511.

[3] Ib. 339.

not last long at this period, for Basil soon went to Constantinople to continue his education, while Gregory and his brother removed to the Palestinian Cæsarea; probably as much for the sake of making a pilgrimage to the Holy Sepulchre, as for the advantage of the schools of that learned resort. Cæsarius soon went on to Alexandria; but Gregory was tempted by the flourishing Palestinian school of rhetoric to remain a while and study that art. One of his fellow-students here was Euzoius, the future heresiarch. From Palestine he too went on to Alexandria, where he found his brother enjoying an excellent character, and highly distinguished among the students of the University. S. Athanasius was at this time the Bishop, and Didymus head of the famous Catechetical School; but as Gregory, though one of his orations is a panegyric on S. Athanasius, does not mention having ever met either of these two great men, we must suppose that the former was at this time suffering one of his many periods of exile—his second banishment lasted from 340 to 347. Gregory does not seem to have remained very long at Alexandria; the fascination exercised on his mind by a yet more famous seat of learning—Athens—soon drew him thither. He could not even wait for a favourable time of year, but must start at once. He took passage in the month of November in a ship bound for Ægina, with some of whose crew he was acquainted. They had a prosperous voyage until they were in sight of Cyprus, when they were assailed by a tremendous storm, and the ship, swept by the heavy seas, became waterlogged, and would not answer her helm. At the same time the violence of the sea burst the water-tanks, and the ship's company were left in dire distress. Gregory, who was not yet baptized, was thrown into terrible distress at thus finding himself in peril of death while yet outside the Covenant of God. In earnest prayer he renewed his self-dedication, and vowed to give himself wholly to the service of God, if his life might be spared to receive Holy Baptism. He tells the story at some length and with great graphic power in his long poem on his own life, from which we subjoin a cento,[4] and also in his oration spoken at his father's funeral (Orat. XVIII, c. 31, p. 352 Ed. Ben.). It is, however, uncertain whether he was baptized immediately after this deliverance, or whether he waited till his return to Nazianzus. At any rate he reached Athens in safety, and shortly afterwards was joined there by Basil; when the early acquaintance which was now renewed soon deepened into an intimacy of brotherly affection, which, though often sorely tried, never grew cold in Gregory's heart. In the funeral oration which he pronounced

[4] What time I parted from Egyptian shores,
Whence I had somewhat culled of ancient lore,
We weighed, and under Cyprus cut the waves
In a straight course for Hellas, when there rose
A mighty strife of winds, and shook the ship:
And all was night; earth, seas, and darkened skies;
And thunders echoed to the lightning's shock.
Whistled the rigging of the swelling sails,
And bent the mast; the helm had lost its power,
For none could hold it in the raging seas.
The ship was filled with overwhelming waves;
Mingled the shout of sailor, and the cries
Of helmsman, captain, and of passenger,
And those who till that fearful hour had been
Unconscious of a God; for fear can teach.
And, worst of all our dread impending woes,
No water had we, for the ship began
To labour, and the beakers soon were broke
Which held our treasure of sweet water scant;
And famine fought with surging and with storm
To slay us. But God sent a swift release.
For Punic sailors suddenly appeared,
Who in their own sore terror soon perceived
By our sad cries our danger, and with oars
(For they were strong) came up and saved our barque
And us, who now all but sea-corpses were;
Like fish forsaken of their native wave,
Or lamp that dies for want of nourishment.

But while we all were fearing sudden death,
Mine was a worse, because a secret, fear.
The cleansing waters ne'er had passed on me,
That slay our foe and join us to our God.
This was my lamentation, this my dread.
For this I stretched my hands and cried to God,
And cried above the noise of surging waves,
And rent my clothes, and lay in misery.
But, though ye scarce believe it, yet 'tis true,
All those on whom our common danger pressed
Forgot themselves, and came and prayed with me.
And Thou wast then, O Christ, my great defence,
Who now deliverest from the storm of life.
For when no good hope dawned upon our eyes,
Nor isle, nor continent, nor mountain top,
Nor torch, nor star to light the mariners,
Nor small nor great of earthly things appeared,
What port was left for troubled sailor-folk?
Despairing of all else, I look to thee;
Life, breath, salvation, light, and strength to men,
Who frightest, smitest, smilest, healest all,
And ever weavest good from human ill.
I call to mind Thy wonders of old time,
By which we recognize Thy mighty hand;
The sea divided—Israel's host brought through—
Their foes defeated by Thy lifted hand—
And Egypt crushed by scourges, chiefs and all—
Nature subdued, and walls thrown down by shout.
And, adding mine to those old famous acts.
Thine own, I said, am I, both erst and now;
Twice shalt Thou take me for Thine own, a gift
Of earth and sea, a doubly hallowed gift,
By prayers of mother and by fateful sea.
To Thee I live, if I escape the waves,
And gain baptismal dews; and Thou wilt lose
A faithful servant if Thou cast me off.
E'en now Thine own disciple, in the deep;
Shake off for me Thy slumber, and arise,
And stay my fear. So prayed I—and the noise
Of winds grew still, the surges ceased, the ship
Held straight upon her course; my prayer was heard.

over his friend, Gregory has left us a most interesting account of University life in the middle of the fourth century, of which we give a summary here, referring the reader for details to the oration itself, which will be found in the present volume. Basil's reputation, he says, preceded him to Athens, where he was received with much enthusiasm. Many of the silliest students there are mad upon Sophists, and are divided upon the respective merits of their teachers with as much excitement as is shown by the partisans of the various chariots in the Hippodromes. And so a new-comer is laid hold of by them in this fashion. First of all, he is entertained by the first who can get hold of him—either a relation or a friend or a fellow-countryman, or a leading Sophister, who is in favour with his master, and touts for him. There he is unmercifully chaffed, and with more or less of rough horseplay, by everybody, to take down his pride; and is then escorted processionally through the streets to the Baths; after which process he is regarded as free of the students' guild. Basil, however, through the good offices of his friend Gregory, was spared this trial of his nerves, out of respect for his great attainments; and this kind action was the beginning of their long and affectionate intimacy. Among the students, however, were a number of young Armenians, some of whom had been at school with Basil, and were very jealous of him. These young men, with the object of destroying his reputation if possible, were continually harassing him with disputations upon hard and sophistical questions. Basil was quite able to hold his own against them; but Gregory, jealous for the honour of his University, and not at first perceiving the malice of these young men, sided with them and made the conflict more equal. As soon, however, as he began to see their real purpose, he forsook them and took his stand by his friend, whose victory was thus made not only assured but easy. The young gentlemen naturally did not like this, and Gregory became, much to Basil's distress, very unpopular among them, as they chose to regard his conduct in the matter as treason against his University, and especially against the students of his own year.

The city of Athens at this time was full of dangerous distractions for young men; feasts, theatres, assemblies, wine parties, etc. Gregory and his friend resolved to renounce all these, and to allow themselves to know only two roads—one, that which led to the Church and its holy teachers; the other, that which took them to their University lectures.[5] Amongst other famous students of Gregory's day was Prince Julian, afterwards the Emperor who apostatized and endeavoured to restore the ancient heathenism, and galvanize it into something like a new life. Gregory claims even at this early period to have foreseen and dreaded the result of Julian's accession. "I had long foreseen," he says, "how matters would be, from the time that I was with him at Athens. He had come there shortly after the violent measures against his brother, having asked permission of the Emperor to do so. He had two reasons for this sojourn—the one more honest, namely, to visit Greece and its schools; the other more secret and known only to a few persons, namely, to consult with the heathen priests and charlatans about his plans; because his wickedness was not as yet declared. Even then I made no bad guess about the man, although I am not one of those skilled in such matters; but I was made a prophet by the unevenness of his disposition and the very unsettled condition of his mind. I used these very words about him: 'What an evil the Roman State is nourishing,' though I prefaced them with a wish that I might prove a false prophet."

[5] Of this early friendship with Basil, Gregory speaks thus:

For God had given me yet one priceless gift
Uniting me with Wisdom's wisest son,
Himself alone above all life and word;
Who this could be, ye soon shall know full well;
Basil his name, our age's great support.
He was the comrade of my words and roof,
And of my thoughts, if I may boast so much.
A pair were we not all unknown in Greece;
All things we shared in common, and one soul
Linked us together, though in body twain.
One thing there was which joined us most of all,
The love of God and of the highest good.
For, soon as courage came to us to speak
Each to the other of that we had at heart,
More closely were our spirits knit in love,
For fellow feeling makes us wondrous kind.

(Carm. de Vita Sua. l. 221.)

(Orat. V. 23, 24.) Gregory must have been a long time at Athens. He seems to have gone there at about the age of eighteen, and not to have left till he was past thirty. Basil left before him and returned to Cappadocia; and as soon as he could follow he went to Constantinople, where he met his brother,[6] who had just come there to practice as a Court Physician, but resolved to throw up his practice and return with his brother to Nazianzus. They found their parents still living and their father occupying the Episcopal Throne. From this time onward Gregory divided his time between his parents and his friend; living partly at Arianzus, and partly with Basil in Pontus, in monastic seclusion. At his Baptism, which it seems most probable took place at this period, he made a solemn vow never to swear, and to devote his whole energies and powers solely to the glory of God, and the defence and spreading of the faith. Cæsarius did not remain long in the retirement of home, but soon returned to the Capital, where a brilliant career seemed opening before him. Gregory, whose mind was strongly impressed with the dangers and temptations of a life at Court, did not altogether approve of this step, yet he does not very severely blame it. He himself, however, felt very strongly drawn to the monastic life; but as retirement from the world did not seem to him to be his vocation, he resolved to continue to live in the world, and to be a help and support to his now aged parents, and especially to his father in the duties of his Episcopate, but at the same time to live under the strictest ascetic rule. He had, however, always a secret hankering after the Solitary life, which he had once (Ep. i.) promised Basil to share with him; and he did find himself able for some years to spend part of his time with his friend in his retirement in the wilds of Pontus. They portioned out their days very carefully between prayer, meditation and study, and manual labour, on the principles laid down by Basil in a letter to his friend, which afterwards were developed into the celebrated Rule still observed by the entire body of the Religious of the Eastern Church.[7] Retirement, he says, does not consist in the act of removal from the world in bodily presence, but in this, that we tear away the soul from those bodily influences which stir up the passions; that we give up our parental city and our father's house, our possessions and goods, friendship and wedlock, business and profession, art and science, and everything, and are quite ready to take into our hearts nothing but the impressions of the divine teaching.

In solitude, Basil thinks, it is possible altogether to tame the passions, like wild beasts, by gentle treatment; to lull them to sleep, to disarm them. By turning away the soul from the enticements of sense, and withdrawing into one's self for the contemplation of God and of Eternal Beauty, it is possible to raise man to a forgetfulness of natural wants, and to a spiritual freedom from care. The means to this spiritual elevation are in his view the reading of Holy Scripture, which sets before us rules of life—but especially the pictures of the lives of godly men; Prayer which draws down the Godhead to us, and makes our mind a pure abode for It; and an earnest silence, more inclined to learn than to teach, but by no means morose or unfriendly. At the same time Basil desires that the outward appearance of one who thus practises solitude shall be in keeping with his inner life; with humble downcast eye, and dishevelled hair, in dirty untidy clothes he must go about, neither lazily loitering nor passionately quick, but quietly. His garment, girt upon his loins with a belt, is to be coarse, not of a bright colour, suited for both summer and winter, close enough to keep the body warm without additional clothing; and his shoes adapted to their purpose, but without ornament. For food, let him use only the most necessary, chiefly vegetables; for drink, water—at least in health. For mealtime, which begins and ends with prayer, one hour is to be fixed. Sleep is to be short, light, and never so dead as to let the soul be open to the impressions of corrupting dreams.[8]

[6] Or. vii. 8. [7] Ullmann G. v. N. [8] Bas. Ep. ii. Ullmann u. s.

They gave themselves especially to the study of Holy Scripture, and to the practice of devotional exercises. In their study their great principle was to interpret the holy writings not by their own individual judgment, but on the lines laid down for them by the authority of ancient interpreters.[9] Of uninspired commentators they had the greatest respect for Origen, whose errors, however, they happily avoided. From his exegetical writings they compiled a book of Extracts, which they published in twenty-seven books, to which they gave the name of Philocalia, *i.e.*, what in modern language is called a Christology. This is happily still extant, and is valuable as preserving for us many passages otherwise lost, or existing only in a Latin translation. Gregory sent a copy of this work to his friend and subsequent companion at Constantinople, Theodore, Bishop of Tyana, as an Easter gift many years afterwards, and accompanied it with a letter,[10] in which he speaks of the work as a memorial of himself and Basil, and as intended for an aid to scholars; and begs that his friend will give a proof of its usefulness, with the help of diligence and the Holy Spirit. Socrates[11] says that this careful study of Origen was of the greatest service to the two friends in their subsequent controversies with the Arians; for these heretics quoted him in support of their errors, but the two Fathers were enabled to confute them readily, by shewing that they were completely ignorant of the meaning of Origen's argument.

But Gregory does not appear to have stayed long in Basil's Monastery;—although Ruffinus speaks of a sojourn of thirteen years. This cannot for chronological reasons have been a continuous stay, although it is true that Basil's monastic life in Pontus, and Gregory's various visits to him there extended over a period of about that length, from his first retirement in 357 to his consecration to the Episcopate in 370. It was after about three years that Gregory returned to Nazianzus (360), possibly, as Ullmann suggests, because of circumstances which had arisen at his home, which seemed to call imperatively for his presence in the interests of the peace of the Diocese, and for the assistance which he might, though a layman, be able to give to his aged Father, who had got into trouble through a piece of imprudent conduct.

The Emperor Constantius, who was an Arian, had in 359 assembled at Ariminum (the modern Rimini) a Council of 400 Western Bishops,[12] and these, partly duped, partly compelled by the Imperial Officers, had put out a Creed, which, while acknowledging the proper Deity of the Son, and confessing Him to be LIKE the Father, omitted to say LIKE IN ALL POINTS, and refused the word CONSUBSTANTIAL; thus, while condemning the extreme followers of Arius, favouring the views of the Semi-Arian party. At the same time another Synod, of 150 Eastern Bishops, was assembled under Court influence at Seleucia, and promulgated a similar formula. The Bishop of Nazianzus, though still as always a staunch upholder of Nicene orthodoxy, was in some way induced to attach his signature to this compromising Creed; and this action led to most important consequences. The Monks of his Diocese took the matter up with the usual earnestness of Religious, and, with several also of the Bishops, withdrew from Communion with their own Bishop. This may have been the reason for his son's return. He induced his Father to apologize for his involuntary error and to put out an orthodox Confession, and so he healed the schism. To this period belongs his first Oration on Peace; in which, after an eloquent encomium on the Religious life, he sets forth the blessings of peace and concord, and contrasts them with the misery of discord; begging the people to be very slow indeed on this account to sever themselves from the Communion of those whom they think to be erring brethren; and thanking God for the restoration of peace. He concludes

[9] Brev. Rom. May 9.

[10] Ep. cxv.

[11] H. E. IV.. xxvi.

[12] The reign of Constantius was, says Dr. Ullmann, in a very special way the age of Synods. By his endless summoning of Synods he not only furthered doctrinal disputes, but also injured the finances of the State, destroyed the existence of the Posts, and brought everything into confusion.

the whole with a splendid setting forth of the Catholic doctrine concerning the Trinity, in the following terms:—

"Would to God that none of us may perish, but that we may all abide in one spirit, with one soul labouring together for the faith of the Gospel, of one mind, minding the same thing, armed with the shield of faith, girt about the loins with truth; knowing only the one war against the Evil One, and those who fight under his orders; not fearing them that kill the body but cannot lay hold of the soul; but fearing Him Who is the Lord both of soul and body; guarding the good deposit which we have received from our fathers; adoring Father, Son, and Holy Ghost; knowing the Father in the Son, and the Son in the Holy Ghost—into which Names we were baptized, in Which we have believed; under Whose banner we have been enlisted; dividing Them before we combine Them, and combining before we divide; not receiving the Three as one Person (for They are not impersonal, or names of one Person, as though our wealth lay in Names alone and not in facts), but the Three as one Thing. For They are One, not in Person, but in Godhead, Unity adored in Trinity, and Trinity summed up in Unity; all adorable, all royal, of one throne and one glory; above the world, above time, uncreated, invisible, impalpable, uncircumscript; in Its relation to Itself known only to Itself; but to us equally venerable and adorable; Alone dwelling in the Holiest, and leaving all creatures outside and shut off, partly by the First Veil, and partly also by the Second;—by the first, the heavenly and angelic host, parted from Godhead; and by the second, we men, severed from the Angels. This let us do; let this be our mind, Brethren; and those that are otherwise minded let us look upon as diseased in regard to the truth, and as far as may be, let us take and cure them; but if they be incurable let us withdraw from them, lest we share their disease before we impart to them our own health. And the God of Peace that passeth all understanding shall be with you in Christ Jesus our Lord. Amen.[13]"

Gregory the Elder was now aged and infirm, and began to feel his need of a Coadjutor in his pastoral duties. So, by the great desire of the people of Nazianzus, he ordained his son to the Priesthood, much against the will of the said son. This Ordination took place at some great Festival, probably at Christmas of the year 361. Gregory the Younger was much aggrieved at this gentle violence, which even in after years he describes as an act of tyranny,[14] and says he cannot bring himself to speak of it in other terms, though he asks pardon of the Holy Spirit for his language. Immediately after his Ordination he made his escape to Pontus, apparently reaching Basil about Epiphany, 362. Here he had time for reflection on the obedience he now owed to his father, not only as son to father, but as Priest to Bishop; and with a truer view of his duty he returned to Nazianzus, where he was present in the Church on Easter day 362, and preached his first Sermon as a Priest, in apology for his reluctance. Strange to say, though it was so great a Festival, and though the preacher was so well known and so much beloved in Nazianzus, the congregation was very small;—probably many refrained from going to Church in order to mark their feeling about Gregory's flight to Pontus. Anyhow he felt the discourtesy keenly, and in his next sermon took occasion to reprove them severely for their inconsistency in receiving him so badly after having compelled him for their sakes to finally renounce the solitude he loved so well. Of this discourse the Abbé Benoît speaks as follows:—

"It is not very long, and it seems to us a model of the tact and art which a Minister of the Gospel ought to use in his speech when just grievances compel him to address deserved reproaches to the faithful. It would be impossible to blame with greater force, to complain with

[13] I have followed Ullmann and Nirschl in placing this occurrence here. The Benedictine Editors, apparently in order to add priestly authority to this Oration (VI.), have put it four years later, on what I cannot but think to be insufficient grounds. Their date would bring it to the close of the reign of Julian or the beginning of that of Jovian, neither of which periods would offer any inducement to Arianizing.

[14] Carm. de vita, l., 345

more frankness, and yet to do it in a way less offensive to the hearers. Praise, indeed, is so mingled with blame in this discourse, and there is in its tone something so earnest and affectionate, that the audience, though sharply reprimanded, not only could not take offence, but was compelled to conceive a yet greater affection and admiration for him who so reproved them."

Gregory took the opportunity to write another very long Oration as his apology for his flight. In it he sets forth at great length his conception of the nature and responsibilities of the Priestly Office, and justifies himself both for having shrunk from such a charge, and for having so soon returned to take it up. It is very improbable that this Oration, numbered II. in the Benedictine Edition, was ever delivered *vivâ voce;* but it was published, and is a complete Treatise on the Priesthood, used both by S. John Chrysostom as the foundation of his Six Books on the Priesthood, and by S. Gregory the Great as the basis of his Treatise on the Pastoral Rule. It has also furnished material to many of the best Ecclesiastical writers of all ages.

Julian had now succeeded to the Empire, and had entered Constantinople in 361. He had by this time completely broken with the Church, and renounced even the outward semblance of Christianity. He persuaded Cæsarius, however, to retain his position at Court; hoping perhaps that he might succeed in perverting him. This was a matter of deep regret to his father and brother, and they felt, the latter says, obliged to keep the fact from the knowledge of his mother. Gregory wrote his brother a letter of most affectionate though earnest remonstrance; with the result that Cæsarius soon made up his mind to retire; and put his resolution in practice on the opportunity afforded by the departure of the Emperor from Constantinople to assume the direction of his campaign against the Persians. Nazianzus was not allowed to remain without attempts being made against its Christianity, for the Prefect of the Province was sent with an armed escort of considerable strength to demand possession of the Church. But the aged Bishop, supported by his son and by his people, boldly refused to comply with the Imperial commands, and there seemed such a probability of powerful resistance that the Prefect felt compelled to withdraw his force, and never came to Nazianzus again on such an errand. The Gregorys, father and son, frequently came into collision with Julian during his stay in Cappadocia on his way to Persia; and indeed it is not too much to say that the firm stand which they made on behalf of the right was, under God, the means of diverting the Emperor from his purpose of making a vehement assault upon the faith and rights of the Church in that Province. As the Abbé Benoît [15] remarks, Julian saw that he must be careful in dealing with a province where Christian faith was such a living power, and where a simple village Bishop could dare to make so stout a stand against Imperial Authority; but he declared his intention of avenging himself upon his opponents on his return from his expedition. The Providence of God, however, interfered, and he never did return, but was defeated and killed.

In 363 or 364 Basil, like Gregory, was ordained Priest much against his will. The Bishop of Cæsarea, Metropolitan of Cappadocia, was Eusebius. He had been elected in 362 by a popular clamour, while yet only a Catechumen, and was very unwillingly consecrated by the Bishops of the Province. He felt it necessary to have at hand a Priest who by his skill in Theology would be a help to him in the controversies of the times, and he selected Basil. But for some unknown reason, possibly no more than a certain jealousy of Basil's superior reputation and influence, within a very short time Eusebius quarrelled with him, and endeavoured to deprive him. This might easily have led to a serious schism, had Basil been a self-seeking man, but as it was, he quietly retired to his Community in Pontus, accompanied

[15] S. G. de N.

by his friend Gregory, who, however, was not able to remain long in that congenial society, as his presence was still much needed by his father. On the succession of Valens, an Arian, to the Throne of the Empire, Eusebius wrote to Gregory, entreating him to come to Cæsarea and give him the benefit of his advice. Gregory, however, respectfully declined the invitation on the grounds of his sense of the wrong which his friend had suffered; and after some correspondence he succeeded in effecting a reconciliation between the latter and his Metropolitan, in the year 365.

Cæsarius meantime had returned to the Court and had received from Valens a valuable piece of preferment in Bithynia; but in the end of 368 or beginning of 369, having been terrified by a great earthquake, during which he had been in considerable danger, he was arranging matters for his final retirement, when he was seized with illness, and very soon died, leaving all his property, which must have amounted to a considerable sum, to his brother in trust for the poor. He was buried at Nazianzus, and on the occasion of his funeral his brother preached the Sermon which is numbered VIII. in the Benedictine Edition. About the same time, but a little later, Gorgonia also departed, and he preached a funeral sermon on her too. Eusebius of Cæsarea died in 370, and Basil at once wrote an urgent letter to Gregory, begging him to come to Cæsarea, probably in order to get him elected Archbishop. Gregory, however, declined to go, and he and his father exerted themselves to the utmost of their power to procure the election of Basil; the elder Gregory writing through his son two letters, one addressed to the people of Cæsarea, the other to the Provincial Synod, urging Basil's claims very strongly. Though ill at the time, he managed to convey himself to the Metropolis in time for the meeting of the Synod; and Basil was elected and consecrated. Gregory wrote him a letter of congratulation; not, however, a very warm one; but when troubles began to arise he spoke out with all the fervour of their early friendship in support of the Archbishop. About this time Valens divided the civil Province of Cappadocia into two, one of which had Cæsarea, the other Tyana, for its Metropolis. Anthimus, Bishop of the latter See, thereupon claimed to be *ipso facto* Metropolitan of the new Province; a claim which Basil strenuously resisted, as savouring of what we call Erastianism. A long dispute followed, in the course of which Basil, to assert his rights as Metropolitan, and to strengthen his own hands, erected several new Bishoprics in the disputed Province; and to one of these, Sasima, a miserable little village [16] he consecrated his friend Gregory, almost by force. Gregory was, not unnaturally, indignant at this treatment; while Basil, whose great object had been to strengthen himself against Anthimus, took it as unkind of Gregory to be so reluctant to comply with his friend's wishes. So the two were for a long time in very strained relations to one another. Although, however, Gregory ultimately yielded to the earnest wish of his father, and submitted to the authority of the Archbishop, yet he did not disguise his reluctance; and in the Sermons which he preached on the occasion (Or. ix. x.) he spoke very strongly on the point. Anthimus, however, occupied the village of Sasima with troops, and prevented Gregory from taking peaceable possession of his See, which it is probable he never actually administered, for his father begged him to remain at Nazianzus and continue his services as coadjutor Bishop. The contest about the Metropolitanate of Tyana went on for some time, but in the end, mainly by Gregory's mediation, it was amicably settled. In 374 Gregory the elder died, and his wife also, and thus our Saint was set free from the charge of the diocese. He spoke a panegyric at his father's funeral, and wrote a number of little "In Memoriam" poems to his mother's memory; and out of respect

[16] The following is Gregory's own description of his new diocese (Carm. de vita sua, 439):
"There is a little station on a high road in Cappadocia, situated where the road is divided into three; without water, without grass, with nothing of freedom about it; a frightfully horrible and narrow little village; everywhere dust and noise and carts, weeping and shouting, lictors and chains. The people are all foreigners and vagabonds. **Such is my Church of Sasima, to which I was presented by a man who is not content with fifty chorepiscopi. What munificence!"**

for his father continued to administer the See of Nazianzus for about a year, making great efforts meanwhile to secure the appointment of a Bishop. But, perceiving that his efforts would be fruitless, because of the devotion of the people to himself, he at length withdrew, after a very serious illness, to Seleucia in Isauria (375,) where he lived three or four years, attached to the famous Church of S. Thecla. Very little is known of his life there; but it must have been at this period that he heard of the death of Basil, upon whom two years later in the Cathedral of Cæsarea he pronounced a splendid panegyric.

In 379 the Church at Constantinople, which for forty years had been oppressed by a succession of Arian Archbishops, and was well nigh crushed out of existence by the multitude of other heresies, Eunomian, Macedonian, Novatian, Apollinarian, etc., which Arian rule had fostered, besought the great Theologian to come to their aid. Theodosius the new Emperor, who was a fervent Catholic, backed their entreaty, as did also numerous Bishops. Gregory resisted the call for a long time; but at last he came to see that it was the will of God that he should accept the Mission, and he consented to go and fill the gap, until such time as the Catholics of the Capital might be able to elect an Archbishop.

The following account of the religious condition of Constantinople at this time is condensed from Ullmann:—

"Religious feeling like everything else had become to the idle and empty mind a subject of joke and amusement. What belonged to the theatre was brought into the Church, and what belonged to the Church into the theatre. The better Christian feelings were not seldom held up in comedies to the sneer of the multitude. Everything was so changed by the Constantinopolitans into light jesting, that earnestness was stripped of its worth by wit, and that which is holy became a subject for banter and scoffing in the refined conversation of worldly people. Yet worse was it that the unbridled delight of these men in dissipating enjoyments threatened to turn the Church into a theatre, and the Preacher into a play actor. If he would please the multitude, he must adapt himself to their taste, and entertain them amusingly in the Church. They demanded also in the preaching something that should please the ear, glittering declamation with theatrical gesticulation; and they clapped with the same pleasure the comedian in the holy place and him on the stage. And alas. there were found at that period too many preachers who preferred the applause of men to their souls' health. At this period the objects of the faith excited, particularly in Constantinople, a very universal and lively interest, which was entertained from the Court downwards, though not always in the most creditable manner; but it was in great part not the interest of the heart, but that of a hypercritical and disputatious intellect, where it was not something far lower, to which the dispute about matters of faith served only as a pretext for attaining the exterior aims of avarice or ambition. While the sanctifying and beatifying doctrines of the Gospel, which are directed to the conversion of the whole inner man were let lie quiet, everyone from the Emperor to the beggar busied himself with incredible interest about a few questions concerning which the Gospel communicates only just so much as is beneficial to the human spirit and necessary to salvation, and whose fuller expression at any rate belongs rather to the school than to practical life. But the more violently these doctrinal disputes were kindled, disturbing and dividing States, cities, and families, so much the more people lost sight of the practical essentials of Christianity; it seemed more important to maintain the Tri-unity of God than to love God with all the heart; to acknowledge the Consubstantiality of the Son, than to follow Him in humility and selfdenial; to defend the Personality of the Holy Spirit, than to bring forth the fruits of the Spirit, love, peace, righteousness. . . . In addition to these religious disputes came also political struggles, namely, the hard-fought wars of the Roman Empire with the Goths; so that the Empire at large presented the picture of a sea, tossed by violent storms. But the unhappy schisms which at this time were severing Christians everywhere, shewed themselves in a particularly discouraging form in the Capital. Under the late reigns several parties had been favoured; but especially those which, though again divided among themselves by differences of opinion, yet agreed in this that they all rejected the Nicene system of doctrine. Constantius had bestowed his favour on the Arians; Julian during his short reign on all parties, at least in appearance,—to crush them all. After Jovian's early death Valens succeeded to power in the East, and with him, even more than with Constantius, Arianism, which he not only protected, but also sought to make predominant by horrible atrocities against the friends of the Nicene Decrees. These had now been forbidden the use of all Churches and Church property; and the Arians had been put in possession of them. But Constantinople still remained the scene of ecclesiastical strifes and partizanships. Here where with a little good so much evil flowed from all three parts of the world, all opinions had their adherents; but the following parties in particular shewed themselves:—The Eunomians, professing an intellectual theology, which claimed to be able completely to explore the Being of God by logical definitions, and maintained in strict Arian fashion the Unlikeness of the Son to the Father, were very numerous in Constantinople (as is shewn by the fact that most of Gregory's polemical utterances were directed against them), and injured earnest religious thought principally by this, that they used the doctrines of the faith exclusively as subjects for an argumentative dialectic. The Macedonians, addicted to the Semi-Arian dogma of the Like Substance, and thereby somewhat more nearly approaching the Orthodox, and distinguished besides by an estimable earnestness of demeanour, and a monk-like strictness of manner, were indeed themselves excluded by the pure Arians from the property of the Church, but were ever being abundantly multiplied, partly in Constantinople itself, partly in the neighbouring regions of the Hellespont, Thrace, Bithynia, and Phrygia. The Novatians, who even overstepped the Macedonians in the strictness of their practical principles, had somewhat earlier been on the point of uniting themselves with the Orthodox, from whom they did not differ on the chief doctrine in dispute, and with whom they found themselves under like oppression from the Arians; but the malevolent disposition of a few of the party leaders had stood in the way, and so they remained separate, and swelled the number of the opponents of Orthodoxy. Lastly the Apollinarians too began to establish themselves there. Their teaching was opposed to the acknowledgment of true and perfect Manhood in Jesus (for true Manhood lies in the reason especially); and there was at that time, as Gregory informs us, a report that an assembly of Apollinarian bishops was to be held at Constantinople, with a view of raising their teaching as to Christ into general notice, and forcing it upon the Churches.

In such a crisis Gregory came most unwillingly to the Capital. At first he lodged in the house of a relation of his own, part of which he arranged as a Chapel, and dedicated under the title Anastasia, as the place where the Catholic faith was to rise again. There he began at once to carry out the rule of the Church as to daily service, to which he added his own splendid preaching.

His constant theme was the worship of the Trinity. After two Sermons in deprecation of religious contentiousness, he preached those famous Five Orations which have won for him the title of the Theologian. To analyse these belongs to another portion of this work; it will be enough in this place to say, that after warning his audience against the frivolity with which the Arians were dragging religious subjects of the most solemn kind into the most unsuitable places and occasions, he proceeds in four magnificent discourses to set forth the Catholic doctrine of the Trinity, shewing carefully the difference between Sabellian confusion of Persons and Tritheistic division of Substance. The Arians, however, persecuted him bitterly; even, on one occasion at least, hiring an assassin to murder him; and their persecution was all the more bitter because of the wonderful success which attended Gregory's preaching. S. Jerome, who came to Constantinople at this time, has left on record the pleasure with which he listened to and conversed with the great Defender of the Faith.

Unfortunately Gregory now let himself be taken in by a plausible adventurer named Maximus, who had come to Constantinople in the hope of obtaining the Bishopric for himself. He attached himself to Gregory and won his confidence, the latter even going so far as to deliver a panegyric upon him as a sufferer for the Faith. After a short time, however, Maximus managed to procure his own consecration secretly from some Egyptian Bishops, who during an illness of Gregory enthroned him at night in the Church. In the morning, when the people discovered what had been done, they were very indignant, and Maximus and his friends were driven out of the Church and forced to leave the City. Meanwhile the rank and fashion of Constantinople began to dislike Gregory, who would not condescend to the arts of the popular preacher, and whose simple retiring life and gentle demeanour were made matter of reproach to him. Gregory was quite willing to retire, and was only prevented from doing so by the earnest remonstrances of his friends, who solemnly assured him that if he went away the Faith would depart with him; so he consented to remain till a fitter man could be found. Late in 380 Theodosius came to Constantinople, where almost his first act was to deprive the Arians of the Churches, and to put Gregory in possession of the Cathedral of S. Sophia. The next year the great Council of Eastern Bishops, which ranks as the Second Ecumenical Council, met at the Capital, under the presidency of Meletius of Antioch. Its first care was to sanction the translation of Gregory from the See of Sasima to that of the Metropolis of the Empire, and to enthrone him in S. Sophia, and thus he became the recognised Archbishop of the Imperial City. Meletius shortly afterwards died, and Gregory assumed the Presidency of the Council. He failed in his endeavours to heal the schism which was troubling the Church of Antioch; and when the Egyptian Bishops on their arrival shewed a disposition to take up the case of Maximus, and were determined at any rate to oust Gregory from the Patriarchal Throne on the ground of a Nicene canon forbidding translations, which had virtually been rescinded by the act of the Council, he made up his mind to resign. He obtained a reluctant assent to this course from the Emperor, and then took leave of the Synod in one of the most magnificent of all his Orations, in which he gives a graphic account of his work in the Metropolis. Nectarius, Prefect of the City, who was only a catechumen, was elected in his place, and Gregory went home to Nazianzus. He administered the affairs of the Church there for a little while, and then, having procured the election of Eulalius as Bishop, he retired to Arianzus, where he passed the few remaining years of his life in seclusion, but still continued to take an active interest in the affairs of the Church. His own city was greatly disturbed by Apollinarian teachers, whose efforts to establish themselves within the Church were very persevering. Apollinarius, or as he is frequently called in the West, Apollinaris, was a Bishop of Laodicea in the latter half of the Fourth Century, and was at one time greatly respected for his learning and orthodoxy by S. Athanasius and S. Basil. He was even an instructor of S. Jerome in 374, but he seceded from the Church in the next year, owing to views which he had come to hold about the nature of our Lord; these really prepared the way for various forms of the Monophysite heresy. He fell into the error of a partial denial of our Lord's true Humanity, attributing to Christ a human body and a human soul, but not a reasoning spirit, whose place, according to him, was supplied by the Divine Logos. This view had first appeared in 362, when it came before a Council at Alexandria. Those who were accused of holding it denied it, and expressed their sense of the absurdity of such a view, pointing out that our Lord could not be said to be really incarnate if He had no human mind; but about 369 it assumed a definite form (though even then it was not known to be the teaching of Apollinarius). Arguing from the Divinity of Christ that He cannot have had a human mind, for if he had He would have had sinful inclinations, and the one Christ would have been two persons, Apollinarius and his followers went on to maintain that the Incarnation only meant a certain converse between God and Man; and that Christ's Body was not really born of Mary, but was a part of the Godhead converted into flesh. S. Athanasius wrote two Books against these two propositions, but did not name Apollinarius, most probably because he did not believe him to be committed to them. The fundamental error of the system was the idea that the Incarnation was, not the Union of the two Natures, but only a *blending* so close, that in the mind of these teachers all the Divine Attributes were transferred to the human nature, and all the human ones to the Divine, and the two were merged in one compound being.

In 377 a Roman Synod excommunicated Apollinarius and his adherents, and S. Damasus wrote a letter containing twenty-five anathemas, which he sent to Paulinus of Antioch and others. This condemnation is in almost the identical words used by S. Gregory in the first of two letters on the question which he wrote to Cledonius, a Priest of Nazianzus, and which were adopted as symbolic at the Councils of Ephesus and Chalcedon. Of these letters Canon Bright[17] says that they belong to that class of documents of the Fourth Century which refuted by anticipation the heresies of the Fifth. Gregory affirmed True Godhead and True Manhood to be combined in the One Person of the Crucified, Who was the adorable Son, Whose Mother was the Mother of God, and Who assumed, in order to redeem it, the entire nature that fell in Adam. In his seclusion, says Mr. Crake, his sole luxuries were a garden and a fountain. He spent his last days in continual devotion. His knees were worn with kneeling, and his whole thoughts and aspirations had gone before to the long home to which he was hastening. After the manner of the Saints, he was very rigorous in his self-denial. His bed was of straw with a covering of sackcloth, and a single tunic was all the outward clothing of him who had been Bishop of Constantinople. Yet his glory was only in the Lord. "As a fish cannot swim without water, and a bird cannot fly without air, he said, so a Christian cannot advance a single step without Christ." He died in 391, and in the same year that he passed from the roll of the earthly episcopate Augustine was ordained Priest at Hippo Regius in Africa.

Ullmann gives the following description of his character and personal appearance:

"Gregory was of middle height and somewhat pale; but his pallor became him. His hair was thick and blanched by age, his short beard and conspicuous eyebrows were thicker. On his right eye he had a scar. His manner was friendly and attractive; his conduct simple. The keynote of his inner being was piety; his soul was full of fiery strength of faith, turned to God and Christ; a lofty zeal for divine things led him all his life. This zeal manifested itself above all in a steadfast adherence to and defence of certain dogmas which that age held to be specially important; as well as in lively conflicts, not always free from partisanship, with opposing convictions; but not less in a hearty and living apprehension of practical Christianity, the establishment and enlargement of which in men's minds was to him all important. His asceticism was overdone; it injured his health; yet it did not degenerate into hypocrisy; it was to him the means for elevating and liberating the mind, but not in and for its own sake a higher virtue. An inborn and inbred love of solitude hindered him from turning all his powers to a publicly useful activity. His seclusion did not allow him to become familiar with the knowledge of men and of the world; lacking in knowledge of men, carelessly confident, sometimes distrustful and bitter in his judgment of others, he demanded

[17] Ch. Hist., 181.

from others much, but from himself most. Susceptible of great resolves, and full of fiery zeal for all good, he was not always steadfast and persevering in carrying them out. In endurance and conflict he was noble and high-minded; in victory moderate; in prosperity humble; never flattering the great, but an ever ready helper to the oppressed and persecuted, and to the poor a loving father. The most excellent qualities were in Gregory mingled with faults; he was not quite free from vanity; he was very irritable and sensitive, but also readily forgave and cherished no grudges. He was a man feeling after holiness, and striving after the highest good, but not perfect, as no man upon earth is."

Before leaving Constantinople he made his will, in which he bequeathed all his property to the Deacon Gregory for life, with reversion to the poor of Nazianzus.

DIVISION II.

The Writings.

I. The Orations.—These—forty-five in number—raise him to equality with the best Orators of antiquity.

a. *The Five Theological Orations.*—These won him the title of The Theologian.[1] They were delivered in Constantinople, in defence of the Church's faith in the Trinity, against Eunomians and Macedonians. In the First and Second he treats of the existence, nature, being, and attributes of God, so far as man's finite intellect can comprehend them. In the Third and Fourth the subject is the Godhead of the Son, which he establishes by exposition of Scripture, and by refutation of the specious arguments brought forward by the heretics. In the Fifth he similarly maintains the Deity and Personality of the Holy Ghost.

b. *The Two Invectives against Julian.*—These were delivered at Nazianzus after the death of the Emperor, and present us with a very dark picture of his character. The orator dwells upon his attempt to rebuild the Temple at Jerusalem, and its failure, and his overthrow in the campaign against Persia. From these facts he demonstrates the power of God's Justice, and sets forth the Christian doctrine of the Divine Providence inculcating a lesson of trust in God.

c. *Moral Orations.*—(1) The Apology for his flight. As was said above, it is most probable that this discourse was never actually spoken; if it was, it certainly must have been considerably enlarged afterwards. In it Gregory dwells on the motive of his flight and his return after his forced ordination; he speaks of his love of retirement, but most of all lays stress upon the difficulty of the Priestly Office, its heavy responsibilities and grave dangers, and upon his own sense of unworthiness. His return, he says, was prompted by respect for his hearers and by care for his aged parents: by the fear of losing his father's blessing; and by the recollection of what befel the Prophet Jonas on account of his resistance to the will of God. The remainder of the Oration is practically a treatise on the Priesthood, and was made use of by S. Chrysostom and S. Gregory the Great in their books on the subject.

(2) The Farewell Oration at Constantinople, containing an account of his work there.

(3) On Love of the Poor.

(4) On the Indissolubility of Marriage, the only Sermon of S. Gregory on a definite text which has come down to us.

(5) Three Orations on Peace.

(6) One on Moderation in theological discussion.

---

[1] In the narrower sense of "Defender of the Godhead of the Word."

d. *The Festal Orations.*—On Christmas, Epiphany (on the Baptism of Christ in the river Jordan, followed up next day by a long one on Holy Baptism), two on Easter (one of these his first sermon, the other almost if not quite his last). On Low Sunday, and on Pentecost.

e. *Panegyrics on Saints.*—The Maccabee Brothers and their Mother; S. Cyprian of Carthage (in which there is evidence of the cultus of the Blessed Virgin Mary and of the practice of invocation of the Saints); and on S. Athanasius.

f. *Funeral Orations on Eminent People.*—On his Father, preached before his Mother and S. Basil. On Cæsarius, in presence of his parents, consoling them by the picture of his brother's virtue, especially in having withstood Julian's efforts to pervert him, and in resigning his post at Court and leaving the Capital. On Gorgonia, whom he praises as a model Christian Matron, and whose wonderful cure before the Altar he relates. On S. Basil.

g. *Occasional Orations*, of which we mention three: (1) On a plague of hail. (2) On the consecration of Eulalius of Doara. (3) On his own consecration to Sasima.

II. The Letters, of which two hundred and forty-three are extant, are characterised by a clear, concise, and pleasant style and spirit. Some of them treat of the theological questions of the day, as for example the two to Cledonius, and one to Nectarius his Successor in the See of Constantinople; these deal with the Apollinarian errors. Most of them however are letters to private friends; sometimes of condolence or congratulation, sometimes of recommendation, sometimes on mere general subjects of interest. To this section must be ascribed his Will, which is probably genuine.

III. The Poems, five hundred and seven in number, are in various metres. While leaving much to be desired, these verses shew much real poetic feeling, and at times rise to genuine beauty. Thirty-eight are dogmatic, on the Trinity, on the works of God in Creation, on Providence, on Angels and Men, on the Fall, on the Decalogue, on the Prophets Elias and Elissæus, on the Incarnation, the Miracles and Parables of our Lord, and the canonical Books of the Bible. Forty are Moral; two hundred and six Historical and Autobiographical; one hundred and twenty-nine are Epitaphs, or rather funeral Epigrams; ninety-four are Epigrams.

There is also a long Tragedy, called Christus Patiens which is the first known attempt at a Christian drama; the parts are sustained by Christ, The Blessed Virgin, S. Joseph, S. Mary Magdalene, Nicodemus, Pontius Pilate, Theologus, Nuntius, and others. The Benedictine Editors however doubt the genuineness of this Tragedy and *Caillau,* who published the second volume of this Edition after the troubles of the French Revolution, thinks it is to be ascribed to another Gregory, Bishop of Antioch in the Sixth Century, and relegates it to an Appendix. None of The Theologian's Odes or Hymns have, however, found a place in the liturgical poetry of the Church.

DIVISION III.

Literature.

There are perhaps more MSS. of the works of Gregory than of any other Father. The great Benedictine Edition of his works contains long lists of MSS., and of Versions, and previous Editions. The most famous of these is that of the Abbat Jacobus Billius in 1589, which was accompanied by the Scholia of Nicetas, etc. In 1571 Leuvenklavius published an edition at Basle containing the Scholia of Elias Cretensis and others. In 1778 appeared the first volume of the great Edition of the Benedictine Fathers of the Abbey of S. Maur near Paris, which had been in preparation ever since 1708. But the Monks were driven away by the French Revolution, and the second volume did not appear till 1842. It has been reprinted in Migne's "Patrologia Græca;" vols. 35–38. Of modern works on the life and writings of our Saint, the best are those of Dr. Ullmann, and that of the Abbé Benoît. A valuable comparison of Gregory and Basil is to be found in Newman's "Church of the Fathers," and last, but not least in value, may be mentioned the long biographical article by Professor Watkins in Smith's "Dictionary of Christian Biography," and a useful short summary in Schaff's Church History (311–600, vol. ii.).

GREGORY NAZIANZEN.

ORATION I.

On Easter and His Reluctance.

I. It is the Day of the Resurrection, and my Beginning has good auspices. Let us then keep the Festival with splendour,[α] and let us embrace one another. Let us say Brethren, even to those who hate us; much more to those who have done or suffered aught out of love for us. Let us forgive all offences for the Resurrection's sake: let us give one another pardon, I for the noble tyranny which I have suffered (for I can now call it noble); and you who exercised it, if you had cause to blame my tardiness; for perhaps this tardiness may be more precious in God's sight than the haste of others. For it is a good thing even to hold back from God for a little while, as did the great Moses of old,[β] and Jeremiah[γ] later on; and then to run readily to Him when He calls, as did Aaron[δ] and Isaiah,[ε] so only both be done in a dutiful spirit;—the former because of his own want of strength; the latter because of the Might of Him That calleth.

II. A Mystery[ς] anointed me; I withdrew a little while at a Mystery, as much as was needful to examine myself; now I come in with a Mystery, bringing with me the Day as a good defender of my cowardice and weakness; that He Who to-day rose again from the dead may renew me also by His Spirit; and, clothing me with the new Man, may give me to His New Creation, to those who are begotten after God, as a good modeller and teacher for Christ, willingly both dying with Him and rising again with Him.

III. Yesterday the Lamb was slain and the door-posts were anointed,[η] and Egypt bewailed her Firstborn, and the Destroyer passed us over, and the Seal was dreadful and reverend, and we were walled in with the Precious Blood.

α Isa. lxvi. 5. β Ex. iv. 10. γ Jer. i. 6. δ Ex. iv. 27. ε Isa. i. 6.

ς *Mystery*, according to Nicetas, is frequently used by S. Gregory in the sense of *Festival*. He also explains the *Anointing* as meaning the Imposition of hands at Ordination.

η Ex. xii. A fine piece of mystical interpretation.

To-day we have clean escaped from Egypt and from Pharaoh; and there is none to hinder us from keeping a Feast to the Lord our God—the Feast of our Departure; or from celebrating that Feast, not in the old leaven of malice and wickedness, but in the unleavened bread of sincerity and truth,[α] carrying with us nothing of ungodly and Egyptian leaven.

IV. Yesterday I was crucified with Him; to-day I am glorified with Him; yesterday I died with Him; to-day I am quickened with Him; yesterday I was buried with Him; to-day I rise with Him. But let us offer to Him Who suffered and rose again for us—you will think perhaps that I am going to say gold, or silver, or woven work or transparent and costly stones, the mere passing material of earth, that remains here below, and is for the most part always possessed by bad men, slaves of the world and of the Prince of the world. Let us offer *ourselves*, the possession most precious to God, and most fitting; let us give back to the Image what is made after the Image. Let us recognize our Dignity; let us honour our Archetype; let us know the power of the Mystery, and for what Christ died.

V. Let us become like Christ, since Christ became like us. Let us become God's for His sake, since He for ours became Man. He assumed the worse that He might give us the better; He became poor that we through His poverty might be rich;[β] He took upon Him the form of a servant that we might receive back our liberty; He came down that we might be exalted; He was tempted that we might conquer; He was dishonoured that He might glorify us; He died that He might save us; He ascended that He might draw to Himself us, who were lying low in the Fall of sin. Let us give *all*, offer *all*, to Him Who gave Himself a Ransom and a Reconciliation for us. But one can give nothing like oneself, understanding the Mystery, and becoming for His sake all that He became for ours.

α 1 Cor. v. 8. β 2 Cor. viii. 9.

VI. As you see, He offers you a Shepherd; for this is what your Good Shepherd,[α] who lays down his life for his sheep, is hoping and praying for, and he asks from you his subjects; and he gives you himself double instead of single, and makes the staff of his old age a staff for your spirit. And he adds to the inanimate temple a living one; to that exceedingly beautiful and heavenly shrine, this poor and small one,[β] yet to him of great value, and built too with much sweat and many labours. Would that I could say it is worthy of his labours. And he places at your disposal all that belongs to him (O great generosity!—or it would be truer to say, O fatherly love!) his hoar hairs, his youth, the temple, the high priest, the testator, the heir, the discourses which you were longing for; and of these not such as are vain and poured out into the air, and which reach no further than the outward ear; but those which the Spirit writes and engraves on tables of stone, or of flesh, not merely superficially graven, nor easily to be rubbed off, but marked very deep, not with ink, but with grace.

VII. These are the gifts given you by this august Abraham, this honourable and reverend Head, this Patriarch, this Restingplace of all good, this Standard of virtue, this Perfection of the Priesthood, who to-day is bringing to the Lord his willing Sacrifice, his only Son,[γ] him of the promise. Do you on your side offer to God and to us obedience to your Pastors, dwelling in a place of herbage, and being fed by water of refreshment;[δ] knowing your Shepherd well, and being known by him;[ε] and following when he calls you as a Shepherd frankly through the door; but not following a stranger climbing up into the fold like a robber and a traitor; nor listening to a strange voice when such would take you away by stealth and scatter you from the truth on mountains,[ζ] and in deserts, and pitfalls, and places which the Lord does not visit; and would lead you away from the sound Faith in the Father, the Son, and the Holy Ghost, the One Power and Godhead, Whose Voice my sheep always heard (and may they always hear it), but with deceitful and corrupt words would tear them from their true Shepherd. From which may we all be kept, Shepherd and flock, as from a poisoned and deadly pasture; guiding and being guided far away from it, that we may all be one in Christ Jesus our Lord, now and unto the heavenly rest. To Whom be the glory and the might for ever and ever. Amen.

α NICETAS says that this refers to S. GREGORY'S Father, who had ordained him Priest, to assist him in the Cure of Souls, and whose one desire was that his Son might succeed him in the Bishopric.

β S. GREGORY'S father had, according to the same authority, rebuilt the Church at Nazianus with great splendour. He thinks that the expression "heavenly" may refer to the great dome. The "living temple" is of course S. Gregory himself.

γ S. GREGORY had an elder sister GORGONIA, and a younger brother CAESARIUS, so that this expression must not be taken too literally, but is rather to be read in connection with the "promise," his Mother having looked upon his birth as a special answer to prayer, and having dedicated him to God from his infancy.

δ Ps. xxiii. 2. ε John x. 14. ζ Ezek. xxxiv. 6.

INTRODUCTION TO ORATION II.

It is generally agreed that this Oration was not intended for oral delivery. Its object was to explain and defend S. Gregory's recent conduct, which had been severely criticised by his friends at Nazianzus. He had been recalled by his father probably during the year A.D. 361 from Pontus, where he had spent several years in monastic seclusion with his friend S. Basil. His father, not content with his son's presence at home as a support for his declining years, and feeling assured of his fitness for the sacred office, had proceeded, with the loudly expressed approval of the congregation, in spite of Gregory's reluctance, to ordain him to the priesthood on Christmas Day A.D. 361. S. Gregory, even after the lapse of many years, speaks of his ordination as an act of tyranny, and at the time, stung almost to madness, as an ox by a gadfly, rushed away again to Pontus, to bury in its congenial solitude, consoled by an intimate friend's deep sympathy, his wounded feelings. Before long the sense of duty reasserted itself, and he returned to his post at his father's side before Easter A.D. 362. On Easter Day he delivered his first Oration before a congregation whose scantiness marked the displeasure with which the people of Nazianzus had viewed his conduct. Accordingly he set himself to supply them in this Oration with a full explanation of the motives which had led to his retirement. At the same time, as the secondary title of the Oration shows, he has supplied an exposition of the obligations and dignity of the Priestly Office which has been drawn upon by all later writers on the subject. S. Chrysostom in his well-known treatise, S. Gregory the Great in his Pastoral Care, and Bossuet in his panegyric on S. Paul, have done little more than summarise the material or develop the considerations contained in this eloquent and elaborate dissertation.

ORATION II.

IN DEFENCE OF HIS FLIGHT TO PONTUS, AND HIS RETURN, AFTER HIS ORDINATION TO THE PRIESTHOOD, WITH AN EXPOSITION OF THE CHARACTER OF THE PRIESTLY OFFICE.

1. I have been defeated, and own my defeat. I subjected myself to the Lord, and

prayed unto Him.[α] Let the most blessed David supply my exordium, or rather let Him Who spoke in David, and even now yet speaks through him. For indeed the very best order of beginning every speech and action, is to begin from God,[β] and to end in God. As to the cause, either of my original revolt and cowardice, in which I got me away far off, and remained[γ] away from you for a time, which perhaps seemed long to those who missed me; or of the present gentleness and change of mind, in which I have given myself up again to you, men may think and speak in different ways, according to the hatred or love they bear me, on the one side refusing to acquit me of the charges alleged, on the other giving me a hearty welcome. For nothing is so pleasant to men as talking of other people's business, especially under the influence of affection or hatred, which often almost entirely blinds us to the truth. I will, however, myself, unabashed, set forth the truth, and arbitrate with justice between the two parties, which accuse or gallantly defend us, by, on the one side, accusing myself, on the other, undertaking my own defence.

2. Accordingly, that my speech may proceed in due order, I apply myself to the question which arose first, that of cowardice. For I cannot endure that any of those who watch with interest the success, or the contrary, of my efforts, should be put to confusion on my account, since it has pleased God that our affairs should be of some consequence to Christians, so I will by my defence relieve, if there be any such, those who have already suffered; for it is well, as far as possible, and as reason allows, to shrink from causing, through our sin or suspicion, any offence or stumbling-block to the community: inasmuch as we know how inevitably even those who offend one of the little ones[δ] will incur the severest punishment at the hands of Him who cannot lie.

3. For my present position is due, my good people, not to inexperience and ignorance, nay indeed, that I may boast myself a little,[ε] neither is it due to contempt for the divine laws and ordinances. Now, just as in the body there is[ζ] one member[η] which rules and, so to say, presides, while another is ruled over and subject; so too in the churches, God has ordained, according either to a law of equality, which admits of an order of merit, or to one of providence, by which He has knit all together, that those for whom such treatment is beneficial, should be subject to pastoral care and rule, and be guided by word and deed in the path of duty; while others should be pastors and teachers,[α] for the perfecting of the church, those, I mean, who surpass the majority in virtue and nearness to God, performing the functions of the soul in the body, and of the intellect in the soul; in order that both may be so united and compacted together, that, although one is lacking and another is pre-eminent, they may, like the members of our bodies, be so combined and knit together by the harmony of the Spirit, as to form one perfect body,[β] really worthy of Christ Himself, our Head.[γ]

4. I am aware then that anarchy[δ] and disorder cannot be more advantageous than order and rule, either to other creatures or to men; nay, this is true of men in the highest possible degree, because the interests at stake in their case are greater; since it is a great thing[ε] for them, even if they fail of their highest purpose—to be free from sin—to attain at least to that which is second best, restoration from sin. Since this seems right and just, it is, I take it, equally wrong and disorderly that all should wish to rule, and that no one should accept[ζ] it. For if all men were to shirk this office, whether it must be called a ministry or a leadership, the fair fulness[η] of the Church would be halting in the highest degree, and in fact cease to be fair. And further, where, and by whom would God be worshipped among us in those mystic and elevating rites which are our greatest and most precious privilege, if there were neither king, nor governor, nor priesthood, nor sacrifice,[θ] nor all those highest offices to the loss of which, for their great sins, men were of old condemned in consequence of their disobedience?

5. Nor indeed is it strange or inconsistent for the majority of those who are devoted to the study of divine things, to ascend to rule from being ruled, nor does it overstep the limits laid down by philosophy,[ι] or involve disgrace;

α Ps. xxxvii. 7 (LXX).

β *Begin from God.* Possibly an adaptation of the exordium of Theocr. Idyll, xvii. 1. ἐκ Διὸς ἀρχώμεσθα, καὶ ἐις Δία λήγετε, μοῖσαι. "Let Zeus inspire our opening strain. And, Muses, end your song in Zeus again." Cf. Demosth. Epist. 1.

γ Ps. lv. 7. δ S. Matt. xviii. 6. ε 2 Cor. xi. 16.

ζ *One member.* The Ben. editors object to this translation (which is that of Rufinus, Billius and Gabriel) as inconsistent with the following allusion to the relation of the *soul* to the body. It seems, however, more in harmony with the figure of S. Paul, who compares the arrangement of the *members* of the body to the hierarchy of the Church. η Rom. xii. 4; 1 Cor. xii. 12.

α Eph. iv. 11. β 1 Cor. xii. 20; Eph. iv. 16. γ Eph. iv. 15.

δ *Anarchy, &c.* Comp. Plato Legg. XII. 2.

ε *A great thing.* The Ben. editors note the obscurity of the original here.

ζ *Accept*, δέχεσθαι. Many MSS. have ἄρχεσθαι, preserving the play upon the word ἄρχειν. The latter reading, the Ben. editors suggest, *may* have an active sense, as Hom. Il. II. 345.

η Eph. i. 23. θ Hos. iii. 4.

ι *Philosophy.* φιλοσοφία is used by S. Greg. and other Fathers in various senses, not always clearly distinguishable. Sometimes it refers to the ancient philosophical teachers and schools: sometimes to the Christian philosophy, which inculcates Divine truth,

any more than for an excellent sailor to become a lookout-man, and for a lookout-man, who has successfully kept watch over the winds, to be entrusted with the helm; or, if you will, for a brave soldier to be made a captain, and a good captain to become a general, and have committed to him the conduct of the whole campaign. Nor again, as perhaps some of those absurd and tiresome people may suppose, who judge of others' feelings by their own, was I ashamed of the rank of this grade from my desire for a higher. I was not so ignorant either of its divine greatness or human low estate, as to think it no great thing for a created nature, to approach in however slight degree to God, Who alone is most glorious and illustrious, and surpasses in purity every nature, material and immaterial alike.

6. What then were my feelings, and what was the reason of my disobedience? For to most men I did not at the time seem consistent with myself, or to be such as they had known me, but to have undergone some deterioration, and to exhibit greater resistance and self-will than was right. And the causes of this you have long been desirous to hear. First, and most important, I was astounded at the unexpectedness of what had occurred, as people are terrified by sudden noises; and, losing the control of my reasoning faculties, my self-respect, which had hitherto controlled me, gave way. In the next place, there came over me an eager longing[α] for the blessings of calm and retirement, of which I had from the first been enamoured to a higher degree, I imagine, than any other student of letters, and which amidst the greatest and most threatening dangers I had promised to God, and of which I had also had so much experience, that I was then upon its threshold, my longing having in consequence been greatly kindled, so that I could not submit to be thrust into the midst of a life of turmoil by an arbitrary act of oppression, and to be torn away by force from the holy sanctuary of such a life as this.

7. For nothing seemed to me so desirable as to close the doors of my senses, and, escaping from the flesh and the world, collected within myself, having no further connection than was absolutely necessary with human affairs, and speaking to myself and to God,[β] to live superior to visible things, ever preserving in myself the divine impressions pure and unmixed with the erring tokens of this lower world, and both being, and constantly growing more and more to be, a real unspotted mirror of God and divine things, as light is added to light, and what was still dark grew clearer, enjoying already by hope the blessings of the world to come, roaming about with the angels, even now being above the earth by having forsaken it, and stationed on high by the Spirit. If any of you has been possessed by this longing, he knows what I mean and will sympathise with my feelings at that time. For, perhaps, I ought not to expect to persuade most people by what I say, since they are unhappily disposed to laugh at such things, either from their own thoughtlessness, or from the influence of men unworthy of the promise, who have bestowed upon that which is good an evil name, calling philosophy nonsense, aided by envy and the evil tendencies of the mob, who are ever inclined to grow worse: so that they are constantly occupied with one of two sins, either the commission of evil, or the discrediting of good.

8. I was influenced besides by another feeling, whether base or noble I do not know, but I will speak out to you all my secrets. I was ashamed of all those others, who, without being better than ordinary people, nay, it is a great thing if they be not worse, with unwashen hands,[α] as the saying runs, and uninitiated souls, intrude into the most sacred offices; and, before becoming worthy to approach the temples, they lay claim to the sanctuary,[β] and they push and thrust around the holy table, as if they thought this order to be a means of livelihood, instead of a pattern of virtue, or an absolute authority, instead of a ministry of which we must give account. In fact they are almost more in number than those whom they govern; pitiable as regards piety,[γ] and unfortunate in their dignity; so that, it seems to me, they will not, as time and this evil alike progress, have any one left to rule, when all are teachers, instead of, as the promise says, taught of God,[δ] and all prophesy,[ε] so that even "Saul is among the prophets,"[ζ] according to the ancient history and proverb. For at no time, either now or in former days, amid the rise and fall of various developments, has there ever been such

and teaches the principles of a good and holy life: sometimes to the practice of these principles, either in regard to some special virtue, *e.g.* patience, or, in general, in the lives of individual Christians, and further, as involving the most careful and extensive reduction of these principles to practice—the discipline of the monastic life. Cf. Suicer. in verb.

α *Eager longing.* Nearly all MSS. read "pity"—which would have to be understood in the sense of "regretful affection."

β 1 Cor. xiv. 28.

α S. Mark vii. 5.

β *The sanctuary.* i.e. That which gave the right to a place in the sanctuary,—the priesthood. Billius wrongly takes it of the episcopate.

γ *Piety*—for it is a mere external pretence, deceiving themselves as well as others. εἰσέβαια here has the double sense of piety and orthodoxy—the former being the more prominent.

δ Is. liv. 13; S. John vi. 45.

ε Numb. xi. 29; 1 Cor. xiv. 24.

ζ 1 Sam. x. 11; xix. 24.

an abundance, as now exists among Christians, of disgrace and abuses of this kind. And, if to stay this current is beyond our powers, at any rate it is not the least important duty of religion to testify the hatred and shame we feel for it.

9. Lastly, there is a matter more serious than any which I have mentioned, for I am now coming to the finale[a] of the question: and I will not deceive you; for that would not be lawful in regard to topics of such moment. I did not, nor do I now, think myself qualified to rule a flock or herd, or to have authority over the souls of men. For in their case it is sufficient to render the herd or flock as stout and fat as possible; and with this object the neatherd and shepherd will look for well watered and rich pastures, and will drive his charge from pasture to pasture, and allow them to rest, or arouse, or recall them, sometimes with his staff, most often with his pipe; and with the exception of occasional struggles with wolves, or attention to the sickly, most of his time will be devoted to the oak and the shade and his pipes, while he reclines on the beautiful grass, and beside the cool water, and shakes down his couch in a breezy spot, and ever and anon sings a love ditty, with his cup by his side, and talks to his bullocks or his flock, the fattest of which supply his banquets or his pay. But no one ever has thought of the virtue of flocks or herds; for indeed of what virtue are they capable? Or who has regarded their advantage as more important than his own pleasure?

10. But in the case of man, hard as it is for him to learn how to submit to rule, it seems far harder to know how to rule over men, and hardest of all, with this rule of ours, which leads them by the divine law, and to God, for its risk is, in the eyes of a thoughtful man, proportionate to its height and dignity. For, first of all, he must, like silver or gold, though in general circulation in all kinds of seasons and affairs, never ring false or alloyed, or give token of any inferior matter, needing further refinement in the fire;[β] or else, the wider his rule, the greater evil he will be. Since the injury which extends to many is greater than that which is confined to a single individual.

11. For it is not so easy to dye deeply a piece of cloth, or to impregnate with odours, foul or the reverse, whatever comes near to them; nor is it so easy for the fatal vapour, which is rightly called a pestilence, to infect the air, and through the air to gain access to living beings, as it is for the vice of a superior to take most speedy possession of his subjects, and that with far greater facility than virtue its opposite. For it is in this that wickedness especially has the advantage over goodness, and most distressing it is to me to perceive it, that vice is something attractive and ready at hand, and that nothing is so easy as to become evil, even without any one to lead us on to it; while the attainment of virtue is rare and difficult, even where there is much to attract and encourage us. And it is this, I think, which the most blessed Haggai had before his eyes, in his wonderful and most true figure:[a]—"Ask the priests concerning the law, saying: If holy flesh borne in a garment touch meat or drink or vessel, will it sanctify what is in contact with it? And when they said No; ask again if any of these things touch what is unclean, does it not at once partake of the pollution? For they will surely tell you that it does partake of it, and does not continue clean in spite of the contact."

12. What does he mean by this? As I take it, that goodness can with difficulty gain a hold upon human nature, like fire upon green wood; while most men are ready and disposed to join in evil, like stubble,[β] I mean, ready for a spark and a wind, which is easily kindled and consumed from its dryness. For more quickly would any one take part in evil with slight inducement to its full extent, than in good which is fully set before him to a slight degree. For indeed a little wormwood most quickly imparts its bitterness to honey; while not even double the quantity of honey can impart its sweetness to wormwood: and the withdrawal of a small pebble would draw headlong a whole river, though it would be difficult for the strongest dam to restrain or stay its course.

13. This then is the first point in what we have said, which it is right for us to guard against, viz.: being found to be bad painters[γ] of the charms of virtue, and still more, if not, perhaps, models for poor painters, poor models for the people, or barely escaping the proverb, that we undertake to heal others[δ] while ourselves are full of sores.

14. In the second place, although a man has kept himself pure from sin, even in a very high degree; I do not know that even this is sufficient for one who is to instruct others in virtue. For he who has received this charge, not only needs to be free from evil, for evil is,

α *The finale of the question*, or "the main conclusion of my subject," lit. "the colophon of my reason." λόγος cannot here mean "of my speech," for it has only just begun.

β Cf. 1 Cor. iii. 12.

α Hagg. ii. 12 *et seq.*

β Job xxi. 18; Ps. lxxxiii. 13; Isai. v. 24; Joel ii. 5.

γ *Painters*, i.e. in our discourses; *models* by our lives and examples.

δ S. Luke iv. 23.

in the eyes of most of those under his care, most disgraceful, but also to be eminent in good, according to the command, "Depart from evil and do good."[α] And he must not only wipe out the traces of vice from his soul, but also inscribe better ones, so as to outstrip men further in virtue than he is superior to them in dignity. He should know no limits in goodness or spiritual progress, and should dwell upon the loss of what is still beyond him, rather than the gain of what he has attained, and consider that which is beneath his feet a step to that which comes next: and not think it a great gain to excel ordinary people, but a loss to fall short of what we ought to be: and to measure his success by the commandment and not by his neighbours, whether they be evil, or to some extent proficient in virtue: and to weigh virtue in no small scales, inasmuch as it is due to the Most High, "from Whom are all things, and to Whom are all things."[β]

15. Nor must he suppose that the same things are suitable to all, just as all have not the same stature, nor are the features of the face, nor the nature of animals, nor the qualities of soil, nor the beauty and size of the stars, in all cases the same: but he must consider base conduct a fault in a private individual, and deserving of chastisement under the hard rule of the law; while in the case of a ruler or leader it is a fault not to attain to the highest possible excellence, and always make progress in goodness, if indeed he is, by his high degree of virtue, to draw his people to an ordinary degree, not by the force of authority, but by the influence of persuasion. For what is involuntary apart from its being the result of oppression, is neither meritorious nor durable. For what is forced, like a plant[γ] violently drawn aside by our hands, when set free, returns to what it was before, but that which is the result of choice is both most legitimate and enduring, for it is preserved by the bond of good will. And so our law and our lawgiver enjoin upon us most strictly that we should "tend the flock not by constraint but willingly."[δ]

16. But granted that a man is free from vice, and has reached the greatest heights of virtue: I do not see what knowledge or power would justify him in venturing upon this office. For the guiding of man, the most variable and manifold of creatures, seems to me in very deed to be the art of arts[ε] and science of sciences. Any one may recognize this, by comparing the work of the physician of souls with the treatment of the body; and noticing that, laborious as the latter is, ours is more laborious, and of more consequence, from the nature of its subject matter, the power of its science, and the object of its exercise. The one labours about bodies, and perishable failing matter, which absolutely must be dissolved and undergo its fate,[α] even if upon this occasion by the aid of art it can surmount the disturbance within itself, being dissolved by disease or time in submission to the law of nature, since it cannot rise above its own limitations.

17. The other is concerned with the soul, which comes from God and is divine, and partakes of the heavenly nobility, and presses on to it, even if it be bound to an inferior nature. Perhaps indeed there are other reasons also for this, which only God, Who bound them together, and those who are instructed by God in such mysteries, can know, but as far as I, and men like myself can perceive, there are two: one, that it may inherit the glory above by means of a struggle and wrestling[β] with things below, being tried as gold in the fire[γ] by things here, and gain the objects of our hope as a prize of virtue, and not merely as the gift of God. This, indeed, was the will of Supreme Goodness, to make the good even our own, not only because sown in our nature, but because cultivated by our own choice, and by the motions of our will,[δ] free to act in either direction. The second reason is, that it may draw to itself and raise to heaven the lower nature, by gradually freeing it from its grossness, in order that the soul may be to the body what God is to the soul, itself leading on the matter which ministers to it, and uniting it, as its fellow-servant, to God.

18. Place and time and age and season and the like are the subjects of a physician's scrutiny; he will prescribe medicines and diet, and guard against things injurious, that the desires of the sick may not be a hindrance to his art. Sometimes, and in certain cases, he will make use of the cautery or the knife or the severer remedies; but none of these, laborious and hard as they may seem, is so difficult as the diagnosis and cure of our habits, passions, lives, wills, and whatever else is within us, by banishing from our compound nature everything brutal and fierce, and introducing and establishing in their stead what is gentle and dear

α Ps. xxxvii. 27. β Rom. xi. 35.
γ *A plant.* Cf. Orat. vi. 8, xxiii. 1. A favourite figure of S. Gregory. δ 1 Pet. v. 2.
ε *The art of arts.* This is the original of the frequently quoted commonplace, which in S. Gregory the Great's Pastoral Care, i. 1, takes the form "ars artium est regimen animarum."

α Gen. iii. 19. β Eph. vi. 12. γ 1 Pet. i. 7.
δ *Our will.* Clémencet compares S. Bernard, de Gratia et Libero Arbitrio, xiv. 47 (tom. i. 1397, Gaume). Petavius, de Incarn., tom. v., p. 416, lib. IX., iii., 11, comments on this passage in treating of free will.

to God, and arbitrating fairly between soul and body; not allowing the superior to be overpowered by the inferior, which would be the greatest injustice; but subjecting to the ruling and leading power that which naturally takes the second place: as indeed the divine law enjoins, which is most excellently imposed on His whole creation, whether visible or beyond our ken.

19. This further point does not escape me, that the nature of all these objects of the watchfulness of the physician remains the same, and does not evolve out of itself any crafty opposition, or contrivance hostile to the appliances of his art, nay, it is rather the treatment which modifies its subject matter,[α] except where some slight insubordination occurs on the part of the patient, which it is not difficult to prevent or restrain. But in our case, human prudence and selfishness, and the want of training and inclination to yield ready submission are a very great obstacle to advance in virtue, amounting almost to an armed resistance to those who are wishful to help us. And the very eagerness with which we should lay bare our sickness to our spiritual physicians, we employ in avoiding this treatment,[β] and shew our bravery by struggling against what is for our own interest, our skill in shunning what is for our health.

20. For we either hide away our sin, cloaking it over in the depth of our soul, like some festering and malignant disease, as if by escaping the notice of men we could escape the mighty eye of God and justice. Or else we allege excuses in our sins,[γ] by devising pleas in defence of our falls, or tightly closing our ears, like the deaf adder that stoppeth her ears, we are obstinate in refusing to hear the voice of the charmer, and be treated with the medicines of wisdom,[δ] by which spiritual sickness is healed. Or, lastly, those of us who are most daring and self-willed shamelessly brazen out our sin before those who would heal it, marching with bared head, as the saying is, into all kinds of transgression. O what madness, if there be no term more fitting for this state of mind! Those whom we ought to love as our benefactors we keep off, as if they were our enemies, hating those who reprove in the gates, and abhorring the righteous word;[ε] and we think that we shall succeed in the war that we are waging against those who are well disposed to us by doing ourselves all the harm we can, like men who imagine they are

α *Its subject matter*, i.e. the affection of the sick body, which it is the object of medicine to change to its opposite. So Combefis.
β *This treatment:* the treatment of the spiritual physician.
γ Ps. cxli. 4 (LXX.). δ Ps. lviii. 5, 6 (LXX.).
ε Amos v. 10.

consuming the flesh of others when they are really fastening upon their own.

21. For these reasons I allege that our office as physicians far exceeds in toilsomeness, and consequently in worth, that which is confined to the body; and further, because the latter is mainly concerned with the surface, and only in a slight degree investigates the causes which are deeply hidden. But the whole of our treatment and exertion is concerned with the hidden man of the heart,[α] and our warfare is directed against that adversary and foe within us, who uses ourselves as his weapons against ourselves, and, most fearful of all, hands us over to the death of sin. In opposition then, to these foes we are in need of great and perfect faith, and of still greater co-operation on the part of God, and, as I am persuaded, of no slight countermanœuvring on our own part, which must manifest itself both in word and deed, if ourselves, the most precious possession we have, are to be duly tended and cleansed and made as deserving as possible.

22. To turn however to the ends in view in each of these forms of healing, for this point is still left to be considered, the one preserves, if it already exists, the health and good habit of the flesh, or if absent, recalls it; though it is not yet clear whether or not these will be for the advantage of those who possess them, since their opposites very often confer a greater benefit on those who have them, just as poverty and wealth, renown or disgrace, a low or brilliant position, and all other circumstances, which are naturally indifferent, and do not incline in one direction more than in another, produce a good or bad effect according to the will of, and the manner in which they are used by the persons who experience them. But the scope of our art is to provide the soul with wings, to rescue it from the world and give it to God, and to watch over that which is in His image,[β] if it abides, to take it by the hand, if it is in danger, or restore it, if ruined, to make Christ to dwell in the heart[γ] by the Spirit: and, in short, to deify, and bestow heavenly bliss upon, one who belongs to the heavenly host.

23. This is the wish of our schoolmaster[δ] the law, of the prophets who intervened between Christ and the law, of Christ who is the fulfiller and end[ε] of the spiritual law; of the emptied Godhead,[ζ] of the assumed flesh,[η] of the novel union between God and man, one consisting[θ] of two, and both in one. This is

α 1 Pet. iii, 4. β Gen. i. 26. γ Eph. iii. 17.
δ Gal. iii. 24. ε Heb. xii. 2. ζ Phil. ii. 7. η Heb. ii. 14.
θ *One consisting*, &c. "These words" says Gabriel, "are indeed a two-edged sword against the heretics, for one clause

why God was united[α] to the flesh by means of the soul,[β] and natures so separate were knit together by the affinity to each of the element which mediated between them: so all became one for the sake of all, and for the sake of one, our progenitor, the soul because of the soul which was disobedient, the flesh because of the flesh which co-operated with it and shared in its condemnation, Christ, Who was superior to, and beyond the reach of, sin, because of Adam, who became subject to sin.

24. This is why the new was substituted for the old,[γ] why He Who suffered was for suffering recalled to life, why each property of His, Who was above us, was interchanged with each of ours, why the new mystery took place of the dispensation, due to loving kindness which deals with him who fell through disobedience. This is the reason for the generation and the virgin, for the manger and Bethlehem; the generation on behalf of the creation,[δ] the virgin on behalf of the woman,[ε] Bethlehem[ς] because of Eden, the manger because of the garden, small and visible things on behalf of great and hidden things. This is why the angels[η] glorified first the heavenly, then the earthly,[θ] why the shepherds saw the glory over the Lamb and the Shepherd, why the star led the Magi to worship and offer gifts,[ι] in order that idolatry might be destroyed. This is why Jesus was baptized,[κ] and received testimony from above, and fasted,[λ] and was tempted, and overcame him who had overcome. This is why devils were cast out,[μ] and diseases healed, and the mighty preaching was entrusted to, and successfully proclaimed by men of low estate.

25. This is why the heathen rage and the peoples imagine vain things;[ν] why tree[ξ] is set over against tree,[ο] hands against hand, the one stretched out in self indulgence,[π] the others in generosity; the one unrestrained, the others fixed by nails,[ρ] the one expelling Adam, the other reconciling the ends of the earth. This is the reason of the lifting up to atone for the fall, and of the gall for the tasting, and of the thorny crown for the dominion of evil, and of death for death, and of darkness for the sake of light, and of burial for the return to the ground, and of resurrection for the sake of resurrection.[α] All these are a training from God for us, and a healing for our weakness, restoring the old Adam to the place whence he fell, and conducting us to the tree of life,[β] from which the tree of knowledge estranged us, when partaken of unseasonably, and improperly.

26. Of this healing we, who are set over others, are the ministers and fellow-labourers;[γ] for whom it is a great thing to recognise and heal their own passions and sicknesses: or rather, not really a great thing, only the viciousness of most of those who belong to this order has made me say so: but a much greater thing is the power to heal and skilfully cleanse those of others, to the advantage both of those who are in want of healing and of those whose charge it is to heal.

27. Again, the healers of our bodies will have their labours and vigils and cares, of which we are aware; and will reap a harvest of pain for themselves from the distresses of others, as one of their wise men[δ] said; and will provide for the use of those who need them, both the results of their own labours and investigations, and what they have been able to borrow from others: and they consider none, even of the minutest details, which they discover, or which elude their search, as having other than an important influence upon health or danger. And what is the object of all this? That a man may live some days longer on the earth, though he is possibly not a good man, but one of the most depraved, for whom it had perhaps been better, because of his badness, to have died long ago, in order to be set free from vice, the most serious of sicknesses. But, suppose he is a good man, how long will he be able to live? For ever? Or what will he gain from life here, from which it is the greatest of blessings, if a man be sane and sensible, to seek to be set free?

28. But we, upon whose efforts is staked the salvation of a soul, a being blessed and immortal, and destined for undying chastisement or praise, for its vice or virtue,—what a struggle ought ours to be, and how great skill do we require to treat, or get men treated properly, and to change their life, and give up the clay to the spirit. For men and women, young

---

mortally wounds Nestorius who separates the Divine from the Human Nature—the other Eutyches, who empties the human into the Divine."

α *Was united*, ἀνεκράθη, lit., "was blended"—cf. Orat. xxxviii. 13. This and similar terms used by Gregory and his contemporaries in an orthodox sense were laid aside by later Fathers, in consequence of their having been perverted in favor of the Eutychian heresy.

β *By means of the soul*, Cf. Orat. xxix. 19; xxxviii. 13; Epist. 101 (tom. 2, p. 90 A.): Poem. Dogmat., x., 55–61 (tom. 2, p. 256); Petavius de Incarn., IV., xiii., 2.

γ Heb. viii. 8–13.

δ Lit. "of the formation"—the substantive here corresponds to the verb in Gen. ii. 7 (LXX.).

ε Gen. ii. 7.

ς S. Luke ii. 7.

η S. Lu. ii. 14.

θ 1 Cor. xv. 49.

ι S. Matt. ii. 9, 11.

κ S. Matt. iii. 13, 17.

λ S. Matt. iv. 2.

μ S. Matt. x. 7, 8.

ν Ps. ii. 1.

ξ Gen. iii. 3. *Why tree*, &c. A striking contrast of the means of Redemption by the Cross of Christ with the circumstances of the Fall.

ο S. John xix. 17.

π Gen. iii. 6–23.

ρ S. Matt. xxvii. 35.

α *For the sake of resurrection.* One translator carries on the contrast, and renders "to atone for the insurrection," sc. of Adam. The preposition ὑπερ seems decisive against this.

β Rev. ii. 7; xxii. 14.

γ 1 Cor. iii. 9; iv. 1; 2 Cor. vi. 1.

δ *One of their wise men*, the author of the treatise περὶ φυσῶν, ascribed to Hippocrates.

and old, rich and poor, the sanguine and despondent, the sick and whole, rulers and ruled, the wise and ignorant, the cowardly and courageous, the wrathful and meek, the successful and failing, do not require the same instruction and encouragement.

29. And if you examine more closely, how great is the distinction between the married and the unmarried, and among the latter between hermits and those who[a] live together in community, between those who are proficient and advanced in contemplation and those who barely hold on the straight course, between townsfolk again and rustics, between the simple and the designing, between men of business and men of leisure, between those who have met with reverses and those who are prosperous and ignorant of misfortune. For these classes differ sometimes more widely from each other in their desires and passions than in their physical characteristics; or, if you will, in the mixtures and blendings of the elements of which we are composed, and, therefore, to regulate them is no easy task.

30. As then the same medicine and the same food are not in every case administered to men's bodies, but a difference is made according to their degree of health or infirmity; so also are souls treated with varying instruction and guidance. To this treatment witness is borne by those who have had experience of it. Some are led by doctrine, others trained by example; some need the spur, others the curb; some are sluggish and hard to rouse to the good, and must be stirred up by being smitten with the word; others are immoderately fervent in spirit, with impulses difficult to restrain, like thoroughbred colts, who run wide of the turning post, and to improve them the word must have a restraining and checking influence.

31. Some are benefited by praise, others by blame, both being applied in season; while if out of season, or unreasonable, they are injurious; some are set right by encouragement, others by rebuke; some, when taken to task in public, others, when privately corrected. For some are wont to despise private admonitions, but are recalled to their senses by the condemnation of a number of people, while others, who would grow reckless under reproof openly given, accept rebuke because it is in secret, and yield obedience in return for sympathy.

32. Upon some it is needful to keep a close watch, even in the minutest details, because if they think they are unperceived (as they would contrive to be), they are puffed up with the idea of their own wisdom. Of others it is better to take no notice, but seeing not to see, and hearing not to hear them, according to the proverb, that we may not drive them to despair, under the depressing influence of repeated reproofs, and at last to utter recklessness, when they have lost the sense of self-respect, the source of persuasiveness.[a] In some cases we must even be angry, without feeling angry, or treat them with a disdain we do not feel, or manifest despair, though we do not really despair of them, according to the needs of their nature. Others again we must treat with condescension[β] and lowliness, aiding them readily to conceive a hope of better things. Some it is often more advantageous to conquer—by others to be overcome, and to praise or deprecate, in one case wealth and power, in another poverty and failure.

33. For our treatment does not correspond with virtue and vice, one of which is most excellent and beneficial at all times and in all cases, and the other most evil and harmful; and, instead of one and the same of our medicines invariably proving either most wholesome or most dangerous in the same cases—be it severity or gentleness, or any of the others which we have enumerated—in some cases it proves good and useful, in others again it has the contrary effect, according, I suppose, as time and circumstance and the disposition of the patient admit. Now to set before you the distinction between all these things, and give you a perfectly exact view of them, so that you may in brief comprehend the medical art, is quite impossible, even for one in the highest degree qualified by care and skill: but actual experience and practice are requisite to form[γ] a medical system and a medical man.

34. This, however, I take to be generally admitted—that just as it is not safe for those who walk on a lofty tight rope to lean to either side, for even though the inclination seems slight, it has no slight consequences, but

---

a *Those who*, &c. μιγάδας, cf. xxi., 10, where μοναδικοὶ and οἱ τῆς ἐρημίας are distinguished from μιγάδες and οἱ τῆς ἐπιμιξίας. Clémencet here holds that οἱ τῆς ἐρημίας are hermits as distinguished from cœnobites, but does not hint at any further subdivision between the κοινωνικοὶ and the μιγάδες. Cf. also xliii. 62; xxi. 19. Montaut, "Revue Critique, &c." (pp. 48–52) attempts to distinguish between the μιγάδες and the κοινωνικοί. But although he confirms the overthrow by Clémencet of the views of previous translators, he leaves Clémencet's own position really unweakened. S. Gregory uses the two terms as practically convertible. In xxi., § 19, (which Montaut misinterprets) he explains that the life of the cœnobite is a hermit-life in its relation to the world which he has forsaken, while it has opportunities in community-life for the growth of those virtues which are required by the relation of man to man. Cf. Bened. edition (Clémencet), Præf. Gener., Pars. II., § iii. sub finem.

a *The source of persuasiveness*, lit., "the medicine of persuasion."

β *condescension*, lit., 'equity,' dealing gently with their weakness, not exacting the literal fulfilment of the law.

γ *Are requisite to form*, lit., by 'actual . . . they become clear to.'

their safety depends upon their perfect balance: so in the case of one of us, if he leans to either side, whether from vice or ignorance, no slight danger of a fall into sin is incurred, both for himself and those who are led by him. But we must really walk in the King's highway,[α] and take care not to turn aside from it either to the right hand or to the left,[β] as the Proverbs say. For such is the case with our passions, and such in this matter is the task of the good shepherd, if he is to know properly the souls of his flock, and to guide them according to the methods of a pastoral care which is right and just, and worthy of our true Shepherd.

35. In regard to the distribution of the word, to mention last the first of our duties, of that divine and exalted word, which everyone now is ready to discourse upon; if anyone else boldly undertakes it and supposes it within the power of every man's intellect, I am amazed at his intelligence, not to say his folly. To me indeed it seems no slight task, and one requiring no little spiritual power, to give in due season[γ] to each his portion of the word, and to regulate with judgment the truth of our opinions, which are concerned with such subjects as the world or worlds,[δ] matter, soul, mind, intelligent natures, better or worse, providence which holds together and guides the universe, and seems in our experience of it to be governed according to some principle, but one which is at variance with those of earth and of men.

36. Again, they are concerned with our original constitution, and final restoration, the types of the truth, the covenants, the first and second coming of Christ, His incarnation, sufferings and dissolution,[ε] with the resurrection, the last day, the judgment and recompense, whether sad or glorious; I, to crown all, with what we are to think of the original[ζ] and blessed Trinity. Now this involves a very great risk to those who are charged with the illumination[η] of others, if they are to avoid contracting[θ] their doctrine to a single Person, from fear of polytheism, and so leave us empty terms, if we suppose the Father and the Son and the Holy Spirit to be one and the same Person only: or, on the other hand, severing It into three, either foreign and diverse, or disordered and unprincipled, and, so to say, opposed divinities, thus falling from the opposite side into an equally dangerous error: like some distorted plant if bent far back in the opposite direction.

37. For, amid the three infirmities in regard to theology, atheism, Judaism, and polytheism, one of which is patronised by Sabellius the Libyan, another by Arius of Alexandria, and the third by some of the ultra-orthodox among us, what is my position, can I avoid whatever in these three is noxious, and remain within the limits of piety; neither being led astray by the new analysis and synthesis into the atheism[α] of Sabellius, to assert not so much that all are one as that each is nothing, for things which are transferred and pass into each other cease to be that which each one of them is, or that we have an unnaturally compound deity, like those mythical creatures, the subject of a picturesque imagination: nor again, by alleging a plurality of severed natures, according to the well named madness[β] of Arius, becoming involved in a Jewish poverty, and introducing envy into the divine nature, by limiting the Godhead to the Unbegotten One alone, as if afraid that our God would perish, if He were the Father of a real God of equal nature: nor again, by arraying three principles in opposition to, or in alliance with, each other, introducing the Gentile plurality of principles from which we have escaped?

38. It is necessary neither to be so devoted to the Father, as to rob Him of His Fatherhood, for whose Father would He be, if the Son were separated and estranged from Him, by being ranked with the creation, (for an alien being, or one which is combined and confounded with his father, and, for the sense is the same, throws him into confusion, is not a son); nor to be so devoted to Christ, as to neglect to preserve both His Sonship, (for whose son would He be, if His origin were not referred to the Father?) and the rank of the Father as origin, inasmuch as He is the Father and Generator; for He would be the origin of petty and unworthy beings, or rather the term would be used in a petty and unworthy sense, if He were not the origin of Godhead and goodness, which are contemplated in the Son and the Spirit: the former being the Son and the Word, the latter the proceeding and indissoluble Spirit. For both the Unity of the Godhead must be preserved, and the Trinity

α Numb. xx. 17. β Prov. iv. 27. γ S. Luke xii. 42.

δ *Worlds*, i.e. the invisible and visible. of which S. Greg. held that the former was created before the latter. cf. Orat. xviii. 3; xxvii. 10; xxviii. 31; xxxviii. 10; xl. 45.

ε *Dissolution*; some translate 'return'—i.e. of the Ascension; referring the 'resurrection, &c.' to mankind in general.

ζ *Original*. Perhaps better 'supreme.'

η *Illumination*. Some apply this to Holy Baptism, with its preliminary instruction.

θ *Contracting*, i.e. by the Sabellian heresy. A parallel passage in almost identical terms is Orat. xx. 6.

α *Atheism*. This term is used of Sabellianism, xviii. 16. xx. 6. xxi. 13. xliii. 30, in the sense in which it is here explained. Cf. Petav. de Trin. I vi. 3, sqq.

β *Madness* of Arianism, xxi. 13. xxxiv. 8. xliii. 30. This term is applied in a letter of Constantine after the Council of Nicæa. It is called Judaism also Orat. xx. 6 as frequently by S. Athanasius. Cf. Petav. de Trin. I. ix. 8.

of Persons confessed, each with His own property.

39. A suitable and worthy comprehension and exposition of this subject demands a discussion of greater length than the present occasion, or even our life, as I suppose, allows, and, what is more, both now and at all times, the aid of the Spirit, by Whom alone we are able to perceive, to expound, or to embrace, the truth in regard to God. For the pure alone can grasp Him Who is pure and of the same disposition as himself; and I have now briefly dwelt upon the subject, to show how difficult it is to discuss such important questions, especially before a large audience, composed of every age and condition, and needing like an instrument of many strings, to be played upon in various ways; or to find any form of words able to edify them all, and illuminate them with the light of knowledge. For it is not only that there are three sources from which danger springs, understanding, speech, and hearing, so that failure in one, if not in all, is infallibly certain; for either the mind is not illuminated, or the language is feeble, or the hearing, not having been cleansed, fails to comprehend, and accordingly, in one or all respects, the truth must be maimed: but further, what makes the instruction of those who profess to teach any other subject so easy and acceptable—viz. the piety[α] of the audience—on this subject involves difficulty and danger.

40. For having undertaken to contend on behalf of God, the Supreme Being, and of salvation, and of the primary hope[β] of us all, the more fervent they are in the faith, the more hostile are they to what is said, supposing that a submissive spirit indicates, not piety, but treason to the truth, and therefore they would sacrifice anything rather than their private convictions, and the accustomed doctrines in which they have been educated. I am now referring to those who are moderate and not utterly depraved in disposition, who, if they have erred in regard to the truth, have erred from piety, who have zeal, though not according to knowledge,[γ] who will possibly be of the number of those not excessively condemned, and not beaten with many stripes,[α] because it is not through vice or depravity that they have failed to do the will of their Lord; and these perchance would be persuaded and forsake the pious opinion which is the cause of their hostility, if some reason either from their own minds, or from others, were to take hold of them, and at a critical moment, like iron from flint, strike fire from a mind which is pregnant and worthy of the light, for thus a little spark would quickly kindle the torch of truth within it.

41. But what is to be said of those who, from vain glory or arrogance, speak unrighteousness against the most High,[β] arming themselves with the insolence of Jannes and Jambres,[γ] not against Moses, but against the truth, and rising in opposition to sound doctrine? Or of the third class, who through ignorance and, its consequence, temerity, rush headlong against every form of doctrine in swinish fashion, and trample under foot the fair pearls[δ] of the truth?

42. What again of those who come with no private idea, or form of words, better or worse, in regard to God, but listen to all kinds of doctrines and teachers, with the intention of selecting from all what is best and safest, in reliance upon no better judges of the truth than themselves? They are, in consequence, borne and turned about hither and thither by one plausible idea after another, and, after being deluged and trodden down by all kinds of doctrine,[ε] and having rung the changes on a long succession of teachers and formulæ, which they throw to the winds as readily as dust, their ears and minds at last are wearied out, and, O what folly! they become equally disgusted with all forms of doctrine, and assume the wretched character of deriding and despising our faith as unstable and unsound; passing in their ignorance from the teachers to the doctrine: as if anyone whose eyes were diseased, or whose ears had been injured, were to complain of the sun for being dim and not shining, or of sounds for being inharmonious and feeble.

43. Accordingly, to impress the truth upon a soul when it is still fresh, like wax not yet subjected to the seal, is an easier task than inscribing pious doctrine on the top of inscriptions—I mean wrong doctrines and dogmas[ζ]—with the result that the former are confused and thrown into disorder by the latter. It is better indeed to tread a road which is smooth and well trodden than one which is untrodden and rough, or to plough land which has often been

α *Piety*, εὐλάβεια. i. e. The pious readily and attentively receive instruction in morality or generally received truth, but are more suspicious and intolerant than ordinary people, if, at a time when any theological question is hotly debated, a preacher touches upon any point connected with it, and so stirs party feeling or personal prejudice.

β *The primary hope*. This term is used of the full knowledge and confession of the doctrine of the Holy Trinity, Orat. xxxii. 23; where its necessary connection with Christianity and the life of the soul is insisted on. For its vital importance cf. Liddon, Bamp. Lect. pp. 435, 6, and its bearing on the Mediatorial Work of Christ, and so on our salvation. Ibid. Lect. VIII. esp. pp. 472-9 (5th ed.). S. Cyr. Hier. Catech. 13. 2. S. Cyr. Alex. de S. Trin. dial. 4. tom v. pp. 508. 509. S. Proclus Hom. in Incarn. 5. 6. 0. Bright. Hist. of the Church. p 149.

γ Rom. x. 2.

α Luke xii. 47. β Ps. lxxiii. 8. (LXX.). γ 2 Tim. iii. 8. δ S. Matt. vii. 6; viii. 32. ε Eph. iv. 14.

ζ *Doctrines and dogmas.* Elias takes the former to refer to morality and the latter to belief.

cleft and broken up by the plough: but a soul to be written upon should be free from the inscription of harmful doctrines, or the deeply cut marks of vice: otherwise the pious inscriber would have a twofold task, the erasure of the former impressions and the substitution of others which are more excellent, and more worthy to abide. So numerous are they whose wickedness is shown, not only by yielding to their passions, but even by their utterances, and so numerous the forms and characters of wickedness, and so considerable the task of one who has been intrusted with this office of educating and taking charge of souls. Indeed I have omitted the majority of the details, lest my speech should be unnecessarily burdensome.

44. If anyone were to undertake to tame and train an animal of many forms and shapes, compounded of many animals of various sizes and degrees of tameness and wildness, his principal task, involving a considerable struggle, would be the government of so extraordinary and heterogeneous a nature, since each of the animals of which it is compounded would, according to its nature or habit, be differently affected with joy, pleasure or dislike, by the same words, or food, or stroking with the hand, or whistling, or other modes of treatment. And what must the master of such an animal do, but show himself manifold and various in his knowledge, and apply to each a treatment suitable for it, so as successfully to lead and preserve the beast? And since the common body of the church is composed of many different characters and minds, like a single animal compounded of discordant parts, it is absolutely necessary that its ruler should be at once simple in his uprightness in all respects, and as far as possible manifold and varied in his treatment of individuals, and in dealing with all in an appropriate and suitable manner.

45. For some need to be fed with the milk[α] of the most simple and elementary doctrines, viz., those who are in habit babes and, so to say, new-made, and unable to bear the manly food of the word: nay, if it were presented to them beyond their strength, they would probably be overwhelmed and oppressed, owing to the inability of their mind, as is the case with our material bodies,[β] to digest and appropriate what is offered to it, and so would lose even their original power. Others require the wisdom which is spoken among the perfect,[α] and the higher and more solid food, since their senses have been sufficiently exercised to discern[β] truth and falsehood, and if they were made to drink milk, and fed on the vegetable diet of invalids,[γ] they would be annoyed. And with good reason, for they would not be strengthened[δ] according to Christ, nor make that laudable increase, which the Word produces in one who is rightly fed, by making him a perfect man, and bringing him to the measure of spiritual stature.[ε]

46. And who is sufficient for these things? For we are not as the many, able to corrupt[ζ] the word of truth, and mix the wine,[η] which maketh glad the heart of man,[θ] with water, mix, that is, our doctrine with what is common and cheap, and debased, and stale, and tasteless, in order to turn the adulteration to our profit, and accommodate ourselves to those who meet us, and curry favor with everyone, becoming ventriloquists[ι] and chatterers, who serve their own pleasures by words uttered from the earth, and sinking into the earth, and, to gain the special good will of the multitude, injuring in the highest degree, nay, ruining ourselves, and shedding the innocent blood of simpler souls, which will be required at our hands.[κ]

47. Besides, we are aware that it is better to offer our own reins to others more skilful than ourselves, than, while inexperienced, to guide the course of others, and rather to give a kindly hearing than stir an untrained tongue; and after a discussion of these points with advisers who are, I fancy, of no mean worth, and, at any rate, wish us well, we preferred to learn those canons of speech and action which we did not know, rather than undertake to teach them in our ignorance. For it is delightful to have the reasoning[λ] of the aged come to one even until the depth of old age, able, as it is, to aid a soul new to piety. Accordingly, to undertake the training of others before being sufficiently trained oneself, and to learn, as men say, the potter's art on a wine-jar, that is, to practise ourselves in piety at the expense of others' souls, seems to me to be excessive folly or excessive rashness—folly, if we are not even aware of our own ignorance; rashness, if in spite of this knowledge we venture on the task.

48. Nay, the wiser of the Hebrews tell us that there was of old among the Hebrews a most excellent and praiseworthy law,[μ] that every

α 1. Cor. iii. 1, 2: Heb. v. 12–14.
β *Our material bodies*, lit., "matter." This, together with "dust," "mire" or "clay" and other similar terms, is often used by S. Gregory as a synonym of "the body."

α 1 Cor. ii. 6. β Heb. v. 14. γ Rom. xiv. 2.
δ Col. i. 11, ii. 19. ε Eph. iv. 13.
ζ 2 Cor. ii. 16, 17. η Isai. i. 22. θ Ps. civ. 15.
ι *Ventriloquists.* Isai. viii. 19, "Wizards."
κ Ezek. iii. 20: xxxiii. 8.
λ I.e., venerable for wisdom due to experience.
μ *Law.* Not definitely enacted, but a custom constantly observed. It applied to the earlier and later chapters of Ezekiel and the Song of Solomon.

age was not entrusted with the whole of Scripture, inasmuch as this would not be the more profitable course, since the whole of it is not at once intelligible to everyone, and its more recondite parts would, by their apparent meaning, do a very great injury to most people. Some portions therefore, whose exterior[α] is unexceptionable, are from the first permitted and common to all; while others are only entrusted to those who have attained their twenty-fifth year, viz., such as hide their mystical beauty under a mean-looking cloak, to be the reward of diligence and an illustrious life; flashing forth and presenting itself only to those whose mind has been purified, on the ground that this age alone[β] can be superior to the body, and properly rise from the letter to the spirit.

49. Among us, however, there is no boundary line between giving and receiving instruction, like the stones of old between the tribes within and beyond the Jordan: nor is a certain part entrusted to some, another to others; nor any rule for degrees[γ] of experience; but the matter has been so disturbed and thrown into confusion, that most of us, not to say all, almost before we have lost our childish curls and lisp, before we have entered the house of God, before we know even the names of the Sacred Books, before we have learnt the character and authors of the Old and New Testaments: (for my present point is not our want of cleansing from the mire and marks of spiritual shame which our viciousness has contracted) if, I say, we have furnished ourselves with two or three expressions of pious authors, and that by hearsay, not by study; if we have had a brief experience of David, or clad ourselves properly in a cloaklet, or are wearing at least a philosopher's girdle, or have girt about us some form and appearance of piety—phew! how we take the chair and show our spirit! Samuel was holy even in his swaddling-clothes:[δ] we are at once wise teachers, of high estimation in Divine things, the first of scribes and lawyers; we ordain ourselves men of heaven and seek to be called Rabbi by men;[ε] the letter is nowhere, everything is to be understood spiritually, and our dreams are utter drivel, and we should be annoyed if we were not lauded to excess. This is the case with the better and more simple of us: what of those who are more spiritual and noble?[α] After frequently condemning us, as men of no account, they have forsaken us, and abhor fellowship with impious people such as we are.

50. Now, if we were to speak gently to one of them, advancing, as follows, step by step in argument: "Tell me, my good sir, do you call dancing anything, and flute-playing?" "Certainly," they would say. "What then of wisdom and being wise, which we venture to define as a knowledge of things divine and human?" This also they will admit. "Are then these accomplishments better than and superior to wisdom, or wisdom by far better than these?" "Better even than all things," I know well that they will say. Up to this point they are judicious. "Well, dancing and flute-playing require to be taught and learnt, a process which takes time, and much toil in the sweat of the brow, and sometimes the payment of fees, and entreaties for inititation, and long absence from home, and all else which must be done and borne for the acquisition of experience: but as for wisdom, which is chief of all things, and holds in her embrace everything which is good, so that even God himself prefers this title to all the names by which He is called; are we to suppose that it is a matter of such slight consequence, and so accessible, that we need but wish, and we would be wise?" "It would be utter folly to do so." If we, or any learned and prudent man, were to say this to them, and try by degrees to cleanse them from their error, it would be sowing upon rocks,[β] and speaking to ears of men who will not hear:[γ] so far are they from being even wise enough to perceive their own ignorance. And we may rightly, in my opinion, apply to them the saying of Solomon: There is an evil which I have seen under the sun,[δ] a man wise in his own conceit;[ε] and a still greater evil is to charge with the instruction of others a man who is not even aware of his own ignorance.

51. This is a state of mind which demands, in special degree, our tears and groans, and has often stirred my pity, from the conviction that imagination robs us in great measure of reality, and that vain glory is a great hindrance to men's attainment of virtue. To heal and stay this disease needs a Peter or Paul, those great disciples of Christ, who in addition to guidance in word and deed, received their grace,[ζ] and

α *Exterior*, Origen, Hom. 5, in Levit., speaks of the 'body, soul, and spirit of Scripture.'

β *Alone.* If, as many MSS. we read μόλις, "with difficulty." This is preferred by the Bened. note.

γ *Degrees, etc.* Heb. v. 14 V. "use" (in the singular). the sense is "any rule for confining the use of difficult passages of Holy Scripture to those whose experience is a guarantee against their abuse."

δ 1 Sam. ii. 11.

ε S. Matt. xxiii. 7.

α "More spiritual and noble."—This is ironical.

β S. Luke viii. 6.

γ Ecclus. xxv. 9.

δ Eccles. x. 5.

ε Prov. xxvi. 12.

ζ *Their grace*, τὸ χάρισμα. Elias takes this of the power to heal diseases. Tillemont of miracles in general. Perhaps better

became all things to all men, that they might gain all.[α] But for other men like ourselves, it is a great thing to be rightly guided and led by those who have been charged with the correction and setting right of things such as these.

52. Since, however, I have mentioned Paul, and men like him, I will, with your permission, pass by all others who have been foremost as lawgivers, prophets, or leaders, or in any similar office—for instance, Moses, Aaron, Joshua, Elijah, Elisha, the Judges, Samuel, David, the company of Prophets, John, the Twelve Apostles, and their successors, who with many toils and labors exercised their authority, each in his own time; all these I pass by, to set forth Paul as the witness to my assertions, and for us to consider by his example how important a matter is the care of souls, and whether it requires slight attention and little judgment. But that we may recognize and perceive this, let us hear what Paul himself says of Paul.

53. I say nothing of his labours, his watchings, his sufferings in hunger and thirst, in cold and nakedness, his assailants from without, his adversaries within.[β] I pass over the persecutions, councils, prisons, bonds, accusers, tribunals, the daily and hourly deaths, the basket, the stonings, beatings with rods, the travelling about, the perils by land and sea, the deep, the shipwrecks, the perils of rivers, perils of robbers, perils from his countrymen, perils among false brethren, the living by his own hands, the gospel without charge,[γ] the being a spectacle to both angels and men,[δ] set in the midst between God and men to champion His cause,[ε] and to unite them to Him, and make them His own peculiar people,[ζ] beside those things that are without.[η] For who could worthily detail these matters, the daily pressure,[θ] the individual solicitude, the care of all the churches, the universal sympathy, and brotherly love? Did anyone stumble, Paul also was weak; did another suffer scandal, it was Paul who was on fire.

54. What of the laboriousness of his teaching? The manifold character of his ministry? His loving kindness? And on the other hand his strictness? And the combination and blending of the two; in such wise that his gentleness should not enervate, nor his severity exasperate? He gives laws for slaves and masters,[ι] rulers and ruled,[κ] husbands and wives,[λ] parents and children,[α] marriage and celibacy,[β] self-discipline and indulgence,[γ] wisdom and ignorance,[δ] circumcision and uncircumcision,[ε] Christ and the world, the flesh and the spirit.[ζ] On behalf of some he gives thanks, others he upbraids. Some he names his joy and crown,[η] others he charges with folly.[θ] Some who hold a straight course he accompanies, sharing in their zeal; others he checks, who are going wrong. At one time he excommunicates,[ι] at another he confirms his love;[κ] at one time he grieves, at another rejoices; at one time he feeds with milk, at another he handles mysteries;[λ] at one time he condescends, at another he raises to his own level; at one time he threatens a rod,[μ] at another he offers the spirit of meekness; at one time he is haughty toward the lofty, at another lowly toward the lowly. Now he is least of the apostles,[ν] now he offers a proof of Christ speaking in him;[ξ] now he longs for departure and is being poured forth as a libation,[ο] now he thinks it more necessary for their sakes to abide in the flesh. For he seeks not his own interests, but those of his children,[π] whom he has begotten in Christ by the gospel.[ρ] This is the aim of all his spiritual authority, in everything to neglect his own in comparison with the advantage of others.

55. He glories in his infirmities and distresses. He takes pleasure in the dying of Jesus,[σ] as if it were a kind of ornament. He is lofty in carnal things,[τ] he rejoices in things spiritual; he is not rude in knowledge,[υ] and claims to see in a mirror, darkly.[φ] He is bold in spirit, and buffets his body,[χ] throwing it as an antagonist. What is the lesson and instruction he would thus impress upon us? Not to be proud of earthly things, or puffed up by knowledge, or excite the flesh against the spirit. He fights for all, prays for all, is jealous for all, is kindled on behalf of all, whether without law, or under the law; a preacher of the Gentiles,[ψ] a patron of the Jews. He even was exceedingly bold on behalf of his brethren according to the flesh,[ω] if I may myself be bold enough to say so, in his loving prayer that they might in his stead be brought to Christ. What magnanimity! what fervor of spirit! He imitates Christ, who became a curse for us,[αα] who took our infirmities and bore our sicknesses;[ββ] or, to use more measured terms, he is

of the special position as Apostles to the Jews and to the Gentiles (Gal. ii. 8, 9), where the term used is χάρις.

α 1 Cor. ix. 22. β 2 Cor. xi. 23 et seq. γ 1 Cor. iv. 12; ix. 18. δ Ib. iv. 9. ε His *cause* reading τοῦ: v. l. τῶν. ζ Tit. ii. 14. η 2 Cor. xi. 28, 29. θ *Pressure* ἐπιστασίαν, 2 Cor. xi. 28, ἐπίστασιν. ι Eph. vi. 5, 9. κ Rom. xiii. 1–3. λ Eph. v. 25, 22.

α Eph. vi. 1–4. β 1 Cor. vii. 3, 8, 25, 31. γ Rom. xiv. 3, 6. δ 1 Cor. i. 27; iii. 18. ε Rom. ii. 25, 29. ζ Gal. v. 16. η Phil. iv. 1. θ Gal. iii. 1. ι 1 Cor. v. 5. κ 2 Cor. ii. 8. λ 1 Cor. ii. 7; iii. 2. μ Ib. iv. 21. ν Ib. xv. 9. ξ 2 Cor. xiii. 3. ο Phil. i. 23; ii. 17. π 1 Cor. x. 33. ρ Ib. iv. 15. σ 2 Cor. iv. 10; xii. 9, 10. τ Rom. v. 3; Phil. iii. 4. υ 2 Cor. xi. 6 φ 1 Cor. xiii. 12. χ Ib. ix. 27. ψ 2 Tim. i. 11. ω Rom. ix. 3. αα Gal. iii. 13. ββ S. Matt. viii. 17.

ready, next to Christ, to suffer anything, even as one of the ungodly, for them, if only they be saved.

56. Why should I enter into detail? He lived not to himself, but to Christ and his preaching. He crucified the world to himself,[α] and being crucified to the world and the things which are seen, he thought all things little,[β] and too small to be desired; even though from Jerusalem and round about unto Illyricum[γ] he had fully preached the Gospel, even though he had been prematurely caught up to the third heaven, and had had a vision of Paradise, and had heard unspeakable words.[δ] Such was Paul, and everyone of like spirit with him. But we fear that, in comparison with them, we may be foolish princes of Zoan,[ε] or extortioners, who exact the fruits of the ground, or falsely bless the people:[ζ] and further make themselves happy, and confuse the way of your feet,[η] or mockers ruling over you, or children in authority,[θ] immature in mind, not even having bread and clothing enough to be rulers over any;[ι] or prophets teaching lies,[κ] or rebellious princes,[λ] deserving to share the reproach of their elders for the straitness of the famine,[μ] or priests very far from speaking comfortably[ν] to Jerusalem, according to the reproaches and protests urged by Isaiah, who was purged by the Seraphim with a live coal.[ξ]

57. Is the undertaking then so serious and laborious to a sensitive and sad heart—a very rottenness to the bones[ο] of a sensible man: while the danger is slight, and a fall not worth consideration? Nay the blessed Hosea inspires me with serious alarm, where he says that to us priests and rulers pertaineth the judgment,[π] because we have been a snare to the watch-tower; and as a net spread upon Tabor, which has been firmly fixed by the hunters of men's souls, and he threatens to cut off the wicked prophets,[ρ] and devour their judges with fire, and to cease for a while from anointing a king and princes,[σ] because they ruled for themselves, and not by Him.[τ]

58. Hence again the divine Micah, unable to brook the building of Zion with blood, however you interpret the phrase, and of Jerusalem with iniquity, while the heads thereof judge for reward, and the priests teach for hire, and the prophets divine for money—what does he say will be the result of this? Zion shall be plowed as a field, and Jerusalem be as a lodge in a garden, and the mountain of the house be reckoned as a glade in a thicket.[α] He bewails also the scarcity of the upright, there being scarcely a stalk or a gleaning grape left, since both the prince asketh, and the judge curries favour,[β] so that his language is almost the same as the mighty David's: Save me, O Lord, for the godly man ceaseth:[γ] and says that therefore their blessings shall fail them, as if wasted by the moth.

59. Joel again summons us to wailing, and will have the ministers of the altar lament under the presence of famine: so far is he from allowing us to revel in the misfortunes of others: and, after sanctifying a fast, calling a solemn assembly, and gathering the old men, the children, and those of tender age,[δ] we ourselves must further haunt the temple in sackcloth and ashes,[ε] prostrated right humbly on the ground, because the field is wasted, and the meat-offering and the drink-offering is cut off from the house of the Lord, till we draw down mercy by our humiliation.

60. What of Habakkuk? He utters more heated words, and is impatient with God Himself, and cries down, as it were our good Lord, because of the injustice of the judges. O Lord, how long shall I cry and Thou wilt not hear? Shall I cry out unto Thee of violence, and Thou wilt not save? Why dost Thou show me toil and labour, causing me to look upon perverseness and impiety? Judgment has been given against me, and the judge is a spoiler. Therefore the law is slacked, and judgment doth never go forth. Then comes the denunciation, and what follows upon it. Behold, ye despisers, and regard, and wonder marvellously, and vanish away, for I work a work.[ζ] But why need I quote the whole of the denunciation? A little further on, however, for I think it best to add this to what has been said, after upbraiding and lamenting many of those who are in some respect unjust or depraved, he upbraids the leaders and teachers of wickedness, stigmatising vice as a foul disorder, and an intoxication and aberration of mind; charging them with giving their neighbours drink in order to look upon the darkness of their soul,[η] and the dens of creeping things and wild beasts, viz.: the dwelling places of wicked thoughts. Such indeed they are, and such teachings do they discuss with us.

61. How can it be right to pass by Malachi, who at one time brings bitter charges against the priests, and reproaches them with despising

α Gal. vi. 14. β Phil. iii. 8. γ Rom. xv. 19. δ 2 Cor. xii. 2, 4. ε Isa. xix. 11. ζ Ib. ix. 16. η Ib. iii. 12. θ Ib. iii. 4. ι Ib. iii. 7. κ Ib. ix. 15. λ Ib. i. 23. μ Ib. viii. 21. ν Ib. xl. 2. ξ Ib. vi. 6, 7. ο Prov. xiv. 30. π Hos. v. 1, 2. ρ Ib. vi. 5. σ Ib. vii. 7. τ Ib. viii. 4.

α Mic. iii. 10–12. β Ib. vii. 1–4. γ Ps. xii. 1. δ Joel i. 13, seq. ε Isa. lviii. 5. ζ Hab. i. 2 et seq. η Ib. ii. 15.

the name of the Lord,[α] and explains wherein they did this, by offering polluted bread upon the altar, and meat which is not firstfruits, which they would not have offered to one of their governors, or, if they had offered it, they would have been dishonoured; yet offering these in fulfilment of a vow to the King of the universe, to wit, the lame and the sick, and the deformed, which are utterly profane and loathsome.[β] Again he reminds them of the covenant of God, a covenant of life and peace, with the sons of Levi, and that they should serve Him in fear, and stand in awe of the manifestation of His Name. The law of truth, he says, was in his mouth, and unrighteousness was not found in his lips; he walked with me uprightly in peace, and turned away many from iniquity: for the priest's lips shall keep knowledge, and they shall seek the law at his mouth. And how honourable and at the same time how fearful is the cause! for he is the messenger of the Lord Almighty.[γ] Although I pass over the following imprecations, as strongly worded,[δ] yet I am afraid of their truth. This however may be cited without offence, to our profit. Is it right, he says, to regard your sacrifice, and receive it with good will at your hands,[ε] as if he were most highly incensed, and rejecting their ministrations owing to their wickedness.

62. Whenever I remember Zechariah, I shudder at the reaping-hook,[ζ] and likewise at his testimony against the priests, his hints in reference to the celebrated Joshua, the high priest, whom he represents as stripped of filthy and unbecoming garments and then clothed in rich priestly apparel.[η] As for the words and charges to Joshua which he puts into the angel's mouth, let them be treated with silent respect, as referring perhaps to a greater[θ] and higher object than those who are many priests:[ι] but even at his right hand stood the devil, to resist him. A fact, in my eyes, of no slight significance, and demanding no slight fear and watchfulness.

63. Who is so bold and adamantine of soul as not to tremble and be abashed at the charges and reproaches deliberately urged against the rest of the shepherds. A voice, he says, of the howling of the shepherds, for their glory is spoiled. A voice of the roaring of lions,[κ] for this hath befallen them. Does he not all but hear the wailing as if close at hand, and himself wail with the afflicted. A little further is a more striking and impassioned strain. Feed, he says, the flock of slaughter, whose possessors slay them without repentance, and they that sell them say, "Blessed be the Lord, for we are rich:" and their own shepherds are without feeling for them. Therefore, I will no more pity the inhabitants of the land, saith the Lord Almighty.[α] And again: Awake, O sword, against the shepherds, and smite the shepherds, and scatter the sheep, and I will turn My Hand upon the shepherds;[β] and, Mine anger is kindled against the shepherds, and I will visit the lambs:[γ] adding to the threat those who rule over the people. So industriously does he apply himself to his task that he cannot easily free himself from denunciations, and I am afraid that, did I refer to the whole series, I should exhaust your patience. This must then suffice for Zechariah.

64. Passing by the elders in the book of Daniel;[δ] for it is better to pass them by, together with the Lord's righteous sentence and declaration concerning them, that wickedness came from Babylon from ancient judges, who seemed to govern the people; how are we affected by Ezekiel, the beholder and expositor of the mighty mysteries and visions? By his injunction to the watchmen[ε] not to keep silence concerning vice and the sword impending over it, a course which would profit neither themselves nor the sinners; but rather to keep watch and forewarn, and thus benefit, at any rate those who gave warning, if not both those who spoke and those who heard?

65. What of his further invective against the shepherds, Woe shall come upon woe, and rumour upon rumour, then shall they seek a vision of the prophet, but the law shall perish from the priest, and counsel from the ancients,[ζ] and again, in these terms, Son of man, say unto her, thou art a land that is not watered, nor hath rain come upon thee in the day of indignation: whose princes in the midst of her are like roaring lions, ravening the prey, devouring souls in their might.[η] And a little further on: Her priests have violated My laws and profaned My holy things, they have put no difference between the holy and profane, but all things were alike to them, and they hid their eyes from My Sabbaths, and I was profaned among them.[θ] He threatens that He will consume both the wall and them that daubed it,[ι] that is, those who sin and those who throw a cloak over them; as the evil

α Mal. i. 6. β Ib. i. 13. γ Ib. ii. 5–7.
δ *Strongly worded*, βλάσφημον, perh. "ill omened."
ε Ib. ii. 13. ζ Zech. v. 1 (LXX.). η Ib. iii. 1 et seq.
θ *A greater*, &c., i.e. they refer to the Person of Jesus Christ Himself.
ι Heb. vii. 23. κ Zech. xi. 3.

α Zech. xi. 5, 6. β Ib. xiii. 7. γ Ib. x. 3.
δ Hist. Susann., 5. ε Ezek. xxxiii. 2. ζ Ib. vii. 26.
η Ib. xxii. 24 seq. θ Ib. xxii. 26. ι Ib. xiii. 14.

rulers and priests have done, who caused the house of Israel to err according to their own hearts which are estranged in their lusts.[α]

66. I also refrain from entering into his discussion of those who feed themselves, devour the milk, clothe themselves with the wool, kill them that are fat, but feed not the flock, strengthen not the diseased, nor bind up that which is broken, nor bring again that which is driven away, nor seek that which is lost, nor keep watch over that which is strong, but oppress them with rigour, and destroy them with their pressure;[β] so that, because there was no shepherd, the sheep were scattered over every plain and mountain, and became meat for all the fowls and beasts,[γ] because there was no one to seek for them and bring them back. What is the consequence? As I live, saith the Lord, because these things are so, and My flock became a prey,[δ] behold I am against the shepherds, and I will require My flock at their hands, and will gather them and make them My own: but the shepherds shall suffer such and such things, as bad shepherds ought.

67. However, to avoid unreasonably prolonging my discourse, by an enumeration of all the prophets, and of the words of them all, I will mention but one more, who was known before he was formed, and sanctified from the womb,[ε] Jeremiah: and will pass over the rest. He longs for water over his head, and a fountain of tears for his eyes, that he may adequately weep for Israel;[ζ] and no less does he bewail the depravity of its rulers.

68. God speaks to him in reproof of the priests: The priests said not, Where is the Lord, and they that handled the law knew Me not; the pastors also transgressed against Me.[η] Again He says to him: The pastors are become brutish, and have not sought the Lord, and therefore all their flock did not understand, and was scattered.[θ] Again, Many pastors have destroyed My vineyard, and have polluted My pleasant portion, till it was reduced to a trackless wilderness.[ι] He further inveighs against the pastors again: Woe be to the pastors that destroy and scatter the sheep of My pasture! Therefore thus saith the Lord against them that feed My people: Ye have scattered My flock, and driven them away, and have not visited them: behold I will visit upon you the evil of your doings.[κ] Moreover he bids the shepherds to howl, and the rams of the flock to lament, because the days of their slaughter are accomplished.[λ]

α Ezek. xiv. 5. β Ib. xxxiv. 2 et seq. γ Ib. xxxix. 17. δ Ib. xxxiv. 8. ε Jer. i. 5. ζ Ib. ix. 1. η Ib. ii. 8. θ Ib. x. 21. ι Ib. xii. 10. κ Ib. xxiii. 1, 2. λ Ib. xxv. 34.

69. Why need I speak of the things of ancient days? Who can test himself by the rules and standards which Paul laid down for bishops and presbyters, that they are to be temperate, soberminded, not given to wine, no strikers, apt to teach, blameless in all things, and beyond the reach of the wicked,[α] without finding considerable deflection from the straight line of the rules? What of the regulations of Jesus for his disciples, when He sends them to preach?[β] The main object of these is—not to enter into particulars—that they should be of such virtue, so simple and modest, and in a word, so heavenly, that the gospel should make its way, no less by their character than by their preaching.

70. I am alarmed by the reproaches of the Pharisees, the conviction of the Scribes. For it is disgraceful for us, who ought greatly surpass them, as we are bidden, if we desire the kingdom of heaven, to be found more deeply sunk in vice: so that we deserve to be called serpents, a generation of vipers, and blind guides, who strain out a gnat and swallow a camel, or sepulchres foul within, in spite of our external comeliness, or platters outwardly clean, and everything else, which they are, or which is laid to their charge.[γ]

71. With these thoughts I am occupied night and day: they waste my marrow, and feed upon my flesh, and will not allow me to be confident or to look up. They depress my soul, and abase my mind, and fetter my tongue, and make me consider, not the position of a prelate, or the guidance and direction of others, which is far beyond my powers; but how I myself am to escape the wrath to come, and to scrape off from myself somewhat of the rust of vice. A man must himself be cleansed, before cleansing others: himself become wise, that he may make others wise; become light, and then give light: draw near to God, and so bring others near; be hallowed, then hallow them; be possessed of hands to lead others by the hand, of wisdom to give advice.

72. When will this be, say they who are swift but not sure in every thing, readily building up, readily throwing down. When will the lamp be upon its stand,[δ] and where is the talent?[ε] For so they call the grace.[ζ] Those who speak thus are more fervent in friendship than in reverence. You ask me, you men of exceeding courage, when these things shall be, and what account I give of them? Not even extreme old age would be too long a limit to

α 1 Tim. iii. 2, 3; Tit. i. 7. β S. Matt. x. 9; S. Luke ix. 3. γ S. Matt. xxiii. 13 et seq. δ Ib. v. 15. ε Ib. xxv. 15. ζ "*The grace*" i.e. the grace of the priesthood.

assign. For hoary hairs combined with prudence are better than inexperienced youth, well-reasoned hesitation than inconsiderate haste, and a brief reign than a long tyranny: just as a small portion honourably won is better than considerable possessions which are dishonourable and uncertain, a little gold than a great weight of lead, a little light than much darkness.

73. But this speed, in its untrustworthiness and excessive haste, is in danger of being like the seeds which fell upon the rock,[α] and, because they had no depth of earth,[β] sprang up at once, but could not bear even the first heat of the sun; or like the foundation laid upon the sand,[γ] which could not even make a slight resistance to the rain and the winds. Woe to thee, O city, whose king is a child,[δ] says Solomon. Be not hasty of speech,[ε] says Solomon again, asserting that hastiness of speech is less serious than heated action. And who, in spite of all this, demands haste rather than security and utility? Who can mould, as clay-figures are modelled in a single day, the defender of the truth, who is to take his stand with Angels, and give glory with Archangels, and cause the sacrifice to ascend to the altar on high, and share the priesthood of Christ, and renew the creature, and set forth the image, and create inhabitants for the world above, aye and, greatest of all, be God, and make others to be God?

74. I know Whose ministers we are, and where we are placed, and whither we are guides. I know the height of God, and the weakness of man, and, on the contrary, his power. Heaven is high, and the earth deep;[ζ] and who of those who have been cast down by sin shall ascend?[η] Who that is as yet surrounded by the gloom here below, and by the grossness of the flesh can purely gaze with his whole mind upon that whole mind, and amid unstable and visible things hold intercourse with the stable and invisible? For hardly may one of those who have been most specially purged, behold here even an image of the Good, as men see the sun in the water. Who hath measured the water with his hand, and the heaven with a span, and the whole earth in a measure? Who hath weighed the mountains in scales, and the hills in a balance?[θ] What is the place of his rest?[ι] and to whom shall he be likened?[κ]

75. Who is it, Who made all things by His Word,[λ] and formed man by His Wisdom, and gathered into one things scattered abroad, and mingled dust with spirit, and compounded an animal visible and invisible, temporal and immortal, earthly and heavenly, able to attain to God but not to comprehend Him, drawing near and yet afar off. I said, I will be wise, says Solomon, but she (i.e. Wisdom) was far from me beyond what is:[α] and, Verily, he that increaseth knowledge increaseth sorrow.[β] For the joy of what we have discovered is no greater than the pain of what escapes us; a pain, I imagine, like that felt by those who are dragged, while yet thirsty, from the water, or are unable to retain what they think they hold, or are suddenly left in the dark by a flash of lightning.

76. This depressed and kept me humble, and persuaded me that it was better to hear the voice of praise[γ] than to be an expounder of truths beyond my power; the majesty, and the height, and the dignity, and the pure natures scarce able to contain the brightness of God, Whom the deep covers, Whose secret place is darkness,[δ] since He is the purest light,[ε] which most men cannot approach unto; Who is in all this universe, and again is beyond the universe; Who is all goodness,[ζ] and beyond all goodness; Who enlightens the mind, and escapes the quickness and height of the mind, ever retiring as much as He is apprehended, and by His flight and stealing away when grasped, withdrawing to the things above one who is enamoured of Him.

77. Such and so great is the object of our longing zeal, and such a man should he be, who prepares and conducts souls to their espousals. For myself, I feared to be cast, bound hand and foot,[η] from the bride-chamber, for not having on a wedding-garment, and for having rashly intruded among those who there sit at meat. And yet I had been invited from my youth, if I may speak of what most men know not, and had been cast upon Him from the womb,[θ] and presented by the promise of my mother, afterwards confirmed in the hour of danger: and my longing grew up with it, and my reason agreed to it, and I gave as an offering my all to Him Who had won me and saved me, my property, my fame, my health, my very words, from which I only gained the advantage of being able to despise them, and of having something in comparison of which I preferred Christ. And the words of God were made sweet as honeycombs[ι] to me, and I cried after knowledge and lifted up my voice for wisdom.[κ] There was moreover the moderation of anger, the curbing of the tongue, the re-

α S. Luke viii. 6. β S. Matt. xiii. 5. γ Ib. vii. 26. δ Eccles. x. 16. ε Prov. xxix. 20. ζ Ib. xxv 3. η Ps. xxiv. 3. θ Isai. xl. 12. ι Ib. lxvi. 1. κ Ib. xl. 18, 25. λ Ps. xxxiii. 6.

α Eccles. vii. 24. β Ib. i. 18. γ Ps. xxvi. 7 (LXX.). δ Ib. xviii. 12; civ. 6. ε 1 Tim. vi. 16. ζ Exod. xxxiii. 19. η S. Matt. xxii. 13. θ Ps. xxii. 11. ι Ib. xix. 10; cxix. 103. κ Prov. ii. 3.

straint of the eyes, the discipline of the belly, and the trampling under foot of the glory which clings to the earth. I speak foolishly,[α] but it shall be said, in these pursuits I was perhaps not inferior to many.

78. One branch of philosophy is, however, too high for me, the commission to guide and govern souls—and before I have rightly learned to submit to a shepherd, or have had my soul duly cleansed, the charge of caring for a flock: especially in times like these, when a man, seeing everyone else rushing hither and thither in confusion, is content to flee from the mêlée and escape, in sheltered retirement, from the storm and gloom of the wicked one: when the members are at war with one another and the slight remains of love, which once existed, have departed, and priest is a mere empty name, since, as it is said, contempt[β] has been poured upon princes.[γ]

79. Would that it were merely empty! And now may their blasphemy fall upon the head of the ungodly! All fear has been banished from souls, shamelessness has taken its place, and knowledge[δ] and the deep things of the Spirit[ε] are at the disposal of anyone who will; and we all become pious by simply condemning the impiety of others; and we claim the services of ungodly judges,[ζ] and fling that which is holy to the dogs, and cast pearls before swine,[η] by publishing divine things in the hearing of profane souls, and, wretches that we are, carefully fulfil the prayers of our enemies, and are not ashamed to go a whoring with our own inventions.[θ] Moabites and Ammonites, who were not permitted even to enter the Church of the Lord,[ι] frequent our most holy rites. We have opened to all not the gates of righteousness,[κ] but, doors of railing and partizan arrogance; and the first place among us is given, not to one who in the fear of God refrains from even an idle word, but to him who can revile his neighbour most fluently, whether explicitly, or by covert allusion; who rolls beneath his tongue mischief and iniquity, or to speak more accurately, the poison of asps.[λ]

80. We observe each other's sins, not to bewail them, but to make them subjects of reproach, not to heal them, but to aggravate them, and excuse our own evil deeds by the wounds of our neighbours. Bad and good men are distinguished not according to personal character, but by their disagreement or friendship with ourselves. We praise one day what we revile the next, denunciation at the hands of others is a passport to our admiration; so magnanimous are we in our viciousness, that everything is frankly forgiven to impiety.

81. Everything has reverted to the original state of things[α] before the world, with its present fair order and form, came into being. The general confusion and irregularity cry for some organising hand and power. Or, if you will, it is like a battle at night by the faint light of the moon, when none can discern the faces of friends or foes; or like a sea fight on the surge, with the driving winds, and boiling foam, and dashing waves, and crashing vessels, with the thrusts of poles, the pipes of boatswains, the groans of the fallen, while we make our voices heard above the din, and not knowing what to do, and having, alas! no opportunity for showing our valour, assail one another, and fall by one another's hands.

82. Nor indeed is there any distinction between the state of the people and that of the priesthood: but it seems to me to be a simple fulfilment of the ancient curse, "As with the people so with the priest."[β] Nor again are the great and eminent men affected otherwise than the majority; nay, they are openly at war with the priests, and their piety is an aid to their powers of persuasion. And indeed, provided that it be on behalf of the faith, and of the highest and most important questions, let them be thus disposed, and I blame them not; nay, to say the truth, I go so far as to praise and congratulate them. Yea! would that I were one of those who contend and incur hatred for the truth's sake: or rather, I can boast of being one of them. For better is a laudable war than a peace which severs a man from God: and therefore it is that the Spirit arms the gentle warrior, as one who is able to wage war in a good cause.

83. But at the present time there are some who go to war even about small matters and to no purpose, and, with great ignorance and audacity, accept, as an associate in their ill-doing, anyone whoever he may be. Then everyone makes the faith his pretext, and this venerable name is dragged into their private quarrels. Consequently, as was probable, we are hated, even among the Gentiles, and, what is harder still, we cannot say that this is without just cause. Nay, even the best of our own people are scandalized, while this result is not surprising in the case of the multitude,

α 2 Cor. xi. 23. β Ps. cvii. 40.
γ *Princes*, ἄρχοντας. i.e. The office of the priesthood, which is one of dignity, has been brought into contempt by the unworthiness of those ordained to it, who have, by their want of the virtues requisite for their office, made it an empty name—and, not only so, but have been actively vicious.
δ *Knowledge*, &c. cf. the ironical passage, §§ 49, 50.
ε 1 Cor. ii. 10. ζ Ib. vi. 1. 7. η S. Matt. vii. 6. θ Ps. cvi. 39.
ι Deut. xxiii. 3. κ Ps. cxviii. 19. λ Ib. x. 7. cxl. 3.

α Gen. i. 2. β Isai. xxiv. 2; Hos. iv. 9.

who are ill-disposed to accept anything that is good.

84. Sinners are planning upon our backs;[α] and what we devise against each other, they turn against us all: and we have become a new spectacle, not to angels and men,[β] as says Paul, that bravest of athletes, in his contest with principalities and powers,[γ] but to almost all wicked men, and at every time and place, in the public squares, at carousals, at festivities, and times of sorrow. Nay, we have already—I can scarcely speak of it without tears—been represented on the stage, amid the laughter of the most licentious, and the most popular of all dialogues and scenes is the caricature of a Christian.

85. These are the results of our intestine warfare, and our extreme readiness to strive about goodness and gentleness, and our inexpedient excess of love for God. Wrestling, or any other athletic contest, is only permitted according to fixed laws, and the man will be shouted down and disgraced, and lose the victory, who breaks the laws of wrestling, or acts unfairly in any other contest, contrary to the rules laid down for the contest, however able and skilful he may be; and shall anyone contend for Christ in an unchristlike manner, and yet be pleasing to peace for having fought unlawfully in her name.

86. Yea, even now, when Christ is invoked, the devils tremble,[δ] and not even by our ill-doing has the power of this Name been extinguished, while we are not ashamed to insult a cause and name so venerable; shouting it, and having it shouted in return, almost in public, and every day; for My Name is blasphemed among the Gentiles because of you.[ε]

87. Of external warfare I am not afraid, nor of that wild beast, and fulness of evil, who has now arisen against the churches, though he may threaten fire, sword, wild beasts, precipices, chasms; though he may show himself more inhuman than all previous madmen, and discover fresh tortures of greater severity. I have one remedy for them all, one road to victory; I will glory in Christ[ζ]—namely, death for Christ's sake.

88. For my own warfare, however, I am at a loss what course to pursue, what alliance, what word of wisdom, what grace to devise, with what panoply to arm myself, against the wiles of the wicked one.[η] What Moses is to conquer him by stretching out his hands upon the mount,[θ] in order that the cross, thus typified and prefigured, may prevail? What Joshua, as his successor, arrayed alongside the Captain of the Lord's hosts?[α] What David, either by harping, or fighting with his sling,[β] and girded by God with strength unto the battle,[γ] and with his fingers trained to war?[δ] What Samuel, praying[ε] and sacrificing for the people, and anointing as king one who can gain the victory? What Jeremiah, by writing lamentations for Israel, is fitly to lament these things?

89. Who will cry aloud, Spare Thy People, O Lord, and give not Thine heritage to reproach, that the nations should rule over them?[ζ] What Noah, and Job,[η] and Daniel, who are reckoned together as men of prayer, will pray for us, that we may have a slight respite from warfare, and recover ourselves, and recognize one another for a while, and no longer, instead of united Israel, be Judah[θ] and Israel, Rehoboam and Jeroboam, Jerusalem and Samaria, in turn delivered up because of our sins, and in turn lamented.

90. For I own that I am too weak for this warfare, and therefore turned my back, hiding my face in the rout, and sat solitary,[ι] because I was filled with bitterness[κ] and sought to be silent, understanding that it is an evil time,[λ] that the beloved had kicked,[μ] that we were become backsliding children,[ν] who are the luxuriant vine,[ξ] the true vine, all fruitful, all beautiful,[ο] springing up splendidly with showers from on high.[π] For the diadem of beauty,[ρ] the signet of glory,[σ] the crown of magnificence[τ] has been changed for me into shame; and if anyone, in face of these things, is daring and courageous, he has my blessing on his daring and courage.

91. I have said nothing yet of the internal warfare within ourselves, and in our passions, in which we are engaged night and day against the body of our humiliation,[υ] either secretly or openly, and against the tide which tosses and whirls us hither and thither, by the aid of our senses and other sources of the pleasures of this life; and against the miry clay[φ] in which we have been fixed; and against the law of sin,[χ] which wars against the law of the spirit, and strives to destroy the royal image in us, and all the divine emanation which has been bestowed upon us; so that it is difficult for anyone, either by a long course of philosophic

α Ps. cxxix. 3 (LXX.). β 1 Cor. iv. 9. γ Eph. vi. 12. δ S. James ii. 19. ε Isai. lii. 5; Rom. ii. 24. ζ Phil. iii. 3. η Eph. vi. 11. θ Exod. xvii. 11.

α Josh. v. 14. β 1 Sam. xvi. 16; xvii. 49. γ Ps. xviii. 39. δ Ib. cxliv. 1. ε 1 Sam. vii. 5. ζ Joel ii. 17. η Ezek. xiv. 14, 20. θ *Judah, etc.*, cf. Orat. vi. 7; xxxii. 4. ι Lam. iii. 28. κ Ib. iii. 19. λ Mic. ii. 3. μ Deut. xxxii. 15. ν Jer. iii. 14. ξ Hos. x. 1. ο Jer. ii. 21; x. 16. π Ps. lxv. 10. ρ Isai. lxii. 3. σ Ezek. xxviii. 12. τ Ib. xxiii. 42. υ Phil. iii. 21. φ Ps. xl. 2; lxix. 2. χ Rom. vii. 23.

training, and gradual separation of the noble and enlightened part of the soul from that which is debased and yoked with darkness, or by the mercy of God, or by both together, and by a constant practice of looking upward, to overcome the depressing power of matter. And before a man has, as far as possible, gained this superiority, and sufficiently purified his mind, and far surpassed his fellows in nearness to God, I do not think it safe for him to be entrusted with the rule over souls, or the office of mediator (for such, I take it, a priest is) between God and man.

92. What is it that has induced this fear in me, that, instead of supposing me to be needlessly afraid, you may highly commend my foresight? I hear from Moses himself, when God spake to him, that, although many were bidden to come to the mount, one of whom was even Aaron, with his two sons who were priests, and seventy elders of the senate, the rest were ordered to worship afar off, and Moses alone to draw near, and the people were not to go up with him.[α] For it is not everyone who may draw near to God, but only one who, like Moses, can bear the glory of God. Moreover, before this, when the law was first given, the trumpet-blasts, and lightnings, and thunders, and darkness, and the smoke of the whole mountain,[β] and the terrible threats that if even a beast touched the mountain it should be stoned,[γ] and other like alarms, kept back the rest of the people, for whom it was a great privilege, after careful purification, merely to hear the voice of God. But Moses actually went up and entered into the cloud,[δ] and was charged with the law, and received the tables, which belong, for the multitude, to the letter, but, for those who are above the multitude, to the spirit.[ε]

93. I hear again that Nadab and Abihu, for having merely offered incense with strange fire, were with strange fire destroyed,[ζ] the instrument of their impiety being used for their punishment, and their destruction following at the very time and place of their sacrilege; and not even their father Aaron, who was next to Moses in the favor of God, could save them. I know also of Eli the priest, and a little later of Uzzah, the former made to pay the penalty for his sons' transgression, in daring to violate the sacrifices by an untimely exaction of the first fruits of the cauldrons, although he did not condone their impiety, but frequently rebuked them;[η] the other, because he only touched the ark, which was being thrown off the cart by the ox,[a] and though he saved it, was himself destroyed, in God's jealousy for the reverence due to the ark.

94. I know also that not even bodily blemishes in either priests[β] or victims[γ] passed without notice, but that it was required by the law that perfect sacrifices must be offered by perfect men—a symbol, I take it, of integrity of soul. It was not lawful for everyone to touch the priestly vesture, or any of the holy vessels; nor might the sacrifices themselves be consumed except by the proper persons, and at the proper time and place;[δ] nor might the anointing oil nor the compounded incense[ε] be imitated; nor might anyone enter the temple who was not in the most minute particular pure in both soul and body; so far was the Holy of holies removed from presumptuous access, that it might be entered by one man only once a year;[ζ] so far were the veil, and the mercy-seat, and the ark, and the Cherubim, from the general gaze and touch.

95. Since then I knew these things, and that no one is worthy of the mightiness of God, and the sacrifice, and priesthood, who has not first presented himself to God, a living, holy sacrifice, and set forth the reasonable, well-pleasing service,[η] and sacrificed to God the sacrifice of praise and the contrite spirit,[θ] which is the only sacrifice required of us by the Giver of all; how could I dare to offer to Him the external sacrifice, the antitype of the great mysteries,[ι] or clothe myself with the garb and name of priest, before my hands had been consecrated by holy works; before my eyes had been accustomed to gaze safely upon created things, with wonder only for the Creator, and without injury to the creature; before my ear had been sufficiently opened to the instruction of the Lord, and He had opened mine ear to hear[κ] without heaviness, and had set a golden earring with precious sardius, that is, a wise man's word in an obedient ear;[λ] before my mouth had been opened to draw in the Spirit,[μ] and opened wide to be filled[ν] with the spirit of speaking mysteries and doctrines;[ξ] and my lips bound,[ο] to use the words of wisdom, by divine knowledge, and, as I would add, loosed in due season: before my tongue had been filled with exultation, and become an instrument of Divine melody, awaking

α Exod. xxiv. 1, 2. β Ib. xix. 16. γ Heb. xii. 18. δ Exod. xxiv. 15, 18. ε 2 Cor. iii. 6, 7. ζ Lev. x. 1. η 1 Sam. ii. 12, 15, 23.

a 2 Sam. vi. 6. β Lev. xxi. 17. γ Ib. xxii. 19. δ Ib. viii. 31. ε Exod. xxx. 33, 38. ζ Lev. xvi. 34; Heb. ix. 7. η Rom. xii. 1. θ Ps. l. 14. ι *The great mysteries, i.e.*, the Sacrificial Death of Christ upon the Cross. κ Isai. l. 4; vi. 10. λ Prov. xxv. 12. μ Ps. cxix. 131. ν Ib. lxxxi. 10. ξ 1 Cor. xiv. 2. ο Prov. xv. 7 (LXX.).

with glory, awaking right early,[α] and laboring till it cleave to my jaws:[β] before my feet had been set upon the rock,[γ] made like hart's feet, and my footsteps directed in a godly fashion so that they should not well-nigh slip,[δ] nor slip at all; before all my members had become instruments of righteousness,[ε] and all mortality had been put off, and swallowed up of life,[ζ] and had yielded to the Spirit?

96. Who is the man, whose heart has never been made to burn,[η] as the Scriptures have been opened to him, with the pure words of God which have been tried in a furnace;[θ] who has not, by a triple[ι] inscription[κ] of them upon the breadth of his heart, attained the mind of Christ;[λ] nor been admitted to the treasures which to most men remain hidden, secret, and dark, to gaze upon the riches therein,[μ] and become able to enrich others, comparing spiritual things with spiritual.[ν]

97. Who is the man who has never beheld, as our duty is to behold it, the fair beauty of the Lord, nor has visited His temple,[ξ] or rather, become the temple of God,[ο] and the habitation of Christ in the Spirit?[π] Who is the man who has never recognized the correlation and distinction between figures and the truth, so that by withdrawing from the former and cleaving to the latter, and by thus escaping from the oldness of the letter and serving the newness of the spirit,[ρ] he may clean pass over to grace from the law, which finds its spiritual fulfilment in the dissolution of the body.[σ]

98. Who is the man who has never, by experience and contemplation, traversed the entire series of the titles[τ] and powers of Christ, both those more lofty ones which originally were His, and those more lowly ones which He later assumed for our sake—viz.: God, the Son, the Image, the Word, the Wisdom, the Truth, the Light, the Life, the Power, the Vapour, the Emanation, the Effulgence, the Maker, the King, the Head, the Law, the Way, the Door, the Foundation, the Rock, the Pearl, the Peace, the Righteousness, the Sanctification, the Redemption, the Man, the Servant, the Shepherd, the Lamb, the High Priest, the Victim, the Firstborn before creation, the Firstborn from the dead, the Resurrection: who is the man who hearkens, but pays no heed, to these names so pregnant with reality, and has never yet held communion with, nor been made partaker of, the Word, in any of the real relations signified by each of these names which He bears?

99. Who, in fine, is the man who, although he has never applied himself to, nor learnt to speak, the hidden wisdom of God in a mystery,[α] although he is still a babe, still fed with milk,[β] still of those who are not numbered in Israel,[γ] nor enrolled in the army of God, although he is not yet able to take up the Cross of Christ like a man, although he is possibly not yet one of the more honorable members, yet will joyfully and eagerly accept his appointment as head of the fulness of Christ?[δ] No one, if he will listen to my judgment and accept my advice! This is of all things most to be feared, this is the extremest of dangers in the eyes of everyone who understands the magnitude of success, the utter ruin of failure.

100. Let others sail for merchandise, I used to say, and cross the wide oceans, and constantly contend with winds and waves, to gain great wealth, if so it should chance, and run great risks in their eagerness for sailing and merchandise; but, for my part, I greatly prefer to stay ashore and plough a short but pleasant furrow, saluting at a respectful distance the sea and its gains, to live as best I can upon a poor and scanty store of barley-bread, and drag my life along in safety and calm, rather than expose myself to so long and great a risk for the sake of great gains.

101. For one in high estate, if he fail to make further progress and to disseminate virtue still more widely, and contents himself with slight results, incurs punishment, as having spent a great light upon the illumination of a little house, or girt round the limbs of a boy the full armor of a man. On the contrary, a man of low estate may with safety assume a light burden, and escape the risk of the ridicule and increased danger which would attend him if he attempted a task beyond his powers. For, as we have heard, it is not seemly for a man to build a tower, unless he has sufficient to finish it.[ε]

102. Such is the defence which I have been able to make, perhaps at immoderate length, for my flight. Such are the reasons which, to my pain and possibly to yours, carried me away from you, my friends and brothers; yet, as it seemed to me at the time, with irresistible force. My longing after you, and the sense of your longing for me, have, more than any-

α Ps. lvii. 9. β Ib. cxxxvii. 6. γ Ib. xviii. 33; xl. 3.
δ Ib. lxxiii. 2. ε Rom. vi. 13. ζ 2 Cor. v. 4.
η S. Luke xxiv. 32. θ Ps. xii. 7.
ι *Triple*, a quotation from Prov. xxii. 20. The meaning of the Hebrew is doubtful. Clémencet, not noticing this, suggests that the allusion is to the law being twice inscribed on tables of stone, once on the heart by the Spirit.
κ Prov. xxii. 20 (LXX.). λ 1 Cor. ii. 16. μ Isai. xlv. 3.
ν 1 Cor. ii. 13. ξ Ps. xxvii. 4. ο 2 Cor. vi. 16.
π Eph. ii. 22. ρ Ib. vii. 6. σ Rom. vi. 6.
τ *Titles*. These are more fully dealt with Orat. xxx. 17–21.

α 1 Cor. ii. 17. β Ib. iii. 2. γ Numb. i. 3.
δ Eph. i. 23 ε S. Luke xiv. 28.

thing else, led to my return, for nothing inclines us so strongly to love as mutual affection.

103. In the next place there was my care, my duty, the hoar hairs and weakness of my holy parents, who were more greatly distressed on my account than by their advanced age—of this Patriarch Abraham whose person is honored by me, and numbered among the angels, and of Sarah, who travailed in my spiritual birth by instructing me in the truth. Now, I had specially pledged myself to become the stay of their old age and the support of their weakness, a pledge which, to the best of my power, I have fulfilled, even at the expense of philosophy itself, the most precious of possessions and titles to me; or, to speak more truly, although I made it the first object of my philosophy to appear to be no philosopher, I could not bear that my labor in consequence of a single purpose should be wasted, nor yet that that blessing should be lost, which one of the saints of old is said to have stolen from his father, whom he deceived by the food which he offered to him, and the hairy appearance he assumed, thus attaining a good object by disgraceful trickery.[α] These are the two causes of my submission and tractability. Nor is it, perchance, unreasonable that my arguments should yield and submit to them both, for there is a time to be conquered, as I also think there is for every purpose,[β] and it is better to be honorably overcome than to win a dangerous and lawless victory.

104. There is a third reason of the highest importance which I will further mention, and then dismiss the rest. I remembered the days of old,[γ] and, recurring to one of the ancient histories, drew counsel for myself therefrom as to my present conduct; for let us not suppose these events to have been recorded without a purpose, nor that they are a mere assemblage of words and deeds gathered together for the pastime of those who listen to them, as a kind of bait for the ears, for the sole purpose of giving pleasure. Let us leave such jesting to the legends and the Greeks, who think but little of the truth, and enchant ear and mind by the charm of their fictions and the daintiness of their style.

105. We however, who extend the accuracy of the Spirit to the merest stroke and tittle,[δ] will never admit the impious assertion that even the smallest matters were dealt with haphazard by those who have recorded them, and have thus been borne in mind down to the present day: on the contrary, their purpose has been to supply memorials and instructions for our consideration under similar circumstances, should such befall us, and that the examples of the past might serve as rules and models, for our warning and imitation.

106. What then is the story, and wherein lies its application? For, perhaps, it would not be amiss to relate it, for the general security. Jonah also was fleeing from the face of God,[α] or rather, thought that he was fleeing: but he was overtaken by the sea, and the storm, and the lot, and the whale's belly, and the three days' entombment, the type of a greater mystery. He fled from having to announce the dread and awful message to the Ninevites, and from being subsequently, if the city was saved by repentance, convicted of falsehood: not that he was displeased at the salvation of the wicked, but he was ashamed of being made an instrument of falsehood, and exceedingly zealous for the credit of prophecy, which was in danger of being destroyed in his person, since most men are unable to penetrate the depth of the Divine dispensation in such cases.

107. But, as I have learned from a man[β] skilled in these subjects, and able to grasp the depth of the prophet, by means of a reasonable explanation of what seems unreasonable in the history, it was not this which caused Jonah to flee, and carried him to Joppa and again from Joppa to Tarshish, when he entrusted his stolen self to the sea:[γ] for it was not likely that such a prophet should be ignorant of the design of God, viz., to bring about, by means of the threat, the escape of the Ninevites from the threatened doom, according to His great wisdom, and unsearchable judgments, and according to His ways which are beyond our tracing and finding out;[δ] nor that, if he knew this he would refuse to co-operate with God in the use of the means which He designed for their salvation. Besides, to imagine that Jonah hoped to hide himself at sea, and escape by his flight the great eye of God, is surely utterly absurd and stupid, and unworthy of credit, not only in the case of a prophet, but

α Gen. xxvii. 21, sq.
β Eccles. iii. 1.
γ Ps. cxliii. 5.
δ S. Matt. v. 18.

α Jonah i. 3.

β *A man*. A Greek scholiast says that this was Origen (ob. A.D. 235), who gives this interpretation in his commentary on the prophecy of Jonah. Elias says that he had read it in the commentary of Methodius (fl. A.D. 300), who usually combats Origen's interpretations. We know that Origen did comment on the book of Job, and that Methodius wrote on one at least of the Minor Prophets: but both these works have been lost, so that we cannot absolutely decide the question, though the assurance with which both the notes are written makes us hesitate to consider either of them merely a happy guess. Combefis thinks that S. Greg. alludes to one of his own instructors: the gen. with ἀκόυω (cf. Plato, Gorg., 503, c.) favours this view, but the interpretation may well have been derived from one of the earlier writers.

γ Jonah i. 3.
δ Rom. xi. 33.

even in the case of any sensible man, who has only a slight perception of God, Whose power is over all.

108. On the contrary, as my instructor said, and as I am myself convinced, Jonah knew better than any one the purpose of his message to the Ninevites, and that, in planning his flight, although he changed his place, he did not escape from God. Nor is this possible for any one else, either by concealing himself in the bosom of the earth, or in the depths of the sea, or by soaring on wings, if there be any means of doing so, and rising into the air, or by abiding in the lowest depths of hell,[α] or by enveloping himself in a thick cloud, or by any other of the many devices for ensuring escape. For God alone of all things cannot be escaped from or contended with; if He wills to seize and bring them under His hand, He outstrips the swift, He outwits the wise, He overthrows the strong, He abases the lofty, He subdues rashness, He represses power.

109. Jonah then was not ignorant of the mighty hand of God, with which he threatened other men, nor did he imagine that he could utterly escape the Divine power; this we are not to believe: but when he saw the falling away of Israel, and perceived the passing over of the grace of prophecy to the Gentiles—this was the cause of his retirement from preaching and of his delay in fulfilling the command; accordingly he left the watchtower of joy, for this is the meaning of Joppa in Hebrew, I mean his former dignity and reputation, and flung himself into the deep of sorrow: and hence he is tempest-tossed, and falls asleep, and is wrecked, and aroused from sleep, and taken by lot, and confesses his flight, and is cast into sea, and swallowed, but not destroyed, by the whale; but there he calls upon God, and, marvellous as it is, on the third day he, like Christ, is delivered: but my treatment of this topic must stand over, and shall shortly, if God permit, be more deliberately worked out.[β]

110. Now however, to return to my original point, the thought and question occurred to me, that although he might possibly meet with some indulgence, if reluctant to prophesy, for the cause which I mentioned—yet, in my own case, what could be said, what defence could be made, if I longer remained restive, and rejected the yoke of ministry, which, though I know not whether to call it light or heavy, had at any rate been laid upon me.

α Ps. cxxxix. 8 et seq.

β *Shall be worked out.* This promise, as Elias tells us, was fulfilled by S. Gregory in his History of Ezekiel the Prophet, a work no longer extant.

111. For if it be granted, and this alone can be strongly asserted in such matters, that we are far too low to perform the priest's office before God, and that we can only be worthy of the sanctuary after we have become worthy of the Church,[α] and worthy of the post of president, after being worthy of the sanctuary, yet some one else may perhaps refuse to acquit us on the charge of disobedience. Now terrible are the threatenings against disobedience, and terrible are the penalties which ensue upon it; as indeed are those on the other side, if, instead of being reluctant, and shrinking back, and concealing ourselves as Saul did among his father's stuff[β]—although called to rule but for a short time—if, I say, we come forward readily, as though to a slight and most easy task, whereas it is not safe even to resign it, nor to amend by second thoughts our first.

112. On this account I had much toilsome consideration to discover my duty, being set in the midst betwixt two fears, of which the one held me back, the other urged me on. For a long while I was at a loss between them, and after wavering from side to side, and, like a current driven by inconstant winds, inclining first in this direction, then in that, I at last yielded to the stronger, and the fear of disobedience overcame me, and has carried me off. Pray, mark how accurately and justly I hold the balance between the fears, neither desiring an office not given to me, nor rejecting it when given. The one course marks the rash, the other the disobedient, both the undisciplined. My position lies between those who are too bold, or too timid; more timid than those who rush at every position, more bold than those who avoid them all. This is my judgment on the matter.

113. Moreover, to distinguish still more clearly between them, we have, against the fear of office, a possible help in the law of obedience, inasmuch as God in His goodness rewards our faith, and makes a perfect ruler of the man who has confidence in Him, and places all his hopes in Him; but against the danger of disobedience I know of nothing which can help us, and of no ground to encourage our confidence. For it is to be feared that we shall have to hear these words concerning those who have been entrusted to us: I will require their souls at your hands;[γ]

α *Of the Church.* S. Gregory seems to describe a series of three steps, (1) the Church, of which all should be worthy members, (2) the Sanctuary, reserved for the Priests, (3) the Throne of the Bishop. Clémencet refers both 1 and 2 to the ministry. If we suppose S. Gregory's own position to be referred to, the third would be applicable to his office under his father, which is held by Thomassin to have been that of Vicar-General (Disc. Eccles., I., ii., 7 §§ 2, 3). A similar post was offered to him by S. Basil (Orat., xliii., 39). β 1 Sam. x. 22. γ Ezek. iii. 18.

and, Because ye have rejected me, and not been leaders and rulers of my people, I also will reject you, that I should not be king over you;[α] and, As ye refused to hearken to My voice, and turned a stubborn back, and were disobedient, so shall it be when ye call upon Me, and I will not regard nor give ear to your prayer.[β] God forbid that these words should come to us from the just Judge, for when we sing of His mercy we must also by all means sing of His judgment.[γ]

114. I resort once again to history, and on considering the men of best repute in ancient days, who were ever preferred by grace to the office of ruler or prophet, I discover that some readily complied with the call, others deprecated the gift, and that neither those who drew back were blamed for timidity, nor those who came forward for eagerness. The former stood in awe of the greatness of the ministry, the latter trustfully obeyed Him Who called them. Aaron was eager, but Moses resisted,[δ] Isaiah readily submitted, but Jeremiah was afraid of his youth,[ε] and did not venture to prophesy until he had received from God a promise and power beyond his years.[ζ]

115. By these arguments I charmed myself, and by degrees my soul relaxed and became ductile, like iron, and time came to the aid of my arguments, and the testimonies of God, to which I had entrusted my whole life, were my counsellors.[η] Therefore I was not rebellious, neither turned away back,[θ] saith my Lord, when, instead of being called to rule, He was led, as a sheep to the slaughter;[ι] but I fell down and humbled myself under the mighty hand of God,[κ] and asked pardon for my former idleness and disobedience, if this is at all laid to my charge. I held my peace,[λ] but I will not hold my peace for ever: I withdrew for a little while,[μ] till I had considered myself and consoled my grief: but now I am commissioned to exalt Him in the congregation of the people, and praise Him in the seat of the elders.[ν] If my former conduct deserved blame, my present action merits pardon.

116. What further need is there of words. Here am I, my pastors and fellow-pastors, here am I, thou holy flock, worthy of Christ, the Chief Shepherd,[ξ] here am I, my father, utterly vanquished, and your subject according to the laws of Christ rather than according to those of the land:[o] here is my obedience, reward it with your blessing. Lead me with your prayers, guide me with your words, establish me with your spirit. The blessing of the father establisheth the houses of children,[α] and would that both I and this spiritual house may be established, the house which I have longed for, which I pray may be my rest for ever,[β] when I have been passed on from the church here to the church yonder, the general assembly of the firstborn, who are written in heaven.[γ]

117. Such is my defence: its reasonableness I have set forth: and may the God of peace,[δ] Who made both one,[ε] and has restored us to each other, Who setteth kings upon thrones, and raiseth up the poor out of the dust and lifteth up the beggar from the dunghill,[ζ] Who chose David His servant and took him away from the sheepfolds,[η] though he was the least and youngest of the sons of Jesse,[θ] Who gave the word[ι] to those who preach the gospel with great power for the perfection of the gospel,—may He Himself hold me by my right hand, and guide me with His counsel, and receive me with glory,[κ] Who is a Shepherd[λ] to shepherds and a Guide to guides: that we may feed His flock with knowledge,[μ] not with the instruments of a foolish shepherd,[ν] according to the blessing, and not according to the curse pronounced against the men of former days: may He give strength and power unto his people,[ξ] and Himself present to Himself[o] His flock resplendent and spotless and worthy of the fold on high, in the habitation of them that rejoice,[π] in the splendour of the saints,[ρ] so that in His temple everyone, both flock and shepherds together may say, Glory,[σ] in Christ Jesus our Lord, to Whom be all glory for ever and ever. Amen.

ORATION III.

To Those Who Had Invited Him, and Not Come to Receive Him.

(About Easter A.D. 362.)

I. How slow you are, my friends and brethren, to come to listen to my words, though you were so swift in tyrannizing over me, and tearing me from my Citadel Solitude, which I had embraced in preference to everything

α 1 Sam. xv. 26; cf. Hos. iv. 6. β Zech. vii. 11, 13. γ Ps. ci. 1. δ Exod. iv. 10, 13, 27. ε Isai. vi. 8. ζ Jer. i. 6. η Ps. cxix. 24. θ Isai. l. 6. ι Ib. liii. 7. κ 1 Pet. v. 6. λ Isai. xlii. 14. μ Ib. xxvi. 20. ν Ps. cvii. 32. ξ 1 Pet. v. 4.

o *Of the land*, lit., "external," i.e.. the Roman laws, which gave absolute power to a father over his children.

α Ecclus. iii. 9. β Ps. cxxxii. 13, 14. γ Heb. xii. 23. δ Heb. xiii. 20. ε Eph. ii. 14. ζ 1 Sam. ii. 8; Ps. cxiii. 7. η Ps. lxxviii. 70. θ 1 Sam. xvii. 14. ι Ps. lxviii. 11. κ Ps. lxxiii. 23, 24. λ Ezek. xxxiv. 12. μ Jer. iii. 15. ν Zech. xi. 15. ξ Ps. lxviii. 35. o Eph. v. 27. π Ps. lxxxvii. 7 (LXX.). ρ Ps. cx. 3 (LXX.). σ Ps. xxix. 9.

else, and as coadjutress and mother of the divine ascent, and as deifying man,[α] I had especially admired, and had set before me as the guide of my whole life.[β] How is it that, now you have got it, you thus despise what you so greatly desired to obtain, and seem to be better able to desire the absent than to enjoy the present; as though you preferred to *possess* my teaching rather than to *profit* by it? Yes, I may even say this to you: "I became a surfeit unto you before you tasted of me, or gave me a trial"[γ]—which is most strange.

II. And neither did you entertain me as a guest, nor, if I may make a remark of a more compassionate kind, did you allow yourselves to be entertained by me, reverencing this command if nothing else; nor did you take me by the hand, as beginning a new task; nor encourage me in my timidity, nor console me for the violence I had suffered; but—I shrink from saying it, though say it I must—you made my festival no festival, and received me with no happy introduction; and you mingled the solemn festival with sorrow, because it lacked that which most of all would have contributed to its happiness, the presence of you my conquerors, for it would not be true to call you people who love me. So easily is anything despised which is easily conquered, and the proud receives attention, while he who is humble before God is slighted.

III. What will ye? Shall I be judged by you, or shall I be your judge? Shall I pass a verdict, or receive one, for I hope to be acquitted if I be judged, and if I give sentence, to give it against you justly? The charge against you is that you do not answer my love with equal measure, nor do you repay my obedience with honour, nor do you pledge the future to me by your present alacrity—though even if you had, I could hardly have believed it. But each of you has something which he prefers to both the old and the new Pastor, neither reverencing the grey hairs of the one, nor calling out the youthful spirit of the other.

IV. There is a Banquet in the Gospels,[δ] and a hospitable Host and friends; and the Banquet is most pleasant, for it is the marriage of His Son, He calleth them, but they come not: He is angry, and—I pass over the interval for fear of bad omen—but, to speak gently, He filleth the Banquet with others. God forbid that this should be your case; but yet you have treated me (how shall I put it gently?) with as much haughtiness or boldness as they who after being called to a feast rise up against it, and insult their host; for you, though you are not of the number of those who are without, or are invited to the marriage, but are yourselves those who invited me, and bound me to the Holy Table, and shewed me the glory of the Bridal Chamber, then deserted me (this is the most splendid thing about you)—one to his field, another to his newly bought yoke of oxen, another to his just-married wife, another to some other trifling matter; you were all scattered and dispersed, caring little for the Bridechamber and the Bridegroom.[α]

V. On this account I was filled with despondency and perplexity—for I will not keep silence about what I have suffered—and I was very near withholding the discourse which I was minded to bestow as a Marriage-gift, the most beautiful and precious of all I had; and I very nearly let it loose upon you, whom, now that the violence had once been done to me, I greatly longed for: for I thought I could get from this a splendid theme, and because my love sharpened my tongue—love which is very hot and ready for accusation when it is stirred to jealousy by grief which it conceives from some unexpected neglect. If any of you has been pierced with love's sting, and has felt himself neglected, he knows the feeling, and will pardon one who so suffers, because he himself has been near the same frenzy.

VI. But it is not permitted to me at the present time to say to you anything upbraiding; and God forbid I ever should. And even now perhaps I have reproached you more than in due measure, the Sacred Flock, the praise-worthy nurselings of Christ, the Divine inheritance; by which, O God, Thou art rich, even wert Thou poor in all other respects. To Thee, I think, are fitting those words, "The lot is fallen unto Thee in a fair ground: yea Thou hast the goodliest heritage."[β] Nor will I allow that the most populous cities or the broadest flocks have any advantage over us, the little ones of the smallest of all the tribes of Israel, of the least of the thousands of Judah,[γ] of the little Bethlehem among cities,[δ] where Christ was born and is from the beginning well-known and wor-

α S. Gregory very frequently uses this very strong expression to bring out the reality and intimacy of the Christian's Union with Christ as the result of the sanctifying grace by which all the Baptized are made "partakers of the Divine Nature" (2 Pet. i. 4).

β The passage might also be rendered "had preferred to every other kind of life."

γ Isa. i. 14.

δ S. Luke xiv. 16.

α S. Matt. xxii. 10.

β Ps. xvi. 6.

γ 1 Sam. xxiii. 23.

δ Mic. v. 2.

shipped; amongst those whom the Father is exalted, and the Son is held to be equal to Him, and the Holy Ghost is glorified with Them: we who are of one soul, who mind the same thing, who in nothing injure the Trinity, neither by preferring One Person above another, nor by cutting off any: as those bad umpires and measurers of the God-head do, who by magnifying One Person more than is fit, diminish and insult the whole.

VII. But do ye also, if you bear me any good will—ye who are my husbandry, my vine-yard, my own bowels, or rather His Who is our common Father, for in Christ he hath begotten you through the Gospels[α]—shew to us also some respect. It is only fair, since we have honoured you above all else: ye are my witnesses, ye, and they who have placed in our hands this—shall I say *Authority*, or *Service?* And if to him that loveth most most is due, how shall I measure the love, for which I have made you my debtors by my own love? Rather, shew respect for yourselves, and the Image committed to your care,[β] and Him Who committed it, and the Sufferings of Christ, and your hopes therefrom, holding fast the faith which ye have received, and in which ye were brought up, by which also ye are being saved, and trust to save others (for not many, be well assured, can boast of what you can), and reckoning piety to consist, not in often speaking about God, but in silence for the most part, for the tongue is a dangerous thing to men, if it be not governed by reason. Believe that listening is always less dangerous than talking, just as learning about God is more pleasant than teaching. Leave the more accurate search into these questions to those who are the Stewards of the Word; and for yourselves, worship a little in words, but more by your actions, and rather by keeping the Law than by admiring the Lawgiver; shew your love for Him by fleeing from wickedness, pursuing after virtue, living in the Spirit, walking in the Spirit, drawing your knowledge from Him, building upon the foundation of the faith, not wood or hay or stubble,[γ] weak materials and easily spent when the fire shall try our works or destroy them; but gold, silver, precious stones, which remain and stand.

VIII. So may ye act, and so may ye honour us, whether present or absent, whether taking your part in our sermons, or preferring to do something else: and may ye be the children of God, pure and unblamable, in the midst of a crooked and perverse generation:[α] and may ye never be entangled in the snares of the wicked that go round about, or bound with the chain of your sins. May the Word in you never be smothered with cares of this life and so ye become unfruitful: but may ye walk in the King's Highway, turning aside neither to the right hand nor to the left,[β] but led by the Spirit through the strait gate. Then all our affairs shall prosper, both now and at the inquest There, in Christ Jesus our Lord, to Whom be the glory for ever. Amen.

α 1 Cor. iv. 15. I.e., the Elder Gregory.
β Gen. i. 27.
γ 1 Cor. iii. 12.

ORATION VII.

PANEGYRIC ON HIS BROTHER S. CÆSARIUS.

The date of this Oration is probably the spring of A.D. 369. It is placed by S. Jerome first among S. Gregory's Orations. Cæsarius, the Saint's younger brother, was born probably about A.D. 330. Educated in his early years at home, he studied later in the schools of Alexandria, where he attained great proficiency in mathematics, astronomy, and, especially, in medicine. On his return from Alexandria, he was offered by the Emperor Constantius, in response to a public petition, an honourable and lucrative post at Byzantium, but was prevailed upon by Gregory to return with him to Nazianzus. After a while he went back to Byzantium, and, on the accession of Julian, was pressed to retain his appointment at court, and did so, in spite of Gregory's reproaches, until Julian, who had long been trying to win him from Christianity, at last invited him to a public discussion. Cæsarius, in spite of the specious arguments of the Emperor, gained the day, but, having now distinctly declared himself a Christian, could no longer remain at court. On the death of Julian, he was esteemed and promoted by successive Emperors, until he received from Valens the office of treasurer of Bithynia. The exact character of this office and its rank are still undecided by historical writers, some of whom attribute to him other offices not mentioned by S. Gregory, which most probably were filled by a namesake. On the 11th of October A.D. 368 the city of Nicæa was almost entirely destroyed by an earthquake and Cæsarius miraculously escaped with his life. Impressed by his escape, he received Holy Baptism, and formed plans for retiring from office and (as

α Phil. ii. 15.
β Num. xxi. 22; Isa. xl. 3.

it seems) devoting himself to a life of ascetic discipline, which were dissipated by his early and sudden death.

1. It may be, my friends, my brethren, my fathers (ye who are dear to me in reality as well as in name) that you think that I, who am about to pay the sad tribute of lamentation to him who has departed, am eager to undertake the task, and shall, as most men delight to do, speak at great length and in eloquent style. And so some of you, who have had like sorrows to bear, are prepared to join in my mourning and lamentation, in order to bewail your own griefs in mine, and learn to feel pain at the afflictions of a friend, while others are looking to feast their ears in the enjoyment of my words. For they suppose that I must needs make my misfortune an occasion for display—as was once my wont, when possessed of a superabundance of earthly things, and ambitious, above all, of oratorical renown—before I looked up to Him Who is the true and highest Word, and gave all up to God, from Whom all things come, and took God for all in all. Now pray do not think this of me, if you wish to think of me aright. For I am neither going to lament for him who is gone more than is good—as I should not approve of such conduct even in others—nor am I going to praise him beyond due measure. Albeit that language is a dear and especially proper tribute to one gifted with it, and eulogy to one who was exceedingly fond of my words—aye, not only a tribute, but a debt, the most just of all debts. But even in my tears and admiration I must respect the law which regards such matters: nor is this alien to our philosophy; for he says The memory of the just is accompanied with eulogies,[α] and also, Let tears fall down over the dead, and begin to lament, as if thou hadst suffered great harm thyself:[β] removing us equally from insensibility and immoderation. I shall proceed then, not only to exhibit the weakness of human nature, but also to put you in mind of the dignity of the soul, and, giving such consolation as is due to those who are in sorrow, transfer our grief, from that which concerns the flesh and temporal things, to those things which are spiritual and eternal.

2. The parents of Cæsarius, to take first the point which best becomes me, are known to you all. Their excellence you are eager to notice, and hear of with admiration, and share in the task of setting it forth to any, if there

α Prov. x. 7 (LXX.). β Ecclus. xxxviii. 16.

be such, who know it not: for no single man is able to do so entirely, and the task is one beyond the powers of a single tongue, however laborious, however zealous. Among the many and great points for which they are to be celebrated (I trust I may not seem extravagant in praising my own family) the greatest of all, which more than any other stamps their character, is piety. By their hoar hairs they lay claim to reverence, but they are no less venerable for their virtue than for their age; for while their bodies are bent beneath the burden of their years, their souls renew their youth in God.

3. His father[α] was well grafted out of the wild olive tree into the good one, and so far partook of its fatness as to be entrusted with the engrafting of others, and charged with the culture of souls, presiding in a manner becoming his high office over this people, like a second Aaron or Moses, bidden himself to draw near to God,[β] and to convey the Divine Voice to the others who stand afar off;[γ] gentle, meek, calm in mien,[δ] fervent in spirit, a fine man in external appearance, but richer still in that which is out of sight. But why should I describe him whom you know? For I could not even by speaking at great length say as much as he deserves, or as much as each of you knows and expects to be said of him. It is then better to leave your own fancy to picture him, than mutilate by my words the object of your admiration.

4. His mother[ε] was consecrated to God by virtue of her descent from a saintly family, and was possessed of piety as a necessary inheritance, not only for herself, but also for her children—being indeed a holy lump from a holy firstfruits.[ζ] And this she so far increased and amplified that some, (bold though the statement be, I will utter it,) have both believed and said that even her husband's perfection has been the work of none other than herself; and, oh how wonderful! she herself, as the reward of her piety, has received a greater and more perfect piety. Lovers of their children and of Christ as they both were, what is most extraordinary, they were far greater lovers of Christ than of their children: yea, even their one enjoyment of their children was that they should be acknowledged and named by Christ, and their one measure of their blessedness in their children was their

α *His father.* S. Gregory the elder. Cf. Orat. xviii., 5, 6, 12–29, 32–39. Also viii., 4, 5; xii., 2, 3; xvi., 1–4, 20.
β Exod. xxiv. 1, 2. γ Exod. xx. 19; Deut. v. 27.
δ *In mien.* v. l. "in disposition."
ε *His mother.* S. Nonna. Cf. Orat. xviii., 7–12, 30, 31, 42, 43. Also viii. 4, 5. ζ Rom. xi. 16.

virtue and close association with the Chief Good.[α] Compassionate, sympathetic, snatching many a treasure from moths and robbers,[β] and from the prince of this world,[γ] to transfer it from their sojourn here to the [true] habitation, laying up in store[δ] for their children the heavenly splendour as their greatest inheritance. Thus have they reached a fair old age, equally reverend both for virtue and for years, and full of days, alike of those which abide and those which pass away; each one failing to secure the first prize here below only so far as equalled by the other; yea, they have fulfilled the measure of every happiness with the exception of this last trial, or discipline, whichever anyone may think we ought to call it; I mean their having to send before them the child who was, owing to his age, in greater danger of falling, and so to close their life in safety, and be translated with all their family to the realms above.

5. I have entered into these details, not from a desire to eulogize them, for this, I know well, it would be difficult worthily to do, if I made their praise the subject of my whole oration, but to set forth the excellence inherited from his parents by Cæsarius, and so prevent you from being surprised or incredulous, that one sprung from such progenitors, should have deserved such praises himself; nay, strange indeed would it have been, had he looked to others and disregarded the examples of his kinsfolk at home. His early life was such as becomes those really well born and destined for a good life. I say little of his qualities evident to all, his beauty, his stature, his manifold gracefulness, and harmonious disposition, as shown in the tones of his voice—for it is not my office to laud qualities of this kind, however important they may seem to others—and proceed with what I have to say of the points which, even if I wished, I could with difficulty pass by.

6. Bred and reared under such influences, we were fully trained in the education afforded here,[ε] in which none could say how far he excelled most of us from the quickness and extent of his abilities—and how can I recall those days without my tears showing that, contrary to my promises, my feelings have overcome my philosophic restraint? The time came when it was decided that we should leave home, and then for the first time we were separated, for I studied rhetoric in the then flourishing schools of Palestine; he went to Alexandria, esteemed both then and now the home of every branch of learning. Which of his qualities shall I place first and foremost, or which can I omit with least injury to my description? Who was more faithful to his teacher than he? Who more kindly to his classmates? Who more carefully avoided the society and companionship of the depraved? Who attached himself more closely to that of the most excellent, and among others, of the most esteemed and illustrious of his countrymen? For he knew that we are strongly influenced to virtue or vice by our companions. And in consequence of all this, who was more honoured by the authorities than he, and whom did the whole city (though[α] all individuals are concealed in it, because of its size), esteem more highly for his discretion, or deem more illustrious for his intelligence?

7. What branch of learning did he not master, or rather, in what branch of study did he not surpass those who had made it their sole study? Whom did he allow even to approach him, not only of his own time and age, but even of his elders, who had devoted many more years to study? All subjects he studied as one, and each as thoroughly as if he knew no other. The brilliant in intellect, he surpassed in industry, the devoted students in quickness of perception; nay, rather he outstripped in rapidity those who were rapid, in application those who were laborious, and in both respects those who were distinguished in both. From geometry and astronomy, that science so dangerous[β] to anyone else, he gathered all that was helpful (I mean that he was led by the harmony and order of the heavenly bodies to reverence their Maker), and avoided what is injurious; not attributing all things that are or happen to the influence of the stars, like those who raise their own fellow-servant, the creation, in rebellion against the Creator, but referring, as is reasonable, the motion of these bodies, and all other things besides, to God. In arithmetic and mathematics, and in the wonderful art of medicine, in so far as it treats of physiology and temperament, and the causes of disease, in order to remove the roots and so destroy their offspring with them, who is there so ignorant or contentious as to think him inferior to himself, and not to be glad to be reckoned next to him, and carry off the second prize? This indeed is no unsupported assertion, but East and West[γ] alike, and every place which he afterward visited, are as

α *The Chief Good.* τὸ κρεῖττον, lit. "that which is better."
β S. Matt. vi. 19; S. John x. 1.
γ S. John xiv. 30.
δ 1 Tim. vi. 19.
ε *Here*, at Nazianzus.

α *Though*, etc. The Ben. ed. translates "Although his teaching was exceedingly sublime and abstruse."
β *Dangerous*, as being so closely connected with astrology.
γ *East and West*, ἑῶά τε ὁμοῦ λῆξις καὶ ἑσπέριος;—λῆξις significat *regionem, locum: culmen* item, seu *fastigium*. Cf. S. Greg. Naz. Orat. xxv. 13. p. 464. S. Chrys. Hom. LVI. in Ioan. p. 786.

pillars inscribed with the record of his learning.

8. But when, after gathering into his single soul every kind of excellence and knowledge, as a mighty merchantman gathers every sort of ware, he was voyaging to his own city, in order to communicate to others the fair cargo of his culture, there befell a wondrous thing, which I must, as its mention is most cheering to me and may delight you, briefly set forth. Our mother,[a] in her motherly love for her children, had offered up a prayer that, as she had sent us forth together, she might see us together return home. For we seemed, to our mother at least, if not to others, to form a pair worthy of her prayers and glances, if seen together, though now, alas, our connection has been severed. And God, Who hears a righteous prayer, and honours the love of parents for well-disposed children, so ordered that, without any design or agreement on our part, the one from Alexandria, the other from Greece, the one by sea, the other by land, we arrived at the same city at the same time. This city was Byzantium, which now presides over Europe, in which Cæsarius, after the lapse of a short time, gained such a repute, that public honours, an alliance with an illustrious family, and a seat in the council of state were offered him; and a mission was despatched to the Emperor by public decision, to beg that the first of cities be adorned and honoured by the first of scholars (if he cared at all for its being indeed the first, and worthy of its name); and that to all its other titles to distinction this further one be added, that it was embellished by having Cæsarius as its physician and its inhabitant, although its brilliancy was already assured by its throngs of great men both in philosophy and other branches of learning. But enough of this. At this time there happened what seemed to others a chance without reason or cause, such as frequently occurs of its own accord in our day, but was more than sufficiently manifest to devout minds as the result of the prayers to god-fearing parents, which were answered by the united arrival of their sons by land and sea.

9. Well, among the noble traits of Cæsarius' character, we must not fail to note one, which perhaps is in others' eyes slight and unworthy of mention, but seemed to me, both at the time and since, of the highest import, if indeed brotherly love be a praiseworthy quality; nor shall I ever cease to place it in the first rank, in relating the story of his life. Although the metropolis strove to retain him by the honours I have mentioned, and declared that it would under no circumstances let him go, my influence, which he valued most highly on all occasions, prevailed upon him to listen to the prayer of his parents, to supply his country's need, and to grant me my own desire. And when he thus returned home in my company, he preferred me not only to cities and peoples, not only to honours and revenues, which had in part already flowed to him in abundance from many sources and in part were within his reach, but even to the Emperor himself and his imperial commands. From this time, then, having shaken off all ambition, as a hard master and a painful disorder, I resolved to practise philosophy and adapt myself to the higher life: or rather the desire was earlier born, the life came later. But my brother, who had dedicated to his country the firstfruits of his learning, and gained an admiration worthy of his efforts, was afterwards led by the desire of fame, and, as he persuaded me, of being the guardian of the city, to betake himself to court, not indeed according to my own wishes or judgment; for I will confess to you that I think it a better and grander thing to be in the lowest rank with God than to win the first place with an earthly king. Nevertheless I cannot blame him, for inasmuch as philosophy is the greatest, so is it the most difficult, of professions, which can be taken in hand by but few, and only by those who have been called forth by the Divine magnanimity, which gives its hand to those who are honoured by its preference. Yet it is no small thing if one, who has chosen the lower form of life, follows after goodness, and sets greater store on God and his own salvation than on earthly lustre; using it as a stage, or a manifold ephemeral mask while playing in the drama of this world, but himself living unto God with that image which he knows that he has received from Him, and must render to Him Who gave it. That this was certainly the purpose of Cæsarius, we know full well.

10. Among physicians he gained the foremost place with no great trouble, by merely exhibiting his capacity, or rather some slight specimen of his capacity, and was forthwith numbered among the friends of the Emperor, and enjoyed the highest honours. But he placed the humane functions of his art at the disposal of the authorities free of cost, knowing that nothing leads to further advancement than virtue and renown for honourable deeds; so that he far surpassed in fame those to whom he was inferior in rank. By his modesty he so won the love of all that they entrusted their

---

[a] *Our mother.* For further detail cf. Orat. xviii. 31.

precious charges to his care, without requiring him to be sworn by Hippocrates, since the simplicity of Crates was nothing to his own: winning in general a respect beyond his rank; for besides the present repute he was ever thought to have justly won, a still greater one was anticipated for him, both by the Emperors[a] themselves and by all who occupied the nearest positions to them. But, most important, neither by his fame, nor by the luxury which surrounded him, was his nobility of soul corrrupted; for amidst his many claims to honour, he himself cared most for being, and being known to be, a Christian, and, compared with this, all other things were to him but trifling toys. For they belong to the part we play before others on a stage which is very quickly set up and taken down again—perhaps indeed more quickly destroyed than put together, as we may see from the manifold changes of life, and fluctuations of prosperity; while the only real and securely abiding good thing is godliness.

11. Such was the philosophy of Cæsarius, even at court: these were the ideas amidst which he lived and died, discovering and presenting to God, in the hidden man, a still deeper godliness than was publicly visible. And if I must pass by all else, his protection of his kinsmen in distress, his contempt for arrogance, his freedom from assumption towards friends, his boldness towards men in power, the numerous contests and arguments in which he engaged with many on behalf of the truth, not merely for the sake of argument, but with deep piety and fervour, I must speak of one point at least as especially worthy of note. The Emperor[β] of unhappy memory was raging against us, whose madness in rejecting Christ, after making himself its first victim, had now rendered him intolerable to others; though he did not, like other fighters against Christ, grandly enlist himself on the side of impiety, but veiled his persecution under the form of equity; and, ruled by the crooked serpent which possessed his soul, dragged down into his own pit his wretched victims by manifold devices. His first artifice and contrivance was, to deprive us of the honour of our conflicts (for, noble man as he was, he grudged this to Christians), by causing us, who suffered for being Christians, to be punished as evil doers: the second was, to call this process persuasion, and not tyranny, so that the disgrace of those who chose to side with impiety might be greater than their danger. Some he won over by money, some by dignities, some by promises, some by various honours, which he bestowed, not royally but in right servile style, in the sight of all, while everyone was influenced by the witchery of his words, and his own example. At last he assailed Cæsarius. How utter was the derangement and folly which could hope to take for his prey a man like Cæsarius, my brother, the son of parents like ours!

12. However, that I may dwell awhile upon this point, and luxuriate in my story as men do who are eyewitnesses in some marvellous event,[a] that noble man, fortified with the sign of Christ, and defending himself with His Mighty Word, entered the lists against an adversary experienced in arms and strong in his skill in argument. In no wise abashed at the sight, nor shrinking at all from his high purpose through flattery, he was an athlete ready, both in word and deed, to meet a rival of equal power. Such then was the arena, and so equipped the champion of godliness. The judge on one side was Christ, arming the athlete with His own sufferings: and on the other a dreadful tyrant,[β] persuasive by his skill in argument, and overawing him by the weight of his authority; and as spectators, on either hand, both those who were still left on the side of godliness and those who had been snatched away by him, watching whether victory inclined to their own side or to the other, and more anxious as to which would gain the day than the combatants themselves.

13. Didst thou not fear for Cæsarius, lest aught unworthy of his zeal should befall him? Nay, be ye of good courage. For the victory is with Christ, Who overcame the world.[γ] Now for my part, be well assured, I should be highly interested in setting forth the details of the arguments and allegations used on that occasion, for indeed the discussion contains certain feats and elegances, which I dwell on with no slight pleasure; but this would be quite foreign to an occasion and discourse like the present. And when, after having torn to shreds all his opponent's sophistries, and thrust aside as mere child's play every assault, veiled or open, Cæsarius in a loud clear voice declared that he was and remained a Christian—not even thus was he finally dismissed. For indeed, the Emperor was possessed by an eager desire to enjoy and be distinguished by his culture,

α *The Emperors.* { Constantius II., A.D. 337–361. Julian, A.D. 361–363. Jovian, A.D. 363–4. Valens, A.D. 364–378. }

β *The Emperor*, *i.e.*, Julian the Apostate.

α Some edd. read "in the spectacle," which would make better sense, but has not MS. authority.

β *A dreadful tyrant.* The Evil One: with Billius and Clémencet. Julian was antagonist, not Judge—unless we consider that he combined unfairly the two offices.

γ S. John xvi. 33.

and then uttered in the hearing of all his famous saying—O happy father, O unhappy sons! thus deigning to honour me, whose culture and godliness[α] he had known at Athens, with a share in the dishonour of Cæsarius, who was remanded for a further trial[β] (since Justice was fitly arming the Emperor against the Persians),[γ] and welcomed by us after his happy escape and bloodless victory, as more illustrious for his dishonour than for his celebrity.

14. This victory I esteem far more sublime and honourable than the Emperor's mighty power and splendid purple and costly diadem. I am more elated in describing it than if he had won from him the half of his Empire. During the evil days he lived in retirement, obedient herein to our Christian law,[δ] which bids us, when occasion offers, to make ventures on behalf of the truth, and not be traitors to our religion from cowardice; yet refrain, as long as may be, from rushing into danger, either in fear for our own souls, or to spare those who bring the danger upon us. But when the gloom had been dispersed, and the righteous sentence had been pronounced in a foreign land, and the glittering sword had struck down the ungodly, and power had returned to the hands of Christians, what boots it to say with what glory and honour, with how many and great testimonies, as if bestowing rather than receiving a favour, he was welcomed again at the Court; his new honour succeeding to that of former days; while time changed its Emperors, the repute and commanding influence of Cæsarius with them was undisturbed, nay, they vied with each other in striving to attach him most closely to themselves, and be known as his special friends and acquaintances. Such was the godliness of Cæsarius, such its results. Let all men, young and old, give ear, and press on through the same virtue to the same distinction, for glorious is the fruit of good labours,[ε] if they suppose this to be worth striving after, and a part of true happiness.

15. Again another wonder concerning him is a strong argument for his parents' piety and his own. He was living in Bithynia, holding an office of no small importance from the Emperor, viz., the stewardship of his revenue, and care of the exchequer: for this had been assigned to him by the Emperor as a prelude to the highest offices. And when, a short time ago, the earthquake[α] in Nicæa occurred, which is said to have been the most serious within the memory of man, overwhelming in a common destruction almost all the inhabitants and the beauty of the city, he alone, or with very few of the men of rank, survived the danger, being shielded by the very falling ruins in his incredible escape, and bearing slight traces of the peril; yet he allowed fear to lead him to a more important salvation, for he dedicated himself entirely to the Supreme Providence; he renounced the service of transitory things, and attached himself to another court. This he both purposed himself, and made the object of the united earnest prayers to which he invited me by letter, when I seized this opportunity to give him warning,[β] as I never ceased to do when pained that his great nature should be occupied in affairs beneath it, and that a soul so fitted for philosophy should, like the sun behind a cloud, be obscured amid the whirl of public life. Unscathed though he had been by the earthquake, he was not proof against disease, since he was but human. His escape was peculiar to himself; his death common to all mankind; the one the token of his piety, the other the result of his nature. The former, for our consolation, preceded his fate, so that, though shaken by his death, we might exult in the extraordinary character of his preservation. And now our illustrious Cæsarius has been restored to us, when his honoured dust and celebrated corse, after being escorted home amidst a succession of hymns and public orations, has been honoured by the holy hands of his parents; while his mother, substituting the festal garments of religion for the trappings of woe, has overcome her tears by her philosophy, and lulled to sleep lamentations by psalmody, as her son enjoys honours worthy of his newly regenerate soul, which has been, through water, transformed by the Spirit.

16. This, Cæsarius, is my funeral offering to thee, this the firstfruits of my words, which thou hast often blamed me for withholding, yet wouldst have stripped off, had they been bestowed on thee; with this ornament I adorn thee, an ornament, I know well, far dearer to thee than all others, though it be not of the soft flowing tissues of silk, in which while living, with virtue for thy sole adorning, thou didst not, like the many, rejoice; nor texture of transparent linen, nor

α *Godliness*, εὐσέβειαν: here, as often, used in the sense of "orthodoxy."

β *A further trial.* Which Julian did not survive to carry out. S. Greg. may allude to Cæsarius' later return to Court.

γ *Persians.* The expedition in which he met his death. Ammian. Marcellin. xxv. 3, 7. Soz. vi. 2. Socr. iii. 21.

δ Matt. x. 23.

ε Wisd. iii. 15.

α *The earthquake*, described by Theodoret, H. E. ii. 26.

β S. Greg. Epist. xx.

outpouring of costly unguents, which thou hadst long resigned to the boudoirs of the fair, with their sweet savours lasting but a single day; nor any other small thing valued by small minds, which would have all been hidden to-day with thy fair form by this bitter stone. Far hence be games and stories of the Greeks, the honours of ill-fated youths, with their petty prizes for petty contests; and all the libations and firstfruits or garlands and newly plucked flowers, wherewith men honour the departed, in obedience to ancient custom and unreasoning grief, rather than reason. My gift is an oration, which perhaps succeeding time will receive at my hand and ever keep in motion, that it may not suffer him who has left us to be utterly lost to earth, but may ever keep him whom we honour in men's ears and minds, as it sets before them, more clearly than a portrait, the image of him for whom we mourn.

17. Such is my offering; if it be slight and inferior to his merit, God loveth that which is according to our power.[a] Part of our gift is now complete, the remainder we will now pay by offering (those of us who still survive) every year our honours and memorials. And now for thee, sacred and holy soul, we pray for an entrance into heaven; mayest thou enjoy such repose as the bosom of Abraham affords, mayest thou behold the choir of Angels, and the glories and splendours of sainted men; aye, mayest thou be united to that choir and share in their joy, looking down from on high on all things here, on what men call wealth, and despicable dignities, and deceitful honours, and the errors of our senses, and the tangle of this life, and its confusion and ignorance, as if we were fighting in the dark; whilst thou art in attendance upon the Great King and filled with the light which streams forth from Him: and may it be ours hereafter, receiving therefrom no such slender rivulet, as is the object of our fancy in this day of mirrors and enigmas, to attain to the fount of good itself, gazing with pure mind upon the truth in its purity, and finding a reward for our eager toil here below on behalf of the good, in our more perfect possession and vision of the good on high: the end to which our sacred books and teachers foretell that our course of divine mysteries shall lead us.

18. What now remains? To bring the healing of the Word to those in sorrow. And a powerful remedy for mourners is sympathy, for sufferers are best consoled by those who have to bear a like suffering. To such, then, I specially address myself, of whom I should be ashamed, if, with all other virtues, they do not show the elements of patience. For even if they surpass all others in love of their children, let them equally surpass them in love of wisdom and love of Christ, and in the special practice of meditation on our departure hence, impressing it likewise on their children, making even their whole life a preparation for death. But if your misfortune still clouds your reason and, like the moisture which dims our eyes, hides from you the clear view of your duty, come, ye elders, receive the consolation of a young man, ye fathers, that of a child, who ought to be admonished by men as old as you, who have admonished many and gathered experience from your many years. Yet wonder not, if in my youth I admonish the aged; and if in aught I can see better than the hoary, I offer it to you. How much longer have we to live, ye men of honoured eld, so near to God? How long are we to suffer here? Not even man's whole life is long, compared with the Eternity of the Divine Nature, still less the remains of life, and what I may call the parting of our human breath, the close of our frail existence. How much has Cæsarius outstripped us? How long shall we be left to mourn his departure? Are we not hastening to the same abode? Shall we not soon be covered by the same stone? Shall we not shortly be reduced to the same dust? And what in these short days will be our gain, save that after it has been ours to see, or suffer, or perchance even to do, more ill, we must discharge the common and inexorable tribute to the law of nature, by following some, preceding others, to the tomb, mourning these, being lamented by those, and receiving from some that meed of tears which we ourselves had paid to others?

19. Such, my brethren, is our existence, who live this transient life, such our pastime upon earth: we come into existence out of non-existence, and after existing are dissolved. We are unsubstantial dreams, impalpable visions,[α] like the flight of a passing bird, like a ship leaving no track upon the sea,[β] a speck of dust, a vapour, an early dew, a flower that quickly blooms, and quickly fades. As for man his days are as grass, as a flower of the field, so he flourisheth.[γ] Well hath inspired David discoursed of our frailty, and again in these words, "Let me know the short-

a Cor. viii. 3; ix. 7.

α Job xx. 8. β Wisd. v. 10 et seq. γ Ps. ciii. 15.

ness of my days;" and he defines the days of man as "of a span long."[α] And what wouldst thou say to Jeremiah, who complains of his mother in sorrow for his birth,[β] and that on account of others' faults? I have seen all things,[γ] says the preacher, I have reviewed in thought all human things, wealth, pleasure, power, unstable glory, wisdom which evades us rather than is won; then pleasure again, wisdom again, often revolving the same objects, the pleasures of appetite, orchards, numbers of slaves, store of wealth, serving men and serving maids, singing men and singing women, arms, spearmen, subject nations, collected tributes, the pride of kings, all the necessaries and superfluities of life, in which I surpassed all the kings that were before me. And what does he say after all these things? Vanity of vanities,[δ] all is vanity and vexation of spirit, possibly meaning some unreasoning longing of the soul, and distraction of man condemned to this from the original fall: but hear, he says, the conclusion of the whole matter, Fear God.[ε] This is his stay in his perplexity, and this is thy only gain from life here below, to be guided through the disorder of the things which are seen[ζ] and shaken, to the things which stand firm and are not moved.[η]

20. Let us not then mourn Cæsarius but ourselves, knowing what evils he has escaped to which we are left behind, and what treasure we shall lay up, unless, earnestly cleaving unto God and outstripping transitory things, we press towards the life above, deserting the earth while we are still upon the earth, and earnestly following the spirit which bears us upward. Painful as this is to the faint-hearted, it is as nothing to men of brave mind. And let us consider it thus. Cæsarius will not reign, but rather will he be reigned over by others. He will strike terror into no one, but he will be free from fear of any harsh master, often himself unworthy even of a subject's position. He will not amass wealth, but neither will he be liable to envy, or be pained at lack of success, or be ever seeking to add to his gains as much again. For such is the disease of wealth, which knows no limit to its desire of more, and continues to make drinking the medicine for thirst. He will make no display of his power of speaking, yet for his speaking will he be admired. He will not discourse upon the dicta of Hippocrates and Galen, and their adversaries, but neither will he be troubled by diseases, and suffer pain at the misfortunes of others. He will not set forth the principles of Eucleides, Ptolemæus, and Heron, but neither will he be pained by the tumid vaunts of uncultured men. He will make no display of the doctrines of Plato, and Aristotle, and Pyrrho, and the names of any Democritus, and Heracleitus, Anaxagoras, Cleanthes and Epicurus, and all the members of the venerable Porch and Academy: but neither will he trouble himself with the solution of their cunning syllogisms. What need of further details? Yet here are some which all men honour or desire. Nor wife nor child will he have beside him, but he will escape mourning for, or being mourned by them, or leaving them to others, or being left behind himself as a memorial of misfortune. He will inherit no property: but he will have such heirs[a] as are of the greatest service, such as he himself wished, so that he departed hence a rich man, bearing with him all that was his. What an ambition! What a new consolation! What magnanimity in his executors! A proclamation has been heard, worthy of the ears of all, and a mother's grief has been made void by a fair and holy promise, to give entirely to her son his wealth as a funeral offering on his behalf, leaving nothing to those who expected it.

21. Is this inadequate for our consolation? I will add a more potent remedy. I believe the words of the wise, that every fair and God-beloved soul, when, set free from the bonds of the body, it departs hence, at once enjoys a sense and perception of the blessings which await it, inasmuch as that which darkened it has been purged away, or laid aside—I know not how else to term it—and feels a wondrous pleasure and exultation, and goes rejoicing to meet its Lord, having escaped as it were from the grievous poison of life here, and shaken off the fetters which bound it and held down the wings of the mind, and so enters on the enjoyment of the bliss laid up for it, of which it has even now some conception. Then, a little later, it receives its kindred flesh, which once shared in its pursuits of things above, from the earth which both gave and had been entrusted with it, and in some way known to God, who knit them together and dissolved them, enters with it upon the inheritance of the glory there. And, as it shared, through their close union, in its hardships, so also it

α Ps. xxxix. 4, 5. β Jer. xv. 10. γ Eccles. i. 14. δ Ib. xii. 8. ε Ib. xii. 13. ζ 2 Cor. iv. 18. η Heb. xii. 27.

a *Heirs*, Cf. S. Basil Ep. 26 (32). Cæsarius left all his property to the poor. This passage shows that his own family welcomed and approved the bequest, which S. Gregory was at much pains to carry out, but was greatly embarrassed by the rapacity of his brother's servants.

bestows upon it a portion of its joys, gathering it up entirely into itself, and becoming with it one in spirit and in mind and in God, the mortal and mutable being swallowed up of life. Hear at least how the inspired Ezekiel discourses of the knitting together of bones and sinews,[α] how after him Saint Paul speaks of the earthly tabernacle, and the house not made with hands, the one to be dissolved, the other laid up in heaven, alleging absence from the body to be presence with the Lord,[β] and bewailing his life in it as an exile, and therefore longing for and hastening to his release. Why am I faint-hearted in my hopes? Why behave like a mere creature of a day? I await the voice of the Archangel,[γ] the last trumpet,[δ] the transformation of the heavens, the transfiguration of the earth, the liberation of the elements, the renovation of the universe.[ε] Then shall I see Cæsarius himself, no longer in exile, no longer laid upon a bier, no longer the object of mourning and pity, but brilliant, glorious, heavenly, such as in my dreams I have often beheld thee, dearest and most loving of brothers, pictured thus by my desire, if not by the very truth.

22. But now, laying aside lamentation, I will look at myself, and examine my feelings, that I may not unconsciously have in myself anything to be lamented. O ye sons of men, for the words apply to you, how long will ye be hard-hearted and gross in mind? Why do ye love vanity and seek after leasing,[ϛ] supposing life here to be a great thing and these few days many, and shrinking from this separation, welcome and pleasant as it is, as if it were really grievous and awful? Are we not to know ourselves? Are we not to cast away visible things? Are we not to look to the things unseen? Are we not, even if we are somewhat grieved, to be on the contrary distressed at our lengthened sojourn,[η] like holy David, who calls things here the tents of darkness, and the place of affliction, and the deep mire,[θ] and the shadow of death;[ι] because we linger in the tombs we bear about with us, because, though we are gods, we die like men[κ] the death of sin? This is my fear, this day and night accompanies me, and will not let me breathe, on one side the glory, on the other the place of correction: the former I long for till I can say, "My soul fainteth for Thy salvation;"[λ] from the latter I shrink back shuddering; yet I am not afraid that this body of mine should utterly perish in dissolution and corruption; but that the glorious creature of God (for glorious it is if upright, just as it is dishonourable if sinful) in which is reason, morality, and hope, should be condemned to the same dishonour as the brutes, and be no better after death; a fate to be desired for the wicked, who are worthy of the fire yonder.

23. Would that I might mortify my members that are upon the earth,[α] would that I might spend my all upon the spirit, walking in the way that is narrow and trodden by few, not that which is broad and easy.[β] For glorious and great are its consequences, and our hope is greater than our desert. What is man, that Thou art mindful of him?[γ] What is this new mystery which concerns me? I am small and great, lowly and exalted, mortal and immortal, earthly and heavenly. I share one condition with the lower world, the other with God; one with the flesh, the other with the spirit. I must be buried with Christ, arise with Christ, be joint heir with Christ, become the son of God, yea, God Himself. See whither our argument has carried us in its progress. I almost own myself indebted to the disaster which has inspired me with such thoughts, and made me more enamoured of my departure hence. This is the purpose of the great mystery for us. This is the purpose for us of God, Who for us was made man and became poor,[δ] to raise our flesh,[ε] and recover His image,[ϛ] and remodel man,[η] that we might all be made one in Christ,[θ] who was perfectly made in all of us all that He Himself is,[ι] that we might no longer be male and female, barbarian, Scythian, bond or free[κ] (which are badges of the flesh), but might bear in ourselves only the stamp of God, by Whom and for Whom we were made,[λ] and have so far received our form and model from Him, that we are recognized by it alone.

24. Yea, would that what we hope for might be, according to the great kindness of our bountiful God, Who asks for little and bestows great things, both in the present and in the future, upon those who truly love Him;[μ] bearing all things, enduring all things[ν] for their love and hope of Him, giving thanks for all things[ξ] favourable and unfavourable alike: I mean pleasant and painful, for reason knows that even these are often instruments of salvation; commending to Him our own souls[ο] and

α Ezek. xxxvii. 3 et seq. β 2 Cor. v. 1, 6; Phil. i. 23. γ 1 Thess. iv. 16. δ 1 Cor. xv. 52. ε 2 Pet. iii. 10. ϛ Ps. iv. 3. η Ib. cxx. 4. θ Ib. xliv. 19 (LXX.); lxix. 2. ι Ib. xliv. 20. κ Ib. lxxii. 6, 7. λ Ib. cxix. 81.

α Col. iii. 5. β S. Matt. vii. 13. γ Ps. viii. 5. δ 2 Cor. viii. 9. ε Rom. viii. 11. ϛ S. Luke xv. 9; 1 Cor. xv. 49. η Col. iii. 10. θ Gal. iii. 28. ι 1 Cor. xv. 28. κ Col. iii. 11. λ Rom. xi. 36. μ 1 Cor. ii. 9. ν Ib. xiii. 7. ξ 1 Thess. v. 18. ο 1 Pet. iv. 19.

the souls of those fellow wayfarers who, being more ready, have gained their rest before us. And, now that we have done this, let us cease from our discourse, and you too from your tears, hastening, as you now are, to your tomb, which as a sad abiding gift you have given to Cæsarius, seasonably prepared as it was for his parents in their old age, and now unexpectedly bestowed on their son in his youth, though not without reason in His eyes Who disposes our affairs. O Lord and Maker of all things, and specially of this our frame! O God and Father and Pilot of men who are Thine! O Lord of life and death! O Judge and Benefactor of our souls! O Maker and Transformer in due time of all things[α] by Thy designing Word,[β] according to the knowledge of the depth of Thy wisdom and providence! do Thou now receive Cæsarius, the firstfruits of our pilgrimage; and if he who was last is first, we bow before Thy Word, by which the universe is ruled; yet do Thou receive us also afterwards, in a time when Thou mayest be found,[γ] having ordered us in the flesh as long as is for our profit; yea, receive us, prepared and not troubled[δ] by Thy fear, not departing from Thee in our last day, nor violently borne away from things here, like souls fond of the world and the flesh, but filled with eagerness for that blessed and enduring life which is in Christ Jesus, our Lord, to whom be glory, world without end. Amen.

ORATION VIII.

On his Sister Gorgonia.

The exact date of this Oration is uncertain. It is certainly (§ 23) later than the death of Cæsarius, A.D. 369, and previous to the death of their father, A.D. 374. So much we gather from the Oration itself, and the references made by some authors to a poem of S. Gregory do not add anything certain to our knowledge (Poem. Hist. I. I. v.v. 108, 227). The place in which it was delivered is, almost without doubt, the city in which her married life had been spent. The public details of that life are familiar to the audience. Gorgonia's parents, and the speaker himself, although known to them, are not spoken of in terms implying intimacy such as we find in Orations known to have been delivered at Nazianzus. The spiritual father and confidant of Gorgonia is present, certainly in a position of authority, probably seated in the Episcopal throne. The husband of Gorgonia (Epitaph. 24) was named Alypius. His home, as Clémencet and Benoît agree, on the authority of Elias, was at Iconium, of which city, at the time, Faustinus was bishop. The names of Gorgonia's two sons are unknown. Elias states that they both became bishops. S. Gregory mentions her three daughters, Alypiana, Eugenia, and Nonna, in his will. The oration is marked by an eloquence, piety, and tender feeling which make it a worthy companion of that on Cæsarius.

Funeral Oration on his Sister Gorgonia.

1. In praising my sister, I shall pay honour to one of my own family; yet my praise will not be false, because it is given to a relation, but, because it is true, will be worthy of commendation, and its truth is based not only upon its justice, but upon well-known facts. For, even if I wished, I should not be permitted to be partial; since everyone who hears me stands, like a skilful critic, between my oration and the truth, to discountenance exaggeration, yet, if he be a man of justice, demanding what is really due. So that my fear is not of outrunning the truth, but, on the contrary, of falling short of it, and lessening her just repute by the extreme inadequacy of my panegyric; for it is a hard task to match her excellences with suitable action and words. Let us not then be so unjust as to praise every characteristic of other folk, and disparage really valuable qualities because they are our own, so as to make some men gain by their absence of kindred with us, while others suffer for their relationship. For justice would be violated alike by the praise of the one and the neglect of the other, whereas if we make the truth our standard and rule, and look to her alone, disregarding all the objects of the vulgar and the mean, we shall praise or pass over everything according to its merits.

2. Yet it would be most unreasonable of all, if, while we refuse to regard it as a righteous thing to defraud, insult, accuse, or treat unjustly in any way, great or small, those who are our kindred, and consider wrong done to those nearest to us the worst of all; we were yet to imagine that it would be an act of justice to deprive them of such an oration as is due most of all to the good, and spend more words upon those who are evil, and beg for

α Amos v. 8 (LXX.). β Ps. xxxiii. 6. γ Ib. xxxii. 6. δ Ib. cxix. 60 (LXX.).

indulgent treatment, than on those who are excellent and merely claim their due. For if we are not prevented, as would be far more just, from praising men who have lived outside our own circle, because we do not know and cannot personally testify to their merits, shall we be prevented from praising those whom we do know, because of our friendship, or the envy of the multitude, and especially those who have departed hence, whom it is too late to ingratiate ourselves with, since they have escaped, amongst all other things, from the reach of praise or blame.

3. Having now made a sufficient defence on these points, and shown how necessary it is for me to be the speaker, come, let me proceed with my eulogy, rejecting all daintiness and elegance of style (for she whom we are praising was unadorned and the absence of ornament was to her, beauty), and yet performing, as a most indispensable debt, all those funeral rites which are her due, and further instructing everyone in a zealous imitation of the same virtue, since it is my object in every word and action to promote the perfection of those committed to my charge. The task of praising the country and family of our departed one I leave to another, more scrupulous in adhering to the rules of eulogy; nor will he lack many fair topics, if he wish to deck her with external ornaments, as men deck a splendid and beautiful form with gold and precious stones, and the artistic devices of the craftsman; which, while they accentuate ugliness by their contrast, can add no attractiveness to the beauty which surpasses them. For my part, I will only conform to such rules so far as to allude to our common parents, for it would not be reverent to pass unnoticed the great blessing of having such parents and teachers, and then speedily direct my attention to herself, without further taxing the patience of those who are eager to learn what manner of woman she was.

4. Who is there who knows not the Abraham and Sarah of these our latter days, Gregory and Nonna his wife? For it is not well to omit the incitement to virtue of mentioning their names. He has been justified by faith, she has dwelt with him who is faithful; he beyond all hope has been the father of many nations,[α] she has spiritually travailed in their birth; he escaped from the bondage of his father's gods,[β] she is the daughter as well as the mother of the free; he went out from kindred and home for the sake of the land of promise,[α] she was the occasion of his exile; for on this head alone I venture to claim for her an honour higher than that of Sarah; he set forth on so noble a pilgrimage, she readily shared with him in its toils; he gave himself to the Lord, she both called her husband lord and regarded him as such, and in part was thereby justified; whose was the promise, from whom, as far as in them lay, was born Isaac, and whose was the gift.

5. This good shepherd was the result of his wife's prayers and guidance, and it was from her that he learned his ideal of a good shepherd's life. He generously fled from his idols, and afterwards even put demons to flight; he never consented to eat salt with idolators: united together with a bond of one honour, of one mind, of one soul, concerned as much with virtue and fellowship with God as with the flesh; equal in length of life and hoary hairs, equal in prudence and brilliancy, rivals of each other, soaring beyond all the rest, possessed in few respects by the flesh, and translated in spirit, even before dissolution: possessing not the world, and yet possessing it, by at once despising and rightly valuing it: forsaking riches and yet being rich through their noble pursuits; rejecting things here, and purchasing instead the things yonder: possessed of a scanty remnant of this life, left over from their piety, but of an abundant and long life for which they have laboured. I will say but one word more about them: they have been rightly and fairly assigned, each to either sex; he is the ornament of men, she of women, and not only the ornament but the pattern of virtue.

6. From them Gorgonia derived both her existence and her reputation; they sowed in her the seeds of piety, they were the source of her fair life, and of her happy departure with better hopes. Fair privileges these, and such as are not easily attained by many of those who plume themselves highly upon their noble birth, and are proud of their ancestry. But, if I must treat of her case in a more philosophic and lofty strain, Gorgonia's native land was Jerusalem above,[β] the object, not of sight but of contemplation, wherein is our commonwealth, and whereto we are pressing on: whose

α Rom. iv. 18.

β *His father's gods.* These words, together with the reference to idols and idolators in § 5 and the lines (Poem, Hist. I. i. 123-4, tome 2. p. 636.) ὑπ' εἰδώλοις πάρος ἦεν ζώων have led some writers (esp. Ullmann and Clericus) to attribute the worship of idols to the Hypsistarii, and Clémencet points out that ζώων is only the Ep. and Ion. partic. of ζάω, and does not mean "of animals." The weakness of a reliance on a poetical expression is shown in Dict. Christ. Biog. Here the words are the mystical application of the actual experience of Abraham, and εἴδωλον does not necessarily connote material idols. It is applied by S. Greg. Nyssen. Orat. funebr. de Placilla, p. 965. B (ed. 1615) to the worship of Jesus Christ by the Arians. Cf. Introd. to Orat. xviii.

α Gen. xii. 1; Heb. xi. 8. β Heb. xii. 22, 23.

citizen Christ is, and whose fellow-citizens are the assembly and church of the first born who are written in heaven, and feast around its great Founder in contemplation of His glory, and take part in the endless festival; her nobility consisted in the preservation of the Image, and the perfect likeness to the Archetype, which is produced by reason and virtue and pure desire, ever more and more conforming, in things pertaining to God, to those truly initiated into the heavenly mysteries; and in knowing whence, and of what character, and for what end we came into being.

7. This is what I know upon these points: and therefore it is that I both am aware and assert that her soul was more noble than those of the East,[a] according to a better than the ordinary rule of noble or ignoble birth, whose distinctions depend not on blood but on character; nor does it classify those whom it praises or blames according to their families, but as individuals. But speaking as I do of her excellences among those who know her, let each one join in contributing some particular and aid me in my speech: for it is impossible for one man to take in every point, however gifted with observation and intelligence.

8. In modesty she so greatly excelled, and so far surpassed, those of her own day, to say nothing of those of old time who have been illustrious for modesty, that, in regard to the two divisions of the life of all, that is, the married and the unmarried state, the latter being higher and more divine, though more difficult and dangerous, while the former is more humble and more safe, she was able to avoid the disadvantages of each, and to select and combine all that is best in both, namely, the elevation of the one and the security of the other, thus becoming modest without pride, blending the excellence of the married with that of the unmarried state, and proving that neither of them absolutely binds us to, or separates us from, God or the world (so that the one from its own nature must be uttely avoided, and the other altogether praised): but that it is mind which nobly presides over wedlock and maidenhood, and arranges and works upon them as the raw material of virtue under the master-hand of reason. For though she had entered upon a carnal union, she was not therefore separated from the spirit, nor, because her husband was her head, did she ignore her first Head: but, performing those few ministrations due to the world and nature, according to the will of the law of the flesh, or rather of Him who gave to the flesh these laws, she consecrated herself entirely to God. But what is most excellent and honourable, she also won over her husband to her side, and made of him a good fellow-servant, instead of an unreasonable master. And not only so, but she further made the fruit of her body, her children and her children's children, to be the fruit of her spirit, dedicating to God not her single soul, but the whole family and household, and making wedlock illustrious through her own acceptability in wedlock, and the fair harvest she had reaped thereby; presenting herself, as long as she lived, as an example to her offspring of all that was good, and when summoned hence, leaving her will behind her, as a silent exhortation to her house.

9. The divine Solomon, in his instructive wisdom, I mean his Proverbs, praises the woman[a] who looks to her household and loves her husband, contrasting her with one who roams abroad, and is uncontrolled and dishonourable, and hunts for precious souls with wanton words and ways, while she manages well at home and bravely sets about her woman's duties, as her hands hold the distaff, and she prepares two coats for her husband, buying a field in due season, and makes good provision for the food of her servants, and welcomes her friends at a liberal table; with all the other details in which he sings the praises of the modest and industrious woman. Now, to praise my sister in these points would be to praise a statue for its shadow, or a lion for its claws, without allusion to its greatest perfections. Who was more deserving of renown, and yet who avoided it so much and made herself inaccessible to the eyes of man? Who knew better the due proportions of sobriety and cheerfulness, so that her sobriety should not seem inhuman, nor her tenderness immodest, but prudent in one, gentle in the other, her discretion was marked by a combination of sympathy and dignity? Listen, ye women addicted to ease and display, who despise the veil of shamefastness. Who ever so kept her eyes under control? Who so derided laughter, that the ripple of a smile seemed a great thing to her? Who more steadfastly closed her ears? And who opened them more to the Divine words, or rather, who installed the mind as ruler of the tongue in uttering the judgments of God? Who, as she, regulated her lips?

a Job i. 3.

a Prov. xxxi. 10.

10. Here, if you will, is another point of her excellence: one of which neither she nor any truly modest and decorous woman thinks anything: but which we have been made to think much of, by those who are too fond of ornament and display, and refuse to listen to instruction on such matters. She was never adorned with gold wrought into artistic forms of surpassing beauty, nor flaxen tresses, fully or partially displayed, nor spiral curls, nor dishonouring designs of men who construct erections on the honourable head, nor costly folds of flowing and transparent robes, nor graces of brilliant stones, which color the neighbouring air, and cast a glow upon the form; nor the arts and witcheries of the painter, nor that cheap beauty of the infernal creator who works against the Divine, hiding with his treacherous pigments the creation of God, and putting it to shame with his honour, and setting before eager eyes the imitation of an harlot instead of the form of God, so that this bastard beauty may steal away that image which should be kept for God and for the world to come. But though she was aware of the many and various external ornaments of women, yet none of them was more precious to her than her own character, and the brilliancy stored up within. One red tint was dear to her, the blush of modesty; one white one, the sign of temperance: but pigments and pencillings, and living pictures, and flowing lines of beauty, she left to women of the stage and of the streets, and to all who think it a shame and a reproach to be ashamed.

11. Enough of such topics. Of her prudence and piety no adequate account can be given, nor many examples found besides those of her natural and spiritual parents, who were her only models, and of whose virtue she in no wise fell short, with this single exception most readily admitted, that they, as she both knew and acknowledged, were the source of her goodness, and the root of her own illumination. What could be keener than the intellect of her who was recognized as a common adviser not only by those of her family, those of the same people and of the one fold, but even by all men round about, who treated her counsels and advice as a law not to be broken? What more sagacious than her words? What more prudent than her silence? Having mentioned silence, I will proceed to that which was most characteristic of her, most becoming to women, and most serviceable to these times. Who had a fuller knowledge of the things of God, both from the Divine oracles, and from her own understanding? But who was less ready to speak, confining herself within the due limits of women? Moreover, as was the bounden duty of a woman who has learned true piety, and that which is the only honourable object of insatiate desire, who, as she, adorned temples with offerings, both others and this one, which will hardly, now she is gone, be so adorned again? Or rather, who so presented herself to God as a living temple? Who again paid such honor to Priests, especially to him who was her fellow soldier and teacher of piety, whose are the good seeds, and the pair of children consecrated to God.

12. Who opened her house to those who live according to God with a more graceful and bountiful welcome? And, which is greater than this, who bade them welcome with such modesty and godly greetings? Further, who showed a mind more unmoved in sufferings? Whose soul was more sympathetic to those in trouble? Whose hand more liberal to those in want? I should not hesitate to honour her with the words of Job: Her door was opened to all comers; the stranger did not lodge in the street. She was eyes to the blind, feet to the lame, a mother to the orphan.[α] Why should I say more of her compassion to widows, than that its fruit which she obtained was, never to be called a widow herself? Her house was a common abode to all the needy of her family; and her goods no less common to all in need than their own belonged to each. She hath dispersed abroad and given to the poor,[β] and according to the infallible truth of the Gospel, she laid up much store in the wine-presses above, and oftentimes entertained Christ in the person of those whose benefactress she was. And, best of all, there was in her no unreal profession, but in secret she cultivated piety before Him who seeth secret things. Everything she rescued from the ruler of this world, everything she transferred to the safe garners. Nothing did she leave behind to earth, save her body. She bartered everything for the hopes above: the sole wealth she left to her children was the imitation of her example, and emulation of her merits.

13. But amid these tokens of incredible magnanimity, she did not surrender her body to luxury, and unrestrained pleasures of the appetite, that raging and tearing dog, as though presuming upon her acts of benevolence, as most men do, who redeem their luxury by compassion to the poor, and instead of healing evil with good, receive evil as a recompense for their good deeds. Nor did she, while

α Job xxix. 15; xxxi. 32. β Ps. cxii. 9.

subduing her dust[a] by fasting, leave to another the medicine of hard lying; nor, while she found this of spiritual service, was she less restrained in sleep than anyone else; nor, while regulating her life on this point as if freed from the body, did she lie upon the ground, when others were passing the night erect, as the most mortified men struggle to do. Nay in this respect she was seen to surpass not only women, but the most devoted of men, by her intelligent chanting of the psalter, her converse with, and unfolding and apposite recollection of, the Divine oracles, her bending of her knees which had grown hard and almost taken root in the ground, her tears to cleanse her stains with contrite heart and spirit of lowliness, her prayer rising heavenward, her mind freed from wandering in rapture; in all these, or in any one of them, is there man or woman who can boast of having surpassed her? Besides, it is a great thing to say, but it is true, that while she was zealous in her endeavour after some points of excellence, of others she was the paragon: of some she was the discoverer, in others she excelled. And if in some single particular she was rivalled, her superiority consists in her complete grasp of all. Such was her success in all points, as none else attained even in a moderate degree in one: to such perfection did she attain in each particular, that any one might of itself have supplied the place of all.

14. O untended body, and squalid garments, whose only flower is virtue! O soul, clinging to the body, when reduced almost to an immaterial state through lack of food; or rather, when the body had been mortified by force, even before dissolution, that the soul might attain to freedom, and escape the entanglements of the senses! O nights of vigil, and psalmody, and standing which lasts from one day to another! O David, whose strains never seem tedious to faithful souls! O tender limbs, flung upon the earth and, contrary to nature, growing hard! O fountains of tears, sowing in affliction that they might reap in joy.[β] O cry in the night, piercing the clouds and reaching unto Him that dwelleth in the heavens! O fervour of spirit, waxing bold in prayerful longings against the dogs of night, and frosts and rain, and thunders, and hail, and darkness! O nature of woman overcoming that of man in the common struggle for salvation, and demonstrating that the distinction between male and female is one of body not of soul! O Baptismal purity, O soul, in the pure chamber of thy body, the bride of Christ! O bitter eating! O Eve mother of our race and of our sin! O subtle serpent, and death, overcome by her self-discipline! O self-emptying of Christ, and form of a servant, and sufferings, honoured by her mortification!

15. Oh! how am I to count up all her traits, or pass over most of them without injury to those who know them not? Here however it is right to subjoin the rewards of her piety, for indeed I take it that you, who knew her life well, have long been eager and desirous to find in my speech not only things present, or her joys yonder, beyond the conception and hearing and sight of man, but also those which the righteous Rewarder bestowed upon her here: a matter which often tends to the edification of unbelievers, who from small things attain to faith in those which are great, and from things which are seen to those which are not seen. I will mention then some facts which are generally notorious, others which have been from most men kept secret; and that because her Christian principle made a point of not making a display of her [Divine] favours. You know how her maddened mules ran away with her carriage, and unfortunately overturned it, how horribly she was dragged along, and seriously injured, to the scandal of unbelievers at the permission of such accidents to the righteous, and how quickly their unbelief was corrected: for, all crushed and bruised as she was, in bones and limbs, alike in those exposed and in those out of sight, she would have none of any physician, except Him Who had permitted it; both because she shrunk from the inspection and the hands of men, preserving, even in suffering, her modesty, and also awaiting her justification from Him Who allowed this to happen, so that she owed her preservation to none other than to Him: with the result that men were no less struck by her unhoped-for recovery than by her misfortune, and concluded that the tragedy had happened for her glorification through sufferings, the suffering being human, the recovery superhuman, and giving a lesson to those who come after, exhibiting in a high degree faith in the midst of suffering, and patience under calamity, but in a still higher degree the kindness of God to them that are such as she. For to the beautiful promise to the righteous "though he fall, he shall not be utterly broken,"[a] has been added one more recent, "though he be utterly broken, he shall speedily be raised up and glorified."[β] For if

[a] *Her dust*, i.e. her body.

[β] Ps. cxxvi. 5.

[a] Ps. xxxvii. 24.

[β] Ib. cxlvi. 8 (LXX.).

her misfortune was unreasonable, her recovery was extraordinary, so that health soon stole away the injury, and the cure became more celebrated than the blow.

16. O remarkable and wonderful disaster! O injury more noble than security! O prophecy, "He hath smitten, and He will bind us up, and revive us, and after three days He will raise us up," [α] portending indeed, as it did, a greater and more sublime event, yet no less applicable to Gorgonia's sufferings! This then, notorious to all, even to those afar off, for the wonder spread to all, and the lesson was stored up in the tongues and ears of all, with the other wonderful works and powers of God. But the following incident, hitherto unknown and concealed from most men by the Christian principle I spoke of, and her pious shrinking from vanity and display, dost thou bid me tell, O best [β] and most perfect of shepherds, pastor of this holy sheep, and dost thou further give thy assent to it, since to us alone has this secret been entrusted, and we were mutual witnesses of the marvel, or are we still to keep our faith to her who is gone? Yet I do think, that as that was the time to be silent, this is the time to manifest it, not only for the glory of God, but also for the consolation of those in affliction.

17. She was sick in body, and dangerously ill of an extraordinary and malignant disease, her whole frame was incessantly fevered, her blood at one time agitated and boiling, then curdling with coma, incredible pallor, and paralysis of mind and limbs: and this not at long intervals, but sometimes very frequently. Its virulence seemed beyond human aid; the skill of physicians, who carefully examined the case, both singly and in consultation, was of no avail; nor the tears of her parents, which often have great power, nor public supplications and intercessions, in which all the people joined as earnestly as if for their own preservation: for her safety was the safety of all, as, on the contrary, her suffering and sickness was a common misfortune.

18. What then did this great soul, worthy offspring of the greatest, and what was the medicine for her disorder, for we have now come to the great secret? Despairing of all other aid, she betook herself to the Physician of all, and awaiting the silent hours of night, during a slight intermission of the disease, she approached the altar with faith, and, calling upon Him Who is honoured thereon, with a mighty cry, and every kind of invocation, calling to mind all His former works of power, and well she knew those both of ancient and of later days, at last she ventured on an act of pious and splendid effrontery: she imitated the woman whose fountain of blood was dried up by the hem of Christ's garment.[α] What did she do? Resting her head with another cry upon the altar, and with a wealth of tears, as she who once bedewed the feet of Christ, [β] and declaring that she would not loose her hold until she was made whole, she then applied her medicine to her whole body, viz., such a portion of the antitypes[γ] of the Precious Body and Blood as she treasured in her hand, mingling therewith her tears, and, O the wonder, she went away feeling at once that she was saved, and with the lightness of health in body, soul, and mind, having received, as the reward of her hope, that which she hoped for, and having gained bodily by means of spiritual strength. Great though these things be, they are not untrue. Believe them all of you, whether sick or sound, that ye may either keep or regain your health. And that my story is no mere boastfulness is plain from the silence in which she kept, while alive, what I have revealed. Nor should I now have published it, be well assured, had I not feared that so great a marvel would have been utterly hidden from the faithful and unbelieving of these and later days.

19. Such was her life. Most of its details I have left untold, lest my speech should grow to undue proportions, and lest I should seem to be too greedy for her fair fame: but perhaps we should be wronging her holy and illustrious death, did we not mention some of its excellences; especially as she so longed for and desired it. I will do so therefore, as concisely as I can. She longed for her dissolution, for indeed she had great boldness towards Him who called her, and preferred to be with Christ, beyond all things on earth.[δ] And there is none of the most amorous and unrestrained, who has such love for his body, as she had to fling away these fetters, and escape from the mire in which we spend our lives, and to associate in purity with Him Who is Fair, and entirely to hold her Beloved, Who is I will even say it, her Lover, by Whose rays, feeble though they now are, we are enlightened, and Whom, though separated from Him, we are able to know. Nor did she fail even of this desire, divine and sublime

α Hos. vi. 1, 2.
β *O best, &c.* Faustinus, bishop of Iconium, must have been present, and S. Gregory, having asked his permission to relate the incident, looks towards him awaiting some sign of his assent.

α S. Matt. ix. 20. β S. Luke vii. 38.
γ *Antitypes*, i.e. the reserved Sacrament. δ Phil. i. 23.

though it was, and, what is still greater, she had a foretaste of His Beauty through her forecast and constant watching. Her only sleep transferred her to exceeding joys, and her one vision embraced her departure at the foreappointed time, having been made aware of this day, so that according to the decision of God she might be prepared and yet not disturbed.

20. She had recently obtained the blessing of cleansing and perfection, which we have all received from God as a common gift and foundation of our *new*[α] life. Or rather all her life was a cleansing and perfecting: and while she received regeneration from the Holy Spirit, its security was hers by virtue of her former life. And in her case almost alone, I will venture to say, the mystery was a seal rather than a gift of grace. And when her husband's perfection was her one remaining desire (and if you wish me briefly to describe the man, I do not know what more to say of him than that he was her husband) in order that she might be consecrated to God in her whole body, and not depart half-perfected, or leave behind her imperfect anything that was hers; she did not even fail of this petition, from Him Who fulfils the desire of them that fear Him,[β] and accomplishes their requests.

21. And now when she had all things to her mind, and nothing was lacking of her desires, and the appointed time drew nigh, being thus prepared for death and departure, she fulfilled the law which prevails in such matters, and took to her bed. After many injunctions to her husband, her children, and her friends, as was to be expected from one who was full of conjugal, maternal, and brotherly love, and after making her last day a day of solemn festival with brilliant discourse upon the things above, she fell asleep, full not of the days of man, for which she had no desire, knowing them to be evil for her, and mainly occupied with our dust and wanderings, but more exceedingly full of the days of God, than I imagine any one even of those who have departed in a wealth of hoary hairs, and have numbered many terms of years. Thus she was set free, or, it is better to say, taken to God, or flew away, or changed her abode, or anticipated by a little the departure of her body.

22. Yet what was I on the point of omitting? But perhaps thou, who art her spiritual father, wouldst not have allowed me, and hast carefully concealed the wonder, and made it known to me. It is a great point for her distinction, and in our memory of her virtue, and regret for her departure. But trembling and tears have seized upon me, at the recollection of the wonder. She was just passing away, and at her last breath, surrounded by a group of relatives and friends performing the last offices of kindness, while her aged mother bent over her, with her soul convulsed with envy of her departure, anguish and affection being blended in the minds of all. Some longed to hear some burning word to be branded in their recollection; others were eager to speak, yet no one dared; for tears were mute and the pangs of grief unconsoled, since it seemed sacrilegious, to think that mourning could be an honour to one who was thus passing away. So there was solemn silence, as if her death had been a religious ceremony. There she lay, to all appearance, breathless, motionless, speechless; the stillness of her body seemed paralysis, as though the organs of speech were dead, after that which could move them was gone. But as her pastor, who in this wonderful scene, was carefully watching her, perceived that her lips were gently moving, and placed his ear to them, which his disposition and sympathy emboldened him to do,—but do you expound the meaning of this mysterious calm, for no one can disbelieve it on your word! Under her breath she was repeating a psalm—the last words of a psalm—to say the truth, a testimony to the boldness with which she was departing, and blessed is he who can fall asleep with these words, "I will lay me down in peace, and take my rest."[α] Thus wert thou singing, fairest of women, and thus it fell out unto thee; and the song became a reality, and attended on thy departure as a memorial of thee, who hast entered upon sweet peace after suffering, and received (over and above the rest which comes to all), that sleep which is due to the beloved,[β] as befitted one who lived and died amid the words of piety.

23. Better, I know well, and far more precious than eye can see, is thy present lot, the song of them that keep holy-day,[γ] the throng of angels, the heavenly host, the vision of glory, and that splendour, pure and perfect beyond all other, of the Trinity Most High, no longer beyond the ken of the captive mind, dissipated by the senses, but entirely contemplated and possessed by the undivided mind, and flashing upon our souls with the whole light of Godhead: Mayest thou enjoy to the

---

α δευτέρον, lit. "second." β Ps. cxlv. 19.

α Ps. iv. 8. β Ib. cxxvii. 2. γ Ib. xlii. 4.

full all those things whose crumbs thou didst, while still upon earth, possess through the reality of thine inclination towards them. And if thou takest any account of our affairs, and holy souls receive from God this privilege, do thou accept these words of mine, in place of, and in preference to many panegyrics, which I have bestowed upon Cæsarius before thee, and upon thee after him—since I have been preserved to pronounce panegyrics upon my brethren. If any one will, after you, pay me the like honour, I cannot say. Yet may my only honour be that which is in God, and may my pilgrimage and my home be in Christ Jesus our Lord, to Whom, with the Father and the Holy Ghost, be glory for ever. Amen.

ORATION XII.

To his Father, when He had Entrusted to Him the Care of the Church of Nazianzus.

This Oration was delivered A.D. 372. Two years earlier Valens had divided Cappadocia into two provinces. Anthimus, Bishop of Tyana, asserting that the ecclesiastical provinces were regulated by those of the empire, claimed metropolitical rights over the churches of Cappadocia Secunda, in opposition to S. Basil, who had hitherto been metropolitan of the undivided province. S. Basil, with the intention of vindicating the permanence of his former rights, created a new see at Sasima, on the borders of the two provinces, and with great difficulty prevailed upon S. Gregory to receive consecration as its first Bishop. S. Gregory, who had "bent his neck, but not his will,"[α] was for a long time reluctant to enter upon his Episcopal duties, and at last was prevailed upon by S. Gregory of Nyssa, S. Basil's brother, to make an attempt to do so. When, however, he found that Anthimus was prepared to bar his entrance by force of arms, he returned home, definitely resigned his see, and once more betook himself to the life of solitude which he so dearly loved. Recalled hence, he consented,[β] at his father's earnest entreaty, to undertake provisionally the duties of Bishop-coadjutor of Nazianzus: and pronounced this short discourse on the occasion of his installation.

1. I opened my mouth, and drew in the Spirit,[γ] and I give myself and my all to the Spirit, my action and speech, my inaction and silence, only let Him hold me and guide me, and move both hand and mind and tongue whither it is right, and He wills: and restrain them as it is right and expedient. I am an instrument of God, a rational instrument, an instrument tuned and struck by that skilful artist, the Spirit. Yesterday His work in me was silence. I mused on abstinence from speech. Does He strike upon my mind to-day? My speech shall be heard, and I will muse on utterance. I am neither so talkative, as to desire to speak, when He is bent on silence; nor so reserved and ignorant as to set a watch before my lips[α] when it is the time to speak: but I open and close my door at the will of that Mind and Word and Spirit, Who is One kindred Deity.

2. I will speak then, since I am so bidden. And I will speak both to the good shepherd here, and to you, his holy flock, as I think is best both for me to speak, and for you to hear to-day. Why is it that you have begged for one to share your shepherd's toil? For my speech shall begin with you, O dear and honoured head, worthy of that of Aaron, down which runs that spiritual and priestly ointment upon his beard and clothing.[β] Why is it that, while yet able to stablish and guide many, and actually guiding them in the power of the Spirit, you support yourself with a staff and prop in your spiritual works? Is it because you have heard and know that even with the illustrious Aaron were anointed Eleazar and Ithamar, the sons of Aaron?[γ] For I pass over Nadab and Abihu,[δ] lest the allusion be ill-omened: and Moses during his lifetime appoints Joshua in his stead, as lawgiver and general over those who were pressing on to the land of promise? The office of Aaron and Hur, supporting the hands of Moses on the mount where Amalek was warred down[ε] by the Cross,[ς] prefigured and typified long before, I feel willing to pass by, as not very suitable or applicable to us: for Moses did not choose them to share his work as lawgiver, but as helpers in his prayer and supports for the weariness of his hands.

3. What is it then that ails you? What is your weakness? Is it physical? I am ready to sustain you, yea I have sustained, and been sustained, like Jacob of old, by your fatherly blessings.[η] Is it spiritual? Who is stronger, and more fervent, especially now, when the

α Carmina Hist., xi., 487.
β Ib., 492–525.
γ Ps. cxix. 131.

α Ps. cxli. 3.
β Ib. cxxxiii. 2.
γ Lev. viii. 2.
δ Ib. x. 1.
ε Exod. xvii. 12.
ς *The Cross.* The stretching out of Moses' hands was a type of the outstretched hands of our Lord Jesus, and His "intercession for the transgressors," upon the Cross.
η Gen. xxvii. 28.

powers of the flesh are ebbing and fading, like so many barriers which interfere with, and dim the brilliancy of a light? For these powers are wont, for the most part, to wage war upon and oppose one another, while the body's health is purchased by the sickness of the soul, and the soul flourishes and looks upward when pleasures are stilled and fade away along with the body. But, wonderful as your simplicity and nobility have seemed to me before, how is it that you have no fear, especially in times like these, that your spirit will be considered a pretext, and that most men will suppose, in spite of our spiritual professions, that we are undertaking this from carnal motives. For most men have made[a] the office to be looked upon as great and princely, and accompanied with considerable enjoyment, even though a man have the charge and rule over a more slender flock than this, and one which affords more troubles than pleasures. Thus far of your simplicity, or parental preference, if it be so, which makes you neither admit yourself, nor readily suspect in others anything disgraceful; for a mind hardly roused to evil, is slow to suspect evil. My second duty is briefly to address this people of yours, or now even of mine.

4. I have been overpowered, my friends and brethren, for I will now, though I did not at the time, ask for your aid. I have been overpowered by the old age of my father, and, to use moderate terms, the kindliness of my friend. So, help me, each of you who can, and stretch out a hand to me who am pressed down and torn asunder by regret and enthusiasm. The one suggests flights, mountains and deserts, and calm of soul and body, and that the mind should retire into itself, and recall its powers from sensible things, in order to hold pure communion with God, and be clearly illumined by the flashing rays of the Spirit, with no admixture or disturbance of the divine light by anything earthly or clouded, until we come to the source of the effulgence which we enjoy here, and regret and desire are alike stayed, when our mirrors[β] pass away in the light of truth. The other wills that I should come forward, and bear fruit for the common good, and be helped by helping others, and publish the Divine light, and bring to God a people for His own possession, a holy nation, a royal priesthood,[γ] and His image cleansed in many souls. And this, because, as a park is better than and preferable to a tree, the whole heaven with its ornaments to a single star, and the body to a limb, so also, in the sight of God, is the reformation of a whole church preferable to the progress of a single soul: and therefore, I ought not to look only on my own interest, but also on that of others.[a] For Christ also likewise, when it was possible for him to abide in His own honour and deity, not only so far emptied Himself as to take the form of a slave,[β] but also endured the cross, despising the shame,[γ] that he might by His own sufferings destroy sin, and by death slay death.[δ] The former are the imaginings of desire, the latter the teachings of the Spirit. And I, standing midway between the desire and the Spirit, and not knowing to which of the two I should rather yield, will impart to you what seems to me the best and safest course, that you may test it with me and take part in my design.

5. It seemed to me to be best and least dangerous to take a middle course between desire and fear, and to yield in part to desire, in part to the Spirit: and that this would be the case, if I neither altogether evaded the office, and so refused the grace, which would be dangerous, nor yet assumed a burden beyond my powers, for it is a heavy one. The former indeed is suited to the person of another, the latter to another's power, or rather to undertake both would be madness. But piety and safety would alike advise me to proportion the office to my power, and as is the case with food, to accept that which is within my power and refuse what is beyond it, for health is gained for the body, and tranquillity for the soul, by such a course of moderation. Therefore I now consent to share in the cares of my excellent father, like an eaglet, not quite vainly flying close to a mighty and high soaring eagle. But hereafter I will offer my wing to the Spirit to be borne whither, and as, He wills: no one shall force or drag me in any direction, contrary to His counsel. For sweet it is to inherit a father's toils, and this flock is more familiar than a strange and foreign one; I would even add, more precious in the sight of God, unless the spell of affection deceives me, and the force of habit robs me of perception: nor is there any more useful or safer course than that willing rulers should rule willing subjects: since it is our practice not to lead by force, or by compulsion, but by good will. For this would not hold together even another form of government, since that which is held in by force is wont, when opportunity offers, to strike for freedom: but freedom of will more than

a *Made*, by the manner in which they have sought for and exercised it. β 1 Cor. xiii. 12. γ 1 Pet. ii. 9.

a Phil. ii. 4. β Ib. ii. 7. γ Heb. xii. 2. δ Ib. ii. 14.

anything else it is, which holds together our—I will not call it rule, but—tutorship. For the mystery of godliness[α] belongs to those who are willing, not to those who are overpowered.

6. This is my speech to you, my good men, uttered in simplicity and with all good will, and this is the secret of my mind. And may the victory rest with that which will be for the profit of both you and me, under the Spirit's guidance of our affairs, (for our discourse comes back again to the same point,)[β] to Whom we have given ourselves, and the head anointed with the oil of perfection, in the Almighty Father, and the Only-begotten Son, and the Holy Spirit, Who is God. For how long shall we hide[γ] the lamp under the bushel,[δ] and withhold from others the full knowledge of the Godhead, when it ought to be now put upon the lampstand and give light to all churches and souls and to the whole fulness of the world, no longer by means of metaphors, or intellectual sketches, but by distinct declaration? And this indeed is a most perfect setting forth of Theology to those who have been deemed worthy of this grace in Christ Jesus Himself, our Lord, to Whom be glory, honour, and power for ever. Amen.

INTRODUCTION TO ORATION XVI.

On his Father's Silence, Because of the Plague of Hail.

This Oration belongs to the year A.D. 373. A series of disasters had befallen the people of Nazianzus. A deadly cattle plague, which had devastated their herds, had been followed by a prolonged drought, and now their just ripened crops had been ruined by a storm of rain and hail. The people flocked to the church, and finding S. Gregory the elder so overwhelmed by his sense of these terrible misfortunes that he was unable to address them, implored his coadjutor to enter the pulpit. The occasion gave no time for preparation, so S. Gregory poured out his feelings in a discourse which was in the fullest sense of the words *ex tempore*. Its present form, however, as Benoît suggests, may be due to a later polishing of notes taken down at the time of delivery.

1. Why do you infringe upon the approved order of things? Why would you do violence to a tongue which is under obligation to the law? Why do you challenge a speech which is in subjection to the Spirit? Why, when you have excused the head, have you hastened to the feet? Why do you pass by Aaron[α] and urge forward Eleazar? I cannot allow the fountain to be dammed up, while the rivulet runs its course; the sun to be hidden, while the star shines forth; hoar hairs to be in retirement, while youth lays down the law; wisdom to be silent, while inexperience speaks with assurance. A heavy rain is not always more useful than a gentle shower. Nay, indeed, if it be too violent, it sweeps away the earth, and increases the proportion of the farmer's loss: while a gentle fall, which sinks deep, enriches the soil, benefits the tiller and makes the corn grow to a fine crop. So the fluent speech is not more profitable than the wise. For the one, though it perhaps gave a slight pleasure, passes away, and is dispersed as soon, and with as little effect, as the air on which it struck, though it charms with its eloquence the greedy ear. But the other sinks into the mind, and opening wide its mouth, fills it[β] with the Spirit, and, showing itself nobler than its origin, produces a rich harvest by a few syllables.

2. I have not yet alluded to the true and first wisdom, for which our wonderful husbandman and shepherd is conspicuous. The first wisdom is a life worthy of praise, and kept pure for God, or being purified for Him Who is all-pure and all-luminous, Who demands of us, as His only sacrifice, purification—that is, a contrite heart and the sacrifice of praise,[γ] and a new creation in Christ,[δ] and the new man,[ε] and the like, as the Scripture loves to call it. The first wisdom is to despise that wisdom which consists of language and figures of speech, and spurious and unnecessary embellishments. Be it mine to speak five words with my understanding in the church, rather than ten thousand words in a tongue,[ζ] and with the unmeaning voice of a trumpet,[η] which does not rouse my soldier to the spiritual combat. This is the wisdom which I praise, which I welcome. By this the ignoble have won renown, and the despised have attained the highest honours. By this a crew of fishermen have taken the whole world in the meshes of the Gospel-net,

α 1 Tim. iii. 16.
β *The same point*, i.e., from which it started, § 1.
γ *Hide*, etc. S. Gregory here alludes to the "economy" which refrained from distinctly declaring the Divinity of the Holy Ghost. Cf. Or. xliii., 68. This declaration of his was afterwards commented on by his audience and others, cf. Epist. 58, in which his mode of teaching is contrasted with that of S. Basil.
δ S. Matt. v. 15.

α *Aaron*, S. Gregory the elder. *Eleazar*, S. Gregory Nazianzen.
β Ps. lxxxi. 11. γ Ib. l. 23; li. 19. δ 2 Cor. v. 17. ε Eph. iv. 24. ζ 1 Cor. xiv. 19. η Ib. xiv. 8.

and overcome by a word finished and cut short [α] the wisdom that comes to naught.[β] I count not wise the man who is clever in words, nor him who is of a ready tongue, but unstable and undisciplined in soul, like the tombs which, fair and beautiful as they are outwardly, are fetid with corpses within,[γ] and full of manifold ill-savours; but him who speaks but little of virtue, yet gives many examples of it in his practice, and proves the trustworthiness of his language by his life.

3. Fairer in my eyes, is the beauty which we can gaze upon than that which is painted in words: of more value the wealth which our hands can hold, than that which is imagined in our dreams; and more real the wisdom of which we are convinced by deeds, than that which is set forth in splendid language. For "a good understanding," he saith, "have all they that do thereafter," [δ] not they who proclaim it. Time is the best touchstone of this wisdom, and "the hoary head is a crown of glory." [ε] For if, as it seems to me as well as to Solomon, we must "judge none blessed before his death," [ς] and it is uncertain "what a day may bring forth," [η] since our life here below has many turnings, and the body of our humiliation [θ] is ever rising, falling and changing; surely he, who without fault has almost drained the cup of life, and nearly reached the haven of the common sea of existence is more secure, and therefore more enviable, than one who has yet a long voyage before him.

4. Do not thou, therefore, restrain a tongue whose noble utterances and fruits have been many, which has begotten many children of righteousness—yea, lift up thine eyes round about and see,[ι] how many are its sons, and what are its treasures; even this whole people, whom thou hast begotten in Christ through the Gospel.[κ] Grudge not to us those words which are excellent rather than many, and do not yet give us a foretaste of our impending loss.[λ] Speak in words which, if few, are dear and most sweet to me, which, if scarcely audible, are perceived from their spiritual cry, as God heard the silence of Moses, and said to him when interceding mentally, "Why criest thou unto Me?" [μ] Comfort this people, I pray thee, I, who was thy nursling, and have since been made Pastor, and now even Chief Pastor. Give a lesson, to me in the Pastor's art, to this people of obedience. Discourse awhile on our present heavy blow, about the just judgments of God, whether we grasp their meaning, or are ignorant of their great deep.[α] How again "mercy is put in the balance," [β] as holy Isaiah declares, for goodness is not without discernment, as the first labourers in the vineyard [γ] fancied, because they could not perceive any distinction between those who were paid alike: and how anger, which is called "the cup in the hand of the Lord," [δ] and "the cup of falling which is drained," [ε] is in proportion to transgressions, even though He abates to all somewhat of what is their due, and dilutes with compassion the unmixed draught of His wrath. For He inclines from severity to indulgence towards those who accept chastisement with fear, and who after a slight affliction conceive and are in pain with conversion, and bring forth [ς] the perfect spirit of salvation; but nevertheless he reserves the dregs,[η] the last drop of His anger, that He may pour it out entire upon those who, instead of being healed by His kindness, grow obdurate, like the hard-hearted Pharaoh,[θ] that bitter taskmaster, who is set forth as an example of the power [ι] of God over the ungodly.

5. Tell us whence come such blows and scourges, and what account we can give of them. Is it some disordered and irregular motion or some unguided current, some unreason of the universe, as though there were no Ruler of the world, which is therefore borne along by chance, as is the doctrine of the foolishly wise, who are themselves borne along at random by the disorderly spirit of darkness? Or are the disturbances and changes of the universe, (which was originally constituted, blended, bound together, and set in motion in a harmony known only to Him Who gave it motion,) directed by reason and order under the guidance of the reins of Providence? Whence come famines and tornadoes and hailstorms, our present warning blow? Whence pestilences, diseases, earthquakes, tidal waves, and fearful things in the heavens? And how is the creation, once ordered for the enjoyment of men, their common and equal delight, changed for the punishment of the ungodly, in order that we may be chastised through that for which, when honoured with it, we did not give thanks, and recognise in

α Isai. x. 22, 23 (LXX.); Rom. ix. 28.
β 1 Cor. ii. 6. γ S. Matt. xxiii. 27. δ Ps. cxi. 10.
ε Prov. xvi. 31. ς Eccles. xi. 28. η Prov. xxvii. 1.
θ Phil. iii. 21. ι Isai. xlix. 18. κ 1 Cor. iv. 15.
λ *Loss*, i.e., the death of his father, which, from his age, could not be long delayed. μ Exod. xiv. 15.

α Ps. xxxvi. 6. β Is. xxviii. 17. (LXX.). γ S. Matt. xx. 12.
δ Ps. lxxv. 9. ε Isai. li. 17 (LXX.). ς Ib. xxvi. 18.
η Ps. lxxv. 10. θ Exod. v. 6.; vii. 22. ι Rom. ix. 17.

our sufferings that power which we did not recognise in our benefits? How is it that some receive at the Lord's hand double for their sins,[α] and the measure of their wickedness is doubly filled up, as in the correction of Israel, while the sins of others are done away by a sevenfold recompense into their bosom?[β] What is the measure of the Amorites that is not yet full?[γ] And how is the sinner either let go, or chastised again, let go perhaps, because reserved for the other world, chastised, because healed thereby in this? Under what circumstances again is the righteous, when unfortunate, possibly being put to the test, or, when prosperous, being observed, to see if he be poor in mind or not very far superior to visible things, as indeed conscience, our interior and unerring tribunal, tells us. What is our calamity, and what its cause? Is it a test of virtue, or a touchstone of wickedness? And is it better to bow beneath it as a chastisement, even though it be not so, and humble ourselves under the mighty hand of God,[δ] or, considering it as a trial, to rise superior to it? On these points give us instruction and warning, lest we be too much discouraged by our present calamity, or fall into the gulf of evil and despise it; for some such feeling is very general; but rather that we may bear our admonition quietly, and not provoke one more severe by our insensibility to this.

6. Terrible is an unfruitful season, and the loss of the crops. It could not be otherwise, when men are already rejoicing in their hopes, and counting on their all but harvested stores. Terrible again is an unseasonable harvest, when the farmers labour with heavy hearts, sitting as it were beside the grave of their crops, which the gentle rain nourished, but the wild storm has rooted up, whereof the mower filleth not his hand, neither he that bindeth up the sheaves his bosom,[ε] nor have they obtained the blessing which passers-by bestow upon the farmers. Wretched indeed is the sight of the ground devastated, cleared, and shorn of its ornaments, over which the blessed Joel wails in his most tragic picture of the desolation of the land, and the scourge of famine;[ζ] while another[η] prophet wails, as he contrasts with its former beauty its final disorder, and thus discourses on the anger of the Lord when He smites the land: before him is the garden of Eden, behind Him a desolate wilderness.[α] Terrible indeed these things are, and more than terrible, when we are grieved only at what is present, and are not yet distressed by the feeling of a severer blow: since, as in sickness, the suffering which pains us from time to time is more distressing than that which is not present. But more terrible still are those which the treasures[β] of God's wrath contain, of which God forbid that you should make trial; nor will you, if you fly for refuge to the mercies of God, and win over by your tears Him Who will have mercy,[γ] and avert by your conversion what remains of His wrath. As yet, this is gentleness and loving-kindness and gentle reproof, and the first elements of a scourge to train our tender years: as yet, the smoke[δ] of His anger, the prelude of His torments; not yet has fallen the flaming fire,[ε] the climax of His being moved; not yet the kindled coals,[ζ] the final scourge, part of which He threatened, when He lifted up the other over us, part He held back by force, when He brought the other upon us; using the threat and the blow alike for our instruction, and making a way for His indignation, in the excess of His goodness; beginning with what is slight, so that the more severe may not be needed; but ready to instruct us by what is greater, if He be forced so to do.

7. I know the glittering sword,[η] and the blade made drunk in heaven, bidden to slay, to bring to naught, to make childless, and to spare neither flesh, nor marrow, nor bones. I know Him, Who, though free from passion, meets us like a bear robbed of her whelps, like a leopard in the way of the Assyrians,[θ] not only those of that day, but if anyone now is an Assyrian in wickedness: nor is it possible to escape the might and speed of His wrath when He watches over our impieties, and His jealousy,[ι] which knoweth to devour His adversaries, pursues His enemies to the death.[κ] I know the emptying, the making void, the making waste, the melting of the heart, and knocking of the knees together,[λ] such are the punishments of the ungodly. I do not dwell on the judgments to come, to which indulgence in this world delivers us, as it is better to be punished and cleansed now than to be transmitted to the torment to come, when it is the time of chastisement, not of cleansing. For as he who remembers God here is conqueror of death (as David[μ] has most excellently

---

α Isai. xl. 2. β Ps. lxxix. 12. γ Gen. xv. 16.
δ 1 Pet. v. 6. ε Ps. cxxix. 7. ζ Joel i. 10.
η *Another*. Either this is a wrong reading, or S. Gregory's memory fails him. The second quotation is also from Joel.

α Joel ii. 3. β Deut. xxxii. 34; Jer. l. 25. γ Hos. vi. 6.
δ Ps. xviii. 8. ε Ib. cv. 32. ζ Ib. lxxviii. 50.
η Ezek. xxi. 9. θ Hos. xiii. 7. 8. ι Isai. xxvi. 11 (LXX.).
κ Hos. viii. 3. λ Nahum ii. 10. μ Ps. vi. 5 (LXX.).

sung) so the departed have not in the grave confession and restoration; for God has confined life and action to this world, and to the future the scrutiny of what has been done.

8. What shall we do in the day of visitation,[α] with which one of the Prophets terrifies me, whether that of the righteous sentence of God against us, or that upon the mountains and hills, of which we have heard, or whatever and whenever it may be, when He will reason with us, and oppose us, and set before us[β] those bitter accusers, our sins, comparing our wrongdoings with our benefits, and striking thought with thought, and scrutinising action with action, and calling us to account for the image[γ] which has been blurred and spoilt by wickedness, till at last He leads us away self-convicted and self-condemned, no longer able to say that we are being unjustly treated—a thought which is able even here sometimes to console in their condemnation those who are suffering.

9. But then what advocate shall we have? What pretext? What false excuse? What plausible artifice? What device contrary to the truth will impose upon the court, and rob it of its right judgment, which places in the balance for us all, our entire life, action, word, and thought, and weighs against the evil that which is better, until that which preponderates wins the day, and the decision is given in favour of the main tendency; after which there is no appeal, no higher court, no defence on the ground of subsequent conduct, no oil obtained from the wise virgins, or from them that sell, for the lamps going out,[δ] no repentance of the rich man wasting away in the flame,[ε] and begging for repentance for his friends, no statute of limitations; but only that final and fearful judgment-seat, more just even than fearful; or rather more fearful because it is also just; when the thrones are set and the Ancient of days takes His seat,[ζ] and the books are opened, and the fiery stream comes forth, and the light before Him, and the darkness prepared; and they that have done good shall go into the resurrection of life,[η] now hid in Christ[θ] and to be manifested hereafter with Him, and they that have done evil, into the resurrection of judgment,[ι] to which they who have not believed have been condemned already by the word which judges them.[κ] Some will be welcomed by the unspeakable light and the vision of the holy and royal Trinity, Which now shines upon them with greater brilliancy and purity and unites Itself wholly to the whole soul, in which solely and beyond all else I take it that the kingdom of heaven consists. The others among other torments, but above and before them all must endure the being outcast from God, and the shame of conscience which has no limit. But of these anon.

10. What are we to do now, my brethren, when crushed, cast down, and drunken but not with strong drink nor with wine,[α] which excites and obfuscates but for a while, but with the blow which the Lord has inflicted upon us, Who says, And thou, O heart, be stirred and shaken,[β] and gives to the despisers the spirit of sorrow and deep sleep to drink:[γ] to whom He also says, See, ye despisers, behold, and wonder and perish?[δ] How shall we bear His convictions; or what reply shall we make, when He reproaches us not only with the multitude of the benefits for which we have continued ungrateful, but also with His chastisements, aud reckons up the remedies with which we have refused to be healed? Calling us His children[ε] indeed, but unworthy children, and His sons, but strange sons[ζ] who have stumbled from lameness out of their paths, in the trackless and rough ground. How and by what means could I have instructed you, and I have not done so? By gentler measures? I have applied them. I passed by the blood drunk in Egypt from the wells and rivers and all reservoirs of water[η] in the first plague: I passed over the next scourges, the frogs, lice, and flies. I began with the flocks and the cattle and the sheep, the fifth plague, and, sparing as yet the rational creatures, I struck the animals. You made light of the stroke, and treated me with less reason and attention than the beasts who were struck. I withheld from you the rain; one piece was rained upon, and the piece whereupon it rained not withered,[θ] and ye said "We will brave it."[ι] I brought the hail upon you, chastising you with the opposite kind of blow, I uprooted your vineyards and shrubberies, and crops, but I failed to shatter your wickedness.

11. Perchance He will say to me, who am not reformed even by blows, I know that thou art obstinate, and thy neck is an iron sinew,[κ] the heedless is heedless and the lawless man acts lawlessly,[λ] naught is the heavenly correction, naught the scourges. The bellows are

α Isai. x. 3. β Ps. l. 21. γ Gen. i. 26. δ S. Matt. xxv. 8. ε S. Luk. xvi. 24. ζ Dan. vii. 9. η S. John v. 29. θ Col. iii. 3. ι S. John v. 29. κ S. John iii. 18; xii. 48.

α Isai. xxix. 9. β Hab. ii. 16. γ Ps. lx. 2, 3; Isai. xxix. 10. δ Hab. i. 5; Acts xiii. 41. ε Deut. xxxii. 5. ζ Ps. xviii. 46. η Exod. vii. 19. θ Amos iv. 7. ι Jer. xviii. 12 (LXX.). κ Isai. xlviii. 4. λ Ib. xxi. 2 (LXX.).

burnt, the lead is consumed,[α] as I once reproached you by the mouth of Jeremiah, the founder melted the silver in vain, your wickednesses are not melted away. Can ye abide my wrath, saith the Lord. Has not My hand the power to inflict upon you other plagues also? There are still at My command the blains breaking forth from the ashes of the furnace,[β] by sprinkling which toward heaven, Moses, or any other minister of God's action, may chastise Egypt with disease. There remain also the locusts, the darkness that may be felt, and the plague which, last in order, was first in suffering and power, the destruction and death of the firstborn, and, to escape this, and to turn aside the destroyer, it were better to sprinkle the doorposts of our mind, contemplation and action, with the great and saving token, with the blood of the new covenant, by being crucified and dying with Christ, that we may both rise and be glorified and reign with Him both now and at His final appearing, and not be broken and crushed, and made to lament, when the grievous destroyer smites us all too late in this life of darkness, and destroys our firstborn, the offspring and results of our life which we had dedicated to God.

12. Far be it from me that I should ever, among other chastisements, be thus reproached by Him Who is good, but walks contrary to me in fury[γ] because of my own contrariness: I have smitten you with blasting and mildew, and blight;[δ] without result. The sword from without[ε] made you childless, yet have ye not returned unto Me, saith the Lord. May I not become the vine of the beloved, which after being planted and entrenched, and made sure with a fence and tower and every means which was possible, when it ran wild and bore thorns, was consequently despised, and had its tower broken down and its fence taken away, and was not pruned nor digged, but was devoured and laid waste and trodden down by all![ζ] This is what I feel I must say as to my fears, thus have I been pained by this blow, and this, I will further tell you, is my prayer. We have sinned, we have done amiss, and have dealt wickedly,[η] for we have forgotten Thy commandments and walked after our own evil thought,[θ] for we have behaved ourselves unworthily of the calling and gospel of Thy Christ, and of His holy sufferings and humiliation for us; we have become a reproach to Thy beloved, priest and people, we have erred together, we have all gone out of the way, we have together become unprofitable, there is none that doeth judgment and justice, no not one.[α] We have cut short Thy mercies and kindness and the bowels and compassion of our God, by our wickedness and the perversity of our doings, in which we have turned away. Thou art good, but we have done amiss; Thou art long-suffering, but we are worthy of stripes; we acknowledge Thy goodness, though we are without understanding, we have been scourged for but few of our faults; Thou art terrible, and who will resist Thee?[β] the mountains will tremble before Thee; and who will strive against the might of Thine arm? If Thou shut the heaven, who will open it? And if Thou let loose Thy torrents, who will restrain them? It is a light thing in Thine eyes to make poor and to make rich, to make alive and to kill, to strike and to heal, and Thy will is perfect action. Thou art angry, and we have sinned,[γ] says one of old, making confession; and it is now time for me to say the opposite, "We have sinned, and Thou art angry:" therefore have we become a reproach to our neighbours.[δ] Thou didst turn Thy face from us, and we were filled with dishonour. But stay, Lord, cease, Lord, forgive, Lord, deliver us not up for ever because of our iniquities, and let not our chastisements be a warning for others, when we might learn wisdom from the trials of others. Of whom? Of the nations which know Thee not, and kingdoms which have not been subject to Thy power. But we are Thy people,[ε] O Lord, the rod of Thine inheritance; therefore correct us, but in goodness and not in Thine anger, lest Thou bring us to nothingness[ζ] and contempt among all that dwell on the earth.

13. With these words I invoke mercy: and if it were possible to propitiate His wrath with whole burnt offerings or sacrifices, I would not even have spared these. Do you also yourselves imitate your trembling priest, you, my beloved children, sharers with me alike of the Divine correction and loving-kindness. Possess your souls in tears, and stay His wrath by amending your way of life. Sanctify a fast, call a solemn assembly,[η] as blessed Joel with us charges you: gather the elders, and the babes that suck the breasts, whose tender age wins our pity, and is specially worthy of the loving-kindness of God. I know also what he enjoins both upon me, the

α Jer. vi. 29. β Exod. ix. 10. γ Lev. xxvi. 27, 28. δ Lev. xxvi. 1 (LXX.); Amos iv. 9. ε Deut. xxxii. 25. ζ Isai. v. 1. η Dan. ix. 5. θ Isai. lxv. 2.

α Ps. xiv. 3. β Ib. lxxvi. 7. γ Isai. lxiv. 5. δ Ps. lxxix. 4. ε Ib. 6, 13. ζ Jer. x. 24. η Joel ii. 15.

minister of God, and upon you, who have been thought worthy of the same honour, that we should enter His house in sackcloth, and lament night and day between the porch and the altar, in piteous array, and with more piteous voices, crying aloud without ceasing on behalf of ourselves and the people, sparing nothing, either toil or word, which may propitiate God: saying "Spare, O Lord, Thy people, and give not Thine heritage to reproach,"[α] and the rest of the prayer; surpassing the people in our sense of the affliction as much as in our rank, instructing them in our own persons in compunction and correction of wickedness, and in the consequent long-suffering of God, and cessation of the scourge.

14. Come then, all of you, my brethren, let us worship and fall down, and weep before the Lord our Maker;[β] let us appoint a public mourning, in our various ages and families, let us raise the voice of supplication; and let this, instead of the cry which He hates, enter into the ears of the Lord of Sabaoth. Let us anticipate His anger by confession;[γ] let us desire to see Him appeased, after He was wroth. Who knoweth, he says, if He will turn and repent, and leave a blessing behind Him?[δ] This I know certainly, I the sponsor of the loving-kindness of God. And when He has laid aside that which is unnatural to Him, His anger, He will betake Himself to that which is natural, His mercy. To the one He is forced by us, to the other He is inclined. And if He is forced to strike, surely He will refrain, according to His Nature. Only let us have mercy on ourselves, and open a road for our Father's righteous affections. Let us sow in tears, that we may reap in joy,[ε] let us show ourselves men of Nineveh, not of Sodom.[ζ] Let us amend our wickedness, lest we be consumed with it; let us listen to the preaching of Jonah, lest we be overwhelmed by fire and brimstone, and if we have departed from Sodom let us escape to the mountain, let us flee to Zoar, let us enter it as the sun rises; let us not stay in all the plain, let us not look around us, lest we be frozen into a pillar of salt, a really immortal pillar, to accuse the soul which returns to wickedness.

15. Let us be assured that to do no wrong[η] is really superhuman, and belongs to God alone. I say nothing about the Angels, that we may give no room for wrong feelings, nor opportunity for harmful altercations. Our unhealed condition arises from our evil and unsubdued nature, and from the exercise of its powers. Our repentance when we sin, is a human action, but an action which bespeaks a good man, belonging to that portion which is in the way of salvation. For if even our dust contracts somewhat of wickedness, and the earthly tabernacle presseth down the upward flight of the soul,[α] which at least was created to fly upward, yet let the image be cleansed from filth, and raise aloft the flesh, its yokefellow, lifting it on the wings of reason; and, what is better, let us neither need this cleansing, nor have to be cleansed, by preserving our original dignity, to which we are hastening through our training here, and let us not by the bitter taste of sin be banished from the tree of life: though it is better to turn again when we err, than to be free from correction when we stumble. For whom the Lord loveth He chasteneth,[β] and a rebuke is a fatherly action; while every soul which is unchastised, is unhealed. Is not then freedom from chastisement a hard thing? But to fail to be corrected by the chastisement is still harder. One of the prophets, speaking of Israel, whose heart was hard and uncircumcised, says, Lord, Thou hast stricken them, but they have not grieved, Thou hast consumed them but they have refused to receive correction;[γ] and again, The people turned not to Him that smiteth them;[δ] and Why is my people slidden back by a perpetual backsliding,[ε] because of which it will be utterly crushed and destroyed?

16. It is a fearful thing, my brethren, to fall into the hands of a living God,[ζ] and fearful is the face of the Lord against them that do evil,[η] and abolishing wickedness with utter destruction. Fearful is the ear of God, listening even to the voice of Abel speaking through his silent blood. Fearful His feet, which overtake evildoing. Fearful also His filling of the universe, so that it is impossible anywhere to escape the action of God,[θ] not even by flying up to heaven, or entering Hades, or by escaping to the far East, or concealing ourselves in the depths and ends of the sea.[ι] Nahum the Elkoshite was afraid before me, when he proclaimed the burden of Nineveh, God is jealous, and the Lord takes vengeance in wrath upon His adversaries,[κ] and uses such abundance of severity that no room is left for further vengeance upon the wicked. For whenever I hear Isaiah threaten the people of Sodom and rulers of Gomorrah,[λ] and say Why will

α Joel ii. 17. β Ps. xcv. 6. γ Ib. xcv. 2 (LXX.). δ Joel ii. 14.
ε Ps. cxxvi. 5. ζ Gen. xix. 17, 23: Jonah iii. 5.
η *To do no wrong*, etc. Clémencet quotes this as an aphorism from Demosth. de Cor.

α Wisd. ix. 15. β Prov. iii. 12. γ Jer. v. 3.
δ Isai. ix. 13. ε Jer. viii. 5. ζ Heb. x. 31.
η Ps. xxxiv. 16. θ Jer. xxiii. 24. ι Ps. cxxxix. 7, 8.
κ Nahum i. 1, 2. λ Isai. i. 10.

ye be smitten any more, adding sin to sin?[α] I am almost filled with horror, and melted to tears. It is impossible, he says, to find any blow to add to those which are past, because of your newly added sins; so completely have you run through the whole, and exhausted every form of chastisement, ever calling upon yourselves some new one by your wickedness. There is not a wound, nor bruise, nor putrefying sore;[β] the plague affects the whole body and is incurable: for it is impossible to apply a plaster, or ointment or bandages. I pass over the rest of the threatenings, that I may not press upon you more heavily than your present plague.

17. Only let us recognise the purpose of the evil. Why have the crops withered, our storehouses been emptied, the pastures of our flocks failed, the fruits of the earth been withheld, and the plains been filled with shame instead of with fatness: why have valleys lamented and not abounded in corn, the mountains not dropped sweetness, as they shall do hereafter to the righteous, but been stript and dishonoured, and received on the contrary the curse of Gilboa?[γ] The whole earth has become as it was in the beginning, before it was adorned with its beauties. Thou visitedst the earth, and madest it to drink[δ]—but the visitation has been for evil, and the draught destructive. Alas! what a spectacle! Our prolific crops reduced to stubble, the seed we sowed is recognised by scanty remains, and our harvest, the approach of which we reckon from the number of the months, instead of from the ripening corn, scarcely bears the firstfruits for the Lord. Such is the wealth of the ungodly, such the harvest of the careless sower; as the ancient curse runs, to look for much, and bring in little,[ε] to sow and not reap, to plant and not press,[ζ] ten acres of vineyard to yield one bath:[η] and to hear of fertile harvests in other lands, and be ourselves pressed by famine. Why is this, and what is the cause of the breach? Let us not wait to be convicted by others, let us be our own examiners. An important medicine for evil is confession, and care to avoid stumbling. I will be first to do so, as I have made my report to my people from on high, and performed the duty of a watcher.[θ] For I did not conceal the coming of the sword that I might save my own soul[ι] and those of my hearers. So will I now announce the disobedience of my people, making what is theirs my own, if I may perchance thus obtain some tenderness and relief.

18. One of us has oppressed the poor, and wrested from him his portion of land, and wrongly encroached upon his landmark by fraud or violence, and joined house to house, and field to field, to rob his neighbour of something, and been eager to have no neighbour, so as to dwell alone on the earth.[α] Another has defiled the land with usury and interest, both gathering where he had not sowed and reaping where he had not strawed,[β] farming, not the land, but the necessity of the needy. Another has robbed God,[γ] the giver of all, of the firstfruits of the barnfloor and winepress, showing himself at once thankless and senseless, in neither giving thanks for what he has had, nor prudently providing, at least, for the future. Another has had no pity on the widow and orphan, and not imparted his bread and meagre nourishment to the needy, or rather to Christ, Who is nourished in the persons of those who are nourished even in a slight degree; a man perhaps of much property unexpectedly gained, for this is the most unjust of all, who finds his many barns too narrow for him, filling some and emptying others, to build greater[δ] ones for future crops, not knowing that he is being snatched away with hopes unrealised, to give an account of his riches and fancies, and proved to have been a bad steward of another's goods. Another has turned aside the way of the meek,[ε] and turned aside the just among the unjust; another has hated him that reproveth in the gates,[ζ] and abhorred him that speaketh uprightly;[η] another has sacrificed to his net which catches much,[θ] and keeping the spoil of the poor in his house,[ι] has either remembered not God, or remembered Him ill—by saying "Blessed be the Lord, for we are rich,"[κ] and wickedly supposed that he received these things from Him by Whom he will be punished. For because of these things cometh the wrath of God upon the children of disobedience.[λ] Because of these things the heaven is shut, or opened for our punishment; and much more, if we do not repent, even when smitten, and draw near to Him, Who approaches us through the powers of nature.

19. What shall be said to this by those of us who are buyers and sellers of corn, and watch the hardships of the seasons, in order to grow prosperous, and luxuriate in the misfor-

α Isai. i. 5 (LXX.). β Ib. i. 6. γ 2 Sam. i. 21. δ Ps. lxv. 9. ε Hag. i. 9. ζ Deut. xxviii. 39. η Isai. v. 10. θ Ib. xxi. 6; lxii. 6; Habak. ii. 1. ι Ezek. xxxiii. 3.

α Isai. v. 8. β S. Matt. xxv. 26. γ Mal. iii. 8. δ S. Luke xii. 18. ε Amos ii. 7. ζ Isai. xxix. 21. η Amos v. 10. θ Habak. i. 16. ι Isai. iii. 14. κ Zech. xi. 5. λ Eph. v. 6.

tunes of others, and acquire, not, like Joseph, the property of the Egyptians,[α] as a part of a wide policy, (for he could both collect and supply corn duly, as he also could foresee the famine, and provide against it afar off,) but the property of their fellow countrymen in an illegal manner, for they say, "When will the new moon be gone, that we may sell, and the sabbaths, that we may open our stores?"[β] And they corrupt justice with divers measures and balances,[γ] and draw upon themselves the ephah of lead.[δ] What shall we say to these things who know no limit to our getting, who worship gold and silver, as those of old worshipped Baal, and Astarte and the abomination Chemosh?[ε] Who give heed to the brilliance of costly stones, and soft flowing garments, the prey of moths, and the plunder of robbers and tyrants and thieves; who are proud of their multitude of slaves and animals, and spread themselves over plains and mountains, with their possessions and gains and schemes, like Solomon's horseleach[ζ] which cannot be satisfied, any more than the grave, and the earth, and fire, and water; who seek for another world for their possession, and find fault with the bounds of God, as too small for their insatiable cupidity? What of those who sit on lofty thrones and raise the stage of government, with a brow loftier than that of the theatre, taking no account of the God over all, and the height of the true kingdom that none can approach unto, so as to rule their subjects as fellow-servants, as needing themselves no less loving-kindness? Look also, I pray you, at those who stretch themselves upon beds of ivory, whom the divine Amos fitly upbraids, who anoint themselves with the chief ointments, and chant to the sound of instruments of music, and attach themselves to transitory things as though they were stable, but have not grieved nor had compassion for the affliction of Joseph;[η] though they ought to have been kind to those who had met with disaster before them, and by mercy have obtained mercy; as the fir-tree should howl, because the cedar had fallen,[θ] and be instructed by their neighbours' chastisement, and be led by others' ills to regulate their own lives, having the advantage of being saved by their predecessors' fate, instead of being themselves a warning to others.

20. Join with us, thou divine and sacred person, in considering these questions, with the store of experience, that source of wisdom, which thou hast gathered in thy long life. Herewith instruct thy people. Teach them to break their bread to the hungry, to gather together the poor that have no shelter, to cover their nakedness and not neglect those of the same blood,[α] and now especially that we may gain a benefit from our need instead of from abundance, a result which pleases God more than plentiful offerings and large gifts. After this, nay before it, show thyself, I pray, a Moses,[β] or Phinehas[γ] to day. Stand on our behalf and make atonement, and let the plague be stayed, either by the spiritual sacrifice,[δ] or by prayer and reasonable intercession.[ε] Restrain the anger of the Lord by thy mediation: avert any succeeding blows of the scourge. He knoweth to respect the hoar hairs of a father interceding for his children. Intreat for our past wickedness: be our surety for the future. Present a people purified by suffering and fear. Beg for bodily sustenance, but beg rather for the angels' food that cometh down from heaven. So doing, thou wilt make God to be our God, wilt conciliate heaven, wilt restore the former and latter rain:[ζ] the Lord shall show loving-kindness[η] and our land shall yield her fruit;[θ] our earthly land its fruit which lasts for the day, and our frame, which is but dust, the fruit which is eternal, which we shall store up in the heavenly winepresses by thy hands, who presentest both us and ours in Christ Jesus our Lord, to whom be glory for evermore. Amen.

INTRODUCTION TO ORATION XVIII.

On the Death of his Father.

This Oration was delivered A. D. 374. S. Gregory the elder died early in that year, according to the Greek Menæa on the 1st of January, though Clémencet and some others place his death a few months later. His wife, S. Nonna, survived him, and was present to hear the Oration, as was also S. Basil, who desired to honour one who had consecrated him to the Episcopate. The aged Saint, who died in his hundredth year, had originally belonged to a sect called Hypsistarii. Our knowledge of the existence and tenets of this sect is due to this Oration[ι] and to a few sentences in that of S. Greg. Nyssen. (c. Eunom. I. ed. 1615, p. 12), by whom they are called Hypsistians. He was converted by the prayers, influence and example of his wife, S. Nonna,

α Gen. xli. 39. β Amos viii. 5. γ Prov. xx. 10. δ Zech. v. 8. ε 1 Kings xi. 33. ζ Prov. xxx. 15. η Amos vi. 4–6. θ Zech. xi. 2.

α Isai. lviii. 7. β Exod. xxxii. 11. γ Ps. cvi. 23. 30. δ 1 Pet. ii. 5. ε Rom. xii. 1. ζ Joel ii. 23. η Ps. lxxxv. 13. θ Ib. lxvii. 6. ι Cf. Orat. viii. § 4, note.

and, soon after his baptism, consecrated Bishop of Nazianzus. He was eminent as an able administrator, a devout Christian, an orthodox teacher, a steadfast Confessor of the faith, a sympathetic Pastor, an affectionate father. In his life and work he was seconded by his wife, and followed by his three children, Gregory, Gorgonia, and Cæsarius, whose names are all to be found upon the roll of the Saints.

Funeral Oration on his Father, in the presence of S. Basil.

1. O man of God,[α] and faithful servant,[β] and steward of the mysteries of God,[γ] and man of desires[δ] of the Spirit:[ε] for thus Scripture speaks of men advanced and lofty, superior to visible things. I will call you also a God to Pharaoh[ς] and all the Egyptian and hostile power, and pillar and ground of the Church[η] and will of God[θ] and light in the world, holding forth the word of life,[ι] and prop of the faith and resting place of the Spirit. But why should I enumerate all the titles which your virtue, in its varied forms, has won for and applied to you as your own?

2. Tell me, however, whence do you come, what is your business, and what favour do you bring us? Since I know that you are entirely moved with and by God, and for the benefit of those who receive you. Are you come to inspect us, or to seek for the pastor, or to take the oversight of the flock? You find us no longer in existence, but for the most part having passed away with him, unable to bear with the place of our affliction, especially now that we have lost our skilful steersman, our light of life, to whom we looked to direct our course as the blazing beacon of salvation above us: he has departed with all his excellence, and all the power of pastoral organization, which he had gathered in a long time, full of days and wisdom, and crowned, to use the words of Solomon, with the hoary head of glory.[κ] His flock is desolate and downcast, filled, as you see, with despondency and dejection, no longer reposing in the green pasture,[λ] and reared up by the water of comfort, but seeking precipices, deserts and pits, in which it will be scattered and perish;[μ] in despair of ever obtaining another wise pastor, absolutely persuaded that it cannot find such an one as he, content if it be one who will not be far inferior.

α Josh. xiv. 6. β Numb. xii. 7.
γ 1 Cor. iv. 1. δ Dan. ix. 23 (LXX.).
ε The first words are addressed to S. Basil, who was present.
ς Exod. vii. 1. η 1. Tim. vii. 15. θ Isai. lxii. 4. (LXX.)
ι Phil. ii. 16. κ Prov. xvi. 31.
λ Ps. xxiii. 2. μ Ezek. xxxiv. 14.

3. There are, as I said, three causes to necessitate your presence, all of equal weight, ourselves, the pastor, and the flock: come then, and according to the spirit of ministry which is in you, assign to each its due, and guide your words in judgment, so that we may more than ever marvel at your wisdom. And how will you guide them? First by bestowing seemly praise upon his virtue, not only as a pure sepulchral tribute of speech to him who was pure, but also to set forth to others his conduct and example as a mark of true piety. Then bestow upon us some brief counsels concerning life and death, and the union and severance of body and soul, and the two worlds, the one present but transitory, the other spiritually perceived and abiding; and persuade us to despise that which is deceitful and disordered and uneven, carrying us and being carried, like the waves, now up, now down; but to cling to that which is firm and stable and divine and constant, free from all disturbance and confusion. For this would lessen our pain because of friends departed before us, nay we should rejoice if your words should carry us hence and set us on high, and hide distress of the present in the future, and persuade us that we also are pressing on to a good Master, and that our home is better than our pilgrimage; and that translation and removal thither is to us who are tempest-tost here like a calm haven to men at sea; or as ease and relief from toil come to men who, at the close of a long journey, escape the troubles of the wayfarer, so to those who attain to the hostel yonder comes a better and more tolerable existence than that of those who still tread the crooked and precipitous path of this life.

4. Thus might you console us; but what of the flock? Would you first promise the oversight and leadership of yourself, a man under whose wings we all would gladly repose, and for whose words we thirst more eagerly than men suffering from thirst for the purest fountain? Secondly, persuade us that the good shepherd who laid down his life for the sheep[a] has not even now left us; but is present, and tends and guides, and knows his own, and is known of his own, and, though bodily invisible, is spiritually recognized, and defends his flock against the wolves, and allows no one to climb over into the fold as a robber and traitor; to pervert and steal away,

a S. John x. 11.

by the voice of strangers, souls under the fair guidance of the truth. Aye, I am well assured that his intercession is of more avail now than was his instruction in former days, since he is closer to God, now that he has shaken off his bodily fetters, and freed his mind from the clay which obscured it, and holds intercourse naked with the nakedness of the prime and purest Mind; being promoted, if it be not rash to say so, to the rank and confidence of an angel. This, with your power of speech and spirit, you will set forth and discuss better than I can sketch it. But in order that, through ignorance of his excellences, your language may not fall very far short of his deserts, I will, from my own knowledge of the departed, briefly draw an outline, and preliminary plan of an eulogy to be handed to you, the illustrious artist of such subjects, for the details of the beauty of his virtue to be filled in and transmitted to the ears and minds of all.

5. Leaving to the laws of panegyric the description of his country, his family, his nobility of figure, his external magnificence, and the other subjects of human pride, I begin with what is of most consequence and comes closest to ourselves. He sprang from a stock unrenowned, and not well suited for piety, for I am not ashamed of his origin, in my confidence in the close of his life, one that was not planted in the house of God,[α] but far removed and estranged, the combined product of two of the greatest opposites—Greek error and legal imposture, some parts of each of which it escaped, of others it was compounded. For, on the one side, they reject idols and sacrifices, but reverence fire and lights; on the other, they observe the Sabbath and petty regulations as to certain meats, but despise circumcision. These lowly men call themselves Hypsistarii, and the Almighty is, so they say, the only object of their worship. What was the result of this double tendency to impiety? I know not whether to praise more highly the grace which called him, or his own purpose. However, he so purged the eye of his mind from the humours[β] which obscured it, and ran towards the truth with such speed that he endured the loss of his mother and his property for a while, for the sake of his heavenly Father and the true inheritance: and submitted more readily to this dishonour, than others to the greatest honours, and, most wonderful as this is, I wonder at it but little. Why? Because this glory is common to him with many others, and all must come into the great net of God, and be caught by the words of the fishers, although some are earlier, some later, enclosed by the Gospel. But what does especially in his life move my wonder, it is needful for me to mention.

6. Even before he was of our fold, he was ours. His character made him one of us. For, as many of our own are not with us, whose life alienates them from the common body, so, many of those without are on our side, whose character anticipates their faith, and need only the name of that which indeed they possess. My father was one of these, an alien shoot, but inclined by his life towards us. He was so far advanced in self control, that he became at once most beloved and most modest, two qualities difficult to combine. What greater and more splendid testimony can there be to his justice than his exercise of a position second to none in the state, without enriching himself by a single farthing, although he saw everyone else casting the hands of Briareus upon the public funds, and swollen with ill-gotten gain? For thus do I term unrighteous wealth. Of his prudence this also is no slight proof, but in the course of my speech further details will be given. It was as a reward[α] for such conduct, I think, that he attained to the faith. How this came about, a matter too important to be passed over, I would now set forth.

7. I have heard the Scripture say: Who can find a valiant woman?[β] and declare that she is a divine gift, and that a good marriage is brought about by the Lord. Even those without are of the same mind; if they say that a man can win no fairer prize than a good wife, nor a worse one than her opposite.[γ] But we can mention none who has been in this respect more fortunate than he. For I think that, had anyone from the ends of the earth and from every race of men attempted to bring about the best of marriages, he could not have found a better or more harmonious one than this. For the most excellent of men and of women were so united that their marriage was a union of virtue rather than of bodies: since, while they excelled all others, they could not excel each other, because in virtue they were quite equally matched.

8. She indeed who was given to Adam as a help meet for him, because it was not good for man to be alone,[δ] instead of an assistant

α Ps. xcii. 13.
β *Humours.* This word is used Aristoph. Plut. 581, of the obscuring effect of old prejudices.

α *Reward.* Faith is, as Clémencet remarks, "the gift of God"—but cf. S. John vii. 17. β Prov. xxxi. 10, 7.
γ Hesiod: Works and Days, 700. δ Gen. ii. 18.

became an enemy, and instead of a yoke-fellow, an opponent, and beguiling the man by means of pleasure, estranged him through the tree of knowledge from the tree of life. But she who was given by God to my father became not only, as is less wonderful, his assistant, but even his leader, drawing him on by her influence in deed and word to the highest excellence; judging it best in all other respects to be overruled by her husband according to the law of marriage, but not being ashamed, in regard of piety, even to offer herself as his teacher. Admirable indeed as was this conduct of hers, it was still more admirable that he should readily acquiesce in it. She is a woman who while others have been honoured and extolled for natural and artificial beauty, has acknowledged but one kind of beauty, that of the soul, and the preservation, or the restoration as far as possible, of the Divine image. Pigments and devices for adornment she has rejected as worthy of women on the stage. The only genuine form of noble birth she recognized is piety, and the knowledge of whence we are sprung and whither we are tending. The only safe and inviolable form of wealth is, she considered, to strip oneself of wealth for God and the poor, and especially for those of our own kin who are unfortunate; and such help only as is necessary, she held to be rather a reminder, than a relief of their distress, while a more liberal beneficence brings stable honour and most perfect consolation. Some women have excelled in thrifty management, others in piety, while she, difficult as it is to unite the two virtues, has surpassed all in both of them, both by her eminence in each, and by the fact that she alone has combined them together. To as great a degree has she, by her care and skill, secured the prosperity of her household, according to the injunctions and laws of Solomon as to the valiant woman, as if she had had no knowledge of piety; and she applied herself to God and Divine things as closely as if absolutely released from household cares, allowing neither branch of her duty to interfere with the other, but rather making each of them support the other.

9. What time or place for prayer ever escaped her? To this she was drawn before all other things in the day; or rather, who had such hope of receiving an immediate answer to her requests? Who paid such reverence to the hand and countenance of the priests? Or honoured all kinds of philosophy? Who reduced the flesh by more constant fast and vigil? Or stood like a pillar at the night long and daily psalmody? Who had a greater love for virginity, though patient of the marriage bond herself? Who was a better patron of the orphan and the widow? Who aided as much in the alleviation of the misfortunes of the mourner? These things, small as they are, and perhaps contemptible in the eyes of some, because not easily attainable by most people (for that which is unattainable comes, through envy, to be thought not even credible), are in my eyes most honourable, since they were the discoveries of her faith and the undertakings of her spiritual fervour. So also in the holy assemblies, or places, her voice was never to be heard except[α] in the necessary responses of the service.

10. And if it was a great thing for the altar never to have had an iron tool lifted upon it,[β] and that no chisel should be seen or heard, with greater reason, since everything dedicated to God ought to be natural and free from artificiality, it was also surely a great thing that she reverenced the sanctuary by her silence; that she never turned her back to the venerable table, nor spat upon the divine pavement; that she never grasped the hand or kissed the lips of any heathen woman, however honourable in other respects, or closely related she might be; nor would she ever share the salt, I say not willingly but even under compulsion, of those who came from the profane and unholy table; nor could she bear, against the law of conscience, to pass by or look upon a polluted house; nor to have her ears or tongue, which had received and uttered divine things, defiled by Grecian tales or theatrical songs, on the ground that what is unholy is unbecoming to holy things; and what is still more wonderful, she never so far yielded to the external signs of grief, although greatly moved even by the misfortunes of strangers, as to allow a sound of woe to burst forth before the Eucharist, or a tear to fall from the eye mystically sealed, or any trace of mourning to be left on the occasion of a festival, however frequent her own sorrows might be; inasmuch as the God-loving soul should subject every human experience to the things of God.

11. I pass by in silence what is still more ineffable, of which God is witness, and those of the faithful handmaidens to whom she has confided such things. That which concerns myself is perhaps undeserving of mention, since I have proved unworthy of the hope

α *Except*, etc. Lit., "except the necessary and mystical (i. e., liturgical) [words]."
β Deut xxvii. 5.

cherished in regard to me: yet it was on her part a great undertaking to promise me to God before my birth, with no fear of the future, and to dedicate me immediately after I was born. Through God's goodness has it been that she has not utterly failed in her prayer, and that the auspicious sacrifice was not rejected. Some of these things were already in existence, others were in the future, growing up by means of gradual additions. And as the sun which most pleasantly casts its morning rays, becomes at midday hotter and more brilliant, so also did she, who from the first gave no slight evidence of piety, shine forth at last with fuller light. Then indeed he, who had established her in his house, had at home no slight spur to piety, possessed, by her origin and descent, of the love of God and Christ, and having received virtue as her patrimony; not, as he had been, cut out of the wild olive and grafted into the good olive, yet unable to bear, in the excess of her faith, to be unequally yoked; for, though surpassing all others in endurance and fortitude, she could not brook this, the being but half united to God, because of the estrangement of him who was a part of herself, and the failure to add to the bodily union, a close connexion in the spirit: on this account, she fell before God night and day, entreating for the salvation of her head with many fastings and tears, and assiduously devoting herself to her husband, and influencing him in many ways, by means of reproaches, admonitions, attentions, estrangements, and above all by her own character with its fervour for piety, by which the soul is specially prevailed upon and softened, and willingly submits to virtuous pressure. The drop[α] of water constantly striking the rock was destined to hollow it, and at length attain its longing, as the sequel shows.

12. These were the objects of her prayers and hopes, in the fervour of faith rather than of youth. Indeed, none was as confident of things present as she of things hoped for, from her experience of the generosity of God. For the salvation of my father there was a concurrence of the gradual conviction[β] of his reason, and the vision of dreams which God often bestows upon a soul worthy of salvation. What was the vision? This is to me the most pleasing part of the story. He thought that he was singing, as he had never done before, though his wife was frequent in her supplications and prayers, this verse from the psalms of holy David: I was glad when they said unto me, we will go into the house of the Lord.[α] The psalm was a strange one to him, and along with its words the desire came to him. As soon as she heard it, having thus obtained her prayer, she seized the opportunity, replying that the vision would bring the greatest pleasure, if accompanied by its fulfilment, and, manifesting by her joy the greatness of the benefit, she urged forward his salvation, before anything could intervene to hinder the call, and dissipate the object of her longing. At that very time it happened that a number of Bishops were hastening to Nicæa, to oppose the madness of Arius, since the wickedness of dividing the Godhead had just arisen; so my father yielded himself to God and to the heralds of the truth, and confessed his desire, and requested from them the common salvation, one of them being the celebrated Leontius, at that time our own metropolitan. It would be a great wrong to grace, were I to pass by in silence the wonder which then was bestowed upon him by grace. The witnesses of the wonder[β] are not few. The teachers of accuracy were spiritually at fault, and the grace was a forecast of the future, and the formula of the priesthood was mingled with the admission of the catechumen. O involuntary initiation! bending his knee, he received the form of admission to the state of a catechumen in such wise, that many, not only of the highest, but even of the lowest, intellect, prophesied the future, being assured by no indistinct signs of what was to be.

13. After a short interval, wonder succeeded wonder. I will commend the account of it to the ears of the faithful, for to profane minds nothing that is good is trustworthy. He was approaching that regeneration by water and the Spirit, by which we confess to God the formation and completion of the Christlike man, and the transformation and reformation from the earthy to the Spirit. He was approaching the laver with warm desire and bright hope, after all the purgation possible, and a far greater purification of soul and body than that of the men who were to receive the tables from Moses. Their purification extended only to their dress, and a slight restriction of the belly, and a temporary continence.[γ] The whole of his past life had been a preparation for the enlightenment, and

α *The drop.* A familiar proverb. Choerilus, 9.
β *Conviction.* Lit., "healing."

α Ps. cxxii. 1.
β *The wonder.* S. Gregory the elder ought, according to the rite of admission to the ranks of the Catechumens, to have remained standing, and in that position have had his ears anointed. He fell upon his knees and the Bishop, in forgetfulness, pronounced over him the form of ordination to the Priesthood.
γ Exod. xix. 10, 15.

a preliminary purification making sure the gift, in order that perfection might be entrusted to purity, and that the blessing might incur no risk in a soul which was confident in its possession of the grace. And as he was ascending out of the water, there flashed around him a light and a glory worthy of the disposition with which he approached the gift of faith;[α] this was manifest even to some others, who for the time concealed the wonder, from fear of speaking of a sight which each one thought had been only his own, but shortly afterwards communicated it to one another. To the baptiser[β] and initiator, however, it was so clear and visible, that he could not even hold back the mystery, but publicly cried out that he was anointing with the Spirit his own successor.

14. Nor indeed would anyone disbelieve this who has heard and knows that Moses, when little in the eyes of men, and not yet of any account, was called from the bush which burned but was not consumed, or rather by Him who appeared in the bush,[γ] and was encouraged by that first wonder: Moses, I say, for whom the sea was divided,[δ] and manna rained down,[ε] and the rock poured out a fountain,[ζ] and the pillar of fire and cloud led the way in turn, and the stretching out of his hands gained a victory, and the representation of the cross overcame tens of thousands. Isaiah, again, who beheld the glory of the Seraphim,[η] and after him Jeremiah, who was entrusted with great power against nations and kings;[θ] the one heard the divine voice and was cleansed by a live coal for his prophetic office, and the other was known before his formation and sanctified before his birth. Paul, also, while yet a persecutor, who became the great herald of the truth and teacher of the Gentiles in faith,[ι] was surrounded by a light[κ] and acknowledged Him whom he was persecuting, and was entrusted with his great ministry, and filled every ear and mind with the gospel.

15. Why need I count up all those who have been called to Himself by God and associated with such wonders as confirmed him in his piety? Nor was it the case that after such and so incredible and startling beginnings, any of the former things was put to shame by his subsequent conduct, as happens with those who very soon acquire a distaste for what is good, and so neglect all further progress, if they do not utterly relapse into vice. This cannot be said of him, for he was most consistent with himself and his early days, and kept in harmony his life before the priesthood with its excellence, and his life after it with what had gone before, since it would have been unbecoming to begin in one way and end in another, or to advance to a different end from that which he had in view at first. He was next entrusted with the priesthood, not with the facility and disorder of the present day, but after a brief interval, in order to add to his own cleansing the skill and power to cleanse others; for this is the law of spiritual sequence. And when he had been entrusted with it, the grace was the more glorified, being really the grace of God, and not of men, and not, as the preacher[α] says, an independent impulse and purpose[β] of spirit.

16. He received a woodland and rustic church, the pastoral care and oversight of which had not been bestowed from a distance, but it had been cared for by one of his predecessors of admirable and angelic disposition, and a more simple man than our present rulers of the people; but, after he had been speedily taken to God, it had, in consequence of the loss of its leader, for the most part grown careless and run wild; accordingly, he at first strove without harshness to soften the habits of the people, both by words of pastoral knowledge, and by setting himself before them as an example, like a spiritual statue, polished into the beauty of all excellent conduct. He next, by constant meditation on the divine words, though a late student of such matters, gathered together so much wisdom within a short time that he was in no wise excelled by those who had spent the greatest toil upon them, and received this special grace from God, that he became the father and teacher of orthodoxy—not, like our modern wise men, yielding to the spirit of the age, nor defending our faith by indefinite and sophistical language, as if they had no fixity of faith, or were adulterating the truth; but, he was more pious than those who possessed rhetorical power, more skilled in rhetoric than those who were upright in mind; or rather, while he took the second place as an orator, he surpassed all in piety. He acknowledged One God worshipped in Trinity, and Three, Who are united in One Godhead; neither Sabellianising[γ] as to the

α *The gift of faith.* One of the questions in some ancient rites of administering Holy Baptism was, "What seekest thou of the Church?" to which the answer was "Faith."

β *The baptiser.* The Bishop of Nazianzus—not Leontius of Cæsarea, who had much to do with Gregory's instruction and had, possibly, admitted him to the order of Catechumens.

γ Exod. iii. 4. δ Ib. xiv. 22. ε Ib. xvi. 4.
ζ Ib. xvii. 6. η Isai. vi. 1 et seq. θ Jer. i. 10.
ι 1 Tim. ii. 7; 2 Tim. i. 11. κ Acts ix. 3.

α Eccles. 1. 17; lxx.

β *Purpose*, etc. A. V. "Vexation of Spirit." R. V. "Striving after wind." γ *Sabellianising*, etc. Cf. II. 36, 37 (notes).

One, nor Arianising as to the Three; either by contracting and so atheistically annihilating the Godhead, or by tearing It asunder by distinctions of unequal greatness or nature. For, seeing that Its every quality is incomprehensible and beyond the power of our intellect, how can we either perceive or express by definition on such a subject, that which is beyond our ken? How can the immeasurable be measured, and the Godhead be reduced to the condition of finite things, and measured by degrees[α] of greater or less?

17. What else must we say of this great man of God, the true Divine, under the influence, in regard to these subjects, of the Holy Ghost, but that through his perception of these points, he, like the great Noah, the father of this second world, made this church to be called the new Jerusalem, and a second ark borne up upon the waters; since it both surmounted the deluge of souls, and the insults of the heretics, and excelled all others in reputation no less than it fell behind them in numbers; and has had the same fortune as the sacred Bethlehem, which can without contradiction be at once said to be a little city and the metropolis of the world, since it is the nurse and mother of Christ, Who both made and overcame the world.

18. To give a proof of what I say. When a tumult of the over-zealous part of the Church was raised against us, and we had been decoyed by a document[β] and artful terms into association with evil, he alone was believed to have an unwounded mind, and a soul unstained by ink, even when he had been imposed upon in his simplicity, and failed from his guilelessness of soul to be on his guard against guile. He it was alone, or rather first of all, who by his zeal for piety reconciled to himself and the rest of the church the faction opposed to us, which was the last to leave us, the first to return, owing to both their reverence for the man and the purity of his doctrine, so that the serious storm in the churches was allayed, and the hurricane reduced to a breeze under the influence of his prayers and admonitions; while, if I may make a boastful remark, I was his partner[γ] in piety and activity, aiding him in every effort on behalf of what is good, accompanying and running beside him, and being permitted on this occasion to contribute a very great share of the toil. Here my account of these matters, which is a little premature, must come to an end.

19. Who could enumerate the full tale of his excellences, or, if he wished to pass by most of them, discover without difficulty what can be omitted? For each trait, as it occurs to the mind, seems superior to what has gone before; it takes possession of me, and I feel more at a loss to know what I ought to pass by, than other panegyrists are as to what they ought to say. So that the abundance of material is to some extent a hindrance to me, and my mind is itself put to the test in its efforts to test his qualities, and its inability, where all are equal, to find one which surpasses the rest. So that, just as when we see a pebble falling into still water, it becomes the centre and starting-point of circle after circle, each by its continuous agitation breaking up that which lies outside of it; this is exactly the case with myself. For as soon as one thing enters my mind, another follows and displaces it; and I am wearied out in making a choice, as what I have already grasped is ever retiring in favour of that which follows in its train.

20. Who was more anxious than he for the common weal? Who more wise in domestic affairs, since God, who orders all things in due variation, assigned to him a house and suitable fortune? Who was more sympathetic in mind, more bounteous in hand, towards the poor, that most dishonoured portion of the nature to which equal honour is due? For he actually treated his own property as if it were another's, of which he was but the steward, relieving poverty as far as he could, and expending not only his superfluities but his necessities—a manifest proof of love for the poor, giving a portion, not only to seven, according to the injunction of Solomon,[α] but if an eighth came forward, not even in his case being niggardly, but more pleased to dispose of his wealth than we know others are to acquire it; taking away the yoke and election (which means, as I think, all meanness in testing as to whether the recipient is worthy or not) and word of murmuring[β] in benevolence. This is what most men do: they give indeed, but without that readiness, which is a greater and more perfect thing than the mere offering. For he thought it much better[γ] to be generous even to the undeserving for the sake of the deserving, than from fear of the undeserving

α *Degrees.* The heretics asserted that the Father, Son and Holy Ghost were arranged in this order according to a real difference in rank.

β *A document.* Benoît (I. p. 179) gives reasons for believing that this was the creed of the council of Antioch, A.D. 363—which accepted the Creed of Nicæa, but explained it in terms capable of a semiarian construction. The "over zealous part" were the monks.

γ *Partner.* S. Gregory had a considerable share in the explanations which made clear his father's real orthodoxy, and re-established peace. Orat. vi. was pronounced by him on the occasion.

α Eccles. xi. 2. β Isai. lviii. 9 (LXX.).

γ *Better.* Clémencet compares Dem. De Corona.

to deprive those who were deserving. And this seems to be the duty of casting our bread upon the waters,[a] since it will not be swept away or perish in the eyes of the just Investigator, but will arrive yonder where all that is ours is laid up, and will meet with us in due time, even though we think it not.

21. But what is best and greatest of all, his magnanimity was accompanied by freedom from ambition. Its extent and character I will proceed to show. In considering their wealth to be common to all, and in liberality in bestowing it, he and his consort rivalled each other in their struggles after excellence; but he intrusted the greater part of this bounty to her hand, as being a most excellent and trusty steward of such matters. What a woman she is? Not even the Atlantic Ocean, or if there be a greater one, could meet her drafts upon it. So great and so boundless is her love of liberality. In the contrary sense she has rivalled the horse-leech[β] of Solomon, by her insatiable longing for progress, overcoming the tendency to backsliding, and unable to satisfy her zeal for benevolence. She not only considered all the property which they originally possessed, and what accrued to them later, as unable to suffice her own longing, but she would, as I have often heard her say, have gladly sold herself and her children into slavery, had there been any means of doing so, to expend the proceeds upon the poor. Thus entirely did she give the rein to her generosity. This is, I imagine, far more convincing than any instance of it could be. Magnanimity in regard to money may be found without difficulty in the case of others, whether it be dissipated in the public rivalries of the state, or lent to God through the poor, the only mode of treasuring it up for those who spend it: but it is not easy to discover a man who has renounced the consequent reputation. For it is desire for reputation which supplies to most men their readiness to spend. And where the bounty must be secret, there the disposition to it is less keen.

22. So bounteous was his hand—further details I leave to those who knew him, so that if anything of the kind is borne witness to in regard to myself, it proceeds from that fountain, and is a portion of that stream. Who was more under the Divine guidance in admitting men to the sanctuary,[γ] or in resenting dishonour done to it, or in cleansing the holy table with awe from the unholy? Who with such unbiassed judgment, and with the scales of justice, either decided a suit, or hated vice, or honoured virtue, or promoted the most excellent? Who was so compassionate for the sinner, or sympathetic towards those who were running well? Who better knew the right time for using the rod and the staff,[a] yet relied most upon the staff? Whose eyes were more upon the faithful in the land,[β] especially upon those who, in the monastic and unwedded life, have despised the earth and the things of earth?

23. Who did more to rebuke pride and foster lowliness? And that in no assumed or external way, as most of those who now make profession of virtue, and are in appearance as elegant as the most mindless women, who, for lack of beauty of their own, take refuge in pigments, and are, if I may say so, splendidly made up, uncomely in their comeliness, and more ugly than they originally were. For his lowliness was no matter of dress, but of spiritual disposition: nor was it expressed by a bent neck, or lowered voice, or downcast look, or length of beard, or close-shaven head, or measured gait, which can be adopted for a while, but are very quickly exposed, for nothing which is affected can be permanent. No! he was ever most lofty in life, most lowly in mind; inaccessible in virtue, most accessible in intercourse. His dress had in it nothing remarkable, avoiding equally magnificence and sordidness, while his internal brilliancy was supereminent. The disease and insatiability of the belly, he, if anyone, held in check, but without ostentation; so that he might be kept down without being puffed up, from having encouraged a new vice by his pursuit of reputation. For he held that doing and saying everything by which fame among externs might be won, is the characteristic of the politician, whose chief happiness is found in the present life: but that the spiritual and Christian man should look to one object alone, his salvation, and think much of what may contribute to this, but detest as of no value what does not; and accordingly despise what is visible, but be occupied with interior perfection alone, and estimate most highly whatever promotes his own improvement, and attracts others through himself to that which is supremely good.

24. But what was most excellent and most characteristic, though least generally recognized, was his simplicity, and freedom from guile, and resentment. For among men of ancient and modern days, each is supposed to have had some special success, as each chanced

a Eccles. xi. 1. β Prov. xxx. 15.
γ *To the Sanctuary*, i.e., To the Priesthood.

a Ps. xxiii. 5. *Rod and Staff*, i.e., Punishment and support.
β Ps. ci. 6.

to have received from God some particular virtue: Job unconquered patience in misfortune,[a] Moses[β] and David[γ] meekness, Samuel prophecy, seeing into the future,[δ] Phineas zeal,[ε] for which he has a name, Peter and Paul eagerness in preaching,[ζ] the sons of Zebedee magniloquence, whence also they were entitled Sons of thunder.[η] But why should I enumerate them all, speaking as I do among those who know this? Now the specially distinguishing mark of Stephen and of my father was the absence of malice. For not even when in peril did Stephen hate his assailants, but was stoned while praying for those who were stoning him[θ] as a disciple of Christ, on Whose behalf he was allowed to suffer, and so, in his long-suffering, bearing for God a nobler fruit than his death: my father, in allowing no interval between assault and forgiveness, so that he was almost robbed of pain itself by the speed of pardon.

25. We both believe in and hear of the dregs[ι] of the anger of God, the residuum of His dealings with those who deserve it: For the Lord is a God of vengeance.[κ] For although He is disposed by His kindness to gentleness rather than severity, yet He does not absolutely pardon sinners, lest they should be made worse by His goodness. Yet my father kept no grudge against those who provoked him, indeed he was absolutely uninfluenced by anger, although in spiritual things exceedingly overcome by zeal: except when he had been prepared and armed and set in hostile array against that which was advancing to injure him. So that this sweet disposition of his would not, as the saying goes, have been stirred by tens of thousands. For the wrath which he had was not like that of the serpent,[λ] smouldering within, ready to defend itself, eager to burst forth, and longing to strike back at once on being disturbed; but like the sting of the bee, which does not bring death with its stroke; while his kindness was superhuman. The wheel and scourge were often threatened, and those who could apply them stood near; and the danger ended in being pinched on the ear, patted on the face, or buffeted on the temple: thus he mitigated the threat. His dress and sandals were dragged off, and the scoundrel was felled to the ground: then his anger was directed not against his assailant, but against his eager succourer, as a minister of evil. How could anyone be more conclusively proved to be good, and worthy to offer the gifts to God? For often, instead of being himself roused, he made excuses for the man who assailed him, blushing for his faults as if they had been his own.

26. The dew would more easily resist the morning rays of the sun, than any remains of anger continue in him; but as soon as he had spoken, his indignation departed with his words, leaving behind only his love for what is good, and never outlasting the sun; nor did he cherish anger which destroys even the prudent, or show any bodily trace of vice within, nay, even when roused, he preserved calmness. The result of this was most unusual, not that he was the only one to give rebuke, but the only one to be both loved and admired by those whom he reproved, from the victory which his goodness gained over warmth of feeling; and it was felt to be more serviceable to be punished by a just man than besmeared by a bad one, for in one case the severity becomes pleasant for its utility, in the other the kindliness is suspected because of the evil of the man's character. But though his soul and character were so simple and divine, his piety nevertheless inspired the insolent with awe: or rather, the cause of their respect was the simplicity which they despised. For it was impossible to him to utter either prayer or curse without the immediate bestowal of permanent blessing or transient pain. The one proceeded from his inmost soul, the other merely rested upon his lips as a paternal reproof. Many indeed of those who had injured him incurred neither lingering requital nor, as the poet[a] says, "vengeance which dogs men's steps;" but at the very moment of their passion they were struck and converted, came forward, knelt before him, and were pardoned, going away gloriously vanquished, and amended both by the chastisement and the forgiveness. Indeed, a forgiving spirit often has great saving power, checking the wrongdoer by the sense of shame, and bringing him back from fear to love, a far more secure state of mind. In chastisement some were tossed by oxen oppressed by the yoke, which suddenly attacked them, though they had never done anything of the kind before; others were thrown and trampled upon by most obedient and quiet horses; others seized by intolerable fevers, and apparitions of their daring deeds; others being punished in different ways, and learning obedience from the things which they suffered.

27. Such and so remarkable being his gentleness, did he yield the palm to others in

α Job i. 21. β Numb. xii. 3. γ Ps. cxxxii. 1 (LXX.). δ 1 Sam. ix. 9. ε Numb. xxxv. 7. ζ Gal. ii. 7. η S. Mark iii. 17. θ Acts vii. 59. ι *Dregs*. Cf. Orat. xvi. 4. κ Ps. lxxv. 8; xciv. 1. λ Ib. lviii. 4 (LXX).

a *The poet*. Pindar.

industry and practical virtue? By no means. Gentle as he was, he possessed, if any one did, an energy corresponding to his gentleness. For although, for the most part, the two virtues of benevolence and severity are at variance and opposed to each other, the one being gentle but without practical qualities, the other practical but unsympathetic, in his case there was a wonderful combination of the two, his action being as energetic as that of a severe man, but combined with gentleness; while his readiness to yield seemed unpractical but was accompanied with energy, in his patronage, his freedom of speech, and every kind of official duty. He united the wisdom of the serpent, in regard to evil, with the harmlessness of the dove, in regard to good, neither allowing the wisdom to degenerate into knavery, nor the simplicity into silliness, but as far as in him lay, he combined the two in one perfect form of virtue. Such being his birth, such his exercise of the priestly office, such the reputation which he won at the hands of all, what wonder if he was thought worthy of the miracles by which God establishes true religion?

28. One of the wonders which concern him was that he suffered from sickness and bodily pain. But what wonder is it for even holy men to be distressed, either for the cleansing of their clay, slight though it may be, or a touchstone of virtue and test of philosophy, or for the education of the weaker, who learn from their example to be patient instead of giving way under their misfortunes? Well, he was sick, the time was the holy and illustrious Easter, the queen of days, the brilliant night which dissipates the darkness of sin, upon which with abundant light we keep the feast of our salvation, putting ourselves to death along with the Light once put to death for us, and rising again with Him who rose. This was the time of his sufferings. Of what kind they were, I will briefly explain. His whole frame was on fire with an excessive, burning fever, his strength had failed, he was unable to take food, his sleep had departed from him, he was in the greatest distress, and agitated by palpitations. Within his mouth, the palate and the whole of the upper surface was so completely and painfully ulcerated, that it was difficult and dangerous to swallow even water. The skill of physicians, the prayers, most earnest though they were, of his friends, and every possible attention were alike of no avail. He himself in this desperate condition, while his breath came short and fast, had no perception of present things, but was entirely absent, immersed in the objects he had long desired, now made ready for him. We were in the temple, mingling supplications with the sacred rites, for, in despair of all others, we had betaken ourselves to the Great Physician, to the power of that night, and to the last succour, with the intention, shall I say, of keeping a feast, or of mourning; of holding festival, or paying funeral honours to one no longer here? O those tears! which were shed at that time by all the people. O voices, and cries, and hymns blended with the psalmody! From the temple they sought the priest, from the sacred rite the celebrant, from God their worthy ruler, with my Miriam [α] to lead them and strike the timbrel [β] not of triumph, but of supplication; learning then for the first time to be put to shame by misfortune, and calling at once upon the people and upon God; upon the former to sympathize with her distress, and to be lavish of their tears, upon the latter, to listen to her petitions, as, with the inventive genius of suffering, she rehearsed before Him all His wonders of old time.

29. What then was the response of Him who was the God of that night and of the sick man? A shudder comes over me as I proceed with my story. And though you, my hearers, may shudder, do not disbelieve: for that would be impious, when I am the speaker, and in reference to him. The time of the mystery was come, and the reverend station and order, when silence is kept for the solemn rites; and then he was raised up by Him who quickeneth the dead, and by the holy night. At first he moved slightly, then more decidedly; then in a feeble and indistinct voice he called by name one of the servants who was in attendance upon him, and bade him come, and bring his clothes, and support him with his hand. He came in alarm, and gladly waited upon him, while he, leaning upon his hand as upon a staff, imitates Moses upon the mount, arranges his feeble hands in prayer, and in union with, or on behalf of,[γ] his people eagerly celebrates the mysteries, in such few words as his strength allowed, but, as it seems to me, with a most perfect intention. What a miracle! In the sanctuary without a sanctuary, sacrificing without an altar, a priest far from the sacred rites: yet all these were present to him in the power of the spirit, recognised by him, though unseen by those who were there. Then, after adding the customary

α *My Miriam.* S. Nonna. β Exod. xv. 20.

γ *On behalf of*, or perhaps "at the head of." The passage does not mean that he actually celebrated the Holy Mysteries, but that he used some of the prayers of the service, and united himself in intention with the service being at the time performed in the church, and invoked the Divine blessing upon his people in his absence.

words of thanksgiving, and after blessing the people, he retired again to his bed, and after taking a little food, and enjoying a sleep, he recalled his spirit, and, his health being gradually recovered, on the new day [α] of the feast, as we call the first Sunday after the festival of the Resurrection, he entered the temple and inaugurated his life which had been preserved, with the full complement of clergy, and offered the sacrifice of thanksgiving. To me this seems no less remarkable than the miracle in the case of Hezekiah,[β] who was glorified by God in his sickness and prayers with an extension of life, and this was signified by the return of the shadow of the degrees,[γ] according to the request of the king who was restored, whom God honoured at once by the favour and the sign, assuring him of the extension of his days by the extension of the day.

30. The same miracle occurred in the case of my mother not long afterwards. I do not think it would be proper to pass by this either: for we shall both pay the meed of honour which is due to her, if to anyone at all, and gratify him, by her being associated with him in our recital. She, who had always been strong and vigorous and free from disease all her life, was herself attacked by sickness. In consequence of much distress, not to prolong my story, caused above all by inability to eat, her life was for many days in danger, and no remedy for the disease could be found. How did God sustain her? Not by raining down manna, as for Israel of old,[δ] or opening the rock, in order to give drink to His thirsting people,[ε] or feasting her by means of ravens, as Elijah,[ζ] or feeding her by a prophet carried through the air, as He did to Daniel when a-hungered in the den.[η] But how? She thought she saw me, who was her favourite, for not even in her dreams did she prefer any other of us, coming up to her suddenly at night, with a basket of pure white loaves, which I blessed and crossed as I was wont to do, and then fed and strengthened her, and she became stronger. The nocturnal vision was a real action. For, in consequence, she became more herself and of better hope, as is manifest by a clear and evident token. Next morning, when I paid her an early visit, I saw at once that she was brighter, and when I asked, as usual, what kind of a night she had passed, and if she wished for anything, she replied, "My child, you most readily and kindly fed me, and then you ask how I am. I am very well and at ease." Her maids too made signs to me to offer no resistance, and to accept her answer at once, lest she should be thrown back into despondency, if the truth were laid bare. I will add one more instance common to them both.

31. I was on a voyage from Alexandria to Greece over the Parthenian Sea. The voyage was quite unseasonable, undertaken in an Æginetan vessel, under the impulse of eager desire; for what specially induced me was that I had fallen in with a crew who were well known to me. After making some way on the voyage, a terrible storm came upon us, and such an one as my shipmates said they had but seldom seen before. While we were all in fear of a common death, spiritual death was what I was most afraid of; for I was in danger of departing in misery, being unbaptised, and I longed for the spiritual water among the waters of death. On this account I cried and begged and besought a slight respite. My shipmates, even in their common danger, joined in my cries, as not even my own relatives would have done, kindly souls as they were, having learned sympathy from their dangers. In this my condition, my parents felt for me, my danger having been communicated to them by a nightly vision, and they aided me from the land, soothing the waves by prayer, as I afterwards learned by calculating the time, after I had landed. This was also shown me in a wholesome sleep, of which I had experience during a slight lull of the tempest. I seemed to be holding a Fury, of fearful aspect, boding danger; for the night presented her clearly to my eyes. Another of my shipmates, a boy most kindly disposed and dear to me, and exceedingly anxious on my behalf, in my then present condition, thought he saw my mother walk upon the sea, and seize and drag the ship to land with no great exertion. We had confidence in the vision, for the sea began to grow calm, and we soon reached Rhodes after the intervention of no great discomfort. We ourselves became an offering in consequence of that peril; for we promised ourselves if we were saved, to God, and, when we had been saved, gave ourselves to Him.

32. Such were their common experiences. But I imagine that some of those who have had an accurate knowledge of his life must have been for a long while wondering why we have dwelt upon these points, as if we thought

α *The new day.* On this feast (in another year) Orat. xliv. was preached. β 2 Kings xx. 1 et seq. γ Isai. xxxviii. 8. δ Exod. xvi. 14; xvii. 6. ε Ps. lxxviii. 24, 15. ζ 1 Kings xvii. 6. η Dan. xiv. 33 (sc. Hist. of Bel. v. 33).

them his only title to renown, and postponed the mention of the difficulties of his times, against which he conspicuously arrayed himself, as though we were either ignorant of them, or thought them to be of no great consequence. Come, then, we will proceed to speak upon this topic. The first, and I think the last, evil of our day, was the Emperor who apostatised from God and from reason, and thought it a small matter to conquer the Persians, but a great one to subject to himself the Christians; and so, together with the demons who led and prevailed upon him, he failed in no form of impiety, but by means of persuasions, threats, and sophistries, strove to draw men to him, and even added to his various artifices the use of force. His design, however, was exposed, whether he strove to conceal persecution under sophistical devices, or manifestly made use of his authority—namely by one means or the other—either by cozening or by violence, to get us into his power. Who can be found who more utterly despised or defeated him? One sign, among many others, of his contempt, is the mission to our sacred buildings of the police and their commissary, with the intention of taking either voluntary or forcible possession of them: he had attacked many others, and came hither with like intent, demanding the surrender of the temple according to the Imperial decree, but was so far from succeeding in any of his wishes that, had he not speedily given way before my father, either from his own good sense or according to some advice given to him, he would have had to retire with his feet mangled, with such wrath and zeal did the priest boil against him in defence of his shrine. And who had a manifestly greater share in bringing about his end, both in public, by the prayers and united supplications which he directed against the accursed one, without regard to the [dangers of] the time; and in private, arraying against him his nightly armoury, of sleeping on the ground, by which he wore away his aged and tender frame, and of tears, with whose fountains he watered the ground for almost a whole year, directing these practices to the Searcher of hearts alone, while he tried to escape our notice, in his retiring piety of which I have spoken. And he would have been utterly unobserved, had I not once suddenly rushed into his room, and noticing the tokens of his lying upon the ground, inquired of his attendants what they meant, and so learned the mystery of the night.

33. A further story of the same period and the same courage. The city of Cæsarea was in an uproar about the election of a bishop; for one[a] had just departed, and another must be found, amidst heated partisanship not easily to be soothed. For the city was naturally exposed to party spirit, owing to the fervour of its faith, and the rivalry was increased by the illustrious position of the see. Such was the state of affairs; several Bishops had arrived to consecrate the Bishop; the populace was divided into several parties, each with its own candidate, as is usual in such cases, owing to the influences of private friendship or devotion to God; but at last the whole people came to an agreement, and, with the aid of a band of soldiers at that time quartered there, seized one of[β] their leading citizens, a man of excellent life, but not yet sealed with the divine baptism, brought him against his will to the sanctuary, and setting him before the Bishops, begged, with entreaties mingled with violence, that he might be consecrated and proclaimed, not in the best of order, but with all sincerity and ardour. Nor is it possible to say whom time pointed out as more illustrious and religious than he was. What then took place, as the result of the uproar? Their[γ] resistance was overcome, they purified him, they proclaimed him, they enthroned him, by external action, rather than by spiritual judgment and disposition, as the sequel shows. They were glad to retire and regain freedom of judgment, and agreed upon a plan—I do not know that it was inspired by the Spirit—to hold nothing which had been done to be valid, and the institution to have been void, pleading violence on the part of him who had had no less violence done to himself, and laying hold of certain words which had been uttered on the occasion with greater vigour than wisdom. But the great high-priest and just examiner of actions was not carried away by this plan of theirs, and did not approve of their judgment, but remained as uninfluenced and unmoved as if no pressure at all had been put upon him. For he saw that, the violence having been common, if they brought any charge against him, they were themselves liable to a counter-charge, or, if they acquitted him, they themselves might be acquitted, or rather with still more justice, they were unable to secure their own acquittal, even by acquitting him: for if they were deserving of excuse, so assuredly was he, and if he was not, much less were they: for it would have been far better to have at the time run the risk

α *One*, i.e. Dianius. β *One of*, etc., Eusebius.
γ *Their*, i.e., of the Bishops.

of resistance to the last extremity, than afterwards to enter into designs against him, especially at such a juncture, when it was better to put an end to existing enmities than to devise new ones. For the state of affairs was as follows.

34. The Emperor [α] had come, raging against the Christians; he was angry at the election and threatened the elect, and the city stood in imminent peril [β] as to whether, after that day it should cease to exist, or escape and be treated with some degree of mercy. The innovation in regard to the election was a new ground of exasperation, in addition to the destruction of the temple of Fortune in a time of prosperity, and was looked upon as an invasion of his rights. The governor of the province also was eager to turn the opportunity to his own account, and was ill disposed to the new bishop, with whom he had never had friendly relations, in consequence of their different political views. Accordingly he sent letters to summon the consecrators to invalidate the election, and in no gentle terms, for they were threatened as if by command of the Emperor. Hereupon, when the letter reached him, without fear or delay, he replied—consider the courage and spirit of his answer—"Most excellent governor, we have one Censor of all our actions, and one Emperor, against whom his enemies are in arms. He will review the present consecration, which we have legitimately performed according to His will. In regard to any other matter, you may, if you will, use violence with the greatest ease against us. But no one can prevent us from vindicating the legitimacy and justice of our action in this case; unless you should make a law on this point, you, who have no right to interfere in our affairs." This letter excited the admiration of its recipient, although he was for a while annoyed at it, as we have been told by many who know the facts well. It also stayed the action of the Emperor, and delivered the city from peril, and ourselves, it is not amiss to add, from disgrace. This was the work of the occupant of an unimportant and suffragan see. Is not a presidency of this kind far preferable to a title derived from a superior see, and a power which is based upon action rather than upon a name.

35. Who is so distant from this world of ours, as to be ignorant of what is last in order, but the first and greatest proof of his power? The same city was again in an uproar for the same reason, in consequence of the sudden removal of the Bishop chosen with such honourable violence, who had now departed to God, on Whose behalf he had nobly and bravely contended in the persecutions. The heat of the disturbance was in proportion to its unreasonableness. The man of eminence was not unknown, but was more conspicuous than the sun amidst the stars, in the eyes not only of all others, but especially of that select and most pure portion of the people, whose business is in the sanctuary, and the Nazarites [α] amongst us, to whom such appointments should, if not entirely, as much as possible belong, and so the church would be free from harm, instead of to the most opulent and powerful, or the violent and unreasonable portion of the people, and especially the most corrupt of them. Indeed, I am almost inclined to believe that the civil government is more orderly than ours, to which divine grace is attributed, and that such matters are better regulated by fear than by reason. For what man in his senses could ever have approached another, to the neglect of your divine [β] and sacred person, who have been beautified by the hands of the Lord, the unwedded, the destitute of property and almost of flesh and blood, who in your words come next to the Word Himself, who are wise among philosophers, superior to the world among worldlings, my companion and workfellow, and to speak more daringly, the sharer with me of a common soul, the partaker of my life and education. Would that I could speak at liberty and describe you before others without being obliged by your presence, in dwelling upon such topics, to pass over the greater part of them, lest I should incur the suspicion of flattery. But, as I began by saying, the Spirit must needs have known him as His own; yet he was the mark of envy, at the hands of those whom I am ashamed to mention, and would that it were not possible to hear their names from others who studiously ridicule our affairs. Let us pass this by like a rock in the midstream of a river, and treat with respectful silence a subject which ought to be forgotten, as we pass on to the remainder of our subject.

36. The things of the Spirit were exactly known to the man of the Spirit, and he felt that he must take up no submissive position, nor side with factions and prejudices which depend upon favour rather than upon God, but must make the advantage of the Church and the common salvation his sole ob-

α *The Emperor*, Julian.
β *In imminent peril*, lit. "on a razor's edge." Homer Il. x. 173.

α *Nazarites*, i.e., "the monks."
β *Your divine*, etc., addressed to S. Basil.

ject. Accordingly he wrote, gave advice, strove to unite the people and the clergy, whether ministering in the sanctuary or not, gave his testimony, his decision and his vote, even in his absence, and assumed, in virtue of his gray hairs, the exercise of authority among strangers no less than among his own flock. At last, since it was necessary that the consecration should be canonical, and there was[a] lacking one of the proper number of Bishops for the proclamation, he tore himself from his couch, exhausted as he was by age and disease, and manfully went to the city, or rather was borne, with his body dead though just breathing, persuaded that, if anything were to happen to him, this devotion would be a noble winding-sheet. Hereupon once more there was a prodigy, not unworthy of credit. He received strength from his toil, new life from his zeal, presided at the function, took his place in the conflict, enthroned the Bishop, and was conducted home, no longer borne upon a bier, but in a divine ark. His long-suffering, over whose praises I have already lingered, was in this case further exhibited. For his colleagues were annoyed at the shame of being overcome, and at the public influence of the old man, and allowed their annoyance to show itself in abuse of him; but such was the strength of his endurance that he was superior even to this, finding in modesty a most powerful ally, and refusing to bandy abuse with them. For he felt that it would be a terrible thing, after really gaining the victory, to be vanquished by the tongue. In consequence, he so won upon them by his long-suffering, that, when time had lent its aid to his judgment, they exchanged their annoyance for admiration, and knelt before him to ask his pardon, in shame for their previous conduct, and flinging away their hatred, submitted to him as their patriarch, lawgiver, and judge.

37. From the same zeal proceeded his opposition to the heretics, when, with the aid of the Emperor's impiety, they made their expedition, in the hope of overpowering us also, and adding us to the number of the others whom they had, in almost all cases, succeeded in enslaving. For in this he afforded us no slight assistance, both in himself, and by hounding us on like well-bred dogs against these most savage beasts, through his training in piety. On one point I blame you both, and pray do not take amiss my plainspeaking, if I should annoy you by expressing the cause of my pain. When I was disgusted at the evils of life, and longing, if anyone of our day has longed, for solitude, and eager, as speedily as possible, to escape to some haven of safety, from the surge and dust of public life, it was you who, somehow or other seized and gave me up by the noble title of the priesthood to this base and treacherous mart of souls. In consequence, evils have already befallen me, and others are yet to be anticipated. For past experience renders a man somewhat distrustful of the future, in spite of the better suggestions of reason to the contrary.

38. Another of his excellences I must not leave unnoticed. In general, he was a man of great endurance, and superior to his robe of flesh: but during the pain of his last sickness, a serious addition to the risks and burdens of old age, his weakness was common to him and all other men; but this fitting sequel to the other marvels, so far from being common, was peculiarly his own. He was at no time free from the anguish of pain, but often in the day, sometimes in the hour, his only relief was the liturgy, to which the pain yielded, as if to an edict of banishment. At last, after a life of almost a hundred years, exceeding David's limit of our age,[a] forty-five of these, the average life of man, having been spent in the priesthood, he brought it to a close in a good old age. And in what manner? With the words and forms of prayer, leaving behind no trace of vice, and many recollections of virtue. The reverence felt for him was thus greater than falls to the lot of man, both on the lips and in the hearts of all. Nor is it easy to find anyone who recollects him, and does not, as the Scripture says, lay his hand upon his mouth[β] and salute his memory. Such was his life, and such its completion and perfection.

39. And since some living memorial of his munificence ought to be left behind, what other is required than this temple, which he reared for God and for us, with very little contribution from the people in addition to the expenditure of his private fortune? An exploit which should not be buried in silence, since in size it is superior to most others, in beauty absolutely to all. It surrounds itself with eight regular equilaterals, and is raised aloft by the beauty of two stories of pillars and porticos, while the statues placed upon them are true to the life; its vault flashes down upon us from above, and it dazzles our eyes with abundant sources of light on every side, being indeed the dwelling-place of light. It

a *There was lacking.* The Council of Nicæa ordered that a Bishop should be consecrated by at least three Bishops.

a Ps. xc. 10.

β Job xl. 4.

is surrounded by excrescent equiangular ambulatories of most splendid material, with a wide area in the midst, while its doors and vestibules shed around it the lustre of their gracefulness, and offer from a distance their welcome to those who are drawing nigh. I have not yet mentioned the external ornament, the beauty and size of the squared and dovetailed stonework, whether it be of marble in the bases and capitals, which divide the angles, or from our own quarries, which are in no wise inferior to those abroad; nor of the belts of many shapes and colours, projecting or inlaid from the foundation to the roof-tree, which robs the spectator by limiting his view. How could anyone with due brevity describe a work which cost so much time and toil and skill: or will it suffice to say that amid all the works, private and public, which adorn other cities, this has of itself been able to secure us celebrity among the majority of mankind? When for such a temple a priest was needed, he also at his own expense provided one, whether worthy of the temple or no, it is not for me to say. And when sacrifices were required, he supplied them also, in the misfortunes of his son, and his patience under trials, that God might receive at his hands a reasonable whole burnt offering and spiritual priesthood, to be honourably consumed, instead of the sacrifice of the Law.

40. What sayest thou, my father? Is this sufficient, and dost thou find an ample recompense for all thy toils, which thou didst undergo for my learning, in this eulogy of farewell or of entombment? And dost thou, as of old, impose silence on my tongue, and bid me stop in due time, and so avoid excess? Or dost thou require some addition? I know thou bidst me cease, for I have said enough. Yet suffer me to add this. Make known to us where thou art in glory, and the light which encircles thee, and receive into the same abode thy partner soon to follow thee, and the children whom thou hadst laid to rest before thee, and me also, after no further, or but a slight addition to the ills of this life: and before reaching that abode receive me in this sweet stone,[a] which thou didst erect for both of us, to the honour even here of thy consecrated namesake, and excuse me from the care both of the people which I have already resigned,[β] and of that which for thy sake I have since accepted: and mayest thou guide and free from peril, as I earnestly entreat, the whole flock and all the clergy, whose father thou art said to be, but especially him who was overpowered by thy paternal and spiritual coercion, so that he may not entirely consider that act of tyranny obnoxious to blame.

41. And what do you think of us, O judge of my words and motions? If we have spoken adequately, and to the satisfaction of your desire, confirm it by your decision, and we accept it: for your decision is entirely the decision of God. But if it falls far short of his glory and of your hope, my ally is not far to seek. Let fall thy voice, which is awaited by his merits like a seasonable shower. And indeed he has upon you the highest claims, those of a pastor upon a pastor and of a father upon his son in grace. What wonder if he, who has[a] through your voice thundered throughout the world, should himself have some enjoyment of it? What more is needed? Only to unite with our spiritual Sarah, the consort and fellow-traveller through life of our great father Abraham, in the last Christian offices.

42. The nature of God, my mother, is not the same as that of men; indeed, to speak generally, the nature of divine things is not the same as that of earthly things. They possess unchangeableness and immortality, and absolute being with its consequences, for sure are the properties of things sure. But how is it with what is ours? It is in a state of flux and corruption, constantly undergoing some fresh change. Life and death, as they are called, apparently so different, are in a sense resolved into, and successive to, each other. For the one takes its rise from the corruption which is our mother, runs its course through the corruption which is the displacement of all that is present, and comes to an end in the corruption which is the dissolution of this life; while the other, which is able to set us free from the ills of this life, and oftentimes translates us to the life above, is not in my opinion accurately called death, and is more dreadful in name than in reality; so that we are in danger of irrationally being afraid of what is not fearful, and courting as preferable what we really ought to fear. There is one life, to look to life. There is one death, sin, for it is the destruction of the soul. But all else, of which some are proud, is a dream-vision, making sport of realities, and a series of phantasms which lead the soul astray. If this be our condition, mother, we shall neither be proud of life, nor greatly hurt by death. What grievance can we find in being transferred hence to the true

a *Stone*, i.e., the tomb in which his father was buried.

β *Which I have resigned*, i.e., Sasima. *Accepted*, i.e., Nazianzus.

a *He who has.* S. Gregory the elder was the principal mover in S. Basil's election and consecration.

life? In being freed from the vicissitudes, the agitation, the disgust, and all the vile tribute we must pay to this life, to find ourselves, amid stable things, which know no flux, while as lesser lights, we circle round the great light?[a]

43. Does the sense of separation cause you pain? Let hope cheer you. Is widowhood grievous to you? Yet it is not so to him. And what is the good of love, if it gives itself easy things, and assigns the more difficult to its neighbour? And why should it be grievous at all, to one who is soon to pass away? The appointed day is at hand, the pain will not last long. Let us not, by ignoble reasonings, make a burden of things which are really light. We have endured a great loss—because the privilege we enjoyed was great. Loss is common to all, such a privilege to few. Let us rise superior to the one thought by the consolation of the other. For it is more reasonable, that that which is better should win the day. You have borne, in a most brave, Christian spirit, the loss of children, who were still in their prime and qualified for life; bear also the laying aside of his aged body by one who was weary of life, although his vigor of mind preserved for him his senses unimpaired. Do you want some one to care for you? Where is your Isaac, whom he left behind for you, to take his place in all respects? Ask of him small things, the support of his hand and service, and requite him with greater things, a mother's blessing and prayers, and the consequent freedom. Are you vexed at being admonished? I praise you for it. For you have admonished many whom your long life has brought under your notice. What I have said can have no application to you, who are so truly wise; but let it be a general medicine of consolation for mourners, so that they may know that they are mortals following mortals to the grave.

INTRODUCTION TO ORATION XXI.

On the Great Athanasius, Bishop of Alexandria.

The reference in § 22 to "the Council which sat first at Seleucia . . . and afterwards at this mighty city," leaves no room for doubting that the Oration was delivered at Constantinople. Further local colour is found in the allusions of § 5. We are assured by the panegyric on S. Cyprian (Orat. xxiv. 1) that it was already the custom of the Church of Constantinople to observe annual festivals in honour of the Saints: and at present two days are kept by the Eastern Church, viz., Jan. 18th, as the day of the actual death of S. Athanasius, and May 2d, in memory of the translation of his remains to the church of S. Sophia at Constantinople. Probably, therefore, this Oration was delivered on the former day, on which Assemani holds that S. Athanasius died. Papebroke and (with some hesitation) Dr. Bright pronounce in favour of May 2d. Tillemont supposes that A.D. 379 is the year of its delivery; in which case it must have been very shortly after S. Gregory's arrival in the city. Since, however, no allusion is made to this, it seems, on the whole, more likely that it should be assigned to A.D. 380. The sermon takes high rank, even among S. Gregory's discourses, as the model of an ecclesiastical panegyric. It lacks, however, the charm of personal affection and intimate acquaintance with the inner life, which is characteristic of the orations concerned with his own relatives and friends.

Oration.

1. In praising Athanasius, I shall be praising virtue. To speak of him and to praise virtue are identical, because he had, or, to speak more truly, has embraced virtue in its entirety. For all who have lived according to God still live unto God, though they have departed hence. For this reason, God is called the God of Abraham, Isaac and Jacob, since He is the God, not of the dead, but of the living.[a] Again, in praising virtue, I shall be praising God, who gives virtue to men and lifts them up, or lifts them up again, to Himself by the enlightenment which is akin to Himself.[β] For many and great as are our blessings—none can say how many and how great—which we have and shall have from God, this is the greatest and kindliest of all, our inclination and relationship to Him. For God is to intelligible things what the sun is to the things of sense. The one lightens the visible, the other the invisible, world. The one makes our bodily eyes to see the sun, the other makes our intellectual natures to see God. And, as that, which bestows on the things which see and are seen the power of seeing and being seen, is itself the most beautiful of visible things; so God, who creates, for those who think, and that which is thought of, the power of thinking and being thought of, is Himself the highest of the objects of thought, in Whom every desire finds its bourne, beyond

a Gen. i. 16.

a S. Matt. xxii. 32. β 1 John i. 5.

Whom it can no further go. For not even the most philosophic, the most piercing, the most curious intellect has, or can ever have, a more exalted object. For this is the utmost of things desirable, and they who arrive at it find an entire rest from speculation.

2. Whoever has been permitted to escape by reason and contemplation from matter and this fleshly cloud or veil (whichever it should be called) and to hold communion with God, and be associated, as far as man's nature can attain, with the purest Light, blessed is he, both from his ascent from hence, and for his deification there, which is conferred by true philosophy, and by rising superior to the dualism of matter, through the unity which is perceived in the Trinity. And whosoever has been depraved by being knit to the flesh, and so far oppressed by the clay that he cannot look at the rays of truth, nor rise above things below, though he is born from above, and called to things above, I hold him to be miserable in his blindness, even though he may abound in things of this world ; and all the more, because he is the sport of his abundance, and is persuaded by it that something else is beautiful instead of that which is really beautiful, reaping, as the poor fruit of his poor opinion, the sentence of darkness, or the seeing Him to be fire, Whom he did not recognize as light.

3. Such has been the philosophy of few, both nowadays and of old—for few are the men of God, though all are His handiwork,—among lawgivers, generals, priests, Prophets, Evangelists, Apostles, shepherds, teachers, and all the spiritual host and band—and, among them all, of him whom now we praise. And whom do I mean by these? Men like Enoch, Noah, Abraham, Isaac, Jacob, the twelve Patriarchs, Moses, Aaron, Joshua, the Judges, Samuel, David, to some extent Solomon, Elijah, Elisha, the Prophets before the captivity, those after the captivity, and, though last in order, first in truth, those who were concerned with Christ's Incarnation or taking of our nature, the lamp [a] before the Light, the voice before the Word, the mediator before the Mediator, the mediator between the old covenant and the new, the famous John, the disciples of Christ, those after Christ, who were set over the people, or illustrious in word, or conspicuous for miracles, or made perfect through their blood.

4. With some of these Athanasius vied, by some he was slightly excelled, and others, if it is not bold to say so, he surpassed : some he made his models in mental power, others in activity, others in meekness, others in zeal, others in dangers, others in most respects, others in all, gathering from one and another various forms of beauty (like men who paint figures of ideal excellence), and combining them in his single soul, he made one perfect form of virtue out of all, excelling in action men of intellectual capacity, in intellect men of action ; or, if you will, surpassing in intellect men renowned for intellect, in action those of the greatest active power ; outstripping those who had moderate reputation in both respects, by his eminence in either, and those who stood highest in one or other, by his powers in both ; and, if it is a great thing for those who have received an example, so to use it as to attach themselves to virtue, he has no inferior title to fame, who for our advantage has set an example to those who come after him.

a S. John i, 23 ; v. 35.

5. To speak of and admire him fully, would perhaps be too long a task for the present purpose of my discourse, and would take the form of a history rather than of a panegyric : a history which it has been the object of my desires to commit to writing for the pleasure and instruction of posterity, as he himself wrote the life of the divine Antony,[a] and set forth, in the form of a narrative, the laws of the monastic life. Accordingly, after entering into a few of the many details of his history, such as memory suggests at the moment as most noteworthy, in order both to satisfy my own longing and fulfil the duty which befits the festival, we will leave the many others to those who know them. For indeed, it is neither pious nor safe, while the lives of the ungodly are honoured by recollection, to pass by in silence those who have lived piously, especially in a city which could hardly be saved by many examples of virtue, making sport, as it does, of Divine things, no less than of the horse-race and the theatre.

6. He was brought up, from the first, in religious habits and practices, after a brief study of literature and philosophy, so that he might not be utterly unskilled in such subjects, or ignorant of matters which he had determined to despise. For his generous and eager soul could not brook being occupied in vanities, like unskilled athletes, who beat the air instead of their antagonists and lose the prize. From meditating on every book of the Old and New Testament, with a depth such as none else has applied even to one of them, he grew

a *Antony*, "the founder of asceticism," the most celebrated of the monks and hermits of the Thebaid desert. His life by S. Athanasius is certainly genuine, and even if, as some suspect, interpolations have been inserted, its substantial integrity is undoubted. (Newman, Ch. of the Fathers, p. 176.)

rich in contemplation, rich in splendour of life, combining them in wondrous sort by that golden bond which few can weave; using life as the guide of contemplation, contemplation as the seal of life. For the fear of the Lord is the beginning of wisdom, and, so to say, its first swathing band; but, when wisdom has burst the bonds of fear and risen up to love, it makes us friends of God, and sons instead of bondsmen.

7. Thus brought up and trained, as even now those should be who are to preside over the people, and take the direction of the mighty body of Christ,[α] according to the will and foreknowledge of God, which lays long before the foundations of great deeds, he was invested with this important ministry, and made one of those who draw near to the God Who draws near to us, and deemed worthy of the holy office and rank, and, after passing through the entire series of orders, he was (to make my story short) entrusted with the chief rule over the people, in other words, the charge of the whole world: nor can I say whether he received the priesthood as the reward of virtue, or to be the fountain and life of the Church. For she, like Ishmael,[β] fainting from her thirst for the truth, needed to be given to drink, or, like Elijah,[γ] to be refreshed from the brook, when the land was parched by drought; and, when but faintly breathing, to be restored to life and left as a seed to Israel,[δ] that we might not become like Sodom and Gomorrah,[ε] whose destruction by the rain of fire and brimstone is only more notorious than their wickedness. Therefore, when we were cast down, a horn of salvation was raised up for us,[ζ] and a chief corner stone,[η] knitting us to itself and to one another, was laid in due season, or a fire[θ] to purify our base and evil matter,[ι] or a farmer's fan[κ] to winnow the light from the weighty in doctrine, or a sword to cut out the roots of wickedness; and so the Word finds him as his own ally, and the Spirit takes possession of one who will breathe on His behalf.

8. Thus, and for these reasons, by the vote of the whole people, not in the evil fashion which has since prevailed, nor by means of bloodshed and oppression, but in an apostolic and spiritual manner, he is led up to the throne[λ] of Saint Mark, to succeed him in piety, no less than in office; in the latter indeed at a great distance from him, in the former, which is the genuine right of succession, following him closely. For unity in doctrine deserves unity in office; and a rival teacher sets up a rival throne; the one is a successor in reality, the other but in name. For it is not the intruder, but he whose rights are intruded upon, who is the successor, not the lawbreaker, but the lawfully appointed, not the man of contrary opinions, but the man of the same faith; if this is not what we mean by successor, he succeeds in the same sense as disease to health, darkness to light, storm to calm, and frenzy to sound sense.

9. The duties of his office he discharged in the same spirit as that in which he had been preferred to it. For he did not at once, after taking possession of his throne, like men who have unexpectedly seized upon some sovereignty or inheritance, grow insolent from intoxication. This is the conduct of illegitimate and intrusive priests, who are unworthy of their vocation; whose preparation for the priesthood has cost them nothing, who have endured no inconvenience for the sake of virtue, who only begin to study religion when appointed to teach it, and undertake the cleansing of others before being cleansed themselves; yesterday sacrilegious, to-day sacerdotal; yesterday excluded from the sanctuary,[α] to-day its officiants; proficient in vice, novices in piety; the product of the favour of man, not of the grace of the Spirit; who, having run through the whole gamut of violence, at last tyrannize over even piety; who, instead of gaining credit for their office by their character, need for their character the credit of their office, thus subverting the due relation between them; who ought to offer more sacrifices[β] for themselves than for the ignorances of the people;[γ] who inevitably fall into one of two errors, either, from their own need of indulgence, being excessively indulgent, and so even teaching, instead of checking, vice, or cloaking their own sins under the harshness of their rule. Both these extremes he avoided; he was sublime in action, lowly in mind; inaccessible in virtue, most accessible in intercourse; gentle, free from anger, sympathetic, sweet in words, sweeter in disposition; angelic in appearance, more angelic in mind; calm in rebuke, persuasive in praise, without spoiling the good effect of either by excess, but rebuking with the tenderness of a father, praising with the dignity of a

α *Body of Christ, i.e.*, the Church, His mystical body.
β Gen. xxi. 19. γ 1 Kings xvii. 4. δ Isai. i. 9.
ε Gen. xix. 24. ζ S. Luke i. 69. η Isai. xxviii. 16.
θ Mal. iii. 2, 3. ι 1 Cor. iii. 13, 15. κ S. Matt. iii. 12.
λ *The throne*, etc., as Patriarch of Alexandria. The date of his consecration is A.D. 326.

α *The Sanctuary*, or "the Sacraments." Exod. xxvi. 33.
β *To offer more sacrifices, i.e.*, These priests are not only "men which have infirmity," who need to offer for their own sins, as well as for those of the people; but because they are even more sinful than their flocks, they need a greater and more frequent atonement.
γ Heb. vii. 27; ix. 7.

ruler, his tenderness was not dissipated, nor his severity sour; for the one was reasonable, the other prudent, and both truly wise; his disposition sufficed for the training of his spiritual children, with very little need of words; his words with very little need of the rod,[α] and his moderate use of the rod with still less for the knife.

10. But why should I paint for you the portrait of the man? St. Paul[β] has sketched him by anticipation. This he does, when he sings the praises of the great High-priest, who hath passed through the heavens[γ] (for I will venture to say even this, since Scripture[δ] can call those who live according to Christ by the name of Christs):[ε] and again when by the rules in his letter to Timothy,[ζ] he gives a model for future Bishops: for if you will apply the law as a test to him who deserves these praises, you will clearly perceive his perfect exactness. Come then to aid me in my panegyric; for I am labouring heavily in my speech, and though I desire to pass by point after point, they seize upon me one after another, and I can find no surpassing excellence in a form which is in all respects well proportioned and beautiful; for each as it occurs to me seems fairer than the rest and so takes by storm my speech. Come then, I pray, you who have been his admirers and witnesses, divide among yourselves his excellences, contend bravely with one another, men and women alike, young men and maidens, old men and children, priests and people, solitaries and cenobites,[η] men of simple or of exact life, contemplatives or practically minded. Let one praise him in his fastings and prayers as if he had been disembodied and immaterial, another his unweariedness and zeal for vigils and psalmody, another his patronage of the needy, another his dauntlessness towards the powerful, or his condescension to the lowly. Let the virgins celebrate the friend of the Bridegroom;[θ] those under the yoke[ι] their restrainer, hermits him who lent wings to their course, cenobites their lawgiver, simple folk their guide, contemplatives the divine, the joyous their bridle, the unfortunate their consolation, the hoary-headed their staff, youths their instructor, the poor their resource, the wealthy their steward. Even the widows will, methinks, praise their protector, even the orphans their father, even the poor their benefactor, strangers their entertainer, brethren the man of brotherly love, the sick their physician, in whatever sickness or treatment you will, the healthy the guard of health, yea all men him who made himself all things to all men that he might gain almost, if not quite, all.

11. On these grounds, as I have said, I leave others, who have leisure to admire the minor details of his character, to admire and extol him. I call them minor details only in comparing him and his character with his own standard, for that which hath been made glorious hath not been made glorious, even though it be exceeding splendid by reason of the glory that surpasseth,[α] as we are told; for indeed the minor points of his excellence would suffice to win celebrity for others. But since it would be intolerable for me to leave the word and serve[β] less important details, I must turn to that which is his chief characteristic; and God alone, on Whose behalf I am speaking, can enable me to say anything worthy of a soul so noble and so mighty in the word.

12. In the palmy days of the Church, when all was well, the present elaborate, far-fetched and artificial treatment of Theology had not made its way into the schools of divinity, but playing with pebbles which deceive the eye by the quickness of their changes, or dancing before an audience with varied and effeminate contortions, were looked upon as all one with speaking or hearing of God in a way unusual or frivolous. But since the Sextuses[γ] and Pyrrhos, and the antithetic style, like a dire and malignant disease, have infected our churches, and babbling is reputed culture, and, as the book of the Acts[δ] says of the Athenians, we spend our time in nothing else but either to tell or to hear some new thing. O what Jeremiah[ε] will bewail our confusion and blind madness; he alone could utter lamentations befitting our misfortunes.

13. The beginning of this madness was Arius (whose name is derived from frenzy[ζ]), who paid the penalty of his unbridled tongue by his death in a profane spot,[η] brought about by prayer not by disease, when he like Judas[θ] burst asunder[ι] for his similar treachery

α 1 Cor. iv. 21.
β *St. Paul.* To whom here the Ep. to the Hebrews is assigned.
γ Heb. iv, 14.
δ Ps. cv. 15.
ε *Christs.* i.e., Ps. cv. 15. "Touch not Mine anointed." (LXX.) and Vulg. "my Christs."
ζ 1 Tim. iii. 2 et seq.
η Cenobites μιγάδες. Cf. Orat. ii. 29; xliii. 62.
θ S. John iii. 29.
ι *Under the yoke*, i.e. "Married." Cf. Orat. xlii. 11.

α 2 Cor. iii. 10.
β Acts vi. 2.
γ *Sextuses.* Sextus Empiricus (cent. 3 A.D.) a leader of the later Sceptic school. Pyrrho of Elis (cent. 4 B.C.) was the founder of the earlier.
δ Acts xvii. 21.
ε Lam. i. 1.
ζ *Frenzy.* Cf. Orat. ii. 37; xxxiv. 8.
η *A profane spot*, lit "profane places"—plural as contrasted with the ἐν τόπῳ ἁγίῳ, Lev. vi. 16. etc., etc.: in which the priests must eat of the sacrifices. The meaning of the phrase is "Arius died excommunicated"—indeed on the eve of the day on which the Emperor Constantine had ordered him to be restored to communion.
θ *Like Judas.* Cf. Epiph. Haer. 68.7; Socr. i. 38. Theodoret i. 4.
ι Acts i. 18.

to the Word. Then others, catching the infection, organized an art of impiety, and, confining Deity to the Unbegotten, expelled from Deity not only the Begotten, but also the Proceeding one, and honoured the Trinity with communion in name[α] alone, or even refused to retain this for it. Not so that blessed one, who was indeed a man of God and a mighty trumpet of truth: but being aware that to contract[β] the Three Persons to a numerical Unity is heretical, and the innovation of Sabellius, who first devised a contraction of Deity; and that to sever the Three Persons by a distinction of nature, is an unnatural mutilation of Deity; he both happily preserved the Unity, which belongs to the Godhead, and religiously taught the Trinity, which refers[γ] to Personality, neither confounding the Three Persons in the Unity, nor dividing the Substance among the Three Persons, but abiding within the bounds of piety, by avoiding excessive inclination or opposition to either side.

14. And therefore, first in the holy Synod of Nicæa,[δ] the gathering of the three hundred and eighteen chosen men, united by the Holy Ghost, as far as in him lay, he stayed the disease. Though not yet ranked among the Bishops, he held the first rank among the members of the Council, for preference was given to virtue just as much as to office. Afterwards, when the flame had been fanned by the blasts of the evil one, and had spread very widely (hence came the tragedies of which almost the whole earth and sea are full), the fight raged fiercely around him who was the noble champion of the Word. For the assault is hottest upon the point of resistance, while various dangers surround it on every side: for impiety is skilful in designing evils, and excessively daring in taking them in hand: and how would they spare men, who had not spared the Godhead? Yet one of the assaults was the most dangerous of all: and I myself contribute somewhat to this scene; yea, let me plead for the innocence of my dear fatherland, for the wickedness was not due to the land that bore them, but to the men who undertook it. For holy indeed is that land, and everywhere noted for its piety, but these men are unworthy of the Church which bore them, and ye have heard of a briar growing in a vine;[α] and the traitor[β] was Judas, one of the disciples.

15. There are some who do not excuse even my namesake[γ] from blame; who, living at Alexandria at the time for the sake of culture, although he had been most kindly treated by him, as if the dearest of his children, and received his special confidence, yet joined in the revolutionary plot against his father and patron: for, though others took the active part in it, the hand of Absalom[δ] was with them, as the saying goes. If any of you had heard of the hand which was produced by fraud against the Saint, and the corpse[ε] of the living man, and the unjust banishment, he knows what I mean. But this I will gladly forget. For on doubtful points, I am disposed to think we ought to incline to the charitable side, and acquit rather than condemn the accused. For a bad man would speedily condemn even a good man, while a good man would not be ready to condemn even a bad one. For one who is not ready to do ill, is not inclined even to suspect it. I come now to what is matter of fact, not of report, what is vouched for as truth instead of unverified suspicion.

16. There was a monster[ζ] from Cappadocia, born on our farthest confines, of low birth, and lower mind, whose blood was not perfectly free, but mongrel, as we know that of mules to be; at first, dependent on the table of others, whose price was a barley-cake, who had learnt to say and do everything with an eye to his stomach, and, at last, after sneaking into public life, and filling its lowest offices, such as that of contractor for swine's flesh, the soldiers' rations, and then having proved himself a scoundrel for the sake of greed in this public trust, and been stripped to the skin, contrived to escape, and after passing, as exiles do, from country to country and city to city, last of all, in an evil hour for the Christian community, like one of the plagues of Egypt, he reached Alexandria. There, his wanderings being stayed, he began his villany. Good for nothing in all other respects, without culture, without fluency in conversation, without even the form and pretence of reverence, his

α *In name*, etc., i.e., They used the name Trinity, although it was rendered meaningless by their false doctrine as to the inequality of the Three Blessed Persons.

β *To contract*, etc. On this whole passage cf. Orat. ii. 36, 37, notes.

γ *Which refers*, etc., or "which consists in personal relations." Cf. on ἰδιότης. Orat. xliii. 30. note.

δ *Nicæa*, A.D. 325. Athanasius was present as theological assistant to Alexander of Alexandria.

α Isai. v. 2 (LXX.); vii. 23, v. l. "in a vineyard."

β S. Luke vi. 16.

γ *Namesake*. Gregory, a Cappadocian, nominated to the see of Alexandria, by the Arian Bishops at Antioch, after the banishment of Athanasius, A.D. 340.

δ ἡ χὲιρ Ἀβεσσαλῶμ "The hand of Absalom," prob. a misquotation of 2 Sam. xiv. 19. "The hand of Joab." 2 Sam. xv. 5.

ε *Corpse*, etc. Athanasius was charged with having murdered Arsenius, and his enemies produced a hand which, they said, had belonged to the dead man.

ζ *Monster*. George of Cappadocia, Arian intruder into the see of Alexandria, A.D. 356–361.

skill in working villany and confusion was unequalled.

17. His acts of insolence towards the saint you all know in full detail. Often were the righteous given into the hands of the wicked,[α] not that the latter might be honoured, but that the former might be tested: and though the wicked come, as it is written, to an awful death,[β] nevertheless for the present the godly are a laughing stock, while the goodness of God and the great treasuries of what is in store for each of them hereafter are concealed. Then indeed word and deed and thought will be weighed in the just balances of God, as He arises to judge the earth,[γ] gathering together counsel and works, and revealing what He had kept sealed up.[δ] Of this let the words and sufferings of Job convince thee, who was a truthful, blameless, just, godfearing man, with all those other qualities which are testified of him, and yet was smitten with such a succession of remarkable visitations, at the hands of him who begged for power over him, that, although many have often suffered in the whole course of time, and some even have, as is probable, been grievously afflicted, yet none can be compared with him in misfortunes. For he not only suffered, without being allowed space to mourn for his losses in their rapid succession, the loss of his money, his possessions, his large and fair family, blessings for which all men care; but was at last smitten with an incurable disease horrible to look upon, and, to crown his misfortunes, had a wife whose only comfort was evil counsel. For his surpassing troubles were those of his soul added to those of the body.[ε] He had also among his friends truly miserable comforters,[ζ] as he calls them, who could not help him. For when they saw his suffering, in ignorance of its hidden meaning, they supposed his disaster to be the punishment of vice and not the touchstone of virtue. And they not only thought this, but were not even ashamed to reproach him with his lot,[η] at a time when, even if he had been suffering for vice, they ought to have treated his grief with words of consolation.

18. Such was the lot of Job: such at first sight his history. In reality it was a contest between virtue and envy:[θ] the one straining every nerve to overcome the good, the other enduring everything, that it might abide unsubdued; the one striving to smooth the way for vice, by means of the chastisement of the upright, the other to retain its hold upon the good, even if they do exceed others in misfortunes. What then of Him who answered Job out of the whirlwind and cloud,[α] Who is slow to chastise and swift to help, Who suffers not utterly the rod of the wicked to come into the lot of the righteous, lest the righteous should learn iniquity?[β] At the end of the contests He declares the victory of the athlete in a splendid proclamation and lays bare the secret of his calamities, saying: "Thinkest thou that I have dealt with thee for any other purpose than the manifestation of thy righteousness?"[γ] This is the balm for his wounds, this is the crown of the contest, this the reward for his patience. For perhaps his subsequent prosperity was small, great as it may seem to some, and ordained for the sake of small minds, even though he received again twice as much as he had lost.

19. In this case then it is not wonderful, if George had the advantage of Athanasius; nay it would be more wonderful, if the righteous were not tried in the fire of contumely; nor is this very wonderful, as it would have been had the flames availed for more than this. Then he was in retirement, and arranged his exile most excellently, for he betook himself to the holy and divine homes[δ] of contemplation in Egypt, where, secluding themselves from the world, and welcoming the desert, men live to God more than all who exist in the body. Some struggle on in an utterly monastic and solitary life, speaking to themselves alone and to God,[ε] and all the world they know is what meets their eyes in the desert. Others, cherishing the law of love in community, are at once Solitaries and Cœnobites, dead to all other men and to the eddies of public affairs which whirl us and are whirled about themselves and make sport of us in their sudden changes, being the world to one another and whetting the edge of their love in emulation. During his intercourse with them, the great Athanasius, who was always the mediator and reconciler of all other men, like Him Who made peace through His blood[ζ] between things which were at variance, reconciled the solitary with the community life: by showing that the Priesthood is capable of contemplation, and that contemplation is in need of a spiritual guide.

20. Thus he combined the two, and so

α Job. ix. 24. β Ib. ix. 23. γ Ps. lxxxii. 8.
δ Dan. xii. 9. ε Job ii. 7 et seq. ζ Ib. xvi. 2.
η *His lot*, lit. "the dreadful (thing)" i.e. "reproach him, as having brought his sufferings upon himself"—or 'reproach him with impiety'—the cause of his sufferings.
θ *Envy*, i.e., of the devil. Wisdom ii. 24. Cf. § 32 of this Oration.

α Job xxxviii. 1. β Ps. cxxv. 3. γ Job xl. 3 (LXX.).
δ *Homes*, etc. The monasteries of lower Egypt and the Thebaid. This was A.D. 356. ε 1 Cor. xiv. 28. ζ Col. 1. 20.

united the partisans of both calm action and of active calm, as to convince them that the monastic life is characterised by steadfastness of disposition rather than by bodily retirement. Accordingly the great David was a man of at once the most active and most solitary life, if any one thinks the verse, I am in solitude, till I pass away,[α] of value and authority in the exposition of this subject. Therefore, though they surpass all others in virtue, they fell further short of his mind than others fell short of their own, and while contributing little to the perfection of his priesthood, they gained in return greater assistance in contemplation. Whatever he thought, was a law for them, whatever on the contrary he disapproved, they abjured: his decisions were to them the tables of Moses,[β] and they paid him more reverence than is due from men to the Saints. Aye, and when men came to hunt the Saint like a wild beast, and, after searching for him everywhere, failed to find him, they vouchsafed these emissaries not a single word, and offered their necks to the sword, as risking their lives for Christ's sake, and considering the most cruel sufferings on behalf of Athanasius to be an important step to contemplation, and far more divine and sublime than the long fasts and hard lying and mortifications in which they constantly revel.

21. Such were his surroundings when he approved the wise counsel of Solomon that their is a time to every purpose:[γ] so he hid himself for a while, escaping during the time of war, to show himself when the time of peace came, as it did soon afterwards. Meanwhile George, there being absolutely no one to resist him, overran Egypt, and desolated Syria, in the might of ungodliness. He seized upon the East also as far as he could, ever attracting the weak, as torrents roll down objects in their course, and assailing the unstable or faint-hearted. He won over also the simplicity of the Emperor, for thus I must term his instability, though I respect his pious motives. For, to say the truth, he had zeal, but not according to knowledge.[δ] He purchased those in authority who were lovers of money rather than lovers of Christ—for he was well supplied with the funds for the poor, which he embezzled—especially the effeminate and unmanly men,[ε] of doubtful sex, but of manifest impiety; to whom, I know not how or why, Emperors of the Romans entrusted authority over men, though their proper function was the charge of women. In this lay the power of that servant[α] of the wicked one, that sower of tares, that forerunner of Antichrist; foremost in speech of the orators of his time among the Bishops; if any one likes to call him an orator who was not so much an impious, as he was a hostile and contentious reasoner,—his name I will gladly pass by: he was the hand of his party, perverting the truth by the gold subscribed for pious uses, which the wicked made an instrument of their impiety.

22. The crowning feat of this faction was the council which sat first at Seleucia, the city of the holy and illustrious virgin Thekla, and afterwards at this mighty city, thus connecting their names, no longer with noble associations, but with these of deepest disgrace; whether we must call that council, which subverted and disturbed everything, a tower of Chalane,[β] which deservedly confounded the tongues—would that theirs had been confounded for their harmony in evil!—or a Sanhedrim of Caiaphas[γ] where Christ was condemned, or some other like name. The ancient and pious doctrine which defended the Trinity was abolished, by setting up a[δ] palisade and battering down the Consubstantial: opening the door to impiety by means of what is written, using as their pretext, their reverence for Scripture and for the use of approved terms, but really introducing unscriptural Arianism. For the phrase "like, according to the Scriptures," was a bait to the simple, concealing the hook of impiety, a figure seeming to look in the direction of all who passed by, a boot fitting either foot, a winnowing with every wind,[ε] gaining authority from the newly written villany and device against the truth. For they were wise to do evil, but to do good they had no knowledge.[ς]

23. Hence came their pretended condemnation[η] of the heretics, whom they renounced in words, in order to gain plausibility for their efforts, but in reality furthered; charging them not with unbounded impiety, but with exaggerated language. Hence came the profane judges of the Saints, and the new combination, and public view and discussion of mysterious questions, and the illegal enquiry into the actions of life, and the hired informers, and the pur-

α Ps. cxli. 10 (LXX.). β Exod. xxxii. 15; xxxiv. 1. γ Eccles. iii. 1. δ Rom. x. 2.

ε *Unmanly men*, the Eunuchs, the chamberlains of Constantius.

α *Servant*, etc., probably, Acacius. β Gen. xi. 4.

γ S. John xi. 47 *et seq.*

δ χάρακα lit. "a pale"—one of the many which formed the palisade. Perhaps there is a play on the word χαρακτηρα "a letter" in reference to the insertion of the letter iota in the Nicene formula—which then became Homoiousion, i.e., "Like in substance." This action on the part of the Semi-Arians (who formed the majority of the Council of Seleucia A.D. 359), was the first step to the Homoion of the Acacian party, who prevailed at the council of Constantinople, A.D. 360, and professed great devotion to the use of Scriptural terms. ε Eccles. v. 9. ς Jer. iv. 22.

η *Condemnation*, i.e., of Aetius, who was banished by Constantius after the Council.

chased sentences. Some were unjustly deposed[a] from their sees, others intruded, and among other necessary qualifications, made to sign the bonds of iniquity: the ink was ready, the informer at hand. This the majority even of us, who were not overcome, had to endure, not falling in mind, though prevailed upon to sign,[β] and so uniting with men who were in both respects wicked, and involving ourselves in the smoke,[γ] if not in the flame. Over this I have often wept, when contemplating the confusion of impiety at that time, and the persecution of the orthodox teaching which now arose at the hands of the patrons of the Word.

24. For in reality, as the Scripture says, the shepherds became brutish,[δ] and many shepherds destroyed My vineyard, and defiled my pleasant portion,[ε] I mean the Church of God, which has been gathered together by the sweat and blood of many toilers and victims both before and after Christ, aye, even the great sufferings of God for us. For with very few exceptions, and these either men who from their insignificance were disregarded, or from their virtue manfully resisted, being left unto Israel,[ζ] as was ordained, for a seed and root,[η] to blossom and come to life again amid the streams of the Spirit, everyone[θ] yielded to the influences of the time, distinguished only by the fact that some did so earlier, some later, that some became the champions and leaders of impiety, while such others were assigned a lower rank, as had been shaken by fear, enslaved by need, fascinated by flattery, or beguiled in ignorance; the last being the least guilty, if indeed we can allow even this to be a valid excuse for men entrusted with the leadership of the people. For just as the force of lions and other animals, or of men and of women, or of old and of young men is not the same, but there is a considerable difference due to age or species—so it is also with rulers and their subjects. For while we might pardon laymen in such a case, and often they escape, because not put to the test, yet how can we excuse a teacher, whose duty it is, unless he is falsely so-called, to correct the ignorance of others. For is it not absurd, while no one, however great his boorishness and want of education, is allowed to be ignorant of the Roman law, and while there is no law in favour of sins of ignorance, that the teachers of the mysteries of salvation should be ignorant of the first principles of salvation, however simple and shallow their minds may be in regard to other subjects. But, even granting indulgence to them who erred in ignorance, what can be said for the rest, who lay claim to subtlety of intellect, and yet yielded to the court-party for the reasons I have mentioned, and after playing the part of piety for a long while, failed in the hour of trial.

25. "Yet once more,"[a] I hear the Scripture say that the heaven and the earth shall be shaken, inasmuch as this has befallen them before, signifying, as I suppose, a manifest renovation of all things. And we must believe S. Paul when he says[β] that this last shaking is none other than the second coming of Christ, and the transformation and changing of the universe to a condition of stability which cannot be shaken. And I imagine that this present shaking, in which[γ] the contemplatives and lovers of God, who before the time exercise their heavenly citizenship, are shaken from us, is of no less consequence than any of former days. For, however peaceful and moderate in other respects these men are, yet they cannot bear to carry their reasonableness so far as to be traitors to the cause of God for quietness' sake: nay on this point they are excessively warlike and sturdy in fight; such is the heat of their zeal, that they would sooner proceed to excess in disturbance, than fail to notice anything that is amiss. And no small portion of the people is breaking away with them, flying away, as a flock of birds does, with those who lead the flight, and even now does not cease to fly with them.

26. Such was Athanasius to us, when present, the pillar of the Church; and such, even when he retired before the insults of the wicked. For those who have plotted the capture of some strong fort, when they see no other easy means of approaching or taking it, betake themselves to arts, and then, after seducing the commander by money or guile, without any effort possess themselves of the stronghold, or, if you will, as those who plotted against Samson first cut off his hair,[δ] in which his strength lay, and then seized upon the judge, and made sport of him at will, to requite him for his former power: so did our foreign foes, after getting rid of our source of strength, and shearing off the glory of the Church, revel in like manner in utterances and deeds of impiety. Then the sup-

---

α *Deposed.* Cyril of Jerusalem, Eustathius of Sebaste, Basil of Ancyra and others.
β *To sign, etc.* Cf. Orat. xviii. 18.
γ *The smoke,* etc. Cf. Orat. xvi. 6; Ps. xviii. 9, cv. 32.
δ Jer. x. 21. ε Ib. ii. 10.
ζ Isai. i. 9. η Ib. xxxvii. 31 (LXX.).
θ *Everyone.* This was the time of which S. Jerome wrote "Ingemuit totus orbis, et miratus est se Arianum esse."

α Hagg. ii. 7; Heb. xii. 26. β Heb. xii. 27.
γ *In which,* etc. This sentence probably alludes to the excessive zeal of the monks of Nazianzus. δ Judges xvi. 19.

porter [α] and patron of the hostile shepherd [β] died, crowning [γ] his reign, which had not been evil, with an evil close, and unprofitably repenting, as they say, with his last breath, when each man, in view of the higher judgement seat, is a prudent judge of his own conduct. For of these three evils, which were unworthy of his reign, he said that he was conscious, the murder of his kinsmen, the proclamation of the Apostate, and the innovation upon the faith; and with these words he is said to have departed. Thus there was once more authority to teach the word of truth, and those who had suffered violence had now undisturbed freedom of speech, while jealousy was whetting the weapons of its wrath. Thus it was with the people of Alexandria, who, with their usual impatience of the insolent, could not brook the excesses of the man, and therefore marked his wickedness by an unusual death, and his death by an unusual ignominy. For you know that camel,[δ] and its strange burden, and the new form of elevation, and the first and, I think, the only procession, with which to this day the insolent are threatened.

27. But when from this hurricane of unrighteousness, this corrupter of godliness, this precursor of the wicked one, such satisfaction had been exacted, in a way I cannot praise, for we must consider not what he ought to have suffered, but what we ought [ε] to do: exacted however it was, as the result of the public anger and excitement: and thereupon, our champion was restored from his illustrious banishment, for so I term his exile on behalf of, and under the blessing of, the Trinity, amid such delight of the people of the city and of almost all Egypt, that they ran together from every side, from the furthest limits of the country, simply to hear the voice of Athanasius, or feast their eyes upon the sight of him, nay even, as we are told of the Apostles, that they might be hallowed by the shadow [ζ] and unsubstantial image of his body: so that, many as are the honours, and welcomes bestowed on frequent occasions in the course of time upon various individuals, not only upon public rulers and bishops, but also upon the most illustrious of private citizens, not one has been recorded more numerously attended or more brilliant than this. And only one honour can be compared with it by Athanasius himself, which had been conferred upon him on his former entrance into the city, when returning from the same exile for the same reasons.

28. With reference to this honour there was also current some such report as the following; for I will take leave to mention it, even though it be superfluous, as a kind of flavouring to my speech, or a flower scattered in honour of his entry. After that entry, a certain officer, who had been twice Consul, was riding into the city; he was one of us, among the most noted of Cappadocians. I am sure that you know that I mean Philagrius, who won upon our affections far beyond any one else, and was honoured as much as he was loved, if I may thus briefly set forth all his distinctions: who had been for a second time entrusted with the government of the city, at the request of the citizens, by the decision of the Emperor. Then one of the common people present, thinking the crowd enormous, like an ocean whose bound no eye can see, is reported to have said to one of his comrades and friends—as often happens in such a case—"Tell me, my good fellow, have you ever before seen the people pour out in such numbers and so enthusiastically to do honour to any one man?" "No!" said the young man, "and I fancy that not even Constantius himself would be so treated;" indicating, by the mention of the Emperor, the climax of possible honour. "Do you speak of that," said the other with a sweet and merry laugh, "as something wonderfully great? I can scarcely believe that even the great Athanasius would be welcomed like this," adding at the same time one of our native oaths in confirmation of his words. Now the point of what he said, as I suppose you also plainly see, is this, that he set the subject of our eulogy before the Emperor himself.

29. So great was the reverence of all for the man, and so amazing even now seems the reception which I have described. For if divided according to birth, age and profession, (and the city is most usually arranged in this way, when a public honour is bestowed on anyone) how can I set forth in words that mighty spectacle? They formed one river, and it were indeed a poet's task to describe that Nile, of really golden stream and rich in crops, flowing back again from the city to the Chaereum, a day's journey, I take it, and more. Permit me to revel a while longer in

α *The Supporter*, Constantius, who died A. D. 360.
β *The hostile shepherd*, George.
γ *Crowning*, Clémencet renders "Appointing an evil head over an empire which was not evil," sc. Julian the Apostate.
δ *Camel*. On the death of Constantius, the pagans of Alexandria murdered George, and carried his mangled body through the streets on the back of a camel.
ε *We ought*, etc. S. Gregory seems to imply that the deed had been done by Christians. Historical writers and Julian's letter to the people make it clear that this was not really the case.
ζ Acts v. 15.

my description: for I am going there, and it is not easy to bring back even my words from that ceremony. He rode upon a colt, almost, blame me not for folly, as my Jesus did upon that other colt,[α] whether it were the people of the Gentiles, whom He mounts in kindness, by setting it free from the bonds of ignorance, or something else, which the Scripture sets forth. He was welcomed with branches of trees, and garments with many flowers and of varied hue were torn off and strewn before him and under his feet: there alone was all that was glorious and costly and peerless treated with dishonour. Like, once more, to the entry of Christ were those that went before with shouts and followed with dances; only the crowd which sung his praises was not of children only, but every tongue was harmonious, as men contended only to outdo one another. I pass by the universal cheers, and the pouring forth of unguents, and the nightlong festivities, and the whole city gleaming with light, and the feasting in public and at home, and all the means of testifying to a city's joy, which were then in lavish and incredible profusion bestowed upon him. Thus did this marvellous man, with such a concourse, regain his own city.

30. He lived then as becomes the rulers of such a people, but did he fail to teach as he lived? Were his contests out of harmony with his teaching? Were his dangers less than those of men who have contended for any truth? Were his honours inferior to the objects for which he contended? Did he after his reception in any way disgrace that reception? By no means. Everything was harmonious, as an air upon a single lyre, and in the same key; his life, his teaching, his struggles, his dangers, his return, and his conduct after his return. For immediately on his restoration to his Church, he was not like those who are blinded by unrestrained passion, who, under the dominion of their anger, thrust away or strike at once whatever comes in their way, even though it might well be spared. But, thinking this to be a special time for him to consult his reputation, since one who is ill-treated is usually restrained, and one who has the power to requite a wrong is ungoverned, he treated so mildly and gently those who had injured him, that even they themselves, if I may say so, did not find his restoration distasteful.

31. He cleansed the temple of those who made merchandise of God, and trafficked in the things of Christ, imitating Christ[β] in this also; only it was with persuasive words, not with a twisted scourge that this was wrought. He reconciled also those who were at variance, both with one another and with him, without the aid of any coadjutor. Those who had been wronged he set free from oppression, making no distinction as to whether they were of his own or of the opposite party. He restored too the teaching which had been overthrown: the Trinity was once more boldly spoken of, and set upon the lampstand, flashing with the brilliant light of the One Godhead into the souls of all. He legislated again for the whole world, and brought all minds under his influence, by letters to some, by invitations to others, instructing some, who visited him uninvited, and proposing as the single law to all—*Good will.*[α] For this alone was able to conduct them to the true issue. In brief, he exemplified the virtues of two celebrated stones—for to those who assailed him he was adamant, and to those at variance a magnet, which by some secret natural power draws iron to itself, and influences the hardest of substances.

32. But yet it was not likely that envy could brook all this, or see the Church restored again to the same glory and health as in former days, by the speedy healing over, as in the body, of the wounds of separation. Therefore it was, that he raised up against Athanasius the Emperor, a rebel like himself,[β] and his peer in villany, inferior to him only from lack of time, the first of Christian Emperors to rage against Christ, bringing forth all at once the basilisk of impiety with which he had long been in labour, when he obtained an opportunity, and shewing himself, at the time when he was proclaimed Emperor, to be a traitor to the Emperor who had entrusted him with the empire, and a traitor double dyed to the God who had saved him. He devised the most inhuman of all the persecutions by blending speciousness with cruelty, in his envy of the honour won by the martyrs in their struggles; and so he called in question their repute for courage, by making verbal twists and quibbles a part of his character, or to speak the real truth, devoting himself to them with an eagerness born of his natural disposition, and imitating in varied craft the Evil one who dwelt within him. The subjugation of the whole race of Christians he thought a simple task; but found it a great one to overcome Atha-

α S. Luke xix. 35.

β S. John ii. 15.

α τὸ βούλεσθαι, lit. "to will"—i.e. be willing to listen to, and understand the interests for which others were contending, in a conciliatory spirit—for the sake of truth, not of victory.

β *He . . . a rebel like himself.* Envy, personifying the Evil one. Cf. supra §18.

nasius and the power of his teaching over us. For he saw that no success could be gained in the plot against us, because of this man's resistance and opposition; the places of the Christians cut down being at once filled up, surprising though it seems, by the accession of Gentiles and the prudence of Athanasius. In full view therefore of this, the crafty perverter and persecutor, clinging no longer to his cloak of illiberal sophistry, laid bare his wickedness and openly banished the Bishop from the city. For the illustrious warrior must needs conquer in three struggles[α] and thus make good his perfect title to fame.

33. Brief was the interval before Justice pronounced sentence, and handed over the offender[β] to the Persians: sending him forth an ambitious monarch—and bringing him back a corpse for which no one even felt pity; which, as I have heard, was not allowed to rest in the grave, but was shaken out and thrown up by the earth which he had shaken: a prelude—I take it—to his future chastisement. Then another king[γ] arose,[δ] not shameless in countenance like the former, nor an oppressor of Israel with cruel tasks and taskmasters, but most pious and gentle. In order to lay the best of foundations for his empire, and begin, as is right, by an act of justice, he recalled from exile all the Bishops, but in the first place him who stood first in virtue and had conspicuously championed the cause of piety. Further, he inquired into the truth of our faith which had been torn asunder, confused, and parcelled out into various opinions and portions by many; with the intention, if it were possible, of reducing the whole world to harmony and union by the co-operation of the Spirit: and, should he fail in this, of attaching himself to the best party, so as to aid and be aided by it, thus giving token of the exceeding loftiness and magnificence of his ideas on questions of the greatest moment. Here too was shown in a very high degree the simple-mindedness of Athanasius, and the steadfastness of his faith in Christ. For, when all the rest who sympathised with us were divided into three parties, and many were faltering in their conception of the Son, and still more in that of the Holy Ghost, (a point on which to be only slightly in error was to be orthodox) and few indeed were sound upon both points, he was the first and only one, or with the concurrence of but a few, to venture to confess in writing, with entire clearness and distinctness, the Unity of Godhead and Essence of the Three Persons, and thus to attain in later days, under the influence of inspiration, to the same faith in regard to the Holy Ghost, as had been bestowed at an earlier time on most of the Fathers in regard to the Son. This confession, a truly royal and magnificent gift, he presented to the Emperor, opposing to the unwritten innovation, a written account[ε] of the orthodox faith, so that an emperor might be overcome by an emperor, reason by reason, treatise by treatise.

34. This confession was, it seems, greeted with respect by all, both in West and East, who were capable of life; some cherishing piety within their own bosoms, if we may credit what they say, but advancing no further, like a still-born child which dies within its mother's womb; others kindling to some extent, as it were, sparks, so far as to escape the difficulties of the time, arising either from the more fervent of the orthodox, or the devotion of the people; while others spoke the truth with boldness, on whose side I would be, for I dare make no further boast; no longer consulting my own fearfulness—in other words, the views of men more unsound than myself (for this we have done enough and to spare, without either gaining anything from others, or guarding from injury that which was our own, just as bad stewards do) but bringing forth to light my offspring, nourishing it with eagerness, and exposing it, in its constant growth, to the eyes of all.

35. This, however, is less admirable than his conduct. What wonder that he, who had already made actual ventures on behalf of the truth, should confess it in writing? Yet this point I will add to what has been said, as it seems to me especially wonderful, and cannot with impunity be passed over in a time so fertile in disagreements as this. For his action, if we take note of him, will afford instruction even to the men of this day. For as, in the case of one and the same quantity of water, there is separated from it, not only the residue which is left behind by the hand when drawing it, but also those drops, once contained in the hand, which trickle out through the fingers; so also there is a separation between us and, not only those who hold aloof in their impiety, but also those who are most pious, and that both in regard to such doctrines as are of small consequence (a matter of less moment) and also in regard to expressions intended to bear the same meaning. We use in an orthodox sense the terms one Essence and three Hypostases, the one to denote the nature of the Godhead, the other the properties[α] of the Three; the Italians[β] mean the same, but, owing to the scantiness of their vocabulary, and its poverty of terms, they are unable to distinguish between Essence and Hypostases, and therefore introduce the term Persons, to avoid being understood to assert three Essences. The result, were it not piteous, would be laughable. This slight difference of sound was taken to indicate a difference of faith. Then, Sabellianism was suspected in the doctrine of Three Persons, Arianism in that of Three Hypostases, both being the offspring of a contentious spirit. And then, from the gradual but constant growth of irritation (the unfailing result of contentiousness) there was a danger of the whole world being torn asunder in the strife about syllables. Seeing and hearing this, our blessed one, true man of God and great steward of souls as he was, felt it inconsistent with his duty to overlook so absurd and unreasonable a rending of the word, and applied his medicine to the disease. In what manner? He conferred in his gentle and sympathetic way with both parties, and after he had carefully weighed the meaning of their expressions, and found that they had the same sense, and were in nowise different in doctrine, by permitting each party to use its own terms, he bound them[γ] together in unity of action.

36. This in itself was more profitable than the long course of labours and teaching on which all writers enlarge, for in it somewhat of ambition mingled, and consequently, perhaps, somewhat of novelty in expressions. This again was of more value than his many vigils and acts of discipline,[δ] the advantage of which is limited to those who perform them. This was worthy of our hero's famous banishments and flights; for the object, in view of which he chose to endure such sufferings, he still pursued when the sufferings

α *In three struggles.* He was thrice banished. A.D. 336 by Constantine, A.D. 356 under Constantius, and A.D. 362 by Julian.

β *The offender.* Julian.

γ *Another king*—the Emperor Jovian.

δ Exod. i. 8.

ε *A written account.* A synodal letter drawn up in council, probably at Alexandria, and conveyed and presented to Jovian at Antioch by S. Athanasius.

α *Properties.* Cf. Orat. xliii. 30. note.

β *The Italians,* etc. Cf. Newman's Arians, pp. 376–384. S. Athanasius' Orations against the Arians, Ed. Bright, p. lxxxi. Pelav. de Trin. IV. ii. 5–10 and iv.

γ *Bound them,* etc. At the Council of Alexandria, A.D. 362. Newman's Arians, pp. 364, sqq.

δ *Acts of discipline.* χαμευνιῶν, "lying on the ground."

were past. Nor did he cease to cherish the same ardour in others, praising some, gently rebuking others; rousing the sluggishness of these, restraining the passion of those; in some cases eager to prevent a fall, in others devising means of recovery after a fall; simple in disposition, manifold in the arts of government; clever in argument, more clever still in mind; condescending to the more lowly, outsoaring the more lofty; hospitable,[α] protector of suppliants, averter of evils, really combining in himself alone the whole of the attributes parcelled out by the sons of Greece among their deities. Further he was the patron of the wedded and virgin state alike, both peaceable and a peacemaker, and attendant upon those who are passing from hence. Oh, how many a title dces his virtue afford me, if I would detail its many-sided excellence.

37. After such a course, as taught and teacher, that his life and habits form the ideal of an Episcopate, and his teaching the law of orthodoxy, what reward does he win for his piety? It is not indeed right to pass this by. In a good old age he closed his life,[β] and was gathered to his fathers, the Patriarchs, and Prophets, and Apostles, and Martyrs, who contended for the truth. To be brief in my epitaph, the honours at his departure surpassed even those of his return from exile; the object of many tears, his glory, stored up in the minds of all, outshines all its visible tokens. Yet, O thou dear and holy one, who didst thyself, with all thy fair renown, so especially illustrate the due proportions of speech and of silence, do thou stay here my words, falling short as they do of thy true meed of praise, though they have claimed the full exercise of all my powers. And mayest thou cast upon us from above a propitious glance, and conduct this people in its perfect worship of the perfect Trinity, which, as Father, Son, Holy Ghost, we contemplate and adore. And mayest thou, if my lot be peaceful, possess and aid me in my pastoral charge, or if it pass through struggles, uphold me, or take me to thee, and set me with thyself and those like thee (though I have asked a great thing) in Christ Himself, our Lord, to whom be all glory, honour, and power for evermore. Amen.

Introduction to the "Theological" Orations.

"It has been said with truth," says the writer of the Article on Gregory of Nazianzus in the Dictionary of Christian Biography, "that these discourses would lose their chief charm in a translation. . . . Critics have rivalled each other in the praises they have heaped upon them, but no praise is so high as that of the many Theologians who have found in them their own best thoughts. A Critic who cannot be accused of partiality towards Gregory has given in a few words perhaps the truest estimate of them: 'A solidity of thought, the concentration of all that is spread through the writings of Hilary, Basil, and Athanasius, a flow of softened eloquence which does not halt or lose itself for a moment, an argument nervous without dryness on the one hand, and

α *Hospitable*, etc., titles given to Zeus, and other Greek gods.
β *Closed his life* A.D. 373.

without useless ornament on the other, give these five Discourses a place to themselves among the monuments of this fine Genius, who was not always in the same degree free from grandiloquence and affectation. In a few pages, and in a few hours, Gregory has summed up and closed the controversy of a whole Century.'"[α] They were preached in the Church called Anastasia,[β] at Constantinople, between 379 and 381, and have gained for their author the title of The Theologian, which he shares with S. John the Evangelist alone. It should perhaps, however, be noted that the word is not here used in the wide and general sense in which we employ it, but in a narrower and more specific way, denoting emphatically the Defender of the Deity of the Logos. His principal opponents were the followers of Eunomius and Macedonius, and it is almost entirely against them that these Orations on Theology, or the Godhead of the Word and the Holy Ghost, are directed. The chief object of the Preacher in these and most other of his public utterances, is to maintain the Nicene Faith of the Trinity or Tri-unity of God; that is, the Doctrine that while there is but One Substance or Essence[γ] in the Godhead, and by consequence God is in the most

α De Broglie, "L'Eglise et l'Empire," v. 385.—"Ce sont autant de modèles dans l'art délicat d'imprimer la forme oratoire aux développements philosophiques. Une pensée substantielle, formée de tous les sucs répandus dans les écrits d'Hilaire, de Basile et d'Athanase; un courant d'éloquence tempérée qui ne se ralentit, ni ne s'égare en aucun moment; une argumentation nerveuse sans sécheresse, mais sans vaine parure d'ornements, font à ces cinq discours une place à part parmi les monuments de ce beau génie, auquel l'emphase et l'affectation ne furent pas toujours aussi étrangers. En quelques pages, et en quelques heures, Grégoire avait résumé et clos la controverse de tout un siècle."

β See Prolegomena p. 171.

γ "There is but one divine Essence or Substance; Father, Son, and Spirit, are one in essence, or consubstantial. They are in one another, inseparable, and cannot be conceived without each other. In this point the Nicene doctrine is thoroughly monotheistic, or monarchian, in distinction from tritheism, which is but a new form of the polytheism of the pagans.

"The terms Essence (οὐσία) and Nature (φύσις), in the philosophical sense, denote not an individual, a personality, but the Genus or Species; not Unum in Numero, but Ens Unum in Multis. All men are of the same substance, partake of the same human nature; though as persons and individuals they are very different. The term Homo-ousion, in its strict grammatical sense, differs from Mono-ousion or Touto-ousion, as well as from Hetero-ousion, and signifies not numerical identity, but equality of essence or community of nature among several beings. It is clearly thus used in the Chalcedonian Symbol, where it is said that Christ is 'consubstantial (Homo-ousios) with the Father as touching the Godhead, and consubstantial with us (and yet individually distinct from us) as touching the Manhood.' But in the Divine Trinity consubstantiality denotes not only sameness of kind, but at the same time Numerical unity; not merely the Unum in Specie, but also the Unum in Numero. The three Persons are related to the Divine Substance not as three individuals to their species, as Abraham, Isaac, and Jacob, or Peter, John, and Paul, to human nature; they are only one God. The divine Substance is absolutely indivisible by reason of its simplicity, and absolutely inextensible and untransferable by reason of its infinity; whereas a corporeal substance can be divided, and the human nature can be multiplied by generation. Three Divine substances would limit and exclude each other, and therefore could not be infinite or absolute. The whole fulness of the one undivided Essence of God, with all its attributes, is in all the Persons of the Trinity, though in each in His own way; in the Father as Original Principle, in the Son by eternal Generation, in the Spirit by eternal Procession. The Church teaches not One Divine Essence *and* Three Persons, but One Essence *In* Three Persons. Father, Son, and Spirit cannot be conceived as absolute sense One, yet God is not Unipersonal, but within this Undivided Unity there are three Self-determining Subjects or Persons, distinguished from one another by special characteristics (ἰδιότητες) or personal properties—Father, Son, and Holy Ghost. With this object he entered into conflict with the heretics named above, who denied either the Consubstantiality of the Son with the Father, or the perfect Godhead and Personality of the Holy Ghost.

Eunomius, whom Ullmann calls one of the most interesting heretics of the Fourth Century, was by birth a Cappadocian, and slightly older than Gregory. As a young man he was a pupil and amanuensis of Aëtius, by whom the Arian heresy was developed to its extreme results. The disciple never shrank from drawing the furthest logical conclusions from his master's premises, or from stating them with a frankness, which to those who regarded the premises themselves from which he reasoned as horrible blasphemies, seemed nothing less than diabolical in its impiety. So precisely did he complete and formulate his teacher's heretical tenets, that the Anomœan Arians were ever afterwards called Eunomians, rather than Aëtians. They asserted the absolute *Unlikeness* of the Being of the Father and of the Son. Starting with the conception of God as Absolute Being, of Whom no Generation can be predicated, Unbegotten and incapable of Begetting, they went on to say that an Eternal Generation is inconceivable, and that the Generation of the Son of God must have had a beginning. Of course, therefore, the Arian conclusion followed, namely, that there was a time when the Son did not exist (ἦν ποτὲ ὅτε οὐκ ἦν), and His Essence is altogether unlike that of the Unbegotten Father. Equality of essence and Similarity of essence, are alike untenable, from the mere fact that the one Essence is Unbegotten, and the other is Begotten. The Son, they said, is the First Creation of the Divine Energy, and is the Instrument by whom God created the world, and in this sense, as the Organ of creative power, may be said to be the Express Image and Likeness of the Energy of the Father.[a]

As they viewed the Holy Ghost as sharing the Divine Nature in an even remoter degree, as being only the noblest production of the Only-begotten Son, Eunomius was the first person heretically to discontinue the practice of threefold immersion in Holy Baptism. He also corrupted the Form of that Sacrament, by setting aside the use of the Name of the Father, Son, and Holy Ghost, and baptizing people "in the name of the Creator, and into the death of Christ." Therefore the Council of Constantinople ordered that converts from Eunomianism should be *baptized*, although those from other forms of Arianism were admitted into the Catholic Church by simple imposition of hands. Through the influence of the followers of Aëtius, Eunomius became, in 360, Bishop of Cyzicus in Mysia, but he does not appear to have occupied the See very long. At any rate when Gregory came, in 379, to Constantinople, he was living in retirement near Chalcedon. All parties concur in representing him as a consummate Dialectician, but the Orthodox declared that he had turned Theology into a mere Technology. Readiness of Dialectic was the great characteristic of his Sect, and it was they who introduced into the Capital that bad spirit of theological disputatiousness which Gregory deplores in the first of these famous Orations. He also differed entirely from Gregory, not merely in the conclusions at which he arrived, but in the method by which he reached them; following the system of Aristotle, rather than of Plato, and using an exclusively intellectual method, while Gregory treated Religion as belonging to the entire man. The point at issue between them, besides this of the Interior relations of the Three Blessed Persons within the Godhead, was mainly the question as to the complete comprehensibility of the Divine Nature, which the Eunomians maintained, and Gregory denied. The latter argued that, while we have a sure conviction that God is, we have not a full understanding of What He is. He would not, however, exclude us from *all* knowledge of God's Nature, only he limits our capacity to so much as God has been pleased to reveal to us of Himself. "In my opinion," he says (Or. xxiv. 4), "it is impossible to express God, and yet more impossible to conceive Him—seeing that the thick covering of the flesh is an obstacle to the full understanding of the truth." Similarly in the Fourth of these Orations (Or. xxx. 17) he says, "The Deity cannot be expressed in words. And this is proved to us, not only by arguments, but by the wisest and most ancient of the Hebrews, so far as they have given us reason for conjecture. For they appropriated certain characters to the honour of the Deity,

Three separate individuals, but are in one another, and form a solidaric Unity." (Schaff, History of the Church, Nic. & Post-Nic. Period, Div. ii. p. 672.)

a Two terms borrowed from Holy Scripture (Heb. i. 3). But observe, borrowed with a difference—not "the Image of His Substance," which they would not admit, but of His "Energy," which is a very different conception.

and would not even allow the name of anything inferior to God to be written with the same letters as that of God, because to their mind it was improper that the Deity should even to that extent admit any of His creatures to a share with Himself. How then could they have admitted that the indivisible and separate Nature can be explained by divisible words?"

In the mind of Gregory, the Orthodox doctrine of the Blessed Trinity is the fundamental dogma of Christianity, in contrast with all other religions, and with all heretical systems. "Remember your confession," he says to his hearers in an Oration against the Arians; "Into what were you baptized? The Father? Good, but still Jewish. The Son? Good; no longer Jewish, but not yet perfect. The Holy Ghost? Very good; this is perfect. Was it then simply into these, or was there some one common Name of these? Yes, there was, and it is God." And in the same oration he calls Arianism a new Judaism, because it ascribes full Deity only to the Father; and he speaks of One Nature in Three Individualities, intelligent, perfect, self-existent, distinct numerically, but one in Godhead. "In created things," says Ullmann, "the several individuals are embraced in a common conception, though in themselves only connected together in thought, while in fact they are not one. Manhood is only an intellectual conception; in fact there exist only Men. But in the Godhead the Three Persons are not only in conception, but in fact, One; and this Unity is not only a relative but an absolute Unity, because the Divine Being is perfect in all Three Persons, and in all in a perfect equality. In this sense therefore Gregory and all orthodox Trinitarians maintain the Unity of God. But within this Unity there is a true Trinity, Father, Son, and Holy Ghost, a Trinity of Persons in a Unity of Nature." We worship, he says (Or. xxxiii. 16), the Father, Son, and Holy Ghost, One Nature in Three Individualities. So that, as he says elsewhere (Or. in laud. Athanasii, xxi. 10), the Trinity is a true Trinity; not a numbering of unlike things, but a binding together of equals. Each of the Persons is God in the fullest sense. The Son and the Holy Ghost have their Source of Being in the Father, but in such sense that They are fully consubstantial with Him, and that neither of Them differs from Him in any particular of Essence. The points of difference lie in the Personal Attributes; the Father Unoriginate, and Source of Deity; the Son deriving His Being eternally from the Father, and Himself the Source of all created existence; the Holy Ghost proceeding eternally from God, and sent into the world.

In the first of these five discourses the Preacher sets himself to clear the ground for the fitting presentation of his great theme. He endeavours to lay down the principles on which Theologians should proceed in such discussions, and very earnestly deprecates the habit of promiscuous argument in all sorts of places, upon all sorts of occasions, and before all sorts of hearers, of the deepest and most sacred truths and mysteries of the Faith. They only should be allowed to engage in such conversation who are fitted for it by the practice of Christian virtue. For others there are many other subjects upon which they can exercise their dialectical attainments, without doing or incurring any injury.

In the second oration Gregory lays down the position referred to above, that it is impossible for even the most exalted human reason fully to grasp the Nature of God, though His Existence is patent to all. We can only, he says, predicate negatives concerning Him. He gives three reasons for this incapacity. First to enhance our estimation of this knowledge, when attained hereafter; secondly to save us from the danger of falling through pride, like Lucifer, if we attained it prematurely; and thirdly, to support and sustain us in the trials and conflicts of this life, by the certainty that its attainment hereafter will be the reward of faithful service in them. The cause of our present inability is the body with which our soul is united, the grossness of whose present condition hinders us from rising to the complete apprehension of the invisible and immaterial. God, out of compassion for our weakness, has been pleased to designate Himself in Holy Scripture by various names taken from material objects, or from moral virtues; but these are only stepping-stones to the truth, and have indeed been sometimes perverted, and made a basis for polytheism. It is, however, only natural that the Divine Essence should be shrouded in Mystery, for the same is the case with the created essences also.

In the Third and Fourth he deals with the question of the Son. His position may be summed up as follows: The Son is absolutely of One Substance with the Father, and shares with Him all the Attributes of Godhead. Yet He is a distinct Person, marked off by the fact that He is begotten of the Father. But we must be careful not to allow this term "Begotten" to suggest to us any analogy with created things. It is wholly independent of time and space and sense.

This position he had to defend against many assailants, and especially against the Eunomians. These heretics maintained that the use of this term necessarily implied a beginning of the Essence of the Son, and they asked the orthodox to tell them when that beginning took place. Gregory replies that the Generation of God the Son is beyond all time; pointing out that Paternity is an Essential attribute of God the Father, and therefore is as eternal as His Essence, so that there never was a time when He was not the Father, and consequently never a time when the Generation of the Son began. He admits that there is a sense in which it is possible to say that the Son and the Spirit are not unoriginate, but then you must be careful not to use the word Origin in the sense of Beginning, but in that of Cause. They derive Their Being eternally from the Father, and all Three Persons are coeternal together. In respect of Cause They are not unoriginate, but the cause is not necessarily prior in time to its effect, just as the Sun is not prior to its own light. In respect of *time*, then, They may be said to be unoriginate, for the Sources of time cannot be subject to time. "If the Father has not ceased to beget, His Generation is an imperfect one; and if He has ceased, He must have begun, for an end implies a beginning." "Not so," says Gregory, "unless you are prepared to admit that what has no end has necessarily no beginning; and in that case what will you say about the Angels, or the human soul? These will have no end; had either of them therefore no beginning?" By a similar process of *Reductio ad absurdum* he dissipates all the quibbles of Eunomian sophistry, and lays down the orthodox Faith of the Church. Then in the remainder of the Third and Fourth Orations he goes on to examine the Scriptural testimony adduced by his opponents, and to shew by a similar catena on the other side that the overwhelming preponderance of the authority of the Bible is clearly against them. In connection with this point he lays down the canon that in the interpretation of Scripture in regard to our Lord, all expressions savouring of humility or weakness are to be referred to that pure Humanity which He assumed for our sake; while all that speaks of Majesty and Power belongs to His Godhead.

In the Fifth he deals with the doctrine of the Holy Ghost. The heresy of Arius was at first directly concerned only with the Person of our Lord, though not without a side-glance at that also of the Holy Ghost. The Council of Nicæa had confined itself to the first question, and its Creed ended with, "We believe in the Holy Ghost." This, it was afterwards argued, was enough to proclaim His Divinity, and so Gregory argues in this Oration, "If He be only a creature, how do we believe on Him, how are we made perfect in Him, for the first of these belongs to Deity, the second may be said of anything" (c. vi.). The reason, however, that the Great Synod made no express definition on the point seems to have been that the controversy had not yet been carried so far in direct terms (cf. S. Basil, Epp. lxxviii. ccclxxxvii.). But fifty years later the growth of the heresy rendered a definition of the Church's faith on this point needful; and in 363, on his return from his fourth period of exile, S. Athanasius held a provincial Synod at Alexandria, in whose Synodical Letter to the Emperor Jovian the Godhead of the Holy Ghost is maintained in terms which, as Canon Bright says, partly anticipate the language of the Creed of Constantinople (Dict. Biog. Art. ATHANASIUS). The new development of the heresy had begun to appear at Constantinople as well as in Thrace and Asia Minor. Macedonius, a Semi-Arian, had been elected Bishop of Constantinople in 341, and in spite of violent opposition, which he met by still more violent measures, had maintained his position till 360, when he was deposed and driven out by the Anomœan Arians. He then in his retirement became the leader of the Semi-Arian party. Accepting the statement that the Son was Like in Essence to the Father, he would not concede even this to the Holy Ghost, but declared Him to be a mere creature (Thdt. Hist. Eccl. ii. 6), and the servant or minister of the Son; applying to Him terms which without error could only be used of the Angels (Sozomen. H. E. iv. 27). His followers were known as Macedonians, or sometimes Marathonians, from a certain Marathonius, formerly a Paymaster of the Prætorian Guards, who had become a Deacon of Constantinople, and, having done much in the way of founding and maintaining Monastic Houses and Houses of Charity in the City, was consecrated by Macedonius as Bishop of Nicomedia. They were also known as Pneumatomachi, from the nature of their Heresy. A controversy had now begun to arise as to the precise position which the true faith was to assign to the Holy Spirit. There were those who left it doubtful whether He had indeed a separate Personality, or whether He were not rather a mere Influence or Activity of the Father and the Son. Gregory tells us how, when he came to the Metropolis, he found the wildest confusion prevalent. Some, he says, conceived of the Holy Ghost as a mere Energy of God, others thought Him a Creature, others believed Him to be God; while many out of an alleged reverence for Holy Scripture, hesitated to give Him the Name of God. To this last class belonged, according to Socrates (H. E. ii. 45), Eustathius, who had been ejected from the Bishopric of Sebasteia in Pontus. He refused to admit that the Holy Spirit is God, while yet He did not dare to affirm that He is a mere creature. When Gregory proceeded to preach the Deity of the Spirit, he was accused of introducing a strange and unscriptural god, because, as he acknowledges, the letter of the Bible is not so clear on the doctrine of the Spirit as it is on that of the Son. But he points out that it is possible to be superstitious in one's reverence for the letter of the Bible, and that such superstition leads directly to heresy. He explains the reticence of the New Testament on this point by shewing (in this Oration, cc. 26, 27) how God's Self-Revelation to man has always been a gradual one; how the Old Testament revealed the Father clearly, with obscure hints about the Son; and the New Testament manifested the Son, but only hinted at the Godhead of the Spirit; but now, he says, the Spirit dwells among us, and allows us to recognize Him more clearly. For it would not have been advisable, as long as the Godhead of the Father was not acknowledged, to proclaim that of the Son; and while the Deity of the Son was not yet accepted, to add another burden in that of the Holy Spirit. Recognizing thus a Divine economy in the Self-Revelations of God, he was not averse to using a similar caution in his own dealings with weak or ill-instructed minds.[a] But yet when real necessity arose, he could speak out with perfect plainness on this subject; and he even incurred danger to life and limb from the violence of the opposing party. He met their opposition by the clearest statements of the Catholic Dogma. "Is the Spirit God?" he asks. "Yes." "But is He consubstantial?" "Yes, if He is God." (Orat. xxxi. 10.) He appeals both to the Bible, and to the experience of the Christian life. If the Spirit is not to be adored, how can He deify me in Baptism? From the Spirit comes our new Birth; from the new Birth our new Life; and from the new Life our knowledge of the Dignity of Him from Whom it is derived (Ibid. c. 29). He is, however, milder in his treatment of these heretics than of the strict Arians, both, as he says, because they approached more nearly to the Orthodox belief on the subject of the Son, and because their conspicuous piety of life shewed that their error was not altogether wilful. In this Oration he shews that though the Name of God may not actually be given in the New Testament to the Holy Ghost, yet all the attributes of God are ascribed to Him, and that therefore the use of the Name is a matter of legitimate inference. He carries on the argument in the Oration on Pentecost (No. XLI. See the Introduction to that Oration in the present Volume).

With regard to the doctrine of the Procession, Gregory gives us no clear information. He is silent as to the Procession from the Son. It is enough for him that the Spirit is not Begotten but Proceeding (in SS. Lumina, c. 12), and that Procession is His distinctive Property, which involves at once His Personality and His Essential Deity.

At length in 381 the work of local Synods and episcopal conferences was completed and clinched by the Ruling of a Second Ecumenical Council. It is true that the Council which Theodosius summoned to meet at Constantinople could scarcely have regarded itself as possessing Ecumenical authority; whilst in the West it certainly was not regarded in this light before the Sixth Century. Nevertheless the honours of Ecumenicity were ultimately awarded to it by the whole Church, because it completes the series of Great Councils by which the Doctrine of the Deity of the Holy Spirit was affirmed; and in fact it expressed the final judgment of the Catholic Church upon the Macedonian controversy. Its first Canon anathematises the Semiarians or Pneumatomachi by name as well as the Eunomians or Anomœan Arians (cf. Dict. Biog. Art. Gregory of Nazianzus, by Dr. H. B. Swete).

XXVII. THE FIRST THEOLOGICAL ORATION.

A Preliminary Discourse against the Eunomians.

I. I am to speak against persons who pride themselves on their eloquence; so, to begin with a text of Scripture, "Behold, I am against thee, O thou proud one,"[a] not only in

[a] In his Fifty-third Epistle, addressed to S. Basil, there is an amusing instance of his defence of this tolerant disposition, which S. Basil also displayed in dealing with minds of this class.

[a] Jer. l. 31.

thy system of teaching, but also in thy hearing, and in thy tone of mind. For there are certain persons who have not only their ears[α] and their tongues, but even, as I now perceive, their hands too, itching for our words; who delight in profane babblings, and oppositions of science falsely so called,[β] and strifes about words, which tend to no profit; for so Paul, the Preacher and Establisher of the "Word cut short,"[γ] the disciple and teacher of the Fishermen,[δ] calls all that is excessive or superfluous in discourse. But as to those to whom we refer, would that they, whose tongue is so voluble and clever in applying itself to noble and approved language, would likewise pay some attention to actions. For then perhaps in a little while they would become less sophistical, and less absurd and strange acrobats of words, if I may use a ridiculous expression about a ridiculous subject.

II. But since they neglect every path of righteousness, and look only to this one point, namely, which of the propositions submitted to them they shall bind or loose, (like those persons who in the theatres perform wrestling matches in public, but not that kind of wrestling in which the victory is won according to the rules of the sport, but a kind to deceive the eyes of those who are ignorant in such matters, and to catch applause), and every marketplace must buzz with their talking; and every dinner party be worried to death with silly talk and boredom; and every festival be made unfestive and full of dejection, and every occasion of mourning be consoled by a greater calamity[ε]—their questions—and all the women's apartments accustomed to simplicity be thrown into confusion and be robbed of its flower of modesty by the torrent of their words . . . since, I say this is so, the evil is intolerable and not to be borne, and our Great Mystery is in danger of being made a thing of little moment. Well then, let these spies[ζ] bear with us, moved as we are with fatherly compassion, and as holy Jeremiah says, torn in our hearts;[η] let them bear with us so far as not to give a savage reception to our discourse upon this subject; and let them, if indeed they can, restrain their tongues for a short while and lend us their ears. However that may be, you shall at any rate suffer no loss. For either we shall have spoken in the ears of them that will hear,[α] and our words will bear some fruit, namely an advantage to you (since the Sower soweth the Word[β] upon every kind of mind; and the good and fertile bears fruit), or else you will depart despising this discourse of ours as you have despised others, and having drawn from it further material for gainsaying and railing at us, upon which to feast yourselves yet more.

And you must not be astonished if I speak a language which is strange to you and contrary to your custom, who profess to know everything and to teach everything in a too impetuous and generous manner . . . not to pain you by saying ignorant and rash.

III. Not to every one, my friends, does it belong to philosophize about God; not to every one; the Subject is not so cheap and low; and I will add, not before every audience, nor at all times, nor on all points; but on certain occasions, and before certain persons, and within certain limits.

Not to all men, because it is permitted only to those who have been examined, and are passed masters in meditation, and who have been previously purified in soul and body, or at the very least are being purified. For the impure to touch the pure is, we may safely say, not safe, just as it is unsafe to fix weak eyes upon the sun's rays. And what is the permitted occasion? It is when we are free from all external defilement or disturbance, and when that which rules within us is not confused with vexatious or erring images; like persons mixing up good writing with bad, or filth with the sweet odours of unguents. For it is necessary to be truly at leisure to know God; and when we can get a convenient season, to discern the straight road of the things divine. And who are the permitted persons? They to whom the subject is of real concern, and not they who make it a matter of pleasant gossip, like any other thing, after the races, or the theatre, or a concert, or a dinner, or still lower employments. To such men as these, idle jests and pretty contradictions about these subjects are a part of their amusement.

IV. Next, on what subjects and to what extent may we philosophize? On matters within our reach, and to such an extent as the mental power and grasp of our audience may extend. No further, lest, as excessively loud sounds injure the hearing, or excess of food the body, or, if you will, as excessive burdens beyond

α Tim. iv. 3. β Ib. ii. 16. γ Rom. ix. 28.

δ S. Paul is called a *disciple of the fishermen*, as having been in some sense their follower (though in fact he was never a literal disciple of any of them); and their *teacher* as having taught such Successors of the Apostles as SS. Timothy and Titus.

ε i.e. be thrown into the shade by something more serious which caused them by comparison to be scarcely felt any longer.

ζ κατάσκοποι quasi ψευδεπίσκοποι. η Jer. iv. 19.

α Ecclus. xxv. 9.

β S. Mark iv. 3 and 14. "He that soweth the Word soweth upon," etc. So Billius and the Benedictines, but the rendering in the text seems preferable.

the strength injure those who bear them, or excessive rains the earth; so these too, being pressed down and overweighted by the stiffness, if I may use the expression, of the arguments should suffer loss even in respect of the strength they originally possessed.[α]

V. Now, I am not saying that it is not needful to remember God at all times; . . . I must not be misunderstood, or I shall be having these nimble and quick people down upon me again. For we ought to think of God even more often than we draw our breath; and if the expression is permissible, we ought to do nothing else. Yea, I am one of those who entirely approve that Word which bids us meditate day and night,[β] and tell at eventide and morning and noon day,[γ] and praise the Lord at every time;[δ] or, to use Moses' words, whether a man lie down, or rise up, or walk by the way, or whatever else he be doing[ε]—and by this recollection we are to be moulded to purity. So that it is not the continual remembrance of God that I would hinder, but only the talking about God; nor even that as in itself wrong, but only when unseasonable; nor all teaching, but only want of moderation. As of even honey repletion and satiety, though it be of honey, produce vomiting;[ς] and, as Solomon says and I think, there is a time for every thing,[η] and that which is good ceases to be good if it be not done in a good way; just as a flower is quite out of season in winter, and just as a man's dress does not become a woman, nor a woman's a man; and as geometry is out of place in mourning, or tears at a carousal; shall we in this instance alone disregard the proper time, in a matter in which most of all due season should be respected? Surely not, my friends and brethren (for I will still call you Brethren, though you do not behave like brothers). Let us not think so nor yet, like hot tempered and hard mouthed horses, throwing off our rider Reason, and casting away Reverence, that keeps us within due limits, run far away from the turning point,[θ] but let us philosophize within our proper bounds, and not be carried away into Egypt, nor be swept down into Assyria,[α] nor sing the Lord's song in a strange land, by which I mean before any kind of audience, strangers or kindred, hostile or friendly, kindly or the reverse, who watch what we do with over great care, and would like the spark of what is wrong in us to become a flame, and secretly kindle and fan it and raise it to heaven with their breath and make it higher than the Babylonian flame which burnt up every thing around it. For since their strength lies not in their own dogmas, they hunt for it in our weak points. And therefore they apply themselves to our—shall I say "misfortunes" or "failings"?—like flies to wounds. But let us at least be no longer ignorant of ourselves, or pay too little attention to the due order in these matters. And if it be impossible to put an end to the existing hostility, let us at least agree upon this, that we will utter Mysteries under our breath, and holy things in a holy manner, and we will not cast to ears profane that which may not be uttered, nor give evidence that we possess less gravity than those who worship demons, and serve shameful fables and deeds; for they would sooner give their blood to the uninitiated than certain words. But let us recognize that as in dress and diet and laughter and demeanour there is a certain decorum, so there is also in speech and silence; since among so many titles and powers of God, we pay the highest honour to The Word. Let even our disputings then be kept within bounds.

VI. Why should a man who is a hostile listener to such words be allowed to hear about the Generation of God, or his creation, or how God was made out of things which had no existence, or of section and analysis and division?[β] Why do we make our accusers judges? Why do we put swords into the hands of our enemies? How, thinkest thou, or with what temper, will the arguments about such subjects be received by one who approves of adulteries, and corruption of children, and who worships the passions and cannot conceive of aught higher than the body . . . who till very lately set up gods for himself, and gods too who were noted for the vilest deeds? Will it not first be from a material standpoint, shamefully and ignorantly, and in the sense to which he has been accustomed? Will he not make thy Theology a defence for his own gods and pas-

α i.e. Should not only fail to be strengthened thereby, but be actually weakened, through their inability to understand the argument. A bad defence weakens a good cause.

β Ps. i. 2. γ Ps. lv. 17. δ Ps. xxxiv. 1.

ε Deut. vi. 7. ς Prov. xxv. 16. η Eccles. iii. 1.

θ The course of the chariot races in the Greek Games was round the Hippodrome a certain number of times. To facilitate this arrangement, a party wall was built down the middle, and at either end of it certain posts were set up called νύσσαι, or in Latin *Metæ*, round which the cars were to turn. The object of the charioteers was to turn round these as close as possible, to save distance; and to do this well it was necessary to have the horses under perfect control, as well as perfectly trained, to make the semicircle at full gallop almost on the axis of the car. The horses that got out of hand and galloped wildly round a large circle would almost certainly lose distance enough to lose the race, while the driver would be laughed at for his unskilfulness.

α Dan. iii. 12.

β The allusion is to the Arian and Eunomian habit of gossiping about the most sacred subjects in every sort of place or company or time, in order to promote their heresy.

sions? For if we ourselves wantonly misuse these words,[α] it will be a long time before we shall persuade them to accept our philosophy. And if they are in their own persons inventors of evil things, how should they refrain from grasping at such things when offered to them? Such results come to us from mutual contest. Such results follow to those who fight for the Word beyond what the Word approves; they are behaving like mad people, who set their own house on fire, or tear their own children, or disavow their own parents, taking them for strangers.

VII. But when we have put away from the conversation those who are strangers to it, and sent the great legion[β] on its way to the abyss into the herd of swine, the next thing is to look to ourselves, and polish our theological self to beauty like a statue. The first point to be considered is—What is this great rivalry of speech and endless talking? What is this new disease of insatiability? Why have we tied our hands and armed our tongues? We do not praise either hospitality, or brotherly love, or conjugal affection, or virginity; nor do we admire liberality to the poor, or the chanting of Psalms, or nightlong vigils,[γ] or tears. We do not keep under the body by fasting, or go forth to God by prayer; nor do we subject the worse to the better—I mean the dust to the spirit—as they would do who form a just judgment of our composite nature; we do not make our life a preparation for death; nor do we make ourselves masters of our passions, mindful of our heavenly nobility; nor tame our anger when it swells and rages, nor our pride that bringeth to a fall, nor unreasonable grief, nor unchastened pleasure, nor meretricious laughter, nor undisciplined eyes, nor insatiable ears, nor excessive talk, nor absurd thoughts, nor aught of the occasions which the Evil One gets against us from sources within ourselves; bringing upon us the death that comes through the windows,[δ] as Holy Scripture saith; that is, through the senses. Nay we do the very opposite, and have given liberty to the passions of others, as kings give releases from service in honour of a victory, only on condition that they incline to our side, and make their assault upon God more boldly, or more impiously. And we give them an evil reward for a thing which is not good, license of tongue for their impiety.

VIII. And yet, O talkative Dialectician, I will ask thee one small question,[α] and answer thou me, as He saith to Job, Who through whirlwind and cloud giveth Divine admonitions.[β] Are there many mansions in God's House, as thou hast heard, or only one? Of course you will admit that there are many, and not only one. Now, are they all to be filled, or only some, and others not; so that some will be left empty, and will have been prepared to no purpose? Of course all will be filled, for nothing can be in vain which has been done by God. And can you tell me what you will consider this Mansion to be? Is it the rest and glory which is in store There for the Blessed, or something else?—No, not anything else. Since then we are agreed upon this point, let us further examine another also. Is there any thing that procures these Mansions, as I think there is; or is there nothing? —Certainly there is—What is it? Is it not that there are various modes of conduct, and various purposes, one leading one way, another another way, according to the proportion of faith, and these we call Ways? Must we, then, travel all, or some of these Ways . . . the same individual along them all, if that be possible; or, if not, along as many as may be; or else along some of them? And even if this may not be, it would still be a great thing, at least as it appears to me, to travel excellently along even one.—"You are right in your conception."—What then when you hear there is but One way, and that a narrow one,[γ] does the word seem to you to shew? That there is but one on account of its excellence. For it is but one, even though it be split into many parts. And narrow because of its difficulties, and because it is trodden by few in comparison with the multitude of the adversaries, and of those who travel along the road of wickedness. "So I think too." Well, then, my good friend, since this is so, why do you, as though condemning our doctrine for a certain poverty, rush headlong down that one which leads through what you call arguments and speculations, but I frivolities and quackeries? Let Paul reprove you with those bitter reproaches, in which, after his list of the Gifts of Grace, he says, Are all Apostles? Are all Prophets? etc.[δ]

IX. But, be it so. Lofty thou art, even beyond the lofty, even above the clouds, if thou wilt, a spectator of things invisible, a hearer

α Such expressions as Generation and the like would certainly be understood in a material sense by the heathen; and so would place an unnecessary stumbling-block in the way of their conversion.

β Luke viii. 31.

γ S. John Chrysostom, consecrated Archbishop of Constantinople in 397, incurred much unpopularity among his clergy by insisting on the revival of the Night Hours of prayer.

δ Jer. ix. 21.

α Job xxxviii. 3.

β Job xxxviii. 1.

γ Matt. vii. 14.

δ 1 Cor. xii. 29.

of things unspeakable; one who hast ascended after Elias, and who after Moses hast been deemed worthy of the Vision of God, and after Paul hast been taken up into heaven; why dost thou mould the rest of thy fellows in one day into Saints, and ordain them Theologians, and as it were breathe into them instruction, and make them many councils of ignorant oracles? Why dost thou entangle those who are weaker in thy spider's web, as if it were something great and wise? Why dost thou stir up wasps' nests against the Faith? Why dost thou suddenly spring a flood of dialectics upon us, as the fables of old did the Giants? Why hast thou collected all that is frivolous and unmanly among men, like a rabble, into one torrent, and having made them more effeminate by flattery, fashioned a new workshop, cleverly making a harvest for thyself out of their want of understanding? Dost thou deny that this is so, and are the other matters of no account to thee? Must thy tongue rule at any cost, and canst thou not restrain the birthpang of thy speech? Thou mayest find many other honourable subjects for discussion. To these turn this disease of thine with some advantage. Attack the silence of Pythagoras,[α] and the Orphic beans, and the novel brag about "The Master said." Attack the ideas of Plato,[β] and the transmigrations and courses of our souls, and the reminiscences, and the unlovely loves of the soul for lovely bodies. Attack the atheism of Epicurus,[γ] and his atoms, and his unphilosophic pleasure; or Aristotle's petty Providence, and his artificial system, and his discourses about the mortality of the soul, and the humanitarianism of his doctrine. Attack the superciliousness of the Stoa,[δ] or the greed and vulgarity of the Cynic.[ε] Attack the "Void and Full" (what nonsense), and all the details about the gods and the sacrifices and the idols and demons, whether beneficent or malignant, and all the tricks that people play with divination, evoking of gods, or of souls, and the power of the stars. And if these things seem to thee unworthy of discussion as petty and already often confuted, and thou wilt keep to thy line, and seek the satisfaction of thy ambition in it; then here too I will provide thee with broad paths. Philosophize about the world or worlds; about matter; about soul; about natures endowed with reason, good or bad; about resurrection, about judgment, about reward, or the Sufferings of Christ. For in these subjects to hit the mark is not useless, and to miss it is not dangerous. But with God we shall have converse, in this life only in a small degree; but a little later, it may be, more perfectly, in the Same, our Lord Jesus Christ, to Whom be glory for ever. Amen.

α The disciples of Pythagoras were made to keep silence absolutely for five years as a qualification for initiation into the mysteries of his order. Further, they were bidden to abstain from eating beans, as these were said to be one receptacle of human souls in the course of their peregrinations; and when asked for proof of their peculiar doctrines, contented themselves with the reply, "*αὐτὸς ἔθα*" "*the master said so.*"

β Plato taught that all things that exist are copies of certain objective archetypal Forms, emanations from the Mind of God, which God copied in creation. He also taught a doctrine of transmigration of souls.

γ Epicurus, an Athenian philosopher, of a materialistic type, taught that God had no existence, and that the world was made by a fortuitous concourse of innumerable atoms of matter, which are self-existent; and he placed the highest good in pleasure, which he defined as the absence of pain.

δ The Stoa, a school of philosophers opposed to the Epicureans, took their name from a certain Colonnade at Athens, in which Zeno, their founder, used to teach. Their highest good consisted in the complete subdual of all feeling; and so they were not unnaturally characterized by a haughty affectation of indifference.

ε The Cynics, so called from their snarling way, were a school founded by Antisthenes. They professed to despise everything human.

ORATION XXVIII.

The Second Theological Oration.

I. In the former Discourse we laid down clearly with respect to the Theologian, both what sort of character he ought to bear, and on what kind of subject he may philosophize, and when, and to what extent. We saw that he ought to be, as far as may be, pure, in order that light may be apprehended by light; and that he ought to consort with serious men, in order that his word be not fruitless through falling on an unfruitful soil; and that the suitable season is when we have a calm within from the whirl of outward things; so as not like madmen[α] to lose our breath; and that the extent to which we may go is that to which we have ourselves advanced, or to which we are advancing. Since then these things are so, and we have broken up for ourselves the fallows of Divinity,[β] so as not to sow upon thorns,[γ] and have made plain the face of the ground,[δ] being moulded and moulding others by Holy Scripture . . . let us now enter upon Theological questions, setting at the head thereof the Father, the Son, and the Holy Ghost, of Whom we are to treat; that the Father may be well pleased, and the Son may help us, and the Holy Ghost may inspire us; or rather that one illumination may come upon us from the One God, One in diversity, diverse in Unity, wherein is a marvel.

α A marginal reading noted by the Benedictines gives "*sobbing*" or "*panting*," which is a better sense.

β Jerem. iv 3. γ Matt. xiii. 7. δ Isa. xxviii. 25.

II. Now when I go up eagerly into the Mount[α]—or, to use a truer expression, when I both eagerly long, and at the same time am afraid (the one through my hope and the other through my weakness) to enter within the Cloud, and hold converse with God, for so God commands; if any be an Aaron, let him go up with me, and let him stand near, being ready, if it must be so, to remain outside the Cloud. But if any be a Nadad or an Abihu, or of the Order of the Elders, let him go up indeed, but let him stand afar off, according to the value of his purification. But if any be of the multitude, who are unworthy of this height of contemplation, if he be altogether impure let him not approach at all,[β] for it would be dangerous to him; but if he be at least temporarily purified, let him remain below and listen to the Voice alone, and the trumpet,[γ] the bare words of piety, and let him see the Mountain smoking and lightening, a terror at once and a marvel to those who cannot get up. But if any is an evil and savage beast, and altogether incapable of taking in the subject matter of Contemplation and Theology, let him not hurtfully and malignantly lurk in his den among the woods, to catch hold of some dogma or saying by a sudden spring, and to tear sound doctrine to pieces by his misrepresentations, but let him stand yet afar off and withdraw from the Mount, or he shall be stoned and crushed, and shall perish miserably in his wickedness. For to those who are like wild beasts true and sound discourses are stones. If he be a leopard let him die with his spots.[δ] If a ravening and roaring lion, seeking what he may devour[ε] of our souls or of our words; or a wild boar, trampling under foot the precious and translucent pearls of the Truth;[ζ] or an Arabian[η] and alien wolf, or one keener even than these in tricks of argument; or a fox, that is a treacherous and faithless soul, changing its shape according to circumstances or necessities, feeding on dead or putrid bodies, or on little vineyards[θ] when the large ones have escaped them; or any other carnivorous beast, rejected by the Law as unclean for food or enjoyment; our discourse must withdraw from such and be engraved on solid tables of stone, and that on both sides because the Law is partly visible, and partly hidden; the one part belonging to the mass who remain below, the other to the few who press upward into the Mount.

III. What is this that has happened to me, O friends, and initiates, and fellow-lovers of the truth? I was running to lay hold on God, and thus I went up into the Mount, and drew aside the curtain of the Cloud, and entered away from matter and material things, and as far as I could I withdrew within myself. And then when I looked up, I scarce saw the back parts of God;[α] although I was sheltered by the Rock, the Word that was made flesh for us. And when I looked a little closer, I saw, not the First and unmingled Nature, known to Itself—to the Trinity, I mean; not That which abideth within the first[β] veil, and is hidden by the Cherubim; but only that Nature, which at last even reaches to us. And that is, as far as I can learn, the Majesty, or as holy David calls it, the Glory[γ] which is manifested among the creatures, which It has produced and governs. For these are the Back Parts of God, which He leaves behind Him, as tokens of Himself[δ] like the shadows and reflection of the sun in the water, which shew the sun to our weak eyes, because we cannot look at the sun himself, for by his unmixed light he is too strong for our power of perception. In this way then shalt thou discourse of God; even wert thou a Moses and a god to Pharaoh;[ε] even wert thou caught up like Paul to the Third Heaven,[ζ] and hadst heard unspeakable words; even wert thou raised above them both, and exalted to Angelic or Archangelic place and dignity. For though a thing be all heavenly, or above heaven, and far higher in nature and nearer to God than we, yet it is farther distant from God, and from the complete comprehension of His Nature, than it is lifted above our complex and lowly and earthward-sinking composition.

IV. Therefore we must begin again thus. It is difficult to conceive God but to define Him in words is an impossibility, as one of the Greek teachers of Divinity[η] taught, not unskilfully, as it appears to me; with the intention that he might be thought to have apprehended Him; in that he says it is a hard thing to do; and yet may escape being convicted of ignorance because of the impossibility of giving expression to the apprehension. But in my opinion it is impossible to express Him, and

α Exod. xxiv. 1. β Ib. xix. 14. γ Ib. xix. 16-18.
δ Jer. xiii. 23. ε 1 Pet. v. 8. ζ Matt. vii. 6.
η *Arabian:* So the LXX. renders the word which in A. V. Jer. v. 6, is translated "*of the evening*," and in the Vulg. "*at evening*." R. V. gives as an alternative, "*of the deserts*."
θ The LXX. in Cant xi. 15, admits of this translation as well as of that followed by A. V.

α Exod. xxxiii. 23.
β This veil of the Mercy Seat, spoken of in Exod. xxvi. 31, signifies in Gregory's sense the denial of contemplation of that Highest Nature. γ Ps. viii. 1.
δ The Face of God signifies His Essence and Deity. which were before all worlds: His back parts are Creation and Providence, by which He reveals Himself.
ε Exod. iv. 2. ζ 2 Cor. xii. 2. η Plato, Tim., 28 E.

yet more impossible to conceive Him. For that which may be conceived may perhaps be made clear by language, if not fairly well, at any rate imperfectly, to any one who is not quite deprived of his hearing, or slothful of understanding. But to comprehend the whole of so great a Subject as this is quite impossible and impracticable, not merely to the utterly careless and ignorant, but even to those who are highly exalted, and who love God, and in like manner to every created nature; seeing that the darkness of this world and the thick covering of the flesh is an obstacle to the full understanding of the truth. I do not know whether it is the same with the higher natures and purer Intelligences[α] which because of their nearness to God, and because they are illumined with all His Light, may possibly see, if not the whole, at any rate more perfectly and distinctly than we do; some perhaps more, some less than others, in proportion to their rank.

V. But enough has been said on this point. As to what concerns us, it is not only the Peace of God[β] which passeth all understanding and knowledge, nor only the things which God hath stored up in promise for the righteous, which "eye hath not seen, nor ear heard, nor mind conceived"[γ] except in a very small degree, nor the accurate knowledge of the Creation. For even of this I would have you know that you have only a shadow when you hear the words, "I will consider the heavens, the work of Thy fingers, the moon and the stars,"[δ] and the settled order therein; not as if he were considering them now, but as destined to do so hereafter. But far before them is That nature Which is above them, and out of which they spring, the Incomprehensible and Illimitable—not, I mean, as to the fact of His being, but as to Its nature. For our preaching is not empty, nor our Faith vain,[ε] nor is this the doctrine we proclaim; for we would not have you take our candid statement as a starting point for a quibbling denial of God, or of arrogance on account of our confession of ignorance. For it is one thing to be persuaded of the existence of a thing, and quite another to know what it is.

VI. Now our very eyes and the Law of Nature teach us that God exists and that He is the Efficient and Maintaining Cause of all things: our eyes, because they fall on visible objects, and see them in beautiful stability and progress, immovably moving and revolving if I may so say; natural Law, because through these visible things and their order, it reasons back to their Author. For how could this Universe have come into being or been put together, unless God had called it into existence, and held it together? For every one who sees a beautifully made lute, and considers the skill with which it has been fitted together and arranged, or who hears its melody, would think of none but the lutemaker, or the luteplayer, and would recur to him in mind, though he might not know him by sight. And thus to us also is manifested That which made and moves and preserves all created things, even though He be not comprehended by the mind. And very wanting in sense is he who will not willingly go thus far in following natural proofs; but not even this which we have fancied or formed, or which reason has sketched for us, proves the existence of a God. But if any one has got even to some extent a comprehension of this, how is God's Being to be demonstrated? Who ever reached this extremity of wisdom? Who was ever deemed worthy of so great a gift? Who has opened the mouth of his mind and drawn in the Spirit,[α] so as by Him that searcheth all things, yea the deep things of God,[β] to take in God, and no longer to need progress, since he already possesses the Extreme Object of desire, and That to which all the social life and all the intelligence of the best men press forward?

VII. For what will you conceive the Deity to be, if you rely upon all the approximations of reason? Or to what will reason carry you, O most philosophic of men and best of Theologians, who boast of your familiarity with the Unlimited? Is He a body? How then is He the Infinite and Limitless, and formless, and intangible, and invisible? or are these attributes of a body? What arrogance for such is not the nature of a body! Or will you say that He has a body, but not these attributes? O stupidity, that a Deity should possess nothing more than we do. For how is He an object of worship if He be circumscribed? Or how shall He escape being made of elements, and therefore subject to be resolved into them again, or even altogether dissolved? For every compound is a starting point of strife, and strife of separation, and

α No one doubts, say the Benedictine Editors, that the Angels do see God, and that men, too, will see Him, when they attain to Eternal Bliss. S. Thomas (Summa I. qu. xii. 4) argues that the Angels have cognition of God's Essence not by nature but by grace: but yet (Ib. qu. lvi. 3) that they have by nature a certain cognition of Him, as represented and as it were mirrored in their own essence; though not the actual vision of His Essence. The Angel, he says again (Ib. qu. lxiv. 1) has a higher cognition of God than man has, on account of the perfection of his intellect; and this cognition remains even in the fallen Angels.

β Phil. iv. 7. γ Isa. lxiv. 4; 1 Cor. ii. 9. δ Ps. viii. 3. ε 1 Cor. xv. 19.

α Ps. cxix. 21. β 1 Cor. ii. 10.

separation of dissolution. But dissolution is altogether foreign to God and to the First Nature. Therefore there can be no separation, that there may be no dissolution, and no strife that there may be no separation, and no composition that there may be no strife. Thus also there must be no body, that there may be no composition, and so the argument is established by going back from last to first.

VIII. And how shall we preserve the truth that God pervades all things and fills all, as it is written "Do not I fill heaven and earth? saith the Lord,"[α] and "The Spirit of the Lord filleth the world,"[β] if God partly contains and partly is contained? For either He will occupy an empty Universe, and so all things will have vanished for us, with this result, that we shall have insulted God by making Him a body, and by robbing Him of all things which He has made; or else He will be a body contained in other bodies, which is impossible; or He will be enfolded in them, or contrasted with them, as liquids are mixed, and one divides and is divided by another;—a view which is more absurd and anile than even the atoms of Epicurus[γ] and so this argument concerning the body will fall through, and have no body and no solid basis at all. But if we are to assert that He is immaterial (as for example that Fifth Element which some[δ] have imagined), and that He is carried round in the circular movement . . . let us assume that He is immaterial, and that He is the Fifth Element; and, if they please, let Him be also bodiless in accordance with the independent drift and arrangement of their argument; for I will not at present differ with them on this point; in what respect then will He be one of those things which are in movement and agitation, to say nothing of the insult involved in making the Creator subject to the same movement as the creatures, and Him That carries all (if they will allow even this) one with those whom He carries. Again, what is the force that moves your Fifth Element, and what is it that moves all things, and what moves that, and what is the force that moves that? And so on *ad infinitum*. And how can He help being altogether contained in space if He be subject to motion? But if they assert that He is something other than this Fifth Element; suppose it is an angelic nature that they attribute to Him, how will they shew that Angels are corporeal, or what sort of bodies they have? And how far in that case could God, to Whom the Angels minister, be superior to the Angels? And if He is above them, there is again brought in an irrational swarm of bodies, and a depth of nonsense, that has no possible basis to stand upon.

IX. And thus we see that God is not a body. For no inspired teacher has yet asserted or admitted such a notion, nor has the sentence of our own Court allowed it. Nothing then remains but to conceive of Him as incorporeal. But this term Incorporeal, though granted, does not yet set before us—or contain within itself His Essence, any more than Unbegotten, or Unoriginate, or Unchanging, or Incorruptible, or any other predicate which is used concerning God or in reference to Him. For what effect is produced upon His Being or Substance[α] by His having no beginning, and being incapable of change or limitation? Nay, the whole question of His Being is still left for the further consideration and exposition of him who truly has the mind of God and is advanced in contemplation. For just as to say "It is a body," or "It was begotten," is not sufficient to present clearly to the mind the various objects of which these predicates are used, but you must also express the subject of which you use them, if you would present the object of your thought clearly and adequately (for every one of these predicates, corporeal, begotten, mortal, may be used of a man, or a cow, or a horse). Just so he who is eagerly pursuing the nature of the Self-existent will not stop at saying what He is *not*, but must go on beyond what He is not, and say what He *is;* inasmuch as it is easier to take in some single point than to go on disowning point after point in endless detail, in order, both by the elimination of negatives and the assertion of positives to arrive at a comprehension of this subject.

But a man who states what God is not without going on to say what He is, acts much in the same way as one would who when asked how many twice five make, should answer, "Not two, nor three, nor four, nor five, nor twenty, nor thirty, nor in short any number below ten, nor any multiple of ten;" but would not answer "ten," nor settle the mind of his questioner upon the firm ground of the answer. For it is much easier, and more concise to shew what a thing is not from what it

α Jer. xxiii. 24. β Wisd. i. 7.

γ Epicurus taught that Matter is eternal, and consists of an indefinite number of Atoms or indivisible units, floating about in space, and mutually attracting and repelling each other; and that all that exists is due to some chance meeting and coalition of these atoms.

δ This is a speculation of Aristotle, who imagined a Fifth Element, consisting of formless matter.

α Petavius (De Trin. IV. ii. 7) notes that ὑπόστασις seems used here of the Essence and Nature common to the Three Persons of the Blessed Trinity.

is, than to demonstrate what it is by stripping it of what it is not. And this surely is evident to every one.

X. Now since we have ascertained that God is incorporeal, let us proceed a little further with our examination. Is He Nowhere or Somewhere. For if He is Nowhere,[α] then some person of a very inquiring turn of mind might ask, How is it then that He can even exist? For if the non-existent is nowhere, then that which is nowhere is also perhaps non-existent. But if He is Somewhere, He must be either in the Universe, or above the Universe. And if He is *in* the Universe, then He must be either in some part or in the whole. If in some part, then He will be circumscribed by that part which is less than Himself; but if everywhere, then by one which is further and greater—I mean the Universal, which contains the Particular; if the Universe is to be contained by the Universe, and no place is to be free from circumscription. This follows if He is contained in the Universe. And besides, where was He before the Universe was created, for this is a point of no little difficulty. But if He is *above* the Universe, is there nothing to distinguish this from the Universe, and where is this *above* situated? And how could this Transcendence and that which is transcended be distinguished in thought, if there is not a limit to divide and define them? Is it not necessary that there shall be some mean to mark off the Universe from that which is above the Universe? And what could this be but Place, which we have already rejected? For I have not yet brought forward the point that God would be altogether circumscript, if He were even comprehensible in thought: for comprehension is one form of circumscription.

XI. Now, why have I gone into all this, perhaps too minutely for most people to listen to, and in accordance with the present manner of discourse, which despises noble simplicity, and has introduced a crooked and intricate[β] style? That the tree may be known by its fruits;[γ] I mean, that the darkness which is at work in such teaching may be known by the obscurity of the arguments. For my purpose in doing so was, not to get credit for myself for astonishing utterances, or excessive wisdom, through tying knots and solving difficulties (this was the great miraculous gift of Daniel),[α] but to make clear the point at which my argument has aimed from the first. And what was this? That the Divine Nature cannot be apprehended by human reason, and that we cannot even represent to ourselves all its greatness. And this not out of envy, for envy is far from the Divine Nature, which is passionless, and only good and Lord of all;[β] especially envy of that which is the most honourable[γ] of all His creatures. For what does the Word prefer to the rational and speaking creatures? Why, even their very existence is a proof of His supreme goodness. Nor yet is this incomprehensibility for the sake of His own glory and honour, Who is full,[δ] as if His possession of His glory and majesty depended upon the impossibility of approaching Him. For it is utterly sophistical and foreign to the character, I will not say of God, but of any moderately good man, who has any right ideas about himself, to seek his own supremacy by throwing a hindrance in the way of another.

XII. But whether there be other causes for it also, let them see who are nearer God, and are eyewitnesses and spectators of His unsearchable judgments;[ε] if there are any who are so eminent in virtue, and who walk in the paths of the Infinite, as the saying is. As far, however, as we have attained, who measure with our little measure things hard to be understood, perhaps one reason is to prevent us from too readily throwing away the possession because it was so easily come by. For people cling tightly to that which they acquire with labour; but that which they acquire easily they quickly throw away, because it can be easily recovered. And so it is turned into a blessing, at least to all men who are sensible, that this blessing is not too easy. Or perhaps it is in order that we may not share the fate of Lucifer, who fell, and in consequence of receiving the full light make our necks stiff against the Lord Almighty, and suffer a fall, of all things most pitiable, from the height we had attained. Or perhaps it may be to give a greater reward hereafter for their labour and glorious life to those who have here been purified, and have exercised long patience in respect of that which they desired.

Therefore this darkness of the body has been placed between us and God, like the cloud of old between the Egyptians and the Hebrews;[ς] and this is perhaps what is meant by "He

α Nowhere is in this passage used in an ambiguous sense. As asserted of God. it means that His Being is in no way limited by place; not that He has no existence in place, for He is everywhere, and He transcends all place. Before the creation of the Universe He existed, and He created Place, which therefore cannot be the seat of His Being.

β v. l. *Affected.* The allusion is especially to the ostentatious dialectics and tedious arguments of Aëtius and his followers, Eunomius and others.

γ Luke vi. 44.

α cf. Dan. v. 12.

β Plato, Tim., 10.

γ v. l. Most Akin to Himself. Combefis.

δ Isa. i. 11.

ε Rom. xi. 33.

ς Exod. xiv. 20.

made darkness His secret place," [α] namely our dulness, through which few can see even a little. But as to this point, let those discuss it whose business it is; and let them ascend as far as possible in the examination. To us who are (as Jeremiah saith), "prisoners of the earth," [β] and covered with the denseness of carnal nature, this at all events is known, that as it is impossible for a man to step over his own shadow, however fast he may move (for the shadow will always move on as fast as it is being overtaken) or, as it is impossible for the eye to draw near to visible objects apart from the intervening air and light, or for a fish to glide about outside of the waters; so it is quite impracticable for those who are in the body to be conversant with objects of pure thought apart altogether from bodily objects. For something in our own environment is ever creeping in, even when the mind has most fully detached itself from the visible, and collected itself, and is attempting to apply itself to those invisible things which are akin to itself.

XIII. This will be made clear to you as follows:—Are not Spirit, and Fire, and Light, Love, and Wisdom, and Righteousness, and Mind and Reason, and the like, the names of the First Nature? What then? Can you conceive of Spirit apart from motion and diffusion; or of Fire without its fuel and its upward motion, and its proper colour and form? Or of Light unmingled with air, and loosed from that which is as it were its father and source? And how do you conceive of a mind? Is it not that which is inherent in some person not itself, and are not its movements thoughts, silent or uttered? And Reason . . . what else can you think it than that which is either silent within ourselves, or else outpoured (for I shrink from saying loosed)? And if you conceive of Wisdom, what is it but the habit of mind which you know as such, and which is concerned with contemplations either divine or human? And Justice and Love, are they not praiseworthy dispositions, the one opposed to injustice, the other to hate, and at one time intensifying themselves, at another relaxed, now taking possession of us, now leaving us alone, and in a word, making us what we are, and changing us as colours do bodies? Or are we rather to leave all these things, and to look at the Deity absolutely, as best we can, collecting a fragmentary perception of It from Its images? What then is this subtile thing, which is of these, and yet is not these, or how can that Unity which is in its Nature uncomposite and incomparable, still be all of these, and each one of them perfectly? Thus our mind faints to transcend corporeal things, and to consort with the Incorporeal, stripped of all clothing of corporeal ideas, as long as it has to look with its inherent weakness at things above its strength. For every rational nature longs for God and for the First Cause, but is unable to grasp Him, for the reasons I have mentioned. Faint therefore with the desire, and as it were restive and impatient of the disability, it tries a second course, either to look at visible things, and out of some of them to make a god . . . (a poor contrivance, for in what respect and to what extent can that which is seen be higher and more godlike than that which sees, that this should worship that?) or else through the beauty and order of visible things to attain to that which is above sight; but not to suffer the loss of God through the magnificence of visible things.

XIV. From this cause some have made a god of the Sun, others of the Moon, others of the host of Stars, others of heaven itself with all its hosts, to which they have attributed the guiding of the Universe, according to the quality or quantity of their movement. Others again of the Elements, earth, air, water, fire, because of their useful nature, since without them human life cannot possibly exist. Others again have worshipped any chance visible objects, setting up the most beautiful of what they saw as their gods. And there are those who worship pictures and images, at first indeed of their own ancestors—at least, this is the case with the more affectionate and sensual—and honour the departed with memorials; and afterwards even those of strangers are worshipped by men of a later generation separated from them by a long interval; through ignorance of the First Nature, and following the traditional honour as lawful and necessary; for usage when confirmed by time was held to be Law. And I think that some who were courtiers of arbitrary power and extolled bodily strength and admired beauty, made a god in time out of him whom they honoured, perhaps getting hold of some fable to help on their imposture.

XV. And those of them who were most subject to passion deified their passions, or honoured them among their gods; Anger and Blood-thirstiness, Lust and Drunkenness, and every similar wickedness; and made out of this an ignoble and unjust excuse for their own sins. And some they left on earth, and some they

α Ps. xviii. 11. β Lam. iii. 34.

hid beneath the earth (this being the only sign of wisdom about them), and some they raised to heaven.[α] O ridiculous distribution of inheritance! Then they gave to each of these concepts the name of some god or demon, by the authority and private judgment of their error, and set up statues whose costliness is a snare, and thought to honour them with blood and the steam of sacrifices, and sometimes even by most shameful actions, frenzies and manslaughter. For such honours were the fitting due of such gods. And before now men have insulted themselves by worshipping monsters, and fourfooted beasts, and creeping things,[β] and of the very vilest and most absurd, and have made an offering to them of the glory of God; so that it is not easy to decide whether we ought most to despise the worshippers or the objects of their worship. Probably the worshippers are far the most contemptible, for though they are of a rational nature, and have received grace from God, they have set up the worse as the better. And this was the trick of the Evil One, who abused good to an evil purpose, as in most of his evil deeds. For he laid hold of their desire in its wandering in search of God, in order to distort to himself[γ] the power, and steal the desire, leading it by the hand, like a blind man asking a road; and he hurled down and scattered some in one direction and some in another, into one pit of death and destruction.

XVI. This was their course. But reason receiving us in our desire for God, and in our sense of the impossibility of being without a leader and guide, and then making us apply ourselves to things visible and meeting with the things which have been since the beginning, doth not stay its course even here. For it was not the part of Wisdom to grant the sovereignty to things which are, as observation tells us, of equal rank. By these then it leads to that which is above these, and by which being is given to these. For what is it which ordered things in heaven and things in earth, and those which pass through air, and those which live in water; or rather the things which were before these, heaven and earth, air and water? Who mingled these, and who distributed them? What is it that each has in common with the other, and their mutual dependence and agreement? For I commend the man, though he was a heathen, who said, What gave movement to these, and drives their ceaseless and unhindered motion? Is it not the Artificer of them Who implanted reason in them all, in accordance with which the Universe is moved and controlled? Is it not He who made them and brought them into being? For we cannot attribute such a power to the Accidental. For, suppose that its existence is accidental, to what will you let us ascribe its order? And if you like we will grant you this: to what then will you ascribe its preservation and protection in accordance with the terms of its first creation. Do these belong to the Accidental, or to something else? Surely not to the Accidental. And what can this Something Else be but God? Thus reason that proceeds from God, that is implanted in all from the beginning and is the first law in us, and is bound up in all, leads us up to God through visible things. Let us begin again, and reason this out.

XVII. What God is in nature and essence, no man ever yet has discovered or can discover. Whether it will ever be discovered is a question which he who will may examine and decide. In my opinion it will be discovered when that within us which is godlike and divine, I mean our mind and reason, shall have mingled with its Like, and the image shall have ascended to the Archetype, of which it has now the desire. And this I think is the solution of that vexed problem as to "We shall know even as we are known."[α] But in our present life all that comes to us is but a little effluence, and as it were a small effulgence from a great Light. So that if anyone has known God, or has had the testimony of Scripture to his knowledge of God, we are to understand such an one to have possessed a degree of knowledge which gave him the appearance of being more fully enlightened than another who did not enjoy the same degree of illumination; and this relative superiority is spoken of as if it were absolute knowledge, not because it is really such, but by comparison with the power of that other.

XVIII. Thus Enos "hoped to call upon the Name of the Lord."[β] Hope was that for which he is commended; and that, not that he should *know* God, but that he should *call upon* him. And Enoch was translated,[γ] but it is not yet clear whether it was because he already comprehended the Divine Nature, or in order that he might comprehend it. And

α Referring to the mythical partition of the Universe, which gave heaven to Zeus, the sea to Poseidon, and the infernal regions to Aidoneus.

β Rom. i. 23.

γ It was a very general belief in the early Church that the gods whom the heathen worshipped were in reality actual evil spirits; and this belief is certainly supported by S. Paul's argument about εἰδωλόθυτον in 1 Cor. x. 19–21.

α 1 Cor. xiii. 12, but with a reading ἐπιγνώσεσθε, which is not in the New Testament.

β Gen. iv. 26. The verb has by some been taken as passive, and not middle, "hoped that the Name of the Lord would be called upon."

γ Ib. v. 24, Ecclus. xlix. 14.

Noah's[α] glory was that he was pleasing to God; he who was entrusted with the saving of the whole world from the waters, or rather of the Seeds of the world, escaped the Deluge in a small Ark. And Abraham, great Patriarch though he was, was justified by faith,[β] and offered a strange victim,[γ] the type of the Great Sacrifice. Yet he saw not God as God, but gave Him food as a man.[δ] He was approved because he worshipped as far as he comprehended.[ε] And Jacob dreamed of a lofty ladder and stair of Angels, and in a mystery anointed a pillar[ζ]—perhaps to signify the Rock that was anointed for our sake—and gave to a place the name of The House of God[η] in honour of Him whom he saw; and wrestled with God in human form; whatever this wrestling of God with man may mean . . . possibly it refers to the comparison of man's virtue with God's; and he bore on his body the marks of the wrestling, setting forth the defeat of the created nature; and for a reward of his reverence he received a change of his name; being named, instead of Jacob, Israel—that great and honourable name. Yet neither he nor any one on his behalf, unto this day, of all the Twelve Tribes who where his children, could boast that he comprehended the whole nature or the pure sight of God.

XIX. To Elias neither the strong wind, nor the fire, nor the earthquake, as you learn from the story,[θ] but a light breeze adumbrated the Presence of God, and not even this His Nature. And who was this Elias? The man whom a chariot of fire took up to heaven, signifying the superhuman excellency of the righteous man. And are you not amazed at Manoah the Judge of yore, and at Peter the disciple in later days; the one being unable to endure the sight even of one in whom was a representation of God; and saying, "We are undone, O wife, we have seen God;"[κ] speaking as though even a vision of God could not be grasped by human beings, let alone the Nature of God; and the other unable to endure the Presence of Christ in his boat and therefore bidding Him depart;[λ] and this though Peter was more zealous than the others for the knowledge of Christ, and received a blessing for this,[α] and was entrusted with the greatest gifts. What would you say of Isaiah or Ezekiel, who was an eyewitness of very great mysteries, and of the other Prophets; for one of these saw the Lord of Sabaoth sitting on the Throne of glory,[β] and encircled and praised and hidden by the sixwinged Seraphim, and was himself purged by the live coal, and equipped for his prophetic office. And the other describes the Cherubic Chariot[γ] of God, and the Throne upon them, and the Firmament over it, and Him that shewed Himself in the Firmament, and Voices, and Forces, and Deeds.[δ] And whether this was an appearance by day, only visible to Saints, or an unerring vision of the night, or an impression on the mind holding converse with the future as if it were the present; or some other ineffable form of prophecy, I cannot say; the God of the Prophets knoweth, and they know who are thus inspired. But neither these of whom I am speaking, nor any of their fellows ever stood before the Council[ε] and Essence of God, as it is written, or saw, or proclaimed the Nature of God.

XX. If it had been permitted to Paul to utter what the Third Heaven[ζ] contained, and his own advance, or ascension, or assumption thither, perhaps we should know something more about God's Nature, if this was the mystery of the rapture. But since it was ineffable, we too will honour it by silence. Thus much we will hear Paul say about it, that we know in part and we prophesy in part.[η] This and the like to this are the confessions of one who is not rude in knowledge,[θ] who threatens to give proof of Christ speaking in him, the great doctor and champion of the truth. Wherefore he estimates all knowledge on earth only as through a glass darkly,[κ] as taking its stand upon little images of the truth. Now, unless I appear to anyone too careful, and over anxious about the examination of this matter, perhaps it was of this and nothing else that the Word Himself intimated

---

α Gen. vi. 8. β Ib. xviii. 18. γ Ib. xxviii. 2.

δ Gen. xviii. 2. Elias Cretensis sees in this occurrence a foreshadowing of the Incarnation; and also with many others, a revelation of the Trinity, in that Abraham saw Three and conversed with One. ε Gen. xxxii. 28. ζ Ib. ver. 28.

η v. l. *The Form of God*, which would refer to the occasion cited below. The reading is grammatically easier, as an accusative is required; but in that case we might have expected the wrestling with the Angel to have been mentioned first, as the name Penuel was given by Jacob on the day following the night in which he wrestled, and received his own change of name. The Benedictines, while retaining *House* in text and version, express a preference for *Form*, because the subject of the argument is the Vision of God.

θ 1 Kgs. xix. 11, 12. LXX. has a Sound of a Light breeze.

κ Judg. xiii. 22. λ Luke v. 8.

α Matt. xvi. 16, 17. β Isa. vi. 1 sqq. γ Ezek. i. 4–28.

δ v. l. Orders, i.e. of angels.

ε This is a quotation from the LXX. of Jer. xxiii. 18, where for ὑποστήματι Aquila has ἀπορρήτῳ, and Symmachus ὁμιλίᾳ, (according to Trommius). ὑπόστημα properly means a Station of troops, and such is the meaning in the other two places where the word occurs in the LXX., viz.:—2 Sam. xxiii. 14, and 1 Chron. xi. 16. The Hebrew word which it represents in this passage is one of frequent use, and means "a Council," or, in a sense derived from this, Familiar Intercourse. In Job xv. 8 it is rendered in A. V. The Secret of God, where the LXX. has σύνταγμα. The Vulgate in both cases has Concilium Dei; the Benedictines however render it Substance. A. V. has Counsel, and in marg. Secret; while R. V. reads Council, with no marginal alternative.

ζ 2 Cor. xii. 2. η 1 Cor. xiii. 9.

θ 2 Cor. xi. 6. κ 1 Cor. xiii. 12.

that there were things which could not now be borne, but which should be borne and cleared up hereafter,[α] and which John the Forerunner of the Word and great Voice of the Truth declared even the whole world could not contain.[β]

XXI. The truth then, and the whole Word is full of difficulty and obscurity; and as it were with a small instrument we are undertaking a great work, when with merely human wisdom we pursue the knowledge of the Self-existent, and in company with, or not apart from, the senses, by which we are borne hither and thither, and led into error, we apply ourselves to the search after things which are only to be grasped by the mind, and we are unable by meeting bare realities with bare intellect to approximate somewhat more closely to the truth, and to mould the mind by its concepts.

Now the subject of God is more hard to come at,[γ] in proportion as it is more perfect than any other, and is open to more objections, and the solutions of them are more laborious. For every objection, however small, stops and hinders the course of our argument, and cuts off its further advance, just like men who suddenly check with the rein the horses in full career, and turn them right round by the unexpected shock. Thus Solomon, who was the wisest of all men,[δ] whether before him or in his own time, to whom God gave breadth of heart, and a flood of contemplation, more abundant than the sand, even he, the more he entered into the depth, the more dizzy he became, and declared the furthest point of wisdom to be the discovery of how very far off she was from him.[ε] Paul also tries to arrive at, I will not say the nature of God, for this he knew was utterly impossible, but only the judgments of God; and since he finds no way out, and no halting place in the ascent, and moreover, since the earnest searching of his mind after knowledge does not end in any definite conclusion, because some fresh unattained point is being continually disclosed to him (O marvel, that I have a like experience), he closes his discourse with astonishment, and calls this the riches of God,[ζ] and the depth, and confesses the unsearchableness of the judgments of God, in almost the very words of David, who at one time calls God's judgments the great deep whose foundations cannot be reached by measure or sense;[η] and at another says that His knowledge of him and of his own constitution was marvellous,[θ] and had attained greater strength than was in his own power or grasp.

XXII. For if, he says, I leave everything else alone, and consider myself and the whole nature and constitution of man, and how we are mingled, and what is our movement, and how the mortal was compounded with the immortal, and how it is that I flow downwards, and yet am borne upwards, and how the soul is circumscribed;[α] and how it gives life and shares in feelings; and how the mind is at once circumscribed and unlimited,[β] abiding in us and yet travelling over the Universe in swift motion and flow; how it is both received and imparted by word, and passes through air, and enters with all things; how it shares in sense, and enshrouds itself away from sense. And even before these questions—what was our first moulding and composition in the workshop of nature, and what is our last formation and completion? What is the desire for and imparting of nourishment, and who brought us spontaneously to those first springs and sources of life? How is the body nourished by food, and the soul by reason? What is the drawing of nature, and the mutual relation between parents and children, that it should be held together by a spell of love? How is it that species are permanent, and are different in their characteristics, although there are so many that their individual marks cannot be described? How is it that the same animal is both mortal and immortal,[γ] the one by decease, the other by coming into being? For one departs, and another takes its place, just like the flow of a river, which is never still, yet ever constant. And you might discuss many more points concerning men's members and parts, and their mutual adaptation both for use and beauty, and how some are connected and others disjoined, some are more excellent and others less comely, some are united and others divided, some contain and others are contained, according to the law and reason of Nature. Much too might be said about voices and ears. How is it that the voice is carried by the vocal organs, and received by the ears, and both are joined by the smiting and resounding of the medium of the air? Much too of the eyes, which have an indescribable communion with visible objects, and which are moved by the will alone, and that together, and are affected exactly as is the mind. For with equal speed the mind is joined to

α John xvi. 12.
β S. John xxi. 25. By a curious slip of the tongue S. Gregory here attributes to the Baptist words of the Evangelist.
γ cf. Petav. de Deo, iii., c. 7. δ 1 Kgs. iii. 12. ε Eccl. vii. 23.
ζ Rom. xi. 23. η Ps. xxxvi. 7. θ Ib. cxxxix. 6.

α v. l. And how the soul is carried round.
β v. l. Invisible
γ Gregory is not here speaking of the immortality of the individual soul, but of that of the Race, which it shares with other animals, and which is effected by continual succession.

the objects of thought, the eye to those of sight. Much too concerning the other senses, not objects of the research of reason. And much concerning our rest in sleep, and the figments of dreams, and of memory and remembrance; of calculation, and anger, and desire; and in a word, all by which this little world called Man is swayed.

XXIII. Shall I reckon up for you the differences of the other animals, both from us and from each other,—differences of nature, and of production, and of nourishment, and of region, and of temper, and as it were of social life? How is it that some are gregarious and others solitary, some herbivorous and others carnivorous, some fierce and others tame, some fond of man and domesticated, others untamable and free? And some we might call bordering on reason and power of learning, while others are altogether destitute of reason, and incapable of being taught. Some with fuller senses, others with less; some immovable, and some with the power of walking, and some very swift, and some very slow; some surpassing in size or beauty, or in one or other of these respects; others very small or very ugly, or both; some strong, others weak, some apt at self-defence, others timid and crafty [a] and others again are unguarded. Some are laborious and thrifty, others altogether idle and improvident. And before we come to such points as these, how is it that some are crawling things, and others upright; some attached to one spot, some amphibious; some delight in beauty and others are unadorned; some are married and some single; some temperate and others intemperate; some have numerous offspring and others not; some are long-lived and others have but short lives? It would be a weary discourse to go through all the details.

XXIV. Look also at the fishy tribe gliding through the waters, and as it were flying through the liquid element, and breathing its own air, but in danger when in contact with ours, as we are in the waters; and mark their habits and dispositions, their intercourse and their births, their size and their beauty, and their affection for places, and their wanderings, and their assemblings and departings, and their properties which so nearly resemble those of the animals that dwell on land; in some cases community, in others contrast of properties, both in name and shape. And consider the tribes of birds, and their varieties of form and colour, both of those which are voiceless and of song-birds. What is the reason of their melody, and from whom came it? Who gave to the grasshopper the lute in his breast, and the songs and chirruping on the branches, when they are moved by the sun to make their midday music, and sing among the groves, and escort the wayfarer with their voices? Who wove the song for the swan when he spreads his wings to the breezes, and makes melody of their rustling? For I will not speak of the forced voices, and all the rest that art contrives against the truth. Whence does the peacock, that boastful bird of Media, get his love of beauty and of praise (for he is fully conscious of his own beauty), so that when he sees any one approaching, or when, as they say, he would make a show before his hens, raising his neck and spreading his tail in circle around him, glittering like gold and studded with stars, he makes a spectacle of his beauty to his lovers with pompous strides? Now Holy Scripture admires the cleverness in weaving even of women, saying, Who gave to woman skill in weaving and cleverness in the art of embroidery? [a] This belongeth to a living creature that hath reason, and exceedeth in wisdom and maketh way even as far as the things of heaven.

XXV. But I would have you marvel at the natural knowledge even of irrational creatures, and if you can, explain its cause. How is it that birds have for nests rocks and trees and roofs, and adapt them both for safety and beauty, and suitably for the comfort of their nurslings? Whence do bees and spiders get their love of work and art, by which the former plan their honeycombs, and join them together by hexagonal and co-ordinate tubes, and construct the foundation by means of a partition and an alternation of the angles with straight lines; and this, as is the case, in such dusky hives and dark combs; and the latter weave their intricate webs by such light and almost airy threads stretched in divers ways, and this from almost invisible beginnings, to be at once a precious dwelling, and a trap for weaker creatures with a view to enjoyment of food? What Euclid ever imitated these, while pursuing philosophical enquiries with lines that have no real existence, and wearying himself with demonstrations? From what Palamedes came the tactics, and, as the saying is, the movements and configurations of cranes, and the systems of their movement in ranks and their complicated flight? Who were their Phidiæ and Zeuxides, and who were the Parrhasii and Aglaophons who knew how to draw and mould excessively beautiful things? What

a The Benedictines here insert Some well protected: but it is their own conjecture, and is not found in the Manuscripts.

a Job xxxviii. 36. LXX.

harmonious Gnossian chorus of Dædalus, wrought for a girl[a] to the highest pitch of beauty? What Cretan Labyrinth, hard to get through, hard to unravel, as the poets say, and continually crossing itself through the tricks of its construction? I will not speak of the ants' storehouses and storekeepers, and of their treasurings of wood in quantities corresponding to the time for which it is wanted, and all the other details which we know are told of their marches and leaders and their good order in their works.

XXVI. If this knowledge has come within your reach and you are familiar with these branches of science, look at the differences of plants also, up to the artistic fashion of the leaves, which is adapted both to give the utmost pleasure to the eye, and to be of the greatest advantage to the fruit. Look too at the variety and lavish abundance of fruits, and most of all at the wondrous beauty of such as are most necessary. And consider the power of roots, and juices, and flowers, and odours, not only so very sweet, but also serviceable as medicines; and the graces and qualities of colours; and again the costly value, and the brilliant transparency of precious stones. Since nature has set before you all things as in an abundant banquet free to all, both the necessaries and the luxuries of life, in order that, if nothing else, you may at any rate know God by His benefits, and by your own sense of want be made wiser than you were. Next, I pray you, traverse the length and breadth of earth, the common mother of all, and the gulfs of the sea bound together with one another and with the land, and the beautiful forests, and the rivers and springs abundant and perennial, not only of waters cold and fit for drinking, and on the surface of the earth; but also such as running beneath the earth, and flowing under caverns, are then forced out by a violent blast, and repelled, and then filled with heat by this violence of strife and repulsion, burst out by little and little wherever they get a chance, and hence supply our need of hot baths in many parts of the earth, and in conjunction with the cold give us a healing which is without cost and spontaneous. Tell me how and whence are these things? What is this great web unwrought by art? These things are no less worthy of admiration, in respect of their mutual relations than when considered separately.

How is it that the earth stands solid and unswerving? On what is it supported? What is it that props it up, and on what does that rest? For indeed even reason has nothing to lean upon, but only the Will of God. And how is it that part of it is drawn up into mountain summits, and part laid down in plains, and this in various and differing ways? And because the variations are individually small, it both supplies our needs more liberally, and is more beautiful by its variety; part being distributed into habitations, and part left uninhabited, namely all the great height of Mountains, and the various clefts of its coast line cut off from it. Is not this the clearest proof of the majestic working of God?

XXVII. And with respect to the Sea even if I did not marvel at its greatness, yet I should have marvelled at its gentleness, in that although loose it stands within its boundaries; and if not at its gentleness, yet surely at its greatness; but since I marvel at both, I will praise the Power that is in both. What collected it? What bounded it? How is it raised and lulled to rest, as though respecting its neighbour earth? How, moreover, does it receive all the rivers, and yet remain the same, through the very superabundance of its immensity, if that term be permissible? How is the boundary of it, though it be an element of such magnitude, only sand? Have your natural philosophers with their knowledge of useless details anything to tell us, those men I mean who are really endeavouring to measure the sea with a wineglass, and such mighty works by their own conceptions? Or shall I give the really scientific explanation of it from Scripture concisely, and yet more satisfactorily and truly than by the longest arguments? "He hath fenced the face of the water with His command."[a] This is the chain of fluid nature. And how doth He bring upon it the Nautilus that inhabits the dry land (i.e., man) in a little vessel, and with a little breeze (dost thou not marvel at the sight of this,—is not thy mind astonished?), that earth and sea may be bound together by needs and commerce, and that things so widely separated by nature should be thus brought together into one for man? What are the first fountains of springs? Seek, O man, if you can trace out or find any of these things. And who was it who cleft the plains and the mountains for the rivers, and gave them an unhindered course? And how comes the marvel on the other side, that the Sea never overflows, nor the Rivers cease to flow? And what is the nourishing power

[a] The allusion is to a group made by Dædalus for Ariadne, representing a chorus of youths and maidens, which seemed to be moving in musical rhythm. It is described by Homer (Il., xviii., 592 sqq.).

[a] Job xxvi. 10. LXX.

of water, and what the difference therein; for some things are irrigated from above, and others drink from their roots, if I may luxuriate a little in my language when speaking of the luxuriant gifts of God.

XXVIII. And now, leaving the earth and the things of earth, soar into the air on the wings of thought, that our argument may advance in due path; and thence I will take you up to heavenly things, and to heaven itself, and things which are above heaven; for to that which is beyond my discourse hesitates to ascend, but still it shall ascend as far as may be. Who poured forth the air, that great and abundant wealth, not measured to men by their rank or fortunes; not restrained by boundaries; not divided out according to people's ages; but like the distribution of the Manna,[a] received in sufficiency, and valued for its equality of distribution; the chariot of the winged creation; the seat of the winds; the moderator of the seasons; the quickener of living things, or rather the preserver of natural life in the body; in which bodies have their being, and by which we speak; in which is the light and all that it shines upon, and the sight which flows through it? And mark, if you please, what follows. I cannot give to the air the whole empire of all that is thought to belong to the air. What are the storehouses of the winds?[β] What are the treasuries of the snow? Who, as Scripture hath said, hath begotten the drops of dew? Out of Whose womb came the ice? and Who bindeth the waters in the clouds, and, fixing part in the clouds (O marvel!) held by His Word though its nature is to flow, poureth out the rest upon the face of the whole earth, and scattereth it abroad in due season, and in just proportions, and neither suffereth the whole substance of moisture to go out free and uncontrolled (for sufficient was the cleansing in the days of Noah; and He who cannot lie is not forgetful of His own covenant); . . . nor yet restraineth it entirely that we should not again stand in need of an Elias[γ] to bring the drought to an end. If He shall shut up heaven, it saith, who shall open it? If He open the floodgates, who shall shut them up?[δ] Who can bring an excess or withhold a sufficiency of rain, unless he govern the Universe by his own measures and balances? What scientific laws, pray, can you lay down concerning thunder and lightning, O you who thunder from the earth, and cannot shine with even little sparks of truth? To what vapours from earth will you attribute the creation of cloud, or is it due to some thickening of the air, or pressure or crash of clouds of excessive rarity, so as to make you think the pressure the cause of the lightning, and the crash that which makes the thunder? Or what compression of wind having no outlet will account to you for the lightning by its compression, and for the thunder by its bursting out?

Now if you have in your thought passed through the air and all the things of air, reach with me to heaven and the things of heaven. And let faith lead us rather than reason, if at least you have learnt the feebleness of the latter in matters nearer to you, and have known reason by knowing the things that are beyond reason, so as not to be altogether on the earth or of the earth, because you are ignorant even of your ignorance.

XXIX. Who spread the sky around us, and set the stars in order? Or rather, first, can you tell me, of your own knowledge of the things in heaven, what *are* the sky and the stars; you who know not what lies at your very feet, and cannot even take the measure of yourself, and yet must busy yourself about what is above your nature, and gape at the illimitable? For, granted that you understand orbits and periods, and waxings and wanings, and settings and risings, and some degrees and minutes, and all the other things which make you so proud of your wonderful knowledge; you have not arrived at comprehension of the realities themselves, but only at an observation of some movement, which, when confirmed by longer practice, and drawing the observations of many individuals into one generalization, and thence deducing a law, has acquired the name of Science (just as the lunar phenomena have become generally known to our sight), being the basis of this knowledge. But if you are very scientific on this subject, and have a just claim to admiration, tell me what is the cause of this order and this movement. How came the sun to be a beacon-fire to the whole world, and to all eyes like the leader of some chorus, concealing all the rest of the stars by his brightness, more completely than some of them conceal others. The proof of this is that they shine against him, but he outshines them and does not even allow it to be perceived that they rose simultaneously with him, fair as a bridegroom, swift and great as a giant[a]—for I will not let his praises be sung from any other source than my own

[a] Exod. xvi. 18.
[β] Job xxxvii. 9, 10.
[γ] 1 Kgs. xviii. 44.
[δ] Job. xii. 14

[a] Ps. xix. 5.

Scriptures—so mighty in strength that from one end to the other of the world he embraces all things in his heat, and there is nothing hid from the feeling thereof, but it fills both every eye with light, and every embodied creature with heat; warming, yet not burning, by the gentleness of its temper, and the order of its movement, present to all, and equally embracing all.

XXX. Have you considered the importance of the fact that a heathen writer [a] speaks of the sun as holding the same position among material objects as God does among objects of thought? For the one gives light to the eyes, as the Other does to the mind; and is the most beautiful of the objects of sight, as God is of those of thought. But who gave him motion at first? And what is it which ever moves him in his circuit, though in his nature stable and immovable, truly unwearied, and the giver and sustainer of life, and all the rest of the titles which the poets justly sing of him, and never resting in his course or his benefits? How comes he to be the creator of day when above the earth, and of night when below it? or whatever may be the right expression when one contemplates the sun? What are the mutual aggressions and concessions of day and night, and their regular irregularities—to use a somewhat strange expression? How comes he to be the maker and divider of the seasons, that come and depart in regular order, and as in a dance interweave with each other, or stand apart by a law of love on the one hand, and of order on the other, and mingle little by little, and steal on their neighbour, just as nights and days do, so as not to give us pain by their suddenness. This will be enough about the sun.

Do you know the nature and phenomena of the Moon, and the measures and courses of light, and how it is that the sun bears rule over the day, and the moon presides over the night; and while She gives confidence to wild beasts, He stirs Man up to work, raising or lowering himself as may be most serviceable? Know you the bond of Pleiades, or the fence of Orion,[β] as He who counteth the number of the stars and calleth them all by their names? [γ] Know you the differences of the glory [δ] of each, and the order of their movement, that I should trust you, when by them you weave the web of human concerns, and arm the creature against the Creator?

XXXI. What say you? Shall we pause here, after discussing nothing further than matter and visible things, or, since the Word knows the Tabernacle of Moses to be a figure of the whole creation—I mean the entire system of things visible and invisible—shall we pass the first veil, and stepping beyond the realm of sense, shall we look into the Holy Place, the Intellectual and Celestial creation? But not even this can we see in an incorporeal way, though it is incorporeal, since it is called—or is—Fire and Spirit. For He is said to make His Angels spirits, and His Ministers a flame of fire [a] . . . though perhaps this "making" means preserving by that Word by which they came into existence. The Angel then is called spirit and fire; Spirit, as being a creature of the intellectual sphere; Fire, as being of a purifying nature; for I know that the same names belong to the First Nature. But, relatively to us at least, we must reckon the Angelic Nature incorporeal, or at any rate as nearly so as possible. Do you see how we get dizzy over this subject, and cannot advance to any point, unless it be as far as this, that we know there are Angels and Archangels, Thrones, Dominions, Princedoms, Powers, Splendours, Ascents, Intelligent Powers or Intelligencies, pure natures and unalloyed, immovable to evil, or scarcely movable; ever circling in chorus round the First Cause (or how should we sing their praises?) illuminated thence with the purest Illumination, or one in one degree and one in another, proportionally to their nature and rank . . . so conformed to beauty and moulded that they become secondary Lights, and can enlighten others by the overflowings and largesses of the First Light? Ministrants of God's Will, strong with both inborn and imparted strength, traversing all space, readily present to all at any place through their zeal for ministry and the agility of their nature . . . different individuals of them embracing different parts of the world, or appointed over different districts of the Universe, as He knoweth who ordered and distributed it all. Combining all things in one, solely with a view to the consent of the Creator of all things; Hymners of the Majesty of the Godhead, eternally contemplating the Eternal Glory, not that God may thereby gain an increase of glory, for nothing can be added to that which is full —to Him, who supplies good to all outside Himself—but that there may never be a cessation of blessings to these first natures after God. If we have told these things as they deserve, it is by the grace of the Trinity, and of the one Godhead in Three Persons; but if less perfectly than we have desired, yet even so our discourse has gained its purpose. For

α Plato.
β Job xxxviii. 31.
γ Ps. cxlvii. 4.
δ 1 Cor. xv. 41.

a Ps. civ. 4.

this is what we were labouring to shew, that even the secondary natures surpass the power of our intellect; much more then the First and (for I fear to say merely That which is above all), the only Nature.

XXIX. THE THIRD THEOLOGICAL ORATION.

On the Son.

I. This then is what might be said to cut short our opponents' readiness to argue and their hastiness with its consequent insecurity in all matters, but above all in those discussions which relate to God. But since to rebuke others is a matter of no difficulty whatever, but a very easy thing, which any one who likes can do; whereas to substitute one's own belief for theirs is the part of a pious and intelligent man; let us, relying on the Holy Ghost, Who among them is dishonoured, but among us is adored, bring forth to the light our own conceptions about the Godhead, whatever these may be, like some noble and timely birth. Not that I have at other times been silent; for on this subject alone I am full of youthful strength and daring; but the fact is that under present circumstances I am even more bold to declare the truth, that I may not (to use the words of Scripture) by drawing back fall into the condemnation of being displeasing to God.[a] And since every discourse is of a twofold nature, the one part establishing one's own, and the other overthrowing one's opponents' position; let us first of all state our own position, and then try to controvert that of our opponents;—and both as briefly as possible, so that our arguments may be taken in at a glance (like those of the elementary treatises which they have devised to deceive simple or foolish persons), and that our thoughts may not be scattered by reason of the length of the discourse, like water which is not contained in a channel, but flows to waste over the open land.

II. The three most ancient opinions concerning God are Anarchia, Polyarchia, and Monarchia. The first two are the sport of the children of Hellas, and may they continue to be so. For Anarchy is a thing without order; and the Rule of Many is factious, and thus anarchical, and thus disorderly. For both these tend to the same thing, namely disorder; and this to dissolution, for disorder is the first step to dissolution.

a Heb. ii. 4; x. 38.

But Monarchy is that which we hold in honour. It is, however, a Monarchy that is not limited to one Person, for it is possible for Unity if at variance with itself to come into a condition of plurality;[a] but one which is made of an equality of Nature and a Union of mind, and an identity of motion, and a convergence of its elements to unity—a thing which is impossible to the created nature—so that though numerically distinct there is no severance of Essence. Therefore Unity[β] having from all eternity arrived by motion at Duality, found its rest in Trinity. This is what we mean by Father and Son and Holy Ghost. The Father is the Begetter and the Emitter;[γ] without passion, of course, and without reference to time, and not in a corporeal manner. The Son is the Begotten, and the Holy Ghost the Emission; for I know not how this could be expressed in terms altogether excluding visible things. For we shall not venture to speak of "an overflow of goodness," as one of the Greek Philosophers dared to say, as if it were a bowl overflowing, and this in plain words in his Discourse on the First and Second Causes.[δ] Let us not ever look on this Generation as involuntary, like some natural overflow, hard to be retained, and by no means befitting our conception of Deity. Therefore let us confine ourselves within our limits, and speak of the Unbegotten and the Begotten and That which proceeds from the Father, as somewhere God the Word Himself saith.

III. When did these come into being? They are above all "When." But, if I am to speak with something more of boldness,—when the Father did. And when did the Father come into being. There never was a time when He was not. And the same thing is true of the Son and the Holy Ghost. Ask me again, and again I will answer you, When was the Son

α Billius and others here read Authority, which is not supported by the best MSS., or by the context.

β Elias explains this to mean that of old men knew only One Person in the Godhead: and until the Incarnation this knowledge was sufficient; but from that time forward they acknowledged a Second Person, and through Him a Third also, the Holy Ghost. But this explanation falls far short of Gregory's meaning, which certainly is that the movement of selfconsciousness in God from all Eternity made the Generation of the Son, and the Procession of the Holy Ghost, a necessity. All is objective in God. cf. Petav. de Deo, II., viii., 16; also, Greg. Naz., Or. xxiii. 5.

γ προβολεὺς–προβολὴ was a term used by the Gnostics to describe the Emanations by which the distance between the Finite and the Infinite was according to them bridged over; and on this account it fell under suspicion. and was rejected by both Arius and Athanasius. Tertullian used it with an explanation which is satisfactory as regards the προβολὴ of the Son; but when he comes to apply it to the Procession of the Holy Ghost he uses an illustration which is in almost the very words rejected by Gregory (c. Prax., 7, 8. See Swete, p. 56). Origen did not admit it. Later when this danger was past, the word came into use again as the equivalent of ἐκπόρευσις, at first with reserve and explanations in the text, but later on as an accepted term. See Swete "On The Doctrine Of The Holy Spirit," p. 36.

δ The expression is from Plato.

begotten? When the Father was not begotten. And when did the Holy Ghost proceed? When the Son was, not proceeding but, begotten—beyond the sphere of time, and above the grasp of reason; although we cannot set forth that which is above time, if we avoid as we desire any expression which conveys the idea of time. For such expressions as "when" and "before" and "after" and "from the beginning" are not timeless, however much we may force them; unless indeed we were to take the Aeon, that interval which is coextensive with the eternal things, and is not divided or measured by any motion, or by the revolution of the sun, as time is measured.

How then are They not alike unoriginate, if They are coeternal? Because They are from Him, though not after Him. For that which is unoriginate is eternal, but that which is eternal is not necessarily unoriginate, so long as it may be referred to the Father as its origin. Therefore in respect of Cause They are not unoriginate; but it is evident that the Cause is not necessarily prior to its effects, for the sun is not prior to its light. And yet They are in some sense unoriginate, in respect of time, even though you would scare simple minds with your quibbles, for the Sources of Time are not subject to time.

IV. But how can this generation be passionless? In that it is incorporeal. For if corporeal generation involves passion, incorporeal generation excludes it. And I will ask of you in turn, How is He God if He is created? For that which is created is not God. I refrain from reminding you that here too is passion if we take the creation in a bodily sense, as time, desire, imagination, thought, hope, pain, risk, failure, success, all of which and more than all find a place in the creature, as is evident to every one. Nay, I marvel that you do not venture so far as to conceive of marriages and times of pregnancy, and dangers of miscarriage, as if the Father could not have begotten at all if He had not begotten thus; or again, that you did not count up the modes of generation of birds and beasts and fishes, and bring under some one of them the Divine and Ineffable Generation, or even eliminate the Son out of your new hypothesis. And you cannot even see this, that as His Generation according to the flesh differs from all others (for where among men do you know of a Virgin Mother?), so does He differ also in His spiritual Generation; or rather He, Whose Existence is not the same as ours, differs from us also in His Generation.

V. Who then is that Father Who had no beginning? One Whose very Existence had no beginning; for one whose existence had a beginning must also have begun to be a Father. He did not then become a Father after He began to be, for His being had no beginning. And He is Father in the absolute sense, for He is not also Son; just as the Son is Son in the absolute sense, because He is not also Father. These names do not belong to us in the absolute sense, because we are both, and not one more than the other; and we are of both, and not of one only; and so we are divided, and by degrees become men, and perhaps not even men, and such as we did not desire, leaving and being left, so that only the relations remain, without the underlying facts.[α]

But, the objector says, the very form of the expression "He begat" and "He was begotten," brings in the idea of a beginning of generation. But what if you do not use this expression, but say, "He had been begotten from the beginning" so as readily to evade your far-fetched and time-loving objections? Will you bring Scripture against us, as if we were forging something contrary to Scripture and to the truth? Why, every one knows that in practice we very often find tenses interchanged when time is spoken of; and especially is this the custom of Holy Scripture, not only in respect of the past tense, and of the present; but even of the future, as for instance "Why did the heathen rage?"[β] when they had not yet raged; and "they shall cross over the river on foot,"[γ] where the meaning is they did cross over. It would be a long task to reckon up all the expressions of this kind which students have noticed.

VI. So much for this point. What is their next objection, how full of contentiousness and impudence? He, they say, either voluntarily begat the Son, or else involuntarily. Next, as they think, they bind us on both sides with cords; these however are not strong, but very weak. For, they say, if it was involuntarily He was under the sway of some one, and who exercised this sway? And how is He, over whom it is exercised, God? But if voluntarily, the Son is a Son of Will; how then is He of the Father?—and they thus invent a new sort of Mother for him,—the Will,—in place of the Father. There is one good point which they may allege about this argument of theirs; namely, that they desert Passion, and take refuge in Will. For Will is not Passion.

α Elias explains this to refer to the fact that children leave and are left by parents; or else to the death of either one or the other.

β Ps. ii. 1.

γ Ps. lxvi. 6.

Secondly, let us look at the strength of their argument. And it were best to wrestle with them at first at close quarters. You yourself, who so recklessly assert whatever takes your fancy; were you begotten voluntarily or involuntarily by your father? If involuntarily, then he was under some tyrant's sway (O terrible violence!) and who was the tyrant? You will hardly say it was nature,—for nature is tolerant of chastity. If it was voluntarily, then by a few syllables your father is done away with, for you are shewn to be the son of Will, and not of your father. But I pass to the relation between God and the creature, and I put your own question to your own wisdom. Did God *create* all things voluntarily or under compulsion? If under compulsion, here also is the tyranny, and one who played the tyrant; if voluntarily, the creatures also are deprived of their God, and you before the rest, who invent such arguments and tricks of logic. For a partition is set up between the Creator and the creatures in the shape of Will. And yet I think that the Person who wills is distinct from the Act of willing; He who begets from the Act of begetting; the Speaker from the speech, or else we are all very stupid. On the one side we have the mover, and on the other that which is, so to speak, the motion. Thus the thing willed is not the child of will, for it does not always result therefrom; nor is that which is begotten the child of generation, nor that which is heard the child of speech, but of the Person who willed, or begat, or spoke. But the things of God are beyond all this, for with Him perhaps the Will to beget is generation, and there is no intermediate action (if we may accept this altogether, and not rather consider generation superior to will).

VII. Will you then let me play a little upon this word Father, for your example encourages me to be so bold? The Father is God either willingly or unwillingly; and how will you escape from your own excessive acuteness? If willingly, when did He begin to will? It could not have been before He began to be, for there was nothing prior to Him. Or is one part of Him Will and another the object of Will? If so, He is divisible. So the question arises, as the result of your argument, whether He Himself is not the Child of Will. And if unwillingly, what compelled Him to exist, and how is He God if He was compelled—and that to nothing less than to be God? How then was He begotten, says my opponent. How was He created, if as you say, He was created? For this is a part of the same difficulty. Perhaps you would say, By Will and Word. You have not yet solved the whole difficulty; for it yet remains for you to shew how Will and Word gained the power of action. For man was not created in this way.

VIII. How then was He begotten? This Generation would have been no great thing, if you could have comprehended it who have no real knowledge even of your own generation, or at least who comprehend very little of it, and of that little you are ashamed to speak; and then do you think you know the whole? You will have to undergo much labour before you discover the laws of composition, formation, manifestation, and the bond whereby soul is united to body,—mind to soul, and reason to mind; and movement, increase, assimilation of food, sense, memory, recollection, and all the rest of the parts of which you are compounded; and which of them belongs to the soul and body together, and which to each independently of the other, and which is received from each other. For those parts whose maturity comes later, yet received their laws at the time of conception. Tell me what these laws are? And do not even then venture to speculate on the Generation of God; for that would be unsafe. For even if you knew all about your own, yet you do not by any means know about God's. And if you do not understand your own, how can you know about God's? For in proportion as God is harder to trace out than man, so is the heavenly Generation harder to comprehend than your own. But if you assert that because you cannot comprehend it, therefore He cannot have been begotten, it will be time for you to strike out many existing things which you cannot comprehend; and first of all God Himself. For you cannot say what He is, even if you are very reckless, and excessively proud of your intelligence. First, cast away your notions of flow and divisions and sections, and your conceptions of immaterial as if it were material birth, and then you may perhaps worthily conceive of the Divine Generation. How was He begotten?—I repeat the question in indignation. The Begetting of God must be honoured by silence. It is a great thing for you to learn that He was begotten. But the manner of His generation we will not admit that even Angels can conceive, much less you. Shall I tell you how it was? It was in a manner known to the Father Who begat, and to the Son Who was begotten. Anything more than this is hidden by a cloud, and escapes your dim sight.

IX. Well, but the Father begat a Son who

either was or was not in existence.[a] What utter nonsense! This is a question which applies to you or me, who on the one hand were in existence, as for instance Levi in the loins of Abraham;[β] and on the other hand came into existence; and so in some sense we are partly of what existed, and partly of what was non-existent; whereas the contrary is the case with the original matter, which was certainly created out of what was non-existent, notwithstanding that some pretend that it is unbegotten. But in this case "to be begotten," even from the beginning, is concurrent with "to be." On what then will you base this captious question? For what is older than that which is from the beginning, if we may place there the previous existence or non-existence of the Son? In either case we destroy its claim to be the Beginning. Or perhaps you will say, if we were to ask you whether the Father was of existent or non-existent substance, that he is twofold, partly pre-existing, partly existing; or that His case is the same with that of the Son; that is, that He was created out of non-existing matter, because of your ridiculous questions and your houses of sand, which cannot stand against the merest ripple.

I do not admit either solution, and I declare that your question contains an absurdity, and not a difficulty to answer. If however you think, in accordance with your dialectic assumptions, that one or other of these alternatives must necessarily be true in every case, let me ask you one little question: Is time in time, or is it not in time? If it is contained in time, then in what time, and what is it but that time, and how does it contain it? But if it is not contained in time, what is that surpassing wisdom which can conceive of a time which is timeless? Now, in regard to this expression, "I am now telling a lie," admit one of these alternatives, either that it is true, or that it is a falsehood, without qualification (for we cannot admit that it is both). But this cannot be. For necessarily he either is lying, and so is telling the truth, or else he is telling the truth, and so is lying. What wonder is it then that, as in this case contraries are true, so in that case they should both be untrue, and so your clever puzzle prove mere foolishness? Solve me one more riddle. Were you present at your own generation, and are you now present to yourself, or is neither the case? If you were and are present, who were you, and with whom are you present? And how did your single self become thus both subject and object? But if neither of the above is the case, how did you get separated from yourself, and what is the cause of this disjoining? But, you will say, it is stupid to make a fuss about the question whether or no a single individual is present to himself; for the expression is not used of oneself but of others. Well, you may be certain that it is even more stupid to discuss the question whether That which was begotten from the beginning existed before its generation or not. For such a question arises only as to matter divisible by time.

X. But they say, The Unbegotten and the Begotten are not the same; and if this is so, neither is the Son the same as the Father. It is clear, without saying so, that this line of argument manifestly excludes either the Son or the Father from the Godhead. For if to be Unbegotten is the Essence of God, to be begotten is not that Essence; if the opposite is the case, the Unbegotten is excluded. What argument can contradict this? Choose then whichever blasphemy you prefer, my good inventor of a new theology, if indeed you are anxious at all costs to embrace a blasphemy. In the next place, in what sense do you assert that the Unbegotten and the Begotten are not the same? If you mean that the Uncreated and the created are not the same, I agree with you; for certainly the Unoriginate and the created are not of the same nature. But if you say that He That begat and That which is begotten are not the same, the statement is inaccurate. For it is in fact a necessary truth that they are the same. For the nature of the relation of Father to Child is this, that the offspring is of the same nature with the parent. Or we may argue thus again. What do you mean by Unbegotten and Begotten, for if you mean the simple fact of being unbegotten or begotten, these are not the same; but if you mean Those to Whom these terms apply, how are They not the same? For example, Wisdom and Unwisdom are not the same in themselves, but yet both are attributes of man, who is the same; and they mark not a difference of essence, but one external to the essence.[a] Are immortality and innocence and immutability also the essence of God? If so God has many essences and not one; or Deity is a compound of these. For He cannot be all these without composition, if they be essences.

XI. They do not however assert this, for these qualities are common also to other beings.

a This is the Arian dilemma, "Did the Son exist before he was begotten?"

β Heb. vii. 10.

a cf. Petavius De Trin., V. ii., 2.

But God's Essence is that which belongs to God alone, and is proper to Him. But they, who consider matter and form to be unbegotten, would not allow that to be unbegotten is the property of God alone (for we must cast away even further the darkness of the Manichæans.[a] But suppose that it is the property of God alone. What of Adam? Was he not alone the direct creature of God? Yes, you will say. Was he then the only human being? By no means. And why, but because humanity does not consist in direct creation? For that which is begotten is also human. Just so neither is He Who is Unbegotten alone God, though He alone is Father. But grant that He Who is Begotten is God; for He is *of* God, as you must allow, even though you cling to your Unbegotten. Then how do you describe the Essence of God? Not by declaring what it is, but by rejecting what it is not. For your word signifies that He is not begotten; it does not present to you what is the real nature or condition of that which has no generation. What then *is* the Essence of God? It is for your infatuation to define this, since you are so anxious about His Generation too; but to us it will be a very great thing, if ever, even in the future, we learn this, when this darkness and dulness is done away for us, as He has promised Who cannot lie. This then may be the thought and hope of those who are purifying themselves with a view to this. Thus much we for our part will be bold to say, that if it is a great thing for the Father to be Unoriginate, it is no less a thing for the Son to have been Begotten of such a Father. For not only would He share the glory of the Unoriginate, since he is of the Unoriginate, but he has the added glory of His Generation, a thing so great and august in the eyes of all those who are not altogether grovelling and material in mind.

XII. But, they say, if the Son is the Same as the Father in respect of Essence, then if the Father is unbegotten, the Son must be so likewise. Quite so—if the Essence of God consists in being unbegotten; and so He would be a strange mixture, begottenly unbegotten. If, however, the difference is outside the Essence, how can you be so certain in speaking of this? Are you also your father's father, so as in no respect to fall short of your father, since you are the same with him in essence? Is it not evident that our enquiry into the Nature of the Essence of God, if we make it, will leave Personality absolutely unaffected? But that Unbegotten is not a synonym of God is proved thus. If it were so, it would be necessary that since God is a relative term, Unbegotten should be so likewise; or that since Unbegotten is an absolute term, so must God be. . . . God of no one. For words which are absolutely identical are similarly applied. But the word Unbegotten is not used relatively. For to what is it relative? And of what things is God the God? Why, of all things. How then can God and Unbegotten be identical terms? And again, since Begotten and Unbegotten are contradictories, like possession and deprivation, it would follow that contradictory essences would co-exist, which is impossible.[a] Or again, since possessions are prior to deprivations, and the latter are destructive of the former, not only must the Essence of the Son be prior to that of the Father, but it must be destroyed by the Father, on your hypothesis.

XIII. What now remains of their invincible arguments? Perhaps the last they will take refuge in is this. If God has never ceased to beget, the Generation is imperfect; and when will He cease? But if He has ceased, then He must have begun. Thus again these carnal minds bring forward carnal arguments. Whether He is eternally begotten or not, I do not yet say, until I have looked into the statement, "Before all the hills He begetteth Me,"[β] more accurately. But I cannot see the necessity of their conclusion. For if, as they say, everything that is to come to an end had also a beginning, then surely that which has no end had no beginning. What then will they decide concerning the soul, or the Angelic nature? If it had a beginning, it will also have an end; and if it has no end, it is evident that according to them it had no beginning. But the truth is that it had a beginning, and will never have an end. Their assertion, then, that that which will have an end had also a beginning, is untrue. Our position, however, is, that as in the case of a horse, or an ox, or a man, the same definition applies to all the individuals of the same species, and whatever shares the definition has also a right to the Name; so in the very same way there is One Essence of God, and One Nature, and One Name; although in accordance with a distinction in our thoughts we use distinct Names; and that whatever is properly called by this Name really is God; and what He is in Nature, That He is truly called—if at

α The Manichæans, who believed in two eternal principles of good and evil, light and darkness, held that darkness too was unbegotten (Elias).

α Because "Son" implies "begotten." But (ex hyp.) "Unbegotten" is synonymous with "God."

β Prov. viii. 25.

least we are to hold that Truth is a matter not of names but of realities. But our opponents, as if they were afraid of leaving any stone unturned to subvert the Truth, acknowledge indeed that the Son is God when they are compelled to do so by arguments[a] and evidences; but they only mean that He is God in an ambiguous sense, and that He only shares the Name.

XIV. And when we advance this objection against them, "What do you mean to say then? That the Son is not properly God, just as a picture of an animal is not properly an animal? And if not properly God, in what sense is He God at all?" They reply, Why should not these terms be ambiguous, and in both cases be used in a proper sense? And they will give us such instances as the land-dog and the dogfish; where the word Dog is ambiguous, and yet in both cases is properly used, for there is such a species among the ambiguously named, or any other case in which the same appellative is used for two things of different nature. But, my good friend, in this case, when you include two natures under the same name, you do not assert that either is better than the other, or that the one is prior and the other posterior, or that one is in a greater degree and the other in a lesser that which is predicated of them both, for there is no connecting link which forces this necessity upon them. One is not a dog more than the other, and one less so; either the dogfish more than the land-dog, or the land-dog than the dogfish. Why should they be, or on what principle? But the community of name is here between things of equal value, though of different nature. But in the case of which we are speaking, you couple the Name of God with adorable Majesty, and make It surpass every essence and nature (an attribute of God alone), and then you ascribe this Name to the Father, while you deprive the Son of it, and make Him subject to the Father, and give Him only a secondary honour and worship; and even if in words you bestow on Him one which is Equal, yet in practice you cut off His Deity, and pass malignantly from a use of the same Name implying an exact equality, to one which connects things which are not equal. And so the pictured and the living man are in your mouth an apter illustration of the relations of Deity than the dogs which I instanced. Or else you must concede to both an equal dignity of nature as well as a common name—even though you introduced these natures into your argument as different; and thus you destroy the analogy of your dogs, which you invented as an instance of inequality. For what is the force of your instance of ambiguity, if those whom you distinguish are not equal in honour? For it was not to prove an equality but an inequality that you took refuge in your dogs. How could anybody be more clearly convicted of fighting both against his own arguments, and against the Deity?

XV. And if, when we admit that in respect of being the Cause the Father is greater than the Son, they should assume the premiss that He is the Cause by Nature, and then deduce the conclusion that He is greater by Nature also, it is difficult to say whether they mislead most themselves or those with whom they are arguing. For it does not absolutely follow that all that is predicated of a class can also be predicated of all the individuals composing it; for the different particulars may belong to different individuals. For what hinders me, if I assume the same premiss, namely, that the Father is greater by Nature, and then add this other, Yet not by nature in every respect greater nor yet Father—from concluding, Therefore the Greater is not in every respect greater, nor the Father in every respect Father? Or, if you prefer it, let us put it in this way: God is an Essence: But an Essence is not in every case God; and draw the conclusion for yourself—Therefore God is not in every case God. I think the fallacy here is the arguing from a conditioned to an unconditioned use of a term,[a] to use the technical expression of the logicians. For while we assign this word Greater to His Nature viewed as a Cause, they infer it of His Nature viewed in itself. It is just as if when we said that such a one was a dead man they were to infer simply that he was a Man.

XVI. How shall we pass over the following point, which is no less amazing than the rest? Father, they say, is a name either of an essence or of an Action, thinking to bind us down on both sides. If we say that it is a name of an essence, they will say that we agree with them that the Son is of another Essence, since there is but one Essence of God, and this, according to them, is preoccupied by the Father. On the other hand, if we say that it is the name of an Action, we shall be

[a] The Benedictines here translate λόγῳ by "Scripture," on the ground that Reason is not competent to assert the Divinity of the Word.

[a] Or as the schoolmen say the fallacy is, A dicto secundum quid ad dictum simpliciter, one of the many forms of Undistributed Middle Term. Petavius, however (De Trin., II., v., 12), pronounces the argument of this section unsatisfactory.

supposed to acknowledge plainly that the Son is created and not begotten. For where there is an Agent there must also be an Effect. And they will say they wonder how that which is made can be identical with That which made it. I should myself have been frightened with your distinction, if it had been necessary to accept one or other of the alternatives, and not rather put both aside, and state a third and truer one, namely, that Father is not a name either of an essence or of an action, most clever sirs. But it is the name of the Relation in which the Father stands to the Son, and the Son to the Father. For as with us these names make known a genuine and intimate relation, so, in the case before us too, they denote an identity of nature between Him That is begotten and Him That begets. But let us concede to you that Father is a name of essence, it will still bring in the idea of Son, and will not make it of a different nature, according to common ideas and the force of these names. Let it be, if it so please you, the name of an action; you will not defeat us in this way either. The Homoousion would be indeed the result of this action, or otherwise the conception of an action in this matter would be absurd. You see then how, even though you try to fight unfairly, we avoid your sophistries. But now, since we have ascertained how invincible you are in your arguments and sophistries, let us look at your strength in the Oracles of God, if perchance you may choose to persuade us out of them.

XVII. For we have learnt to believe in and to teach the Deity of the Son from their great and lofty utterances. And what utterances are these? These: God—The Word—He That Was In The Beginning and With The Beginning, and The Beginning. "In the Beginning was The Word, and the Word was with God, and the Word was God,"[α] and "With Thee is the Beginning,"[β] and "He who calleth her The Beginning from generations."[γ] Then the Son is Only-begotten: The only "begotten Son which is in the bosom of the Father, it says, He hath declared Him."[δ] The Way, the Truth, the Life, the Light. "I am the Way, the Truth, and the Life;" and "I am the Light of the World."[ε] Wisdom and Power, "Christ, the Wisdom of God, and the Power of God."[ζ] The Effulgence, the Impress, the Image, the Seal; "Who being the Effulgence of His glory and the Impress of His Essence,"[α] and "the Image of His Goodness,"[β] and "Him hath God the Father sealed."[γ] Lord, King, He That Is, The Almighty. "The Lord rained down fire from the Lord;"[δ] and "A sceptre of righteousness is the sceptre of Thy Kingdom;"[ε] and "Which is and was and is to come, the Almighty"[ζ]—all which are clearly spoken of the Son, with all the other passages of the same force, none of which is an afterthought, or added later to the Son or the Spirit, any more than to the Father Himself. For Their Perfection is not affected by additions. There never was a time when He was without the Word, or when He was not the Father, or when He was not true, or not wise, or not powerful, or devoid of life, or of splendour, or of goodness.

But in opposition to all these, do you reckon up for me the expressions which make for your ignorant arrogance, such as "My God and your God,"[η] or greater, or created, or made, or sanctified;[θ] Add, if you like, Servant[κ] and Obedient[λ] and Gave[μ] and Learnt,[ν] and was commanded,[ξ] was sent,[ο] can do nothing of Himself, either say, or judge, or give, or will.[π] And further these,—His ignorance,[ρ] subjection,[σ] prayer,[τ] asking,[υ] increase,[φ] being made perfect.[χ] And if you like even more humble than these; such as speak of His sleeping,[ψ] hungering,[ω] being in an agony,[αα] and fearing;[ββ] or perhaps you would make even His Cross and Death a matter of reproach to Him. His Resurrection and Ascension I fancy you will leave to me, for in these is found something to support *our* position. A good many other things too you might pick up, if you desire to put together that equivocal and intruded god of yours, Who to us is True God, and equal to the Father. For every one of these points, taken separately, may very easily, if we go through them one by one, be explained to you in the most reverent sense, and the stumbling-block of the letter be cleansed away—that is, if your stumbling at it be honest, and not wilfully malicious. To give you the explanation in one sentence. What is lofty you are to apply to the Godhead, and to that Nature in Him which is superior to sufferings and incorporeal; but all that is lowly to the composite condition[γγ] of Him who for your

α John i. 1. β Ps. cx. 3. γ Isa. xli. 4. δ John i. 18. ε John vii. 12; ix. 5; xiv. 6. ζ 1 Cor. i. 24.

α Heb. i. 3 R. V. β Wisd. vii. 26. γ John vi. 27. δ Gen. xix. 24. ε Ps. xlv. 6 ζ Rev. i. 8. η John xx. 17, 28. θ Prov. viii. 22; John x. 36; Acts ii. 36. κ Phil. ii. 7. λ Phil. ii. 8. μ John i. 12. ν Heb. v. 8. ξ John x. 18; xiv. 31. ο Ib. iv. 34; v. 23, sq. π Ib. v. 19, 30. ρ Mark xiii. 32. σ 1 Cor. xv. 28. τ Luke vi. 12. υ John xiv. 16. φ Luke ii. 52. χ Heb. v. 9, etc. ψ Matt. viii. 24; Mark iv. 38. ω Matt. iv. 2; Luke iv. 2. αα Luke xxii. 44. ββ Heb. v. 7.

γγ S. Gregory often speaks of Human Nature as *our composite*

sakes made Himself of no reputation and was Incarnate—yes, for it is no worse thing to say, was made Man, and afterwards was also exalted. The result will be that you will abandon these carnal and grovelling doctrines, and learn to be more sublime, and to ascend with His Godhead, and you will not remain permanently among the things of sight, but will rise up with Him into the world of thought, and come to know which passages refer to His Nature, and which to His assumption of Human Nature.[α]

XIX. For He Whom you now treat with contempt was once above you. He Who is now Man was once the Uncompounded. What He was He continued to be; what He was not He took to Himself.[β] In the beginning He was, uncaused; for what is the Cause of God? But afterwards for a cause He was born. And that cause was that you might be saved, who insult Him and despise His Godhead, because of this, that He took upon Him your denser nature, having converse with Flesh by means of Mind.[γ] While His inferior Nature, the Humanity, became God, because it was united to God, and became One Person[δ] because the Higher Nature prevailed . . . in order that I too might be made God so far as He is made Man.[ε] He was born—but He had been begotten: He was born of a woman—but she was a Virgin. The first is human the second Divine. In His Human nature He had no Father, but also in His Divine Nature no Mother.[α] Both these[β] belong to Godhead. He dwelt in the womb—but He was recognized by the Prophet,[γ] himself still in the womb, leaping before the Word, for Whose sake He came into being. He was wrapped in swaddling clothes[δ]—but He took off the swathing bands of the grave by His rising again. He was laid in a manger—but He was glorified by Angels, and proclaimed by a star, and worshipped by the Magi. Why are you offended by that which is presented to your sight, because you will not look at that which is presented to your mind? He was driven into exile into Egypt—but He drove away the Egyptian idols.[ε] He had no form nor comeliness in the eyes of the Jews[ζ]—but to David He is fairer than the children of men.[η] And on the Mountain He was bright as the lightning, and became more luminous than the sun,[θ] initiating us into the mystery of the future.

XX. He was baptized as Man—but He remitted sins as God[ι]—not because He needed purificatory rites Himself, but that He might sanctify the element of water. He was tempted as Man, but He conquered as God; yea, He bids us be of good cheer, for He has overcome the world.[κ] He hungered—but He fed thousands;[λ] yea, He is the Bread that giveth life, and That is of heaven. He thirsted—but He cried, If any man thirst, let him come unto Me and drink.[μ] Yea, He promised that foun-

being; and here he means the Sacred Humanity exclusively; there is no shadow of suspicion of Nestorianism or Eutychianism attaching to his name.

α The word οἰκονομία is used in four principal senses: (a) The ministry of the Gospel, cf. Ephes. iii. 2. Col. i 25, etc., and S. Cyril Hieros., has the expression "Economy of the Mystery" (Cat., xxv.). It is also used absolutely by S. Chrysostom and others. (b) The Providence of God, as by Epiphanius, Greg. Nyss., and others. (c) The Incarnation, as in the text, without any epithet—in which use it is opposed to ἡ θεότης. Sometimes however epithets are added. (d) The whole Mystery of Redemption, including the Passion.

β cf. S. Leo, Serm. xxi., De Nativ. Dei, c. ii. "Remaining what He was, and putting on what He was not, He united the true form of a servant to that form in which He was equal to God the Father, and combined both natures in a union so close that the lower was not consumed by receiving glory, nor the higher lessened by assuming lowliness.

γ "Mediante anima," cf. Orat. xxxviii., 13. S. T. Aq., Summa, III., vi. Jungmann, de Verbo Incarn., c. 68. Forbes, On Nicene Creed, p. 188. Petav. de Incarn., IV., xiii., 2.

δ γενόμενος ἄνθρωπος ὁ κάτω θεός. The passage is one of great difficulty. Elias Cretensis renders the words as follows:—"Becoming Man, the inferior God, because humanity was" etc.; but his rendering is rejected as impossible by Petavius (de Incarn., IV., ix., 2. 3). (i.) It is grammatically possible (Madvig, Gk. Syntax, 9 a. rem. 3) for ὁ κάτω, standing as it does, to qualify ἄνθρωπος. (ii) But the καὶ γενόμενος . . . θεός may be taken as a nom. absolute, which would have been expressed by a gen. if ἄνθρωπος had not been the same Person as ὁμιλήσας.

ε As by the Incarnation He who was God was made perfect Man, so Man was made perfect God, and each nature retained its own qualities. Or it may mean that God Incarnate was made Man in respect of body, soul, and mind; that is, in all points: and the Humanity which He assumed was in all these points Deified; and therefore they who are His kindred and imitators share to that extent the Deification (Elias). In the First Epistle to Cledonius (v. infra) the Priest, against Apollinarius, which is sometimes reckoned as the 51st Oration, S. Gregory says, "The Godhead and the Manhood are two natures, just as soul and body are. But there are not two Sons or two Gods; although Paul did thus entitle the outward man and the inward. And, to speak succinctly, the Natures which make our Saviour are distinct, for the Invisible is not the same as the visible, nor the Timeless as that which is subject to time; but He is not two Persons, God forbid, for both these are one in the union, God being made Man, and Man being made God, or however else you may express it." And upon this S. Thomas Aquinas remarks that it is true, if by Man you understand simply Human Nature, and not a Human Person; in this sense it was brought to pass that Man was God; or in other words Human Nature was made that of the Son of God. (Summa, III., xvi., 7.)

α "If any does not admit Mary to be the Mother of God (θεοτόκον), he is separated from God. If any say that He passed through the Virgin as through a conduit, and that He was not formed in her both divinely and humanly (divinely, because without a human father; humanly, because in accordance with the laws of gestation), he is in like manner atheistic. If any assert that the Humanity was thus formed, and the Deity subsequently added, he is condemned; for this is not a generation of God, but an evasion of generation" (S. G. N. ad Cled., Ep. i.) S. Thomas Aquinas explains the fitness of the title thus: The Blessed Virgin could be denied to be the Mother of God only if either His Humanity had been conceived and born before That Man was the Son of God;—which was the position taken up by Photinus; or else if the Humanity had not been assumed into the unity of the Person (or Hypostasis) of the Son of God;—which was the position of Nestorius. Both these positions are erroneous. Therefore to deny that the Blessed Virgin is the Mother of God is heretical (Summa, III., xxxv., 4). In the text S. Gregory merely means that the Godhead of our Lord was not derived from His Blessed Mother, just as his Manhood was not derived from any man; but, as the extract at the beginning of this Note shews, he would be the last to take up the Nestorian notion, which was afterwards condemned at the Council of Ephesus.

β Both These, i e., the being without Father, and without Mother is a condition which belongs only to the Godhead.

γ S. John the Baptist (S. Luke i.). δ Luke ii. 41.

ε Referring, perhaps, to the tradition that at the coming of Christ into Egypt all the Idols in the land fell down and were broken. ζ Isa. liii. 2. η Ps. xlv. 2. θ Matt. xvii. 2.

ι Matt. iii. 13; ix. 6. κ John xvi. 33. λ Ib. vi. 10. μ Ib. vii. 37.

tains should flow from them that believe. He was wearied, but He is the Rest of them that are weary and heavy laden.[α] He was heavy with sleep, but He walked lightly over the sea.[β] He rebuked the winds, He made Peter light as he began to sink.[γ] He pays tribute, but it is out of a fish;[δ] yea, He is the King of those who demanded it.[ε]

He is called a Samaritan and a demoniac;[ζ]—but He saves him that came down from Jerusalem and fell among thieves;[η] the demons acknowledge Him, and He drives out demons, and sinks in the sea legions of foul spirits,[θ] and sees the Prince of the demons falling like lightning.[ι] He is stoned, but is not taken. He prays, but He hears prayer. He weeps, but He causes tears to cease. He asks where Lazarus was laid, for He was Man; but He raises Lazarus, for He was God.[κ] He is sold, and very cheap, for it is only for thirty pieces of silver;[λ] but He redeems the world, and that at a great price, for the Price was His own blood.[μ] As a sheep He is led to the slaughter,[ν] but He is the Shepherd of Israel, and now of the whole world also. As a Lamb He is silent, yet He is the Word, and is proclaimed by the Voice of one crying in the wilderness.[ξ] He is bruised and wounded, but He healeth every disease and every infirmity.[ο] He is lifted up and nailed to the Tree, but by the Tree of Life He restoreth us; yea, He saveth even the Robber crucified with Him;[π] yea, He wrapped the visible world in darkness. He is given vinegar to drink mingled with gall. Who? He who turned the water into wine,[ρ] who is the destroyer of the bitter taste, who is Sweetness and altogether desire.[σ] He lays down His life, but He has power to take it again;[τ] and the veil is rent, for the mysterious doors of Heaven are opened; the rocks are cleft, the dead arise.[υ] He dies, but He gives life, and by His death destroys death. He is buried, but He rises again; He goes down into Hell, but He brings up the souls; He ascends to Heaven, and shall come again to judge the quick and the dead, and to put to the test such words as yours. If the one give you a starting point for your error, let the others put an end to it.

XXI. This, then, is our reply to those who would puzzle us; not given willingly indeed (for light talk and contradictions of words are not agreeable to the faithful, and one Adversary is enough for us), but of necessity, for the sake of our assailants (for medicines exist because of diseases), that they may be led to see that they are not all-wise nor invincible in those superfluous arguments which make void the Gospel. For when we leave off believing, and protect ourselves by mere strength of argument, and destroy the claim which the Spirit has upon our faith by questionings, and then our argument is not strong enough for the importance of the subject (and this must necessarily be the case, since it is put in motion by an organ of so little power as is our mind), what is the result? The weakness of the argument appears to belong to the mystery, and thus elegance of language makes void the Cross, as Paul also thought.[α] For faith is that which completes our argument. But may He who proclaimeth unions and looseth those that are bound, and who putteth into our minds to solve the knots of their unnatural dogmas, if it may be, change these men and make them faithful instead of rhetoricians, Christians instead of that which they now are called. This indeed we entreat and beg for Christ's sake. Be ye reconciled to God,[β] and quench not the Spirit;[γ] or rather, may Christ be reconciled to you, and may the Spirit enlighten you, though so late. But if you are too fond of your quarrel, we at any rate will hold fast to the Trinity, and by the Trinity may we be saved, remaining pure and without offence, until the more perfect shewing forth of that which we desire, in Him, Christ our Lord, to Whom be the glory for ever.

AMEN.

THE FOURTH THEOLOGICAL ORATION, WHICH IS THE SECOND CONCERNING THE SON.

I. Since I have by the power of the Spirit sufficiently overthrown the subtleties and intricacies of the arguments, and already solved in the mass the objections and oppositions drawn from Holy Scripture, with which these sacrilegious robbers of the Bible and thieves of the sense of its contents draw over the multitude to their side, and confuse the way of truth; and that not without clearness, as I believe all candid persons will say; attributing to the Deity the higher and diviner expressions, and the lower and more human to Him Who for us men was the Second Adam, and was God made capable of suffering to strive against sin;

α Matt. xi. 28. β Ib. viii. 24. γ Ib. xiv. 25, 30. δ Ib. xvii. 24. ε John xix. 19. ζ Ib. viii. 48. η Luke x. 30, etc. θ Luke viii. 28-33. ι Ib. x. 18. κ John xi. 43. λ Matt. xxvi. 15. μ 1 Pet. i. 19. ν Isa. liii. 7. ξ John i. 23. ο Isa. liii. 23. π Luke xxiii. 43. ρ John ii. 1-11. σ Cant. v. 16. τ John x. 18. υ Matt. xxvii. 51.

α 1 Cor. i. 17. β 2 Cor. v. 20. γ 1 Thess. v. 19.

yet we have not yet gone through the passages in detail, because of the haste of our argument. But since you demand of us a brief explanation of each of them, that you may not be carried away by the plausibilities of their arguments, we will therefore state the explanations summarily, dividing them into numbers for the sake of carrying them more easily in mind.

II. In their eyes the following is only too ready to hand "The LORD created me at the beginning of His ways with a view to His works." [α] How shall we meet this? Shall we bring an accusation against Solomon, or reject his former words because of his fall in after-life? Shall we say that the words are those of Wisdom herself, as it were of Knowledge and the Creator-word, in accordance with which all things were made? For Scripture often personifies many even lifeless objects; as for instance, "The Sea said" [β] so and so; and, "The Depth saith, It is not in me;" [γ] and "The Heavens declare the glory of God;" [δ] and again a command is given to the Sword; [ε] and the Mountains and Hills are asked the reason of their skipping.[ζ] We do not allege any of these, though some of our predecessors used them as powerful arguments. But let us grant that the expression is used of our Saviour Himself, the true Wisdom. Let us consider one small point together. What among all things that exist is unoriginate? The Godhead. For no one can tell the origin of God, that otherwise would be older than God. But what is the cause of the Manhood, which for our sake God assumed? It was surely our Salvation. What else could it be? Since then we find here clearly both the Created and the Begetteth Me, the argument is simple. Whatever we find joined with a cause we are to refer to the Manhood, but all that is absolute and unoriginate we are to reckon to the account of His Godhead. Well, then, is not this "Created" said in connection with a cause? He created Me, it so says, as the beginning of His ways, with a view to his works. Now, the Works of His Hands are verity and judgment; [α] for whose sake He was anointed with Godhead; [β] for this anointing is of the Manhood; but the "He begetteth Me" is not connected with a cause; or it is for you to shew the adjunct. What argument then will disprove that Wisdom is called a creature, in connection with the lower generation, but Begotten in respect of the first and more incomprehensible?

III. Next is the fact of His being called Servant [γ] and serving many well, and that it is a great thing for Him to be called the Child of God. For in truth He was in servitude to flesh and to birth and to the conditions of our life with a view to our liberation, and to that of all those whom He has saved, who were in bondage under sin. What greater destiny can befall man's humility than that he should be intermingled with God, and by this intermingling should be deified,[δ] and that we should be so visited by the Dayspring from on high,[ε] that even that Holy Thing that should be born should be called the Son of the Highest,[ζ] and that there should be bestowed upon Him a Name which is above every name? And what else can this be than God?—and that every knee should bow to Him That was made of no reputation for us, and That mingled the Form of God with the form of a servant, and that all the House of Israel should know that God hath made Him both Lord and Christ? [η] For all this was done by the action of the Begotten, and by the good pleasure of Him That begat Him.

IV. Well, what is the second of their great irresistible passages? "He must reign," [θ] till such and such a time . . . and "be received by heaven until the time of restitution," [ι] and "have the seat at the Right Hand until the overthrow of His enemies." [κ] But after this? Must He cease to be King, or be removed from Heaven? Why, who shall make Him cease, or for what cause? What a bold and very anarchical interpreter you are; and yet you have heard that Of His Kingdom *there shall be no end*.[λ] Your mistake arises from not understanding that Until is not always exclusive of that which comes after, but asserts *up to* that time, without denying what comes

---

α Prov. viii. 22. The A. V. has in this place Possessed, and this has very high authority: but the Hebrew word in almost every case signifies to Acquire. It is used, says Bp. Wordsworth (ad h. l.), about eighty times in the O. T., and in only five places is it rendered in our Translation by Possess;—in two of which (Gen. xiv. 10, 22, and Ps. cxxxix. 13) it might well have the sense of Creating, and in two (Jer. xxxii. 15, and Zech. xi. 5) of Getting. In some ancient Versions (LXX. and Syr.) it is rendered by Create. S. Jerome in his Ep. ad Cypr. (ii. 697) says that the word may here be understood of possession, but in his Comm. on Ephes. ii. (p. 342) he adopts the rendering Create, which he applies to the Incarnation, as in several places does S. Athanasius. But Wordsworth thinks it better to apply the words to the Eternal Generation, as S. Hilary expounds it (c. Arianos, who argued from it that Christ was a creature): "quia Filius Dei non corporalis parturitionis est genitus exemplo, sed ex perfecto Deo perfectus Deus natus; et ideo ait creatam se esse Sapientia; omnem in generatione sua notionem passionis corporalis excludens." β Is. xxiii. 4.

γ Job xxviii. 14. δ Ps. xix. 1. ε Zech. xiii. 7. ζ Ps. cxiv. 6.

α Ps. cxi. 7. β Ps. xlv. 7.

γ Isa. xlix. 6: liii. 11. The LXX. here mistranslates; the Hebrew and the Latin have the same word in all the passages quoted below, while the LXX. varies, as follows: Isa. xlii. 1. παῖς. 19. παῖδες, δοῦλοι. xliv. 2. παῖς. 21. παῖς. xlviii. 29. δοῦλον. xlix. 3. δοῦλος. 5. δοῦλον. 6. παῖδα. 7. δοῦλον. lii. 13. παῖς. liii. 11. δουλεύοντα.

δ See Prolegomena, sec. ii. and 2 Pet. i. 4. ε Luke i. 78.

ζ Phil. ii. 9 η Acts ii. 36. θ 1 Cor. xv. 35. ι Acts iii. 21.

κ Ps. cx. 1. λ Luke i. 33. Cf. Nic. Creed.

after it. To take a single instance—how else would you understand, "Lo, I am with you always, even unto the end of the world?"[α] Does it mean that He will no longer be so afterwards. And for what reason? But this is not the only cause of your error; you also fail to distinguish between the things that are signified. He is said to reign in one sense as the Almighty King, both of the willing and the unwilling; but in another as producing in us submission, and placing us under His Kingship as willingly acknowledging His Sovereignty. Of His Kingdom, considered in the former sense, there shall be no end. But in the second sense, what end will there be? His taking us as His servants, on our entrance into a state of salvation. For what need is there to Work Submission in us when we have already submitted? After which He arises to judge the earth, and to separate the saved from the lost. After that He is to stand as God in the midst of gods,[β] that is, of the saved, distinguishing and deciding of what honour and of what mansion each is worthy.

V. Take, in the next place, the subjection by which you subject the Son to the Father. What, you say, is He not now subject, or must He, if He is God, be subject to God?[γ] You are fashioning your argument as if it concerned some robber, or some hostile deity. But look at it in this manner: that as for my sake He was called a curse,[δ] Who destroyed my curse; and sin,[ε] who taketh away the sin of the world; and became a new Adam[ζ] to take the place of the old, just so He makes my disobedience His own as Head of the whole body. As long then as I am disobedient and rebellious, both by denial of God and by my passions, so long Christ also is called disobedient on my account. But when all things shall be subdued unto Him on the one hand by acknowledgment of Him, and on the other by a reformation, then He Himself also will have fulfilled His submission, bringing me whom He has saved to God. For this, according to my view, is the subjection of Christ; namely, the fulfilling of the Father's Will. But as the Son subjects all to the Father, so does the Father to the Son; the One by His Work, the Other by His good pleasure, as we have already said. And thus He Who subjects presents to God that which he has subjected, making our condition His own. Of the same kind, it appears to me, is the expression, "My God, My God, why hast Thou forsaken Me?"[α] It was not He who was forsaken either by the Father, or by His own Godhead, as some have thought, as if It were afraid of the Passion, and therefore withdrew Itself from Him in His Sufferings (for who compelled Him either to be born on earth at all, or to be lifted up on the Cross?) But as I said, He was in His own Person representing us. For we were the forsaken and despised before, but now by the Sufferings of Him Who could not suffer, we were taken up and saved. Similarly, He makes His own our folly and our transgressions; and says what follows in the Psalm, for it is very evident that the Twenty-first[β] Psalm refers to Christ.

VI. The same consideration applies to another passage, "He learnt obedience by the things which He suffered,"[γ] and to His "strong crying and tears," and His "Entreaties," and His "being heard," and His "Reverence," all of which He wonderfully wrought out, like a drama whose plot was devised on our behalf. For in His character of the Word He was neither obedient nor disobedient. For such expressions belong to servants, and inferiors, and the one applies to the better sort of them, while the other belongs to those who deserve punishment. But, in the character of the Form of a Servant, He condescends to His fellow servants, nay, to His servants, and takes upon Him a strange form, bearing all me and mine in Himself, that in Himself He may exhaust the bad, as fire does wax, or as the sun does the mists of earth; and that I may partake of His nature by the blending. Thus He honours obedience by His action, and proves it experimentally by His Passion. For to possess the disposition is not enough, just as it would not be enough for us, unless we also proved it by our acts; for action is the proof of disposition.

And perhaps it would not be wrong to assume this also, that by the art[δ] of His love for man He gauges our obedience, and measures all by comparison with His own Sufferings, so that He may know our condition by His own, and how much is demanded of us, and how much we yield, taking into the account, along with our environment, our weakness also. For if the Light shining through the veil[ε] upon the darkness, that is upon this life, was persecuted by the other darkness (I mean, the Evil

α Matt. xxviii. 20. β Ps. lxxxii. 1.
γ S. Gregory would here shew that the subjection of Christ of which S. Paul speaks in the passage quoted, is that of the Head of the Church, representing the members of His body. Cf. S. Ambrose, de Fide V. vi., quoted by Petavius, de Trin. III. v. 2.
δ Gal. iii. 13. ζ 2 Cor. v. 21. ε 1 Cor. xv. 45.

α Ps. xxii. 1. β I.e. Ps. xxii. A. V. γ Heb. v. 8, etc.
δ Leuvenclavius translates "The art of this lovingkindness gauges," etc.
ε The Benedicitnes render, "In darkness, that is, in this life, because of the veil of the body."

One and the Tempter), how much more will the darkness be persecuted, as being weaker than it? And what marvel is it, that though He entirely escaped, we have been, at any rate in part, overtaken? For it is a more wonderful thing that He should have been chased than that we should have been captured;—at least to the minds of all who reason aright on the subject. I will add yet another passage to those I have mentioned, because I think that it clearly tends to the same sense. I mean "In that He hath suffered being tempted, He is able to succour them that are tempted."[α] But God will be all in all in the time of restitution; not in the sense that the Father alone will Be; and the Son be wholly resolved into Him, like a torch into a great pyre, from which it was reft away for a little space, and then put back (for I would not have even the Sabellians injured[β] by such an expression); but the entire Godhead . . . when we shall be no longer divided (as we now are by movements and passions), and containing nothing at all of God, or very little, but shall be entirely like.

VII. As your third point you count the Word Greater;[γ] and as your fourth, To My God and your God.[δ] And indeed, if He had been called greater, and the word equal had not occurred, this might perhaps have been a point in their favour. But if we find both words clearly used what will these gentlemen have to say? How will it strengthen their argument? How will they reconcile the irreconcilable? For that the same thing should be at once greater than and equal to the same thing is an impossibility; and the evident solution is that the Greater refers to origination, while the Equal belongs to the Nature; and this we acknowledge with much good will. But perhaps some one else will back up our attack on your argument, and assert, that That which is from such a Cause is not inferior to that which has no Cause; for it would share the glory of the Unoriginate, because it is from the Unoriginate. And there is, besides, the Generation, which is to all men a matter so marvellous and of such Majesty. For to say that he is greater than the Son considered as man, is true indeed, but is no great thing. For what marvel is it if God is greater than man? Surely that is enough to say in answer to their talk about Greater.

VIII. As to the other passages, My God would be used in respect, not of the Word, but of the Visible Word. For how could there be a God of Him Who is properly God? In the same way He is Father, not of the Visible, but of the Word; for our Lord was of two Natures; so that one expression is used properly, the other improperly in each of the two cases; but exactly the opposite way to their use in respect of us. For with respect to us God is properly our God, but not properly our Father. And this is the cause of the error of the Heretics, namely the joining of these two Names, which are interchanged because of the Union of the Natures. And an indication of this is found in the fact that wherever the Natures are distinguished in our thoughts from one another, the Names are also distinguished; as you hear in Paul's words, "The God of our Lord Jesus Christ, the Father of Glory."[α] The God of Christ, but the Father of glory. For although these two terms express but one Person, yet this is not by a Unity of Nature, but by a Union of the two. What could be clearer?

IX. Fifthly, let it be alleged that it is said of Him that He receives life,[β] judgment,[γ] inheritance of the Gentiles,[δ] or power over all flesh,[ε] or glory,[ζ] or disciples, or whatever else is mentioned. This also belongs to the Manhood; and yet if you were to ascribe it to the Godhead, it would be no absurdity. For you would not so ascribe it as if it were newly acquired, but as belonging to Him from the beginning by reason of nature, and not as an act of favour.

X. Sixthly, let it be asserted that it is written, The Son can do nothing of Himself, but what He seeth the Father do.[η] The solution of this is as follows:—Can and Cannot are not words with only one meaning, but have many meanings. On the one hand they are used sometimes in respect of deficiency of strength, sometimes in respect of time, and sometimes relatively to a certain object; as for instance, A Child cannot be an Athlete, or, A Puppy cannot see, or fight with so and so. Perhaps some day the child will be an athlete, the puppy will see, will fight with that other, though it may still be unable to fight with Any other. Or again, they may be used of that which is Generally true. For instance,—A city that is set on a hill cannot be hid;[θ] while yet it might possibly be hidden by another higher hill being in a line with it. Or in another sense they are used of a thing which is not reasonable; as, Can the Children of the Bridechamber fast while the

α Heb. ii. 18.
β The Benedictines take παρα φθειρέσθωσαν in an active sense: "I would not let even the Sabellians wrest such an expression."
γ John xiv. 28
δ Ib., xx. 17.

α Ephes. i. 17. β John viii. 54. γ John v. 22. δ Ps. ii. 8. ε John xvii. 2. ζ 2 Pet. i. 17, etc. η John v. 19. θ Matt. v. 14.

Bridegroom is with them;[α] whether He be considered as visible in bodily form (for the time of His sojourning among us was not one of mourning, but of gladness), or, as the Word. For why should they keep a bodily fast who are cleansed by the Word?[β] Or, again, they are used of that which is contrary to the will; as in, He could do no mighty works there because of their unbelief,[γ]—i.e. of those who should receive them. For since in order to healing there is need of both faith in the patient and power in the Healer,[δ] when one of the two failed the other was impossible. But probably this sense also is to be referred to the head of the unreasonable. For healing is not reasonable in the case of those who would afterwards be injured by unbelief. The sentence The world cannot hate you,[ε] comes under the same head, as does also How can ye, being evil, speak good things?[ζ] For in what sense is either impossible, except that it is contrary to the will? There is a somewhat similar meaning in the expressions which imply that a thing impossible by nature is possible to God if He so wills;[η] as that a man cannot be born a second time,[θ] or that a needle will not let a camel through it.[κ] For what could prevent either of these things happening, if God so willed?

XI. And besides all this, there is the absolutely impossible and inadmissible, as that which we are now examining. For as we assert that it is impossible for God to be evil, or not to exist—for this would be indicative of weakness in God rather than of strength—or for the non-existent to exist, or for two and two to make both four and ten,[λ] so it is impossible and inconceivable that the Son should do anything that the Father doeth not.[μ] For all things that the Father hath are the Son's;[ν] and on the other hand, all that belongs to the Son is the Father's. Nothing then is peculiar, because all things are in common. For Their Being itself is common and equal, even though the Son receive it from the Father. It is in respect of this that it is said I live by the Father;[ξ] not as though His Life and Being were kept together by the Father, but because He has His Being from Him beyond all time, and beyond all cause. But how does He see the Father doing, and do likewise? Is it like those who copy pictures and letters, because they cannot attain the truth unless by looking at the original, and being led by the hand by it? But how shall Wisdom stand in need of a teacher, or be incapable of acting unless taught? And in what sense does the Father "Do" in the present or in the past? Did He make another world before this one, or is He going to make a world to come? And did the Son look at that and make this? Or will He look at the other, and make one like it? According to this argument there must be Four worlds, two made by the Father, and two by the Son. What an absurdity! He cleanses lepers, and delivers men from evil spirits, and diseases, and quickens the dead, and walks upon the sea, and does all His other works; but in what case, or when did the Father do these acts before Him? Is it not clear that the Father impressed the ideas of these same actions, and the Word brings them to pass, yet not in slavish or unskilful fashion, but with full knowledge and in a masterly way, or, to speak more properly, like the Father? For in this sense I understand the words that whatsoever is done by the Father, these things doeth the Son likewise; not, that is, because of the likeness of the things done, but in respect of the Authority. This might well also be the meaning of the passage which says that the Father worketh hitherto and the Son also;[α] and not only so but it refers also to the government and preservation of the things which He has made; as is shewn by the passage which says that He maketh His Angels Spirits,[β] and that the earth is founded upon its steadfastness (though once for all these things were fixed and made) and that the thunder is made firm and the wind created.[γ] Of all these things the Word was given once, but the Action is continuous even now.

XII. Let them quote in the seventh place that The Son came down from Heaven, not to do His own Will, but the Will of Him That sent Him.[δ] Well, if this had not been said by Himself Who came down, we should say that the phrase was modelled as issuing from the Human Nature, not from Him who is conceived of in His character as the Saviour, for His Human Will cannot be opposed to God, seeing it is altogether taken into God; but conceived of simply as in our nature, inasmuch as the human will does not completely follow the Divine, but for the most part struggles against and resists it. For we understand in the same way the words, Father, if

α Mark ii. 19. β John xv. 3. γ Mark vi. 5.
δ Note with the Benedictines that S. Gregory is here speaking of our Lord alone, not of ordinary Physicians; hence he uses the singular. ε John vii. 7. ζ Matt. xii. 34.
η Matt. xix. 26. θ John iii. 4. κ Matt. xix. 24.
λ One MS. reads "to be fourteen."
μ John v. 19. ν Ib. xvi. 15. ξ Ib. vi. 57.

α John v. 17. β Ps. civ. 4, 5, LXX.
γ cf. Amos iv. 13, where A. V. reads, He That formed the mountains and created the wind.
δ John vi. 38.

it be possible, let this cup pass from Me; Nevertheless let not what I will but Thy Will prevail.[α] For it is not likely that He did not know whether it was possible or not, or that He would oppose will to will. But since, as this is the language of Him Who assumed our Nature (for He it was Who came down), and not of the Nature which He assumed, we must meet the objection in this way, that the passage does not mean that the Son has a special will of His own, besides that of the Father, but that He has not; so that the meaning would be, "not to do Mine own Will, for there is none of Mine apart from, but that which is common to, Me and Thee; for as We have one Godhead, so We have one Will."[β] For many such expressions are used in relation to this Community, and are expressed not positively but negatively; as, e.g., God giveth not the Spirit by measure,[γ] for as a matter of fact He does not *give* the Spirit to the Son, nor does He *measure* It, for God is not measured by God; or again, Not my transgression nor my sin.[δ] The words are not used because He has these things, but because He has them not. And again, Not for our righteousness which we have done,[ε] for we have not done any. And this meaning is evident also in the clauses which follow. For what, says He, is the Will of My Father? That everyone that believeth on the Son should be saved,[ζ] and obtain the final Resurrection.[η] Now is this the Will of the Father, but not of the Son? Or does He preach the Gospel, and receive men's faith against His will? Who could believe that? Moreover, that passage, too, which says that the Word which is heard is not the Son's[θ] but the Father's has the same force. For I cannot see how that which is common to two can be said to belong to one alone, however much I consider it, and I do not think any one else can. If then you hold this opinion concerning the Will, you will be right and reverent in your opinion, as I think, and as every right-minded person thinks.

XIII. The eighth passage is, That they may know Thee, the only true God, and Jesus Christ Whom Thou hast sent;[κ] and There is none good save one, that is, God.[λ] The solution of this appears to me very easy. For if you attribute this only to the Father, where will you place the Very Truth? For if you conceive in this manner of the meaning of To the only wise God,[α] or Who only hath Immortality, Dwelling in the light which no man can approach unto,[β] or of to the king of the Ages, immortal, invisible, and only wise God,[γ] then the Son has vanished under sentence of death, or of darkness, or at any rate condemned to be neither wise nor king, nor invisible, nor God at all, which sums up all these points. And how will you prevent His Goodness, which especially belongs to God alone, from perishing with the rest? I, however, think that the passage That they may know Thee the only true God, was said to overthrow those gods which are falsely so called, for He would not have added and Jesus Christ Whom Thou hast sent, if The Only True God were contrasted with Him, and the sentence did not proceed upon the basis of a common Godhead. The "None is Good" meets the tempting Lawyer, who was testifying to His Goodness viewed as Man. For perfect goodness, He says, is God's alone, even if a man is called perfectly good. As for instance, A good man out of the good treasure of his heart bringeth forth good things.[δ] And, I will give the kingdom to one who is good above Thee.[ε] . . . Words of God, speaking to Saul about David. Or again, Do good, O Lord, unto the good[ζ] . . . and all other like expressions concerning those of us who are praised, upon whom it is a kind of effluence from the Supreme Good, and has come to them in a secondary degree. It will be best of all if we can persuade you of this. But if not, what will you say to the suggestion on the other side, that on your hypothesis the Son has been called the only God. In what passage? Why, in this: —This is your God; no other shall be accounted of in comparison with Him, and a little further on, after this did He shew Himself upon earth, and conversed with men.[η] This addition proves clearly that the words are not used of the Father, but of the Son; for it was He Who in bodily form companied with us, and was in this lower world. Now, if we should determine to take these words as said in contrast with the Father, and not with the imaginary gods, we lose the Father by the very terms which we were pressing against the Son. And what could be more disastrous than such a victory?

XIV. Ninthly, they allege, seeing He ever

α Matt. xxvi. 39.

β Observe that S. Gregory expressly limits this paraphrase to the Divine Nature of our Lord, and is not in any way denying to Him a Human Will also;—indeed in the preceding sentence he distinctly asserts it. The whole passage makes very strongly against the heresy of Apollinarius, which adopted the Arian tenet that in our Lord the Divine Logos supplied the place of the human soul.

γ John iii. 34.

δ Ps. lix. 3.

ε Dan. ix. 18.

ζ John vi. 40.

η V. l. Restoration.

θ John xiv. 24.

κ Ib. xvii. 3.

λ Luke xviii. 19.

α 1 Tim. i. 17.

β Ib. vi. 16.

γ Ib. i. 17.

δ Mat. xii. 35.

ε 1 Sam. xv. 28.

ζ Ps. cxxv. 4.

η Baruch iii. 35, 37.

liveth to make intercession for us.[α] O, how beautiful and mystical and kind. For to intercede does not imply to seek for vengeance, as is most men's way (for in that there would be something of humiliation), but it is to plead for us by reason of His Mediatorship, just as the Spirit also is said to make intercession for us.[β] For there is One God, and One Mediator between God and Man, the Man Christ Jesus.[γ] For He still pleads even now as Man for my salvation; for He continues to wear the Body which He assumed, until He make me God by the power of His Incarnation; although He is no longer known after the flesh [δ]—I mean, the passions of the flesh, the same, except sin, as ours. Thus too, we have an Advocate,[ε] Jesus Christ, not indeed prostrating Himself for us before the Father, and falling down before Him in slavish fashion . . . Away with a suspicion so truly slavish and unworthy of the Spirit! For neither is it seemly for the Father to require this, nor for the Son to submit to it; nor is it just to think it of God. But by what He suffered as Man, He as the Word and the Counsellor persuades Him to be patient. I think this is the meaning of His Advocacy.

XV. Their tenth objection is the ignorance, and the statement that Of the last day and hour knoweth no man, not even the Son Himself, but the Father.[ζ] And yet how can Wisdom be ignorant of anything — that is, Wisdom Who made the worlds, Who perfects them, Who remodels them, Who is the Limit of all things that were made, Who knoweth the things of God as the spirit of a man knows the things that are in him?[η] For what can be more perfect than this knowledge? How then can you say that all things before that hour He knows accurately, and all things that are to happen about the time of the end, but of the hour itself He is ignorant? For such a thing would be like a riddle; as if one were to say that he knew accurately all that was in front of the wall, but did not know the wall itself; or that, knowing the end of the day, he did not know the beginning of the night — where knowledge of the one necessarily brings in the other. Thus everyone must see that He knows as God, and knows not as Man; — if one may separate the visible from that which is discerned by thought alone. For the absolute and unconditioned use of the Name "The Son" in this passage, without the addition of whose Son, gives us this thought, that we are to understand the ignorance in the most reverent sense, by attributing it to the Manhood, and not to the Godhead.

XVI. If then this argument is sufficient, let us stop here, and not enquire further. But if not, our second argument is as follows: — Just as we do in all other instances, so let us refer His knowledge of the greatest events, in honour of the Father, to The Cause. And I think that anyone, even if he did not read it in the way that one of our own Students[α] did, would soon perceive that not even the Son knows the day or hour otherwise than as the Father does. For what do we conclude from this? That since the Father knows, therefore also does the Son, as it is evident that this cannot be known or comprehended by any but the First Nature. There remains for us to interpret the passage about His receiving commandment,[β] and having kept His Commandments, and done always those things that please Him; and further concerning His being made perfect,[γ] and His exaltation,[δ] and His learning obedience by the things which He suffered; and also His High Priesthood, and His Oblation, and His Betrayal, and His prayer to Him That was able to save Him from death, and His Agony and Bloody Sweat and Prayer,[ε] and such like things; if it were not evident to every one that such words are concerned, not with That Nature Which is unchangeable and above all capacity of suffering, but with the passible Humanity. This, then, is the argument concerning these objections, so far as to be a sort of foundation and memorandum for the use of those who are better able to conduct the enquiry to a more complete working out. It may, however, be worth while, and will be consistent with what has been already said, instead of passing over without remark the actual Titles of the Son (there are many of them, and they are concerned with many of His Attributes), to set before you the meaning of each of them, and to point out the mystical meaning of the names.

XVII. We will begin thus. The Deity cannot be expressed in words. And this is proved to us, not only by argument, but by the wisest and most ancient of the Hebrews, so far as they have given us reason for conjecture. For they appropriated certain characters to the honour of the Deity, and would not even allow the name of anything inferior to God to be written with the same letters as that of

α Heb. vii. 25. β Rom. viii. 26. γ 1 Tim. ii. 5. δ 2 Cor. v. 16. ε 1 John ii. 1. ζ Mark xiii. 32. η 1 Cor. ii. 11.

α Elias thinks that the great S. Basil is here referred to. Petavius thinks the first argument of c. xvi. forced and unsatisfactory.
β John xii. 49. γ Heb. v. 7, etc. δ Phil. ii. 9. ε Luke xii. 44.

God, because to their minds it was improper that the Deity should even to that extent admit any of His creatures to a share with Himself. How then could they have admitted that the invisible and separate Nature can be explained by divisible words? For neither has any one yet breathed the whole air, nor has any mind entirely comprehended, or speech exhaustively contained the Being of God. But we sketch Him by His Attributes, and so obtain a certain faint and feeble and partial idea concerning Him, and our best Theologian is he who has, not indeed discovered the whole, for our present chain does not allow of our seeing the whole, but conceived of Him to a greater extent than another, and gathered in himself more of the Likeness or adumbration of the Truth, or whatever we may call it.

XVIII. As far then as we can reach, He Who Is, and God, are the special names of His Essence; and of these especially He Who Is, not only because when He spake to Moses in the mount, and Moses asked what His Name was, this was what He called Himself, bidding him say to the people "I Am hath sent me,"[α] but also because we find that this Name is the more strictly appropriate. For the Name Θεός (God), even if, as those who are skilful in these matters say, it were derived from Θέειν[β] (to run) or from Αἴθειν (to blaze), from continual motion, and because He consumes evil conditions of things (from which fact He is also called A Consuming Fire),[γ] would still be one of the Relative Names, and not an Absolute one; as again is the case with Lord,[δ] which also is called a name of God. I am the Lord Thy God, He says, that is My name;[ε] and, The Lord is His name.[ζ] But we are enquiring into a Nature Whose Being is absolute and not into Being bound up with something else. But Being is in its proper sense peculiar to God, and belongs to Him entirely, and is not limited or cut short by any Before or After, for indeed in him there is no past or future.

XIX. Of the other titles, some are evidently names of His Authority, others of His Government of the world, and of this viewed under a twofold aspect, the one before the other in the Incarnation. For instance the Almighty, the King of Glory, or of The Ages, or of The Powers, or of The Beloved, or of Kings. Or again the Lord of Sabaoth, that is of Hosts, or of Powers, or of Lords; these are clearly titles belonging to His Authority. But the God either of Salvation or of Vengeance, or of Peace, or of Righteousness; or of Abraham, Isaac, and Jacob, and of all the spiritual Israel that seeth God,—these belong to His Government. For since we are governed by these three things, the fear of punishment, the hope of salvation and of glory besides, and the practice of the virtues by which these are attained, the Name of the God of Vengeance governs fear, and that of the God of Salvation our hope, and that of the God of Virtues our practice; that whoever attains to any of these may, as carrying God in himself, press on yet more unto perfection, and to that affinity which arises out of virtues. Now these are Names common to the Godhead, but the Proper Name of the Unoriginate is Father, and that of the unoriginately Begotten is Son, and that of the unbegottenly Proceeding or going forth is The Holy Ghost. Let us proceed then to the Names of the Son, which were our starting point in this part of our argument.

XX. In my opinion He is called Son because He is identical with the Father in Essence; and not only for this reason, but also because He is Of Him. And He is called Only-Begotten, not because He is the only Son and of the Father alone, and only a Son; but also because the manner of His Sonship is peculiar to Himself and not shared by bodies. And He is called the Word, because He is related to the Father as Word to Mind; not only on account of His passionless Generation, but also because of the Union, and of His declaratory function. Perhaps too this relation might be compared to that between the Definition and the Thing defined[α] since this also is called Λόγος.[β] For, it says, he that hath mental perception of the Son (for this is the meaning of Hath Seen) hath also perceived the Father;[γ] and the Son is a concise demonstration and easy setting forth of the Father's Nature. For every thing that is begotten is a silent word of him that begat it. And if any one should say that this Name was given Him because

α Exod. iii. 14.

β The derivation of Θεός from Θέειν (to run) is given by Plato (Crat., 397c). That from Αἴθειν (to blaze) is found also in S. John Damascene (De Fide Orth., I., 12), who however may have borrowed it from S. Gregory, or from the source whence the latter took it. S. Athanasius also admits it (De Defin., 11). Other definitions are, according to Suicer, (1) Θεᾶσθαι (to see), e. g. Greg. Nyss. in Cant. Hom., V. (2) Θεωρεῖν (to contemplate), Athan. Quaest Misc., Qu. XI., Θεὸς λέγεται ἀπὸ τὸ θεωρεῖν τὰ πάντα, οἱονεὶ θεωρὸς καὶ θεος, ἤγουν θεάτης πάντων. (3) Τιθέναι (to place), Clem., Al. Strom., I. s. fin., θεὸς παρὰ τὴν θέσιν εἴρηται.

γ Deut. iv. 24.

δ Lord (Κύριος) is simply the LXX. rendering of the word which in reading Hebrew is substituted for the Ineffable Name. Thus in the passages quoted, had the original language been used, the Four-Lettered Name would have appeared.

ε Isa. xlii. 8.

ζ Amos, ix. 6.

α Of the oration on Christmas Day, where He is called ὁ τοῦ Πατρὸς ὅρος καὶ λόγος, and see Note there.

β Ratio (relation; sometimes reason) Sermo (discourse) and Verbum (Word) are all renderings of Λόγος.

γ John xiv. 9.

He exists in all things that are, he would not be wrong. For what is there that consists but by the word? He is also called Wisdom, as the Knowledge of things divine and human. For how is it possible that He Who made all things should be ignorant of the reasons of what He has made? And Power, as the Sustainer of all created things, and the Furnisher to them of power to keep themselves together. And Truth, as being in nature One and not many (for truth is one and falsehood is manifold), and as the pure Seal of the Father and His most unerring Impress. And the Image as of one substance with Him, and because He is of the Father, and not the Father of Him. For this is of the Nature of an Image, to be the reproduction of its Archetype, and of that whose name it bears; only that there is more here. For in ordinary language an image is a motionless representation of that which has motion; but in this case it is the living reproduction of the Living One, and is more exactly like than was Seth to Adam,[α] or any son to his father. For such is the nature of simple Existences, that it is not correct to say of them that they are Like in one particular and Unlike in another; but they are a complete resemblance, and should rather be called Identical than Like. Moreover he is called Light as being the Brightness of souls cleansed by word and life. For if ignorance and sin be darkness, knowledge and a godly life will be Light. . . . And He is called Life, because He is Light, and is the constituting and creating Power of every reasonable soul. For in Him we live and move and have our being,[β] according to the double power of that Breathing into us; for we were all inspired by Him with breath,[γ] and as many of us as were capable of it, and in so far as we open the mouth of our mind, with God the Holy Ghost. He is Righteousness, because He distributes according to that which we deserve, and is a righteous Arbiter both for those who are under the Law and for those who are under Grace, for soul and body, so that the former should rule, and the latter obey, and the higher have supremacy over the lower; that the worse may not rise in rebellion against the better. He is Sanctification, as being Purity, that the Pure may be contained by Purity. And Redemption, because He sets us free, who were held captive under sin, giving Himself a Ransom for us, the Sacrifice to make expiation for the world. And Resurrection, because He raises up from hence, and brings to life again us, who were slain by sin.

XXI. These names however are still common to Him Who is above us, and to Him Who came for our sake. But others are peculiarly our own, and belong to that nature which He assumed. So He is called Man, not only that through His Body He may be apprehended by embodied creatures, whereas otherwise this would be impossible because of His incomprehensible nature; but also that by Himself He may sanctify humanity, and be as it were a leaven to the whole lump; and by uniting to Himself that which was condemned may release it from all condemnation, becoming for all men all things that we are, except sin;—body, soul, mind and all through which death reaches—and thus He became Man, who is the combination of all these; God in visible form, because He retained that which is perceived by mind alone. He is Son of Man, both on account of Adam, and of the Virgin from Whom He came; from the one as a forefather, from the other as His Mother, both in accordance with the law of generation, and apart from it. He is Christ, because of His Godhead. For this is the Anointing of His Manhood, and does not, as is the case with all other Anointed Ones, sanctify by its action, but by the Presence in His Fulness of the Anointing One; the effect of which is that That which anoints is called Man, and makes that which is anointed God. He is The Way, because He leads us through Himself; The Door, as letting us in; the Shepherd, as making us dwell in a place of green pastures,[α] and bringing us up by waters of rest, and leading us there, and protecting us from wild beasts, converting the erring, bringing back that which was lost, binding up that which was broken, guarding the strong, and bringing them together in the Fold beyond, with words of pastoral knowledge. The Sheep, as the Victim: The Lamb, as being perfect: the Highpriest, as the Offerer; Melchisedec, as without Mother in that Nature which is above us, and without Father in ours; and without genealogy above (for who, it says, shall declare His generation?) and moreover, as King of Salem, which means Peace, and King of Righteousness, and as receiving tithes from Patriarchs, when they prevail over powers of evil. They are the titles of the Son. Walk through them, those that are lofty in a godlike manner; those that belong to the body in a manner suitable to them; or rather, altogether in a godlike manner, that thou mayest become a god, ascending from

α Gen. v. 3. β Acts xvii. 28. γ Gen. ii. 7.

α Ps. xxiii. 2.

below, for His sake Who came down from on high for ours. In all and above all keep to this, and thou shalt never err, either in the loftier or the lowlier names; Jesus Christ is the Same yesterday and to-day in the Incarnation, and in the Spirit for ever and ever. Amen.

THE FIFTH THEOLOGICAL ORATION.

On The Holy Spirit.

I. Such then is the account of the Son, and in this manner He has escaped those who would stone Him, passing through the midst of them.[α] For the Word is not stoned, but casts stones when He pleases; and uses a sling against wild beasts—that is, words—approaching the Mount[β] in an unholy way. But, they go on, what have you to say about the Holy Ghost? From whence are you bringing in upon us this strange God, of Whom Scripture is silent? And even they who keep within bounds as to the Son speak thus. And just as we find in the case of roads and rivers, that they split off from one another and join again, so it happens also in this case, through the superabundance of impiety, that people who differ in all other respects have here some points of agreement, so that you never can tell for certain either where they are of one mind, or where they are in conflict.

II. Now the subject of the Holy Spirit presents a special difficulty, not only because when these men have become weary in their disputations concerning the Son, they struggle with greater heat against the Spirit (for it seems to be absolutely necessary for them to have some object on which to give expression to their impiety, or life would appear to them no longer worth living), but further because we ourselves also, being worn out by the multitude of their questions, are in something of the same condition with men who have lost their appetite; who having taken a dislike to some particular kind of food, shrink from all food; so we in like manner have an aversion from all discussions. Yet may the Spirit grant it to us, and then the discourse will proceed, and God will be glorified. Well then, we will leave to others[γ] who have worked upon this subject for us as well as for themselves, as we have worked upon it for them, the task of examining carefully and distinguishing in how

α Luke iv. 29, 30. β Exod. xix. 13.
γ E.g. S. Basil and S. Gregory of Nyssa.

many senses the word Spirit or the word Holy is used and understood in Holy Scripture, with the evidence suitable to such an enquiry; and of shewing how besides these the combination of the two words—I mean, Holy Spirit—is used in a peculiar sense; but we will apply ourselves to the remainder of the subject.

III. They then who are angry with us on the ground that we are bringing in a strange or interpolated God, viz.:—the Holy Ghost, and who fight so very hard for the letter, should know that they are afraid where no fear is;[α] and I would have them clearly understand that their love for the letter is but a cloak for their impiety, as shall be shewn later on, when we refute their objections to the utmost of our power. But we have so much confidence in the Deity of the Spirit Whom we adore,[β] that we will begin our teaching concerning His Godhead by fitting to Him the Names which belong to the Trinity, even though some persons may think us too bold. The Father was the True Light which lighteneth every man coming into the world. The Son was the True Light which lighteneth every man coming into the world. The Other Comforter was the True Light which lighteneth every man coming into the world.[γ] Was and Was and Was, but Was One Thing. Light thrice repeated; but One Light and One God. This was what David represented to himself long before when he said, In Thy Light shall we see Light.[δ] And now we have both seen and proclaim concisely and simply the doctrine[ε] of God the Trinity, comprehending out of Light (the Father), Light (the Son), in Light (the Holy Ghost). He that rejects it, let him reject it;[ζ] and he that doeth iniquity, let him do iniquity; we proclaim that which we have understood. We will get us up into a high mountain,[η] and will shout, if we be not heard, below; we will exalt the Spirit; we will not be afraid; or if we are afraid, it shall be of keeping silence, not of proclaiming.

IV. If ever there was a time when the Father was not, then there was a time when the Son was not. If ever there was a time when the Son was not, then there was a time when the Spirit was not. If the One was from the beginning, then the Three were so too. If you

α Ps. liii. 5.

β πρεσβεύειν is not commonly used in this sense, but there are classical instances of it (e.g. Æsch. Choeph., 488; Soph., Trach., 1065, and it occurs also in Plato), and this is the sense in which it is here rendered by Billius; but a V. L. of some MSS. gives the meaning, whose cause we are pleading, which is a more frequent use of the word. γ John i. 9. δ Ps. xxxvi. 9.

ε Al. The Confession. ζ Isa. xxi. 2. η Ib. xl. 9.

throw down the One, I am bold to assert that you do not set up the other Two. For what profit is there in an imperfect Godhead? Or rather, what Godhead can there be if It is not perfect? And how can that be perfect which lacks something of perfection? And surely there is something lacking if it hath not the Holy, and how would it have this if it were without the Spirit? For either holiness is something different from Him, and if so let some one tell me what it is conceived to be; or if it is the same, how is it not from the beginning, as if it were better for God to be at one time imperfect and apart from the Spirit? If He is not from the beginning, He is in the same rank with myself, even though a little before me; for we are both parted from Godhead by time. If He is in the same rank with myself, how can He make me God, or join me with Godhead?

V. Or rather, let me reason with you about Him from a somewhat earlier point, for we have already discussed the Trinity. The Sadducees altogether denied the existence of the Holy Spirit, just as they did that of Angels and the Resurrection; rejecting, I know not upon what ground, the important testimonies concerning Him in the Old Testament. And of the Greeks those who are more inclined to speak of God, and who approach nearest to us, have formed some conception of Him, as it seems to me, though they have differed as to His Name, and have addressed Him as the Mind of the World, or the External Mind, and the like. But of the wise men amongst ourselves, some have conceived of him as an Activity, some as a Creature, some as God; and some have been uncertain which to call Him, out of reverence for Scripture, they say, as though it did not make the matter clear either way. And therefore they neither worship Him nor treat Him with dishonour, but take up a neutral position, or rather a very miserable one, with respect to Him. And of those who consider Him to be God, some are orthodox in mind only, while others venture to be so with the lips also. And I have heard of some who are even more clever, and measure Deity; and these agree with us that there are Three Conceptions; but they have separated these from one another so completely as to make one of them infinite both in essence and power, and the second in power but not in essence, and the third circumscribed in both; thus imitating in another way those who call them the Creator, the Co-operator, and the Minister, and consider that the same order and dignity which belongs to these names is also a sequence in the facts.

VI. But we cannot enter into any discussion with those who do not even believe in His existence, nor with the Greek babblers (for we would not be enriched in our argument with the oil of sinners).[a] With the others, however, we will argue thus. The Holy Ghost must certainly be conceived of either as in the category of the Self-existent, or as in that of the things which are contemplated in another; of which classes those who are skilled in such matters call the one Substance and the other Accident. Now if He were an Accident, He would be an Activity of God, for what else, or of whom else, could He be, for surely this is what most avoids composition? And if He is an Activity, He will be effected, but will not effect and will cease to exist as soon as He has been effected, for this is the nature of an Activity. How is it then that He acts and says such and such things, and defines, and is grieved, and is angered, and has all the qualities which belong clearly to one that moves, and not to movement? But if He is a Substance and not an attribute of Substance, He will be conceived of either as a Creature of God, or as God. For anything between these two, whether having nothing in common with either, or a compound of both, not even they who invented the goat-stag could imagine. Now, if He is a creature, how do we believe in Him, how are we made perfect in Him? For it is not the same thing to believe IN a thing and to believe ABOUT it. The one belongs to Deity, the other to—any thing. But if He is God, then He is neither a creature, nor a thing made, nor a fellow servant, nor any of these lowly appellations.

VII. There—the word is with you. Let the slings be let go; let the syllogism be woven. Either He is altogether Unbegotten, or else He is Begotten. If He is Unbegotten, there are two Unoriginates. If he is Begotten, you must make a further subdivision. He is so either by the Father or by the Son. And if by the Father, there are two Sons, and they are Brothers. And you may make them twins if you like, or the one older and the other younger, since you are so very fond of the bodily conceptions. But if by the Son, then such a one will say, we get a glimpse of a Grandson God, than which nothing could be more absurd. For my part however, if I saw the necessity of the distinction, I should

[a] Ps. cxli. 5.

have acknowledged the facts without fear of the names. For it does not follow that because the Son is the Son in some higher relation (inasmuch as we could not in any other way than this point out that He is of God and Consubstantial), it would also be necessary to think that all the names of this lower world and of our kindred should be transferred to the Godhead. Or may be you would consider our God to be a male, according to the same arguments, because he is called God and Father, and that Deity is feminine, from the gender of the word, and Spirit neuter, because It has nothing to do with generation; But if you would be silly enough to say, with the old myths and fables, that God begat the Son by a marriage with His own Will, we should be introduced[α] to the Hermaphrodite god of Marcion and Valentinus[β] who imagined these newfangled Æons.

VIII. But since we do not admit your first division, which declares that there is no mean between Begotten and Unbegotten, at once, along with your magnificent division, away go your Brothers and your Grandsons, as when the first link of an intricate chain is broken they are broken with it, and disappear from your system of divinity. For, tell me, what position will you assign to that which Proceeds, which has started up between the two terms of your division, and is introduced by a better Theologian than you, our Saviour Himself? Or perhaps you have taken that word out of your Gospels for the sake of your Third Testament, The Holy Ghost, which proceedeth from the Father;[γ] Who, inasmuch as He proceedeth from That Source, is no Creature; and inasmuch as He is not Begotten is no Son; and inasmuch as He is between the Unbegotten and the Begotten is God. And thus escaping the toils of your syllogisms, He has manifested himself as God, stronger than your divisions. What then is Procession? Do you tell me what is the Unbegottenness of the Father, and I will explain to you the physiology of the Generation of the Son and the Procession of the Spirit, and we shall both of us be frenzy-stricken for prying into the mystery of God.[α] And who are we to do these things, we who cannot even see what lies at our feet, or number the sand of the sea, or the drops of rain, or the days of Eternity, much less enter into the Depths of God, and supply an account of that Nature which is so unspeakable and transcending all words?

IX. What then, say they, is there lacking to the Spirit which prevents His being a Son, for if there were not something lacking He would be a Son? We assert that there is nothing lacking—for God has no deficiency. But the difference of manifestation, if I may so express myself, or rather of their mutual relations one to another, has caused the difference of their Names. For indeed it is not some deficiency in the Son which prevents His being Father (for Sonship is not a deficiency), and yet He is not Father. According to this line of argument there must be some deficiency in the Father, in respect of His not being Son. For the Father is not Son, and yet this is not due to either deficiency or subjection of Essence; but the very fact of being Unbegotten or Begotten, or Proceeding has given the name of Father to the First, of the Son to the Second, and of the Third, Him of Whom we are speaking, of the Holy Ghost that the distinction of the Three Persons may be preserved in the one nature and dignity of the Godhead. For neither is the Son Father, for the Father is One, but He is what the Father is; nor is the Spirit Son because He is of God, for the Only-begotten is One, but He is what the Son is. The Three are One in Godhead, and the One Three in properties; so that neither is the Unity a Sabellian one,[β] nor

α Irenæus. I.. 6.

β It would seem that S. Gregory commonly confused Marcion with Marcus, one of the leaders of the Gnostic School of Valentinus. In another place he speaks of the Æons of Marcion and Valentinus, evidently meaning Marcus; for the system of Marcion is characterized by an entire absence of any theory of Emanations (Æons). Similarly there is no trace in Marcion of this notion of a hermaphrodite Deity, but there is something very like it in the account of Marcus given by S. Irenæus.

γ John xv. 26. "It did not fall within this Father's (Greg. Naz.) province to develop the doctrine of the Procession. He is content to shew that the Spirit was not Generated, seeing that according to Christ's own teaching He Proceeds from the Father. The question of His relation to the Son is alien to S. Gregory Nazianzen's purpose; nor does it seem to have once been raised in the great battle between Arianism and Catholicity which was fought out at Constantinople during Gregory's Episcopate" (Swete on the Procession, p. 107).

α Ecclus i. 2.

β Sabellius, who taught at Rome during the Pontificate of Callistus, was by far the most important heresiarch of his period, and his opinions by far the most dangerous. While strongly emphasizing the fundamental doctrine of the Divine Unity, he also admitted in terms a Trinity, but his Trinity was not that of the Catholic dogma, for he represented it as only a threefold manifestation of the one Divine Essence. The Father, Son, and Holy Ghost are in his view only temporary phænomena, which fulfil their mission, and then return into the abstract Monad. Dr Schaff (Hist. of the Church, Ante-Nicene Period, p. 582) gives the following concise account of his teaching:

"The unity of God, without distinction in itself, unfolds or extends itself in the course of the word's development, in three different forms and periods of revelation, and after the completion of redemption returns into Unity. The Father reveals Himself in the giving of the Law or the Old Testament Economy (not in the creation also, which in his view precedes the Trinitarian revelation); the Son in the Incarnation; the Holy Ghost in inspiration; the revelation of the Son ends with the Ascension; that of the Spirit goes on in generation and sanctification. He illustrates the Trinitarian revelation by comparing the Father to the disc of the sun, the Son to its enlightening power, the Spirit to its warming influence. He is also said to have likened the Father to the body, the Son to the soul, the Holy Ghost to the spirit of man: but this is unworthy of his evident speculative discrimination. His view of the Logos too is peculiar. The Logos is not identical with the Son, but is the Monad itself in its transition to Triad; that is, God conceived as vital motion and creating principle; the Speaking God, as distinguished from the Silent God. Each Person (or

does the Trinity countenance the present evil distinction.

X. What then? Is the Spirit God? Most certainly. Well then, is He Consubstantial? Yes, if He is God. Grant me, says my opponent, that there spring from the same Source One who is a Son, and One who is not a Son, and these of One Substance with the Source, and I admit a God and a God. Nay, if you will grant me that there is another God and another nature of God I will give you the same Trinity with the same name and facts. But since God is One and the Supreme Nature is One, how can I present to you the Likeness? Or will you seek it again in lower regions and in your own surroundings? It is very shameful, and not only shameful, but very foolish, to take from things below a guess at things above, and from a fluctuating nature at the things that are unchanging, and as Isaiah says, to seek the Living among the dead.[α] But yet I will try, for your sake, to give you some assistance for your argument, even from that source. I think I will pass over other points, though I might bring forward many from animal history, some generally known, others only known to a few, of what nature has contrived with wonderful art in connection with the generation of animals. For not only are likes said to beget likes, and things diverse to beget things diverse, but also likes to be begotten by things diverse, and things diverse by likes. And if we may believe the story, there is yet another mode of generation, when an animal is self-consumed and self-begotten.[β] There are also creatures which depart in some sort from their true natures, and undergo change and transformation from one creature into another, by a magnificence of nature. And indeed sometimes in the same species part may be generated and part not; and yet all of one substance; which is more like our present subject. I will just mention one fact of our own nature which every one knows, and then I will pass on to another part of the subject.

XI. What was Adam? A creature of God. What then was Eve? A fragment of the creature. And what was Seth? The begotten of both. Does it then seem to you that Creature and Fragment and Begotten are the same thing? Of course it does not. But were not these persons consubstantial? Of course they were. Well then, here it is an acknowledged fact that different persons may have the same substance. I say this, not that I would attribute creation or fraction or any property of body to the Godhead (let none of your contenders for a word be down upon me again), but that I may contemplate in these, as on a stage, things which are objects of thought alone. For it is not possible to trace out any image exactly to the whole extent of the truth. But, they say, what is the meaning of all this? For is not the one an offspring, and the other a something else of the One? Did not both Eve and Seth come from the one Adam? And were they both begotten by him? No; but the one was a fragment of him, and the other was begotten by him. And yet the two were one and the same thing; both were human beings; no one will deny that. Will you then give up your contention against the Spirit, that He must be either altogether begotten, or else cannot be consubstantial, or be God; and admit from human examples the possibility of our position? I think it will be well for you, unless you are determined to be very quarrelsome, and to fight against what is proved to demonstration.

XII. But, he says, who in ancient or modern times ever worshipped the Spirit? Who ever prayed to Him? Where is it written that we ought to worship Him, or to pray to Him, and whence have you derived this tenet of yours? We will give the more perfect reason hereafter, when we discuss the question of the unwritten; for the present it will suffice to say that it is the Spirit in Whom we worship, and in Whom we pray. For Scripture says, God is a Spirit, and they that worship Him must worship Him in Spirit and in truth.[α] And again,—We know not what we should pray for as we ought; but the Spirit Itself maketh intercession for us with groanings which cannot be uttered;[β] and I will pray with the Spirit and I will pray with the understanding also;[γ]—that is, in the mind and in the Spirit. Therefore to adore or to pray to the Spirit seems to me to be simply Himself offering prayer or adoration to Himself. And what godly or learned man would disapprove of this, because in fact the adoration of One is the adoration of the Three, because of the equality of honour and Deity between the Three? So I will not be frightened by the argument that all things are said to have been made by the Son;[δ] as if the Holy Spirit also were one of these things. For it says all things that were

Aspect—the word is ambiguous) is another Uttering; and the Three Persons together are only successive evolutions of the Logos, or world-ward aspect of the Divine Nature. As the Logos proceeded from God, so He at last returns into Him, and the process of Trinitarian development closes."

α Isa. viii. 19. β i.e. the Phœnix. Hdt., ii. 37.

α John iv. 24. β Rom. viii. 26.
γ 1 Cor. xiv. 15. δ John i. 2.

made, and not simply all things. For the Father was not, nor were any of the things that were not made. Prove that He was made, and then give Him to the Son, and number Him among the creatures; but until you can prove this you will gain nothing for your impiety from this comprehensive phrase. For if He was made, it was certainly through Christ; I myself would not deny that. But if He was not made, how can He be either one of the All, or through Christ? Cease then to dishonour the Father in your opposition to the Only-begotten (for it is no real honour, by presenting to Him a creature to rob Him of what is more valuable, a Son), and to dishonour the Son in your opposition to the Spirit. For He is not the Maker of a Fellow servant, but He is glorified with One of co-equal honour. Rank no part of the Trinity with thyself, lest thou fall away from the Trinity; cut not off from Either the One and equally august Nature; because if thou overthrow any of the Three thou wilt have overthrown the whole. Better to take a meagre view of the Unity than to venture on a complete impiety.

XIII. Our argument has now come to its principal point; and I am grieved that a problem that was long dead, and that had given way to faith, is now stirred up afresh; yet it is necessary to stand against these praters, and not to let judgment go by default, when we have the Word on our side, and are pleading the cause of the Spirit. If, say they, there is God and God and God, how is it that there are not Three Gods, or how is it that what is glorified is not a plurality of Principles? Who is it who say this? Those who have reached a more complete ungodliness, or even those who have taken the secondary part; I mean who are moderate in a sense in respect of the Son. For my argument is partly against both in common, partly against these latter in particular. What I have to say in answer to these is as follows:—What right have you who worship the Son, even though you have revolted from the Spirit, to call us Tritheists? Are not you Ditheists? For if you deny also the worship of the Only Begotten, you have clearly ranged yourself among our adversaries. And why should we deal kindly with you as not *quite* dead? But if you do worship Him, and are so far in the way of salvation, we will ask you what reasons you have to give for your ditheism, if you are charged with it? If there is in you a word of wisdom answer, and open to us also a way to an answer. For the very same reason with which you will repel a charge of Ditheism will prove sufficient for us against one of Tritheism. And thus we shall win the day by making use of you our accusers as our Advocates, than which nothing can be more generous.

XIV. What is our quarrel and dispute with both? To us there is One God, for the Godhead is One, and all that proceedeth from Him is referred to One, though we believe in Three Persons. For one is not more and another less God; nor is One before and another after; nor are They divided in will or parted in power; nor can you find here any of the qualities of divisible things; but the Godhead is, to speak concisely, undivided in separate Persons; and there is one mingling of Light, as it were of three suns joined to each other. When then we look at the Godhead, or the First Cause, or the Monarchia, that which we conceive is One; but when we look at the Persons in Whom the Godhead dwells, and at Those Who timelessly and with equal glory have their Being from the First Cause—there are Three Whom we worship.

XV. What of that, they will say perhaps; do not the Greeks also believe in one Godhead, as their more advanced philosophers declare? And with us Humanity is one, namely the entire race; but yet they have many gods, not One, just as there are many men. But in this case the common nature has a unity which is only conceivable in thought; and the individuals are parted from one another very far indeed, both by time and by dispositions and by power. For we are not only compound beings, but also contrasted beings, both with one another and with ourselves; nor do we remain entirely the same for a single day, to say nothing of a whole lifetime, but both in body and in soul are in a perpetual state of flow and change. And perhaps the same may be said of the Angels[a] and the whole of that superior nature which is second to the Trinity alone; although they are simple in some measure and more fixed in good, owing to their nearness to the highest Good.

XVI. Nor do those whom the Greeks worship as gods, and (to use their own expression) dæmons, need us in any respect for their accusers, but are convicted upon the testimony of their own theologians, some as subject to passion, some as given to faction, and full of innumerable evils and changes, and in a state of opposition, not only to one another, but even to their first causes, whom they call Oceani

a "Similarly it is clear concerning the Angels, that they have a being incapable of change, so far as pertains to their nature, with a capacity of change as to choice, and of intelligence and affections and places, in their own manner" (S. Thomas Aq., Summa, I., x., 5).

and Tethyes and Phanetes, and by several other names; and last of all a certain god who hated his children through his lust of rule, and swallowed up all the rest through his greediness that he might become the father of all men and gods whom he miserably devoured, and then vomited forth again. And if these are but myths and fables, as they say in order to escape the shamefulness of the story, what will they say in reference to the dictum that all things are divided into three parts,[α] and that each god presides over a different part of the Universe, having a distinct province as well as a distinct rank? But our faith is not like this, nor is this the portion of Jacob, says my Theologian.[β] But each of these Persons possesses Unity, not less with that which is United to it than with itself, by reason of the identity of Essence and Power.[γ] And this is the account of the Unity, so far as we have apprehended it. If then this account is the true one, let us thank God for the glimpse He has granted us; if it is not let us seek for a better.

XVII. As for the arguments with which you would overthrow the Union which we support, I know not whether we should say you are jesting or in earnest. For what is this argument? "Things of one essence, you say, are counted together," and by this "counted together," you mean that they are collected into one number.[δ] But things which are not of one essence are not thus counted . . . so that you cannot avoid speaking of three gods, according to this account, while we do not run any risk at all of it, inasmuch as we assert that they are not consubstantial. And so by a single word you have freed yourselves from trouble, and have gained a pernicious victory, for in fact you have done something like what men do when they hang themselves for fear of death. For to save yourselves trouble in your championship of the Monarchia you have denied the Godhead, and abandoned the question to your opponents. But for my part, even if labor should be necessary, I will not abandon the Object of my adoration. And yet on this point I cannot see where the difficulty is.

XVIII. You say, Things of one essence are counted together, but those which are not consubstantial are reckoned one by one. Where did you get this from? From what teachers of dogma or mythology? Do you not know that every number expresses the quantity of what is included under it, and not the nature of the things? But I am so oldfashioned, or perhaps I should say so unlearned, as to use the word Three of that number of things, even if they are of a different nature, and to use One and One and One in a different way of so many units, even if they are united in essence, looking not so much at the things themselves as at the quantity of the things in respect of which the enumeration is made. But since you hold so very close to the letter (although you are contending against the letter), pray take your demonstrations from this source. There are in the Book of Proverbs three things which go well, a lion, a goat, and a cock; and to these is added a fourth;—a King making a speech before the people,[α] to pass over the other sets of four which are there counted up, although things of various natures. And I find in Moses two Cherubim[β] counted singly. But now, in your technology, could either the former things be called three, when they differ so greatly in their nature, or the latter be treated as units when they are so closely connected and of one nature? For if I were to speak of God and Mammon, as two masters, reckoned under one head, when they are so very different from each other, I should probably be still more laughed at for such a connumeration.

XIX. But to my mind, he says, those things are said to be connumerated and of the same essence of which the names also correspond, as Three Men, or Three gods, but not Three this and that. What does this concession amount to? It is suitable to one laying down the law as to names, not to one who is asserting the truth. For I also will assert that Peter and James and John are not three or consubstantial, so long as I cannot say Three Peters, or Three Jameses, or Three Johns; for what you have reserved for common names we demand also for proper names, in accordance with your arrangement; or else you will be unfair in not conceding to others what you assume for yourself. What about John then, when in his Catholic Epistle he says that there are Three that bear witness,[γ] the Spirit

α Homer, Il., xiv., 189. β Jer. x. 16.

γ Petavius praises this dictum, De Trin., IV., xiii., 9.

δ συναριθμεῖται, as when you say Three Gods, or Three Men, and the like, as you do when you reckon up things of the same sort. On the other hand, you must use the plural number in reckoning up things which differ in kind.

α Prov. xxx. 29, 30, 31. β Exod. xxxvii. 7.

γ This is the famous passage of the Witnesses in 1 John v. 8. In some few later codices of the Vulgate are found the words which form verse 7 of our A. V. But neither verse 7 nor these words are to be found in any Greek MS. earlier than the Fifteenth Century; nor are they quoted by any Greek Father, and by very few and late Latin ones. They have been thought to be cited by S. Cyprian in his work on the Unity of the Church; and this citation, if a fact, would be a most important one, as it would throw back their reception to an early date. But Tischendorf (Gk. Test., Ed. viii., ad. loc.) gives reasons for believing that the quotation is only apparent, and is really of the last clause of verse 8.

and the Water and the Blood? Do you think he is talking nonsense? First, because he has ventured to reckon under one numeral things which are not consubstantial, though you say this ought to be done only in the case of things which are consubstantial. For who would assert that these are consubstantial? Secondly, because he has not been consistent in the way he has happened upon his terms; for after using Three in the masculine gender he adds three words which are neuter, contrary to the definitions and laws which you and your grammarians have laid down. For what is the difference between putting a masculine Three first, and then adding One and One and One in the neuter, or after a masculine One and One and One to use the Three not in the masculine but in the neuter, which you yourself disclaim in the case of Deity? What have you to say about the Crab, which may mean either an animal, or an instrument, or a constellation? And what about the Dog, now terrestrial, now aquatic, now celestial? Do you not see that three crabs or dogs are spoken of? Why of course it is so. Well then, are they therefore of one substance? None but a fool would say that. So you see how completely your argument from connumeration has broken down, and is refuted by all these instances. For if things that are of one substance are not always counted under one numeral, and things not of one substance are thus counted, and the pronunciation of the name[a] once for all is used in both cases, what advantage do you gain towards your doctrine?

XX. I will look also at this further point, which is not without its bearing on the subject. One and One added together make Two; and Two resolved again becomes One and One, as is perfectly evident. If, however, elements which are added together must, as your theory requires, be consubstantial, and those which are separate be heterogeneous, then it will follow that the same things must be both consubstantial and heterogeneous. No: I laugh at your Counting Before and your Counting After, of which you are so proud, as if the facts themselves depended upon the order of their names. If this were so, according to the same law, since the same things are in consequence of the equality of their nature counted in Holy Scripture, sometimes in an earlier, sometimes in a later place, what prevents them from being at once more honourable and less honourable than themselves? I say the same of the names God and Lord, and of the prepositions Of Whom, and By Whom, and In Whom, by which you describe the Deity according to the rules of art for us, attributing the first to the Father, the second to the Son, and the third to the Holy Ghost. For what would you have done, if each of these expressions were constantly allotted to Each Person, when, the fact being that they are used of all the Persons, as is evident to those who have studied the question, you even so make them the ground of such inequality both of nature and dignity. This is sufficient for all who are not altogether wanting in sense. But since it is a matter of difficulty for you after you have once made an assault upon the Spirit, to check your rush, and not rather like a furious boar to push your quarrel to the bitter end, and to thrust yourself upon the knife until you have received the whole wound in your own breast; let us go on to see what further argument remains to you.

XXI. Over and over again you turn upon us the silence of Scripture. But that it is not a strange doctrine, nor an afterthought, but acknowledged and plainly set forth both by the ancients and many of our own day, is already demonstrated by many persons who have treated of this subject, and who have handled the Holy Scriptures, not with indifference or as a mere pastime, but have gone beneath the letter and looked into the inner meaning, and have been deemed worthy to see the hidden beauty, and have been irradiated by the light of knowledge. We, however in our turn will briefly prove it as far as may be, in order not to seem to be over-curious or improperly ambitious, building on another's foundation. But since the fact, that Scripture does not very clearly or very often write Him God in express words (as it does first the Father and afterwards the Son), becomes to you an occasion of blasphemy and of this excessive wordiness and impiety, we will release you from this inconvenience by a short discussion of things and names, and especially of their use in Holy Scripture.

XXII. Some things have no existence, but are spoken of; others which do exist are not spoken of; some neither exist nor are spoken of, and some both exist and are spoken of. Do you ask me for proof of this? I am ready to give it. According to Scripture God sleeps and is awake, is angry, walks, has the Cherubim for His Throne. And yet when did He become liable to passion, and have you ever

[a] i.e. Though the things referred to may differ essentially, yet if the name by which they are known is the same, one utterance of it with one numeral is enough to express a collection of them all.

heard that God has a body? This then is, though not really fact, a figure of speech. For we have given names according to our own comprehension from our own attributes to those of God. His remaining silent apart from us, and as it were not caring for us, for reasons known to Himself, is what we call His sleeping; for our own sleep is such a state of inactivity. And again, His sudden turning to do us good is the waking up; for waking is the dissolution of sleep, as visitation is of turning away. And when He punishes, we say He is angry; for so it is with us, punishment is the result of anger. And His working, now here now there, we call walking; for walking is change from one place to another. His resting among the Holy Hosts, and as it were loving to dwell among them, is His sitting and being enthroned; this, too, from ourselves, for God resteth nowhere as He doth upon the Saints. His swiftness of moving is called flying, and His watchful care is called His Face, and his giving and bestowing[α] is His hand; and, in a word, every other of the powers or activities of God has depicted for us some other corporeal one.

XXIII. Again, where do you get your Unbegotten and Unoriginate, those two citadels of your position, or we our Immortal? Show me these in so many words, or we shall either set them aside, or erase them as not contained in Scripture; and you are slain by your own principle, the names you rely on being overthrown, and therewith the wall of refuge in which you trusted. Is it not evident that they are due to passages which imply them, though the words do not actually occur? What are these passages?—I am the first, and I am the last,[β] and before Me there was no God, neither shall there be after Me.[γ] For all that depends on that Am makes for my side, for it has neither beginning nor ending. When you accept this, that nothing is before Him, and that He has not an older Cause, you have implicitly given Him the titles Unbegotten and Unoriginate. And to say that He has no end of Being is to call Him Immortal and Indestructible. The first pairs, then, that I referred to are accounted for thus. But what are the things which neither exist in fact nor are said? That God is evil; that a sphere is square; that the past is present; that man is not a compound being. Have you ever known a man of such stupidity as to venture either to think or to assert any such thing? It remains to shew what are the things which exist, both in fact and in language. God, Man, Angel, Judgment, Vanity (viz., such arguments as yours), and the subversion of faith and emptying of the mystery.

XXIV. Since, then, there is so much difference in terms and things, why are you such a slave to the letter, and a partisan of the Jewish wisdom, and a follower of syllables at the expense of facts? But if, when you said twice five or twice seven, I concluded from your words that you meant Ten or Fourteen; or if, when you spoke of a rational and mortal animal, that you meant Man, should you think me to be talking nonsense? Surely not, because I should be merely repeating your own meaning; for words do not belong more to the speaker of them than to him who called them forth. As, then, in this case, I should have been looking, not so much at the terms used, as at the thoughts they were meant to convey; so neither, if I found something else either not at all or not clearly expressed in the Words of Scripture to be included in the meaning, should I avoid giving it utterance, out of fear of your sophistical trick about terms. In this way, then, we shall hold our own against the semi-orthodox—among whom I may not count you. For since you deny the Titles of the Son, which are so many and so clear, it is quite evident that even if you learnt a great many more and clearer ones you would not be moved to reverence. But now I will take up the argument again a little way further back, and shew you, though you are so clever, the reason for this entire system of secresy.

XXV. There have been in the whole period of the duration of the world two conspicuous changes of men's lives, which are also called two Testaments,[α] or, on account of the wide fame of the matter, two Earthquakes; the one from idols to the Law, the other from the Law to the Gospel. And we are taught in the Gospel of a third earthquake, namely, from this Earth to that which cannot be shaken or moved.[β] Now the two Testaments are alike in this respect, that the change was not made on a sudden, nor at the first movement of the endeavour. Why not (for this is a point on which we must have information)? That no violence might be done to us, but that we might be moved by persuasion. For nothing that is involuntary is durable; like streams or trees which are kept back by force. But that which is voluntary is more durable and safe.

α var. lect., receiving. β Isa. xli. 4. γ Ib. xliii. 10.

α Heb. xii. 26.

β Referring to the earthquake at the giving of the Law on Mt. Sinai (Heb. xiii.), and to the prophesy of Haggai (ii. 6), with reference to the Incarnation. The third great earthquake is that of the end of the world (Heb. xii. 26).

The former is due to one who uses force, the latter is ours; the one is due to the gentleness of God, the other to a tyrannical authority. Wherefore God did not think it behoved Him to benefit the unwilling, but to do good to the willing. And therefore like a Tutor or Physician He partly removes and partly condones ancestral habits, conceding some little of what tended to pleasure, just as medical men do with their patients, that their medicine may be taken, being artfully blended with what is nice. For it is no very easy matter to change from those habits which custom and use have made honourable. For instance, the first cut off the idol, but left the sacrifices; the second, while it destroyed the sacrifices did not forbid circumcision.[α] Then, when once men had submitted to the curtailment, they also yielded that which had been conceded to them;[β] in the first instance the sacrifices, in the second circumcision; and became instead of Gentiles, Jews, and instead of Jews, Christians, being beguiled into the Gospel by gradual changes. Paul is a proof of this; for having at one time administered circumcision, and submitted to legal purification, he advanced till he could say, and I, brethren, if I yet preach circumcision, why do I yet suffer persecution?[γ] His former conduct belonged to the temporary dispensation, his latter to maturity.

XXVI. To this I may compare the case of Theology[δ] except that it proceeds the reverse way. For in the case by which I have illustrated it the change is made by successive subtractions; whereas here perfection is reached by additions. For the matter stands thus. The Old Testament proclaimed the Father openly, and the Son more obscurely. The New manifested the Son, and suggested the Deity of the Spirit. Now the Spirit Himself dwells among us, and supplies us with a clearer demonstration of Himself. For it was not safe, when the Godhead of the Father was not yet acknowledged, plainly to proclaim the Son; nor when that of the Son was not yet received to burden us further (if I may use so bold an expression) with the Holy Ghost; lest perhaps people might, like men loaded with food beyond their strength, and presenting eyes as yet too weak to bear it to the sun's light, risk the loss even of that which was within the reach of their powers; but that by gradual additions, and, as David says, Goings up, and advances and progress from glory to glory,[α] the Light of the Trinity might shine upon the more illuminated. For this reason it was, I think, that He *gradually* came to dwell in the Disciples, measuring Himself out to them according to their capacity to receive Him, at the beginning of the Gospel, after the Passion, after the Ascension, making perfect their powers, being breathed upon them, and appearing in fiery tongues. And indeed it is by little and little that He is declared by Jesus, as you will learn for yourself if you will read more carefully. I will ask the Father, He says, and He will send you another Comforter, even the spirit of Truth.[β] This He said that He might not seem to be a rival God, or to make His discourses to them by another authority. Again, He shall send Him, but it is in My Name. He leaves out the I will ask, but He keeps the Shall send,[γ] then again, I will send,—His own dignity. Then shall come,[δ] the authority of the Spirit.

XXVII. You see lights breaking upon us, gradually; and the order of Theology, which it is better for us to keep, neither proclaiming things too suddenly, nor yet keeping them hidden to the end. For the former course would be unscientific, the latter atheistical; and the former would be calculated to startle outsiders, the latter to alienate our own people. I will add another point to what I have said; one which may readily have come into the mind of some others, but which I think a fruit of my own thought. Our Saviour had some things which, He said, could not be borne at that time by His disciples[ε] (though they were filled with many teachings), perhaps for the reasons I have mentioned; and therefore they were hidden. And again He said that all things should be taught us by the Spirit when He should come to dwell amongst us.[ς] Of these things one, I take it, was the Deity of the Spirit Himself, made clear later on when such knowledge should be seasonable and capable of being received after our Saviour's restoration, when it would no longer be received with incredulity because of its marvellous character. For what greater thing than this did either He promise, or the Spirit teach. If indeed anything is to be considered great and worthy of the Majesty of God, which was either promised or taught.

XXVIII. This, then, is my position with regard to these things, and I hope it may be always my position, and that of whosoever is dear

α Acts xvi. 3. β Ib. xxi. 26. γ Galat. vii. 7–17.

δ Theology is here used in a restricted sense, as denoting simply the doctrine of the Deity of the Son or Logos. It is very frequently used in this limited sense; examples of which may readily be found in Gregory of Nyssa, Basil, Chrysostom, and others. A similar use occurs in Orat. XXXVIII., c. 8, in which passage θεολογία is contrasted with οἰκονομία, the doctrine of our Lord's Divinity with that of the Incarnation.

α Ps. lxxxiv. 7, and 2 Cor. iii. 18. β John xiv. 16, 17. γ John xvi. 7. δ Ib. xvi. 8 ε Ib. xvi. 12. ς Ib. xiv. 26.

to me; to worship God the Father, God the Son, and God the Holy Ghost, Three Persons, One Godhead, undivided in honour and glory and substance and kingdom, as one of our own inspired philosophers[α] not long departed shewed. Let him not see the rising of the Morning Star, as Scripture saith,[β] nor the glory of its brightness, who is otherwise minded, or who follows the temper of the times, at one time being of one mind and of another at another time, and thinking unsoundly in the highest matters. For if He is not to be worshipped, how can He deify me by Baptism? but if He is to be worshipped, surely He is an Object of adoration, and if an Object of adoration He must be God; the one is linked to the other, a truly golden and saving chain. And indeed from the Spirit comes our New Birth, and from the New Birth our new creation, and from the new creation our deeper knowledge of the dignity of Him from Whom it is derived.

XXIX. This, then, is what may be said by one who admits the silence of Scripture. But now the swarm of testimonies shall burst upon you from which the Deity of the Holy Ghost[γ] shall be shewn to all who are not excessively stupid, or else altogether enemies to the Spirit, to be most clearly recognized in Scripture. Look at these facts:—Christ is born; the Spirit is His Forerunner. He is baptized; the Spirit bears witness. He is tempted; the Spirit leads Him up.[δ] He works miracles; the Spirit accompanies them. He ascends; the Spirit takes His place. What great things are there in the idea of God which are not in His power?[ε] What titles which belong to God are not applied to Him, except only Unbegotten and Begotten? For it was needful that the distinctive properties of the Father and the Son should remain peculiar to Them, lest there should be confusion in the Godhead Which brings all things, even disorder[ζ] itself, into due arrangement and good order. Indeed I tremble when I think of the abundance of the titles, and how many Names they outrage who fall foul of the Spirit. He is called the Spirit of God, the Spirit of Christ, the Mind of Christ, the Spirit of The Lord, and Himself The Lord, the Spirit of Adoption, of Truth, of Liberty; the Spirit of Wisdom, of Understanding, of Counsel, of Might, of Knowledge, of Godliness, of the Fear of God. For He is the Maker of all these, filling all with His Essence, containing all things, filling the world in His Essence, yet incapable of being comprehended in His power by the world; good, upright, princely, by nature not by adoption; sanctifying, not sanctified; measuring, not measured; shared, not sharing; filling, not filled; containing, not contained; inherited, glorified, reckoned with the Father and the Son; held out as a threat;[α] the Finger of God; fire like God; to manifest, as I take it, His consubstantiality); the Creator-Spirit, Who by Baptism and by Resurrection creates anew; the Spirit That knoweth all things, That teacheth, That bloweth where and to what extent He listeth; That guideth, talketh, sendeth forth, separateth, is angry or tempted; That revealeth, illumineth, quickeneth, or rather is the very Light and Life; That maketh Temples; That deifieth; That perfecteth so as even to anticipate Baptism,[β] yet after Baptism to be sought as a separate gift;[γ] That doeth all things that God doeth; divided into fiery tongues; dividing gifts; making Apostles, Prophets, Evangelists, Pastors, and Teachers; understanding manifold, clear, piercing, undefiled, unhindered, which is the same thing as Most wise and varied in His actions; and making all things clear and plain; and of independent power, unchangeable, Almighty, all-seeing, penetrating all spirits that are intelligent, pure, most subtle (the Angel Hosts I think); and also all prophetic spirits and apostolic in the same manner and not in the same places; for they lived in different places; thus showing that He is uncircumscript.

XXX. They who say and teach these things, and moreover call Him another Paraclete in the sense of another God, who know that blasphemy against Him alone cannot be forgiven,[δ] and who branded with such fearful infamy Ananias and Sapphira for having lied to the Holy Ghost, what do you think of these men?[ε] Do they proclaim the Spirit God, or something else? Now really, you must be extraordinarily dull and far from the Spirit if you have any doubt about this and need some one to teach you. So important then, and so vivid are His Names. Why is it necessary to lay before you the testimony contained in the very

α Perhaps S. Gregory Thaumaturgus is meant. He was born about A.D. 210. The date of his death is uncertain, but was probably not before 270. He was Bishop of Neocæsarea in Pontus. Amongst his works was an Exposition of the Faith, which he is said to have received by direct revelation, and in it the words in the text were contained. S. Gregory in another Oration refers to the closing sentences as the substance of the Formula itself: "There is nothing created or servile in the Trinity, nor anything superinduced, as though previously non-existing and introduced afterwards. Never, therefore, was the Son wanting to the Father, nor the Spirit to the Son; but there is ever the same Trinity, unchangeable and unalterable (Reynolds, in Dict. Biog.).

β Job iii. 9. γ Luke i. 35; iii. 22; iv. 1. δ Luke iv. 1, 18.

ε Acts ii. 4. ζ v. l. Yea, even disorder.

α Viz.:—where we are told that Blasphemy against Him hath never forgiveness.

β As in the case of the Centurion Cornelius, Acts x. 9.

γ i. e. in Confirmation. δ Matt. xii. 31. ε Acts v. 3, etc.

words? And whatever in this case also[a] is said in more lowly fashion, as that He is Given, Sent, Divided; that He is the Gift, the Bounty, the Inspiration, the Promise, the Intercession for us, and, not to go into any further detail, any other expressions of the sort, is to be referred to the First Cause, that it may be shewn from Whom He is, and that men may not in heathen fashion admit Three Principles. For it is equally impious to confuse the Persons with the Sabellians, or to divide the Natures with the Arians.

XXXI. I have very carefully considered this matter in my own mind, and have looked at it in every point of view, in order to find some illustration of this most important subject, but I have been unable to discover any thing on earth with which to compare the nature of the Godhead. For even if I did happen upon some tiny likeness it escaped me for the most part, and left me down below with my example. I picture to myself an eye,[β] a fountain, a river, as others have done before, to see if the first might be analogous to the Father, the second to the Son, and the third to the Holy Ghost. For in these there is no distinction in time, nor are they torn away from their connexion with each other, though they seem to be parted by three personalities. But I was afraid in the first place that I should present a flow in the Godhead, incapable of standing still; and secondly that by this figure a numerical unity would be introduced. For the eye and the spring and the river are numerically one, though in different forms.

XXXII. Again I thought of the sun and a ray and light. But here again there was a fear lest people should get an idea of composition in the Uncompounded Nature, such as there is in the Sun and the things that are in the Sun. And in the second place lest we should give Essence to the Father but deny Personality to the Others, and make Them only Powers of God, existing in Him and not Personal. For neither the ray nor the light is another sun, but they are only effulgences from the Sun, and qualities of His essence. And lest we should thus, as far as the illustration goes, attribute both Being and Not-being to God, which is even more monstrous. I have also heard that some one has suggested an illustration of the following kind. A ray of the Sun flashing upon a wall and trembling with the movement of the moisture which the beam has taken up in mid air, and then, being checked by the hard body, has set up a strange quivering. For it quivers with many rapid movements, and is not one rather than it is many, nor yet many rather than one; because by the swiftness of its union and separating it escapes before the eye can see it.

XXXIII. But it is not possible for *me* to make use of even this; because it is very evident what gives the ray its motion; but there is nothing prior to God which could set Him in motion; for He is Himself the Cause of all things, and He has no prior Cause. And secondly because in this case also there is a suggestion of such things as composition, diffusion, and an unsettled and unstable nature . . . none of which we can suppose in the Godhead. In a word, there is nothing which presents a standing point to my mind in these illustrations from which to consider the Object which I am trying to represent to myself, unless one may indulgently accept one point of the image while rejecting the rest. Finally, then, it seems best to me to let the images and the shadows go, as being deceitful and very far short of the truth; and clinging myself to the more reverent conception, and resting upon few words, using the guidance of the Holy Ghost, keeping to the end as my genuine comrade and companion the enlightenment which I have received from Him, and passing through this world to persuade all others also to the best of my power to worship Father, Son, and Holy Ghost, the One Godhead and Power. To Him belongs all glory and honour and might for ever and ever. Amen.

ORATION XXXIII.

Against the Arians, and Concerning Himself.

Delivered at Constantinople about the middle of the year 380.

I. Where are they who reproach us with our poverty, and boast themselves of their own riches; who define the Church by numbers,[a] and scorn the little flock; and who measure Godhead,[β] and weigh the people in the balance, who honour the sand, and despise the luminaries of heaven; who treasure pebbles and overlook pearls; for they know not that sand is not in a greater degree more abundant than stars, and pebbles than lustrous stones—

[a] As before in the case of the Son. See above, Theol., iii. 18.

[β] Elias Cretensis says that the Eye in this passage is not to be understood of the member of the body so called, but as the Eye or the centre of a spring, the point from which the water flows.

[a] Shewing the absurdity of defining the Church by counting heads.

[β] This refers to the distinction drawn by the Arians in degree as to the Godhead, asserting the Spirit to be great, the Son greater, and the Father greatest (cf. Or. xlii., 16).

that the former are purer and more precious than the latter? Are you again indignant? Do you again arm yourselves? Do you again insult us?[α] Is this a new faith? Restrain your threats a little while that I may speak. We will not insult you, but we will convict you; we will not threaten, but we will reproach you; we will not strike, but we will heal. This too appears an insult! What pride! Do you here also regard your equal as your slave? If not, permit me to speak openly; for even a brother chides his brother if he has been defrauded by him.

II. Would you like me to utter to you the words of God to Israel, stiff-necked and hardened? "O my people what have I done unto thee, or wherein have I injured thee, or wherein have I wearied thee?"[β] This language indeed is fitter from me to you who insult me. It is a sad thing that we watch for opportunities against each other, and having destroyed our fellowship of spirit by diversities of opinion have become almost more inhuman and savage to one another than even the barbarians who are now engaged in war against us, banded together against us by the Trinity whom we have separated; with this difference that we are not foreigners making forays and raids upon foreigners, nor nations of different language, which is some little consolation in the calamity, but are making war upon one another, and almost upon those of the same household; or if you will, we the members of the same body are consuming and being consumed by one another. Nor is this, bad though it be, the extent of our calamity, for we even regard our diminution as a gain. But since we are in such a condition, and regulate our faith by the times, let us compare the times with one another; you your Emperor,[γ] and I my Sovereigns;[δ] you Ahab and I Josias. Tell me of your moderation, and I will proclaim my violence. But indeed yours is proclaimed by many books and tongues, which I think future ages will accept as an immortal pillory for your actions and I will declare my own.

III. What tumultuous mob have I led against you? What soldiers have I armed? What general boiling with rage, and more savage than his employers, and not even a Christian, but one who offers his impiety against us as his private worship to his own gods?[ε] Whom have I besieged while engaged in prayer and lifting up their hands to God? When have I put a stop to psalmody with trumpets? or mingled the Sacramental Blood with blood of massacre? What spiritual sighs have I put an end to by cries of death, or tears of penitence by tears of tragedy? What House of prayer have I made a burialplace? What liturgical vessels which the multitude may not touch have I given over to the hands of the wicked, of a Nebuzaradan,[α] chief of the cooks, or of a Belshazzar, who wickedly used the sacred vessels for his revels,[β] and then paid a worthy penalty for his madness? "Altars beloved" as Holy Scripture saith, but "now defiled."[γ] And what licentious youth has insulted you for our sake with shameful writhings and contortions? O precious Throne, seat and rest of precious men, which hast been occupied by a succession of pious Priests, who from ancient times have taught the divine Mysteries, what heathen popular speaker and evil tongue hath mounted thee to inveigh against the Christian's faith? O modesty and majesty of Virgins, that cannot endure the looks of even virtuous men, which of us hath shamed thee, and outraged thee by the exposure of what may not be seen, and showed to the eyes of the impious a pitiable sight, worthy of the fires of Sodom? I say nothing of deaths, which were more endurable than this shame.

IV. What wild beasts have we let loose upon the bodies of Saints,—like some who have prostituted human nature,—on one single accusation, that of not consenting to their impiety; or defiled ourselves by communion with them, which we avoid like the poison of a snake, not because it injures the body, but because it blackens the depths of the soul? Against whom have we made it a matter of criminal accusation that they buried the dead, whom the very beasts reverenced? And what a charge, worthy of another theatre and of other beasts! What Bishop's aged flesh have we carded with hooks in the presence of their disciples, impotent to help them save by tears, hung up with Christ, conquering by suffering, and sprinkling the people with their

α The beginning of the Oration was apparently disturbed by hostile demonstrations on the part of Arian hearers.

β Mic. vi. 3. γ Valens. δ Theodosius and Gratian.

ε Dr. Ullmann makes this passage refer to outrages perpetrated in Constantinople itself on Gregory, by his Arian opponents. On one occasion, he says, in the night time the meetingplace of the Orthodox was assailed; a mob of Arians, and in particular women of the lowest stamp, set on by monks, armed themselves with sticks and stones, and forced an entrance into the peaceful place of holy worship. The champion of orthodoxy well nigh became a martyr to his convictions; the Altar was profaned, the consecrated wine was mixed with blood; the house of prayer was made a scene of outrage and unbridled licentiousness. The Benedictine Editors, however, whom Benoit follows, think the reference is to the disturbances in Alexandria when the Arian Lucius was forcibly intruded into the Chair of Athanasius by the Prefect Palladius. A full account of the atrocities by which his installation was marked is to be found in a letter of Peter, the expelled or orthodox Patriarch, preserved in Theodoret (H. E. IV. 22). This Lucius was living in Constantinople and abetting the Arian party there at the time when Gregory pronounced this Oration.

α 2 Kings xxv. 11. β Dan. v. 3. γ Hos. viii. 11 (LXX.).

precious blood, and at last carried away to death, to be both crucified and buried and glorified with Christ; with Christ Who conquered the world by such victims and sacrifices? What priests have those contrary elements fire and water divided, raising a strange beacon over the sea, and set on fire together with the ship in which they put to sea?[α] Who (to cover the more numerous part of our woes with a veil of silence) have been accused of inhumanity by the very magistrates who conferred such favour on them? For even if they did obey the lusts of those men, yet at any rate they hated the cruelty of their purpose. The one was opportunism, the other calculation; the one came of the lawlessness of the Emperor, the other of a consciousness of the laws by which they had to judge.

V. And to speak of older things, for they too belong to the same fraternity; whose hands living or dead have I cut off—to bring a lying accusation against Saints,[β] and to triumph over the faith by bluster? Whose exiles have I numbered as benefits, and failed to reverence even the sacred colleges of sacred philosophers, whence I sought their suppliants? Nay the very contrary is the case; I have reckoned as Martyrs those who incurred anger for the truth. Upon whom have I, whom you accuse of licentiousness of language, brought harlots when they were almost fleshless and bloodless? Which of the faithful have I exiled from their country and given over to the hands of lawless men, that they might be kept like wild beasts in rooms without light, and (for this is the saddest part of the tragedy) left separated from each other to endure the hardships of hunger and thirst, with food measured out to them, which they had to receive through narrow openings, so that they might not be permitted even to see their companions in misery. And what were they who suffered thus? Men of whom the world was not worthy.[γ] Is it thus that you honour faith? Is this your kind treatment of it? Ye know not the greater part of these things, and that reasonably, because of the number of these facts and the pleasure of the action. But he who suffers has a better memory. There have been even some more cruel than the times themselves, like wild boars hurled against a fence. I demand your victim of yesterday[α] the old man, the Abraham-like Father, whom on his return from exile you greeted with stones in the middle of the day and in the middle of the city. But we, if it is not invidious to say so, begged off even our murderers from their danger. God says somewhere in Scripture, How shall I pardon thee for this?[β] Which of these things shall I praise; or rather for which shall I bind a wreath upon you?

VI. Now since your antecedents are such, I should be glad if you too will tell me of my crimes, that I may either amend my life or be put to shame. My greatest wish is that I may be found free from wrong altogether; but if this may not be, at least to be converted from my crime; for this is the second best portion of the prudent. For if like the just man I do not become my own accuser in the first instance,[γ] yet at any rate I gladly receive healing from another. "Your City, you say to me, is a little one, or rather is no city at all, but only a village, arid, without beauty, and with few inhabitants." But, my good friend, this is my misfortune, rather than my fault;—if indeed it be a misfortune; and if it is against my will, I am to be pitied for my bad luck, if I may put it so; but if it be willingly, I am a philosopher. Which of these is a crime? Would anyone abuse a dolphin for not being a land animal, or an ox because it is not aquatic, or a lamprey because it is amphibious? But we, you go on, have walls and theatres and racecourses and palaces, and beautiful great Porticoes, and that marvellous work the underground and overhead river,[δ] and the splendid and admired column,[ε] and the crowded marketplace and a restless people, and a famous senate of highborn men.

VII. Why do you not also mention the convenience of the site, and what I may call the contest between land and sea as to which owns the City, and which adorns our Royal City with all their good things? This then is our crime, that while you are great and splendid, we are small and come from a small place? Many others do you this wrong, indeed all those whom you excel; and must we die be-

α Socrates (H. E. IV. 16) gives an account of the murder of eighty Priests by order of Valens. The Prefect of Nicomedia, being afraid to execute the Emperor's commands by a public action, put these men on board a ship, as if to send them into exile, but gave orders to the crew to set the vessel on fire on the high seas, and leave the prisoners to their fate.

Billius, however, thinks that the reference is to the martyrdom of a single Priest, whose death in this way is described by S. Gregory in his panegyric on Maximus (Or. xxv. 10, p. 461, 462).

β S. Athanasius was accused by the Arians of having murdered a Meletian Bishop named Arsenius, and cut off his hand to use for magical purposes; and at a Synod held at Tyre in 334 they produced the alleged hand in a box. Athanasius, however, was able to produce Arsenius alive and unmutilated; but even so his accusers were not satisfied. γ Heb. xi. 38.

α The reference is perhaps to Eusebius of Samosata, who was killed by a tile thrown at him by an Arian woman. In dying he bound his friends by an oath not to allow the murderess to be punished. β Jer. v. 7. γ Prov. xviii. 17.

δ Valens had constructed an Aqueduct, partly subterranean, partly raised on arches, for the supply of water to the Capital.

ε A magnificent column on which stood an equestrian statue of Constantine the Great.

cause we have not reared a city, nor built walls around it, nor can boast of our racecourse, or our stadia, and pack of hounds, and all the follies that are connected with these things; nor have to boast of the beauty and splendour of our baths, and the costliness of their marbles and pictures and golden embroideries of all sorts of species, almost rivalling nature? Nor have we yet rounded off the sea for ourselves, or mingled the seasons, as of course you, the new Creators, have done, that we may live in what is at once the pleasantest and the safest way. Add if you like other charges, you who say, The silver is mine and the gold is mine,[α] those words of God. We neither think much of riches, on which, if they increase, our Law forbids us to set our hearts, nor do we count up yearly and daily revenues; nor do we rival one another in loading our tables with enchantments for our senseless belly. For neither do we highly esteem those things which after we have swallowed them are all of the same worth, or rather I should say worthlessness, and are rejected. But we live so simply and from hand to mouth, as to differ but little from beasts whose sustenance is without apparatus and inartificial.

VIII. Do you also find fault with the raggedness of my dress, and the want of elegance in the disposition of my face? for these are the points upon which I see that some persons who are very insignificant pride themselves. Will you leave my head alone, and not jeer at it, as the children did at Elissæus? What followed I will not mention. And will you leave out of your allegations my want of education, and what seems to you the roughness and rusticity of my elocution? And where will you put the fact that I am not full of small talk, nor a jester popular with company, nor great hunter of the marketplace, nor given to chatter and gossip with any chance people upon all sorts of subjects, so as to make even conversation grievous; nor a frequenter of Zeuxippus, that new Jerusalem;[β] nor one who strolls from house to house flattering and stuffing himself; but for the most part staying at home, of low spirits and with a melancholy cast of countenance, quietly associating with myself, the genuine critic of my actions; and perhaps worthy of imprisonment for my uselessness? How is it that you pardon me for all this, and do not blame me for it? How sweet and kind you are.

IX. But I am so old fashioned and such a philosopher as to believe that one heaven is common to all; and that so is the revolution of the sun and the moon, and the order and arrangement of the stars; and that all have in common an equal share and profit in day and night, and also change of seasons, rains, fruits, and quickening power of the air; and that the flowing rivers are a common and abundant wealth to all; and that one and the same is the Earth, the mother and the tomb, from which we were taken, and to which we shall return, none having a greater share than another. And further, above this, we have in common reason, the Law, the Prophets, the very Sufferings of Christ, by which we were all without exception created anew, who partake of the same Adam, and were led astray by the serpent and slain by sin, and are saved by the heavenly Adam and brought back by the tree of shame to the tree of life from whence we had fallen.

X. I was deceived too by the Ramah of Samuel, that little fatherland of the great man; which was no dishonour to the Prophet, for it drew its honour not so much from itself as from him; nor was he hindered on its account from being given to God before his birth, or from uttering oracles, and foreseeing the future; nor only so, but also anointing Kings and Priests, and judging the men of illustrious cities. I heard also of Saul, how while seeking his father's asses he found a kingdom. And even David himself was taken from the sheepfolds to be the shepherd of Israel. What of Amos? Was he not, while a goatherd and scraper of sycamore fruit entrusted with the gifts of prophecy? How is it that I have passed over Joseph, who was both a slave and the giver of corn to Egypt, and the father of many myriads who were promised before to Abraham? Aye and I was deceived by the Carmel of Elias, who received the car of fire; and by the sheepskin of Elissæus that had more power than a silken web or than gold forced into garments. I was deceived by the desert of John, which held the greatest among them that are born of women, with that clothing, that food, that girdle, which we know. And I ventured even beyond these, and found God Himself the Patron of my rusticity. I will range myself with Bethlehem, and will share the ignominy of the Manger; for since you refuse on this account honour to God, it is no wonder that on the same account you despise His herald also. And I will bring up to you the Fishermen, and the poor to whom the Gospel is preached, as preferred before many rich. Will you ever leave off priding yourselves upon your cities?

α Hagg. ii. 8

β It is not certain what is the allusion here. Some think a great Circus or Hippodrome for chariot races; others say an institution in which were heretical schools; others again, the great baths of Zeuxippus.

Will you ever revere that wilderness which you abominate and despise? I do not yet say that gold has its birthplace in sand; nor that translucent stones are the product and gifts of rocks; for if to these I should oppose all that is dishonourable in cities perhaps it would be to no good end that I should use my freedom of speech.

XI. But perhaps some one who is very circumscribed and carnally minded will say, "But our herald is a stranger and a foreigner." What of the Apostles? Were not they strangers to the many nations and cities among whom they were divided, that the Gospel might have free course everywhere, that nothing might miss the illumination of the Threefold Light, or be unenlightened by the Truth; but that the night of ignorance might be dissolved for those who sat in darkness and the shadow of death? You have heard the words of Paul, "that we might go the Gentiles, and they to the Circumcision." [α] Be it that Judæa is Peter's home; what has Paul in common with the Gentiles, Luke with Achaia, Andrew with Epirus, John with Ephesus, Thomas with India, Marc with Italy, or the rest, not to go into particulars, with those to whom they went? So that you must either blame them or excuse me, or else prove that you, the ambassadors of the true Gospel, are being insulted by trifling. But since I have argued with you in a petty way about these matters, I will now proceed to take a larger and more philosophic view of them.

XII. My friend, every one that is of high mind has one Country, the Heavenly Jerusalem, in which we store up our Citizenship. All have one family—if you look at what is here below the dust—or if you look higher, that Inbreathing of which we are partakers, and which we were bidden to keep, and with which I must stand before my Judge to give an account of my heavenly nobility, and of the Divine Image. Everyone then is noble who has guarded this through virtue and consent to his Archetype. On the other hand, everyone is ignoble who has mingled with evil, and put upon himself another form, that of the serpent. And these earthly countries and families are the playthings of this our temporary life and scene. For our country is whatever each may have first occupied, either as tyrant, or in misfortune; and in this we are all alike strangers and pilgrims, however much we may play with names. And the family is accounted noble which is either rich from old days, or is recently raised; and of ignoble birth that which is of poor parents, either owing to misfortune or to want of ambition. For how can a nobility be given from above which is at one time beginning and at another coming to an end; and which is not given to some, but is bestowed on others by letters patent? Such is my mind on this matter. Therefore I leave it to you to pride yourself on tombs or in myths, and I endeavour as far as I can, to purify myself from deceits, that I may keep if possible my nobility, or else may recover it.

XIII. It is thus then and for these reasons that I, who am small and of a country without repute, have come upon you, and that not of my own accord, nor self-sent, like many of those who now seize upon the chief places; but because I was invited, and compelled, and have followed the scruples of my conscience and the Call of the Spirit. If it be otherwise, may I continue to fight here to no purpose, and deliver no one from his error, but may they obtain their desire who seek the barrenness of my soul, if I lie. But since I am come, and perchance with no contemptible power (if I may boast myself a little of my folly), which of those who are insatiable have I copied, what have I emulated of opportunism, although I have such examples, even apart from which it is hard and rare not to be bad? Concerning what churches or property have I disputed with you; though you have more than enough of both, and the others too little? What imperial edict have we rejected and emulated? What rulers have we fawned upon against you? Whose boldness have we denounced? And what has been done on the other side against me? "Lord, lay not this sin to their charge," even then I said, for I remembered in season the words of Stephen,[α] and so I pray now. Being reviled, we bless: being blasphemed we retreat.[β]

XIV. And if I am doing wrong in this, that when tyrannized over I endure it, forgive me this wrong; I have borne to be tyrannized over by others too; and I am thankful that my moderation has brought upon me the charge of folly. For I reckon thus, using considerations altogether higher than any of yours; what a mere fraction are these trials of the spittings and blows which Christ, for Whom and by Whose aid we encounter these dangers, endured. I do not count them, taken altogether, worth the one crown of thorns which robbed our conqueror of his crown, for whose sake also I learn that I am crowned for the

α Galat. ii. 9.

α Acts vii. 59. β 1 Cor. iv. 12.

hardness of life. I do not reckon them worth the one reed by which the rotten empire was destroyed; of the gall alone, the vinegar alone, by which we were cured of the bitter taste; of the gentleness alone which He shewed in His Passion. Was He betrayed with a kiss? He reproves with a kiss, but smites not. Is he suddenly arrested? He reproaches indeed, but follows; and if through zeal thou cuttest off the ear of Malchus with the sword, He will be angry, and will restore it. And if one flee in a linen sheet,[a] he will defend him. And if you ask for the fire of Sodom upon his captors, he will not pour it forth; and if he take a thief hanging upon the cross for his crime, he will bring him into Paradise through His Goodness. Let all the acts of one that loves men be loving, as were all the sufferings of Christ, to which we could add nothing greater than, when God even died for us, to refuse on our part to forgive even the smallest wrongs of our fellow-men.

XV. Moreover this also I reckoned and still reckon with myself; and do you see if it is not quite correct. I have often discussed it with you before. These men have the houses, but we the Dweller in the house; they the Temples, we the God; and besides it is ours to be living temples of the Living God, lively sacrifices, reasonable burnt-offerings, perfect sacrifices, yea, gods through the adoration of the Trinity. They have the people, we the Angels; they rash boldness, we faith; they threatenings, we prayer; they smiting, we endurance; they gold and silver, we the pure word. "Thou hast built for thyself a wide house and large chambers (recognize the words of Scripture), a house ceiled and pierced with windows."[β] But not yet is this loftier than my faith, and than the heavens to which I am being borne onwards. Is mine a little flock? But it is not being carried over a precipice. Is mine a narrow fold? But it is unapproachable by wolves; it cannot be entered by a robber, nor climbed by thieves and strangers. I shall yet see it, I know well, wider. And many of those who are now wolves, I must reckon among my sheep, and perhaps even amongst the shepherds. This is the glad tidings brought me by the Good Shepherd, for Whose sake I lay down my life for the sheep. I fear not for the little flock, for it is seen at a glance. I know my sheep and am known of mine. Such are they that know God and are known of God. My sheep hear my voice, which I have heard from the oracles of God, which I have been taught by the Holy Fathers, which I have taught alike on all occasions, not conforming myself to the opportune, and which I will never cease to teach; in which I was born, and in which I will depart.

a Mark xiv. 51. β Jer. xxii. 14.

XVI. These I call by name (for they are not nameless like the stars which are numbered and have names),[a] and they follow me, for I rear them up beside the waters of rest; and they follow every such shepherd, whose voice they love to hear, as you see; but a stranger they will not follow, but will flee from him, because they have a habit of distinguishing the voice of their own from that of strangers. They will flee from Valentinus[β] with his division of one into two, refusing to believe that the Creator is other than the Good. They will flee from Depth and Silence, and the mythical Æons, that are verily worthy of Depth and Silence. They will flee from Marcion's[γ] god, compounded of elements and numbers; from Montanus'[δ] evil and feminine spirit; from the matter and darkness of Manes;[ε] from Novatus'[ς] boasting and wordy assumption of purity; from the analysis and confusion of Sabellius,[η] and if I may use the expression,

a Ps. cxlvii. 4.

β VALENTINUS, a celebrated Gnostic leader of the Second Century, was one of the first Gnostics who taught in Rome. He was probably of Ægypto-Jewish descent, and was educated at Alexandria. He died in Cyprus about 160. His system is a very curious one, giving the reins to the wildest vagaries of the imagination. The original eternal Being, or Absolute Existence, he called Bythos or Depth; and to this he assigned as a wife Sige or Silence. From this union there sprang thirty Æons or Emanations, who unfolded the Attributes of the Deity and created the world.

γ MARCION was a contemporary of Valentinus. He was a native of Sinope in Pontus, of which city his father was Bishop. He supposed Three Principles, the Good God, Who was first revealed by Christ; the Just Creator, Who is the "hot-tempered and imperfect" God of the Jews; and the intrinsically evil Hyle or Matter, which is ruled by the Devil He also distinguished two Messiahs; one a mere warrior prince sent by the Jewish God to restore Israel; the other sent by the Good God for the delivery of the whole human race.

δ MONTANUS, a Phrygian enthusiast of the middle of the Second Century, imagined himself the inspired Organ of the Paraclete. Connected with him were two Prophetesses, Priscilla and Maximilla, who left their husbands to follow him. His heresy, or rather his schism, spread to Rome and Northern Africa, and threw the whole Church into confusion. He was very early anathematized by Bishops and Synods of Asia, but he carried the great African, Tertullian, away by his frenzy.

ε MANES or MANI, a Persian philosopher, astronomer, and painter of the Third Century, who introduced into Christianity some elements drawn from the religion of Zoroaster, especially its πρῶτον ψεῦδος, Dualism, the co-eternity of two contradictory principles, Light and Darkness, Spirit and Matter, Good and Evil. This heresy flourished till the Sixth Century, S. Augustine himself having been for nine years led away by it. It is believed not to be wholly extinct even now in some parts of Eastern Christendom.

ς NOVATUS was a Carthaginian Priest, who at first rebelled against his Bishop, S. Cyprian, on account of his severity in the treatment of persons who had lapsed in the Decian persecution. At Rome, however, this same Novatus, either out of simple antagonism to constituted authority, or because he had really changed his views, adopted the extremest rigorism, and became one of the most violent partisans of the Priest Novatian, whom his followers contrived to get consecrated as a rival Bishop of Rome, in opposition to Cornelius, the reigning Pope. They set up a new "church," and arrogated to themselves an exclusive claim to the title of Cathari, the Pure.

η SABELLIUS, a native of the Libyan Pentapolis, rejected the Catholic Faith of the Trinity of Persons in God, and would only allow a Trinity of manifestations.

his absorption, contracting the Three into One, instead of defining the One in Three Personalities; from the difference of natures taught by Arius[a] and his followers, and their new Judaism, confining the Godhead to the Unbegotten; from Photinus'[β] earthly Christ, who took his beginning from Mary. But they worship the Father and the Son and the Holy Ghost, One Godhead; God the Father, God the Son and (do not be angry) God the Holy Ghost, One Nature in Three Personalities, intellectual, perfect, Self-existent, numerically separate, but not separate in Godhead.

XVII. These words let everyone who threatens me to-day concede to me; the rest let whoever will claim. The Father will not endure to be deprived of the Son, nor the Son of the Holy Ghost. Yet that must happen if They are confined to time, and are created Beings . . . for that which is created is not God. Neither will I bear to be deprived of my consecration; One Lord, One Faith, One Baptism. If this be cancelled, from whom shall I get a second? What say you, you who destroy Baptism or repeat it? Can a man be spiritual without the Spirit? Has he a share in the Spirit who does not honour the Spirit? Can he honour Him who is baptized into a creature and a fellow-servant? It is not so; it is not so; for all your talk. I will not play Thee false, O Unoriginate Father, or Thee O Only-begotten Word, or Thee O Holy Ghost. I know Whom I have confessed, and whom I have renounced, and to Whom I have joined myself. I will not allow myself, after having been taught the words of the faithful, to learn also those of the unfaithful; to confess the truth, and then range myself with falsehood; to come down for consecration and to go back even less hallowed; having been baptised that I might live, to be killed by the water, like infants who die in the very birthpangs, and receive death simultaneously with birth. Why make me at once blessed and wretched, newly enlightened and unenlightened, Divine and godless, that I may make shipwreck even of the hope of regeneration? A few words will suffice. Remember your confession. Into what were you baptised? The Father? Good but Jewish still. The Son? . . . good . . . but not yet perfect. The Holy Ghost? . . . Very good . . . this is perfect. Now was it into these simply, or some common name of Them? The latter. And what was the common Name? Why, God. In this common Name believe, and ride on prosperously and reign,[a] and pass on from hence into the Bliss of Heaven. And that is, as I think, the more distinct apprehension of These; to which may we all come, in the same Christ our God, to Whom be the glory and the might, with the Unoriginate Father, and the Lifegiving Spirit, now and for ever and to ages of ages. Amen.

a It is hardly necessary here to dwell on the Arian tenets; cf. Prolegomena to the Theological Oration.

β PHOTINUS was a Galatian by birth, and flourished in the fourth century, a little earlier than S. Gregory. He seems to have taught that our Lord Jesus Christ was a mere man, and had no existence previous to His Birth of the Virgin Mary. He made Jesus rise on the basis of His human nature, by a course of moral improvement, to the divine dignity, so that the Divine in Him is a thing of growth: cf. Schaff, H. E. Nicene Period, vol. ii. p. 653.

ORATION XXXIV.

ON THE ARRIVAL OF THE EGYPTIANS.

THIS Oration was preached at Constantinople in 380, under the following circumstances:

Peter, Patriarch of Alexandria, had sent a mission of five of his Suffragans to consecrate the impostor Maximus to the Throne occupied by Gregory. This had led to much trouble, but in the end the intruder had been expelled and banished. Shortly afterwards an Egyptian fleet, probably the regular corn ships, had arrived at Constantinople, apparently on the day before a Festival. The crews of the ships, landing next day to go to Church, passed by the numerous Churches held by the Arians, and betook themselves to the little Anastasia. S. Gregory felt himself moved to congratulate them specially on such an act, after what had recently passed, and accordingly pronounced the following discourse.

I. I WILL address myself as is right to those who have come from Egypt; for they have come here eagerly, having overcome illwill by zeal; from that Egypt which is enriched by the River, raining out of the earth, and like the sea in its season,—if I too may follow in my small measure those who have so eloquently spoken of these matters; and which is also enriched by Christ my Lord, Who once was a fugitive into Egypt, and now is supplied by Egypt; the first, when He fled from Herod's massacre of the children;[β] and now by the love of the fathers for their children, by Christ the new Food of those who hunger after good;[γ] the greatest alms of corn of which history speaks and men believe; the Bread which came down from heaven and giveth life to the world, that life which is indestructible and indissoluble, concerning Whom I now seem to hear the Father saying, Out of Egypt have I called My Son.[δ]

II. For from you hath sounded forth the Word to all men; healthfully believed and preached; and you are the best bringers of fruit of all men, specially of those who now hold the

a Ps. xlv. 4. β Matt. ii. 13. γ John vi. 33. δ Hos. xi. 1.

right faith, as far as I know, who am not only a lover of such food, but also its distributor, and not at home only but also abroad. For you indeed supply bodily food to peoples and cities so far as your lovingkindness reaches; and you supply spiritual food also, not to a particular people, nor to this or that city, circumscribed by narrow boundaries, though its people may think it very illustrious, but to almost the whole world. And you bring the remedy not for famine of bread or thirst of water,[α] which is no very terrible famine—and to avoid it is easy; but to a famine of hearing the Word of the Lord, which it is most miserable to suffer, and a most laborious matter to cure at the present time, because iniquity hath abounded,[β] and scarce anywhere do I find its genuine healers.

III. Such was Joseph your Superintendent of corn measures, whom I may call ours also; who by his surpassing wisdom was able both to foresee the famine and to cure it by decrees of government, healing the ill-favoured and starving kine by means of the fair and fat.[γ] And indeed you may understand by Joseph which you will, either the great lover and creator and namesake of immortality or his successor in throne and word and hoary hair, our new Peter,[δ] not inferior in virtue or fame to him by whom the middle course was destroyed and crushed, though it still wriggles a little weakly, like the tail of a snake after it is cut off; the one of whom, after having departed this life in a good old age after many conflicts and wrestlings, looks upon us from above, I well know, and reaches a hand to those who are labouring for the right: and this the more, in proportion as he is freed from his bonds; and the other is hastening to the same end or dissolution of life, and is already drawing near the dwellers in heaven, but is still so far in the flesh as is needed to give the last aids to the Word, and to take his journey with richer provision.

IV. Of these great men and doctors and soldiers of the truth and victors, you are the nurslings and offspring; of these neither times nor tyrants, reason nor envy, nor fear, nor accuser, nor slanderer, whether waging open war against them, or plotting secretly; nor any who appeared to be of our side, nor any stranger, nor gold—that hidden tyrant, through which now almost everything is turned upside down and made to depend on the hazard of a die; nor flatteries nor threats, nor long and distant exiles (for they only could not be affected by confiscation, because of their great riches, which were—to possess nothing) nor anything else, whether absent or present or expected, could induce to take the worse part, and to be anywise traitor to the Trinity, or to suffer loss of the Godhead. On the contrary indeed, they grew strong by dangers, and became more zealous for true religion. For to suffer thus for Christ adds to one's love, and is as it were an earnest to high-souled men of further conflicts. These, O Egypt, are thy present tales and wonders.

V. Once thou didst praise me thy Mendesian Goats, and thy Memphite Apis, a fatted and fleshy calf, and the rites of Isis, and the mutilations of Osiris, and thy venerable Serapis, a log that was honoured by myths and ages and the madness of its worshippers, as some unknown and heavenly matter, however it may have been aided by falsehood; and things yet more shameful than these, multiform images of monstrous beasts and creeping things, all of which Christ and the heralds of Christ have conquered, both the others who have been illustrious in their own times, and also the Fathers whom I have named just now; by whom, O admirable country, thou art more famous today than all others put together, whether in ancient or modern history.

VI. Wherefore I embrace and salute thee, O noblest of peoples and most Christian, and of warmest piety, and worthy of thy leaders; for I can find nothing greater to say of thee than this, nor anything by which better to welcome thee. And I greet thee, to a small extent with my tongue, but very heartily with the movements of my affections.[α] O my people, for I call you mine, as of one mind and one faith, instructed by the same Fathers, and adoring the same Trinity. My people, for mine thou art, though it seem not so to those who envy me. And that they who are in this case may be the deeper wounded, see, I give the right hand of fellowship before so many witnesses, seen and unseen. And I put away the old calumny by this new act of kindness. O my people, for mine thou art, though in saying so I, who am least of all men, am claiming for myself that which is greatest. For such is the grace of the Spirit that it makes of equal honour those who are of one mind. O my people, for mine thou art, though it be afar, because we are divinely joined together,[β] and in a manner wholly different to the unions of carnal people; for bodies are united in place, but souls are fitted together by the Spirit. O my people, who didst formerly study how to suffer for Christ, but now

α Amos viii. 11.
β Matt. xxiv. 12.
γ Gen. xli. 29 sq.
δ Athanasius.

α Galat. ii. 9.
β Isa. lxii. 4.

if thou wilt hearken unto me, wilt study not to do aught, but to consider the power of doing to be a sufficient gain, and to deem that thou art offering a sacrifice to Christ, as in those days of thy endurance so in these of meekness. O people to whom the Lord hath prepared Himself to do good, as to do evil to thine enemies.[α] O people, whom the Lord hath chosen to Himself out of all peoples; O people who art graven upon the hands of the Lord, to whom saith the Lord, Thou art My Will; and, Thy gates are carved work, and all the rest that is said to them that are being saved. O people;—nay, marvel not at my insatiability that I repeat your name so often; for I delight in this continual naming of you, like those who can never have enough of their enjoyment of certain spectacles or sounds.

VII. But, O people of God and mine, beautiful also was your yesterday's assembly, which you held upon the sea, and pleasant, if any sight ever was, to the eyes, when I saw the sea like a forest, and hidden by a cloud made with hands, and the beauty and speed of your ships, as though ordered for a procession, and the slight breeze astern, as though purposely escorting you, and wafting to the City your city of the Sea. Yet the present assembly which we now behold is more beautiful and more magnificent. For you have not hastened to mingle with the larger number, nor have you reckoned religion by numbers, nor endured to be a mere unorganized rabble, rather than a people purified by the Word of God; but having, as is right, rendered to Cæsar the things that are Cæsar's, ye have offered besides to God the things that are God's; to the former Custom, to the latter Fear; and after feeding the people with your cargoes, you yourselves have come to be fed by us. For we also distribute corn, and our distribution is perhaps not worth less than yours. Come eat of my Bread and drink of the Wine which I have mingled for you.[β] I join with Wisdom in bidding you to my table. For I commend your good feeling, and I hasten to meet your ready mind, because ye came to us as to your own harbour, running to your like; and ye valued the kindred Faith, and thought it monstrous that, while they who insult higher things are in harmony with each other and think alike, and think to make good each man's individual falsehood by their common conspiracy, like ropes which get strength from being twisted together; yet you should not meet nor combine with those who are of the same mind, with whom it is more reasonable that you should associate, for we gather in the Godhead also. And that you may see that not in vain have you come to us, and that you have not brought up in a port among strangers and foreigners, but amongst your own people, and have been well guided by the Holy Ghost; we will discourse to you briefly concerning God; and do you recognize your own, like those who distinguish their kindred by the ensigns of their arms.

VIII. I find two highest differences in things that exist, viz.:—Rule, and Service; not such as among us either tyranny has cut or poverty has severed, but which nature has distinguished, if any like to use this word. For That which is First is also above nature. Of these the former is creative, and originating, and unchangeable; but the other is created, and subject and changing; or to speak yet more plainly, the one is above time, and the other subject to time. The Former is called God, and subsists in Three Greatest, namely, the Cause, the Creator, and the Perfecter; I mean the Father, the Son, and the Holy Ghost, who are neither so separated from one another as to be divided in nature, nor so contracted as to be circumscribed by a single person; the one alternative being that of the Arian madness, the other that of the Sabellian heresy; but they are on the one hand more single than what is altogether divided, and on the other more abundant than what is altogether singular. The other division is with us, and is called Creation, though one may be exalted above another according to the proportion of their nearness to God.

IX. This being so, if any be on the Lord's side let him come with us,[α] and let us adore the One Godhead in the Three; not ascribing any name of humiliation to the unapproachable Glory, but having the exaltations of the Triune God continually in our mouth.[β] For since we cannot properly describe even the greatness of Its Nature, on account of Its infinity and undefinableness, how can we assert of It humiliation? But if any one be estranged from God, and therefore divideth the One Supreme Substance into an inequality of Natures, it were marvellous if such an one were not cut in sunder by the sword, and his portion appointed with the unbelievers,[γ] reaping any evil fruit of his evil thought both now and hereafter.

X. What must we say of the Father, Whom by common consent all who have been preoccupied with natural conceptions share, although

α Isai. lxiv. 12, etc. β Prov. ix. 5.

α Exod. xxxii. 26. β Ps. cxlix. 6. γ Luke xii. 46.

He hath endured the beginnings of dishonour, having been first divided by ancient innovation into the Good and the Creator. And of the Son and of the Holy Ghost, see how simply and concisely we shall discourse. If any one could say of Either that He was mutable or subject to change; or that either in time, or place, or power, or energy He could be measured; or that He was not naturally good, or not Self-moved, or not a free agent, or a Minister, or a Hymnsinger; or that He feared, or was a recipient of freedom, or was not counted with God; let him prove this and we will acquiesce, and will be glorified by the Majesty of our Fellow Servants, though we lose our God. But if all that the Father has belongs likewise to the Son, except Causality; and all that is the Son's belongs also to the Spirit, except His Sonship, and whatsoever is spoken of Him as to Incarnation for me a man, and for my salvation, that, taking of mine, He may impart His own by this new commingling; then cease your babbling, though so late, O ye sophists of vain talk that falls at once to the ground; for why will ye die O House of Israel? [a]—if I may mourn for you in the words of Scripture.

XI. For my part I revere also the Titles of the Word, which are so many, and so high and great, which even the demons respect. And I revere also the Equal Rank of the Holy Ghost; and I fear the threat pronounced against those who blaspheme Him. And blasphemy is not the reckoning Him God, but the severing Him from the Godhead. And here you must remark that That which is blasphemed is Lord, and That which is avenged is the Holy Ghost, evidently as Lord. I cannot bear to be unenlightened after my Enlightenment, by marking with a different stamp any of the Three into Whom I was baptized; and thus to be indeed buried in the water, and initiated not into Regeneration, but into death.

XII. I dare to utter something, O Trinity; and may pardon be granted to my folly, for the risk is to my soul. I too am an Image of God, of the Heavenly Glory, though I be placed on earth. I cannot believe that I am saved by one who is my equal. If the Holy Ghost is not God, let Him first be made God, and then let Him deify me His equal. But now what deceit this is on the part of grace, or rather of the givers of grace, to believe in God and to come away godless; by one set of questions and confessions leading to another set of conclusions. Alas for this fair fame, if after the Laver I am blackened, if I am to see those who are not yet cleansed brighter than myself; if I am cheated by the heresy of my Baptizer; if I seek for the stronger Spirit and find Him not. Give me a second Font before you think evil of the first. Why do you grudge me a complete regeneration? Why do you make me, who am the Temple of the Holy Ghost as of God, the habitation of a creature? Why do you honour part of what belongs to me, and dishonour part, judging falsely of the Godhead, to cut me off from the Gift, or rather to cut me in two by the gift? Either honour the Whole, or dishonour the Whole, O new Theologian, that, if you are wicked, you may at any rate be consistent with yourself, and not judge unequally of an equal nature.

XIII. To sum up my discourse:—Glorify Him with the Cherubim, who unite the Three Holies into One Lord,[a] and so far indicate the Primal Substance as their wings open to the diligent. With David be enlightened, who said to the Light, In Thy Light shall we see Light,[β] that is, in the Spirit we shall see the Son; and what can be of further reaching ray? With John thunder, sounding forth nothing that is low or earthly concerning God, but what is high and heavenly, Who is in the beginning, and is with God, and is God the Word,[γ] and true God of the true Father, and not a good fellow-servant honoured only with the title of Son; and the Other Comforter (other, that is, from the Speaker, Who was the Word of God). And when you read, I and the Father are One,[δ] keep before your eyes the Unity of Substance; but when you see, "We will come to him, and make Our abode with him," [ε] remember the distinction of Persons; and when you see the Names, Father, Son, and Holy Ghost, think of the Three Personalities.

XIV. With Luke be inspired as you study the Acts of the Apostles. Why do you range yourself with Ananias and Sapphira, those vain embezzlers (if indeed the theft of one's own property be a vain thing) and that by appropriating, not silver nor any other cheap and worthless thing, like a wedge of gold,[ζ] or a didrachma, as did of old a rapacious soldier; but stealing the Godhead Itself, and lying, not to men but to God, as you have heard. What? Will you not reverence even the authority of the Spirit Who breathes upon whom, and when, and as He wills? He comes upon Cornelius and his companions before Baptism, to others after Baptism, by the hands of the Apostles; so that from both

a Ezek. xviii. 31.

a Isai. vi. 3. β Ps. xxxvi. 9. γ John i. 1.
δ Ib. x. 30. ε John xiv. 23. ζ Josh. vii. 21.

sides, both from the fact that He comes in the guise of a Master and not of a Servant, and from the fact of His being sought to make perfect, the Godhead of the Spirit is testified.

XV. Speak of God with Paul, who was caught up to the third Heaven,[α] and who sometimes counts up the Three Persons, and that in varied order, not keeping the same order, but reckoning one and the same Person now first, now second, now third; and for what purpose? Why, to shew the equality of the Nature. And sometimes he mentions Three, sometimes Two or One, because That which is not mentioned is included. And sometimes he attributes the operation of God to the Spirit, as in no respect different from Him, and sometimes instead of the Spirit he brings in Christ; and at times he separates the Persons saying, "One God, of whom are all things, and we in Him; and one Lord Jesus Christ, by whom are all things, and we by Him;" [β] at other times he brings together the one Godhead, "For of Him and through Him and in Him are all things;" [γ] that is, through the Holy Ghost, as is shown by many places in Scripture. To Him be glory for ever and ever. Amen.

ORATION XXXVII.

On the Words of the Gospel, "When Jesus had Finished these Sayings," etc.—S. Matt. xix. 1.

I. Jesus Who Chose The Fishermen, Himself also useth a net, and changeth place for place. Why? Not only that He may gain more of those who love God by His visitation; but also, as it seems to me, that He may hallow more places. To the Jews He becomes as a Jew that He may gain the Jews; to them that are under the Law as under the Law, that He may redeem them that are under the Law; to the weak as weak, that He may save the weak. He is made all things to all men that He may gain all. Why do I say, All things to all men? For even that which Paul could not endure to say of himself I find that the Saviour suffered. For He is made not only a Jew, and not only doth He take to Himself all monstrous and vile names, but even that which is most monstrous of all, even very sin and very curse; not that He it such, but He is called so. For how can He be sin, Who setteth us free from sin; and how can He be a curse, Who redeemeth us from the curse of the Law? [δ] But it is in order that He may carry His display of humility even to this extent, and form us to that humility which is the producer of exaltation. As I said then, He is made a Fisherman; He condescendeth to all; He casteth the net; He endureth all things, that He may draw up the fish from the depths, that is, Man who is swimming in the unsettled and bitter waves of life.

II. Therefore now also, when He had finished these sayings He departed from Galilee and came into the coasts of Judea beyond Jordan; He dwelleth well in Galilee, in order that the people which sat in darkness may see great Light.[α] He removeth to Judea in order that He may persuade people to rise up from the Letter and to follow the Spirit. He teacheth, now on a mountain; now He discourseth on a plain; now He passeth over into a ship; now He rebuketh the surges. And perhaps He goes to sleep, in order that He may bless sleep also; perhaps He is tired that He may hallow weariness also; perhaps He weeps that He may make tears blessed. He removeth from place to place, Who is not contained in any place; the timeless, the bodiless, the uncircumscript, the same Who was and is; Who was both above time, and came under time, and was invisible and is seen. He was in the beginning and was with God, and was God.[β] The word Was occurs the third time to be confirmed by number. What He was He laid aside; what He was not He assumed; not that He became two, but He deigned to be One made out of the two. For both are God, that which assumed, and that which was assumed; two Natures meeting in One, not two Sons (let us not give a false account of the blending). He who is such and so great—but what has befallen me? I have fallen into human language. For how can So Great be said of the Absolute, and how can That which is without quantity be called Such? But pardon the word, for I am speaking of the greatest things with a limited instrument. And That great and long-suffering and formless and bodiless Nature will endure this, namely, my words as if of a body, and weaker than the truth. For if He condescended to Flesh, He will also endure such language.

III. And great multitudes followed Him, and He healed them there, where the multitude was greater. If He had abode upon His own eminence, if He had not condescended to infirmity, if He had remained what He was, keeping Himself unapproachable and incomprehensible, a few perhaps would have followed Him—perhaps not even a few, possibly

α 2 Cor. xii. 2.
β 1 Cor. viii. 6.
γ Rom. xi. 36.
δ Gal. iii. 10, 13.

α Isa. ix. 1.
β John i. 1.

only Moses—and He only so far as to see with difficulty the Back Parts of God.[α] For He penetrated the cloud, either being placed outside the weight of the body or being withdrawn from his senses; for how could he have gazed upon the subtlety, or the incorporeity, or I know not how one should call it, of God, being incorporate and using material eyes? But inasmuch as He strips Himself for us, inasmuch as He comes down (and I speak of an exinanition, as it were, a laying aside and a diminution of His glory), He becomes by this comprehensible.

IV. And pardon me meanwhile that I again suffer a human affection. I am filled with indignation and grief for my Christ (and I would that you might sympathize with me) when I see my Christ dishonoured on this account on which He most merited honour. Is He on this account to be dishonoured, tell me, that for you He was humble? Is He therefore a Creature, because He careth for the creature? Is He therefore subject to time, because He watches over those who are subject to time? Nay, He beareth all things, He endureth all things.[β] And what marvel? He put up with blows, He bore spittings, He tasted gall for my taste. And even now He bears to be stoned, not only by those who deal despitefully with Him, but also by ourselves who seem to reverence Him. For to use corporeal names when discoursing of the incorporeal is perhaps the part of those who deal despitefully and stone Him; but pardon, I say again to our infirmity, for I do not willingly stone Him; but having no other words to use, we use what we have. Thou art called the Word, and Thou art above Word; Thou art above Light, yet art named Light; Thou art called Fire not as perceptible to sense, but because Thou purgest light and worthless matter; a Sword, because Thou severest the worse from the better; a Fan, because Thou purgest the threshing-floor, and blowest away all that is light and windy, and layest up in the garner above all that is weighty and full; an Axe, because Thou cuttest down the worthless fig-tree, after long patience, because Thou cuttest away the roots of wickedness; the Door, because Thou bringest in; the Way, because we go straight; the Sheep, because Thou art the Sacrifice; the High Priest, because Thou offerest the Body; the Son, because Thou art of the Father. Again I stir men's tongues; again some men rave against Christ, or rather against me, who have been deemed worthy to be a herald of the Word. I am like John, The Voice of one crying in the wilderness[α]—a wilderness that once was dry, but now is only too populous.

V. But, as I was saying, to return to my argument; for this reason great multitudes followed Him, because He condescended to our infirmities. What next? The Pharisees also, it says, came unto Him, tempting Him, and saying unto Him, is it lawful for a man to put away his wife for every cause? Again the Pharisees tempt Him; again they who read the Law do not know the Law; again they who are expounders of the Law need others to teach them. It was not enough that Sadducees should tempt Him concerning the Resurrection, and Lawyers question Him about perfection, and the Herodians about the poll-tax, and others about authority; but some one must also ask about Marriage at Him who cannot be tempted, the Creator of wedlock, Him who from the First Cause made this whole race of mankind. And He answered and said unto them, Have ye not read that He which made them at the beginning made them male and female? He knoweth how to solve some of their questions and to bridle others. When He is asked, By what authority doest thou these things? He Himself, because of the utter ignorance of those who asked Him, replies with another question; The baptism of John, was it from Heaven or of men? He on both sides entangles His questioners, so that we also are able, following the example of Christ, sometimes to check those who argue with us over-officiously, and with still more absurd questions to solve the absurdity of their questions. For we too are wise in vanity at times, if I may boast of the things of folly. But when He sees a question that calls for reasoning, then He does not deem His questioners unworthy of prudent answers.

VI. The question which you have put seems to me to do honour to chastity, and to demand a kind reply. Chastity, in respect of which I see that the majority of men are ill-disposed, and that their laws are unequal and irregular. For what was the reason why they restrained the woman, but indulged the man, and that a woman who practises evil against her husband's bed is an adulteress, and the penalties of the law for this are very severe; but if the husband commits fornication against his wife, he has no account to give? I do not accept this legislation; I do not approve this custom. They who made the Law were men,

α Exod. xx. 21; xxxiii. 20, 23. β 1 Cor. xiii. 7.

α Matt. iii. 3.

and therefore their legislation is hard on women, since they have placed children also under the authority of their fathers, while leaving the weaker sex uncared for. God doth not so; but saith Honour thy father and thy mother, which is the first commandment with promise; that it may be well with thee; and, He that curseth father or mother, let him die the death. Similarly He gave honour to good and punishment to evil. And, The blessing of a father strengtheneth the houses of children, but the curse of a mother uprooteth the foundations.[α] See the equality of the legislation. There is one Maker of man and woman; one debt is owed by children to both their parents.

VII. How then dost thou demand Chastity, while thou dost not thyself observe it? How dost thou demand that which thou dost not give? How, though thou art equally a body, dost thou legislate unequally? If thou enquire into the worse—The Woman Sinned, and so did Adam.[β] The serpent deceived them both; and one was not found to be the stronger and the other the weaker. But dost thou consider the better? Christ saves both by His Passion. Was He made flesh for the Man? So He was also for the woman. Did He die for the Man? The Woman also is saved by His death. He is called of the seed of David;[γ] and so perhaps you think the Man is honoured; but He is born of a Virgin, and this is on the Woman's side. They two, He says, shall be one Flesh; so let the one flesh have equal honour." And Paul legislates for chastity by His example. How, and in what way? This Sacrament is great, he says, But I speak concerning Christ and the Church.[δ] It is well for the wife to reverence Christ through her husband: and it is well for the husband not to dishonor the Church through his wife. Let the wife, he says, see that she reverence her husband, for so she does Christ; but also he bids the husband cherish his wife, for so Christ does the Church.[ε] Let us, then, give further consideration to this saying.

VIII. Churn milk and it will be butter;[ζ] examine this and perhaps you may find something more nourishing in it. For I think that the Word here seems to deprecate second marriage. For, if there were two Christs, there may be two husbands or two wives; but if Christ is One, one Head of the Church, let there be also one flesh, and let a second be rejected; and if it hinder the second what is to be said for a third? The first is law, the second is indulgence, the third is transgression, and anything beyond this is swinish, such as has not even many examples of its wickedness. Now the Law grants divorce for every cause; but Christ not for every cause; but He allows only separation from the whore; and in all other things He commands patience. He allows to put away the fornicatress, because she corrupts the offspring; but in all other matters let us be patient and endure; or rather be ye[α] enduring and patient, as many as have received the yoke of matrimony. If you see lines or marks upon her, take away her ornaments; if a hasty tongue, restrain it; if a meretricious laugh, make it modest; if immoderate expenditure or drink, reduce it; if unseasonable going out, shackle it; if a lofty eye, chastise it. It is uncertain which is in danger, the separator or the separated. Let thy fountain of water, it says, be only thine own, and let no stranger share it with thee;[β] and, let the colt of thy favours and the stag of thy love company with thee; do thou then take care not to be a strange river, nor to please others better than thine own wife. But if thou be carried elsewhere, then thou makest a law of lewdness for thy partner also. Thus saith the Saviour.

IX. But what of the Pharisees? To them this word seems harsh. Yes, for they are also displeased at other noble words—both the older Pharisees, and the Pharisees of the present day. For it is not only race, but disposition also that makes a Pharisee. Thus also I reckon as an Assyrian or an Egyptian him who is ranged among these by his character. What then say the Pharisees? If the case of the man be so with his wife, it is not good to marry. Is it only now, O Pharisee, that thou understandest this, It is not good to marry?[γ] Didst thou not know it before when thou sawest widowhoods, and orphanhoods, and untimely deaths, and mourning succeeding to shouting, and funerals coming upon weddings, and childlessness, and all the comedy or tragedy that is connected with this? Either is most appropriate language. It is good to marry; I too admit it, for marriage is honourable in all, and the bed undefiled.[δ] It is good for the temperate, not for those who are insatiable, and who desire to give more than due honour to the flesh. When marriage is only marriage and conjunction and the desire for a succession of children, marriage is honourable, for it brings into the world more to please God. But

α Ecclus. iii. 11. β Gen. iii. 6. γ Rom. i. 3.
δ Ephes. v. 32. ε Ib. v. 22 seq. ζ Prov. xxx. 33.

α An indication that S. Gregory was himself unmarried.
β Prov. v. 17. γ Matt. xix. 10. δ Heb. xiii. 4.

when it kindles matter, and surrounds us with thorns, and as it were discovers the way of vice, then I too say, It is not good to marry.

X. Marriage is honourable; but I cannot say that it is more lofty than virginity; for virginity were no great thing if it were not better than a good thing. Do not however be angry, ye women that are subject to the yoke. We must obey God rather than man. But be ye bound together, both virgins and wives, and be one in the Lord, and each others' adornment. There would be no celibate if there were no marriage. For whence would the virgin have passed into this life? Marriage would not have been venerable unless it had borne virgin fruit to God and to life. Honour thou also thy mother, of whom thou wast born. Honour thou also her who is of a mother and is a mother.[α] A mother she is not, but a Bride of Christ she is. The visible beauty is not hidden, but that which is unseen is visible to God. All the glory of the King's Daughter is within,[β] clothed with golden fringes, embroidered whether by actions or by contemplation. And she who is under the yoke, let her also in some degree be Christ's; and the virgin altogether Christ's. Let the one be not entirely chained to the world,[γ] and let the other not belong to the world at all. For that which is a part to the yoked, is to the virgin all in all. Hast thou chosen the life of Angels? Art thou ranked among the unyoked? Sink not down to the flesh; sink not down to matter; be not wedded to matter, while otherwise thou remainest unwedded. A lascivious eye guardeth not virginity; a meretricious tongue mingles with the Evil One; feet that walk disorderly accuse of disease or danger. Let the mind also be virgin; let it not rove about; let it not wander; let it not carry in itself forms of evil things (for the form is a part of harlotry); let it not make idols in its soul of hateful things.

XI. But He said unto them, All men cannot receive this saying, save they to whom it is given. Do you see the sublimity of the matter? It is found to be nearly incomprehensible. For surely it is more than carnal that that which is born of flesh should not beget to the flesh. Surely it is Angelic that she who is bound to flesh should live not according to flesh, but be loftier than her nature. The flesh bound her to the world, but reason led her up to God. The flesh weighed her down, but reason gave her wings; the flesh bound her, but desire loosed her. With thy whole soul, O Virgin, be intent upon God (I give this same injunction to men and to women); and do not take the same view in other respects of what is honourable as the mass of men do; of family, of wealth, of throne, of dynasty, of that beauty which shews itself in complexion and composition of members, the plaything of time and disease. If thou hast poured out upon God the whole of thy love; if thou hast not two objects of desire, both the passing and the abiding, both the visible and the invisible, then thou hast been so pierced by the arrow of election, and hast so learned the beauty of the Bridegroom, that thou too canst say with the bridal drama and song, thou art sweetness and altogether loveliness.

XII. You see how streams confined in lead pipes, through being much compressed and carried to one point, often so far depart from the nature of water that that which is pushed from behind will often flow constantly upwards. So if thou confine thy desire, and be wholly joined to God, thou wilt not fall downward; thou wilt not be dissipated; thou wilt remain entirely Christ's, until thou see Christ thy Bridegroom. Keep thyself unapproachable, both in word and work and life, and thought and action. From all sides the Evil One interferes with thee; he spies thee everywhere, where he may strike, where wound thee; let him not find anything bared and ready to his stroke. The purer he sees thee, the more he strives to stain thee, for the stains on a shining garment are more conspicuous. Let not eye draw eye, nor laughter laughter, nor familiarity night, lest night bring destruction. For that which is gradually drawn away and stolen, works a mischief which is unperceived at the time, but yet attains to the consummation of wickedness.

XIII. All men, He saith, cannot receive this saying, but they to whom it is given. When you hear this, It is given, do not understand it in a heretical fashion, and bring in differences of nature, the earthly and the spiritual and the mixed. For there are people so evilly disposed as to think that some men are of an utterly ruined nature, and some of a nature which is saved, and that others are of such a disposition as their will may lead them to, either to the better, or to the worse. For that men may have a certain aptitude, one more, another less, I too admit; but not that this aptitude alone suffices for perfection, but that it is reason which calls this out, that

α The passage is obscure. Combefis reads, "Though she be not a mother" but the MSS are against him.

β Ps. xlv. 14.

γ Luke viii. 14.

nature may proceed to action, just as fire is produced when a flint is struck with iron. When you hear To whom it is given, add, And it is given to those who are called and to those who incline that way. For when you hear, Not of him that willeth, nor of him that runneth, but of God that sheweth mercy,[a] I counsel you to think the same. For since there are some who are so proud of their successes that they attribute all to themselves and nothing to Him that made them and gave them wisdom and supplied them with good; such are taught by this word that even to wish well needs help from God; or rather that even to choose what is right is divine and a gift of the mercy of God. For it is necessary both that we should be our own masters and also that our salvation should be of God. This is why He saith not of him that willeth; that is, not of him that willeth only, nor of him that runneth only, but also of God. That sheweth mercy. Next; since to will also is from God, he has attributed the whole to God with reason. However much you may run, however much you may wrestle, yet you need one to give the crown. Except the Lord build the house, they laboured in vain that built it: Except the Lord keep the city, in vain they watched that keep it.[β] I know, He says, that the race is not to the swift, nor the battle to the strong,[γ] nor the victory to the fighters, nor the harbours to the good sailors; but to God it belongs both to work victory, and to bring the barque safe to port.

XIV. In another place it is also said and understood, and perhaps it is necessary that I should add it as follows to what has already been said, in order that I may impart to you also my wealth. The Mother of the Sons of Zebedee, in an impulse of parental affection, asked a thing in ignorance of the measure of what she was asking,[δ] but pardonably, through the excess of her love and of the kindness due to her children. For there is nothing more affectionate than a Mother,—and I speak of this that I may lay down a law for honouring Mothers. Their mother, then, asked Jesus that they might sit, the one on His right hand, the other on his left. But what saith the Saviour? He first asks if they can drink the Cup which He Himself was about to drink; and when this was professed, and the Saviour accepted the profession (for He knew that they were being perfected by the same, or rather that they would be perfected thereby); what saith He? "They shall drink the cup; but to sit on My right hand and on My left—it is not Mine, He saith, to give this, but to whom it hath been given." Is then the ruling mind nothing? Nothing the labour? Nothing the reasoning? Nothing the philosophy? Nothing the fasting? Nothing the vigils, the sleeping on the ground, the shedding floods of tears? Is it for nothing of these, but in accordance with some election by lot, that a Jeremias is sanctified, and others are estranged from the womb?

XV. I fear lest some monstrous reasoning may come in, as of the soul having lived elsewhere, and then having been bound to this body, and that it is from that other life that some receive the gift of prophecy, and others are condemned, namely, those who lived badly. But since such a conception is too absurd, and contrary to the traditions of the Church (others if they like may play with such doctrines, but it is unsafe for us to play with them); we must in this place too add to the words "To whom it hath been given," this, "who are worthy;" who have not only received this character from the Father, but have given it to themselves.

XVI. For there are eunuchs which were made eunuchs from their mother's womb, etc. I should very much like to be able to say something bold about eunuchs. Be not proud, ye who are eunuchs by nature. For, in point of self-restraint, this is perhaps unwilling. For it has not come to the test, nor has your self-restraint been proved by trial. For the good which is by nature is not a subject of merit; that which is the result of purpose is laudable. What merit has fire for burning, for it is its nature to burn? What merit has water for falling, a property given to it by its Maker? What thanks does the snow get for its coldness, or the sun for its shining?—It shines even if it does not wish. Claim merit if you please by willing the better things. You will claim it if, being carnal, you make yourself yourself spiritual; if, while drawn down by the leaden flesh, you receive wings from reason; if though lowly born, you are found to be heavenly; if while chained down to the flesh, you shew yourself superior to the flesh.

XVII. Since then, natural chastity is not meritorious, I demand something else from the eunuchs. Do not go a whoring in respect of the Godhead. Having been wedded to Christ, do not dishonour Christ. Being perfected by the spirit, do not make the Spirit your own equal. If I yet pleased men, says

α Rom. ix. 16. β Ps. cxxvii. 1.
γ Eccles. ix., 11. δ Matt. xx. 20, etc.

Paul, I should not be the servant of Christ.[a] If I worshipped a creature, I should not be called a Christian. For why is Christianity precious? Is it not that Christ is God, unless my mingling with Him in love is a mere human passion? And yet I honour Peter, but I am not called a Petrine; and Paul, but have never been called a Pauline. I cannot allow myself to be named after a man, who am born of God. So then, if it is because you believe Him to be God that you are called a Christian, may you ever be so called, and may you remain in both the name and the thing; but if you are called from Christ only because you have an affection for Him, you attribute no more to him than other names which are given from some practice or fact.

XVIII. Consider those men who are devoted to horse racing. They are named after the colours and the sides on which they have placed themselves. You know the names without my mentioning them. If it is thus that you have got the name of Christian, the mere title is a very small thing even though you pride yourself upon it. But if it is because you believe Him to be God, shew your faith by your works. If the Son is a creature, even now also you are worshipping the creature instead of the Creator. If the Holy Ghost is a creature, you are baptized in vain, and are only sound on two sides, or rather not even on them; but on one you are altogether in danger. Imagine the Trinity to be a single pearl, alike on all sides and equally glistening. If any part of the pearl be injured, the whole beauty of the stone is gone. So when you dishonour the Son in order to honour the Father, He does not accept your honour. The Father doth not glory in the dishonour of the Son. If a wise Son maketh a glad Father,[β] how much more doth the honour of the Son become that of the Father! And if you also accept this saying, My Son, glory not in the dishonour of thy Father,[γ] similarly the Father doth not glory in the Son's dishonour. If you dishonour the Holy Ghost, the Son receiveth not your honour. For though He be not of the Father in the same way as the Son, yet He is of the same Father. Either honour the whole or dishonour the whole, so as to have a consistent mind. I cannot accept your half piety. I would have you altogether pious, but in the way that I desire. Pardon my affection: I am grieved even for those who hate me. You were one of my members, even though you are now cut off: perhaps you will again become a member; and therefore I speak kindly. Thus much for the sake of the Eunuchs, that they may be chaste in respect of the Godhead.

XIX. For it is not only bodily sin which is called fornication and adultery, but any sin you have committed, and especially transgression against that which is divine. Perhaps you ask how we can prove this:—They went a whoring, it says, with their own inventions.[a] Do you see an impudent act of fornication? And again, They committed adultery in the wood.[β] See you a kind of adulterous religion? Do not then commit spiritual adultery, while keeping your bodies chaste. Do not shew that it is unwillingly you are chaste in body, by not being chaste where you *can* commit fornication. Why have you done your impiety? Why are you hurried to vice, so that it is all one to call a man a Eunuch or a villain? Place yourselves on the side of men, and, even though so late, have some manly thoughts. Avoid the women's apartments; do not let the disgrace of proclamation be added to the disgrace of the name. Would you have us persevere a little longer in this discourse, or are you tired with what we have said? Nay, by what follows let even the eunuchs be honoured. For the word is one of praise.

XX. There are, He says, some eunuchs which were so born from their mother's womb; and there are some eunuchs which were made eunuchs of men; and there be eunuchs which have made themselves eunuchs for the Kingdom of Heaven's sake. He that is able to receive it, let him receive it. I think that the discourse would sever itself from the body, and represent higher things by bodily figures; for to stop the meaning at bodily eunuchs would be small and very weak, and unworthy of the Word; and we must understand in addition something worthy of the Spirit. Some, then, seem by nature to incline to good. And when I speak of nature, I am not slighting free will, but supposing both—an aptitude for good, and that which brings the natural aptitude to effect. And there are others whom reason cleanses, by cutting them off from the passions. These I imagine to be meant by those whom men have made Eunuchs, when the word of teaching distinguishing the better from the worse and rejecting the one and commanding the other (like the verse, Depart from evil and do good),[γ] works spiritual chastity. This sort of making eunuchs I ap-

a Galat. i. 10. β Prov. x. 1 γ Ecclus. iii. 10.

a Ps. cvi. 39. β Jer. iii. 9 (Libere). γ Ps. xxxvii. 27.

prove; and I highly praise both teachers and taught, that the one have nobly effected, and the other still more nobly endured, the cutting off.

XXI. And there be eunuchs which have made themselves eunuchs for the Kingdom of Heaven's sake. Others, too, who have not met with teachers, have been laudable teachers to themselves. No father nor mother, no Priest or Bishop, nor any of those commissioned to teach, taught you your duty; but by moving reason in yourself and by kindling the spark of good by your free will, you made yourself a eunuch, and acquired such a habit of virtue that impulse to vice became almost an impossibility to you. Therefore I praise this kind of Eunuch-making also, and perhaps even above the others. He that is able to receive it let him receive it. Choose which part you will; either follow the Teacher or be your own teacher. One thing alone is shameful—that the passions be not extirpated. It matters not how they are extirpated. The teacher is God's creature; and you also have the same origin; and whether the teacher grasp this grace, or the good be your own—it is equally good.

XXII. Only let us cut ourselves off from passion, lest any root of bitterness springing up trouble us;[a] only let us follow the image; only let us reverence our Archetype. Cut off the bodily passions; cut off also the spiritual. For by how much the soul is more precious than the body, by so much more precious is it to cleanse the soul than the body. And if cleansing of the body be a praiseworthy act, see, I pray you, how much greater and higher is that of the soul. Cut away the Arian impiety; cut away the false opinion of Sabellius; do not join more than is right, or wrongly sever; do not either confuse the Three Persons into One, or make Three diversities of Nature. The One is praiseworthy if rightly understood; and the Three when rightly divided, when the division is of Persons, not of Godhead.

XXIII. I enact this for Laymen too, and I enjoin it also upon all Priests, and upon those commissioned to rule. Come to the aid of the Word, all of you to whom God has given power to aid. It is a great thing to check murder, to punish adultery, to chastise theft; much more to establish piety by law, and to bestow sound doctrine. My word will not be able to do as much in fighting for the Holy Trinity as your Edict, if you will bridle the ill disposed, if you will help the persecuted, if you will check the slayers, and prevent people from being slain. I am speaking not merely of bodily but of spiritual slaughter. For all sin is the death of the soul. . . . Here let my discourse end.

XXIV. But it remains that I speak a prayer for those who are assembled. Husbands alike and wives, rulers and ruled, old men, and young men, and maidens, every sort of age, bear ye every loss whether of money or of body, but one thing alone do not endure—to lose the Godhead. I adore the Father, I adore the Son, I adore the Holy Ghost; or rather We adore them; I, who am speaking, before all and after all and with all, in the same Christ our Lord, to whom be the glory and the might for ever. Amen.

a Heb. xii. 15.

INTRODUCTION TO THE ORATION ON THE THEOPHANY.

THE Title of this Oration has given rise to a doubt whether it was preached on Dec. 25, 380, or on Jan. 6, 381. The word Theophania is well known as a name for the Epiphany; which, however, according to Schaff,[a] was originally a celebration both of the Nativity and the Baptism of our Lord. The two words seem both to have been used in the simplest sense of the Manifestation of God, and certainly were applied to Christmas Day. Thus Suidas, "The Epiphany is the Incarnation of the Saviour;" and Epiphanius (Hær., 53), "The Day of the Epiphany is the day on which Christ was born according to the flesh." But S. Jerome applies the word to the Baptism of Christ; "The day of the Epiphany is still venerable; not, as some think, on account of His Birth in the flesh; for then He was hidden, not manifested; but it agrees with the time at which it was said, This is My beloved Son (In Ezech. I.). There is also a Sermon, attributed to S. Chrysostom, "On the Baptism of Christ," in which it is expressly denied that the name Theophany applies to Christmas. The Oration itself, however, contains evidence to shew that the Festival of our Lord's Birth was kept at the earlier date; for in c. 16 the Preacher says, "A little later you shall see Jesus submitting to be purified in the river Jordan for my purification." And another piece of evidence occurs in the oration In Sancta Lumina, c. 14, "At His Birth we duly kept festival, both I the leader of the feast,

a H. E., Nic Per., p. 399.

and you. Now we are come to another action of Christ and another Mystery."

The Oration is thus analysed by Abbé Bénoît:

"After an exordium which is full of the enthusiasm and joy which such a subject naturally inspires the Orator recommends his hearers to celebrate the Festival by a pious gladness, and by hearing the Word of God; and not as the heathen celebrated their feasts, by profane amusements and all kinds of excess. He will try to satisfy their desires by speaking to them of God. God is infinite, ineffable, eternal, the Sovereign Good. He created the Angels in the beginning out of goodness. The fall of the Angels was followed by the creation of the material world. Man too fell, and God shewed His mercy even in the punishment. He used various means to raise him again; and at length He came Himself. Then the speaker forcibly argues against those who misuse the infinite condescension of the Word to contest His Godhead; he rapidly traces the principal features of His Life—at once human and Divine; and ends with a recommendation to his hearers to imitate in all things the Life of Christ, so that they may have a share in His Kingdom in Heaven."

It is considered one of the best of Gregory's discourses. "By the grandeur of the plan," says Bénoît, "the elevation of the ideas, and the rich fund of doctrine, this discourse is incontestably one of S. Gregory's most remarkable efforts."

ORATION XXXVIII.

On the Theophany, or Birthday of Christ.

I. Christ is born, glorify ye Him. Christ from heaven, go ye out to meet Him. Christ on earth; be ye exalted. Sing unto the Lord all the whole earth;[a] and that I may join both in one word, Let the heavens rejoice, and let the earth be glad, for Him Who is of heaven and then of earth. Christ in the flesh, rejoice with trembling and with joy; with trembling because of your sins, with joy because of your hope. Christ of a Virgin; O ye Matrons live as Virgins, that ye may be Mothers of Christ. Who doth not worship Him That is from the beginning? Who doth not glorify Him That is the Last?

α Ps. xcvi. 1, 11.

II. Again the darkness is past; again Light is made; again Egypt is punished with darkness; again Israel is enlightened by a pillar.[α] The people that sat in the darkness of ignorance, let it see the Great Light of full knowledge.[β] Old things are passed away, behold all things are become new.[γ] The letter gives way, the Spirit comes to the front. The shadows flee away, the Truth comes in upon them. Melchisedec is concluded.[δ] He that was without Mother becomes without Father (without Mother of His former state, without Father of His second). The laws of nature are upset; the world above must be filled. Christ commands it, let us not set ourselves against Him. O clap your hands together all ye people,[ε] because unto us a Child is born, and a Son given unto us, Whose Government is upon His shoulder (for with the Cross it is raised up), and His Name is called The Angel of the Great Counsel of the Father.[ζ] Let John cry, Prepare ye the way of the Lord:[η] I too will cry the power of this Day. He Who is not carnal is Incarnate; the Son of God becomes the Son of Man, Jesus Christ the Same yesterday, and to-day, and for ever.[θ] Let the Jews be offended, let the Greeks deride;[κ] let heretics talk till their tongues ache. Then shall they believe, when they see Him ascending up into heaven; and if not then, yet when they see Him coming out of heaven and sitting as Judge.

III. Of these on a future occasion; for the present the Festival is the Theophany or Birth-day, for it is called both, two titles being given to the one thing. For God was manifested to man by birth. On the one hand Being, and eternally Being, of the Eternal Being, above cause and word, for there was no word before The Word; and on the other hand for our sakes also Becoming, that He Who gives us our being might also give us our Wellbeing, or rather might restore us by His Incarnation, when we had by wickedness fallen from wellbeing. The name Theophany is given to it in reference to the Manifestation, and that of Birthday in respect of His Birth.

IV. This is our present Festival; it is this which we are celebrating to-day, the Coming of God to Man, that we might go forth,[λ] or

α Exod. xiv. 20. β Isa. ix. 6. γ 1 Cor. v. 17.

δ The meaning clearly is that the type presented by Melchisedec (Heb. vii. 3) is fulfilled in Christ. The explanation here given by S. Gregory is the ordinary one found in the Fathers. Thus, e.g., Theodoret says, "Christ our Lord is without Mother as God, for He was begotten of the Father alone; and without Father as Man, for He was born of a pure Virgin." Oecumenius has almost the exact words of Gregory. So also S. Augustine (Tract in Joann, 8), "Christ was singularly born of a Father without a Mother, of a Mother without a Father; without Mother as God, without Father as Man." ε Ps. xlvii. 1. ζ Isa. ix. 6. η Matt. iii. 3.

θ Heb. xiii. 8. κ 1 Cor. i. 23. λ Ephes. iv. 22, 24.

rather (for this is the more proper expression) that we might go back to God—that putting off the old man, we might put on the New; and that as we died in Adam, so we might live in Christ,[α] being born with Christ and crucified with Him and buried with Him and rising with Him.[β] For I must undergo the beautiful conversion, and as the painful succeeded the more blissful, so must the more blissful come out of the painful. For where sin abounded Grace did much more abound;[γ] and if a taste condemned us, how much more doth the Passion of Christ justify us? Therefore let us keep the Feast, not after the manner of a heathen festival, but after a godly sort; not after the way of the world, but in a fashion above the world; not as our own, but as belonging to Him Who is ours, or rather as our Master's; not as of weakness, but as of healing; not as of creation, but of re-creation.

V. And how shall this be? Let us not adorn our porches, nor arrange dances, nor decorate the streets; let us not feast the eye, nor enchant the ear with music, nor enervate the nostrils with perfume, nor prostitute the taste, nor indulge the touch, those roads that are so prone to evil and entrances for sin; let us not be effeminate in clothing soft and flowing, whose beauty consists in its uselessness, nor with the glittering of gems or the sheen of gold[δ] or the tricks of colour, belying the beauty of nature, and invented to do despite unto the image of God; Not in rioting and drunkenness, with which are mingled, I know well, chambering and wantonness, since the lessons which evil teachers give are evil; or rather the harvests of worthless seeds are worthless. Let us not set up high beds of leaves, making tabernacles for the belly of what belongs to debauchery. Let us not appraise the bouquet of wines, the kickshaws of cooks, the great expense of unguents. Let not sea and land bring us as a gift their precious dung, for it is thus that I have learnt to estimate luxury; and let us not strive to outdo each other in intemperance (for to my mind every superfluity is intemperance, and all which is beyond absolute need),—and this while others are hungry and in want, who are made of the same clay and in the same manner.

VI. Let us leave all these to the Greeks and to the pomps and festivals of the Greeks, who call by the name of gods beings who rejoice in the reek of sacrifices, and who consistently worship with their belly; evil inventors and worshippers of evil demons. But we, the Object of whose adoration is the Word, if we must in some way have luxury, let us seek it in word, and in the Divine Law, and in histories; especially such as are the origin of this Feast; that our luxury may be akin to and not far removed from Him Who hath called us together. Or do you desire (for to-day I am your entertainer) that I should set before you, my good Guests, the story of these things as abundantly and as nobly as I can, that ye may know how a foreigner can feed[a] the natives of the land, and a rustic the people of the town, and one who cares not for luxury those who delight in it, and one who is poor and homeless those who are eminent for wealth?

We will begin from this point; and let me ask of you who delight in such matters to cleanse you mind and your ears and your thoughts, since our discourse is to be of God and Divine; that when you depart, you may have had the enjoyment of delights that really fade not away. And this same discourse shall be at once both very full and very concise, that you may neither be displeased at its deficiencies, nor find it unpleasant through satiety.

VII. God always was,[β] and always is, and always will be. Or rather, God always Is. For Was and Will be are fragments of our time, and of changeable nature, but He is Eternal Being. And this is the Name that He gives to Himself when giving the Oracle to Moses in the Mount. For in Himself He sums up and contains all Being, having neither beginning in the past nor end in the future; like some great Sea of Being, limitless and unbounded, transcending all conception of time and nature, only adumbrated by the mind, and that very dimly and scantily . . . not by His Essentials, but by His Environment; one image being got from one source and another from another, and combined into some sort of presentation of the truth, which escapes us before we have caught it, and takes to flight before we have conceived it, blazing forth upon our Master-part, even when that is cleansed, as the lightning flash which will not stay its course, does upon our sight . . . in order as I conceive by that part of it which we can comprehend to draw us to itself (for that which is altogether incom-

α 1 Cor. xv. 22. β Col. ii. 11. γ Rom. v. 20. δ Rom. xiii. 13.

a Alluding to his own recent arrival at Constantinople, after a life spent in the distant country of Cappadocia, and in ministering in small and insignificant places like Nazianzus.

β The whole of this passage occurs again verbatim in the second Oration for Easter Day, cc. iii.–ix.

prehensible is outside the bounds of hope, and not within the compass of endeavour), and by that part of It which we cannot comprehend to move our wonder, and as an object of wonder to become more an object of desire, and being desired to purify, and by purifying to make us like God;[a] so that when we have thus become like Himself, God may, to use a bold expression, hold converse with us as Gods, being united to us, and that perhaps to the same extent as He already knows those who are known to Him. The Divine Nature then is boundless and hard to understand; and all that we can comprehend of Him is His boundlessness; even though one may conceive that because He is of a simple nature He is therefore either wholly incomprehensible, or perfectly comprehensible. For let us further enquire what is implied by "is of a simple nature." For it is quite certain that this simplicity is not itself its nature, just as composition is not by itself the essence of compound beings.

VIII. And when Infinity is considered from two points of view, beginning and end (for that which is beyond these and not limited by them is Infinity), when the mind looks to the depth above, not having where to stand, and leans upon phenomena to form an idea of God, it calls the Infinite and Unapproachable which it finds there by the name of Unoriginate. And when it looks into the depths below, and at the future, it calls Him Undying and Imperishable. And when it draws a conclusion from the whole it calls Him Eternal (αἰώνιος). For Eternity (αἰών) is neither time nor part of time; for it cannot be measured. But what time, measured by the course of the sun, is to us, that Eternity is to the Everlasting, namely, a sort of time-like movement and interval co-extensive with their existence. This, however, is all I must now say about God; for the present is not a suitable time, as my present subject is not the doctrine of God, but that of the Incarnation. But when I say God, I mean Father, Son, and Holy Ghost. For Godhead is neither diffused beyond these, so as to bring in a mob of gods; nor yet is it bounded by a smaller compass than these, so as to condemn us for a poverty-stricken conception of Deity; either Judaizing to save the Monarchia, or falling into heathenism by the multitude of our gods. For the evil on either side is the same, though found in contrary directions. This then is the Holy of Holies,[β] which is hidden even from the Seraphim, and is glorified with a thrice repeated Holy,[a] meeting in one ascription of the Title Lord and God, as one of our predecessors has most beautifully and loftily pointed out.

IX. But since this movement of self-contemplation alone could not satisfy Goodness, but Good must be poured out and go forth beyond Itself to multiply the objects of Its beneficence, for this was essential to the highest Goodness, He first conceived the Heavenly and Angelic Powers. And this conception was a work fulfilled by His Word, and perfected by His Spirit. And so the secondary Splendours came into being, as the Ministers of the Primary Splendour; whether we are to conceive of them as intelligent Spirits, or as Fire of an immaterial and incorruptible kind, or as some other nature approaching this as near as may be. I should like to say that they were incapable of movement in the direction of evil, and susceptible only of the movement of good, as being about God, and illumined with the first rays from God—for earthly beings have but the second illumination; but I am obliged to stop short of saying that, and to conceive and speak of them only as difficult to move because of him,[β] who for his splendour was called Lucifer, but became and is called Darkness through his pride; and the apostate hosts who are subject to him, creators of evil[γ] by their revolt against good and our inciters.

X. Thus, then, and for these reasons, He gave being to the world of thought, as far as I can reason upon these matters, and estimate great things in my own poor language. Then when His first creation was in good order, He conceives a second world, material and visible; and this a system and compound of earth and sky, and all that is in the midst of them—an admirable creation indeed, when we look at the fair form of every part, but yet more worthy of admiration when we consider the harmony and the unison of the whole, and how each

a John x. 15.

β The Holy of Holies here means the Holy Trinity.

a The reference is to the Ter Sanctus or Triumphal Hymn, which is found in every Liturgy. The previous writer referred to is thought by some to be S. Athanasius, but by others S. Dionysius the Areopagite, who has some words on this point in his treatise De Cœlest. Hier., c. 7. But the most competent scholars deny the authenticity of the works attributed to S. Dionysius, and place them from one hundred to one hundred and fifty years later than S. Gregory's time.

β S. Thomas Aquinas (Summa I., qu. 63, art. 7) gives reasons for thinking that Satan was originally the highest of all the angelic hosts. This, however, is an opinion in which many high authorities differ from him. At any rate, Satan as Lucifer must have held a very high place.

γ Evil, says Nicetas here, has no positive existence, but is the negation of good. "The faculties of mind and body which are used in a sinful action are indeed things, and are the creatures of God; but the sin itself is not a thing, and consequently not a creature. God is indeed the Author of all that is, of every substance; but sin is not a substance, and is not. It is a declination from substance and from being, and not a part of it. (Mozley, Treatise on the Augustinian doctrine of predestination.)

part fits in with every other, in fair order, and all with the whole, tending to the perfect completion of the world as a Unit. This was to shew that He could call into being, not only a Nature akin to Himself, but also one altogether alien to Himself. For akin to Deity are those natures which are intellectual, and only to be comprehended by mind; but all of which sense can take cognisance are utterly alien to It; and of these the furthest removed are all those which are entirely destitute of soul and of power of motion. But perhaps some one of those who are too festive and impetuous may say, What has all this to do with us? Spur your horse to the goal. Talk to us about the Festival, and the reasons for our being here to-day. Yes, this is what I am about to do, although I have begun at a somewhat previous point, being compelled to do so by love, and by the needs of my argument.

XI. Mind, then, and sense, thus distinguished from each other, had remained within their own boundaries, and bore in themselves the magnificence of the Creator-Word, silent praisers[α] and thrilling heralds of His mighty work. Not yet was there any mingling of both, nor any mixtures of these opposites, tokens of a greater Wisdom and Generosity in the creation of natures; nor as yet were the whole riches of Goodness made known. Now the Creator-Word, determining to exhibit this, and to produce a single living being out of both—the visible and the invisible creations, I mean—fashions Man; and taking a body from already existing matter, and placing in it a Breath taken from Himself[β] which the Word knew to be an intelligent soul and the Image of God, as a sort of second world. He placed him, great in littleness[γ] on the earth; a new Angel, a mingled worshipper, fully initiated into the visible creation, but only partially into the intellectual; King of all upon earth, but subject to the King above; earthly and heavenly; temporal and yet immortal; visible and yet intellectual; half-way between greatness and lowliness; in one person combining spirit and flesh; spirit, because of the favour bestowed on him; flesh, because of the height to which he had been raised; the one that he might continue to live and praise his Benefactor, the other that he might suffer, and by suffering be put in remembrance, and corrected if he became proud of his greatness. A living creature trained here, and then moved elsewhere; and, to complete the mystery, deified by its inclination to God. For to this, I think, tends that Light of Truth which we here possess but in measure, that we should both see and experience the Splendour of God, which is worthy of Him Who made us, and will remake us again after a loftier fashion.

α Ps. xix. 1, 3. β Gen. ii. 7. γ Sc. a microcosm.

XII. This being He placed in Paradise, whatever the Paradise may have been, having honoured him with the gift of Free Will (in order that God might belong to him as the result of his choice, no less than to Him who had implanted the seeds of it), to till the immortal plants, by which is meant perhaps the Divine Conceptions, both the simpler and the more perfect; naked in his simplicity and inartificial life, and without any covering or screen; for it was fitting that he who was from the beginning should be such. Also He gave him a Law, as a material for his Free Will to act upon. This Law was a Commandment as to what plants he might partake of, and which one he might not touch. This latter was the Tree of Knowledge; not, however, because it was evil from the beginning when planted; nor was it forbidden because God grudged it to us . . Let not the enemies of God wag their tongues in that direction, or imitate the Serpent . . . But it would have been good if partaken of at the proper time, for the tree was, according to my theory, Contemplation, upon which it is only safe for those who have reached maturity of habit to enter; but which is not good for those who are still somewhat simple and greedy in their habit; just as solid food is not good for those who are yet tender, and have need of milk.[α] But when through the Devil's malice and the woman's caprice, to which she succumbed as the more tender, and which she brought to bear upon the man, as she was the more apt to persuade, alas for my weakness! (for that of my first father was mine), he forgot the Commandment which had been given to him;[β] he yielded to the baleful fruit; and for his sin he was banished, at once from the Tree of Life, and from Paradise, and from God; and put on the coats of skins . . that is, perhaps, the coarser flesh, both mortal and contradictory. This was the first thing that he learnt—his own shame;[γ] and he hid himself from God. Yet here too he makes a gain, namely death, and the cutting off of sin, in order that evil may not be immortal. Thus his punishment is changed into a mercy; for it is in mercy, I am persuaded, that God inflicts punishment.

XIII. And having been first chastened by

α Heb. v. 12. β Gen. iii. 5. γ Rom. i. 22–31.

many means (because his sins were many, whose root of evil sprang up through divers causes and at sundry times), by word, by law, by prophets, by benefits, by threats, by plagues, by waters, by fires, by wars, by victories, by defeats, by signs in heaven and signs in the air and in the earth and in the sea, by unexpected changes of men, of cities, of nations (the object of which was the destruction of wickedness), at last he needed a stronger remedy, for his diseases were growing worse; mutual slaughters, adulteries, perjuries, unnatural crimes, and that first and last of all evils, idolatry and the transfer of worship from the Creator to the Creatures. As these required a greater aid, so also they obtained a greater. And that was that the Word of God Himself—Who is before all worlds, the Invisible, the Incomprehensible, the Bodiless, Beginning of Beginning,[α] the Light of Light, the Source of Life and Immortality, the Image of the Archetypal Beauty, the immovable Seal, the unchangeable Image, the Father's Definition[β] and Word, came to His own Image, and took on Him flesh for the sake of our flesh, and mingled Himself with an intelligent soul for my soul's sake, purifying like by like; and in all points except sin was made man. Conceived by the Virgin,[γ] who first in body and soul was purified by the Holy Ghost[δ] (for it was needful both that Childbearing should be honoured, and that Virginity should receive a higher honour), He came forth then as God with that which He had assumed, One Person in two Natures, Flesh and Spirit, of which the latter deified the former.[ε] O new commingling; O strange conjunction; the Self-Existent comes into being, the Uncreate is created, That which cannot be contained is contained, by the intervention of an intellectual soul, mediating between the Deity and the corporeity of the flesh. And He Who gives riches becomes poor, for He assumes the poverty of my flesh, that I may assume the richness of His Godhead. He that is full empties Himself, for He empties Himself of His glory for a short while, that I may have a share in His Fulness. What is the riches of His Goodness? What is this mystery that is around me? I had a share in the image; I did not keep it; He partakes of my flesh that He may both save the image and make the flesh immortal. He communicates a second Communion far more marvellous than the first, inasmuch as then He imparted the better Nature, whereas now Himself partakes of the worse. This is more godlike than the former action, this is loftier in the eyes of all men of understanding.

XIV. To this what have those cavillers to say, those bitter reasoners about Godhead, those detractors of all that is praiseworthy, those darkeners of light, uncultured in respect of wisdom, for whom Christ died in vain, those unthankful creatures, the work of the Evil One? Do you turn this benefit into a reproach to God? Wilt thou deem Him little on this account, that He humbled Himself for thee; because the Good Shepherd,[α] He who lays down His life for His sheep, came to seek for that which had strayed upon the mountains and the hills, on which thou wast then sacrificing, and found the wanderer; and having found it,[β] took it upon His shoulders—on which He also took the Wood of the Cross; and having taken it, brought it back to the higher life; and having carried it back, numbered it amongst those who had never strayed. Because He lighted a candle—His own Flesh—and swept the house, cleansing the world from sin; and sought the piece of money, the Royal Image that was covered up by passions. And He calls together His Angel friends on the finding of the coin, and makes them sharers in His joy,[γ] whom He had made to share also the secret of the Incarnation? Because on the candle of the Forerunner there follows the light that exceeds in brightness; and to the Voice the Word succeeds; and to the Bridegroom's friend the Bridegroom; to him that prepared for the Lord a peculiar people, cleansing them by water in preparation for the Spirit? Dost thou reproach God with all this? Dost thou on this account deem Him lessened, because He girds Himself with a towel and washes His disciples' feet, and shows that humiliation is the best road to exaltation? Because for the soul that was bent to the ground He humbles Himself, that He may raise up with Himself the soul that was tottering to a fall under a weight of sin? Why dost thou not also charge upon Him as a

α Cf. Light of Light Begotten. Christ our Lord is called "The Beginning of the Creation of God, because by Him all things were made; and He is of the Beginning, inasmuch as God the Father is the Unoriginate Principle of all, and the Origin and Fount of Godhead. The Scholiast here refers to Ps. cx. 3, which in the Vulgate and LXX. runs "With Thee is the Beginning in the day of Thy Power."

β Cf. Theol.: IV. xx., where S. Gregory says "Perhaps this Relation might be compared to that between the Definition and the thing defined" Nicetas remarks that, just as the definition declares the nature of the defined, so the Personal Word shows forth the Nature of the Father. Suidas (in voce ὅρος) says that the phrase is used to show the Unity of Nature between the Father and the Son. It is not, however, of frequent occurrence.

γ Luke i. 35.

δ S. Gregory does not seem to have been aware of the doctrine of the "Immaculate Conception."

ε See note on In Sancta Lumina, c. xiv.

α John x. 11. β Luke xv. 4, sq. γ Ib. xv. 8, 10.

crime the fact that He eats with Publicans and at Publicans' tables,[α] and that He makes disciples of Publicans, that He too may gain somewhat . . . and what? . . . the salvation of sinners. If so, we must blame the physician for stooping over sufferings, and enduring evil odours that he may give health to the sick; or one who as the Law commands bent down into a ditch to save a beast that had fallen into it.[β]

XV. He was sent, but as man, for He was of a twofold Nature; for He was wearied, and hungered, and was thirsty, and was in an agony, and shed tears, according to the nature of a corporeal being. And if the expression be also used of Him as God, the meaning is that the Father's good pleasure is to be considered a Mission, for to this He refers all that concerns Himself; both that He may honour the Eternal Principle, and because He will not be taken to be an antagonistic God. And whereas it is written both that He was betrayed, and also that He gave Himself up[γ] and that He was raised up by the Father, and taken up into heaven; and on the other hand, that He raised Himself and *went* up; the former statement of each pair refers to the good pleasure of the Father, the latter to His own Power. Are you then to be allowed to dwell upon all that humiliates Him, while passing over all that exalts Him, and to count on your side the fact that He suffered, but to leave out of the account the fact that it was of His own will? See what even now the Word has to suffer. By one set He is honoured as God, but is confused with the Father,[δ] by another He is dishonoured as mere flesh[α] and severed from the Godhead. With which of them will He be most angry, or rather, which shall He forgive, those who injuriously confound Him or those who divide Him? For the former ought to have distinguished, and the latter to have united Him; the one in number, the other in Godhead. Stumblest Thou at His flesh? So did the Jews. Or dost thou call Him a Samaritan, and . . . I will not say the rest. Dost thou disbelieve in His Godhead? This did not even the demons, O thou who art less believing than demons and more stupid than Jews. Those did perceive that the name of Son implies equality of rank; these did know that He who drove them out was God, for they were convinced of it by their own experience. But you will admit neither the equality nor the Godhead. It would have been better for you to have been either a Jew or a demoniac (if I may utter an absurdity), than in uncircumcision and in sound health to be so wicked and ungodly in your attitude of mind.

XVI. A little later on you will see Jesus submitting to be purified in the River Jordan for my Purification, or rather, sanctifying the waters by His Purification (for indeed He had no need of purification Who taketh away the sin of the world) and the heavens cleft

α Luke v. 29.

β S. Gregory is referring to the provision of the Law, which orders a man, if he see his friend's or his enemy's ox or ass fallen under a burden or going astray, to lend assistance; but the terms of his reference are rather to the reasoning of our Lord with the Pharisees about the Sabbath. Luke xiii. 15 and xiv. 5.

γ Cf. ἐν τῇ νυκτὶ ἐν ᾗ παρεδίδοτο, μᾶλλον δε ἑαυτὸν παρεδίδου. Canon of Liturgy of S. Mark (Swainson p. 517). Ea nocte qua tradidit seipsum. Lit. Copt. S. Basil (Ib.). Cum statuisset se tradere. Coptic S. Basil (Hammond, p. 209) Rot. Vatic. and Cod. Ross. of S. Mark, has only τ. ν. ᾗ ἑαυτ, παρεδ. (Swainson, 50); so too S. Basil (Ib., 81) in Cod. B. M., 22749 and Barberini of S. Chrys. (Ib., 91); but the whole expression is in Chrys. (cent. xi., ib., 129) and in Greek S. James (78. 272–3), but Syriac S. James has "in qua nocte tradendus erat." (Canon. Univ., Æthiop. Hammond, 258). *Pridie quam pateretur* is the form in the Canon of the Roman, Ambrosian, and Sarum Missals; but the Mozarabic, which is largely of an Eastern character, has *in qua nocte tradebatur*. (Hammond, 333).

δ The Sabellian heresy may be briefly described as the doctrine of One God exercising three offices, as opposed to the Catholic Faith of One God in three Persons. Sabellius himself was a Priest of the Libyan Pentapolis, who at Rome in the time of Pope Zephyrinus embraced the heresy of Notus, which maintained that God the Father suffered for us on the cross in the form of Christ. His followers, who openly declared themselves first about A.D. 357, thought that God, to Whom as the Source of all things the name of Father is given, is called the Son when He united Himself to the humanity of Jesus for the work of our redemption; and in like manner He is the Holy Spirit when manifested for the work of sanctification. Sabellius was condemned by a Council held at Rome, probably in 258; again at Nicea, and again at Constantinople, where Sabellian Baptism was pronounced invalid.

α Arianism was the result of a strong opposition to Sabellianism, coupled with a misunderstanding of the argument against it. There was, no doubt, a danger of falling into the opposite error of Tritheism, to avoid which Arianism "divided the Substance" and virtually—and in the end explicitly—denied the Godhead of our Lord Jesus Christ. Arius was a Priest of Alexandria, and it was there that he began to publish his opinions, in the early years of the Fourth Century (318); but Newman traces the origin of the heresy to Antioch and its Judaizing tendency. At a meeting of the clergy in Alexandria the Bishop, S. Alexander, gave an address on the coeternity, and coequality of the Father and the Son, and used the expression τὴν αὐτὴν οὐσίαν ἔχειν, that They had the same Substance. Arius protested against this as a Sabellian statement, and used the words κτίσμα (creature) and ποίημα (a thing made) of the Son, adding the sentence which became so famous, ἦν ὅτε οὐκ ἦν,—there was a time when the Son did not exist. Having ineffectually tried private remonstrance, S. Alexander brought the matter in 321 before his Provincial Synod, in which were present about 100 Egyptian and Pentapolitan Bishops, who after giving the matter a patient hearing, excommunicated Arius and his principal adherents. But it was too late to undo the mischief. The heresy spread widely, and the whole Eastern Church was stirred by the controversy. At last a great Council of the whole Church met at Nicæa in 325, summoned by the Emperor; and there the heresy was unequivocally condemned, and the great Creed propounded with its watchword, the Homoousion. The false teaching had however struck its roots deep and wide; and though now banned by the anathema of the Church, it was long in dying; and indeed at one time it seemed as if—humanly speaking—it must swamp the whole Catholic Church. Under various forms the Semi-Arians who claimed to differ from the faith of Nicæa only by a single letter, the Aetians and Eunomians, who went to the furthest extreme of the falsehood (Anomoeans), and many others, the heresy spread far and wide; and when S. Gregory came to Constantinople there was not one Catholic Church or Priest to be found in the place, and only a few scattered folk who still held to the Faith of the Consubstantial. Gregory's wonderful discourses however came to their aid, and partly under his presidency was held the Second Oecumenical Synod, which condemned the heresy of Macedonius, a still further development of Arianism, which denied also the Deity of the Holy Ghost. Arianism survived for another two centuries among the Goths and Vandals, the Burgundians and Lombards; but it never rose again as a power in the Church.

asunder, and witness borne to him by the Spirit That is of one nature with Him;[α] you shall see Him tempted and conquering and served by Angels,[β] and healing every sickness[γ] and every disease,[δ] and giving life to the dead (O that He would give life to you who are dead because of your heresy), and driving out demons,[ε] sometimes Himself, sometimes by his disciples; and feeding vast multitudes with a few loaves;[ζ] and walking dryshod upon seas;[η] and being betrayed and crucified, and crucifying with Himself my sin; offered as a Lamb, and offering as a Priest; as a Man buried in the grave, and as God rising again; and then ascending, and to come again in His own glory. Why what a multitude of high festivals there are in each of the mysteries of the Christ; all of which have one completion, namely, my perfection and return to the first condition of Adam.

XVII. Now then I pray you accept His Conception, and leap before Him; if not like John from the womb,[θ] yet like David, because of the resting of the Ark.[ι] Revere the enrolment on account of which thou wast written in heaven, and adore the Birth by which thou wast loosed from the chains of thy birth,[κ] and honour little Bethlehem, which hath led thee back to Paradise; and worship the manger through which thou, being without sense, wast fed by the Word. Know as Isaiah bids thee, thine Owner, like the ox, and like the ass thy Master's crib;[λ] if thou be one of those who are pure and lawful food, and who chew the cud of the word and are fit for sacrifice. Or if thou art one of those who are as yet unclean and uneatable and unfit for sacrifice, and of the gentile portion, run with the Star, and bear thy Gifts with the Magi, gold and frankincense and myrrh,[μ] as to a King, and to God, and to One Who is dead for thee. With Shepherds glorify Him;[ν] with Angels join in chorus; with Archangels sing hymns. Let this Festival be common to the powers in heaven and to the powers upon earth.[ξ] For I am persuaded that the Heavenly Hosts join in our exultation and keep high Festival with us to-day[ο] . . . because they love men, and they love God . . . just like those whom David introduces after the Passion ascending with Christ[π] and coming to meet Him, and bidding one another to lift up the gates.

XVIII. One thing connected with the Birth of Christ I would have you hate . . . the murder of the infants by Herod.[α] Or rather you must venerate this too, the Sacrifice of the same age as Christ, slain before the Offering of the New Victim. If He flees into Egypt,[β] joyfully become a companion of His exile. It is a grand thing to share the exile of the persecuted Christ. If He tarry long in Egypt, call Him out of Egypt by a reverent worship of Him there. Travel without fault through every stage and faculty of the Life of Christ. Be purified; be circumcised; strip off the veil which has covered thee from thy birth. After this teach in the Temple, and drive out the sacrilegious traders.[γ] Submit to be stoned if need be, for well I wot thou shalt be hidden from those who cast the stones; thou shalt escape even through the midst of them, like God.[δ] If thou be brought before Herod, answer not for the most part.[ε] He will respect thy silence more than most people's long speeches. If thou be scourged,[ζ] ask for what they leave out. Taste gall for the taste's sake;[η] drink vinegar;[θ] seek for spittings; accept blows, be crowned with thorns,[ι] that is, with the hardness of the godly life; put on the purple robe, take the reed in hand, and receive mock worship from those who mock at the truth; lastly, be crucified with Him, and share His Death and Burial gladly, that thou mayest rise with Him, and be glorified with Him and reign with Him. Look at and be looked at by the Great God, Who in Trinity is worshipped and glorified, and Whom we declare to be now set forth as clearly before you as the chains of our flesh allow, in Jesus Christ our Lord, to Whom be the glory for ever. Amen.

α Matt. iii. 13, 17. β Ib. iv. 1–11. γ Ib. iv. 23.
δ Nicetas distinguishes between Νόσος and Μαλακία, saying that the first is actual disease, and the second the premonitory failing of health which prognosticates a disease. And, so, he says, in reference to the soul, Νόσος is actual sin, while Μαλακία is the relaxation of the will which leads and assents to actual sin.
ε Ib. ix. 33. ζ Ib. ix. 14. η Ib. ix. 25.
θ Luke i. 41. ι 2 Sam. vi. 14. κ Luke ii. 1–5.
λ I. e., original sin (Ps. li. 5). μ Isa. i. 3.
ν Matt. ii. ξ Luke ii. 14, 15. ο The Liturgy. π Ps. xxiv.

INTRODUCTION TO THE ORATIONS ON THE HOLY LIGHTS AND ON HOLY BAPTISM.

THE Oration on the Holy Lights was preached on the Festival of the Epiphany 381, and was followed the next day by that on Baptism. In the Eastern Church this Festival is regarded as more particularly the commemoration of our Lord's Baptism, and is accordingly one of the great days for the solemn ministration of the Sacrament. It is generally called Theophania,

α Matt. ii. 16. β Ib. v. 13. γ John ii. 15. δ Ib. viii. 59.
ε Luke xxiii. 9. ζ John xix. 1. η Matt. xxvii. 34.
θ John xix. 29. ι Matt. xxvi. 67, and xxvii. 28.

and the Gospel in the Liturgy is S. Matthew iii. 13-17. The Sunday in the Octave is called μετὰ τὰ φῶτα (After The Lights), pointing to a time when the Feast was known as the "Holy Lights," as seems to have been the case in S. Gregory's day. This name is derived from Baptism, which was often in ancient days called Illumination, in reference to which name (derived from the spiritual grace of the Sacrament) lighted torches or candles were carried by the neophytes. It would appear that the solemnites of the Festival lasted two days, of which the second was devoted to the solemn conferring of the Sacrament. Accordingly we find two Orations belonging to the Festival. In the first, delivered on the Day itself he dwells more especially on the Feast and the Mystery of our Lord's Baptism therein commemorated; and proceeds to speak of the different kinds of Baptism, of which he enumerates Five, viz.:—

1. The figurative Baptism of Israel by Moses in the cloud and in the Sea.

2. The preparatory Baptism of repentance ministered by S. John the Baptist.

3. The spiritual Baptism of water and the Holy Ghost given us by our Lord.

4. The glorious Baptism of Martyrdom.

5. The painful Baptism of Penance.

In speaking of this last he takes occasion to refute the extreme rigorism of the followers of Novatus, who denied absolution to certain classes of sins committed after Baptism.

In the second Oration, delivered next day, he dwells on the Sacrament of Baptism and its spiritual effects; and takes occasion to reprove the then still prevalent practice of deferring Baptism till the near approach of death. He likewise dwells on the truth that the validity and spiritual effect of the Sacrament is wholly independent of the rank or worthiness of the Priest who may minister it; and he concludes with a sketch of the obligations which its reception involves, with a very valuable exposition of the Creed, and of the Ceremonies which accompanied the administration of the Sacrament.

ORATION XXXIX.

Oration on the Holy Lights.

I. Again My Jesus, and again a mystery; not deceitful nor disorderly, nor belonging to Greek error or drunkenness (for so I call their solemnities, and so I think will every man of sound sense); but a mystery lofty and divine, and allied to the Glory above. For the Holy Day of the Lights, to which we have come, and which we are celebrating to-day, has for its origin the Baptism of my Christ, the True Light That lighteneth every man that cometh into the world,[α] and effecteth my purification, and assists that light which we received from the beginning from Him from above, but which we darkened and confused by sin.

II. Therefore listen to the Voice of God, which sounds so exceeding clearly to me, who am both disciple and master of these mysteries, as would to God it may sound to you; I Am The Light Of The World.[β] Therefore approach ye to Him and be enlightened, and let not your faces be ashamed,[γ] being signed with the true Light. It is a season of new birth,[δ] let us be born again. It is a time of reformation, let us receive again the first Adam.[ε] Let us not remain what we are, but let us become what we once were. The Light Shineth In Darkness,[ζ] in this life and in the flesh, and is chased by the darkness, but is not overtaken by it:—I mean the adverse power leaping up in its shamelessness against the visible Adam, but encountering God and being defeated;—in order that we, putting away the darkness, may draw near to the Light, and may then become perfect Light, the children of perfect Light. See the grace of this Day; see the power of this mystery. Are you not lifted up from the earth? Are you not clearly placed on high, being exalted by our voice and meditation? and you will be placed much higher when the Word shall have prospered the course of my words.

III. Is there any such among the shadowy purifications of the Law, aiding as it did with temporary sprinklings, and the ashes of an heifer sprinkling the unclean;[η] or do the gentiles celebrate any such thing in their mysteries, every ceremony and mystery of which to me is nonsense, and a dark invention of demons, and a figment of an unhappy mind, aided by time, and hidden by fable? For what they worship as true, they veil as mythical. But if these things are true, they ought not to be called myths, but to be proved not to be shameful;[θ] and if they are false, they ought not to be objects of wonder; nor ought people so inconsiderately to hold the most contrary opinions about the same thing, as if they were playing in the market-place with boys or really ill-disposed men, not engaged

α John i. 9. β John viii. 12. γ Ps. xxxiv. 5. δ John iii. 3.
ε I.e., the condition of man before the fall. ζ Ib. i. 5.
η This is the same word which in S. John i. 5, is rendered by "comprehend." θ Heb. vii. 13.

in discussion with men of sense, and worshippers of the Word, though despisers of this artificial plausibility.

IV. We are not concerned in these mysteries with births of Zeus and thefts of the Cretan Tyrant[α] (though the Greeks may be displeased at such a title for him), nor with the name of Curetes, and the armed dances, which were to hide the wailings of a weeping god, that he might escape from his father's hate. For indeed it would be a strange thing that he who was swallowed as a stone should be made to weep as a child.[β] Nor are we concerned with Phrygian mutilations and flutes and Corybantes,[γ] and all the ravings of men concerning Rhea, consecrating people to the mother of the gods, and being initiated into such ceremonies as befit the mother of such gods as these. Nor have we any carrying away of the Maiden,[δ] nor wandering of Demeter, nor her intimacy with Celei and Triptolemi and Dragons; nor her doings and sufferings . . for I am ashamed to bring into daylight that ceremony of the night, and to make a sacred mystery of obscenity. Eleusis knows these things, and so do those who are eyewitnesses of what is there guarded by silence, and well worthy of it. Nor is our commemoration one of Dionysus, and the thigh that travailed with an incomplete birth, as before a head had travailed with another;[ε] nor of the hermaphrodite god, nor a chorus of the drunken and enervated host; nor of the folly of the Thebans which honours him; nor the thunderbolt of Semele which they adore. Nor is it the harlot mysteries of Aphrodite, who, as they themselves admit, was basely born and basely honoured; nor have we here Phalli and Ithyphalli,[ζ] shameful both in form and action; nor Taurian massacres of strangers;[α] nor blood of Laconian youths shed upon the altars, as they scourged themselves with the whips;[β] and in this case alone use their courage badly, who honour a goddess, and her a virgin. For these same people both honour effeminacy, and worship boldness.

V. And where will you place the butchery of Pelops,[γ] which feasted hungry gods, that bitter and inhuman hospitality? Where the horrible and dark spectres of Hecate, and the underground puerilities and sorceries of Trophonius, or the babblings of the Dodonæan Oak, or the trickeries of the Delphian tripod, or the prophetic draught of Castalia, which could prophesy anything, except their own being brought to silence?[δ] Nor is it the sacrificial art of Magi, and their entrail forebodings, nor the Chaldæan astronomy and horoscopes, comparing our lives with the movements of the heavenly bodies, which cannot know even what they are themselves, or shall be. Nor are these Thracian orgies, from which the word Worship (θρησκεία) is said to be derived; nor rites and mysteries of Orpheus, whom the Greeks admired so much for his wisdom that they devised for him a lyre which draws all things by its music. Nor the tortures of Mithras[ε] which it is just that those who can endure to be initiated into such things should suffer; nor the manglings of Osiris,[ζ] another calamity honoured by the Egyptians; nor the ill-fortunes of Isis[η] and the goats more venerable than the Mendesians, and the stall of Apis,[θ] the calf that luxuriated in the folly of the Memphites, nor all those honours with which they outrage the Nile, while themselves proclaiming it in song to be the Giver of fruits and corn, and the measurer of happiness by its cubits.[ι]

VI. I pass over the honours they pay to rep-

α I.e., Zeus, who was said by some to be a deified man, once tyrant of Crete, where his tomb was shown.

β The allusion is to the birth of Zeus. Kronos the Titan, father of the gods, was the husband of Rhea, who bore him children. But an oracle having declared that Kronos should be dethroned by his children, he swallowed them immediately after they were born. Rhea, however, on the birth of Zeus, aided by the Curetes, a wild band of Cretan Priests, concealed the child, and substituted a stone, which Kronos swallowed in his haste without perceiving the difference. The stone made him very sick, and he vomited forth the children whom he had previously swallowed; and by them and Zeus the prophecy was fulfilled. Kronos was deposed and imprisoned in Tartarus.

γ There was a temple of Rhea in Phrygia, in which at her festivals people mutilated themselves to do her honour. The flutes alluded to served to turn the thoughts of the sufferers from the pain of the operation. The Corybantes were the ministers of the goddess, who led the wild orgies of her worship. It is believed that there is an allusion to this practice of self-mutilation in Galat. v. 12. So at least S. Jerome, S. Ambrose, and all the Greek Fathers take the passage. S. Thomas Aquinas, understanding the word in the same sense, applies it mystically; and Estius, who here follows Erasmus, refers the "cutting off" merely to excommunication, a sense which he calls "Apostolico sensu dignior," though why "*dignior*" it is not easy to see. Yet he acknowledges that those who interpret it literally do so "*non immerito*."

δ The mythus of the Rape of Persephone and its consequences.

ε Dionysus was said to have been born from the thigh of Zeus, as Athene to have sprung full-grown and armed at all points from his head.

ζ These myths and practices are too shameful to be described.

α See the Iphigenia In Tauris of Euripides.

β It was a custom of the Spartans that at their great festival of Artemis the youths who were just coming of age (Ephebi) should scourge themselves cruelly on her altar in honour of the goddess, and to prove their manhood.

γ The gods came to dine with Tantalus, and he, to do them honour, boiled his son Pelops for their food. They, however, found it out, and restored him to life; not, however, before Demeter had unwittingly eaten his shoulder, in the place of which they substituted one of ivory.

δ S. Jerome, commenting on Isaiah xli. 22, says: "Why could they never predict anything concerning Christ and His Apostles, or the ruin and destruction of their own temples? If then they could not foretell their own destruction, how can they foretell anything good or bad?"

ε These Mysteries were of Persian origin, connected it is said with the worship of the Sun. The neophytes were made to undergo twelve different kinds of torture.

ζ The Egyptian Mysteries.

η Zeus fell in love with Isis, and carried her off in the form of a heifer. Here, discovering the fraud, sent a gadfly, which drove Isis mad.

θ Apis, the sacred bull, worshipped at Memphis.

ι i.e., that the prosperity of the country was proportionate to the annual rise of the River.

tiles, and their worship of vile things, each of which has its peculiar cultus and festival, and all share in a common devilishness; so that, if they were absolutely bound to be ungodly, and to fall away from honouring God, and to be led astray to idols and works of art and things made with hands, men of sense could not imprecate anything worse upon themselves than that they might worship just such things, and honour them in just such a way; that, as Paul says, they might receive in themselves that recompense of their error which was meet,[α] in the very objects of their worhip; not so much honouring them as suffering dishonour by them; abominable because of their error, and yet more abominable from the vileness of the objects of their adoration and worship; so that they should be even more without understanding than the objects of their worship; being as excessively foolish as the latter are vile.

VII. Well, let these things be the amusement of the children of the Greeks and of the demons to whom their folly is due, who turn aside the honour of God to themselves, and divide men in various ways in pursuit of shameful thoughts and fancies, ever since they drove us away from the Tree of Life, by means of the Tree of Knowledge unseasonably[β] and improperly imparted to us, and then assailed us as now weaker than before; carrying clean away the mind, which is the ruling power in us, and opening a door to the passions. For, being of a nature envious and man-hating, or rather having become so by their own wickedness, they could neither endure that we who were below should attain to that which is above, having themselves fallen from above upon the earth; nor that such a change in their glory and their first natures should have taken place. This is the meaning of their persecution of the creature. For this God's Image was outraged; and as we did not like to keep the Commandments,[γ] we were given over to the independence of our error. And as we erred we were disgraced by the objects of our worship. For there was not only this calamity, that we who were made for good works[δ] to the glory and praise of our Maker, and to imitate God as far as might be, were turned into a den of all sorts of passions, which cruelly devour and consume the inner man; but there was this further evil, that man actually made gods the advocates of his passions, so that sin might be reckoned not only irresponsible, but even divine, taking refuge in the objects of his worship as his apology.

VIII. But since to us grace has been given to flee from superstitious error and to be joined to the truth and to serve the living and true God, and to rise above creation, passing by all that is subject to time and to first motion; let us look at and reason upon God and things divine in a manner corresponding to this Grace given us. But let us begin our discussion of them from the most fitting point. And the most fitting is, as Solomon laid down for us; us; The beginning of wisdom, he says, is to get wisdom.[α] And what this is he tells us; the beginning of wisdom is fear.[β] For we must not begin with contemplation and leave off with fear (for an unbridled contemplation would perhaps push us over a precipice), but we must be grounded and purified and so to say made light by fear, and thus be raised to the height. For where fear is there is keeping of commandments; and where there is keeping of commandments there is purifying of the flesh, that cloud which covers the soul and suffers it not to see the Divine Ray. And where there is purifying there is Illumination; and Illumination is the satisfying of desire to those who long for the greatest things, or the Greatest Thing, or That Which surpasses all greatness.

IX. Wherefore we must purify ourselves first, and then approach this converse with the Pure; unless we would have the same experience as Israel,[γ] who could not endure the glory of the face of Moses, and therefore asked for a veil;[δ] or else would feel and say with Manoah "We are undone O wife, we have seen God,"[ε] although it was God only in his fancy; or like Peter would send Jesus out of the boat,[ζ] as being ourselves unworthy of such a visit; and when I say Peter, I am speaking of the man who walked upon the waves;[η] or like Paul would be stricken in eyes,[θ] as he was before he was cleansed from the guilt of his persecution, when he conversed with Him Whom he was persecuting—or rather with a short flash of That great Light; or like the Centurion[ι] would seek for healing, but would not, through a praiseworthy fear, receive the Healer into his house. Let each one of us also speak so, as

α Rom. i. 27.

β cf. Orat. in Theoph. c. 12. The explanation seems to be, that the "Knowledge of good and evil" was a necessary part of the development of man's intellect, but that a premature attempt to attain it *per saltum* instead of by a gradual progress would prove fatal. Had human nature gone through its originally intended educational stages, it might have reached to the knowledge of evil without having that knowledge alloyed and deteriorated by the experience of evil, but might have known it, as God does, without taint. (Blount, Ann. Bible on Gen. ii. 7.)

γ Ibid. i. 28. δ Eph. ii. 10; Phil. i. 11.

α Prov. iv. 7. β Ib. i. 7 sq. γ Exod. xxxiv. 30.
δ 2 Cor. iii. 7. ε Judg. xiii. 23. ζ Luke v. 8.
η Matt. xiv. 29. θ Acts ix. 3–8. ι Matt. viii. 8.

long as he is still uncleansed, and is a Centurion still, commanding many in wickedness, and serving in the army of Cæsar, the World-ruler of those who are being dragged down; "I am not worthy that thou shouldest come under my roof." But when he shall have looked upon Jesus, though he be little of stature like Zaccheus[α] of old, and climb up on the top of the sycamore tree by mortifying his members which are upon the earth,[β] and having risen above the body of humiliation, then he shall receive the Word, and it shall be said to him, This day is salvation come to this house.[γ] Then let him lay hold on the salvation, and bring forth fruit more perfectly, scattering and pouring forth rightly that which as a publican he wrongly gathered.

X. For the same Word is on the one hand terrible through its nature to those who are unworthy, and on the other through its loving kindness can be received by those who are thus prepared, who have driven out the unclean and worldly spirit from their souls, and have swept and adorned their own souls by self-examination, and have not left them idle or without employment, so as again to be occupied with greater armament by the seven spirits of wickedness . . . the same number as are reckoned of virtue (for that which is hardest to fight against calls for the sternest efforts) . . . but besides fleeing from evil, practise virtue, making Christ entirely, or at any rate to the greatest extent possible, to dwell within them, so that the power of evil cannot meet with any empty place to fill it again with himself, and make the last state of that man worse than the first, by the greater energy of his assault, and the greater strength and impregnability of the fortress. But when, having guarded our soul with every care, and having appointed goings up in our heart,[δ] and broken up our fallow ground,[ε] and sown unto righteousness,[ζ] as David and Solomon and Jeremiah bid us, let us enlighten ourselves with the light of knowledge, and then let us speak of the Wisdom of God that hath been hid in a mystery,[η] and enlighten others. Meanwhile let us purify ourselves, and receive the elementary initiation of the Word, that we may do ourselves the utmost good, making ourselves godlike, and receiving the Word at His coming; and not only so, but holding Him fast and shewing Him to others.

XI. And now, having purified the theatre by what has been said, let us discourse a little about the Festival, and join in celebrating this Feast with festal and pious souls. And, since the chief point of the Festival is the remembrance of God, let us call God to mind. For I think that the sound of those who keep Festival *There*, where is the dwelling of all the Blissful, is nothing else than this, the hymns and praises of God, sung by all who are counted worthy of that City. Let none be astonished if what I have to say contains some things that I have said before; for not only will I utter the same words, but I shall speak of the same subjects, trembling both in tongue and mind and thought when I speak of God for you too, that you may share this laudable and blessed feeling. And when I speak of God you must be illumined at once by one flash of light and by three. Three in Individualities or Hypostases, if any prefer so to call them, or persons,[a] for we will not quarrel about names so long as the syllables amount to the same meaning; but One in respect of the Substance—that is, the Godhead. For they are divided without division, if I may so say; and they are united in division. For the Godhead is one in three, and the

α Luke xix. 3. β Col. iii. 5. γ Luke xix. 9. δ Ps. lxxxiv. 5. ε Jer. iv. 3. ζ Prov. xi. 18. η 2 Cor. ii. 6.

a The sense of Person (here πρόσωπον), which is the usual post-Nicene equivalent of ὑπόστασις, was by no means generally attached to that word during the first Four Centuries, though here and there there are traces of such a use. Throughout the Arian controversy a great deal of trouble and misunderstanding was caused by the want of a precise definition of the meaning of ὑπόστασις. It seems to have been at first understood by the Eastern Church to mean Real Personal Existence—Reality being the fundamental idea. In this fundamental sense it was used in Theology as expressing the distinct individuality and relative bearing of the Three "Persons" of the Blessed Trinity to each other (τὸ ἴδίον πὰρα τὸ κοινόν, Suidas). But Arius gave it a heretical twist, and said that there are Three Hypostases, in the sense of Natures or Substances: and this doctrine was anathematized by the Nicene Council, which, apparently regarding the term ὑπόστασις as exactly equivalent to οὐσία (as Arius tried to make it) condemned the proposition that the Son is ἐξ ἑτέρας ὑποστάσεως ἢ οὐσίας (Symb. Nic.). Similar is the use of the word in S. Athanasius. As against Sabellius, however, who taught that in the Godhead there are τρία πρόσωπα (using this word in the sense of Aspects only) but would not allow τρεῖς ὑποστάσεις (i. e., Self-existent Personalities), the post-Nicene Church regarded ὑπόστασις as designating the Person, and spoke freely of τρεῖς ὑποστάσεις. The Western Church increased the confusion by continuing to regard ὑπόστασις as equivalent to οὐσία, and translating it by Substantia or Subsistentia. It was not till the word Essentia came into use to express οὐσία that the Western Church grasped the difference, so long accepted in the East, so as to use the words accurately. Meantime, however, there would seem to have grown up a difference in the use of the two words supposed to represent ὑπόστασις, of the same kind as that between ὑπόστασις and οὐσία; Substantia being appropriated to the Essence of a thing, that which is the foundation of its being; while Subsistentia came rather to connote a limitation, i.e., Personality. Thus the West also became confused, and Substantia was held to be the true equivalent of ὑπόστασις. Hence the condemnation at Sardica (A.D. 347) by the Western Bishops of the doctrine of Three Hypostases as Arian. The confusion lasted long, but in 362 a Council was held at Alexandria, when this difference was seen to be a mere logomachy, and it was pronounced orthodox to confess either τρεῖς ὑποστάσεις in the sense of "Persons," or μίαν ὑπόστασιν in that of "Substance." Our author in his Oration to the Fathers of the Council of Constantinople fully acknowledges this. "What do you mean," he says, "by ὑποστάσεις or πρόσωπα? You mean that the Three are distinct, not in Nature, but in Personality" And in the Panegyric on S. Athanasius (Or. xxi. c. 35), he remarks on the orthodoxy of the phrase μία οὐσία, τρεῖς ὑποστάσεις, that the first expression refers to the Nature of the Godhead, the second to the special properties of the Persons. With this, he says, the Italians agree, but the poverty of their language is such that it does not admit of the distinction between οὐσία and ὑπόστασις, and therefore has to call in the word πρόσωπον, which if misunderstood is liable to be charged with Sabellianism.

three are one, in whom the Godhead is, or to speak more accurately, Who are the Godhead. Excesses and defects we will omit, neither making the Unity a confusion, nor the division a separation. We would keep equally far from the confusion of Sabellius and from the division of Arius, which are evils diametrically opposed, yet equal in their wickedness. For what need is there heretically to fuse God together, or to cut Him up into inequality?

XII. For to us there is but One God, the Father, of Whom are all things, and One Lord Jesus Christ, by Whom are all things; and One Holy Ghost, in Whom are all things;[α] yet these words, of, by, in, whom, do not denote a difference of nature (for if this were the case, the three prepositions, or the order of the three names would never be altered), but they characterize the personalities of a nature which is one and unconfused. And this is proved by the fact that They are again collected into one, if you will read—not carelessly—this other passage of the same Apostle, "Of Him and through Him and to Him are all things; to Him be glory forever, Amen."[β] The Father is Father, and is Unoriginate, for He is of no one; the Son is Son, and is not unoriginate, for He is of the Father. But if you take the word Origin in a temporal sense, He too is Unoriginate, for He is the Maker of Time, and is not subject to Time. The Holy Ghost is truly Spirit, coming forth from the Father indeed, but not after the manner of the Son, for it is not by Generation but by Procession (since I must coin a word for the sake of clearness[γ]); for neither did the Father cease to be Unbegotten because of His begetting something, nor the Son to be begotten because He is of the Unbegotten (how could that be?), nor is the Spirit changed into Father or Son because He proceeds, or because He is God—though the ungodly do not believe it. For Personality is unchangeable; else how could Personality remain, if it were changeable, and could be removed from one to another? But they who make "Unbegotten" and "Begotten" natures of equivocal gods would perhaps make Adam and Seth differ in nature, since the former was not born of flesh (for he was created), but the latter was born of Adam and Eve. There is then One God in Three, and These Three are One, as we have said.

XIII. Since then these things are so, or rather since This is so; and His Adoration ought not to be rendered only by Beings above, but there ought to be also worshippers on earth, that all things may be filled with the glory of God (forasmuch as they are filled with God Himself); therefore man was created and honored with the hand[α] and Image of God. But to despise man, when by the envy of the Devil and the bitter taste of sin he was pitiably severed from God his Maker—this was not in the Nature of God. What then was done, and what is the great Mystery that concerns us? An innovation is made upon nature, and God is made Man. "He that rideth upon the Heaven of Heavens in the East"[β] of His own glory and Majesty, is glorified in the West of our meanness and lowliness. And the Son of God deigns to become and to be called Son of Man; not changing what He was (for It is unchangeable); but assuming what He was not (for He is full of love to man), that the Incomprehensible[γ] might be comprehended, conversing with us through the mediation of the Flesh as through a veil; since it was not possible for that nature which is subject to birth and decay to endure His unveiled Godhead. Therefore the Unmingled is mingled; and not only is God mingled with birth and Spirit[δ] with flesh, and the Eternal with time, and the Uncircumscribed with measure;

α 2 Cor. viii. 6. β Rom. xi. 36.

γ The Coining is simply of the adverbial form; the Substantive is found in earlier writings. S. Gregory himself uses it Orat. Theol. V. He uses other words also, as ἔκπεμψις, πρόοδος, and the verbs προέρχεσθαι, προϊέναι.

As to the question of the Double Procession (Filioque) see Introd. to Orat. Theol. V. Dr. Swete (Doctr. of H. S. p. 118) says, "It is instructive to notice how at this period the two great Sees of Rome and Constantinople seem to have agreed in abstaining from a minuter definition of the Procession. Both in East and West the relations of the Spirit to the Son were being examined by individual theologians: but S. Gregory and S. Damasus appear to have alike refrained from entering upon a question which did not touch the essentials of the Faith." He adds in a note "This is the more remarkable because Damasus was of Spanish origin."

α "The rest of the Creation was made by the command of God, but Man was formed by the hand of God." (Wordsworth in Gen. ii. 7.)

"There was a peculiar glory in the creation of Man, distinguishing him from the rest of the creatures. The creatures inferior to man were called into being by a simple act of the Divine Will; but in the case of man, bearing as he does the nature and the form which God was about to assume as His own, and which, once assumed, was never again to be laid aside, the process of creation was markedly different. Then for the first time the Most Holy Persons of the Blessed Trinity appear upon the scene. They are manifested as in mutual consultation and common action personally engaged. . . . 'Let Us make Man in Our Image after Our Likeness' . . . Then followed the exercise of creative power as a personal act, the putting forth the Hand of God to fashion the body of Man; 'The Lord God formed Man of the dust of the earth.' Afterwards came the yet higher work in the infusion of the immaterial invisible life enshrined in the body, perfecting the work of God: 'He breathed into his nostrils the breath of life and Man became a living soul.'" (T. T. Carter, The Divine Dispensations, p. 44.) β Ps. lxviii. 4.

γ Ullmann comments on this passage as follows: There is in it, as follows especially from what comes after, the double sense that the Infinite Godhead entered in Christ into the limitations of a finite human life; and in consequence of this, since otherwise as an infinite Being it was not fully cognisable by the finite human soul, became in this limitation cognisable in some degree to it, as it was not before this special manifestation in Christ.

δ "In this and several other places πνεῦμα and νοῦς evidently denote the Divine the Spiritual, taken in the highest and purest sense, in which it is lifted above the σάρξ, and generally above all that is material; in which sense S. John says, πνεῦμα ὁ θεός." Ullmann.

but also Generation with Virginity, and dishonour with Him who is higher than all honour; He who is impassible with Suffering,[α] and the Immortal with the corruptible. For since that Deceiver thought that he was unconquerable in his malice, after he had cheated us with the hope of becoming gods, he was himself cheated by God's assumption of our nature; so that in attacking Adam as he thought, he should really meet with God, and thus the new Adam should save the old, and the condemnation of the flesh should be abolished, death being slain by flesh.

XIV. At His birth we duly kept Festival, both I, the leader of the Feast, and you, and all that is in the world and above the world. With the Star we ran, and with the Magi we worshipped, and with the Shepherds we were illuminated, and with the Angels we glorified Him, and with Simeon we took Him up in our arms, and with Anna the aged and chaste we made our responsive confession. And thanks be to Him who came to His own in the guise of a stranger, because He glorified the stranger.[β] Now, we come to another action of Christ, and another mystery. I cannot restrain my pleasure; I am rapt into God. Almost like John I proclaim good tidings; for though I be not a Forerunner, yet am I from the desert.[γ] Christ is illumined, let us shine forth with Him. Christ is baptized, let us descend with Him that we may also ascend with Him. Jesus is baptized; but we must attentively consider not only this but also some other points. Who is He, and by whom is He baptized, and at what time? He is the All-pure; and He is baptized by John; and the time is the beginning of His miracles. What are we to learn and to be taught by this? To purify ourselves first; to be lowly minded; and to preach only in maturity both of spiritual and bodily stature. The first[δ] has a word especially for those who rush to Baptism off hand, and without due preparation, or providing for the stability of the Baptismal Grace by the disposition of their minds to good. For since Grace contains remission of the past (for it is a *grace*), it is on that account more worthy of reverence, that we return not to the same vomit again. The second speaks to those who rebel against the Stewards of this Mystery, if they are their superiors in rank. The third is for those who are confident in their youth, and think that any time is the right one to teach or to preside. Jesus is purified, and dost thou despise purification? . . . and by John, and dost thou rise up against thy herald? . . . and at thirty years of age, and dost thou before thy beard has grown presume to teach the aged, or believe that thou teachest them, though thou be not reverend on account of thine age, or even perhaps for thy character? But here it may be said, Daniel, and this or that other, were judges in their youth, and examples are on your tongues; for every wrongdoer is prepared to defend himself. But I reply that that which is rare is not the law of the Church. For one swallow does not make a summer, nor one line a geometrician, nor one voyage a sailor.

XV. But John baptizes, Jesus comes to Him[α] . . . perhaps to sanctify the Baptist himself, but certainly to bury the whole of the old Adam in the water; and before this and for the sake of this, to sanctify Jordan; for as He is Spirit and Flesh, so He consecrates us by Spirit and water.[β] John will not receive Him; Jesus contends. "I have need to be baptized of Thee"[γ] says the Voice to the Word, the Friend to the Bridegroom;[δ] he that is above all among them that are born of women,[ε] to Him Who is the Firstborn of every creature;[ζ] he that leaped in the womb,[η] to Him Who was adored in the womb; he who was and is to be the Forerunner[θ] to Him Who was and is to be manifested. "I have need to be baptized of Thee;" add to this "and for Thee;" for he knew that he would be baptized by Martyrdom, or, like Peter, that he would be cleansed not only as to his feet.[ι] "And comest Thou to me?" This also was prophetic; for he knew that after Herod would come the madness of Pilate, and so that when he had gone before Christ would follow him. But what saith Jesus? "Suffer it to be so now," for this is the time of His Incarnation; for He knew that yet a little while and He should baptize the Baptist. And what is the "Fan?" The Purification. And what is the "Fire?" The consuming of the chaff, and the heat

---

α "In a double sense:—either that the Godhead is, in union with the Man Jesus, subjected to suffering (cf. Or. XXI. 24), or that the Divine Substance, which is unapproachable by any passion or suffering, combined itself with a Man, whose nature cannot be free from such emotions." Ullmann.

β i.e., human nature, which was severed from and made hostile to God by sin.

γ i.e., Sasima.

δ That the All-pure was baptized is to remind us of our need of preparation. That He was baptized by John is to teach us humility towards the Priesthood, even if the Priest be socially our inferior. That He was baptized at thirty years of age shews that the Teachers and Rulers of the Church ought not to be very young men. Scholiast.

α Matt. iii. 14. β John v. 35. γ Matt. iii. 17. δ John iii. 39. ε Matt. xi. 11. ζ Col. i. 5. η Luke i. 41.

θ "He who was the forerunner on earth, and was to be the forerunner in Hades of Christ, Who manifested Himself on earth, and manifested Himself also in Hades." Elias Cretensis.

ι John xiii. 9.

of the Spirit. And what the "Axe?" The excision of the soul which is incurable even after the dung.[α] And what the Sword? The cutting of the Word, which separates the worse from the better,[β] and makes a division between the faithful and the unbeliever;[γ] and stirs up the son and the daughter and the bride against the father and the mother and the mother in law,[δ] the young and fresh against the old and shadowy. And what is the Latchet of the shoe, which thou John who baptizest Jesus mayst not loose?[ε] thou who art of the desert, and hast no food, the new Elias,[ζ] the more than Prophet, inasmuch as thou sawest Him of Whom thou didst prophesy, thou Mediator of the Old and New Testaments. What is this? Perhaps the Message of the Advent, and the Incarnation, of which not the least point may be loosed, I say not by those[η] who are yet carnal and babes in Christ, but not even by those who are like John in spirit.

XVI. But further—Jesus goeth up out of the water . . . for with Himself He carries up the world . . . and sees the heaven opened which Adam had shut against himself and all his posterity,[θ] as the gates of Paradise by the flaming sword. And the Spirit bears witness to His Godhead, for he descends upon One that is like Him, as does the Voice from Heaven (for He to Whom the witness is borne came from thence), and like a Dove, for He honours the Body (for this also was God, through its union with God) by being seen in a bodily form; and moreover, the Dove has from distant ages been wont to proclaim the end of the Deluge.[ι] But if you are to judge of Godhead by bulk and weight, and the Spirit seems to you a small thing because He came in the form of a Dove, O man of contemptible littleness of thought concerning the greatest of things, you must also to be consistent despise the Kingdom of Heaven, because it is compared to a grain of mustard seed;[κ] and you must exalt the adversary above the Majesty of Jesus, because he is called a great Mountain,[λ] and Leviathan[μ] and King of that which lives in the water, whereas Christ is called the Lamb,[ν] and the Pearl,[ξ] and the Drop[ο] and similar names.

XVII. Now, since our Festival is of Baptism, and we must endure a little hardness with Him Who for our sake took form, and was baptized, and was crucified; let us speak about the different kinds of Baptism, that we may come out thence purified. Moses baptized[α] but it was in water, and before that in the cloud and in the sea.[β] This was typical as Paul saith; the Sea of the water, and the Cloud of the Spirit; the Manna, of the Bread of Life; the Drink, of the Divine Drink. John also baptized; but this was not like the baptism of the Jews, for it was not only in water, but also "unto repentance." Still it was not wholly spiritual, for he does not add "And in the Spirit." Jesus also baptized, but in the Spirit. This is the perfect Baptism. And how is He not God, if I may digress a little, by whom you too are made God? I know also a Fourth Baptism—that by Martyrdom and blood, which also Christ himself underwent;—and this one is far more august than all the others, inasmuch as it cannot be defiled by after-stains. Yes, and I know of a Fifth also, which is that of tears, and is much more laborious, received by him who washes his bed every night and his couch with tears;[γ] whose bruises stink through his wickedness;[δ] and who goeth mourning and of a sad countenance; who imitates the repentance of Manasseh[ε] and the humiliation of the Ninevites[ζ] upon which God had mercy; who utters the words of the Publican in the Temple, and is justified rather than the stiff-necked Pharisee;[η] who like the Canaanite woman bends down and asks for mercy and crumbs, the food of a dog that is very hungry.[θ]

XVIII. I, however, for I confess myself to be a man,—that is to say, an animal shifty and of a changeable nature,—both eagerly receive this Baptism, and worship Him Who has given it me, and impart it to others; and by shewing mercy make provision for mercy. For I know that I too am compassed with infirmity,[ι] and that with what measure I mete it shall be measured to me again.[κ] But what sayest thou, O new Pharisee pure[λ] in title but not in intention, who dischargest upon us the sentiments of Novatus,[μ] though thou sharest the

α Luke xiii. 8. β Heb. iv. 12. γ Matt. x. 35.
δ Micah vii. 6. ε John i. 27. ζ Luke vii. 26.
η One important MS. reads "Us Who."
θ Gen. iii. 24. ι Ib. viii. 11. κ Matt. xiii. 31.
λ Zech. iv. 7
μ The word Leviathan does not occur in the LXX., though it is found twice in other Greek Versions of the Book of Job, viz.:—iii. 8 and xl. 20. ν Isa. liii. 7.
ξ Matt. xiii. 46. ο Ps. lxxii. 6.

α Lev. xi. β 1 Cor. x. 2. γ Ps. vi. 6. δ Ib. xxxviii. 5.
ε 2 Chron. xxxviii. 12. ζ Jon. iii. 7–10. η Luke xviii. 13.
θ Matt. xv. 27. ι Heb. v. 2. κ Matt. vii. 2.
λ The Novatians were known as Cathari or Puritans.
μ In A.D. 251 Novatus, a Presbyter of the Church of Carthage, who with others had formed a party against S. Cyprian. their Bishop, came to Rome, and excited Novatian to become leader in a similar schism against Cornelius, the recently elected Bishop of the Apostolic See. The plea urged on behalf of the schism was that Cornelius, who was of one accord with Cyprian, had lapsed in the time of the persecution under Decius, A.D. 250. and that he had relaxed the discipline of the Church by admitting to Communion on too easy terms those who had been guilty of a similar offence; and that therefore he ought not to be recognized as a true Bishop of the Church, but a faithful Pastor should be chosen in his place. Consequently Novatian was elected by some who held these views, and was consecrated by three Bishops. There seem to

same infirmities? Wilt thou not give any place to weeping? Wilt thou shed no tear? Mayest thou not meet with a Judge like thyself? Art thou not ashamed by the mercy of Jesus, Who took our infirmities and bare our sicknesses;[α] Who came not to call the righteous but sinners to repentance;[β] Who will have mercy rather than sacrifice; who forgiveth sins till seventy times seven.[γ] How blessed would your exaltation be if it really were purity, not pride, making laws above the reach of men, and destroying improvement by despair. For both are alike evil, indulgence not regulated by prudence, and condemnation that will never forgive; the one because it relaxes all reins, the other because it strangles by its severity. Shew me your purity, and I will approve your boldness. But as it is, I fear that being full of sores you will render them incurable. Will you not admit even David's repentance, to whom his penitence preserved even the gift of prophecy? nor the great Peter himself, who fell into human weakness at the Passion of our Saviour? Yet Jesus received him, and by the threefold question and confession healed the threefold denial.[δ] Or will you even refuse to admit that he was made perfect by blood (for your folly goes even as far as that)? Or the transgressor at Corinth? But Paul confirmed love towards him when he saw his amendment, and gives the reason, "that such an one be not swallowed up by overmuch sorrow,"[ε] being overwhelmed by the excess of the punishment.[ζ] And will you refuse to grant liberty of marriage to young widows on account of the liability of their age to fall? Paul ventured to do so; but of course you can teach him; for you have been caught up to the Fourth heaven, and to another Paradise, and have heard words more unspeakable, and comprehend a larger circle in your Gospel.

XIX. But these sins were not after Baptism, you will say. Where is your proof? Either prove it—or refrain from condemning; and if there be any doubt, let charity prevail. But Novatus, you say, would not receive those who lapsed in the persecution. What do you mean by this? If they were unrepentant he was right; I too would refuse to receive those who either would not stoop at all or not sufficiently, and who would refuse to make their amendment counterbalance their sin; and when I do receive them, I will assign them their proper place;[α] but if he refused those who wore themselves away with weeping, I will not imitate him. And why should Novatus's want of charity be a rule for me? He never punished covetousness, which is a second idolatry; but he condemned fornication as though he himself were not flesh and body. What say you? Are we convincing you by these words? Come and stand here on our side, that is, on the side of humanity. Let us magnify the Lord together. Let none of you, even though he has much confidence in himself, dare to say, Touch me not for I am pure, and who is so pure as I? Give us too a share in your brightness. But perhaps we are not convincing you? Then we will weep for you. Let these men then if they will, follow our way, which is Christ's way; but if they will not, let them go their own. Perhaps in it they will be baptized with Fire, in that last Baptism which is more painful and longer, which devours wood like grass,[β] and consumes the stubble of every evil.

XX. But let us venerate to-day the Baptism of Christ; and let us keep the feast well, not in pampering the belly, but rejoicing in spirit. And how shall we luxuriate? "Wash you, make you clean."[γ] If ye be scarlet with sin and less bloody, be made white as snow; if ye be red, and men bathed in blood, yet be ye brought to the whiteness of wool. Anyhow be purified, and you shall be clean (for God rejoices in nothing so much as in the amendment and salvation of man, on whose behalf is every discourse and every Sacrament), that you may be like lights in the world, a quickening force to all other men; that you may stand as perfect lights beside That great Light, and may learn the mystery of the illumination of Heaven, enlightened by the Trinity more purely and clearly, of Which even now you are receiving in a measure the One Ray from the One Godhead in Christ Jesus our Lord; to Whom be the glory and the might for ever and ever. Amen.

have been a good many of his followers in Constantinople at this time. There had been at one time a disposition among them to reunite themselves to the Catholic Church, for they were orthodox in faith; but it had been hindered by the malevolence of their party leaders; so that the schism continued, and the Novatians must be added to the opponents with whom S. Gregory had to deal.

α Matt. viii. 17. β Ib. ix. 13.

γ Ib. xviii. 22. δ John xxi. 15 sq. ε 2 Cor. ii. 7.

ζ "This too often ignored page gives a solemn contradiction to those who, falsifying history as well as theology, pretended two centuries ago to revive by their extravagant rigour the spirit of the primitive Church. The spirit of the Church never changes. Inflexible against error, it is full of gentleness and kindliness for repentant sinners. The spirit of the Church is that of the Saints of all times; or rather it is that of the Divine Shepherd, Who made Himself known above all by His unspeakable tenderness and His inexhaustible mercy to lost sheep." (Benoit S. G. de N.)

α i.e., their proper class among the Penitents.

β 1 Cor. iii. 12–19. γ Isa. i. 17, 18.

ORATION XL.

The Oration on Holy Baptism.

Preached at Constantinople Jan. 6, 381, being the day following the delivery of that on the Holy Lights.

I. Yesterday we kept high Festival on the illustrious Day of the Holy Lights; for it was fitting that rejoicings should be kept for our Salvation, and that far more than for weddings and birthdays, and namedays, and house-warmings, and registrations of children, and anniversaries, and all the other festivities that men observe for their earthly friends. And now to-day let us discourse briefly con-concerning Baptism, and the benefits which accrue to us therefrom, even though our discourse yesterday spoke of it cursorily; partly because the time pressed us hard, and partly because the sermon had to avoid tediousness. For too great length in a sermon is as much an enemy to people's ears, as too much food is to their bodies. . . . It will be worth your while to apply your minds to what we say, and to receive our discourse on so important a subject not perfunctorily, but with ready mind, since to know the power of this Sacrament is itself Enlightenment.[α]

II. The Word recognizes three Births for us; namely, the natural birth, that of Baptism, and that of the Resurrection. Of these the first is by night, and is servile, and involves passion; but the second is by day, and is destructive of passion, cutting off all the veil[β] that is derived from birth, and leading on to the higher life; and the third is more terrible and shorter, bringing together in a moment all mankind,[γ] to stand before its Creator, and to give an account of its service and conversation here; whether it has followed the flesh, or whether it has mounted up with the spirit, and worshipped the grace of its new creation. My Lord Jesus Christ has showed that He honoured all these births in His own Person; the first, by that first and quickening Inbreathing;[δ] the second by His Incarnation and the Baptism wherewith He Himself was baptized; and the third by the Resurrection of which He was the Firstfruits; condescending, as He became the Firstborn[α] among many brethren, so also to become the Firstborn from the dead.[β]

III. Concerning two of these births, the first and the last, we have not to speak on the present occasion. Let us discourse upon the second, which is now necessary for us, and which gives its name to the Feast of the Lights. Illumination is the splendour of souls, the conversion of the life, the question put to the Godward conscience.[γ] It is the aid to our weakness, the renunciation of the flesh, the following of the Spirit, the fellowship of the Word, the improvement of the creature, the overwhelming of sin, the participation of light, the dissolution of darkness. It is the carriage to God, the dying with Christ, the perfecting of the mind, the bulwark of Faith, the key of the Kingdom of heaven, the change of life, the removal of slavery, the loosing of chains, the remodelling of the whole man. Why should I go into further detail? Illumination is the greatest and most magnificent of the Gifts of God. For just as we speak of the Holy of Holies, and the Song of Songs, as more comprehensive and more excellent than others, so is this called Illumination, as being more holy than any other illumination which we possess.

IV. And as Christ the Giver of it is called by many various names, so too is this Gift, whether it is from the exceeding gladness of its nature (as those who are very fond of a thing take pleasure in using its name), or that the great variety of its benefits has reacted for us upon its names. We call it, the Gift, the Grace, Baptism, Unction, Illumination, the Clothing of Immortality, the Laver of Regeneration, the Seal, and everything that is honourable. We call it the Gift, because it is given to us in return for nothing on our part; Grace, because it is conferred even on debtors; Baptism, because sin is buried with it in the water; Unction, as Priestly and Royal, for such were they who were anointed; Illumination, because of its splendour; Clothing, because it hides our shame; the Laver, because it washes us; the Seal because it preserves us, and is moreover the indication of Dominion. In it the heavens rejoice; it is glorified by Angels, because of its kindred splendour. It is the image of the heavenly bliss. We long

α Enlightenment (φωτισμός) is one of the most ancient names for Holy Baptism; the name, in fact, which S. Gregory uses throughout this Oration, and which his Latin translator almost invariably renders by Baptismus.

β This Veil is Original Sin, by which the soul is darkened and as it were covered.

γ All Mankind (πᾶν τὸ πλάσμα). πλάσμα would not be correctly rendered by Creation. It is a word belonging solely to Man, who was formed by the Hand of God, and who, alone among creatures, has to give an account of his past life to his Creator at the Last Day. (Edd. Bened.)

δ Gen. ii. 7.

α Rom. viii. 29.

β Col. i. 18.

γ This is the literal version of the passage, which is somewhat loosely quoted from 1 S. Peter iii. 21, where the A. V. renders "the answer of a good conscience towards God," and the R. V., "The interrogation (Marg. inquiry) of a good conscience, etc." The passage is usually explained as referring to the Interrogatories in Holy Baptism, answered by the threefold Vow which enlists us "under Christ's banner against sin, the world, and the Devil," professes the Faith, and promises obedience.

indeed to sing out its praises, but we cannot worthily do so.

V. God is Light:[α] the highest, the unapproachable, the ineffable, That can neither be conceived in the mind nor uttered with the lips,[β] That giveth life to every reasoning creature.[γ] He is in the world of thought, what the sun is in the world of sense; presenting Himself to our minds in proportion as we are cleansed; and loved in proportion as He is presented to our mind; and again, conceived in proportion as we love Him; Himself contemplating and comprehending Himself, and pouring Himself out upon what is external to Him. That Light, I mean, which is contemplated in the Father and the Son and the Holy Ghost, Whose riches is Their unity of nature, and the one outleaping of Their brightness. A second Light is the Angel, a kind of outflow or communication of that first Light, drawing its illumination from its inclination and obedience thereto; and I know not whether its illumination is distributed according to the order of its state, or whether its order is due to the respective measures of its illumination.[δ] A third Light is man; a light which is visible to external objects. For they call man light[ε] because of the faculty of speech in us. And the name is applied again to those of us who are more like God, and who approach God more nearly than others. I also acknowledge another Light, by which the primeval darkness was driven away or pierced. It was the first of all the visible creation to be called into existence; and it irradiates the whole universe, the circling orbit of the stars, and all the heavenly beacon fires.

VI. Light was also the firstborn commandment given to the firstborn man (for the commandment of the Law is a lamp and a light;[ζ] and again, Because Thy judgments are a light upon the earth);[η] although the envious darkness crept in and wrought wickedness. And a Light typical and proportionate to those who were its subjects was the written law, adumbrating the truth and the sacrament of the great Light, for Moses' face was made glorious by it.[θ] And, to mention more Lights—it was Light that appeared out of Fire to Moses, when it burned the bush indeed, but did not consume it,[ι] to shew its nature and to declare the power that was in it. And it was Light that was in the pillar of fire that led Israel and tamed the wilderness.[α] It was Light that carried up Elias in the car of fire,[β] and yet did not burn him as it carried him. It was Light that shone round the Shepherds[γ] when the Eternal Light was mingled with the temporal. It was Light that was the beauty of the Star that went before to Bethlehem to guide the Wise Men's way,[δ] and to be the escort of the Light That is above us, when He came amongst us. Light was That Godhead Which was shewn upon the Mount to the disciples—and a little too strong for their eyes.[ε] Light was That Vision which blazed out upon Paul,[ζ] and by wounding his eyes healed the darkness of his soul. Light is also the brilliancy of heaven to those who have been purified here, when the righteous shall shine forth as the Sun,[η] and God shall stand in the midst of them,[θ] gods and kings, deciding and distinguishing the ranks of the Blessedness of heaven. Light beside these in a special sense is the illumination of Baptism of which we are now speaking; for it contains a great and marvellous sacrament of our salvation.

VII. For since to be utterly sinless belongs to God, and to the first and uncompounded nature (for simplicity is peaceful, and not subject to dissension), and I venture to say also that it belongs to the Angelic nature too; or at least, I would affirm that nature to be very nearly sinless, because of its nearness to God; but to sin is human and belongs to the Compound on earth (for composition is the beginning of separation); therefore the master did not think it right to leave His creature unaided, or to neglect its danger of separation from Himself; but on the contrary, just as He gave existence to that which did not exist, so He gave new creation to that which did exist, a diviner creation and a loftier than the first, which is to those who are beginning life a Seal, and to those who are more mature in age both a gift and a restoration of the image which had fallen through sin, that we may not, by becoming worse through despair, and ever being borne downward to that which is more evil, fall altogether from good and from virtue, through despondency; and having fallen into a depth of evil (as it is said) despise Him;[ι] but that like those who in the course of a long journey make a brief rest from labour at an inn, we should be enabled to accomplish the rest of the road fresh and full of courage. Such is the grace and power of baptism; not an overwhelming of the world as of old, but a

α 1 John i. 5. β 1 Tim. vi. 16. γ John i. 9.
δ S. Thomas Aquinas (Summa I qu. 108) seems to solve this question in accordance with the second of these alternatives.
ε φώς (masc) is a common poetical word for Man. It is probably derived from the root (Indo-Eur. Bha) of φάω, which also appears in φημί, and modified in φαίνω. ζ Prov. vi. 23.
η Ps. cxix. 105. θ Exod. xxxiv. 30. ι Ib. iii. 2.

α Ex. xiii. 21. β 2 Kings ii. 11. γ Luke ii. 9.
δ Matt. ii. 9. ε Luke ix. 32, 34. ζ Acts ix. 3.
η Matt. xiii. 43. θ Wisd. iii. 7. ι Prov. xviii. 3 (LXX.).

purification of the sins of each individual, and a complete cleansing from all the bruises and stains of sin.

VIII. And since we are double-made, I mean of body and soul, and the one part is visible, the other invisible, so the cleansing also is twofold, by water and the spirit; the one received visibly in the body, the other concurring with it invisibly and apart from the body; the one typical, the other real and cleansing the depths. And this which comes to the aid of our first birth, makes us new instead of old, and like God instead of what we now are; recasting us without fire, and creating us anew without breaking us up, For, to say it all in one word, the virtue of Baptism is to be understood as a covenant with God for a second life and a purer conversation. And indeed all need to fear this very much, and to watch our own souls, each one of us, with all care, that we do not become liars in respect of this profession. For if God is called upon as a Mediator to ratify human professions, how great is the danger if we be found transgressors of the covenant which we have made with God Himself; and if we be found guilty before the Truth Himself of that lie, besides our other transgressions . . . and that when there is no second regeneration, or recreation, or restoration to our former state, even though we seek it with all our might, and with many sighs and tears, by which it is cicatrized over (with great difficulty in my opinion, though we all believe that it may be cicatrized). Yet if we might wipe away even the scars I should be glad, since I too have need of mercy. But it is better not to stand in need of a second cleansing, but to stop at the first, which is, I know, common to all, and involves no labour, and is of equal price to slaves, to masters, to poor, to rich, to humble, to exalted, to gentle, to simple, to debtors, to those who are free from debt; like the breathing of the air, and the pouring forth of the light, and the changes of the seasons, and the sight of creation, that great delight which we all share alike, and the equal distribution of the faith.

IX. For it is a strange thing to substitute for a painless remedy one which is more painful; to cast away the grace of mercy, and owe a debt of punishment; and to measure our amendment against sin. For how many tears must we contribute before they can equal the fount of baptism; and who will be surety for us that death shall wait for our cure, and that the judgment seat shall not summon us while still debtors, and needing the fire of the other world? You perhaps, as a good and pitiful husbandman, will entreat the Master still to spare the figtree,[α] and not yet to cut it down, though accused of unfruitfulness; but to allow you to put dung about it in the shape of tears, sighs, invocations, sleepings on the ground, vigils, mortifications of soul and body, and correction by confession and a life of humiliation. But it is uncertain if the Master will spare it, inasmuch as it cumbers the ground of another asking for mercy, and becoming deteriorated by the longsuffering shewn to this one. Let us then be buried with Christ by Baptism,[β] that we may also rise with Him; let us descend with Him, that we may also be exalted with Him; let us ascend with Him, that we may also be glorified together.

X. If after baptism the persecutor and tempter of the light assail you (for he assailed even the Word my God through the veil,[γ] the hidden Light through that which was manifested), you have the means to conquer him. Fear not the conflict; defend yourself with the Water; defend yourself with the Spirit, by Which all the fiery darts of the wicked shall be quenched.[δ] It is Spirit, but That Spirit which rent the Mountains.[ε] It is Water, but that which quenches fire. If he assail you by your want (as he dared to assail Christ), and asks that stones should be made bread, do not be ignorant of his devices.[ς] Teach him what he has not learnt. Defend yourself with the Word of life, Who is the Bread sent down from heaven, and giving life to the world.[η] If he plot against you with vain glory (as he did against Christ when he led Him up to the pinnacle of the temple and said to Him, Cast Thyself down[θ] as a proof of Thy Godhead), be not overborne by elation. If you be taken by this he will not stop here. For he is insatiable, he grasps at every thing. He fawns upon you with fair pretences, but he ends in evil; this is the manner of his fighting. Yes, and the robber is skilled in Scripture. On the one side was that It is written about the Bread, and on the other that it Is written about the Angels. It is written, quoth he, He shall give His Angels charge concerning thee, and they shall bear thee in their hands.[ι] O vile sophist! now was it that thou didst suppress the words that follow, for I know it well, even if thou passest it by in silence? I will make thee to go upon the asp and basilisk, and I will tread upon serpents and scorpions, being fenced by the Trinity.

α Luke xiii. 8. β Rom. vi. 4; Col. ii. 12. γ i.e., the Sacred Manhood. δ Ephes. vi. 16. ε 1 Ki. xix. 11. ς 2 Cor. ii. 11. η John vi. 33. θ Matt. iv. 6. ι Ps. xci. 14.

If he wrestle against thee to a fall through avarice, shewing thee all the Kingdoms at one instant and in the twinkling of an eye, as belonging to himself, and demand thy worship, despise him as a beggar. Say to him relying on the Seal, "I am myself the Image of God; I have not yet been cast down from the heavenly Glory, as thou wast through thy pride; I have put on Christ; I have been transformed into Christ by Baptism; worship thou me." Well do I know that he will depart, defeated and put to shame by this; as he did from Christ the first Light, so he will from those who are illumined by Christ. Such blessings does the laver bestow on those who apprehend it; such is the rich feast which it provides for those who hunger aright.

XI. Let us then be baptized that we may win the victory; let us partake of the cleansing waters, more purifying than hyssop, purer than the legal blood, more sacred than the ashes of the heifer sprinkling the unclean,[α] and providing a temporary cleansing of the body, but not a complete taking away of sin; for if once purged, why should they need further purification? Let us be baptized today, that we suffer not violence[β] to-morrow; and let us not put off the blessing as if it were an injury, nor wait till we get more wicked that more may be forgiven us; and let us not become sellers and traffickers of Christ, lest we become more heavily burdened than we are able to bear, that we be not sunk with all hands[γ] and make shipwreck of the Gift, and lose all because we expected too much. While thou art still master of thy thoughts run to the Gift. While thou art not yet sick in body or in mind, nor seemest so to those who are with thee (though thou art really of sound mind); while thy good is not yet in the power of others, but thou thyself art still master of it; while thy tongue is not stammering or parched, or (to say no more) deprived of the power of pronouncing the sacramental words; while thou canst still be made one of the faithful, not conjecturally but confessedly; and canst still receive not pity but congratulation; while the Gift is still clear to thee, and there is no doubt about it; while the grace can reach the depth of thy soul, and it is not merely thy body that is washed for burial; and before tears surround thee announcing thy decease—and even these restrained perhaps for thy sake—and thy wife and children would delay thy departure, and are listening for thy dying words; before the physician is powerless to help thee, and is giving thee but hours to live—hours which are not his to give—and is balancing thy salvation with the nod of his head, and discoursing learnedly on thy disease after thou art dead, or making his charges heavier by withdrawals, or hinting at despair; before there is a struggle between the man who would baptize thee and the man who seeks thy money, the one striving that thou mayest receive thy Viaticum, the other that he may be inscribed in thy Will as heir—and there is no time for both.

XII. Why wait for a fever to bring you this blessing, and refuse it from God? Why will you have it through lapse of time, and not through reason? Why will you owe it to a plotting friend, and not to a saving desire? Why will you receive it of force and not of free will; of necessity rather than of liberty? Why must you hear of your death from another, rather than think of it as even now present? Why do you seek for drugs which will do no good, or the sweat of the crisis, when the sweat of death is perhaps upon you? Heal yourself before your extremity; have pity upon yourself the only true healer of your disease; apply to yourself the really saving medicine; while you are still sailing with a favouring breeze fear shipwreck, and you will be in less danger of it, if you make use of your terror as a helper. Give yourself occasion to celebrate the Gift with feasting, not with mourning; let the talent be cultivated, not buried in the ground; let some time intervene between the grace and death, that not only may the account of sins be wiped out, but something better may be written in its place; that you may have not only the Gift, but also the Reward; that you may not only escape the fire, but may also inherit the glory, which is bestowed by cultivation of the Gift. For to men of little soul it is a great thing to escape torment; but men of great soul aim also at attaining reward.

XIII. I know of three classes among the saved; the slaves, the hired servants, the sons.

α Heb. x. 4.

β There is here an untranslateable play upon words.

γ Again a play upon words. Βαπτίζεσθαι is sometimes used in the sense of to be drowned. The word primarily means to Immerse, and this of course, when applied to a ship, is to sink her. The practice of immersion in Holy Baptism was undoubtedly universal in the primitive ages, except where in cases of necessity persons were baptized in sickness, or in prison under sentence of death; and in such cases this "Clinic" Baptism, though recognized as valid, and therefore not to be repeated, was viewed as irregular, and disqualified its recipient from subsequently receiving Holy Orders. Affusion was gradually allowed, probably for climatic reasons, to become the prevailing practice of the West, though immersion predominated as late as the Twelfth Century. It is, however, a remarkable fact that the Didache, a Manual of instruction which some date within the lifetime of the Apostles, and nearly all are agreed in placing not later than the early years of the Second Century, expressly permits affusion, without any hint of irregularity, or mention of any circumstance of necessity except scarcity of water.

If you are a slave, be afraid of the whip; if you are a hired servant, look only to receive your hire; if you are more than this, a son, revere Him as a Father, and work that which is good, because it is good to obey a Father; and even though no reward should come of it for you, this is itself a reward, that you please your Father. Let us then take care not to despise these things. How absurd it would be to grasp at money and throw away health; and to be lavish of the cleansing of the body, but economical over the cleansing of the soul; and to seek for freedom from earthly slavery, but not to care about heavenly freedom; and to make every effort to be splendidly housed and dressed, but to have never a thought how you yourself may become really very precious; and to be zealous to do good to others, without any desire to do good to yourself. And if good could be bought, you would spare no money; but if mercy is freely at your feet, you despise it for its cheapness. Every time is suitable for your ablution, since any time may be your death. With Paul I shout to you with that loud voice, "Behold now is the accepted time; behold Now is the day of salvation;"[α] and that Now does not point to any one time, but is every present moment. And again "Awake, thou that sleepest, and Christ shall give thee light,"[β] dispelling the darkness of sin. For as Isaiah says,[γ] In the night hope is evil, and it is more profitable to be received in the morning.

XIV. Sow in good season, and gather together, and open thy barns when it is the time to do so; and plant in season, and let the clusters be cut when they are ripe, and launch boldly in spring, and draw thy ship on shore again at the beginning of winter, when the sea begins to rage. And let there be to thee also a time for war and a time for peace; a time to marry, and a time to abstain from marrying; a time for friendship, and a time for discord, if this be needed; and in short a time for everything, if you will follow Solomon's advice.[δ] And it is best to do so, for the advice is prôfitable. But the work of your salvation is one upon which you should be engaged at all times; and let every time be to you the definite one for Baptism. If you are always passing over to-day and waiting for to-morrow, by your little procrastinations you will be cheated without knowing it by the Evil One, as his manner is. Give to me, he says, the present, and to God the future; to me your youth, and to God old age; to me your pleasures, and to Him your uselessness. How great is the danger that surrounds you. How many the unexpected mischances. War has expended you; or an earthquake overwhelmed you; or the sea swallowed you up; or a wild beast carried you off; or a sickness killed you; or a crumb going the wrong way (a most insignificant thing, but what is easier than for a man to die, though you are so proud of the divine image); or a too freely indulged drinking bout;[α] or a wind knocked you down; or a horse ran away with you; or a drug maliciously scheming against you, or perhaps found to be deleterious when meant to be wholesome; or an inhuman judge; or an inexorable executioner; or any of the things which make the change swiftest and beyond the power of human aid.

α 2 Cor. vi. 2. β Ephes. v. 14. γ Isa. xxviii. 19, LXX. δ Eccl. iii. 1 sq.

XV. But if you would fortify yourself beforehand with the Seal, and secure yourself for the future with the best and strongest of all aids, being signed both in body and in soul with the unction, as Israel was of old with that blood and unction of the firstborn at night that guarded him,[β] what then can happen to you, and what has been wrought out for you? Listen to the Proverbs. "If thou sittest, he says, thou shalt be without fear; and if thou sleepest, thy sleep shall be sweet."[γ] And listen to David giving thee the good news, "Thou shalt not be afraid for the terror by night, for mischance or noonday demon."[δ] This, even while you live, will greatly contribute to your sense of safety (for a sheep that is sealed is not easily snared, but that which is unmarked is an easy prey to thieves), and at your death a fortunate shroud, more precious than gold, more magnificent than a sepulchre, more reverent than fruitless libations,[ε] more seasonable than ripe firstfruits, which the dead bestow on the dead, making a law out of custom. Nay, if all things forsake thee,[ς] or be taken violently away from thee; money, possessions, thrones, distinctions, and everything that belongs to this early turmoil, yet you will be able to lay down your life in safety, having suffered no loss of the helps which God gave you unto salvation.

XVI. But are you afraid lest you should destroy the Gift, and do you therefore put off your cleansing, because you cannot have it a second time? What? Would you not be afraid of danger in time of persecution, and of losing

α Some MSS. read "A flooded river."
β Exod. xii. 22. γ Prov. iii. 24. δ Ps. xci. 5.
ε Billius suggests, though without adopting it in his text, a slight conjectural alteration, which would read "Than funeral games and libations;" but this, though it gives a very good sense, is a needless departure from the MSS. ς Luke ix. 60.

the most precious Thing you have—Christ? Would you then on this account avoid becoming a Christian? Perish the thought. Such a fear is not for a sane man; such an argument argues insanity. O incautious caution, if I may so. O trick of the Evil One! Truly he is darkness and pretends to be light; and when he can no longer prevail in open war, he lays snares in secret, and gives advice, apparently good, really evil, if by some trick at least he may prevail, and we find no escape from his plotting. And this is clearly what he is aiming at in this instance. For, being unable to persuade you to despise Baptism, he inflicts loss upon you through a fictitious security; that in consequence of your fear you may suffer unconsciously the very thing you are afraid of; and because you fear to destroy the Gift, you may for this very reason fail of the Gift altogether. This is his character; and he will never cease his duplicity as long as he sees us pressing onwards towards heaven from which he has fallen. Wherefore, O man of God, do thou recognize the plots of thine adversary; for the battle is against him that hath, and it is concerned with the most important interests. Take not thine enemy to be thy counsellor; despise not to be and to be called Faithful. As long as you are a Catechumen you are but in the porch of Religion; you must come inside, and cross the court, and observe the Holy Things, and look into the Holy of Holies, and be in company with the Trinity. Great are the interests for which you are fighting, great too the stability which you need. Protect yourself with the shield of faith. He fears you, if you fight armed with this weapon, and therefore he would strip you of the Gift, that he may the more easily overcome you unarmed and defenceless. He assails every age, and every form of life; he must be repelled by all.

XVII. Art thou young? stand against thy passions; be numbered with the alliance in the army of God:[α] do valiantly against Goliath.[β] Take your thousands or your myriads;[γ] thus enjoy your manhood; but do not allow your youth to be withered, being killed by the imperfection of your faith. Are you old and near the predestined necessity? Aid your few remaining days. Entrust the purification to your old age. Why do you fear youthful passion in deep old age and at your last breath? Or will you wait to be washed till you are dead, and not so much the object of pity as of dislike? Are you regretting the dregs of pleasure, being yourself in the dregs of life? It is a shameful thing to be past indeed the flower of your age, but not past your wickedness; but either to be involved in it still, or at least to seem so by delaying your purification. Have you an infant child? Do not let sin get any opportunity, but let him be sanctified from his childhood; from his very tenderest age let him be consecrated by the Spirit. Fearest thou the Seal on account of the weakness of nature? O what a small-souled mother, and of how little faith! Why, Anna even before Samuel was born[α] promised him to God, and after his birth consecrated him at once, and brought him up in the priestly habit, not fearing anything in human nature, but trusting in God. You have no need of amulets or incantations, with which the Devil also comes in, stealing worship from God for himself in the minds of vainer men. Give your child the Trinity, that great and noble Guard.

XVIII. What more? Are you living in Virginity? Be sealed by this purification; make this the sharer and companion of your life. Let this direct your life, your words, every member, every movement, every sense. Honour it, that it may honour you; that it may give to your head a crown of graces, and with a crown of delights may shield you.[β] Art thou bound by wedlock? Be bound also by the Seal; make it dwell with you as a guardian of your continence, safer than any number of eunuchs or of doorkeepers. Art thou not yet wedded to flesh? Fear not this consecration; thou art pure even after marriage. I will take the risk of that. I will join you in wedlock. I will dress the bride. We do not dishonour marriage because we give a higher honour to virginity. I will imitate Christ, the pure Groomsman and Bridegroom, as He both wrought a miracle at a wedding, and honours wedlock with His Presence.[γ] Only let marriage be pure and unmingled with filthy lusts. This only I ask; receive safety from the Gift, and give to the Gift the oblation of chastity in its due season, when the fixed time of prayer comes round, and that which is more precious than business. And do this by common consent and approval. For we do not command, we exhort; and we would receive something of you for your own profit, and the common security of you both. And in one word,

α The Benedictine Editors punctuate differently, and render "Stand against passions with the assistance (of Baptism), be numbered in the army of God," remarking that David fought Goliath without allies, leaning on God's assistance; and that S. Gregory here certainly means that a Christian who relies on the aid of his Baptism is to stand firm in the battle against the Devil.

β 1 Sam. xvii. 32. γ Ib. xviii. 7.

α 1 Sam. i. 10. β Ecclus. xxxii. 3. γ John ii. 1–11.

there is no state of life and no occupation to which Baptism is not profitable. You who are a free man,[α] be curbed by it; you who are in slavery, be made of equal rank; you who are in grief, receive comfort; let the gladsome be disciplined; the poor receive riches that cannot be taken away; the rich be made capable of being good stewards of their possessions. Do not play tricks or lay plots against your own salvation. For even if we can delude others we cannot delude ourselves. And so to play against oneself is very dangerous and foolish.

XIX. But you have to live in the midst of public affairs, and are stained by them; and it would be a terrible thing to waste this mercy. The answer is simple. Flee, if you can, even from the forum, along with the good company, making yourself the wings of an eagle, or, to speak more suitably, of a dove . . . for what have you to do with Cæsar or the things of Cæsar? . . . until you can rest where there is no sin, and no blackening, and no biting snake in the way to hinder your godly steps. Snatch your soul away from the world; flee from Sodom; flee from the burning; travel on without turning back, lest you should be fixed as a pillar of salt.[β] Escape to the Mountain lest you be destroyed with the plain. But if you are already bound and constrained by the chain of necessity, reason thus with yourself; or rather let me reason thus with you. It is better both to attain the good and to keep the purification. But if it be impossible to do both it is surely better to be a little stained with your public affairs than to fall altogether short of grace; just as I think it better to undergo a slight punishment from father or master than to be put out of doors; and to be a little beamed upon than to be left in total darkness. And it is the part of wise men to choose, as in good things the greater and more perfect, so in evils the lesser and lighter. Wherefore do not overmuch dread the purification. For our success is always judged by comparison with our place in life by our just and merciful Judge; and often one who is in public life and has had small success has had a greater reward than one who in the enjoyment of liberty has not completely succeeded; as I think it more marvellous for a man to advance a little in fetters, than for one to run who is not carrying any weight; or to be only a little spattered in walking through mud, than to be perfectly clean when the road is clean. To give you a proof of what I have said:—Rahab the harlot was justified by one thing alone, her hospitality,[α] though she receives no praise for the rest of her conduct; and the Publican was exalted by one thing, his humility,[β] though he received no testimony for anything else; so that you may learn not easily to despair concerning yourself.

XX. But some will say, What shall I gain, if, when I am preoccupied by baptism, and have cut off myself by my haste from the pleasures of life, when it was in my power to give the reins to pleasure, and then to obtain grace? For the labourers in the vineyard who had worked the longest time gained nothing thereby, for equal wages were given to the very last.[γ] You have delivered me from some trouble, whoever you are who say this, because you have at last with much difficulty told the secret of your delay; and though I cannot applaud your shiftiness, I do applaud your confession. But come hither and listen to the interpretation of the parable, that you may not be injured by Scripture for want of information. First of all, there is no question here of baptism, but of those who believe at different times and enter the good vineyard of the Church. For from the day and hour at which each believed, from that day and hour he is required to work. And then, although they who entered first contributed more to the measure of the labour yet they did not contribute more to the measure of the purpose; nay perhaps even more was due to the last in respect of this, though the statement may seem paradoxical. For the cause of their later entrance was their later call to the work of the vineyard. In all other respects let us see how different they are. The first did not believe or enter till they had agreed on their hire; but the others came forward to do the work without an agreement, which is a proof of greater faith. And the first were found to be of an envious and murmuring nature, but no such charge is brought against the others. And to the first, that which was given was wages, though they were worthless fellows; to the last it was the free gift. So that the first were convicted of folly, and with reason deprived of the greater reward. Let us see what would have happened to them if they had been late. Why, the equal pay, evidently. How then can they blame the employer as unjust because of their equality? For all these things take away the merit of their labour from the first, although they were at work first; and therefore it turns out that the distribution of

α ἐν ἐξουσίᾳ evidently means Tui juris—your own master.
β Gen. xix. 26.

α Josh. vi. 25; James ii. 25.
β Luke xviii. 14.
γ Matt. xx. 1 sq.

equal pay was just, if you measure the good will against the labour.

XXI. But supposing that the Parable does sketch the power of the font according to your interpretation, what would prevent you, if you entered first, and bore the heat, from avoiding envy of the last, that by this very lovingkindness you might obtain more, and receive the reward, not as of grace but as of debt? And next, the workmen who receive the wages are those who have entered, not those who have missed, the vineyard; which last is like to be your case. So that if it were certain that you would obtain the Gift, though you are of such a mind, and maliciously keep back some of the labour, you might be forgiven for taking refuge in such arguments, and desiring to make unlawful gain out of the kindness of the master; though I might assure you that the very fact of being able to labour is a greater reward to any who is not altogether of a huckstering mind. But since there is a risk of your being altogether shut out of the vineyard through your bargaining, and losing the capital through stopping to pick up little gains, do let yourselves be persuaded by my words to forsake the false interpretations and contradictions, and to come forward without arguing to receive the Gift, lest you should be snatched away before you realize your hopes, and should find out that it was to your own loss that you devised these sophistries.

XXII. But then, you say, is not God merciful, and since He knows our thoughts and searches out our desires, will He not take the desire of Baptism instead of Baptism? You are speaking in riddles, if what you mean is that because of God's mercy the unenlightened is enlightened in His sight; and he is within the kingdom of heaven who merely desires to attain to it, but refrains from doing that which pertains to the kingdom. I will, however, speak out boldly my opinion on these matters; and I think that all other sensible men will range themselves on my side. Of those who have received the gift, some were altogether alien from God and from salvation, both addicted to all manner of sin, and desirous to be bad; others were semivicious, and in a kind of mean state between good and bad; others again, while they did that which was evil, yet did not approve their own action, just as men in a fever are not pleased with their own sickness. And others even before they were illuminated were worthy of praise; partly by nature, and partly by the care with which they prepared themselves for Baptism. These after their initiation became evidently better, and less liable to fall; in the one case with a view to procuring good, and in the other in order to preserve it. And amongst these, those who gave in to *some* evil are better than those who were altogether bad; and better still than those who yielded a little, are those who were more zealous, and broke up their fallow ground before Baptism; they have the advantage over the others of having already laboured; for the font does not do away with good deeds as it does with sins. But better even than these are they who are also cultivating the Gift, and are polishing themselves to the utmost possible beauty.

XXIII. And so also in those who fail to receive the Gift, some are altogether animal or bestial, according as they are either foolish or wicked; and this, I think, has to be added to their other sins, that they have no reverence at all for this Gift, but look upon it as a mere gift—to be acquiesced in if given them, and if not given them, then to be neglected. Others know and honour the Gift, but put it off; some through laziness, some through greediness. Others are not in a position to receive it, perhaps on account of infancy,[a] or some perfectly involuntary circumstance through which they are prevented from receiving it, even if they wish. As then in the former case we found much difference, so too in this. They who altogether despise it are worse than they who neglect it through greed or carelessness. These are worse than they who have lost the Gift through ignorance or tyranny, for tyranny is nothing but an involuntary error.[β] And I think that the first will have to suffer punishment, as for all their sins, so for their contempt of baptism; and that the second will also have to suffer, but less, because it was not so much through wickedness as through folly that they wrought their failure; and that the third will be neither glorified nor punished by the righteous Judge, as unsealed and yet not wicked, but persons who have suffered rather than done wrong. For not every one who is not bad enough to be punished is good enough to be honoured; just as not every one who is not good enough to be honoured is bad enough to be punished. And I look upon it as well from another point of view. If you judge the murderously disposed man by his will alone, apart from the

[a] That S. Gregory did not reject infant Baptism is clear, from the directions given later on in this Oration (c. xxviii; and cf. c. xvii. s. fin.). He is here referring simply to the inability of infants to bring themselves to the font whereby through the mistaken scruples of parents many must have died unbaptized.

[β] i.e., The sins which are due altogether to external tyranny do not involve guilt, inasmuch as they are involuntary, whereas the guilt of sin is in the will.

act of murder, then you may reckon as baptized him who desired baptism apart from the reception of baptism. But if you cannot do the one how can you do the other? I cannot see it. Or, if you like, we will put it thus:—If desire in your opinion has equal power with actual baptism, then judge in the same way in regard to glory, and you may be content with longing for it, as if that were itself glory. And what harm is done you by your not attaining the actual glory, as long as you have the desire for it?

XXIV. Therefore since you have heard these words, come forward to it, and be enlightened, and your faces shall not be ashamed[α] through missing the Grace. Receive then the Enlightenment in due season, that darkness pursue you not, and catch you, and sever you from the Illumining. The night cometh when no man can work[β] after our departure hence. The one is the voice of David, the other of the True Light which lighteth every man that cometh into the world.[γ] And consider how Solomon reproves you who are too idle or lethargic, saying, How long wilt thou sleep, O sluggard,[δ] and when wilt thou arise out of thy sleep? You rely upon this or that, and "pretend pretences in sins;"[ε] I am waiting for Epiphany; I prefer Easter; I will wait for Pentecost.[ζ] It is better to be baptized with Christ, to rise with Christ on the Day of His Resurrection,[η] to honour the Manifestation of the Spirit. And what then? The end will come suddenly in a day for which thou lookest not, and in an hour that thou art not aware of; and then you will have for a companion lack of grace; and you will be famished in the midst of all those riches of goodness, though you ought to reap the opposite fruit from the opposite course, a harvest by diligence, and refreshment from the font, like the thirsty hart[θ] that runs in haste to the spring, and quenches the labour of his race by water; and not to be in Ishmael's case, dried up for want of water,[α] or as the fable has it, punished by thirst in the midst of a spring.[β] It is a sad thing to let the market day go by and then to seek for work. It is a sad thing to let the Manna pass and then to long for food. It is a sad thing to take a counsel too late, and to become sensible of the loss only when it is impossible to repair it; that is, after our departure hence, and the bitter closing of the acts of each man's life, and the punishment of sinners, and the glory of the purified. Therefore do not delay in coming to grace, but hasten, lest the robber outstrip you, lest the adulterer pass you by, lest the insatiate be satisfied before you, lest the murderer seize the blessing first, or the publican or the fornicator, or any of these violent ones who take the Kingdom of heaven by force.[γ] For it suffers violence willingly, and is tyrannized over through goodness.

XXV. Take my advice, my friend, and be slow to do evil, but swift to your salvation; for readiness to evil and tardiness to good are equally bad. If you are invited to a revel, be not swift to go; if to apostasy, leap away; if a company of evildoers say to you, "Come with us, share our bloodguiltiness, let us hide in the earth a righteous man unjustly,"[δ] do not lend them even your ears. Thus you will make two very great gains; you will make known to the other his sin, and you will deliver yourself from evil company. But if David the Great say unto you, Come and let us rejoice in the Lord;[ε] or another Prophet, Come and let us ascend into the Mountain of the Lord;[ζ] or our Saviour Himself, Come unto me all ye that labour and are heavy laden, and I will give you rest;[η] or, Arise, let us go hence, shining brightly, glittering above snow, whiter than milk,[θ] shining above the sapphire stone; let us not resist or delay. Let us be like Peter and John, and let us hasten;[κ] as they did to the Sepulchre and the Resurrection, so we to the Font; running together, racing against each other, striving to be first to obtain this Blessing. And say not, "Go away, and come again, and tomorrow I will be baptized,"[λ] when you may have the blessing today. "I

α Ps. xxxiv. 5. β John xii 35. γ Ib. i. 4. δ Prov. vi. 9. ε Ps. cxli. 4.

ζ The Festivals of Easter and Pentecost were set apart as early as the Second Century for the solemn administration of Holy Baptism; and S. Siricius Bishop of Rome about the time of S. Gregory of Nazianzus, states that all the Churches agreed in keeping these exclusively. But this is a mistake (though Van Espen says (II., c. i., tit. 2, c. 4) that S. Siricius acknowledges the existence of the different custom, but condemns it, and gives reference to ad. Himerum Tarraconensem, c. 2), for there is evidence that in many Churches the Epiphany also was thus observed, and in some Christmas also. But Tertullian (De Bapt.) says that no time is unsuitable. In the Western Church, however. Papal decrees, Conciliar Canons, and Imperial Capitularies from the VIth to the XIIIth. Centuries abound, limiting the administration, except in cases of sickness, to the two seasons of Easter and Pentecost, on the Vigils of which it is still provided for in the Missals. No doubt it was felt to be a very useful limitation, when most persons who were presented for Baptism were adults, and required preparation. When this ceased to be the case the rule gradually became obsolete, and has long ceased to be observed.

η Matt. xxiv. 50. θ Ps. xlii. 1.

α Gen. xix. 15. sqq

β The allusion is to the well known story of Tantalus, whose punishment in hell was said to be that, being tormented with hunger and thirst, he was condemned to stand for ever in water up to his lips, but to be unable to drink, and to have a tree laden with luscious fruit within easy reach, but to be unable to gather of it.

γ Matt. xi. 12. δ Prov. i. 11. ε Ps. xcv. 1.

ζ Mic. iv. 2. η Matt. xi. 28.

θ The A. V. is here used, as more accurate than the LXX. The passage is quoted freely from Lam. iv. 7.

κ John xx. 3. λ Prov. iii. 28.

will have with me father, mother, brothers, wife, children, friends, and all whom I value, and then I will be saved; but it is not yet the fitting time for me to be made bright;" for if you say so, there is reason to fear lest you should have as sharers of your sorrow those whom you hoped to have as sharers of your joy. If they will be with you, well;—but do not wait for them. For it is base to say, "But where is my offering for my baptism, and where is my baptismal robe, in which I shall be made bright, and where is what is wanted for the entertainment of my baptizers, that in these too I may become worthy of notice? For, as you see, all these things are necessary, and on account of this the Grace will be lessened." Do not thus trifle with great things, or allow yourself to think so basely. The Sacrament is greater than the visible environment. Offer *yourself;* clothe yourself with Christ, feast me with your conduct; I rejoice to be thus affectionately treated, and God Who gives these great gifts rejoices thus. Nothing is great in the sight of God, but what the poor may give, so that the poor may not here also be outrun, for they cannot contend with the rich. In other matters there is a distinction between poor and rich, but here the more willing is the richer.

XXVI. Let nothing hinder you from going on, nor draw you away from your readiness. While your desire is still vehement, seize upon that which you desire. While the iron is hot, let it be tempered by the cold water, lest anything should happen in the interval, and put an end to your desire. I am Philip; do you be Candace's Eunuch.[a] Do you also say, "See, here is water, what doth hinder me to be baptized?" Seize the opportunity; rejoice greatly in the blessing; and having spoken be baptized; and having been baptized be saved; and though you be an Ethiopian body, be made white in soul. Do not say, "A Bishop shall baptize me,—and he a Metropolitan,—and he of Jerusalem (for the Grace does not come of a place, but of the Spirit),—and he of noble birth, for it would be a sad thing for my nobility to be insulted by being baptized by a man of no family." Do not say, "I do not mind a mere Priest, if he is a celibate, and a religious, and of angelic life; for it would be a sad thing for me to be defiled even in the moment of my cleansing." Do not ask for credentials of the preacher or the baptizer. For another is his judge,[a] and the examiner of what thou canst not see. For man looketh on the outward appearance, but the Lord looketh on the heart. But to thee let every one be trustworthy for purification, so only he is one of those who have been approved, not of those who are openly condemned, and not a stranger to the Church. Do not judge your judges, you who need healing; and do not make nice distinctions about the rank of those who shall cleanse you, or be critical about your spiritual fathers. One may be higher or lower than another, but all are higher than you. Look at it this way. One may be golden, another iron, but both are rings and have engraved on them the same royal image; and thus when they impress the wax, what difference is there between the seal of the one and that of the other? None. Detect the material in the wax, if you are so very clever. Tell me which is the impression of the iron ring, and which of the golden. And how do they come to be one? The difference is in the material and not in the seal. And so anyone can be your baptizer; for though one may excel another in his life, yet the grace of baptism is the same, and any one may be your consecrator who is formed in the same faith.

XXVII. Do not disdain to be baptized with a poor man, if you are rich; or if you are noble, with one who is lowborn; or if you are a master, with one who is up to the present time your slave. Not even so will you be humbling yourself as Christ, unto Whom you are baptized today, Who for your sake took upon Himself even the form of a slave. From the day of your new birth all the old marks were effaced, and Christ was put upon all in one form. Do not disdain to confess your sins, knowing how John baptized, that by present shame you may escape from future shame (for this too is a part of the future punishment); and prove that you really hate sin by making a shew of it openly, and triumphing over it as worthy of contempt. Do not reject the medicine of exorcism, nor refuse it because of its length. This too is a touchstone of your right disposition for grace. What labour have you to do compared with that of the Queen of Ethiopia,[β] who arose and came from the utmost part of the earth to see the wisdom of Solomon? And behold a Greater than Solomon is here[γ] in the judgment of those who reason maturely. Do not hesitate either at length of journey, or distance by sea; or fire, if this too lies before

a Acts viii. 36.

a 1 Sam. xvi. 7. β 1 Kgs. x. 1. γ Matt. xii. 42.

you; or of any other, small or great, of the hindrances that you may attain to the gift. But if without any labour and trouble at all you may obtain that which you desire, what folly it is to put off the gift: "Ho, every one that thirsteth, come ye to the waters," [α] Esaias invites you, "and he that hath no money, come buy wine and milk, without money and without price." O swiftness of His mercy: O easiness of the Covenant: This blessing may be bought by you merely for willing it; He accepts the very desire as a great price; He thirsts to be thirsted for; He gives to drink to all who desire to drink; He takes it as a kindness to be asked for the kindness; He is ready and liberal; He gives with more pleasure than others receive.[β] Only let us not be condemned for frivolity by asking for little, and for what is unworthy of the Giver. Blessed is he from whom Jesus asks drink, as He did from that Samaritan woman, and gives a well of water springing up unto eternal life.[γ] Blessed is he that soweth beside all waters, and upon every soul, tomorrow to be ploughed and watered, which today the ox and the ass tread, while it is dry and without water,[δ] and oppressed with unreason. And blessed is he who, though he be a "valley of rushes," [ε] is watered out of the House of the Lord; for he is made fruitbearing instead of rushbearing, and produces that which is for the food of man, not that which is rough and unprofitable. And for the sake of this we must be very careful not to miss the Grace.

XXVIII. Be it so, some will say, in the case of those who ask for Baptism; what have you to say about those who are still children, and conscious neither of the loss nor of the grace? Are we to baptize them too? Certainly, if any danger presses. For it is better that they should be unconsciously sanctified than that they should depart unsealed and uninitiated.

A proof of this is found in the Circumcision on the eighth day, which was a sort of typical seal, and was conferred on children before they had the use of reason. And so is the anointing of the doorposts,[ζ] which preserved the firstborn, though applied to things which had no consciousness. But in respect of others[η] I give my advice to wait till the end of the third year, or a little more or less, when they may be able to listen and to answer something about the Sacrament; that, even though they do not perfectly understand it, yet at any rate they may know the outlines; and then to sanctify them in soul and body with the great sacrament of our consecration. For this is how the matter stands; at that time they begin to be responsible for their lives, when reason is matured, and they learn the mystery of life (for of sins of ignorance owing to their tender years they have no account to give), and it is far more profitable on all accounts to be fortified by the Font, because of the sudden assaults of danger that befall us, stronger than our helpers.

XXIX. But, one says, Christ was thirty years old when He was baptized,[α] and that although He was God; and do you bid us hurry our Baptism?—You have solved the difficulty when you say He was God. For He was absolute cleansing; He had no need of cleansing; but it was for you that He was purified, just as it was for you that, though He had not flesh, yet He is clothed with flesh. Nor was there any danger to Him from putting off Baptism, for He had the ordering of His own Passion as of His own Birth. But in your case the danger is to no small interests, if you were to depart after a birth to corruption alone, and without being clothed with incorruption. And there is this further point for me to consider, that that particular time of baptism was a necessity for Him, but your case is not the same. He manifested Himself in the thirtieth year after His birth and not before; first, in order that He might not appear ostentatious, which is a condition belonging to vulgar minds; and next, because that age tests virtue thoroughly, and is the right time to teach. And since it was needful for Him to undergo the passion which saves the world, it was needful also that all things which belong to the passion should fit into the passion; the Manifestation, the Baptism, the Witness from Heaven, the Proclamation, the concourse of the multitude, the Miracles; and that they should be as it were one body, not torn asunder, nor broken apart by intervals. For out of the Baptism and Proclamation arose that earthquake of people coming together,[β] for so Scripture calls that time;[γ] and out of the multitude arose the shewing of the signs and the miracles that lead up to the Gospel. And out of these came the jealousy, and from this the hatred, and out of the hatred the circumstance of the plot against Him, and the betrayal; and out of these the Cross, and the other events by which our Salvation has been effected. Such are the

α Isa. lv. 1. β Acts xx. 35. γ John iv. 7. δ Isa. xxxii. 20.
ε Joel iii. 18; The Hebrew word rendered "rushes" by the LXX. is in our Hebrew text Shittim—acacia trees.
ζ Exod. xii. 22. η i.e. when there is no danger.

α Luke iii. 23.
β "All the City was moved." A. V., lit. "shaken as by earthquake." γ Matt. xxi. 10.

reasons in the case of Christ[α] so far as we can attain to them. And perhaps another more secret reason might be found.

XXX. But for you, what necessity is there that by following the examples which are far above you, you should do a thing so ill-advised for yourself? For there are many other details of the Gospel History which are quite different to what happens nowadays, and the seasons of which do not correspond. For instance Christ fasted a little before His temptation, we before Easter. As far as the fasting days are concerned it is the same,[β] but the difference in the seasons is no little one. He armed Himself with them against temptation; but to us this fast is symbolical of dying with Christ, and it is a purification in preparation for the festival. And He fasted absolutely for forty days, for He was God; but we measure our fasting by our power, even though some are led by zeal to rush beyond their strength. Again, He gave the Sacrament of the Passover to His Disciples in an upper chamber, and after supper, and one day before He suffered; but we celebrate it in Houses of Prayer, and before food,[γ] and after His resurrection. He rose again the third day; our resurrection is not till after a long time. But matters which have to do with Him are neither abruptly separated from us, nor yet yoked together with those which concern us in point of time; but they were handed down to us just so far as to be patterns of what we should do, and then they carefully avoided an entire and exact resemblance.

XXXI. If then you will listen to me, you will bid a long farewell to all such arguments, and you will jump at this Blessing, and begin to struggle in a twofold conflict; first, to prepare yourself for baptism by purifying yourself; and next, to preserve the baptismal gift; for it is a matter of equal difficulty to obtain a blessing which we have not, and to keep it when we have gained it. For often what zeal has acquired sloth has destroyed; and what hesitation has lost diligence has regained. A great assistance to the attainment of what you desire are vigils, fasts, sleeping on the ground, prayers, tears, pity of and almsgiving to those who are in need. And let these be your thanksgiving for what you have received, and at the same time your safeguard of them. You have the benefit to remind you of many commandments; so do not transgress them. Does a poor man approach you? Remember how poor you once were, and how rich you were made. One in want of bread or of drink, perhaps another Lazarus,[α] is cast at your gate; respect the Sacramental Table to which you have approached, the Bread of Which you have partaken, the Cup in Which you have communicated,[β] being consecrated by the Sufferings of Christ. If a stranger fall at your feet, homeless and a foreigner, welcome in him Him who for your sake was a stranger, and that among His own,[γ] and who came to dwell in you by His grace, and who drew you towards the heavenly dwelling place. Be a Zaccheus,[δ] who yesterday was a Publican, and is to-day of liberal soul; offer all to the coming in of Christ, that though small in bodily stature you may show yourself great, nobly contemplating Christ. A sick or a wounded man lies before you; respect your own health, and the wounds from which Christ delivered you. If you see one naked clothe him, in honour of your own garment of incorruption, which is Christ, for as many as were baptized into Christ have put on Christ.[ε] If you find a debtor falling at your feet,[ζ] tear up every document, whether just or unjust. Remember the ten thousand talents which Christ forgave you, and be not a harsh exactor of a smaller debt—and that from whom? From your fellow servant, you who were forgiven so much more by the Master. Otherwise you will have to give satisfaction to His mercy, which you would not imitate and take as your copy.

XXXII. Let the laver be not for your body only, but also for the image of God in you; not merely a washing away of sins in you, but also a correction of your temper; let it not only wash away the old filth, but let it purify the fountainhead. Let it not only move you to honourable acquisition, but let it teach you also honourably to lose possession; or, which is more easy, to make restitution of what you have wrongfully acquired. For what profit is it that your sin should have been forgiven you, but the loss which you have inflicted should not be repaired to him whom you have injured? Two sins are on your conscience, the one that you made a dishonest gain, the

α i.e., the reasons why He was not baptized till He was thirty.

β Here is an indication that the Forty Days of Lent were a well known observance in S. Gregory's time. At the Council of Nicæa this period was taken for granted. The Great Fast of the Eastern Church begins on the Monday after the Sunday corresponding to our Quinquagesima, and the Fast is kept to some extent even on Sunday.

γ Note the rule of Fasting Communion here recognized as universal.

α Luke xvi. 19 sq.

β Note that this allusion implies that Communion in both Kinds was given separately, as in the Anglican Church, not by intinction, as in the present Orthodox Eastern Church.

γ John i. 11.

δ Luke xix. 1 sq.

ε Galat. iii. 27.

ζ Matt. xviii. 23, &c.

other that you retained the gains; you received forgiveness for the one, but in respect of the other you are still in sin, for you have still possession of what belongs to another; and your sin has not been put to an end, but only divided by the time which has elapsed. Part of it was perpetrated before your Baptism, but part remains after your Baptism; for Baptism carries forgiveness of Past, not of Present sins; and its purification must not be played with, but be genuinely impressed upon you; you must be made perfectly bright, and not be merely coloured; you must receive the gift, not of a mere covering of your sins, but of a taking them clean away. Blessed are they whose iniquities are forgiven[α] . . . this is done by the complete cleansing . . . and whose sins are hidden . . . this belongs to those who are not yet healed in their deepest soul. Blessed is the man to whom the Lord will not impute sin. . . . This is a third class of sinners, whose actions are not praiseworthy, but who are innocent of intention.

XXXIII. What say I then, and what is my argument? Yesterday you were a Canaanite soul bent together[β] by sin; today you have been made straight by the Word. Do not be bent again, and condemned to the earth, as if weighed down by the Devil with a wooden collar, nor get an incurable curvature. Yesterday you were being dried up[γ] by an abundant hæmorrhage, for you were pouring out crimson sin; today stanched and flourishing again, for you have touched the hem of Christ and your issue has been stayed. Guard, I pray you, the cleansing lest you should again have a hæmorrhage, and not be able to lay hold of Christ to steal salvation; for Christ does not like to be stolen from often, though He is very merciful. Yesterday you were flung upon a bed, exhausted and paralyzed, and you had no one when the water should be troubled to put you into the pool.[δ] Today you have Him Who is in one Person Man and God, or rather God and Man. You were raised up from your bed, or rather you took up your bed, and publicly acknowledged the benefit. Do not again be thrown upon your bed by sinning, in the evil rest of a body paralyzed by its pleasures. But as you now are, so walk, mindful of the command,[ε] Behold thou art made whole; sin no more lest a worse thing happen unto thee if thou prove thyself bad after the blessing thou hast received. You have heard the loud voice, Lazarus, come forth,[α] as you lay in the tomb; not, however, after four days, but after many days; and you were loosed from the bonds of your graveclothes. Do not again become dead, nor live with those who dwell in the tombs;[β] nor bind yourself with the bonds of your own sins;[γ] for it is uncertain whether you will rise again from the tomb till the last and universal resurrection, which will bring every work into judgment,[δ] not to be healed, but to be judged, and to give account of all which for good or evil it has treasured up.

XXXIV. If you were full of leprosy, that shapeless evil, yet you scraped off the evil matter, and received again the Image whole. Shew your cleansing to me your Priest, that I may recognize how much more precious it is than the legal one. Do not range yourself with the nine unthankful men, but imitate the tenth.[ε] For although he was a Samaritan, yet he was of better mind than the others. Make certain that you will not break out again with evil ulcers, and find the indisposition of your body hard to heal. Yesterday meanness and avarice were withering your hand; to-day let liberality and kindness stretch it out.[ζ] It is a noble cure for a weak hand to disperse abroad, to give to the poor,[η] to pour out the things which we possess abundantly, till we reach the very bottom; and perhaps this will gush forth food for you, as for the woman of Sarepta,[θ] and especially if you happen to be feeding an Elias, to recognize that it is a good abundance to be needy for the sake of Christ, Who for our sakes became poor. If you were deaf and dumb, let the Word sound[κ] in your ears, or rather keep there Him Who hath sounded. Do not shut your ears to the Instruction of the Lord, and to His Counsel, like the adder to charms.[λ] If you are blind and unenlightened, lighten your eyes that you sleep not in death.[μ] In God's Light see light,[ν] and in the Spirit of God be enlightened by the Son, That Threefold and Undivided Light. If you receive all the Word, you will bring therewith upon your own soul all the healing powers of Christ, with which separately these individuals were healed. Only be not ignorant of the measure of grace; only let not the enemy, while you sleep, maliciously sow tares.[ξ] Only take care that as by your cleansing you have become an object of enmity to the Evil One, you do not again make yourself

α Ps. xxxii. 1.
β Luke xiii. 11, which S. Gregory has apparently mixed with a recollection of Matt. xv. 21.
γ Matt. ix. 20. δ John v. 1, &c. ε Ib. v. 14.

α John xi. 43. β Mark v. 3. γ Ps. lxviii. 9 δ Eccles. xii. 14. ε Luke xvii. 12, &c. ζ Ib. vi. 6. η Ps. cxii. 9. θ 1 Kgs. xvii. 8, &c. κ Mark vii. 32. λ Ps. lviii. 4, 5. μ Ib. xiii. 3. ν Ib. xxxvi. 9. ξ Matt. xiii. 25.

an object of pity by sin. Only be careful lest, while rejoicing and lifted up above measure by the blessing, you fall again through pride. Only be diligent as to your cleansing, "setting ascensions in your heart,"[α] and keep with all diligence the remission which you have received as a gift, in order that, while the remission comes from God, the preservation of it may come from yourself also.

XXXV. How shall this be? Remember always the parable,[β] and so will you best and most perfectly help yourself. The unclean and malignant spirit is gone out of you, being chased by baptism. He will not submit to the expulsion, he will not resign himself to be houseless and homeless: He goes through waterless places, dry of the Divine Stream, and there he desires to abide. He wanders, seeking rest; he finds none. He lights on baptized souls, whose sins the font has washed away. He fears the water; he is choked with the cleansing, as the Legion were in the sea.[γ] Again he returns to the house whence he came out. He is shameless, he is contentious, he makes a fresh assault upon it, he makes a new attempt. If he finds that Christ has taken up His abode there, and has filled the place which he had vacated, he is driven back again, and goes off without success and is become an object of pity in his wandering state. But if he finds in you a place, swept and garnished indeed, but empty and idle, equally ready to take in this or that which shall first occupy it, he makes a leap into it, he takes up his abode there with a larger train; and the last state is worse than the first, inasmuch as then there was a hope of amendment and safety, but now the evil is rampant, and drags in sin by its flight from good, and therefore the possession is more secure to him who dwells there.

XXXVI. I will remind you again about Illuminations, and that often, and will reckon them up from Holy Scripture. For I myself shall be happier for remembering them (for what is sweeter than light to those who have tasted light?) and I will dazzle you with my words. There is sprung up a light for the righteous, and its partner joyful gladness.[δ] And, The light of the righteous is everlasting;[ε] and Thou art shining wondrously from the everlasting mountains, is said to God, I think of the Angelic powers which aid our efforts after good. And you have heard David's words; The Lord is my Light and my Salvation, whom then shall I fear?[α] And now he asks that the Light and the Truth may be sent forth for him,[β] now giving thanks that he has a share in it, in that the Light of God is marked upon him;[γ] that is, that the signs of the illumination given are impressed upon him and recognized. One light alone let us shun—that which is the offspring of the baleful fire; let us not walk in the light of our fire,[δ] and in the flame which we have kindled. For I know a cleansing fire which Christ came to send upon the earth,[ε] and He Himself is anagogically[ζ] called a Fire. This Fire takes away whatsoever is material and of evil habit; and this He desires to kindle with all speed, for He longs for speed in doing us good, since He gives us even coals of fire to help us.[η] I know also a fire which is not cleansing, but avenging; either that fire of Sodom[θ] which He pours down on all sinners,[κ] mingled with brimstone and storms, or that which is prepared for the Devil and his Angels[λ] or that which proceeds from the face of the Lord, and shall burn up his enemies round about;[μ] and one even more fearful still than these, the unquenchable fire[ν] which is ranged with the worm that dieth not but is eternal for the wicked. For all these belong to the destroying power; though some may prefer even in this place to take a more merciful view[ξ] of this fire, worthily of Him That chastises.

XXXVII. And as I know of two kinds of fire, so also do I of light. The one is the light of our ruling power directing our steps according to the will of God; the other is a deceitful and meddling one, quite contrary to the true light, though pretending to be that light, that it may cheat us by its appearance. This really is darkness, yet has the appearance of noonday, the high perfection of light. And so I read that passage of those who continually flee in darkness at noonday;[ο] for this is really night, and yet is thought to be bright light by those who have been ruined by luxury. For what saith David? "Night was around me and I knew it not, for I thought that my

α Ps. lxxxiv. 6. So LXX. and Vulgate. Various interpretations are given of these Steps, but they differ only by indicating different virtues and good works as especially intended, and may well be summed up under the three heads of the purgative, illuminative, and unitive ways of salvation. A man can set in his heart such a "going up" by the co-operation of grace and free will.—NEALE & LITTLEDALE in Pss. β Luke xi. 24. γ Mark v. 13. δ Ps. xcvii. 11. ε Prov. xiii. 9.

α Ps. lxxvi. 4. β Ib. xliii. 3. γ Ib. iv. 7. δ Isa. l. 11. ε Luke xii. 49.
ζ Anagoge is one of the three methods of mystical interpretation, according to the distich,

Littera scripta docet: Quid credas allegoria:
Quid speres anagoge: Quid agas tropologia.

η cf. Isa. xlvii. 14, LXX. θ Gen. xix. 24. κ Ps. xi. 6. λ Matt. xxv. 41. μ Ps. xcvii. 3. ν Mark ix. 44, &c.
ξ i.e. To view the Fire there spoken of as Temporal punishment, with a purpose of correcting and reforming the sinner. This is not S. Gregory's own view of the meaning of the passage, though he admits it to be tenable. ο Isa. xvi. 3.

luxury was enlightenment."[α] But such are they, and in this condition; but let us kindle for ourselves the light of knowledge.[β] This will be done by sowing unto righteousness, and reaping the fruit of life, for action is the patron of contemplation, that amongst other things we may learn also what is the true light, and what the false, and be saved from falling unawares into evil wearing the guise of good. Let us be made light, as it was said to the disciples by the Great Light, ye are the light of the world.[γ] Let us be made lights in the world, holding forth the Word of Life;[δ] that is, let us be made a quickening power to others. Let us lay hold of the Godhead; let us lay hold of the First and Brightest Light. Let us walk towards Him shining, before our feet stumble upon dark and hostile mountains.[ε] While it is day let us walk honestly as in the day, not in rioting and drunkenness, not in chambering and wantonness,[ζ] which are the dishonesties of the night.

XXXVIII. Let us cleanse every member, Brethren, let us purify every sense; let nothing in us be imperfect or of our first birth; let us leave nothing unilluminated. Let us enlighten our eyes,[η] that we may look straight on, and not bear in ourselves any harlot idol through curious and busy sight; for even though we might not worship lust, yet our soul would be defiled. If there be beam or mote,[θ] let us purge it away, that we may be able to see those of others also. Let us be enlightened in our ears; let us be enlightened in our tongue, that we may hearken what the Lord God will speak,[κ] and that He may cause[λ] us to hear His lovingkindness in the morning, and that we may be made to hear of joy and gladness,[μ] spoken into godly ears, that we may not be a sharp sword, nor a whetted razor,[ν] nor turn under our tongue labour and toil,[ξ] but that we may speak the Wisdom of God in a mystery, even the hidden Wisdom,[ο] reverencing the fiery tongues.[π] Let us be healed also in the smell, that we be not effeminate; and be sprinkled with dust instead of sweet perfumes,[ρ] but may smell the Ointment that was poured out for us,[ς] spiritually receiving it; and so formed and transformed by it, that from us too a sweet odour may be smelled. Let us cleanse our touch, our taste, our throat, not touching them over gently, nor delighting in smooth things, but handling them as is worthy of Him, the Word That was made flesh for us; and so far following the example of Thomas,[α] not pampering them with dainties and sauces, those brethren of a more baleful pampering,[β] but tasting and learning that the Lord is good,[γ] with the better and abiding taste; and not for a short while refreshing that baneful and thankless dust, which lets pass and does not hold that which is given to it; but delighting it with the words which are sweeter than honey.[δ]

XXXIX. And in addition to what has been said, it is good with our head cleansed, as the head which is the workshop of the senses is cleansed, to hold fast the Head of Christ,[ε] from which the whole body is fitly joined together and compacted; and to cast down our sin that exalted itself, when it would exalt us above our better part. It is good also for the shoulder to be sanctified and purified that it may be able to take up the Cross of Christ, which not everyone can easily do. It is good for the hands to be consecrated, and the feet; the one that they may in every place be lifted up holy;[ζ] and that they may lay hold of the discipline[η] of Christ, lest the Lord at any time be angered; and that the Word may gain credence by action, as was the case with that which was given in the hand of a prophet;[θ] the other, that they be not swift to shed blood, nor to run to evil,[κ] but that they be prompt to run to the Gospel and the Prize[λ] of the high Calling, and to receive Christ Who washes and cleanses them. And if there be also a cleansing of that belly which receiveth and digesteth the food of the Word, it were good also; not to make it a god by luxury and the meat that perisheth,[μ] but rather to give it all possible cleansing, and to make it more spare, that it may receive the Word of God at the very heart, and grieve honourably over the sins of Israel.[ν] I find also the heart and inward parts deemed worthy of honour. David convinces me of this, when he prays that a clean heart may be created in him, and a right spirit renewed in his inward parts;[ξ] meaning, I think, the mind and its movements or thoughts.

XL. And what of the loins, or reins, for we must not pass these over? Let the purification take hold of these also. Let our loins be girded about and kept in check by conti-

α A strange paraphrase of the last clause of Ps. cxxxix. 11, in the LXX., "And I said, then the darkness shall swallow me, and night is enlightenment in my luxury."
β Thus LXX. in Hosea x. 12, where we read "Break up your fallow ground." γ Matt. v. 14. δ Phil. ii. 15, 16.
ε Jer. xlii. 16. ζ Rom. xiii. 13. η Prov. iv. 25.
θ Matt. vii. 2. κ Ps. lxxxv. 8. λ Ib. cxliii. 8. μ Ib. li. 8.
ν Ib. lvii. 4; lii. 2. ξ Ib. x. 7. ο 1 Cor. ii. 7.
π Acts ii. 3. ρ Isa. iii. 34. ς Cant. i. 3.

α John xx. 28. β Quia gula est parens immunditiæ et luxuriæ.
γ Ps. xxxiv. 8. δ Ps. cxix. 103.
ε Ephes iv. 16. ζ 1 Tim. ii. 8. η Ps. ii. 12. θ Hag. i. 1.
κ Mal. i. 1 sq.; Prov. i. 16. λ Phil. iii. 14.
μ John vi. 27. ν Jer. iv. 19. ξ Ps. li. 10.

nence, as the Law bade Israel of old when partaking of the Passover.[α] For none comes out of Egypt purely, or escapes the Destroyer, except he who has disciplined these. And let the reins be changed by that good conversion by which they transfer all the affections to God, so that they can say, Lord, all my desire is before Thee,[β] and the day of man have I not desired ;[γ] for you must be a man of desires,[δ] but they must be those of the spirit. For thus you would destroy the dragon that carries the greater part of his strength upon his navel and his loins,[ε] by slaying the power that comes to him from these. Do not be surprised at my giving a more abundant honour to our uncomely parts,[ζ] mortifying them and making them chaste by my speech, and standing up against the flesh. Let us give to God all our members which are upon the earth ;[η] let us consecrate them all ; not the lobe of the liver[θ] or the kidneys with the fat, nor some part of our bodies now this now that (why should we despise the rest?); but let us bring ourselves entire, let us be reasonable holocausts,[κ] perfect sacrifices ; and let us not make only the shoulder or the breast a portion for the Priest to take away,[λ] for that would be a small thing, but let us give ourselves entire, that we may receive back ourselves entire ; for this is to receive entirely, when we give ourselves to God and offer as a sacrifice our own salvation.

XLI. Besides all this and before all, keep I pray you the good deposit, by which I live and work, and which I desire to have as the companion of my departure ; with which I endure all that is so distressful, and despise all delights ; the confession of the Father and the Son and the Holy Ghost. This I commit unto you to-day ; with this I will baptize you and make you grow. This I give you to share, and to defend all your life, the One Godhead and Power, found in the Three in Unity, and comprising the Three separately, not unequal, in substances or natures, neither increased nor diminished by superiorities or inferiorities ; in every respect equal, in every respect the same ; just as the beauty and the greatness of the heavens is one ; the infinite conjunction of Three Infinite Ones, Each God when considered in Himself ; as the Father so the Son, as the Son so the Holy Ghost ; the Three One God when contemplated together ; Each God because Consubstantial ; One God because of the Monarchia. No sooner do I conceive of the One than I am illumined by the Splendour of the Three ; no sooner do I distinguish Them than I am carried back to the One. When I think of any One of the Three I think of Him as the Whole, and my eyes are filled, and the greater part of what I am thinking of escapes me.[α] I cannot grasp the greatness of That One so as to attribute a greater greatness to the Rest. When I contemplate the Three together, I see but one torch, and cannot divide or measure out the Undivided Light.

XLII. Do you fear to speak of Generation lest you should attribute aught of passion to the impassible God? I on the other hand fear to speak of Creation, lest I should destroy God by the insult and the untrue division, either cutting the Son away from the Father, or from the Son the Substance of the Spirit. For this paradox is involved, that not only is a created Life foisted into the Godhead by those who measure Godhead badly ; but even this created life is divided against itself. For as these low earthly minds make the Son subject to the Father, so again is the rank of the Spirit made inferior to that of the Son, until both God and created life are insulted by the new Theology. No, my friends, there is nothing servile in the Trinity, nothing created, nothing accidental, as I have heard one of the wise[β] say. If I yet pleased men I should not be the servant of Christ, says the Apostle ;[γ] and if I yet worshipped a creature, or were baptized into a creature, I should not be made divine, nor have changed my first birth. What shall I say to those who worship Astarte or Chemosh, the abomination of the Sidonians, or the likeness of a star,[δ] a god a little above them to these idolaters, but yet a creature and a piece of workmanship, when I myself either do not worship Two of Those into Whose united Name I am baptized, or else worship my fellow-servants, for they are fellow-servants, even if a little higher in the scale ; for differences must exist among fellow-servants.

XLIII. I should like to call the Father the

α Exod. xii. 11. β Ps. xxxviii. 9. γ Job xvii. 16.
δ Dan. x. 11. ε Job xxxix. 16. ζ 1 Cor. xii. 23. η Col. iii. 5.
θ Levit. iii. 4. The Mosaic Law ordered that the upper part of the liver and the kidneys, together with the fat, should in certain sacrifices be consecrated to God ; signifying that anger (which was intimated by the liver, which produces bile), and lust (signified by the kidneys and the fat) should especially be sacrificed to God. Again Moses assigned the shoulder and the breast of some sacrifices to the Priests, hinting obscurely at this, that we ought to take care to offer our hearts to the Priests by confession (for the heart is signified by the breast which protects it) and also our actions, which are intended by the shoulder, that by the Priest they may be presented to God. But the Apostle bids us mortify all our members which are upon the earth, and offer ourselves entire as a sacrifice to God, destroying with the sword of the Word of God all our evil and corrupt affections.—NICETAS.
κ Rom. xii. 1. λ Levit. vii. 34.

α i.e. If I think of One Blessed Person, the other Two are not in my mind, and so the greater part of God escapes me.
β S. Gregory Thaumaturgus. γ Galat. i. 10. δ Amos v. 26.

greater, because from him flows both the Equality and the Being of the Equals (this will be granted on all hands), but I am afraid to use the word Origin, lest I should make Him the Origin of Inferiors, and thus insult Him by precedencies of honour. For the lowering of those Who are from Him is no glory to the Source. Moreover, I look with suspicion at your insatiate desire, for fear you should take hold of this word Greater, and divide the Nature, using the word Greater in *all* senses, whereas it does not apply to the Nature, but only to Origination. For in the Consubstantial Persons there is nothing greater or less in point of Substance. I would honour the Son as Son before the Spirit, but Baptism consecrating me through the Spirit does not allow of this. But are you afraid of being reproached with Tritheism? Do you take possession of this good thing, the Unity in the Three, and leave me to fight the battle. Let me be the shipbuilder, and do you use the ship; or if another is the builder of the ship, take me for the architect of the house, and do you live in it with safety, though you spent no labour upon it. You shall not have a less prosperous voyage, or a less safe habitation than I who built them, because you have not laboured upon them. See how great is my indulgence; see the goodness of the Spirit; the war shall be mine, yours the achievement; I will be under fire, and you shall live in peace; but join with your defender in prayer, and give me your hand by the Faith. I have three stones which I will sling at the Philistine;[α] I have three inspirations against the son of the Sareptan,[β] with which I will quicken the slain; I have three floods against the faggots with which I will consecrate the Sacrifice with water, raising the most unexpected fire;[γ] and I will throw down the prophets of shame by the power of the Sacrament.

XLIV. What need have I any more of speech? It is the time for teaching, not for controversy. I protest before God and the elect Angels,[δ] be thou baptized in this faith. If thy heart is written upon in some other way than as my teaching demands, come and have the writing changed; I am no unskilled caligrapher of these truths. I write that which is written upon my own heart; and I teach that which I have been taught, and have kept from the beginning up to these hoar hairs.[ε] Mine is the risk; be mine also the reward of being the Director of your soul, and consecrating you by Baptism. But if you are already rightly disposed, and marked with the good inscription, see that you keep what is written, and remain unchanged in a changing time concerning an unchanging Thing. Follow Pilate's example in the better sense; you who are rightly written on, imitate him who wrote wrongfully. Say to those who would persuade you differently, what I have written, I have written.[α] For indeed I should be ashamed if, while that which was wrong remained inflexible, that which is right should be so easily bent aside; whereas we ought to be easily bent to that which is better from that which is worse, but immovable from the better to the worse. If it be thus, and according to this teaching that you come to Baptism, lo I will not refrain my lips,[β] lo I lend my hands to the Spirit; let us hasten your salvation. The Spirit is eager, the Consecrator is ready, the Gift is prepared. But if you still halt and will not receive the perfectness of the Godhead, go and look for someone else to baptize—or rather to drown you: I have no time to cut the Godhead, and to make you dead in the moment of your regeneration, that you should have neither the Gift nor the Hope of Grace, but should in so short a time make shipwreck of your salvation. For whatever you may subtract from the Deity of the Three, you will have overthrown the whole, and destroyed your own being made perfect.

XLV. But not yet perhaps is there formed upon your soul any writing good or bad; and you want to be written upon today, and formed by us unto perfection. Let us go within the cloud. Give me the tables of your heart; I will be your Moses, though this be a bold thing to say; I will write on them with the finger of God a new Decalogue.[γ] I will write on them a shorter method of salvation. And if there be any heretical or unreasoning beast, let him remain below, or he will run the risk of being stoned by the Word of truth. I will baptize you and make you a disciple in the Name of the Father and of the Son and of the Holy Ghost;[δ] and These Three have One common name, the Godhead. And you shall know, both by appearances[ε] and by words that you reject all ungodliness, and are united to all the Godhead. Believe that all that is in the world, both all that is seen and all that

α 1 Sam. xvii. 49. β 1 Kgs. xvii. 21.
γ Ib. xviii 33. δ 1 Tim. v. 21.
ε Supposing S. Gregory's birth to have been in 325, the earliest date which seems at all probable, he would be under 60 in 381, when this Oration was delivered; so that the expression on the text must be held to be a rhetorical exaggeration. Suidas, however, pushes back the date of his birth as far as 299 or 300; which does not fit in well with the chronology of his life, as given by himself.

α John xix. 22. β Ps. xl. 9. γ Exod. xxxviii. 28.
δ Ib. xix. 13. ε Matt. xxviii. 19.

is unseen, was made out of nothing by God, and is governed by the Providence of its Creator, and will receive a change to a better state. Believe that evil has no substance or kingdom, either unoriginate or self-existent or created by God; but that it is our work, and the evil one's, and came upon us through our heedlessness, but not from our Creator. Believe that the Son of God, the Eternal Word, Who was begotten of the Father before all time and without body, was in these latter days for your sake made also Son of Man, born of the Virgin Mary ineffably and stainlessly (for nothing can be stained where God is, and by which salvation comes), in His own Person at once entire Man and perfect God, for the sake of the entire sufferer, that He may bestow salvation on your whole being, having destroyed the whole condemnation of your sins: impassible in His Godhead, passible in that which He assumed; as much Man for your sake as you are made God for His. Believe that for us sinners He was led to death; was crucified and buried, so far as to taste of death; and that He rose again the third day, and ascended into heaven, that He might take you with Him who were lying low; and that He will come again with His glorious Presence to judge the quick and the dead; no longer flesh, nor yet without a body, according to the laws which He alone knows of a more godlike body, that He may be seen by those who pierced Him,[α] and on the other hand may remain as God without carnality. Receive besides this the Resurrection, the Judgment and the Reward according to the righteous scales of God; and believe that this will be Light to those whose mind is purified (that is, God—seen and known) proportionate to their degree of purity, which we call the Kingdom of heaven; but to those who suffer from blindness of their ruling faculty, darkness, that is estrangement from God, proportionate to their blindness here. Then, in the tenth place, work that which is good upon this foundation of dogma; for faith without works is dead,[β] even as are works apart from faith. This is all that may be divulged of the Sacrament, and that is not forbidden to the ear of the many. The rest you shall learn within the Church by the grace of the Holy Trinity; and those matters you shall conceal within yourself, sealed and secure.

XLVI. But one thing more I preach unto you. The Station in which you shall presently stand after your Baptism before the Great Sanctuary[α] is a foretype of the future glory. The Psalmody with which you will be received is a prelude to the Psalmody of Heaven; the lamps which you will kindle are a Sacrament of the illumination there with which we shall meet the Bridegroom, shining and virgin souls, with the lamps of our faith shining, not sleeping through our carelessness, that we may not miss Him that we look for if He come unexpectedly; nor yet unfed, and without oil, and destitute of good works, that we be not cast out of the Bridechamber. For I see how pitiable is such a case. He will come when the cry demands the meeting, and they who are prudent shall meet Him, with their light shining and its food abundant, but the others seeking for oil too late from those who possess it. And He will come with speed, and the former shall go in with Him, but the latter shall be shut out, having wasted in preparations the time of entrance; and they shall weep sore when all too late they learn the penalty of their slothfulness, when the Bridechamber can no longer be entered by them for all their entreaties, for they have shut it against themselves by their sin, following in another fashion the example of those who missed the Wedding feast[β] with which the good Father feasts the good Bridegroom; one on account of a newly wedded wife; another of a newly purchased field; another of a yoke of oxen; which he and they acquired to their misfortune, since for the sake of the little they lose the great. For none are there of the disdainful, nor of the slothful, nor of those who are clothed in filthy rags and not in the Wedding garment even though here they may have thought themselves worthy of wearing the bright robe there, and secretly intruded themselves, deceiving themselves with vain hopes. And then, What? When we have entered, then the Bridegroom knows what He will teach us, and how He will converse with the souls that have come in with Him. He will converse with them, I think in teaching things more perfect and more pure. Of which may we all, both Teachers and Taught, have share, in the Same Christ our Lord, to Whom be the Glory and the Empire, for ever and ever. Amen.

α Rev. i. 7.

β James ii. 17.

α The word here used is Bema, which properly means a Platform. In an Oriental Church the East end of the building is raised by one or more steps above the choir. A little distance East of these steps is a great Screen called the Iconostasis, from the pictures (Icons) with which it is covered. It has three doors, one in the centre, called the Royal Gates, leading to the Altar; one on the left hand, leading to the Prothesis, or Credence; and one on the right to the Sacristy. The whole raised portion is called the Bema, or sometimes the Altar, the Altar proper being known as the Throne.

β Luke xiv. 16, &c.

INTRODUCTION TO THE ORATION ON PENTECOST.

It is uncertain to what year the following Oration belongs. It was, however, certainly delivered at Constantinople; the Benedictine Editors think in the year 381, in which case the day would be May 16. An indication tending to establish this date is found in c. 14, in the expression of apprehension of personal danger to himself for his boldness in setting forth the true faith. In fact, in the earlier part of this year, after the Emperor Theodosius had put him in possession of the Patriarchal Throne, vacant by the expulsion and deposition of the Arian Demophilus, he had narrowly escaped assassination at the hands of the Arians.

The Oration deals again with the subject of the Fifth Theological Oration, the question of the Deity of the Holy Ghost, but proceeds to establish the point by quite a different set of arguments from those adopted in the former discourse, none of whose points are here repeated.

The Preacher begins by commenting on the various ways in which Festivals are kept by Jews, by Heathen and by Christians. Then he remarked on the mystical significance of the number Seven, which he illustrates by several instances; and next proceeds with his principal Subject.

God the Holy Ghost, he says, completes the work of Christ. Those who regard Him as a Created Being, as did the followers of Macedonius, are thereby guilty of blasphemy and impiety. The true Faith recognizes Him as God; and this belief is necessary to salvation; yet some reserve must be employed in applying that Name to Him. We must indeed insist on the recognition of His possession of all the attributes of Godhead; and we must at any rate bear with those who, like the Orator himself, also give Him the Name of God, which he hopes all his hearers will receive from the Holy Ghost grace to do. Then he proceeds to shew from Holy Scripture that in fact all the Attributes of Deity do belong to the Holy Spirit; and that His distinctive Personal Mark is that He is neither Unbegotten like the Father, nor Begotten like the Son. He does not touch on the question of the double Procession.

It would seem from some expressions in c. 8 that this Discourse was not delivered to his usual audience, but to an Assembly of "Religious."

The Title of the Oration varies in different MSS. Thus some have it "Of The Same On Pentecost," to which one adds "And On The Holy Spirit;" and another puts it "Of The Same, a Homily on Pentecost." The printed Editions before the Benedictine have "On The Holy Pentecost."

ORATION XLI.

On Pentecost.

I. Let us reason a little about the Festival, that we may keep it spiritually. For different persons have different ways of keeping Festival; but to the worshipper of the Word a discourse seems best; and of discourses, that which is best adapted to the occasion. And of all beautiful things none gives so much joy to the lover of the beautiful, as that the lover of festivals should keep them spiritually. Let us look into the matter thus. The Jew keeps festival as well as we, but only in the letter. For while following after the bodily Law, he has not attained to the spiritual Law. The Greek too keeps festival, but only in the body, and in honour of his own gods and demons, some of whom are creators of passion by their own admission, and others were honoured out of passion. Therefore even their manner of keeping festival is passionate, as though their very sin were an honour to God, in Whom their passion takes refuge as a thing to be proud of.[a] We too keep festival, but we keep it as is pleasing to the Spirit. And it is pleasing to Him that we should keep it by discharging some duty, either of action or speech. This then is our manner of keeping festival, to treasure up in our soul some of those things which are permanent and will cleave to it, not of those which will forsake us and be destroyed, and which only tickle our senses for a little while; whereas they are for the most part, in my judgment at least, harmful and ruinous. For sufficient unto the body is the evil thereof. What need has that fire of further fuel, or that beast of more plentiful food, to make it more uncontrollable, and too violent for reason?

II. Wherefore we must keep the feast spiritually. And this is the beginning of our discourse; for we must speak, even if our speech do seem a little too discursive; and we must be diligent for the sake of those who love

[a] They deify bad passions, and then act as if the gratification of them were an honour to the gods in whom they have personified them.

learning, that we may as it were mix up some seasoning with our solemn festival. The children of the Hebrews do honour to the number Seven, according to the legislation of Moses (as did the Pythagoreans in later days to the number Four, by which indeed they were in the habit of swearing[α] as the Simonians and Marcionites[β] do by the number Eight and the number Thirty, inasmuch as they have given names to and reverence a system of Æons of these numbers); I cannot say by what rules of analogy, or in consequence of what power of this number; anyhow they do honour to it. One thing indeed is evident, that God, having in six days created matter, and given it form, and having arranged it in all kinds of shapes and mixtures, and having made this present visible world, on the seventh day rested from all His works, as is shewn by the very name of the Sabbath, which in Hebrew means Rest. If there be, however, any more lofty reason than this, let others discuss it. But this honour which they pay to it is not confined to days alone, but also extends to years. That belonging to days the Sabbath proves, because it is continually observed among them; and in accordance with this the removal of leaven is for that number of days.[γ] And that belonging to years is shewn by the seventh year, the year of Release;[δ] and it consists not only of Hebdomads, but of Hebdomads of Hebdomads, alike in days and years. The Hebdomads of days give birth to Pentecost, a day called holy among them; and those of years to what they call the Jubilee, which also has a release of land, and a manumission of slaves, and a release of possessions bought. For this nation consecrates to God, not only the firstfruits of offspring, or of firstborn, but also those of days and years. Thus the veneration paid to the number Seven gave rise also to the veneration of Pentecost. For seven being multiplied by seven generates fifty all but one day, which we borrow from the world to come, at once the Eighth and the first, or rather one and indestructible. For the present sabbatism of our souls can find its cessation there, that a portion may be given to seven and also to eight[α] (so some of our predecessors have interpreted this passage of Solomon).

III. As to the honour paid to Seven there are many testimonies, but we will be content with a few out of the many. For instance, seven precious spirits are named; for I think Isaiah[β] loves to call the activities of the Spirit spirits; and the Oracles of the Lord are purified seven times according to David,[γ] and the just is delivered from six troubles and in the seventh is not smitten.[δ] But the sinner is pardoned not seven times, but seventy times seven.[ε] And we may see it by the contrary also (for the punishment of wickedness is to be praised), Cain being avenged seven times, that is, punishment being exacted from him for his fratricide, and Lamech seventy times seven,[ζ] because he was a murderer after the law and the condemnation.[η] And wicked neighbours

α The followers of Pythagoras swore by their master, who taught them the mystic properties of the number Four, which he called the Fountain of the Universe, because all things were made of four elements.

β The Simonians and Marcionites were two Gnostic sects, the one deriving its name from Simon Magus, the other from Marcion of Sinope. Simon, of whom we read in the Acts c. viii., is generally regarded by the Fathers as the precursor of the Gnostic Heresies. He maintained a system of Emanations from God, of which he claimed to be himself the chief. In his teaching the first cause of all things was an Ineffable Existence or Non-existence, which he sometimes called Silence and sometimes Fire, from which the Universe was generated by a series of six Emanations called Roots, which he arranged in pairs, male and female; and these six contained among them the whole Essence of his first Principle Silence. These Roots with Simon himself and his consort Helena, made up the Ogdoad referred to in the text.

Marcion was a native of Sinope in Pontus, and flourished about the middle of the Second Century. His system of teaching was mainly rationalistic, and did not recognize (Dr. Mansel tells us, "Gnostic Heresies," p. 203) any theory of Emanations as connecting links between God and the world; for from his point of view the Supreme God was not, even indirectly, the Author of the world. It would seem that S. Gregory is confusing Marcion with Valentinus, an Egyptian heresiarch who flourished about the same time. In his theory we first find a system of "Æons," divided into an Ogdoad, a Decad, and a Dodecad. Or he may mean Marcus, a follower of Valentinus, and founder of the subordinate sect of the Marcosians. γ Exod. xii. 15. δ Ib. xxi. 2.

α Eccles. xi. 2. S. Gregory himself (Or. xviii. "in laudem Patris," c. 20) comments upon this passage as enjoining liberal almsgiving. S. Ambrose (in Luc. vi.) has a mystical interpretation somewhat resembling that here referred to; but I cannot find a predecessor of Gregory on the verse. Some later commentators, according to Cornelius and Lapide, take the Seven of the poor in this life, and the Eight of the souls in Purgatory, following a common interpretation of these numbers. β Isa. xi. 2. γ Ps. xix. 6. δ Job v. 19. ε Matt. xviii. 22. ζ Gen. iv. 24.

η It will be worth while, says Nicetas, to add S. John Chrysostom's account of the sevenfold punishment which was inflicted on Cain. The number Seven he says (Hom. in Gen. xix. 5, p. 168 c.) is often used in Holy Scripture in the sense of multitude, as e.g., in such places as, "The barren hath borne seven," and the like. So here; the greatness of the crime is implied, and that it is not a simple and single crime, but seven sins; and those of such a sort that every one of them must be avenged by a very severe punishment. First, that he envied his brother when he saw that God loved him, a sin which without any other added to it was sufficient to be deadly. The next was that this sin was against a brother. The third that he compassed a deceit. The fourth that he perpetrated a murder. The fifth that it was his brother that he slew. The sixth that he was the first man to commit a murder. The seventh that he lied to God. You have followed these steps with your mind, or do you desire that I should repeat the enumeration in a fuller way, to make you understand how each of these sins would be visited with a very severe penalty, even if it stood alone. Who would judge a man worthy of pardon who envies another simply because he enjoys the favour and love of God? Here then is one very great and inexpiable sin. And this is shewn to be even more atrocious when he who is envied is a brother, and has done him no wrong. Further, he contrived a deceit, bringing his brother out by a trick into the field, without reverence for nature herself. The fourth crime is the murder which he committed. The fifth is that it was his brother whom he put to death; his brother, I say, that came out of the same womb. Sixthly, he was the first inventor of murder. Seventhly, when questioned by God he did not hesitate to lie. And therefore because he dared to lay hands on his brother, he draws upon himself severe punishments. He then proceeds to shew how Lamech's crime was worse than Cain's, and is therefore said to be punished seventy times; that is, in manifold ways. Lamech slew a man and a young man, and this, after the law against murder had been given; that is, after God had punished Cain. Cain's punishment he says was

receive sevenfold into their bosom;[α] and the House of Wisdom rests on seven pillars,[β] and the Stone of Zerubbabel is adorned with seven eyes;[γ] and God is praised seven times a day.[δ] And again the barren beareth seven,[ε] the perfect number, she who is contrasted with her who is imperfect in her children."[ζ]

IV. And if we must also look at ancient history, I perceive that Enoch,[η] the seventh among our ancestors, was honoured by translation. I perceive also that the twenty-first, Abraham,[θ] was given the glory of the Patriarchate, by the addition of a greater mystery. For the Hebdomad thrice repeated brings out this number. And one who is very bold might venture even to come to the New Adam, my God and Lord Jesus Christ, Who is counted the Seventy-seventh from the old Adam who fell under sin, in the backward genealogy according to Luke.[κ] And I think of the seven trumpets of Jesus, the son of Nave, and the same number of circuits and days and priests, by which the walls of Jericho were shaken down.[λ] And so too the seven compassings of the City; in the same way as there is a mystery in the threefold breathings of Elias, the Prophet, by which he breathed life into the son of the Sareptan widow,[μ] and the same number of his floodings of the wood,[ν] when he consumed the sacrifice with fire sent from God, and condemned the prophets of shame, who could not do the like at his challenge. And the sevenfold looking for the cloud imposed upon the young servant; and Elissæus stretching himself that number of times upon the child of the Shunammite, by which stretching the breath of life was restored.[ξ] To the same doctrine belongs, I think (if I may omit the seven-stemmed and seven-lamped candlestick of the Temple[α]) that the ceremony of the Priests' consecration lasted seven days;[β] and seven that of the purifying of a leper,[γ] and that of the Dedication of the Temple[δ] the same number, and that in the seventieth year the people returned from the Captivity;[ε] that whatever is in Units may appear also in Decads, and the mystery of the Hebdomad be reverenced in a more perfect number. But why do I speak of the distant past? Jesus Himself who is pure perfection, could in the desert and with five loaves feed five thousand, and again with seven loaves four thousand. And the leavings after they were satisfied were in the first case twelve baskets full, and in the other seven baskets;[ζ] neither, I imagine, without a reason or unworthy of the Spirit. And if you read for yourself you may take note of many numbers which contain a meaning deeper than appears on the surface. But to come to an instance which is most useful to us on the present occasion, not that for these reasons or others very similar or yet more divine, the Hebrews honour the Day of Pentecost, and we also honour it; just as there are other rites of the Hebrews which we observe . . . they were typically observed by them, and by us they are sacramentally reinstated. And now having said so much by way of preface about the Day, let us proceed to what we have to say further.

V. We are keeping the feast of Pentecost and of the Coming of the Spirit, and the appointed time of the Promise, and the fulfilment of our hope. And how great, how august, is the Mystery. The dispensations of the Body of Christ are ended; or rather, what belongs to His Bodily Advent (for I hesitate to say the Dispensation of His Body, as long as no discourse persuades me that it is better to have put off the body[η]), and that of the Spirit is beginning. And what were the things pertaining to the Christ? The Virgin, the Birth, the Manger, the Swaddling, the Angels glorifying Him, the Shepherds running to Him, the course of the Star, the Magi worshipping Him and bringing Gifts, Herod's

---

sevenfold, corresponding to his seven sins:—1. Cursed is the ground for thy sake. 2. Thou shalt till the ground; i.e., thou shalt never rest from the toils of husbandry. 3. It shall not yield unto thee its strength; 4. thy labours shall be barren, and 5. "sighing and trembling" shalt thou be. And the sixth is from the lips of Cain himself:—"If Thou castest me out from the earth," i.e., from all earthly conveniences, "from Thy face shall I be hid." And God put a mark upon Cain; this is the seventh punishment—a mark of infamy declaring his guilt and shame to all that should see him. Others according to the same authority (and Bishop Wordsworth adopts the explanation) explains it thus. From Cain to the Deluge are seven generations, and then the world was punished because sin had spread far and wide. But Lamech's sin could not be cured by the Deluge, but only by Him Who taketh away the sin of the world. Then count all the generations from Adam to Christ, and according to the Genealogy in Luke, you will find that our Lord was born in the seventieth generation. This is S. Jerome's explanation. α Ps. lxxix. 12.

β Prov. ix. i. γ Zech. iii. 9. δ Ps. cxix. 164. ε 1 Sam. ii. 5.

ζ Peninnah who had "many" children is called Imperfect in her children, because Many is an indefinite word; whereas Hannah's one child Samuel was so perfect a man that he was as it were seven to his mother. For Seven is mystically, as Six or Ten is arithmetically, the perfect number. (Six because it is the sum of its own factors 1, 2, 3; Ten, because it is the basis of numeration; Seven because it is the number of Creation; for God rested on the Sabbath Day.)

η Jude 14. θ Gen. v. 22. κ Luke iii. 34.

λ Josh. vi. 4. &c. μ 1 Kgs. xvii. 21. ν Ib. xviii. 33.

ξ 2 Kgs. iv. 25, where the LXX. has "he contracted himself upon the child until seven times, and the child opened his eyes;" saying nothing about the sneezing of the child, which the Hebrew and Vulgate mention, while they omit the number in the case of Elisha's similar action. S. Bernard has a curious explanation of the seven sneezes of the child (in Cant. xvi).

α Ex. xxv. 32, 37. β Levit. viii. 33. γ Ib. xiv, 8.

δ 1 Kings viii. 6. ε 2 Chron. xxxvi. 32.

ζ Different words are used here as in the New Testament for Baskets. The second implies a larger size: it is the word used for the "basket" in which St. Paul was let down from the wall of Damascus, Acts ix. 25.

η S. Gregory makes this explanation because there were certain heretics who taught that our Lord at His Ascension laid aside His Humanity. It is said that this was held by certain Manichæans, who based their idea on Ps. xix. 4, where the LXX. and Vulgate read, "He hath set His Tabernacle in the Sun."

murder of the children, the Flight of Jesus into Egypt, the Return from Egypt, the Circumcision, the Baptism, the Witness from Heaven, the Temptation, the Stoning for our sake (because He had to be given as an Example to us of enduring affliction for the Word), the Betrayal, the Nailing, the Burial, the Resurrection, the Ascension; and of these even now He suffers many dishonours at the hands of the enemies of Christ; and He bears them, for He is longsuffering. But from those who love Him He receives all that is honourable. And He defers, as in the former case His wrath, so in ours His kindness; in their case perhaps to give them the grace of repentance, and in ours to test our love; whether we do not faint in our tribulations[α] and conflicts for the true Religion, as was from of old the order of His Divine Economy, and of his unsearchable judgments, with which He orders wisely all that concerns us. Such are the mysteries of Christ. And what follows we shall see to be more glorious; and may we too be seen. As to the things of the Spirit, may the Spirit be with me, and grant me speech as much as I desire; or if not that, yet as is in due proportion to the season. Anyhow He will be with me as my Lord; not in servile guise, nor awaiting a command, as some think.[β] For He bloweth where He wills and on whom He wills, and to what extent He wills.[γ] Thus we are inspired both to think and to speak of the Spirit.

VI. They who reduce the Holy Spirit to the rank of a creature are blasphemers and wicked servants, and worst of the wicked. For it is the part of wicked servants to despise Lordship, and to rebel against dominion, and to make That which is free their fellow-servant. But they who deem Him God are inspired by God[δ] and are illustrious in their mind; and they who go further and *call* Him so, if to well disposed hearers are exalted; if to the low, are not reserved enough, for they commit pearls to clay, and the noise of thunder to weak ears, and the sun to feeble eyes, and solid food to those who are still using milk;[α] whereas they ought to lead them little by little up to what lies beyond them, and to bring them up to the higher truths; adding light to light, and supplying truth upon truth. Therefore we will leave the more mature discourse, for which the time has not yet come, and will speak with them as follows.

VII. If, my friends, you will not acknowledge the Holy Spirit to be uncreated, nor yet eternal; clearly such a state of mind is due to the contrary spirit—forgive me, if in my zeal I speak somewhat over boldly. If, however, you are sound enough to escape this evident impiety, and to place outside of slavery Him Who gives freedom to yourselves, then see for yourselves with the help of the Holy Ghost and of us what follows. For I am persuaded that you are to some extent partakers of Him, so that I will go into the question with you as kindred souls. Either shew me some mean between lordship and servitude, that I may there place the rank of the Spirit; or, if you shrink from imputing servitude to Him, there is no doubt of the rank in which you must place the object of your search. But you are dissatisfied with the syllables, and you stumble at the word, and it is to you a stone of stumbling and a rock of offence;[β] for so is Christ to some minds. It is only human after all. Let us meet one another in a spiritual manner; let us be full rather of brotherly than of self love. Grant us the Power of the Godhead, and we will give up to you the use of the Name. Confess the Nature in other words for which you have greater reverence, and we will heal you as infirm people, filching from you some matters in which you delight. For it is shameful, yes, shameful and utterly illogical, when you are sound in soul, to draw petty distinctions about the sound, and to hide the Treasure, as if you envied it to others, or were afraid lest you should sanctify your own tongue too. But it is even more shameful for us to be in the state of which we accuse you, and, while condemning your petty distinctions of words to make petty distinctions of letters.

VIII. Confess, my friends, the Trinity to be of One Godhead; or if you will, of One Nature; and we will pray the Spirit to give you this word God. He will give it to you, I well know, inasmuch as He has already granted you the first portion and the second;[γ] and especially

α Ephes. iii. 13.

β The reference is to the Macedonians or Pneumatomachi, followers of Macedonius, Patriarch of Constantinople, who had passed from extreme or Anomœan Arianism to Semi-Arianism, and was forcibly intruded on the See by order of Constantius in 343, but was afterwards deposed. After his deposition he broached the heresy known by his name, denying the Deity of the Holy Ghost; some of its adherents, with Macedonius himself, maintaining Him to be a mere creature; others stopping short of this; and others calling Him a creature and servant of the Son. The heresy was formally condemned in the Ecumenical Council of Constantinople in 381.

γ John iii. 8.

δ S. Gregory here commends the practice of reserve in respect of the Deity of the Holy Ghost. To *believe* it is necessary to salvation, he would say; but in view of the prevailing ignorance it is well to be careful before whom we give Him the Name of God. But he demands that his hearers should give to the Holy Ghost all the Attributes of Godhead, and should bear with those who, like himself, gave Him also the Name, as he prays that they all may have grace to do (Bênoît).

α Heb. v. 12.

β Isa. viii. 14; Rom. ix. 33; 1 Pet. ii. 8.

γ i.e., inasmuch as He has granted you a right faith in the Consubstantiality and Unity of the Trinity, I am sure He will in time grant you the grace also to call Him by the Name of God.

if that about which we are contending is some spiritual cowardice, and not the devil's objection. Yet more clearly and concisely, let me say, do not you call us to account for our loftier word (for envy has nothing to do with this ascent), and we will not find fault with what you have been able to attain, until by another road you are brought up to the same resting place. For we are not seeking victory, but to gain brethren, by whose separation from us we are torn. This we concede to you in whom we do find something of vital truth, who are sound as to the Son. We admire your life, but we do not altogether approve your doctrine. Ye who have the things of the Spirit, receive Himself in addition, that ye may not only strive, but strive lawfully,[α] which is the condition of your crown. May this reward of your conversation be granted you, that you may confess the Spirit perfectly and proclaim with us, aye and before us, all that is His due. Yes, and I will venture even more on your behalf; I will even utter the Apostle's wish. So much do I cling to you, and so much do I revere your array, and the colour of your continence, and those sacred assemblies, and the august Virginity, and purification, and the Psalmody that lasts all night[β] and your love of the poor, and of the brethren, and of strangers, that I could consent to be Anathema from Christ, and even to suffer something as one condemned, if only you might stand beside us, and we might glorify the Trinity together. For of the others why should I speak, seeing they are clearly dead (and it is the part of Christ alone to raise them, Who quickeneth the dead by His own Power), and are unhappily separated in place as they are bound together by their doctrine; and who quarrel among themselves as much as a pair of squinting eyes in looking at the same object, and differ with one another, not in sight but in position—if indeed we may charge them only with squinting, and not with utter blindness. And now that I have to some extent laid down your position, come, let us return again to the subject of the Spirit, and I think you will follow me now.

IX. The Holy Ghost, then, always existed, and exists, and always will exist. He neither had a beginning, nor will He have an end; but He was everlastingly ranged with and numbered with the Father and the Son. For it was not ever fitting that either the Son should be wanting to the Father, or the Spirit to the Son. For then Deity would be shorn of Its Glory in its greatest respect, for It would seem to have arrived at the consummation of perfection as if by an afterthought. Therefore He was ever being partaken, but not partaking; perfecting, not being perfected; sanctifying, not being sanctified; deifying, not being deified; Himself ever the same with Himself, and with Those with Whom He is ranged; invisible, eternal, incomprehensible, unchangeable, without quality, without quantity, without form, impalpable, self-moving, eternally moving, with free-will, self-powerful, All-powerful (even though all that is of the Spirit is referable to the First Cause, just as is all that is of the Only-begotten); Life and Lifegiver; Light and Lightgiver; absolute Good, and Spring of Goodness; the Right, the Princely Spirit; the Lord, the Sender, the Separator; Builder of His own Temple; leading, working as He wills; distributing His own Gifts; the Spirit of Adoption, of Truth, of Wisdom, of Understanding, of Knowledge, of Godliness, of Counsel, of Fear (which are ascribed to Him[α]) by Whom the Father is known and the Son is glorified; and by Whom *alone* He is known; one class, one service, worship, power, perfection, sanctification. Why make a long discourse of it? All that the Father hath the Son hath also, except the being Unbegotten; and all that the Son hath the Spirit hath also, except the Generation. And these two matters do not divide the Substance, as I understand it, but rather are divisions within the Substance.[β]

X. Are you labouring to bring forth objections? Well, so am I to get on with my discourse. Honour the Day of the Spirit; restrain your tongue if you can a little. It is the time to speak of other tongues—reverence them or fear them, when you see that they are of fire. To-day let us teach dogmatically; to-morrow we may discuss. To-day let us keep the feast; to-morrow will be time enough to behave ourselves unseemly—the first mystically, the second theatrically; the one in the Churches, the other in the marketplace; the one among the sober, the other among the drunken; the one as befits those who vehemently desire, the other, as among those who

α 2 Tim. ii. 5.

β The Constantinopolitan followers of Macedonius at the period were noted for their strict asceticism. The attempt to revive the Night Office among the secular Clergy of the Diocese brought great odium on S. John Chrysostom a few years later.

α i.e., by Isaiah.

β Job xxxviii. 4, Ps. v. 10, xxxvi., cxxxix. 7–15, cxlii., Isa. xi. 1–3, xlviii. 16, Mal. iii. 6, Wisd. i. 2, John i. 14, iii. 24, xv. 26, xvi. 14, 15, Acts xiii. 2, Rom. iv. 17, xv. 16, 19, 1 Cor. ii. 10, vi. 19, viii. 2, 2 Cor. iii. 1, 6, xiii. 4, 2 Thess. iii. 5, 1 Tim. vi. 10, Heb. ix. 14.

make a joke of the Spirit. Having then put an end to the element that is foreign to us, let us now thoroughly furnish our own friends.

XI. He wrought first in the heavenly and angelic powers, and such as are first after God and around God. For from no other source flows their perfection and their brightness, and the difficulty or impossibility of moving them to sin, but from the Holy Ghost. And next, in the Patriarchs and Prophets, of whom the former saw Visions of God, or knew Him, and the latter also foreknew the future, having their master part moulded by the Spirit, and being associated with events that were yet future as if present, for such is the power of the Spirit. And next in the Disciples of Christ (for I omit to mention Christ Himself, in Whom He dwelt, not as energizing, but as accompanying His Equal), and that in three ways, as they were able to receive Him, and on three occasions; before Christ was glorified by the Passion, and after He was glorified by the Resurrection; and after His Ascension, or Restoration, or whatever we ought to call it, to Heaven. Now the first of these manifests Him—the healing of the sick and casting out of evil spirits, which could not be apart from the Spirit; and so does that breathing upon them after the Resurrection, which was clearly a divine inspiration; and so too the present distribution of the fiery tongues, which we are now commemorating. But the first manifested Him indistinctly, the second more expressly, this present one more perfectly, since He is no longer present only in energy, but as we may say, substantially, associating with us, and dwelling in us. For it was fitting that as the Son had lived with us in bodily form—so the Spirit too should appear in bodily form; and that after Christ had returned to His own place, He should have come down to us—*Coming* because He is the Lord; *Sent*, because He is not a rival God. For such words no less manifest the Unanimity than they mark the separate Individuality.

XII. And therefore He came after Christ, that a Comforter should not be lacking unto us; but *Another* Comforter, that you might acknowledge His co-equality. For this word Another marks an Alter Ego, a name of equal Lordship, not of inequality. For Another is not said, I know, of different kinds, but of things consubstantial. And He came in the form of Tongues because of His close relation to the Word. And they were of Fire, perhaps because of His purifying Power (for our Scripture knows of a purifying fire, as any one who wishes can find out), or else because of His Substance. For our God is a consuming Fire, and a Fire[α] burning up the ungodly;[β] though you may again pick a quarrel over these words, being brought into difficulty by the Consubstantiality. And the tongues were cloven, because of the diversity of Gifts; and they sat to signify His Royalty and Rest among the Saints, and because the Cherubim are the Throne of God. And it took place in an Upper Chamber (I hope I am not seeming to any one over tedious), because those who should receive it were to ascend and be raised above the earth; for also certain upper chambers[γ] are covered with Divine Waters,[δ] by which the praise of God are sung. And Jesus Himself in an Upper Chamber gave the Communion of the Sacrament to those who were being initiated into the higher Mysteries, that thereby might be shewn on the one hand that God must come down to us, as I know He did of old to Moses; and on the other that we must go up to Him, and that so there should come to pass a Communion of God with men, by a coalescing of the dignity. For as long as either remains on its own footing, the One in His Glory[ε] the other in his lowliness, so long the Goodness of God cannot mingle with us, and His lovingkindness is incommunicable, and there is a great gulf between, which cannot be crossed; and which separates not only the Rich Man from Lazarus and Abraham's Bosom which he longs for, but also the created and changing natures from that which is eternal and immutable.

XIII. This was proclaimed by the Prophets in such passages as the following:—The Spirit of the Lord is upon me;[ζ] and, There shall rest upon Him Seven Spirits; and The Spirit of the Lord descended and led them;[η] and The spirit of Knowledge filling Bezaleel,[θ] the Master-builder of the Tabernacle; and, The Spirit provoking to anger;[κ] and the Spirit carrying away Elias in a chariot,[λ] and sought in double measure by Elissæus; and David led and strengthened by the Good and Princely Spirit.[μ] And He was promised by the mouth of Joel first, who said, And it shall be in the last days that I will pour out of My Spirit upon all flesh (that is, upon all that believe), and upon your sons and upon your daughters,[ν] and

α Heb. xii. 29. β Deut. iv. 24 γ Ps. civ. 3. δ Ps. cxlviii. 4.

ε ἐπὶ περιοπῆς; Billius renders "In specula sua," "On His watch tower," and the meaning is admissible, but the context seems rather to point to the passive sense of Majesty or Glory. The word is not in the Lexicon, and Suicer does not notice it; but the corresponding adjective has *only* the passive sense. Specula, however, is used in the sense of Eminence, but apparently only geographically.

ζ Isa. lxi. 1.

η Ib. xi. 2; lxiii. 14. θ Exod. xxxi. 3. κ Isa. lxiii. 10.

λ 2 Kgs. ii. 11. μ Ps. li. 12; cxliii. 10. ν Joel ii. 28.

the rest; and then afterwards by Jesus, being glorified by Him, and giving back glory to Him, as He was glorified by and glorified the Father.[α] And how abundant was this Promise. He shall abide for ever, and shall remain with you, whether now with those who in the sphere of time are worthy, or hereafter with those who are counted worthy of that world, when we have kept Him altogether by our life here, and not rejected Him in so far as we sin.

XIV. This Spirit shares with the Son in working both the Creation and the Resurrection, as you may be shewn by this Scripture; By the Word of the Lord were the heavens made, and all the power of them by the breath of His Mouth;[β] and this, The Spirit of God that made me, and the Breath of the Almighty that teacheth me;[γ] and again, Thou shalt send forth Thy Spirit and they shall be created, and Thou shalt renew the face of the earth.[δ] And He is the Author of spiritual regeneration. Here is your proof:—None can see or enter into the Kingdom, except he be born again of the Spirit,[ε] and be cleansed from the first birth, which is a mystery of the night, by a remoulding of the day and of the Light, by which every one singly is created anew. This Spirit, for He is most wise and most loving,[ς] if He takes possession of a shepherd makes him a Psalmist, subduing evil spirits by his song,[η] and proclaims him King; if he possess a goatherd and scraper[θ] of sycamore fruit,[κ] He makes him a Prophet. Call to mind David and Amos. If He possess a goodly youth, He makes him a Judge of Elders,[λ] even beyond his years, as Daniel testifies, who conquered the lions in their den.[μ] If He takes possession of Fishermen, He makes them catch the whole world in the nets of Christ, taking them up in the meshes of the Word. Look at Peter and Andrew and the Sons of Thunder, thundering the things of the Spirit. If of Publicans, He makes gain of them for discipleship, and makes them merchants of souls; witness Matthew, yesterday a Publican, today an Evangelist. If of zealous persecutors, He changes the current of their zeal, and makes them Pauls instead of Sauls, and as full of piety as He found them of wickedness. And He is the Spirit of Meekness, and yet is provoked by those who sin. Let us therefore make proof of Him as gentle, not as wrathful, by confessing His Dignity; and let us not desire to see Him implacably wrathful. He too it is who has made me today a bold herald to you;—if without rest to myself, God be thanked; but if with risk, thanks to Him nevertheless; in the one case, that He may spare those that hate us; in the other, that He may consecrate us, in receiving this reward of our preaching of the Gospel, to be made perfect by blood.

XV. They spoke with strange tongues, and not those of their native land; and the wonder was great, a language spoken by those who had not learnt it. And the sign is to them that believe not,[α] and not to them that believe, that it may be an accusation of the unbelievers, as it is written, With other tongues and other lips will I speak unto this people, and not even so will they listen to Me[β] saith the Lord. But they heard. Here stop a little and raise a question, how you are to divide the words. For the expression has an ambiguity, which is to be determined by the punctuation. Did they each hear in their own dialect[γ] so that if I may so say, one sound was uttered, but many were heard; the air being thus beaten and, so to speak, sounds being produced more clear than the original sound; or are we to put the stop after "they Heard," and then to add "them speaking in their own languages" to what follows, so that it would be speaking in languages their own to the hearers, which would be foreign to the speakers? I prefer to put it this latter way; for on the other plan the miracle would be rather of the hearers than of the speakers; whereas in this it would be on the speakers' side; and it was they who were reproached for drunkenness, evidently because they by the Spirit wrought a miracle in the matter of the tongues.

XVI. But as the old Confusion of tongues was laudable, when men who were of one language in wickedness and impiety, even as some now venture to be, were building the Tower;[δ] for by the confusion of their language the unity of their intention was broken up, and their undertaking destroyed; so much more worthy of praise is the present miraculous one. For being poured from One Spirit upon many men, it brings them again into harmony. And there is a diversity of Gifts, which stands in need of yet another Gift to

α John xiv. 16. β Ps. xxxiii. 6. γ Job xxxiii. 4.
δ Ps. civ. 30. ε John iii. 3. ς Wisd. i. 6. η 1 Sam. xvi. 23.
θ The Hebrew word means "a cultivator of sycamores." The LXX. rendering is due to the process of maturing the fruit, which grows on the stem of the trunk and is made to mature by puncturing it with an iron instrument, when after three days the fruit is fit to eat. The Hebrew word occurs only this once in the Bible; Aquila renders it by "Looking for;" Symmachus by "propping with stakes."
κ Amos vii. 14. λ Susannah. μ Dan. vi. 22.

α 1 Cor. xiv. 22. β Isa. xxviii. 11.
γ The actual order of the words in the Greek of Acts ii. 6 is, They heard each individual in his own dialect them speaking; so that the position of the comma affects the meaning.
δ Gen. xi. 7.

discern which is the best, where all are praiseworthy. And that division also might be called noble of which David says, Drown O Lord and divide their tongues.[α] Why? Because they loved all words of drowning, the deceitful tongue.[β] Where he all but expressly arraigns the tongues of the present day[γ] which sever the Godhead. Thus much upon this point.

XVII. Next, since it was to inhabitants of Jerusalem, most devout Jews, Parthians, Medes, and Elamites, Egyptians, and Libyans, Cretans too, and Arabians, and Mesopotamians, and my own Cappadocians, that the tongues spake, and to Jews (if any one prefer so to understand it), out of every nation under heaven thither collected; it is worth while to see who these were and of what captivity. For the captivity in Egypt and Babylon was circumscribed, and moreover had long since been brought to an end by the Return; and that under the Romans, which was exacted for their audacity against our Saviour, was not yet come to pass, though it was in the near future. It remains then to understand it of the captivity under Antiochus, which happened not so very long before this time. But if any does not accept this explanation, as being too elaborate, seeing that this captivity was neither ancient nor widespread over the world, and is looking for a more reliable—perhaps the best way to take it would be as follows. The nation was removed many times, as Esdras related; and some of the Tribes were recovered, and some were left behind; of whom probably (dispersed as they were among the nations) some would have been present and shared the miracle.

XVIII. These questions have been examined before by the studious, and perhaps not without occasion; and whatever else any one may contribute at the present day, he will be joined with us. But now it is our duty to dissolve this Assembly, for enough has been said. But the Festival is never to be put an end to; but kept now indeed with our bodies; but a little later on altogether spiritually *there*, where we shall see the reasons of these things more purely and clearly, in the Word Himself, and God, and our Lord Jesus Christ, the True Festival and Rejoicing of the Saved —to Whom be the glory and the worship, with the Father and the Holy Ghost, now and for ever. Amen.

α Ps. lv. 9. β Ib. lii 4.
γ Arians, Macedonians, and kindred sects.

INTRODUCTION TO ORATION XLII.

"The Last Farewell."

This Oration was delivered during the Second Œcumenical Council, held at Constantinople A.D. 381. Historical as well as personal motives render the occasion of the deepest interest. The audience consisted of the one hundred and fifty Bishops of the Eastern Church who took part in the Council, and of the speaker's own flock, the orthodox Christians of Constantinople. He had by his own exertions gathered that flock together, after it had been ravaged by heretical teachers. He had won the admiration and affection of its members, by his courageous championship of the Faith, his lucid teaching, and his fatherly care for their spiritual needs. He had been, against his will, enthroned with acclamation in the highest ecclesiastical position in the Eastern Church, and called to preside over the Synod of its assembled Bishops. Finding himself unable to guide the deliberations of the Council in regard to a question of the highest importance, and perceiving that he himself and his position were made by some of the Bishops a fresh cause of dissension, he felt bound to resign his high office, and endeavour by this personal sacrifice to restore peace to the Church. His language is worthy of the occasion. Obliged to deal with the topics which had caused dissension, he handles them with gentle and discriminating tact; he speaks with great self-restraint in his own defence; he sets forth with tenderest feeling the common experiences of himself and his flock: he gives with dignity and clearness his last public exposition of the Faith; and finally, in language of exquisite beauty, spoken with the quivering tones of an aged man, he bids a tender farewell to his flock, his cathedral, and his throne, with all their affecting associations. It was an occasion whose pathos is unsurpassed in history. Orator and audience were alike deeply moved, and the emotion has been renewed in all those who have read his words, and realised the scene of their delivery.

"The Last Farewell" in the Presence of the One hundred and fifty Bishops.

1. What think ye of our affairs, dear shepherds and fellow-shepherds: whose feet are beautiful, for you bring glad tidings of peace

and of the good things[α] with which ye have come; beautiful again in our eyes, to whom ye have come in season, not to convert a wandering sheep,[β] but to converse with a pilgrim shepherd? What think ye of this our pilgrimage? And of its fruit, or rather of that of the Spirit[γ] within us,[δ] by Whom we are ever moved,[ε] and specially have now been moved, desiring to have, and perhaps having, nothing of our own? Do you of yourselves understand and perceive—and are you kindly critics of our actions? Or must we, like those from whom a reckoning is demanded as to their military command, or civil government, or administration of the exchequer, publicly and in person submit to you the accounts of our administration? Not indeed that we are ashamed of being judged, for we are ourselves judges in turn, and both with the same charity. But the law is an ancient one: for even Paul communicated to the Apostles his Gospel:[ζ] not for the sake of ostentation, for the Spirit is far removed from all ostentation, but in order to establish his success and correct his failure, if indeed there were any such in his words or actions, as he declares when writing of himself. Since even the Spirits of the Prophets are subject to the prophets,[η] according to the order of the Spirit who regulates and divides all things well. And do not wonder that, while he rendered his account privately and to some, I do so publicly, and to all. For my need is greater than his, of being aided by the freedom of my censors, if I am proved to have failed in my duty, lest I should run, or have run, in vain.[θ] And the only possible mode of self-defence is speech in the presence of men who know the facts.

2. What then is my defence?[ι] If it be false, you must convict me, but if true, you on behalf of whom[κ] and in whose presence I speak, must bear witness to it. For you are my defence, my witnesses, and my crown of rejoicing,[λ] if I also may venture to boast myself a little in the Apostle's language. This flock was, when it was small and poor, as far as appearances went, nay, not even a flock, but a slight trace and relic of a flock, without order, or shepherd, or bounds, with neither right to pasturage, nor the defence of a fold, wandering upon the mountains and in caves and dens of the earth,[μ] scattered and dispersed hither and thither as each one could find shelter or pasture, or could gratefully secure its own safety; like that flock which was harassed by lions, dispersed by tempest, or scattered in darkness, the lamentation of prophets who compared it to the misfortunes of Israel,[α] given up to the Gentiles; over which we also lamented, so long as our lot was worthy of lamentation. For in very deed we also were thrust out and cast off, and scattered upon every mountain and hill, from the need of a shepherd:[β] and a dreadful storm fell upon the Church, and fearful beasts assailed her, who do not even now, after the calm, spare us, but without being ashamed of themselves, wield a greater power than the time should allow; while a gloomy darkness, far more oppressive than the ninth plague of Egypt, the darkness which might be felt,[γ] enveloped and concealed everything, so that we could scarcely even see one another.

3. To speak in a more feeling strain, trusting in Him Who then forsook me, as in a Father, "Abraham has been ignorant of us, Israel has acknowledged us not, but Thou art our Father, and unto Thee do we look;[δ] beside Thee we know none else, we make mention of Thy name."[ε] Therefore, says Jeremiah, I will plead with Thee, I will reason the cause with Thee.[ζ] We are become as at the beginning, when Thou barest not rule[η] over us, and Thou hast forgotten Thy holy covenant, and shut up Thy mercies from us. Therefore we, the worshippers of the Trinity, the perfect suppliants of the perfect Deity, became a reproach to Thy Beloved, neither daring to bring down to our own level any of the things above us, nor in such wise to rise up against the godless tongues which fought against God, as to make His Majesty a fellow servant with ourselves; but, as is plain, we were delivered up on account of our other sins, and because our conduct had been unworthy of Thy commandments, and we had walked after our own evil mind. For what other reason can there be for our being delivered up to the most unrighteous and wicked men of all the dwellers upon the earth? First Nebuchadnezzar[θ] afflicted us,[ι] possessed during the Christian era with an anti-Christian rage, hating Christ just because he had through Him gained salvation, and having bartered the sacred books for sacrifices to those who are no gods. He devoured me, he tore me in pieces, a slight darkness enveloped me,[κ] if I may even in my lamentation

α Isai. lii. 7; Rom. x. 15. β S. Matt. xviii. 12. γ Gal. v. 22. δ 2 Tim. i. 14. ε Acts xvii. 28. ζ Gal. ii. 2. η 1 Cor. xiv. 32. θ Gal. ii. 2. ι 1 Cor. ix. 3.
κ *On behalf of*, i.e., the Christians of Constantinople, whose Pastor he had been, who were present at the time in the church.
λ 1 Thess. ii. 19. μ Heb. xi. 38.

α Ezek. xxxi. ii. β Ib. xxxiv. 6. γ Exod. x. 21. δ Isai. lxiii. 16. ε Ib. xxvi. 13 (LXX.). ζ Jer. xii. 1. η Isai. lxiii. 19. θ *Nebuchadnezzar*, i.e., Julian. ι Jer. li. 34. κ Ps. lv. 6 (LXX.).

keep to the language of Scripture. If the Lord had not helped me,[α] and righteously delivered him to the hands of the lawless, by casting him off (such are the judgments of God) to the Persians, by whom his blood was righteously shed for his unholy sheddings of blood, since in this case alone justice could not afford even to be longsuffering, my soul had shortly dwelt in the grave.[β] The second [γ] no more kindly, if he were not even more grievous still, for while he bore the name of Christ, he was a false Christ, and at once a burden and a reproach to the Christians, for, while to obey him was ungodly, to suffer at his hands was inglorious, since they did not even seem to be wronged, nor to gain by their sufferings the glorious title of martyr, inasmuch as the truth was in this case perverted, for while they suffered as Christians, they were supposed to be punished as heretics. Alas! how rich we were in misfortunes, for the fire consumed the beauties of the world.[δ] That which the palmerworm left did the locust eat, and that which the locust left did the caterpillar eat: then came the cankerworm,[ε] then, what next I know not, one evil springing up after another. But for what purpose should I give a tragic description of the evils of the time, and of the penalty exacted from us, or, if I must rather call it so, the testing and refining we endured? At any rate, we went through fire and water,[ζ] and have attained a place of refreshment by the good pleasure of God our Saviour.

4. To return to my original startingpoint. This was my field, when it was small and poor, unworthy not only of God, Who has been, and is cultivating the whole world with the fair seeds and doctrines of piety, but, apparently, even of any poor and needy man of slender means. Nay it did not deserve to be called a field, requiring neither barn nor threshingfloor, and not even worthy of the sickle; with neither heap nor sheaves, or small and untimely sheaves, like those on the housetop, which do not fill the hand of the reaper, nor call forth a blessing from them which go by.[η] Such was my field, such my harvest; great and well-eared and fat in the eyes of Him Who beholdeth hidden things, and becoming such a husbandman, its abundance springing from the valleys of souls well tilled with the Word: unrecognized however in public, and not collected together, but gathered in fragments, as an ear gleaned in the stubble,[θ] as gleaning-grapes in the vintage, where there is no cluster left. I think I may add, only too appropriately, I found Israel like a figtree in the wilderness,[α] and like one or two ripe grapes in an unripe cluster, preserved as a blessing from the Lord,[β] and a consecrated firstfruit, though small as yet and scanty, and not filling the mouth of the eater: and as an ensign on a hill,[γ] and as a beacon on a mountain, or any other solitary thing visible only to few. Such was its former poverty and dejection.

5. But since God, Who maketh poor and maketh rich, Who killeth and maketh alive;[δ] Who maketh and transformeth all things; Who turneth night into day,[ε] winter into spring, storm into calm, drought into abundance of rain; and often for the sake of the prayers[ζ] of one righteous man[η] sorely persecuted; Who lifteth up the meek on high, and bringeth the ungodly down to the ground;[θ] since God said to Himself, I have surely seen the affliction of Israel;[ι] and they shall no longer be further vexed with clay and brickmaking; and when He spake He visited, and in His visitation He saved, and led forth His people with a mighty hand and outstretched arm,[κ] by the hand of Moses and Aaron,[λ] His chosen—what is the result, and what wonders have been wrought? Those which books and monuments contain. For besides all the wonders by the way, and that mighty roar, to speak most concisely, Joseph came into Egypt alone,[μ] and soon after six hundred thousand depart from Egypt.[ν] What more marvellous than this? What greater proof of the generosity of God, when from men without means He wills to supply the means for public affairs? And the land of promise is distributed through one who was hated, and he who was sold[ξ] dispossesses nations, and is himself made a great nation, and that small offshoot becomes a luxuriant vine,[ο] so great that it reaches to the river, and is stretched out to the sea,[π] and spreads from border to border, and hides the mountains with the height of its glory and is exalted above the cedars, even the cedars of God, whatever we are to take these mountains and cedars to be.

6. Such then was once this flock, and such it is now, so healthy and well grown, and if it be not yet in perfection, it is advancing towards it by constant increase, and I pro-

α Ps. xciv. 17. β Ib. xciv. 17. γ *The second*, i.e., Valens. δ Joel i. 19. ε Ib. i. 4. ζ Ps. lxvi. 12. η Ib. cxxix. 6 sqq. θ Mic. vii. 1 (LXX.).

α Hos. ix. 10 (LXX.). β Isai. lxv. 8. γ Ib. xxx. 17. δ 1 Sam. ii. 6 sqq. ε Amos v. 8. ζ 1 Kings xviii. 42. η S. James v. 16, 17. θ Ps. cxlvii. 6. ι Exod. iii. 7. κ Ps. cxxxvi. 12. λ Ib. lxxvii. 20. μ Gen. xxxvii. 28. ν Exod. xii. 37. ξ Gen. xlix. 22. ο Hos. x. 1. π Ps. lxxx. 8 et seq.

phesy that it will advance. This is foretold me by the Holy Spirit, if I have any prophetic instinct and insight into the future. And from what has preceded I am able to be confident, and recognize this by reasoning, being the nursling of reason. For it was much more improbable that, from that condition, it should reach its present development, than that, as it now is, it should attain to the height of renown. For ever since it began to be gathered together, by Him Who quickeneth the dead,[α] bone to its bone, joint to joint, and the Spirit of life and regeneration was given to it in their dryness,[β] its entire resurrection has been, I know well, sure to be fulfilled: so that the rebellious should not exalt themselves,[γ] and that those who grasp at a shadow, or at a dream when one awaketh,[δ] or at the dispersing breezes, or at the traces of a ship in the water,[ε] should not think that they have anything. Howl, firtree, for the cedar is fallen![ζ] Let them be instructed by the misfortunes of others, and learn that the poor shall not alway be forgotten,[η] and that the Deity will not refrain, as Habakkuk says, from striking through the heads of the mighty ones[θ] in His fury—the Deity, Who has been struck through and impiously divided into Ruler and Ruled, in order to insult the Deity in the highest degree by degrading It, and oppress a creature by equality with Deity.

7. I seem indeed to hear that voice, from Him Who gathers together those who are broken, and welcomes the oppressed: Enlarge thy cords, break forth on the right hand and on the left, drive in thy stakes, spare not thy curtains.[ι] I have given thee up, and I will help thee. In a little wrath I smote thee, but with everlasting mercy I will glorify thee.[κ] The measure of His kindness exceeds the measure of His discipline. The former things were owing to our wickedness, the present things to the adorable Trinity: the former for our cleansing, the present for My glory, Who will glorify them that glorify Me,[λ] and I will move to jealousy them that move Me to jealousy. Behold this is sealed up with Me,[μ] and this is the indissoluble law of recompense. But thou didst surround thyself with walls and tablets and richly set stones, and long porticos and galleries, and didst shine and sparkle with gold, which thou didst, in part pour forth like water, in part treasure up like sand; not knowing that better is faith, with no other roof but the sky to cover it, than impiety rolling in wealth, and that three gathered together in the Name of the Lord[α] count for more with God than tens of thousands of those who deny the Godhead. Would you prefer the whole of the Canaanites to Abraham alone?[β] or the men of Sodom to Lot?[γ] or the Midianites to Moses,[δ] when each of these was a pilgrim and a stranger? How do the three hundred men with Gideon, who bravely lapped,[ε] compare with the thousands who were put to flight? Or the servants of Abraham, who scarcely exceeded them in number, with the many kings and the army of tens of thousands whom, few as they were, they overtook and defeated?[ζ] Or how do you understand the passage that though the number of the children of Israel be as the sand of the sea, a remnant shall be saved?[η] And again, I have left me seven thousand men, who have not bowed the knee to Baal?[θ] This is not the case; it is not? God has not taken pleasure in numbers.

8. Thou countest tens of thousands, God counts those who are in a state of salvation; thou countest the dust which is without number, I the vessels of election. For nothing is so magnificent in God's sight as pure doctrine, and a soul perfect in all the dogmas of the truth.—For there is nothing worthy of Him Who made all things, of Him by Whom are all things, and for Whom are all things,[ι] so that it can be given or offered to God: not merely the handiwork or means of any individual, but even if we wished to honour Him, by uniting together all the property and handiwork of all mankind. Do not I fill heaven and earth?[κ] saith the Lord! and what house will ye build Me? or what is the place of My rest?[λ] But, since man must needs fall short of what is worthy, I ask of you, as approaching it most nearly, piety, the wealth which is common to all and equal in My eyes, wherein the poorest may, if he be nobleminded, surpass the most illustrious. For this kind of glory depends upon purpose, not upon affluence. These things be well assured, I will accept at your hands.[μ] To tread[ν] My courts ye shall not proceed, but the feet of the meek[ξ] shall tread them, who have duly and sincerely acknowledged Me, and My only-begotten Word, and the Holy Spirit. How long will ye inherit My holy Mountain?[ο] How long

α Rom. iv. 17. β Ezek. xxxvii. 7, 10. γ Ps. lxvi. 7.
δ Ps. lxxiii. 20. ε Wisd. v. 9 sqq. ζ Zech. xi. 2.
η Ps. ix. 18. θ Hab. iii. 13. ι Isai. liv. 2.
κ Ib. liv. 8. λ 1 Sam. ii. 30. μ Deut. xxxii. 21, 34.

α S. Matt. xviii. 20. β Gen. xii. 6; xiii. 12. γ Ib. xix. 1.
δ Exod. ii. 15. ε Judg. vii. 5. ζ Gen. xiv. 14.
η Isai. x. 22; Rom. ix. 27. θ 1 Kings xix. 18; Rom. xi. 4.
ι 1 Cor. viii. 6. κ Jer. xxiii. 24. λ Isai. lxvi. 1. μ Ib. i. 12.
ν *To tread.* etc. The Arians for a time had been in possession of the churches of Constantinople.
ξ Isai. xxvi. 6 (LXX.). ο Ib. lvii. 13; lxv. 9.

shall My ark be among the heathen?[α] Now for a little longer ye indulge yourselves in that which belongs to others, and gratify your desires. For as ye have devised to reject Me, so will I also reject you,[β] saith the Lord Almighty.

9. This I seemed to hear Him say, and to see Him do, and besides, to hear Him shouting to His people, which once were few and scattered and miserable, and have now become many, and compact enough and enviable, Go through[γ] My gates[δ] and be ye enlarged. Must you always be in trouble and dwell in tents, while those who vex you rejoice exceedingly? And to the presiding Angels, for I believe, as John teaches me in his Revelation, that each Church has its guardian,[ε] Prepare ye the way of My people, and cast away the stones from the way,[ζ] that there may be no stumblingblock or hindrance for the people[η] in the divine road and entrance, now, to the temples made with hands,[θ] but soon after, to Jerusalem above,[ι] and the Holy of holies there,[κ] which will, I know, be the end of suffering and struggle to those who here bravely travel on the way. Among whom are ye also called to be Saints,[λ] a people of possession, a royal priesthood,[μ] the most excellent portion of the Lord, a whole river from a drop, a heavenly lamp from a spark, a tree from a grain of mustard seed,[ν] on which the birds come and lodge.

10. These we present to you, dear shepherds, these we offer to you, with these we welcome our friends, and guests, and fellow pilgrims. We have nothing fairer or more splendid to offer to you, for we have selected the greatest of all our possessions, that you may see that, strangers as we are, we are not in want, but though poor are making many rich.[ξ] If these things are small and unworthy of notice, I would fain learn what is greater and of more account. For, if it be no great thing to have established and strengthened with wholesome doctrines a city which is the eye of the universe, in its exceeding strength by sea and land, which is, as it were, the link between the Eastern and Western shores, in which the extremities of the world from every side meet together, and from which, as the common mart of the faith, they take their rise, a city borne hither and thither on the eddying currents of so many tongues, it will be long ere anything be considered great or worthy of esteem. But if it be indeed a subject for praise, allow to us some glory on this account, since we have contributed in some portion to these results which ye see.

11. Lift up thine eyes round about, and see,[α] thou critic of my words! See the crown which has been platted in return for the hirelings of Ephraim[β] and the crown of insolence; see the assembly of the presbyters, honoured for years and wisdom, the fair order of the deacons, who are not far from the same Spirit, the good conduct of the readers, the people's eagerness for teaching, both of men and women, who are equally renowned for virtue: the men, whether philosophers or simple folk, being alike wise in divine things, whether rulers or ruled, being all in this respect duly under rule; whether soldiers or nobles, students or men of letters, being all soldiers[γ] of God, though in all other respects meek, ready to fight for the Spirit, all reverencing the assembly above, to which we obtain an entrance, not by the mere letter, but by the quickening Spirit, all in very deed being men of reason, and worshippers of Him Who is in truth the Word: the women, if married, being united by a Divine rather than by a carnal bond; if unwedded and free, being entirely dedicated to God; whether young or old, some honourably advancing towards old age, others eagerly striving to remain immortal, being renewed by the best of hopes.

12. To those who platted this crown—that which I speak, I speak it not after the Lord,[δ] nevertheless I will say it—I also have given assistance. Some of them are the result of my words, not of those which we have uttered at random, but of those which we have loved—nor again of those which are meretricious, though the language and manners of the harlot have been slanderously attributed to me, but of those which are most grave. Some of them are the offspring and fruit of my Spirit, as the Spirit can beget those who rise superior to the body. To this I have no doubt that those who are kindly among you, nay all of you, will testify, since I have been the husbandman of all: and my sole reward is your confession. For we neither have, nor have had, any other object. For virtue, that it may remain virtue, is without reward, its eyes fixed alone on that which is good.

13. Would you have me say something still more venturesome? Do you see the tongues of the enemy made gentle, and those

α 1 Sam. vi. 1. β Hos. iv. 6.
γ *Go through*, etc. This passage refers to the restoration of the churches to the orthodox by Theodosius, Jan. 10, A.D. 381.
δ Isai. lxii. 10. ε Rev. ii. 1. ζ Isai. lxii. 10.
η Ib. lvii. 14. θ Acts vii. 48. ι Gal. iv. 26.
κ Heb. ix. 3, 24. λ Rom. i. 6.
μ 1 Pet. ii. 9. ν S. Matt. xiii. 21. ξ 2 Cor. vi. 10.

α Isai. lx. 4. β Ib. xxviii. 1 (LXX.).
γ 2 Tim. ii. 3. δ 2 Cor. xi. 17.

who made war upon the Godhead against me tranquillised? This also is the result of our Spirit, of our husbandry. For we are not undisciplined in our exercise of discipline, nor do we hurl insults, as many do, who assail not the argument but the speaker, and sometimes strive by their invective to hide the weakness of their reasoning; as the cuttlefish are said to cast forth ink before them, in order to escape from their pursuers, or themselves to hunt others when unperceived. But we show that our warfare is in behalf of Christ by fighting as Christ, the peaceable and meek,[α] Who has borne our infirmities, fought.[β] Though peaceable, we do not injure the word of truth, by yielding a jot, to gain a reputation for reasonableness; for we do not pursue that which is good by means of ill: and we are peaceable by the legitimate character of our warfare, confined as it is to our own limits, and the rules of the Spirit. Upon these points, this is my decision, and I lay down the law for all stewards of souls and dispensers of the Word: neither to exasperate others by their harshness, nor to render them arrogant by submissiveness: but to be of good words in treating of the Word, and in neither direction to overstep the mean.

14. But you are perhaps longing for me to give an exposition of the faith, in so far as I am able. For I shall myself be sanctified by the effort of memory, and the people also will be benefited, by its special delight in such discussions, and you will fully acknowledge it—unless we are the objects of groundless envy, as the rivals, in the manifestation of the truth, of those whom we do not excel. For as, of deep waters, some in the depths are utterly hidden, some foam against any obstruction, and hesitate a while before breaking (as they promise to our ears), some do actually break; so also, of those who are professors of the Divine philosophy—setting aside the utterly misguided—some keep their piety entirely secret and hidden within themselves, some are not far from the birth pangs, avoiding impiety, yet not speaking out their piety, either from cautious reserve in their teaching, or under pressure of fear, being themselves sound, as they say, in mind, but not making sound their people, as if they had been entrusted with the government of their own souls, but not of those of others; while there are some who make public their treasure, unable to restrain themselves from giving birth to their piety, and not considering that to be salvation which saves themselves alone, without bestowing upon others the overflow of their blessings. Among these would I range myself, and all who by my side have nobly dared to confess the truth.

15. One concise proclamation of our teaching, an inscription intelligible to all, is this people, which so sincerely worships the Trinity, that it would sooner sever anyone from this life, than sever one of the three from the Godhead: of one mind, of equal zeal, and united to one another, to us and to the Trinity by unity of doctrine. Briefly to run over its details: That which is without beginning, and is the beginning, and is with the beginning, is one God. For the nature of that which is without beginning does not consist in being without beginning or being unbegotten, for the nature of anything lies, not in what it is not but in what it is. It is the assertion of what is, not the denial of what is not. And the Beginning is not, because it is a beginning, separated from that which has no beginning. For its beginning is not its nature, any more than the being without beginning is the nature of the other. For these are the accompaniments of the nature, not the nature itself. That again which is with that which has no beginning, and with the beginning, is not anything else than what they are. Now, the name of that which has no beginning is the Father, and of the Beginning the Son, and of that which is with the Beginning, the Holy Ghost, and the three have one Nature—God. And the union is the Father from Whom and to Whom the order of Persons runs its course, not so as to be confounded, but so as to be possessed, without distinction of time, of will, or of power. For these things in our case produce a plurality of individuals, since each of them is separate both from every other quality, and from every other individual possession of the same quality. But to Those who have a simple nature, and whose essence is the same, the term One belongs in its highest sense.

16. Let us then bid farewell to all contentious shiftings and balancings of the truth on either side, neither, like the Sabellians, assailing the Trinity in the interest of the Unity, and so destroying the distinction by a wicked confusion; nor, like the Arians, assailing the Unity in the interest of the Trinity, and by an impious distinction overthrowing the Oneness. For our object is not to exchange one evil for another, but to ensure our attainment of that which is good. These are the playthings of the Wicked One,

α S. Matt. xi. 29. β Ib. viii. 17; Isai. liii. 4.

who is ever swaying our fortunes towards the evil. But we, walking along the royal road which lies between the two extremes, which is the seat of the virtues, as the authorities say, believe in the Father, the Son and the Holy Ghost, of one Substance and glory; in Whom also baptism has its perfection, both nominally and really (thou knowest who hast been initiated!); being a denial of atheism and a confession of Godhead; and thus we are regenerated, acknowledging the Unity in the Essence and in the undivided worship, and the Trinity in the Hypostases or Persons (which term some prefer.) And let not those who are contentious on these points utter their scandalous taunts, as if our faith depended on terms and not on realities. For what do you mean who assert the three Hypostases? Do you imply three Essences by the term? I am assured that you would loudly shout against those who do so. For you teach that the Essence of the Three is One and the same. What do you mean, who assert the Three Persons? Do you imagine a single compound sort of being, with three faces,[α] or of an entirely human form? Perish the thought! You too will loudly reply that he who thinks thus, will never see the face of God, whatever it may be. What is the meaning of the Hypostases of the one party, of the Persons of the other, to ask this further question? That They are three, Who are distinguished not by natures, but by properties.[β] Excellent. How could men agree and harmonize better than you do, even if there be a difference between the syllables you use? You see what a reconciler I am, bringing you back from the letter to the sense, as we do with the Old and New Testaments.

17. But, to resume: let us speak of the Unbegotten, the Begotten, and the Proceeding, if anyone likes to create names: for we shall have no fear of bodily conceptions attaching to Those who are not embodied, as the calumniators of the Godhead think. For the creature must be called God's, and this is for us a great thing, but God never. Otherwise I shall admit that God is a creature, if I become God, in the strict sense of the term. For this is the truth. If God, He is not a creature; for the creature ranks with us who are not Gods. And if a creature, he is not God, for he had a beginning in time. And there was a time when he who had a beginning was not. And that of which non-existence was its prior condition, has not being in the strict sense of the term. And how can that, which strictly has not being, be God? Not one single one, then, of the Three is a creature, nor, what is worse, came into being for my sake; for in that case he would be not only a creature, but inferior in honour to us. For, if I am for the glory of God, and he is for my sake, as the tongs for the waggon, the saw for the door, I am his superior in causality. For in whatever degree God is superior to creatures, in the same degree is he, who came into being for my sake, inferior to me who exist for God's sake.

18. Moreover, the Moabites and Ammonites must not even be allowed to enter[a] into the Church of God, I mean those sophistical, mischievous arguments which enquire curiously into the generation and inexpressible procession of God, and rashly set themselves in array against the Godhead: as if it were necessary that those things which it is beyond the power of language to set forth, must either be accessible to them alone, or else have no existence because they have not comprehended them. We however, following the Divine Scriptures, and removing out of the way of the blind the stumbling blocks contained in them, will cling to salvation, daring any and every thing rather than arrogance against God. As for the evidences, we leave them to others, since they have been set forth by many, and by ourselves also with no little care. And indeed, it would be a very shameful thing for me at this time to be gathering together proofs for what has all along been believed. For it is not the best order of things, first to teach and then to learn, even in matters which are small and of no consequence, and much more in those which are Divine and of such great importance. Nor, again, is it proper to the present occasion to explain and disentangle the difficulties of Scripture, a task requiring fuller and more careful consideration than our present purpose will allow. Such then, to sum up, is our teaching. I have entered into these details, with no intention of contending against the adversaries: for I have already often, even if it be imperfectly, fought out the question with them: but in order that I might exhibit to you the character of my teaching, that you might see whether I have not a share in the defence of your own, and do not take my stand on the same side, and opposed to the same enemies as yourselves.

α *With three faces* (or masks). A play upon the word πρόσωπον which is used in theology in the sense of Person.
β *Properties.* Cf. xliii. 30, note.

a Deut. xxiii. 3.

19. You have now, my friends, heard the defence of my presence here: if it be deserving of praise, thanks are due for it to God, and to you who called me; if it has fallen below your expectation, I give thanks even on this behalf. For I am assured that it has not been altogether deserving of censure, and am confident that you also admit this. Have we at all made a gain[α] of this people? Have we consulted at all our own interests, as I see is most often the case? Have we caused any vexation to the Church? To others possibly, with whose idea that they had gained judgment against us by default, we have joined issue in our argument; but in no wise, as far as I am aware, to you. I have taken no ox of yours,[β] says the great Samuel, in his contention against Israel on the subject of the king, nor any propitiation for your souls, the Lord is witness among you, nor this, nor that, proceeding at greater length, that I may not count up every particular; but I have kept the priesthood pure and unalloyed. And if I have loved power, or the height of a throne, or to tread Kings' courts, may I never possess any distinction, or if I gain it, may I be hurled from it.

20. What then do I mean? I am no proficient in virtue without reward, having not attained to so high a degree of virtue. Give me the reward of my labours. What reward? Not that which some, prone to any suspicion would suppose, but that which it is safe for me to seek. Give me a respite from my long labours; give honour to my foreign service; elect another in my place, the one who is being eagerly sought on your behalf, someone who is clean of hands, someone who is not unskilled in voice, someone who is able to gratify you on all points, and share with you the ecclesiastical cares; for this is especially the time for such. But behold, I pray you, the condition of this body, so drained by time, by disease, by toil. What need have you of a timid and unmanly old man, who is, so to speak, dying day by day, not only in body, but even in powers of mind, who finds it difficult to enter into these details before you? Disobey not the voice of your teacher: for indeed you have never yet disobeyed it. I am weary of being charged with my gentleness. I am weary of being assailed in words and in envy by enemies, and by our own. Some aim at my breast, and are less successful in their effort, for an open enemy can be guarded against. Others lie in wait for my back, and give greater pain, for the unsuspected blow is the more fatal. If again I have been a pilot, I have been one of the most skilful; the sea has been boisterous around us, boiling about the ship, and there has been considerable uproar among the passengers, who have always been fighting about something or another, and roaring against one another and the waves. What a struggle I have had, seated at the helm, contending alike with the sea and the passengers, to bring the vessel safe to land through this double storm? Had they in every way supported me, safety would have been hardly won, and when they were opposed to me, how has it been possible to avoid making shipwreck?

21. What more need be said? But how can I bear this holy war? For there has been said to be a holy, as well as a Persian, war.[α] How shall I unite and join together the hostile occupants of sees, and hostile pastors, and the people broken up along with, and opposed to them, as if by some chasms caused by earthquakes between neighbouring and adjoining places; or as, in pestilential diseases, befalls servants and members of the family, when the sickness readily attacks in succession one after another; and besides the very quarters of the globe are affected by the spirit of faction, so that East and West are arrayed on opposite sides, and bid fair to be severed in opinion no less than in position. How long are parties to be mine and yours, the old and the new, the more rational and the more spiritual, the more noble and the more ignoble, the more and the less numerous? I am ashamed of my old age, when, after being saved by Christ, I am called by the name of others.

22.[β] I cannot bear your horse races and theatres, and this rage for rivalry in expense and party spirit. We unharness, and harness ourselves on the other side, we neigh against each other, we almost beat the air, as they do, and fling the dust towards heaven, like those which are excited; and under other masks satisfy our own rivalry, and become evil arbiters of emulation, and senseless judges of affairs. To-day sharing the same thrones and opinions, if our leaders thus carry us along; to-morrow hostile alike in position and opinion, if the wind blows in the contrary direction. Amid the variations of friendship and hatred, our names also vary: and what is most

α 2 Cor. xii. 17.

β 1 Kings xii. 2.

α *A Holy War.* That against the Phocians to avenge their sacrilege at Delphi.

β § 22 is a comparison of Ecclesiastical partisanship to the emulation and party spirit connected with the horse races in the amphitheatre.

terrible, we are not ashamed to set forth contrary doctrines to the same audience; nor are we constant to the same objects, being rendered different at different times by our contentiousness. They are like the ebb and flow of some narrow strait.[α] For as when the children are at play in the midst of the market place, it would be most disgraceful and unbecoming for us to leave our household business, and join them; for children's toys are not becoming for old age: so, when others are contending, even if I am better informed than the majority, I could not allow myself to be one of them, rather than, as I now do, enjoy the freedom of obscurity. For, besides all this, my feeling is that I do not, on most points, agree with the majority, and cannot bear to walk in the same way. Rash and stupid though it may be, such is my feeling. That which is pleasant to others causes pain to me, and I am pleased with what is painful to others. So that I should not be surprised if I were even imprisoned as a disagreeable man, and thought by most men to be out of my senses, as is said to have been the case with one of the Greek philosophers, whose moderation exposed him to the charge of madness, because he laughed at everything, since he saw that the objects of the eager pursuit of the majority were ridiculous; or even be thought full of new wine as were in later days the disciples of Christ, because they spoke with tongues,[β] since men knew not that it was the power of the Spirit, and not a distraction of mind.

23. Now, consider the charges laid against us. You have been ruler of the church, it is said, for so long, and favoured by the course of time, and the influence of the sovereign, a most important matter. What change have we been able to notice? How many men have in days gone by used us outrageously? What sufferings have we failed to undergo? Ill-usage? Threats? Banishment? Plunder? Confiscation? The burning[γ] of priests at sea? The desecration of temples by the blood of the saints, till, instead of temples, they became charnel-houses? The public slaughter of aged Bishops, to speak more accurately, of Patriarchs? The denial of access to every place in the case of the godly alone? In fact any kind of suffering which could be mentioned? And for which of these have we requited the wrongdoers? For the wheel of fortune gave us the power of rightly treating those who so treated us, and our persecutors ought to have received a lesson. Apart from all other things, speaking only of our experiences, not to mention your own, have we not been persecuted, maltreated, driven from churches, houses, and, most terrible of all, even from the deserts? Have we not had to endure an enraged people, insolent governors, the disregard of Emperors and their decrees? What was the result? We became stronger, and our persecutors took to flight. That was actually the case. The power to requite them seemed to me a sufficient vengeance on those who had wronged us. These men thought otherwise; for they are exceedingly exact and just in requiting: and accordingly they demand[α] what the state of things permits. What governor, they say, has been fined? What populace chastised? What ringleaders of the populace? What fear of ourselves have we been able to inspire for the future?

24. Perhaps[β] we may be reproached, as we have been before, with the exquisite character of our table, the splendour of our apparel, the officers who precede us, our haughtiness to those who meet us. I was not aware that we ought to rival the consuls, the governors, the most illustrious generals, who have no opportunity of lavishing their incomes; or that our belly ought to hunger for the enjoyment of the goods of the poor, and to expend their necessaries on superfluities, and belch forth over the altars. I did not know that we ought to ride on splendid horses, and drive in magnificent carriages, and be preceded by a procession and surrounded by applause, and have everyone make way for us, as if we were wild beasts, and open out a passage so that our approach might be seen afar. If these sufferings have been endured, they have now passed away: Forgive me this wrong.[γ] Elect another who will please the majority: and give me my desert, my country life, and my God, Whom alone I may have to please, and shall please by my simple life. It is a painful thing to be deprived of speeches and conferences, and public gatherings, and applause like that which now lends wings to my thoughts, and relatives, and friends and honours, and the beauty and grandeur of the city, and its brilliancy which dazzles those who look at the surface without investigating the inner nature of things; but yet not so painful as being clamoured against and besmirched amid public disturbances and agitations, which trim their sails to the popular breeze. For they seek not for priests, but for orators, not

α *Narrow strait*, lit. Euripus. β Acts ii. 4.
γ *The burning*, etc., cf. This was by order of Valens.

α *Demand.* After all these persecutions, some thought S. Gregory ought to have used his influence with Theodosius to requite or punish the former persecutors of the orthodox.
β *Perhaps*, an ironical passage. γ 2 Cor. xii. 13.

for stewards of souls, but for treasurers of money, not for pure offerers of the sacrifice, but for powerful patrons. I will say a word in their defence: we have thus trained them, by becoming all things to all men,[α] whether to save or destroy all, I know not.

25. What say you? Are you persuaded, have you been overcome by my words? Or must I use stronger terms in order to persuade you? Yea by the Trinity Itself, Whom you and I alike worship, by our common hope, and for the sake of the unity of this people, grant me this favour; dismiss me with your prayers; let this be the proclamation of my contest; give me my certificate of retirement, as sovereigns do to their soldiers; and, if you will, with a favourable testimony, that I may enjoy the honour of it; if not, just as you please; this will make no difference to me, until God sees what my case really is. What successor then shall we elect? God will provide Himself[β] a shepherd for the office, as He once provided a lamb for a burnt-offering. I only make this further request,—let him be one who is the object of envy, not the object of pity; not one who yields everything to all, but one who can on some points offer resistance for the sake of what is best: for though the one is most pleasant, the other is most profitable. So do you prepare for me your addresses of dismissal: I will now bid you farewell.

26. Farewell my Anastasia,[γ] whose name is redolent of piety: for thou hast raised up for us the doctrine which was in contempt: farewell, scene of our common victory, modern Shiloh,[δ] where the tabernacle was first fixed, after being carried about in its wanderings for forty years in the wilderness. Farewell likewise, grand and renowned temple, our new inheritance, whose greatness is now due to the Word, which once wast a Jebus,[ε] and hast now been made by us a Jerusalem. Farewell, all ye others, inferior only to this in beauty, scattered through the various parts of the city, like so many links, uniting together each your own neighbourhood, which have been filled with worshippers of whose existence we had despaired, not by me, in my weakness, but by the grace which was with me.[ζ] Farewell, ye Apostles,[η] noble settlers here, my masters in the strife; if I have not often kept festival with you, it has been possibly due to the Satan[α] which I, like S. Paul,[β] who was one of you, carry about in my body for my own profit, and which is the cause of my now leaving you. Farewell, my throne, envied and perilous height; farewell assembly of high priests, honoured by the dignity and age of its priests, and all ye others ministers of God round the holy table, drawing nigh to the God Who draws nigh to you.[γ] Farewell, choirs of Nazarites, harmonies of the Psalter, night-long stations, venerable virgins, decorous matrons, gatherings of widows and orphans, and ye eyes of the poor, turned towards God and towards me. Farewell, hospitable and Christ-loved dwellings, helpers of my infirmity. Farewell, ye lovers of my discourses, in your eagerness and concourse, ye pencils seen and unseen, and thou balustrade, pressed upon by those who thrust themselves forward to hear the word. Farewell, Emperors, and palace, and ministers and household of the Emperor, whether faithful or not to him, I know not, but for the most part, unfaithful to God. Clap your hands, shout aloud, extol your orator to the skies. This pestilent and garrulous tongue has ceased to speak to you. Though it will not utterly cease to speak: for it will fight with hand and ink: but for the present we have ceased to speak.

27. Farewell, mighty Christ-loving city. I will testify to the truth, though thy zeal be not according to knowledge.[δ] Our separation renders us more kindly. Approach the truth: be converted at this late hour. Honour God more than you have been wont to do. It is no disgrace to change, while it is fatal to cling to evil. Farewell, East and West, for whom and against whom I have had to fight; He is witness, Who will give you peace, if but a few would imitate my retirement. For those who resign their thrones will not also lose God, but will have the seat on high, which is far more exalted and secure. Last of all, and most of all, I will cry,—farewell ye Angels, guardians of this church, and of my presence and pilgrimage, since our affairs are in the hands of God. Farewell, O Trinity, my meditation, and my glory. Mayest Thou be preserved by those who are here, and preserve them, my people: for they are mine, even if I have my place assigned elsewhere; and may I learn that Thou art ever extolled and glorified in word and conduct.

α 1 Cor. ix. 22. β Gen. xxii. 8.
γ *Anastasia.* The little church "of the Resurrection" in which the orthodox Christians worshipped with S. Gregory at first on his arrival, while the churches of the city were held by the heretics.
δ Josh. xviii. 1. ε 1 Chron. xi. 4. ζ 1 Cor. xv. 10.
η *Apostles.* The Church of the Holy Apostles, to which Constantius translated the relics of SS. Andrew, Luke and Timothy.

α *Satan, i.e.,* "Thorn in the flesh, a messenger of Satan"—in S. Gregory's case serious ill health.
β Cor. xvii. 7. γ S. James iv. 8. δ Rom. x. 2.

My children, keep, I pray you, that which is committed to your trust.[α] Remember my stonings.[β] The grace of our Lord Jesus Christ be with you all. Amen.

INTRODUCTION TO ORATION XLIII.

The Panegyric on S. Basil.

S. Basil died January 1, A.D. 379. A serious illness, in addition to other causes, prevented S. Gregory from being present at his funeral (Epist. 79). Benoît holds that an expression (Epitaph, cxix. 38) in which S. Gregory says that his "lips are fettered" proves that he was still in retirement at Seleucia. This is an unwarranted deduction. In this Oration, § 2, the Saint, alluding to his illness in disparaging terms, alleges his labours at Constantinople as a more pressing reason for his absence: and says that he undertook the task according to the judgment of S. Basil. This implies that S. Gregory went to Constantinople before the death of S. Basil, or that he had then been influenced by his friend's advice and was on the point of setting out—more probably the former, as we may be sure that, if S. Gregory had been still at Seleucia, no reason but physical incapacity would have kept him from his friend's side. His pressing duties at Constantinople and the difficulties of the long journey were the "other causes" of his letter to S. Gregory of Nyssa: and we know that he suffered from serious illness at Constantinople (Carm. xi. 887. Orat. xxiii. 1). S. Gregory left Constantinople in June, A.D. 381, and Tillemont places the date of this Oration soon after his return to Nazianzus. Benoît thinks that it was probably delivered on the anniversary of S. Basil's death. The Oration, as all critics are agreed, is one of great power and beauty. Its length (62 pages folio), the physical weakness of the speaker, and the limits of the endurance of even an interested audience, incline us to suppose that it was not spoken in its present form. We cannot well set aside expressions which clearly point to actual delivery, but it may have been amplified later.

Funeral Oration on the Great S. Basil, Bishop of Cæsarea in Cappadocia.

1. It has then been ordained that the great Basil, who used so constantly to furnish me with subjects for my discourses, of which he was quite as proud as any other man of his own, should himself now furnish me with the grandest subject which has ever fallen to the lot of an orator. For I think that if anyone desired, in making trial of his powers of eloquence, to test them by the standard of that one of all his subjects which he preferred (as painters do with epoch-making pictures), he would choose that which stood first of all others, but would set aside this as beyond the powers of human eloquence. So great a task is the praise of such a man, not only to me, who have long ago laid aside all thought of emulation, but even to those who live for eloquence, and whose sole object is the gaining of glory by subjects like this. Such is my opinion, and, as I persuade myself, with perfect justice. But I know not what subject I can treat with eloquence, if not this; or what greater favour I can do to myself, to the admirers of virtue, or to eloquence itself, than express our admiration for this man. To me it is the discharge of a most sacred debt. And our speech is a debt beyond all others due to those who have been gifted, in particular, with powers of speech. To the admirers of virtue a discourse is at once a pleasure and an incentive to virtue. For when[a] I have learned the praises of men, I have a distinct idea of their progress: now, there is none of us all, within whose power it is not to attain to any point whatsoever in that progress. As for eloquence itself, in either case, all must go well with it. For, if the discourse be almost worthy of its subject—eloquence will have given an exhibition of its power: if it fall far short of it, as must be the case when the praises of Basil are being set forth, by an actual demonstration of its incapacity, it will have declared the superiority of the excellences of its subject to all expression in words.

2. These are the reasons which have urged me to speak, and to address myself to this contest. And at my late appearance, long after his praises have been set forth by so many, who have publicly and privately done him honour, let no one be surprised. Yea, may I be pardoned by that divine soul, the object of my constant reverence! And as, when he was amongst us, he constantly corrected me in many points, according to the rights of a friend and the still higher law; for I am not ashamed to say this, for he was a standard of virtue to us all; so now, looking down upon me from above, he will treat me with indul-

α 1 Tim. vi. 20.

β Col. iv. 18.

a *For when*, etc. This seems to be the sense of an admittedly difficult sentence.

gence. I ask pardon too of any here who are among his warmest admirers, if indeed anyone can be warmer than another, and we are not all abreast in our zeal for his good fame. For it is not contempt which has caused me to fall short of what might have been expected of me: nor have I been so regardless of the claims of virtue or of friendship; nor have I thought that to praise him befitted any other more than me. No! my first reason was, that I shrunk from this task, for I will say the truth, as priests[α] do, who approach their sacred duties before being cleansed both in voice and mind. In the second place, I remind you, though you know it well, of the task[β] in which I was engaged on behalf of the true doctrine, which had been properly forced upon me, and had carried me from home, according, as I suppose, to the will of God, and certainly according to the judgment of our noble champion of the truth, the breath of whose life was pious doctrine alone, such as promotes the salvation of the whole world. As for my bodily health, I ought not, perhaps, to dare to mention it, when my subject is a man so doughty in his conquest of the body, even before his removal hence, and who maintained that no powers of the soul should suffer hindrance from this our fetter.[γ] So much for my defence. I do not think I need labour it further, in speaking of him to you who know so clearly my affairs. I must now proceed with my eulogy, commending myself to his God, in order that my commendations may not prove an insult to the man, and that I may not lag far behind all others; even though we all equally fall as far short of his due, as those who look upon the heavens or the rays of the Sun.

3. Had I seen him to be proud of his birth, and the rights of birth, or any of those infinitely little objects of those whose eyes are on the ground, we should have had to inspect a new catalogue of the Heroes. What details as to his ancestors might I not have laid under contribution! Nor would even history have had any advantage over me, since I claim this advantage, that his celebrity depends, not upon fiction or legend, but upon actual facts attested by many witnesses. On his father's side Pontus offers to me many details, in no wise inferior to its wonders of old time, of which all history and poesy are full;[δ] there are many others concerned with this my native land, of illustrious men of Cappadocia, renowned for its youthful progeny,[α] no less than for its horses. Accordingly we match with his father's family that of his mother. What family owns more numerous, or more illustrious generals and governors, or court officials, or again, men of wealth, and lofty thrones, and public honours, and oratorical renown? If it were permitted me to wish to mention them, I would make nothing of the Pelopidæ and Cecropidæ, the Alcmæonids, the Æacidæ, and Heracleidæ, and other most noble families: inasmuch as they, in default of public merit in their house, betake themselves to the region of uncertainty, claiming demigods and divinities, merely mythical personages, as the glory of their ancestors, whose most vaunted details are incredible, and those which we can believe are an infamy.

4. But since our subject is a man who has maintained that each man's nobility is to be judged of according to his own worth, and that, as forms and colours, and likewise our most celebrated and most infamous horses, are tested by their own properties, so we too ought not to be depicted in borrowed plumes; after mentioning one or two traits, which, though inherited from his ancestors, he made his own by his life, and which are specially likely to give pleasure to my hearers, I will then proceed to deal with the man himself. Different families and individuals have different points of distinction and interest, great or small, which, like a patrimony of longer or shorter descent, come down to posterity: the distinction of his family on either side was piety, which I now proceed to display.

5. There was a persecution, the most frightful and severe of all; I mean, as you know, the persecution of Maximinus, which, following closely upon those which immediately preceded it, made them all seem gentle, by its excessive audacity, and by its eagerness to win the crown of violence in impiety. It was overcome by many of our champions, who wrestled with it to the death, or well-nigh to the death, with only life enough left in them to survive their victory, and not pass away in the midst of the struggle; remaining to be trainers[β] in virtue, living witnesses, breathing trophies, silent exhortations, among whose numerous ranks were found Basil's paternal ancestors, upon whom,

α *As priests*, or, more generally, "as those who approach our temples." In the E. there were lavers at the entrance to the churches for the ablutions of intending worshippers.

β *Of the task*, i.e., of restoring the orthodox faith in Constantinople.

γ *Fetter*, i.e., the body.

δ *History and poesy*, e.g., Xenophon, Polybius, and Apollonius.

α *Renowned*, etc. Cf. Homer, Od. ix. 27.

β *Trainers*, lit. "anointers"—those who physically and by their advice prepared athletes for their exercises.

in their practice of every form of piety, that period bestowed many a fair garland. So prepared and determined were they to bear readily all those things on account of which Christ crowns those who have imitated His struggle on our behalf.

6. But since their strife must needs be lawful, and the law of martyrdom alike forbids us voluntarily to go to meet it (in consideration for the persecutors, and for the weak) or to shrink from it if it comes upon us; for the former shows foolhardiness, the latter cowardice; in this respect they paid due honour to the Lawgiver; but what was their device, or rather, to what were they led by the Providence which guided them in all things? They betook themselves to a thicket on the mountains of Pontus, of which there are many deep ones of considerable extent, with very few comrades of their flight, or attendants upon their needs. Let others marvel at the length of time, for their flight was exceedingly prolonged, to about seven years, or a little more, and their mode of life, delicately nurtured as they were, was straitened and unusual, as may be imagined, with the discomfort of its exposure to frost and heat and rain: and the wilderness allowed no fellowship or converse with friends: a great trial to men accustomed to the attendance and honour of a numerous retinue. But I will proceed to speak of what is still greater and more extraordinary: nor will anyone fail to credit it, save those who, in their feeble and dangerous judgment, think little of persecutions and dangers for Christ's sake.

7. These noble men, suffering from the lapse of time, and feeling a distaste for ordinary food, felt a longing for something more appetising. They did not indeed speak as Israel did,[α] for they were not murmurers[β] like them, in their afflictions in the desert, after the escape from Egypt—that Egypt would have been better for them than the wilderness, in the bountiful supply of its flesh-pots, and other dainties which they had left behind them there, for the brickmaking and the clay seemed nothing to them then in their folly—but in a more pious and faithful manner. For why, said they, is it incredible that the God of wonders, who bountifully fed[γ] in the wilderness his homeless and fugitive people, raining bread upon them, and abounding in quails, nourishing them not only with necessaries, but even with luxuries: that He, Who divided the sea,[δ] and stayed the sun,[ε] and parted the river, with all the other things that He has done; for under such circumstances the mind is wont to recur to history, and sing the praises of God's many wonders: that He, they went on, should feed us champions of piety with dainties to-day? Many animals which have escaped the tables of the rich, have their lairs in these mountains, and many eatable birds fly over our longing heads, any of which can surely be caught at the mere fiat of Thy will! At these words, their quarry lay before them, with food come of its own accord, a complete banquet prepared without effort, stags appearing all at once from some place in the hills. How splendid they were! how fat! how ready for the slaughter! It might almost be imagined that they were annoyed at not having been summoned earlier. Some of them made signs to draw others after them, the rest followed their lead. Who pursued and drove them? No one. What riders? What kind of dogs, what barking, or cry, or young men who had occupied the exits according to the rules of the chase? They were the prisoners of prayer and righteous petition. Who has known such a hunt among men of this, or any day?

8. O what a wonder! They were themselves stewards of the chase; what they would, was caught by the mere will to do so; what was left, they sent away to the thickets, for another meal. The cooks were extemporised, the dinner exquisite, the guests were grateful for this wonderful foretaste of their hopes. And hence they grew more earnest in their struggle, in return for which they had received this blessing. Such is my history. And do thou, my persecutor, in thy admiration for legends, tell of thy huntresses,[α] and Orions, and Actæons, those ill-fated hunters, and the hind substituted for the maiden,[β] if any such thing rouses thee to emulation, and if we grant that this story is no legend. The sequel of the tale is too disgraceful. For what is the benefit of the exchange, if a maiden is saved to be taught to murder her guests, and learn to requite humanity with inhumanity? Let this one instance, such as it is, chosen out of many, represent the rest, as far as I am concerned. I have not related it to contribute to his reputation: for neither does the sea stand in need of the rivers which flow into it, many and great though they be, nor does the present subject of my praises need any contributions to his fair fame. No! my object is to exhibit

α Exod. xvi. 2 et seq. β 1 Cor. x. 10. γ Exod. xvi. 13. δ Ib. xiv. 21. ε Josh. iii. 16; x. 12.

α *Huntresses*, esp. Artemis, a passion for whom was fatal to Orion and Actæon.
β *The maiden*, Iphigenia, daughter of Agamemnon.

the character of his ancestors, and the example before his eyes, which he so far excelled. For if other men find it a great additional advantage to receive somewhat of their honour from their forefathers, it is a greater thing for him to have made such an addition to the original stock that the stream seems to have run uphill.

9. The union of his parents, cemented as it was by a community of virtue, no less than by cohabitation, was notable for many reasons, especially for generosity to the poor, for hospitality, for purity of soul as the result of self-discipline, for the dedication to God of a portion of their property, a matter not as yet so much cared for by most men, as it now has grown to be, in consequence of such previous examples, as have given distinction to it, and for all those other points, which have been published throughout Pontus and Cappadocia, to the satisfaction of many: in my opinion, however, their greatest claim to distinction is the excellence of their children. Legend indeed has its instances of men whose children were many and beautiful, but it is practical experience which has presented to us these parents, whose own character, apart from that of their children, was sufficient for their fair fame, while the character of their children would have made them, even without their own eminence in virtue, to surpass all men by the excellence of their children. For the attainment of distinction by one or two of their offspring might be ascribed to their nature; but when all are eminent, the honour is clearly due to those who brought them up. This is proved by the blessed roll of priests and virgins, and of those who, when married, have allowed nothing in their union to hinder them from attaining an equal repute, and so have made the distinction between them to consist in the condition, rather than in the mode of their life.

10. Who has not known Basil, our archbishop's father, a great name to everyone, who attained a father's prayer, if anyone, I will not say as no one, ever did? For he surpassed all in virtue, and was only prevented by his son from gaining the first prize. Who has not known Emmelia, whose name was a forecast of what she became, or else whose life was an exemplification of her name? For she had a right to the name which implies gracefulness, and occupied, to speak concisely, the same place among women, as her husband among men. So that, when it was decided that he, in whose honour we are met, should be given to men to submit to the bondage of nature, as anyone of old has been given by God for the common advantage, it was neither fitting that he should be born of other parents, nor that they should possess another son: and so the two things suitably concurred. I have now, in obedience to the Divine law which bids us to pay all honour to parents, bestowed the firstfruits of my praises upon those whom I have commemorated, and proceed to treat of Basil himself, premising this, which I think will seem true to all who knew him, that we only need his own voice to pronounce his eulogium. For he is at once a brilliant subject for praise, and the only one whose powers of speech make him worthy of treating it. Beauty indeed and strength and size, in which I see that most men rejoice, I concede to anyone who will—not that even in these points he was inferior to any of those men of small minds who busy themselves about the body, while he was still young, and had not yet reduced the flesh by austerity—but that I may avoid the fate of unskilful athletes, who waste their strength in vain efforts after minor objects, and so are worsted in the crucial struggle, whose results are victory and the distinction of the crown. The praise, then, which I shall claim for him is based upon grounds which no one, I think, will consider superfluous, or beyond the scope of my oration.

11. I take it as admitted by men of sense, that the first of our advantages is education; and not only this our more noble form of it, which disregards rhetorical ornaments and glory, and holds to salvation, and beauty in the objects of our contemplation: but even that external culture which many Christians ill-judgingly abhor, as treacherous and dangerous, and keeping us afar from God. For as we ought not to neglect the heavens, and earth, and air, and all such things, because some have wrongly seized upon them, and honour God's works instead of God: but to reap what advantage we can from them for our life and enjoyment, while we avoid their dangers; not raising creation, as foolish men do, in revolt against the Creator, but from the works of nature apprehending the Worker,[α] and, as the divine apostle says, bringing into captivity every thought to Christ:[β] and again, as we know that neither fire, nor food, nor iron, nor any other of the elements, is of itself most useful, or most harmful, except according to the will of those who use it; and as we have compounded healthful drugs from certain of the reptiles; so from secular literature we

α Rom. i. 20, 25. β 2 Cor. x. 5.

have received principles of enquiry and speculation, while we have rejected their idolatry, terror, and pit of destruction. Nay, even these have aided us in our religion, by our perception of the contrast between what is worse and what is better, and by gaining strength for our doctrine from the weakness of theirs. We must not then dishonour education, because some men are pleased to do so, but rather suppose such men to be boorish and uneducated, desiring all men to be as they themselves are, in order to hide themselves in the general, and escape the detection of their want of culture. But come now, and, after this sketch of our subject and these admissions, let us contemplate the life of Basil.

12. In his earliest years he was swathed and fashioned, in that best and purest fashioning which the Divine David speaks of as proceeding day by day,[a] in contrast with that of the night, under his great father, acknowledged in those days by Pontus, as its common teacher of virtue. Under him then, as life and reason grew and rose together, our illustrious friend was educated: not boasting of a Thessalian mountain cave, as the workshop of his virtue, nor of some braggart Centaur,[β] the tutor of the heroes of his day: nor was he taught under such tuition to shoot hares, and run down fawns, or hunt stags, or excel in war, or in breaking colts, using the same person as teacher and horse at once; nor nourished on the fabulous marrows of stags and lions, but he was trained in general education, and practised in the worship of God, and, to speak concisely, led on by elementary instructions to his future perfection. For those who are successful in life or in letters only, while deficient in the other, seem to me to differ in nothing from one-eyed men, whose loss is great, but their deformity greater, both in their own eyes, and in those of others. While those who attain eminence in both alike, and are ambidextrous, both possess perfection, and pass their life with the blessedness of heaven. This is what befell him, who had at home a model of virtue in well-doing, the very sight of which made him excellent from the first. As we see foals and calves skipping beside their mothers from their birth, so he too, running close beside his father in foal-like wantonness, without being left far behind in his lofty impulses toward virtue, or, if you will, sketching out and showing traces of the future beauty of his virtue, and drawing the outlines of perfection before the time of perfection arrived.

13. When sufficiently trained at home, as he ought to fall short in no form of excellence, and not be surpassed by the busy bee, which gathers what is most useful from every flower, he set out for the city of Cæsarea,[a] to take his place in the schools there, I mean this illustrious city of ours, for it was the guide and mistress of my studies, the metropolis of letters, no less than of the cities which she excels and reigns over: and if any one were to deprive her of her literary power, he would rob her of her fairest and special distinction. Other cities take pride in other ornaments, of ancient or of recent date, that they may have something to be described or to be seen. Letters form our distinction here, and are our badge, as if upon the field of arms or on the stage. His subsequent life let those detail who trained him, or enjoyed his training, as to what he was to his masters, what he was to his classmates, equalling the former, surpassing the latter in every form of culture, what renown he won in a short time from all, both of the common people, and of the leaders of the state; by showing both a culture beyond his years, and a steadfastness of character beyond his culture. An orator among orators, even before the chair of the rhetoricians,[β] a philosopher among philosophers, even before the doctrines of philosophers: highest of all a priest among Christians even before the priesthood. So much deference was paid to him in every respect by all. Eloquence was his by-work, from which he culled enough to make it an assistance to him in Christian philosophy, since power of this kind is needed to set forth the objects of our contemplation. For a mind which cannot express itself is like the motion of a man in a lethargy. His pursuit was philosophy, and breaking from the world, and fellowship with God, by concerning himself, amid things below, with things above, and winning, where all is unstable and fluctuating, the things which are stable and remain.

14. Thence to Byzantium, the imperial city of the East, for it was distinguished by the eminence of its rhetorical and philosophic teachers, whose most valuable lessons he soon assimilated by the quickness and force of his powers: thence he was sent by God, and by his generous craving for culture, to Athens the home of letters. Athens, which has been to me, if to

a Ps. cxxxix. 16.
β *Centaur*. Alluding to Chiron, the tutor of Achilles.

a *Cæsarea*. the Cappadocian city, as seems plain from the context. Yet Tillemont and Billius incline to think Cæsarea in Palestine is meant.
β *Chair*, etc., Before he had studied rhetoric and philosophy.

any one, a city truly of gold, and the patroness of all that is good. For it brought me to know Basil more perfectly, though he had not been unknown to me before; and in my pursuit of letters, I attained to happiness; and in another fashion had the same experience as Saul,[α] who, seeking his father's asses, found a kingdom, and gained incidentally what was of more importance than the object which he had in view. Hitherto my course has been clear, leading me in my encomiums along a level and easy, in fact, a king's highway: henceforth I know not how to speak or whither to turn: for my task is becoming arduous. For here I am anxious, and seize this opportunity to add from my own experience somewhat to my speech, and to dwell a little upon the recital of the causes and circumstances which originated our friendship, or to speak more strictly, our unity of life and nature. For as our eyes are not ready to turn from attractive objects, and, if we violently tear them away, are wont to return to them again; so do we linger in our description of what is most sweet to us. I am afraid of the difficulty of the undertaking. I will try, however, to use all possible moderation. And if I am at all overpowered by my regret, pardon this most righteous of all feelings, the absence of which would be a great loss, in the eyes of men of feeling.

15. We were contained by Athens, like two branches of some river-stream, for after leaving the common fountain of our fatherland, we had been separated in our varying pursuit of culture, and were now again united by the impulsion of God no less than by our own agreement. I preceded him by a little, but he soon followed me, to be welcomed with great and brilliant hope. For he was versed in many languages, before his arrival, and it was a great thing for either of us to outstrip the other in the attainment of some object of our study. And I may well add, as a seasoning to my speech, a short narrative, which will be a reminder to those who know it, a source of information to those who do not. Most of the young men at Athens in their folly are mad after rhetorical skill—not only those who are ignobly born and unknown, but even the noble and illustrious, in the general mass of young men difficult to keep under control. They are just like men devoted to horses and exhibitions, as we see, at the horse-races; they leap,[β] they shout, raise clouds of dust, they drive in their seats, they beat the air, (instead of the horses) with their fingers as whips, they yoke and unyoke the horses, though they are none of theirs: they readily exchange with one another drivers, horses, positions, leaders: and who are they who do this? Often poor and needy fellows, without the means of support for a single day. This is just how the students feel in regard to their own tutors, and their rivals, in their eagerness to increase their own numbers and thereby enrich them. The matter is absolutely absurd and silly. Cities, roads, harbours, mountain tops, coastlines, are seized upon—in short, every part of Attica, or of the rest of Greece, with most of the inhabitants; for even these they have divided between the rival parties.

16. Whenever any newcomer arrives, and falls into the hands of those who seize upon him, either by force or willingly, they observe this Attic law, of combined jest and earnest. He is first conducted to the house of one of those who were the first to receive him, or of his friends, or kinsmen, or countrymen, or of those who are eminent in debating power, and purveyors of arguments, and therefore especially honoured among them; and their reward consists in the gain of adherents. He is next subjected to the raillery of any one who will, with the intention I suppose, of checking the conceit of the newcomers, and reducing them to subjection at once. The raillery is of a more insolent or argumentative kind, according to the boorishness or refinement of the railer: and the performance, which seems very fearful and brutal to those who do not know it, is to those who have experienced it very pleasant and humane: for its threats are feigned rather than real. Next, he is conducted in procession through the market place to the bath. The procession is formed by those who are charged with it in the young man's honour, who arrange themselves in two ranks separated by an interval, and precede him to the bath. But when they have approached it, they shout and leap wildly, as if possessed, shouting that they must not advance, but stay, since the bath will not admit them; and at the same time frighten the youth by furiously knocking at the doors: then allowing him to enter, they now present him with his freedom, and receive him after the bath as an equal, and one of themselves. This they consider the most pleasant part of the ceremony, as being a speedy exchange and relief from annoyances. On this occasion I not only refused to put to shame my friend the great Basil, out of respect for the gravity of

α 1 Sam. ix. 3.

β *They leap*, etc. This passage refers to the spectators who unite in sympathy with, and imitate as far as possible, in their excitement, the actions of, those who drive the chariots in the races.

his character, and the ripeness of his reasoning powers, but also persuaded all the rest of the students to treat him likewise, who happened not to know him. For he was from the first respected by most of them, his reputation having preceded him. The result was that he was the only one to escape the general rule, and be accorded a greater honour than belongs to a freshman's position.

17. This was the prelude of our friendship. This was the kindling spark of our union: thus we felt the wound of mutual love. Then something of this kind happened, for I think it right not to omit even this. I find the Armenians to be not a simple race, but very crafty and cunning. At this time some of his special comrades and friends, who had been intimate with him even in the early days of his father's instruction, for they were members of his school, came up to him under the guise of friendship, but with envious, and not kindly intent, and put to him questions of a disputatious rather than rational kind, trying to overwhelm him at the first onset, having known his original natural endowments, and unable to brook the honour he had then received. For they thought it a strange thing that they who had put on their gowns, and been exercised in shouting, should not get the better of one who was a stranger and a novice. I also, in my vain love for Athens, and trusting to their professions without perceiving their envy, when they were giving way, and turning their backs, since I was indignant that in their persons the reputation of Athens should be destroyed, and so speedily put to shame, supported the young men, and restored the argument; and by the aid of my additional weight, for in such cases a small addition makes all the difference, and, as the poet says, "made equal their heads in the fray." [α] But, when I perceived the secret motive of the dispute, which could no longer be kept under, and was at last clearly exposed, I at once drew back, and retired from their ranks, to range myself on his side, and made the victory decisive. He was at once delighted at what had happened, for his sagacity was remarkable, and being filled with zeal, to describe him fully in Homer's language, he pursued in confusion [β] with argument those valiant youths, and, smiting them with syllogisms, only ceased when they were utterly routed, and he had distinctly won the honours due to his power. Thus was kindled again, no longer a spark, but a manifest and conspicuous blaze of friendship.

18. Their efforts having thus proved fruitless, while they severely blamed their own rashness, they cherished such annoyance against me that it broke out into open hostility, and a charge of treachery, not only to them, but to Athens herself: inasmuch as they had been confuted and put to shame at the first onset, by a single student, who had not even had time to gain confidence. He moreover, according to that human feeling, which makes us, when we have all at once attained to the high hopes which we have cherished, look upon their results as inferior to our expectation, he, I say, was displeased and annoyed, and could take no delight in his arrival. He was seeking for what he had expected, and called Athens an empty happiness. I however tried to remove his annoyance, both by argumentative encounter, and by the enchantments of reasoning; alleging, as is true, that the disposition of a man cannot at once be detected, without a long time and more constant association, and that culture likewise is not made known to those who make trial of her, after a few efforts and in a short time. In this way I restored his cheerfulness, and by this mutual experience, he was the more closely united to me.

19. And when, as time went on, we acknowledged our mutual affection, and that philosophy [a] was our aim, we were all in all to one another, housemates, messmates, intimates, with one object in life, or an affection for each other ever growing warmer and stronger. Love for bodily attractions, since its objects are fleeting, is as fleeting as the flowers of spring. For the flame cannot survive, when the fuel is exhausted, and departs along with that which kindles it, nor does desire abide, when its incentive wastes away. But love which is godly and under restraint, since its object is stable, not only is more lasting, but, the fuller its vision of beauty grows, the more closely does it bind to itself and to one another the hearts of those whose love has one and the same object. This is the law of our superhuman love. I feel that I am being unduly borne away, and I know not how to enter upon this point, yet I cannot restrain myself from describing it. For if I have omitted anything, it seems, immediately afterwards, of pressing importance, and of more consequence than what I had preferred to mention. And if any one would carry me tyrannically forward, I become like the polyps, which when they are being dragged from their holes, cling with their suckers to the rocks,

α Homer Il. xi. 72.

β Ib. xi. 496.

a *Philosophy*, here, a truly Christian life.

and cannot be detached, until the last of these has had exerted upon it its necessary share of force. If then you give me leave, I have my request, if not I must take it from myself.

20. Such were our feelings for each other, when we had thus supported, as Pindar[α] has it, our "well-built chamber with pillars of gold," as we advanced under the united influences of God's grace and our own affection. Oh! how can I mention these things without tears.

We were impelled by equal hopes, in a pursuit especially obnoxious to envy, that of letters. Yet envy we knew not, and emulation was of service to us. We struggled, not each to gain the first place for himself, but to yield it to the other; for we made each other's reputation to be our own. We seemed to have one soul, inhabiting two bodies. And if we must not believe those whose doctrine is "All things[β] are in all;" yet in our case it was worthy of belief, so did we live in and with each other. The sole business of both of us was virtue, and living for the hopes to come, having retired from this world, before our actual departure hence. With a view to this, were directed all our life and actions, under the guidance of the commandment, as we sharpened upon each other our weapons of virtue; and if this is not a great thing for me to say, being a rule and standard to each other, for the distinction between what was right and what was not. Our associates were not the most dissolute, but the most sober of our comrades; not the most pugnacious, but the most peaceable, whose intimacy was most profitable: knowing that it is more easy to be tainted with vice, than to impart virtue; just as we can more readily be infected with a disease, than bestow health. Our most cherished studies were not the most pleasant, but the most excellent; this being one means of forming young minds in a virtuous or vicious mould.

21. Two ways were known to us, the first of greater value, the second of smaller consequence: the one leading to our sacred buildings and the teachers there, the other to secular instructors. All others we left to those who would pursue them—to feasts, theatres, meetings, banquets. For nothing is in my opinion of value, save that which leads to virtue and to the improvement of its devotees. Different men have different names, derived from their fathers, their families, their pursuits, their exploits: we had but one great business and name—to be and to be called Christians—of which we thought more than Gyges[α] of the turning of his ring, if this is not a legend, on which depended his Lydian sovereignty: or than Midas[β] did of the gold through which he perished, in answer to his prayer that all he had might turn to gold—another Phrygian legend. For why should I speak of the arrow of the Hyperborean Abaris,[γ] or of the Argive Pegasus,[δ] to whom flight through the air was not of such consequence as was to us our rising to God, through the help of, and with each other? Hurtful as Athens was to others in spiritual things, and this is of no slight consequence to the pious, for the city is richer in those evil riches—idols—than the rest of Greece, and it is hard to avoid being carried along with their devotees and adherents, yet we, our minds being closed up and fortified against this, suffered no injury. On the contrary, strange as it may seem, we were thus the more confirmed in the faith, from our perception of their trickery and unreality, which led us to despise these divinities in the very home of their worship. And if there is, or is believed to be, a river[ε] flowing with fresh water through the sea, or an animal[ζ] which can dance in fire, the consumer of all things, such were we among all our comrades.

22. And, best of all, we were surrounded by a far from ignoble band, under his instruction and guidance, and delighting in the same objects, as we ran on foot beside that Lydian car,[η] his own course and disposition: and so we became famous, not only among our own teachers and comrades, but even throughout Greece, and especially in the eyes of its most distinguished men. We even passed beyond its boundaries, as was made clear by the evidence of many. For our instructors were known to all who knew Athens, and all who knew them, knew us, as the subject of conversation, being actually looked upon, or heard of by report, as an illustrious pair. Orestes and Pylades[θ] were in their eyes nothing to

α Olymp. Od. vi. 1.

β *All things*, etc., i.e. Empedocles and Anaxagoras.

α *Gyges* is said to have had a ring by means of which he could make himself invisible, and by thus using it was able to seize on the Kingdom of Lydia.

β *Midas*. said to have had the power granted of turning everything he touched to gold. Accordingly, as this power took effect on his food, he died of hunger.

γ *Abaris*, a Hyperborean priest of Apollo, who was said to have given him an arrow, on which he rode through the air.

δ *Pegasus*, called Argive, because caught near to Argos, the winged horse, by the aid of which Bellerophon was said to have destroyed the Chimæra.

ε *A river*, etc. The Alpheus, a river of Arcadia.

ζ *Animal*. The salamander, a lizard said to be impervious to the action of fire. Plin. N. H. x. 67.

η *Lydian car*, proverbial expression for anything whose speed distances all competitors.

θ *Orestes and Pylades*, types of close comradeship in Greek tragedies.

us, or the sons of Molione,[a] the wonders of the Homeric scroll, celebrated for their union in misfortune, and their splendid driving, as they shared in reins and whip alike. But I have been unawares betrayed into praising myself, in a manner I would not have allowed in another. And it is no wonder that I gained here in some advantage from his friendship, and that, as in life he aided me in virtue, so since his departure he has contributed to my renown. But I must return to my proper course.

23. Who possessed such a degree of the prudence of old age, even before his hair was gray? Since it is by this that Solomon defines old age.[β] Who was so respectful to both old and young, not only of our contemporaries, but even of those who long preceded him? Who, owing to his character, was less in need of education? Yet who, even with his character, was so imbued with learning? What branch of learning did he not traverse; and that with unexampled success, passing through all, as no one else passed through any one of them: and attaining such eminence in each, as if it had been his sole study? The two great sources of power in the arts and sciences, ability and application, were in him equally combined. For, because of the pains he took, he had but little need of natural quickness, and his natural quickness made it unnecessary for him to take pains; and such was the coöperation and unity of both, that it was hard to see for which of the two he was more remarkable. Who had such power in Rhetoric, which breathes[γ] with the might of fire, different as his disposition was from that of rhetoricians? Who in Grammar, which perfects our tongues in Greek and compiles history, and presides over metres and legislates for poems? Who in Philosophy, that really lofty and high reaching science, whether practical and speculative, or in that part of it whose oppositions and struggles are concerned with logical demonstrations; which is called Dialectic, and in which it was more difficult to elude his verbal toils, if need required, than to escape from the Labyrinths?[δ] Of Astronomy, Geometry, and numerical proportion he had such a grasp, that he could not be baffled by those who are clever in such sciences: excessive application to them he despised, as useless to those whose desire is godliness: so that it is possible to admire what he chose more than what he neglected, or what he neglected more than what he chose. Medicine, the result of philosophy and laboriousness, was rendered necessary for him by his physical delicacy, and his care of the sick. From these beginnings he attained to a mastery of the art, not only in its empirical and practical branches, but also in its theory and principles. But what are these, illustrious though they be, compared with the moral discipline of the man? To those who have had experience of him, Minos and Rhadamanthus[a] were mere trifles, whom the Greeks thought worthy of the meadows of Asphodel and the Elysian plains, which are their representations of our Paradise, derived from those books of Moses which are also ours, for though their terms are different, this is what they refer to under other names.

24. Such was the case, and his galleon was laden with all the learning attainable by the nature of man; for beyond Cadiz[β] there is no passage. There was left no other need but that of rising to a more perfect life, and grasping those hopes upon which we were agreed. The day of our departure was at hand, with its attendant speeches of farewell, and of escort, its invitations to return, its lamentations, embraces and tears. For there is nothing so painful to any one, as is separation from Athens and one another, to those who have been comrades there. On that occasion was seen a piteous spectacle, worthy of record. Around us were grouped our fellow students and classmates and some of our teachers, protesting amid entreaties, violence, and persuasion, that, whatever happened, they would not let us go; saying and doing everything that men in distress could do. And here I will bring an accusation against myself, and also, daring though it be, against that divine and irreproachable soul. For he, by detailing the reasons of his anxiety to return home, was able to prevail over their desire to retain him, and they were compelled, though with reluctance, to agree to his departure. But I was left behind at Athens, partly, to say the truth, because I had been prevailed on—partly because he had betrayed me, having been persuaded to forsake and hand over to his captors one who refused to forsake him. A thing incredible, before it happened. For

α *Sons of Molione*, Eurytus and Cteatus. Hom. Il. ii. 621. Their father was Actor.

β Wisd. iv. 8.

γ *Which breathes*, a phrase used Hom. Il. vi. 182 of the Chimæra.

δ *Labyrinths*, the mythical mazes of Crete, the home of the Minotaur.

α *Minos and Rhadamanthus*, Kings of Crete and Lycia, fabled to have been made judges in the lower world because of their justice when on earth.

β *Beyond Cadiz.* The Atlantic Ocean beyond Cadiz was reputed impassable by the ancients.

it was like cutting one body into two, to the destruction of either part, or the severance of two bullocks who have shared the same manger and the same yoke, amid pitiable bellowings after one another in protest against the separation. However, my loss was not of long duration, for I could not long bear to be seen in piteous plight, nor to have to account to every one for our separation: so, after a brief stay at Athens, my longing desire made me, like the horse in Homer, to burst the bonds of those who restrained me, and prancing o'er the plains, rush to my mate.

25. Upon our return, after a slight indulgence to the world and the stage, sufficient to gratify the general desire, not from any inclination to theatrical display, we soon became independent, and, after being promoted from the rank of beardless boys to that of men, made bold advances along the road of philosophy, for though no longer together, since envy would not allow this, we were united by our eager desire. The city of Cæsarea took possession of him, as a second founder and patron, but in course of time he was occasionally absent, as a matter of necessity due to our separation, and with a view to our determined course of philosophy. Dutiful attendance on my aged parents, and a succession of misfortunes kept me apart from him, perhaps without right or justice, but so it was. And to this cause I am inclined to ascribe all the inconsistency and difficulty which have befallen my life, and the hindrances in the way of philosophy, which have been unworthy of my desire and purpose. But as for my fate, let it lead whither God pleases, only may its course be the better for his intercessions. As regards himself, the manifold love of God toward man,[a] and His providential care for our race did, after shewing forth his merits under many intervening circumstances with ever greater brilliancy, set him up as a conspicuous and celebrated light for the Church, by advancing him to the holy thrones of the priesthood, to blaze forth, through the single city of Cæsarea, to the whole world. And in what manner? Not by precipitate advancement, nor by at once cleansing and making him wise, as is the wont of many present candidates for preferment: but bestowing upon him the honour in the due order of spiritual advancement.

26. For I do not praise the disorder and irregularity which sometimes exist among us, even in those who preside over the sanctuary. I do not venture, nor is it just, to accuse them all. I approve the nautical custom, which first gives the oar to the future steersman, and afterward leads him to the stern, and entrusts him with the command, and seats him at the helm, only after a long course of striking the sea and observing the winds. As is the case again in military affairs: private, captain, general. This order is the best and most advantageous for their subordinates. And if it were so in our case, it would be of great service. But, as it is, there is a danger of the holiest of all offices being the most ridiculous among us. For promotion depends not upon virtue, but upon villany; and the sacred thrones fall not to the most worthy, but to the most powerful. Samuel, the seer into futurity, is among the prophets: but Saul, the rejected one, is also there. Rehoboam, the son of Solomon, is among the kings, but so also is Jeroboam, the slave and apostate. And there is not a physician, or a painter who has not first studied the nature of diseases, or mixed many colours, or practised drawing: but a prelate is easily found, without laborious training, with a reputation of recent date, being sown and springing up in a moment, as the legend [a] of the giants goes. We manufacture those who are holy in a day, and bid those to be wise, who have had no instruction, and have contributed nothing before to their dignity, except the will. So one man is content with an inferior position, and abides in his low estate, who is worthy of a lofty one, and has meditated much on the inspired words, and has reduced the flesh by many laws into subjection to the spirit: while the other haughtily takes precedence, and raises his eyebrow over his betters, and does not tremble at his position, nor is he appalled at the sight, seeing the disciplined man beneath him; and wrongly supposes himself to be his superior in wisdom as well as in rank, having lost his senses under the influence of his position.

27. Not so our great and illustrious Basil. In this grace, as in all others, he was a public example. For he first read to the people the sacred books, while already able to expound them, nor did he deem himself worthy of this rank [β] in the sanctuary, and thus proceeded to praise the Lord in the seat of the Presbyters, [γ] and next in that of the Bishops, attaining the office neither by stealth nor by violence, instead of seeking for the honour, being sought

a Tit. iii. 4.

a *The legend*, i.e., of Cadmus who sowed at Thebes the dragon's teeth from which sprung giants.

β *This rank*, i.e., the office of Lector, or Reader.

γ Ps. cvii. 32.

for by it, and receiving it not as a human favour, but as from God and divine. The account of his bishopric must be deferred: over his subordinate ministry let us linger a while, for indeed it had almost escaped me, in the midst of my discourse.

28. There arose a disagreement between him and his predecessor [α] in the rule over this Church: its source and character it is best to pass over in silence, yet it arose. He was a man in other respects far from ignoble, and admirable for his piety, as was proved by the persecution of that time, and the opposition to him, yet his feeling against Basil was one to which men are liable. For Momus seizes not only upon the common herd, but on the best of men, so that it belongs to God alone to be utterly uninfluenced by and proof against such feelings. All the more eminent and wise portion of the Church was roused against him, if those are wiser than the majority who have separated themselves from the world and consecrated their life to God. I mean the Nazarites [β] of our day, and those who devote themselves to such pursuits. They were annoyed that their chief [γ] should be neglected, insulted, and rejected, and they ventured upon a most dangerous proceeding. They determined to revolt and break off from the body of the Church, which admits of no faction, severing along with themselves no small fraction of the people, both of the lower ranks, and of those of position. This was most easy, owing to three very strong reasons. In the first place, the man was held in repute, beyond any other, I think, of the philosophers of our time, and able, if he wished, to inspire with courage the conspirators. Next, his opponent [δ] was suspected by the city, in consequence of the tumult which accompanied his institution, of having obtained his preferment in an arbitrary manner, not according to the laws and canons. Also there were present some of the bishops [ε] of the West, drawing to themselves all the orthodox members of the Church.

29. What then did our noble friend, the disciple of the Peaceable One? It was not his habit to resist his traducers or partisans, nor was it his part to fight, or rend the body of the Church, which was from other reasons the subject of attack, and hardly bestead, from the great power of the heretics. With my advice and earnest encouragement on the point, he set out from the place with me into Pontus, and presided over the abodes of contemplation there. He himself too founded one [α] worthy of mention, as he welcomed the desert together with Elijah and John,[β] those professors of austerity; thinking this to be more profitable for him than to form any design in reference to the present juncture unworthy of his philosophy, and to ruin in a time of storm the straight course which he was making, where the surges of disputation were lulled to a calm. Yet wonderfully philosophic though his retirement was, we shall find his return still more wonderful. For thus it was.

30. While we were thus engaged, there suddenly arose a cloud full of hail, with destructive roar, overwhelming every Church upon which it burst and seized: an Emperor,[γ] most fond of gold and most hostile to Christ, infected with these two most serious diseases, insatiate avarice and blasphemy; a persecutor in succession to the persecutor, and, in succession to the apostate, not indeed an apostate, though no better to Christians, or rather, to the more devout and pure party of Christians, who worship the Trinity, which I call the only true devotion and saving doctrine. For we do not measure out the Godhead into portions, nor banish from Itself by unnatural estrangements the one and unapproachable Nature; nor cure one evil by another, destroying the godless confusion of Sabellius by a more impious severance and division; which was the error of Arius, whose name declares his madness,[δ] the disturber and destroyer of a great part of the Church. For he did not honour the Father, by dishonouring His offspring with his unequal degrees of Godhead. But we recognize one glory [ε] of the Father, the equality of the Only-begotten; and one glory of the Son, that of the Spirit. And we hold that, to subordinate any of the Three, is to destroy the whole. For we worship and acknowledge Them as Three in their properties,[ζ] but One in their Godhead. He however had no such idea, being unable to look

α *His predecessor*, Eusebius, Archbishop of Cæsarea.

β *Nazarites*, i.e.. the monks. γ *Their chief*. i.e. Basil.

δ *His opponent*, lit. "the man who was vexing him," i.e., Eusebius.

ε *Bishops*. It is uncertain who these bishops were. Clémencet thinks they were Lucifer and Eusebius of Vercellæ. But a separation had ere this taken place between them in consequence of Lucifer's rash action at Antioch. Nor is it certain that Eusebius had not already returned to Italy.

α *One*, a monastery. The rule of S. Basil is widely observed to this day in Eastern monasteries. Cf. § 34.

β *John*, Saint John Baptist. γ *An Emperor*, Valens.

δ *Madness*. cf. ii. 37. Note.

ε *Glory*. The word δόξα means both "doctrine" and "glory."

ζ *Properties*. ἰδιότητες. Petav. de Trin. iv. Proem. §2 gives other Greek equivalent terms. The Latin terms are "*notiones*" (S. Thom. Aq. Summa. I. xxxii. qu. 2), "*proprietates*" or *relationes*. They denote those relative "attributes ad intra" which distinguish the Persons, if they do not actually constitute the Personality of each of the Three Divine Persons. They are five in number, Unbegottenness. Paternity, Filiation, active and passive Spiration. Perhaps the nearest English equivalent is "characteristic (or distinctive) relations."—Cf. Orat. xlii. 15.

up, but being debased by those who led him, he dared to debase along with himself even the Nature of the Godhead, and became a wicked creature reducing Majesty to bondage, and aligning with creation the uncreated and timeless Nature.

31. Such was his mind, and with such impiety he took the field against us. For we must consider it to be nothing else than a barbaric inroad which, instead of destroying walls, cities and houses, and other things of little worth, made with hands and capable of restoration, spent its ravages upon men's souls. A worthy army joined in his assault, the evil rulers of the Churches, the bitter governors of his world-wide Empire. Some of the Churches they now held, some they were assaulting, others they hoped to gain by the already exercised influence of the Emperor, and the violence which he threatened. But in their purpose of perverting our own, their confidence was specially based on the smallness of mind of those whom I have mentioned, the inexperience of our prelate, and the infirmities which prevailed among us. The struggle would be fierce: the zeal of numerous troops was far from ignoble, but their array was weak, from the want of a leader and strategist to contend for them with the might of the Word and of the Spirit. What then did this noble and magnanimous and truly Christ-loving soul? No need of many words to urge his presence and aid. At once when he saw me on my mission, for the struggle on behalf of the faith was common to us both, he yielded to my entreaty; and decided by a most excellent distinction, based on spiritual reasons, that the time for punctiliousness (if indeed we may give way to such feelings at all) is a time of security, but that forbearance is required in the hour of necessity. He immediately returned with me from Pontus, and as a zealous volunteer took his place in the fight for the endangered truth, and devoted himself to the service of his mother, the Church.

32. Did then his actual efforts fall short of his preliminary zeal? Were they directed by courage, but not by prudence, or by skill, while he shrank from danger? Or, in spite of their unexampled perfection on all these points, was there left in him some trace of irritation? Far from it. He was at once completely reconciled, and took part in every plan and effort. He removed all the thorns and stumbling blocks which were in our way, upon which the enemy relied in their attack upon us. He took hold of one, grasped another, thrust away a third. He became to some a stout wall and rampart,[α] to others an axe breaking the rock in pieces,[β] or a fire among the thorns,[γ] as the divine Scripture says, easily destroying those fagots who were insulting the Godhead. And if his Barnabas, who speaks and records these things, was of service to Paul in the struggle, it is to Paul that thanks are due, for choosing and making him his comrade in the strife.

33. Thus the enemy failed, and, base men as they were, for the first time were then basely put to shame and worsted, learning not to be ready to despise the Cappadocians, of all men in the world, whose special qualities are firmness in the faith, and loyal devotion to the Trinity; to Whom is due their unity and strength, and from Whom they receive an even greater and stronger assistance than they are able to give. Basil's next business and purpose was to conciliate the prelate, to allay suspicion, to persuade all men that the irritation which had been felt was due to the temptation and effort of the Evil one, in his envy of virtuous concord: carefully complying with the laws of obedience and spiritual order. Accordingly he visited him, with instruction and advice. While obedient to his wishes, he was everything to him, a good counsellor, a skilful assistant, an expounder of the Divine Will, a guide of conduct, a staff for his old age, a support of the faith, most trusty of those within, most practical of those without, in a word, as much inclined to goodwill, as he had been thought to hostility. And so the power of the Church came into his hands almost, if not quite, to an equal degree with the occupant of the see. For in return for his good-will, he was requited with authority. And their harmony and combination of power was wonderful. The one was the leader of the people, the other of their leader, like a lion-keeper, skilfully soothing the possessor of power. For, having been recently installed in the see, and still somewhat under the influence of the world, and not yet furnished with the things of the Spirit, in the midst of the eddying tide of enemies assaulting the Church, he was in need of some one to take him by the hand and support him. Accordingly he accepted the alliance, and imagined himself the conqueror of one who had conquered him.

34. Of his care for and protection of the Church, there are many other tokens; his boldness towards the governors and other

α Jer. i. 18. β Ib. xxiii. 29. γ Ps. cxviii. 12.

most powerful men in the city: the decisions of disputes, accepted without hesitation, and made effective by his simple word, his inclination being held to be decisive: his support of the needy, most of them in spiritual, not a few also in physical distress: for this also often influences the soul and reduces it to subjection by its kindness; the support of the poor, the entertainment of strangers, the care of maidens; legislation[α] written and unwritten for the monastic life: arrangements of prayers,[β] adornments of the sanctuary, and other ways in which the true man of God, working for God, would benefit the people: one being especially important and noteworthy. There was a famine, the most severe one ever recorded. The city was in distress, and there was no source of assistance, or relief for the calamity. For maritime cities are able to bear such times of need without difficulty, by an exchange of their own products for what is imported: but an inland city like ours can neither turn its superfluity to profit, nor supply its need, by either disposing of what we have, or importing what we have not: but the hardest part of all such distress is, the insensibility and insatiability of those who possess supplies. For they watch their opportunities, and turn the distress to profit, and thrive upon misfortune: heeding not that he who shows mercy to the poor, lendeth to the Lord,[γ] nor that he that withholdeth corn, the people shall curse him:[δ] nor any other of the promises to the philanthropic, and threats against the inhuman. But they are too insatiate, in their ill-judged policy; for while they shut up their bowels against their fellows, they shut up those of God against themselves, forgetting that their need of Him is greater than others' need of them. Such are the buyers and sellers of corn, who neither respect their fellows, nor are thankful to God, from Whom comes what they have, while others are straitened.

35. He indeed could neither rain bread from heaven by prayer,[ε] to nourish an escaped people in the wilderness,[ζ] nor supply fountains of food without cost from the depth of vessels which are filled by being emptied,[η] and so, by an amazing return for her hospitality, support one who supported him; nor feed thousands of men with five loaves whose very fragments were a further supply for many tables.[α] These were the works of Moses and Elijah, and my God, from Whom they too derived their power. Perhaps also they were characteristic of their time and its circumstances: since signs are for unbelievers not for those who believe.[β] But he did devise and execute with the same faith things which correspond to them, and tend in the same direction. For by his word and advice he opened the stores of those who possessed them, and so, according to the Scripture dealt food to the hungry,[γ] and satisfied the poor with bread,[δ] and fed them in the time of dearth,[ε] and filled the hungry souls with good things.[ζ] And in what way? for this is no slight addition to his praise. He gathered together the victims of the famine with some who were but slightly recovering from it, men and women, infants, old men, every age which was in distress, and obtaining contributions of all sorts of food which can relieve famine, set before them basins of soup and such meat as was found preserved among us, on which the poor live. Then, imitating the ministry of Christ, Who, girded with a towel, did not disdain to wash the disciples' feet, using for this purpose the aid of his own servants, and also of his fellow servants, he attended to the bodies and souls of those who needed it, combining personal respect with the supply of their necessity, and so giving them a double relief.

36. Such was our young furnisher of corn, and second Joseph: though of him we can say somewhat more. For the one made a gain from the famine, and bought up Egypt[η] in his philanthropy, by managing the time of plenty with a view to the time of famine, turning to account the dreams of others for that purpose. But the other's services were gratuitous, and his succour of the famine gained no profit, having only one object, to win kindly feelings by kindly treatment, and to gain by his rations of corn the heavenly blessings. Further he provided the nourishment of the Word, and that more perfect bounty and distribution, which is really heavenly and from on high—if the word be that bread of angels,[θ] wherewith souls are fed and given to drink, who are a hungered for God,[ι] and seek for a food which does not pass away or fail, but abides forever. This food he, who was the poorest and most needy man whom I have known, supplied in rich abundance to the relief not of a famine of bread,

α *Legislation.* Cf. §30.

β *Prayers.* The liturgy of S. Basil together with that of S. Chrysostom are still the authorized liturgies of the Eastern Church. γ Prov. xix. 17. δ Ib. xi. 26.

ε Exod. xvi. 15. ζ Ps. lxxviii. 24. η 1 Kings xvii. 14.

α S. Matt. xiv. 19. β 1 Cor. xiv. 22. γ Isai. lviii. 7. δ Ps. cxxxii. 15. ε Ib. xxxiii. 19. ζ Ib. cvii. 9; S. Luke i. 53. η Gen. xli. 1 et seq. θ Ps. lxxviii. 25. ι Ib. lxiii. 1; S. Matt. v. 6.

nor of a thirst for water, but a longing for that Word[α] which is really lifegiving and nourishing, and causes to grow to spiritual manhood him who is duly fed thereon.

37. After these and similar actions—why need I stay to mention them all?—when the prelate whose name[β] betokened his godliness had passed away, having sweetly breathed his last in Basil's arms, he was raised to the lofty throne of a Bishop, not without difficulty or without the envious struggles of the prelates of his native land, on whose side were found the greatest scoundrels of the city. But the Holy Spirit must needs win the day—and indeed the victory was decisive. For He brought from a distance, to anoint him, men[γ] illustrious and zealous for godliness, and with them the new Abraham, our Patriarch, I mean my father, in regard to whom an extraordinary thing happened. For, failing as he was from the number of his years, and worn away almost to his last breath by disease, he ventured on the journey to give assistance by his vote, relying on the aid of the Spirit. In brief, he was placed in his litter, as a corpse is laid in its tomb, to return in the freshness and strength of youth, with head erect, having been strengthened by the imposition of hands and unction, and, it is not too much to say by the head of him who was anointed. This must be added to the instances of old time, which prove that labour bestows health, zealous purpose raises the dead, and old age leaps up when anointed by the Spirit.

38. Having thus been deemed worthy of the office of prelate, as it is seemly that men should who have lived such a life, and won such favour and consideration, he did not disgrace, by his subsequent conduct, either his own philosophy, or the hopes of those who had trusted him. But he ever so far surpassed himself as he has been shown hitherto to have surpassed others, his ideas on this point being most excellent and philosophic. For he held that, while it is virtuous in a private individual to avoid vice, and be to some extent good, it is a vice in a chief and ruler, especially in such an office, to fail to surpass by far the majority of men, and by constant progress to make his virtue correspond to his dignity and throne: for it is difficult for one in high position to attain the mean, and by his eminence in virtue raise up his people to the golden mean. Or rather to treat this question more satisfactorily, I think that the result is the same as I see in the case of our Saviour, and of every specially wise man, I fancy, when He was with us in that form which surpassed us and yet is ours. For He also, the gospel says, increased in wisdom and favour, as well as in stature,[α] not that these qualities in Him were capable of growth: for how could that which was perfect from the first become more perfect, but that they were gradually disclosed and displayed? So I think that the virtue of Basil, without being itself increased, obtained at this time a wider exercise, since his power provided him with more abundant material.

39. He first of all made it plain that his office had been bestowed upon him, not by human favour, but by the gift of God. This will also be shown by my conduct. For in what philosophic research did he not, about that time, join with me? So every one thought that I should run to meet him after what had happened, and show my delight at it (as would, perhaps, have been the case with any one else) and claim a share in his authority, rather than rule beside him, according to the inferences they drew from our friendship. But, in my exceeding anxiety to avoid the annoyance and jealousy of the time, and specially since his position was still a painful and troubled one, I remained at home, and forcibly restrained my eager desire, while, though he blamed me, Basil accepted my excuse. And when, on my subsequent arrival, I refused, for the same reason the honour of this chair, and a dignified position[β] among the Presbyters, he kindly refrained from blaming, nay he praised me, preferring to be charged with pride by a small clique, in their ignorance of our policy, rather than do anything contrary to reason and his own resolutions. And indeed, how could a man have better shown his soul to be superior to all fawning and flattery, and his single object to be the law of right, than by thus treating me, whom he acknowledged as among the first of his friends and associates?

40. His next task was to appease, and allay by magnanimous treatment, the opposition to himself: and that without any trace of flattery or servility, but in a most chivalrous and magnanimous way; with a view, not merely to present exigencies, but also to the fostering of future obedience. For, seeing that, while tenderness leads to laxity and slackness, severity gives rise to stubbornness and self-will, he was able to avoid the dangers of each course

α Amos viii. 11. β *Name*, Eusebius, i.e., "pious," "godly." γ *Men*. Eusebius of Samosaba and S. Gregory the Elder.

α S. Luke ii. 52.
β *Dignified position*, known later as that of Vicar General. Thomassin. Disc. Eccl. I. ii. 7. § 3.

by a combination of both, blending his correction with consideration, and gentleness with firmness, influencing men in most cases principally by his conduct rather than by argument: not enslaving them by art, but winning them by good nature, and attracting them by the sparing use, rather than by the constant exercise, of his power. And, most important of all, they were brought to recognize the superiority of his intellect and the inaccessibility of his virtue, to consider their only safety to consist in being on his side and under his command, their sole danger to be in opposition to him, and to think that to differ from him involved estrangement from God. Thus they willingly yielded and surrendered, submitting themselves, as if in a thunder-clap, and hastening to anticipate each other with their excuses, and exchange the intensity of their hostility for an equal intensity of good-will, and advance in virtue, which they found to be the one really effective defence. The few exceptions to this conduct were passed by and neglected, because their ill-nature was incurable, and they expended their powers in wearing out themselves, as rust consumes itself together with the iron on which it feeds.

41. Affairs at home being now settled to his mind, in a way that faithless men who did not know him would have thought impossible, his designs became greater and took a loftier range. For, while all others had their eyes on the ground before them, and directed attention to their own immediate concerns, and, if these were safe, troubled themselves no further, being incapable of any great and chivalrous design or undertaking; he, moderate as he was in all other respects, could not be moderate in this, but with head erect, casting his mental eye about him, took in the whole world over which the word of salvation has made its way. And when he saw the great heritage of God, purchased by His own words and laws and sufferings, the holy nation, the royal priesthood,[α] in such evil plight that it was torn asunder into ten thousand opinions and errors: and the vine brought out of Egypt and transplanted,[β] the Egypt of impious and dark ignorance, which had grown to such beauty and boundless size that the whole earth was covered with the shadow of it, while it overtopped mountains and cedars, now being ravaged by that wicked wild boar, the devil, he could not content himself with quietly lamenting the misfortune, and merely lifting up his hands to God, and

α 1 Pet. ii. 9. β Ps. lxxx. 9.

seeking from Him the dispersion of the pressing misfortunes, while he himself was asleep, but felt bound to come to her aid at some expense to himself.

42. For what could be more distressing than this calamity, or call more loudly on one whose eyes were raised aloft for exertions on behalf of the common weal? The good or ill success of an individual is of no consequence to the community, but that of the community involves of necessity the like condition of the individual. With this idea and purpose, he who was the guardian and patron of the community (and, as Solomon says with truth, a perceptive heart is a moth to the bones,[α] unsensitiveness is cheerily confident, while a sympathetic disposition is a source of pain, and constant consideration wastes away the heart), he, I say, was consequently in agony and distress from many wounds; like Jonah and David, he wished in himself to die[β] and gave not sleep to his eyes, nor slumber to his eyelids,[γ] he expended what was left of his flesh upon his reflections, until he discovered a remedy for the evil: and sought for aid from God and man, to stay the general conflagration, and dissipate the gloom which was lowering over us.

43. One of his devices was of the greatest service. After a period of such recollection as was possible, and private spiritual conference, in which, after considering all human arguments, and penetrating into all the deep things of the Scriptures, he drew up a sketch of pious doctrine, and by wrestling with and attacking their opposition he beat off the daring assaults of the heretics: overthrowing in hand to hand struggles by word of mouth those who came to close quarters, and striking those at a distance by arrows winged with ink, which is in no wise inferior to inscriptions on tablets; not giving directions for one small nation only like that of the Jews, concerning meats and drinks, temporary sacrifices, and purifications of the flesh;[δ] but for every nation and part of the world, concerning the Word of truth, the source of our salvation. Again, since unreasoning action and unpractical reasoning are alike ineffectual, he added to his reasoning the succour which comes from action; he paid visits, sent messages, gave interviews, instructed, reproved, rebuked,[ε] threatened, reproached, undertook the defence of nations, cities and individuals, devising every kind of succour, and procuring from every source specifics for disease: a second Bezaleel, an

α Prov. xiv. 30 (LXX). β Jonah iv. 8. γ Ps. cxxxii. 4. δ Heb. ix. 10. ε 2 Time iv. 2.

architect of the Divine tabernacle,[α] applying every material and art to the work, and combining all in a harmonious and surpassing beauty.

44. Why need I enter into further detail? We were assailed again by the Anti-Christian Emperor,[β] that tyrant of the faith, with more abundant impiety and a hotter onset, inasmuch as the dispute must be with a stronger antagonist, like that unclean and evil spirit, who when sent forth upon his wanderings from man, returns to take up his abode in him again with a greater number of spirits, as we have heard in the Gospels.[γ] This spirit he imitated, both in renewing the contest in which he had formerly been worsted, and in adding to his original efforts. He thought that it was a strange and insufferable thing that he, who ruled over so many nations and had won so much renown, and reduced under the power of impiety all those round about him, and overcome every adversary, should be publicly worsted by a single man, and a single city, and so incur the ridicule not only of those patrons of ungodliness by whom he was led, but also, as he supposed, of all men.

45. It is said that the King[δ] of Persia, on his expedition into Greece, was not only urged to immoderate threats, by elation at the numbers of every race of men which in his wrath and pride he was leading against them: but thought to terrify them the more, by making them afraid of him, in consequence of his novel treatment of the elements. A strange land and sea were heard of, the work of the new creator; and an army which sailed over the dry land, and marched over the ocean, while islands were carried off, and the sea was scourged, and all the other mad proceedings of that army and expedition, which, though they struck terror into the ignoble, were ridiculous in the eyes of men of brave and steadfast hearts. There was no need of anything of this kind in the expedition against us, but what was still worse and more harmful, this was what the Emperor was reported to say and do. He stretched forth his mouth unto heaven, speaking blasphemy against the most High, and his tongue went through the world.[ε] Excellently did the inspired David before our days thus describe him who made heaven to stoop to earth, and reckoned with the creation that supermundane nature, which the creation cannot even contain, even though in kindness to man it did to some extent come among us, in order to draw to itself us who were lying upon the ground.

46. Furious indeed were his first acts of wantonness, more furious still his final efforts against us. What shall I speak of first? Exiles, banishments, confiscations, open and secret plots, persuasion, where time allowed, violence, where persuasion was impossible. Those who clung to the orthodox faith, as we did, were extruded from their churches; others were intruded, who agreed with the Imperial soul-destroying doctrines, and begged for testimonials of impiety, and subscribed to statements still harder than these. Burnings[α] of Presbyters at sea, impious generals, not those who conquered the Persians, or subdued the Scythians, or reduced any other barbaric nation, but those who assailed churches, and danced in triumph upon altars, and defiled the unbloody sacrifices with the blood of man and victims, and offered insult to the modesty of virgins. With what object? The extrusion of the Patriarch Jacob,[β] and the intrusion in his place of Esau, who was hated,[γ] even before his birth. This is the description of his first acts of wantonness, the mere recollection and mention of which even now, rouses the tears of most of us.

47. Accordingly, when, after passing through all quarters, he made his attack in order to enslave this impregnable and formidable mother of the Churches, the only still remaining unquenched spark of the truth, he discovered that he had been for the first time ill advised. For he was driven back like a missile which strikes upon some stronger body, and recoiled like a broken hawser. Such was the prelate of the Church that he met with, such was the bulwark by which his efforts were broken and dissipated. Other particulars may be heard from those who tell and recount them, from their own experience—and none of those who recount them is destitute of this full experience. But all must be filled with admiration who are aware of the struggles of that time, the assaults, the promises, the threats, the commissioners sent before him to try to prevail upon us, men of judicial and military rank, men from the harem, who are men among women, women among men, whose only manliness consisted in their impiety, and being incapable of natural licentiousness, commit fornication in the only way they can, with their tongues; the chief cook

α Exod. xxxi. 2. β *Emperor.* Valens. γ S. Luke xi. 24. δ *King.* Xerxes. ε Ps. lxxiii. 9.

α *Burnings.* A.D. 370. Eighty ecclesiastics, sent on a mission to Valens at Nicomedia, were by his orders sent to sea off the coast of Bithynia, and, the vessel being set on fire, were burnt to death.
β *Jacob*, i.e., Athanasius. Esau = George. γ Rom. ix. 11.

Nebuzaradan,[a] who threatened us with the weapons of his art, and was despatched by his own fire. But what especially excites my wonder, and what I could not, even if I would, pass by, I will describe as concisely as possible.

48. Who has not heard of the prefect[β] of those days, who, for his own part, treated us with such excessive arrogance, having himself been admitted, or perhaps committed, to baptism by the other party; and strove by exceeding the letter of his instructions, and gratifying his master in every particular, to guarantee and preserve his own possession of power. Though he raged against the Church, and assumed a lion-like aspect, and roared like a lion till most men dared not approach him, yet our noble prelate was brought into or rather entered his court, as if bidden to a feast, instead of to a trial. How can I fitly describe, either the arrogance of the prefect or the prudence with which it was met by the Saint. "What is the meaning, Sir Basil," he said, addressing him by name, and not as yet deigning to term him Bishop, "of your daring, as no other dares, to resist and oppose so great a potentate?" "In what respect?" said our noble champion, "and in what does my rashness consist? For this I have yet to learn." "In refusing to respect the religion of your Sovereign, when all others have yielded and submitted themselves?" "Because," said he, "this is not the will of my real Sovereign; nor can I, who am the creature of God, and bidden myself to be God, submit to worship any creature." "And what do we," said the prefect, "seem to you to be? Are we, who give you this injunction, nothing at all? What do you say to this? Is it not a great thing to be ranged with us as your associates?" "You are, I will not deny it," said he, "a prefect, and an illustrious one, yet not of more honour than God. And to be associated with you is a great thing, certainly; for you are yourself the creature of God; but so it is to be associated with any other of my subjects. For faith, and not personal importance, is the distinctive mark of Christianity."

49. Then indeed the prefect became excited, and rose from his seat, boiling with rage, and making use of harsher language. "What?" said he, "have you no fear of my authority?" "Fear of what?" said Basil, "How could it affect me?" "Of what? Of any one of the resources of my power." "What are these?" said Basil, "pray, inform me." "Confiscation, banishment, torture, death." "Have you no other threat?" said he, "for none of these can reach me." "How indeed is that?" said the prefect. "Because," he replied, "a man who has nothing, is beyond the reach of confiscation; unless you demand my tattered rags, and the few books, which are my only possessions. Banishment is impossible for me, who am confined by no limit of place, counting my own neither the land where I now dwell, nor all of that into which I may be hurled; or, rather, counting it all God's, whose guest and dependent I am. As for tortures, what hold can they have upon one whose body has ceased to be? Unless you mean the first stroke, for this alone is in your power. Death is my benefactor, for it will send me the sooner to God, for Whom I live, and exist, and have all but died, and to Whom I have long been hastening."

50. Amazed at this language, the prefect said, "No one has ever yet spoken thus, and with such boldness, to Modestus." "Why, perhaps," said Basil, "you have not met with a Bishop, or in his defence of such interests he would have used precisely the same language. For we are modest in general, and submissive to every one, according to the precept of our law. We may not treat with haughtiness even any ordinary person, to say nothing of so great a potentate. But where the interests of God are at stake, we care for nothing else, and make these our sole object. Fire and sword and wild beasts, and rakes which tear the flesh, we revel in, and fear them not. You may further insult and threaten us, and do whatever you will, to the full extent of your power. The Emperor himself may hear this—that neither by violence nor persuasion will you bring us to make common cause with impiety, not even though your threats become still more terrible."

51. At the close of this colloquy, the prefect, having been convinced by the attitude of Basil, that he was absolutely impervious to threats and influence, dismissed him from the court, his former threatening manner being replaced by somewhat of respect and deference. He himself with all speed obtained an audience of the Emperor, and said: "We have been worsted, Sire, by the prelate of this Church. He is superior to threats, invincible in argument, uninfluenced by persuasion. We must make trial of some more feeble character; and in this case resort to open violence,

α *Nebuzaradan.* Demosthenes, a creature of Valens, sent to persuade Basil to yield to the Emperor.
β *Prefect.* Modestus.

or submit to the disregard of our threatenings." Hereupon the Emperor, forced by the praises of Basil to condemn his own conduct (for even an enemy can admire a man's excellence), would not allow violence to be used against him: and, like iron, which is softened by fire, yet still remains iron, though turned from threatening to admiration, would not enter into communion with him, being prevented by shame from changing his course, but sought to justify his conduct by the most plausible excuse he could, as the sequel will show.

52. For he entered the Church attended by the whole of his train; it was the festival of the Epiphany, and the Church was crowded, and, by taking his place among the people, he made a profession of unity. The occurrence is not to be lightly passed over. Upon his entrance he was struck by the thundering roll of the Psalms, by the sea of heads of the congregation, and by the angelic rather than human order which pervaded the sanctuary and its precincts: while Basil presided over his people, standing erect, as the Scripture says of Samuel,[α] with body and eyes and mind undisturbed, as if nothing new had happened, but fixed upon God and the sanctuary, as if, so to say, he had been a statue, while his ministers stood around him in fear and reverence. At this sight, and it was indeed a sight unparalleled, overcome by human weakness, his eyes were affected with dimness and giddiness, his mind with dread. This was as yet unnoticed by most people. But when he had to offer the gifts at the Table of God, which he must needs do himself, since no one would, as usual, assist him, because it was uncertain whether Basil would admit him, his feelings were revealed. For he was staggering, and had not some one in the sanctuary reached out a hand to steady his tottering steps, he would have sunk to the ground in a lamentable fall. So much for this.

53. As for the wisdom of his conference with the Emperor, who, in his quasi-communion with us entered within the veil to see and speak to him, as he had long desired to do, what else can I say but that they were inspired words, which were heard by the courtiers and by us who had entered with them? This was the beginning and first establishment of the Emperor's kindly feeling towards us; the impression produced by this reception put an end to the greater part of the persecution which assailed us like a river.

α 1 Sam. xix. 20.

54. Another incident is not of less importance than those I have mentioned. The wicked were victorious, and the decree for his banishment was signed, to the full satisfaction of those who furthered it. The night had come, the chariot was ready, our haters were exultant, the pious in despair, we surrounded the zealous traveller, to whose honourable disgrace nothing was wanting. What next? It was undone by God. For He Who smote the first-born of Egypt,[α] for its harshness towards Israel, also struck the son of the Emperor with disease. How great was the speed! There was the sentence of banishment, here the decree of sickness: the hand of the wicked scribe was restrained, and the saint was preserved, and the man of piety presented to us, by the fever which brought to reason the arrogance of the Emperor. What could be more just or more speedy than this? This was the series of events: the Emperor's child was sick and in bodily pain. The father was pained for it, for what can the father do? On all sides he sought for aid in his distress, he summoned the best physicians, he betook himself to intercessions with the greatest fervour, and flung himself upon the ground. Affliction humbles even emperors, and no wonder, for the like sufferings of David in the case of his child are recorded for us.[β] But as no cure for the evil could anywhere be found, he applied to the faith of Basil, not personally summoning him, in shame for his recent ill treatment, but entrusting the mission to others of his nearest and dearest friends. On his arrival, without the delay or reluctance which any one else might have shown, at once the disease relaxed, and the father cherished better hopes; and had he not blended salt water with the fresh, by trusting to the heterodox at the same time that he summoned Basil, the child would have recovered his health and been preserved for his father's arms. This indeed was the conviction of those who were present at the time, and shared in the distress.

55. The same mischance is said to have befallen the prefect. He also was obliged by sickness to bow beneath the hands of the Saint, and, in reality, to men of sense a visitation brings instruction, and affliction is often better than prosperity. He fell sick, was in tears, and in pain, he sent for Basil, and entreated him, crying out, "I own that you were in the right; only save me!" His request was granted, as he himself acknowledged, and convinced many who had known

α Exod. xii. 29. β 2 Sam. xii. 16.

nothing of it; for he never ceased to wonder at and describe the powers of the prelate. Such was his conduct in these cases, such its result. Did he then treat others in a different way, and engage in petty disputes about trifles, or fail to rise to the heights of philosophy in a course of action which merits no praise and is best passed over in silence? By no means. He who once stirred up the wicked Hadad against Israel,[α] stirred up against him the prefect[β] of the province of Pontus; nominally, from annoyance connected with some poor creature of a woman, but in reality as a part of the struggle of impiety against the truth. I pass by all his other insults against Basil, or, for it is the same thing, against God; for it is against Him and on His behalf that the contest was waged. One instance of it, however, which brought special disgrace upon the assailant, and exalted his adversary, if philosophy and eminence for it be a great and lofty thing, I will describe at length.

56. The assessor of a judge was attempting to force into a distasteful marriage a lady of high birth whose husband was but recently dead. At a loss to escape from this high-handed treatment, she resorted to a device no less prudent than daring. She fled to the holy table, and placed herself under the protection of God against outrage. What, in the Name of the Trinity Itself, if I may introduce into my panegyric somewhat of the forensic style, ought to have been done, I do not say, by the great Basil, who laid down the law for us all in such matters, but by any one who, though far inferior to him, was a priest? Ought he not to have allowed her claim, to have taken charge of, and cared for, her; to have raised his hand in defence of the kindness of God and the law which gives honour to the altar? Ought he not to have been willing to do and suffer anything, rather than take part in any inhuman design against her, and outrage at once the holy table, and the faith in which she had taken sanctuary? No! said the baffled judge, all ought to yield to my authority, and Christians should betray their own laws. The suppliant whom he demanded, was at all hazards retained. Accordingly, in his rage, he at last sent some of the magistrates to search the saint's bedchamber, with the purpose of dishonouring him, rather than from any necessity. What! Search the house of a man so free from passion, whom the angels revere, at whom women do not venture even to look? And, not content with this, he summoned him, and put him on his defence; and that, in no gentle or kindly manner, but as if he were a convict. Upon Basil's appearance, standing, like my Jesus, before the judgment seat of Pilate, he presided at the trial, full of wrath and pride. Yet the thunderbolts did not fall, and the sword of God still glittered, and waited, while His bow, though bent, was restrained. Such indeed is the custom of God.

57. Consider another struggle between our champion and his persecutor. His ragged pallium having been ordered to be torn away, "I will also, if you wish it, strip off my coat," said he. His fleshless form was threatened with blows, and he offered to submit to be torn with combs, and he said, "By such laceration you will cure my liver, which, as you see, is wearing me away." Such was their argument. But when the city perceived the outrage and the common danger of all—for each one considered this insolence a danger to himself, it became all on fire with rage; and, like a hive roused by smoke, one after another was stirred and arose, every race and every age, but especially the men from the small-arms factory and from the imperial weaving-sheds. For men at work in these trades are specially hot-tempered and daring, because of the liberty allowed them. Each man was armed with the tool he was using, or with whatever else came to hand at the moment. Torch in hand, amid showers of stones, with cudgels ready, all ran and shouted together in their united zeal. Anger makes a terrible soldier or general. Nor were the women weaponless, when roused by such an occasion. Their pins were their spears, and no longer remaining women, they were by the strength of their eagerness endowed with masculine courage. It is a short story. They thought that they would share among themselves the piety of destroying him, and held him to be most pious who first laid hands on one who had dared such deeds. What then was the conduct of this haughty and daring judge? He begged for mercy in a pitiable state of distress, cringing before them to an unparalleled extent, until the arrival of the martyr without bloodshed, who had won his crown without blows, and now restrained the people by the force of his personal influence, and delivered the man who had insulted him and now sought his protection. This was the doing of the God of Saints, Who worketh and changeth all things for the best, who resisteth the proud, but giveth grace to

---

α 1 Kings xi. 14.

β *The prefect.* Eusebius.

the humble.[a] And why should not He, Who divided the sea and stayed the river, and ruled the elements, and by stretching out set up a trophy, to save His exiled people, why should not He have also rescued this man from his perils?

58. This was the end and fortunate close, in the Providence of God, of the war with the world, a close worthy of his faith. But here at once is the beginning of the war with the Bishops, and their allies, which involved great disgrace, and still greater injury to their subjects. For who could persuade others to be temperate, when such was the conduct of their prelates? For a long time they had been unkindly disposed towards him, on three grounds. They neither agreed with him in the matter of the faith, except in so far as they were absolutely obliged to yield to the majority of the faithful. Nor had they altogether laid aside the grudge they owed him for his election. And, what was most grievous of all to them, though they would have been most ashamed to own it—he so far outshone them in reputation. There was also a further cause of dissension which stirred up again the others. When our country had been divided into two provinces and metropolitical sees, and a great part of the former was being added to the new one, this again roused their factious spirit. The one[β] thought it right that the ecclesiastical boundaries should be settled by the civil ones: and therefore claimed those newly added, as belonging to him, and severed from their former metropolitan. The other[γ] clung to the ancient custom, and to the division which had come down from our fathers. Many painful results either actually followed, or were struggling in the womb of the future. Synods were wrongfully gathered by the new metropolitan, and revenues seized upon. Some of the presbyters of the churches refused obedience, others were won over. In consequence the affairs of the churches fell into a sad state of dissension and division. Novelty indeed has a certain charm for men, and they readily turn events to their own advantage, and it is easier to overthrow something which is already established, than to restore it when overthrown. What however enraged him most was, that the revenues[δ] of the Taurus, which passed along before his eyes, accrued to his rival, as also the offerings at Saint Orestes',[a] of which he was greatly desirous to reap the fruits. He even went so far as, on one occasion when Basil was riding along his own road, to seize his mules by the bridle and bar the passage with a robber band. And with how specious a pretext, the care of his spiritual children and of the souls entrusted to him, and the defence of the faith—pretexts which veiled that most common vice, insatiable avarice—and further, the wrongfulness of paying dues to heretics, a heretic being any one who had displeased him.

59. The holy man of God however, metropolitan as he was of the true Jerusalem above, was neither carried away with the failure of those who fell, nor allowed himself to overlook this conduct, nor did he desire any inadequate remedy for the evil. Let us see how great and wonderful it was, or, I would say, how worthy of his soul. He made of the dissension a cause of increase to the Church, and the disaster, under his most able management, resulted in the multiplication of the Bishops of the country. From this ensued three most desirable consequences; a greater care for souls, the management by each city of its own affairs, and the cessation of the war in this quarter. I am afraid that I myself was treated as an appendage to this scheme. By no other term can I readily describe the position. Greatly as I admire his whole conduct, to an extent indeed beyond my powers of expression, of this single particular I find it impossible to approve, for I will acknowledge my feelings in regard to it, though these are from other sources not unknown to most of you. I mean the change and faithlessness of his treatment of myself, a cause of pain which even time has not obliterated. For this is the source of all the inconsistency and tangle of my life; it has robbed me of the practice, or at least the reputation, of philosophy; of small moment though the latter be. The defence, which you will perhaps allow me to make for him, is this; his ideas were superhuman, and having, before his death, become superior to worldly influences, his only interests were those of the Spirit: while his regard for friendship was in no wise lessened by his readiness then, and then only, to disregard its claims, when they were in conflict with his paramount duty to God, and when the end he had in view was of greater importance than the interests he was compelled to set aside.

60. I am afraid that, in avoiding the imputation of indifference at the hands of those

α S. James iv. 6.
β *The one*, i.e., Anthimus, Bishop of Tyana.
γ *The other*, i.e., Basil.
δ *Revenues.* The dues and offerings of the people of the diocese.

a *Orestes.* A chapel dedicated to S. Orestes at the foot of Mt. Taurus, where the offerings were collected.

who desire to know all that can be said about him, I shall incur a charge of prolixity from those whose ideal is the golden mean. For the latter Basil himself had the greatest respect, being specially devoted to the adage "In all things the mean [a] is the best," and acting upon it throughout his life. Nevertheless, disregarding alike those who desire undue conciseness or excessive prolixity, I proceed thus with my speech. Different men attain success in different ways, some applying themselves to one alone of the many forms of excellence, but no one, of those hitherto known to me, arriving at the highest eminence in all respects; he being in my opinion the best, who has won his laurels on the widest field, or gained the highest possible renown in some single particular. Such however was the height of Basil's fame, that he became the pride of human kind. Let us consider the matter thus. Is any one devoted to poverty and a life devoid of property, and free from superfluity? What did he possess besides his body, and the necessary coverings of the flesh? His wealth was the having nothing, and he thought the cross, with which he lived, more precious than great riches. For no one, however much he may wish, can obtain possession of all things, but any one can learn to despise, and so prove himself superior to, all things. Such being his mind, and such his life, he had no need of an altar and of vainglory, nor of such a public announcement as "Crates [β] sets Crates the Theban free." For his aim was ever to be, not to seem, most excellent. Nor did he dwell in a tub,[γ] and in the midst of the market-place, and so by luxuriating in publicity turn his poverty into riches: but was poor and unkempt, yet without ostentation: and taking cheerfully the casting overboard of all that he ever had, sailed lightly across the sea of life.

61. A wondrous thing is temperance, and fewness of wants, and freedom from the dominion of pleasures, and from the bondage of that cruel and degrading mistress, the belly. Who was so independent of food, and, without exaggeration, more free from the flesh? For he flung away all satiety and surfeit to creatures destitute of reason, whose life is slavish and debasing. He paid little attention to such things as, next to the appetite, are of equal rank, but, as far as possible, lived on the merest necessaries, his only luxury being to prove himself not luxurious, and not, in consequence, to have greater needs: but he looked to the lilies and the birds,[a] whose beauty is artless, and their food casual, according to the important advice of my Christ, who made Himself poor [β] in the flesh for our sakes, that we might enjoy the riches of His Godhead. Hence came his single coat and well worn cloak, and his bed on the bare ground, his vigils, his unwashedness (such were his decorations) and his most sweet food and relish, bread, and salt, his new dainty, and the sober and plentiful drink, with which fountains supply those who are free from trouble. The result, or the accompaniment, of these things were the attendance on the sick and practice of medicine, our common intellectual pursuit. For, though inferior to him in all other respects, I must needs be his equal in distress.

62. A great thing is virginity, and celibacy, and being ranked with the angels, and with the single nature; for I shrink from calling it Christ's, Who, though He willed to be born for our sakes who are born, by being born of a Virgin, enacted [γ] the law of virginity, to lead us away from this life, and cut short the power of the world, or rather, to transmit one world to another, the present to the future. Who then paid more honour to virginity, or had more control of the flesh, not only by his personal example, but in those under his care? Whose are the convents, and the written regulations, by which he subdued every sense, and regulated every member, and won to the real practice of virginity, turning inward the view of beauty, from the visible to the invisible; and by wasting away the external, and withdrawing fuel from the flame, and revealing the secrets of the heart to God, Who is the only bridegroom of pure souls, and takes in with himself the watchful souls, if they go to meet him with lamps burning and a plentiful supply of oil?[δ] Moreover he reconciled most excellently and united the solitary and the community life. These had been in many respects at variance and dissension, while neither of them was in absolute and unalloyed possession of good or evil: the one being more calm and settled, tending to union with God, yet not free from pride, inasmuch as its virtue lies beyond the means of testing or comparison; the other, which is of more practical service, being not free from the tendency to turbulence. He founded cells [ε] for ascetics

α *The mean, etc.* A saying of Cleobulus, one of the seven Sages.

β *Crates.* He made this proclamation when he had stripped himself of all his possessions.

γ *In a tub*, like Diogenes, the Cynic.

α S. Matt. vi. 26. β 2 Cor. viii. 9.

γ *Enacted* by his religious rule, or as some say by a treatise on Virginity. δ S. Matt. xxv. 2.

ε *Cells, etc.* This passage strongly favours the view of Clemencet that S. Gregory uses μοναστήρια in the literal sense of "the

and hermits, but at no great distance from his cenobitic communities, and, instead of distinguishing and separating the one from the other, as if by some intervening wall, he brought them together and united them, in order that the contemplative spirit might not be cut off from society, nor the active life be uninfluenced by the contemplative, but that, like sea and land, by an interchange of their several gifts, they might unite in promoting the one object, the glory of God.

63. What more? A noble thing is philanthropy, and the support of the poor, and the assistance of human weakness. Go forth a little way from the city, and behold the new city,[α] the storehouse of piety, the common treasury of the wealthy, in which the superfluities of their wealth, aye, and even their necessaries, are stored, in consequence of his exhortations, freed from the power of the moth,[β] no longer gladdening the eyes of the thief, and escaping both the emulation of envy, and the corruption of time: where disease is regarded in a religious light, and disaster is thought a blessing, and sympathy is put to the test. Why should I compare with this work Thebes[γ] of the seven portals, and the Egyptian Thebes, and the walls of Babylon, and the Carian tomb of Mausolus, and the Pyramids, and the bronze without weight of the Colossus, or the size and beauty of shrines that are no more, and all the other objects of men's wonder, and historic record, from which their founders gained no advantage, except a slight meed of fame. My subject is the most wonderful of all, the short road to salvation, the easiest ascent to heaven. There is no longer before our eyes that terrible and piteous spectacle of men who are living corpses, the greater part of whose limbs have mortified, driven away from their cities and homes and public places and fountains, aye, and from their own dearest ones, recognizable by their names rather than by their features: they are no longer brought before us at our gatherings and meetings, in our common intercourse and union, no longer the objects of hatred, instead of pity on account of their disease; composers of piteous songs, if any of them have their voice still left to them. Why should I try to express in tragic style all our experiences, when no language can be adequate to their hard lot? He however it was, who took the lead in pressing upon those who were men, that they ought not to despise their fellowmen, nor to dishonour Christ, the one Head of all, by their inhuman treatment of them; but to use the misfortunes of others as an opportunity of firmly establishing their own lot, and to lend to God that mercy of which they stand in need at His hands. He did not therefore disdain to honour with his lips this disease, noble and of noble ancestry and brilliant reputation though he was, but saluted them as brethren, not, as some might suppose, from vainglory, (for who was so far removed from this feeling?) but taking the lead in approaching to tend them, as a consequence of his philosophy, and so giving not only a speaking, but also a silent, instruction. The effect produced is to be seen not only in the city, but in the country and beyond, and even the leaders of society have vied with one another in their philanthropy and magnanimity towards them. Others have had their cooks, and splendid tables, and the devices and dainties of confectioners, and exquisite carriages, and soft, flowing robes; Basil's care was for the sick, and the relief of their wounds, and the imitation of Christ, by cleansing leprosy, not by a word, but in deed.

64. As to all this, what will be said by those who charge him with pride and haughtiness? Severe critics they are of such conduct, applying to him, whose life was a standard, those who were not standards at all. Is it possible that he who kissed the lepers, and humiliated himself to such a degree, could treat haughtily those who were in health: and, while wasting his flesh by abstinence, puff out his soul with empty arrogance? Is it possible to condemn the Pharisee, and expound the debasing effect of haughtiness, to know Christ, Who condescended to the form of a slave, and ate with publicans, and washed the disciples' feet, and did not disdain the cross, in order to nail my sin to it: and, more incredible still, to see God crucified, aye, along with robbers also, and derided by the passers by, impassible, and beyond the reach of suffering as He is; and yet, as his slanderers imagine, soar himself above the clouds, and think that nothing can be on an equality with him. Nay, what they term pride is, I fancy, the firmness and steadfastness and stability of his character. Such persons would readily, it seems to me, call bravery rashness, and the circumspect a coward, and the temperate misanthropic, and the just illiberal. For indeed this philosophic axiom is excellent, which says that the vices[α] are settled close to the

abodes of solitaries." and that there is no great distinction between κοινωνικοί and μιγάδες. Cf. ii. 29. xxi. 10–19.

α *New city*—a hospital for the sick.

β S. Matt. vi. 19.

γ *Thebes, etc.* The "seven wonders of the world."

α *The vices.* This was the doctrine of Menander and Aristotle.

virtues, and are, in some sense, their next-door neighbours: and it is most easy, for those whose training in such subjects has been defective, to mistake a man for what he is not. For who honoured virtue and castigated vice more than he, or showed himself more kind to the upright, more severe to the wrong doers? His very smile often amounted to praise, his silence to rebuke, racking the evil in the secret conscience. And if a man have not been a chatterer, and jester, and gossip, nor a general favourite, because of having pleased others by becoming all things to all men,[α] what of that? Is he not in the eyes of sensible men worthy of praise rather than of blame? Unless it is a fault in the lion that he is terrible and royal, and does not look like an ape, and that his spring is noble, and is valued for its wonderfulness: while stage-players ought to win our admiration for their pleasant and philanthropic characters, because they please the vulgar, and raise a laugh by their sounding slaps in the face. And if this indeed be our object, who was so pleasant when you met him, as I know, who have had the longest experience? Who was more kindly in his stories, more refined in his wit, more tender in his rebukes? His reproofs gave rise to no arrogance, his relaxation to no dissipation, but avoiding excess in either, he made use of both in reason and season, according to the rules of Solomon, who assigns to every business a season.[β]

65. But what are these to his renown for eloquence, and his powers of instruction, which have won the favour of the ends of the world? As yet we have been compassing the foot of the mountain, to the neglect of its summit, as yet we have been crossing a strait, paying no heed to the mighty and deep ocean. For I think that if any one ever has become, or can become, a trumpet, in his far sounding resonance, or a voice of God, embracing the universe, or an earthquake of the world, by some unheard of miracle, it is his voice and intellect which deserve these titles, for surpassing and excelling all men as much as we surpass the irrational creatures. Who, more than he, cleansed himself by the Spirit, and made himself worthy to set forth divine things? Who was more enlightened by the light of knowledge, and had a closer insight into the depths of the Spirit, and by the aid of God beheld the things of God? Whose language could better express intellectual truth, without, as most men do, limping on one foot, by either failing to express his ideas, or allowing his eloquence to outstrip his reasoning powers? In both respects he won a like distinction, and showed himself to be his own equal, and absolutely perfect. To search all things, yea, the deep things of God[α] is, according to the testimony of S. Paul, the office of the Spirit, not because He is ignorant of them, but because He takes delight in their contemplation. Now all the things of the Spirit Basil had fully investigated, and hence he drew his instructions for every kind of character, his lessons in the sublime, and his exhortations to quit things present, and adapt ourselves to things to come.

66. The sun is extolled by David for its beauty, its greatness, its swift course, and its power, splendid as a bridegroom, majestic as a giant;[β] while, from the extent of its circuit, it has such power that it equally sheds its light from one end of heaven to the other, and the heat thereof is in no wise lessened by distance. Basil's beauty was virtue, his greatness theology, his course the perpetual motion reaching even to God by its ascents, and his power the sowing and distribution of the Word. So that I will not hesitate to say even this, his utterance went out into all lands,[γ] and the power of his words to the ends of the world: as S. Paul says of the Apostles,[δ] borrowing the words from David. What other charm is there in any gathering to-day? What pleasure in banquets, in the courts, in the churches? What delight in those in authority, and those beneath them? What in the hermits, or the cenobites? What in the leisured classes, or those busied in affairs? What in profane schools of philosophy or in our own? There is one, which runs through all, and is the greatest—his writings and labours. Nor do writers require any supply of matter besides his teaching or writings. All the laborious studies of old days in the Divine oracles are silent, while the new ones are in everybody's mouth, and he is the best teacher among us who has the deepest acquaintance with his works, and speaks of them and explains them in our ears. For he alone more than supplies the place of all others to those who are specially eager for instruction.

67. I will only say this of him. Whenever I handle his Hexaemeron, and take its words on my lips, I am brought into the presence of the Creator, and understand the words of creation, and admire the Creator more than before, using my teacher as my only means of

α 1 Cor. ix. 22. β Eccles. iii. 1.

α 1 Cor. ii. 10. β Ps. xix. 6. γ Ps. xix. 5. δ Rom. x. 18.

sight. Whenever I take up his polemical works, I see the fire of Sodom,[a] by which the wicked and rebellious tongues are reduced to ashes, or the tower of Chalane,[β] impiously built,[γ] and righteously destroyed. Whenever I read his writings on the Spirit, I find the God Whom I possess, and grow bold in my utterance of the truth, from the support of his theology and contemplation. His other treatises, in which he gives explanations for those who are shortsighted, by a threefold inscription on the solid tablets of his heart, lead me on from a mere literal or symbolical interpretation to a still wider view, as I proceed from one depth to another, calling upon deep[δ] after deep, and finding light after light, until I attain the highest pinnacle. When I study his panegyrics on our athletes, I despise the body, and enjoy the society of those whom he is praising, and rouse myself to the struggle. His moral and practical discourses purify soul and body, making me a temple fit for God, and an instrument struck by the Spirit, to celebrate by its strains the glory and power of God. In fact, he reduces me to harmony and order, and changes me by a Divine transformation.

68. Since I have mentioned theology, and his most sublime treatises in this science, I will make this addition to what I have already said. For it is of great service to the community, to save them from being injured by an unjustifiably low opinion of him. My remarks are directed against those evil disposed persons who shelter their own vices under cover of their calumnies against others. In his defence of orthodox teaching, and of the union and coequal divinity of the Holy Trinity, to use terms which are, I think, as exact and clear as possible, he would have eagerly welcomed as a gain, and not a danger, not only expulsion from his see, in which he had originally no desire to be enthroned, but even exile, and death, and its preliminary tortures. This is manifest from his actual conduct and sufferings. For when he had been sentenced to banishment on behalf of the truth, the only notice which he took of it was, to bid one of his servants to take his writing tablet and follow him. He held it necessary, according to the divine David's advice, to guide his words with discretion,[ε] and to endure for a while the time of war, and the ascendency of the heretics, until it should be succeeded by a time of freedom and calm, which would admit of freedom of speech. The enemy were on the watch for the unqualified statement "the Spirit is God;" which, although it is true, they and the wicked patron of their impiety imagined to be impious; so that they might banish him and his power of theological instruction from the city, and themselves be able to seize upon the church, and make it the starting point and citadel, from which they could overrun with their evil doctrine the rest of the world. Accordingly, by the use of other terms, and by statements which unmistakably had the same meaning, and by arguments necessarily leading to this conclusion, he so overpowered his antagonists, that they were left without reply, and involved in their own admissions,—the greatest proof possible of dialectical power and skill. His treatise on this subject makes it further manifest, being evidently written by a pen borrowed from the Spirit's store. He postponed for the time the use of the exact term, begging as a favour from the Spirit Himself and his earnest champions, that they would not be annoyed at his economy,[a] nor, by clinging to a single expression, ruin the whole cause, from an uncompromising temper, at a crisis when religion was in peril. He assured them that they would suffer no injury from a slight change in their expressions, and from teaching the same truth in other terms. For our salvation is not so much a matter of words as of actions; for we would not reject the Jews, if they desired to unite with us, and yet for a while sought to use the term "Anointed" instead of "Christ:" while the community would suffer a very serious injury, if the church were seized upon by the heretics.

69. That he, no less than any other, acknowledged that the Spirit is God, is plain from his often having publicly preached this truth, whenever opportunity offered, and eagerly confessed it when questioned in private. But he made it more clear in his conversations with me, from whom he concealed nothing during our conferences upon this subject. Not content with simply asserting it, he proceeded, as he had but very seldom done before, to imprecate upon himself that most terrible fate of separation from the Spirit, if he did not adore the Spirit as consubstantial and coequal with the Father and the Son. And if any one would accept me as having been his fellow labourer in this cause, I will set forth one point hitherto unknown to most men. Under the pressure of the difficulties

a Gen. xix. 24. β *Chalane.* LXX. for Babel.
γ Gen. xi. 4. δ Ps. xlii. 8. ε Ib. cxii. 5.

a *Economy.* In refraining from the express assertion "The Holy Ghost is God"—some have blamed S. Basil for this: but his conduct has the approval of S. Athanasius. Ep. ad Palladium.

of the period, he himself undertook the economy, while allowing freedom of speech to me, whom no one was likely to drag from obscurity to trial or banishment, in order that by our united efforts our Gospel might be firmly established. I mention this, not to defend his reputation, for the man is stronger than his assailants, if there are any such; but to prevent men from thinking that the terms found in his writings are the utmost limit of the truth, and so have their faith weakened, and consider that their own error is supported by his theology, which was the joint result of the influences of the time and of the Spirit, instead of considering the sense of his writings, and the object with which they were written, so as to be brought closer to the truth, and enabled to silence the partisans of impiety. At any rate let his theology be mine, and that of all dear to me! And so confident am I of his spotlessness in this respect, that I take him for my partner in this, as in all else: and may what is mine be attributed to him, what is his to me, both at the hands of God, and of the wisest of men! For we would not say that the Evangelists are at variance with one another, because some are more occupied with the human side of the Christ, and others pay attention to His Divinity; some having commenced their history with what is within our own experience, others with what is above us; and by thus sharing the substance of their message, they have procured the advantage of those who receive it, and followed the impressions of the Spirit Who was within them.

70. Come then, there have been many men of old days illustrious for piety, as lawgivers, generals, prophets, teachers, and men brave to the shedding of blood. Let us compare our prelate with them, and thus recognize his merit. Adam was honoured by the hand of God,[α] and the delights of Paradise,[β] and the first legislation:[γ] but, unless I slander the reputation of our first parent, he kept not the command. Now Basil both received and observed it, and received no injury from the tree of knowledge, and escaped the flaming sword, and, as I am well assured, has attained to Paradise. Enos first ventured to call upon the Lord.[δ] Basil both called upon Him himself, and, what is far more excellent, preached Him to others. Enoch was translated,[ε] attaining to his translation as the reward of a little piety (for the faith was still in shadow) and escaped the peril of the remainder of life, but Basil's whole life was a translation, and he was completely tested in a complete life. Noah was entrusted with the ark,[α] and the seeds of a new world committed to a small house of wood, in their preservation from the waters. Basil escaped the deluge of impiety and made of his own city an ark of safety, which sailed lightly over the heretics, and afterwards recovered the whole world.

α Gen. i. 27. β Ib. ii. 8. γ Ib. ii. 16. δ Ib. iv. 26. ε Ib. v. 21.

71. Abraham was a great man, a patriarch, the offerer of the new sacrifice,[β] by presenting to Him who had given it the promised seed, as a ready offering, eager for slaughter. But Basil's offering was no slight one, when he offered himself to God, without any equivalent being given in his stead, (for how could that have been possible?) so that his sacrifice was consummated. Isaac was promised even before his birth,[γ] Basil promised himself, and took for his spouse Rebekah, I mean the Church, not fetched from a distance by the mission of a servant,[δ] but bestowed upon and entrusted to him by God close at home: nor was he outwitted in the preference of his children, but bestowed upon each what was due to him, without any deception, according to the judgment of the Spirit. I extol the ladder of Jacob,[ε] and the pillar which he anointed to God, and his wrestling with Him, whatever it was; and, in my opinion, it was the contrast and opposition of the human stature to the height of God, resulting in the tokens of the defeat[ζ] of his race. I extol also his clever devices and success in cattle-breeding, and his children, the twelve Patriarchs, and the distribution of his blessings, with their glorious prophecy of the future. But I still more extol Basil for the ladder which he did not merely see, but which he ascended by successive steps towards excellence, and the pillar which he did not anoint, but which he erected to God, by pillorying the teaching of the ungodly; and the wrestling with which he wrestled, not with God, but, on behalf of God, to the overthrow of the heretics; and his pastoral care, whereby he grew rich, through gaining for himself a number of marked sheep greater than that of the unmarked, and his illustrious fruitfulness in spiritual children, and the blessing with which he established many.

72. Joseph was a provider of corn,[η] but in Egypt only, and not frequently, and of bodily food. Basil did so for all men, and at all

α Gen. vi. 13. β Ib. xxii. i. γ Ib. xviii. 10. δ Ib. xxiv. 3. ε Ib. xxviii. 12. ζ *Defeat* or "loss of generative power." η Gen. xli. 40.

times, and in spiritual food, and therefore, in my opinion, his was the more honourable function. Like Job, the man of Uz,[α] he was both tempted, and overcame, and at the close of his struggles gained splendid honour, having been shaken by none of his many assailants, and having gained a decisive victory over the efforts of the tempter, and put to silence the unreason of his friends, who knew not the mysterious character of his affliction. "Moses and Aaron among His priests."[β] Truly was Moses great, who inflicted the plagues upon Egypt,[γ] and delivered the people among many signs and wonders, and entered within the cloud, and sanctioned the double law, outward in the letter, and inward in the Spirit. Aaron was Moses' brother,[δ] both naturally and spiritually, and offered sacrifices and prayers for the people, as the hierophant of the great and holy tabernacle, which the Lord pitched, and not man.[ε] Of both of them Basil was a rival, for he tortured, not with bodily but with spiritual and mental plagues, the Egyptian race of heretics, and led to the land of promise[ς] the people of possession, zealous of good works;[η] he inscribed laws, which are no longer obscure, but entirely spiritual, on tables[θ] which are not broken but are preserved; he entered the Holy of holies,[ι] not once a year, but often, I may say every day, and thence he revealed to us the Holy Trinity; and cleansed the people, not with temporary sprinklings, but with eternal purifications. What is the special excellence of Joshua?[κ] His generalship, and the distribution of the inheritance, and the taking possession of the Holy Land. And was not Basil an Exarch?[λ] Was he not a general of those who are saved by faith?[μ] Did he not assign the different inheritances and abodes, according to the will of God, among his followers? So that he too could use the words, "The lot is fallen unto me in pleasant places;"[ν] and "my fortunes are in Thy hands,"[ξ] fortunes more precious than those which come to us on earth, and can be snatched away.

73. Further, to run over the Judges, or the most illustrious of the Judges, there is "Samuel among those that call upon His Name,"[ο] who was given to God before his birth,[π] and sanctified immediately after his birth, and the anointer with his horn of kings and priests.[ρ] But was not Basil as an infant consecrated to God from the womb, and offered with a coat[α] at the altar, and was he not a seer of heavenly things, and anointed of the Lord, and the anointer of those who are perfected by the Spirit? Among the kings, David is celebrated, whose victories and trophies[β] gained from the enemy are on record, but his most characteristic trait was his gentleness,[γ] and, before his kingly office, his power with the harp, able to soothe even the evil spirit. Solomon asked of God and obtained breadth of heart,[δ] making the furthest possible progress in wisdom and contemplation, so that he became the most famous man of his time. Basil, in my opinion, was in no wise, or but little inferior, to the one in gentleness, to the other in wisdom, so that he soothed the arrogance of infuriated sovereigns; and did not merely bring the queen of the south from the ends of the earth, or any other individual, to visit him because of his renown for wisdom, but made his wisdom known in all the ends of the world. I pass over the rest of Solomon's life. Even if we spare it, it is evident to all.

74. Do you praise the courage of Elijah[ε] in the presence of tyrants, and his fiery translation?[ς] Or the fair inheritance of Elisha, the sheepskin mantle, accompanied by the spirit of Elijah?[η] You must also praise the life of Basil, spent in the fire. I mean in the multitude of temptations, and his escape through fire, which burnt, but did not consume, the mystery of "the bush,"[θ] and the fair cloak of skin from on high, his indifference to the flesh. I pass by the rest, the three young men bedewed in the fire,[ι] the fugitive prophet praying in the whale's belly,[κ] and coming forth from the creature, as from a chamber; the just man in the den, restraining the lions' rage,[λ] and the struggle of the seven Maccabees,[μ] who were perfected with their father and mother in blood, and in all kinds of tortures. Their endurance he rivalled, and won their glory.

75. I now turn to the New Testament, and comparing his life with those who are here illustrious, I shall find in the teachers a source of honour for their disciple. Who was the forerunner of Jesus?[ν] John, the voice of the Word,[ξ] the lamp of the Light,[ο] before Whom he even leaped in the womb,[π] and Whom he preceded to Hades, whither he was despatched by the rage of Herod,[ρ] to herald even there

α Job i. 1. β Ps. xcix. 6. γ Exod. vii. 8 et seq. δ Ib. xxix. 4. ε Heb. viii. 2. ς Ib. xi. 9. η Tit. ii. 14. θ 2 Cor. iii. 3. ι Exod. xxiv. 8; Heb. ix. 19. κ Josh. i. 2. λ *Exarch* or Metropolitan. μ Eph. ii. 8. ν Ps. xvi. 6. ξ Ib. xxxi. 16. ο Ib. cxix. 6. π 1 Sam. i. 20. ρ Ib. xvi. 13.

α Cf. 1 Sam. ii. 19. β 2 Sam. v. 1. γ Ps. cxxxii. 1 (LXX.). δ 1 Kings iv. 29. ε 2 Kings i. 1. ς Ib. ii. 11. η Ib. ii. 13, 15. θ Exod. iii. 1. ι Dan. iii. 5. κ Jonah ii. 1. λ Dan. vi. 22. μ 2 Macc. vii. 1. ν S. Luke i. 76. ξ Ib. iii. 4. ο S. John v. 35; i. 8. π S. Luke ii. 41. ρ S. Matt. xiv. 10.

Him who was coming. And, if my language seems audacious to anyone, let me assure him beforehand, that in making this comparison, I neither prefer Basil, nor imply that he is equal to him who surpasses all who are born of women,[α] but only show that he was stirred to emulation, and possessed to some extent his striking features. For it is no slight thing for the earnest to imitate the greatest of men, even in a slight degree. Is it not indeed manifest that Basil was a copy of John's asceticism? He also lived in the wilderness, and wore in nightly watchings a ragged garb, during his shrinking retirement; he also loved a similar food, purifying himself for God by abstinence; he also was thought worthy to be a herald, if not a forerunner, of Christ, and there went out to him not only all the region round about,[β] but also that which was beyond its borders; he also stood between the two covenants, abolishing the letter of the one by administering the spirit of the other, and bringing about the fulfilment of the hidden law through the dissolution of that which was apparent.

76. He emulated the zeal of Peter,[γ] the intensity of Paul, the faith of both these men of name and of surname, the lofty utterance of the sons of Zebedee, the frugality and simplicity of all the disciples. Therefore he was also entrusted with the keys of the heavens,[δ] and not only from Jerusalem and round about unto Illyricum,[ε] but he embraces a wider circle in the Gospel; he is not named, but becomes, a Son of thunder; and lying upon the breast of Jesus, he draws thence the power of his word, and the depth of his thoughts. He was prevented from becoming a Stephen,[ς] eager though he was, since reverence stayed the hands of those who would have stoned him. I am able to sum up still more concisely, to avoid treating in detail on these points of each individual. In some respects he discovered, in some he emulated, in others he surpassed the good. In his many-sided virtues he excelled all men of this day. I have but one thing left to say, and in few words.

77. So great was his virtue, and the eminence of his fame, that many of his minor characteristics, nay, even his physical defects, have been assumed by others with a view to notoriety. For instance his paleness, his beard, his gait, his thoughtful, and generally meditative, hesitation in speaking, which, in the ill-judged, inconsiderate imitation of many, took the form of melancholy. And besides, the style of his dress, the shape of his bed, and his manner of eating, none of which was to him a matter of consequence, but simply the result of accident and chance. So you might see many Basils in outward semblance, among these statues in outline, for it would be too much to call them his distant echo. For an echo, though it is the dying away of a sound, at any rate represents it with great clearness, while these men fall too far short of him to satisfy even their desire to approach him. Nor was it a slight thing, but a matter with good reason held in the highest estimation, to chance to have met him or done him some service, or to carry away the souvenir of something which he had said or done in jest or in earnest: as I know that I have myself often taken pride in doing; for his improvisations were much more precious and brilliant than the laboured efforts of other men.

78. But when, after he had finished his course, and kept the faith,[α] he longed to depart, and the time for his crown was approaching,[β] he did not hear the summons: "Get thee up into the mountain and die,"[γ] but "Die, and come up to us." And here again he wrought a wonder in no wise inferior to those mentioned before. For when he was almost dead, and breathless, and had lost the greater part of his powers, he grew stronger in his last words, so as to depart with the utterances of religion, and, by ordaining the most excellent of his attendants, bestowed upon them both his hand and the Spirit: so that his disciples, who had aided him in his priestly office, might not be defrauded of the priesthood. The remainder of my task I approach, but with reluctance, as it would fall more fitly from the mouths of others than from my own. For I cannot philosophise over my misfortune, even if I greatly longed to do so, when I recollect that the loss is common to us all, and that the misfortune has befallen the whole world.

79. He lay, drawing his last breath, and awaited by the choir on high, towards which he had long directed his gaze. Around him poured the whole city, unable to bear his loss, inveighing against his departure, as if it had been an oppression, and clinging to his soul, as though it had been capable of restraint or compulsion at their hands or their prayers. Their suffering had driven them distracted, all were eager, were it possible, to add to his life a portion of their own. And when they failed, for it must needs be proved that he was a man, and, with his last words "Into thy Hands I commend my spirit,"[δ] he had joyfully resigned his soul to the care of the angels who carried him away; not without having some religious instructions and injunctions for the benefit of those who were present—then occurred a wonder more remarkable than any which had happened before.

80. The saint was being carried out, lifted high by the hands of holy men, and everyone was eager, some to seize the hem of his garment,[ε] others only just to touch the shadow,[ς] or the bier which bore his holy remains (for what could be more holy or pure than that body), others to draw near to those who were carrying

α S. Matt. xi. 11. β Ib. iii. 5. γ Acts iv. 8. δ S. Matt. xvi. 1. ε Rom. xv. 1. ς Acts vii. 58.

α 2 Tim. iv. 7. β Phil. i. 23. γ Deut. xxxii. 49. δ Ps. xxxi. 6. ε S. Luke viii. 44. ς Acts v. 15.

it, others only to enjoy the sight, as if even this were beneficial. Market places, porticos, houses of two or three stories were filled with people escorting, preceding, following, accompanying him, and trampling upon each other; tens of thousands of every race and age, beyond all previous experience. The psalmody was overborne by the lamentations, philosophic resignation sank beneath the misfortune. Our own people vied with strangers, Jews, Greeks, and foreigners, and they with us, for a greater share in the benefit, by means of a more abundant lamentation. To close my story, the calamity ended in danger; many souls departed along with him, from the violence of the pushing and confusion, who have been thought happy in their end, departing together with him, "funeral victims," perhaps some fervid orator might call them. The body having at last escaped from those who would seize it, and made its way through those who went before it, was consigned to the tomb of his fathers, the high priest being added to the priests, the mighty voice which rings in my ears to the heralds, the martyr to the martyrs. And now he is in heaven, where, if I mistake not, he is offering sacrifices for us, and praying for the people, for though he has left us, he has not entirely left us. While I, Gregory, who am half dead, and, cleft in twain, torn away from our great union, and dragging along a life of pain which runs not easily, as may be supposed, after separation from him, know not what is to be my end now that I have lost my guidance. And even now I am admonished and instructed in nightly visions, if ever I fall short of my duty. And my present object is not so much to mingle lamentations with my praises, or to portray the public life of the man, or publish a picture of virtue common to all time, and an example salutary to all churches, and to all souls, which we may keep in view, as a living law, and so rightly direct our lives as to counsel you, who have been completely initiated into his doctrine, to fix your eyes upon him, as one who sees you and is seen by you, and thus to be perfected by the Spirit.

81. Come hither then, and surround me, all ye members of his choir, both of the clergy and the laity, both of our own country and from abroad; aid me in my eulogy, by each supplying or demanding the account of some of his excellences. Regard, ye occupants of the bench, the lawgiver; ye politicians, the statesman; ye men of the people, his orderliness; ye men of letters, the instructor; ye virgins, the leader of the bride; ye who are yoked in marriage, the restrainer; ye hermits, him who gave you wings; ye cenobites, the judge; ye simple men, the guide; ye contemplatives, the divine; ye cheerful ones, the bridle; ye unfortunate men, the consoler, the staff of hoar hairs, the guide of youth, the relief of poverty, the steward of abundance. Widows also will, I imagine, praise their protector, orphans their father, poor men their friend, strangers their entertainer, brothers the man of brotherly love, the sick their physician, whatever be their sickness and the healing they need, the healthy the preserver of health, and all men him who made himself all things to all that he might gain the majority, if not all.

82. This is my offering to thee, Basil, uttered by the tongue which once was the sweetest of all to thee, of him who was thy fellow in age and rank. If it have approached thy deserts, thanks are due to thee, for it was from confidence in thee that I undertook to speak of thee. But if it fall far short of thy expectations, what must be our feelings, who are worn out with age and disease and regret for thee? Yet God is pleased, when we do what we can. Yet mayest thou gaze upon us from above, thou divine and sacred person; either stay by thy entreaties our thorn in the flesh,[α] given to us by God for our discipline, or prevail upon us to bear it boldly, and guide all our life towards that which is most for our profit. And if we be translated, do thou receive us there also in thine own tabernacle, that, as we dwell together, and gaze together more clearly and more perfectly upon the holy and blessed Trinity, of Which we have now in some degree received the image, our longing may at last be satisfied, by gaining this recompense for all the battles we have fought and the assaults we have endured. Such are our words on thy behalf: who will there be to praise us, since we leave this life after thee, even if we offer any topic worthy of words or praise in Christ Jesus our Lord, to Whom be glory forever? Amen.

INTRODUCTION TO THE SECOND ORATION ON EASTER.

THIS Oration was not, as its title would perhaps lead us to suppose, delivered immediately after the first; but an interval of many years elapsed between them, and the two have no connection with each other. Chronologically they are the first and last of S. Gregory's Sermons. The Second was delivered in the Church of Arianzus, a village near Nazianzus, where he had inherited some property, to which he withdrew after resigning the Archbishopric of Constantinople, and then, finding the administration even of the little Bishopric of Nazianzus too much for his advancing years and declining strength, he retired to Arianzus about the end of A.D. 383, dying there in 389 or 390. "The exordium of this discourse is quite in the style of the Bible; the Orator here describes and puts words into the mouth of the Angel of the Resurrection. His object is to show the importance of the day's solemnities, and to explain allegorically all the circumstances of the ancient Passover, applying them to Christ and the Christian life. Two passages are borrowed verbatim from the discourse on the Nativity, preached at Constantinople" (Bénoît).

The Benedictine Editors profess themselves unable to determine whether this repetition is due to S. Gregory himself—or to the carelessness of some amanuensis.

ORATION XLV.

THE SECOND ORATION ON EASTER.

I. I will stand upon my watch,[β] saith the venerable Habakkuk; and I will take my post beside him today on the authority and observation which was given me of the Spirit; and I will look forth, and will observe what shall be said to me. Well, I have taken my stand, and looked forth; and behold a man riding on the clouds and he is very high, and his countenance is as the countenance of an Angel,[γ] and his vesture as the brightness of piercing lightning; and he lifts his hand toward the East, and cries with a loud voice. His voice is like the voice of a trumpet; and round about Him is as it were a multitude of the Heavenly Host; and he saith, Today is salvation come unto the world, to that which

α 2 Cor. xii. 7. β Hab. ii. 1. γ Jud. xiii. 6.

is visible, and to that which is invisible. Christ is risen from the dead, rise ye with Him. Christ is returned again to Himself, return ye. Christ is freed from the tomb, be ye freed from the bond of sin. The gates of hell are opened, and death is destroyed, and the old Adam is put aside, and the New is fulfilled; if any man be in Christ he is a new creature;[α] be ye renewed. Thus he speaks; and the rest sing out, as they did before when Christ was manifested to us by His birth on earth, their glory to God in the highest, on earth, peace, goodwill among men.[β] And with them I also utter the same words among you. And would that I might receive a voice that should rank with the Angel's, and should sound through all the ends of the earth.

II. The Lord's Passover, the Passover, and again I say the Passover to the honour of the Trinity. This is to us a Feast of feasts and a Solemnity of solemnities[γ] as far exalted above all others (not only those which are merely human and creep on the ground, but even those which are of Christ Himself, and are celebrated in His honour) as the Sun is above the stars. Beautiful indeed yesterday was our splendid array, and our illumination, in which both in public and private we associated ourselves, every kind of men, and almost every rank, illuminating the night with our crowded fires, formed after the fashion of that great light, both that with which the heaven above us lights its beacon fires, and that which is above the heavens, amid the angels (the first luminous nature, next to the first nature of all, because springing directly from it), and that which is in the Trinity, from which all light derives its being, parted from the undivided light and honoured. But today's is more beautiful and more illustrious; inasmuch as yesterday's light was a forerunner of the rising of the Great Light, and as it were a kind of rejoicing in preparation for the Festival; but today we are celebrating the Resurrection itself, no longer as an object of expectation, but as having already come to pass, and gathering the whole world unto itself. Let then different persons bring forth different fruits and offer different offerings at this season, smaller or greater . . such spiritual offerings as are dear to God . . as each may have power. For scarcely Angels themselves could offer gifts worthy of its rank, those first and intellectual and pure beings, who are also eye-witnesses of the Glory That is on high; if even these can attain the full strain of praise. We will for our part offer a discourse, the best and most precious thing we have—especially as we are praising the Word for the blessing which He hath bestowed on the reasoning creation. I will begin from this point. For I cannot endure, when I am engaged in offering the sacrifice of the lips concerning the Great Sacrifice and the greatest of days, to fail to recur to God, and to take my beginning from Him. Therefore I pray you, cleanse your mind and ears and thoughts, all you who delight in such subjects, since the discourse will be concerning God, and will be divine; that you may depart filled with delights of a sort that do not pass away into nothingness. And it shall be at once very full and very concise, so as neither to distress you by its deficiencies, nor to displease you by satiety.

III. God[α] always was and always is, and always will be; or rather, God always Is[β] For Was and Will Be are fragments of our time, and of changeable nature. But He is Eternal Being; and this is the Name He gives Himself when giving the Oracles to Moses in the Mount. For in Himself He sums up and contains all Being, having neither beginning in the past nor end in the future . . like some great Sea of Being, limitless and unbounded, transcending all conception of time and nature, only adumbrated by the mind, and that very dimly and scantily . . not by His Essentials but by His Environment,[γ] one image being got from one source and another from another, and combined into some sort of presentation of the truth, which escapes us before we have caught it, and which takes to flight before we have conceived it, blazing forth upon our master-part, even when that is cleansed, as the lightning flash which will not stay its

α 2 Cor. v. 17.

β The reading εὐδοκία of the Received Text is pronounced by Tischendorf to have less authority than εὐδοκίας, which he adopts on the testimony of important MSS., but chiefly on the strength of a citation and comment three times in Origen, and because all the Latin Fathers read *bonæ voluntatis*. Lachmann, Tregelles, Westcott, and with some hesitation Alford follow him; though Tregelles and Westcott allow εὐδοκίας a place in the margin. Wordsworth (giving no reason); and Scrivener because he thinks it makes better sense, read εὐδοκια, and scout εὐδοκίας; which, however, is found in four of the five oldest MSS., and in all the Latin versions and Fathers. The Greek Fathers, however, all but unanimously support the Received Text.

γ ἑορτὴ ἑορτῶν, καὶ πανήγυρις πανηγύριον. ἑορτή says Nicetas, is one thing, πανήγυρις another. ἑορτή is the Commemoration of a Saint; πανήγυρις is Easter, or Ascension, or some other mystical festival. Thus Synesius calls the Paschal Letters of the Alexandrian Patriarch πανηγυρικὰ γράμματα.

α This passage to the end of c. ix. occurs verbatim in the oration on the Theophany, cc.vii.–xiii.

β "There is no Past in Eternity, and no Future; for that which is past has ceased to be, and that which is future has not yet come into existence; but Eternity is only Present; it has no Past which does not still exist nor any Future which does not yet exist" (S. Augustine de Vera Rel., c. 49).

γ The Environment here spoken of seems to mean those created Existences of which God is the Self-Existent Cause.

course does upon our sight . . in order, as I conceive, by that part of it which we can comprehend to draw us to itself (for that which is altogether incomprehensible is outside the bounds of hope, and not within the compass of endeavour); and by that part of It which we cannot comprehend to move our wonder; and as an object of wonder to become more an object of desire; and being desired, to purify; and purifying to make us like God; so that, when we have become like Himself, God may, to use a bold expression, hold converse with us as God; being united to us, and known by us; and that perhaps to the same extent as He already knows those who are known to Him.[a] The Divine Nature, then, is boundless and hard to understand, and all that we can comprehend of Him is His boundlessness; even though one may conceive that because He is of a simple Nature He is therefore either wholly incomprehensible or perfectly comprehensible. For let us further enquire what is implied by "is of a simple Nature?" For it is quite certain that this simplicity is not itself its nature, just as composition is not by itself the essence of compound beings.

IV. And when Infinity is considered from two points of view, beginning and end (for that which is beyond these and not limited by them is Infinity), when the mind looks into the depths above, not having where to stand, and leans upon phænomena to form an idea of God it calls the Infinite and Unapproachable which it finds there by the name of Unoriginate. And when it looks into the depth below and at the future, it calls Him Undying and Imperishable. And when it draws a conclusion from the whole, it calls Him Eternal. For Eternity is neither time nor part of time; for it cannot be measured. But what time measured by the course of the sun is to us, that Eternity is to the Everlasting; namely a sort of timelike movement and interval, coextensive with Their Existence. This however is all that I must now say of God; for the present is not a suitable time, as my present subject is not the doctrine of God, but that of the Incarnation. And when I say God, I mean Father, Son, and Holy Ghost; for Godhead is neither diffused beyond These, so as to introduce a mob of gods, nor yet bounded by a smaller compass than These, so as to condemn us for a poverty stricken conception of Deity, either Judaizing to save the Monarchia, or falling into heathenism by the multitude of our gods. For the evil on either side is the same, though found in contrary directions. Thus then is the Holy of Holies, Which is hidden even from the Seraphim, and is glorified with a thrice-repeated Holy meeting in one ascription of the title Lord and God, as one of our predecessors has most beautifully and loftily reasoned out.

V. But since this movement of Self-contemplation alone could not satisfy Goodness, but Good must be poured out and go forth beyond Itself, to multiply the objects of Its beneficence (for this was essential to the highest Goodness), He first conceived the Angelic and Heavenly Powers. And this conception was a work fulfilled by His Word and perfected by His Spirit. And so the Secondary Splendours came into being, as the ministers of the Primary Splendour (whether we are to conceive of them as intelligent Spirits, or as Fire of an immaterial and incorporeal kind, or as some other nature approaching this as near as may be). I should like to say that they are incapable of movement in the direction of evil, and susceptible only of the movement of good, as being about God and illuminated with the first Rays from God (for earthly beings have but the second illumination), but I am obliged to stop short of saying that they are immovable, and to conceive and speak of them as only difficult to move, because of him who for His Splendour was called Lucifer, but became and is called Darkness through his pride; and the Apostate Hosts who are subject to him, creators of evil by their revolt against good, and our inciters.

VI. Thus then and for these reasons, He gave being to the world of thought, as far as I can reason on these matters, and estimate great things in my own poor language. Then, when His first Creation was in good order, He conceives a second world, material and visible; and this a system of earth and sky and all that is in the midst of them; an admirable creation indeed when we look at the fair form of every part, but yet more worthy of admiration when we consider the harmony and unison of the whole, and how each part fits in with every other in fair order, and all with the whole, tending to the perfect completion of the world as a Unit. This was to shew that He could call into being not only a nature akin to Himself, but also one altogether alien to Him. For akin to Deity are those natures which are intellectual, and only to be comprehended by mind; but all of which sense can take cognizance are utterly alien to It;

a John x. 15; 1 Cor. xiii. 12.

and of these the furthest removed from It are all those which are entirely destitute of soul and power of motion.

VII. Mind then and sense, thus distinguished from each other, had remained within their own boundaries, and bore in themselves the magnificence of the Creator-Word, silent praisers and thrilling heralds of His mighty work. Not yet was there any mingling of both, nor any mixture of these opposites, tokens of a greater wisdom and generosity in the creation of natures; nor as yet were the whole riches of goodness made known. Now the Creator-Word, determining to exhibit this, and to produce a single living being out of both (the invisible and the visible creation, I mean) fashions Man; and taking a body from already existing matter, and placing in it a Breath taken from Himself (which the Word knew to be an intelligent soul, and the image of God), as a sort of second world, great in littleness, He placed him on the earth, a new Angel, a mingled worshipper, fully initiated into the visible creation, but only partially into the intellectual; king of all upon earth, but subject to the King above; earthly and heavenly; temporal and yet immortal; visible and yet intellectual; half-way between greatness and lowliness; in one person combining spirit and flesh; spirit because of the favour bestowed on him, flesh on account of the height to which he had been raised; the one that he might continue to live and glorify his benefactor, the other that he might suffer, and by suffering be put in remembrance, and be corrected if he became proud in his greatness; a living creature, trained here and then moved elsewhere; and to complete the mystery, deified by its inclination to God . . . for to this, I think, tends that light of Truth which here we possess but in measure; that we should both see and experience the Splendour of God, which is worthy of Him Who made us, and will dissolve us, and remake us after a loftier fashion.

VIII. This being He placed in paradise—whatever that paradise may have been (having honoured him with the gift of free will, in order that good might belong to him as the result of his choice, no less than to Him Who had implanted the seeds of it)—to till the immortal plants, by which is perhaps meant the Divine conceptions, both the simpler and the more perfect; naked in his simplicity and inartificial life; and without any covering or screen; for it was fitting that he who was from the beginning should be such. And He gave Him a Law, as material for his free will to act upon. This Law was a commandment as to what plants he might partake of, and which one he might not touch. This latter was the Tree of Knowledge; not, however, because it was evil from the beginning when planted; nor was it forbidden because God grudged it to men—let not the enemies of God wag their tongues in that direction, or imitate the serpent. But it would have been good if partaken of at the proper time; for the Tree was, according to my theory, Contemplation, which it is only safe for those who have reached maturity of habit to enter upon; but which is not good for those who are still somewhat simple and greedy; just as neither is solid food good for those who are yet tender and have need of milk. But when through the devil's malice and the woman's caprice,[a] to which she succumbed as the more tender, and which she brought to bear upon the man, as she was the more apt to persuade—alas for my weakness, for that of my first father was mine; he forgot the commandment which had been given him, and yielded to the baleful fruit; and for his sin was banished at once from the tree of life, and from paradise, and from God; and put on the coats of skins, that is, perhaps, the coarser flesh, both mortal and contradictory. And this was the first thing which he learnt—his own shame—and he hid himself from God. Yet here too he makes a gain, namely death and the cutting off of sin, in order that evil may not be immortal. Thus, his punishment is changed into a mercy, for it is in mercy, I am persuaded, that God inflicts punishment.

IX. And having first been chastened by many means because his sins were many, whose root of evil sprang up through divers causes and sundry times, by word, by law, by prophets, by benefits, by threats, by plagues, by waters, by fires, by wars, by victories, by defeats, by signs in heaven, and signs in the air, and in the earth, and in the sea; by unexpected changes of men, of cities, of nations (the object of which was the destruction of wickedness) at last he needed a stronger remedy, for his diseases were growing worse; mutual slaughters, adulteries, perjuries, unnatural crimes, and that first and last of all evils, idolatry, and the transfer of worship from the Creator to the creatures. As these required a greater aid, so they also obtained a greater. And that was that the Word of God Himself, Who is before all worlds, the Invisible, the Incomprehensible, the Bodiless, the Begin-

a Wisd. ii. 24.

ning of beginning, the Light of Light, the Source of Life and Immortality, the Image of the Archetype, the Immovable Seal, the Unchangeable Image, the Father's Definition and Word, came to His own Image, and took on Him Flesh for the sake of our flesh, and mingled Himself with an intelligent soul for my soul's sake, purifying like by like; and in all points except sin was made Man; conceived by the Virgin, who first in body and soul was purified by the Holy Ghost, for it was needful both That Child-bearing should be honoured and that Virginity should receive a higher honour. He came forth then, as God, with That which He had assumed; one Person in two natures, flesh and Spirit, of which the latter deified the former. O new commingling; O strange conjunction! the Self-existent comes into Being, the Uncreated is created, That which cannot be contained is contained by the intervention of an intellectual soul mediating between the Deity and the corporeity of the flesh. And He who gives riches becomes poor; for He assumes the poverty of my flesh, that I may assume the riches of His Godhead. He that is full empties Himself; for He empties Himself of His Glory for a short while, that I may have a share in His Fulness. What is the riches of His Goodness? What is this mystery that is around me? I had a share in the Image and I did not keep it; He partakes of my flesh that He may both save the Image and make the flesh immortal. He communicates a Second Communion, far more marvellous than the first, inasmuch as then He imparted the better nature, but now He Himself assumes the worse. This is more godlike than the former action; this is loftier in the eyes of all men of understanding.

X. But perhaps some one of those who are too impetuous and festive may say, "What has all this to do with us? Spur on your horse to the goal; talk to us about the Festival and the reasons for our being here to-day." Yes, this is what I am about to do, although I have begun at a somewhat previous point, being compelled to do so by the needs of my argument. There will be no harm in the eyes of scholars and lovers of the beautiful if we say a few words about the word Pascha itself, for such an addition will not be useless in their ears. This great and venerable Pascha is called Phaska by the Hebrews in their own language; and the word means Passing Over. Historically, from their flight and migration from Egypt into the Land of Canaan; spiritually, from the progress and ascent from things below to things above and to the Land of Promise. And we observe that a thing which we often find to have happened in Scripture, the change of certain nouns from an uncertain to a clearer sense, or from a coarser to a more refined, has taken place in this instance. For some people, supposing this to be a name of the Sacred Passion, and in consequence Grecizing the word by changing Phi and Kappa into Pi and Chi, called the Day Pascha.[α] And custom took it up and confirmed the word, with the help of the ears of most people, to whom it had a more pious sound.

XI. But before our time the Holy Apostle declared that the Law was but a shadow of things to come,[β] which are conceived by thought. And God too, who in still older times gave oracles to Moses, said when giving laws concerning these things, See thou make all things according to the pattern shewed thee in the Mount,[γ] when He shewed him the visible things as an adumbration of and design for the things that are invisible. And I am persuaded that none of these things has been ordered in vain, none without a reason, none in a grovelling manner or unworthy of the legislation of God and the ministry of Moses, even though it be difficult in each type to find a theory descending to the most delicate details, to every point about the Tabernacle itself, and its measures and materials, and the Levites and Priests who carried them, and all the particulars which were enacted about the Sacrifices and the purifications and the Offerings;[δ] and though these are only to be understood by those who rank with Moses in virtue, or have made the nearest approach to his learning. For in that Mount itself God is seen by men; on the one hand through His own descent from His lofty abode, on the other through His drawing us up from our abasement on earth, that the Incomprehensible may be in some degree, and as far as is safe, comprehended by a mortal nature. For in no other way is it possible for the denseness of a material body and an

α Pascha represents the Hebrew PHSKH. Throughout 2 Chron. the LXX. represents the word by Phasek, which like Pascha is a transliteration of the Hebrew word. The form which the transliteration takes is due to the fact that the Greek language does not tolerate these two aspirates in juxtaposition. S. Gregory is correct in remarking that Pascha has no real connection with πάσχω (to suffer), though it might appear to unlearned ears that it has.

β Heb. x. 1.

γ Exod. xxv. 40.

δ ἀφαίρεμα is given by the Lexicons as the Heave-Offering, and it is certainly used in that sense among others (all sacrificial) in the LXX. Suicer, however, follows Suidas in regarding the word as quite general; he also quotes Zonaras' definition, "Quod offertur ἀφαίρεμα dicitur, quod a toto mactatæ animantis corpore abstractum sit." Balsamon, according to the same authority, makes it the portion which was severed from the carcase of the victim and set apart for the Priest (*i.e.*, the heave-offering, Lev. vii. 14, 32).

imprisoned mind to come into consciousness of God, except by His assistance. Then therefore all men do not seem to have been deemed worthy of the same rank and position; but one of one place and one of another, each, I think, according to the measure of his own purification. Some have even been altogether driven away, and only permitted to hear the Voice from on high, namely those whose dispositions are altogether like wild beasts, and who are unworthy of divine mysteries.

XII. But we, standing midway between those whose minds are utterly dense on the one side, and on the other those who are very contemplative and exalted, that we may neither remain quite idle and immovable, nor yet be more busy than we ought, and fall short of and be estranged from our purpose—for the former course is Jewish and very low, and the latter is only fit for the dream-soothsayer, and both alike are to be condemned—let us say our say upon these matters, so far as is within our reach, and not very absurd, or exposed to the ridicule of the multitude. Our belief is that since it was needful that we, who had fallen in consequence of the original sin, and had been led away by pleasure, even as far as idolatry and unlawful bloodshed, should be recalled and raised up again to our original position through the tender mercy of God our Father, Who could not endure that such a noble work of His own hands as Man should be lost to Him; the method of our new creation, and of what should be done, was this:—that all violent remedies were disapproved, as not likely to persuade us, and as quite possibly tending to add to the plague, through our chronic pride; but that God disposed things to our restoration by a gentle and kindly method of cure. For a crooked sapling will not bear a sudden bending the other way, or violence from the hand that would straighten it, but will be more quickly broken than straightened; and a horse of a hot temper and above a certain age will not endure the tyranny of the bit without some coaxing and encouragement. Therefore the Law is given to us as an assistance, like a boundary wall between God and idols, drawing us away from one and to the Other. And it concedes a little at first, that it may receive that which is greater. It concedes the Sacrifices for a time, that it may establish God in us, and then when the fitting time shall come may abolish the Sacrifices also; thus wisely changing our minds by gradual removals, and bringing us over to the Gospel when we have already been trained to a prompt obedience.

XIII. Thus then and for this cause the written Law came in, gathering us into Christ; and this is the account of the Sacrifices as I account for them. And that you may not be ignorant of the depth of His Wisdom and the riches of His unsearchable judgments,[α] He did not leave even these unhallowed altogether, or useless, or with nothing in them but mere blood.[β] But that great, and if I may say so, in Its first nature unsacrificeable Victim, was intermingled with the Sacrifices of the Law, and was a purification, not for a part of the world, nor for a short time, but for the whole world and for all time. For this reason a Lamb was chosen for its innocence, and its clothing of the original nakedness. For such is the Victim, That was offered for us, Who is both in Name and fact the Garment of incorruption. And He was a perfect Victim not only on account of His Godhead, than which nothing is more perfect; but also on account of that which He assumed having been anointed with Deity, and having become one with That which anointed It, and I am bold to say, made equal with God. A Male, because offered for Adam; or rather the Stronger for the strong, when the first Man had fallen under sin; and chiefly because there is in Him nothing feminine, nothing unmanly; but He burst from the bonds of the Virgin-Mother's womb with much power, and a Male was brought forth by the Prophetess,[γ] as Isaiah declares the good tidings. And of a year old, because He is the Sun of Righteousness[δ] setting out from heaven, and circumscribed by His visible Nature, and returning unto Himself.[ε] And "The blessed crown of Goodness,"—being on every side equal to Himself and alike; and not only this, but also as giving life to all the circle of the virtues, gently commingled and intermixed with each other, according to the Law of Love and Order.[ζ] And Immaculate and

---

α Rom. xi. 33.

β The Jewish Sacrifices had a deep inner meaning and mystery. In a limited sense they may be called Sacraments of the future Atonement, which they prefigured and appealed to. But only in a limited sense can they be so called, because they did not convey grace to the soul, but only appealed to the grace to come; and so the Sin-offerings of the Law are only said to *cover*, not to *take away* sin. They removed the spiritual disqualification for worship: but they did not restore full Spiritual Communion with God. Still they were not altogether unhallowed or useless like those of the heathen, inasmuch as they did point forward and plead the merits of the One true Sacrifice.

γ Isa. xiii. 3. δ Mal. iv. 2.

ε The Greek here is very obscure. The meaning seems to be that which Nicetas suggests, viz.:—that our Lord in coming to earth and becoming Incarnate did not in His Divine Nature leave Heaven, but was, while still here on earth in His own words, "The Son of Man Which is in Heaven."

ζ Christ is "a blessed crown of goodness" according to the

guileless, as being the Healer of faults, and of the defects and taints that come from sin. For though He both took on Him our sins and bare our diseases,[α] yet He did not Himself suffer aught that needed healing. For He was tempted in all points like as we are yet without sin.[β] For he that persecuted the Light that shineth in darkness could not overtake Him.

XIV. What more? The First Month is introduced, or rather the beginning of months, whether it was so among the Hebrews from the beginning, or was made so later on this account, and became the first in consequence of the Mystery; and the tenth of the Month, for this is the most complete number, of units the first perfect unit, and the parent of perfection. And it is kept until the fifth day, perhaps because the Victim, of Whom I am speaking, purifies the five senses, from which comes falling into sin, and around which the war rages, inasmuch as they are open to the incitements to sin. And it was chosen, not only out of the lambs, but also out of the inferior species, which are placed on the left hand [γ]—the kids; because He is sacrificed not only for the righteous, but also for sinners; and perhaps even more for these, inasmuch as we have greater need of His mercy. And we need not be surprised that a lamb for a house should be required as the best course, but if that could not be, then one might be obtained by contributions (owing to poverty) for the houses of a family; because it is clearly best that each individual should suffice for his own perfecting, and should offer his own living sacrifice holy unto God Who called him, being consecrated at all times and in every respect. But if that cannot be, then that those who are akin in virtue and of like disposition should be made use of as helpers. For I think this provision means that we should communicate of the Sacrifice to those who are nearest, if there be need.

XV. Then comes the Sacred Night, the Anniversary of the confused darkness of the present life, into which the primæval darkness is dissolved, and all things come into life and rank and form, and that which was chaos is reduced to order. Then we flee from Egypt, that is from sullen persecuting sin; and from Pharaoh the unseen tyrant, and the bitter taskmasters, changing our quarters to the world above; and are delivered from the clay and the brickmaking, and from the husks and dangers of this fleshly condition, which for most men is only not overpowered by mere husklike calculations. Then the Lamb is slain, and act and word are sealed with the Precious Blood; that is, habit and action, the sideposts of our doors; I mean, of course, of the movements of mind and opinion, which are rightly opened and closed by contemplation, since there is a limit even to thoughts. Then the last and gravest plague upon the persecutors, truly worthy of the night; and Egypt mourns the first-born of her own reasonings and actions which are also called in the Scripture the Seed of the Chaldeans[α] removed, and the children of Babylon dashed against the rocks and destroyed;[β] and the whole air is full of the cry and clamour of the Egyptians; and then the Destroyer of them shall withdraw from us in reverence of the Unction. Then the removal of leaven; that is, of the old and sour wickedness, not of that which is quickening and makes bread; for seven days, a number which is of all the most mystical,[γ] and is co-ordinate with this present world, that we may not lay in provision of any Egyptian dough, or relic of Pharisaic or ungodly teaching.

XVI. Well, let them lament; we will feed on the Lamb toward evening—for Christ's Passion was in the completion of the ages; because too He communicated His Disciples in the evening with His Sacrament, destroying the darkness of sin; and not sodden, but roast—that our word may have in it nothing that is unconsidered or watery, or easily made away with; but may be entirely consistent and solid, and free from all that is impure and from all vanity. And let us be aided by the good coals,[δ] kindling and purifying our minds from Him

saying of David, Thou shalt bless the crown of the year with Thy goodness (Ps. lxv. 11). The idea of a year is taken from the Sun; that of the crown from the year (for the year is a circle guarded with four seasons), and from the circle again equality. Therefore the crown is Christ, as adorning and beautifying the minds of believers. But the year of Goodness was that time when Christ moved by goodness was declaring the Gospel, as Isaiah saith of Him, "He hath sent Me to preach the Gospel to the poor, to proclaim the acceptable year of the Lord" (Isa. lxi. 1, 2). Thus the Crown is on every side equal. For if one draw a line from the upper side to the lower, and the same in a transverse direction, all the intervals will be equal. And the Crown is like itself, because its figure is seen alike on every side, for on every side it is seen as a round. Therefore Christ as to His Humanity is called a Crown of Righteousness, as composed of all the virtues, and having no end of His goodness and righteousness; and of that righteousness one quality is equality, that is, it allows neither excess nor defect. For excess and defect do not arise from virtue and righteousness, but from fault and unrighteousness (Nicetas).

α Isa. liii. 4. β Heb. iv. 15. γ Matt. xxv. 33.

α Judith v. 6. β Ps. cxxxviii. 9.

γ We are to part with leaven for seven days (Exod. xii. 15), that is, with sin for the whole week of this life. The number Seven Days signifies the passing of time which revolves in weeks. And this number is mystical, because it is virgin and signifies virginity and the angelic life: for it alone, as arithmeticians teach, of all the numbers within the decade, is neither a multiple nor a measure, and also contains in itself the Four and the Three. For there are four elements of the world, and the Trinity is their Creator. He calls it co-ordinate with the world, because the world was made in seven days, and again because when seven thousand years are completed the end of the world is to come (Nicetas). S. Augustine (Civ. Dei. c. ii. 31) says that the number Seven often stands for the Universe, because it is made up of Four which is altogether even (2 and 2 the sum of two even numbers) and Three which is altogether uneven (1 and 1 and 1).

δ Isa. vi. 6.

That cometh to send fire on the earth,[a] that shall destroy all evil habits, and to hasten its kindling. Whatsoever then there be, of solid and nourishing in the Word, shall be eaten with the inward parts and hidden things of the mind, and shall be consumed and given up to spiritual digestion; aye, from head to foot, that is, from the first contemplations of Godhead to the very last thoughts about the Incarnation. Neither let us carry aught of it abroad, nor leave it till the morning; because most of our Mysteries may not be carried out to them that are outside, nor is there beyond this night any further purification; and procrastination is not creditable to those who have a share in the Word. For just as it is good and well-pleasing to God not to let anger last through the day,[β] but to get rid of it before sunset, whether you take this of time or in a mystical sense, for it is not safe for us that the Sun of Righteousness should go down upon our wrath; so too we ought not to let such Food remain all night, nor to put it off till to-morrow. But whatever is of bony nature and not fit for food and hard for us even to understand, this must not be broken; that is, badly divined and misconceived (I need not say that in the history not a bone of Jesus was broken, even though His death was hastened by His crucifiers on account of the Sabbath);[γ] nor must it be stripped off and thrown away, lest that which is holy should be given to the dogs,[δ] that is, to the evil hearers of the Word; just as the glorious pearl of the Word is not to be cast before swine; but it shall be consumed with the fire with which the burnt offerings also are consumed, being refined and preserved by the Spirit That searcheth and knoweth all things, not destroyed in the waters, nor scattered abroad as the calf's head which was hastily made by Israel was by Moses,[ε] for a reproach for their hardness of heart.

XVII. Nor would it be right for us to pass over the manner of this eating either, for the Law does not do so, but carries its mystical labour even to this point in the literal enactment. Let us consume the Victim in haste, eating It with unleavened bread, with bitter herbs, and with our loins girded, and our shoes on our feet, and leaning on staves like old men; with haste, that we fall not into that fault which was forbidden to Lot[ζ] by the commandment, that we look not around, nor stay in all that neighbourhood, but that we escape to the mountain, that we be not overtaken by the strange fire of Sodom, nor be congealed into a pillar of salt in consequence of our turning back to wickedness; for this is the result of delay. *With bitter herbs*, for a life according to the Will of God is bitter and arduous, especially to beginners, and higher than pleasures. For although the new yoke is easy and the burden light,[a] as you are told, yet this is on account of the hope and the reward, which is far more abundant than the hardships of this life. If it were not so, who would not say that the Gospel is more full of toil and trouble than the enactments of the Law? For, while the Law prohibits only the completed acts of sin, we are condemned for the causes also, almost as if they were acts. The Law says, *Thou shalt not commit adultery;* but *you* may not even *desire*, kindling passion by curious and earnest looks. *Thou shalt not kill*, says the Law; but *you* are not even to return a blow, but on the contrary are to offer yourself to the smiter. How much more ascetic is the Gospel than the Law! *Thou shalt not forswear thyself* is the Law; but *you* are not to swear at all, either a greater or a lesser oath, for an oath is the parent of perjury. *Thou shalt not join house to house, nor field to field, oppressing the poor;*[β] but *you* are to set aside willingly even your just possessions, and to be stripped for the poor, that without encumbrance you may take up the Cross[γ] and be enriched with the unseen riches.

XVIII. And let the loins of the unreasoning animals be unbound and loose, for they have not the gift of reason which can overcome pleasure (it is not needful to say that even they know the limit of natural movement). But let that part of your being which is the seat of passion, and which neighs,[δ] as Holy Scripture calls it, when sweeping away this shameful passion, be restrained by a girdle of continence, so that you may eat the Passover purely, having mortified your members which are upon the earth,[ε] and copying the girdle[ζ] of John, the Hermit and Forerunner and great Herald of the Truth. Another girdle I know, the soldierly and manly one, I mean, from which the Euzoni of Syria and certain Monozoni[η] take their name. And it is in respect of this too that God saith in an oracle to Job, "Nay, but gird up thy loins like a

α Luke xii. 49. β Ephes. iv. 26.
γ S. Gregory does not mean to say that our Lord's death was actually hastened by violent actions on the part of the Jews, which we know was not the case; but that they were anxious that it should take place before the Sabbath began. The two thieves, who were still living, received the *coup de grace* from the Roman soldiers, who broke their legs; but our Lord, much to their astonishment, was dead already, so this course was not taken with Him, but His side was pierced with a spear.
δ Matt. vii. 6. ε Exod. xxxii. 20. ζ Gen. xix. 17.

α Matt. xi. 20. β Isa. v. 8. γ Mark x. 21.
δ Jer. v. 8. ε Col. iii. 5. ζ Matt. iii. 4.
η The expression is often used in the LXX. to represent the word גדוד, translated A Band, especially in 2 Kings.

man, and give a manly answer."[α] With this also holy David boasts that he is girded with strength from God,[β] and speaks of God Himself as clothed with strength[γ] and girded about with power—against the ungodly of course—though perhaps some may prefer to see in this a declaration of the abundance of His power, and, as it were, its restraint, just as also He clothes Himself with Light as with a garment.[δ] For who shall endure His unrestrained power and light? Do I enquire what there is common to the loins and to truth? What then is the meaning to S. Paul of the expression, "Stand, therefore, having your loins girt about with truth?"[ε] Is it perhaps that contemplation is to restrain concupiscence, and not to allow it to be carried in another direction? For that which is disposed to love in a particular direction will not have the same power towards other pleasures.

XIX. And as to *shoes*, let him who is about to touch the Holy Land which the feet of God have trodden, put them off, as Moses did upon the Mount,[ζ] that he may bring there nothing dead; nothing to come between Man and God. So too if any disciple is sent to preach the Gospel, let him go in a spirit of philosophy and without excess, inasmuch as he must, besides being without money and without staff and with but one coat, also be barefooted,[η] that the feet of those who preach the Gospel of Peace and every other good may appear beautiful.[θ] But he who would flee from Egypt and the things of Egypt must put on shoes for safety's sake, especially in regard to the scorpions and snakes in which Egypt so abounds, so as not to be injured by those which watch the heel,[κ] which also we are bidden to tread under foot.[λ] And concerning *the staff* and the signification of it, my belief is as follows. There is one I know to lean upon, and another which belongs to Pastors and Teachers, and which corrects human sheep. Now the Law prescribes to you the staff to lean upon, that you may not break down in your mind when you hear of God's Blood, and His Passion, and His death; and that you may not be carried away to heresy in your defence of God; but without shame and without doubt may eat the Flesh and drink the Blood, if you are desirous of true life, neither disbelieving His words about His Flesh, nor offended at those about His Passion. Lean upon this, and stand firm and strong, in nothing shaken by the adversaries nor carried away by the plausibility of their arguments. Stand upon thy High Place; in the Courts of Jerusalem[α] place thy feet; lean upon the Rock, that thy steps in God be not shaken.

XX. What sayest thou? Thus it hath pleased Him that thou shouldest come forth[β] out of Egypt, the iron furnace; that thou shouldest leave behind the idolatry of that country, and be led by Moses and his lawgiving and martial rule. I give thee a piece of advice which is not my own, or rather which is very much my own, if thou consider the matter spiritually. Borrow from the Egyptians vessels of gold and silver;[γ] with these take thy journey; supply thyself for the road with the goods of strangers, or rather with thine own. There is money owing to thee, the wages of thy bondage and of thy brickmaking; be clever on thy side too in asking retribution; be an honest robber. Thou didst suffer wrong there whilst thou wast fighting with the clay (that is, this troublesome and filthy body) and wast building cities foreign and unsafe, whose memorial perishes with a cry.[δ] What then? Dost thou come out for nothing and without wages? But why wilt thou leave to the Egyptians and to the powers of thine adversaries that which they have gained by wickedness, and will spend with yet greater wickedness? It does not belong to them: they have ravished it, and have sacrilegiously taken it as plunder from Him who saith, The silver is Mine and the gold is Mine,[ε] and I give it to whom I will. Yesterday it was theirs, for it was permitted to be so; to-day the Master takes it and gives it to thee,[ζ] that thou mayest make a good and saving use of it. Let us make to ourselves friends of the Mammon of unrighteousness,[η] that when we fail, they may receive us in the time of judgment.

XXI. If you are a Rachel or a Leah, a patriarchal and great soul, steal whatever idols of your father you can find;[θ] not, however, that you may keep them, but that you may destroy them; and if you are a wise Israelite remove them to the Land of the Promise, and let the persecutor grieve over the loss of them, and learn through being outwitted that it was vain for him to tyrannize over and keep in bondage better men than himself. If thou doest this, and comest out of Egypt thus, I know well that thou shalt be guided by the pillar of fire and cloud by night and day.[κ] The wilderness shall be tamed for thee, and the Sea divided;[λ]

α Job xxxviii. 3. β Ps. xviii. 32. γ Ib. xciii. 1. δ Ib. civ. 2. ε Eph. v. 14. ζ Exod. iii. 5. η Matt. x. 9. θ Isa. lii. 7. κ Gen. iii. 15. λ Luke x. 19.

α Ps. cxxii. 2.
β ἐξελθεῖν c. acc. loci; a very rare use, but found in classical authors. γ Exod. xi. 2. δ Ps. ix. 6. ε Hag. ii. 8. ζ Matt. xx. 14. η Luke xvi. 9. θ Gen. xxxi. 19. κ Exod. xiii. 20. λ Ib. xiv. 21.

Pharaoh shall be drowned;[α] bread shall be rained down;[β] the rock shall become a fountain;[γ] Amalek shall be conquered, not with arms alone, but with the hostile hand of the righteous forming both prayers and the invincible trophy of the Cross;[δ] the River shall be cut off; the sun shall stand still; and the moon be restrained;[ε] walls shall be overthrown even without engines;[ζ] swarms of hornets shall go before thee to make a way for Israel, and to hold the Gentiles in check;[η] and all the other events which are told in the history after these and with these (not to make a long story) shall be given thee of God. Such is the feast thou art keeping to-day; and in this manner I would have thee celebrate both the Birthday and the Burial of Him Who was born for thee and suffered for thee. Such is the Mystery of the Passover; such are the mysteries sketched by the Law and fulfilled by Christ, the Abolisher of the letter, the Perfecter of the Spirit, who by His Passion taught us how to suffer, and by His glorification grants us to be glorified with Him.

XXII.[θ] Now we are to examine another fact and dogma, neglected by most people, but in my judgment well worth enquiring into. To Whom was that Blood offered that was shed for us, and why was It shed? I mean the precious and famous Blood of our God and Highpriest and Sacrifice. We were detained in bondage by the Evil One, sold under sin, and receiving pleasure in exchange for wickedness. Now, since a ransom belongs only to him who holds in bondage, I ask to whom was this offered, and for what cause? If to the Evil One, fie upon the outrage! If the robber receives ransom, not only from God, but a ransom which consists of God Himself, and has such an illustrious payment for his tyranny, a payment for whose sake it would have been right for him to have left us alone altogether. But if to the Father, I ask first, how? For it was not by Him that we were being oppressed; and next, On what principle did the Blood of His Only begotten Son delight the Father, Who would not receive even Isaac, when he was being offered by his Father, but changed the sacrifice, putting a ram in the place of the human victim?[κ] Is it not evident that the Father accepts Him, but neither asked for Him nor demanded Him; but on account of the Incarnation, and because Humanity must be sanctified by the Humanity of God,[λ] that He might deliver us Himself, and overcome the tyrant, and draw us to Himself by the mediation of His Son, Who also arranged this to the honour of the Father, Whom it is manifest that He obeys in all things? So much we have said of Christ; the greater part of what we might say shall be reverenced with silence. But that brazen serpent[α] was hung up as a remedy for the biting serpents, not as a type of Him that suffered for us, but as a contrast; and it saved those that looked upon it, not because they believed it to live, but because it was killed, and killed with it the powers that were subject to it, being destroyed as it deserved. And what is the fitting epitaph for it from us? "O death, where is thy sting? O grave, where is thy victory?"[β] Thou art overthrown by the Cross; thou art slain by Him who is the Giver of life; thou art without breath, dead, without motion, even though thou keepest the form of a serpent lifted up on high on a pole.

XXIII. Now we will partake of a Passover which is still typical, though it is plainer than the old one. For that is ever new which is now becoming known. It is ours to learn what is that drinking and that enjoyment, and His to teach and communicate the Word to His disciples. For teaching is food, even to the Giver of food. Come hither then, and let us partake of the Law, but in a Gospel manner, not a literal one; perfectly, not imperfectly; eternally, not temporarily. Let us make our Head, not the earthly Jerusalem, but the heavenly City;[γ] not that which is now trodden under foot by armies,[δ] but that which is glorified by Angels. Let us sacrifice not young calves, nor lambs that put forth horns and hoofs,[ε] in which many parts are destitute of life and feeling; but let us sacrifice to God the sacrifice of praise upon the heavenly Altar, with the heavenly dances; let us hold aside the first veil; let us approach the second, and look into the Holy of Holies.[ζ] Shall I say that which is a greater thing yet? Let us sacrifice *ourselves* to God; or rather let us go on sacrificing throughout every day and at every moment. Let us accept anything for the Word's sake. By sufferings let us imitate His Passion: by our blood let us reverence His Blood: let us gladly mount upon the Cross. Sweet are the nails, though they be very painful. For to suffer with Christ and for Christ is better than a life of ease with others.

XXIV. If you are a Simon of Cyrene,[η] take

α Exod. xiv. 28. β Ib. xvi. 15. γ Ib. xvii. 6. δ Ib. xvii. 10, 11. ε Josh. iii. 15, 16. ζ Ib. x. 13. η Ib. vi. 20. θ Ib. xxiv. 12. κ Gen. xxii. 11, &c.

λ Have we not here the germ of the idea, afterwards known as the Scotist, that the Incarnation was the purpose of God independently of the Fall, for the perfecting of Humanity; but that the Passion and death of Incarnate God were the direct result of the sin of man?

α Num. xxi. 9. β Hos. xiii. 14 and 1 Cor. xv. 55. γ Heb. xii. 22. δ Luke xxi. 20–24. ε Ps. lxiv. 32. ζ Heb. xiii. 15 and x. 20. η Mark xv. 21.

up the Cross and follow. If you are crucified with Him as a robber,[α] acknowledge God as a *penitent* robber. If even He was numbered among the transgressors[β] for you and your sin, do you become law-abiding for His sake. Worship Him Who was hanged for you, even if you yourself are hanging; make some gain even from your wickedness; purchase salvation by your death; enter with Jesus into Paradise,[γ] so that you may learn from what you have fallen.[δ] Contemplate the glories that are there; let the murderer die outside with his blasphemies; and if you be a Joseph of Arimathaea,[ε] beg the Body from him that crucified Him, make thine own that which cleanses the world.[ζ] If you be a Nicodemus, the worshipper of God by night, bury Him with spices.[η] If you be a Mary, or another Mary, or a Salome, or a Joanna, weep in the early morning. Be first to see the stone taken away,[θ] and perhaps you will see the Angels and Jesus Himself. Say something; hear His Voice. If He say to you, Touch Me not,[κ] stand afar off; reverence the Word, but grieve not; for He knoweth those to whom He appeareth first. Keep the feast of the Resurrection; come to the aid of Eve who was first to fall, of Her who first embraced the Christ, and made Him known to the disciples. Be a Peter or a John; hasten to the Sepulchre, running together, running against one another, vying in the noble race.[λ] And even if you be beaten in speed, win the victory of zeal; not Looking into the tomb, but Going in. And if, like a Thomas, you were left out when the disciples were assembled to whom Christ shews Himself, when you do see Him be not faithless;[μ] and if you do not believe, then believe those who tell you; and if you cannot believe them either, then have confidence in the print of the nails. If He descend into Hell,[ν] descend with Him. Learn to know the mysteries of Christ there also, what is the providential purpose of the twofold descent, to save all men absolutely by His manifestation, or there too only them that believe.

XXV. And if He ascend up into Heaven,[ξ] ascend with Him. Be one of those angels who escort Him, or one of those who receive Him. Bid the gates be lifted up,[ο] or be made higher, that they may receive Him, exalted after His Passion. Answer to those who are in doubt because He bears up with Him His body and the tokens of His Passion, which He had not when He came down, and who therefore inquire, "Who is this King of Glory?"

α Luke xxiii. 42. β Isa. liii. 12. γ Luke xxiii. 43.
δ Rev. ii. 5. ε Luke xxiii. 52. ζ 1 John i. 7.
η John xix. 39. θ Ib. xx. 11, etc. κ Ib. xxi. 17.
λ Ib. xx. 3, 4. μ Ib. xx. 25. ν 1 Pet. iii. 19.
ξ Luke xxiv. 51. ο Ps. xxiv. 7, 10.

that it is the Lord strong and mighty, as in all things that He hath done from time to time and does, so now in His battle and triumph for the sake of Mankind. And give to the doubting of the question the twofold answer. And if they marvel and say as in Isaiah's drama Who is this that cometh from Edom and from the things of earth? Or How are the garments red of Him that is without blood or body, as of one that treads in the full winepress?[α] Set forth the beauty of the array of the Body that suffered, adorned by the Passion, and made splendid by the Godhead, than which nothing can be more lovely or more beautiful.

XXVI.[β] To this what will those cavillers say, those bitter reasoners about Godhead, those detractors of all things that are praiseworthy, those darkeners of Light, uncultured in respect of Wisdom, for whom Christ died in vain, unthankful creatures, the work of the Evil One. Do you turn this benefit into a reproach to God? Will you deem Him little on this account, that He humbled Himself for your sake, and because to seek for that which had wandered the Good Shepherd, He who layeth down His life for the sheep,[γ] came upon the mountains and hills upon which you used to sacrifice,[δ] and found the wandering one; and having found it, took it upon His shoulders,[ε] on which He also bore the wood; and having borne it, brought it back to the life above; and having brought it back, numbered it among those who have never strayed. That He lit a candle,[ζ] His own flesh, and swept the house, by cleansing away the sin of the world, and sought for the coin, the Royal Image that was all covered up with passions, and calls together His friends, the Angelic Powers, at the finding of the coin, and makes them sharers of His joy, as He had before made them sharers of the secret of His Incarnation? That the Light that is exceeding bright should follow the Candle-Forerunner,[η] and the Word, the Voice, and the Bridegroom, the Bridegroom's friend,[θ] that prepared for the Lord a peculiar people[κ] and cleansed them by the water[λ] in preparation for the Spirit? Do you Reproach God with this? Do you conceive of Him as less because He girds Himself with a towel and washes His disciples,[μ] and shows that humiliation is the best road to exaltation;[ν] because He humbles Himself for the sake of the soul that

α Isa. lxiii. 1.
β This passage, to nearly the end of c. XXVII., is taken from the Oration on the Nativity, cc. XIII.–XIV. γ John x. 11.
δ John v. 35. ε Hos. iv. 13. ζ Luke xv. 4, 5.
η Ib. xv. 8, 9. θ Ib. i. 23; iii. 9, 29.
κ A reminiscence of S. Luke i. 17. λ Matt. iii. 11.
μ John xiii. 4, 5. ν Matt. xxiii. 12.

is bent down to the ground,[α] that He may even exalt with Himself that which is bent double under a weight of sin? How comes it that you do not also charge it upon Him as a crime that He eateth with Publicans[β] and at Publicans' tables, and makes disciples of Publicans[γ] that He too may make some gain. And what gain? The salvation of sinners. If so, one must blame the physician for stooping over suffering and putting up with evil smells in order to give health to the sick; and him also who leans over the ditch, that he may, according to the Law, save the beast that has fallen into it.

XXVII. He was sent, but sent according to His Manhood (for He was of two Natures), since He was hungry and thirsty and weary, and was distressed and wept, according to the Laws of human nature. But even if He were sent also as God, what of that? Consider the Mission to be the good pleasure of the Father, to which He refers all that concerns Himself, both that He may honour the Eternal Principle, and that He may avoid the appearance of being a rival God. For He is said on the one hand to have been betrayed, and on the other it is written that He gave Himself up; and so too that He was raised and taken up by the Father, and also that of His own power He rose and ascended. The former belongs to the Good Pleasure, the latter to His own Authority; but you dwell upon all that diminishes Him, while you ignore all that exalts Him. For instance, you score that He suffered, but you do not add "of His own Will." Ah, what things has the Word even now to suffer! By some He is honoured as God but confused with the Father; by others He is dishonoured as Flesh, and is severed from God. With whom shall He be most angry—or rather which shall He forgive—those who falsely contract Him, or those who divide Him? For the former ought to have made a distinction, and the latter to have made a Union, the one in number, the other in Godhead. Do you stumble at His Flesh? So did the Jews. Do you call Him a Samaritan,[δ] and the rest which I will not utter? This did not even the demons, O man more unbelieving than demons, and more stupid than Jews. The Jews recognized the title Son as expressing equal rank; and the demons knew that He who drove them out was God, for they were persuaded by their own experience. But you will not either admit the equality or confess the Godhead. It would have been better for you to have been circumcised and a demoniac—to reduce the matter to an absurdity—than in uncircumcision and robust health to be thus ill and ungodly disposed. But for our war with such men, let it be brought to an end by their returning, however late, to a sound mind, if they will; or else if they will not, let it be postponed to another occasion, if they continue as they are. Anyhow, we will have no fear when contending for the Trinity with the help of the Trinity.

XXVIII. It is now needful for us to sum up our discourse as follows: We were created that we might be made happy. We were made happy when we were created. We were entrusted with Paradise that we might enjoy life. We received a Commandment that we might obtain a good repute by keeping it; not that God did not know what would take place, but because He had laid down the law of Free Will. We were deceived because we were the objects of envy. We were cast out because we transgressed. We fasted because we refused to fast, being overpowered by the Tree of Knowledge. For the Commandment was ancient, coeval with ourselves, and was a kind of education of our souls and curb of luxury, to which we were reasonably made subject, in order that we might recover by keeping it that which we had lost by not keeping it. We needed an Incarnate God, a God put to death, that we might live. We were put to death together with Him, that we might be cleansed; we rose again with Him because we were put to death with Him; we were glorified with Him, because we rose again with Him.

XXIX. Many indeed are the miracles of that time: God crucified; the sun darkened and again rekindled; for it was fitting that the creatures should suffer with their Creator; the veil rent; the Blood and Water shed from His Side; the one as from a man, the other as above man; the rocks rent for the Rock's sake; the dead raised for a pledge of the final Resurrection of all men; the Signs at the Sepulchre and after the Sepulchre, which none can worthily celebrate; and yet none of these equal to the Miracle of my salvation. A few drops of Blood recreate the whole world, and become to all men what rennet is to milk, drawing us together and compressing us into unity.

XXX. But, O Pascha, great and holy and purifier of all the world—for I will speak to thee as to a living person—O Word of God and Light and Life and Wisdom and Might—for I rejoice in all Thy names—O Offspring and Expression and Signet of the Great Mind; O Word conceived and Man contemplated, Who bearest all things, binding them by the Word of Thy power; receive this discourse,

α Luke xiii. 10, etc.
β Mark ii. 15, 16.
γ Luke xv. 2.
δ John viii. 48.

not now as firstfruits, but perhaps as the completion of my offerings, a thanksgiving, and at the same time a supplication, that we may suffer no evil beyond those necessary and sacred cares in which our life has been passed; and stay the tyranny of the body over us; (Thou seest, O Lord, how great it is and how it bows me down) or Thine own sentence, if we are to be condemned by Thee. But if we are to be released, in accordance with our desire, and be received into the Heavenly Tabernacle, there too it may be we shall offer Thee acceptable Sacrifices upon Thine Altar, to Father and Word and Holy Ghost; for to Thee belongeth all glory and honour and might, world without end. Amen.

SELECT LETTERS

OF

SAINT GREGORY NAZIANZEN.

ARCHBISHOP OF CONSTANTINOPLE.

A SELECTION FROM THE LETTERS OF SAINT GREGORY NAZIANZEN, SOMETIME ARCHBISHOP OF CONSTANTINOPLE.

DIVISION I.

LETTERS ON THE APOLLINARIAN CONTROVERSY.

Introduction.

The circumstances which called forth the two letters to Cledonius have already been described in the first section of the General Prolegomena, and it will not be necessary here to add much to what was there said. In the letter to Nectarius, his own successor on the throne of Constantinople, written about A.D. 383, and sometimes reckoned as Orat. XLVI., S. Gregory gives extracts from a work of Apollinarius himself, but without mentioning the title of the book. In this treatise the fundamental errors of the heresy (see Proleg. c. 1, p. 172) are laid down. Apollinarius, according to S. Gregory, declares that the Son of God was from all eternity clothed with a human body, and not from the time of His conception only by the Blessed Virgin; but that this humanity of God is without human mind, the place of which was supplied by the Godhead of the Only-begotten. And he goes even further and ascribes passibility and mortality to the very Godhead of Christ. Therefore S. Gregory earnestly protests against any toleration being granted to these heretics, or even permission to hold their assemblies; for, he says, toleration or permission would certainly be regarded by them as a condonation of their doctrinal position, and a condemnation of that of the Church. Dr. Ullman, however, thinks that while S. Gregory was certainly speaking the truth in saying that he had in his hands a pamphlet by Apollinarius, yet that he, perhaps unconsciously, exaggerated the heretical character of its contents, pushing its statements to consequences which Apollinarius would have repudiated. The one purpose of the latter was, in Dr. Ullman's view, to safeguard the doctrine of the Unity of Christ; and he thought that the orthodox expression of Two Whole and Perfect Natures tended to a Nestorian division of the Person of Christ; and so he used language which certainly seemed to confound the natures, or at any rate to make the Incarnation imperfect, inasmuch as a Christ in Whom the human mind is absent, and its place filled up by the Godhead of the Son, cannot be said to be perfect Man. But while Epiphanius mentions these extravagances of the heresy, and does so with a lingering feeling of regret for the lapse of so good a man whose services in the past had been of so much value to the Church, yet, in the spirit common to Ecclesiastical authorities of the time, he would rather ascribe them to an expansion of Apollinarius' teaching by his younger disciples who did not really understand what Apollinarius himself meant.

Olympius, to whom the last of this series is addressed, was Governor of Cappadocia Secunda in A.D. 382. He was a man for whom S. Gregory had a very high esteem, and with whom he was upon terms of close friendship, as will be seen from other letters of Gregory to him in another division of this Selection. The occasion of the present letter was the necessity to appeal to the secular power for aid to punish a sect of Apollinarians at Nazianzus, who had ventured to take advantage of S. Gregory's absence at the Baths of Xanxaris to procure the consecration of a Bishop of their own way of thinking. Technically the See was vacant, but the administration had been committed to Gregory by the Bishops of the Province, and though he, foreseeing some such attempt on the part of the heretics, had been very earnest in pressing upon the Metropolitan and his Comprovincials the necessity of filling this throne by a canonical election, yet he was by no means prepared to hand over the authority, with which he had been invested, to an irregularly elected and uncanonically consecrated heretic.

To Nectarius, Bishop of Constantinople. (Ep. CCII.)

The Care of God, which throughout the time before us guarded the Churches, seems to have utterly forsaken this present life. And my soul is immersed to such a degree by calamities that the private sufferings of my own life hardly seem to be worth reckoning among evils (though they are so numerous and great, that if they befel anyone else I should think them unbearable); but I can only look at the common sufferings of the Churches; for if at the present crisis some pains be not taken to find a remedy for them, things will gradually get into an altogether desperate condition. Those who follow the heresy of Arius or Eudoxius (I cannot say who stirred them up to this folly) are making a display of their disease, as if they had attained some degree of confidence by collecting congregations as if by permission. And they of the Macedonian party have reached such a pitch of folly that they are arrogating to themselves the name of Bishops, and are wandering about our districts babbling of Eleusius[a] as to their ordinations. Our bosom evil, Eunomius, is no longer content with merely existing; but unless he can draw away everyone with him to his ruinous heresy, he thinks himself an injured man. All this, however, is endurable. The most grievous item of all in the woes of the Church is the boldness of the Apollinarians, whom your Holiness has overlooked, I know not how, when providing themselves with authority to hold meetings on an equality with myself. However, you being, as you are, thoroughly instructed by the grace of God in the Divine Mysteries on all points, are well informed, not only as to the advocacy of the true faith, but also as to all those arguments which have been devised by the heretics against the sound faith; and yet perhaps it will not be unseasonable that your Excellency should hear from my littleness that a pamphlet by Apollinarius has come into my hands, the contents of which surpass all heretical pravity. For he asserts that the Flesh which the Only-begotten Son assumed in the Incarnation for the remodelling of our nature was no new acquisition, but that that carnal nature was in the Son from the beginning. And he puts forward as a witness to this monstrous assertion a garbled quotation from the Gospels, namely, No man hath Ascended up into Heaven save He which came down from Heaven, even the Son of Man which is in Heaven.[α] As though even before He came down He was the Son of Man, and when He came down He brought with Him that Flesh, which it appears He had in Heaven, as though it had existed before the ages, and been joined with His Essence. For he alleges another saying of an Apostle, which he cuts off from the whole body of its context, that The Second Man is the Lord from Heaven.[β] Then he assumes that that Man who came down from above is without a mind, but that the Godhead of the Only-begotten fulfils the function of mind, and is the third part of this human composite, inasmuch as soul and body are in it on its human side, but not mind, the place of which is taken by God the Word. This is not yet the most serious part of it; that which is most terrible of all is that he declares that the Only-begotten God, the Judge of all, the Prince of Life, the Destroyer of Death, is mortal, and underwent the Passion in His proper Godhead; and that in the three days' death of His body, His Godhead also was put to death with His body, and thus was raised again from the dead by the Father. It would be tedious to go through all the other propositions which he adds to these monstrous absurdities. Now, if they who hold such views have authority to meet, your Wisdom approved in Christ must see that, inasmuch as we do not approve their views, any permission of assembly granted to them is nothing less than a declaration that their view is thought more true than ours. For if they are permitted to teach their view as godly men, and with all confidence to preach their doctrine, it is manifest that the doctrine of the Church has been condemned, as though the truth were on their side. For nature does not admit of two contrary doctrines on the same subject being both true. How then could your noble and lofty mind submit to suspend your usual courage in regard to the correction of so great an evil? But even though there is no precedent for such a course, let your inimitable perfection in virtue stand up at a crisis like the present, and teach our most pious

[a] Eleusius was Bishop of Cyzicus, a prominent leader of the Semi-Arian party. He bore a very high character for personal holiness, and approached more nearly to orthodoxy than most of his associates, men like Basil of Ancyra, Eustathius of Sebaste, etc. He obstinately maintained, however, Macedonian views on the Deity of the Holy Ghost, even after their condemnation by the Council of Constantinople.

[α] John iii. 13. [β] Cor. xv. 47.

Emperor, that no gain will come from his zeal for the Church on other points if he allows such an evil to gain strength from freedom of speech for the subversion of sound faith.

To Cledonius the Priest Against Apollinarius. (Ep. CI.)

TO OUR MOST REVEREND AND GOD-BELOVED BROTHER AND FELLOW-PRIEST CLEDONIUS, GREGORY, GREETING IN THE LORD.

I desire to learn what is this fashion of innovation in things concerning the Church, which allows anyone who likes, or the passer-by,[a] as the Bible says, to tear asunder the flock that has been well led, and to plunder it by larcenous attacks, or rather by piratical and fallacious teachings. For if our present assailants had any ground for condemning us in regard of the faith, it would not have been right for them, even in that case, to have ventured on such a course without giving us notice. They ought rather to have first persuaded us, or to have been willing to be persuaded by us (if at least any account is to be taken of us as fearing God, labouring for the faith, and helping the Church), and then, if at all, to innovate; but then perhaps there would be an excuse for their outrageous conduct. But since our faith has been proclaimed, both in writing and without writing, here and in distant parts, in times of danger and of safety, how comes it that some make such attempts, and that others keep silence?

The most grievous part of it is not (though this too is shocking) that the men instil their own heresy into simpler souls by means of those who are worse; but that they also tell lies about us and say that we share their opinions and sentiments; thus baiting their hooks, and by this cloak villainously fulfilling their will, and making our simplicity, which looked upon them as brothers and not as foes, into a support of their wickedness. And not only so, but they also assert, as I am told, that they have been received by the Western Synod, by which they were formerly condemned, as is well known to everyone. If, however, those who hold the views of Apollinarius have either now or formerly been received, let them prove it and we will be content. For it is evident that they can only have been so received as assenting to the Orthodox Faith, for this were an impossibility on any other terms. And they can surely prove it, either by the minutes of the Synod, or by Letters of Communion, for this is the regular custom of Synods. But if it is mere words, and an invention of their own, devised for the sake of appearances and to give them weight with the multitude through the credit of the persons, teach them to hold their tongues, and confute them; for we believe that such a task is well suited to your manner of life and orthodoxy. Do not let the men deceive themselves and others with the assertion that the "Man of the Lord," as they call Him, Who is rather our Lord and God, is without human mind. For we do not sever the Man from the Godhead, but we lay down as a dogma the Unity and Identity of Person, Who of old was not Man but God, and the Only Son before all ages, unmingled with body or anything corporeal; but Who in these last days has assumed Manhood also for our salvation; passible in His Flesh, impassible in His Godhead; circumscript in the body, uncircumscript in the Spirit; at once earthly and heavenly, tangible and intangible, comprehensible and incomprehensible; that by One and the Same Person, Who was perfect Man and also God, the entire humanity fallen through sin might be created anew.

If anyone does not believe that Holy Mary is the Mother of God, he is severed from the Godhead. If anyone should assert that He passed through the Virgin as through a channel, and was not at once divinely and humanly formed in her (divinely, because without the intervention of a man; humanly, because in accordance with the laws of gestation), he is in like manner godless. If any assert that the Manhood was formed and afterward was clothed with the Godhead, he too is to be condemned. For this were not a Generation of God, but a shirking of generation. If any introduce the notion of Two Sons, one of God the Father, the other of the Mother, and discredits the Unity and Identity, may he lose his part in the adoption promised to those who believe aright. For God and Man are two natures, as also soul and body are; but there are not two Sons or two Gods. For neither in this life are there two manhoods; though Paul speaks in some such language of the inner and outer man. And (if I am to speak concisely) the Saviour is made of elements which are distinct from one another (for the invisible is not the same with the visible, nor the timeless with that which is subject to time), yet He is not two Persons. God forbid! For both natures are one by the combination, the Deity being made Man, and the Manhood

a Ps. lxxx. 12.

deified or however one should express it. And I say different Elements, because it is the reverse of what is the case in the Trinity; for There we acknowledge different Persons so as not to confound the persons; but not different Elements, for the Three are One and the same in Godhead.

If any should say that it wrought in Him by grace as in a Prophet, but was not and is not united with Him in Essence—let him be empty of the Higher Energy, or rather full of the opposite. If any worship not the Crucified, let him be Anathema and be numbered among the Deicides. If any assert that He was made perfect by works, or that after His Baptism, or after His Resurrection from the dead, He was counted worthy of an adoptive Sonship, like those whom the Greeks interpolate as added to the ranks of the gods, let him be anathema. For that which has a beginning or a progress or is made perfect, is not God, although the expressions may be used of His gradual manifestation. If any assert that He has now put off His holy flesh, and that His Godhead is stripped of the body, and deny that He is now with His body and will come again with it, let him not see the glory of His Coming. For where is His body now, if not with Him Who assumed it? For it is not laid by in the sun, according to the babble of the Manichaeans, that it should be honoured by a dishonour; nor was it poured forth into the air and dissolved, as is the nature of a voice or the flow of an odour, or the course of a lightning flash that never stands. Where in that case were His being handled after the Resurrection, or His being seen hereafter by them that pierced Him, for Godhead is in its nature invisible. Nay; He will come with His body—so I have learnt—such as He was seen by His Disciples in the Mount, or as he shewed Himself for a moment, when his Godhead overpowered the carnality. And as we say this to disarm suspicion, so we write the other to correct the novel teaching. If anyone assert that His flesh came down from heaven, and is not from hence, nor of us though above us, let him be anathema. For the words, The Second Man is the Lord from Heaven;[α] and, As is the Heavenly, such are they that are Heavenly; and, No man hath ascended up into Heaven save He which came down from Heaven, even the Son of Man which is in Heaven;[β] and the like, are to be understood as said on account of the Union with the heavenly; just as that All Things were made by Christ,[γ] and that Christ dwelleth in your hearts[α] is said, not of the visible nature which belongs to God, but of what is perceived by the mind, the names being mingled like the natures, and flowing into one another, according to the law of their intimate union.

If anyone has put his trust in Him as a Man without a human mind, he is really bereft of mind, and quite unworthy of salvation. For that which He has not assumed He has not healed; but that which is united to His Godhead is also saved. If only half Adam fell, then that which Christ assumes and saves may be half also; but if the whole of his nature fell, it must be united to the whole nature of Him that was begotten, and so be saved as a whole. Let them not, then, begrudge us our complete salvation, or clothe the Saviour only with bones and nerves and the portraiture of humanity. For if His Manhood is without soul, even the Arians admit this, that they may attribute His Passion to the Godhead, as that which gives motion to the body is also that which suffers. But if He has a soul, and yet is without a mind, how is He man, for man is not a mindless animal? And this would necessarily involve that while His form and tabernacle was human, His soul should be that of a horse or an ox, or some other of the brute creation. This, then, would be what He saves; and I have been deceived by the Truth, and led to boast of an honour which had been bestowed upon another. But if His Manhood is intellectual and not without mind, let them cease to be thus really mindless. But, says such an one, the Godhead took the place of the human intellect. How does this touch me? For Godhead joined to flesh alone is not man, nor to soul alone, nor to both apart from intellect, which is the most essential part of man. Keep then the whole man, and mingle Godhead therewith, that you may benefit me in my completeness. But, he asserts, He could not contain Two perfect Natures. Not if you only look at Him in a bodily fashion. For a bushel measure will not hold two bushels, nor will the space of one body hold two or more bodies. But if you will look at what is mental and incorporeal, remember that I in my one personality can contain soul and reason and mind and the Holy Spirit; and before me this world, by which I mean the system of things visible and invisible, contained Father, Son, and Holy Ghost. For such is the nature of intellectual Existences, that they can mingle with one another and with bodies, in-

α Cor. xv. 47. β John iii. 13. γ John i. 3.

α Ephes. iii. 17.

corporeally and invisibly. For many sounds are comprehended by one ear; and the eyes of many are occupied by the same visible objects, and the smell by odours; nor are the senses narrowed by each other, or crowded out, nor the objects of sense diminished by the multitude of the perceptions. But where is there mind of man or angel so perfect in comparison of the Godhead that the presence of the greater must crowd out the other? The light is nothing compared with the sun, nor a little damp compared with a river, that we must first do away with the lesser, and take the light from a house, or the moisture from the earth, to enable it to contain the greater and more perfect. For how shall one thing contain two completenesses, either the house, the sunbeam and the sun, or the earth, the moisture and the river? Here is matter for inquiry; for indeed the question is worthy of much consideration. Do they not know, then, that what is perfect by comparison with one thing may be imperfect by comparison with another, as a hill compared with a mountain, or a grain of mustard seed with a bean or any other of the larger seeds, although it may be called larger than any of the same kind? Or, if you like, an Angel compared with God, or a man with an Angel. So our mind is perfect and commanding, but only in respect of soul and body; not absolutely perfect; and a servant and a subject of God, not a sharer of His Princedom and honour. So Moses was a God to Pharaoh,[α] but a servant of God,[β] as it is written; and the stars which illumine the night are hidden by the Sun, so much that you could not even know of their existence by daylight; and a little torch brought near a great blaze is neither destroyed, nor seen, nor extinguished; but is all one blaze, the bigger one prevailing over the other.

But, it may be said, our mind is subject to condemnation. What then of our flesh? Is that not subject to condemnation? You must therefore either set aside the latter on account of sin, or admit the former on account of salvation. If He assumed the worse that He might sanctify it by His incarnation, may He not assume the better that it may be sanctified by His becoming Man? If the clay was leavened and has become a new lump, O ye wise men, shall not the Image be leavened and mingled with God, being deified by His Godhead? And I will add this also: If the mind was utterly rejected, as prone to sin and subject to damnation, and for this reason He assumed a body but left out the mind, then there is an excuse for them who sin with the mind; for the witness of God—according to you—has shewn the impossibility of healing it. Let me state the greater results. You, my good sir, dishonour my mind (you a Sarcolater, if I am an Anthropolater[α] that you may tie God down to the Flesh, since He cannot be otherwise tied; and therefore you take away the wall of partition. But what is my theory, who am but an ignorant man, and no Philosopher. Mind is mingled with mind, as nearer and more closely related, and through it with flesh, being a Mediator between God and carnality.

Further let us see what is their account of the assumption of Manhood, or the assumption of Flesh, as they call it. If it was in order that God, otherwise incomprehensible, might be comprehended, and might converse with men through His Flesh as through a veil, their mask and the drama which they represent is a pretty one, not to say that it was open to Him to converse with us in other ways, as of old, in the burning bush[β] and in the appearance of a man.[γ] But if it was that He might destroy the condemnation by sanctifying like by like, then as He needed flesh for the sake of the flesh which had incurred condemnation, and soul for the sake of our soul, so, too, He needed mind for the sake of mind, which not only fell in Adam, but was the first to be affected, as the doctors say of illnesses. For that which received the command was that which failed to keep the command, and that which failed to keep it was that also which dared to transgress; and that which transgressed was that which stood most in need of salvation; and that which needed salvation was that which also He took upon Him. Therefore, Mind was taken upon Him. This has now been demonstrated, whether they like it or no, by, to use their own expression, geometrical and necessary proofs. But you are acting as if, when a man's eye had been injured and his foot had been injured in consequence, you were to attend to the foot and leave the eye uncared for; or as if, when a painter had drawn something badly, you were to alter the picture, but to pass over the artist as if he had succeeded. But if they, overwhelmed by these arguments, take refuge in the proposition that it is possible for God to save man even apart

α Exod. vii. 1. β Num. xii. 7.

α The Apollinarians seem to have charged the Orthodox with being Anthropolaters, or worshippers of a mere Man. S. Gregory retorts upon them that if so, they are worse themselves, being actually Sarcolaters, or worshippers of mere flesh, denying Mind to Him whom they adore as Lord and Saviour.

β Exod. iii. 2. γ Gen. xviii. 5.

from mind, why, I suppose that it would be possible for Him to do so also apart from flesh by a mere act of will, just as He works all other things, and has wrought them without body. Take away, then, the flesh as well as the mind, that your monstrous folly may be complete. But they are deceived by the latter, and, therefore, they run to the flesh, because they do not know the custom of Scripture. We will teach them this also. For what need is there even to mention to those who know it, the fact that everywhere in Scripture he is called Man, and the Son of Man?

If, however, they rely on the passage, The Word was made Flesh and dwelt among us,[a] and because of this erase the noblest part of Man (as cobblers do the thicker part of skins) that they may join together God and Flesh, it is time for them to say that God is God only of flesh, and not of souls, because it is written, "As Thou hast given Him power over all Flesh," [β] and "Unto Thee shall all Flesh come;" [γ] and "Let all Flesh bless His holy Name," [δ] meaning every Man. Or, again, they must suppose that our fathers went down into Egypt without bodies and invisible, and that only the Soul of Joseph was imprisoned by Pharaoh, because it is written, "They went down into Egypt with threescore and fifteen Souls," [ε] and "The iron entered into his Soul," [ζ] a thing which could not be bound. They who argue thus do not know that such expressions are used by Synecdoche, declaring the whole by the part, as when Scripture says that the young ravens call upon God,[η] to indicate the whole feathered race; or Pleiades, Hesperus, and Arcturus [θ] are mentioned, instead of all the Stars and His Providence over them.

Moreover, in no other way was it possible for the Love of God toward us to be manifested than by making mention of our flesh, and that for our sake He descended even to our lower part. For that flesh is less precious than soul, everyone who has a spark of sense will acknowledge. And so the passage, The Word was made Flesh, seems to me to be equivalent to that in which it is said that He was made sin,[κ] or a curse [λ] for us; not that the Lord was transformed into either of these, how could He be? But because by taking them upon Him He took away our sins and bore our iniquities.[μ] This, then, is sufficient to say at the present time for the sake of clearness and of being understood by the many. And I write it, not with any desire to compose a treatise, but only to check the progress of deceit; and if it is thought well, I will give a fuller account of these matters at greater length.

But there is a matter which is graver than these, a special point which it is necessary that I should not pass over. I would they were even cut off that trouble you,[a] and would reintroduce a second Judaism, and a second circumcision, and a second system of sacrifices. For if this be done, what hinders Christ also being born again to set them aside, and again being betrayed by Judas, and crucified and buried, and rising again, that all may be fulfilled in the same order, like the Greek system of cycles, in which the same revolutions of the stars bring round the same events? For what the method of selection is, in accordance with which some of the events are to occur and others to be omitted, let these wise men who glory in the multitude of their books shew us.

But since, puffed up by their theory of the Trinity, they falsely accuse us of being unsound in the Faith and entice the multitude, it is necessary that people should know that Apollinarius, while granting the Name of Godhead to the Holy Ghost, did not preserve the Power of the Godhead. For to make the Trinity consist of Great, Greater, and Greatest, as of Light, Ray, and Sun, the Spirit and the Son and the Father (as is clearly stated in his writings), is a ladder of Godhead not leading to Heaven, but down from Heaven. But we recognize God the Father and the Son and the Holy Ghost, and these not as bare titles, dividing inequalities of ranks or of power, but as there is one and the same title, so there is one nature and one substance in the Godhead.

But if anyone who thinks we have spoken rightly on this subject reproaches us with holding communion with heretics, let him prove that we are open to this charge, and we will either convince him or retire. But it is not safe to make any innovation before judgment is given, especially in a matter of such importance, and connected with so great issues. We have protested and continue to protest this before God and men. And not even now, be well assured, should we have written this, if we had not seen that the Church was being torn asunder and divided, among their other tricks, by their present synagogue of vanity.[β] But if anyone when we say and protest this, either from some advantage they will thus gain, or through fear of men, or monstrous littleness of

---

a John i. 14. β Ib. xvii. 2. γ Ps. lxv. 2. δ Ib. cxlv. 21. ε Acts vii. 14. ζ Ps. cv. 18. η Ps. cxlvii. 8. θ Job ix. 9. κ 2 Cor. v. 21. λ Gal. iii. 13. μ Isa. liii. 7 LXX.

a Galat. v. 12. β Ps. xxvi. 4 LXX.

mind, or through some neglect of pastors and governors, or through love of novelty and proneness to innovations, rejects us as unworthy of credit, and attaches himself to such men, and divides the noble body of the Church, he shall bear his judgment, whoever he may be,[α] and shall give account to God in the day of judgment.[β] But if their long books, and their new Psalters, contrary to that of David, and the grace of their metres, are taken for a third Testament, we too will compose Psalms, and will write much in metre. For we also think we have the spirit of God,[γ] if indeed this is a gift of the Spirit, and not a human novelty. This I will that thou declare publicly, that we may not be held responsible, as overlooking such an evil, and as though this wicked doctrine received food and strength from our indifference.

AGAINST APOLLINARIUS; THE SECOND LETTER TO CLEDONIUS. (Ep. CII.)

Forasmuch as many persons have come to your Reverence seeking confirmation of their faith, and therefore you have affectionately asked me to put forth a brief definition and rule of my opinion, I therefore write to your Reverence, what indeed you knew before, that I never have and never can honour anything above the Nicene Faith, that of the Holy Fathers who met there to destroy the Arian heresy; but am, and by God's help ever will be, of that faith; completing in detail that which was incompletely said by them concerning the Holy Ghost; for that question had not then been mooted, namely, that we are to believe that the Father, Son, and Holy Ghost are of one Godhead, thus confessing the Spirit also to be God. Receive then to communion those who think and teach thus, as I also do; but those who are otherwise minded refuse, and hold them as strangers to God and the Catholic Church. And since a question has also been mooted concerning the Divine Assumption of humanity, or Incarnation, state this also clearly to all concerning me, that I join in One the Son, who was begotten of the Father, and afterward of the Virgin Mary, and that I do not call Him two Sons, but worship Him as One and the same in undivided Godhead and honour. But if anyone does not assent to this statement, either now or hereafter, he shall give account to God at the day of judgment.

α Galat. v. 10. β Matt. xii. 36. γ 1 Cor. vii. 40.

Now, what we object and oppose to their mindless opinion about His Mind is this, to put it shortly; for they are almost alone in the condition which they lay down, as it is through want of mind that they mutilate His mind. But, that they may not accuse us of having once accepted but of now repudiating the faith of their beloved Vitalius[α] which he handed in in writing at the request of the blessed Bishop Damasus of Rome, I will give a short explanation on this point also. For these men, when they are theologizing among their genuine disciples, and those who are initiated into their secrets, like the Manichaeans among those whom they call the "Elect," expose the full extent of their disease, and scarcely allow flesh at all to the Saviour. But when they are refuted and pressed with the common answers about the Incarnation which the Scripture presents, they confess indeed the orthodox words, but they do violence to the sense; for they acknowledge the Manhood to be neither without soul nor without reason nor without mind, nor imperfect, but they bring in the Godhead to supply the soul and reason and mind, as though It had mingled Itself only with His flesh, and not with the other properties belonging to us men; although His sinlessness was far above us, and was the cleansing of our passions.

Thus, then, they interpret wrongly the words, But we have the Mind of Christ,[β] and very absurdly, when they say that His Godhead is the mind of Christ, and not understanding the passage as we do, namely, that they who have purified their mind by the imitation of the mind which the Saviour took of us, and, as far as may be, have attained conformity with it, are said to have the mind of Christ; just as they might be testified to have the flesh of Christ who have trained their flesh, and in this respect have become of the same body and partakers of Christ; and so he says "As we have borne the image of the earth[γ] we shall also bear the image of the heavenly." And so they declare that the Perfect Man is not

α Vitalius or Vitalis was one of the principal followers of Apollinarius, and by him was consecrated schismatical Bishop of Antioch, where, while yet orthodox, he had been ordained a priest by Meletius. But he quarrelled with his Bishop through jealousy of another priest, and then fell under the influence of Apollinarius. He was summoned to Rome to clear himself of the charge of heresy; and by a clever manipulation of language he produced a confession which the Pope, Damasus, accepted as orthodox; but the Pope remitted the whole case to Paulinus, who was at that time recognized by the Western Church as rightful Bishop. Vitalius, however, was unable to accept the test required, and seceded. On his return from Rome he had visited Nazianzus, where S. Gregory received him as a brother in the faith, though further acquaintance compelled him to withdraw from this position. Vitalius, while admitting that our Lord had both a human body and a human soul, denied Him a human mind; whose place, according to his teaching, was supplied by the Divinity. β 1 Cor. ii. 16. γ 1 Cor. xv. 49.

He who was in all points tempted like as we are yet without sin;[α] but the mixture of God and Flesh. For what, say they, can be more perfect than this?

They play the same trick with the word that describes the Incarnation, viz.: He was made Man, explaining it to mean, not, He was in the human nature with which He surrounded Himself, according to the Scripture, He knew what was in man;[β] but teaching that it means, He consorted and conversed with men, and taking refuge in the expression which says that He was seen on Earth and conversed with Men.[γ] And what can anyone contend further? They who take away the Humanity and the Interior Image cleanse by their newly invented mask only our outside,[δ] and that which is seen; so far in conflict with themselves that at one time, for the sake of the flesh, they explain all the rest in a gross and carnal manner (for it is from hence that they have derived their second Judaism and their silly thousand years delight in paradise, and almost the idea that we shall resume again the same conditions after these same thousand years); and at another time they bring in His flesh as a phantom rather than a reality, as not having been subjected to any of our experiences, not even such as are free from sin; and use for this purpose the apostolic expression, understood and spoken in a sense which is not apostolic, that our Saviour was made in the likeness of Men and found in fashion as a Man,[ε] as though by these words was expressed, not the human form, but some delusive phantom and appearance.

Since then these expressions, rightly understood, make for orthodoxy, but wrongly interpreted are heretical, what is there to be surprised at if we received the words of Vitalius in the more orthodox sense; our desire that they should be so meant persuading us, though others are angry at the intention of his writings? This is, I think, the reason why Damasus himself, having been subsequently better informed, and at the same time learning that they hold by their former explanations, excommunicated them and overturned their written confession of faith with an Anathema; as well as because he was vexed at the deceit which he had suffered from them through simplicity.

Since, then, they have been openly convicted of this, let them not be angry, but let them be ashamed of themselves; and let them not slander us, but abase themselves and wipe off from their portals that great and marvellous proclamation and boast of their orthodoxy, meeting all who go in at once with the question and distinction that we must worship, not a God-bearing Man, but a flesh-bearing God. What could be more unreasonable than this, though these new heralds of truth think a great deal of the title? For though it has a certain sophistical grace through the quickness of its antithesis, and a sort of juggling quackery grateful to the uninstructed, yet it is the most absurd of absurdities and the most foolish of follies. For if one were to change the word *Man* or *Flesh* into *God* (the first would please us, the second them), and then were to use this wonderful antithesis, so divinely recognized, what conclusion should we arrive at? That we must worship, not a God-bearing Flesh, but a Man-bearing God. O monstrous absurdity! They proclaim to us to-day a wisdom hidden ever since the time of Christ—a thing worthy of our tears. For if the faith began thirty years ago, when nearly four hundred years had passed since Christ was manifested, vain all that time will have been our Gospel, and vain our faith; in vain will the Martyrs have borne their witness, and in vain have so many and so great Prelates presided over the people; and Grace is a matter of metres and not of the faith.

And who will not marvel at their learning, in that on their own authority they divide the things of Christ, and assign to His Manhood such sayings as He was born, He was tempted, He was hungry, He was thirsty, He was wearied, He was asleep; but reckon to His Divinity such as these: He was glorified by Angels, He overcame the Tempter, He fed the people in the wilderness, and He fed them in such a manner, and He walked upon the sea; and say on the one hand that the "Where have ye laid Lazarus?"[α] belongs to us, but the loud voice "Lazarus, Come Forth"[β] and the raising him that had been four days dead, is above our nature; and that while the "He was in an Agony, He was crucified, He was buried," belongs to the Veil, on the other hand, "He was confident, He rose again, He ascended," belong to the Inner Treasure; and then they accuse us of introducing two natures, separate or conflicting, and of dividing the supernatural and wondrous Union. They ought, either not to do that of which they accuse us, or not to accuse us of that which they do; so at least if they are resolved to be consistent and not to propound at once their own and their opponents' principles. Such is their want of reason; it conflicts both with itself and with the

α Heb. iv. 15. β John ii. 25. γ Baruch iii. 37. δ Matt. xxiii. 25, 26. ε Phil. ii. 7.

α John xi. 34. β Ib. xi. 43.

truth to such an extent that they are neither conscious nor ashamed of it when they fall out with themselves. Now, if anyone thinks that we write all this willingly and not upon compulsion, and that we are dissuading from unity, and not doing our utmost to promote it, let him know that he is very much mistaken, and has not made at all a good guess at our desires, for nothing is or ever has been more valuable in our eyes than peace, as the facts themselves prove; though their actions and brawlings against us altogether exclude unanimity.

Ep. CXXV.

To Olympius.

Even hoar hairs have something to learn; and old age, it would seem, cannot in all respects be trusted for wisdom. I at any rate, knowing better than anyone, as I did, the thoughts and the heresy of the Apollinarians, and seeing that their folly was intolerable; yet thinking that I could tame them by patience and soften them by degrees, I let my hopes make me eager to attain this object. But, as it seems, I overlooked the fact that I was making them worse, and injuring the Church by my untimely philosophy. For gentleness does not put bad men out of countenance. And now if it had been possible for me to teach you this myself, I should not have hesitated, you may be sure, even to undertake a journey beyond my strength to throw myself at the feet of your Excellency. But since my illness has brought me too far, and it has become necessary for me to try the hot baths of Xanxaris at the advice of my medical men, I send a letter to represent me. These wicked and utterly abandoned men have dared, in addition to all their other misdeeds, either to summon, or to make a bad use of the passage (I am not prepared to say precisely which) of certain Bishops, deprived by the whole Synod of the Eastern and Western Church; and, in violation of all Imperial Ordinances, and of your commands, to confer the name of Bishop on a certain individual of their own misbelieving and deceitful crew; encouraged to do so, as I believe, by nothing so much as my great infirmity; for I must mention this. If this is to be tolerated, your Excellency will tolerate it, and I too will bear it, as I have often before. But if it is serious, and not to be endured by our most august Emperors, pray punish what has been done—though more mildly than such madness merits.

DIVISION II.

CORRESPONDENCE WITH SAINT BASIL THE GREAT, ARCHBISHOP OF CAESAREA.

Ep. I.

(Perhaps about A.D. 357 or 358; in answer to a letter which is not now extant.)

To Basil his Comrade.

I have failed, I confess, to keep my promise. I had engaged even at Athens, at the time of our friendship and intimate connection there (for I can find no better word for it), to join you in a life of philosophy. But I failed to keep my promise, not of my own will, but because one law prevailed against another; I mean the law which bids us honour our parents overpowered the law of our friendship and intercourse. Yet I will not fail you altogether, if you will accept this offer. I shall be with you half the time, and half of it you will be with me, that we may have the whole in common, and that our friendship may be on equal terms; and so it will be arranged in such a way that my parents will not be grieved, and yet I shall gain you.

Ep. II.

(Written about the same time, in reply to another letter now lost.)

I do not like being joked about Tiberina and its mud and its winters, O my friend, who are so free from mud, and who walk on tiptoe, and trample on the plains. You who have wings and are borne aloft, and fly like the arrows of Abaris, in order that, Cappadocian though you are, you may flee from Cappadocia. Have we done you an injury, because while you are pale and breathing hard and measuring the sun, we are sleek and well fed and not pressed for room? Yet this is your condition. You are luxurious and rich, and go to market. I do not approve of this. Either then cease to reproach us with our mud (for you did not build your city, nor we make our winter), or else for our mud we will bring against you your hucksters, and the rest of the crop of nuisances which infest cities.

Ep. IV.

(In answer to Ep. XIV., of Basil, about 361.)

You may mock and pull to pieces my affairs, whether in jest or in earnest. This is a matter of no consequence; only laugh, and take your fill of culture, and enjoy my friendship. Everything that comes from you is pleasant to me, no matter what it may be, and how it may look. For I think you are chaffing about things here, not for the sake of chaffing, but that you may draw me to yourself, if I understand you at all; just like people who block up streams in order to draw them into another channel. That is how your sayings always seem to me.

For my part I will admire your Pontus and your Pontic darkness, and your dwelling place so worthy of exile, and the hills over your head, and the wild beasts which test your faith, and your sequestered spot that lies under them . . . or as I should say your mousehole with the stately names of Abode of Thought, Monastery, School; and your thickets of wild bushes, and crown of precipitous mountains, by which may you be, not crowned but, cloistered; and your limited air; and the sun, for which you long, and can only see as through a chimney, O sunless Cimmerians of Pontus, who are condemned not only to a six months' night, as some are said to be, but who have not even a part of your life out of the shadow, but all your life is one long night, and a real shadow of death, to use a Scripture phrase. And I admire your strait and narrow road, leading . . . I know not if it be to the Kingdom, or to Hades, but for your sake I hope it is the Kingdom. . . And as for the intervening country, what is your wish? Am I falsely to call it Eden, and the fountain divided into four heads, by which the world is watered, or the dry and waterless wilderness (only what Moses will come to tame it, bringing water out of the rock with his staff)? For all of it which has escaped the rocks is full of gullies; and that which is not a gully is a thicket of thorns; and whatever is above the thorns is a precipice; and the road above that is precipitous, and slopes both ways, exercising the mind of travellers, and calling for gymnastic exercises for safety. And the river rushes roaring down, which to you is a Strymon of Amphipolis for quietness, and there are not so many fishes in it as stones, nor does it flow into a lake, but it dashes into abysses, O my grandiloquent friend and inventor of new names. For it is great and terrible, and overwhelms the psalmody of those who live above it; like the Cataracts and Catadoupa of the Nile, so does it roar you down day and night. It is rough and fordless; and it has only this morsel of kindness about it, that it does not sweep away your dwelling when the torrents and winter storms make it mad. This then is what I think of those Fortunate Islands and of you happy people. And you are not to admire the crescent-shaped curves which strangle rather than cut off the accessible parts of your Highlands, and the strip of mountain ridge that hangs over your heads, and makes your life like that of Tantalus; and the draughty breezes, and the vent-holes of the earth, which refresh your courage when it fails; and your musical birds that sing (but only of famine), and fly about (but only about the desert). No one visits it, you say, except for hunting; you might add, and except to look upon your dead bodies. This is perhaps too long for a letter, but it is too short for a comedy. If you can take my jokes kindly you will do well, but if not, I will send you some more.

Ep. V.

(Circa A.D. 361.)

Since you do take my jokes kindly, I send you the rest. My prelude is from Homer.

> "Come now and change thy theme,
> And sing of the inner adornment."
> —Od. viii. 492.

Your roofless and doorless hut, your fireless and smokeless hearth, your walls dried by fire, that we may not be hit by the drops of the mud, condemned like Tantalus thirsting in the midst of waters, and that pitiable feast with nothing to eat, to which we were invited from Cappadocia, not as to a Lotus-eater's poverty, but to a table of Alcinous—we young and miserable survivors of a wreck. For I remember those loaves and the broth (so it was called), yes, and I shall remember them too, and my poor teeth that slipped on your hunks of bread, and then braced themselves up, and pulled themselves as it were out of mud. You yourself will raise these things to a higher strain of tragedy, having learnt to talk big through your own sufferings. . . for if we had not been quickly delivered by that great supporter of the poor —I mean your mother—who appeared opportunely like a harbour to men tossed by a storm, we should long ago have been dead, rather pitied than admired for our faith in Pontus. How shall I pass over that garden which was no garden and had no vegetables, and the Augean dunghill which we cleared out of the house, and with which we filled it up (sc. the garden), when we drew that mountainous wagon, I the vintager, and you the valiant, with our necks and hands, which still bear the traces of our labours. "O earth and sun, O air and virtue" (for I will indulge a little in tragic tones), not that we might bridge the Hellespont, but that we might level a precipice. If you are not put out by the mention of the circumstances, no more am I; but if you are, how much more was I by the reality. I pass by the rest, through respect for the others from whom I received much enjoyment.

Ep. VI.

(Written about the same time, in a more serious vein.)

What I wrote before about our stay in Pontus was in joke, not in earnest; what I write now is very much in earnest. O that one would place me as in the month of those former days,[a] in which I luxuriated with you in hard living; since voluntary pain is more valuable than involuntary delight. O that one would give me back those psalmodies

---

[a] Job xxix. 2.

and vigils and those sojournings with God in prayer, and that immaterial, so to speak, and unbodied life. O for the intimacy and one-souledness of the brethren who were by you divinized and exalted: O for the contest and incitement of virtue which we secured by written Rules and Canons; O for the loving labour in the Divine Oracles, and the light we found in them by the guidance of the Holy Ghost. Or, if I may speak of lesser and slighter matters, O for the daily courses and experiences; O for the gatherings of wood, and the cutting of stone; O for the golden plane-tree, more precious than that of Xerxes, under which sat, not a King enfeebled by luxury, but a Monk worn out by hard life, which I planted and Apollos (I mean your honourable self) watered;[α] but God gave the increase to our honour, that a memorial might remain among you of my diligence, as in the Ark we read and believe, did Aaron's rod that budded.[β] To long for all this is very easy, but it is not easy to attain it. But do you come to me, and conspire with me in virtue, and co-operate with me, and aid me by your prayers to keep the profit which we used to get together, that I may not perish by little and little, like a shadow as the day draws to its close. I would rather breathe you than the air, and only live while I am with you, either actually in your presence, or virtually by your likeness in your absence.

Ep. VIII.

(Written to S. Basil shortly after his Ordination as Priest, probably toward the end of A.D. 362.)

I approve the beginning of your letter; but what is there of yours that I do not approve? And you are convicted of having written just like me;[γ] for I, too, was forced into the rank of the Priesthood, for indeed I never was eager for it. We are to one another, if ever any men were, trustworthy witnesses of our love for a humble and lowly philosophy. But perhaps it would have been better that this had not happened, or I know not what to say, as long as I am in ignorance of the purpose of the Holy Ghost. But since it has come about, we must bear it, at least so it seems clear to me; and especially when we take the times into consideration, which are bringing in upon us so many heretical tongues, and must not put to shame either the hopes of those who have trusted us thus, or our own lives.

α 1 Cor. iii. 6. β Num. xvii. 8, 10.
γ The Editors render "And you were captured just as I also was circumscribed," etc., but the Greek hardly bears this rendering.

Ep. XIX.

(This Epistle should be read in connection with the three addressed to Eusebius of Cæsarea, to which it refers. For the circumstances see General Prolegomena, § 1, p. 194.)

It is a time for prudence and endurance, and that we should not let anyone appear to be of higher courage than ourselves, or let all our labours and toils be in an instant brought to nothing. Why do I write this, and wherefore? Our Bishop Eusebius, very dear to God (for so we must for the future both think and write of him), is very much disposed to agreement and friendship with us; and as fire softens iron, so has time softened him; and I think a letter of appeal and invitation will come to you from him, as he intimated to me, and as many persons who are well acquainted with his affairs assure me. Let us be beforehand with him then, either by going to him, or by writing to him; or rather by first writing and then going; in order that we may not by and by be put to shame by being defeated when it was in our power to secure a victory by being honourably and philosophically beaten, which so many are asking from us. Be persuaded by me then, and come; both on this account and on account of the bad times; for a conspiracy of heretics is assailing the Church; some of them are here now, and are troubling us; and others, rumour says, are coming; and there is reason to fear lest the Word of Truth should be swept away, unless there be stirred up very soon the spirit of a Bezaleel, the wise Master builder of such arguments and dogmas. If you think I ought to go too, to stay with you and travel with you, I will not refuse to do even this.

(We insert here the three letters to Eusebius, which are so closely connected with the above as not to seem out of place.)

Ep. XVI.

To Eusebius, Bishop of Cæsarea.

Since I am addressing a man who does not love falsehood, and who is the keenest man I know at detecting it in another, however it may be twined in skilful and varied labyrinths; and, moreover, on my own part I will say it, though against the grain I do not like artifice, either, both from my natural constitution, and because God's Word has formed me so. Therefore I write what presents itself to my mind; and I beg you to excuse my plain speaking, or you will wrong the truth by depriving me of my liberty, and forcing me to restrain within myself the pain of my grief, like some secret and malignant disease. I rejoice that I have your respect (for I am a man, as some one has said before), and that I am summoned to Synods and spiritual conferences. But I am troubled at the slight which has been inflicted on my most Reverend brother Basil, and is still inflicted on him by Your Reverence; for I chose him as the companion of my life and words and highest philosophy, and he is so still; and I never had reason to regret my judgment of him. It is more temperate to speak thus of him, that I may not seem to be praising myself in admiring him. You, however, I think, by honouring me and dishonouring him, seem to be acting like a man who should with one hand stroke a man's head, and with the other hand strike him on the face; or while tearing up the foundations of a house should paint the walls and decorate the exterior. If then you will listen to me, this is what you will do, and I claim to be listened to, for this is justice. If you will pay due attention to him, he will do the like by you. And I will follow him as a shadow does the body, being of little worth and inclined to peace. For I am not so mean as to be willing in other respects to philosophize, and to be of the better part, but to overlook a matter which is the end of all our teaching, namely love; especially in regard to a Priest, and one of so high a character, and one whom I know of all my acquaintances to be the best both in life and doctrine and conduct. For my pain shall not obscure the truth.

Ep. XVII.

To Eusebius, Archbishop of Cæsarea.

I did not write in an insolent spirit, as you complain of my letter, but rather in a spiritual and philosophical one, and as was fitting, unless this too wrongs "your most eloquent Gregory." For though you are my Superior in rank, yet you will grant me something of liberty and just freedom of speech. Therefore be kinder to me. But if you regard my letter as coming from a servant, and from one who has not the right even to look you in the face, I will in this instance accept your stripes and not even shed a tear. Will you blame me for this also? That would befit anyone rather than your Reverence. For it is the part of a high-souled man to accept more readily the freedom of a friend than the flattery of an enemy.

Ep. XVIII.

To Eusebius of Cæsarea.

I was never meanly disposed towards your Reverence; do not find me guilty. But after allowing myself a little liberty and boldness, just to relieve and heal my grief, I at once bowed and submitted, and willingly subjected myself to the Canon. What else could I have done, knowing both you and the Law of the Spirit? But if I had been ever so mean and ignoble in my sentiments, yet the present time would not allow such feelings, nor the wild beasts which are rushing on the Church, nor your own courage and manliness, so purely and genuinely fighting for the Church. I will come then, if you wish it, and take part with you in prayers and in conflict, and will serve you, and like cheering boys will stir up the noble athlete by my exhortations.

Ep. XL.

To the Great Basil.

(About the middle of the year 370. On the death of Eusebius Basil seems to have formed a desire that his friend Gregory should succeed to the vacant Metropolitanate; and so he wrote to him, without mentioning the death of the Archbishop, to come to him at Cæsarea, representing himself as dangerously ill. Gregory, deeply grieved at the news, set off at once, but had not proceeded far on his way when he learned that Basil was in his usual health, and that the Bishops of the Province were assembling at Cæsarea for the Election of a Metropolitan. He saw through the artifice at once; and thinking that Basil had wished to secure his presence at the Metropolis in order that his influence might bring about his own (Basil's) Election, he wrote him the following indignant letter. Nevertheless both he and his father felt that no one was so well fitted to succeed to the vacant throne; and so Gregory wrote in his father's name the three letters which we have placed next, addressed respectively to the people of Cæsarea, to the Bishops attending the Synod, and to Eusebius Bishop of Samosata.)

Do not be surprized if I say something strange, which has not been said before by anyone. I think you have the reputation of being a steady safe and strong-minded man, but also of being more simple than safe in much that you plan and do. For that which is free from evil is also in proportion slow to suspect evil, as is shewn by what has just occurred. You have summoned me to the Metropolis at the moment when a council has been called for the election of a Bishop, and your pretext is very seemly and plausible. You pretend to be very ill, indeed at your last breath, and to long to see me and to bid me a last farewell; I do not know with what object, even what my presence can effect in the matter. I started in great grief at what had happened; for what could be of higher value to me than your life, or more distressing than your departure? And I shed a fountain of tears; and I wailed aloud; and I felt myself now for the first time unphilosophically disposed. What did I leave unperformed of all that befits a funeral? But as soon as I found that the Bishops were assembling at the City, at once I stopped short in my course; and I wondered first that you had not perceived what was proper, or guarded against people's tongues, which are so given to slander the guileless; and secondly that you did not think the same course to be fitting for me as for yourself, though our life and our rule and everything is common to us both, who have been so closely associated by God from the first. Thirdly, for I must say this also, I wondered whether you remembered that such nominations are worthy of the more religious, not of the more powerful, nor of those most in favour with the multitude. For these reasons then I backed water, and held back. Now, if you think as I do, come to this determination, to avoid these public turmoils and evil suspicions. I shall see your Reverence when the matters are settled and time allows, and I shall have more and graver reproaches to address to you.

Ep. XLI.

To the People of Cæsarea, in his Father's name.

I am a little shepherd, and preside over a tiny flock, and I am among the least of the servants of the Spirit. But Grace is not narrow, or circumscribed by place. Wherefore let freedom of speech be given even to the small,—especially when the subject matter is of such great importance, and one in which all are interested—even to deliberate with men of hoary hairs, who speak with perhaps greater wisdom than the ordinary run of men. You are deliberating on no ordinary or unimportant matter, but on one by which the common interest must necessarily be promoted or injured according to the decision at which you arrive. For our subject matter is the Church, for which Christ died, and the guide who is to present it and lead it to God. For the light of the body is the eye,[a] as we have heard; not only the bodily eye which sees and is seen, but that which contemplates and is contemplated spiritually. But the light of the Church is the Bishop, as is evident to you even without our writing it. As then the straightness or crookedness of the course of the body depends upon the clearness or dulness of the eye, so must the Church necessarily share the peril or safety incurred by the conduct of its Chief. You must then take thought for the whole Church as the Body of Christ, but more especially for your own, which was from the beginning and is now the Mother of almost all the Churches, to which all the Commonwealth looks, like a circle described round a centre, not only because of its orthodoxy proclaimed of old to all, but also because of the grace of unanimity so evidently bestowed upon it by God. You then have summoned us also to your discussion of this matter, and so are acting rightly and canonically. But we are oppressed by age and infirmity, and if we by the strength given us by the Holy Ghost could be present (nothing is incredible to them that believe), this would be best for the common welfare and most pleasant to ourselves, that we might confer something on you, and ourselves have a part of the blessing; but if I should be kept away through weakness, I will give at any rate whatever can be given by one who is absent.

I believe that there are others among you worthy of the Primacy, both because of the greatness of your city, and because it has been governed in times past so excellently and by such great men; but there is one man among you to whom I cannot prefer any, our son well beloved of God, Basil the Priest (I speak before God as my witness); a man of pure life and word, and alone, or almost alone, of all qualified in both respects to stand against the present times, and the prevailing wordiness of the heretics. I write this to men of the priestly and monastic Orders, and also to the dignitaries and councillors, and to the whole people. If you should approve it, and my vote should prevail, being so just and right, and given with God's aid, I am and will be with you in spirit; or rather I have already set my hand to the work—and am bold in

[a] Matt. vi. 22.

the Spirit. But if you should not agree with me, but determine something else, and if the matter is to be settied by cliques and relationships, and if the hand of the mob is again to disturb the sincerity of your vote, do what pleases you—I shall stay at home.

Ep. XLIII.

(The comprovincial Bishops had notified the elder Gregory of their Synod, but without mentioning its date or purpose or inviting him to take part in it—probably because they knew how strongly he would support the election of Basil, to which they were unfavourable. S. Gregory therefore wrote the following letter in his father's name.)

To The Bishops.

How sweet and kind you are, and how full of love. You have invited me to the Metropolis, because, as I imagine, you are going to take some counsel about a Bishop. So much I learn from you, though you have not told me either that I am to be present, or why, or when, but have merely announced to me suddenly that you were setting out, as though resolved not to respect me, and as not desirous that I should share your counsels, but rather putting a hindrance in the way of my coming, that you may not meet me even against my will. This is your way of action, and I will put up with the insult, but I will set before you my view and how I feel. Various people will put forward various candidates, each according to his own inclinations and interests, as is usually the case at such times. But I cannot prefer anyone, for my conscience would not allow it, to my dear son and fellow priest Basil. For whom of all my acquaintance do I find more approved in his life, or more powerful in his word, or more furnished altogether with the beauty of virtue? But if you allege weak health against him, I reply that we are choosing not an athlete but a teacher. And at the same time is seen in this case the power of Him that strengthens and supports the weak, if such they be. If you accept this vote I will come and take part, either in spirit or in body. But if you are marching to a foregone conclusion, and faction is to overrule justice, I shall rejoice to have been overlooked. The work must be yours; but pray for me.[a]

[a] There is here a various reading (the difference being merely the result of itacism) which seems to give a better sense; "Ours is to pray for you."

Ep. XLII.

(There still seemed a probability that intrigues and party spirit would carry the day, and so the two Gregories determined to call in the aid of Eusebius of Samosata, though he did not belong to the Province. He had been a conspicuous champion of orthodoxy against the Arian Emperor Valens, and the Gregories hoped much from his presence at the Synod. He responded to their appeal, and undertook the three hundred miles of very difficult travelling to throw in his influence with the cause which they had at heart. He saw, however, that it was necessary that the aged Bishop of Nazianzus, notwithstanding his years and infirmities, should make the effort, and he persuaded him to go. The result was all that could be desired; for Basil was elected by a unanimous vote. The letter, which S. Gregory wrote in his own name to thank him, will be found later on.)

To Eusebius, Bishop of Samosata.

O that I had the wings of a dove, or that my old age could be renewed, that I might be able to go to your charity, and to satisfy the longings that I have to see you, and to tell you the troubles of my soul, and in you to find some comfort for my afflictions. For since the death of the blessed Bishop Eusebius I am not a little afraid lest they who on a former occasion set traps for our Metropolis, and wanted to fill it with heretical tares, should now seize the opportunity, and uproot by their evil teaching the piety which has with so much labour been sown in the hearts of men, and should tear asunder its unity, as they have done in many Churches. As soon as I received letters from the Clergy asking me not to forget them in their present circumstances, I looked round about me, and remembered your love and your right faith and the zeal with which you are ever possessed for the Churches of God; and therefore I sent my beloved Eustathius, my Deacon and helper, to warn your Reverence, and to entreat you, in addition to all your toils for the Churches, to meet me, and both to refresh my old age by your coming, and to establish in the Orthodox Church that piety which is so famous, by giving her with us (if we may be deemed worthy to have a share with you in the good work) a Shepherd according to the will of the Lord, who shall be able to rule His people. For we have a man before our eyes, and you are not unacquainted with him; and if we are permitted to obtain him I know that we shall acquire great boldness towards God, and shall confer a very great benefit upon the people who have called upon our aid. I beg you again and again to put away all delay, and to come to us before the bad weather of the winter sets in.

Ep. XLV.

(After the Consecration every one thought that Gregory would at once join his friend; and Basil himself much wished for his assistance. But Gregory thought it better to restrain his desire to see his friend until jealousies had had time to calm down. So he wrote the following letter to explain the reasons for his staying away at this juncture.)

To Basil.

When I learnt that you had been placed on the lofty throne, and that the Spirit had prevailed to publish the candle upon the candlestick, which even before shone with no dim light, I was glad, I confess. Why should I not be, seeing as I did that the commonwealth of the Church was in sorry plight, and needed such a guiding hand? Yet I did not run to you off hand, nor shall I run to you, not even if you ask me yourself. First, in order that I may be careful of your dignity, and that you may not seem to be collecting partisans under the influence of bad taste and hot temper, as your calumniators would say; and secondly that I may make for myself a reputation for stability, and above illwill. When then will you come, perhaps you will ask, and how long will you put it off? As long as God shall bid me, and until the shadow of the present enmity and slander shall have passed away. For the lepers, I well know, will not hold out very long to keep our David out of Jerusalem.

Ep. XLVI.

(The new Archbishop seems not to have been satisfied with the reasons given in Gregory's last letter; so the latter writes again.)

To Basil.

How can any affairs of yours be mere grape-gleanings to me, O dear and sacred friend? "What a word has escaped the fence of your teeth," or how could you dare to say such a thing, if I too may be somewhat daring? How could your mind set it going, or your ink write it, or your paper receive it, O lectures and Athens and virtues and literary labours! You almost make me write a tragedy by what you have written. Do you not know me or yourself, you eye of the world, and great voice and trumpet and palace of learning? Your affairs trifles to Gregory? What then on earth could any one admire, if Gregory admire not you? There is one spring among the seasons, one sun among the stars, and one heaven that embraces all things; and so your voice is unique among all things, if I am capable of judging such things, and not deceived by my affection—and this I do not think to be the case. But if it is because I do not value you according to your worth that you blame me, you must also blame all mankind; for no one else has or will sufficiently admire you, unless it be yourself, and your own eloquence, at least if it were possible to praise oneself, and if such were the custom of our speech. But if you are accusing me of despising you, why not rather of being mad? Or are you vexed because I am acting like a philosopher? Give me leave to say that this and this alone is higher than even your conversation.

Ep. XLVII.

(The division of the civil Province of Cappadocia into two Provinces in the year 372 was followed by ecclesiastical troubles. Anthimus, the Bishop of Tyana, the civil metropolis of the new division of Cappadocia Secunda, maintained that the Ecclesiastical divisions must necessarily follow the civil, and by consequence claimed for himself that the purely civil action of the State had *ipso facto* elevated him to the dignity of Metropolitan of the new Province; and this pretension was supported by the Bishops of that district, who were as a rule not well disposed towards the great Archbishop. The next three letters are connected with this dispute.)

To Basil.

I hear that you are being troubled by this fresh innovation, and are being worried by some sophistical and not unusual officiousness on the part of those in power; and it is not to be wondered at. For I was not ignorant of their envy, or of the fact that many of those around you are making use of you to further their own interests, and are kindling the spark of meanness. I have no fear of seeing you unphilosophically affected by your troubles, or in any way unworthy of yourself and me. Nay, I think that it is now above all that my Basil will be known, and that the philosophy which all your life you have been collecting will shew itself, and will overcome the abuse as with a high wave; and that you will remain unshaken while others are being troubled. If you think it well, I will come myself and perhaps shall be able to give you some assistance by my counsel (if the sea needs water, you do counsel!); but in any case I shall derive benefit, and shall learn philosophy by bearing my part of the abuse.

Ep. XLVIII.

(Shortly after the events described above, Basil determined to strengthen his own hands by creating a number of new Bishoprics in the disputed Province, to one of which, Sasima, he consecrated Gregory, very much against the will of the latter, who felt that he had been hardly used, and did not attempt to disguise his reluctance. See Gen. Prolegg. p. 195.)

To Basil.

Do leave off speaking of me as an ill-educated and uncouth and unfriendly man, not even worthy to live, because I have ventured to be conscious of the way in which I have been treated. You yourself would admit that I have not done wrong in any other respect, and my own conscience does not reproach me with having been unkind to you in either great or small matters; and I hope it never may. I only know that I saw that I had been deceived—too late indeed, but I saw it—and I throw the blame on your throne, as having on a sudden lifted you above yourself; and I am weary of being blamed for faults of yours, and of having to make excuses for them to people who know both our former and our present relations. For of all that I have to endure this is the most ridiculous or most pitiable thing, that the same person should have both to suffer the wrong and to bear the blame, and this is my present case. Different people blame me for different things according to the tastes of each, or each man's disposition, or the measure of their ill feeling on my account; but the kindest reproach me with contempt and disdain, and they throw me on one side after making use of me, like the most valueless vessels, or those frames upon which arches are built, which after the building is complete are taken down and cast aside. We will let them be and say what they please; no one shall curb their freedom of speech. And do you, as my reward, pay off those blessed and empty hopes, which you devised against the evil speakers, who accused you of insulting me on pretence of honouring me, as though I were lightminded and easily taken in by such treatment. Now I will plainly speak out the state of my mind, and you must not be angry with me. For I will tell you just what I said at the moment of the suffering, not in a fit of anger or so much in the sense of astonishment at what had happened as to lose my reason or not to know what I said. I will not take up arms, nor will I learn tactics which I did not learn in former times, when the occasion seemed more suitable, as every one was arming and in frenzy (you know the illness of the weak), nor will I face the martial Anthimus, though he be an untimely warrior, being myself unarmed and unwarlike, and thus the more exposed to wounds. Fight with him yourself if you wish (for necessity often makes warriors even of the weak), or look out for some one to fight when he seizes your mules, keeping guard over a defile, and like Amalek of old, barring the way against Israel. Give me before all things quiet. Why should I fight for sucking pigs and fowls, and those not my own, as though for souls and canons? Why should I deprive the Metropolis of the celebrated Sasima, or lay bare and unveil the secret of your mind, when I ought to join in concealing it? Do you then play the man and be strong and draw all parties to your own conclusion, as the rivers do the winter torrents, without regard for friendship or intimacy in good, or for the reputation which such a course will bring you. Give yourself up to the Spirit alone. I shall gain this only from your friendship, that I shall learn not to trust in friends, or to esteem anything more valuable than God.

Ep. XLIX.

(The Praises of Quiet.)

To Basil.

You accuse me of laziness and idleness, because I did not accept your Sasima, and because I have not bestirred myself like a Bishop, and do not arm you against each other like a bone thrown into the midst of dogs. My greatest business always is to keep free from business. And to give you an idea of one of my good points, so much do I value freedom from business, that I think I might even be a standard to all men of this kind of magnanimity, and if only all men would imitate me the Churches would have no troubles; nor would the faith, which every one uses as a weapon in his private quarrels, be pulled in pieces.

Ep. L.

(At the request of Anthimus it would appear that S. Gregory wrote to S. Basil a letter, not now extant, proposing a conference between the rival Metropolitans. Basil took umbrage at the well-meant proposal, and wrote a stiff letter to S. Gregory, to which the following is the reply.)

To Basil.

How hotly and like a colt you skip in your letters. Nor do I wonder that when you have just become the property of glory you should wish to shew me what you find glory to be, so that you may make yourself more majestic, like those painters who picture the seasons. But, to explain the whole matter about the Bishops, and the letter by which you were annoyed; what was my starting point, and how far I went, and where I stopped, appears to me to be too long a matter for a letter, and to be a subject not so much for an apology as for a history. To explain it to you concisely:—the most noble Anthimus came to us with certain Bishops, whether to visit my Father (this at least was the pretext), or to act as he did act. He sounded me in many ways and on many subjects; dioceses, the marshes of Sasima, my ordination, . . . flattering, questioning, threatening, pleading, blaming, praising, drawing circles round himself, as though I ought only to look at him and his new Metropolis, as being the greater. Why, I said, do you draw your line to include our city, for we too deem our Church to be really a Mother of Churches, and that too from ancient times? In the end he went away without having gained his object, much out of breath, and reproaching me with Basilism, as if it were a kind of Philipism. Do you think I did you wrong in this? And now look at the letter from me, who, you say, insulted you. They fashioned a Synodal summons to me; and when I declined it and said that the thing was an insult, they then asked as an alternative that through me you should be invited to deliberate upon these matters. This I promised, in order to prevent their first plan being carried out; placing the whole matter in your hands, if you choose to call them together, and where and when. And if I have not injured you in this, tell me where there is room for injury. If you have to learn this from me, I will read you the letter which Anthimus sent me, after invading the marshes, notwithstanding my prohibitions and threats, insulting and reviling me, and as it were singing a song of triumph over my defeat. And what reason is there that I should offend him for your sake and at the same time displease you, as though I were currying favour with him? You ought to have learnt this first, my dear friend; and even if it had been so, you should not have insulted me,—if only because I am a Priest. But if you are very much disposed to ostentation and quarrelsomeness, and speak as my Superior—as the Metropolitan to an insignificant Suffragan, or even as to a Bishop without a See—I too have a little pride to set against yours. That is very easy to anybody, and is perhaps the most suitable course.

Ep. LVIII.

(An attack had been made in Gregory's presence on the orthodoxy of Basil in respect of the Deity of God the Holy Ghost; and in this letter he gives his friend an account of the way in which he had defended him. Unfortunately Basil was not pleased with the letter, taking it as intended to convey reproach under the guise of friendly sympathy.)

To Basil.

From the first I have taken you, and I take you still, for my guide of life and my teacher of the faith, and for every thing honourable that can be said; and if any one else praises your merits, he is altogether with me, or even behind me, so far am I surpassed by your piety, and so thoroughly am I yours. And no wonder; for the longer the intimacy the greater the experience; and where the experience is more abundant the testimony is more perfect. And if I get any profit in life it is from your friendship and company. This is my disposition in regard to these matters, and I hope always will be. What I now write I write unwillingly, but still I write it. Do not be angry with me, or I shall be very angry myself, if you do not give me credit for both saying and writing it out of goodwill to you.

Many people have condemned us as not firm in our faith; those, I mean, who think and think rightly that we thoroughly agree. Some openly charge us with heresy, others with cowardice; with heresy, those who believe that our language is not sound; with cowardice, they who blame our reserve. I need not report what other people say; I will tell you what has recently happened.

There was a party here at which a great many distinguished friends of ours were present, and amongst them was a man who wore the name and dress which betoken piety (i.e. a Monk). They had not yet begun to drink, but were talking about us, as often happens at such parties, and made us rather than anything else the subject of their conversation. They admired everything connected with you, and they brought me in as professing the same philosophy; and they spoke of our friendship, and of Athens, and of our conformity of views and feelings on all points. Our Philosopher was annoyed by this. "What is this, gentlemen?" he said, with a very mighty shout, "what liars and flatterers you are. You may praise these men for other reasons if you like, and I will not contradict you; but I cannot concede to you the most important point, their orthodoxy. Basil and Gregory are falsely praised; the former, because his words are a betrayal of the faith, the latter, because his toleration aids the treason."

What is this, said I, O vain man and new Dathan and Abiram in folly? Where do you come from to lay down the law for us? How do you set yourself up as a judge of such great matters? "I have just come," he replied, "from the festival of the Martyr Eupsychius[a], (and so it really was), and there I heard the great Basil speak most beautifully and perfectly upon the Godhead of the Father and the Son, as hardly anyone else could speak; but he slurred over the Spirit." And he added a sort of illustration from rivers, which pass by rocks and hollow out sand. "As for you my good sir," he said, looking at me, "you do now express yourself openly on the Godhead of the Spirit," and he referred to some remarks of mine in speaking of God at a largely attended Synod, as having added in respect of the Spirit that expression which has made a noise, (how long shall we hide the candle under the bushel?) "but the other man hints obscurely, and as it were, merely suggests the doctrine, but does not openly speak out the truth; flooding people's ears with more policy than piety, and hiding his duplicity by the power of his eloquence."

"It is," I said, "because I (living as I do in a corner, and unknown to most men who do not know what I say, and hardly that I speak at all) can philosophize without danger; but his word is of greater weight, because he is better known, both on his own account and on that of his Church. And everything that he says is public, and the war around him is great, as the heretics try to snatch every naked word from Basil's lips, to get him expelled from the Church; because he is almost the only spark of truth left and the vital force, all else around having been destroyed; so that evil may be rooted in the city, and may spread over the whole world as from a centre in that Church. Surely then it is better to use some reserve in the truth, and ourselves to give way a little to circumstances as to a cloud, rather than by the openness of the proclamation to risk its destruction. For no harm will come to us if we recognize the Spirit as God from other phrases which lead to this conclusion (for the truth consists not so much in sound as in sense), but a very great injury would be done to the Church if the truth were driven away in the person of one man." The company present would not receive my economy, as out of date and mocking them; but they shouted me down as practising it rather from cowardice than for reason. It would be much better, they said, to protect our own people by the truth, than by your so-called Economy to weaken them while failing to win over the others. It would be a long business and perhaps unnecessary to tell you all the details of what I said, and of what I heard, and how vexed I was with the opponents, perhaps immoderately and contrary to my own usual temper. But, in fine, I sent them away in the same fashion. But do you O divine and sacred head, instruct me how far I ought to go in setting forth the Deity of the Spirit; and what words I ought to use, and how far to use reserve; that I may be furnished against opponents. For if I, who more than any one else know both you and your opinions, and have often both given and received assurance on this point, still need to be taught the truth of this matter, I shall be of all men the most ignorant and miserable.

---

[a] He suffered under the Emperor Hadrian. The Festival was Sept. 7.

Ep. LIX.

(The reply to Basil's somewhat angry answer to the last.)

To Basil.

This was a case which any wiser man would have foreseen; but I who am very simple and foolish did not fear it in writing to you. My letter grieved you; but in my opinion neither rightly nor justly, but quite unreasonably. And whilst you did not acknowledge that you were hurt, neither did you conceal it, or if you did it was with great skill, as with a mask, hiding your vexation under an appearance of respect. But as to myself if I acted in this deceitfully or maliciously, I shall be punished not more by your vexation than by the truth itself; but if in simplicity and with my accustomed good-will, I will lay the blame on my own sins rather than on your temper. But it would have been better to have set this matter straight, rather than to be angry with those who offer you counsel. But you must see to your own affairs, inasmuch as you are quite capable of giving the same advice to others. You may look upon me as very ready, if God will, both to come to you, and to join you in the conflict, and to contribute all that I can. For who would flinch, who would not rather take courage in speaking and contending for the truth under you and by your side?

Ep. LX.

(Gregory was not able, owing to the serious illness of his Mother, to carry out the promise at the end of Ep. LIX.; so he writes to explain and excuse himself.)

To Basil.

The Carrying Out of your bidding depends partly on me; but partly, and I venture to think principally, on your Reverence. What depends on me is the good will and eagerness, for I never yet avoided meeting you, but have always sought opportunities, and at the present moment am even more desirous of doing so. What depends on your Holiness is that my affairs be set straight. For I am sitting by my lady Mother, who has for a long time been suffering from illness. And if I could leave her out of danger you might be well assured that I would not deprive myself of the pleasure of going to you. So give me the help of your prayers for her restoration to health, and for my journey to you.

DIVISION III.

MISCELLANEOUS LETTERS.

---

§ 1. Letters to His Brother Cæsarius.

Ep. VII.

(On the death of the Emperor Constantius the undisputed succession devolved on his cousin Julian the Apostate, who at once began to employ all the power of the Empire to discourage, while not absolutely persecuting, Christianity, and to restore the supremacy of the ancient Paganism. One of his first acts was to dismiss all the men who had held high dignities under his predecessor. S. Cæsarius, Gregory's brother, was however to be excepted; Julian, who had perhaps known and esteemed him at Athens, did all that he could to keep him at Court, and to attach him to himself. This caused much anxiety to Gregory and other friends of Cæsarius, who foresaw that Julian would do his utmost to shake the young man's faith, and could not feel sure that he would have courage to resist such assaults. In his trouble Gregory wrote him the following letter. Shortly afterwards the expected attempt was made. S. Cæsarius bravely held his ground against the Emperor, and after declaring his unalterable determination to hold firm to his faith, resigned his office at Court and withdrew to Nazianzus.)

I have had enough to blush for in you; that I was grieved, it is hardly necessary to say to him who of all men knows me best. But, not to speak of my own feelings, or of the distress with which the rumour about you filled me (and let me say also the fear), I should have liked you, had it been possible, to have heard what was said by others, both relations and outsiders, who are any way acquainted with us (Christians I mean, of course,) about you and me; and not only some of them, but everyone in turn alike; for men are always more ready to philosophize about strangers than about their own relations. Such speeches as the following have become a sort of exercise among them: Now a Bishop's son takes service in the army; now he covets exterior power and fame; now he is a slave of money, when the fire is being rekindled for all, and men are running the race for life; and he does not deem the one only glory and safety and wealth to be to stand nobly against the times, and to place himself as far as possible out of reach of every abomination and defilement. How then can the Bishop exhort others not to be carried along with the times, or to be mixed up with idols? How can he rebuke those who do wrong in other ways, seeing his own home takes away his right to speak freely? We have every day to hear this, and even more severe things, some of the speakers perhaps saying them from a motive of friendship, and others with unfriendly feelings. How do you think we feel, and what is the state of mind with which we, men professing to serve God, and to deem the only good to be to look forward to the hopes of the future, hear such things as these? Our venerable Father is very much distressed by all that he hears, which even disgusts him with life. I console and comfort him as best I can, by making myself surety for your mind, and assuring him that you will not continue thus to grieve us. But if our dear Mother were to hear about you (so far we have kept her in the dark by various devices), I think she would be altogether inconsolable; being, as a woman, of a weak mind, and besides unable, through her great piety, to control her feelings on such matters. If then you care at all for yourself and us, try some better and safer course. Our means are certainly enough for an independent life, at least for a man of moderate desires, who is not insatiable in his lust for more. Moreover, I do not see what occasion for your settling down we are to wait for, if we let this one pass. But if you cling to the same opinion, and every thing seems to you of small account in comparison with your own desires, I do not wish to say anything else that may vex you, but this I foretell and protest, that one of two things must happen; either you, remaining a genuine Christian, will be ranked among the lowest, and will be in a position unworthy of yourself and your hopes; or in grasping at honours you will injure yourself in what is more important, and will have a share in the smoke, if not actually in the fire.

Ep. XIV. and XXIII.

(Under the Emperor Valens Cæsarius returned to public life and was made Quæstor of Bithynia. While he was in this office the following letters were written to him by his brother on behalf of two cousins, Eulalius, who afterwards succeeded Gregory in the Bishopric of Nazianzus, and with whom Gregory was on terms of intimate friendship, and Amphilochius, who, through the roguery of a partner, had got into some trouble at Constantinople about money matters, and for whom he asks aid and advice. Some however think that this letter is not addressed to his brother (who may have been at Constantinople at the time), but to some other officer of high rank at the Imperial Court. Amphilochius soon after retired from the world, and by A.D. 347 was already bishop of the important See of Iconium. Gregory's letters to him are given later in this division.)

Do a kindness to yourself and to me, of a kind that you will not often have an opportunity of doing, because opportunities for such kindnesses do not often occur. Undertake a most righteous protection of my dear cousins, who are worried more than enough about a property which they bought as suitable for retirement, and capable of providing them with some means of living; but after having completed the purchase they have fallen into many troubles, partly through finding the vendors dishonest, and partly through being plundered and robbed by their neighbours, so that it would be a gain to them to get rid of their acquisition for the price they gave for it, *plus* the not small sum they have spent on it besides. If, then, you would like to transfer the business to yourself, after examining the contract to see how it may be best and most securely done, this course would be most acceptable both to them and me; but if you would rather not, the next best course would be to oppose yourself to the officiousness and dishonesty of the man, that he may not succeed in gaining one advantage over their want of business habits, either by wronging them if they retain their property, or by inflicting loss upon them if they part with it. I am really ashamed to write to you on such a subject. All the same, since we owe it to them, on account both of their relationship and of their profession (for of whom would one rather take care than of such, or what would one be more ashamed of than of being unwilling to confer such a benefit?) do you either for your own sake, or for mine, or for the sake of the men themselves, or for all these sakes put together, by all means do them this kindness.

Ep. XXIII.

Do not be surprized if I ask of you a great favour; for it is from a great man that I am asking it, and the request must be measured by him of whom it is made; for it is equally absurd to ask great things from a small man, and small things from a great man, the one being unseasonable, and the other mean. I therefore present to you with my own hand my most precious son Amphilochius, a man so famous (even beyond his years) for his gentlemanly bearing, that I myself, though an old man, and a Priest, and your friend, would be quite content to be as much esteemed. What wonder is it if he was cheated by a man's pretended friendship, and did not suspect the swindle? For not being himself a rogue, he did not suspect roguery, but thought that correction of language rather than of character was what was wanted, and therefore entered into partnership with him in business. What blame can attach to him for this with honest men? Do not then allow wickedness to get the better of virtue; and do not dishonour my grey hairs, but do honour to my testimony, and add your kindness to my benedictions, which are perhaps of some account with God before Whom we stand.

Ep. XX.

(In A.D. 368 the City of Nicæa in Bithynia was almost entirely destroyed by a terrible earthquake. Cæsarius lost his house, and his personal escape was almost miraculous. Gregory writes (as also did Basil) to congratulate him on his escape, and profits by the occasion to urge upon him retirement from his secular avocations. Cæsarius soon resolved to follow this advice, and was taking steps to carry this resolution into effect, when he died suddenly, early in A.D. 369, aged only 40. He left the whole of his large property to the poor, but it fell for a time into the hands of designing persons, and Gregory, who was his brother's executor, had much difficulty in recovering it for the purpose for which it had been intended. (See the letter to Sophronius, Prefect of Constantinople on this subject.) He was buried at Nazianzus in the Church of the Martyrs, in a vault which his parents had prepared for themselves. Gregory preached the funeral sermon, which is given in the former part of this volume. These four are the only letters known to have passed between the brothers.)

Even frights are not without use to the wise; or, as I should say, they are very valuable and salutary. For, although we pray that they may not happen, yet when they do they instruct us. For the afflicted soul, as Peter[a] somewhere admirably says, is near to God; and every man who escapes a danger is brought into nearer relation to Him Who preserved him. Let us not then be vexed that we had a share in the calamity, but let us give thanks that we were delivered. And let us not shew ourselves one thing to God in the time of peril, and another when the danger is over, but let us resolve, whether at home or abroad, whether in private life or in public office (for I must say this and may not omit it), to follow Him Who has preserved us, and to attach ourselves to His side, thinking little of the little concerns of earth; and let us furnish a tale to those who come after us, great for our glory and the benefit of our soul, and at the same time a very useful lesson to all, that danger is better than security, and that misfortune is preferable to success, at least if before our fears we belonged to the world, but after them we belong to God. Perhaps I seem to you somewhat of a bore, by writing to you so often on the same subject, and you will think my letter a piece not of exhortation but of ostentation, so enough of this. You will know that I desire and wish especially that I might be with you and share your joy at your preservation, and to talk over these matters later on. But since that cannot be, I hope to receive you here as soon as may be, and to celebrate our thanksgiving together.

§ 2. To S. Gregory of Nyssa.

(Gregory, Bishop of Nyssa, was a younger brother of Basil the Great. Ordained a Reader at an early age he grew tired of his vocation, and became a professor of Rhetoric. This gave scandal in the Church and occasioned much grief to his friends. Gregory of Nazianzus, wrote him the following letter of remonstrance, which was not without effect, for shortly afterwards he gave up his secular avocation, and retired to the Monastery which his brother Basil had founded in Pontus. Here he spent several years in the study of Holy Scripture and the best Commentators.)

Ep. I.

There is one good point in my character, and I will boast myself of one point out of many. I am equally vexed with myself and my friends over a bad plan. Since, then, all are friends and kinsfolk who live according to God, and walk by the same Gospel, why should you not hear from me in plain words what all men are saying in whispers? They do not approve your inglorious glory (to borrow a phrase from your own art), and your gradual descent to the lower life, and your ambition, the worst of demons, according to Euripides.[a] For what has happened to you, O wisest of men, and for what do you condemn yourself, that you have cast away the sacred and delightful books which you used once to read to the people (do not be ashamed to hear this), or have hung them up over the chimney, as men do in winter with rudders and hoes, and have applied yourself to salt and bitter ones, and preferred to be called a Professor of Rhetoric rather than of Christianity? I, thank God, would rather be the latter than the former. Do not, my dear friend, do not let this be longer the case, but, though it is full late, become sober again, and come to yourself once more, and make your apology to the faithful, and to God, and to His Altars and Sacraments, from which you have withdrawn yourself. And do not say to me in proud rhetorical style, What, was I not a Christian when I practised rhetoric? Was I not a believer when I was engaged among the boys? And perhaps you will call God to witness. No, my friend, not as thoroughly as you ought to have been, even if I grant it you in part. What of the offence to others given by your present employment—to others who are prone naturally to evil—and of the opportunity afforded them both to think and to speak the worst of you? Falsely, I grant, but where

a Source of the quotation unknown.

a Phœn., 534.

was the necessity? For a man lives not for himself alone but also for his neighbour; nor is it enough to persuade yourself, you must persuade others also. If you were to practise boxing in public, or to give and receive blows in the theatre, or to writhe and twist yourself shamefully, would you speak of yourself as having a temperate soul? Such an argument does not befit a wise man; it is frivolous to accept it. If you make a change I shall rejoice even now, said one of the Pythagorean philosophers, lamenting the fall of a friend; but, he wrote, if not you are dead to me. But I will not yet say this for your sake. Being a friend, he became an enemy, yet still a friend, as the Tragedy says. But I shall be grieved (to speak gently), if you do neither yourself see what is right, which is the highest method of all, nor will follow the advice of others, which is the next. Thus far my counsel. Forgive me that my friendship for you makes me grieve, and kindles me both on your behalf and on behalf of the whole priestly Order, and I may add on that of all Christians. And if I may pray with you or for you, may God who quickeneth the dead aid your weakness.

Ep. LXXII.

(When S. Gregory was consecrated Bishop of Nyssa the Imperial Throne was occupied by Valens, an ardent Arian, whose mind was bent on the destruction of the Nicene Faith. He appointed, with this object, one Demosthenes, a former clerk of the Imperial Kitchen, to be Vicar of the civil Diocese of Pontus. An old quarrel with Basil had made this man unfriendly to Gregory, and after persecuting him in various small ways for some time he procured, A.D. 275, the summoning of a Synod to enquire into some allegations of irregularity in his consecration, and to try Gregory on some frivolous charges of malversation of Church funds. Gregory was unable to attend this Synod, which met at Ancyra, on account of an attack of pleurisy; and another was summoned to meet at Nyssa itself. Gregory however refused to appear, and was deposed as contumacious. Thereupon Valens banished him, and he seems to have fallen into very low spirits, almost into despondency at the apparent triumph of the heretical party. The three letters which follow throw some light upon his state at this time. They were written in answer to letters of his now lost, and their object was to comfort him in his trouble and to encourage him to take heart again in the hope of a good day coming. This more cheerful tone was justified by the event, for on the death of Valens, A.D. 378, the exiled Bishops were restored by Gratian, and Gregory was replaced in his Episcopal Throne, to the great joy of the faithful of his Diocese.)

Do not let your troubles distress you too much. For the less we grieve over things, the less grievous they are. It is nothing strange that the heretics have thawed, and are taking courage from the springtime, and creeping out of their holes, as you write. They will hiss for a short time, I know, and then will hide themselves again, overcome both by the truth and the times, and all the more so the more we commit the whole matter to God.

Ep. LXXIII.

As to the subject of your letter, these are my sentiments. I am not angry at being overlooked, but I am glad when I am honoured. The one is my own desert, the other is a proof of your respect. Pray for me. Excuse this short letter, for anyhow, though it is short, it is longer than silence.

Ep. LXXIV.

Although I am at home, my love is expatriated with you, for affection makes us have all things common. Trusting in the mercy of God, and in your prayers, I have great hopes that all will turn out according to your mind, and that the hurricane will be turned into a gentle breeze, and that God will give you this reward for your orthodoxy, that you will overcome your opponents. Most of all I long to see you shortly, and to have a good time with you, as I pray. But if you delay owing to the pressure of affairs, at any rate cheer me by a letter, and do not disdain to tell me all about your circumstances, and to pray for me, as you are accustomed to do. May God grant you health and good spirits in all circumstances,—you who are the common prop of the whole Church.

Ep. LXXVI.

(Basil the Great died Jan. 1, A.D. 379. Gregory of Nazianzus was prevented by very serious illness from attending his funeral, and therefore wrote as follows to Gregory of Nyssa.)

This, then, was also reserved for my sad life, to hear of the death of Basil, and the departure of that holy soul, which has gone from us that it may be with the Lord, for which he had been preparing himself all his life. And among all the other losses I have had to endure this is the greatest, that by reason of the bodily sickness from which I am still suffering and in great danger, I cannot kiss that holy dust, or be with you to enjoy the consolations of a just philosophy, and to comfort our common friends. But to see the desolation of the Church, shorn of such a glory, and bereft of such a crown, is what no one, at least no one of any feeling, can bear to let his eyes look upon, or his ear hearken to. But you, I think, though you have many friends and will receive many words of condolence, yet will not derive comfort so much from any as from yousrelf and your memory of him; for you two were a pattern to all of philosophy, a kind of spiritual standard, both of discipline in prosperity, and of endurance in adversity; for philosophy bears prosperity with moderation and adversity with dignity. This is what I have to say to Your Excellency. But for myself who write so, what time or what words shall comfort me, except your company and conversation, which our blessed one has left me in place of all, that seeing his character in you as in a bright and shining mirror, I may think myself to possess him also!

Ep. LXXXI.

You are distressed by your travels, and think yourself unsteady, like a stick carried along by a stream. But, my dear friend, you must not let yourself feel so at all. For the travels of the stick are involuntary, but your course is ordained by God, and your stability is in doing good to others, even though you are not fixed to a place; unless indeed one ought to find fault with the sun, for going about the world scattering his rays, and giving life to all things on which he shines; or, while praising the fixed stars, one should revile the planets, whose very wandering is harmonious.

Ep. CLXXXII.

(Gregory after his resignation of the Patriarchal See of Constantinople had retired to Nazianzus, and had been persuaded to undertake the administration of the diocese then vacant, until the vacancy should be filled. The Bishops of the Province wished him to retain it altogether, and therefore were in no hurry to proceed to election. At length however they yielded to the continually expressed wishes of Gregory and chose his cousin Eulalius. Soon however Gregory's enemies spread abroad a report that this election had been made against his wishes, and with the intention of unfairly ousting him from the administration of that Church. The following letter was written in consequence of this slander.)

Woe is me that my sojourning is prolonged, and, which is the greatest of my misfortunes, that war and dissensions are among us, and that we have not kept the peace which we received from our holy fathers. This I doubt not you will restore, in the power of the Spirit who upholds you and yours. But let no one, I beg, spread false reports about me and my lords the bishops, as though they had proclaimed another bishop in my place against my will. But being in great need, owing to my feeble health, and fearing the responsibility of a Church neglected, I asked this favour of them, which was not opposed to the Canon Law, and was a relief to me, that they would give a Pastor to the Church. He has been given to your prayers, a man worthy of your piety, and I now place him in your hands, the most reverend Eulalius, a bishop very dear to God, in whose arms I should like to die. If any be of opinion that it is not right to ordain another in the lifetime of a Bishop, let him know that he will not in this matter gain any hold upon us. For it is well known that I was appointed, not to Nazianzus, but to Sasima, although for a short time out of reverence for my father, I as a stranger undertook the government.

Ep. CXCVII.

A Letter of Condolence on the Death of His Sister Theosebia.

(The writer of the article on Gregory Nyssen in the Dict. Biogr. supposes her to have been his wife, but produces no evidence of this beyond the ambiguous expression in this letter which speaks of her as "the true consort of a priest," but on the other hand she is expressly called his Sister in the same letter. Some writers have imagined that she was the wife of Gregory Nazianzen himself, but there is no evidence to show that he was ever married. The date of her death is uncertain, but it was probably subsequent to A.D. 381. It would seem that the term Consort might have a general application to those who shared in the same work, and consequently the Benedictine Editors regard Theosebia as a Deaconess of the Church of Nyssa.)

I had started in all haste to go to you, and had got as far as Euphemias, when I was delayed by the festival which you are celebrating in honour of the Holy Martyrs; partly because I could not take part in it, owing to my bad health, partly because my coming at so unsuitable a time might be inconvenient to you. I had started partly for the sake of seeing you after so long, and partly that I might admire your patience and philosophy (for I had heard of it) at the departure of your holy and blessed sister, as a good and perfect man, a minister of God, who knows better than any the things both of God and man; and who regards as a very light thing that which to others would be most heavy, namely to have lived with such a soul, and to send her away and store her up in the safe garners, like a shock of the threshingfloor gathered in due season,[α] to use the words of Holy Scripture; and that in such time that she, having tasted the joys of life, escaped its sorrows through the shortness of her life; and before she had to wear mourning for you, was honoured by you with that fair funeral honour which is due to such as she. I too, believe me, long to depart, if not as you do, which were much to say, yet only less than you. But what must we feel in presence of a long prevailing law of God which has now taken my Theosebia (for I call her mine because she lived a godly life; for spiritual kindred is better than bodily), Theosebia, the glory of the church, the adornment of Christ, the helper of our generation, the hope of woman; Theosebia, the most beautiful and glorious among all the beauty of the Brethren; Theosebia, truly sacred, truly consort of a priest, and of equal honour and worthy of the Great Sacraments,[β] Theosebia, whom all future time shall receive, resting on immortal pillars, that is, on the souls of all who have known her now, and of all who shall be hereafter. And do not wonder that I often invoke her name. For I rejoice even in the remembrance of the blessed one. Let this, a great deal in few words, be her epitaph from me, and my word of condolence for you, though you yourself are quite able to console others in this way through your philosophy in all things. Our meeting (which I greatly long for) is prevented by the reason I mentioned. But we pray with one another as long as we are in the world, until the common end, to which we are drawing nigh, overtake us. Wherefore we must bear all things, since we shall not for long have either to rejoice or to suffer.

α Job. v. 26. β Referring to her office as a Deaconess.

§ 3. To Eusebius Bishop of Samosata.

Ep. XLII.

(This letter, urging his friend to attend at Cæsarea for the election of a Metropolitan in succession to Eusebius, has been already given in the second division of this Selection.)

Ep. XLIV.

(Eusebius, having in response to the appeal referred to above, betaken himself to Cæsarea, the Elder Gregory, though in very feeble health, resolved to attend the Synod in person, that Basil's Election might be secured by their joint exertions, Gregory the Younger sent the following letter by his father to explain to his friend the reason why he had not come too. The date is about September of the year 379.)

Whence shall I begin your praises, and by what name shall I give you your right appellation? The pillar and ground of the church, or a light in the world, using the very words of the apostle, or a crown of glory to the remaining portion of christendom;[α] or a gift of God, or the bulwark of your country, or the standard of faith, or the ambassador of truth, or all these at once, and more than all? And these excessive praises I will prove by what we shall see. What rain ever came so seasonably to a thirsty land, what water flowing out of the rock to those in the wilderness? What such Bread of Angels did ever man eat? When did Jesus the common Lord ever so seasonably present Himself to His drowning disciples, and tame the sea, and save the perishing, as you have shewn yourself to us in our weariness and distress, and in our immediate danger as it were of shipwreck? I need not speak of other points, with what courage and joy you filled the souls of the orthodox, and how many you delivered from despair.

But our mother church, Cæsarea I mean, is now really putting off the garments of her widowhood at the sight of you, and putting on again her robe of cheerfulness, and will be yet more resplendent when she receives a pastor

α Alluding to his work in opposing the prevalence of Arianism.

worthy of herself and of her former Bishops and of your hands. For you yourself see what is the state of our affairs, and what a miracle your zeal has wrought, and your toil, and your godly plainness of speech. Age is renewed, disease is conquered,[a] they leap who were in their beds, and the weak are girded with power. By all this I guess that our matters too will turn out as we desire. You have my father, moreover, representing both himself and me, to put a glorious close to his whole life and to his venerable age by this present struggle on behalf of the Church. And I shall receive him back, I am well assured, strengthened by your prayers, and with youth renewed, for one must confidently commit all in faith to them. But if he should end his life in this anxiety, it would be no calamity to attain to such an end in such a cause. Pardon me, I beg of you, if I give way a little to the tongues of evil men, and delay a little to come and embrace you, and to complete in person what I now pass over of the praises due to you.

Ep. LXIV.

(In the year 374 Eusebius and other orthodox Bishops of the East were banished by Valens and their thrones filled with Arian intruders. Eusebius was ordered to retire to Thrace, and his journey lay through Cappadocia, where he saw Basil, but Gregory to his great grief was too unwell to leave his house and go to meet him. Instead he sent the following letter.)

When Your Reverence was passing through our country I was so ill as not to be able even to *look* out of my house. And I was grieved not so much on account of the illness, though it brought about the fear of the worst, as by the inability to meet your holiness and goodness. My longing to see your venerable face was like that which a man would naturally feel who needed healing of spiritual wounds, and expected to receive it from you. But though at that time the effect of my sins was that I missed the meeting with you, it is now by your goodness possible for me to find a remedy for my trouble, for if you will deign to remember me in your acceptable prayers, this will be to me a store of every blessing from God, both in this my life and in the age to come. For that such a man, such a combatant for the Faith of the Gospel, one who has endured such persecutions, and won for himself such confidence before the all-righteous God by his patience in tribulation—that such a man should deign to be my patron also in his prayers will gain for me, I am persuaded, as much strength as I should have gained through one of the holy martyrs. Therefore let me entreat you to remember your Gregory without ceasing in all the matters in which I desire to be worthy of your remembrance.

Ep. LXV.

(Eusebius having replied to the former letter Gregory wrote again, having an opportunity of communicating with his friend through one Eupraxius, a disciple of Eusebius, who passed through Cappadocia on his way to visit his master. This letter is sometimes attributed to Basil.)

Our reverend brother Eupraxius has always been dear to me and a true friend, but he has shewn himself dearer and truer through his affections for you, inasmuch as even at the present time he has hurried to your reverence, like, to use David's words, a hart to quench his great and unendurable thirst[a] with a sweet and pure spring at your patience in tribulations. Deign then to be his patron and mine.

Happy indeed are they who are permitted to come near you, and happier still is he who can place upon his sufferings for Christ's sake and upon his labours for the truth, a crown such as few of those who fear God have obtained. For it is not an untested virtue that you have shown, nor is it only in a time of calm that you have sailed aright and steered the souls of others, but you have shone in the difficulties of temptations, and have been greater than your persecutors, having nobly departed from the land of your birth. Others possess the threshold of their fathers,—we the heavenly City; others perhaps hold our throne, but we Christ. O what a profitable exchange! How little we give up, to receive how much! We went through fire and water, and I believe that we shall also come out into a place of refreshment. For God will not forsake us for ever, or abandon the true faith to persecution, but according to the multitude of our pains His comforts shall make us glad. This at any rate we believe and desire. But do you, I beg, pray for our humility. And as often

a Alluding to the effort made by his father.

a Ps. xliii. 1.

as occasion shall present itself bless us without hesitation by a letter, and cheer us up by news of yourself, as you have just been good enough to do.

Ep. LXVI.

(The following letter is sometimes attributed to Basil, and is found in his works as well as in those of Gregory. The MSS. however, with only a single exception, give it to the latter.)

You give me pleasure both by writing and remembering me, and a much greater pleasure by sending me your blessing in your letter. But if I were worthy of your sufferings and of your conflicts for Christ and through Christ I should have been counted worthy also to come to you, to embrace Your Piety, and to take example by your patience in your sufferings. But since I am not worthy of this, being troubled with many afflictions and hindrances I do what is next best. I address Your Perfection, and I beg you not to be weary of remembering me. For to be deemed worthy of your letters is not only profitable to me, but is also a matter to boast of to many people, and is an honour, because I am considered by a man of so great virtue, and such near relations with God, that he can bring others also by word and example into relation to Him.

§ 4. To Sophronius, Prefect of Constantinople.

(Sophronius, a native of the Cappadocian Cæsarea, was an early friend and fellow-student of Gregory and Basil. He entered the Civil Service, and soon rose to high office. In A.D. 365 he was appointed Prefect of Constantinople, as a reward for timely intimation which he gave to the Emperor Valens of the usurpation attempted by Procopius. He is chiefly known to us by the letters of Gregory and Basil, invoking his good offices for various persons. Ep. 21 was written in A.D. 369 to commend to him Nicobulus, Gregory's nephew by marriage, the husband of Alypiana, daughter of his sister Gorgonia. This Nicobulus was a man of great wealth and ability, but much disinclined for public life. Gregory constantly writes to one and another high official to get him excused from appointments which had been thrust upon him.)

Ep. XXI.

Gold is changed and transformed into various forms at various times, being fashioned into many ornaments, and used by art for many purposes; yet it remains what it is—gold; and it is not the substance but the form which admits of change. So also, believing that your kindness will remain unchanged for your friends, although you are ever climbing higher, I have ventured to send you this request, because I do not more reverence your high rank than I trust your kind disposition. I entreat you to be favourable to my most respectable son Nicobulus, who is in all respects allied with me, both by kindred and by intimacy, and, which is more important, by disposition. In what matters, and to what extent? In whatever he may ask your aid, and as far as may seem to you to befit your Magnanimity. I on my part will repay you the best I have. I have the power of speech, and of proclaiming your goodness, if not nearly according to its worth, at any rate to the best of my ability.

Ep. XXII.

(Is for Amphilochius, written at the same time and in consequence of the same trouble as that which we have placed second of the letters to Cæsarius.)

As we know gold and stones by their look, so too we may distinguish good men from bad in the same way, and do not need a very long trial. For I should not have needed many words in pleading for my most honourable son Amphilochius with Your Magnanimity. I should rather have expected some strange and incredible thing to happen than that he would do anything dishonourable, or think of such a thing, in a matter of money; such a universal reputation has he as a gentleman, and as wiser than his years. But what must he suffer? Nothing escapes envy, for some word of blame has touched even him, a man who has fallen under accusation of crime through simplicity rather than depravity of disposition. But do not allow it to be tolerable to you to overlook him in his vexations and trouble. Not so, I entreat your sacred and great mind, but honour your country[a] and aid his virtue, and have a respect for me who have attained to glory by and through you; and be everything to this man, adding the will to the power, for I know that there is nothing of equal power with Your Excellency.

Ep. XXIX.

(Of the same year. Here Cæsarius had bequeathed all his property to the poor; but

[a] Sophronius and Amphilochius were natives of Cæsarea.

his house had been looted by his servants, and his friends could only find a comparatively small sum. Besides this a number of persons, shortly afterwards, presented themselves as creditors of his estate, and their claims, though incapable of proof, were paid. Then others kept coming forward, until at last the family refused to admit any more. Then a lawsuit was threatened. Gregory intensely disliking all this, and dreading moreover the scandal which might be caused by legal proceedings, writes as follows to the Prefect.)

You see how matters stand with me, and how the circle of human affairs goes round, now some now others flourishing or the reverse, and neither prosperity nor adversity remaining constant with us, as the saying is, but ever changing and altering, so that one might trust the breezes, or letters written in the waters, rather than human prosperity. For what reason is this? I think it is in order that by the contemplation of the uncertainty and anomaly of all these things we may learn the rather to have recourse to God and to the future, giving scanty thoughts to shadows and dreams. But what has produced this talk, for it is not without a cause that I thus philosophize, and I am not idly boasting?

Cæsarius was once one of your not least distinguished friends; indeed, unless my brotherly affection deceives me, he was one of your most distinguished, for he was remarkably well informed, and for gentlemanly conduct was above the average, and was celebrated for the number of his friends; among the very first of these, as he always thought and as he persuaded me, Your Excellency held the first place. These are old stories, and you will add to them of your own accord in rendering honours to his memory; for it is human nature to add something to the praises of the departed. But now (that you may not pass over this story without a tear, or that you may weep to some good and useful purpose), he lies dead, friendless, solitary, pitiable, deemed worthy of a little myrrh (if even of so much), and of the last small coverings, and it is much that he has found even thus much compassion. But his enemies, as I hear, have fallen upon his estate, and from all quarters with great violence are plundering it, or are about to do so. O cruelty! O savagery! And there is no one to hinder them; but even the kindest of his friends only calls upon the laws as his utmost favour. If I may put it concisely, I am become a mere drama, who once was wont to be happy. Do not let this seem to you to be tolerable, but help me by sympathy and by sharing my indignation, and do right by the dead Cæsarius. Yes, in the name of friendship herself; yes, by all that you hold dearest; by your hope (which may you make secure by shewing yourself faithful and true to the departed), I pray you do this kindness to the living, and make them of good hope. Do you think that I am grieved about the money? It would have been a more intolerable disgrace to me if Cæsarius alone, who thought he had so many friends, turned out to have none. Such is my request, and from such a cause does it arise, for perhaps my affairs are not altogether matters of indifference to you. In what you will assist me, and by what means, and how, the matter itself will suggest and your wisdom will consider.

Ep. XXXVII.

(A letter of recommendation for Eudoxius a Rhetorician for whom Gregory had a warm regard.)

To honour a mother is a religious duty. Now, different individuals have different mothers; but the common mother of all is our country. This mother you have honoured by the splendour of your whole life; and you will honour her again now by obtaining for me that which I entreat. And what is my request? You certainly know Eudoxius the Rhetorician, the most learned of her sons. His son, to speak concisely, another Eudoxius both in life and learning, now approaches you through me. In order then to get yourself a yet better name, be helpful to him in the matters for which he asks your assistance. For it were a shame were you, who are the universal Patron of our Country, and who have done good to so many, and I will add, who will yet continue to do so, should not honour above all him who is most excellent in learning and in his eloquence, which you ought to honour, if for no other reason, because he uses it to praise your goodness.

Ep. XXXIX.

(About the same date. A recommendation of one Amazonius, whose learning was much respected by Gregory.)

I wish well to all my friends. And when I speak of friends, I mean honourable and good men, linked with me in virtue, if indeed I myself have any claim to it. Therefore at the present time when seeking how I might do a kindness to my excellent brother Amazonius (for I was very much pleased with the man in some intercourse which has lately taken place between us), I thought I might return him one favour for all,—in your friendship and protection. For in a short time he shewed proof of an extensive education, both of the kind which I used once to be very zealous for, when I was shortsighted, and of that for which I am zealous in its place since I have been able to contemplate the summit of virtue. Whether I in my turn have appeared to him to be worth anything in respect of virtue is his affair. At any rate I shewed him the best things I have, namely, my friends to him as my friend. Of these I reckon you as the first and truest, and want you to shew yourself so to him—as your common Country demands, and my desire and promise begs; for I promised him your patronage in return for all his kindness.

Ep. XCIII.

(Written soon after Gregory's resignation of the Archbishopric.)

Our retreat and leisure and quiet have about them something very agreeable to me; but the fact that they cut me off from your friendship and society is not so advantageous but rather the other way. Others enjoy your Perfection, to me it would be really a great boon if I might have just that shadow of conversation which comes in a letter. Shall I see you again? Shall I embrace again him of whom I am so proud, and shall this be granted to the remnant of my life? If so, all thanks to God: if not, the best part of my life is over. Pray remember your friend Gregory and pray for him.

Ep. CXXXV.

(About the middle of A.D. 382 Theodosius, on the recommendation of S. Damasus, summoned a new Synod of Eastern Bishops to meet at Constantinople, to try and heal the schism which had been embittered by the election of Flavian at Antioch. As soon as Gregory heard of the convocation of this Synod he wrote to several of his influential friends at Court, to beg them to do their utmost for the promotion of peace.)

I am philosophizing at leisure. That is the injury my enemies have done me, and I should be glad if they would do more of the same sort, that I might look upon them still more as benefactors. For it often happens that those who are wronged get a benefit, while they, whom we would treat well, suffer injury. That is the state of my affairs. But if I cannot make every one believe this, I am very anxious, that at all events you, for them all, to whom I most willingly give an account of my affairs, should know, or rather I feel certain that you do know it, and can persuade those who do not. You, however, I beg to give all diligence, now at any rate, if you have not done so before, to bring together to one voice and mind the sections of the world that are so unhappily divided; and above all if you should perceive, as I have observed, that they are divided not on account of the Faith, but by petty private interests. To succeed in doing this would earn you a reward; and my retirement would have less to grieve over if I could see that I did not grasp at it to no purpose, but was like a Jonas, willingly casting myself into the sea, that the storm might cease and the sailors be saved. If, however, they are still as storm-tost as ever, I at all events have done what I could.

§ 5. To Amphilochius The Younger.

Ep. IX.

(Constantine and Constantius had granted exemption from the military tax to all clerics. This privilege was, however, abolished by Julian, and was restored by Valentinian and Valens: but the collectors of revenue often tried to levy it on them in spite of the exemption. The collector at Nazianzus tried to do this in the case of a Deacon named Euthalius, in whose behalf Gregory wrote the following letter to Amphilochius, who was at the time one of the principal magistrates of the province. The date of the letter is given as A.D. 372, the year of Gregory's Ordination to the Priesthood. For further particulars about this Amphilochius, see introd. to letters II. and III. to Cæsarius Epp. 22, 23.)

Support a wellbuilt chamber with columns of gold, as Pindar[a] says, and make yourself from the beginning known to us on the right side in our present anxiety, that you may build yourself a notable palace, and shew yourself in it with a good fame. But how will you do this? By honouring God and the things of God, than Whom there can be nothing greater in your

[a] Olymp., Od. vi., 1.

eyes. But how, and by what act can you honour Him? By this one act, by protecting the servants of God and ministers of the altar. One of these is our fellow deacon Euthalius, on whom, I know not how, the officers of the Prefecture are trying to impose a payment of gold after his promotion to the higher rank. Pray do not allow this. Reach a hand to this deacon and to the whole clergy, and above all to me, for whom you care; for otherwise he would have to endure a grievous wrong, alone of men deprived of the kindness of the time and the privilege granted by the Emperor to the Clergy, and would even be insulted and fined, possibly on account of my weakness. It would be well for you to prevent this even if others are not well disposed.

Ep. XIII.

(See the first letter to Sophronius. The nature of the trouble here alluded to is unknown. There are several letters to various persons in reference to his troubles and difficulties, many of them coming from his reluctance to undertake the duties of any public office. He died at an early age, leaving his widow, Alypiana, with a large family to bring up in very reduced circumstances. Her troubles and the education of her children were matters of much concern to Gregory, whose frequent letters on the subject will be found below.)

I approve the statement of Theognis, who, while not praising the friendship which goes no further than cups and pleasures, praises that which extends to actions in these words,

> Beside a full wine cup a man has many friends:
> But they are fewer when grave troubles press.

We, however, have not shared winecups with each other, nor indeed have we often met (though we ought to have been very careful to do so, both for our own sake, and for the sake of the friendship which we inherited from our fathers), but we do ask for the goodwill which shews itself in acts. A struggle is at hand, and a very serious struggle. My son Nicobulus has got into unexpected troubles, from a quarter from which troubles would least be looked for. Therefore I beg you to come and help us as soon as you can, both to take part in trying the case, and to plead our cause, if you find that a wrong is being done us. But if you cannot come, at any rate do not let yourself be previously retained by the other side, or sell for a small gain the freedom which we know from everybody's testimony has always characterized you.

Ep. XXV.

(Amphilochius was acquitted of the charges made against him, referred to in former letters; but the result of the accusation on his own mind was such that he resigned his office, and retired to a sort of hermitage at a place called Ozizala, not far from Nazianzus, where he devoted his hours of labour to the cultivation of vegetables. The four letters which follow are of no special importance, and are only given as specimens of the lighter style which Gregory could use with his intimate friends.)

I did not ask you for bread, just as I would not ask for water from the inhabitants of Ostracine. But if I were to ask for vegetables from a man of Ozizala it were no strange thing, nor too great a strain on friendship; for you have plenty of them, and we a great dearth. I beg you then to send me some vegetables, and plenty of them, and the best quality, or as many as you can (for even small things are great to the poor); for I am going to receive the great Basil, and you, who have had experience of him full and philosophical, would not like to know him hungry and irritated.

Ep. XXVI.

What a very small quantity of vegetables you have sent me! They must surely be golden vegetables! And yet your whole wealth consists of orchards and rivers and groves and gardens, and your country is productive of vegetables as other lands are of gold, and

> You dwell among meadowy leafage.

But corn is for you a fabulous happiness, and your bread is the bread of angels, as the saying is, so welcome is it, and so little can you reckon upon it. Either, then, send me your vegetables less grudgingly, or—I won't threaten you with anything else, but I won't send you any corn, and will see whether there is any truth in the saying that grasshoppers live on dew!

Ep. XXVII.

You make a joke of it; but I know the danger of an Ozizalean starving when he has taken most pains with his husbandry. There is only this praise to be given them, that even if they die of hunger they smell sweet, and have a gorgeous funeral. How so? Because they are covered with plenty of all sorts of flowers.

Ep. XXVIII.

In visiting the mountain cities which border on Pamphylia I fished up in the Mountains a sea Glaucus; I did not drag the fish out of the depths with a net of flax, but I snared my game with the love of a friend. And having once taught my Glaucus to travel by land, I sent him as the bearer of a letter to Your Goodness. Please receive him kindly, and honour him with the hospitality commended in the Bible, not forgetting the vegetables.

Ep. LXII.

(The Armenian referred to is probably Eustathius Bishop of Sebaste, the capital of Armenia Minor. He had been a disciple of Arius, but more than once professed the Nicene Faith, changing his opinions with his company. His personal character however stood very high, and for a long time S. Basil regarded him with affectionate esteem. Indeed S. Basil's Rule for Monks is based on one drawn up by him. But after Basil's elevation to the Episcopate Eustathius began to oppose him and to calumniate him on all sides, and even entered openly into communion with the Arians. It would seem that this man tried to get Amphilochius round to his side, and through him Gregory.)

The Injunction of your inimitable Honour is not barbaric, but Greek, or rather christian; but as for the Armenian on whom you pride yourself so, he is a downright barbarian, and far from our honour.

Ep. LXIII.

To Amphilochius the Elder.

(In A.D. 374 Amphilochius was made Bishop of Iconium; and his father, a man of the same name, was deeply aggrieved at being thus deprived of his son, to whom he had looked to support him in his old age, and accused Gregory of being the cause. Gregory, who had just lost his own father, writes to undeceive him, and to convince him how much he dreads the burden of the responsibilities of the episcopate for his friend as well as for himself.)

Are you grieving? I, of course, am full of joy! Are you weeping? I, as you see, am keeping festival and glorying in the present state of things! Are you grieved because your son is taken from you and promoted to honour on account of his virtue, and do you think it a terrible misfortune that he is no longer with you to tend your old age, and, as his custom is, to bestow on you all due care and service? But it is no grief to me that my father has left me for the last journey, from which he will return to me no more, and I shall never see him again! Then I for my part do not blame you, nor do I ask you for due condolence, knowing as I do that private troubles allow no leisure for those of strangers; for no man is so friendly and so philosophical as to be above his own suffering and to comfort another when needing comfort himself. But you on the contrary heap blow on blow, when you blame me, as I hear you do, and think that your son and my brother is neglected by us, or even betrayed by us, which is a still heavier charge; or that we do not recognize the loss which all his friends and relatives have suffered, and I more than all, because I had placed in him my hopes of life, and looked upon him as the only bulwark, the only good counsellor, and the only sharer of my piety. And yet, on what grounds do you form this opinion? If on the first, be assured that I came over to you on purpose, and because I was troubled by the rumour, and I was ready to share your deliberations while it was still time for consultation about the matter; and you imparted anything to me rather than this, whether because you were in the same distress, or with some other purpose, I know not what. But if the last, I was prevented from meeting you again by my grief, and the honour I owed my father, and his funeral, over which I could not give anything precedence, and that when my sorrow was fresh, and it would not only have been wrong but also quite improper to be unseasonably philosophical, and above human nature. Moreover, I thought that I was previously engaged by the circumstances, especially as his had come to such a conclusion as seemed good to Him who governs all our affairs. So much concerning this matter. Now I beg you to put aside your grief, which is most unreasonable I am sure; and if you have any further grievance, bring it forward that you may not grieve both me in part and yourself, and put yourself in a position unworthy of your nobility, blaming me instead of others, though I have done you no wrong, but, if I must say the truth, have been equally tyrannized over by our common friend, although you used to think me your only benefactor.

Ep. CLXXI.

To Amphilochius, Bishop of Iconium.

Scarcely yet delivered from the pains of my illness, I hasten to you, the guardian of my cure. For the tongue of a priest meditating of the Lord raises the sick. Do then the greater thing in your priestly ministration, and loose the great mass of my sins when you lay hold of the Sacrifice of Resurrection. For your affairs are a care to me waking or sleeping, and you are to me a good plectrum, and have made a welltuned lyre to dwell within my soul, because by your numerous letters you have trained my soul to science. But, most reverend friend, cease not both to pray and to plead for me when you draw down the Word by your word, when with a bloodless cutting you sever the Body and Blood of the Lord, using your voice for the glaive.[a]

Ep. CLXXXIV.

(Bosporius, Bishop of Colonia in Cappadocia Secunda, who had apparently taken a prominent part in the election and consecration of Eulalius to the See of Nazianzus, was accused of heresy by Helladius Archbishop of Cæsarea, and a Council met at Parnassus to try him, A.D. 383. Gregory, not being able personally to attend this Synod, writes to Amphilochius, to beg him to undertake the defence of the accused. The letter is lost, but Gregory's friend carried out his mission with success, and the following letter is to thank him for his kindness.)

The Lord fulfil all thy petitions (do not despise a father's prayer), for you have abundantly refreshed my age, both by having gone to Parnassus, as you were invited to do, and by having refuted the calumny against the most Reverend and God-beloved Bishop. For evil men love to set down their own faults to those who convict them. For the age of this man is stronger than all the accusations, and so is his life, and we too who have often heard from him and taught others, and those whom he has recovered from error and added to the common body of the church; but yet the present evil times called for more accurate proof on account of the slanderers and evil-disposed; and this you have supplied us with, or rather you have supplied it to those who are of fickler mind and easily led away by such men. But if you will undertake a longer journey, and will personally give testimony, and settle the matter with the other bishops, you will be doing a spiritual work worthy of your Perfection. I and those with me salute your Fraternity.

a A very clear assertion of the Real Presence.

§ 6. To Nectarius Archbishop of Constantinople.

(Gregory, having failed to persuade the Council of A.D. 381 to end the schism at Antioch by recognizing Paulinus as successor to Meletius, thought it best for the sake of peace to resign the Archbishopric. The Council elected in his place Nectarius, a catechumen at the time, who was Prætor of Constantinople, and he was consecrated and enthroned June 9, A.D. 381. Gregory always maintained cordial relations with him; and the following letter was written in answer to the formal announcement of his election.)

Ep. LXXXVIII.

It was needful that the Royal Image should adorn the Royal City. For this reason it wears you upon its bosom, as was fitting, with the virtues and the eloquence, and the other beauties with which the Divine Favour has conspicuously enriched you. Us it has treated with utter contempt, and has cast away like refuse and chaff or a wave of the sea. But since friends have a common interest in each other's affairs, I claim a share in your welfare, and feel myself a partaker in your glory and the rest of your prosperity. Do you also, as is fitting, partake of the anxieties and reverses of your exiles, and not only (as the tragedians say) hold and stick to happy circumstances, but also take your part with your friend in troubles; that you may be perfectly just, living justly and equally in respect of friendship and of your friends. May good fortune abide with you long, that you may do yet more good; yes, may it be with you irrevocably and eternally, after your prosperity here, unto the passage to that other world.

Ep. XCI.

(A letter of no great importance, except as shewing the friendly feelings which Gregory continued to maintain towards his successor.)

Affairs with us go on as usual: we are quiet without strifes and disputes, valuing as we do the reward (which has no risk attaching to it) of silence, beyond everything. And we have derived some profit from this rest, having by God's mercy fairly recovered from our illness. Do you ride on and reign, as holy David says,[a] and may God, Who has honoured you with Priesthood, accompany you throughout, and set it for you above all slander. And that we may give each other a proof of our courage, and may not suffer any human calamity as we stand before God, I send this message to you, and do you promptly assent to it. There are many reasons which make me very anxious about our very dear Pancratius. Be good enough to receive him kindly, and to commend him to the best of your friends, that he may attain his object. His object is through some kind of military service to obtain relief from public office, though there is no single kind of life that is unexposed to the slanders of worthless men, as you very well know.

Ep. CLI.

(Written about A.D. 382, commending his friend George, a deacon of Nazianzus, to the good offices of the Archbishop and the Count of the Domestics, or Master of the Imperial Household, on account of his private troubles and anxieties.)

People in general make a very good guess at your disposition—or rather, they do not conjecture, but they do not refuse to believe me when I pride myself on the fact that you deem me worthy of no small respect and honour. One of these people is my very precious son George, who having fallen into many losses, and being very much overwhelmed by his troubles, can find only one harbour of safety, namely, to be introduced to you by us, and to obtain some favour at the hands of the Most Illustrious the Count of the Domestics. Grant them this favour, either to him and his need, or else, if you prefer it, to me, to whom I know you have resolved to grant all favours; and facts also persuade me that this is true of you.

Ep. CLXXXV.

(See Introduction to Ep. CLXXXIV. above, p. 469. Bosporius was to be sent to Constantinople that his cause might there be tried in the Civil Courts. Gregory therefore writes to the Archbishop to point out what a serious infringement of the rights of the Church this would be. Probably the attitude which Nectarius took up at the suggestion of Gregory was the occasion of the Edict which Theodosius addressed in February, A.D. 384 or 5, to the Augustal Prefect, withdrawing all clerics from the jurisdiction of the civil tribunals, and placing them under the exclusive control of the episcopal courts.)

Whenever different people praise different points in you, and all are pushing forward your good fame, as in a marketplace, I contribute whatever I can, and not less than any of them, because you deign also to honour me, to cheer my old age, as a well-beloved son does that of his father. For this reason I now also venture to offer to you this appeal on behalf of the Most Reverend and God-beloved Bishop Bosporius; though ashamed on the one hand that such a man should need any letter from me, since his venerable character is assured both by his daily life and by his age; and on the other hand not less ashamed to keep silence and not to say a word for him, while I have a voice, and honour faith, and know the man most intimately. The controversy about the dioceses you will no doubt yourself resolve according to the grace of the Spirit which is in you, and to the order of the canons. But I hope Your Reverence will see that it is not to be endured that our affairs are to be posted up in the secular courts. For even if they who are judges of such courts are Christians, as by the mercy of God they are, what is there in common between the Sword and the Spirit? And even if we yield this point, how or where can it be just that a dispute concerning the faith should be interwoven with the other questions? Is our God-beloved Bishop Bosporius to-day a heretic? Is it to-day that his hoar hair is set in the balance, who has brought back so many from their error, and has given so great proof of his orthodoxy, and is a teacher of us all? No, I entreat you, do not give place to such slanders; but if possible reconcile the opposing parties and add this to your praises; but if this may not be, at all events do not allow us all, (with whom he has lived, and with whom he has grown old,) to be outraged by such insolence,—us whom you know to be accurate preachers of the Gospel, both when to be so was dangerous, and when it is free from risk; and to be unable to endure any detraction from the One Unapproachable Godhead. And I beg you to pray for me who am suffering from serious illness. I and all who are with me salute the brethren who surround you. May you, strong and of good courage and of good fame in the Lord, grant to us and the Churches the support which all in common demand.

Ep. CLXXXVI.

(A letter of introduction for a relative.)

What would you have done if I had come in person and taken up your time? I am quite certain you would have undertaken with all

[a] Ps. xlv. 4.

zeal to deliver me from the slander, if I may take as a token what has happened before. Do me this favour, then, through my most discreet kinswoman who approaches you through me, reverencing first the age of your petitioner, and next her disposition and piety, which is more than is ordinarily found in a woman; and besides this, her ignorance in business-matters, and the troubles now brought upon her by her own relations; and above all, my entreaty. The greatest favour you can do me is speed in the benefit for which I am asking. For even the unjust judge in the Gospel [a] shewed kindness to the widow, though only after long beseeching and importunity. But from you I ask for speed, that she may not be overwhelmed by being long burdened with anxieties and miseries in a foreign land; though I know quite well that Your Piety will make that alien land to be a fatherland to her.

Ep. CCII.

(An important letter on the Apollinarian controversy has already been given above.)

§ 7. To Theodore, Bishop of Tyana.

(Theodore, a native of Arianzus, and an intimate friend of Gregory, accompanied him to Constantinople A.D. 379, and shared his persecution by the Arians, who broke into their church during the celebration of the divine liturgy, and pelted the clergy with stones. Theodore could not bring himself to put up with this, and declared his intention of prosecuting the aggressors. Gregory wrote the following letter to dissuade him from this course, by shewing him how much more noble it is to forgive than to revenge.)

Ep. LXXVII.

I hear that you are indignant at the outrages which have been committed on us by the Monks and the Mendicants. And it is no wonder, seeing that you never yet had felt a blow, and were without experience of the evils we have to endure, that you did feel angry at such a thing. But we as experienced in many sorts of evil, and as having had our share of insult, may be considered worthy of belief when we exhort Your Reverence, as old age teaches and as reason suggests. Certainly what has happened was dreadful, and more than dreadful,—no one will deny it: that our altars were insulted, our mysteries disturbed, and that we ourselves had to stand between the communicants and those who would stone them, and to make our intercessions a cure for stonings; that the reverence due to virgins was forgotten, and the good order of monks, and the calamity of the poor, who lost even their pity through ferocity. But perhaps it would be better to be patient, and to give an example of patience to many by our sufferings. For argument is not so persuasive of the world in general as is practice, that silent exhortation.

We think it an important matter to obtain penalties from those who have wronged us: an important matter, I say, (for even this is sometimes useful for the correction of others)—but it is far greater and more Godlike, to bear with injuries. For the former course curbs wickedness, but the latter makes men good, which is much better and more perfect than merely being not wicked. Let us consider that the great pursuit of mercifulness is set before us, and let us forgive the wrongs done to us that we also may obtain forgiveness, and let us by kindness lay up a store of kindness.

Phineas was called Zelotes because he ran through the Midianitish woman with the man who was committing fornication with her,[a] and because he took away the reproach from the children of Israel: but he was more praised because he prayed for the people when they had transgressed.[β] Let us then also stand and make propitiation, and let the plague be stayed, and let this be counted unto us for righteousness. Moses also was praised because he slew the Egyptian that oppressed the Israelite;[γ] but he was more admirable because he healed by his prayer his sister Miriam when she was made leprous for her murmuring.[δ] Look also at what follows. The people of Nineve are threatened with an overthrow, but by their tears they redeem their sin.[ε] Manasses was the most lawless of Kings,[ς] but is the most conspicuous among those who have attained salvation through mourning.

O Ephraim what shall I do unto thee,[η] saith God. What anger is here expressed—and yet protection is added. What is swifter than Mercy? The Disciples ask for flames of Sodom upon those who drive Jesus away, but He deprecates revenge.[θ] Peter cuts off the ear of Malchus, one of those who outraged Him, but Jesus restores it.[κ] And what of him who asks whether he must seven times forgive a brother if he has trespassed, is he not condemned for

a S. Luke xviii. 1, etc.

a Num. xxiv. 7. β Ps. cvi. 30, 31. γ Exod. ii. 12. δ Num. xii. 40. ε Jon. iii. 10. ς 2 Chron. xxxiii. 12, 13. η Hos. vi. 4. θ S. Luke ix. 54. κ Ib. xxii. 50.

his niggardliness, for to the seven is added seventy times seven?[α] What of the debtor in the Gospel who will not forgive as he has been forgiven?[β] Is it not more bitterly exacted of him for this? And what saith the pattern of prayer? Does it not desire that forgiveness may be earned by forgiveness?

Having so many examples let us imitate the mercy of God, and not desire to learn from ourselves how great an evil is requital of sin. You see the sequence of goodness. First it makes laws, then it commands, threatens, reproaches, holds out warnings, restrains, threatens again, and only when forced to do so strikes the blow, but this little by little, opening the way to amendment. Let us then not strike suddenly (for it is not safe to do so), but being selfrestrained in our fear let us conquer by mercy, and make them our debtors by our kindness, tormenting them by their conscience rather than by anger. Let us not dry up a fig tree which may yet bear fruit,[γ] nor condemn it as useless and cumbering the ground, when possibly the care and diligence of a skilful gardener may yet heal it. And do not let us so quickly destroy so great and glorious a work through what is perhaps the spite and malice of the devil; but let us choose to shew ourselves merciful rather than severe, and lovers of the poor rather than of abstract justice; and let us not make more account of those who would enkindle us to this than of those who would restrain us, considering, if nothing else, the disgrace of appearing to contend against mendicants who have this great advantage that even if they are in the wrong they are pitied for their misfortune. But as things are, consider that all the poor and those who support them, and all the Monks and Virgins are falling at your feet and praying you on their behalf. Grant to all these for them this favour (since they have sufferred enough as is clear by what they have asked of us) and above all to me who am their representative. And if it appear to you monstrous that we should have been dishonoured by them, remember that it is far worse that we should not be listened to by you when we make this request of you. May God forgive the noble Paulus his outrages upon us.

Ep. CXV.

(Sent about Easter A.D. 382 with a copy of the Philocalia, or Chrestomathy of Origen's works edited by himself and S. Basil.)

You anticipate the Festival, and the letters, and, which is better still, the time by your eagerness, and you bestow on us a preliminary festival. Such is what Your Reverence gives us. And we in return give you the greatest thing we have, our prayers. But that you may have some small thing to remember us by, we send you the volume of the Philocalia of Origen, containing a selection of passages useful to students of literature. Deign to accept this, and give us a proof of its usefulness, being aided by diligence and the Spirit.

α S. Matt. xviii. 21. β Ib. xviii. 28 sq. γ S. Luke xiii. 7.

Ep. CXXI.

(Written a little later, as a letter of thanks for an Easter Gift. Theodore had quite recently been made Archbishop of Tyana.)

We rejoice in the tokens of love, and especially at such a season, and from one at once so young a man, and so perfect; and, to greet you with the words of Scripture, stablished in your youth,[α] for so it calls him who is more advanced in wisdom than his years lead us to expect. The old Fathers prayed for the dew of heaven and fatness of the earth[β] and other such things for their children, though perhaps some may understand these things in a higher sense; but we will give you back all in a spiritual sense. The Lord fulfil all thy requests,[γ] and mayest thou be the father of such children[δ] (if I may pray for you concisely and intimately) as you yourself have shewn yourself to your own parents, so that we, as well as every one else, may be glorified concerning you.

Ep. CXXII.

You owe me, even as a sick man, tending, for one of the commandments is the visitation of the sick. And you also owe to the Holy Martyrs their annual honour, which we celebrate in your own Arianzus on the 23rd of the month which we call Dathusa.[ε] And at the same time there are ecclesiastical affairs not a few which need our common examination. For all these reasons then, I beg you to come at once: for though the labour is great, the reward is equivalent.

Ep. CXXIII.

(To excuse himself for postponing his acceptance of an invitation.)

I reverence your presence, and I delight in your company; although otherwise I counsel-

α Ps. cxliv. 2. β Gen. xxvii. 28. γ Ps. xx. 7.
δ It seems clear, as Benoît remarks, that this expression refers to Spiritual fatherhood. Theodore does not appear to have been married. ε Probably July.

led myself to remain at home and philosophize in quiet, for I found this of all courses the most profitable for myself. And since the winds are still somewhat rough, and my infirmity has not yet left me, I beg you to bear with me patiently for a little while, and to join me in my prayers for health; and as soon as the fit season comes I will attend upon your requests.

Ep. CXXIV.

(A little later on, when the weather was more settled, Gregory accepts the invitation and proposes to come at once, but declines to attend the Provincial Synod.)

You call me? And I hasten, and that for a private visit. Synods and Conventions I salute from afar, since I have experienced that most of them (to speak moderately) are but sorry affairs. What then remains? Help with your prayers my just desires that I may obtain that for which I am anxious.

Ep. CLII.

(On his retirement from Constantinople Gregory had at the request of the Bishops of the Province, and especially of Theodore of Tyana the Metropolitan, and Bosporius Bishop of Colonia (see letters above) and at the earnest solicitation of the people, undertaken the charge of the Diocese of Nazianzus; but he very soon found that his health was not equal to so great a task, and that he could not fulfil its calls upon him. He struggled on for some time, but at length, finding himself quite unequal to it, he wrote as follows to the Metropolitan:)

It is time for me to use these words of Scripture, To whom shall I cry when I am wronged?[α] Who will stretch out a hand to me when I am oppressed? To whom shall the burden of this Church pass, in its present evil and paralysed condition? I protest before God and the Elect Angels that the Flock of God is being unrighteously dealt with in being left without a Shepherd or a Bishop, through my being laid on the shelf. For I am a prisoner to my ill health and have been very quickly removed thereby from the Church, and made quite useless to everybody, every day breathing my last, and getting more and more crushed by my duties. If the Province had any other head, it would have been my duty to cry out and protest to it continually. But since Your Reverence is the Superior, it is to you I must look. For, to leave out everything else, you shall learn from my fellow-priests, Eulalius the Chorepiscopus[α] and Celeusius, whom I have specially sent to Your Reverence, what these robbers[β] who have now got the upper hand, are both doing and threatening. To repress them is not in the power of my weakness, but belongs to your skill and strength; since to you, with His other gifts God has given that of strength also for the protection of His Church. If in saying and writing this I cannot get a hearing, I shall take the only course remaining to me, that of publicly proclaiming and making known that this Church needs a Bishop, in order that it may not be injured by my feeble health. What is to follow is matter for your consideration.

Ep. CLIII.

(S. Gregory had to carry out his threat. He resigned the care of Nazianzus, and nothing would induce him to withdraw his resignation. Bosporius wrote him an urgent letter with this object, but he replied as follows:)

To Bosporius, Bishop of Colonia.

Twice I have been tripped up by you, and have been deceived (you know what I mean), and if it was justly, may the Lord smell from you an odour of sweet savour;[γ] if unjustly, may the Lord pardon it. For so it is reasonable for me to speak of you, seeing we are commanded to be patient when injuries are inflicted on us. But as you are master of your own opinions, so am I of mine. That troublesome Gregory will no longer be troublesome to you. I will withdraw myself to God, Who alone is pure and guileless. I will retire into myself. This I have determined; for to stumble twice on the same stone is attributed by the proverb to fools alone.

To Theodore, Archbishop of Tyana.

Ep. CLVII.

(S. Gregory succeeded at the end of A.D. 382 in convincing the Metropolitan and his Comprovincials of his sincerity in desiring to retire; and so they began to cast about for a Successor. Gregory desired that his cousin the

α Hab. ii. 1.

α Chorepiscopi;—a grade of clergy called into existence in the latter part of the Third Century, first in Asia Minor, to meet the difficulty of providing Episcopal supervision in the country districts of large Dioceses. They seemed to have been allowed to confer the Minor, but not the Holy Orders, unless by special commission from the Diocesan, on the ground of their lack of original Jurisdiction. That they were originally possessed of full Episcopal Orders there can be no doubt, but eventually the position was allowed to be held by Priests, and in the West the office became practically merged in that of the Archdeacon.

β The Apollinarians.

γ Gen. viii. 21.

Chorepiscopus Eulalius should be nominated, but the Bishops felt some jealousy at what they took to be an attempt on his part to dictate to them, and refused to allow him to take any part in the election, on the ground that he either never had been, or at any rate had ceased to be one of the Bishops of the Province. He protested, but finding that he could not convince them he withdrew his claim to a vote and wrote to Theodore, as follows:—)

Our spiritual affairs have reached their limit: I will not trouble you any further. Join together: take your precautions: take counsel against us: let our enemies have the victory: let the canons be accurately observed, beginning with us, the most ignorant of men. There is no ill-will in accuracy; only do not let the rights of friendship be impeded. The children of my very honoured son Nicobulus have come to the city to learn shorthand. Be kind enough to look upon them with a fatherly and kindly eye (for the canons do not forbid this), but especially take care that they live near the Church. For I desire that they should be moulded in character to virtue by continual association with Your Perfectness.

Ep. CLXIII.

(George a layman of Paspasus, was sent by Theodore of Tyana to Saint Gregory that the latter might convince him of his error and sin in repudiating an oath which he had taken, on the ground that it was taken in writing and not *viva voce*. Gregory seems to have brought him to a better mind, and sent him back to the Metropolitan with the following letter, requesting that due penance be imposed upon him, and have its length regulated by his contrition. This letter was read to the Second Council of Constantinople in 553, by Euphrantes, a successor of Theodore in the See of Tyana, and was accepted by the Fathers, wherefore it is regarded as having almost the force of a Canon of the Church Universal.)

God grant you to the Churches, both for our glory, and for the benefit of many, being as you are so circumspect and cautious in spiritual matters as to make us also more cautious who are considered to have some advantage over you in years. Since, however, you have wished to take us as partners in your spiritual inquiry (I mean about the oath which George of Paspasus appears to have sworn), we will declare to Your Reverence what presents itself to our mind. Very many people, as it seems to me, delude themselves by considering oaths which are taken with the sanction of spoken imprecations to be real oaths, but those which are written and not verbally uttered, to be mere matter of form, and no oaths at all. For how can we suppose that while a written schedule of debts is more binding than a verbal acknowledgment, yet a written oath is something other than an oath? Or to speak concisely, we hold an oath to be the assurance given to one who asked for and obtained it. Nor is it sufficient to say that he suffered violence (for the violence was the Law by which he bound himself), nor that afterwards he won the cause in the Law Court—for the very fact that he went to law was a breach of his oath. I have persuaded our brother George of this, not to pretend excuses for his sin, and not to seek out arguments to defend his transgression, but to recognize the writing as an oath, and to bewail his sin before God and Your Reverence, even though he formerly deceived himself and took a different view of it. This is what we have personally argued with him; and it is evident that if you will discourse with him more carefully, you will deepen his contrition, since you are a great healer of souls, and having treated him according to the Canon for as long a time as shall seem right, you will afterwards be able to confer indulgence upon him in the matter of time. And the measure of the time must be the measure of his compunction.

Ep. CLXXXIII.

(Helladius, Archbishop of Cæsarea, contested the validity of the election of Eulalius to the Bishopric of Nazianzus, and accused Bosporius of heresy. S. Gregory here throws the whole weight of his authority into the other scale. It is however manifest from the very terms of the letter that the person addressed is not Theodore of Tyana. It was conjectured by Clemencet that perhaps he was Theodore of Mopsuestia.)

Envy, which no one easily escapes, has got some foothold amongst us. See, even we Cappadocians are in a state of faction, so to speak—a calamity never heard of before, and not to be believed—so that no flesh may glory[a] in the sight of God, but that we may be careful, since we are all human, not to condemn each other rashly. For myself, there is some gain even from the misfortune (if I may speak somewhat

[a] 1 Cor. i. 29.

paradoxically), and I really gather a rose out of thorns, as the proverb has it. Hitherto I have never met Your Reverence face to face, nor conversed with you by letter, but have only been illuminated by your reputation; but now I am of necessity compelled to approach you by letter, and I am very grateful to him who has procured me this privilege. I omit to write to the other Bishops about whom you wrote to me, as the opportunity has not yet arisen. Moreover my weak health makes me less active in this matter; but what I write to you I write to them also through you. My Lord the God-beloved Bishop Helladius[a] must cease to waste his labour on our concerns. For it is not through spiritual earnestness, but through party zeal, that he is seeking this; and not for the sake of accurate compliance with the canons, but for the satisfaction of anger, as is evident by the time he has chosen, and because many have moved with him unreasonably, for I must say this, and not trouble myself about it. If I were physically in a condition to govern the Church of Nazianzus, to which I was originally appointed, and not to Sasima as some would falsely persuade you, I should not have been so cowardly or so ignorant of the Divine Constitutions as either to despise that Church, or to seek for an easy life in preference to the prizes which are in store for those who labour according to God's will, and work with the talent committed to their care. For what profit should I have from my many labours and my great hopes, if I were ill advised in the most important matters? But since my bodily health is bad, as everyone can plainly see, and I have not any responsibility to fear on account of this withdrawal, for the reason I have mentioned, and I saw that the Church through cleaving to me was suffering in its best interests and almost being destroyed through my illness, I prayed both before and now again my Lords the God-beloved Bishops (I mean those of our own Province) to give the Church a head, which they have done by God's Grace, worthy both of my desire and of your prayers. This I would have you both know yourself, most honourable Lord, and also inform the rest of the Bishops, that they may receive him and support him by their votes, and not bear heavily on my old age by believing the slander. Let me add this to my letter. If your examination finds my Lord the God-beloved Priest Bosporius guilty concerning the faith—a thing which it is not lawful even to suggest—(I pass over his age and my personal testimony) judge him so yourselves. But if the discussion about the dioceses is the cause of this evil report and this novel accusation, do not be led away by the slander, and do not give to falsehoods a greater strength than to the truth, I beg you, lest you should cast into despair those who desire to do what is right. May you be granted good health and spirits and courage and continual progress in the things of God to us and to the Church, whose common boast you are.

a Basil's successor.

Ep. CXXXIX.

(This letter is written at a somewhat earlier date in reference to the consent he had been induced to give to remaining for some time longer as administrator of the See of Nazianzus. It is certainly not addressed to Theodore of Tyana, and it is not known who this Theodore is.)

He Who raised David His servant from the Shepherd's work to the Throne, and Your Reverence from the flock to the Work of the Shepherd: He that orders our affairs and those of all who hope in Him according to His own Will: may He now put it into the mind of Your Reverence to know the dishonour which I have suffered at the hands of my Lords the Bishops in the matter of their votes, in that they have agreed to the Election,[a] but have excluded us. I will not lay the blame on Your Reverence, because you have but recently come to preside over our affairs, and are, as is to be expected, for the most part unacquainted with our history. This is quite enough: for I have no mind to trouble you further, that I may not seem burdensome at the very beginning of our friendship. But I will tell you what suggests itself to me in taking counsel with God. I retired from the Church at Nazianzus, not as either despising God, or looking down on the littleness of the flock (God forbid that a philosophic[β] soul should be so disposed); but first because I am not bound by any such appointment: and secondly because I am broken down by my ill health, and do not think myself equal to such anxieties. And since you too have been heavy on me, in reproaching me with my resignation, and I myself could not endure the clamours against me, and since the times are hard, threatening us with an inroad of enemies to the injury of the commonwealth of the whole Church, I finally made up my mind to suffer a defeat which is painful to my body, but perhaps not

a See Introd. to Ep. 157.
β Probably equivalent to A Monk.

bad for my soul. I make over this miserable body to the Church for as long as it may be possible, thinking it better to suffer any distress to the flesh rather than to incur a spiritual injury myself or to inflict it upon others, who have thought the worst of us, judging from their own experience. Knowing this, do pray for me, and approve my resolution: and perhaps it is not out of place to say, mould yourself to piety.

§ 8. To Nicobulus.

(See the introduction to the first letter to Sophronius above.)

Ep. XII. (about A.D. 365).

You joke me about Alypiana as being little and unworthy of your size, you tall and immense and monstrous fellow both in form and strength. For now I understand that soul is a matter of measure, and virtue of weight, and that rocks are more valuable than pearls, and crows more respectable than nightingales. Well, well! rejoice in your bigness and your cubits, and be in no respect inferior to the famed sons of Aloeus.[α] You ride a horse, and shake a spear, and concern yourself with wild beasts. But she has no such work; and no great strength is needed to carry a comb,[β] or to handle a distaff, or to sit by a loom, "For such is the glory of woman."[γ] And if you add this, that she has become fixed to the ground on account of prayer, and by the great movement of her mind has constant communion with God, what is there here to boast of in your bigness or the stature of your body? Take heed to seasonable silence: listen to her voice: mark her unadornment, her womanly virility, her usefulness at home, her love of her husband. Then you will say with the Laconian, that verily soul is not a subject for measure, and the outer must look to the inner man. If you look at the things in this way you will leave off joking and deriding her as little, and you will congratulate yourself on your marriage.

Ep. LI.

(An answer to a request made by Nicobulus for a treatise on the art of writing letters. Benoît thinks this and the following ones were written to the Younger Nicobulus.)

Of those who write letters, since this is what you ask, some write at too great a length, and others err on the side of deficiency; and both miss the mean, like archers shooting at a mark and sending some shafts short of it and others beyond it; for the missing is the same though on opposite sides. Now the measure of letters is their usefulness: and we must neither write at very great length when there is little to say, nor very briefly when there is a great deal. What? Are we to measure our wisdom by the Persian Schœne, or by the cubits of a child, and to write so imperfectly as not to write at all but to copy the midday shadows, or lines which meet right in front of you, whose lengths are foreshortened and which show themselves in glimpses rather than plainly, being recognized only by certain of their extremities? We must in both respects avoid the want of moderation and hit off the moderate. This is my opinion as to brevity; as to perspicuity it is clear that one should avoid the oratorical form as much as possible and lean rather to the chatty: and, to speak concisely, that is the best and most beautiful letter which can convince either an unlearned or an educated reader; the one, as being within the reach of the many; the other, as above the many; and it should be intelligible in itself. It is equally disagreeable to think out a riddle and to have to interpret a letter. The third point about a letter is grace: and this we shall safeguard if we do not write in any way that is dry and unpleasing or unadorned and badly arranged and untrimmed, as they call it; as for instance a style destitute of maxims and proverbs and pithy sayings, or even jokes and enigmas, by which language is sweetened. Yet we must not seem to abuse these things by an excessive employment of them. Their entire omission shews rusticity, but the abuse of them shews insatiability. We may use them about as much as purple is used in woven stuffs. Figures of speech we shall admit, but few and modest. Antitheses and balanced clauses and nicely divided sentences, we shall leave to the sophists, or if we do sometimes admit them, we shall do so rather in play than in earnest. My final remark shall be one which I heard a clever man make about the eagle, that when the birds were electing a king, and came with various adornment, the most beautiful point about him was that he did not think himself beautiful. This point is to be especially attended to in letter-writing, to be without adventitious orna-

α Otus and Ephialtes, the two Homeric Giants, who piled Pelion on Ossa and Olympus on Pelion in the vain endeavour to reach heaven and dethrone Zeus, but were slain by Apollo. (See Hom., Odyss., xi., 305–320.)

β An instrument used in weaving to make the web firm and close.

γ From his own Poem against women who take too much pains about adorning themselves (i., 267).

ment and as natural as possible. So much about letters I send you by a letter; but perhaps you had better not apply it to myself, who am busied about more important matters. The rest you will work out for yourself, as you are quick at learning, and those who are clever in these matters will teach you.

Ep. LII.

(Nicobulus asked Gregory to publish a collection of his letters. Gregory forwards a copy.)

You are asking flowers from an autumn meadow, and arming Nestor in his old age, in demanding from me now something clever in the way of language, after I have long neglected all that is enjoyable in language and in life. But yet (since it is not an Eurysthean or Herculean labour that you are imposing on me, but rather one which is very agreeable and quiet, to collect for you as many of my own letters as I can), do you place this volume among your books—a work not amatory but oratorical, and not for display so much as for use, and that for our own home.[a] For different authors have different characteristics, greater or smaller. Mine is a tendency to instruct by maxims and positive statements wherever opportunity occurs. And as in a legitimate child, so also in language, the father is always visible, not less than parents are shewn by bodily characteristics. Mine are such as I have mentioned. You may repay me both by writing and by deriving profit from what I have written. I cannot ask for or request any better reward than this, either more profitable to the asker, or more becoming him who gives it.

Ep. LIII.

(Gregory put a collection of Basil's letters with his own, and gave them the first place. Nicobulus seems to have been surprised at this, and asked the reason. Gregory explains as follows.)

I have always preferred the Great Basil to myself, though he was of the contrary opinion; and so I do now, not less for truth's sake than for friendship's. This is the reason why I have given his letters the first place and my own the second. For I hope we two will always be coupled together; and also I would supply others with an example of modesty and submission.

Ep. LIV.

On Laconicism. To be laconic is not merely, as you suppose, to write few words, but to say a great deal in few words. Thus I call Homer very brief and Antimachus lengthy. Why? Because I measure the length by the matter and not by the letters.

Ep. LV.

An Invitation. You flee when I pursue you: perhaps in accordance with the laws of love, to make yourself more valuable. Come then, and fill up at last the loss I have suffered by your long delay. And if any home affairs detain you, you shall leave us again, and so make yourself more precious as an object of desire.

§ 9. To Olympius.

(Olympius was Prefect of Cappadocia Secunda in 382. One letter to him against the Apollinarians, has already been given; the rest, which are to follow are mainly recommendations of various persons to his patronage.)

Ep. CIV.

All The Other favours which I have received I know to be due to your kindness; and may God reward you for them with His own mercies; and may one of these be, that you may discharge your office of prefect with good fame and splendour from beginning to end. In what I now ask I come rather to give than to receive, if it is not arrogant to say so. I personally introduce poor Philumena to you, to entreat your justice, and to move you to the tears with which she afflicts my soul. She herself will explain to you in what and by whom she has been wronged, for it would not be right for me to bring accusations against any one. But this much it is necessary for me to say, that widowhood and orphanhood have a right to the assistance of all right-minded men, and especially of those who have wife and children, those great pledges of pity, since we—ourselves only men—are set to judge men. Pardon me that I plead with you for these by letter, since it is by ill health that I am deprived of seeing a ruler so kind and so conspicuous for virtue that even the prelude of your administration is more precious than the good fame of others even at the end of their term.

Ep. CV.

The time is swift, the struggle great, and my sickness severer, reducing me almost to immovability. What is left but to pray to God, and to supplicate your kindness, the one, that

a I.e. as a model of Christian style.

He will incline your mind to gentler counsels, the other that you will not roughly dismiss our intercession, but will receive kindly the wretched Paulus, whom justice has brought under your hands, perhaps in order that it may make you more illustrious by the greatness of your kindness, and may commend our prayers (such as they are) to your mercy.

Ep. CVI.

Here is another laying before you a letter, of which, if the truth may be said, you are the cause yourself, for you provoke them by the honour you do them. Here too is another petitioner for you, a prisoner of fear, our kinsman Eustratius, who with us and by us entreats your goodness, inasmuch as he cannot endure to be in perpetual rebellion against your government, even though a just terror has frightened him, nor does he choose to entreat you by anyone else than me, that he may make your mercy to him more conspicuous through his use of such intercessors, whom at all events you yourself make great by thus accepting their appeal. I will say one thing, and that briefly. All the other favours you conferred upon me; but this you will confer upon your own judgment, since once you purposed to comfort our age and infirmity with such honours. And I will add that you are continually rendering God more propitious to you.

Ep. CXXV.

(Given above, § 1.)

Ep. CXXVI.

(While Gregory was at Xantharis an opportunity presented itself for seeing Olympius, but a return of illness prevented him from taking advantage of it. He writes to express his regret, and takes the opportunity also to request that Nicobulus may be exempted from the charge of the Imperial Posts.)

I was happy in a dream. For having been brought as far as the Monastery to obtain some comfort from the bath, and then hoping to meet you, and having this good fortune almost in my hands, and having delayed a few days, I was suddenly carried away by my illness, which was already painful in some respects and threatening in others. And, if one must find some conjecture to account for the misfortune, I suffered in the same way as the polypods do, which if torn by force from the rocks risk the loss of the suckers by which they attach themselves to the rocks, or carry off some portion of the latter. Something of this kind is my case. And what I should have asked Your Excellency for had I seen you, I now venture to ask for though I am absent. I found my son Nicobulus much worried by the care of the Post, and by close attention to the Monastery. He is not a strong man, and has great distaste for solitude. Make use of him for anything else you please, for he is eager to serve your authority in all things; but if it be possible set him free from this charge, if for no other reason, at any rate to do him honour as my Hospitaller. Since I have asked many favours from you for many people, and have obtained them, I need also your kindness for myself.

Ep. CXXXI.

(In 382 Gregory was summoned to a Synod at Constantinople; he wrote to Procopius, the Prefectus Urbi, and declined to go, on the ground of his great dislike to Episcopal Synods, from which, he said, he had never known any good to result. However he seems to have received a more urgent summons through Icarius and Olympius. His reply to Icarius has been lost; that to Olympius is as follows.)

It is more serious to me than my illness, that no one will believe that I am ill, but that so long a journey is enjoined upon me, and I am pushed into the midst of troubles from which I rejoiced to have withdrawn, and almost thought that I ought to be grateful for this to my bodily affliction. For quiet and freedom from affairs is more precious than the splendour of a busy life. I wrote this yesterday to the Most Illustrious Icarius, from whom I received the same summons: and I now beg your Magnanimity also to write this for me, for you are a very trustworthy witness of my ill health. Another proof of my inability is the loss which I have now suffered in having been unable even to come and enjoy your society, who are so kind a Governor, and so admirable for virtue that even the preludes of your term of office are more honourable than the good fame which others can earn by the end of theirs.

Ep. CXL.

Again I write when I ought to come: but I gain confidence to do so from yourself, O Umpire of spiritual matters (to put the first thing first), and Corrector of the Commonweal—and both by Divine Providence: who have also received as the reward of your piety that your affairs would prosper to your mind, and that you alone should find attainable what to every one else is out of reach. For wisdom and courage conduct your government, the one discovering what is to be done, and the other easily carrying out what has been discovered. And the greatest of all is the purity of your hands with which all is directed. Where is your ill-gotten gold? There never was any; it was the first thing you condemned to exile as an invisible tyrant. Where is illwill? It is condemned. Where is favour? Here you do bend somewhat (for I will accuse you a little), but it is in imitating the Divine Mercy, which at the present time your soldier Aurelius entreats of you by me. I call him a foolish fugitive, because he has placed himself in our hands, and through ours in yours, sheltering himself under our gray hair and our Priesthood (for which you have often professed your veneration) as if it were under some Imperial Image. See, this sacrificing and unbloodstained hand leads this man to you; a hand which has written often in your praise, and will I am sure write yet more, if God continue your term of government—yours, I mean, and that of your colleague Themis.

Ep. CXLI.

(The people of Nazianzus had in some way incurred the loss of civic rights; and the Order for the forfeiture of the title of City had been signed by Olympius. This led to something like a revolt on the part of a certain number of the younger citizens: and this Olympius determined to punish by the total destruction of the place. S. Gregory was again prevented by sickness from appearing in person before the Governor: but he pleaded the cause of his native city (using its official Latin name of Diocæsarea) in the following letters so successfully as to induce Olympius to pardon the outbreak.)

Again an opportunity for kindness: and again I am bold enough to commit to a letter my entreaty about so important a matter. My illness makes me thus bold, for it does not even allow me to go out, and it does not permit me to make a fitting entrance to you. What then is my Embassy? Pray receive it from me gently and kindly. The death of a single man, who to-day is and to-morrow will not be and will not return to us is of course a dreadful thing. But it is much more dreadful for a City to die, which Kings founded, and time compacted, and a long series of years has preserved. I speak of Diocæsarea, once a City, a City no longer, unless you grant it mercy. Think that this place now falls at your feet by me: let it have a voice, and be clothed in mourning and cut off its hair as in a tragedy, and let it speak to you in such words as these:

Give a hand to me that lie in the dust: help the strengthless: do not add the weight of your hand to time, nor destroy what the Persians have left me. It is more honourable to you to raise up cities than to destroy those that are distressed. Be my founder, either by adding to what I possess, or by preserving me as I am. Do not suffer that up to the time of your administration I should be a City, and after you should be so no longer: do not give occasion to after times to speak evil of you, that you received me numbered among cities, and left me an uninhabited spot, which was once a city, only recognizable by mountains and precipices and woods.

This let the City of my imagination do and say to your mercy. But deign to receive an exhortation from me as your friend: certainly chastise those who have rebelled against the Edict of your authority. On this behalf I am not bold to say anything, although this piece of audacity was not, they say, of universal design, but was only the unreasoning anger of a few young men. But dismiss the greater part of your anger, and use a larger reasoning. They were grieved for their Mother's being put to death; they could not endure to be called citizens, and yet to be without political rights: they were mad: they committed an offence against the law: they threw away their own safety: the unexpectedness of the calamity deprived them of reason. Is it really necessary that for this the city should cease to be a city? Surely not. Most excellent, do not write the order for this to be done. Rather respect the supplication of all citizens and statesmen and men of rank—for remember the calamity will touch all alike—even if the greatness of your authority keeps them silent, sighing as it were in secret. Respect also my gray hair: for it would be dreadful to me, after having had a great city, now to have none at all, and that after your government the Temple which we have raised to God, and our love for its adornment, is to become a dwelling for beasts. It is not a terrible thing if some statues were thrown down —though in itself it would be so—but I would not have you think that I am speaking of this, when all my care is for more important things: but it is dreadful if an ancient city is to be destroyed with them—one which has splendidly endured, as I, who am honoured by you, and am supposed to have some influence, have lived to see. But this is enough upon such a subject, for I shall not, if I speak at greater length, find anything stronger than your own reasons, by which this nation is governed—and may more and greater ones be governed by them too, and that in greater commands. This however it was needful that Your Magnanimity should know about those who have fallen before your feet, that they are altogether wretched and despairing, and have not shared in any disorder with those who have broken the law, as I am certified by many who were then present. Therefore deliberate what you may think expedient, both for your own reputation in this world, and your hopes in the next. We will bear what you determine—not indeed without grief—but we will bear it: for what else can we do? If the worse determination prevail, we shall be indignant, and shall shed a tear over our City that has ceased to be.

Ep. CXLII.

Though my desire to meet you is warm, and the need of your petitioners is great, yet my illness is invincible. Therefore I am bold to commit my intercession to writing. Have respect to our gray hair, which you have already often reverenced by good actions. Have respect also to my infirmity, to which my labours for God have in part contributed, if I may swagger a little. For this cause spare the citizens who look to me because I use some freedom of speech with you. And spare also the others who are under my care. For public affairs will suffer no damage through mercy, since you can do more by fear than others by punishment. May you, as your reward for this, obtain such a Judge as you shew yourself to your petitioners and to me their intercessor.

Ep. CXLIII.

What does much experience, and experience of good do for men? It teaches kindness, and inclines them to those who entreat them. There is no such education in pity as the previous reception of goodness. This has happened to myself among others. I have learned compassion by the things which I have suffered. And do you see my greatness of soul when I myself need your gentleness in my own affairs? I intercede for others, and do not fear lest I should exhaust all your kindness on other men's concerns. I am writing thus on behalf of the Presbyter Leontius—or, if I may so describe him, the ex-Presbyter. If he has suffered sufficiently for what he has done, let us stop there, lest excess become injustice. And if there is still any balance of punishment due, and the consequences of his crime have not yet equalled his offence, yet remit it for our sake and God's, and that of the sanctuary, and the general assembly of the priests, among whom he was once numbered, even though he has now shewn himself unworthy of them, both by what he has done and by what he has suffered. If I can prevail with you it will be best; but if not, I will bring to you a more powerful intercessor, her who is the partner both of your rule and of your good fame.

Ep. CXLIV.

(Verianus, a citizen of Nazianzus, had been offended by his son-in-law, and on this account wished his daughter to sue for a divorce. Olympius referred the matter to the Episcopal arbitration of S. Gregory, who refused to countenance the proceeding, and writes the two following letters, the first to the Prefect, the second to Verianus himself.)

Haste is not always praiseworthy. For this reason I have deferred my answer until now about the daughter of the most honourable Verianus, both to allow for time setting matters right, and also because I conjecture that Your Goodness does not approve of the divorce, inasmuch as you entrusted the enquiry to me, whom you knew to be neither hasty nor uncircumspect in such matters. Therefore I have refrained myself till now, and, I venture to think, not without reason. But since we have come nearly to the end of the allotted time, and it is necessary that you should be informed of the result of the examination I will inform you. The young lady seems to me to be of two minds, divided between reverence for her parents and affection for her husband. Her words are on their side, but her mind, I rather think, is with her husband, as is shewn by her tears. You will do what commends itself to your justice, and to God who directs you in all things. I should most willingly have given my opinion to my son Verianus that he should pass over much of what is in question, with a view not to confirm the divorce, which is entirely contrary to our law,[a] though the Roman law may determine otherwise. For it is necessary that justice be observed—which I pray you may ever both say and do.

---

a The law of the Church.

To Verianus.

Ep. CXLV.

Public executioners commit no crime, for they are the servants of the laws: nor is the sword unlawful with which we punish criminals. But nevertheless, the public executioner is not a laudable character, nor is the death-bearing sword received joyfully. Just so neither can I endure to become hated by confirming the divorce by my hand and tongue. It is far better to be the means of union and of friendship than of division and parting of life. I suppose it was with this in his mind that our admirable Governor entrusted me with the enquiry about your daughter, as one who could not proceed to divorce abruptly or unfeelingly. For he proposed me not as Judge, but as Bishop, and placed me as a mediator in your unhappy circumstances. I beg you therefore, to make some allowance for my timidity, and if the better prevail, to use me as a servant of your desire: I rejoice in receiving such commands. But if the worse and more cruel course is to be taken, seek for some one more suitable to your purpose. I have not time, for the sake of favouring your friendship (though in all respects I have the highest regard for you), to offend against God, to Whom I have to give account of every action and thought. I will believe your daughter (for the truth shall be told) when she can lay aside her awe of you, and boldly declare the truth. At present her condition is pitiable—for she assigns her words to you, and her tears to her husband.

To Olympius.

Ep. CXLVI.

This is what I said as if by a sort of prophecy, when I found you favourable to every request, and was making insatiable use of your gentleness, that I fear I shall exhaust your kindness upon the affairs of others. For see, a contest of my own has come (if that is mine which concerns my own relations), and I cannot speak with the same freedom. First, because it is my own. For to entreat for myself, though it may be more useful, is more humiliating. And next, I am afraid of excess as destroying pleasure, and opposing all that is good. So matters stand, and I conjecture only too rightly. Nevertheless with confidence in God before Whom I stand, and in your magnanimity in doing good, I am bold to present this petition.

Suppose Nicobulus to be the worst of men:—though his only crime is that through me he is an object of envy, and more free than he ought to be. And suppose that my present opponent is the most just of men. For I am ashamed to accuse before Your Uprightness one whom yesterday I was supporting: but I do not know if it will seem to you just that punishment should be demanded for one man's crimes from another, though these were quite strange to him, and had not even his consent; from the man who has so stirred his household and been so upset as to have surrendered to his accuser more readily than the latter wished. Must Nicobulus or his children be reduced to slavery as his persecutors desire? I am ashamed both of the ground of the persecution and of the time, if this is to be done while both you are in power and I have influence with you. Not so, most admirable friend, let not this be suggested to Your Integrity. But recognizing by the winged swiftness of your mind the malice from which this proceeds, and having respect to me your admirer, shew yourself a merciful judge to those who are being disturbed—for to-day you are not merely judging between man and man, but between virtue and vice; and to this more consideration than by an ordinary man must be given by those who are like you in virtue and are skilful governors. And in return for this you shall have from me not only the matter of my prayers, which I know you do not, like so many men, despise; but also that I will make your government famous with all to whom I am known.

Ep. CLIV.

To me you are Prefect even after the expiry of your term of office—for I judge things differently from the run of men—because you embrace in yourself every prefectoral virtue. For many of those who sit on lofty thrones are to me base, all those whose hand makes them base and slaves of their subjects.[a] But many are high and lofty though they stand low, whom virtue places on high and makes worthy of greater government. But what have I to do with this? No longer is the great Olympius with us, nor does he bear our rudder-lines. We are undone, we are betrayed, we have become again the Second Cappadocia, after having been made the First by you. Of other men's

[a] I. e. who are accessible to bribery.

matters why should I speak? but who will cherish the old age of your Gregory, and administer to his weakness the enchantment of honours, and make him more honourable because he obtains kindness for many from you? Now then depart on your journey with escort and greater pomp, leaving behind for us many tears, and carrying with you much wealth, and that of a kind which few Prefects do, good fame, and the being inscribed on all hearts, pillars not easily moved. If you preside over us again with greater and more illustrious rule, (this is what our longing augurs), we shall offer to God more perfect thanks.

INDICES.

S. GREGORY NAZIANZEN.

INDEX OF SUBJECTS.

[Including the Introduction and Notes.]

S. GREGORY NAZIANZEN.

INDEX OF TEXTS.